Tolley's
Health and Safety
at Work
Handbook
2002

# Tolley's Health and Safety at Work Handbook 2002

Fourteenth Edition

Tolley

A Member of the LexisNexis Group

# Members of the LexisNexis Group worldwide

| | |
|---|---|
| United Kingdom | Butterworths Tolley, a Division of Reed Elsevier (UK) Ltd, 2 Addiscombe Road, CROYDON CR9 5AF |
| Argentina | Abeledo Perrot, Jurisprudencia Argentina and Depalma, BUENOS AIRES |
| Australia | Butterworths, a Division of Reed International Books Australia Pty Ltd, CHATSWOOD, New South Wales |
| Austria | ARD Betriebsdienst and Verlag Orac, VIENNA |
| Canada | Butterworths Canada Ltd, MARKHAM, Ontario |
| Chile | Publitecsa and Conosur Ltda, SANTIAGO DE CHILE |
| Czech Republic | Orac sro, PRAGUE |
| France | Editions du Juris-Classeur SA, PARIS |
| Hong Kong | Butterworths Asia (Hong Kong), HONG KONG |
| Hungary | Hvg Orac, BUDAPEST |
| India | Butterworths India, NEW DELHI |
| Ireland | Butterworths (Ireland) Ltd, DUBLIN |
| Italy | Giuffré, MILAN |
| Malaysia | Malayan Law Journal Sdn Bhd, KUALA LUMPUR |
| New Zealand | Butterworths of New Zealand, WELLINGTON |
| Poland | Wydawnictwa Prawnicze PWN, WARSAW |
| Singapore | Butterworths Asia, SINGAPORE |
| South Africa | Butterworths Publishers (Pty) Ltd, DURBAN |
| Switzerland | Stämpfli Verlag AG, BERNE |
| USA | LexisNexis, DAYTON, Ohio |

© Reed Elsevier (UK) Ltd 2001

A CIP Catalogue record for this book is available from the British Library.

ISBN 0 75451 260-6

Typeset by Letterpart Limited, Reigate, Surrey
Printed in Great Britain by Clays Ltd, St Ives plc

**Visit Butterworths LexisNexis *direct* at www.butterworths.com**

# List of Contributors

Sally Andrews, LLB, LLM, Solicitor, Cartwrights

Roger Barrowcliffe, Head of ERM's Air Quality Group

Mike Bateman, BSc, MIOSH, RSP, Independent Health and Safety Consultant

Alison Brown, LLB, MIOSH, Solicitor, CMS Cameron McKenna

David Brown, BA, Partner, Zyda Brown

Martin Bruffell, LLB, Partner, Berrymans Lace Mawer

David Clarke, CIBiol, Food Safety Consultant

Nicola Coote, FIOSH, MIIRSM, MRSH, MCIPD, RSP, Director of Personnel Health and Safety Consultants Ltd

Kitty Debenham, BA (Oxon), Solicitor, Simmons & Simmons

Christopher Eskell, TD, LLB, MIMgt, Partner, Cartwrights

Janet Gaymer, MA (Oxon), LLM (Lond), Partner, Simmons & Simmons

Andrew Gilbert, LLB, Partner, Kennedys

Dorothy Henderson, BA, Partner, Travers Smith Braithwaite

Jo Hilliard, LLB, Solicitor, Cartwrights

Rhiannon Hughes, BA, Solicitor, CMS Cameron McKenna

Nick Humphreys, LLB, LLM, Solicitor, Barrister, Richards Butler

Mariel Irvine, BA (Dubl), Dip Law, Solicitor, Kennedys

Ian Jerome, BSc, Senior Consultant, Education and Training, Loss Prevention Council

Raj Lakha, BA, MBA, MIIRSM, MIOSH, MInstD, AIMC, Director of Safety Solutions (UK) Ltd, Director of COASST International Ltd

David Leckie, LLB, Barrister, Maclay Murray & Spens

Deborah Lloyd, BSc, LLB, LLM, Solicitor, Herbert Smith

Subash Ludhra, BSc, RSP, FIOSH, Dip Env Man, Director Quality Assurance & Training, Initial Catering Services Ltd

Peter Neild, MPhil, FCII, Berrymans Lace Mawer

Andrea Oates, BSc, Health and Safety Researcher, Labour Research Department

George Pitblado, I Eng, MI Plant E, MIIRSM, MWM Soc, Partner, GMP Support Services Consultants

Laura Pitman, BA (Cantab), Solicitor, Travers Smith Braithwaite

Mark Rutter, BSc, PhD, Environmental Advisor, CMS Cameron McKenna

Frank Saxon, Manager Gas Services, Blackburn College

Mary Spear, BA (Cantab), Solicitor, Cartwrights

Roger Tompsett, BSc(Eng), MIOA, Head of Acoustics, WS Atkins Noise & Vibration

Mark Tyler, MA, LLM, MIOSH, Partner, CMS Cameron McKenna

George Ventris, formerly secretary of the HSC's Construction Industry Advisory Committee (CONIAC) and a leader of HSE's Construction National Interest Group

Jeffrey Wale, LLB, Partner, Berrymans Lace Mawer

# Contents

## Contents

# List of Tables

# List of Illustrations/Diagrams

# Abbreviations and References

Many abbreviations occur only in one section of the book and are set out in full there. The following is a list of abbreviations used more frequently or throughout the book.

## Organisations/Publications

| | | |
|---|---|---|
| ACAS | = | Advisory, Conciliation and Arbitration Service |
| ACOP | = | Approved Code of Practice |
| BS | = | British Standard |
| BSC | = | British Safety Council |
| CBI | = | Confederation of British Industry |
| Cmnd | = | Command Paper |
| COIT | = | Central Office of the Industrial Tribunals |
| CPS | = | Crown Prosecution Service |
| DSS | = | Department of Social Security |
| EU | = | European Union |
| HMIP | = | HM Inspectorate of Pollution (now part of the Environment Agency) |
| HSC | = | Health and Safety Commission |
| HSE | = | Health and Safety Executive |
| HMSO | = | Her Majesty's Stationery Office |
| HSIB | = | Health and Safety Information Bulletin |
| ILO | = | International Labour Office |
| IOSH | = | Institution of Occupational Safety and Health |
| JCT | = | Joint Contracts Tribunal |
| MoD | = | Ministry of Defence |
| RoSPA | = | Royal Society for the Prevention of Accidents |
| TUC | = | Trades Union Congress |

## Statutes/Statutory Instruments

| | | |
|---|---|---|
| CHIP | = | Chemicals (Hazard Information and Packaging for Supply) Regulations 1994 as amended |
| COSHH | = | Control of Substances Hazardous to Health Regulations 1994 |
| CPA | = | Consumer Protection Act 1987 |
| EA | = | Environment Act 1995 |
| EPA 1990 | = | Environmental Protection Act 1990 |
| EPCA | = | Employment Protection (Consolidation) Act 1978 |
| ERA | = | Employment Rights Act 1996 |
| FA | = | Factories Act 1961 |
| FSA 1990 | = | Food Safety Act 1990 |
| HSWA | = | Health and Safety at Work etc. Act 1974 |
| OLA | = | Occupiers' Liability Act 1957 |
| OSRPA | = | Offices, Shops and Railway Premises Act 1963 |
| TURERA | = | Trade Union Reform and Employment Rights Act 1993 |
| UCTA | = | Unfair Contract Terms Act 1977 |
| Reg | = | Regulation (or Statutory Instrument) |
| SI | = | Statutory Instrument |
| SR&O | = | Statutory Rule and Order |
| Sch | = | Schedule |
| s or Sec | = | Section |

## Case citations

| | | |
|---|---|---|
| AC | = | Appeal Cases |
| AER | = | All England Reports |
| ALJR | = | Australian Law Journal Reports |
| Camp | = | Campbell Reports |
| CB, NS | = | Common Bench, New Series (ended 1865) |
| Ch | = | Chancery Reports |
| CL | = | Current Law |
| CLY | = | Current Law Year Book |
| CMLR | = | Community Law Reports |
| COD | = | Crown Office Digest |
| Con LR | = | Construction Law Reports |
| Cr App R | = | Criminal Appeal Reports |
| Crim LR | = | Criminal Law Review |
| East | = | East's Term Reports |
| EG | = | Estates Gazette |
| Env LR | = | Environmental Law Reports |
| Exch | = | Exchequer Reports |
| F & F | = | Foster & Finlayson (ended 1867) |
| H & C | = | Hurlstone & Norman |
| HSIB | = | Health and Safety Information Bulletin |
| ICR | = | Industrial Cases Reports |
| IRLR | = | Industrial Relations Law Reports |
| JP | = | Justice of the Peace and Local Government Review |
| KB/QB | = | Law Reports, King's (Queen's) Bench Division |
| KIR | = | Knight's Industrial Reports |
| LGR | = | Local Government Reports |
| LJKB | = | Law Journal Reports – New Series, Kings Bench |
| Lloyd's Rep | = | Lloyd's List Reports |
| M & W | = | Meeson & Welby |
| Med LR | = | Medical Law Reports |
| NLJ | = | New Law Journal |
| PIQR | = | Personal Injuries and Quantum Reports |
| RTR | = | Road Traffic Reports |
| SCCR | = | Scottish Criminal Case Reports |
| SJ | = | Solicitors' Journal |
| SLT/SLT (Notes) | = | Scots Law Times/(Notes) |
| Taunt | = | Taunton Reports |
| TLR | = | Times Law Reports |
| WLR | = | Weekly Law Reports |

## Legal terminology

| | | |
|---|---|---|
| ECJ | = | European Court of Justice |
| HL | = | House of Lords |
| CA | = | Court of Appeal |
| EAT | = | Employment Appeal Tribunal |
| IT | = | Industrial Tribunal |
| J | = | Mr Justice, a junior judge, normally sitting in a court of first instance |
| LJ | = | Lord Justice, a senior judge, normally sitting in a court of appeal |
| plaintiff | = | the person presenting a claim in a civil action |
| defendant | = | the person against whom a claim is brought in a civil action |
| appellant | = | the person bringing an appeal in a civil action |
| respondent | = | the person against whom an appeal is brought in a civil action |

| | | |
|---|---|---|
| **tort** | = | a species of civil action for injury or damage where the remedy or redress is an award of unliquidated damages |
| **volenti non fit injuria** | = | 'to one who is willing no harm is done'; a complete defence in a civil action |
| **novus actus interveniens** | = | supervening act of third party |
| **obiter dicta** | = | words said by the way |
| **ratio decidendi** | = | principle of a case |
| **res ipsa loquitur** | = | the event itself is evidence of negligence (a principle in the law of tort); the assertion can be rebutted by the defendant |

# Introduction

**1.**

## This Introduction is in three main parts

— recent trends in UK health and safety law and its enforcement (this starts at paragraph 2);

— the structure of UK health and safety law (starting at paragraph 15);

— the management of health and safety at work (starting at paragraph 21).

## Recent trends in UK health and safety law

### The role of the European Union

**2.** For the past decade the European Union (EU) has provided the principal motor for changes in UK health and safety legislation. Article 118A in the Treaty of Rome gives health and safety prominence in the objectives of the EU. The Social Charter also contains a declaration on health and safety, although this has no legal force. Whilst the EU can issue its own regulations, it mainly operates through directives requiring Member States to pass their own legislation. The 'Framework Directive' adopted in 1989 contained many broad duties, including the requirement to assess risks and introduce appropriate control measures. Other directives have since been adopted or proposed, including many relating to technical standards and safety requirements for specific products.

### Implementation of EU Directives

**3.** The UK, along with other Member States, must implement EU directives by designated dates. This is normally overseen by the Health and Safety Commission (HSC) which first circulates consultative documents incorporating the proposed regulations together with a related Approved Code of Practice (ACoP) and/or guidance to interested parties (trades unions, employers' organisations, professional bodies, local authorities etc.). Following the consultation process, the HSC submits a final version to the Secretary of State who then lays the regulations before Parliament. It is at this stage that a date for their coming into force is determined – usually that stipulated by the original EU directive.

### The 'six pack' and beyond

**4.** This process peaked on 1 January 1993 when six sets of regulations came into operation on the same day. These were:

- the *Management of Health and Safety at Work Regulations 1992* (since replaced by the *Management of Health and Safety at Work Regulations 1999 (SI 1999 No 3242)*);

- the *Provision and Use of Work Equipment Regulations 1992 (PUWER)* (since replaced by the *Provision and Use of Work Equipment Regulations 1998*) *(SI 1998 No 2306)*;

- the *Workplace (Health, Safety and Welfare) Regulations 1992 (SI 1992 No 3004)*;

- the *Personal Protective Equipment at Work Regulations 1992 (SI 1992 No 2966)*;

- the *Manual Handling Operations Regulations 1992 (SI 1992 No 2793)*; and

- the *Health and Safety (Display Screen Equipment) Regulations 1992 (SI 1992 No 2792)*.

Some of the requirements of these regulations are discussed later in this Introduction and many aspects of them are dealt with elsewhere in this publication.

5.     Although the pace has slackened since, new regulations and changed requirements continue to appear on a regular basis. Two of the original six pack have been replaced in the last two years – *PUWER*, in 1998 and the *Management of Health and Safety at Work Regulations* in 1999. A summary of the more significant changes since the last edition of this chapter is provided at paragraph 14. Application of the requirements of some of the more specific EU directives has resulted in some quite detailed regulations or ACoPs, which runs counter to the original objective-setting approach of the *Health and Safety at Work etc. Act 1974 (HSWA 1974)*. Concerns have been expressed (not least within the UK) in relation to the variable standards of implementation and enforcement within EU Member States. There have been moves recently to address these concerns and also to evaluate the impact of EU directives. Late in1999 the European Commission announced its intention to censure Luxembourg, Sweden and Ireland for failing to comply with health and safety directives.

## Deregulation

6.     The latter stages of the Conservative Government of 1979–1997 saw a drive towards deregulation because of the perceived burden of legislation on business and particularly on small employers. As part of this process the HSC was asked to review health and safety regulations and its report was published in May 1994. However, the scope of its recommendations was limited by the need to comply with EU directives and by the requirement contained in *HSWA 1974, s 1(2)* that any new regulations or orders must maintain or improve health and safety standards.

Consequently the report recommended no major changes; its main effect has been the repeal of some outdated legislation which had limited application anyway because alternative legislation already existed. Also the HSE was to attempt to make its Approved Codes of Practice and Guidance publications more 'user friendly'.

Many people, however – both inside and outside the HSC and HSE – were concerned that political pressure was being brought to bear on the enforcement of health and safety legislation. Criticisms particularly centred around the so-called 'minded to' procedure which required inspectors to advise employers in writing of their intention to issue an improvement notice.

## The Labour Government

7.     The present Labour Government came to power in May 1997 and one of its early actions was to remove the 'minded to' procedure. Responsibility for the HSE passed

to the newly created Department of Environment, Transport and the Regions (DETR) early in 1998 which announced an increase in HSE funding. Early in 2000 the DETR's select committee published a report recommending the creation of a new offence of corporate killing and an increase in the level of fines for health and safety offences. The committee also recommended that the HSE should act to increase the reporting of workplace injuries (studies have demonstrated significant non-compliance with RIDDOR obligations – see paragraph 19) and also to increase the number of reported injuries it investigates.

Public pressure for manslaughter prosecutions following work-related fatalities has been building in recent years. The highly publicised 'corporate manslaughter' prosecution following the *Herald of Free Enterprise* disaster was unsuccessful and manslaughter charges relating to the Southall rail crash were also eventually ruled out by the judge. However, both the company and a director involved in the Lyme Bay canoeing tragedy were convicted of manslaughter charges.

The Home Secretary has responded to this pressure and the DETR committee recommendations by proposing a new Bill including offences of corporate killing, reckless killing and killing by gross carelessness. Penalties would include life prison terms, unlimited fines and company directors being struck off. Consultation on these proposals continues until September 2000.

## Health and Safety Executive

8. In July 1999 the Health and Safety Commission (HSC) published a consultation document *'Revitalising Health and Safety'* and, after a lengthy consultation period, a ten year strategy statement with the same title was launched by the Deputy Prime Minister in June 2000. The statement included targets for reducing incidence rates for fatal and major injury accidents and for work-related ill health by 10% and 20% respectively and also for reducing the proportion of working days lost due to work-related injury and ill health.

The ten point strategy for achieving these reductions included:

— positive engagement of small firms;

— motivation of employers through insurance incentives;

— cultivation of a more deeply engrained culture of self regulation (see paragraph 11);

— more partnerships with workers on health and safety issues;

— government leading by example (including promoting best practice through the supply chain – see paragraph 13);

— improved education on health and safety;

— introduction of a new occupational health strategy.

In the strategy document the Government refers to the significantly increased resources it has made available to the HSC/HSE and increasing numbers of inspections and prosecutions. Whilst the aim is clearly to make progress through education and encouragement, the process is intended to be underpinned by enforcement. Reference is made to the Home Secretary's proposals on corporate killing (see paragraph 7), and also to the Government's intention to increase maximum fines, extend the range of offences which may be subject to custodial sentences and introduce other more innovative penalties. Such penalties might include fines linked to turnover or profit, prohibition of director bonuses, suspension of managers without pay or compulsory health and safety training. As part of this strategy the HSE is introducing measures to 'name and shame' companies and individuals convicted of offences.

The HSE has already been active in introducing initiatives to improve occupational health with asbestos, back problems, hand-arm vibration and occupational stress all receiving significant attention. Another relatively new topic which has received attention from the HSE is work-related violence.

## Other Influences

9.    Both the Government and the HSC/HSE are subject to pressure from public opinion and lobby groups. The spate of rail accidents and incidents, particularly the disasters at Southall and Paddington have done much to fuel this pressure. Trade Unions are also once again being more actively involved in the consultation processes.

Many civil actions for work-related injuries or ill health are supported by Trade Unions and these often bring issues into the public eye. Following the successful action by a social worker against Northumberland County Council, many more claims have been made for work-related stress. The TUC reported 783 cases against employers in 1999 – 70% up on 1998.

Settlements and awards have included £203,000 to the warden of a travellers' site, £67,000 to a council clerical worker and £47,000 to a teacher, whist another council employee received £200,000 following a breakdown alleged to have been caused by management bullying.

## Penalties and prosecutions

10.    As stated earlier, the number of prosecutions being brought by the HSE is increasing and so are the penalties being imposed by the courts. Although the manslaughter charges relating to the Southall rail crash were unsuccessful, Great Western Trains pleaded guilty to a charge under *s 3* of the *HSWA 1974* and were fined £1.5 million (plus £680,000 costs) – a record for a single offence under health and safety legislation.

In September 1994 six people were killed and seven seriously injured when a pedestrian walkway at the port of Ramsgate collapsed. After a twenty-five day trial early in 1997, two Swedish companies which had constructed and designed the walkway were fined £750,000 and £250,000 respectively, Lloyds Register of Shipping (which inspected the walkway) was fined £500,000 and Port Ramsgate, the client, was fined £200,000. With costs added to the total fines of £1.7 million, the bill to the defendants for the criminal proceedings alone came to a total of just under £2.5 million.

The collapse in October 1994 of a rail tunnel being constructed at Heathrow did not result in any injuries but was described in court as one of the 'biggest near misses' in years. When the prosecution came to court in 1999, Balfour Beatty Civil Engineering were fined £700,000 plus £100,000 costs, with the tunnelling sub-contractor, Geoconsult GES MBH, fined £500,000 plus £100,000 costs.

Both of these cases show how responsibilities for health and safety are often shared between companies, with the Ramsgate prosecution illustrating, in particular, the importance of exerting control throughout the 'supply chain'.

Fines in excess of £100,000 for health and safety offences have now become relatively commonplace although both the Government and the HSE believe that some courts continue to impose relatively lenient punishments. Guidelines on appropriate levels of penalties for breaches of health and safety legislation were laid down by the Court of Appeal in *R v F Howe & Son (Engineering) Ltd [1999] 2 AER* and endorsed by the same court in *R v Rollco Screw and Rivet Co. Ltd [1999] IRLR 439.*

The first custodial sentence for a health and safety offence, one of three months, was imposed on Roy Hill by Bristol Crown Court, whilst Paul Evans received a nine-month term of imprisonment from Birmingham Crown Court in September 1998. Both penalties resulted from carrying out work involving asbestos without the necessary licence.

## Self-regulation

11.

The *Health and Safety at Work etc. Act 1974* resulted from the findings of a committee chaired by Lord Alf Robens, who died in 1999. The report of the Robens Committee (which met from 1970 to 1972) recommended that the emphasis of legislation should switch from prescriptive requirements (often relating to specific industries, equipment or processes) to more general obligations. This approach is typified by the all-embracing nature of *HSWA 1974, ss 2 and 3*, albeit qualified by the phrase 'so far as is reasonably practicable'.

It was felt that this would encourage much more 'self-regulation' by employers who would address all of the health and safety risks involved in their activities rather than just dealing with those for which there were specific legal provisions. Whilst this approach has been partially successful, there are always those employers who require an external stimulus to take appropriate action. In a tribute to the first Director General of the HSE, the late John Locke, it was said by the HSE's former Director of Field Operations, Jim Hammer, that 'John knew . . . that legislation without effective inspection is no more than an essay in ethics'.

This theme is further developed as part of the DETR 10 point Strategy Statement which states 'A more deeply engrained culture of self-regulation needs to be cultivated, most crucially in the 3.7 million businesses with less than 250 employees. We must demonstrate and promote the business case for effective health and safety management. We must provide financial incentives which motivate, and change the law to secure penalties which deter. This culture must be further supported through the full integration of health and safety within general management systems'.

## Risk assessments

12.

Much recent UK legislation has included a requirement for some type of risk assessment. The concept was introduced in the early 1980s in regulations applying to asbestos and lead but it came to wider prominence as a core requirement of the *Control of Substances Hazardous to Health Regulations 1988 ('COSHH')*. The 'Six Pack' of regulations which came into force on 1 January 1993 (see 4. above) continued this trend with four sets of regulations requiring an assessment of one kind or another. The most important of these was the general requirement for risk assessment contained in *Reg 3* of the *Management of Health and Safety at Work Regulations 1992* ('the *Management Regulations*'). Other important regulations requiring more specific types of risk assessment relate to noise, manual handling operations, personal protective equipment, display screen equipment and fire precautions.

In practice a less formal type of risk assessment was already required by health and safety legislation – an assessment of the level of risk, the adequacy of existing precautions and the costs of additional precautions was necessary in order to determine what was 'reasonably practicable'. Risk assessment takes the concept of self-regulation somewhat further – employers must be able to demonstrate that they have identified relevant risks together with appropriate precautions and in most cases must have records available to prove this. To make a rather paradoxical statement, this makes enforcement of self-regulation considerably easier.

### Supply-chain pressure

13.  Since the introduction of *HSWA 1974*, many court decisions, most notably those involving Swan Hunter Shipbuilders and Associated Octel, have emphasised that employers often have responsibilities for the activities of employees of other organisations. The structure of *HSWA 1974* and much subsidiary legislation is such that responsibilities overlap between employers rather than being neatly apportioned between them. Employers must do more than simply not turn a blind eye to the obvious health and safety failings of those with whom they come into contact: they must often take a pro-active interest in the health and safety standards of others.

This principle is exemplified by the Ramsgate prosecution (see paragraph 10). Despite having engaged specialists to carry out the design, construction and checking of the passenger walkway, Port Ramsgate was still convicted of an offence. Mr Justice Clark stated that 'the jury has found, in my judgement correctly, that an owner and operator of a port cannot simply sit back and do nothing and rely on others, however expert'.

In recent years a growing number of larger companies, local authorities and other public bodies have had increasingly formalised procedures for checking the health and safety standards of contractors wishing to work for them. This process has been accelerated by the demands of the *Construction (Design and Management) Regulations 1994 (SI 1994 No 3140)* ('*CDM*') which require clients to satisfy themselves (via their planning supervisors) that potential principal contractors are capable of dealing with the health and safety issues associated with projects. The regulations also place responsibilities on principal contractors in respect of sub-contractors. Consequently contractors are frequently required to provide details of their health and safety policies and generic risk assessments together with risk assessments and/or method statements for specific projects or activities. Many clients also take an extremely hands-on approach in policing the work of contractors on their premises. The importance of supply chain pressure is stressed in the DETR Strategy Statement which states 'All public bodies must demonstrate best practice in health and safety management, Public procurement must lead the way on achieving effective action on health and safety considerations and promoting best practice right through the supply chain'.

### Recent changes in legislation

14.  The more significant changes in health and safety legislation since the last edition of this Introduction are summarised below.

- *Ionising Radiations Regulations 1999 (SI 1999 No 3232)*

  The Regulations (which replace the Ionising Radiations Regulations 1985) implement the majority of the *Basic Safety Standards Directive 96/29/Euratom* and also consolidate The requirements of other domestic regulations, including two sets made under the *Factories Act 1961*. The aim of the Regulations and the accompanying Approved Code of Practice (ACoP) is stated as being 'to establish a framework for ensuring that exposure to ionising radiation arising from work activities, whether from man-made or natural radiation and from external radiation (e.g. X ray sets) or internal radiation (e.g. inhalation of a radio-active substance), is kept as low as reasonably practicable and does not exceed dose limits specified for individuals'. The HSE have published a booklet L121 *'Work with ionising radiation'* which incorporates the regulations, ACoP and guidance.

● *Management of Health and Safety at Work Regulations 1999 (SI 1999 No 3242)*

The Regulations consolidate a number of previous amendments to the *Management of Health and Safety at Work Regulations 1992* relating to new or expectant mothers, young persons and fire precautions. The main changes to the original 1992 regulations are:

— specific requirements for risk assessments in relat*ion to fire precautions, young persons and new or expectant mothers (Regs 3, 16* and *19)*;

— certain principles of preventing risks must be applied in precautions adopted by employers (*Reg 4 and Sch 1)*;

— competent health and safety assistance to employers should be provided by employees in preference to outside sources e.g. consultants (*Reg 7)*;

— contacts with external services must be arranged where necessary for first-aid, emergency medical care and rescue work (*Reg 9)*;

— specific provisions relating to new or expectant mothers (*Regs 17* and *18)*.

The HSE have published the Regulations, a new AcoP and guidance in their booklet, L 21 *'Management of Health and Safety at Work'*.

● *Pressure Systems Safety Regulations 2000 (SI 2000 No 128)*

These Regulations replace similar regulations introduced in 1989 which had been subject to a number of amendments. The aim of the regulations is to prevent serious injury from energy stored in pressure systems through the failure of the system or one of its components. The main changes from the 1989 Regulations are that reports of examinations of pressure systems may now be made in electronic form.

● *New 'Health and Safety Law' Poster*

Another change of relevance to all employers is that the HSE have published new versions of the statutory 'Health and Safety Law' poster and the alternative leaflet for distribution to employees. One or other of these must be provided in accordance with the *Health and Safety Information for Employees Regulations 1989 (SI 1989 No 682)*. The new versions (obtainable from HSE Books) should have been in use from 1 July 2000.

Other changes of relevance to a more limited range of workplaces include:

● *Asbestos (Prohibitions)(Amendment) Regulations 1999 (SI 1999 No 2373)*

These Regulations extend the prohibitions affecting the importation and supply of chrysotile (white asbestos) and products to which it has intentionally been added e.g. asbestos cement products and boards, tiles, and panels containing asbestos. They came into force on 24 November 1999, implementing a European Directive five years ahead of its deadline.

- *Chemicals (Hazard Information and Packaging for Supply) (Amendment) (No 2) Regulations 1999 (SI 1999 No 3165)*

  This latest change to the CHIP Regulations introduces a 4th edition of the *'Approved Classification and Labelling Guide'* and a 5th edition of the *'Approved Supply List'* (both obtainable from HSE Books).

- *Mines (Control of Ground Movement) Regulations 1999 (SI 1999 No 2463)*

  The Regulations require mine managers to ensure the assessment, design and implementation of ground control measures appropriate to their mine. HSE booklet L119 *'The control of ground movement in mines'* includes the Regulations, an AcoP and guidance.

- *Quarries Regulations 1999 (SI 1999 No 2024)*

  These Regulations replace twelve previous pieces of legislation. They cover risk control in quarries, use of explosives and safety of excavations and tips. Provisions affecting the duties of employers and people at work in quarries and involvement of the workforce in health and safety are also included.

- *Railway Safety Regulations 1999 (SI 1999 No 2244)*

  These Regulations establish timetables for the introduction of safety improvements on trains. A train protection system which applies the brakes if the train passes signals at danger must be installed by 1 January 2004. 'Mark 1' slam doors on carriages must be modified or replaced.

## The structure of UK health and safety law

15. Health and safety in the workplace involves two different branches of the law – criminal law (dealt with below) and civil law (referred to in paragraph 20).

### Criminal law

16. Criminal law is the process by which society, through the courts, punishes organisations or individuals for breaches of its rules. These rules, known as 'statutory duties', are comprised in Acts passed by Parliament (e.g. *Health and Safety at Work etc. Act 1974*) or regulations which are made by Government Ministers using powers given to them by virtue of Acts (e.g. the *Manual Handling Operations Regulations 1992*).

Cases involving breaches of criminal law may be brought before the courts by the enforcement authorities which, in the case of health and safety law, are the Health and Safety Executive (HSE) and local authorities via their environmental health departments (see ENFORCEMENT). Magistrates' courts hear the vast majority of health and safety prosecutions although more serious cases can be heard by the Crown Courts. The maximum fine which can be imposed by the magistrates' courts is currently £20,000 for breaches of certain sections of *HSWA 1974* and £5,000 for most other offences.

Where cases are heard by the Crown Court there is no limit on the fines which can be imposed. Paragraph 10 details some significant fines resulting from recent cases. There are also a limited number of health and safety offences which can result in prison sentences of up to two years. These include:

— contravention of licensing requirements (e.g. for asbestos removal);

— explosives-related offences;

— contravention of an improvement or prohibition notice;

—    contravention of a court remedy order.

As in all criminal prosecutions the case must be proved 'beyond all reasonable doubt'. There is a right of appeal to the Court of Appeal (Criminal Division) and eventually to the House of Lords or even the European courts, although in practice very few health and safety cases go to appeal. A death involving work activities might result in manslaughter charges which could lead to more severe penalties, although hitherto such cases have been rare. (Paragraphs 7 and 8 refer to recent developments in relation to 'corporate killing' etc. and also to likely extensions to the range of penalties available for health and safety offences.)

## The Health and Safety at Work etc. Act 1974 (HSWA 1974)

17.

*HSWA 1974* is the most important Act of Parliament relating to health and safety. It applies to everyone 'at work' – employers, self-employed and employees (with the exception of domestic servants in private households). It also protects the general public who may be affected by work activities. HSE has published a booklet, '*A guide to the Health and Safety at Work etc. Act 1974*' (ref L1).

Some of the key sections of the Act are listed below.

### Section 2 – Duties of employers

*Section 2(1)* is the catch-all provision: 'It shall be the duty of every employer to ensure, so far as is reasonably practicable, the health, safety and welfare at work of all his employees.' See below for further discussion of the term 'reasonably practicable'.

*Section 2(2)* goes on to detail more specific requirements relating to:

—    the provision and maintenance of plant and systems of work;

—    the use, handling, storage and transport of articles and substances;

—    the provision of information, instruction, training and supervision;

—    places of work and means of access and egress;

—    the working environment, facilities and welfare arrangements.

These are also qualified by the term 'reasonably practicable'.

*Section 2(3)* provides that an employer with five or more employees must prepare a written health and safety policy statement, together with the organisation and arrangements for carrying it out, and bring this to the notice of employees (see paragraph 23).

### Section 3 – Duties to others

*Section 3(1)* provides: 'It shall be the duty of every employer to conduct his undertaking in such a way as to ensure, so far as is reasonably practicable, that persons not in his employment who may be affected thereby are not exposed to risks to their health or safety.'

Employers thus have duties to contractors (and their employees), visitors, customers, members of the emergency services, neighbours, passers-by and the public at large. This may extend to include trespassers, particularly if it is 'reasonably foreseeable' that they could be endangered, for example where high-risk workplaces are left unfenced.

Individuals who are self-employed are placed under a similar duty and must also take care of themselves. (If they have employees, they must comply with *section 2*).

### Section 4 – Duties relating to premises

Under this section persons in total or partial control of work premises (and plant or substances within them) must take 'reasonable' measures to ensure the health and safety of those who are not their employees. These responsibilities might be held by landlords or managing agents etc., even if they have no presence on the premises.

### Section 6 – Duties of manufacturers, suppliers etc.

Those who design, manufacture, import, supply, erect or install any article, plant, machinery, equipment or appliances for use at work, or who manufacture, import or supply any substance for use at work, have duties under this section.

### Section 7 – Duties of employees

> 'It shall be the duty of every employee while at work:
>
> (a)  to take reasonable care for the health and safety of himself and of other persons who may be affected by his acts or omissions at work; and
>
> (b)  as regards any duty or requirement imposed on his employer or any other person by or under any of the relevant statutory provisions, to co-operate with him so far as is necessary to enable that duty or requirement to be complied with.'

Consequently employees must not do, or fail to do, anything which could endanger themselves or others. It should be noted that managers and supervisors also hold these duties as employees.

### Section 8 – Interference and misuse

> 'No person shall intentionally or recklessly interfere with or misuse anything provided in the interests of health, safety or welfare in pursuance of any of the relevant statutory provisions.'

### Section 9 – Duty not to charge

'No employer shall levy or permit to be levied on any employee of his any charge in respect of anything done or provided in pursuance of any specific requirement of the relevant statutory provisions.'

## Levels of duty

Health and safety law contains different levels of duty:

### Absolute

Absolute requirements must be complied with whatever the practicalities of the situation or the economic burden.

### Practicable

The term 'practicable' means that measures must be possible in the light of current knowledge and invention.

*Reasonably practicable*

This term is contained in the main sections of *HSWA 1974* and many important Regulations. It requires the risk to be weighed against the costs necessary to avert it (including time and trouble as well as financial cost). If, compared with the costs involved, the risk is small then the precautions need not be taken – it should be noted that such a comparison should be made before any incident has occurred. The burden of proof, however, rests on the person with the duty (usually the employer) – they must prove why something was not reasonably practicable at a particular point in time. The duty holder's ability to meet the cost is not a factor to be taken into account.

In effect, considering what is 'reasonably practicable' requires that a risk assessment be carried out. The existence of a well-documented and carefully considered risk assessment would go a long way towards supporting a case on what was or was not reasonably practicable. Neither risks nor costs remain the same forever and what is practicable or reasonably practicable will change with time – hence the need to keep risk assessments up to date.

## The 'six pack'

18.

The term 'six pack' is often used to describe the six sets of Regulations which all came into operation on 1 January 1993 to implement EC Directives, two of which have since been replaced. The updated 'six pack' consists of:

*Management of Health and Safety at Work Regulations 1999 (SI 1999 No 3242)*

Employers and the self-employed are required to manage the health and safety aspects of their activities in a systematic and responsible way. The Regulations include requirements for risk assessment, the availability of competent health and safety advice and emergency procedures – several of these management issues are dealt with later in this Introduction (see paragraph 21). Changes introduced by the 1999 Regulations are summarised in paragraph 14.

*Provision and Use of Work Equipment Regulations 1998 (PUWER 1998) (SI 1998 No 2306)*

These Regulations cover equipment safety, including the guarding of machinery. The definition of 'work equipment' also includes hand tools, vehicles, laboratory apparatus, lifting equipment, access equipment etc. The 1998 Regulations introduced additional requirements in respect of mobile work equipment and also replaced previous specific regulations relating to power presses, woodworking machines and abrasive wheels.

*Workplace (Health, Safety and Welfare) Regulations 1992 (SI 1992 No 3004)*

Physical working conditions, safe access for pedestrians and vehicles, and welfare provisions are covered by these Regulations.

*Personal Protective Equipment at Work Regulations 1992 (SI 1992 No 2966)*

Employers must assess the personal protective equipment (PPE) needs created by their work activities, provide the necessary PPE, and take reasonable steps to ensure its use.

*Manual Handling Operations Regulations 1992 (SI 1992 No 2793)*

Manual handling operations involving risk of injury must either be avoided or be assessed by the employer with steps taken to reduce the risk, so far as is reasonably practicable.

*Health and Safety (Display Screen Equipment) Regulations 1992 (SI 1992 No 2792)*

Where there is significant use of display screen equipment (DSE), employers must assess DSE workstations and offer 'users' eye and eyesight tests (which may necessitate provision of spectacles for DSE work).

19.  ## Other important Regulations

*Construction (Design and Management) Regulations 1994 (SI 1994 No 3140)*

The broad definition of 'construction work' used in the Regulations means that they apply to many medium-sized engineering and maintenance projects as well as to traditional construction activities and all demolition work. The Regulations provide for specific duties to be carried out by the 'client' (who must appoint a 'planning supervisor') and by the 'principal contractor' (who may in some cases also be the client). Key requirements of the Regulations are for the development and implementation of a formal 'health and safety plan' and the creation of a 'health and safety file' for the project.

*Control of Substances Hazardous to Health Regulations 1999 (COSHH) (SI 1999 No 437)*

These require an assessment to be made of all substances hazardous to health in order to identify means of preventing or controlling exposure. There are also requirements for the proper use and maintenance of control measures and for workplace monitoring and health surveillance in certain circumstances.

*Electricity at Work Regulations 1989 (SI 1989 No 635)*

These Regulations contain requirements relating to the construction and maintenance of all electrical systems and work activities on or near such systems. They apply to all electrical equipment, from a battery-operated torch to a high-voltage transmission line.

*Health and Safety (Consultation with Employees) Regulations 1996 (SI 1996 No 1513)*

These Regulations extended the previous requirements (contained in the *Safety Representatives and Safety Committees Regulations 1977*) so that employers must now also consult workers not covered by trade union safety representatives.

*Health and Safety (First-Aid) Regulations 1981 (SI 1981 No 917)*

Basic first-aid equipment controlled by an 'appointed person' must be provided for all workplaces. Higher risk activities or larger numbers of employees may require additional equipment and fully trained first-aiders.

*Health and Safety (Safety Signs and Signals) Regulations 1996 (SI 1996 No 341)*

These Regulations require safety signs to be provided, where appropriate, for risks which cannot adequately be controlled by other means. Signs must be of the prescribed design and colours.

*Health and Safety (Training for Employment) Regulations 1990 (SI 1990 No 1380)*

Those receiving 'relevant training' (through training for employment schemes or work experience programmes) are treated as being 'at work' for the purposes of health and safety law. The provider of the 'relevant training' is deemed to be their employer – youth trainees and students on work experience placements therefore have the status of employees and must be protected accordingly.

*Noise at Work Regulations 1989 (SI 1989 No 1790)*

Employers must carry out an assessment to determine the level of exposure to noise of their employees. The precautions required include noise reduction measures, provision of hearing protection and the establishment of hearing protection zones.

*Reporting of Injuries, Diseases and Dangerous Occurrences Regulations 1995 (RIDDOR) (SI 1995 No 3163)*

Fatal accidents, major injuries (as defined) and dangerous occurrences (as defined) must be reported immediately to the enforcing authority. Accidents involving four or more days' absence must be reported in writing within seven days.

*Safety Representatives and Safety Committees Regulations 1977 (SI 1977 No 500)*

Members of recognised trade unions may appoint safety representatives to represent them formally in consultations with their employer in respect of health and safety issues. The functions and rights of safety representatives are detailed in the Regulations. The employer must establish a safety committee if at least two representatives request this in writing.

## Civil law

20. A civil action can be initiated by an employee who has suffered injury or damage to health caused by their work. This may be based upon the law of negligence, i.e. where the employer has been in breach of the duty of care which he owes to the employee. Being part of the common law, the law of negligence has evolved, and continues to evolve, by virtue of decisions in the courts – Parliament has had virtually no role to play in its development.

Civil actions may also be brought on the grounds of breach of statutory duty – it should be noted, however, that *HSWA 1974* and most of the provisions in the *Management of Health and Safety at Work Regulations 1999* do not confer a right of civil action, although the statutory duties owed by employers to employees under *HSWA 1974* have their equivalent obligations at common law.

## Duty of care

Every member of society is under a 'duty of care', i.e. to take reasonable care to avoid acts or omissions which they can reasonably foresee are likely to injure their neighbour (anyone who ought reasonably to have been kept in mind). What is 'reasonable' will depend upon the circumstances.

Employers owe a duty of care not only to employees but also to such people as contractors, visitors, customers, and people on neighbouring property. In the case of the duty of care owed by employers to employees, it includes the duty to provide:

— safe premises;

— a safe system of work;

— safe plant, equipment and tools; and

— safe fellow workers.

Occupiers of premises are under statutory duties comprised in the *Occupiers' Liability Acts* of 1957 and 1984 (see OCCUPIERS' LIABILITY), and those suffering injury because of a defect in a product may sue the producer or importer under the *Consumer Protection Act 1987* (see PRODUCT SAFETY).

## Vicarious liability

Employers are liable to persons injured by the wrongful acts of their employees, if such acts are committed in the course of their employment. Thus if an employee's careless driving of a forklift truck injures another employee (or a contractor or customer), the employer is likely to be liable. There is no vicarious liability if the act is not committed in the course of employment – thus the employer is not likely to be held liable if one employee assaults another.

## Civil procedure

Civil actions must commence within three years from the time of knowledge of the cause of action. In an action for negligence, this will be the date on which the plaintiff knew or should have known that there was a significant injury and that it was caused by the employer's negligence. The plaintiff must be prepared to prove his case in the courts, but in practice most cases are settled out of court following negotiations between the plaintiff's legal representatives and the employer's insurers or their representatives. The *Employers' Liability (Compulsory Insurance) Act 1969* requires employers to be insured against such actions (see EMPLOYERS' LIABILITY INSURANCE), although some public bodies, for example local authorities, are exempt from the provisions of this Act.

As the result of recommendations made by Lord Woolf in his '*Access to Justice*' report of 1996, the *Civil Procedure Rules 1998* introduced widespread changes to civil procedure on 26 April 1999, affecting the progress of civil claims from their commencement to their conclusion. The rules involve a 'pre-action protocol' and govern the conduct of litigation in a way that is intended to limit delay. In most cases a single expert, medical or non-medical, will be instructed rather than each party using separate experts. Even if the case goes to court, the expert's report will usually be in writing, with both parties able to ask written questions of the expert and to see the replies. The new arrangements include a fast track system for personal injury claims up to a value of £15,000.

## *Damages*

Damages are assessed under a number of headings including:

— loss of earnings (prior to trial);

— damage to clothing, property etc.;

— pain and suffering (before and after trial);

— future loss of earnings;

— disfigurement;

— medical or nursing expenses; and

— inability to pursue personal or social interests or activities.

## *Defences*

The plaintiff must prove breach of a statutory duty or of the duty of care on a balance of probabilities. However, a number of defences are available to the employer, including:

● contributory negligence

   The employer may claim that the injured person was careless or reckless – for example, that he ignored clear safety rules or disobeyed instructions. Accidental errors are distinguished from a failure to take reasonable care. Damages will be reduced by the percentage of contributory negligence established, which will vary with the facts of each case.

● injuries not reasonably foreseeable

   The employer may claim that the injuries were beyond normal expectation or control (an act of God). In cases of noise-induced hearing damage, mesothelioma (an asbestos-related cancer) or vibration-induced white finger, the courts have established dates after which a reasonable employer should have been aware of the relevant risks and taken precautions.

● voluntary assumption of risk

   If an employee consents to take risks as part of the job, the employer may escape liability. However, this defence (*volenti non fit injuria*) cannot be used for cases involving breach of statutory duty – no one can contract out of their statutory obligations or be deprived of statutory protection.

## *Other civil actions*

Other health and safety related situations may result in civil actions by employees. Employment protection legislation has recently been strengthened in relation to dismissals or redundancies resulting from health and safety activities (including refusal to work in situations of serious and imminent danger). Suspension or dismissal on maternity or medical grounds may also give a right of action. See EMPLOYMENT PROTECTION.

## Management of health and safety at work

21. The Robens doctrine of self-regulation (see paragraph 11) has been developed considerably in recent years by the HSE as it has paid increasing attention to the way health and safety is managed. Its Accident Prevention Advisory Unit (APAU) worked with a number of large organisations from the late 1970s onwards, steadily building up its expertise. This culminated in the publication by the HSE in 1991 of *'Successful Health and Safety Management'*. A revised edition of the booklet (reference HS(G) 65) was published in 1997.

*'Successful Health and Safety Management'* drew together much of what was already known about management techniques and the principles on which they are based. This included the earlier work of H L Heinrich and Frank Bird in the United States. The introduction to the booklet included the paragraph:

> *'Many of the features of effective health and safety management are indistinguishable from the sound management practices advocated by proponents of quality and business excellence. Indeed, commercially successful companies often also excel at health and safety management, precisely because they bring efficient business expertise to bear on health and safety as on all other aspects of their operations. The general principles of good management are therefore a sound basis for deciding how to bring about improved health and safety performance.'*

However, the then Chief Inspector of Factories, Tony Linehan, stated in his Foreword:

> *'The path described is neither easy nor short. There are no short cuts to successful health and safety management. It cannot be sidelined. It must not be delegated out of sight. The clearest lesson from practical experience is that the starting point is the genuine and thoughtful commitment of top management. I believe firmly that such commitment is beneficial and worthwhile.'*

Since the publication of *'Successful Health and Safety Management'*, several of its principles have found their way into statutory obligations – particularly through the requirements for risk assessments included in a number of Regulations, and in *Reg 5* of the *Management of Health and Safety at Work Regulations 1999* which requires the application of the 'management cycle' to health and safety precautions (see paragraph 24). The requirement for preventive and protective measures to follow certain principles (as introduced by *Reg 4* of the 1999 Regulations) is also compatible with its thinking.

*Managment cycle?*

### The costs of accidents

22. Their own humanitarian attitudes together with social pressures and the possibility of legal sanctions have for many years acted as powerful motivational factors for employers to avoid accidents at work. *'Successful Health and Safety Management'* drew attention to the high costs to employers of failing to manage health and safety effectively. This theme was developed further by the publication by the HSE in 1993 of *'The Costs of Accidents at Work'*.

The APAU carried out five detailed case studies in different industrial sectors in order to determine the full cost of accidents. Employers often believe that most accident costs are covered by insurance but the studies demonstrated the opposite. The ratio between insured and uninsured costs varied from 1:8 to 1:36.

Whilst insurance is likely to cover employer's liability and public liability claims and major damage costs, together with major losses due to business interruption, there are a host of uninsured costs associated with accidents, many of which go unrecorded.

Employee sick pay can usually be quantified but the costs of minor accident repairs are often hidden within much larger maintenance figures, and loss or damage of product due to accidents is seldom separated out from other wastage statistics. Indirect losses due to the unavailability of staff or equipment while both are being 'repaired' are difficult to quantify as are other indirect costs such as the administrative time involved and the possible damage to the employer's image (to staff, customers or the wider public, including investors).

Statistical analysis has shown that for all businesses the number of serious accidents is small in relation to the number of minor accidents and damage incidents – although these latter types may not be fully recorded or investigated. Whilst minor accidents and damage incidents seldom result in insurance claims, their cumulative effects result in significant uninsured costs to the employer. Accidents were found to be costing one of the companies in the APAU study 37 per cent of its annual profits.

A second edition of the study was published in 1997. A separate HSE report '*The costs to Britain of workplace accidents and work-related ill health*', published in 1999, estimates the total losses to society at between £14.5 and £18.1 billion per annum (2.1 to 2.6 % of the GDP).

## Health and safety policies

23.

'*Successful Health and Safety Management*' stated that 'accidents are caused by the absence of adequate management control' and stressed the importance of effective health and safety policies in establishing such control. *Section 2(3)* of the *Health and Safety at Work etc. Act 1974* requires employers to prepare in writing:

- a statement of their general policy with respect to the health and safety at work of their employees; and

- the organisation and arrangements for carrying out the policy.

It also requires the statement to be brought to the notice of all employees – employers with fewer than five employees are exempt from this requirement.

Policies are normally divided into three sections, to meet the three separate demands of *HSWA 1974*:

### (i) The statement of intent

This involves a general statement of good intent, usually linked to a commitment to comply with relevant legislation. Many employers extend their policies so as to relate also to the health and safety of others affected by their activities. In order to demonstrate clearly that there is commitment at a high level, the statement should preferably be signed by the chairman, chief executive or someone in a similar position of seniority.

### (ii) Organisational responsibilities

It is vitally important that the responsibilities for putting the good intentions into practice are clearly identified. In a small organisation this may be relatively simple but larger employers should identify the responsibilities held by those at different levels in the management structure. Whilst reference to employees' responsibilities may be included, it should be emphasised that the law requires the employer's organisation to be detailed in writing. Types of responsibilities to be covered in the policy might include:

— making adequate resources available to implement the policy;

—    setting health and safety objectives;

—    developing suitable procedures and safe systems;

—    delegating specific responsibilities to others;

—    monitoring the effectiveness of others in carrying out their responsibilities;

—    monitoring standards within the workplace; and

—    feeding concerns up through the organisation.

### (iii) Arrangements

The policy need not contain all of the organisation's arrangements relating to health and safety but should contain information as to where they might be found, for example in a separate health and safety manual or within various procedural documents. Topics which may require detailed arrangements to be specified are:

—    operational procedures relating to health and safety;

—    training;

—    personal protective equipment;

—    health and safety inspection programmes;

—    accident and incident investigation arrangements;

—    fire and other emergency procedures;

—    first aid;

—    occupational health;

—    control of contractors and visitors;

—    consultation with employees; and

—    audits of health and safety arrangements.

Employees must be aware of the policy and, in particular, must understand the arrangements which affect them and what their own responsibilities might be. They may be given their own copy (for example, within an employee handbook) or the policy might be displayed around the workplace. With regard to some arrangements detailed briefings may be necessary, for example as part of induction training.

Employers must revise their policies as often 'as may be appropriate'. Larger employers are likely to need to arrange for formal review and, where necessary, for revision to take place on a regular basis (e.g. by way of an ISO 9000 procedure). Dating of the policy document is an important part of this process.

## Application of the 'management cycle'

24.   As stated in paragraph 12, a requirement for a risk assessment has been included in many recent health and safety regulations. Even where there is no explicit require-ment, it is often implicit within the wording of regulations that compliance will involve a risk assessment process. This is frequently stated in the accompanying ACoP or guidance – the *Provision and Use of Work Equipment Regulations 1998*, the *Lifting Operations and Lifting Equipment Regulations 1998* and the *Confined Spaces Regulations 1997* all provide examples of this.

Whilst risk assessment involves the identification of risks and an assessment of their significance, its purpose is to identify the measures necessary to eliminate the risks or to control them to a satisfactory degree. There is, however, little point in going through the process of risk assessment if these precautions are not actually implemented in the workplace. The 'theory' of the risk assessment must become reality in a practical setting.

The importance of this is recognised by the proximity in the *Management of Health and Safety at Work Regulations 1999* (the *Management Regulations*) of *Reg 3* requiring 'risk assessment' and *Reg 5* entitled 'Health and safety arrangements'. *Paragraph (1)* of *Reg 5* states that:

> *'Every employer shall make and give effect to such arrangements as are appropriate, having regard to the nature of his activities and the size of his undertaking for the effective planning, organising, control, monitoring and review of the preventive and protective measures.'*

*Paragraph (2)* of *Reg 5* requires employers with five or more employees to record these arrangements.

Such a 'management cycle' has long been applied to other areas of business activity, such as finance, but relatively few employers have utilised it in relation to health and safety. Managers have often stated their good intentions but have not always set up the organisational structure and control to implement those intentions and have failed to monitor what is actually happening in the workplace.

The cycle can be applied to an employer's overall approach to health and safety:

*Plan* — through the statement of intent within the health and safety policy;

*Organise* — by allocating responsibilities for implementing the policy and making the necessary resources available;

*Control* — through application of relevant management systems and techniques and the use of performance standards;

*Monitor* — through health and safety audits and inspections;

*Review* — in health and safety committee and management meetings.

At a different level the cycle can be applied to management systems or procedures, such as those for carrying out health and safety inspections:

*Plan* — through a statement of intent to conduct regular inspections;

*Organise* — by having a formal procedure relating to inspections – where, who by, how often;

*Control* — by specifying arrangements for reporting on inspections and implementing remedial actions, and by providing training in inspection techniques;

*Monitor* — through checking that inspections are being carried out as scheduled, reviewing the quality of inspection reports and making sure that remedial action is being implemented;

*Review* — by investigating the reasons for any shortcomings in the system (and looping back to the start of the cycle to plan how to correct these).

British Standard 8800 '*Guide to Occupational Health and Safety Management Systems*' and many other commercially available management systems are based upon similar application of the management cycle. However, whether or not employers use such formal systems, the principles of the cycle should always be applied to all aspects of health and safety management. The *Management Regulations* have made this a statutory obligation.

### Sources of health and safety advice

25.

Within '*Successful Health and Safety Management*' the HSE emphasised the importance of establishing a positive health and safety culture within an organisation as a prerequisite of effective health and safety management. It referred to the 'four Cs' as key components in establishing such a culture: control, competence, communication and co-operation.

While competence in health and safety matters is relevant throughout any workforce, it is particularly important at management levels. The *Management Regulations* have taken this concept further by requiring (in *Reg 7*) every employer to appoint one or more competent persons to assist him in complying with the law. The ACoP accompanying the Regulations states that the size and type of resource required will be relative to the size of the organisation and the risks present in its activities. Full-time or part-time specialists may be appointed, or use may be made of external consultants, although the 1999 Management Regulations state a preference for employees. Smaller employers may appoint themselves, provided that they are competent – the ACoP refers to competence as comprising both the possession of theoretical knowledge and the capacity to put it into practice in the work situation. An awareness of the limits of one's own knowledge and capabilities is also important.

Health and safety training is available from many different sources. The following organisations either provide training themselves or oversee training through accredited training centres.

- National Examination Board in Occupational Safety and Health (NEBOSH)

  tel: 0116 288 8858

- Institution of Occupational Safety and Health (IOSH)

  tel: 0116 257 3100

- Chartered Institution of Environmental Health (CIEH)

  tel: 0207 928 6006

- Royal Society for the Prevention of Accidents (RoSPA)

  tel: 0121 248 2000

- British Safety Council (BSC)

  tel: 0208 741 1231

There are many independent consultants who can provide advice and assistance on health and safety matters. Consultants are listed in the Yellow Pages and the Institution of Occupational Safety and Health (see above) maintains a consultants' register. A free HSE leaflet, '*Need help on Health and Safety?*' (IND(G) 322) provides guidance for employers on when and how to get advice on health and safety.

The HSE itself can also be a valuable source of information and advice:

- HSE Books

  tel: 01787 881165

  fax: 01787 313995

  website: www.hse books.co.uk

The HSE has a huge range of priced publications and free leaflets, some of which are referred to elsewhere in this Introduction. '*The Essentials of Health and Safety at Work*' is a useful starting point for the small employer.

- HSE Infoline

  tel: 08701 545500

  Open Monday to Friday 8.30am to 5pm to provide information on workplace health and safety.

- HSE Home Page on the Internet

  http://www.hse.gov.uk

  An online enquiry service can be accessed from the home page.

- '*Escaping the Maze*'

  This video guide, designed to help companies through the maze of health and safety information and its different sources, is available from HSE Videos (tel: 0845 741 9411; fax: 01937 541083). HSE Videos also offer a range of videos on specific health and safety topics.

Of course, within this issue of *Tolley's Health and Safety at Work* you will find it easy to access much valuable information and practical advice, designed to keep you up-to-date with the law and all recent and relevant developments.

# Access, Traffic Routes and Vehicles

## Introduction

A1001    With the regular daily flow of labour to and from the workplace and vehicles making deliveries and collecting items, access and egress points constitute potentially hazardous situations. For this reason there is a duty on employers and factory occupiers to 'provide and maintain' safe access to and egress from a place of work both under statute and at common law. As part and parcel of compliance with the *Building Regulations 1991 (SI 1991 No 2768)*. This includes access facilities for disabled workers and visitors (that is, persons who have difficulty walking or are wheelchair users, or, alternatively, have a hearing problem or impaired vision) (see further W11043 WORKPLACES – HEALTH, SAFETY AND WELFARE), as well as proper precautions to effect entry or exit to or from confined spaces, where a build-up of gas/combustible substances can be a real though not obvious danger (see A1022 below). Statutory requirements consist of general duties under *HSWA*, which apply to all employers, and the more specific duties of the *Workplace (Health, Safety and Welfare) Regulations 1992 (SI 1992 No 3004)*.

The term 'access' is a comprehensive one and refers to just about anything that can reasonably be regarded as means of entrance/exit to a workplace, even if it is not the usual method of access/egress. Unreasonable means of access/egress would not be included, such as a dangerous short-cut, particularly if management has drawn a worker's attention to the danger, though the fact that a worker is a trespasser has not prevented recovery of damages (*Westwood v The Post Office [1973] 3 AER 184*). Access to a fork lift truck qualified, for the purposes of *Sec 29(1)* of the *Factories Act 1961* (repealed as from 1 January 1996), the fork lift truck being a 'place' (*Gunnion v Roche Products Ltd, The Times, 4 November 1994*). The proper procedure is for the employer/factory occupier to designate points of access/egress for workers and see that they are safe, well-lit, maintained and (if necessary) manned and de-iced. Moreover, the statutory duties apply to access/egress points to any place where any employees have to work, and not merely their normal workplace.

This chapter summarises key statutory and common law duties in connection with:

(*a*)    access and egress;

(*b*)    vehicular traffic routes for internal traffic and deliveries;

(*c*)    work vehicles and delivery vehicles – with particular emphasis on potentially hazardous activities involving such vehicles; and

(*d*)    work in confined spaces, of necessity involving access and egress points.

## Statutory duties concerning workplace access and egress – Workplace (Health, Safety and Welfare) Regulations 1992 (SI 1992 No 3004)

A1002    Statutory duties centre around:

(*a*)     the organisation of safe workplace transport systems;

(*b*)     the suitability of traffic routes for vehicles and pedestrians; and

(*c*)     the need to keep vehicles and pedestrians separate.

### Organisation of safe workplace transport systems

A1003     Every workplace must (so far as is reasonably practicable) be so organised that pedestrians and vehicles can circulate in a safe manner. [*Reg 17(1)*].

### Suitability of traffic routes

A1004     Traffic routes in a workplace must be suitable for the persons or vehicles using them, sufficient in number, in suitable positions and of sufficient size. [*Reg 17(2)*].

More particularly:

(*a*)     pedestrians or vehicles must be able to use traffic routes without endangering those at work;

(*b*)     there must be sufficient separation of traffic routes from doors, gates and pedestrian traffic routes, in the case of vehicles;

(*c*)     where vehicles and pedestrians use the same traffic routes, there must be sufficient space between them; and

(*d*)     where necessary, all traffic routes must be suitably indicated.

[*Reg 17(3)(4)*].

Compliance with these statutory duties involves provision of safe access for:

(i)     vehicles, with attention being paid to design and layout of road systems, loading bays and parking spaces for employees and visitors; and

(ii)     pedestrians, so as to avoid their coming into contact with vehicles.

### Traffic routes for vehicles

A1005     There should be sufficient traffic routes to allow vehicles to circulate safely and without difficulty. As for internal traffic, lines marked on roads/access routes in and between buildings should clearly indicate where vehicles are to pass e.g. fork lift trucks. Obstructions, such as limited headroom, are acceptable if clearly indicated. Temporary obstacles should be brought to the attention of drivers by warning signs or hazard cones or, alternatively, access prevented or restricted. Both internal and delivery traffic should be subject to sensible speed limits (e.g. 10 mph), which should be clearly displayed. Speed ramps (sleeping policemen), preceded by a warning sign or mark, are necessary, save for fork lift trucks, on workplace approaches. The traffic route should be wide enough to allow vehicles to pass and repass oncoming or parked traffic, and it may be advisable to introduce one way systems or parking restrictions. Traffic signs on roads, for example speed limit signs, must conform with those on public roads, whether or not the road is subject to the *Road Traffic Regulations Act 1984*.

### *Checklist – safe traffic routes*

A1006     Safe traffic routes should:

(*a*)     provide the safest route possible between places where vehicles have to call or deliver;

(*b*) be wide enough for the safe movement of the largest vehicle, including visiting vehicles (e.g. articulated lorries, ambulances etc.) and should allow vehicles to pass oncoming or parked vehicles safely. One way systems or parking restrictions are desirable;

(*c*) avoid vulnerable areas/items, such as fuel or chemical tanks or pipes, open or unprotected edges, and structures likely to collapse;

(*d*) incorporate safe areas for loading/unloading;

(*e*) avoid sharp or blind bends; if this is not possible, hazards should be indicated (e.g. blind corner);

(*f*) ensure that road/rail crossings are kept to a minimum and are clearly signed;

(*g*) ensure that entrances/gateways are wide enough; if necessary, to accommodate a second vehicle that may have stopped, without causing obstruction;

(*h*) set sensible speed limits, which are clearly signposted. Where necessary, ramps should be used to retard speed, and road humps or bollards to restrict the width of the road. These should be preceded by a warning sign or mark on the road;

(*i*) ensure that fork lift trucks should not have to pass over road humps, unless of a type capable of doing so;

(*j*) give prominent warning of limited headroom, both in advance and at an obstruction. Overhead electric cables or pipes containing flammable/hazardous chemicals should be shielded, i.e. using goal posts, height gauge posts or barriers;

(*k*) ensure that routes on open manoeuvring areas/yards are marked and signposted, and banksmen are employed to supervise the safe movement of vehicles;

(*l*) ensure that people at risk from exhaust fumes or material falling from vehicles are screened or protected; and

(*m*) restrict vehicle access where high-risk substances are stored (e.g. LPG) and where refuelling takes place.

(*n*) consider installation of refuge points (safe havens) where vehicles need to reverse into delivery areas or dead ends, or position barriers to prevent vehicles reversing from colliding into people.

## Traffic routes for pedestrians

*Checklist – safe traffic routes*

A1007  In the case of pedestrians, the main object of the traffic route is to prevent their coming into contact with vehicles. Safe traffic routes should:

(*a*) provide separate routes/pavements for pedestrians, to keep them away from vehicles;

(*b*) where necessary, provide suitable barriers/guard rails at entrances/exits and at the corners of buildings;

(*c*) where traffic routes are used by both pedestrians and vehicles, be wide enough to allow vehicles to pass pedestrians safely;

(*d*) where pedestrian and vehicle routes cross, provide appropriate crossing points. These should be clearly marked and signposted. If necessary, barriers or rails should be provided to prevent pedestrians crossing at dangerous points and to direct them to designated crossing points;

*(e)*   where traffic volume is high, traffic lights, bridges or subways should be used to control movement and ensure a smooth, safe flow;

*(f)*   where crowds use or are likely to use roadways, e.g. at the end of a shift, stop vehicles from using them at such times;

*(g)*   provide separate vehicle and pedestrian doors in premises, with vision panels on all doors;

*(h)*   provide high visibility clothing for people permitted in delivery areas (e.g. bright jackets/overalls);

*(i)*   where the public has access (e.g. at a farm or factory shop), public access points should be as near as possible to shops and separate from work activities.

(See also W11014 WORKPLACES.)

## Vehicles

A1008   Vehicles account for a high percentage of deaths and injuries at work. In 1994, 77 people were killed, including six members of the public; there were 1,363 major injuries and 4,698 workers had to take three or more days off work as a result of vehicle injury. Many of these casualties occur whilst vehicles are reversing, though activities such as loading and unloading, sheeting and unsheeting, as well as cleaning, can similarly lead to injuries, especially where employees are struck by a falling load or a fall from a height on, say, a tanker or HGV. So, too, climbing and descending ladders on tankers during delivery and 'dipping' at petrol forecourts can be hazardous, access onto vehicles and egress being as important as design and construction. Tipping, too, has its dangers, with tipping vehicles, tipping trailers and tankers overturning in considerable numbers. Also, sheeting and unsheeting operations have led to sheeters slipping or losing their grip or falling whilst walking on top of loads or in consequence of ropes breaking; absence of, or inadequate, training being an additional factor in injuries involving work vehicles. This part of the chapter considers the general statutory requirements relating to vehicles at work, precautions in connection with potentially hazardous operations involving vehicles, as well as providing a checklist for vehicle safety. Specific construction and use requirements are not considered.

### General statutory requirements

A1009   Both work and private vehicles come within the parameters of health and safety at work. Regarding work vehicles, employers have the direct responsibilities of provision and maintenance generally under *HSWA s 2*, and, more specifically, under the *Provision and Use of Work Equipment Regulations 1998 (SI 1998 No 2306)* (*PUWER*), vehicles qualifying as 'work equipment'. Regarding private vehicles, employers have much less control – at least, as far as design, construction and use are concerned – but should, nevertheless, endeavour to ensure regulated use via:

*(a)*   restricted routes and access;

*(b)*   provision of clearly signposted parking areas away from hazardous activities and operations; and

*(c)*   enforcement of speed limits.

**Work vehicles**

A1010   Generally, work vehicles should be as safe, stable, efficient and roadworthy as private vehicles on public roads. As work equipment, they are subject to the controls of *PUWER*, which specifies provision, maintenance, access and safety provisions in the event of rolling or falling over, whilst employers must also ensure that drivers are suitably trained in conformity with the requirements of the *Management of Health and Safety at Work Regulations 1999 (SI 1999 No 3242)*.

*Provision*

A1011   All employers must ensure that vehicles:

(*a*)   are constructed and adapted as to be suitable for its purpose;

(*b*)   when selected, caters for risks to the health and safety of persons where the vehicles are to be used; and

(*c*)   are only used for operations specified and under suitable conditions.

[*PUWER, Reg 5*].

Compliance with these requirements on the part of operators of HGVs, fork lift trucks, dump trucks and mobile cranes presupposes conformity with the following checklist, namely:

(i)   a high level of stability;

(ii)   safe means of access and egress to and from the cab;

(iii)   suitable and effective service and parking brakes;

(iv)   windscreens with wipers and external mirrors giving optimum all-round visibility;

(v)   a horn, vehicle lights, reflectors, reversing lights, reversing alarms;

(vi)   suitable painting/markings so as to be conspicuous;

(vii)   provision of a seat and seat belts;

(viii)   guards on dangerous parts (e.g. power take-offs);

(ix)   driver protection to prevent injury from overturning, and from falling objects or materials; and

(x)   driver protection from adverse weather.

*Maintenance*

A1012   All employers must ensure that work equipment (including vehicles) is maintained in an efficient state, in efficient working order and in good repair. [*PUWER, Reg 6*]. This combines the need for basic daily safety checks by the driver before using the vehicle, as well as preventive inspections and services carried out at regular intervals of time and/or mileage, in accordance with manufacturers recommendations. As regards basic daily safety checks, employers should provide drivers with a log book in which to record visual inspections undertaken and the findings of the following:

–   brakes, tyres, steering, mirrors, windscreen washers and wipers, warning signals and specific safety systems (e.g. control interlocks)

Employers should see that drivers carry out the checks.

*Training of drivers*

A1013   All employers must:

(*a*)   in entrusting tasks to employees, take into account their capabilities as regards health and safety; and

(*b*)   ensure that employees are provided with adequate health and safety training on recruitment and exposure to new or increased risks.

[*Management of Health and Safety at Work Regulations 1999*].

In order to conform with these requirements, employers should ensure that, for general purposes, drivers of work vehicles are over 17 and have passed their driving test or, in the case of drivers of HGVs, that they are over 21 and have passed the HGV test. Moreover, to ensure continued competence, or to accommodate new risks at work or a changing work environment, employers should provide safety updates on an on-going basis as well as refresher training, and require approved drivers to report any conviction for a driving offence, whether or not involving a company vehicle. One method for ensuring this is to require all drivers to submit their licence annually so that a copy can be held in their personnel file.

*Contractors and subcontractors*

A1014   Similar assurances (see A1013 above) should be obtained from drivers of contractors and subcontractors visiting an employer's workplace. If they are not forthcoming, permission to work on site or in-house should be refused until either the contractor's vehicles comply with statutory requirement and/or his drivers are adequately trained. Training of contractor's drivers would normally be undertaken by contractors themselves, though site or in-house hazards, routes to be used etc. should be communicated to contractors by employers or occupiers. Contractors should be left in no doubt of the penalties involved for failure to conform with safe working practices – a useful way of ensuring enforcement on the part of contractors and subcontractors is to issue a licence.

*Access to vehicles*

A1015   In addition to *Regulation 5* of *PUWER* (see A1011 above), employers (and others having control, to any extent, of workplaces (see OCCUPIERS' LIABILITY)), who operate/use vehicles, are subject to:

(*a*)   the fall prevention requirements of *Regulation 13* of the *Workplace (Health, Safety and Welfare) Regulations 1992* (see W9003 WORK AT HEIGHTS). As far as possible, compliance with this regulation would obviate the need for climbing on top of vehicles (by bottom-filling) and also require vehicle operators to ensure that loads are evenly distributed, packaged properly and secured in the interests of drivers going down slopes and up steep hills (see further A1018 below).

(*b*)   the co-operation requirements of *Regulation 9* of the *Management of Health and Safety at Work Regulations 1999*, specifying that where activities of different employers interact, different employers may need to co-operate with each other and co-ordinate preventive and protective measures. This regulation is particularly relevant for example, to tanker deliveries and 'dipping' at petrol forecourts as well as loading and/or unloading operations. For 'dipping' purposes or gaining top access to tankers, access should be by a ladder at the front or rear, such ladders being properly constructed, maintained and securely fixed; ideally, they should incline inwards towards the top.

There should be a means of preventing people from falling whilst on top of the tanker. Failing this, employers of tanker drivers and forecourt owners should liaise on potential risks involved in tanker deliveries, e.g. the provision of suitable step-ladders on the part of the latter. As for carriage of goods and loading/unloading operations, consignors should ensure that goods are evenly distributed, properly packaged and secured.

## Potentially hazardous operations

A1016    The following activities and operations are potentially hazardous in connection with vehicles.

### Reversing

A1017    Approximately a quarter of all deaths at work are caused by reversing vehicles; in addition, negligent reversing can result in costly damage to premises, plant and goods. Where possible, workplace design should aspire to obviate the need for reversing by the incorporation of one-way traffic systems. Failing this, reversing areas should be clearly identified and marked, and non-essential personnel excluded from the area. Ideally, banksmen wearing high-visibility clothing should be in attendance to guide drivers through, and keep non-essential personnel and pedestrians away from, the reversing area. Refuge points, also known as safe havens, should be constructed where possible to enable an escape route or safe place for people to stay in the event of a vehicle reversing in an unsafe manner. Vehicles should be fitted with external side-mounted and rear-view mirrors – as, indeed, many now are. Closed-circuit television systems are also advisable for enabling drivers to see round 'blind spots' and corners.

### Loading and unloading

A1018    Because employees can be seriously injured by falling loads or overturning vehicles, loading/unloading should not be carried out:

(*a*)    near passing traffic, pedestrians and other employees;

(*b*)    where there is a possibility of contact with overhead electric cables;

(*c*)    on steep gradients;

(*d*)    unless the load is spread evenly (racking will assist load stability);

(*e*)    unless the vehicle has its brakes applied or is stabilised (similarly with trailers); or

(*f*)    with the driver in the cab.

(See also OFFICES AND SHOPS.)

### Tipping

A1019    Overturning of lorries and trailers is the main hazard associated with tipping. In order to minimise the potential for injuries, tipping operations should only occur:

(*a*)    after drivers have consulted with site operators and checked that loads are evenly distributed;

(*b*)    when non-essential personnel are not present;

(*c*)    on level and stable ground away from power lines and pipework; and (*d*)     with the driver in the cab and the cab door closed.

Moreover, after discharge, drivers should ensure that the body of the vehicle is completely empty and should not drive the vehicle in an endeavour to free a stuck load.

### Giving unauthorised lifts

A1020     Giving unauthorised lifts in work vehicles is both a criminal offence and can lead to employers being involved in civil liability. Thus, 'every employer shall ensure that work equipment is used only for operations for which, and under conditions for which, it is suitable'. [*PUWER, Reg 5*].

Where a driver of a work vehicle gives employees and/or others unauthorised lifts, his employer could find himself prosecuted for breach of the above regulation, whilst the driver himself may be similarly prosecuted for breach of *Sec 7* of *HSWA*, as endangering co-employees and members of the public. In addition, although acting in an unauthorised manner and contrary to instructions, the employee may well involve his employer in vicarious liability for any subsequent injury to a co-employee and/or member of the public (see further *Rose v Plenty* at E11004 EMPLOYERS' DUTIES TO THEIR EMPLOYEES).

Where instructions to employees not to give unauthorised lifts are clearly displayed in a work vehicle, but an employee nevertheless gives an unauthorised lift and a co-employee or member of the public is injured or killed as a result of the employee's negligent driving, it can be argued that the employee has exceeded the scope of his employment and so the employer is absolved from liability. (In *Twine v Bean's Express [1946] 1 AER 202* a driver gave a lift to a third party who was killed in consequence of his negligent driving. There was a notice in the van prohibiting drivers from giving lifts. It was held that the employer was not liable, as the driver was acting outside the parameters of his employment when giving a lift. The injured passenger knew that the driver should not give lifts.)

Conversely, courts have taken the view that such conduct, on the part of drivers, does not circumscribe the scope of employment but rather constitutes performance of work in an unauthorised manner, so leaving the employer liable as the employee is doing what he is employed to do but doing it wrongly (see further *Rose v Plenty and Century Insurance Co v Northern Ireland Road Transport Board* at E11004 EMPLOYERS' DUTIES TO THEIR EMPLOYEES). Yet again, if the passenger, having seen the prohibition on unauthorised lifts in the vehicle, nevertheless accepted a lift and was injured, arguably, if an adult rather than a minor, he has agreed to run the risk of negligent injury and so will forfeit the right to compensation.

## Common law duty of care

A1021     At common law every employer owes all his employees a duty to provide and maintain safe means of access to and egress from places of work. Moreover, this duty extends to the workforce of another employer/contractor who happens to be working temporarily on the premises. Hence the common law duty covers all workplaces, out of doors as well as indoors, above ground or below, and extends to factories, mines, schools, universities, aircraft, ships, buses and even fire engines and appliances (*Cox v Angus [1981] ICR 683*, where a fireman injured in a cab was entitled to damages at common law).

## Confined spaces

A1022 Accidents and fatalities such as drowning, poisoning by fumes or gassing, have happened as a result of working in confined spaces. See, for instance, the case of *Baker v T E Hopkins & Son Ltd [1959] 3 AER 225* where a doctor was overcome by carbon monoxide fumes while going to rescue two workmen down a well – the defence of *volenti non fit injuria* failed). Normal safe practice is a formalised permit to work system or checklist tailored to a particular task and requiring appropriate and sufficient personal protective equipment. Hazards typical of this sort of operation are:

(*a*) atmospheric hazards – oxygen deficiency, enrichment (see *R v Swan Hunter Shipbuilders Ltd* at C8060 CONSTRUCTION AND BUILDING OPERATIONS), toxic gases (e.g. carbon monoxide), explosive atmospheres (e.g. methane in sewers);

(*b*) physical hazards – low entry headroom or low working headroom, protruding pipes, wet surfaces underfoot as well as any electrical or mechanical hazards;

(*c*) chemical hazards – concentration of toxic gas can quickly build up, where there is a combination of chemical cleaning substances and restricted air flow or movement.

In order to combat this variety of hazards peculiar to work in confined spaces, use of both gas detection equipment and suitable personal protective equipment are a prerequisite, since entry/exit paths are necessarily restricted.

Prior to entry, gas checks should test for (*a*) oxygen deficiency/enrichment, then (*b*) combustible gas and (*c*) toxic gas, by detection equipment being lowered into the space. This will determine the nature of personal protective equipment necessary. If gas is present in any quantity, the offending space should then be either naturally or mechanically ventilated. Where gas is present, entry should only take place in emergencies, subject to the correct respiratory protective equipment being worn. Assuming gas checks establish that there is no gaseous atmosphere, entry can then be made without use of respiratory equipment. Gas detection equipment should continue to be used whilst people are in the confined space so that any atmospheric change can subsequently be registered on the gas detection equipment. It is essential that an emergency plan is devised when gaining access to confined spaces, which includes effective two way communication between people inside and immediately outside the confined space, contact with emergency services and first aid, and fire prevention personnel on hand.

### Statutory requirements

A1023 It should be noted that the *Confined Spaces Regulations 1997 (SI 1997 No 1713)* came into force on 28 January 1998. These repeal *Factories Act 1961, s 30*, and impose requirements and prohibitions with respect to the health and safety of persons carrying out work in confined spaces.

A 'confined space' is defined in *reg 1(2)* as 'any place, including any chamber, tank, vat, silo, pit, trench, pipe, sewer, flue, well or other similar space in which, by virtue of its enclosed nature, there arises a reasonably foreseeable specified risk'.

A 'specified risk' means a risk of:

(*a*) serious injury to any person at work arising from a fire or explosion;

(*b*) without prejudice to paragraph (*a*) –

(i)    the loss of consciousness of any person at work arising from an increase in body temperature;

(ii)    the loss of consciousness or asphyxiation of any person at work arising from gas, fume, vapour or the lack of oxygen;

(c)    the drowning of any person at work arising from an increase in the level of a liquid; or

(d)    the asphyxiation of any person at work arising from a free flowing solid or the inability to reach a respirable environment due to entrapment by a free flowing solid.

*Regulation 4* prohibits a person from entering a confined space to carry out work for any purpose where it is reasonably practicable to carry out the work by other means.

If, however, a person is required to work in a confined space, a risk assessment must be undertaken to comply with the requirements of the *Management of Health and Safety at Work Regulations 1999, Reg 3.* The risk assessment must be undertaken by a competent person and the outcome of the risk assessment process will then provide the basis for the development of a safe system of work (*Confined Spaces Regulations 1997, Reg 3*).

The risk assessment process should make use of all available information such as engineering drawings, working plans, soil or geological information and take into consideration factors such as the general condition of the confined space, work to be undertaken in the space to minimise hazards produced in the area, need for isolation of the space and the requirements for emergency rescue. In particular, information should be collected and assessed on the previous contents of the confined space, residues that still may be present, contamination that may arise from adjacent plant, processes, gas mains, surrounding soil, land or strata; oxygen level and physical dimensions of the space that may limit safe access and/or egress. The work to be undertaken should be assessed to determine if additional risks will be produced as a result of this work and systems developed to control these risks. All information collected should be recorded and a safe system of work developed for safe entry.

The main elements to consider when designing a safe system of work include the following:

(a)    supervision,

(b)    competence levels for personnel working in confined spaces,

(c)    communications,

(d)    testing/monitoring the atmosphere,

(e)    gas purging,

(f)    ventilation,

(g)    removal of residues,

(h)    isolation from gases, liquids and other flowing materials,

(j)    isolation from mechanical and electrical equipment,

(k)    selection and use of suitable equipment,

(l)    personal protective equipment (PPE) and respiratory protective equipment (RPE),

(m)    portable gas cylinders and internal combustion engines,

(n)    gas supplied by pipes and hoses,

(*o*)   access and egress,

(*p*)   fire prevention,

(*q*)   lighting,

(*r*)   static electricity,

(*s*)   smoking,

(*t*)   emergencies and rescue,

(*u*)   limited working time.

[*Confined Spaces Regulations 1997, Reg 4*].

*Regulation 6* provides for circumstances allowing the Health and Safety Executive to grant exemption certificates.

# Accident Reporting

## Introduction

A3001 Employers (both onshore and offshore [*Reporting of Injuries, Diseases and Dangerous Occurrences Regulations 1995* (*RIDDOR*) *(SI 1995 No 3163)*, *Reg 12*]) and other 'responsible persons' (see A3003 below) who have control over employees and work premises are required to notify and report to the relevant enforcing authority (see A3004 below) the following specified events occurring at work:

(*a*) accidents causing injuries, fatal and non-fatal, including:

   (i) acts of non-consensual physical violence committed at work, and

   (ii) acts of suicide occurring on, or in the course of, the operation of a railway, tramway, trolley or guided transport system

   [*RIDDOR (SI 1995 No 3163), Reg 2(1)*];

(*b*) occupational diseases; and

(*c*) dangerous occurrences, even where no injury results.

The duty to report applies not only in the case of incidents involving employees, but also to visitors, customers and members of the public killed or injured by work activities [*RIDDOR (SI 1995 No 3163), Reg 3(1)*].

Employees also have certain obligations to report accidents to their employers.

## Reporting of Injuries, Diseases and Dangerous Occurrences Regulations 1995 (RIDDOR) – (SI 1995 No 3163)

A3002 The *Reporting of Injuries, Diseases and Dangerous Occurrences Regulations 1995* cover:

(*a*) reportable work injuries (see A3007 below);

(*b*) reportable occupational diseases (see Appendix B at A3030 below) – now 47 in all;

(*c*) reportable dangerous occurrences (see A3009 and Appendix A at A3029 below) – now 83 in all;

(*d*) road accidents involving work (see A3019 below); and

(*e*) gas incidents (see A3020 below).

Records must be kept by employers and other 'responsible persons' (see A3005) of such injuries, diseases and dangerous occurrences for a minimum of three years from the date they were made. In addition, employers must also keep an Accident Book (Form BI 510).

Two reporting routes now exist:

- Injuries and dangerous occurrences are reportable to the relevant enforcing authority on Form F2508 and diseases on Form F2508A (see A3012 and Appendices C and D at A3031, A3032 below); or

- Reports can be made by telephone or electronically to the national Incident Contact Centre (ICC) (see A3004).

As for notification of major accident hazards (see C10009 CONTROL OF MAJOR ACCIDENT HAZARDS), notification and reporting under RIDDOR is sufficient for the purposes of the *Control of Industrial Major Accident Hazards Regulations 1984 (CIMAH) (SI 1984 No 1902)*.

## Relevant enforcing authority

A3003    Health and safety law is separately enforced either by the Health and Safety Executive (HSE), or by local authorities, through their environmental health departments, depending on the nature of the business activity in question. Under *RIDDOR*, notifications and reports should be directed to the authority responsible for the premises where the reportable event occurs (or in connection with which the work causing the event is being carried out). Details of HSE offices are listed in Appendix E to this chapter.

## Incident Reporting Centre

A3004    For all incidents occurring after 1 April 2001, employers and others who are subject to the reporting requirements, can comply with their obligations by contacting the Incident Contact Centre (ICC). This will eliminate the need to identify the local agency or other local enforcing authority. The ICC will then pass the report on to them. Reporting to the local HSE office or local enforcement authority by phone and on the current statutory forms is still an option and this information will be forwarded to the ICC.

Incidents may be reported to the ICC through the following channels:

- By telephone: Telephone 0845 300 9923 (Monday to Friday, 8.30 a.m. to 5.30 p.m.)

- By facsimile: Fax 0845 300 9923

- By email: riddor@gov.uk

- By internet: www.riddor.gov.uk

- By post: Incident Contact Centre, Caerphilly Business Park, Caerphilly CF83 3GG

In taking advantage of these arrangements, the employer or other reporting person will not have a record of a statutory RIDDOR form, so the ICC will send out confirmation copies of reports which should be checked for accuracy and retained.

## Persons responsible for notification and reporting

A3005    The person generally responsible for reporting injury-causing accidents, deaths or diseases is the employer. Failing that, the person having control of the work premises or activity will be the responsible person. [*RIDDOR (SI 1995 No 3163), Reg 2(1)*]. In certain cases these normal rules are displaced and there are specifically designated 'responsible persons', e.g. in the case of mines, quarries, offshore installations, vehicles, diving operations and pipelines (see Table 1 below).

## Table 1

## Persons generally responsible for reporting accidents

| | | |
|---|---|---|
| Death, major injury, over-3-day injury or specified occupational disease: | of an employee at work | that person's employer |
| | of a person receiving training for employment | the person whose undertaking makes immediate provision of the training |
| | of a self-employed person at work in premises under the control of someone else | the person for the time being having control of the premises in connection with the carrying on by him of any trade, business or undertaking |
| Specified major injury or condition, or over-3-day injury: | of a self-employed person at work in premises under his control | the self-employed person or someone acting on his behalf |
| Death, or specified major injury or condition: | of a person who is not himself at work (but is affected by the work of someone else), e.g. a member of the public, a shop customer, a resident of a nursing home | the person for the time being having control of the premises in connection with the carrying on by him of any trade, business or undertaking at which, or in connection with the work at which, the accident causing the injury happened |

[*Reg 2(1)(b)*].

## Persons responsible for reporting accidents in specific locations

| | |
|---|---|
| A mine | the mine manager |
| A quarry | the quarry owner |
| A closed tip | the owner of the mine or quarry with which the tip is associated |
| An offshore installation (except in the case of reportable diseases) | the duty holder |
| A dangerous occurrence at a pipeline | the owner of the pipeline |
| A dangerous occurrence at a well | the appointed person or, failing that, the concession owner |

| | |
|---|---|
| A diving operation (except in the case of reportable diseases) | the diving contractor |
| A vehicle | the vehicle operator |
| [*Reg 2(1)(a)*]. | |

In situations where the responsible person is difficult to identify because of the shared control of a site or operations, arrangements should be made to determine who will deal with *RIDDOR* reporting in line with the duty to co-operate and co-ordinate under the *Management of Health and Safety at Work Regulations 1999 (SI 1999 No 3242), Reg 11*.

## What is covered?

A3006    Covered by these Regulations are events involving:

(*a*)    employees;

(*b*)    self-employed persons;

(*c*)    trainees (see E11017 EMPLOYERS' DUTIES TO THEIR EMPLOYEES);

(*d*)    any person, not an employee or trainee, on premises under the control of another, or who was otherwise involved in an accident (e.g. a visitor, customer, passenger or bystander) (see A3004 above).

## Major injuries or conditions

A3007    Where any person dies or suffers a major injury as a result of, or in connection with, work, such an incident must be notified immediately and details formally reported. The person who dies or suffers injury need not be at work; it is enough if the death or injury arose from a work activity. For example, reporting requirements would apply to a shopper who fell and was injured on an escalator, so long as the injury was connected with the escalator (*Woking Borough Council v British Home Stores [1995] 93 LGR 396*); a member of the public overcome by fumes on a visit to a factory and who lost consciousness; a patient in a nursing home who fell over an electrical cable lying across the floor and was injured; or a pupil or student killed or injured in the course of his curricular work which was supervised by a lecturer or teacher.

Reportable major injuries and conditions are as follows:

(*a*)    any fracture (other than to fingers, thumb or toes);

(*b*)    any amputation;

(*c*)    dislocation of shoulder, hip, knee or spine;

(*d*)    loss of sight (whether temporary or permanent);

(*e*)    a chemical or hot metal burn to the eye or any penetrating eye injury;

(*f*)    any injury resulting from an electrical shock or electrical burn (including one caused by arcing or arcing products) leading to unconsciousness or requiring resuscitation or admittance to hospital for more than 24 hours;

(*g*)    any other injury

   (i)    leading to hypothermia, heat-induced illness or unconsciousness,

   (ii)    requiring resuscitation, or

(iii)   requiring admittance to hospital for more than 24 hours;

(*h*)   loss of consciousness caused by asphyxia or by exposure to a harmful substance or biological agent;

(*j*)   either

(i)   acute illness requiring medical treatment, or

(ii)   loss of consciousness

resulting from the absorption of any substance by inhalation, ingestion or through the skin;

(*k*)   acute illness requiring medical treatment where there is reason to believe that this resulted from exposure to a biological agent or its toxins or infected material.

[*RIDDOR (SI 1995 No 3163), Reg 2(1), Sch 1*].

## Injuries incapacitating for more than three consecutive days

A3008   Where a person at work is incapacitated for more than three consecutive days from their normal contractual work (excluding the day of the accident but including any days which would not have been working days) owing to an injury resulting from an accident at work (other than an injury reportable as a major injury listed in A3007 above), a report of the accident must be made direct to the ICC or sent in writing on Form F2508 to the enforcing authority as soon as is practicable and in any event within ten days of the accident. [*RIDDOR (SI 1995 No 3163), Reg 3(2)*].

## Specified dangerous occurrences

A3009   83 types of reportable dangerous occurrences are specified in *RIDDOR (SI 1995 No 3163), Sch 2*, ranging from general dangerous occurrences (e.g. the collapse of a building or structure, the explosion of a pressure vessel, and accidental releases of significant quantities of dangerous substances) to more specific dangerous occurrences in mines, quarries, transport systems and offshore installations (see Appendix A at A3028 below).

## Specified diseases

A3010   Where a worker suffers from an occupational disease related to a particular activity or process (as specified in *Schedule 3*), a report must be sent to the enforcing authority. [*RIDDOR (SI 1995 No 3163), Reg 5(1)*].

This duty arises only when an employer has received information in writing from a registered medical practitioner diagnosing one of the reportable diseases. (In the case of the self-employed, the duty is triggered regardless of whether or not the information is given to him in writing.) Many of these diseases are those for which disablement benefit is ordinarily prescribed (see O1043 OCCUPATIONAL HEALTH AND DISEASES). (In respect of offshore workers, such diseases tend to be communicable.)

Moreover, the *Industrial Diseases (Notification) Act 1981* and the *Registration of Births and Deaths Regulations 1987 (SI 1987 No 2088)* require that particulars are to be included on the death certificate as to whether death might have been due to, or contributed to by, the deceased's employment. Such particulars are to be supplied by the doctor who attended the deceased during the last illness. (The full list of specified diseases is contained in Appendix B at A3030 below.)

## Duty to notify/report

### Duty to notify

A3011    'Responsible persons' must notify enforcing authorities (see A3003 and A3004 above) by the quickest means practicable (normally by telephone) of the following:

(*a*)    death as a result of an accident arising out of, or in connection with, work;

(*b*)    'major injury' (see A3007 above) of a person at work as a result of an accident arising out of, or in connection with, work;

(*c*)    injury suffered by a person not at work (e.g. a visitor, customer, client, passenger or bystander) as a result of an accident arising out of, or in connection with, work, where that person is taken from the accident site to a hospital for treatment;

(*d*)    major injury suffered by a person not at work, as a result of an accident arising out of, or in connection with, work at a hospital;

(*e*)    a dangerous occurrence (see A3009 above)

[*RIDDOR (SI 1995 No 3163), Reg 3(1)*];

(*f*)    road injuries or deaths [*RIDDOR (SI 1995 No 3163), Reg 10(2)*] (see A3019 below); and

(*g*)    gas incidents [*RIDDOR (SI 1995 No 3163), Reg 6(1)*] (see A3020 below).

### Duty to report

A3012    Responsible persons must also formally report events causing death or major injury, dangerous occurrences and details associated with workers' occupational diseases. In cases of death, major injury and accidents leading to hospitalisation, the duty to report extends to visitors, bystanders and other non-employees. More particularly, within ten days of the incident, responsible persons must send a written report form to the relevant enforcing authority in relation to:

(*a*)    all events which require notification (listed in (*a*) to (*g*) at A3011 above);

(*b*)    the death of an employee if it occurs within a year following a reportable injury (whether or not reported under (*a*)) [*RIDDOR (SI 1995 No 3163), Reg 4*] (see A3018 below);

(*c*)    incapacitation for work of a person at work for more than three consecutive days as a result of an injury caused by an accident at work [*RIDDOR (SI 1995 No 3163), Reg 3(2)*] (see A3008 above);

(*d*)    specified occupational diseases relating to persons at work (see A3009 ABOVE and Appendix B Part I at A3029 below), and also specifically those suffered by workers on offshore installations (see Appendix B Part II at A3029 below) [*RIDDOR (SI 1995 No 3163), Reg 5(1)*], provided that, in both cases,

   (i)    the responsible person has received a written statement by a doctor diagnosing the specified disease, in the case of an employee, or

   (ii)    a self-employed person has been informed by a doctor that he is suffering from a specified disease.

[*RIDDOR (SI 1995 No 3163), Reg 5(2)*].

### Exceptions to notification and reporting

A3013    There is no requirement to notify or report the injury or death of:

(*a*)    a patient undergoing treatment in a hospital or a doctor's or dentist's surgery [*RIDDOR (SI 1995 No 3163), Reg 10(1)*]; or

(*b*)    a member of the armed forces of the Crown [*RIDDOR (SI 1995 No 3163), Reg 10(3)*].

## Duty to keep records

A3014    Records of injury-causing accidents, dangerous occurrences and specified diseases must be kept by responsible persons for at least three years. [*RIDDOR (SI 1995 No 3163), Reg 7*].

### Injuries and dangerous occurrences

A3015    In the case of injuries and dangerous occurrences, such records must contain:

(*a*)    date and time of the accident or dangerous occurrence;

(*b*)    if an accident is suffered by a person at work –

(i)    full name,

(ii)    occupation, and

(iii)    nature of the injury;

(*c*)    in the event of an accident suffered by a person not at work –

(i)    full name,

(ii)    status (e.g. passenger, customer, visitor or bystander), and

(iii)    nature of injury;

(*d*)    place where the accident or dangerous occurrence happened;

(*e*)    a brief description of the circumstances;

(*f*)    the date that the event was first reported to the enforcing authority;

(*g*)    the method by which the event was reported.

[*RIDDOR (SI 1995 No 3163), Sch 4, Part I*].

### Disease

A3016    In the case of specified diseases, such records must contain:

(*a*)    date of diagnosis;

(*b*)    name of the person affected;

(*c*)    occupation of the person affected;

(*d*)    name or nature of the disease;

(*e*)    the date on which the disease was first reported to the enforcing authority; and

(*f*)    the method by which disease was reported.

[*RIDDOR (SI 1995 No 3163), Sch 4, Part II*].

**Action to be taken by employers and others when accidents occur at work**

A3017    *fig. 1*

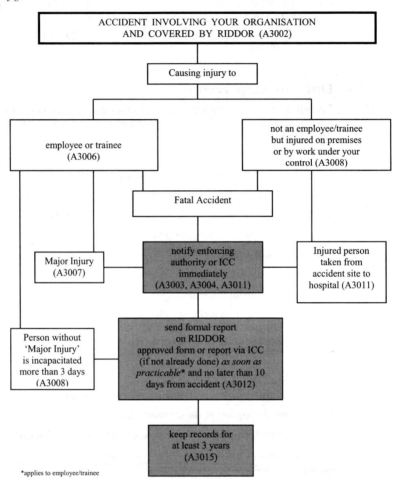

*applies to employee/trainee

# Reporting the death of an employee

A3018    Where an employee, as a result of an accident at work, has suffered a reportable injury/condition which is the cause of his death within one year of the date of the accident, the employer must inform the enforcing authority in writing of the death as soon as it comes to his attention, whether or not the accident has been reported under *Regulation 3*. [*RIDDOR (SI 1995 No 3163), Reg 4*].

# Road accidents

A3019    Road accident deaths and injuries are notifiable and reportable if the death or major injury is caused by or connected with:

(*a*)    exposure to any substance conveyed by road;

(*b*)    loading or unloading vehicles;

(c)    construction, demolition, alteration or maintenance activities on public roads; or

(d)    an accident involving a train.

[*RIDDOR (SI 1995 No 3163), Reg 10(2)*].

The person injured, whether fatally or not, may or may not be engaged in the above-mentioned activities. Thus, an employee struck by a passing vehicle or a motorist injured by falling scaffolding, are covered. In addition, certain dangerous occurrences on public highways and private roads are covered (see Appendix A at A3029 below).

## Duty to report gas incidents

### Gas suppliers

A3020    Where:

(a)    a conveyor of flammable gas through a fixed pipe distribution system, or

(b)    a filler, importer or supplier (not by way of the retail trade) of a refillable container containing liquefied petroleum gas

receives notification of any death, injury or condition (see A3012 above) which has arisen out of, or in connection with, the gas supplied, filled or imported, he must immediately notify the HSE and then send a report of the incident within 14 days. [*RIDDOR (SI 1995 No 3163), Reg 6(1)*].

### Gas fitters

A3021    Where an employer or self-employed person who is an approved gas fitter has information that a gas fitting, flue or ventilation is, or is likely to cause, death or major injury, he is required to report that fact to the HSE on a prescribed form within 14 days. [*RIDDOR (SI 1995 No 3163), Reg 6(2)*].

## Penalties

A3022    Contravention of any of the provisions of *RIDDOR* is an offence. The maximum penalty on summary conviction is a fine of £5,000. Conviction on indictment in the Crown Court carries an unlimited fine.

### Defence in proceedings for breach of Regulations

A3023    It is a defence under the Regulations for a person to prove that:

(a)    he was not aware of the event requiring him to notify or send a report to the enforcing authority; and

(b)    he had taken all reasonable steps to have all such events brought to his notice.

[*RIDDOR (SI 1995 No 3163), Reg 11*].

## Obligations on employees

A3024    There are reporting requirements on employees by the *Social Security (Claims and Payments) Regulations 1979 (SI 1979 No 628)*. Although not actually bound in with the separate scheme of health and safety legislation, these reporting requirements complement those which employers have under *RIDDOR*, and there is an overlap in the record keeping requirements for both sets of provisions – see further below.

An accident to which the employees' reporting requirements apply is one 'in respect of which benefit may be payable . . .'. [*Social Security (Claims and Payments) Regulations 1979 (SI 1979 No 628), Reg 24(1)*]. Under *Regulation 24*, every 'employed earner' who suffers personal injury by an accident for the purposes of the Regulations is required by to give either *oral or written* notice to the employer in one of number of different ways. These ways include notice given to any supervisor or direct to a person designated by the employer. The method that has probably become the norm through custom and practice is by way of an entry of the appropriate particulars in a 'book kept specifically for these purposes' under the Regulations. These books are available from the Stationary Office as form BI 510. As well as containing sections for completing details of accidents etc. form BI 150 includes pages of instructions to employees and employers about their responsibilities.

The entry in an Accident Book is to be made soon as practicable after the happening of an accident by the employed earner or by some other person acting on his behalf. [*Social Security (Claims and Payments) Regulations 1979 (SI 1979 No 628), Reg 24(3)*]. Failure to so is an offence punishable by a fine. [*Social Security (Claims and Payments) Regulations 1979 (SI 1979 No 628), Reg 31*].

Under *Reg 25* of the 1979 Regulations, once an accident is reported by the employee, the employer must take reasonable steps to investigate the circumstances and, if there appear to be any discrepancies between the circumstances reported and the findings in these investigations, these should be recorded.

Where the accident in question is one to which *RIDDOR* applies there is, as well as the usual reporting requirements (see A3014 above), a requirement to keep a record of the accident. [*RIDDOR (SI 1995 No 3163, Reg 7*]. The HSE guide to *RIDDOR* provides (at paragraph 86) that an employer may choose to utilise the form BI 150 Accident Book as this record, and the format of the form includes space for the employer to initial the report as being one reportable under *RIDDOR*.

# Objectives of accident reporting

A3025

There should be an effective accident reporting and investigation system in all organisations. Accident reporting procedures should be clearly established in writing with individual reporting responsibilities specified. Staff should be trained in the system and disciplinary action may have to be taken where there is a failure to comply with it. Moreover, there is a case for all accidents, no matter how trivial they may seem, being reported through the internal reporting procedures.

The principal objectives of an accident reporting procedure are:

(*a*)    to ensure compliance with current legislation, e.g. *RIDDOR*;

(*b*)    to enable prompt remedial action to be taken;

(*c*)    to assist in monitoring the implementation of statements of health and safety policy (see further STATEMENTS OF HEALTH AND SAFETY POLICY);

(*d*)    to assist decision-making, planning and future resource allocation;

(*e*)    to provide feedback information which can be used in the development of future safety strategies and safe systems of work; and

(*f*)    to provide information to other interested parties.

# Duty of disclosure of accident data

A3026     Employers are under a duty to disclose accident data to works safety representatives and, in the course of litigation, to legal representatives of persons claiming damages for death or personal injury.

*Safety representatives*

A3027     An employer must make available to safety representatives of both unionised and non-unionised workforces the information within the employer's knowledge necessary to enable them to fulfil their functions. [*Safety Representatives and Safety Committees Regulations 1977 (SI 1977 No 500), Reg 7(2)*; *Health and Safety (Consultation with Employees) Regulations 1996 (SI 1996 No 1513), Reg 5(1)*]. The Approved Code of Practice in association with these Regulations states that such information should include information which the employer keeps relating to the occurrence of any accident, dangerous occurrence or notifiable industrial disease and any associated statistical records. (Code of Practice: Safety Representatives and Safety Committees 1976, para 6(c)). See JOINT CONSULTATION – SAFETY REPRESENTATIVES AND SAFETY COMMITTEES.

*Legal representatives*

A3028     In the course of litigation (and sometimes before proceedings have actually begun) obligations may arise to give disclosure of relevant documents concerning an accident – even if they are confidential. Legal representatives of an injured party would expect reasonable access to *RIDDOR* information. The decision in *Waugh v British Railways Board [1979] 2 AER 1169* established that where an employer seeks to withhold on grounds of privilege a report made following an accident, he can only do so if its dominant purpose is related to actual or potential hostile legal proceedings. In *Waugh* a report was commissioned for two purposes following the death of an employee: (*a*) to recommend improvements in safety measures, and (*b*) to gather material for the employer's defence. It was held that the report was not privileged.

Employees who suffer an accident at work can also contact the Law Society's Accident Line on (0800) 192939 or email at www.accidentlinedirect.co.uk

# Appendix A

## List of Reportable Dangerous Occurrences

PART I(A) – GENERAL

*Lifting machinery, etc.*

1.  The collapse of, the overturning of, or the failure of any load-bearing part of any –

    (a)  lift or hoist;

    (b)  crane or derrick;

    (c)  mobile powered access platform;

    (d)  access cradle or window-cleaning cradle;

    (e)  excavator;

    (f)  pile-driving frame or rig having an overall height, when operating, of more than 7 metres; or

    (g)  fork lift truck.

*Pressure systems*

2.  The failure of any closed vessel (including a boiler or boiler tube) or of any associated pipework, in which the internal pressure was above or below atmospheric pressure, where the failure has the potential to cause the death of any person.

*Freight containers*

3.  (a)  The failure of any freight container in any of its load-bearing parts while it is being raised, lowered or suspended.

    (b)  In this paragraph, 'freight container' means a container as defined in regulation 2(1) of the Freight Containers (Safety Convention) Regulations 1984.

*Overhead electric lines*

4.  Any unintentional incident in which plant or equipment either –

    (a)  comes into contact with an uninsulated overhead electric line in which the voltage exceeds 200 volts; or

    (b)  causes an electrical discharge from such an electric line by coming into close proximity to it.

*Electrical short circuit*

5.  Electrical short circuit or overload attended by fire or explosion which results in the stoppage of the plant involved for more than 24 hours or which has the potential to cause the death of any person.

*Explosives*

6. (1) Any of the following incidents involving explosives –

   (a) the unintentional explosion or ignition of explosives other than one –

       (i) caused by the unintentional discharge of a weapon where, apart from that unintentional discharge, the weapon and explosives functioned as they were designed to do; or

       (ii) where a fail-safe device or safe system of work functioned so as to prevent any person from being injured in consequence of the explosion or ignition;

   (b) a misfire (other than one at a mine or quarry or inside a well or one involving a weapon) except where a fail-safe device or safe system of work functioned so as to prevent any person from being endangered in consequence of the misfire;

   (c) the failure of the shots in any demolition operation to cause the intended extent of collapse or direction of fall of a building or structure;

   (d) the projection of material (other than at a quarry) beyond the boundary of the site on which the explosives are being used or beyond the danger zone in circumstances such that any person was or might have been injured thereby;

   (e) any injury to a person (other than at a mine or quarry or one otherwise reportable under these Regulations) involving first-aid or medical treatment resulting from the explosion or discharge of any explosives or detonator.

   (2) In this paragraph 'explosives' means any explosive of a type which would, were it being transported, be assigned to class 1 within the meaning of the Classification and Labelling of Explosives Regulations 1983 and 'danger zone' means the area from which persons have been excluded or forbidden to enter to avoid being endangered by any explosion or ignition of explosives.

*Biological agents*

7. Any accident or incident which resulted or could have resulted in the release or escape of a biological agent likely to cause severe human infection or illness.

*Malfunction of radiation generators, etc.*

8. (1) Any incident in which –

   (a) the malfunction of a radiation generator or its ancillary equipment used in fixed or mobile industrial radiography, the irradiation of food or the processing of products by irradiation, which causes it to fail to de-energise at the end of the intended exposure period; or

   (b) the malfunction of equipment used in fixed or mobile industrial radiography or gamma irradiation causes a radioactive source to fail to return to its safe position by the normal means at the end of the intended exposure period.

(2)    In this paragraph 'radiation generator' has the same meaning as in regulation 2 of the Ionising Radiations Regulations 1985.

*Breathing apparatus*

**9.**    (1)    Any incident in which breathing apparatus malfunctions –

(a)    while in use, or

(b)    during testing immediately prior to use in such a way that had the malfunction occurred while the apparatus was in use it would have posed a danger to the health or safety of the user.

(2)    This paragraph shall not apply to breathing apparatus while it is being –

(a)    used in a mine; or

(b)    maintained or tested as part of a routine maintenance procedure.

*Diving operations*

**10.**    Any of the following incidents in relation to a diving operation –

(a)    the failure or the endangering of –

(i)    any lifting equipment associated with the diving operation, or

(ii)    life support equipment, including control panels, hoses and breathing apparatus,

which puts a diver at risk;

(b)    any damage to, or endangering of, the dive platform, or any failure of the dive platform to remain on station, which puts a diver at risk;

(c)    the trapping of a diver;

(d)    any explosion in the vicinity of a diver; or

(e)    any uncontrolled ascent or any omitted decompression which puts a diver at risk.

*Collapse of scaffolding*

**11.**    The complete or partial collapse of –

(a)    any scaffold which is –

(i)    more than 5 metres in height which results in a substantial part of the scaffold falling or overturning; or

(ii)    erected over or adjacent to water in circumstances such that there would be a risk of drowning to a person falling from the scaffold into the water; or

(b)    the suspension arrangements (including any outrigger) of any slung or suspended scaffold which causes a working platform or cradle to fall.

*Train collisions*

12.    Any unintended collision of a train with any other train or vehicle, other than one reportable under Part IV of this Schedule, which caused, or might have caused, the death of, or major injury to, any person.

*Wells*

13.    Any of the following incidents in relation to a well (other than a well sunk for the purpose of the abstraction of water) –

(a)    a blow-out (that is to say an uncontrolled flow of well-fluids from a well);

(b)    the coming into operation of a blow-out prevention or diversion system to control a flow from a well where normal control procedures fail;

(c)    the detection of hydrogen sulphide in the course of operations at a well or in samples of well-fluids from a well where the presence of hydrogen sulphide in the reservoir being drawn on by the well was not anticipated by the responsible person before that detection;

(d)    the taking of precautionary measures additional to any contained in the original drilling programme following failure to maintain a planned minimum separation distance between wells drilled from a particular installation; or

(e)    the mechanical failure of any safety critical element of a well (and for this purpose the safety critical element of a well is any part of a well whose failure would cause or contribute to, or whose purpose is to prevent or limit the effect of, the unintentional release of fluids from a well or a reservoir being drawn on by a well).

*Pipelines or pipeline works*

14.    The following incidents in respect of a pipeline or pipeline works –

(a)    the uncontrolled or accidental escape of anything from, or inrush of anything into, a pipeline which has the potential to cause the death of, major injury or damage to the health of any person or which results in the pipeline being shut down for more than 24 hours;

(b)    the unintentional ignition of anything in a pipeline or of anything which, immediately before it was ignited, was in a pipeline;

(c)    any damage to any part of a pipeline which has the potential to cause the death of, major injury or damage to the health of any person or which results in the pipeline being shut down for more than 24 hours;

(d)    any substantial and unintentional change in the position of a pipeline requiring immediate attention to safeguard the integrity or safety of a pipeline;

(e)    any unintentional change in the subsoil or seabed in the vicinity of a pipeline which has the potential to affect the integrity or safety of a pipeline;

    (f)     any failure of any pipeline isolation device, equipment or system which has the potential to cause the death of, major injury or damage to the health of any person or which results in the pipeline being shut down for more than 24 hours; or

    (g)     any failure of equipment involved with pipeline works which has the potential to cause the death of, major injury or damage to the health of any person.

*Fairground equipment*

**15.**    The following incidents on fairground equipment in use or under test –

    (a)     the failure of any load-bearing part;

    (b)     the failure of any part designed to support or restrain passengers; or

    (c)     the derailment or the unintended collision of cars or trains.

*Carriage of dangerous substances by road*

**16.**    (1)    Any incident involving a road tanker or tank container used for the carriage of a dangerous substance in which –

    (a)     the road tanker or vehicle carrying the tank container overturns (including turning onto its side);

    (b)     the tank carrying the dangerous substance is seriously damaged;

    (c)     there is an uncontrolled release or escape of the dangerous substance being carried; or

    (d)     there is a fire involving the dangerous substance being carried.

    (2)    In this paragraph 'carriage', 'dangerous substance', 'road tanker' and 'tank container' have the same meanings as in Part I: INTERPRETA TION AND APPLICATION of the Carriage of Dangerous Goods by Road Regulations 1996 (SI 1996 No 2095).

**17.**    (1)    Any incident involving a vehicle used for the carriage of a dangerous substance, other than a vehicle to which paragraph 16 applies, where there is –

    (a)     an uncontrolled release or escape of the dangerous substance being carried in such a quantity as to have the potential to cause the death of, or major injury to, any person; or

    (b)     a fire which involves the dangerous substance being carried.

    (2)    In this paragraph, 'carriage' and 'dangerous substance' have the same meaning as in Part I: INTERPRETATION AND APPLICATION of the Carriage of Dangerous Goods by Road Regulations 1996 (SI 1996 No 2095).

## PART I(B) – DANGEROUS OCCURRENCES WHICH ARE REPORTABLE EXCEPT IN RELATION TO OFFSHORE WORKPLACES

*Collapse of building or structure*

18.   Any unintended collapse or partial collapse of –

(a)   any building or structure (whether above or below ground) under construction, reconstruction, alteration or demolition which involves a fall of more than 5 tonnes of material;

(b)   any floor or wall of any building (whether above or below ground) used as a place of work; or

(c)   any false-work.

*Explosion or fire*

19.   An explosion or fire occurring in any plant or premises which results in the stoppage of that plant or as the case may be the suspension of normal work in those premises for more than 24 hours, where the explosion or fire was due to the ignition of any material.

*Escape of flammable substances*

20.   (1)   The sudden, uncontrolled release –

(a)   inside a building –

(i)   of 100 kilograms or more of a flammable liquid,

(ii)   of 10 kilograms or more of a flammable liquid at a temperature above its normal boiling point, or

(iii)   of 10 kilograms or more of a flammable gas; or

(b)   in the open air, of 500 kilograms or more of any of the substances referred to in sub-paragraph (a) above.

(2)   In this paragraph, 'flammable liquid' and 'flammable gas' means respectively a liquid and a gas so classified in accordance with regulation 5(2), (3) or (5) of the Chemicals (Hazard Information and Packaging for Supply) Regulations 1994.

*Escape of substances*

21.   The accidental release or escape of any substance in a quantity sufficient to cause the death, major injury or any other damage to the health of any person.

## PART II – DANGEROUS OCCURRENCES WHICH ARE REPORTABLE IN RELATION TO MINES

*Fire or ignition of gas*

22.   The ignition, below ground, of any gas (other than gas in a safety lamp) or of any dust.

23.   The accidental ignition of any gas in part of a firedamp drainage system on the surface or in an exhauster house.

24.   The outbreak of any fire below ground.

25.   An incident where any person in consequence of any smoke or any other indication that a fire may have broken out below ground has been caused to leave any place pursuant to either Regulation 11(1) of the Coal and Other Mines (Fire and Rescue) Regulations 1956 or section 79 of the Mines and Quarries Act 1954.

26.   The outbreak of any fire on the surface which endangers the operation of any winding or haulage apparatus installed at a shaft or unwalkable outlet or of any mechanically operated apparatus for producing ventilation below ground.

*Escape of gas*

27.   Any violent outburst of gas together with coal or other solid matter into the mine workings except when such outburst is caused intentionally.

*Failure of plant or equipment*

28.   The breakage of any rope, chain, coupling, balance rope, guide rope, suspension gear or other gear used for or in connection with the carrying of persons through any shaft or staple shaft.

29.   The breakage or unintentional uncoupling of any rope, chain, coupling, rope tensioning system or other gear used for or in connection with the transport of persons below ground, or breakage of any belt, rope or other gear used for or in connection with a belt conveyor designated by the mine manager as a man-riding conveyor.

30.   An incident where any conveyance being used for the carriage of persons is overwound; or any conveyance not being so used is overwound and becomes detached from its winding rope; or any conveyance operated by means of the friction of a rope on a winding sheave is brought to rest by the apparatus provided in the headframe of the shaft or in the part of the shaft below the lowest landing for the time being in use, being apparatus provided for bringing the conveyance to rest in the event of its being overwound.

31.   The stoppage of any ventilating apparatus (other than an auxiliary fan) which causes a substantial reduction in ventilation of the mine lasting for a period exceeding 30 minutes, except when for the purpose of planned maintenance.

32.   The collapse of any headframe, winding engine house, fan house or storage bunker.

*Breathing apparatus*

33.   At any mine an incident where –

(a)   breathing apparatus or a smoke helmet or other apparatus serving the same purpose or a self-rescuer, while being used, fails to function safely or develops a defect likely to affect its safe working; or

(b)   immediately after using and arising out of the use of breathing apparatus or a smoke helmet or other apparatus serving the same purpose or a self-rescuer, any person receives first-aid or medical treatment by reason of his unfitness or suspected unfitness at the mine.

*Injury by explosion of blasting material etc.*

**34.** An incident in which any person suffers an injury (not being a major injury or one reportable under regulation 3(2)) which results from an explosion or discharge of any blasting material or device within the meaning of section 69(4) of the Mines and Quarries Act 1954 for which he receives first-aid or medical treatment at the mine.

*Use of emergency escape apparatus*

**35.** An incident where any apparatus is used (other than for the purpose of training and practice) which has been provided at the mine in accordance with regulation 4 of the Mines (Safety of Exit) Regulations 1988 or where persons leave the mine when apparatus and equipment normally used by persons to leave the mine is unavailable.

*Inrush of gas or water*

**36.** Any inrush of noxious or flammable gas from old workings.

**37.** Any inrush of water or material which flows when wet from any source.

*Insecure tip*

**38.** Any movement of material or any fire or any other event which indicates that a tip to which Part I of the Mines and Quarries (Tips) Act 1969 applies, is or is likely to become insecure.

*Locomotives*

**39.** Any incident where an underground locomotive when not used for testing purposes is brought to rest by means other than its safety circuit protective devices or normal service brakes.

*Falls of ground*

**40.** Any fall of ground, not being part of the normal operations at a mine, which results from a failure of an underground support system and prevents persons travelling through the area affected by the fall or which otherwise exposes them to danger.

## PART III – DANGEROUS OCCURRENCES WHICH ARE REPORTABLE IN RELATION TO QUARRIES

*Collapse of storage bunkers*

**41.** The collapse of any storage bunker.

*Sinking of craft*

**42.** The sinking of any water-borne craft or hovercraft.

*Injuries*

**43.** (1) An incident in which any person suffers an injury (not otherwise reportable under these Regulations) which results from an explosion or from the discharge of any explosives for which he receives first-aid or medical treatment at the quarry.

(2)    In this paragraph, 'explosives' has the same meaning as in regulation 2(1) of the Quarries (Explosives) Regulations 1988.

*Projection of substances outside quarry*

**44.**    Any incident in which any substance is ascertained to have been projected beyond a quarry boundary as a result of blasting operations in circumstances in which any person was or might have been endangered.

*Misfires*

**45.**    Any misfire, as defined by regulation 2(1) of the Quarries (Explosives) Regulations 1988.

*Insecure tips*

**46.**    Any event (including any movement of material or any fire) which indicates that a tip, to which Part I of the Mines and Quarries (Tips) Act 1969 applies, is or is likely to become insecure.

*Movement of slopes or faces*

**47.**    Any movement or failure of an excavated slope or face which –

(a)    has the potential to cause the death of any person; or

(b)    adversely affects any building, contiguous land, transport system, footpath, public utility or service, watercourse, reservoir or area of public access.

*Explosions or fires in vehicles or plant*

**48.**    (1)    Any explosion or fire occurring in any large vehicle or mobile plant which results in the stoppage of that vehicle or plant for more than 24 hours and which affects –

(a)    any place where persons normally work; or

(b)    the route of egress from such a place.

(2)    In this paragraph, 'large vehicle or mobile plant' means –

(a)    a dump truck having a load capacity of at least 50 tonnes; or

(b)    an excavator having a bucket capacity of at least 5 cubic metres.

## PART IV – DANGEROUS OCCURRENCES WHICH ARE REPORTABLE IN RESPECT OF RELEVANT TRANSPORT SYSTEMS

*Accidents to passenger trains*

**49.**    Any collision in which a passenger train collides with another train.

**50.**    Any case where a passenger train or any part of such a train unintentionally leaves the rails.

*Accidents not involving passenger trains*

51.   Any collision between trains, other than one between a passenger train and another train, on a running line where any train sustains damage as a result of the collision, and any such collision in a siding which results in a running line being obstructed.

52.   Any derailment, of a train other than a passenger train, on a running line, except a derailment which occurs during shunting operations and does not obstruct any other running line.

53.   Any derailment, of a train other than a passenger train, in a siding which results in a running line being obstructed.

*Accidents involving any kind of train*

54.   Any case of a train striking a buffer stop, other than in a siding, where damage is caused to the train.

55.   Any case of a train striking any cattle or horse, whether or not damage is caused to the train, or striking any other animal if, in consequence, damage (including damage to the windows of the driver's cab but excluding other damage consisting solely in the breakage of glass) is caused to the train necessitating immediate temporary or permanent repair.

56.   Any case of a train on a running line striking or being struck by any object which causes damage (including damage to the windows of the driver's cab but excluding other damage consisting solely in the breakage of glass) necessitating immediate temporary or permanent repair or which might have been liable to derail the train.

57.   Any case of a train, other than one on a railway, striking or being struck by a road vehicle.

58.   Any case of a passenger train, or any other train not fitted with continuous self-applying brakes, becoming unintentionally divided.

59.   (1)   Any of the following classes of accident which occurs or is discovered whilst the train is on a running line –

(a)   the failure of an axle;

(b)   the failure of a wheel or tyre, including a tyre loose on its wheel;

(c)   the failure of a rope or the fastenings thereof or of the winding plant or equipment involved in working an incline;

(d)   any fire, severe electrical arcing or fusing in or on any part of a passenger train or a train carrying dangerous goods;

(e)   in the case of any train other than a passenger train, any severe electrical arcing or fusing, or any fire which was extinguished by a fire-fighting service; or

(f)   any other failure of any part of a train which is likely to cause an accident to that or any other train or to kill or injure any person.

(2)   In this paragraph 'dangerous goods' has the same meaning as in regulation 1(2) of the Carriage of Dangerous Goods by Rail Regulations 1994.

*Accidents and incidents at level crossings*

60.   Any case of a train striking a road vehicle or gate at a level crossing.

61.   Any case of a train running onto a level crossing when not authorised to do so.

62.   A failure of the equipment at a level crossing which could endanger users of the road or path crossing the railway.

*Accidents involving the permanent way and other works on or connected with a relevant transport system*

63.   The failure of a rail in a running line or of a rack rail, which results in –

(a)   a complete fracture of the rail through its cross-section; or

(b)   in a piece becoming detached from the rail which necessitates an immediate stoppage of traffic or the immediate imposition of a speed restriction lower than that currently in force.

64.   A buckle of a running line which necessitates an immediate stoppage of traffic or the immediate imposition of a speed restriction lower than that currently in force.

65.   Any case of an aircraft or a vehicle of any kind landing on, running onto or coming to rest foul of the line, or damaging the line, which causes damage which obstructs the line or which damages any railway equipment at a level crossing.

66.   The runaway of an escalator, lift or passenger conveyor.

67.   Any fire or severe arcing or fusing which seriously affects the functioning of signalling equipment.

68.   Any fire affecting the permanent way or works of a relevant transport system which necessitates the suspension of services over any line, or the closure of any part of a station or signal box or other premises, for a period –

(a)   in the case of a fire affecting any part of a relevant transport system below ground, of more than 30 minutes, and

(b)   in any other case, of more than 1 hour.

69.   Any other fire which causes damage which has the potential to affect the running of a relevant transport system.

*Accidents involving failure of the works on or connected with a relevant transport system*

70.   (1)   The following classes of accident where they are likely either to cause an accident to a train or to endanger any person –

(a)   the failure of a tunnel, bridge, viaduct, culvert, station, or other structure or any part thereof including the fixed electrical equipment of an electrified relevant transport system;

(b)   any failure in the signalling system which endangers or which has the potential to endanger the safe passage of trains other than a failure of a traffic light controlling the movement of vehicles on a road;

(c)   a slip of a cutting or of an embankment;

(d)   flooding of the permanent way;

(e)    the striking of a bridge by a vessel or by a road vehicle or its load; or

(f)    the failure of any other portion of the permanent way or works not specified above.

*Incidents of serious congestion*

71.    Any case where planned procedures or arrangements have been activated in order to control risks arising from an incident of undue passenger congestion at a station unless that congestion has been relieved within a period of time allowed for by those procedures or arrangements.

*Incidents of signals passed without authority*

72.    (1)    Any case where a train, travelling on a running line or entering a running line from a siding, passes without authority a signal displaying a stop aspect unless –

(a)    the stop aspect was not displayed in sufficient time for the driver to stop safely at the signal; or

(b)    the line is equipped with automatic train protection equipment which is in operation.

(2)    In this paragraph 'automatic train protection equipment' means equipment which automatically controls the speed of a train, either by bringing it to a halt or reducing its speed, in the event that the train passes a signal without authority or exceeds a prescribed speed limit.

## PART V – DANGEROUS OCCURRENCES WHICH ARE REPORTABLE IN RESPECT OF AN OFFSHORE WORKPLACE

*Release of petroleum hydrocarbon*

73.    Any unintentional release of petroleum hydrocarbon on or from an offshore installation which –

(a)    results in –

(i)    a fire or explosion; or

(ii)    the taking of action to prevent or limit the consequences of a potential fire or explosion; or

(b)    has the potential to cause death or major injury to any person.

*Fire or explosion*

74.    Any fire or explosion at an offshore installation, other than one to which paragraph 73 above applies, which results in the stoppage of plant or the suspension of normal work.

*Release or escape of dangerous substances*

75.    The uncontrolled or unintentional release or escape of any substance (other than petroleum hydrocarbon) on or from an offshore installation which has the potential to cause the death of, major injury to or damage to the health of any person.

### Collapses

**76.**   Any unintended collapse of any offshore installation or any unintended collapse of any part thereof or any plant thereon which jeopardises the overall structural integrity of the installation.

### Dangerous occurrences

**77.**   Any of the following occurrences having the potential to cause death or major injury –

(a)   the failure of equipment required to maintain a floating offshore installation on station;

(b)   the dropping of any object on an offshore installation or on an attendant vessel or into the water adjacent to an installation or vessel; or

(c)   damage to or on an offshore installation caused by adverse weather conditions.

### Collisions

**78.**   Any collision between a vessel or aircraft and an offshore installation which results in damage to the installation, the vessel or the aircraft.

**79.**   Any occurrence with the potential for a collision between a vessel and an offshore installation where, had a collision occurred, it would have been liable to jeopardise the overall structural integrity of the offshore installation.

### Subsidence or collapse of seabed

**80.**   Any subsidence or local collapse of the seabed likely to affect the foundations of an offshore installation or the overall structural integrity of an offshore installation.

### Loss of stability or buoyancy

**81.**   Any incident involving loss of stability or buoyancy of a floating offshore installation.

### Evacuation

**82.**   Any evacuation (other than one arising out of an incident reportable under any other provision of these Regulations) of an offshore installation, in whole or part, in the interests of safety.

### Falls into water

**83.**   Any case of a person falling more than 2 metres into water (unless the fall results in death or injury required to be reported under sub-paragraphs (a)–(d) of regulation 3(1)).

[*The Reporting of Injuries, Diseases and Dangerous Occurrences Regulations 1995, Reg 2(1), 2 Sch*].

# *Appendix B*

## List of Reportable Diseases

A3030   **PART I – OCCUPATIONAL DISEASES**

| Column 1 | Column 2 |
|---|---|
| **Diseases** | **Activities** |

*Conditions due to physical agents and the physical demands of work*

| | | |
|---|---|---|
| 1. | Inflammation, ulceration or malignant disease of the skin due to ionising radiation. | |
| 2. | Malignant disease of the bones due to ionising radiation. | Work with ionising radiation. |
| 3. | Blood dyscrasia due to ionising radiation. | |
| 4. | Cataract due to electromagnetic radiation. | Work involving exposure to electromagnetic radiation (including radiant heat). |
| 5. | Decompression illness. | |
| 6. | Barotrauma resulting in lung or other organ damage. | Work involving breathing gases at increased pressure (including diving). |
| 7. | Dysbaric osteonecrosis. | |
| 8. | Cramp of the hand or forearm due to repetitive movements. | Work involving prolonged periods of handwriting, typing or other repetitive movements of the fingers, hand or arm. |
| 9. | Subcutaneous cellulitis of the hand (beat hand). | Physically demanding work causing severe or prolonged friction or pressure on the hand. |
| 10. | Bursitis or subcutaneous cellulitis arising at or about the knee due to severe or prolonged external friction or pressure at or about the knee (beat knee). | Physically demanding work causing severe or prolonged friction or pressure at or about the knee. |
| 11. | Bursitis or subcutaneous cellulitis arising at or about the elbow due to severe or prolonged external friction or pressure at or about the elbow (beat elbow). | Physically demanding work causing severe or prolonged friction or pressure at or about the elbow. |
| 12. | Traumatic inflammation of the tendons of the hand or forearm or of the associated tendon sheaths. | Physically demanding work, frequent or repeated movements, constrained postures or extremes of extension or flexion of the hand or wrist. |

| Column 1 | Column 2 |
|---|---|
| **Diseases** | **Activities** |
| 13. Carpal tunnel syndrome. | Work involving the use of hand-held vibrating tools. |
| 14. Hand-arm vibration syndrome. | Work involving: |
| | (a) the use of chain saws, brush cutters or hand-held or hand-fed circular saws in forestry or wood-working; |
| | (b) the use of hand-held rotary tools in grinding material or in sanding or polishing metal; |
| | (c) the holding of material being ground or metal being sanded or polished by rotary tools; |
| | (d) the use of hand-held percussive metal-working tools or the holding of metal being worked upon by percussive tools in connection with riveting, caulking, chipping, hammering, fettling or swaging; |
| | (e) the use of hand-held powered percussive drills or hand-held powered percussive hammers in mining, quarrying or demolition, or on roads or footpaths (including road construction); or |
| | (f) the holding of material being worked upon by pounding machines in shoe manufacture. |
| *Infections due to biological agents* | |
| 15. Anthrax. | (a) Work involving handling infected animals, their products or packaging containing infected material; or |
| | (b) work on infected sites. |

| Column 1 | Column 2 |
|---|---|
| **Diseases** | **Activities** |
| 16.  Brucellosis. | Work involving contact with: |
| | (a)  animals or their carcasses (including any parts thereof) infected by brucella or the untreated products of same; or |
| | (b)  laboratory specimens or vaccines of or containing brucella. |
| 17.  (a)  Avian chlamydiosis. | Work involving contact with birds infected with chlamydia psittaci, or the remains or untreated products of such birds. |
| (b)  Ovine chlamydiosis. | Work involving contact with sheep infected with chlamydia psittaci or the remains or untreated products of such sheep. |
| 18.  Hepatitis. | Work involving contact with: |
| | (a)  human blood or human blood products; or |
| | (b)  any source of viral hepatitis. |
| 19.  Legionellosis. | Work on or near cooling systems which are located in the workplace and use water; or work on hot water service systems located in the workplace which are likely to be a source of contamination. |
| 20.  Leptospirosis. | (a)  Work in places which are or are liable to be infested by rats, fieldmice, voles or other small mammals; |
| | (b)  work at dog kennels or involving the care or handling of dogs; or |
| | (c)  work involving contact with bovine animals or their meat products or pigs or their meat products. |
| 21.  Lyme disease. | Work involving exposure to ticks (including in particular work by forestry workers, rangers, dairy farmers, game keepers and other persons engaged in countryside management). |

| Column 1 | Column 2 |
| --- | --- |
| **Diseases** | **Activities** |
| 22.  Q fever. | Work involving contact with animals, their remains or their untreated products. |
| 23.  Rabies. | Work involving handling or contact with infected animals. |
| 24.  Streptococcus suis. | Work involving contact with pigs infected with streptococcus suis, or with the carcasses, products or residues of pigs so affected. |
| 25.  Tetanus. | Work involving contact with soil likely to be contaminated by animals. |
| 26.  Tuberculosis. | Work with persons, animals, human or animal remains or any other material which might be a source of infection. |
| 27.  Any infection reliably attributable to the performance of the work specified in the entry opposite hereto. | Work with micro-organisms; work with live or dead human beings in the course of providing any treatment or service or in conducting any investigation involving exposure to blood or body fluids; work with animals or any potentially infected material derived from any of the above. |

*Conditions due to substances*

28.  Poisonings by any of the following:        Any activity.

    (a)    acrylamide monomer;

    (b)    arsenic or one of its compounds;

    (c)    benzene or a homologue of benzene;

    (d)    beryllium or one of its compounds;

    (e)    cadmium or one of its compounds;

    (f)    carbon disulphide;

    (g)    diethylene dioxide (dioxan);

    (h)    ethylene oxide;

    (i)    lead or one of its compounds;

| Column 1 | Column 2 |
|---|---|
| **Diseases** | **Activities** |
| (j)  manganese or one of its compounds; | |
| (k)  mercury or one of its compounds; | |
| (l)  methyl bromide; | |
| (m)  nitrochlorobenzene, or a nitro-or amino-or chloro-derivative of benzene or of a homologue of benzene; | |
| (n)  oxides of nitrogen; | |
| (o)  phosphorus or one of its compounds. | |
| 29.  Cancer of a bronchus or lung. | (a)  Work in or about a building where nickel is produced by decomposition of a gaseous nickel compound or where any industrial process which is ancillary or incidental to that process is carried on; or |
| | (b)  work involving exposure to bis(chloromethyl) ether or any electrolytic chromium processes (excluding passivation) which involve hexavalent chromium compounds, chromate production or zinc chromate pigment manufacture. |
| 30.  Primary carcinoma of the lung where there is accompanying evidence of silicosis. | Any occupation in: |
| | (a)  glass manufacture; |
| | (b)  sandstone tunnelling or quarrying; |
| | (c)  the pottery industry; |
| | (d)  metal ore mining; |
| | (e)  slate quarrying or slate production; |
| | (f)  clay mining; |
| | (g)  the use of siliceous materials as abrasives; |
| | (h)  foundry work; |

| Column 1 | Column 2 |
|---|---|
| **Diseases** | **Activities** |
| | (i)   granite tunnelling or quarrying; or |
| | (j)   stone cutting or masonry. |
| 31.   Cancer of the urinary tract. | 1. Work involving exposure to any of the following substances: |
| | (a)   beta-naphthylamine or methylene-bis-orthochloroaniline; |
| | (b)   diphenyl substituted by at least one nitro or primary amino group or by at least one nitro and primary amino group (including benzidine); |
| | (c)   any of the substances mentioned in sub-paragraph (b) above if further ring substituted by halogeno, methyl or methoxy groups, but not by other groups; or |
| | (d)   the salts of any of the substances mentioned in sub-paragraphs (a) to (c) above. |
| | 2. The manufacture of auramine or magenta. |
| 32.   Bladder cancer. | Work involving exposure to aluminium smelting using the Soderberg process. |
| 33.   Angiosarcoma of the liver. | (a)   Work in or about machinery or apparatus used for the polymerisation of vinyl chloride monomer, a process which, for the purposes of this sub-paragraph, comprises all operations up to and including the drying of the slurry produced by the polymerisation and the packaging of the dried product; or |
| | (b)   work in a building or structure in which any part of the process referred to in the foregoing sub-paragraph takes place. |

| Column 1 | Column 2 |
|---|---|
| **Diseases** | **Activities** |
| 34. Peripheral neuropathy. | Work involving the use or handling of or exposure to the fumes of or vapour containing n–hexane or methyl n–butyl ketone. |
| 35. Chrome ulceration of:<br><br>(a)  the nose or throat; or<br><br>(b)  the skin of the hands or forearm. | Work involving exposure to chromic acid or to any other chromium compound. |
| 36. Folliculitis.<br><br>37. Acne.<br><br>38. Skin cancer. | Work involving exposure to mineral oil, tar, pitch or arsenic. |
| 39. Pneumoconiosis (excluding asbestosis). | 1.    The mining, quarrying or<br>(a)  working of silica rock or the working of dried quartzose sand, any dry deposit or residue of silica or any dry admixture containing such materials (including any activity in which any of the aforesaid operations are carried out incidentally to the mining or quarrying of other minerals or to the manufacture of articles containing crushed or ground silica rock); or<br><br>(b)  the handling of any of the materials specified in the foregoing sub–paragraph in or incidentally to any of the operations mentioned therein or substantial exposure to the dust arising from such operations.<br><br>2. The breaking, crushing or grinding of flint, the working or handling of broken, crushed or ground flint or materials containing such flint or substantial exposure to the dust arising from any of such operations. |

| Column 1 | Column 2 |
|----------|----------|
| **Diseases** | **Activities** |

3. Sand blasting by means of compressed air with the use of quartzose sand or crushed silica rock or flint or substantial exposure to the dust arising from such sand blasting.

4. Work in a foundry or the performance of, or substantial exposure to the dust arising from, any of the following operations:

(a)  the freeing of steel castings from adherent siliceous substance or;

(b)  the freeing of metal castings from adherent siliceous substance:

   (i)  by blasting with an abrasive propelled by compressed air, steam or a wheel, or

   (ii)  by the use of power-driven tools.

5. The manufacture of china or earthenware (including sanitary earthenware, electrical earthenware and earthenware tiles) and any activity involving substantial exposure to the dust arising therefrom.

6. The grinding of mineral graphite or substantial exposure to the dust arising from such grinding.

7. The dressing of granite or any igneous rock by masons, the crushing of such materials or substantial exposure to the dust arising from such operations.

8. The use or preparation for use of an abrasive wheel or substantial exposure to the dust arising therefrom.

| Column 1 | Column 2 |
|---|---|
| **Diseases** | **Activities** |
| | 9. (a) Work underground in any mine in which one of the objects of the mining operations is the getting of any material; |
| | (b) the working or handling above ground at any coal or tin mine of any materials extracted therefrom or any operation incidental thereto; |
| | (c) the trimming of coal in any ship, barge, lighter, dock or harbour or at any wharf or quay; or |
| | (d) the sawing, splitting or dressing of slate or any operation incidental thereto. |
| | 10. The manufacture or work incidental to the manufacture of carbon electrodes by an industrial undertaking for use in the electrolytic extraction of aluminium from aluminium oxide and any activity involving substantial exposure to the dust therefrom. |
| | 11. Boiler scaling or substantial exposure to the dust arising therefrom. |
| 40. Byssinosis. | The spinning or manipulation of raw or waste cotton or flax or the weaving of cotton or flax, carried out in each case in a room in a factory, together with any other work carried out in such a room. |
| 41. Mesothelioma. | (a) The working or handling of asbestos or any admixture of asbestos; |
| 42. Lung cancer. | (b) the manufacture or repair of asbestos textiles or other articles containing or composed of asbestos; |

| Column 1 | Column 2 |
|----------|----------|
| **Diseases** | **Activities** |
| 43.  Asbestosis. | (c)  the cleaning of any machinery or plant used in any of the foregoing operations and of any chambers, fixtures and appliances for the collection of asbestos dust; or |
| | (d)  substantial exposure to the dust arising from any of the foregoing operations. |
| 44.  Cancer of the nasal cavity or associated air sinuses. | 1.  Work in or about a building<br>(a)  where wooden furniture is manufactured; |
| | (b)  work in a building used for the manufacture of footwear or components of footwear made wholly or partly of leather or fibre board; or |
| | (c)  work at a place used wholly or mainly for the repair of footwear made wholly or partly of leather or fibre board. |
| | 2. Work in or about a factory building where nickel is produced by decomposition of a gaseous nickel compound or in any process which is ancillary or incidental thereto. |
| 45.  Occupational dermatitis. | Work involving exposure to any of the following agents: |
| | (a)  epoxy resin systems; |
| | (b)  formaldehyde and its resins; |
| | (c)  metalworking fluids; |
| | (d)  chromate (hexavalent and derived from trivalent chromium); |
| | (e)  cement, plaster or concrete; |
| | (f)  acrylates and methacrylates; |
| | (g)  colophony (rosin) and its modified products; |
| | (h)  glutaraldehyde; |

| Column 1 | Column 2 |
|---|---|
| **Diseases** | **Activities** |
| | (i) mercaptobenzothiazole, thiurams, substituted paraphenylene-diamines and related rubber processing chemicals; |
| | (j) biocides, anti-bacterials, preservatives or disinfectants; |
| | (k) organic solvents; |
| | (l) antibiotics and other pharmaceuticals and therapeutic agents; |
| | (m) strong acids, strong alkalis, strong solutions (e.g. brine) and oxidising agents including domestic bleach or reducing agents; |
| | (n) hairdressing products including in particular dyes, shampoos, bleaches and permanent waving solutions; |
| | (o) soaps and detergents; |
| | (p) plants and plant-derived material including in particular the daffodil, tulip and chrysanthemum families, the parsley family (carrots, parsnips, parsley and celery), garlic and onion, hardwoods and the pine family; |
| | (q) fish, shell-fish or meat; |
| | (r) sugar or flour; or |
| | (s) any other known irritant or sensitising agent including in particular any chemical bearing the warning 'may cause sensitisation by skin contact' or 'irritating to the skin'. |
| 46. Extrinsic alveolitis (including farmer's lung). | Exposure to moulds, fungal spores or heterologous proteins during work in: |
| | (a) agriculture, horticulture, forestry, cultivation of edible fungi or malt-working; |

| Column 1 | Column 2 |
|---|---|
| **Diseases** | **Activities** |
| | (b) loading, unloading or handling mouldy vegetable matter or edible fungi whilst same is being stored; |
| | (c) caring for or handling birds; or |
| | (d) handling bagasse. |
| 47. Occupational asthma. | Work involving exposure to any of the following agents: |
| | (a) isocyanates; |
| | (b) platinum salts; |
| | (c) fumes or dust arising from the manufacture, transport or use of hardening agents (including epoxy resin curing agents) based on phthalic anhydride, tetrachlorophthalic anhydride, trimellitic anhydride or triethylene-tetramine; |
| | (d) fumes arising from the use of rosin as a soldering flux; |
| | (e) proteolytic enzymes; |
| | (f) animals including insects and other arthropods used for the purposes of research or education or in laboratories; |
| | (g) dusts arising from the sowing, cultivation, harvesting, drying, handling, milling, transport or storage of barley, oats, rye, wheat or maize or the handling, milling, transport or storage of meal or flour made therefrom; |
| | (h) antibiotics; |
| | (i) cimetidine; |
| | (j) wood dust; |
| | (k) ispaghula; |
| | (l) castor bean dust; |
| | (m) ipecacuanha; |

| Column 1 | Column 2 |
|----------|----------|
| Diseases | Activities |
| | (n) azodicarbonamide; |
| | (o) animals including insects and other arthropods (whether in their larval forms or not) used for the purposes of pest control or fruit cultivation or the larval forms of animals used for the purposes of research or education or in laboratories; |
| | (p) glutaraldehyde; |
| | (q) persulphate salts or henna; |
| | (r) crustaceans or fish or products arising from these in the food processing industry; |
| | (s) reactive dyes; |
| | (t) soya bean; |
| | (u) tea dust; |
| | (v) green coffee bean dust; |
| | (w) fumes from stainless steel welding; |
| | (x) any other sensitising agent, including in particular any chemical bearing the warning 'may cause sensitisation by inhalation'. |

## PART II – DISEASES ADDITIONALLY REPORTABLE IN RESPECT OF OFFSHORE WORKPLACES

48. Chickenpox.
49. Cholera.
50. Diphtheria.
51. Dysentery (amoebic or bacillary).
52. Acute encephalitis.
53. Erysipelas.
54. Food poisoning.
55. Legionellosis.
56. Malaria.
57. Measles.
58. Meningitis.
59. Meningococcal septicaemia (without meningitis).
60. Mumps.
61. Paratyphoid fever.

62.    Plague.
63.    Acute poliomyelitis.
64.    Rabies.
65.    Rubella.
66.    Scarlet fever.
67.    Tetanus.
68.    Tuberculosis.
69.    Typhoid fever.
70.    Typhus.
71.    Viral haemorrhagic fevers.
72.    Viral hepatitis.

[*The Reporting of Injuries, Diseases and Dangerous Occurrences Regulations 1995, Reg 5(1)(2), Sch 3*].

*Appendix C*

## Prescribed Form for Reporting an Injury or Dangerous Occurrence

A3031

---

Health and Safety at Work etc Act 1974
The Reporting of Injuries, Diseases and Dangerous Occurrences Regulations 1995

**HSE**
Health & Safety
Executive

# Report of an injury or dangerous occurrence

**Filling in this form**
This form must be filled in by an employer or other responsible person.

## Part A

### About you
1 What is your full name?

2 What is your job title?

3 What is your telephone number?

### About your organisation
4 What is the name of your organisation?

5 What is its address and postcode?

6 What type of work does the organisation do?

## Part B

### About the incident
1 On what date did the incident happen?

    /    /

2 At what time did the incident happen?
(Please use the 24-hour clock eg 0600)

3 Did the incident happen at the above address?

Yes ☐ Go to question 4

No ☐ Where did the incident happen?
☐ elsewhere in your organisation – give the name, address and postcode
☐ at someone else's premises – give the name, address and postcode
☐ in a public place – give details of where it happened

If you do not know the postcode, what is the name of the local authority?

4 In which department, or where on the premises, did the incident happen?

F2508 (01/96)

## Part C

### About the injured person
If you are reporting a dangerous occurrence, go to Part F.
If more than one person was injured in the same incident, please attach the details asked for in Part C and Part D for each injured person.

1 What is their full name?

2 What is their home address and postcode?

3 What is their home phone number?

4 How old are they?

5 Are they
☐ male?
☐ female?

6 What is their job title?

7 Was the injured person (tick only one box)
☐ one of your employees?
☐ on a training scheme? Give details:

☐ on work experience?
☐ employed by someone else? Give details of the employer:

☐ self-employed and at work?
☐ a member of the public?

## Part D

### About the injury
1 What was the injury? (eg fracture, laceration)

2 What part of the body was injured?

*Continued overleaf*

A30/39

3 Was the injury (tick the one box that applies)

☐ a fatality?

☐ a major injury or condition? (see accompanying notes)

☐ an injury to an employee or self-employed person which prevented them doing their normal work for more than 3 days?

☐ an injury to a member of the public which meant they had to be taken from the scene of the accident to a hospital for treatment?

4 Did the injured person (tick all the boxes that apply)

☐ become unconscious?

☐ need resuscitation?

☐ remain in hospital for more than 24 hours?

☐ none of the above.

## Part E

### About the kind of accident

Please tick the one box that best describes what happened, then go to Part G.

☐ Contact with moving machinery or material being machined

☐ Hit by a moving, flying or falling object

☐ Hit by a moving vehicle

☐ Hit something fixed or stationary

☐ Injured while handling, lifting or carrying

☐ Slipped, tripped or fell on the same level

☐ Fell from a height
How high was the fall?

| | metres |
|---|---|

☐ Trapped by something collapsing

☐ Drowned or asphyxiated

☐ Exposed to, or in contact with, a harmful substance

☐ Exposed to fire

☐ Exposed to an explosion

☐ Contact with electricity or an electrical discharge

☐ Injured by an animal

☐ Physically assaulted by a person

☐ Another kind of accident (describe it in Part G)

## Part F

### Dangerous occurrences

Enter the number of the dangerous occurrence you are reporting. (The numbers are given in the Regulations and in the notes which accompany this form)

## Part G

### Describing what happened

Give as much detail as you can. For instance

• the name of any substance involved
• the name and type of any machine involved
• the events that led to the incident
• the part played by any people.

If it was a personal injury, give details of what the person was doing. Describe any action that has since been taken to prevent a similar incident. Use a separate piece of paper if you need to.

## Part H

### Your signature

Signature

Date

| / | / |
|---|---|

**Where to send the form**

Please send it to the Enforcing Authority for the place where it happened. If you do not know the Enforcing Authority, send it to the nearest HSE office.

# *Appendix D*

## Prescribed Form for Reporting a Case of Disease

A3032

Health and Safety at Work etc Act 1974
The Reporting of Injuries, Diseases and Dangerous Occurrences Regulations 1995

**HSE**
Health & Safety
Executive

# Report of a case of disease

**Filling in this form**
This form must be filled in by an employer or other responsible person.

## Part A

### About you

1  What is your full name?

2  What is your job title?

3  What is your telephone number?

### About your organisation

4  What is the name of your organisation?

5  What is its address and postcode?

6  Does the affected person usually work at this address?

Yes ☐ Go to question 7

No ☐ Where do they normally work?

7  What type of work does the organisation do?

## Part B

### About the affected person

1  What is their full name?

2  What is their date of birth?

/  /

3  What is their job title?

4  Are they
☐ male?
☐ female?

5  Is the affected person (tick one box)
☐ one of your employees?
☐ on a training scheme? Give details:

☐ on work experience?
☐ employed by someone else? Give details:

☐ other? Give details:

F2508A (01/96)

*Continued overleaf*

A30/41

## Part C

### The disease you are reporting

1 Please give:

- the name of the disease, and the type of work it is associated with; or

- the name and number of the disease *(from Schedule 3 of the Regulations – see the accompanying notes).*

2 What is the date of the statement of the doctor who first diagnosed or confirmed the disease?

    /    /

3 What is the name and address of the doctor?

## Part D

### Describing the work that led to the disease

Please describe any work done by the affected person which might have led to them getting the disease.

If the disease is thought to have been caused by exposure to an agent at work *(eg a specific chemical)* please say what that agent is.

Give any other information which is relevant.

**Give your description here**

**Continue your description here**

## Part E

### Your signature

Signature

Date

    /    /

**Where to send the form**

Please send it to the Enforcing Authority for the place where the affected person works. If you do not know the Enforcing Authority, send it to the nearest HSE office.

| For official use | |
|---|---|
| Client number | Location number |
| | |
| Event number | |
| | ☐ INV  REP ☐ Y ☐ N |

# *Appendix E*

## Health and Safety Executive Regional Offices

### London and South East Region

Covers the counties of Kent, Surrey, East Sussex and West Sussex, and all London Boroughs.

St Dunstans House
201–211 Borough High Street
London SE1 1GZ
*Telephone*: 020 7556 2100
*Fax*: 020 7556 2200

3 East Grinstead House
London Road
East Grinstead RH19 1RR
*Telephone*: 01342 334 200
*Fax*: 01342 334 222

### Home Counties Region

Covers the counties of Bedfordshire, Berkshire, Buckinghamshire, Cambridgeshire, Dorset, Essex (except London Boroughs in Essex), Hampshire, Hertfordshire, Isle of Wight, Norfolk, Suffolk and Wiltshire.

14 Cardiff Road
Luton LU1 1PP
*Telephone*: 01582 444 200
*Fax*: 01582 444 320

Priestley House
Priestley Road
Basingstoke RG24 9NW
*Telephone*: 01256 404 000
*Fax*: 01256 404 100

39 Baddow Road
Chelmsford CM2 0HL
*Telephone*: 01245 706 200
*Fax*: 01245 706 222

### Midlands Region

Covers the counties of West Midlands, Leicestershire, Northamptonshire, Oxfordshire, Warwickshire, Derbyshire, Lincolnshire and Nottinghamshire.

McLaren Building
35 Dale End
Birmingham B4 7NP
*Telephone*: 0121 607 6200
*Fax*: 0121 607 6349

5th Floor
Belgrave House
1 Greyfriars
Northampton NN1 2BS
*Telephone*: 01604 738 300
*Fax*: 01604 738 333

1st Floor
The Pearson Building
55 Upper Parliament Street
Nottingham NG1 6AU
*Telephone*: 0115 971 2800
*Fax*: 0115 971 2802

## Yorkshire and North East Region

Covers the counties and unitary authorities of Hartlepool, Middlesbrough, Redcar and Cleveland, Stockton-on-Tees, Durham, Hull, North Lincolnshire, North East Lincolnshire, East Riding, York, North Yorkshire, Northumberland, West Yorkshire, Tyne and Wear and the Metropolitan Boroughs of Barnsley, Doncaster, Rotherham and Sheffield.

Marshalls Mill
Marshall Street
Leeds LS11 9YJ
*Telephone*: 0113 283 4200
*Fax*: 0113 283 4296

Sovereign House
110 Queen Street
Sheffield S1 2ES
*Telephone*: 0114 291 2300
*Fax*: 0114 291 2379

Arden House
Regent Centre
Regent Farm Road
Gosforth
Newcastle upon Tyne NE3 3JN
*Telephone*: 0191 202 6200
*Fax*: 0191 202 6300

## North West Region

Covers the counties of Cheshire, Cumbria, Greater Manchester, Lancashire and Merseyside.

Grove House
Skerton Road
Manchester M16 ORB
*Telephone*: 0161 952 8200
*Fax*: 0161 952 8222

Victoria House
Ormskirk Road
Preston PR1 1HH
*Telephone*: 01772 836 200
*Fax*: 01772 836 222

## Wales and West Region

Covers Wales, and the unitary authorities of Cornwall, Devon, Somerset, North West Somerset, Bath and North East Somerset, Bristol, South Gloucestershire, Gloucestershire, Hereford and Worcester, Shropshire and Staffordshire.

Government Buildings
Phase 1
Ty GlasLlanishen
Cardiff CF14 5SH
*Telephone*: 029 2026 3000
*Fax*: 029 2026 3120

Inter City House
Mitchell Lane
Victoria Street
Bristol BS1 6AN
*Telephone*: 0117 988 6000
*Fax*: 0117 926 2998

The Marches House
Midway
Newcastle-under-Lyme
Staffordshire ST5 1DT
*Telephone*: 01782 602 300
*Fax*: 01782 602 400

## Scotland

Belford House
59 Belford Road
Edinburgh EH4 3UE
*Telephone*: 0131 247 2000
*Fax*: 0131 247 2121

Offshore Safety Division
Lord Cullen House
Fraser Place
Aberdeen AB25 3UB
*Telephone*: 01224 252 500
*Fax*: 01224 252 662

375 West George Street
Glasgow G2 4LW
*Telephone*: 0141 275 3000
*Fax*: 0141 276 3100

# Asbestos

## Introduction

A5001 Asbestos (Greek meaning 'unburnable', 'unquenchable') is a naturally-occurring dangerous substance found throughout industry. It is a generic term for a variety of silicates of iron, magnesium, calcium, sodium and aluminium which naturally exist in fibrous form. Defined as 'any of the following minerals . . . crocidolite, amosite, chrysotile, fibrous actinolite, fibrous anthophyllite, fibrous tremolite and any mixture containing any of those minerals' (by the *Asbestos (Licensing) Regulations 1983 (SI 1983 No 1649)* as amended by the *Control of Asbestos at Work Regulations 1987 (SI 1987 No 2115)*), asbestos has emerged in the last decade as one of the most significant occupational health hazards worldwide.

Exposure to asbestos can lead to asbestosis or mesothelioma. Asbestosis is a widespread pneumoconiosis or fibrosis of the lungs, caused by inhalation of asbestos fibres deep into the lungs, thus impairing their capacity to absorb oxygen. As a result, victims become increasingly breathless and physical activity is curtailed. Asbestosis is exacerbated by tobacco smoking, particularly cigarettes. Mesothelioma is a tumour which attacks the pleura or the membrane covering both lungs and lining the inner wall of the chest cavity. It develops quickly and is normally fatal, as there is no cure.

Asbestosis together with mesothelioma accounted for 32 deaths in 1968, 74 in 1976 and 88 in 1983; and mesothelioma of the pleura accounted for 98 deaths in 1968, 198 in 1976, 400 in 1983 and 1,010 in 1991. More spectacularly, in North America the avalanche of product liability litigation involving asbestosis/mesothelioma resulted in America's biggest manufacturer of asbestos, Johns-Manville Corporation of Denver, filing for voluntary liquidation in the early eighties. As usual, developments have been more prosaic over here but asbestosis/mesothelioma claims, the flagship of 'long tail liability', have caused major headaches for liability insurance companies, including Lloyds and its 'names'.

Asbestos-related disease is currently responsible for about 3,000 deaths annually, and will probably increase to between 5,000 and 10,000 annually in the next few years – exposure to asbestos dust being the salient cause. For every death from mesothelioma, it is estimated that there is one from asbestos-related lung cancer. Although use of asbestos peaked in the 1970s, many buildings still contain asbestos materials, with the result that there may still be substantial exposure in building renovation/maintenance work, particularly amongst plumbers, gas fitters, carpenters and electricians.

The Health and Safety Executive (HSE) estimate that there could be as many as 1.5 million workplace properties with asbestos in them. Because of this, the Trade Unions Congress (TUC) has set up the first ever national asbestos register of UK buildings. This is accessible at the following website: www.asbestosregister.com. Eventually the TUC aim to list every property in the UK containing asbestos.

By logging onto the above website, builders, surveyors, property developers and planners will be able to tell whether there is an asbestos register for the building on which they are about to start work. The website will then put them in touch with the building's owner or manager who will in turn be able to provide them with further information.

# Pathological effects of exposure to asbestos

A5002    Health risks are associated with the inhalation of fibrous dust and its dispersion within the lungs and other parts of the body. Workers engaged in extracting the fibre and processing it, along with those manufacturing asbestos products, are particularly vulnerable. However, exposure to asbestos alone is uncommon; in practice other mineral dusts are normally inhaled along with asbestos and the effect of these and other pollutants, such as cigarette smoke, often combine to produce diseases such as asbestosis. Inhalation of asbestos can give rise to the following three medical conditions namely, asbestosis, cancer of the bronchial tubes and cancer of the pleural surface (see further A5031 below).

Asbestos social security awards peaked in 1986 at 329, whereas mesothelioma awards escalated from 93 in 1981 and 462 in 1990 to 1,010 in 1991.

Unlike many occupational diseases, asbestos-related diseases manifest themselves over an incubation period of anything from 20 to 30 years. In consequence, current incidence of asbestos-related disease is not a measure of the effects of present dust levels, but rather of past dust exposures, which were (obviously) too high. In addition, this 'long tail' liability has strained the application of the three year rule for personal injury claims operating under the *Limitation Act 1980* (see A5035 below and E11029 EMPLOYERS' DUTIES TO THEIR EMPLOYEES).

# Control of exposure – control limits

A5003    Exposure to all forms of asbestos should be reduced to the minimum reasonably practicable (for the meaning of this expression, see E15017 ENFORCEMENT). Moreover, personal exposure should not exceed the *control limits* (formerly TLVs – threshold limit values). Control limits are the *upper* level of permitted exposure, for each species of asbestos. The following control limits apply (see also A5008 below):

(*a*)    for dust consisting of/containing chrysotile:

– 0.3 fibres per millilitre of air averaged over any continuous period of 4 hours,

– 0.9 fibres per millilitre of air averaged over any continuous period of 10 minutes;

(*b*)    for dust consisting of/containing any other form of asbestos, including mixtures of chrysotile and other asbestos:

– 0.2 fibres per millilitre of air averaged over any continuous period of 4 hours,

– 0.6 fibres per millilitre of air averaged over any continuous period of 10 minutes.

[*Reg 2 of the Control of Asbestos at Work Regulations 1987 (SI 1987 No 2115) as amended by the Control of Asbestos at Work (Amendment) Regulations 1998 (SI 1998 No 3235), Sch*].

(N.B. These measurements represent the concentration of fibres per millilitre of air sampled by routine atmospheric monitoring, e.g. by use of a static sampling device.)

### Control limits

A5004    Replacing TLVs, a control limit is the limit which is 'judged, after detailed consideration of the available evidence, to be "reasonably practicable" for the whole spectrum of work activities in Great Britain'. They are 'those exposure limits contained in regulations, approved codes of practice and EU Directives, or those agreed by the Health and Safety Commission'. (For the legal effect of approved codes of practice as distinct from regulations, see 42 INTRODUCTION.) Characteristically, they:

(a)    are set at a level which it would be reasonably practicable for relevant sectors of industry to achieve;

(b)    provide a clear indication of what the law requires as a maximum standard, so that when they are exceeded, employers know that they are in breach of *HSWA*; and

(c)    are based on a full review of medical/scientific evidence by the HSE and agreed by employers'/employees' organisations as acceptable.

A5005    Hence, as distinct from TLVs or recommended limits (which indicate the highest tolerable level of exposure), control limits represent the lowest exposure technically and economically possible. For this reason, control limits are not synonymous with safe levels of exposure which, once attained, make further improvements in dust control unnecessary. Rather they are gradually self-updating (see further, *Qualcast Ltd v Haynes* at 29 INTRODUCTION). *Failure to comply with control limits, or to put it another way, reduce exposure to the minimum reasonably practicable, can result in prosecution or some other form of enforcement action (see ENFORCEMENT).*

## Statutory requirements governing exposure to asbestos

A5006    Compliance with control limits is only part of an employer's duty towards his employees under *HSWA* and the *Control of Asbestos at Work Regulations 1987* as amended. The statutory requirements are as follows.

(a)    *General.* All employers must provide a safe working environment for their employees. [*HSWA s 2(2)(e)*]. This includes preventing the exposure of their employees to asbestos or, where it is not reasonably practicable to prevent such exposure, the provision of an environment in which exposure of employees to asbestos dust is reduced to the lowest levels reasonably practicable.

(b)    *Specific.* Specific statutory requirements relating to protection against exposure to asbestos are contained in the *Control of Asbestos at Work Regulations 1987 (SI 1987 No 2115)* as amended by the *Control of Asbestos at Work (Amendment) Regulations 1998 (SI 1998 No 3235)*, the *Asbestos (Licensing) Regulations 1983 (SI 1983 No 1649)* as amended and the *Special Waste Regulations 1996 (SI 1996 No 972)*. Moreover, labelling of asbestos products used at work is required by the *Chemicals (Hazard Information and Packaging for Supply) Regulations 1994 (SI 1994 No 3247)* (*CHIP 2*), the *Carriage of Dangerous Goods by Road Regulations 1996 (SI 1996 No 2095)* and the *Carriage of Dangerous Goods (Classification, Packaging and Labelling) and Use of Transportable Pressure Receptacles Regulations 1996 (SI 1996 No 2092)*.

### History of statute law on asbestos

A5007    The first regulations on asbestos, the *Asbestos Industry Regulations 1931*, were passed to control asbestosis in asbestos textile factories. These regulations were confined to asbestos factories handling and processing raw fibre. The purpose of these regulations was to prevent workers contracting asbestosis (see O1031 OCCUPATIONAL HEALTH AND DISEASES), since the dangers of lung cancer and mesothelioma were not then fully documented, nor were the varying levels of hazard associated with the three main species of asbestos, i.e. crocidolite, amosite and chrysotile – and so the regulations applied to all three species. The regulations protected workers in asbestos textile factories, manufacture of brake linings and asbestos cement works, usually against the least harmful species of asbestos, namely chrysotile. Significantly, however, workers in the thermal insulation industry exposed to the most harmful kind of asbestos, namely crocidolite, were not covered and their employers were under no statutory duties. Indeed, it was not until the *Asbestos Regulations 1969* were passed that these workers were covered for the first time.

## Action levels and control limits

A5008    Being limited in operation to factories, the *Asbestos Regulations 1969* were replaced by the wider *Control of Asbestos at Work Regulations 1987*, extending to all work-places where asbestos is made, used or handled. The basic duty of employers, whose employees are, or are liable to be exposed to above 'action level' asbestos, is to *prevent* the exposure of employees to asbestos. However, where *prevention* of exposure is not reasonably practicable in cost/benefit terms, employers must *reduce* exposure of their employees, by means other than use of respiratory protective equipment, to the lowest level reasonably practicable [*Reg 8(1)*]. 'Action level' refers to one of the following cumulative exposures to asbestos over a continuous 12 week period, namely:

(a)    where exposure is solely to chrysotile (white asbestos), 72 fibre-hours per millilitre of air;

(b)    where exposure is to any other form of asbestos including crocidolite (blue asbestos) or amosite (brown asbestos) either alone or in conjunction with chrysotile (white asbestos), 48 fibre-hours per millilitre of air; or

(c)    where both types of exposure occur separately during the 12 week period concerned, a proportionate number of fibre-hours per millilitre of air.

[*Control of Asbestos at Work Regulations 1987, Reg 2(1) as amended* by the *Control of Asbestos at Work (Amendment) Regulations 1998 (SI 1998 No 3235)*].

In determining whether an employee is exposed to asbestos or whether the extent of such exposure exceeds the action level or any control limit, no account shall be taken of any respiratory protective equipment which may be worn by that employee. [*Reg 2(2)* as amended].

However, where reduction of the exposure of employees below both the specified 'control limits' is not reasonably practicable in cost/benefit terms, employees must be supplied additionally with suitable and approved respiratory protective equipment in order to reduce the concentration of airborne asbestos inhaled by employees to a level below the specified 'control limit' [*Reg 8(2)*] (see A5003 above).

A5009    In addition, employers must designate asbestos areas (where exposure of employees might exceed the action level) and respirator zones (where concentrations of asbestos might exceed any control limit) [*Reg 14*], monitor the exposure of employees to asbestos [*Reg 15*], ensure that employees undergo regular periodic medical checks and keep health records for a minimum of 40 years [*Reg 16*]. Breach of these regulations is an offence under the *Health and Safety at Work etc. Act 1974*, punishable by a maximum fine of £5,000 on summary conviction and an unlimited fine and/or up to two years' imprisonment on conviction on indictment. Moreover, many of the duties exist for the benefit not just of employees but also of other workers and the general public who may be affected by exposure to asbestos. The duties also apply to self-employed persons. [*Reg 3(2)*].

# Control of Asbestos at Work Regulations 1987 (SI 1987 No 2115) (As amended by SI 1992 No 3068 and SI 1998 No 3235)

## Duty to assess risks

A5010    Contractors who undertake work on materials containing asbestos are on notice, as from 1988 at the latest, when these Regulations came into force, that there are serious health hazards connected with such work. In consequence, contractors are under a duty to find out about the risks associated with asbestos and take corresponding precautions. In *Barclays Bank plc v Fairclough Building Ltd (No 2) [1995] 1 AER 289*, BB contracted F to carry out maintenance work. F subcontracted the cleaning of corrugated asbestos roofs to C who, in turn, subcontracted it to T. Neither C nor T was experienced in cleaning asbestos roofs. T did the work using a high-pressure hose, which caused asbestos-contaminated slurry to enter buildings, leaving dangerous levels of asbestos dust and fibres. A prohibition notice required remedial work costing £4,000,000. BB obtained judgment against F; meanwhile C paid F £1,250,000. In C's action against T, the Court of Appeal overturned judgment given for T, holding that:

(*a*)    neither T nor C had exercised reasonable care and skill in the contractual chain for cleaning the asbestos roof, risks associated with asbestos being well publicised by the HSE and trade journals;

(*b*)    contractors cleaning asbestos roofs with high-pressure hoses undertake to do so safely and without causing extensive contamination of the surrounding area, therefore T was liable to C; *but*

(*c*)    because of (*a*) T's liability would be reduced by 50% to reflect the extent of C's contributory negligence.

The Health and Safety Commission's (HSC) proposals to modify the 1997 Regulations are currently out for consultation. If the proposals are adopted they would introduce a duty to manage asbestos in non-domestic premises. To support this proposal, HSE is developing new technical guidance on the Methods for Determining Hazardous Substances (MDHS) Series on surveying workplace premises for materials containing asbestos.

The modifications to the Regulations will, if accepted, require those responsible for workplace premises to:

●    find out whether asbestos is present in their buildings and its location;

●    work on the assumption that asbestos is present unless they can be certain otherwise;

●    record their findings;

●    prepare and implement plans to manage the risks from such asbestos; and

●    provide information to anyone liable to come into contact with asbestos.

The '*MDHS technical guidance on surveying*' (MDHS 100) will give advice on how to recognise materials containing asbestos, how to take samples of these materials and how to assess the risk from their presence in the building.

Bill MacDonald, Head of Asbestos Policy at HSE explained: 'Copies of the draft MDHS document have been circulated to external specialists as part of the development process. I would stress that the published MDHS 100 may differ from the draft on points of detail and emphasis. It is also possible that changes may have to be made as a result of HSC's consultation on the new duty under the Control of Asbestos at Work Regulations'.

For the same reasons, HSE considers that it would be more appropriate to publish the guidance at the time that the modified Regulations are introduced, which is likely to be Spring 2002.

### Prohibitions on asbestos activities

A5011    No employer must carry out work which:

(*a*)    exposes, or

(*b*)    is liable to expose,

his employees to asbestos, unless first:

(i)    he has identified the type of asbestos involved in the work activity; or

(ii)    he has assumed that the asbestos is not chrysotile alone and treated it accordingly

[*Reg 4*];

(iii)    he has made and regularly reviewed an adequate assessment of that exposure. Such assessment must:

    (*a*)    identify the type of asbestos;

    (*b*)    determine the nature and degree of exposure expected in the course of the work; and

    (*c*)    specify the steps to be taken to prevent or to reduce exposure to the lowest level reasonably practicable. The assessment must be reviewed regularly and a new assessment substituted when there is reason to suspect that the existing assessment is no longer valid or there is a significant change in working conditions.

    (*d*)    be kept on the premises where, and for the period which, the work is being carried out.

[*Reg 5*],

(iv)    he has, if the work involves removal of asbestos from any building, structure, plant, installation or ship, prepared a written plan detailing how the work is to be carried out prior to the commencement of removal activities, a copy to be kept on the premises where, and for the period during which, the work is being carried out. The plan must include details of:

    (*a*)    the nature and probable duration of the work;

    (*b*)    the location of the place where the work is to be carried out;

    (*c*)    the methods to be applied where the work involves the handling of asbestos or materials containing asbestos;

    (*d*)    the characteristics of the equipment to be used for:

        (1)    protection and decontamination of those carrying out the work;

        (2)    protection of other persons on or near the work site.

The employer must also ensure, so far as is reasonably practicable, that the work to which the plan relates is carried out in accordance with that plan. [*Reg 5A*] (see A5015, A5016 below);

(v)  he has notified the 'enforcing authority' (see E15003, E15004 ENFORCEMENT for the meaning of this expression) at least 14 days before commencing work, of:

(*a*)  his name, address and telephone number;

(*b*)  his usual place of business;

(*c*)  types of asbestos used or handled;

(*d*)  maximum quantity of asbestos on the premises (see A5015 below);

(*e*)  activities/processes involved on the premises;

(*f*)  products (if any) manufactured (see A5017 below);

(*g*)  date when work activity is to start.

Also any material change(s) in work activity involving asbestos must be notified. [*Reg 6* as amended].

## Notification of work with asbestos: specimen form

A5012    To comply with *Regulation 6* of the *Control of Asbestos at Work Regulations 1987* the following particulars are to be sent to the relevant Enforcing Authority.

To comply with *Regulation 6* of the *Control of Asbestos at Work Regulations 1987* the following particulars are to be sent to the relevant Enforcing Authority.

Name ...........................................................................................................................

Company.....................................................................................................................

Usual place of business.............................................................................................

..................................................................................................................................

Telephone number .....................................................................................................

## Brief description of work with asbestos

1    Type(s) of asbestos used or handled (crocidolite, amosite, chrysotile or other)

..................................................................................................................................

..................................................................................................................................

..................................................................................................................................

2    Maximum quantity of asbestos held on the premises at any one time

..................................................................................................................................

..................................................................................................................................

..................................................................................................................................

3    Activities or processes involved

..................................................................................................................................

..................................................................................................................................

..................................................................................................................................

4    Products manufactured

..................................................................................................................................

..................................................................................................................................

..................................................................................................................................

5    Date of commencement of work activity where work has yet to begin

..................................................................................................................................

..................................................................................................................................

..................................................................................................................................

*fig. 1*

# Duties in connection with asbestos activities

## Employers

**A5013**    All employers whose employees are, or are liable to be, exposed to asbestos (see A5008 above), must:

(*a*)    provide adequate information, instruction and training to such employees, so that they are aware of the risks and precautions to be taken (see A5021 below) [*Control of Asbestos at Work Regulations 1987, Reg 7* as amended]. This must be provided at suitable intervals and adapted to take account of any significant changes in the type of work carried out or methods of working used by the employer;

(*b*)    (i)    prevent exposure of employees to asbestos, but where prevention of exposure is not reasonably practicable, reduce exposure to the lowest level reasonably practicable by means other than use of respiratory protective equipment (that is, by substituting for asbestos a substance not creating a health risk or lesser health risk to employees) [*Reg 8(1A)* as amended],

(ii)    where reduction to below both the applicable 'control limits' (see A5008 above) is not reasonably practicable, supply employees in addition with suitable and HSE-approved respiratory protective equipment in order to reduce the concentration of airborne asbestos inhaled by employees to a concentration which is as low as reasonably practicable in and any event below the specified 'control limit'

[*Reg 8(2) and (3),* as amended],

(iii)    if an unforeseen event occurs, resulting in escape of asbestos into the workplace at a concentration that is liable to exceed any applicable control limit, ensure that only persons responsible for carrying out repairs are permitted in the affected area and are provided with respiratory protective equipment/clothing *and* that employees and other persons who may have been affected are notified immediately

[*Reg 8(4)* as amended];

(*c*)    ensure that personal protective equipment is properly used or applied [*Reg 9*];

(*d*)    and is maintained in a clean and efficient state and in good working order and is regularly examined/tested by a competent person (see 48 INTRODUCTION). A record of such maintenance must be kept for at least five years [*Reg 10* as amended];

(*e*)    provide adequate and suitable protective clothing and see that such clothing is disposed of as asbestos waste or, alternatively, cleaned at regular intervals. The clothing must first be packed in a suitable container labelled 'Warning. Contains asbestos. Breathing asbestos dust is dangerous to health. Follow safety instructions' [*Reg 11* as amended];

(*f*)    prevent the spread of asbestos from any place where work under his control is carried out, but where prevention is not reasonably practicable, reduce its spread to the lowest level reasonably practicable [*Reg 12* as amended] (see A5017 below);

(*g*)    keep work premises and plant clean and, in the case of new premises, ensure that they are:

(i)    designed and constructed to facilitate cleaning, and

      (ii)   equipped with an adequate and suitable vacuum cleaning system which ideally should be a fixed system

[*Reg 13*].

(Under the previous *Asbestos Regulations 1969 (SI 1969 No 690)*, dry-sweeping asbestos dust qualified as a process, so that dust containing asbestos in excess of the threshold limit value was a breach of the regulations (*Edgson v Vickers plc, The Times, 8 April 1994*). It is likely that it would qualify as 'work' under the current regulations.)

## Designated areas/air monitoring/health records

### Designated asbestos areas/respirator zones

A5014    All employers must:

(*a*)    designate asbestos areas where exposure to asbestos of an employee exceeds, or is liable to exceed, the 'action level' (see A5008 above);

(*b*)    designate respirator zones where the concentration of asbestos exceeds, or is liable to exceed, any 'control limit' (see A5008 above);

(*c*)    ensure that employees (other than employees whose work so requires) do not either (i) enter or (ii) remain in any designated areas/zones;

(*d*)    ensure that employees do not eat/drink/smoke in designated areas/zones.

Both (*a*) asbestos areas and (*b*) respirator zones must be separately demarcated and identified by notices, and in the case of a respirator zone, the notice must require an employee entering the zone to wear respiratory protective equipment. [*Reg 14*].

### Written assessments

A5015    Written assessments should specify:

(i)    type of work involved;

(ii)    reasons for not using a substitute material;

(iii)    type and quantity of asbestos and results of analysis;

(iv)    details of expected exposures – and, in particular,

    (*a*)    likelihood of action level being exceeded (see A5008 above),

    (*b*)    likelihood of control limit being exceeded (see A5008 above),

    (*c*)    if above either relevant control limit, expected exposure, for selection of respiratory protective equipment,

    (*d*)    frequency and duration of exposure,

    (*e*)    expected exposure of non-employees,

    (*f*)    air monitoring results,

    (*g*)    measures to control exposure and release of asbestos to the environment,

    (*h*)    procedures relating to provision and use of respiratory protective equipment and other protective equipment,

    (*j*)    in case of demolition, procedures for asbestos to be removed before demolition begins, (*k*)    procedures for dealing with emergencies,

(*l*)    procedures for removal of waste from the workplace.

(Approved Code of Practice to these Regulations).

## Plan of work

A5016    An employer must not undertake any work involving the removal of asbestos from any building, structure, plant, installation or ship unless he has prepared a suitable written plan of work, giving details of:

(*a*)    nature/duration of work;

(*b*)    address/location of work;

(*c*)    methods for handling asbestos; and

(*d*)    equipment for protection and decontamination of employees, and protection of other persons on or near the worksite.

The plan, which must be submitted to the HSE on request, should indicate that, so far as reasonably practicable, asbestos/asbestos products have been removed prior to work commencement. [*Reg 5A*].

## Reduction of exposure to asbestos

A5017    Exposure to asbestos can be reduced by technical measures (including local exhaust ventilation) and a suitable work system – the latter varying according to whether the working environment is construction or manufacturing.

In the case of *construction*, a suitable work system consists of:

(*a*)    removal of asbestos materials before other major work begins;

(*b*)    methods of work which minimise breakage, abrasion, machining or cutting of asbestos;

(*c*)    suppression of dust by wetting;

(*d*)    segregation of work with asbestos; and

(*e*)    prompt removal of off-cuts, waste and dust.

In the case of *manufacturing*, a suitable work system involves:

(i)    limiting quantity of asbestos used;

(ii)    limiting number of persons exposed;

(iii)    ensuring collection of waste and removal from work area as soon as possible in suitably labelled containers;

(iv)    ensuring that damaged containers of raw fibre or waste are repaired forthwith or placed inside another suitable container;

(v)    avoiding manual handling of raw fibre or intermediate products; and

(vi)    intermediate cleaning/sealing of all products containing asbestos.

[*Approved Code of Practice, paras 28, 29*].

## Maintenance and inspection

A5018    Exhaust ventilation equipment should be:

(*a*)    inspected weekly, and

(*b*)    examined and tested by a competent person every six months.

[*Approved Code of Practice, para 38*].

### Weekly inspections

A5019    Weekly inspections should include a check of position and condition of exhaust hoods and any visible signs of malfunction (e.g. dust deposits).

In particular,

(*a*)    if dust seems to be escaping, this should be checked using a dust lamp;

(*b*)    pressure drop across the filter should be checked in the case of manometers fitted to dust collectors;

(*c*)    filter hoppers/bins should be checked to ensure proper routine emptying;

(*d*)    records of weekly inspections should be kept and any faults logged; and

(*e*)    faults should be rectified quickly and a written note made of action taken.

[*Approved Code of Practice, para 40*].

### Six-monthly examination and test

A5020    This should include:

(*a*)    *New equipment – Part I examination*

(i)    confirmation that system is satisfactorily controlling airborne asbestos;

(ii)    measurement of pressures and air velocities (including static and dynamic pressures, face and duct velocities as well as static pressure differences across fans and filters);

(iii)    checks on dust collection.

(*b*)    *Previously examined machinery – Part II examination*

(i)    visual check for deterioration/leakage;

(ii)    verification that method of use of system is satisfactory;

(iii)    check on dust collection;

(iv)    measurement of pressures/velocities.

This done, a report of the examination should be completed and signed within 14 days.

[*Approved Code of Practice, paras 41–47*].

### Maintenance schedules

A5021    Maintenance procedures for all control measures and personal protective equipment should be drawn up including, as appropriate:

(*a*)    cleaning equipment – particularly vacuum cleaners (to BS 5145);

(*b*)    washing and changing facilities;

(*c*)   controls (including enclosures) to prevent contamination.

The maintenance schedule should specify:

(i)    what control measures require maintenance;

(ii)   when and how maintenance is to be carried out;

(iii)  who is responsible for maintenance; and

(iv)   how defects are to be remedied.

[*Approved Code of Practice, paras 48, 49*].

## Asbestos premises and hot work

A5022   Cleaning of asbestos-contaminated premises should be frequent, and for inside walls and ceilings at least once a year, though not by dry manual brushing or sweeping. Hosing is permissible if residues are suitably disposed of. Ideally, a fixed vacuum system should be installed, using high efficiency filters and venting (preferably) outside. Small amounts of asbestos dust can be removed with a well-dampened cloth.

Asbestos stripping should not be carried out on hot plant until absolutely necessary, and preferably on a scheduled basis during shutdowns or holidays, since the risk of heat stress is greater at such times, leading possibly to heat stroke which can be fatal. The main reason for this is that, as insulation material is progressively removed, heat input into the working area will increase; in addition, protective equipment is normally hooded with elasticated cuffs and ankles, restricting air movement over the body and minimising evaporation of sweat. Moreover, respiratory protective equipment often restricts breathing. Work in such high temperatures can cause burns, swelling of ankles and feet, fainting, muscle cramps, heat exhaustion, breathing difficulties and thirst; and so periodical break-offs are advisable as follows:

Work at 26.0°C – 27.5°C – 15 minutes rest after 45 minutes work

Work at 27.5°C – 29.0°C – 30 minutes rest after 30 minutes work

Work at 29.0°C – 31.0°C – 45 minutes rest after 15 minutes work.

## Air monitoring

A5023   All employers must monitor the exposure of employees to asbestos and keep a record of such monitoring for:

(*a*)   forty years, if a health record (see A5024 below);

(*b*)   otherwise, five years.

[*Reg 15 as amended by Control of Asbestos at Work (Amendment) Regulations 1992, Sch*].

## Compliance with EN 45001

A5024   All employers must ensure that any measurement of the concentration of asbestos fibres in the air complies with the requirements of European Standard EN 45001 'General Criteria for the operating of testing laboratories'. [*Reg 15A as inserted by the Control of Asbestos at Work (Amendment) Regulations 1998 (SI 1998 No 3235*].

## Health records/medical surveillance

A5025   All employers must:

(*a*)   keep health records of all employees exposed to asbestos exceeding 'action level' (see above) for at least forty years (the incubation period of many asbestos-related diseases) [*Reg 16(1) as amended by Control of Asbestos at Work (Amendment) Regulations 1992, Sch*];

(*b*)   require employees exposed to above 'action level' asbestos, to undergo a periodic medical examination at least every two years.

Employers must be issued with a certificate of examination and keep it for at least four years, giving a copy to the employee. Such medical examinations, carried out by Employment Medical Advisers (EMAs), during working hours and on work premises, are at the expense of the employer, who must provide suitable facilities. On being given reasonable notice, employers must allow employees access to health records. [*Reg 16*].

## Washing facilities/storage/distribution/labelling etc.

A5026   All employers must:

(*a*)   provide employees exposed or liable to be exposed to asbestos with adequate and suitable facilities for

(i)   washing/changing,

(ii)   storage of protective clothing and personal clothing not worn during working hours, and

(iii)   separate storage of respiratory protective equipment

[*Reg 17* as amended];

(*b*)   ensure that raw asbestos or waste containing asbestos is not

(i)   stored,

(ii)   received into or despatched from any place of work, or

(iii)   distributed (unless in a totally enclosed distribution system) within any place of work,

unless it is in a suitable and sealed container clearly labelled and marked [*Reg 18*].

## Labelling/marking of raw asbestos, asbestos waste and asbestos products

A5027   (*a*)   Raw asbestos must be labelled in the prescribed form, using the words: 'Warning. Contains asbestos. Breathing asbestos dust is dangerous to health. Follow safety instructions'.

(*b*)   Waste containing asbestos must be labelled:

(i)   in accordance with the *Chemicals (Hazard Information and Packaging for Supply) Regulations 1994 (SI 1994 No 3247) (CHIP 2)* or the *Carriage of Dangerous Goods (Classification, Packaging and Labelling) and Use of Transportable Pressure Receptacles Regulations 1996 (SI 1996 No 2092)* (see D1013–D1016 DANGEROUS SUBSTANCES I and D3006–D3014 DANGEROUS SUBSTANCES II);

(ii)     if conveyed by road in a road tanker or tank container, in accordance with the *Carriage of Dangerous Goods by Road Regulations 1996 (SI 1996 No 2095)* (see D3018–D3034 DANGEROUS SUBSTANCES II).

(c)     Asbestos products must be labelled: 'Warning. Contains asbestos. Breathing asbestos dust is dangerous to health. Follow safety instructions' [*Reg 19*]. If the product contains crocidolite, the words 'Contains asbestos' are replaced by 'Contains crocidolite/blue asbestos'.

(For the effect of 'warnings' on civil liability in connection with defective products, see P9032 PRODUCT SAFETY.)

## Employees' duties

A5028     Every employee must:

(a)     make full and proper use of any control measures, personal protective equipment or other facility provided by the employer [*Reg 9(2)*];

(b)     report to the employer any defect in personal protective equipment or control measures [*Reg 9(2)*];

(c)     not enter/remain in (i) asbestos areas (ii) respirator zones (unless his work requires him to do so) [*Reg 14*]; and

(d)     when required by his employer, present himself during working hours for medical examination/checks [*Reg 16(4)*].

## Offences and defences

A5029     By *section 33(1)(c) HSWA* it is an offence for a person to contravene any health and safety regulations or any requirement or prohibition imposed under any such regulations.

A new *Reg 21A* inserted by the *Control of Asbestos at Work (Amendment) Regulations 1998 (SI 1998 No 3235)*, provides that in any proceedings for such an offence it shall be a defence for the person charged to prove that he took all reasonable precautions and exercised all due diligence to avoid the commission of the offence.

The penalties imposed for offences relating to asbestos tend to be severe. In *R v Brintons (1999) (unreported)*, the Court of Appeal upheld the imposition of a fine of £100,000 plus costs on an employer who contravened *Reg 8(1)*, by failing to prevent the exposure of his employees to asbestos, even though the exemplary record of the employer on health and safety matters before the incident was acknowledged, as was the promptness with which the employer took action after being informed of the presence of asbestos on his premises: the fault lay in his doing nothing about investigating the possible presence of asbestos.

# Prohibitions on the use of asbestos products – the Asbestos (Prohibitions) Regulations 1992 (SI 1992 No 3067) as amended by SI 1999 No 2373 and SI 1999 No 2977

A5030     (a)     *Amphibole asbestos*

The *Asbestos (Prohibitions) Regulations 1992 (SI 1992 No 3067)* as amended prohibit:

(i)     importation into the United Kingdom of all forms of amphibole asbestos, namely crocidolite ('blue asbestos'), amosite ('brown asbestos'), fibrous actinolite, fibrous anthophyllite, fibrous tremolite and any mixture containing any of those minerals and any product containing amphibole asbestos [*Reg 3*];

(ii)    supply (other than solely for the purposes of disposal) of amphibole asbestos or any product to which it has been added [*Reg 4*];

(iii)   use of amphibole asbestos or any product to which it has been intentionally added, except products containing:

— crocidolite or amosite, which were in use before 1 January 1986; or

— other forms of amphibole asbestos, which were in use before 1 January 1993

[Reg 5];

(iv)   asbestos spraying [*Reg 6*].

*(b)    Chrysotile asbestos*

Supply and use of chrysotile and any product to which chrysotile has been intentionally added unless it was in use before 24 November 1999 or was installed in or has formed part of any premises or plant since that date. [*Reg 7*, as amended].

## Working with asbestos insulation or asbestos coating – Asbestos (Licensing) Regulations 1983 (SI 1983 No 1649) as amended by SI 1998 No 3233

A5031    A system of licensing or advance notification applies to work with asbestos insulation or coating carried out by an employer or a self-employed person.

A licence is not necessary for such work where:

(*a*)    (i)    any person who carries out such work will not spend more than one hour on the work in seven consecutive days; and

(ii)   the total time spent on the work by all persons involved in it does not exceed two hours; or

(*b*)    (i)    the employer or self-employed person is the occupier of the premises on which the work is carried out; and

(ii)   he has given at least 28 days' notice to the HSE in advance, specifying the type of work to be carried out and the address of the premises at which it is to be done; or

(*c*)    the work consists solely of air monitoring or collecting samples.

[*Reg 3*].

Even if a licence is not necessary, employers (or self-employed persons) must still comply with the *Control of Asbestos at Work Regulations 1987* and in particular, should:

(i)    give to employees the necessary instruction and training;

(ii)   provide adequate information to others (e.g. workforce of an outside contractor) who may be affected by the work;

(iii)  achieve the lowest level of asbestos exposure reasonably practicable; and

(iv)   ensure that employees are under medical surveillance.

### Issue of licence

A5032  Licence applications must be made to the HSE at least 28 days before the work is due to start [*Reg 4(1)*]. A fee is payable (currently £505.00 – *Health and Safety (Fees) Regulations 1999 (SI 1999 No 645), Reg 6, 5 Sch*).

The HSE can:

(*a*)  impose a time limit on the period for which a licence is granted;

(*b*)  impose other conditions;

(*c*)  refuse to issue a licence;

(*d*)  vary conditions on a licence already granted; or

(*e*)  revoke a licence, if it is considered appropriate to do so.

[*Reg 4(2)–(4)*].

There is a right of appeal to the Secretary of State under *HSWA s 44*.

Any conditions imposed will depend upon the applicant's previous track record with asbestos work; and companies with limited experience will receive more restrictive licences than companies with greater experience. In particular,

(i)  new applicants will receive a one year licence;

(ii)  renewal licensees will receive a licence for 30 months;

(iii)  licensees who have been the recipient of enforcement action but who are considered likely to improve, will be required to comply with an agreed method statement for each job;

(iv)  licensees with a poor first year record, but not bad enough for refusal, will receive a similar restrictive licence, but for one year.

For medical surveillance requirements, see A5025(*b*) above.

## Occupational diseases associated with asbestos

A5033  There are three occupational diseases associated with working with asbestos, i.e.:

—  diffuse mesothelioma (D3);

—  primary carcinoma of the lung (D8); and

—  bilateral diffuse pleural thickening (D9).

The occupations for which these three conditions are prescribed are as follows:

(*a*)  working or handling asbestos, or any admixture of asbestos;

(*b*)  manufacture or repair of asbestos textiles or other articles containing or composed of asbestos;

(*c*)  cleaning of any machinery or plant used for (*a*) and (*b*), and of any chambers, fixtures and appliances for the collection of asbestos dust;

(*d*)  substantial exposure to dust arising from operations (*a*), (*b*) and (*c*).

[*Social Security (Industrial Injuries) (Prescribed Diseases) Regulations 1985 (SI 1985 No 967), 1 Sch as amended by the Social Security (Industrial Injuries) (Miscellaneous Amendments) Regulations 1997 (SI 1997 No 810)*].

## Actions against the employer for asbestos-related diseases

A5034
In addition to being prescribed occupational diseases, asbestosis and mesothelioma may give rise to actions against the employer for breach of statutory duty and the common law duty of care (negligence) (*Bryce v Swan Hunter Group [1987] 2 Lloyd's Rep 426* concerning a painter, employed for most of his working life by various shipbuilding employers, who died, aged 60, from mesothelioma. The defendant employers were held liable for breach of statutory duty for failing to take all practical measures to reduce exposure of employees to asbestos dust (under the *Asbestos Regulations 1969*), but not for breach of duty at common law because, applying the standards of knowledge of the time (1947), it could not be suggested that the defendants had to prevent the employee from all exposure to dangerous quantities of asbestos dust).

Businesses carrying out operations involving asbestos may also be liable in negligence to members of the public who suffer foreseeable pulmonary injury, following exposure to airborne dust (*Margereson and Hancock v JW Roberts Ltd, The Times, 17 April 1996* where the defendant, a former factory owner, was held liable to two plaintiffs who contracted mesothelioma as a result of playing, when children, in a factory loading bay, where there were high concentrations of asbestos dust. As stated by Lord Lloyd in *Page v Smith, The Times, 12 May 1995*, 'the test in every case ought to be whether the defendant can reasonably foresee that his conduct will expose the plaintiff to the risk of personal injury'. On this basis, the defendant was liable if, as here, he should reasonably have foreseen the risk of some pulmonary injury, not necessarily mesothelioma).

## Time limitation problems

A5035
Symptom manifestation can take anything from 20-30 years after exposure and consequently the possibility arises that actions for damages, being actions in respect of 'personal injuries', may become statute-barred.

The *Limitation Act 1980* states that the period for initiating action is three years from:

(a)    the date on which the cause of action accrued; or

(b)    the date of knowledge (if later) of the person injured.

[*Limitation Act 1980, s 11(4)*].

In *Central Asbestos Co Ltd v Dodd [1973] AC 518*, a workman was employed in a workshop where various processes connected with asbestos were carried out from 1952 to 1965. Throughout that period the employer was in breach of the *Asbestos Industry Regulations 1931* and, in consequence, the employee was exposed to asbestos dust and contracted asbestosis, leading eventually to his death. The employee's condition was diagnosed in January 1964, when he was advised by the Pneumoconiosis Medical Panel not to carry on working with asbestos. Therefore, from that time he had actual knowledge that the disease had been caused by the inhalation of asbestos dust. He did not, however, feel ill then and so continued working for the company. In March 1964 he was awarded disability benefit based on 10 per cent disablement. In September 1965 he left the company on his doctor's advice. By then, he knew that (a) he was suffering from asbestosis, (b) the company had been convicted for breach of the *Asbestos Industry Regulations 1931* during all the period he had worked there, and (c) the nature of his condition meant that he had to stop working with asbestos. He did not, however, know he had a good cause of action against his employer, having been told by the works manager (who was also suffering from asbestosis) that if he received disability benefit he could not sue his employer. When he learned in April 1967 that a co-employee was suing the company, he also started legal action, in October 1967.

The employer argued that the claim was statute-barred under the *Limitation Act 1963* because the action had been begun more than three years from the date the employee had knowledge of the injury (January 1964). It was held (by the House of Lords) that the action was not statute-barred because the employee's ignorance of his legal rights was a 'material fact' of a 'decisive character'. Significantly, claims for asbestosis/mesothelioma cannot begin to run before a claimant has knowledge, both medical and legal, of his condition and liability for it.

Although employers can be sued for the death of employees caused by asbestos-related conditions, this does not necessarily extend to wives of asbestos workers (*Gunn v Wallsend Slipway and Engineering Co Ltd, The Times, 23 January 1989* where the wife of the plaintiff died as a result of mesothelioma caused by inhalation of asbestos from the plaintiff's working clothes, and it was held that the employers owed no duty of care to the deceased because in 1965 when the plaintiff ceased to be exposed to asbestos dust, medical knowledge did not extend to an appreciation that the condition could be contracted in that way, that is, by washing contaminated clothes).

### Discretionary exclusion of time limits – asbestosis claims

A5036 Statutory time limits can be excluded if the court thinks it equitable to allow an action to proceed. [*Limitation Act 1980, s 33*].

# Practical control measures

A5037 Asbestos has been the standard form of thermal insulation since the turn of the century and may be found in numerous locations in industrial, commercial and domestic premises. In its various forms, it may be present in lagging to pipework, tanks and boilers, or as a component of structural finishes, such as walls and ceilings. In most cases, the presence of asbestos is not considered until it is actually exposed through normal wear and tear on plant and structural finishes, through structural damage or during redevelopment work.

In order to prevent further exposure, a practical control system is necessary, which incorporates procedures for sampling, treatment or removal, and disposal of asbestos waste.

Asbestos has been used widely for the following industrial purposes:

(*a*)    as fire protection on structures, protected exits, doors and in fire breaks in service ducts;

(*b*)    in the construction of inner walls and partitions;

(*c*)    in switchgear areas;

(*d*)    in ceiling tiles and linings for semi-exposed areas e.g. loading bay canopies;

(*e*)    for thermal and acoustic insulation of buildings; and

(*f*)    for thermal insulation of cold stores.

It may be applied in several forms, namely:

—    *Sprayed asbestos coating.* The asbestos content is not normally less than 55%, and such coating usually contains amosite or crocidolite.

— *Thermal insulation material.* Thermal insulation of services or process plant frequently consists of sectional insulation, such as asbestos insulation board, which may contain a considerable proportion of asbestos. In some cases asbestos may be a minor constituent of the mixture together with materials such as magnesia and diatomaceous earth. The asbestos content of insulation board is typically 16.25%, amosite being the most common form of asbestos used.

### Sampling

A5038  An asbestos removal contractor should initially commence operation by taking a series of 10 gm samples in areas where asbestos is suspected. In large buildings this may entail taking several hundred samples for analysis. Once the results of these samples have been received a decision to remove or seal the asbestos must be taken. The actual sampling procedure needs a high degree of control in terms of site preparation for sampling, the use of personal protective equipment, the actual sampling process and despatch of samples. Specific provisions apply to those persons taking the sample, in exactly the same way as those engaged in removal or sealing of the asbestos.

### Disposal of asbestos waste

A5039  Relevant to disposal of asbestos are:

(*a*)  the provision and use of suitable receptacles;

(*b*)  transfer procedures from surface to receptacles;

(*c*)  transfer procedures from working area to disposal point; and

(*d*)  action to be taken in the event of asbestos spillage.

Asbestos waste must be disposed of only at a suitably licensed disposal site and in accordance with specific requirements laid down by the waste regulation authority (in England and Wales, the Environment Agency; in Scotland, SEPA).

### Transport of asbestos waste

A5040  Before transporting any asbestos waste, the haulier must ensure that, so far as is reasonably practicable:

(*a*)  suitable vehicles are available;

(*b*)  the release of asbestos dust is prevented;

(*c*)  effective arrangements exist for dealing with accidental spillage; and

(*d*)  effective arrangements exist for decontamination of the vehicle used for transport.

Such arrangements should ensure that asbestos dust is not released during decontamination.

## Special Waste Regulations 1996 (SI 1996 No 972)

A5041  Duties under the *Special Waste Regulations 1996 (SI 1996 No 972)* are placed on:

(*a*)  persons who cause special waste (which includes asbestos) to be removed from premises ('consignors');

(*b*)  carriers; and

(*c*)    persons to whom such waste is delivered ('consignees').

The standard procedure is as follows:

(*a*)    the consignor must prepare five copies of a 'consignment note' (see A5044 below), complete Parts A and B of the note and enter a code, unique to that consignment, which has been obtained from the Environment Agency or SEPA. The consignor must send a copy of the note, as so completed, to the Agency for the place to which the consignment is to be transported (i.e. the Environment Agency for sites in England and Wales, and SEPA for sites in Scotland);

(*b*)    the carrier must complete Part C on each of the four remaining copies;

(*c*)    the consignor:

   (i)    must complete Part D on each of those copies;

   (ii)    must retain one copy (on which Parts A to D have been completed and the relevant unique code entered); and

   (iii)    must give the three remaining copies to the carrier;

(*d*)    the carrier must ensure that the copies which he has received:

   (i)    travel with the consignment; and

   (ii)    are given to the consignee on delivery of the consignment;

(*e*)    the consignee, on receiving the consignment, must:

   (i)    complete Part E on the three copies of the consignment note given to him;

   (ii)    retain one copy;

   (iii)    give one copy to the carrier; and

   (iv)    send one copy to the Agency for the place to which the consignment has been transported.

[Reg 5].

For at least three years consignors and carriers must keep a register containing copies of all consignment notes; a consignee must keep a register containing copies of all consignment notes until his waste management licence for the site is surrendered or revoked, when he must send the register to the Agency which must retain the register for at least three years [*Reg 15*].

Any person who deposits special waste on land must record the location of each deposit, keep such records until his waste management licence is surrendered or revoked and then send the records to the Agency [*Reg 16*].

## Offences/penalties

A5042    Any consignor, carrier or consignee who fails to comply with the regulations is liable:

(*a*)    on summary conviction, to a fine of not more than £5,000; and

(*b*)    on conviction on indictment to an unlimited fine or imprisonment for up to two years, or both.

[*Reg 18*].

# HSE Guidance Notes

A5043   A number of HSE Guidance Notes dealing with this subject are available and should be consulted, together with the Approved Codes of Practice which give practical guidance with regard to the *Asbestos (Licensing) Regulations 1983* and the *Control of Asbestos at Work Regulations 1987*, before any work involving asbestos is undertaken. These Guidance Notes are:

EH 10 – Asbestos: exposure limits and measurement of airborne dust concentrations. (1995)

EH 47 – Provision, use and maintenance of hygiene facilities for work with asbestos insulation and coatings. (1990)

EH 50 – Training operatives and supervisors for work with asbestos insulation and coatings. (1988)

EH 51 – Enclosures provided for work with asbestos insulation, coatings and insulation board. (1999)

EH 57 – The problems of asbestos removal at high temperatures. (1993)

L 11 – A guide to the *Asbestos (Licensing) Regulations 1983* as amended. (1999)

L 27 – The control of asbestos at work. *Control of Asbestos at Work Regulations 1987* – approved code of practice. (1999)

L 28 – Work with asbestos insulation, asbestos coating and asbestos board. *Control of Asbestos at Work Regulations 1987* – approved code of practice. (1999)

INDG 107 – Asbestos and you. (1996)

INDG 188 – Asbestos alert for building maintenance, repair and refurbishment workers. (2000)

INDG 223 – Managing asbestos in workplace buildings.(1996)

INDG 255 – Asbestos dust kills – keep your mask on. (1999)

INDG 288 – Selection of suitable respiratory protective equipment for work with asbestos. (1999)

INDG 289 – Working with asbestos in buildings. (1999)

HSG 189/1 – Controlled asbestos stripping techniques for work requiring a licence. (1999)

HSG 189/2 – Working with asbestos cement. (1999)

In addition, HSE has published two related guidance booklets as part of its ongoing campaign to highlight the dangers of asbestos.

'*Introduction to asbestos essentials*', HSG 213, is aimed at anyone who is liable to control or carry out maintenance work with asbestos-containing materials (ACMs). That includes employers, contract managers, site agents, safety representatives and self-employed contractors.

'*Asbestos essentials task manual*', HSG 210, is aimed at workers and provides clear and concise assistance to those likely to come into contact with asbestos during the course of their work e.g. plumbers, electricians, computer installers, telecommunications engineers etc. It explains how asbestos enters and affects the body and how individuals can best protect themselves. The booklet is designed to be taken on site and includes 25 task sheets and 8 additional sheets. The former focus on common tasks associated with the above trades and the latter describe the equipment pinpointed in the task sheets. To help workers identify ACMs and know what to do should they accidentally disturb them, the building diagram and flow diagrams are again included.

Copies of these publications are available from HSE Books, PO Box 1999, Sudbury, Suffolk CO10 6FS (tel: 01787 881165; fax: 01787 313995).

# Form for consignment note

A5044

## CONSIGNMENT NOTE

| | |
|---|---|
| **SPECIAL WASTE REGULATIONS 1996** | Consignment Note No _____ |

No of prenotice (*if different*) _____   Sheet        of

---

**A   CONSIGNMENT DETAILS**                    PLEASE TICK IF YOU ARE A TRANSFER STATION ☐

1.   The waste described below is to be removed from (name, address
     and postcode)

2.   The waste will be taken to (address & postcode)

3.   The consignment(s) will be:     one single ☐ a succession ☐ carrier's round ☐ other ☐

4.   Expected removal date of first consignment:              last consignment:

5.   Name                                       On behalf of (company)

     Signature                                  Date

6.   ☎                        7.   The waste producer was (if different from 1)

**B   DESCRIPTION OF THE WASTE**     *No of additional sheet(s)* ☐

1.   The waste is                          2.   Classification

3.   Physical Form: Liquid ☐ Powder ☐ Sludge ☐ Solid ☐ Mixed ☐     4.   Colour

5.   Total quality for removal   quantity          units (eg kg/ltrs/tonnes)          Container type, number and size:

6.   The chemical/biological components that make the waste special are:

| Component | Concentration (% or mg/kg) | Component | Concentration (% or mg/kg) |
|---|---|---|---|
| | | | |
| | | | |
| | | | |

7.   The hazards are:

8.   The process giving rise to waste is:

**C   CARRIER'S CERTIFICATE**     I certify that I today collected the consignment and that the details in A1, A2 and B1 above
                                 are correct. The Quantity collected in the load is:

     Name                                       On behalf of (company) (name & address)

     Signature                                  Date        at      hrs.

1.   Carrier registration no/reason for exemption          2.   Vehicle registration no (or mode of transport, if not road)

**D   CONSIGNOR'S CERTIFICATE**

     I certify that the information in B and C above are correct, that the carrier is registered or exempt and was advised of the appropriate
     precautionary measures.

     Name                                       On behalf of (company)

     Signature                                  Date

**E   CONSIGNEE'S CERTIFICATE**

1.   I received this waste on        at        hrs.     2.   Quantity received     quantity     units (eg kg/ltrs/tonnes)

3.   Vehicle registration no                            4.   Management Operation

I certify that waste management licence/authorisation/exemption no     authorises the management of the waste described in B

Name                                       On behalf of (company)

Signature                                  Date

# FORM OF SCHEDULE

SPECIAL WASTE REGULATIONS 1996:    Carrier Schedule:    Consignment Note No _____

Sheet        of

| Name and address of premises from which waste was removed | I certify that today I collected the quantity of waste shown from the address given here and will take it to the address given in A2 on the consignment note |
|---|---|
| | Quantity of waste removed / Carrier's signature and Date |
| | I certify that the waste collected is as detailed above and conforms with the description given in B on the relevant consignment note |
| Consignment Note No | Name of Consignor / Signature and Date |

| Name and address of premises from which waste was removed | I certify that today I collected the quantity of waste shown from the address given here and will take it to the address given in A2 on the consignment note |
|---|---|
| | Quantity of waste removed / Carrier's signature and Date |
| | I certify that the waste collected is as detailed above and conforms with the description given in B on the relevant consignment note |
| Consignment Note No | Name of Consignor / Signature and Date |

| Name and address of premises from which waste was removed | I certify that today I collected the quantity of waste shown from the address given here and will take it to the address given in A2 on the consignment note |
|---|---|
| | Quantity of waste removed / Carrier's signature and Date |
| | I certify that the waste collected is as detailed above and conforms with the description given in B on the relevant consignment note |
| Consignment Note No | Name of Consignor / Signature and Date |

| Name and address of premises from which waste was removed | I certify that today I collected the quantity of waste shown from the address given here and will take it to the address given in A2 on the consignment note |
|---|---|
| | Quantity of waste removed / Carrier's signature and Date |
| | I certify that the waste collected is as detailed above and conforms with the description given in B on the relevant consignment note |
| Consignment Note No | Name of Consignor / Signature and Date |

| Name and address of premises from which waste was removed | I certify that today I collected the quantity of waste shown from the address given here and will take it to the address given in A2 on the consignment note |
|---|---|
| | Quantity of waste removed / Carrier's signature and Date |
| | I certify that the waste collected is as detailed above and conforms with the description given in B on the relevant consignment note |
| Consignment Note No | Name of Consignor / Signature and Date |

# Children and Young Persons

## Introduction

C3001     For many years work done by children and young persons has been subject to an often bewildering array of prohibitions – equipment that children and young persons are not allowed to use or processes or activities that they must not be involved in. However, first the *Health and Safety (Young Persons) Regulations 1997 (SI 1997 No 135)* – and now the *Management of Health and Safety at Work Regulations 1999 (SI 1999 No 3242)* – have switched the emphasis from such prohibitions towards restrictions, based upon a process of risk assessment as described later in this chapter.

Many of the previous age-related prohibitions have been revoked (some of the more significant revocations are listed in Appendix B) but a significant number still remain. The more important prohibitions still existing are referred to later in the chapter or listed in Appendix A. It must be noted, however, that the ongoing programme of modernisation of health and safety legislation being conducted by the Health and Safety Executive (HSE) is sweeping away many residual prohibitions. Any cases of doubt should be referred to the HSE.

## Definitions

C3002     The term 'child' and 'young person' are defined in *regulation 1(2) of the Management of Health and Safety at Work Regulations 1999 ('Management Regulations')*.

'Child' is defined as a person who is not over compulsory school age in accordance with:

—    *section 8 of the Education Act 1996* (for England and Wales); and

—    *section 31 of the Education (Scotland) Act 1980* (for Scotland).

(In practice, this is just under or just over the age of sixteen.)

'Young person' is defined as 'any person who has not attained the age of eighteen'.

Some of the prohibitions remaining from older health and safety regulations use different cut-off ages – where relevant these are referred to in Appendix A. Further detail is also provided in the HSE guidance booklet HS(G) 165: *Young People at Work*.

## Health and Safety (Training for Employment) Regulations 1990

C3003     These regulations have the effect of giving students on work experience training programmes and trainees on training for employment programmes the status of 'employees'. The immediate provider of their training is treated as the 'employer'. (There are exceptions for courses at educational establishments, i.e. universities, colleges, schools etc.)

Consequently, employers have duties in respect of all children and young persons at work in their undertaking: full-time employees, part-time and temporary employees and also students or trainees on work placement with them.

# Prohibitions and restrictions on the employment of children

C3004    Work by children is still subject to a series of prohibitions imposed by the following:

- *Children and Young Persons Act 1933*;

- *Children and Young Persons (Scotland) Act 1937*;

- *Children and Young Persons Act 1963*.

All of these Acts were subjected to amendments contained in the *Children (Protection at Work) Regulations 1998 (SI 1998 No 276)*. Amongst other changes these regulations raised the ages at which young people are allowed to be employed in many types of work. This implemented requirements contained in an EC Directive (94/33/EC). The main requirements are:

- Children under 14 may not be employed in any work, except:

    — when employed by their parent or guardian in light agricultural or horticultural work on an occasional basis;

    — children over 13 may work in categories of light work specified in local authority by-laws.

- Children may only be employed in light work, i.e. work which does not jeopardise the child's safety, health or development and is not harmful to their school attendance or participation in work experience.

- Hours of employment of children are severely limited.

    The main limitations are that children may not be employed:

    — before the end of school hours;

    — before 7 am or after 7 pm on any day;

    — for more than two hours on any school day or on a Sunday;

    — for more than four hours in any day without a rest break of one hour;

    — without at least one two-week period during their school holidays in each calendar year which is free from any employment.

    Hours of employment for children on days other than school days and Sundays are limited to 5 hours for under-15s and 8 hours for over-15s.

    Maximum hours permitted for children in any week (i.e. a period of seven consecutive days) are 25 hours for under-15s and 35 hours for over-15s.

- Licences are required for certain types of work.

    A licence must be obtained from the local authority (or a JP) where a child:

    — goes abroad for the purposes of performing for profit; or

    — takes part in public performances within the UK (where payment is made).

    These licensing requirements now include circumstances where the child takes part in a sport or works as a model.

*The Children and Young Persons Act 1993* has recently been further amended by *The Children (Protection at Work) Regulations 2000 (SI 2000 No 1333)* which came into force on 7 June 2000.

*Regulation 2(1)* amends *section 18* raising to 13 the minimum age at which children may be authorised by local authority bylaws to be employed in light agricultural or horticultural work.

*Regulation 2(2)* amends *section 20* so that local authority bylaws authorising children to take part in street trading must contain provisions determining the days and hours during which, and the places at which, they may do so.

*Regulation 2(3)* amends *section 23* so that only persons aged at least sixteen and who are also over compulsory school age may take part in performances of a dangerous nature.

# The Management of Health and Safety at Work Regulations 1999

C3005    These Regulations *(SI 1999 No 3242)* came into force on 29 December 1999. They revoke, among other things, the *Management of Health and Safety at Work Regulations 1992, the Management of Health and Safety at Work (Amendment) Regulations 1994* and the *Health and Safety (Young Persons) Regulations 1997*. Provisions requiring employers to carry out risk assessments are now contained in *Reg 3 of the Management of Health and Safety at Work Regulations 1999. Regulation 3(4) and 3(5)* provide as follows:

'(4)    An employer shall not employ a young person unless he has, in relation to risks to the health and safety of young persons, made or reviewed an assessment in accordance with paragraphs (1) and (5).

(5)    In making or reviewing the assessment, an employer who employs or is to employ a young person shall take particular account of –

(a)    the inexperience, lack of awareness of risks and immaturity of young persons;

(b)    the fitting-out and layout of the workplace and the workstation;

(c)    the nature, degree and duration of exposure to physical, biological and chemical agents;

(d)    the form, range, and use of work equipment and the way in which it is handled;

(e)    the organisation of processes and activities;

(f)    the extent of the health and safety training provided or to be provided to young persons; and

(g)    risks from agents, processes and work listed in the Annex to Council Directive 94/33/EC on the protection of young people at work.'

*(Paragraph (1) of Reg 3* contains the substantive requirement for employers to carry out risk assessments in respect of all their employees and of others who may be affected by their undertaking.)

In assessing the risks to young persons, the employer must take particular note of *Reg 19* which states:

'(1)    Every employer shall ensure that young persons employed by him are protected at work from any risks to their health or safety which are a consequence of their lack of experience, or absence of awareness of existing or potential risks or the fact that young persons have not yet fully matured.

(2)    Subject to paragraph (3), no employer shall employ a young person for work –

    (a)    which is beyond his physical or psychological capacity;

    (b)    involving harmful exposure to agents which are toxic or carcinogenic, cause heritable genetic damage or harm to the unborn child or which in any other way chronically affect human health;

    (c)    involving harmful exposure to radiation;

    (d)    involving the risk of accidents which it may reasonably be assumed cannot be recognised or avoided by young persons owing to their insufficient attention to safety or lack of experience or training; or

    (e)    in which there is a risk to health from –

        (i)    extreme cold or heat;

        (ii)    noise; or

        (iii)    vibration,

    and in determining whether work will involve harm or risks for the purposes of this paragraph, regard shall be had to the results of the assessment.

(3)    Nothing in paragraph (2) shall prevent the employment of a young person who is no longer a child for work –

    (a)    where it is necessary for his training;

    (b)    where the young person will be supervised by a competent person; and

    (c)    where any risk will be reduced to the lowest level that is reasonably practicable.

(4)    The provisions contained in this regulation are without prejudice to –

    (a)    the provisions contained elsewhere in these Regulations; and

    (b)    any prohibition or restriction, arising otherwise than by this regulation, on the employment of any person.'

Some of the practical implications of these provisions are considered later in this chapter.

Important provisions relating to the employment of children are contained in *paragraphs (2) and (3) of Reg 10*, which deals with information for employees. These provide:

'(2)    Every employer shall, before employing a child, provide a parent of the child with comprehensible and relevant information on –

    (a)    the risks to his health and safety identified by the assessment;

    (b)    the preventive and protective measures; and

    (c)    the risks notified to him in accordance with regulation 11(1)(c).

(3)    The reference in paragraph (2) to a parent of the child includes –

    (a)    in England and Wales, a person who has parental responsibility, within the meaning of section 3 of the Children Act 1989, for him; and

    (b)    in Scotland, a person who has parental rights, within the meaning of section 8 of the Law Reform (Parent and Child) (Scotland) Act 1986 for him.'

This requirement to provide information to parents includes situations where children are on work experience programmes (where they have the status of employees by virtue of the *Health and Safety (Training for Employment) Regulations 1990*) and also includes part-time or temporary work. Some of the practical implications of this provision are considered later in this chapter.

The wide-ranging impact of these provisions is lessened to a certain extent by the inclusion of *paragraph (2)* in *Reg 2*, 'Disapplication of these Regulations'. This states:

'(2)     Regulations 3(4), (5), 10(2) and 19 shall not apply to occasional work or short-term work involving –

(a)     domestic service in a private household; or

(b)     work regarded as not being harmful, damaging or dangerous to young people in a family undertaking.'

However, the key term 'family undertaking' is not defined in the regulations. HSE guidance indicates that this should be interpreted as meaning 'small and medium-sized firms, owned by, and employing members of the same family'. They suggest family members should include – 'husbands, wives, fathers, mothers, grandfathers, grandmothers, stepfathers, stepmothers, sons, daughters, grandsons, granddaughters, stepsons, stepdaughters, brothers, sisters, half-brothers and half-sisters'.

As far as is known, this narrow interpretation of 'family undertaking' has not been tested in the courts. Common usage of the term would suggest that it comprises small and medium-sized businesses controlled and managed by members of the same family but not necessarily only employing family members, as implied by the words used by the HSE. Further guidance may be provided when the Approved Code of Practice on the 1999 Regulations is published by the HSE.

*Regulation 22 of the Management of Health and Safety at Work Regulations 1999* specifically state that a breach of a duty imposed by the regulations does not confer a right of action in any civil proceedings. However, this exclusion does not apply in respect of duties imposed by *Reg 19*, i.e. *Reg 19 can* be cited as a breach of statutory duty in civil proceedings should employers fail to observe its fairly detailed requirements in respect of the protection of young persons.

*Regulation 13 of the Management Regulations* is also relevant. *Paragraph (1)* provides that every employer must, in entrusting tasks to his employees, take into account their capabilities as regards health and safety. Quite clearly the capabilities of children and young persons are rather different from those of more experienced and mature employees.

HSE has published updated guidance for employers of under-18s, which will also be helpful for parents, guardians, teachers and people who organise work experience.

*'Young people at work – a guide for employers'*, (second edition), explains employers' duties to protect young people at work, as well as offer specific guidance on the risks that young people are likely to encounter.

Copies of *'Young people at work – a guide for employers'*, HSG(G) 165 (rev), ISBN 0 7176 1889 7, price £7.95, and *'Managing health and safety at work – a guide for organisers'*, price £6.50, can be ordered online at www.hsebooks.co.uk or are available from HSE Books, PO Box 1999, Sudbury, Suffolk, CO10 2WA (tel: 01787 881165; fax: 01787 313995).

## Risk assessments with respect to children and young persons

C3006    The requirements of *Regs 3(4)-(5) and 19* are based upon the contents of a European Directive (94/33/EC), and it is not particularly easy for the employer to identify exactly what he or she must (or must not) do.

A good starting point is to consider the three characteristics associated with young people which are mentioned in both *Regs 3(5)(a)* and *19(1)*:

- lack of experience;

- lack of awareness of existing or potential risks; and

- immaturity (in both the physical and psychological sense).

All young people share these characteristics but to differing extents – for example, one would have different expectations of a school leaver who had already been playing a prominent role in a family business such as a farm, as opposed to a work experience student with no previous exposure to the world of work. Employers need to be aware that the degrees of physical and psychological maturity of young people vary hugely.

These three characteristics must then be considered in respect of the risks involved in the employer's work activities and particularly those identified in *Reg 3(5)(b)-(g)* and *Reg 19(2)*.

The contents of those regulations (including the risks listed in the Annex to Council Directive 94/33/EC) have been consolidated into a single checklist for employers in Appendix C to this chapter.

The purpose of all risk assessments is to identify what measures the employer needs to take in order to comply with the law. Additional measures which the employer must consider in order to provide adequate protection for young persons are:

- not exposing the young person to the risk at all;

- providing additional training;

- providing close supervision by a competent person;

- carrying out additional health surveillance (as required by *Reg 6 of the Management Regulations* or other regulations, e.g. *COSHH 1999*);

- taking other additional precautions.

*Regulation 19(3)* allows more latitude in respect of young persons who are no longer children in relation to the requirement to exclude them completely from the types of risks specified in *Reg 19(2)*.

In deciding what precautions are required, the employer must consider both young people generally and the characteristics of individual young persons. For example, higher levels of training and/or supervision may be necessary in respect of young people with 'special needs'.

Young people should gradually acquire more experience, awareness of risks and maturity, particularly as they pass through formal training programmes within the NVQ system. As this occurs, restrictions on their activities may be progressively removed.

# Provision of information

C3007    *Regulation 10(1) of the Management Regulations 1999* requires employers to provide *all* employees with comprehensible and relevant information on:

- risks to their health and safety as identified by the risk assessment (or notified by other employers);

- preventive and protective measures (i.e. appropriate precautions);

- emergency procedures and arrangements.

This requirement is of particular importance in relation to young persons. *Regulation 10(2)* requires employers *also* to provide information to parents of children (under the minimum school leaving age) on the risks to health and safety that the children will be exposed to and the precautions which are in place.

The information may be provided either orally or in writing or possibly both. Key items (for example, critical restrictions or prohibitions) should be recorded. Means of providing information might include:

- induction training programmes;

- employee handbooks or rulebooks;

- job descriptions;

- formal operating procedures;

- trainee agreement forms (increasingly common for young persons on formal training programmes, e.g. modern apprenticeships);

- information forms for parents (commonly used by organisations managing work experience programmes).*

* Further guidance on work experience is provided in the HSE booklet HSG 199, '*Managing health and safety on work experience – a guide for organisers*'.

The information must be comprehensible – special arrangements may be necessary for young people whose command of English is poor or for those with special needs. The type of information required to be provided will obviously relate to the work activities and the risks involved. The content must be relevant – both to the workplace and the young person. It might include the following types of information:

- general risks present in the workplace, e.g. fork lift trucks are widely used in the warehouse;

- general precautions taken in respect of those risks, e.g. all fork lift drivers are trained to the standard required by the ACOP;

- specific precautions in respect of the young person, e.g. the induction tour includes identification of areas where fork lift trucks operate and indication of warning signs;

- restrictions or prohibitions on the young person, e.g. X will not be allowed to drive fork lift trucks or any other vehicles (he will be considered for fork lift truck training after attaining the age of 17);

- supervision arrangements, e.g. X will be supervised by the warehouse foreman (or other persons designated by him)

- PPE (personal protective equipment) requirements, e.g. safety footwear must be worn by all employees working in the warehouse (this is supplied by the company).

Where restrictions or prohibitions are removed (e.g. after successful completion of training programmes), an appropriate record should be made, either on the original restriction/prohibition or upon the individual's training record.

## Restrictions on the hours of work of young persons

C3008

The *Working Time Regulations 1998* implemented both the European Working Time Directive (93/104/EC) and parts of the Protection of Young People at Work Directive (94/33/EC). Although some work sectors (transport, sea fishing, offshore work) are excluded from the regulations in respect of adults, the special provisions relating to young persons are not excluded for these sectors. Detailed guidance on the regulations is provided in the Department of Trade and Industry booklet, *A Guide to Working Time Regulations*.

The special provisions applying to young persons entitle them to:

- a health and capacities assessment, if they work during the period 10 pm to 6 am. This must take into account such factors as physique, maturity, experience and competence;

- an uninterrupted period of 12 hours' rest in each 24 hour period during which they work* (unless work periods are split up over the day or are of short duration);

- two days' rest in each week (this cannot be averaged over a two-week period but may be reduced to 36 hours, 'where justified by technical or organisational reasons');

- a rest break of 30 minutes where daily working time is more than 4½ hours* (working time is aggregated should the young person be employed by more than one employer).

* Rest entitlements may be modified or excluded in the case of:

- occurrences 'due to unusual or unforeseeable circumstances';

- when the work is of a temporary nature and must be performed immediately; *and*

- no adult worker is available to do the work in place of the young person.

All three conditions must apply, i.e. there is no alternative but for the young person to deal with a short-term emergency situation which was unexpected. Equivalent compensatory rest must be allowed within the following three weeks.

The entitlements to rest periods may also be disapplied in respect of young people serving as members of the armed forces.

# Appendix A

## Prohibitions on children and young persons

C3009 These prohibitions were still in place following the introduction of the *Management of Health and Safety at Work Regulations 1999*. However, the HSE continue to modernise legislation and some of these are likely to be revoked.

- **Explosives**

  Under-16s may not enter rooms where explosives are made, or where explosives (or their ingredients) are stored.

  Under-18s may only be employed in explosives buildings in the presence, and under the supervision, of a person aged 21 or over.

  [*Explosives Act 1875 as amended by the Explosives Act 1923*].

  Under-18s may not be employed as a driver or attendant of an explosives vehicle and may only enter the vehicle under supervision of someone over 18. (There are exceptions where the risks are slight.)

  [*Carriage of Explosives by Road Regulations 1996*].

- **Ionising radiation**

  Under-18s may not be designated as 'classified persons'. Dose exposure limits are lower for under-18s.

  [*Ionising Radiation Regulations 1985*].

- **Lead**

  Various old regulations and two sections of the *Factories Act 1961* (*s 74 and s 131*) prohibit young persons from working with lead and lead compounds. Some requirements only apply to under-16s or females under 18.

- **Carriage of dangerous goods**

  Under-18s may not supervise road tankers or vehicles carrying dangerous goods nor supervise the unloading of petrol from a road tanker at a petrol filling station.

  [*Carriage of Dangerous Goods by Road Regulations 1996*].

- **Agriculture**

  Under-13s may not ride on vehicles and machines including tractors, trailers etc. Children (under the minimum school leaving age) may not operate certain machines and tractors carrying out certain operations.

  [*Agriculture (Avoidance of Accidents to Children) Regulations 1958 and associated ACoP*].

- **Mines and quarries**

  Various restrictions exist for under-18s and under-16s relating to the use of winding and rope haulage equipment, locomotives, shunting, quarry vehicles and shot firing. Some restrictions also apply to under-21s and under-22s.

- **Shipbuilding and shiprepairing**

  Under-18s, until they have been employed in a shipyard for six months, may not be employed on staging or in any part of a ship where they are liable to fall more than two metres or into water where there is a risk of drowning.

  [*Shipbuilding and Shiprepairing Regulations 1960*].

- **Docks**

  Under-18s may not operate powered lifting appliances in dock operations unless undergoing a suitable course of training under proper supervision of a competent person (serving members of HM Forces are exempt).

  [*Docks Regulations 1988*].

## Appendix B

### Age-related prohibitions now repealed or revoked

C3010 Various age-related prohibitions were contained in the statutes listed below which have now been repealed or revoked. However, work by young people in activities previously controlled by these statutes must be subjected to the risk assessment based approach required by the *Management of Health and Safety at Work Regulations 1999.*

- *Factories Act 1961, sections 20 and 21;*

- *Dangerous Machines (Training of Young Persons) Order 1954;*

- *Offices, Shops and Railway Premises Act 1963, section 18;*

- *Agriculture (Circular Saws) Regulations 1959;*

- *Construction (Lifting Operations) Regulations 1961;*

- *Locomotives and Wagons (Used on Lines and Sidings) Regulations 1906;*

- *Offshore Installations (Operational Safety, Health and Welfare) Regulations 1976;*

- *Power Presses Regulations 1965;*

- *Woodworking Machines Regulations 1974.*

# Appendix C

## Work presenting increased risks for children and young persons

C3011   This checklist is based upon *Regs 3(5) and 19(2) of the Management of Health and Safety at Work Regulations 1999* and the Annex to the European Council Directive 94/33/EC. It is intended to assist employers conducting risk assessments in respect of work by children and young persons.

These types of work are not necessarily prohibited, although the requirements of *Reg 19(2)* must be taken into account. However, such work is likely to require restrictions for most young persons (particularly children) and additional precautions are likely to be required to provide them with adequate protection from risk.

### Excessively physically demanding work

● Manual handling operations where the force required or the repetitive nature could injure someone whose body is still developing (including production line work);

● Certain types of piece work.

### Excessively psychologically demanding work

● Work with difficult clients or situations where there is a possibility of violence or aggression;

● Difficult emotional situations, e.g. dealing with death, serious illness or injury;

● Decision-making under stress.

### Harmful exposure to physical agents

● Ionising radiation;

● Non-ionising radiation, e.g. lasers, UV from welding;

● Risks to health from extreme cold or heat;

● Excessive noise;

● Hand-arm vibration, e.g. from portable tools;

● Whole-body vibration, e.g. from off-road vehicles;

● Work in pressurised atmospheres and diving work.

### Harmful exposure to biological or chemical agents

● Toxic or carcinogenic substances (including lead and asbestos);

● Substances causing heritable genetic damage or harming the unborn child;

● Substances chronically affecting human health;

● Other hazardous substances (harmful, corrosive, irritant).

## Work equipment

Where there is an increased risk of injury due to the complexity of precautions required or the level of skill required for safe operation, for example:

- Woodworking machines;

- Food slicers and other food processing machinery;

- Certain types of portable tools such as chainsaws;

- Setting of power presses;

- Vehicles such as fork lift trucks, mobile cranes, construction vehicles;

- Firearms.

## Dangerous processes or activities

- Work with explosives, including fireworks;

- Work with fierce or poisonous animals, for example on farms, in zoos or veterinary work;

- Certain types of electrical work, e.g. exposure to high voltage or live electrical equipment;

- Handling of highly flammable materials, e.g. petrol, other flammable liquids, flammable gases;

- Work with pressurised gases;

- Work in large slaughterhouses.

## Dangerous workplaces or workstations

- Work at heights, for example on high ladders or other unprotected forms of access;

- Work in confined spaces, particularly where the risks specified in the *Confined Spaces Regulations 1997* are present;

- Work where there is a risk of structural collapse, e.g. in construction or demolition activities or inside old buildings.

# Compensation for Work Injuries/Diseases

## Introduction

C6001 Compensation for work injuries, diseases and death is payable under two interrelated but nevertheless independent systems, namely, under the social security system and in the form of damages for civil wrongs (torts). The former is a form of public insurance, funded by employers/employees and taxpayers, and benefit is payable irrespective of liability on the part of an employer, i.e. 'no fault' – though connection with employment must be established. The social security system is bound by legislation, such as the various *Social Security Acts*, culminating in the present *Social Security Administration Act 1992* and the *Social Security Contributions and Benefits Act 1992 (SSCBA 1992)*, the *Statutory Sick Pay Act 1994*, the *Social Security (Incapacity for Work) Act 1994*, the *Social Security (Industrial Injuries) (Prescribed Diseases) Regulations 1985 (SI 1985 No 967)*, the *Social Security (Incapacity for Work) (General) Regulations 1995 (SI 1995 No 311)*, the *Social Security (Recoupment of Benefits) Act 1997*, and sundry other legislation.

The tort system relevant to personal injuries is a form of private insurance, funded by employers' liability insurance premiums (see EMPLOYERS' LIABILITY INSURANCE), and awards of damages in tort depend on proof of negligence against an employer. Current law relating to work injuries and diseases is to be found in a variety of Acts, such as the *Law Reform (Personal Injuries) Act 1948*, the *Employers' Liability (Compulsory Insurance) Act 1969*, the *Employers' Liability (Defective Equipment) Act 1969*, the *Damages Act 1996* and the common law of tort, particularly negligence. This section examines the two concurrent systems and interaction between them.

'*Guidelines for the Assessment of General Damages*', 5th edition, 2000 (ISBN 1 841740314) issued by the Judicial Studies Board, is a publication which aims to unify judicial approaches to awards of damages. These Guidelines are not a legal document, do not and are not expected to obviate the need for a full examination of the law applicable to each case.

A useful handbook, '*Industrial Injuries Handbook for Adjudicating Medical Officers*', was published in 1997. It sets out medical examination procedures, and points out that unlawful discrimination in the discharge of officers' duties must be avoided. It also offers guidance on the legislation, and discusses the effect of case law to help the reader with those matters which are not covered by the legislation. From the case law, for example, loss of faculty is described as a total loss of power or function of an organ of the body, including disfigurement.

## Social security benefits

C6002 Changes were introduced by the provisions of the *Social Security (Incapacity for Work) Act 1994*, and regulations made under that Act, which came into force in April 1995, affected those on industrial injuries benefits. Sickness benefit and invalidity benefit were replaced by incapacity benefit which is payable at different rates, as before, but the higher rate is not be payable until after 364 days, instead of after 168 days.

The effect that this has had on industrial injuries benefits, including disablement benefit, is that industrial benefits continue to be payable after 90 days, but the benefits which are payable before and at the same time, that is, any national insurance benefits, are less for the relevant period. The higher adult dependant's allowance is delayed for 364 days when the long-term incapacity benefit increases begin. Claimants whose industrial injuries benefit is lower than the rate of incapacity for work benefit and who are thus entitled to claim this benefit are also affected. (See C6015–C6017 below for details of these changes.)

Entitlement to industrial injuries benefits now requires compliance with national insurance contribution conditions for incapacity benefit. The incapacity for work tests under the *Social Security (Incapacity for Work) Act 1994* do not apply to industrial disablement benefits. The medical adjudication procedures for these benefits continue with some modifications as before. The incapacity for work tests will apply to sufferers from industrial disablement if they apply for incapacity benefit before the ninety qualifying days for industrial disablement benefits begin, or if they do not qualify for industrial disablement benefit under the percentage or other rules, or if incapacity benefit is payable at a higher rate than industrial disablement pension rates and incapacity benefit is chosen by the claimant.

Under the rules for claimants for incapacity benefit, the employee has to supply information and evidence of sickness and be prepared to submit to a medical examination to decide the question of whether he is fit to work. If he has worked for more than eight weeks in the twenty-one weeks immediately preceding the first day of sickness, a test relevant to his incapacity to do work which he could reasonably be expected to do in the course of his occupation applies. This test criterion continues to the 197th day of incapacity. After that date, and for all claimants who do not qualify for the required period, an 'all work' test arises. Regulations provide for prescribed activities and a person's incapacity, by reason of a specific disease, or bodily or mental disablement, to perform these activities. These tests are detailed and are outside the scope of this book. [*SSCBA 1992, ss 171(A)-(G) as inserted by Social Security (Incapacity for Work) Act 1994, s 5*].

The *Social Security (Incapacity for Work) (General) Regulations 1995 (SI 1995 No 311)* as amended by the *Social Security (Incapacity for Work) (General) Regulations 1996 (SI 1996 No 484)*, provide that certain people are deemed to be incapable of work, including those suffering from a severe condition as defined in the Regulations or those receiving certain regular treatment (such as chronic renal failure, hospital in-patients and those suffering from an infectious or contagious disease). 'Welfare to work beneficiaries' will also be treated as incapable of work in the circumstances prescribed by *Regulation 13A* of the 1995 Regulations. A pregnant woman may also be deemed incapable of work if there is a serious risk to her health, or that of her unborn child, if she does not refrain from work, in the case of the 'own occupation' test; or in the case of the 'all work' test, if she does not refrain from work in any occupation. If she has no entitlement to maternity allowance or statutory maternity pay and the actual date of confinement has been certified, she is deemed to be incapable of work beginning with the first day of the sixth week before the expected week of confinement until the fourteenth day after the actual date of confinement and during this period she will therefore be entitled to claim incapacity benefit.

Whilst most actual work by a claimant disqualifies him from receiving this benefit on any day of such work, certain work does not stop benefit. [*Social Security (Incapacity for Work) (General) Regulations 1995 (SI 1995 No 311), Reg 17*]. Earnings from such work must not exceed £60.50 per week (2001/2002) and in most cases must be for less than 16 hours per week. The exempt work is work done on the advice of a doctor which:

(*a*)   helps to improve, or to prevent or delay deterioration in the disease or bodily or mental disablement which causes that person's incapacity for work; or

(*b*)   is part of the treatment programme undertaken as a hospital in-patient or out-patient under medical supervision; or

(*c*)   is done when the claimant is attending a sheltered workshop for people with disabilities.

Voluntary work and duties as a member of a disability appeal tribunal or the Disability Living Allowance Advisory Board are also exempt work.

Under the *Social Security (Incapacity Benefit) (Transitional) Regulations 1995 (SI 1995 No 310)*, those who claimed and were in receipt of sickness benefit or invalidity benefit were automatically transferred to the new benefits without the need for a fresh claim, and a claim for industrial injuries was also transferred in the same way. These Transitional Regulations also preserved increases of allowances for those who were in receipt of the former benefits which will continue to be payable provided the spouse is residing with the beneficiary, or if the beneficiary is contributing to the maintenance of his spouse. Long-term incapacity benefit is paid to existing beneficiaries at the differential rates applicable to invalidity benefit before the changeover and adult dependency allowances will continue to be paid. Except in circumstances which are set out in the Regulations, including assessment of industrial injuries, all of the transitional rights have been made subject to satisfaction of the stricter tests of incapacity for work.

## Industrial injuries benefit

C6003   The benefits which are currently available to new claimants for industrial injuries benefits are industrial injuries disablement pension, constant attendance allowance and exceptionally severe disablement allowance. Disabled person's tax credit may also be claimed in some circumstances (see C6016 below). Some older benefits continue to be payable to recipients who were receiving them when they were otherwise abolished, or whose entitlement arose before the relevant dates. Reduced earnings allowance was one of these benefits. (For details of these older benefits and more detailed social security benefits information, see *Tolley's Social Security and State Benefits Handbook.*)

## Accident and personal injuries provisions

C6004   The employed earner must have suffered personal injury caused after 4 July 1948 by an accident arising out of and in the course of his employment, being employed earner's employment. [*SSCBA 1992, s 94*]. The *Reporting of Injuries, Diseases and Dangerous Occurrences Regulations 1995 (SI 1995 No 3163)* require reports to be made on prescribed forms to the Health and Safety Executive forthwith after the occurrence of an accident or on receipt of a report from a registered medical practitioner of his diagnosis of a prescribed disease. A self-employed person may arrange for this report to be sent by someone else. Records must be kept for three years containing prescribed details of accidents, or the date of diagnosis of the disease, the occupation of the person affected and the nature of the disease. For more information on these Regulations see ACCIDENT REPORTING.

Industrial accident and disease records may be kept for these three years on:

- a B510 Accident Book;
- photocopies of completed form F2508; or
- computerised records.

## Personal injury caused by accident

C6005　'Personal injury' includes physical and mental impairment, a hurt to body or mind, which includes nervous disorders or shocks (R(I) 22/52; R(I) 22/59). Damage to artificial limbs or appendages is not included unless the additional aid has become part of the body. Damage to a crutch, hearing aid, false teeth, a pair of glasses or an artificial leg is not included (R(I) 7/56).

The personal injury must have been caused by an accident. Although this is usually an unintended and unexpected occurrence, such as a fall, if a victim is injured by someone else, that may be an accident from the point of view of the victim (*Trim Joint District School Board v Kelly [1914] AC 667*). Where the employee injures himself, there is no need for there to have been any exceptional exertion on his part. For example, a labourer pushing a truck 'felt something go' and was incapable of work thereafter by reason of heart trouble. This counted as an industrial injury (C 27/49). The effect of the injury may be immediate or delayed if the full extent of the damage inflicted is not immediately apparent.

A relevant accident may still have occurred where a series of accidents without separate definite times cause personal injuries. An office worker was held to have suffered a series of accidents on each occasion she had been obliged to inhale her colleagues' tobacco smoke and this was held to have caused personal injuries. The fact that she was asthmatic did not debar benefit rights because of a pre-existing condition, or susceptibility in a victim does not affect benefits (R(I) 24/54; R(I) 43/55). However, where more than one accident gives rise to entitlement to industrial injuries benefit, the pensions will be aggregated so that the combined rate does not exceed the maximum rate. [*SSCBA 1992, s 107*]. (See Table 1 at C6017 below.)

'Accident' must be distinguished from 'process', that is, bodily or mental derangement not ascribable to a particular event. Injuries to health caused by processes are not industrial injuries, unless they lead to prescribed industrial diseases (see C6010 below). 'There must come a time when the indefinite number of so-called accidents and the length of time over which they occur, take away the name of accident and substitute that of process' (*Roberts v Dorothea Slate Quarries Co Ltd (No 1) [1948] 2 AER 201*). In *Chief Adjudication Officer v Faulds [2000] 1 WLR 1035*, the House of Lords, in disallowing a claim for damages for psychological injury suffered by a fireman, held there must be at least one identifiable accident that caused the injury. The fact that an employee might develop stress from a stressful occupation would not satisfy the definition of 'accident'.

## Accident arising out of and in the course of employment

C6006　There is no need to show a cause for the relevant accident, such as a fall, provided that the employee was working in the employer's premises at the time of the accident. An accident arising in the course of employment is presumed to have arisen out of that employment, in the absence of any evidence to the contrary. What runs through all the case law is the common requirement giving rise to industrial injuries rights; namely, that the employee was doing something reasonably incidental to and within the scope of his employment, and this includes extra-mural activities which the employee has agreed to do (R(I) 39/56). A male nurse who was injured in a football match watched by patients in the hospital grounds succeeded in a claim for benefit as this was reasonably incidental to and within the scope of his employment (R(I) 3/57), but a policeman who was injured whilst playing football for his force was unable to recover benefit despite the fact that his employers had encouraged him to play in the game (*R v National Insurance Commissioner, ex parte Michael [1977] 1 WLR 109*). Also, in *Faulkner v Chief Adjudication Officer [1994] PIQR P244*, a police officer who was injured whilst playing for a police football team was not entitled to industrial injuries benefit despite the benefit to the community resulting from his participation. He was not on duty at the time. *Social Security Case 7/97/14111/96* concerned a clerical officer who was employed at the Benefits Agency. The officer correctly reported a neighbour for benefits fraud. This led to an assault by the neighbour on the officer. It was held that the officer was entitled to disablement benefit, since the assault was held to have occurred in the course of employment. Further guidance can be found in *Chief Adjudication Officer v Rhodes [1999] ICR 178* where it was held that the two main questions to be asked are what are the employee's duties and was he discharging them at the time of the accident.

Whilst most claims will not cause much difficulty with respect to accidents arising out of and in the course of employment, a great deal of litigation has centred on cases where the employee is on the premises, but not working at his usual tasks, when he is injured. The effect of the case law concerning meal breaks, for example, shows that an accident during a meal break will be covered if the meal break is at a set time within a shift, and the employee is actually taking a meal; or if the employee has a set duty, such as keeping an eye on a vehicle during a meal break, and is carrying out this duty at the time of the accident.

## Supplementary rules

**C6007**    Five statutory provisions establish rules under which the employee is deemed to be acting in the course of his employment duties. If the occurrence falls within these rules, the employee will be covered by industrial injuries benefit. These provisions are as follows:

(*a*)    Illegal employment – if the employee was not lawfully employed, or his employment was actually void because of some contravention of employment legislation. [*SSCBA 1992, s 97*].

(*b*)    Acting in breach of regulations, or orders of the employer – if the employee is not acting outside his authority under his employment duties, and an accident occurs while the employee is doing something for the purposes of, and in connection with, the employer's business [*SSCBA 1992, s 98*], he will be covered. For instance, a kitchen porter hung up his apron to dry in a recess near to the ovens where he was forbidden to go. He was injured when he fell into a shallow pit. The hanging up of the apron was for the purposes of his employment, so the accident was deemed to have arisen out of, and in the course of, his employment duties (R(I) 6/55).

Moreover, where a dock labourer was employed on loading a ship by the method of two slings, but he instead used a truck which he had not been authorised to use for this purpose, he was held to be acting in the course of his employment. It was held that he could recover benefit (R(I) 1/70B). This contrasts with the earlier case of *R v D'Albuquerque, ex parte Bresnahan [1966] 1 Lloyd's Rep 69*, where a dock labourer was killed in an accident whilst driving a forklift truck, which he had no authority or permission to use to remove an obstruction. His widow was unable to recover industrial injuries benefit as her husband was held not to have been acting in the course of his employment.

(c)　　Travelling in an employer's transport – travel to and from work is not covered except where the employee is travelling in transport provided by the employer with his express or implied permission, whether or not the employee was bound to travel in this transport. [*SSCBA 1992, s 99*]. Outside this express provision, the employee will, in most cases, both be required to be on the employer's premises doing what he was authorised to do, unless his work takes him off the premises. A postman was able to recover benefit when he was bitten by a dog on the street, as his job required him to walk along streets (R(I) 10/57). If the journey is preparatory to the start of timed itinerant duties, for example, as a home help, there will be no entitlement to benefit in respect of injury sustained on the way to the first home, though if the employee has more discretion about his movements, he may be entitled to benefit on the way to his first call.

(d)　　An injury incurred while an employee is trying to prevent a danger to other people, or serious damage to property during an emergency. [*SSCBA 1992, s 100*].

(e)　　Accidents caused by another's misconduct, boisterousness or negligence (provided that the claimant did not directly induce or contribute to the accident by his own conduct), the behaviour of animals (including birds, fish and insects), if these cause an accident, or if a person is struck by lightning or by any object, respectively confer entitlement to industrial injuries benefit. [*SSCBA 1992, s 101*].

## Relevant employment

C6008　　'Employed earner's employment' includes all persons who are gainfully employed in Great Britain under a contract of service, or as an office holder, and who are subject to income tax under Schedule E. Self-employed people and private contractors are thus not entitled to industrial injuries benefits.

Certain classes of person are expressly included for the purposes of industrial injuries benefits. They include unpaid apprentices, members of fire brigades (or other rescue brigades), first-aid, salvage or air raid precautions parties, inspectors of mines, special constables, certain off-shore oil and gas workers and certain mariners and air crew. Most trainees on Government training schemes are excluded from the scheme. [*SSCBA 1992, ss 2, 95*].

If an industrial accident occurs outside Great Britain, industrial injuries benefit has since 1 October 1986 been payable when the employee returns to Great Britain, provided the employer is paying UK national insurance contributions, or if the claimant is a voluntary worker overseas and is himself paying UK contributions. Accidents which occur, or prescribed diseases which develop in other EU countries are covered by common rules. An employee who is entitled to make a claim for industrial benefit in another EU member state should make his claim for benefit in that state, regardless of the country which will actually pay the benefit.

Certain types of employment are excluded from cover. [*SSCBA 1992, s 95; Employed Earners' Employments for Industrial Injuries Purposes Regulations 1975 (SI 1975 No 467), Regs 2–7 and Sch 1, 2*].

## Persons treated as employers

C6009　　The *Employed Earners' Employments for Industrial Injuries Purposes Regulations 1975 (SI 1975 No 467), Sch 3* also provide for cases where certain people who may not have a contract with the employee, or who may be an agency employer, to be the relevant employer for the person who has suffered the industrial injury, or who has developed a prescribed disease. An agency that supplies an office cleaner, or a typist, will be the relevant employer. For casual employees of clubs, the club will be the relevant employer. The Head of Chambers in barristers' chambers is deemed to be the barristers' clerk's employer.

### Benefits for prescribed industrial diseases

C6010 The rules for certain prescribed diseases (namely deafness, asthma and asbestos related diseases), differ in some respects from the provisions affecting prescribed diseases outlined below. (See C6045, C6046 below for details of these differing provisions.) The different rules applicable to diseases resulting from exposure to asbestos at work are dealt with for industrial injuries purposes by a special medical board and there is a separate state scheme for statutory compensation where one of these diseases develops and there is no remedy against an employer, or entitlement to state benefits (see C6048 below). (See leaflets NI 12, NI 207 and NI 272 for help with making a claim.)

To obtain the right to industrial injuries benefits for all other prescribed diseases, the claimant must show:

—  that he is suffering from the prescribed disease;

—  that the disease is prescribed for his particular occupation (where a disease is prescribed for a general activity, for example, contact with certain substances, he must clearly show that this was more than to a minimal extent); and

—  that he contracted the disease through engaging in the particular occupation (there is a presumption that if the disease is prescribed for a particular occupation, the disease was caused by it, in the absence of evidence to the contrary).

(See also OCCUPATIONAL HEALTH AND DISEASES.)

Claims are made on Form BI 100B and there is a right to, and it is advisable to, claim immediately after the disease starts. The 90-day waiting period for receipt of benefit applies as for accidents, as do the percentage disabilities and aggregated assessment rules, except in the case of loss of faculty resulting from diffuse mesothelioma when entitlement begins on the first day of the claim. Assessments are made by two doctors who will decide on the percentage disability and how long the disability will last. Benefit will then be payable for the period stated in the assessment, but if the doctors are not sure of the period, benefit will be paid for a while with a further review. If the disease recurs during that period, there will be no need to make a further claim, but if the condition has worsened, the assessment may be reviewed. If there is a further attack after the period of the assessment, a fresh claim will have to be made, which will be subject to a further 90-day waiting period.

# Industrial injuries disablement benefit

## Entitlement and assessment

C6011 A person is entitled to an industrial injuries disablement pension if he suffers as a result of the relevant accident, a loss of physical or mental faculty such that the assessed extent of the resulting disablement amounts to not less than 14 per cent. [*SSCBA 1992, s 103, Sch 6*]. See leaflet NI 6 (July 1999). He will be similarly entitled if he suffers from a prescribed industrial disease (see C6010 above). An assessment of the percentage disablement up to 100 per cent will be made by an adjudicating medical practitioner who, in the case of accidents, looks at the claimant's physical and mental condition, comparing him in those respects with those of a normal person of the same age and sex. No other factors are relevant. The assessment may cover a fixed period/or the life of the claimant. The degrees of disablement are laid down in a scale so that, for example, loss of one hand is normally 60 per cent and loss of both hands 100 per cent. Disfigurement is included even if this causes no bodily handicap.

Where the claimant suffered from a pre-existing disability before the happening of the industrial accident at the onset of the industrial disease, benefit will only be payable in respect of the industrial accident or disease itself, and the medical adjudicators will compare the original disability with the industrial disability for this purpose. Where one or more disabilities result from industrial accidents or diseases, the level of resulting disability may be aggregated, but not so as to exceed the 100 per cent disability and its corresponding rate of benefit. [*Social Security (General Benefit) Regulations 1982 (SI 1982 No 1408), Reg 11*].

A list of initial application forms is supplied in NI 6 (July 1999) Industrial Injuries Disablement Benefit. Once a claim for industrial injuries benefit has been made, the Secretary of State will send Form B1/76 to the claimant. This form asks for full details of the accident or disease. The claimant must then submit to examination by at least two adjudicating medical practitioners and must agree to follow any appropriate medical treatment. If he fails to comply with these requirements, he will be disqualified from receiving this benefit for six months. A decision in writing will be sent to the claimant. It is possible to appeal a refusal of industrial benefit; details of how to appeal will be sent with the decision if it is negative.

This benefit can only be paid 90 days after the date of the accident excluding Sundays. [*SSCBA 1992, s 103*].

### Claims in accident cases

C6012    Claims should be made on Form BI 100A obtainable from the post office, job centre, or from the Benefits Agency, by claimants disabled by the accident for nine weeks. Claims should be made within six months of the accident to avoid loss of benefit, as the usual period for which benefit will be backdated is three months. [*Social Security (Claims and Payments) Regulations 1987 (SI 1987 No 1968), Reg 19, Sch 4, para 3*]. It is possible to apply to the DSS for a declaration from an adjudicating officer that an accident is covered by the scheme if a claimant suspects that an accident at work may have lasting effects which may not become apparent until some time later. If a positive finding is made, this will bind the DSS on any later claim for benefit. [*Social Security Act 1998, s 29(4)*]. Form BI 95 should be used for making this application. (Claims in respect of prescribed diseases are mentioned at C6010 above; appeals at C6018 below.)

### Rate of industrial injuries disablement benefit

C6013    Benefit is paid at one of two rates with the higher being paid to claimants aged over 18. (See C6017 below for current rates and injury percentages.)

# Constant attendance allowance and exceptionally severe disablement allowance

C6014    Constant attendance allowance is available if the claimant is receiving industrial injuries disablement benefit based on 100 per cent disablement, or aggregated disablements that total 100 per cent or more. It requires, in addition, that the claimant needs constant care and attention as a result of the effects of an industrial accident or disease. If the carer of the claimant spends at least 35 hours a week looking after him and is of working age and is not earning more than £50 (before tax but after deduction of national insurance and other reasonable expenses) per week, invalid care allowance of £41.75 per week with allowances for the carer's own dependants (if any) may be granted to that person. Claims for industrial injuries benefit are made on Form BI 104. It is granted for a fixed period and may be renewed from time to time. There are four rates of payment: part-time (where full-time care is unnecessary); normal maximum rate (if the above conditions are fulfilled and full-time care is required); intermediate (if the claimant is exceptionally disabled and the degree of attendance required is greater, and the care necessary is greater than under the 'normal' classification, the benefit is limited to one and a half times the normal rate); and an exceptional rate (if the claimant is so exceptionally disabled as to be entirely dependent on full-time attendance for the necessities of life). If the intermediate or exceptional rates are payable, an additional allowance (known as exceptionally severe disablement allowance) will be due if the condition is likely to be permanent. Constant attendance allowance may continue to be paid for up to four weeks if the claimant goes into hospital for free medical treatment.

## Other sickness/disability benefits

**C6015**  However, most applicants for industrial injuries benefit will, as their incapacity results from accidents or diseases contracted during their employment, be able to claim statutory sick pay or incapacity benefit up to the date of commencement of industrial injuries benefit as 90 days is less than 28 weeks. The rate of statutory sick pay is higher than that for incapacity benefit for 28 weeks when they are then paid at the same rate. Incapacity benefit rates in the first 28 weeks apply to the self-employed and to the unemployed, or those with too few contributions. For the purposes of claiming incapacity benefit before being entitled to claim a disablement benefit, it should be noted that the presumption that a claimant for benefit for industrial or prescribed diseases has satisfied the contribution requirements for incapacity benefit (as was the case with sickness benefit), has been removed. An age addition is added to incapacity benefit where the claimant is under certain age limits. Claims for incapacity benefit for the first time claimant should be made on Form BI 202. Where entitlement to industrial injuries benefit is below the incapacity benefit rates, then that benefit may be claimed to top up industrial injuries benefit to the current rate of incapacity benefit.

It is possible to claim extra for a spouse or person looking after children if the spouse is over 60, or, if younger, child benefit is being paid, and the claimant was maintaining the family to at least the extent of the dependency benefit being claimed. None of these restrictive rules apply to industrial injuries benefit claims.

If the carer of the claimant spends at least 35 hours a week looking after him and is of working age and is not earning more than £50 per week (before tax but after deduction of national insurance and other reasonable expenses), invalid care allowance of £41.75 per week (2000/2001) with allowances for the carer's own dependants (if any) may be granted to that carer.

If the adult dependant does not live with the claimant, there will be no increase if he is earning more than £51.40 per week. Also, dependant's earnings of over £150 per week in the case of one child, and an extra £20 earnings for each extra child affect dependency benefits.

Income support and other state benefits such as housing benefit and council tax benefit may be available if the claimant with or without dependants does not have sufficient to live on.

## Disabled person's tax credit

C6016    This benefit is for people aged 16 years or over who wish to work, but have a physical or mental disability which puts them at a disadvantage in securing a job under criteria set out in the regulations. The applicant must work for at least 16 hours a week to qualify and he receives a credit if he works for 30 hours or more a week. Self-employed people may qualify. This benefit is intended to help those on low incomes, so there are income and capital limits to entitlement. To receive the maximum allowance, the claimant's capital must not exceed £3,000. Capital above £16,000 disqualifies an applicant. An amount between these two figures attracts the maximum allowance less 70 per cent of the difference between the income and applicable amounts where an income of £1 for every £250 is assumed.

In addition to these criteria, he must be in receipt of certain benefits for at least eight weeks before his claim is made. With respect to industrial injuries, the relevant benefits to which he must have been entitled are constant attendance allowance, an increase in disablement pension, higher rate incapacity benefit, housing benefit, or council tax with a higher pensioner premium or he has an invalid carriage or other vehicle provided under the DSS Vehicle Scheme.

## Payment

C6017    Statutory sick pay is normally paid in the same way and on the same day as the employee's wages; or by credit transfer, cheque or postal order; or it can be collected by a representative of the employee.

Incapacity benefit is paid direct into a bank or building society account every two weeks, four weeks, or thirteen weeks.

Disablement benefit is either paid direct into a bank or building society account every four weeks or paid at a Post Office every week.

Industrial injuries benefits are paid weekly in advance on Wednesdays, either by order book cashable at a local post office, or by direct credit transfer if the claimant opts for this.

## Table 1

## Benefit rates

For financial year 2001/2002 the following weekly benefit rates are payable [*Social Security Benefits Up-rating Order 2001 (SI 2001 No 207)*].

| Benefit | Per Week |
|---|---|
| **Statutory sick pay** | |
| Single weekly rate | £62.20 |
| **Incapacity benefit** | |
| Up to 28 weeks | £52.60 |
| After 28 weeks to 52 weeks | £62.20 |
| *Long-term incapacity benefit* | |
| After 52 weeks | £69.75 |

| *Age addition* | | |
|---|---|---|
| Under 35 | | £14.65 |
| 35-49 | | £9.30 |

| *Increase for dependants* | *Increase for dependent child* | *Increase for Adult dependant* |
|---|---|---|
| Short-term dependency: | | |
| (a) where beneficiary is under pension age | 11.35 | £32.55 |
| (b) where the beneficiary is over pension age | 11.35 | £40.10 |
| Long-term dependency | 11.35 | £41.75 |

**Industrial injuries disablement benefit**

| *Disablement* | *Over 18* | *Under 18 with no dependants* |
|---|---|---|
| 100% | £112.90 | £69.15 |
| 90% | £101.61 | £62.24 |
| 80% | £90.32 | £55.32 |
| 70% | £79.03 | £48.41 |
| 60% | £67.74 | £41.49 |
| 50% | £56.45 | £34.58 |
| 40% | £45.16 | £27.66 |
| 30% | £33.87 | £20.75 |
| 20%* | £22.58 | £13.83 |

**Constant attendance increase**

| | |
|---|---|
| Normal maximum rate | £45.20 |

**Constant attendance allowance**

| | |
|---|---|
| Part-time rate | £22.60 |
| Intermediate rate | £67.80 |
| Exceptional rate | £90.40 |
| In any case, maximum benefit | £90.40 |

**Exceptionally severe disablement increase**

| | |
|---|---|
| Rate | £45.20 |
| Disabled person's tax credit | |
| Single weekly rate | £61.05 |
| Couples or lone parent** | £91.05 |
| Credit for working 30 hours or more per week | £11.45 |

> \* Disability must be assessed as at least 14% to be able to claim this 20% payment for a disablement pension.
>
> \*\*Additional £26 increase for each dependant child

## Appeals

C6018    Appeals relating to all industrial injuries are made to an appeal tribunal and should be made within three months of the decision of the adjudicating medical officer(s).

## Change of circumstances and financial effects of receipt of benefit

C6019    *Hospital* – if a claimant enters hospital, industrial injuries disablement pension continues to be payable, as does exceptionally severe disablement allowance. Constant attendance allowance will stop after four weeks. Statutory sick pay will be reduced after six weeks.

*Taxation* – industrial injuries disablement benefit, constant attendance allowance, exceptionally severe disablement allowance and disabled person's tax credit are not taxable. Incapacity benefit is taxable for all claimants who have claimed after 13 April 1995. Those who were in receipt of invalidity benefit before that date are not liable to tax on it. Statutory sick pay is taxable under the PAYE system.

## Benefit overlaps

C6020    Industrial injuries benefits may be taken at the same time as incapacity for work benefit with no reduction. Disability living allowance and attendance allowance may not be received at the same time as constant attendance allowance, but if the claimant should receive a higher rate of either of those benefits, constant attendance allowance will be topped-up to bring it up to the higher benefit rate. (For recoupment of benefit after awards of damages see C6041 below.)

# Damages for occupational injuries and diseases

C6021    When a person is injured or killed at work in circumstances indicating negligence on the part of an employer, he may be entitled to an award of damages. Damages are normally of two kinds, i.e. liquidated and unliquidated damages. *Liquidated damages* are damages where the amount and circumstances of payment have been agreed in advance by the contracting parties; awards are generally confined to cases of breach of contract.

Where negligent injury and/or death occur, compensation by way of prior agreement is not possible. In other words, employers and employees cannot agree beforehand a set amount of damages for injury, disease or death at work. Such damages, i.e. *unliquidated damages*, are assessed by judges in accordance with precedent; very exceptionally they may be assessed by a jury. Damages are also categorised as general and special damages, according to whether they reflect pre-trial or post-trial losses. Calculation of damages is often made by reference to Kemp and Kemp, *The Quantum of Damages* and to the Judicial Studies Board's document, *Guidelines for the Assessment of General Damages in Personal Injury Cases* (5th edition, 2000).

Damages normally take the form of a lump sum; however, 'structured settlements', whereby accident victims are paid a variable sum for the rest of their lives, are now a viable alternative [*Damages Act 1996, s 2*] (see C6025 below). This may well involve greater reliance on actuarial evidence and a rate of return of interest provided by index-linked government securities. Moreover, the rule in *British Transport Commission v Gourley* (see C6022 below), to the effect that damages are paid *net* of tax, may have to be modified, as offering a fiscal subsidy to defendants.

Legal Aid is currently the subject of extensive Government reform. The Legal Services Commission (LSC) replaced the Legal Aid Board in April 2000. Legal aid is no longer available in negligence personal injury cases. It is now only available in non-negligence personal injury claims, i.e. where the injury has been intentionally as opposed to negligently caused. There is one further exception, legal aid may be available where the personal injury claims forms a small part of another claim for which legal aid is available. Only law firms with a General Civil Contract for personal injury or clinical negligence will be able to do such publicly funded work. Legal aid is still available for clinical negligence. The *Access to Justice Act 1999* introduced the conditional fee system whereby solicitors represent clients on a 'no win no fee' basis. In the absence of legal aid, such a system will be the way in which most personal injury actions are brought.

To the extent that legal aid is still available for personal injury and clinical negligence cases, the following limits apply: legal help (formerly known as Green Form legal advice) is now only available to those who are on income support or whose disposable income is £87 per week or less and whose disposable capital is £1,000 or less. The lower income limit for non-contributory legal aid is £2,767 (2001/2002) and the upper income limit for contributory legal aid is £8,196 (2001/2002). The lower disposable capital limit for non-contributory legal aid is £3,000 and the upper disposable capital limit for contributory legal aid is £6,750. Disposable capital over these limits disqualifies an applicant from funding unless the LSC regional office considers the probable costs would exceed the contribution payable. Capital limits are now subject to an upper limit of £100,000 in relation to the equitable value of the applicant's dwelling-house, that is, after deduction of any mortgage or charge on the property. Stricter rules also apply to financial support from friends and relatives which may be taken into account.

Accident Line, which is part of a scheme run by solicitors who are members of a specialist panel of personal injuries lawyers, provides a free half-hour consultation for claimants who have suffered personal injuries, including industrial accidents. The telephone number is 0500 192 939. In addition, the Association of Personal Injuries Lawyers has a helpful website at www.apil.com.

## Basis of claim for damages for personal injuries at work

**C6022**    The basis of an award of unliquidated damages is that an injured employee should be entitled to recoup the loss which he has suffered in consequence of the injury/disease at work. 'The broad general principle which should govern the assessment in cases such as this is that the Tribunal should award the injured party such a sum of money as will put him in the same position as he would have been in if he had not sustained the injuries' (per Earl Jowitt in *British Transport Commission v Gourley [1956] AC 185*). Normally, a lump sum must be awarded. Courts could not order periodical payments instead of a lump sum, unless both parties consented (*Burke v Tower Hamlets Health Authority, The Times, 10 August 1989*). However, following the *Damages Act 1996*, periodical payments may be made in some cases.

It is not necessary that a particular injury be foreseeable, although it normally would be (see further *Smith v Leech Brain & Co Ltd [1962] 2 QB 405*). Moreover, if the original injury has made the claimant susceptible to further injury (which would not otherwise have happened), damages will be awarded in respect of such further injuries, unless the injuries were due to the negligence of the claimant himself

(*Wieland v Cyril Lord Carpets Ltd [1969] 3 AER 1006*). In this case, a woman, who had earlier injured her neck, was fitted with a surgical collar. She later fell on some stairs, injuring herself, because her bifocal glasses had been dislodged slightly by the surgical collar. It was held that damages were payable in respect of this later injury by the perpetrator of the original act of negligence. Conversely, where, in spite of having suffered an injury owing to an employer's negligence, an employee contracts a disease which has no causal connection with the earlier injury, and the subsequent illness prevents the worker from working, any damages awarded in respect of the injury will stop at that point, since the supervening illness would have prevented (and, indeed, has prevented) the worker from going on working.

A dustman who had injured his wrist in the course of his employment made a complaint of breach of statutory duty against D2. His contract of employment with D2 was transferred to D1 by virtue of the *Transfer of Undertakings (Protection of Employment) Regulations 1981*. On a preliminary question of the effect of these Regulations, it was held that potential liability for the claimant's claim had been transferred to D1. This case highlights the need to consider outstanding litigation on the transfer of a business. [*Taylor v Serviceteam and London Borough of Waltham Forest [1998] PIQR P201*].

C6023     Listed below are the various losses for which the employee can expect to be compensated. Losses are classified as non-pecuniary and pecuniary.

*(a) Non-pecuniary losses*

The principal non-pecuniary losses are:

(i)     pain and suffering prior to the trial;

(ii)    disability and loss of amenity (i.e. faculty) before the trial;

(iii)   pain and suffering in the future, whether permanent or temporary;

(iv)    disability and loss of amenity in the future, whether permanent or temporary;

(v)     bereavement.

(Damages for loss of expectation of life were abolished by the *Administration of Justice Act 1982, s 1(1)* (see further 'Loss of amenity' at C6031 below).)

There are four main compensatable types of injury, namely (*a*) maximum severity injuries (or hopeless cases), e.g. irreversible brain damage, quadraplegia; (*b*) very serious injuries but not hopeless cases, e.g. severe head injuries/loss of sight in both eyes/injury to respiratory and/or excretory systems; (*c*) serious injuries, e.g. loss of arm, hand, leg; (*d*) less serious injuries, e.g. loss of a finger, thumb, toe etc. There is a scale of rates applicable to the range of disabilities accompanying injury to workers but it is nowhere as precise as the scale for social security disablement benefit. The general (perhaps obvious) principle is that the more serious the disability the greater the damages. Damages for maximum severity cases can vary from several hundred thousand pounds to millions of pounds. In *Biesheuval v Birrell [1999] PIQR Q40*, the High Court awarded total damages of £9,200,000 (see C6024 below) to a student who was almost completely paralysed in all four limbs after a car crash. In *Dashiell v Luttitt [2000] 3 QR 4* a settlement of £5,000,000 was reached for brain damage sustained by a child aged 14 at the time of a school minibus crash. In *Capocci v Bloomsbury Health Authority (21 January 2000)* the High Court awarded £2,275,000 damages to a 13-year-old boy who had been asphyxiated at birth and as a result suffered cerebral palsy and other severe physical and mental handicaps. Less serious injuries attract lower damages – for example, in *Williams v Gloucestershire*

*County Council (10 September 1999)* an out of court settlement of £3,639 was reached in a case where a 6-year-old lost the top of her little finger in an accident.

*(b) Pecuniary losses*

These consist chiefly of:

(i)   loss of earnings prior to trial (i.e. special damages);

(ii)  expenses prior to the trial, e.g. medical expenses;

(iii) loss of future earnings (see below);

(iv)  loss of earning capacity, i.e. the handicap on the open labour market following disability.

In actions for pecuniary losses, employees can be required to disclose the general medical records of the whole of their medical history to the employer's medical advisers (*Dunn v British Coal Corporation [1993] ICR 591*).

## General and special damages

*(a) General damages*

C6024   General damages are awarded for loss of future earnings, earning capacity and loss of amenity. They are, therefore, awarded in respect of both pecuniary and non-pecuniary losses. An award of general damages normally consists of:

(i)   damages for loss of future earnings;

(ii)  pain and suffering (before and after the trial); and

(iii) loss of amenity (including disfigurement).

*(b) Special damages*

Special damages are awarded for itemised expenses and loss of earnings incurred prior to the trial. Unlike general damages, this amount is normally agreed between the parties' solicitors. When making an award, judges normally specify separately awards for general and special damages. A statement of special damage must be served with the statement of claim which should suffice to give the defendant a fair idea of the case he has to answer. More detailed information must be supplied after the exchange of medical and expert reports.

*(c) Example*

An example of the way in which damages awards are assessed and broken down is the case of *Biesheuval v Birrell* (referred to in C6023 above) where the High Court awarded £9,200,000 damages consisting of:

| | |
|---|---:|
| Pain and suffering and loss of amenity | £137,000 |
| Interest on general damages | £6,617 |
| Past loss of earnings | £80,700 |
| Interest on past loss of earnings | £14,929 |
| Other special damages | £360,113 |
| Interest on special damages | £54,516 |

| | |
|---|---|
| Tax on interest | £41,215 |
| Loss of future earnings | £3,700,000 |
| Loss of pension rights | £67,491 |
| Initial capital expenditure | £551,803 |
| Recurring costs and future care | £4,267,000 |

## Structured settlements

C6025   A structured settlement is an agreement for settling a claim or action for damages on terms that the award is made wholly or partly in the form of periodic payments. Such settlements are expected to become more usual in the case of larger awards of damages. Under the *Damages Act 1996*, these periodic payments must be payable in the form of an annuity for life, or for a specified period, and may be held on trust for the claimant if that should be necessary. Provision may be added to the settlements for increases, percentages or adjustments where the court or claimant's advisers secure these variations in his interest. Structured settlements in favour of claimants may be made for the duration of their life. Knowledge of the claimant's special needs is thus vital for the structure to be successful – it should be recognised that structured settlements will not be suitable for all cases. If the claimant dies while in receipt of periodic payments, they pass under his estate. Structured settlements may also be made in awards of damages in respect of fatal accidents. Tax-free annuities are payable directly to the claimant by the Life Office.

Structured settlements have received special protection in the case of the bankruptcy of the insurer. Under the administration of the Policy Holders Protection Board, the fund collected from other insurers is set at 100 per cent, rather than the usual 90 per cent, of other policy holders' losses (*Damages Act 1996, s 4*).

Structured settlement awards made by the Criminal Injuries Compensation Authority are also tax free.

When agreeing a settlement (whether structured or not), it is better to agree whether payments are net of repayable benefits. If a settlement offer is silent as to repayable benefits, then a deduction will have to be made in respect of them, possibly with unplanned results for the claimant.

Structured settlements are advisable where brain damage makes the injured person at risk and suggestible to pressure from relatives. They are also useful where the injured person has little experience or interest in investment, or dislikes the possibility of becoming dependent on the State or relatives should funds run out. Disadvantages are that annuities only last for the lifetime of the injured person. There is also a loss of flexibility to deal with changed circumstances and of the better return gained with the skilful investment of a lump sum.

## Assessment of pecuniary losses (i.e. loss of future earnings)

C6026   Assessing loss of future earnings can be a chancy affair, subject, as it is, to the vagaries and vicissitudes of human life. As was authoritatively said, 'If (the claimant) had not been injured, he would have had the prospect of earning a continuing income, it may be, for many years, but there can be no certainty as to what would have happened. In many cases the amount of that income may be doubtful, even if he had remained in good health, and there is always the possibility that he might have died or suffered from some incapacity at any time. The loss which he has suffered between the date of the accident and the date of the trial (i.e. special damages (see above)) may be certain, but his prospective loss is not. Yet damages must be assessed as a lump sum once and for all (see, however, 'Provisional awards' at C6037 below), not only in respect of loss accrued before the trial but also in respect of a prospective loss' (per Lord Reid in *British Transport Commission v Gourley [1956] AC 185*). Moreover, if, at the time of injury, a worker earns at a particular rate, it is presumed that this will remain the same. If, therefore, he wishes to claim more, he must show that his earnings were going to rise, for example, in line with a likely increase in productivity – a probable rise in *national* productivity is not enough.

When the court assesses loss of earnings, the claimant has to mitigate his loss by taking work if he can. In *Larby v Thurgood [1993] ICR 66*, the defendant applied to the court to dismiss an action brought by a fireman who was severely injured in a road traffic accident and who had taken employment as a driver earning £6,000 per annum, unless he agreed to be interviewed by an employment consultant who would then give expert evidence on whether the claimant could have obtained better paid employment. This application was refused. Evidence of whether the claimant could have obtained better paid employment depended partly on medical evidence of his capabilities and the present and future state of the job market where he lived, which could be established by an employment consultant. His general suitability for employment, his willingness and motivation, were matters of fact for the judge; thus expert opinion was not required for that purpose.

A claimant may be earning practically as much as he was before his accident, but may be more at risk of losing his present job, of not achieving expected promotion, or of disadvantages in the labour market. Damages may be claimed for such prospective losses and are known as *Smith v Manchester* damages (after *Smith v Manchester City Council (1974) 118 SJ 597*). In *Thorn v Powergen plc [1997] PIQR Q73*, it was advised that it is good practice to plead for *Smith v Manchester* damages in the statement of claim, but it is not essential if the facts already include such a claim.

Where the injured claimant was a company director or a member of a partnership and will not work again or as well as before, damages for diminution of the value of shares or profits are limited to the injured party's proportionate share (*Anderson v Davis [1995] PIQR Q87*).

Where a marriage has broken down as a result of the personal injury, damages may be recovered if the facts support this conclusion (*Oakley v Walker (1977) 121 SJ 619*).

## Capitalisation of future losses

**C6027**  Loss of future earnings, often spanning many years ahead, is awarded normally as a once-and-for-all capital sum for the maintenance of the injured victim. The House of Lords have recently considered the way in which lump sums should be calculated in the leading case of *Wells v Wells; Thomas v Brighton Health Authority [1999] 1 AC 345*. This also applies in Scotland (*McNulty v Marshall's Food Group Ltd [1999] SC 195*).

The award of damages is calculated on the basis of the *present* value of future losses – a sum less than the aggregate of prospective earnings because the final amount has to be discounted (or reduced) to give the *present* value of the future losses. Inflation is ignored when assessing future losses in the majority of cases (e.g. pension rights), since this was best left to prudent investment (*Lim Poh Choo v Camden and Islington Area Health Authority [1980] AC 174*). And where injury shortens the life of a worker, he can recover losses for the whole period for which he would have been working (net of income tax and social security contributions, which he would have had to pay), if his life had not been shortened by the accident. The present value of future losses can be gauged from actuarial or annuity tables. Indeed, it is necessary to identify a capital sum which, as income is progressively and periodically deducted for maintenance of the injured victim (with the necessary statutory deductions for income tax and social security contributions), will equate with the net loss of earnings over the working life of the injured victim.

More particularly, the net annual loss (based on rate of earnings at the time of trial) (the multiplicand) has to be multiplied by a suitable number of years (multiplier) which takes account of factors such as the claimant's life expectancy and the number of years that the disability or loss of earnings is expected to last. The multiplier normally ranges between 6 and 18, and is set out in actuarial tables. Both the multiplier and the multiplicand can vary for different periods; for example, where medical evidence shows that the need for care could increase or decrease over time – *Wells v Wells; Thomas v Brighton Health Authority [1998] 3 AER 481*. In *McIlgrew v Devon County Council [1995] PIQR Q66*, the maximum multiplier of 18 was applied for permanent general losses, and the multiplier of 12 was applied to loss of earnings.

The multiplier is calculated on the assumption that the claimant will invest the lump sum prudently. Before *Wells v Wells; Thomas v Brighton Health Authority*, the assumption was that the claimant would invest in equities and the net discount rate was accordingly 4–5 per cent. In *Wells v Wells; Thomas v Brighton Health Authority*, the House of Lords held that the court should fix the award by assuming that claimants will invest their damages in index-linked government stock and not in higher risk equities. The net discount rate was changed to 3 per cent. However, the Ogden working party has recommended that the net discount rate should be reduced to 2 per cent (*The Times*, 3 May 1999) and it is likely that there will be a fourth edition of the Ogden Tables to reflect the changes. Under *section 1(1) of the Damages Act 1996*, the Lord Chancellor may by order prescribe a rate of return which the courts must have regard to. No such order has yet been made under this provision, although now that the House of Lords have clarified the position it is likely that the Lord Chancellor will fix the rate under the provisions of the *Damages Act 1996*.

*Example*

In the case of a male worker, aged 30 at the date of trial, and earning £15,000 per year net, on a 3 per cent interest yield, the multiplier will be 21.22. Hence, general damages will be about £318,300, assuming incapacity to work up to age 65.

In the case of a male worker, aged 50 at date of trial, earning £25,000 net, on a 3 per cent interest yield, the multiplier will be 11.63. Hence, general damages will be about £290,750 assuming incapacity to work until age 65. (The corresponding multipliers for similar female workers are 21.4 (£321,000) and 11.78 (£294,500), assuming same earnings.)

Deductions from awards under this head are made for the actual earnings of the injured claimant. Where the claimant takes a lighter, less well paid job, and thus suffers a loss of earnings, the courts have held that the fact that he gains more leisure through working shorter hours is not to be taken into account to reduce the amount of damages awarded for loss of earnings (*Potter v Arafa [1995] IRLR 316*).

## Inflation-proof compensation – actuarial tables and index-linked government stock

C6028   It is for an injured claimant to invest a lump sum award prudently so as to replace the lost income for which he is being compensated. Since *Wells v Wells; Thomas v Brighton Health Authority*, it is now assumed that claimants will invest in index-linked government stock, which is fully protected against inflation, and as a result current multipliers assume a discount rate of 3 per cent (see C6027 above).

Actuarial tables (for use in personal injury and fatal accident cases), first published in 1984 by the Government Actuary's Department, list multipliers calculated on the basis of non-speculative investment in index-linked government stock, showing rates of interest between 1½ per cent and 5 per cent. The current Actuarial Tables were published on 25 August 1998 by the Stationery Office. Though hitherto not binding on the judiciary, these Tables have been widely used by judges at first instance and such evidence is now accepted by the courts. The Actuarial Tables are admissible in evidence for the purposes of assessing sums to be awarded as general damages for future pecuniary loss [*Civil Evidence Act 1995, s 10(1)*].

The 1st edition of the Actuarial Tables (HMSO 1984) took account only of mortality risks but not other common risks, such as redundancy, early retirement, child birth or ill-health. These latter risks were taken into account in the 2nd edition of Actuarial Tables (HMSO 1994). As earlier editions of the Actuarial Tables failed to take account of a number of important factors, the courts in the past tended to make deductions from the final figures of up to 10 per cent. The result of the most recent edition of the Actuarial Tables and the acceptance by the courts of the use of such tables means that awards of damages are greater, particularly for young workers injured at work.

## Institutional care and home care

C6029   Expenses of medical treatment may be claimed, except where the victim is maintained at public expense in a hospital or a local authority financed nursing home, in which case any saving of income during his stay will be set off against the claim for pecuniary loss. Alterations to a home, purchase of a bungalow accessible to a wheelchair, adaptations to a car and equipment (such as lifting equipment), which are necessary for care, may be claimed. Nursing and care requiring constant or less attendance may be claimed whether or not the carer is a professional or voluntary carer. It was confirmed by the House of Lords in *Hunt v Severs [1994] AC 350*, that where an injured claimant is cared for by a voluntary carer, such as a member of his family, that damages could be recovered for this care, but the claimant should hold them in trust for the voluntary carer. In the final ruling on this case, where the person who had caused the injury was the carer, it was held that in these unusual circumstances, damages for the cost of this voluntary care could not be recovered by the claimant.

Where voluntary care is undertaken by relatives, compensation for the cost of this care is assessed as a percentage of the Crossroads rate agreed from time to time for community care by most local authorities; the actual percentage awarded being about two-thirds of that rate. A higher percentage of that rate will be awarded where the care being given is beyond the level of care normally provided by home helps (*Fairhurst v St Helens and Knowsley Health Authority [1995] PIQR 41*).

Where a relative gave up work to look after her injured daughter, she could not claim compensation both for the care she had given and has to give and also for her own loss of earnings as this would constitute double recovery which the law does not allow (*Fish v Wilcox [1994] 5 Med LR 230*).

## Damages for lost years

C6030    Damages may be payable up to retirement age for lost earnings resulting from the shortening of the claimant's life expectancy by reason of the industrial accident or disease. Estimated costs of living expenses are deductible from these damages. Damages under this head may also be awarded to dependants if the victim has died.

Normally no damages are awarded for loss of the ability to do DIY and gardening. An exception was made in *Gabriel v Nuclear Electric [1996] PIQR Q1*. The claimant had been remarkably adept at DIY including home alterations, car maintenance, electrical and plumbing work and had been exceptionally fit for his age until mesothelioma led to his grave illness and very much shortened life expectancy.


## Non-pecuniary losses (i.e. loss of amenity)

C6031    It is generally accepted by the courts that quantification of non-pecuniary losses is considerably more difficult than computing pecuniary losses. Clearly, it is more difficult to attach a figure to the loss of a foot or eye than to two years' wages or salary. This becomes even more difficult where loss of sense of taste and smell are involved, or loss of reproductive or excretory organs. Unlike pecuniary losses, loss of amenity generally consists of two awards, i.e. an award for (i) actual loss of amenity and (ii) the impairment of the quality of life suffered in consequence (i.e the psychic loss). That judges recognise the inadequacy of damages here is much in evidence. (In the case of a claimant who had suffered grave injuries, 'He is deprived of much that makes his life worthwhile. No money can compensate for the loss. Yet compensation has to be given in money. The problem is insoluble' (per Lord Denning MR in *Ward v James [1966] 1 QB 273*).) Given that damages for non-pecuniary loss have tended to lag behind inflation in recent years, the Law Commission has suggested in its Consultation Paper No 140 (1996), the establishment of a Compensation Advisory Board, consisting of representatives from the medical profession, insurers and employers, to assess such damages. However, the recommendations have not yet been implemented.

Victims are generally conscious of their predicament, but in very serious cases they may not be, a distinction underlined in the leading case of *H West & Son Ltd v Shephard [1964] AC 326*. Thus, damages are payable for loss of amenity, whether or not a claimant is aware of his predicament. In other words, it is not just subjective or psychic losses which are compensatable. If, however, a victim's injuries are of the maximum severity kind (e.g. tetraplegia) and he is conscious of his predicament, his damages will be greater, since a person who is mentally anguished about his condition, suffers more than one who is not. However, where, as is often the case, the injuries shorten the life of an accident victim, his damages for non-pecuniary losses will be reduced to take into account the fact of shortened life.


## Types of non-pecuniary losses recoverable

C6032    The following are the non-pecuniary losses which are recoverable by way of damages:

(a)    pain and suffering;

(b)    loss of amenity;

(c)    bereavement.

## (a) Pain and suffering

This refers principally to actual pain and suffering at the time of the injury and later. Since, however, modern drugs can easily remove acute distress, actual pain and suffering is not likely to be great and so damages awarded will be relatively small.

Additionally, 'pain and suffering' includes 'mental distress' and related psychic conditions; more specifically (i) nervous shock, (ii) concomitant pain or illness following post-accident surgery and embarrassment or humiliation following disfigurement. Claustrophobia and fear are within the normal human emotional experience, but even if causing sweating and vomiting, are not compensatable, unless amounting to a recognised psychiatric condition, such as post-traumatic stress syndrome (*Reilly v Merseyside Regional Health Authority [1995] 6 Med LR 246*).

In *Heil v Rankin & anr and joined appeals [2001] QB 272*, the Court of Appeal, reviewed the current awards for pain, suffering and loss of amenity. The court held that whilst payments under £10,000 should not increase, there would be a tapered increase for awards above that up to a maximum of 33 per cent for the highest level of damages.

(i)    Nervous shock

Nervous shock refers to actual and quantifiable damage to the nervous system, affecting nerves, glands and blood; and, although normally consequent upon earlier negligent physical injury, an action is nevertheless maintainable, even if shock is caused by property damage (*Attia v British Gas plc [1988] QB 304* where a house caught fire following a gas explosion. The claimant, who suffered nervous shock, was held entitled to damages).

Claimants fall into two categories, namely, (*a*) primary and (*b*) secondary victims, the former being directly involved in an accident and normally (though not necessarily) having suffered earlier negligent physical injury; the latter are essentially spectators, bystanders or rescuers (who have not been victims of earlier negligent physical injury). *Primary* victims can sue for damages for nervous shock/psychiatric injury, even if they have not suffered earlier physical injury (*Page v Smith [1996] AC 155* in which the appellant, who was physically uninjured in a collision between his car and that of the respondent, had developed myalgic encephalomyelitis and chronic fatigue syndrome, which became permanent. It was held by the House of Lords that the respondent was liable for this condition in consequence of his negligent driving). Foreseeability of physical injury is sufficient to enable a claimant directly involved in an accident to recover damages for nervous shock. Thus, in the historic case of *Bourhill v Young [1943] AC 92* a pregnant woman, whilst getting off a tram, heard an accident some fifteen yards away between a motor cyclist and a car, in which the motor cyclist, driving negligently, was killed. In consequence, the claimant gave birth to a stillborn child. It was held on the facts of the case that the unknown motor cyclist could not have foreseen injury to the claimant who was unknown to him. As for secondary victims, defendants are taken to foresee the likelihood of nervous shock to rescuers attending to an injured person and to their close relatives, though the precise extent of nervous shock need not have been foreseen (*Brice v Brown [1984] 1 AER 997*). Persons who witness distressing personal injuries, who are not related in either of these ways to the victim, are not only considered not to have been foreseen by the defendant, but are expected to be possessed of sufficient fortitude to be able to withstand the calamities of modern life. Only persons with a close tie with the victim or their rescuers who are within sight or sound of the accident or its immediate aftermath will be awarded damages for nervous shock as the law stands at the present.

Husbands and wives will be presumed to have a sufficiently proximate tie whilst other relationships are considered on the evidence of the proximity of the relationship.

In *Chadwick v British Railways Board [1967] 1 WLR 912*, following a serious railway accident, for which the defendant was held to be liable, a volunteer rescue worker suffered nervous shock and became psychoneurotic. As administratrix of the rescuer's estate, the claimant sued for nervous shock. It was held that (i) damages were recoverable for nervous shock, even though shock was not caused by fear for one's own safety or for that of one's children, (ii) the shock was foreseeable, and (iii) the defendant should have foreseen that volunteers might well offer to rescue and so owed them a duty of care.

The class of persons who can sue for damages for nervous shock is limited, depending on proximity of the claimant's relationship with the deceased or injured person (*McLoughlin v O'Brian [1983] 1 AC 410* where the claimant's husband and three children were involved in a serious road accident, owing to the defendant's negligence. One child was killed and the husband and other two children were badly injured. At the time of the accident, the claimant was two miles away at home, being told of the accident by a neighbour and taken to the hospital, where she saw the injured members of her family and heard that her daughter had been killed. In consequence of hearing and seeing the results of the road accident, the claimant suffered severe and recurrent shock. It was held that she was entitled to damages for nervous shock as she was present in the immediate aftermath). This approach was confirmed by the House of Lords in *Alcock v Chief Constable of South Yorkshire Police [1992] 1 AC 310*, where it was stated that the class of persons to whom this duty of care was owed as being sufficiently proximate, was not limited to particular relationships such as husband and wife or parent and child, but was based on ties of love and affection, the closeness of which would need to be proved in each case, except that of spouse or parent, when such closeness would be assumed. Similarly, in *Hinz v Berry [1970] 2 QB 40* the appellant left her husband and children in a lay-by while she crossed over the road to pick bluebells. The respondent negligently drove his car into the rear of the car of the appellant. The appellant heard the crash and later saw her husband and children lying severely injured, the former fatally. She became ill from nervous shock and successfully sued the respondent for damages. On this basis, an employee who suffers nervous shock as a result of witnessing the death of a co-employee at work, will be unlikely to be able to claim damages against his employer for nervous shock, as being a 'bystander who happens to be an employee', as distinct from an active participant in rescue (*Robertson v Forth Bridge Joint Board [1995] IRLR 251* where an employee was blown off the Forth Bridge in a high gale and fell to his death; a co-employee who watched this was unable to sue for damages for nervous shock).

Moreover, in *Vernon v Bosley [1997] 1 AER 577 and 614*, the defendant to a claim for nervous shock argued unsuccessfully that the claimant who had been present at the death of his children would have suffered the same psychiatric illness from grief and bereavement if he had not been at the scene. The children's nanny was with the children in a car which she negligently drove into a river. She escaped, but the children were trapped and died despite a rescue attempt at which both parents were present. Although grief and bereavement are not actionable at common law, there was no doubt that the claimant had suffered nervous shock in accordance with common law principles. The majority of the Court of Appeal rejected the defendant's appeal, but reduced the damages awarded.

In *Young v Charles Church (Southern) Ltd (1998) 39 BMLR 146* an employee suffered a psychiatric illness after seeing a workmate electrocuted; the claimant was working close to the victim, and the circumstances were such that he himself was in similar danger. The claimant recovered damages from his employer for breach of statutory duty under electricity regulations – employees are protected by these Regulations against foreseeable injury when electrical cable or equipment could become a source of danger to them. It was held in this case that a mental illness was included as a foreseeable injury when the claimant was so close to the electrical shock that killed his workmate.

By contrast, the following cases are concerned with nervous shock to relatives who were not within sight of the tragic event or its aftermath. In *Taylor v Somerset Health Authority [1993] 4 Med LR 34* the claimant's husband suffered a heart attack at work and died. The claimant went to the hospital where, on learning of his death, she suffered nervous shock. Refusing to believe he was dead, she visited his corpse in the mortuary. Her action for damages, on the ground that the defendant had failed to diagnose and treat his heart condition, failed because the main purpose of viewing the corpse was to settle disbelief as to death, and so was not part of the 'immediate aftermath'. Moreover, the viewing related to the death itself rather than the circumstances leading up to it. Similarly, where the mother of an employee crushed to death by a forklift truck sought damages for psychiatric illness resulting from nervous shock, her claim failed, as she had neither seen nor heard the accident or been involved with its immediate aftermath (*Ravenscroft v Rederiaktiebolaget Transatlantic [1992] 2 AER 470*). Nor will viewing a disaster on television, involving friends/relatives, qualify for entitlement (*Alcock v Chief Constable of South Yorkshire Police* (above)).

In *Hunter v British Coal Corporation [1999] QB 140*, a claimant who was 30 metres away from the scene of a fatal accident and was told of the victim's death 15 minutes later was unable to recover damages for the psychiatric injury he suffered because he felt responsible for the accident. It was held that he was neither physically nor temporarily close enough to the accident to be a primary victim.

In any event, reasonable fortitude, on the part of the claimant, will be assumed, thereby *ipso facto* disqualifying claims on the part of hypersensitive persons (*McFarlane v EE Caledonia [1994] 2 AER 1* where the owner of a rig did not owe a duty of reasonable care to avoid causing psychiatric injury to a crew member of a rescue vessel who witnessed horrific scenes at the Piper Alpha disaster). (Had he suffered physical injury as well, a claim for additional psychiatric injury might have succeeded.) In rescue situations a distinction is drawn between nervous/post-traumatic stress suffered by voluntary unpaid rescuers, on the one hand, and uniformed or paid rescuers, on the other, the former, in principle, being entitled to damages, ever since *Chadwick's* case, the latter not being so, in that they are 'fortitudinous bystanders'.

In *White v Chief Constable of South Yorkshire Police [1999] 1 AER 1*, the House of Lords considered the question of psychiatric injury to police officers on duty during the Hillsborough football stadium disaster when 95 spectators were crushed to death. It was held that police officers were not entitled to recover damages against the Chief Constable for psychiatric injury suffered as a result of assisting with the aftermath of a disaster, either as employees or as rescuers. An employee who suffered psychiatric injury in the course of his employment had to prove liability under the general rules of negligence, including the rules restricting the recovery of damages for psychiatric injury.

(ii)    Illness following post-accident surgery

The claimant was employed by the defendant as a train driver. Whilst operating a passenger train, he saw two employees less than thirty yards away on the line he was passing along. He blew the horn but the employees only moved when the train was a few yards away. As a result, the claimant suffered shock and was admitted to hospital where he was diagnosed as having suffered a heart attack. He was off work for nine months. When he returned to work he was not able to drive main-line trains because of his heart condition, and was engaged on shunting operations. This in turn revived a serious back injury from which he had suffered for a long time. Eighteen months later he stopped work and several months afterwards he was readmitted to hospital for a laminectomy. Following this back surgery, the claimant suffered a further heart attack. It was held that nervous shock was a reasonably foreseeable consequence of the employer's breach of duty; in addition, the employer had to take his victim as he found him, i.e. with a pre-existing symptomless back condition, pre-disposing him to heart attacks, and the employer had to pay damages in respect of both these conditions as well (*Galt v British Railways Board (1983) 133 NLJ 870*).

## (b) Loss of amenity

This is a loss, permanent or temporary, of a bodily or mental function, coupled with gradual deterioration in health, e.g. loss of finger, eye, hand etc. Traditionally, there are three kinds of loss of amenity, ranging from maximum severity injury (quadraplegias and irreversible brain damage), multiple injuries (very severe injuries but not hopeless cases) to less severe injuries (i.e. loss of sight, hearing etc.). Obviously, the more grave the injury the greater the award of damages. Moreover, it is clear that, on balance, damages reflect the actual amenity loss rather than the concomitant psychic loss, at least in hopeless cases. Though, if a claimant is aware that his life has been shortened, he will be compensated for this loss. Thus, the *Administration of Justice Act 1982, s 1(1)* states:

' (i)    *damages are not recoverable in respect of loss of expectation of life caused to the injured person by the injuries; but*

(ii)    *if the injured person's expectation of life has been reduced by injuries, there shall be taken into account any pain and suffering caused or likely to be caused by awareness that his expectation of life has been reduced.*'

## (c) Bereavement

A statutory sum of £7,500 is awardable for bereavement by the *Fatal Accidents Act 1976, s 1A* (as amended by the *Administration of Justice Act 1982, s 3(1)* and the *Damages for Bereavement (Variation of Sum) Order 1990 (SI 1990 No 2575)*). This sum is awardable at the suit of husband or wife, or of parents provided the deceased was under eighteen at the date of death if the deceased was legitimate; or of the deceased's mother, if the deceased was illegitimate. (In *Doleman v Deakin, (1990) 87 (13) LSG 43* it was held that where an injury was sustained before the deceased's eighteenth birthday, but the deceased actually died after his eighteenth birthday, bereavement damages were not recoverable by his parents.)

## Fatal injuries

**C6033**     Death at work can give rise to two types of action for damages, i.e.

(*a*)     damages in respect of death itself, payable under the *Fatal Accidents Act 1976* (as later amended); and

(*b*)     damages in respect of liability which an employer would have incurred had the employee lived; here the action is said to 'survive' for the benefit of the deceased worker's estate, payable under the *Law Reform (Miscellaneous Provisions) Act 1934*.

Actions of both kinds are, in practice, brought by the deceased's dependants, though actions of the second kind technically survive for the benefit of the deceased's *estate*. Moreover, previously paid state benefits are *not* deductible from damages for fatal injuries. [*Social Security Act 1989, s 22(4)(c)*]. Nor are insurance moneys payable on death deductible e.g. life assurance moneys. [*Fatal Accident Act 1976, s 4*]. This also includes any amounts passing to dependants as a result of intestacy (*Wood v Bentall Simplex Ltd [1992] PIQR P332* in which an annual income of £5,000, receivable on intestacy, was not to be deducted from damages for fatal accident).

### *Damages under the Fatal Accidents Act 1976*

**C6034**     'If death is caused by any wrongful act, neglect or default which is such as would (if death had not ensued) have entitled the person injured to maintain an action and recover damages, the person who would have been liable if death had not ensued, shall be liable . . . for damages . . . '. [*Administration of Justice Act 1982, s 3(1), amending the Fatal Accidents Act 1976*].

Only dependants, which normally means the deceased's widow (or widower) and children and grandchildren can claim – the claim generally being brought by the bereaved spouse on behalf of him/herself and children. [*Administration of Justice Act 1982, s 1(2)*]. The basis of a successful claim is *dependency*, i.e. the claimant must show that he was, prior to the fatality, being maintained out of the income of the deceased. If, therefore, a widow had lived on her own private moneys prior to her husband's death, the claim will fail, as there is no dependency. The fact that both the deceased and his partner were at the time of the accident on state benefits is irrelevant to the question of loss in assessing damages – *Cox v Hockenhull [2000] 1 WLR 750*. Nominal damages for loss of life expectancy are abolished. [*Administration of Justice Act 1982, s 1(1)*].

In *Jameson and Another v Central Electricity Generating Board and Another [2000] AC 455*, the House of Lords, overturning the decision of the Court of Appeal, held that 'full and final settlement' of a claim for compensation following exposure to asbestos prevented dependants bringing an action against a concurrent tortfeasor. This case concerned a dependency claim brought by the executors of a deceased employee (J) of a company (B) against another company (C), whom B had sent J to work for. B had already paid J £80,000 before his death in 'full and final settlement' of his claim for breach of statutory duty by exposing J to asbestos at various workplaces (including at C), resulting in his suffering from malignant mesothelioma. C argued that this settlement prevented J's executors subsequently bringing the present claim and that, failing this, C was entitled to recover a contribution towards the damages from B. J's executors contended that J's settlement did not represent full satisfaction of J's claim against B and consequently J was not barred from an action against a concurrent tortfeasor. The judge agreed with this argument and allowed the claim. C appealed.

The House of Lords allowed the appeal (Lord Lloyd dissenting). It held that a compromise had the effect of fixing the amount of the claimant's claim in the same way as if the matter had gone to trial and judgement had been given in his favour. Where an action was subsequently brought against a concurrent tortfeasor, there was no scope for inquiry as to whether the agreed amount represented the full value of the claim. Consequently, the only question was whether the sum received by J was intended to be in full satisfaction of the cause of action and, as it clearly was, the terms of the settlement extinguished J's claim against C as from the date of the settlement.

Originally at common law if a widow remarried, or if her marriage prospects were good, this was taken into account in assessing damages for fatal injuries, since remarriage or its prospects lessened the financial hardship caused by death of a breadwinner. This rule has, however, been abolished. The *Fatal Accidents Act 1976, s 3* provides that remarriage or remarriage prospects are not to be taken into account in assessing fatal damages though likelihood of divorce may be taken into account in some circumstances (see *Martin v Owen* at C6036 below).

However, contributory negligence on the part of the deceased will result in damages on the part of the dependants being reduced. [*Fatal Accidents Act 1976, s 5*].

## Survival of actions

C6035    Actions for injury at work which the deceased worker might have had, had he lived, survive for the benefit of his estate, normally for the benefit of his widow, but not necessarily, as he might have willed his estate to someone else, e.g. a mistress. This is provided for in the *Law Reform (Miscellaneous Provisions) Act 1934*. Any damages paid or payable under one Act are 'set off' when damages are awarded under the other Act, as in practice actions in respect of deceased workers are brought simultaneously under both Acts.

## Assessment of damages in fatal injuries cases

C6036    Damages in respect of a fatal injury are calculated by multiplying the net annual loss (i.e. earnings minus tax, social security contributions and deductions necessary for personal living (i.e. dependency)) by a suitable number of years' purchase. There is no deduction for things used jointly, such as a house or car. However, where a widow also works, this will reduce the dependency and she cannot claim a greater dependency in future on the ground that she and her deceased husband intended to have children (*Malone v Rowan [1984] 3 AER 402*). In *Crabtree (Administratrix of the Estate of Crabtree) v Wilson [1993] PIQR Q24*, it was confirmed that a wife's net dependency percentage of expenditure in an assessment of the damages due to the Crabtree estate must be reduced from the conventional net dependency by the amount of any earnings she makes. The conventional net dependencies, which are based on the assumed expenditure of a male deceased person which is no longer required, leave a dependency of 75 per cent for his dependants if there are children, and 66⅔ per cent where the family was husband and wife. Moreover, if, at the time of death, a widow is separated from her husband, her claim for dependency depends on the likelihood of either being reconciled, or, alternatively, receiving maintenance (*Davies v Taylor [1974] AC 207*). Under *s 3* (see C6034 above) what has to be valued is the expectation of continuing dependency on the deceased, had he lived. Anything that might affect that expectation was relevant including the likelihood of divorce in this particular case (*Martin v Owen, [1992] PIQR Q151*). However, damages for loss of moonlighting (i.e. dependency in respect of undeclared earnings) or for loss of housing or supplementary benefit cannot be recovered (*Hunter v Butler [1996] RTR 396*).

It is possible to agree that fatal injury damages should be paid in the form of a structured settlement (see C6025 above).

Where both parents are dead as a result of negligence or a mother dies, dependency is assessed on the cost of supplying a nanny (*Watson v Willmott [1991] 1 QB 140; Cresswell v Eaton [1991] 1 WLR 1113*).

Moreover, benefits accruing to a person, such as a widow's pension, are not taken into account in assessing damages. [*Fatal Accidents Act 1976, s 4*].

### Provisional awards

C6037      Because medical prognosis can only *estimate* the chance of a victim's recovery, whether partial or total, or alternatively, deterioration or death, it is accepted that there is too much chance and uncertainty in the system of lump sum damages paid on a once-and-for-all basis. 'Chance' refers to 'measurable probabilities' rather than 'fanciful probabilities'. Serious deterioration denotes clear risk of deterioration beyond the norm that could be expected, ruling out pure speculation (*Willson v Ministry of Defence [1991] 1 AER 638*). Similarly in the case of dependency awards under the *Fatal Accidents Act 1976* it can never be known what the deceased's future would have been, yet courts are expected and called upon to make forecasts as to future income. Therefore, if the doctors get it wrong and a seriously ill victim makes a miraculous recovery, or a victim who was expected to do well suddenly and unforeseeably deteriorates, injustice results from the previous over and under compensation. To meet this problem it is provided that provisional awards may be made. Thus, 'This section applies to an action for damages for personal injuries in which there is proved or admitted to be a chance that at some definite or indefinite time in the future the injured person will, as a result of the act or omission, which gave rise to the cause of action, develop some serious disease or suffer some serious deterioration in his physical or mental condition'. [*Administration of Justice Act 1982, s 6(1)*]. Moreover, 'Provision may be made by rules of the court for enabling the court to award the injured person:

(*a*)      damages assessed on the assumption that the injured person will not develop the disease or suffer the deterioration in his condition; and

(*b*)      further damages at a future date if he develops the disease or suffers the deterioration'.

[*Administration of Justice Act 1982, s 6(2)*].

A claim in respect of provisional damages must be included in the statement of claim to entitle the claimant to such damages. The disease or type of deterioration in respect of which any future applications may be made must be stated (the *Civil Procedure Rules 1998 (SI 1998 No 3132),Part 41 rule 2(2)*). The defendant may make a written offer if the statement of claim includes a claim for provisional damages, offering a specified sum on the basis that the claimant's condition will not deteriorate and agreeing to make an award of provisional damages in that sum.

The mere fact that there is a disagreement over future medical prognosis does not necessarily prevent a sufficient basis of agreement for provisional damages (*Hurditch v Sheffield Health Authority [1989] QB 562* where the plaintiff, suffering from asbestosis, claimed provisional damages against his employer. Part of the medical statement was disputed. It was held that the offer and acceptance of a 'provisional figure' was sufficient for the purposes of *s 6* of the *Administration of Justice Act 1982*).

### Interim awards

C6038   In certain limited circumstances a successful claimant can apply to the court for an interim payment. This enables a claimant to recover *part* of the compensation to which he is entitled before the trial rather than waiting till the result of the trial is known – which may be some time away. This procedure is provided for in the *Civil Procedure Rules 1998 (SI 1998 No 3132), Part 25*, but it only applies where the defendant is either (*a*) insured, (*b*) a public authority, or (*c*) a person whose resources are such as to enable him to make the interim payment. Interim orders cannot be made in 'chance' and 'forecast' cases (see C6034 above). Prior to making an interim payment a judge is under an obligation to take into account any effect the payment may have on whether there is a 'level playing field' for the hearing – see *Campbell v Mylchreest [1999] PIQR Q17*.

In *Stringman v McArdle [1994] 1 WLR 1653*, it was held, provided that the usual procedural requirements were fulfilled, that it was not the concern of the judge as to what is to be done with the interim damages awarded to a victim. However, in this case the judge expressed the view that plans for conversion of a dwelling were too elaborate and he doubted that there would be enough left for the maintenance of the victim.

Compensation recovery applies to interim payments as well as to payments into court. Care needs to be taken when applying for interim payments to avoid putting the claimant at a disadvantage. Capital of over £8,000, which could include an interim award, removes entitlement to means tested benefits, particularly income support, and there are also reductions on a sliding scale in such benefits for any capital above £3,000. In the recent judgement of *Beattie v Department of Social Security ([2001] EWCA Civ 498)* the Court of Appeal held that payments from structured annuity funds constitutes 'income' for the purposes of the *Income Support (General) Regulations 1987*. In order to avoid such loss of benefits claimants would be well advised to put in place properly constituted trusts.

### Payments into court

C6039   A payment into court ('Part 36 payment') may be made in satisfaction of a claim even where liability is disputed. From the defendant's point of view, costs from the date of the Part 36 payment may be saved if the court does not order a higher payment of damages than that paid into court. The claimant may accept a Part 36 payment or Part 36 offer not less than 21 days before the start of the trial without needing the court's permission if he gives the defendant written notice of the acceptance not later than 21 days after the offer or payment was made. If the defendant's Part 36 offer or Part 36 payment is made less than 21 days before the start of the trial, or the claimant does not accept it within the specified period, then the court's permission is only required if liability for costs is not agreed between the parties. [*Civil Procedure Rules 1998 (SI 1998 No 3132), Part 36 rule 11*]. A defendant may accept a Part 36 offer on the same terms. [*Civil Procedure Rules 1998 (SI 1998 No 3132), Part 36 rule 12*]. Where the claimant is legally aided, he should be advised that the legal aid statutory charge will apply to the defendant's costs if the claimant recovers less than the sum paid into court.

Payments into court in settlement of personal injury claims are now statutory subject to recovery of relevant benefits paid to the claimant. The liability of the defendant to pay and benefit recovery does not commence until the injured party takes the payment out of court. Practitioners should avoid paying small settlements into court in view of the wide provisions of *s 6* of the *Administration of Justice Act 1982* as the compensator might become liable for all of the relevant benefits payments which have been made.

The defendant may, instead of making a Part 36 payment, make a Part 36 offer (formerly known as a Calderbank letter) in which he sets out his terms for settling the action (or makes certain offers). From a defendant's point of view, a Part 36 offer is helpful in that he may reserve the right to produce it to the attention of the trial judge after judgment on the question of costs. From the claimant's point of view, these letters should be studied with care because of applicability of the legal aid statutory charge to the defendant's costs where the defendant recovers less than the amount offered in the letter.

### Interest on damages

C6040    Damages constitute a judgment debt; such debt carries interest at 8 per cent (currently) up to date of payment. Courts have a discretion to award interest on any damages, total or partial, prior to date of payment (and this irrespective of whether part payment has already been made [*Administration of Justice Act 1982, s 15*]), though this does not apply in the case of damages for loss of earnings, since they are not yet due. Moreover, a claimant is entitled to interest at 2 per cent on damages relating to non-pecuniary losses (except bereavement), even though the actual damages themselves take into account inflation (*Wright v British Railways Board [1983] 2 AC 773*). Under *s 17* of the *Judgments Act 1838* (and *s 35A* of the *Supreme Court Act 1981* and *Schedule 1* to the *Administration of Justice Act 1982*), interest runs from the date of the damages judgment. Thus, where, as sometimes happens, there is a split trial, interest is payable from the date that the damages are quantified or recorded, rather than from the date (earlier) that liability is determined (*Thomas v Bunn, Wilson v Graham, Lea v British Aerospace plc [1991] 1 AC 362*). Moreover, interest at the recommended rate (of 8 per cent) is recoverable only after damages have been assessed, and not (earlier) when liability has been established (*Lindop v Goodwin Steel Castings Ltd, The Times, 19 June 1990*). The current rate of interest was reduced in 1993 from 15 per cent to 8 per cent [*Judgment Debts (Rate of Interest) Order 1993 (SI 1993 No 564)*] – this interest being tax-free [*Income and Corporation Taxes Act 1988, s 329*].

## Awards of damages and the new scheme for recovery of state benefits

C6041    The *Social Security (Recovery of Benefits) Act 1997* and accompanying regulations have made some important changes to the rules for recoupment of benefit from compensation payments. Total costs to business for compliance with the new Scheme have been estimated at between £54 and £70 million.

One key change is that recoupment will not be taken from general damages for pain and suffering and for loss of amenity which it has been accepted should be paid in full. With respect to the other heads of compensation, namely loss of earnings, cost of care and compensation for loss of mobility, they are only to be subject to recoupment from specified benefits relevant to each of these heads of compensation. [*Social Security (Recovery of Benefits) Act 1997, s 8*].

These heads of compensation and relevant benefits are set out below.

# Table 2

## Calculation of compensation payment

| (1) | (2) |
|---|---|
| *Head of compensation* | *Benefit* |
| 1.  Compensation for earnings lost during the relevant period | Industrial injuries disablement pension payable under s 103 of the 1992 Act |
| | Incapacity benefit |
| | Income support |
| | Invalidity pension and allowance |
| | Jobseeker's allowance |
| | Reduced earnings allowance |
| | Severe disablement allowance |
| | Sickness benefit |
| | Statutory sick pay |
| | Unemployability supplement |
| | Unemployment benefit |
| 2.  Compensation for cost of care incurred during the relevant period | Attendance allowance |
| | Care component of disability living allowance |
| | Disablement pension increase payable under s 104 or 105 of the 1992 Act |
| 3.  Compensation for loss of mobility during the relevant period | Mobility allowance |
| | Mobility component of disability living allowance |

The former sum of £2,500, which was exempt from compensation recovery, is no longer so exempt. The Secretary of State does have the power to exempt small payments under *s 24* of the *Social Security (Recovery of Benefits) Act 1997.*

The retrospective effect of the new provisions should be noted. The new scheme applies to compensation for accidents, injuries or diseases from the date of commencement of the Act unless compensation was made in pursuance of a court order or agreement before the commencement date. Under the *Social Security Administration Act 1992*, the following payments remain exempt from the recoupment of benefits:

(*a*)   any payment made out of property held for the purpose of the charitable trust called the Macfarlane Trust and established partly out of funds provided by the Secretary of State to the Haemophilia Society for the relief of poverty or distress among those suffering from haemophilia;

(*b*)   any compensation payment made by British Coal in accordance with the NCB Pneumoconiosis Compensation Scheme set out in the Schedule to an agreement made on 13 September 1974 between the National Coal Board, the

National Union of Mine Workers, the National Association of Colliery Overmen Deputies and Shot-firers and the British Association of Colliery Management;

(c)   any payment made to the victim in respect of sensorineural hearing loss where the loss is less than 50 db in one or both ears;

(d)   any contractual amount paid to an employee by an employer of his in respect of a day of incapacity for work;

(e)   any payment made from the Macfarlane (Special Payments) Trust established on 29 January 1990 partly out of funds provided by the Secretary of State for the benefit of certain persons suffering from haemophilia;

(f)   any payment made from the Macfarlane (Special Payments) (No 2) Trust established on 3 May 1991 partly out of funds provided by the Secretary of State, for the benefit of certain persons suffering from haemophilia and other beneficiaries;

(g)   any payment made under the *National Health Service (Injury Benefits) Regulations 1974* or the *National Health Service (Scotland) (Injury Benefits) Regulations 1974;*

(h)   any payment made by or on behalf of the Secretary of State for the benefit of persons eligible for payment in accordance with the provisions of a scheme established by him on 24 April 1992 or, in Scotland, on 10 April 1992;

(j)   Any payment made from the Eileen Trust established on 29 March 1993 out of funds provided by the Secretary of State for the benefit of persons eligible for payment in accordance with its provisions.

Statutory sick pay will not normally be deductible, as most employers are liable to pay in full. Where this is not so in the case of small employers, it will be deductible like other state benefits. [*Statutory Sick Pay Act 1994 (Consequential) Regulations 1994 (SI 1994 No 730)*].

## Duties of the compensator

C6042   Before the compensator makes a compensation payment, he must apply to the Secretary of State for a certificate of recoverable benefits. [*Social Security (Recovery of Benefits) Act 1997, s 4*]. The Secretary of State must send a written acknowledgement of receipt of the application and must supply the certificate within four weeks of receipt of the application. [*Social Security (Recovery of Benefits) Act 1997, s 4*].

He must supply the following information with his application:

•   full name and address of the injured person;

•   his date of birth or national insurance number, if known;

•   date of accident or injury when liability arose (or is alleged to have arisen);

•   nature of the accident or disease;

•   his payroll number (where known), if the injured person is employed under a contract of service and the period of five years during which benefits can be recouped includes a period prior to 1994 [*Social Security (Recovery of Benefits) Regulations 1997 (SI 1997 No 2205), Reg 5*]; and

- the amount of statutory sick pay paid to the injured person for five years since the date when liability first arose, as well as any statutory sick pay before 1994, if the compensator is also the injured person's employer. The causes of his incapacity for work must also be stated.

The certificate of recoverable benefits will show the benefits which have been paid.

The compensator must pay the sum certified within 14 days of the date following the date of issue of the certificate of recoverable benefits (*Social Security (Recovery of Benefits) Act 1997, s 6*). If the compensator makes a compensation payment without having applied for a certificate, or fails to pay within the prescribed fourteen days, the Secretary of State may issue a demand for payment immediately. A county court execution may be issued against the compensator to recover the sum as though under a court order. It is wise for the compensator to check the benefits required to be set off against the heads of compensation payment so that he is sure that the correct reduced compensation is paid to the injured person. Adjustments of recoupable benefits and the issue of fresh certificates are possible.

Where the compensator makes a reduced compensation payment to the injured person, he must inform him that the payment has been reduced. Statements that compensation has been reduced to nil must be made in a specific form. Once the compensator has paid the Secretary of State the correct compensation recovery amount and has made the statement as required, he is treated as having discharged his liability. [*Social Security (Recovery of Benefits) Act 1997, s 9*].

# Complications

## Contributory negligence

C6043    Where damages have been reduced as the result of the claimant's contributory negligence, the reduction of compensation is ignored and recovery of benefits is set-off against the full compensation sum.

## Structured settlements

The original sum agreed or awarded is subject to compensation recovery and for this purpose, the terms of the structured settlement are ignored and this original sum is treated as a single compensation payment. [*Social Security (Recovery of Benefits) Regulations 1997 (SI 1997 No 2205), Reg 10*].

## Complex cases

Where a lump sum payment has been made followed by a later lump sum, both payments are subject to recoupment of benefits where those benefits were recoupable. If the compensator has overpaid the Benefits Agency, he can seek a partial refund. [*Social Security (Recovery of Benefits) Regulations 1997 (SI 1997 No 2205), Reg 9*].

## Information provisions

Under *s 23* of the *Social Security (Recovery of Benefits) Act 1997*, anyone who is liable in respect of any accident, injury or disease must supply the Secretary of State with the following information within 14 days of the receipt of the claim against him:

- full name and address of the injured person;

- his date of birth or national insurance number, if known;

- date of accident or injury when liability arose (or is alleged to have arisen); and

- nature of the accident, or disease.

Where the injured person is employed under a contract of service, his employer should also supply the injured person's payroll number (if known) if the period of five years during which benefits may be recouped includes a period prior to 1994 and this is requested by the Secretary of State. [*Social Security (Recovery of Benefits) Regulations 1997 (SI 1997 No 2205), Regs 3, 5 and 6*].

If the Secretary of State requests prescribed information from the injured person, it must be supplied within 14 days of the date of the request. This information includes details of the name and address of the person accused of the default which led to the accident, injury or disease, the name and address of the maker of any compensation claim and a list of the benefits received from the date of the claim. If statutory sick pay was received by the injured person, the name and address of the employer who has paid statutory sick pay during the five-year period from the date of the claim or before 6 April 1994.

## Appeals against certificates of recoverable benefits

**C6044**     Appeals against the certificate of recoverable benefits must be in writing and made not less than three months after the compensation payment was made. The appeal should be made to the Compensation Recovery Unit for a hearing before a tribunal. Leave to appeal to a Commissioner against the decision of the tribunal should be made not later than three months after notice of the tribunal's decision.

In *Hassall and Pether v Secretary of State for Social Security [1995] 1 WLR 812*, Hassall and Pether were unemployed and in receipt of non-recoupable benefits before they were both injured in an accident. They received exactly the same amount of weekly benefits after the accident but, by contrast, from recoupable benefits. This amount was recouped. The unfairness of this recoupment could have been avoided if the statement of claim had included a claim for special damages for loss of non-recoupable pre-accident benefits.

### Treatment of deductible and non-deductible payments from awards of damages

There are three well established exceptions to deductibility of financial gains:

- recovery under an insurance policy to which the claimant has contributed all or part of the premiums paid on the policy;

- retirement pensions;

- charitable or ex-gratia payments prompted by sympathy for the claimant's misfortune.

### (a) Deductible financial gains

The courts, applying the principles outlined above, have ruled that the following financial gains are deductible:

(i) tax rebates where the employee has been absent from work as a result of his injuries (*Hartley v Sandholme Iron Co [1975] QB 600*);

(ii)   domestic cost of living expenses (estimated) must be set off against the cost of care (*Lim Poh Choo v Camden and Islington Area Health Authority [1980] AC 174*);

(iii)  estimated living expenses must be set off against loss of earnings (*Lim Poh Choo*, above);

(iv)   payment from a job release scheme must be set off against loss of earnings (*Crawley v Mercer, The Times, 9 March 1984*);

(v)    statutory sick pay must be set off against loss of earnings (*Palfrey v GLC [1985] ICR 437*);

(vi)   sick pay provided under an insurance policy must be set off against loss of earnings not paid as a lump sum (*Hussain v New Taplow Paper Mills [1988] AC 514*);

(vii)  health insurance payment under an occupational pension plan paid before retirement must be set off against loss of earnings where no separate premium had been paid by the employee who had paid contributions to the pension scheme (*Page v Sheerness Steel plc [1996] PIQR Q26*);

(viii) reduced earnings allowance (not a disability benefit) must be set off against loss of earnings (*Flanagan v Watts Blake Bearne & Co plc [1992] PIQR Q144*);

(ix)   payments under *s* 5 of the *Administration of Justice Act 1982* of any saving to the person who has sustained personal injuries through maintenance at the public expense must be set off against loss of earnings.


*(b) Non-deductible financial gains against loss of wages*

(i)    accident insurance payments under a personal insurance policy taken out by the employee (*Bradburn v Great Western Railway Co (1874) LR 10 Exch 1*) (contributory);

(ii)   lump-sum wage-related accident insurance payment under a personal accident group policy payable regardless of the fault of the employee (*McCamley v Cammell Laird Shipbuilders [1990] 1 WLR 963*) (benevolent);

(iii)  incapacity pension (from contributory insurance scheme) both before and after retirement age (*Longden v British Coal Corporation [1998] AC 653*). It should be noted that even though the incapacity pension was triggered by the accident, benefit flows from the prior contributions paid by the injured party (contributory);

(iv)   private retirement pensions (*Parry v Cleaver [1970] AC 1; Hewson v Downs [1970] 1 QB 73; Smoker v London Fire and Civil Defence Authority [1991] 2 AC 502*) (contributory or benevolent);

(v)    redundancy payment unconnected with the accident or disease (*Mills v Hassal [1983] ICR 330*). Where the claimant was made redundant because he was unfit to take up employment in the same trade, however, the redundancy payment was deductible from damages for lost earnings (*Wilson v National Coal Board [1981] SLT 67*);

(vi)   ex-gratia payment by an employer (*Cunningham v Harrison [1973] QB 942; Bews v Scottish Hydro-Electric plc [1992] SLT 749*) (benevolent);

(vii) ill health award and higher pension benefits provided by the employer (*Smoker v London Fire and Civil Defence Authority [1991] 2 AC 502*) (benevolent);

(viii) moneys from a benevolent fund, paid through trustees (not directly to the injured person or dependant) in respect of injuries;

(ix) charitable donations (but not where the tortfeasor is the donor);

(*c*) *Non-deductible financial gains against cost of care*

(i) Loss of board and lodging expenses awarded despite their being provided voluntarily by parents where the claimant had formerly paid such expenses herself (*Liffen v Watson [1940] 1 KB 556*).

## Social security and damages for prescribed diseases

C6045  The claims for social security benefits are similar to those for personal injuries. Claims for damages are also similar, with more latitude for late court applications because of recurrence of, or worsening of, industrial diseases. Lists of prescribed diseases are contained in social security leaflet NI 2. It is advisable always to refer to the latest edition of the leaflet, as the list of diseases is subject to amendment from time to time. There are special provisions applicable to asthma and deafness resulting from industrial processes, and also for pneumoconiosis and similar diseases.

(*a*) *Occupational deafness (see DSS leaflet 207)*

If the claimant's deafness was caused by an accident at work, then to qualify for disablement benefit his average hearing loss must have been at least 50 decibels in both ears due to damage of the inner ear. The claimant's disablement must be at least 20 per cent or more for him to qualify for disablement benefit (total deafness being 100 per cent). The claimant must have worked for at least the five years immediately before making his claim, or for at least ten years, in one of the listed jobs set out in the current edition of the leaflet. A claimant who has been refused benefit because the rules were not complied with will have to wait for three more years when he may qualify if he has worked in one of the listed occupations for five years. Leaflet NI 196 '*Social Security Benefits Rates*' shows the rates payable, relevant to each percentage of loss, for a weekly disablement pension.

The claim will be decided by a Medical Board, whose members will also decide on reviews if the claimant believes that his deafness has worsened. They will inform the claimant in detail of their decision. Awards will be made for a period of five years, and there will be a review at the end of that period with another hearing test to determine whether benefit should continue, or be reduced.

Claims must be made on Form BI 100 (OD) which may be obtained free from the Department of the Environment HS ORI Level 4, Caxton House, London SW1H 9NA (tel: 020 7273 5248), or from a post office and some borough libraries.

(*b*) *Asthma because of a job (see DSS leaflet NI 237)*

As is well known, there has been an increase in the number of sufferers from asthma. To be able to claim disablement benefit because of asthma, a claimant must have worked for an employer for at least ten years and have been in contact with prescribed substances, and his disability must amount to at least 14 per cent. In the list of substances, item 23 includes 'any other sensitising agent encountered at work', so claims may be possible even if the offending sensitising substance is not yet on the list.

Claims must be made on Form BI 100 (OA) which may be obtained from the Department of the Environment (see address and telephone number above), or from a post office and some borough libraries.

Once a claim has been made, the claimant will be seen by a Medical Board whose members will decide whether he has asthma because of his job and, if so, how disabled he is by the asthma. They will also determine how long his disability is likely to last and the extent of his disability, and will then communicate all of this information to the claimant. If they consider that no change is likely, they may award benefit for life. If they expect that there will be changes, there will be a review at the end of the period for which benefit was awarded.

*(c) Repetitive strain injuries*

Repetitive strain injuries are included in the *Social Security (Industrial Injuries) (Prescribed Diseases) Regulations 1985 (SI 1985 No 967), Sch 1,* as item A4. [See OCCUPATIONAL HEALTH AND DISEASES]. The difficulties in establishing causation can be seen from the case of *Pickford v Imperial Chemical Industries [1998] 1 WLR 1189,* where the House of Lords reversed the decision of the Court of Appeal and upheld the trial judge's decision that a secretary was not entitled to damages for repetitive strain injury as she had failed to establish the cause of the injury and that the condition was not reasonably foreseeable. However, in many other cases damages for repetitive strain injury have been awarded – for example, *Ping v Esselte-Letraset Ltd [1992] PIQR P74* where nine claimants who worked at a printing factory were awarded damages ranging from £3,000 to £8,000. In *Fish v British Tissues* (Sheffield County Court, 29 November 1994), damages of £57,482 were awarded to a factory packer for repetitive strain injuries to arms, hands and elbows.

# Pneumoconiosis

C6046    Pneumoconiosis is compensatable under different heads; first, as a ground for disablement benefit, under the *Social Security Contributions and Benefits Act 1992* and, secondly, by way of claim made under the *Pneumoconiosis etc. (Workers' Compensation) Act 1979* – the latter being in addition to any disablement benefit previously paid. See the Department of Environment guidance on the *Pneumoconiosis etc. (Workers' Compensation) Act 1979* on the DETR website: www.environment.detr.gov.uk//pneumo/index.htm

### Pneumoconiosis/tuberculosis-pneumoconiosis/emphysema – disablement benefit

C6047    Where a person is suffering from pneumoconiosis accompanied by tuberculosis, then, for benefit purposes, tuberculosis is to be treated as pneumoconiosis. [*Social Security Contributions and Benefits Act 1992, s 110*]. This applies also to pneumoconiosis accompanied by emphysema or chronic bronchitis, provided that disablement from pneumoconiosis, or pneumoconiosis and tuberculosis, is assessed at, at least, 50 per cent. [*Social Security Contributions and Benefits Act 1992, s 110*]. However, a person suffering from byssinosis is not entitled to disablement, unless he is suffering from loss of faculty which is likely to be permanent. [*Social Security Contributions and Benefits Act 1992, s 110*].

Benefit may be payable if the claimant's disablement is assessed at 1 per cent or more, instead of the usual minimum of 14 per cent. If the assessment of disablement is 10 per cent or less (but at least 1 per cent), then the industrial injuries disablement pension will be payable at one-tenth of the 100 per cent rate.

See Table 3(C) at the end of this chapter for details of sums payable to the dependants of sufferers who have died from one of these diseases.

If the disease dies down and recrudescence questions arise later, the decision on the recrudescence must be determined by qualified adjudicating medical practitioners.

## Pneumoconiosis – payment of compensation under the Pneumoconiosis etc. (Workers' Compensation) Act 1979

C6048    Claims made under the *Pneumoconiosis etc. (Workers' Compensation) Act 1979* are in addition to any disablement benefit paid or payable under the *Social Security (Industrial Injuries) (Prescribed Diseases) Regulations 1985 (SI 1985 No 967).* Indeed, whereas the latter consists of periodical payments, the former resemble damages awarded against an employer at common law and/or for breach of statutory duty, except that under the above Act fault (or negligence) need not be proved. This statutory compensation is available only if the employee is unable to claim compensation from any of his former employers (for example, if the employer has become insolvent). There are no requirements that the employee must have worked in a particular industry to be able to claim compensation under the scheme. Claimants are entitled to benefits from the date of claim. There is no ninety day waiting period under the scheme; it is sufficient if the claimant suffers from the prescribed disease. Coal miners are excluded from the scheme because they have their own statutory scheme. Claims made under the *Pneumoconiosis etc. (Workers' Compensation) Act 1979* must be made in the manner set out in the *Pneumoconiosis etc. (Workers' Compensation) (Determination of Claims) Regulations 1985 (SI 1985 No 1645).* The claim must be made (except in the case of a 'specified disease' – see C6049 below) within 12 months from the date on which disablement benefit (under the *Social Security Regulations*) first become payable; or if the claim is by a dependant, within 12 months from the date of the deceased's death. [*Pneumoconiosis etc (Workers' Compensation) (Determination of Claims) Regulations 1985 (SI 1985 No 1645), Reg 4(1), (2)*]. Awards for pneumoconiosis/byssinosis have slowly declined recently.

## Claims for specified diseases

C6049    Claims for a 'specified disease', i.e.:

(*a*)    pneumoconiosis, including (i) silicosis, (ii) asbestosis and kaolinosis;

(*b*)    byssinosis (caused by cotton or flax dust);

(*c*)    diffuse mesothelioma;

(*d*)    primary carcinoma of the lung coupled with evidence of (i) asbestosis and/or (ii) bilateral diffuse pleural thickening

[*Pneumoconiosis etc. (Workers' Compensation) (Specified Diseases) Order 1985 (SI 1985 No 2034)*], must be made within 12 months from the date when disablement benefit first became payable, or, in the case of a dependant, within 12 months from the date of the deceased's death [*Pneumoconiosis etc. (Workers' Compensation) (Determination of Claims) Regulations 1985 (SI 1985 No 1645), Reg 4(3)(4)*]. These time periods can be extended at the discretion of the Secretary of State. Moreover, where a person has already made a claim and has been refused payment, he can apply for a reconsideration of determination, on the ground that there has been a material change of circumstances since determination was made, or that determination was made in ignorance of, or based on, a mistake as to material fact.

### The Pneumoconiosis etc. (Workers' Compensation) (Payment of Claims) (Amendment) Regulations 2000 (SI 2000 No 1118)

**C6050**     The *Pneumoconiosis etc. (Workers' Compensation) (Payment of Claims) (Amendment) Regulations 2000 (SI 2000 No 1118)* which came into force on 1 June 2000 specify the following payments for sufferers of 'specified diseases'.

# Table 3

(A) Payments in respect of a prescribed disease to sufferers from pneumoconiosis or byssinosis.

| Age of disabled person | Percentage assessment for the relevant period | | | | | | | | | |
|---|---|---|---|---|---|---|---|---|---|---|
| | 10% or less | 11–20% | 21–30% | 31–40% | 41–50% | 51–60% | 61–70% | 71–80% | 81–90% | 91–100% |
| | £ | £ | £ | £ | £ | £ | £ | £ | £ | £ |
| 37 and under | 23,066 | 41,192 | 48,330 | 49,703 | 51,076 | 52,174 | 53,274 | 54,371 | 55,470 | 56,568 |
| 38 | 22,407 | 39,542 | 46,874 | 48,552 | 49,976 | 51,076 | 52,174 | 53,274 | 54,371 | 55,470 |
| 39 | 21,747 | 37,894 | 45,419 | 47,396 | 48,880 | 49,976 | 51,076 | 52,174 | 53,274 | 54,371 |
| 40 | 21,090 | 36,246 | 43,964 | 46,242 | 47,779 | 48,880 | 49,976 | 51,076 | 52,174 | 53,274 |
| 41 | 20,430 | 34,600 | 42,509 | 45,088 | 46,683 | 47,779 | 48,880 | 49,976 | 51,076 | 52,174 |
| 42 | 19,768 | 32,953 | 41,053 | 43,938 | 45,584 | 46,683 | 47,779 | 48,880 | 49,976 | 51,076 |
| 43 | 18,783 | 31,030 | 39,597 | 43,058 | 44,817 | 46,134 | 47,231 | 48,330 | 49,429 | 50,528 |
| 44 | 17,794 | 29,107 | 38,141 | 42,179 | 44,046 | 45,584 | 46,683 | 47,779 | 48,880 | 49,976 |
| 45 | 16,807 | 27,185 | 36,687 | 41,300 | 43,279 | 45,034 | 46,134 | 47,231 | 48,330 | 49,429 |
| 46 | 15,817 | 25,264 | 35,232 | 40,422 | 42,509 | 44,486 | 45,584 | 46,683 | 47,779 | 48,880 |
| 47 | 14,830 | 23,341 | 33,776 | 39,542 | 41,740 | 43,938 | 45,034 | 46,134 | 47,231 | 48,330 |
| 48 | 13,977 | 22,571 | 32,624 | 37,785 | 40,422 | 42,396 | 43,498 | 44,595 | 45,692 | 46,793 |
| 49 | 13,126 | 21,804 | 31,470 | 36,028 | 39,106 | 40,860 | 41,959 | 43,058 | 44,158 | 45,256 |
| 50 | 12,275 | 21,035 | 30,338 | 34,271 | 37,785 | 39,322 | 40,422 | 41,520 | 42,617 | 43,716 |
| 51 | 11,425 | 20,266 | 29,161 | 32,513 | 36,467 | 37,785 | 38,895 | 39,980 | 41,081 | 42,179 |
| 52 | 10,572 | 19,497 | 28,010 | 30,755 | 35,148 | 36,246 | 37,348 | 38,444 | 39,542 | 40,640 |
| 53 | 9,775 | 18,125 | 26,251 | 29,218 | 33,830 | 35,148 | 36,246 | 37,348 | 38,444 | 39,542 |
| 54 | 8,979 | 16,752 | 24,493 | 27,682 | 32,513 | 34,052 | 35,148 | 36,246 | 37,348 | 38,444 |
| 55 | 8,183 | 15,378 | 22,739 | 26,142 | 31,194 | 32,953 | 34,052 | 35,148 | 36,246 | 37,348 |
| 56 | 7,386 | 14,044 | 20,980 | 24,605 | 29,878 | 31,854 | 32,953 | 34,052 | 35,148 | 36,246 |
| 57 | 6,591 | 12,631 | 19,223 | 23,066 | 28,563 | 30,756 | 31,854 | 32,953 | 34,052 | 35,148 |
| 58 | 6,069 | 11,480 | 17,165 | 20,703 | 25,701 | 27,735 | 28,915 | 30,070 | 31,194 | 32,294 |
| 59 | 5,546 | 10,324 | 15,102 | 18,344 | 22,845 | 24,714 | 25,977 | 27,185 | 28,339 | 29,435 |
| 60 | 5,027 | 9,171 | 13,043 | 15,981 | 19,993 | 21,694 | 23,038 | 24,303 | 25,485 | 26,583 |
| 61 | 4,503 | 8,018 | 10,985 | 13,619 | 17,136 | 18,673 | 20,099 | 21,419 | 22,628 | 23,725 |
| 62 | 3,982 | 6,865 | 8,925 | 11,258 | 14,281 | 15,653 | 17,165 | 18,536 | 19,768 | 20,869 |
| 63 | 3,706 | 6,205 | 8,018 | 10,066 | 12,702 | 14,058 | 15,488 | 16,807 | 18,013 | 19,112 |
| 64 | 3,437 | 5,546 | 7,111 | 8,869 | 11,121 | 12,467 | 13,814 | 15,076 | 16,255 | 17,353 |
| 65 | 3,159 | 4,887 | 6,205 | 7,678 | 9,543 | 10,874 | 12,137 | 13,347 | 14,500 | 15,598 |
| 66 | 2,884 | 4,231 | 5,300 | 6,479 | 7,965 | 9,281 | 10,463 | 11,615 | 12,743 | 13,840 |
| 67 | 2,610 | 3,569 | 4,392 | 5,286 | 6,385 | 7,691 | 8,787 | 9,886 | 10,985 | 12,083 |
| 68 | 2,539 | 3,458 | 4,242 | 5,066 | 6,167 | 7,386 | 8,444 | 9,584 | 10,640 | 11,725 |
| 69 | 2,471 | 3,350 | 4,093 | 4,848 | 5,947 | 7,086 | 8,103 | 9,281 | 10,300 | 11,367 |
| 70 | 2,403 | 3,241 | 3,939 | 4,627 | 5,726 | 6,781 | 7,758 | 8,979 | 9,954 | 11,013 |
| 71 | 2,335 | 3,129 | 3,790 | 4,406 | 5,505 | 6,479 | 7,415 | 8,679 | 9,612 | 10,397 |
| 72 | 2,266 | 3,022 | 3,639 | 4,189 | 5,286 | 6,180 | 7,070 | 8,376 | 9,266 | 10,300 |
| 73 | 2,210 | 2,968 | 3,584 | 4,106 | 5,203 | 6,041 | 6,934 | 8,157 | 8,993 | 9,996 |
| 74 | 2,156 | 2,910 | 3,529 | 4,023 | 5,123 | 5,903 | 6,798 | 7,937 | 8,720 | 9,687 |
| 75 | 2,102 | 2,857 | 3,475 | 3,939 | 5,038 | 5,767 | 6,659 | 7,716 | 8,444 | 9,390 |
| 76 | 2,046 | 2,799 | 3,417 | 3,859 | 4,956 | 5,631 | 6,523 | 7,498 | 8,168 | 9,091 |
| 77 and over | 1,992 | 2,745 | 3,364 | 3,775 | 4,874 | 5,492 | 6,385 | 7,280 | 7,895 | 8,787 |

(B) Payments to sufferers from pneumoconiosis or byssinosis under the statutory scheme (see C6048).

| Age of disabled person | Extent of incapacity for the relevant period | |
|---|---|---|
| | Partial | Total |
| | £ | £ |
| 37 and under | 41,192 | 56,568 |
| 38 | 39,542 | 55,470 |
| 39 | 37,894 | 54,371 |
| 40 | 36,246 | 53,274 |
| 41 | 34,600 | 52,174 |
| 42 | 32,953 | 51,076 |
| 43 | 31,030 | 50,528 |
| 44 | 29,107 | 49,976 |
| 45 | 27,185 | 49,429 |
| 46 | 25,264 | 48,880 |
| 47 | 23,341 | 48,330 |
| 48 | 22,571 | 46,793 |
| 49 | 21,804 | 45,256 |
| 50 | 21,035 | 43,716 |
| 51 | 20,266 | 42,179 |
| 52 | 19,497 | 40,640 |
| 53 | 18,125 | 39,542 |
| 54 | 16,752 | 38,444 |
| 55 | 15,378 | 37,348 |
| 56 | 14,004 | 36,246 |
| 57 | 12,631 | 35,148 |
| 58 | 11,480 | 32,294 |
| 59 | 10,324 | 29,435 |
| 60 | 9,171 | 26,583 |
| 61 | 8,018 | 23,725 |
| 62 | 6,865 | 20,869 |
| 63 | 6,205 | 19,112 |
| 64 | 5,546 | 17,353 |
| 65 | 4,887 | 15,598 |
| 66 | 4,231 | 13,840 |
| 67 | 3,569 | 12,083 |
| 68 | 3,458 | 11,725 |
| 69 | 3,350 | 11,367 |
| 70 | 3,241 | 11,013 |
| 71 | 3,129 | 10,657 |
| 72 | 3,022 | 10,300 |
| 73 | 2,968 | 9,996 |
| 74 | 2,910 | 9,687 |
| 75 | 2,857 | 9,390 |
| 76 | 2,799 | 9,091 |
| 77 and over | 2,745 | 8,787 |

(C) Payments to dependants of a deceased former sufferer from the prescribed diseases of pneumoconiosis or byssinosis (see C6047).

| *Age of disabled person at his last birthday preceding death* | *Percentage assessment for the relevant period* | | | | |
|---|---|---|---|---|---|
| | 10% or less | 11%-20% | 21%-30% | 31%-49% | 50% and over |
| | £ | £ | £ | £ | £ |
| 37 and under | 10,847 | 21,147 | 24,164 | 24,990 | 25,676 |
| 38 | 10,517 | 20,212 | 23,342 | 24,164 | 25,043 |
| 39 | 10,190 | 19,277 | 22,518 | 23,341 | 24,412 |
| 40 | 9,856 | 18,344 | 21,694 | 22,518 | 23,780 |
| 41 | 9,528 | 17,411 | 20,869 | 21,694 | 23,149 |
| 42 | 9,201 | 16,480 | 20,045 | 20,869 | 22,518 |
| 43 | 8,607 | 15,269 | 19,304 | 20,128 | 21,915 |
| 44 | 8,018 | 14,058 | 18,561 | 19,387 | 21,303 |
| 45 | 7,429 | 12,851 | 17,822 | 18,646 | 20,703 |
| 46 | 6,837 | 11,641 | 17,016 | 17,903 | 20,099 |
| 47 | 6,247 | 10,433 | 16,341 | 17,165 | 19,497 |
| 48 | 5,795 | 10,104 | 15,792 | 16,857 | 18,755 |
| 49 | 5,340 | 9,775 | 15,240 | 16,011 | 18,013 |
| 50 | 4,887 | 9,445 | 14,693 | 15,432 | 17,272 |
| 51 | 4,435 | 9,116 | 14,143 | 14,856 | 16,532 |
| 52 | 3,982 | 8,787 | 13,594 | 14,281 | 15,792 |
| 53 | 3,775 | 8,8018 | 12,551 | 13,483 | 15,184 |
| 54 | 3,569 | 7,249 | 11,506 | 12,687 | 14,582 |
| 55 | 3,364 | 6,479 | 10,463 | 11,891 | 13,977 |
| 56 | 3,159 | 5,711 | 9,419 | 11,096 | 13,371 |
| 57 | 2,951 | 4,944 | 8,376 | 10,300 | 12,768 |
| 58 | 2,759 | 4,392 | 7,182 | 8,899 | 11,096 |
| 59 | 2,565 | 3,844 | 5,987 | 7,498 | 9,419 |
| 60 | 2,376 | 3,296 | 4,791 | 6,096 | 7,745 |
| 61 | 2,185 | 2,745 | 3,598 | 4,697 | 6,069 |
| 62 | 1,992 | 2,198 | 2,403 | 3,296 | 4,392 |
| 63 | 1,992 | 2,156 | 2,322 | 3,033 | 3,914 |
| 64 | 1,992 | 2,114 | 2,237 | 2,774 | 3,437 |
| 65 | 1,992 | 2,075 | 2,156 | 2,512 | 2,951 |
| 66 | 1,992 | 2,034 | 2,075 | 2,252 | 2,471 |
| 67 and over | 1,992 | 1,992 | 1,992 | 1,992 | 1,992 |

(D) Payments to dependants of a deceased former sufferer from pneumoconiosis or byssinosis under the statutory scheme (see C6048).

| Age of disabled person at his last birthday preceding death | Extent of incapacity for the relevant period | |
|---|---|---|
| | Partial | Total |
| | £ | £ |
| 37 and under | 21,147 | 25,676 |
| 38 | 20,212 | 25,043 |
| 39 | 19,277 | 24,412 |
| 40 | 18,344 | 23,780 |
| 41 | 17,411 | 23,149 |
| 42 | 16,480 | 22,518 |
| 43 | 15,269 | 21,915 |
| 44 | 14,058 | 21,303 |
| 45 | 12,851 | 20,703 |
| 46 | 11,641 | 20,099 |
| 47 | 10,433 | 19,497 |
| 48 | 10,104 | 18,755 |
| 49 | 9,775 | 18,013 |
| 50 | 9,445 | 17,272 |
| 51 | 9,116 | 16,532 |
| 52 | 8,787 | 15,792 |
| 53 | 8,018 | 15,184 |
| 54 | 7,249 | 14,582 |
| 55 | 6,479 | 13,977 |
| 56 | 5,711 | 13,371 |
| 57 | 4,944 | 12,768 |
| 58 | 4,392 | 11,096 |
| 59 | 3,844 | 9,419 |
| 60 | 3,296 | 7,745 |
| 61 | 2,745 | 6,069 |
| 62 | 2,198 | 4,392 |
| 63 | 2,156 | 3,914 |
| 64 | 2,114 | 3,437 |
| 65 | 2,075 | 2,951 |
| 66 | 2,034 | 2,471 |
| 67 and over | 1,992 | 1,992 |

(E) Payments to dependants of persons who died as a result of diffuse mesothelioma.

| Age of disabled person at his last birthday preceding death | Payment |
|---|---|
| | £ |
| 37 and under | 25,676 |
| 38 | 25,043 |
| 39 | 24,412 |
| 40 | 23,780 |
| 41 | 23,149 |
| 42 | 22,518 |
| 43 | 21,915 |
| 44 | 21,303 |
| 45 | 20,703 |
| 46 | 20,099 |
| 47 | 19,497 |
| 48 | 18,755 |
| 49 | 18,013 |
| 50 | 17,272 |
| 51 | 16,532 |
| 52 | 15,792 |
| 53 | 15,184 |
| 54 | 14,582 |
| 55 | 13,977 |
| 56 | 13,371 |
| 57 | 12,768 |
| 58 | 11,096 |
| 59 | 9,419 |
| 60 | 7,745 |
| 61 | 6,069 |
| 62 | 4,392 |
| 63 | 3,914 |
| 64 | 3,437 |
| 65 | 2,951 |
| 66 | 2,471 |
| 67 and over | 1,992 |

# Construction and Building Operations

## Introduction to construction work

The main causes of accidents and ill-health in the construction industry are:

*(a)* *Falls* – particularly through fragile roofs and roof lights, from ladders and from scaffolds and other work;

*(b)* *Falling material and collapses;*

*(c)* *Electrical accidents;*

*(d)* *Mobile plant* – causing people to be struck by excavators, lift trucks, dumpers and other vehicles;

*(e)* *Exposure to dusts* – including asbestos, and other hazardous substances;

*(f)* *Lifting heavy and awkward loads;* and

*(g)* *Exposure to high noise levels and vibration.*

A recent Health and Safety Executive (HSE) campaign focused on the following health and safety aspects of construction work:

- Eliminating hazards and controlling risks through compliance with the *Construction (Design and Management) Regulations 1994 (SI 1994 No 3140)* (see C8015), for example, by eliminating the use of fragile roof lights in new and refurbished buildings;

- Controlling risks to scaffolders and to the public and other workers from falling material and scaffold collapses;

- Segregating people from vehicles and plant, and eliminating reversing and/or ensuring the use of suitable reversing aids;

- Ensuring appropriate precautions are taken during work by licensed contractors, including work with asbestos insulation board (see further ASBESTOS);

- Eliminating handling of heavy blocks over 20kg, or reducing the risk from single-person repetitive lifting of these blocks. HSE has recently published '*Backs for the future: Safe manual handling in construction*', which explains the principles for managing manual handling risks, provides an example of a manual handling risk assessment, and describes the role and lists the key points for designers, planning supervisors, principal contractors, contractors and manufacturers and suppliers. It also contains details of case studies where manual handling risks were identified and solutions to the problems found. (See further MANUAL HANDLING); and

- Eliminating or reducing risk from hand-arm vibration and noise at the design stage, and managing residual risk, particularly during scabbling, pile head removal by breaker and hand tunnelling. (See further NOISE AND VIBRATION)

## Practical safety criteria

Good safety practice dictates the following.

## Ladders

**C8003**    (*a*)    Only ladders in a sound condition should be used.

(*b*)    The 'one out four up' rule should be strictly adhered to in all situations (i.e. that the vertical height from the ground to the ladder's point of rest should be four times the distance between the base of the vertical dimension and the foot of the ladder).

(*c*)    Ladders should be securely fixed near to their upper resting place or, where this is impracticable, 'footed' by an individual or securely fixed at the base to prevent slipping.

(*d*)    Ladders should be inspected on a regular basis and a record of such inspections maintained.

(See W9018 WORK AT HEIGHTS for statutory requirements.)

## Working platforms

**C8004**    (*a*)    Working platforms should be adequately fenced by means of guard-rails and toe-boards.

(*b*)    Platforms should be adequately covered with sound boards.

(*c*)    Where mobile platforms are used, they should be stationed on a firm level base and, where possible, tied to the structure to prevent sideways movement. Wheel-locking devices should be provided and used.

(*d*)    The following height to base ratios should be applied for all mobile working platforms:

outdoor work – 3:1; indoor work – 3.5:1.

(See W9013 WORK AT HEIGHTS for statutory requirements.)

## Materials

**C8005**    (*a*)    Meticulous standards of housekeeping must be maintained on working platforms and other elevated working positions to prevent materials, tools and other items falling on to people working directly below. The correct positioning of toe-boards is most important here.

(*b*)    Lifting operations should ensure correct hooking and slinging prior to raising, correct assembly of gin-wheels and a high degree of supervision.

(*c*)    Catchment platforms or 'fans' should be installed to catch small items which may fall during construction, particularly where work is undertaken above a public thoroughfare.

## Excavations

**C8006**    (*a*)    Trenches should be adequately timbered with regard to the depth and width of the trench, the nature of the surrounding ground and the load imposed by subsoil.

(*b*)    Excavated ground and building materials should be stored well away from the verge of any excavation.

## Powered hand tools and machinery

C8007    (*a*)    Electrically operated hand tools, such as drills, should comply with British Standard 2769: Series and, unless 'all insulated' or 'double insulated', must be effectively earthed.

(*b*)    Portable tools and temporary lighting arrangements should operate through reduced voltages, using 110 volt mains isolation transformers with the secondary winding centre tapped to earth.

(*c*)    Power take-offs, cooling fans, belt drives and other items of moving machinery should be securely fenced to prevent workers coming into contact with them. All machinery should comply with the *Provision and Use of Work Equipment Regulations 1998 (SI 1998 No 2306)* (see further MACHINERY SAFETY AND ELECTRICITY). The HSE booklet, '*Electrical safety on construction sites*', provides more detailed guidance in this area.

(d)    The health risks associated with vibration should be assessed when buying or hiring hand-held power tools, and existing power tools should also be checked (see further NOISE AND VIBRATION).

## Site transport

C8008    (*a*)    Employees should not travel on site transport, such as dumper trucks, and notices should be affixed to such vehicles to that effect.

(*b*)    All vehicle movement and tipping operations on site should be supervised by a person outside the driver's cab.

(*c*)    Site vehicles should be subject to regular maintenance, particular attention being paid to braking and reversing systems.

(*d*)    Only competent and trained drivers should be allowed to drive site vehicles.

(*e*)    Site roadways should be maintained in a sound condition, free from mud, debris, obstructions and large puddles. The verges of the roadway should be clearly defined and adequate lighting provided, particularly at tipping points, reversing and turning areas.

(*f*)    Site speed limits should be established and clearly marked with signs corresponding to speed limit signs on public roads.

## Demolition

C8009    (*a*)    A pre-demolition survey should always be undertaken, making use of the original plans if available.

(*b*)    Catching platforms should be installed not more than 6 m below the working level wherever there is a risk to the public.

(*c*)    Employees should be provided with safety helmets incorporating chin straps, goggles, heavy duty gloves and safety boots with steel insoles. In certain cases, respiratory protection, safety belts or harnesses may also be necessary.

(*d*)    Demolition should be undertaken, wherever possible, in the reverse order of erection.

(*e*)    When using working platforms, all debris should be removed on a regular basis.

(*f*)    Members of framed structures should be adequately supported and temporary props, bracing or guys installed to restrain remaining parts of the building.

(*g*)    Employees should not work from the floor of a building which is currently being demolished.

(*h*)    Where pulling arrangements, demolition ball, explosives or pusher arms are to be used, employees should be kept well away until these stages have been completed.

(*i*)    Frequent inspections must be made of the demolition site to detect dangers which may have arisen following commencement of demolition.

## Fire

**C8010**    (*a*)    All sources of ignition should be carefully controlled, e.g. welding activities, the use of blow lamps, gas or liquid fuel fired appliances.

(*b*)    All flammable materials, including waste materials, should be carefully stored away from the main construction activity.

(*c*)    All employees should be aware of the fire warning system, training sessions being undertaken according to need.

(*d*)    There should be sufficient access for fire brigade appliances in the event of fire.

(*e*)    There should be adequate space between buildings, e.g. site huts, canteen, etc.

(*f*)    High-risk buildings should be separated from low-risk buildings.

(*g*)    Controlled areas, where smoking and the use of naked lights are forbidden, should be established and suitably marked with warning signs.

(*h*)    An adequate supply of water should be available for fire brigade appliances and on-site fire-fighting.

(*i*)    Fire wardens should be appointed to undertake routine site inspections, together with the operation of a fire patrol, particularly at night and weekends.

(See also FIRE AND FIRE PRECAUTIONS.)

## Asbestos

**C8011**    (*a*)    It should be assumed that buildings constructed or refurbished before the 1980s will contain asbestos-based materials.

(*b*)    No work should be carried out which is likely to expose employees to asbestos unless an adequate assessment of exposure has been made.

(*c*)    The area where work is to be carried out should be checked to identify the location, type and condition of any asbestos likely to be disturbed.

Two new guidance booklets from the HSE, '*Introduction to Asbestos Essentials*' (aimed at anyone who is liable to control or carry out maintenance work with asbestos-containing materials) and '*Asbestos Essentials Task Manual*' (aimed at workers), provide information on ensuring that building maintenance work involving asbestos-containing materials is carried out safely and in accordance with the law. (Also see further ASBESTOS.)

# The Regulations

C8012    The series of construction Regulations made under the *Factories Act 1961* referred to 'building operations' and 'works of engineering construction'. A major revision of these Regulations gives a more comprehensive definition of 'construction work', which is based on a much broader concept and also includes the installation and removal of services which are part of a structure and the installation and removal of fixed plant where there is a risk of falling two metres or more (see also WORK AT HEIGHTS).

All construction activities are now contained in three sets of Regulations bearing the prefix 'Construction'.

—    the *Construction (Head Protection) Regulations 1989 (SI 1989 No 2209 as amended)* (see C8097 below);

—    the *Construction (Design and Management) Regulations 1994 (CDM) (SI 1994 No 3140)* (see C8015 below);

—    the *Construction (Health, Safety and Welfare) Regulations 1996 (CHSW) (SI 1996 No 1592)* (see C8031 below).

Generally, the definition of construction work covers the activities on all kinds of construction sites, from the smallest internal jobs to large-scale complex projects including:

—    general building and construction work;

—    refurbishment work;

—    maintenance and repair work;

—    engineering construction work;

—    civil engineering work.

The exploration and extraction of mineral resources and the preparatory activities are excluded from the definition of construction work, which is extensively defined in the principal regulations. Reference to the full definitions should be made in any case of doubt or for litigation purposes. [*CDM (SI 1994 No 3140), Reg 2(1); CHSW (SI 1996 No 1592), Reg 2(1)*].

The two principal sets of Regulations have different applications:

—    *CDM* applies to construction sites only when the 'construction work' is notifiable to the HSE (see C8016) and where more than five people are likely to be employed at any one time;

—    *CHSW* applies to all construction sites (that is, any place where the principal activity carried on is 'construction work') and when a person is at work on a construction site.

## Associated statutory requirements

C8013    The protection of the workforce who carry out construction work stems from the *HSWA 1974* and the *Management of Health and Safety at Work Regulations 1999 (MHSWR) (SI 1999 No 3242)*.

In particular, under the Act itself:

(*a*)    contractors (as employers) owe health and safety duties to their employees [*HSWA 1974, s 2*];

(*b*)    employees owe such duties to their employers (i.e. contractors/ subcontractors) [*HSWA 1974, s 7*];

(*c*)    building owners (i.e contractors' employers) owe health and safety duties to subcontractors and their employees [*HSWA 1974, s 3(1)*] (also see *R v Associated Octel Co Ltd at* C8136);

(*d*)    self-employed contractors/workmen owe health and safety duties to other self-employed persons (e.g. building owners to main contractors), and to employees (of other organisations) [*HSWA 1974, s 3(2)*].

Self-styled 'labour-only' subcontractors have been held to be employees of a large main contractor and so were entitled to the protection of some of the *Construction Regulations* (*Ferguson v John Dawson & Partners (Contractors) Ltd [1976] IRLR 346* where a nominated subcontractor was liable to a 'self-employed labour-only subcontractor' for breach of *Reg 28(1)* of the *Construction (Working Places) Regulations 1966* (now repealed), requiring provision of guard-rails and toe-boards at working platforms and places);

(*e*)    building owners and occupiers have duties to employees of contractors and subcontractors. [*HSWA 1974, s 4(1), (2)*]. Thus, *HSWA 1974, s 4* states that anyone 'having control to any extent' of premises, must take reasonable care in respect of persons working there, who are *not* employees. This duty can be subject to indemnity clauses in a lease and/or contract (see further OCCUPIERS' LIABILITY), it is strict and must be carried out so far as is reasonably practicable, that is, subject to cost-effective constraints;

(*f*)    although ostensibly applicable to all workplaces, the *Workplace (Health, Safety and Welfare) Regulations 1992 (SI 1992 No 3004)* do *not* extend to building operations and works of engineering construction, unless some other activity is being carried on there (see further WORKPLACES – HEALTH, SAFETY AND WELFARE).

## Main Regulations relating to the construction industry

C8014      The most relevant legislation relating to construction work is listed below:

—    *Construction (Design and Management) Regulations 1994 (SI 1994 No 3140);*

—    *Construction (Health, Safety and Welfare) Regulations 1996 (SI 1996 No 1592);*

—    *Management of Health and Safety at Work Regulations 1999 (SI 1999 No 3242);*

—    *Provision and Use of Work Equipment Regulations 1998 (SI 1998 No 2306);*

—    *Control of Substances Hazardous To Health Regulations 1999 (SI 1999 No 437);*

—    *Control of Asbestos at Work Regulations 1987 (SI 1987 No 2115);*

—    *Asbestos (Licensing) Regulations 1983 (SI 1983 No 1649);*

—    *Manual Handling Operations Regulations 1992 (SI 1992 No 2793);*

—    *Personal Protective Equipment Regulations 1992 (SI 1992 No 2966);*

—    *Noise at Work Regulations 1989 (SI 1989 No 1790);*

—    *Confined Spaces Regulations 1997 (SI 1997 No 1713);*

—    *Work in Compressed Air Regulations 1996 (SI 1996 No 1656);*

— *Lifting Operations and Lifting Equipment Regulations 1998 (SI 1998 No 2307);*

— *Reporting of Injuries Diseases and Dangerous Occurrences Regulations 1995 (SI 1995 No 3163);*

— *Workplaces (Health, Safety and Welfare) Regulations 1992 (SI 1992 No 3004);*

— *Health and Safety (Enforcing Authority) Regulations 1998 (SI 1998 No 494);*

— *Safety Representatives and Safety Committees Regulations 1977 (SI 1977 No 500);*

— *Health and Safety (Consultation with Employees) Regulations 1996 (SI 1996 No 1513).*

## Construction (Design and Management) Regulations 1994 (SI 1994 No 3140)

C8015     The *Construction (Design and Management) Regulations 1994 (CDM) (SI 1994 No 3140)* implement (with minor exceptions) EU Directive 92/57/EEC on the minimum safety and health requirements at temporary or mobile construction sites. The Regulations are supported by an Approved Code of Practice, L54: *Managing construction for health and safety* (ISBN 0 7176 0792 5). This will be replaced by a new Approved Code of Practice (ACoP) on the Regulations, *Managing construction for health and safety*. The ACoP is expected to come into force (at the earliest) in summer 2002. The revision is intended to focus the duty holders on managing health and safety while avoiding unnecessary bureaucracy. It clarifies the duties involved in complying with the legislation and concentrates on the role of duty holders and particular topics including:

- Assessing competence and resources;

- Preparing health and safety plans; and

- Giving advice on the contents of the health and safety file.

Generally, the *CDM Regulations* apply to construction work (as defined) carried out on a construction site which is notifiable to the HSE, that is, a construction project which:

— is scheduled to last for more than 30 days; or

— will involve more than 500 man-days of work; or

— includes any demolition work regardless of the size or duration of the work; or

— involves five or more workers being on site at any one time.

The Regulations always apply when construction design work is involved.

### Notification of project

C8016     Notification of a construction project (where notifiable) (see 'Exclusions' at C8017 below) should be given to HSE in writing (ideally) as soon as practicable after appointment of the planning supervisor, or (failing that), after the appointment of the principal contractor, but before construction work starts, specifying:

(*a*)     date of forwarding;

(*b*)     exact address of construction site;

(*c*)     name and address of client(s);

(*d*)    type of project;

(*e*)    name and address of the planning supervisor;

(*f*)    declaration of appointment by the planning supervisor;

(*g*)    name and address of principal contractor;

(*h*)    declaration of appointment of the principal contractor;

(*i*)    date planned for start of the construction phase;

(*j*)    planned duration of the construction phase;

(*k*)    estimated maximum number of people at work on the construction site;

(*l*)    planned number of contractors on construction site;

(*m*)    name and address of any contractor(s) already chosen.

[*CDM (SI 1994 No 3140), Reg 3, Sch 1*].


## Exclusions

C8017    These Regulations are inapplicable (mainly) to construction work:

(*a*)    where a client reasonably believes that

    (i)    a project is not notifiable, and

    (ii)    no more than four people are working at any one time (except for demolition and dismantling)

    [*CDM (SI 1994 No 3140), Reg 3(2), (3)*];

(*b*)    of a minor nature where the local authority is the enforcing authority [*CDM (SI 1994 No 3140), Reg 3(4)*];

(*c*)    carried out for a domestic client, unless (as a result of agreement/ arrangement with the developer):

    (i)    land is transferred to the client,

    (ii)    the developer undertakes to build on the land, or

    (iii)    after construction, the land will incorporate premises to be occupied by the client

    [*CDM (SI 1994 No 3140), Reg 3(8)*].


## Objectives of the CDM Regulations

C8018    The *CDM Regulations* introduce a control framework which requires the effective management of all stages of a construction project from conception, design, commissioning of work, its planning and execution, and in particular construction activities which are likely to pose significant risks to workers.

The overall aim of the *CDM Regulations* is to raise construction safety standards by improving co-ordination between various parties involved at both preparation and execution stage. More particularly, clients are required to appoint co-ordinators for preparation (planning supervisors) and execution stages (principal contractors), the co-ordinators being required to prepare and update the health and safety plan, which is the key to the operation of *CDM Regulations*, planning supervisors dealing mainly with designers and principal contractors dealing mainly with other contractors. The health and safety plan (see C8025 below) is initiated by the planning supervisor and forms part of tendering documentation. Before actual construction work begins, the plan should be scrutinised by the principal contractor in order to ensure that it is properly adjusted to contractors and site activities. Under *CDM (SI 1994 No 3140), Reg 6*, clients must ensure that adequate financial provision is made and adequate time allowed for completion of the project, with the main health and safety costs being assessed and included in tenders, the basis of this assessment being the health and safety plan. Under *CDM (SI 1994 No 3140), Reg 14*, planning supervisors must be competent to assess the project and advise the client, who must then set the budget and timescale and finance the project. As companies, individuals or partnerships, they will often be the lead member of the design team (e.g. architect or engineer); sometimes a main contractor may be a planning supervisor, sometimes even a client. But both planning supervisors and principal contractors should be appointed as early as possible during the planning stage of the project.

It is incumbent on clients to specify that contractors comply with the health and safety plan; in turn, contractors should price compliance, with clients requiring that contractors include in tender identifiable sums for the management of health and safety and to deal with specific hazards. For that reason, tenderers should advise clients of any hazards not identified in the plan which appear in their assessments. It is then for the planning supervisor to advise the client on adequacy of tender (and provision for health and safety), who should take this into account when awarding contracts. In this way, contracts should only be awarded to contractors/tenderers prepared to comply with health and safety requirements and standards.

## Duties and responsibilities

C8019    Because the United Kingdom construction industry has characteristics which were not recognised by the EU Temporary or Mobile Construction Sites Directive, it was necessary to specify that the 'client' (a term which includes clients' agents and developers) must appoint other principals for the planning and the carrying out of the construction work within the scope of the Directive. These are the 'planning supervisor' and the 'principal contractor'.

The *CDM Regulations* give detailed 'job descriptions' for the various parties involved in the construction contract. It should be noted that the following duties imposed by the Regulations are additional to those imposed by the *Management of Health and Safety at Work Regulations 1999 (SI 1999 No 3242) (MHSWR)* and other similar health and safety legislation.

### Clients

C8020    Clients (including clients' agents) [*CDM (SI 1994 No 3140), Reg 4(1)*] must, prior to construction work, and in respect of each project:

(*a*)    appoint

(i)    a competent planning supervisor [*CDM (SI 1994 No 3140), Reg 6(1), (3)*], and

(ii)    a competent principal contractor (who must be a contractor) [*CDM (SI 1994 No 3140), Reg 6(1)–(3)*].

Such appointments can be terminated, changed or renewed (where necessary) to ensure that these roles are filled until construction is completed [*CDM (SI 1994 No 3140), Reg 6(5)*]. So long as competent to perform both roles, planning supervisors can also be principal contractors; and clients can be planning supervisors or principal contractors (or both) [*CDM (SI 1994 No 3140), Reg 6(6)*]. However, clients must not appoint planning supervisors, designers and contractors, unless satisfied as to their competence [*CDM (SI 1994 No 3140), Reg 8(1)–(3)*], and that all three have allocated, or will allocate, appropriate resources for the performance of their respective roles [*CDM (SI 1994 No 3140), Reg 9*];

(*b*)   so far as is reasonably practicable, ensure that the construction phase of any project does not begin without preparation of a satisfactory health and safety plan [*CDM (SI 1994 No 3140), Reg 10*];

(*c*)   as soon as is reasonably practicable but before commencement of work, ensure that the planning supervisor is provided with information relevant to the state of the premises on which construction work is to take place [*CDM (SI 1994 No 3140), Reg 11*];

(*d*)   ensure that information in the health and safety file is kept available for inspection by any person, for the purposes of compliance with statutory requirements and prohibitions [*Reg 12(1)*].

*Designers*

**C8021**   Designers must:

(1)   advise clients as to their duties; and

(2)   ensure that any design has regard to the need:

(*a*)   to avoid foreseeable risks to the health and safety of any person involved in construction or cleaning work in or on the structure at any time, or anyone who may be affected by the work of such person (e.g. a member of the public);

(*b*)   to combat at source risks to the health and safety of any person at work involved in construction, cleaning work or any person who may be affected by such work;

(*c*)   to give priority to measures for protecting those involved in construction, cleaning and those who may be affected;

(*d*)   to ensure that the design includes adequate information about any aspect of the project or structure of materials which might affect construction or cleaning workers or those who may be affected by their work; and

(*e*)   to co-operate with the planning supervisor (and any other designer preparing a design in connection with the project) for the purposes of compliance with statutory requirements and prohibitions.

[*CDM (SI 1994 No 3140), Reg 13(2)*].

The Regulations concerning the definition of and duties of designers were amended by the *Construction (Design and Management) (Amendment) Regulations 2000 (SI 2000 No 2380)*.

The amending Regulations were made as a result of a Court of Appeal decision in *R v Paul Wurth SA, The Times, 29 March 2000*, in which HSE had prosecuted Paul Wurth SA following a fatality during the installation of a conveyor at the British Steel Port Talbot works in 1997.

The HSE had alleged that the company had failed in its duties as designers under *Regulation 13(2)* of the 1994 Regulations. This places a duty on a designer to ensure that any design he prepares, and which he is aware will be used for the purposes of construction work, includes among its design considerations adequate regard to the need to avoid foreseeable risks to the health and safety of people as a result of construction work and subsequent cleaning work.

However, the Court of Appeal held that designers do not have responsibilities for designs which are prepared by others under their control, including their employees. This was contrary to the aim of the original provisions of the Regulations, and hence the need for the amendment.

*Regulations 2* (concerning the definition of 'designer'), *3* (regarding a person preparing a design), and *12* (concerning the client's duty to ensure the health and safety file is available for inspection) and *13* (concerning requirements on designers), have all been amended. The amended Regulations ensure that legal duties on designers to build safety into a design, apply not only to a design prepared by them personally, but also to a design prepared by an employee or other person under their control.

### Planning supervisors

C8022 Planning supervisors must:

(a) ensure that the project is notified to the HSE (unless it is reasonably believed that the project is not notifiable (see 'Exclusions' at C8017 above));

(b) ensure that the design of a project includes

   (i) reference to health and safety management, and

   (ii) adequate information regarding structure and materials;

(c) ensure co-operation between designers, for the purposes of compliance with their duties as designers (under *CDM (SI 1994 No 3140), Reg 13*);

(d) be able to give adequate advice to

   (i) any client/contractor regarding competence of personnel/allocation of resources, and

   (ii) any client regarding competence of a contractor and a contractor's allocation of resources as well as the health and safety plan;

(e) ensure preparation of a health and safety file, containing

   (i) information concerning aspects of the project, structure or materials that may affect health and safety, and

   (ii) any other information which, foreseeably, will be necessary to ensure health and safety of persons involved in construction, cleaning and maintenance or demolition work;

(f) ensure that, on completion of the project, the health and safety file is delivered to the client

[*CDM (SI 1994 No 3140), Reg 14*]; and

(g) ensure that the health and safety plan is made available to every contractor before arrangements are made for them to manage or carry out construction work.

[*CDM (SI 1994 No 3140), Reg 15(1)(2)*].

*Principal contractors*

C8023    Principal contractors must:

(*a*)    take reasonable steps to ensure co-operation between all contractors, for the purposes of compliance with statutory requirements and/or prohibitions;

(*b*)    so far as is reasonably practicable, ensure that every contractor and every employee complies with the health and safety plan;

(*c*)    take reasonable steps to ensure that only authorised persons are allowed where construction work is carried on;

(*d*)    ensure that notification particulars (see C8016 above) are displayed prominently so that they can be read by construction personnel; and

(*e*)    provide the planning supervisor promptly with any of the following information,

(i)    which is in possession of the principal contractor, or which the latter could ascertain by making reasonable enquiries of a contractor,

(ii)    which, reasonably, the planning supervisor would include in the health and safety file (in order to comply with his duties (under *Reg 14* above)), and

(iii)    which is not in possession of the planning supervisor.

[*CDM (SI 1994 No 3140), Reg 16(1)*].

For the purposes of compliance with *Reg 16(1)*, principal contractors can

(i)    give any necessary directions to any contractor, and

(ii)    include in the health and safety plan rules for the management of construction work reasonably required for health and safety management; such rules being in writing and brought to the attention of those affected.

[*CDM (SI 1994 No 3140), Reg 16(2)(3)*];

(*f*)    so far as is reasonably practicable, ensure that every contractor is provided with comprehensible information on health and safety risks to that contractor or to employees or other persons under that contractor's control;

(*g*)    so far as is reasonably practicable, ensure that every contractor who is an employer provides his employees engaged in construction work with:

(i)    information relating to

—    health and safety risks,

—    protective measures,

—    procedures to be followed in imminent danger and in danger areas, and

—    persons appointed to implement those procedures, and

(ii)    health and safety training, both on recruitment and/or exposure to new/increased risks; such training to be repeated periodically

[*CDM (SI 1994 No 3140), Reg 17*];

(*h*)    ensure that:

    (i)    employees/self-employed personnel are able to discuss, and offer advice on, matters foreseeably affecting their health and safety, and

    (ii)   there are arrangements for the co-ordination of employees' views (or their representatives')

[*CDM (SI 1994 No 3140), Reg 18*].

*Contractors*

**C8024**    Contractors must:

(*a*)    co-operate with the principal contractor, so that both can comply with their statutory duties;

(*b*)    so far as is reasonably practicable, provide the principal contractor promptly with any information (including risk assessments for the purposes of the *Management of Health and Safety at Work Regulations 1999*) *(SI 1999 No 3242)*, which might affect the health and safety of construction workers, or those who might be affected by construction work, or which might justify a review of the health and safety plan;

(*c*)    comply with directions given by the principal contractor, for the purposes of compliance by contractors;

(*d*)    comply with rules applicable to them in the health and safety plan;

(*e*)    provide the principal contractor promptly with information relating to deaths, injuries, conditions and dangerous occurrences notifiable under the *Reporting of Injuries, Diseases and Dangerous Occurrences Regulations 1995 (SI 1995 No 3163)* (see further ACCIDENT REPORTING);

(*f*)    provide the principal contractor promptly with any information which:

    (i)    is in the possession of the contractor, or which he could ascertain by reasonable enquiries, and

    (ii)   it is reasonable to suppose the principal contractor would provide to the planning supervisor, for the purposes of inclusion in the health and safety file, which is not in the possession of the planning supervisor or the principal contractor

[*CDM (SI 1994 No 3140), Reg 19(1)*];

(*g*)    not allow any employee to work on construction work, unless provided with:

    (i)    the name of the planning supervisor,

    (ii)   the name of the principal contractor, and

    (iii)  the contents of the health and safety plan relating to work being carried out by the employee.

Self-employed personnel must also be provided with this information [*Reg 19(2)-(4)*].

## Health and safety plan

**C8025**    Before construction work starts, a duty is placed on the 'client' (as defined) to ensure that the appointed planning supervisor prepares a document known as the 'health and safety plan' which is to serve two purposes:

(*a*)    during the pre-construction phase, to bring together the health and safety information obtained from the client and designers;

(*b*)    during the construction phase, to include the principal contractor's health and safety policy and risk assessments.

The health and safety plan will continue to evolve and provide a focus for the co-ordination of health and safety matters as the construction work progresses.

The health and safety plan forms the basis of the health and safety management structure, being part of the tender documents. It should:

(*a*)    indicate (in general terms) the approach to health and safety to be adopted by everyone (as per the *Management of Health and Safety at Work Regulations 1999 (SI 1999 No 3242)*);

(*b*)    identify the main health and safety hazards likely to occur to employees, self-employed operatives and the general public – these having been specified earlier by the client and/or designers (e.g. work in compressed air);

(*c*)    specify precautions to be taken; and

(*d*)    require work to be done to recognised technical standards and in accordance with published guidance (which should be specified in the plan).

Before the commencement of work, the planning supervisor should acquaint both principal contractor and contractors with the health and safety plan, so that they can agree to it or to modifications in it, and then draw up tenders.

### The planning supervisor

**C8026**    Planning supervisors should:

— prepare the health and safety plan;

— ensure that the plan forms part of the tender documentation;

— investigate significant differences in tender documents relating to the plan;

— assess the adequacy of sums specified in tenders vis-à-vis the plan;

— advise the client on the adequacy of tenders; and

— review the plan if the basis of the original advice changes.

### The principal contractor

**C8027**    Principal contractors should ensure that the health and safety plan:

— translates into an intelligible working document for all those involved in the construction phase;

— incorporates arrangements submitted by individual contractors for the overall management of health and safety; and

— includes arrangements for compliance with the duties of the principal contractor (see C8022 above);

— specifies detailed arrangements for monitoring compliance with health and safety law;

— includes arrangements for assessing competence of subcontractors; and

— can be modified/updated in the light of the experience and information of contractors.

### Health and safety file

C8028 The health and safety file is a permanent record containing information about the particulars and arrangements relating to the design, methods and materials, maintenance and other information relating to the construction. In practice, the 'file' amounts to a manual to alert those who will be responsible for the structure after construction on safety matters which must be managed after handover. The manual should contain appropriate information regarding maintenance, repair, renovation and demolition.

### Prosecution – defence and civil liability

*Defence*

C8029 A defence is provided against prosecution where it can be shown that an employer or a self-employed person made all reasonable enquiries and reasonably believed either that the Regulations did not apply to the work in question or that he had been given the names of the planning supervisor and the principal contractor together with the relevant contents of the health and safety plan [*CDM (SI 1994 No 3140), Reg 19(5)*].

*Civil liability*

C8030 Generally, breach of the *CDM Regulations* is not actionable, except as regards:

(*a*)   the preparation of the health and safety plan, prior to construction work, under *Reg 10*; or

(*b*)   allowing only authorised personnel onto premises where construction work is going on, under *Reg 16(1)(c)*.

[*CDM (SI 1994 No 3140), Reg 21*].

## Construction (Health, Safety and Welfare) Regulations 1996 (SI 1996 No 1592)

C8031 The *Construction (Health, Safety and Welfare) Regulations 1996 (CHSW) (SI 1996 No 1592)* promote the health and safety of everyone carrying out 'construction work' (as defined, and see also C8012 above) but the Regulations do not apply to workplaces on construction sites which are set aside for non-construction purposes. However, the *CHSW Regulations* give protection to other people who may be affected by the construction work.

A 'construction site' is defined in the Regulations as 'any place where the principal work activity being carried out is construction work' [*CHSW (SI 1996 No 1592), Reg 2(1)*].

For details of the requirements and standards of protection regarding falls from access equipment [*CHSW (SI 1996 No 1592), Reg 6*], see:

*Schedule 1:* Requirements for guardrails etc;

*Schedule 2:* Requirements for working platforms;

*Schedule 3:* Requirements for personal suspension equipment;

*Schedule 4:* Requirements for means of arresting falls;

*Schedule 5:* Requirements for ladders.

For details of the requirements for welfare facilities [*CHSW (SI 1996 No 1592), Reg 22*] see:

*Schedule 6:* Welfare facilities.

Training and site inspection by competent persons followed by preparation of a report to be kept on site and available for inspection by HSE inspectors are especially important requirements. In particular, anyone involved in construction work, which requires training, technical knowledge or experience for reduction of risk of injury, must possess such training, knowledge etc. or be under the supervision of a person with such knowledge. In addition, places of work on construction sites must only be used following inspection by competent persons and preparation of a report to the effect that such place is safe (see C8055 below).

These Regulations implement Annex IV of the Temporary or Mobile Construction Sites Directive, thereby extending to construction sites the health, safety and welfare requirements imposed on all other workplaces by the *Workplace (Health, Safety and Welfare) Regulations 1992 (SI 1992 No 3004)*. The Regulations revoke the *Construction Regulations 1961–1966* (with the exception of the *Construction (Lifting Operations) Regulations 1961* – which have been replaced by the *Lifting Operations and Lifting Equipment Regulations 1998 (SI 1998 No 2307)*.

These Regulations lay duties principally on employers, self-employed contractors and employees, and, to a lesser extent, on persons in control of construction sites. [*CHSW (SI 1996 No 1592), Regs 4, 22, 29(2)*]. All contractors, big or small, are covered. Breach of duty, followed by conviction, will be visited with criminal sanction (normally payment of a fine). There is also strict civil liability where breach of the Regulations results in injury or damage (see ENFORCEMENT and INTRODUC-TION). Characteristically, 'I find it necessary to make some general observations about the interpretation of regulations of this kind. They are addressed to practical people skilled in the particular trade or industry, and their primary purpose is to prevent accidents by prescribing appropriate precautions. Any failure to take prescribed precautions is a criminal offence. The right to compensation, which arises when an accident is caused by a breach is a secondary matter. The Regulations supplement, but in no way supersede the ordinary common law obligations of an employer to care for the safety of his men, and they ought not to be expected to cover every possible kind of danger' (*Gill v Donald Humberstone & Co Ltd [1963] 3 AER 180*, as per Lord Reid).

### Duties under the regulations

C8032    The following duties are laid on employers (and self-employed persons) in respect of employees involved in construction work and any persons under their control.

*Safe place of work*

C8033    Except in the case of a person making such place safe [*CHSW (SI 1996 No 1592), Reg 5(4)*]:

(*a*)    every place of work must be made and kept safe and free from health risks for any person at work there, so far as is reasonably practicable [*CHSW (SI 1996 No 1592), Reg 5(2)*];

(*b*)    so far as is reasonably practicable, suitable and sufficient safe access/egress, to/from, every place of work and any other place provided for use of a person at work, must be provided and properly maintained [*CHSW (SI 1996 No 1592), Reg 5(1)*];

(*c*) so far as is reasonably practicable, suitable and sufficient steps must be taken to deny access to any place not complying with (*a*) and (*b*) above [*CHSW (SI 1996 No 1592), Reg 5(3)*]; and

(*d*) so far as is reasonably practicable, every place of work must have sufficient working space and be so arranged as to be suitable for any person working or likely to work there [*CHSW (SI 1996 No 1592), Reg 5(5)*].

(For requirements relating to falls, fall-preventative equipment, scaffolds, personal suspension equipment, working platforms and ladders, set out in *Regs 6, 7* and *8*, see WORK AT HEIGHTS.)

### Stability of structures

C8034    The Regulations require that:

(*a*) in order to prevent danger to any person, all practicable steps must be taken to ensure that any new or existing structure which may become unstable through construction work (including excavations) does not accidentally collapse [*CHSW (SI 1996 No 1592), Reg 9(1)*];

(*b*) no part of a structure must be so loaded as to make it unsafe [*CHSW (SI 1996 No 1592), Reg 9(2)*]; and

(*c*) any buttress, temporary support or structure (used to support a permanent structure) must be erected or dismantled under the surveillance of a competent person [*CHSW (SI 1996 No 1592), Reg 9(3)*].

### Demolition or dismantling

C8035    Suitable and sufficient steps must be taken to ensure that demolition or dismantling of structures is planned and executed so as to prevent, so far as practicable, danger to any person. Planning and execution of demolition must be carried out under the supervision of a competent person [*CHSW (SI 1996 No 1592), Reg 10*].

### Explosives

C8036    Explosive charges can only be used or fired if suitable and sufficient steps have been taken to ensure that no one is exposed to any risk of injury from the explosion or flying material [*CHSW (SI 1996 No 1592), Reg 11*].

### Excavations

C8037    The Regulations require that:

(*a*) to prevent danger to any person, all practicable steps must be taken to ensure that new or existing excavations which are temporarily unstable due to the carrying out of construction work (including other excavation work) do not collapse accidentally [*CHSW (SI 1996 No 1592), Reg 12(1)*];

(*b*) so far as is reasonably practicable, suitable and sufficient steps must be taken to prevent any person being buried or trapped by a fall or dislodgement of material. [*CHSW (SI 1996 No 1592), Reg 12(2)*]. In particular, as early as practicable in the course of the work, the excavation must be sufficiently supported so as to prevent, so far as reasonably practicable, that fall or dislodgement of material [*CHSW (SI 1996 No 1592), Reg 12(3)*]; suitable and sufficient supporting equipment must be provided [*CHSW (SI 1996 No*

1592), *Reg 12(4)*]; and installation, alteration or dismantling must be carried out only under the supervision of a competent person [*CHSW (SI 1996 No 1592), Reg 12(5)*];

(*c*)     suitable and sufficient steps must be taken to prevent any person, vehicle, plant and equipment, accumulation of earth or other material, from falling into an excavation [*CHSW (SI 1996 No 1592), Reg 12(6)*];

(*d*)     where collapse of an excavation would endanger a person, no material, vehicle or plant and equipment must be placed or moved near any excavation [*CHSW (SI 1996 No 1592), Reg 12(7)*]; and

(*e*)     no excavation work must be carried out unless suitable and sufficient steps have been taken to identify and, so far as reasonably practicable, to prevent any risk of injury arising from any underground cable or service [*CHSW (SI 1996 No 1592), Reg 12(8)*].

A HSE guidance booklet, '*Health and safety in excavations: Be safe and shore*', provides practical guidance on working in the ground without placing anyone at risk. It is intended for all those who may be involved with excavation works, e.g. clients, designers, planning supervisors, contractors, site managers and foremen. It aims to help identify the main failings which lead to injury and how to take the necessary measures, at the planning stage, to avoid them. It deals with:

—     Hazards and control measures;

—     Planning, design and management;

—     Legal requirements; and

—     Sources of further information.

It covers pipe and cable laying, manhole construction, foundations, small retaining walls, and other structures where earthworks are required.

*Cofferdams and caissons*

C8038    The Regulations require that:

(*a*)     every cofferdam or caisson must be:

(i)     of suitable design and construction,

(ii)     of suitable and sound material,

(iii)     of sufficient strength and capacity for the purpose used, and

(iv)     properly maintained

[*CHSW (SI 1996 No 1592), Reg 13(1)*]; and

(*b*)     construction, installation, alteration or dismantling must be under the supervision of a competent person [*CHSW (SI 1996 No 1592), Reg 13(2)*].

*Prevention of drowning*

C8039    The Regulations require that where:

(*a*)     after falling, any person is liable to fall into water (or other liquid) with a risk of drowning, suitable and sufficient steps must be taken to:

(i)     prevent, so far as is reasonably practicable, such person from falling,

(ii)     minimise the risk of drowning, and

(iii)   ensure the provision and maintenance of suitable rescue equipment

[*CHSW (SI 1996 No 1592), Reg 14(1)*]; and

(*b*)   where there are conveyances by water, there must be provision of safe transport to or from a place of work by water [*CHSW (SI 1996 No 1592), Reg 14(2)*]. Vessels used for conveyance purposes must be:

    (i)   of suitable construction,

    (ii)   properly maintained,

    (iii)   under the control of a competent person, and

    (iv)   not overcrowded or overloaded

[*CHSW (SI 1996 No 1592), Reg 14(3)*].

*Traffic routes*

**C8040**   Pedestrians and vehicles should be able to move safely and without health risks. To that end, traffic routes should be:

(*a*)   suitable for persons and vehicles using them;

(*b*)   sufficient in number;

(*c*)   in suitable positions;

(*d*)   of sufficient size; and

(*e*)   indicated by suitable signs (see WORKPLACES – HEALTH, SAFETY AND WELFARE).

[*CHSW (SI 1996 No 1592), Reg 15(1), (2), (6)*].

These requirements are not satisfied unless:

    (i)   pedestrians or vehicles can use a traffic route without causing danger to the health or safety of persons near it;

    (ii)   any door or gate (intended for use by pedestrians) leading on to a traffic route for vehicles is so separated from that traffic route as to enable pedestrians to see any approaching vehicle or plant from a place of safety;

    (iii)   there is sufficient separation between vehicles and pedestrians to ensure safety, or if that is not reasonably practicable that:

        (1)   other means are provided for the protection of pedestrians, and

        (2)   effective arrangements are made for warning a person liable to be crushed or trapped by a vehicle of the vehicle's approach;

    (iv)   a loading bay has at least one exit point for exclusive use of pedestrians; and

    (v)   where it is unsafe for pedestrians to use any gate intended primarily for vehicles, one or more doors for pedestrians is provided in the immediate vicinity of such gate (such door(s) being clearly marked and obstruction free).

[*CHSW (SI 1996 No 1592), Reg 15(3)*].

Vehicles must not be driven on traffic routes unless, so far as is reasonably practicable, the route is free from obstruction and permits sufficient clearance [*CHSW (SI 1996 No 1592), Reg 15(4)*]. Where this is not reasonably practicable, drivers and persons riding on vehicles must be warned of any approaching obstruction or lack of clearance, e.g. by a sign. (For requirements relating to traffic routes generally, see ACCESS, TRAFFIC ROUTES AND VEHICLES.)

*Vehicles*

**C8041**    The Regulations require:

(*a*)    unintended movement of vehicles (including mobile plant, locomotives and towed vehicles) must be either prevented or controlled [*CHSW (SI 1996 No 1592), Reg 17(1)*];

(*b*)    where persons may be endangered by vehicle movement, the person in effective control of the vehicle must warn any person at work of the risk of injury [*CHSW (SI 1996 No 1592), Reg 17(2)*];

(*c*)    construction work vehicles, when being driven, operated or towed, must be:

    (i)    driven, operated or towed safely, and

    (ii)    be so loaded as to be able to be driven, operated or towed safely

[*CHSW (SI 1996 No 1592), Reg 17(3)*];

(*d*)    no person must ride or be required or permitted to ride on any construction work vehicle other than in a safe place provided for that purpose [*CHSW (SI 1996 No 1592), Reg 17(4)*]. (For civil liability consequences of failure to do so, see ACCESS, TRAFFIC ROUTES AND VEHICLES.);

(*e*)    no person must remain or be required or permitted to remain on a vehicle during the loading or unloading of loose material unless a safe place is provided and maintained [*CHSW (SI 1996 No 1592), Reg 17(5)*];

(*f*)    excavating, handling and tipping vehicles must be prevented from:

    (i)    falling into an excavation, pit or water, or

    (ii)    overturning the edge of an embankment or earthwork

[*CHSW (SI 1996 No 1592), Reg 17(6)*]; and

(*g*)    in the case of rail vehicles, plant and equipment must be provided for replacing them on their track, or moving them, if derailed [*CHSW (SI 1996 No 1592), Reg 17(7)*].

The HSE publication, '*The safe use of vehicles on construction sites*', provides guidance for clients, designers, contractors, managers, and workers involved with construction transport. It provides guidance on how to establish safe workplaces for vehicle operations, vehicle selection, inspection and maintenance, safe driving and work practices, and managing construction transport.

*Doors and gates (not forming part of mobile plant and equipment)*

**C8042**    The Regulations require that:

(*a*)    where necessary to prevent risk of injury, any door, gate, hatch (including temporary ones) – must incorporate (or be fitted with) suitable safety devices [*CHSW (SI 1996 No 1592), Reg 16(1)*]; and

(*b*)    compliance with the Regulations presupposes that:

    (i)    any sliding door, gate or hatch has a device to prevent it coming off its track during use,

(ii)   any upward opening door, gate or hatch has a device to prevent it falling back,

(iii)   any powered door, gate or hatch has suitable and effective features to prevent it trapping persons, and

(iv)   any powered door, gate or hatch can be operated manually unless it opens automatically if the power fails

[*CHSW (SI 1996 No 1592), Reg 16(2)*].

## Prevention of fire risks

**C8043**   The Regulations require that:

(*a*)   so far as reasonably practicable, suitable and sufficient steps must be taken to prevent risk of injury from:

(i)   fire or explosion,

(ii)   flooding, or

(iii)   substances liable to cause asphyxiation

[*CHSW (SI 1996 No 1592), Reg 18*];

(*b*)   if a work activity gives rise to risk of fire, such activity must not be carried out unless the worker is suitably instructed to prevent risk [*CHSW (SI 1996 No 1592), Reg 21(6)*];

(*c*)   there must also be provision of:

(i)   suitable and sufficient fire-fighting equipment, suitably located (e.g. in emergency routes),

(ii)   suitable and sufficient fire detectors and alarm systems, suitably located (e.g. in emergency routes);

(iii)   training of all persons on site in the correct use of appliances

[*CHSW (SI 1996 No 1592), Reg 21(5)*];

(*d*)   fire-fighting equipment, detectors and alarm systems must be:

(i)   properly maintained, examined and tested [*CHSW (SI 1996 No 1592), Reg 21(3)*],

(ii)   indicated by suitable signs [*Reg 21(7)*], and

(iii)   easily accessible, if not designed to come into use automatically [*CHSW (SI 1996 No 1592), Reg 21(4)*].

## Emergency routes and exits

**C8044**   The Regulations require:

(*a*)   a sufficient number of suitable emergency routes and exits, indicated by suitable signs (see WORKPLACES – HEALTH, SAFETY AND WELFARE), must be provided to enable any person to reach a place of safety quickly in the event of danger. [*CHSW (SI 1996 No 1592), Reg 19(1)*]. This should lead, as directly as possible, to an identified safe area [*CHSW (SI 1996 No 1592), Reg 19(2)*]; and (*b*)    emergency routes (and traffic routes or doors thereto) must be kept clear and obstruction free and, if necessary, be provided with emergency lighting [*CHSW (SI 1996 No 1592), Reg 19(3)*].

### Emergency procedures

**C8045**    There must be prepared and implemented suitable and sufficient arrangements (to be tested by being put into effect at regular intervals) for dealing with any foreseeable emergency, including procedures for site evacuation. Moreover, persons likely to be affected must be acquainted with such arrangements. [*CHSW (SI 1996 No 1592), Reg 20(1)(3)*].

### Welfare facilities

**C8046**    Duties in connection with the provision of welfare facilities on construction sites are laid principally on those in control of sites (i.e. occupiers, see generally C8131 below, and OCCUPIERS' LIABILITY). The fact that occupation (or control) of construction sites can be, and frequently is, shared between the building owner and contractor(s) means that both have obligations to see that welfare facilities are provided. In practice, actual provision would be made by the contractor(s). Hence, although overall duties are imposed on occupiers, employers (and self-employed persons) must ensure that workers under their control are provided with welfare facilities.

Facilities to be provided are:

(*a*)    suitable and sufficient sanitary conveniences at readily accessible places [*CHSW (SI 1996 No 1592), Reg 22(3)*]. So far as is reasonably practicable, such conveniences must be:

    (i)    adequately ventilated and lit,

    (ii)    kept in a clean and orderly condition, with

    (iii)    separate rooms containing sanitary conveniences provided for men and women (except where each convenience is in a separate room, the door of which can be secured from the inside)

[*CHSW (SI 1996 No 1592), Sch 6*];

(*b*)    suitable and sufficient washing facilities (including, where necessary, showers) at readily accessible places. So far as is reasonably practicable, washing facilities must:

    (i)    be provided in the immediate vicinity of sanitary conveniences (except showers), and in the vicinity of changing rooms (whether or not provided elsewhere),

    (ii)    include a supply of clean hot and cold (or warm) water (ideally running water), and soap, towels etc.

Rooms containing washing facilities must be:

    (iii)    sufficiently ventilated and lit,

    (iv)    kept in a clean and orderly condition, and

    (v)    must have separate washing facilities provided for men and women (except for washing hands, forearms and face only) unless provided in a room the door of which can be secured from the inside and the facilities in each such room are intended for use by only one person at a time

[*CHSW (SI 1996 No 1592), Sch 6*];

(c)     an adequate supply of wholesome drinking water at readily accessible places [*Reg 22(5)*]. So far as is reasonably practicable, every supply of drinking water must:

   (i)    be conspicuously marked, and

   (ii)   be provided with a sufficient number of suitable cups or other drinking vessels, unless the supply is from a jet

   [*CHSW (SI 1996 No 1592), Sch 6*];

(d)     suitable and sufficient accommodation for:

   (i)    accommodating the clothing of any person at work which is not worn during working hours, and

   (ii)   special clothing worn by a person at work but which is not taken home

   [*CHSW (SI 1996 No 1592), Reg 22(6)*].

   So far as is reasonably practicable, clothing accommodation should include facilities for drying clothing [*CHSW (SI 1996 No 1592), Sch 6*];

(e)     suitable and sufficient accommodation for changing clothing where:

   (i)    a person has to wear special clothing at work, and

   (ii)   that person cannot be expected to change elsewhere

   [*CHSW (SI 1996 No 1592), Reg 22(7)*].

   (See *Post Office v Footitt [2000] IRLR 243* in W11026.)

   Where necessary, facilities for changing clothing must be separate facilities for men and women [*CHSW (SI 1996 No 1592), Sch 6*];

(f)     suitable and sufficient rest facilities at readily accessible places [*Reg 22(8)*]. So far as reasonably practicable, rest facilities must include:

   (i)    suitable arrangements to protect non-smokers from discomfort caused by tobacco smoke, and where necessary

   (ii)   facilities for pregnant women or nursing mothers

   [*CHSW (SI 1996 No 1592), Sch 6*].

   (For welfare facilities generally, see WELFARE FACILITIES.)

## Fresh air

**C8047**     Every workplace on a construction site must, so far as reasonably practicable, have a supply of fresh or purified air so as to ensure safety and absence of health risks; and plant used for supply purposes must, where necessary, contain effective devices for giving visible or audible warning of failure. [*CHSW (SI 1996 No 1592), Reg 23*].

(For ventilation requirements generally, see VENTILATION.)

## Temperature

**C8048**     During working hours, so far as reasonably practicable, temperature at any indoor place of work must be reasonable, having regard to the purpose of the workplace. [*CHSW (SI 1996 No 1592), Reg 24(1)*].

(For temperature requirements generally, see WORKPLACES – HEALTH, SAFETY AND WELFARE.)

### Weather protection

**C8049**   Every place of work outdoors must, where necessary, be so arranged, so far as is reasonably practicable, as to provide protection from adverse weather. [*CHSW (SI 1996 No 1592), Reg 24(2)*].

### Lighting

**C8050**   Every place of work and traffic route must have suitable and sufficient lighting. In the case of artificial lighting where there would be a risk to a person's health or safety from failure of primary artificial lighting, suitable and sufficient secondary lighting must be provided. [*CHSW (SI 1996 No 1592), Reg 25(1)(3)*].

(For lighting requirements generally see LIGHTING.)

### Plant and equipment

**C8051**   The regulations require that, so far as is reasonably practicable, all plant and equipment used for construction work must be safe and without health risks, and be:

(*a*)    of good construction,

(*b*)    of suitable and sound materials,

(*c*)    of sufficient strength and suitability for its intended purpose, and

(*d*)    so used and maintained that it remains safe and without health risks

[*CHSW (SI 1996 No 1592), Reg 27*].

### Good order

**C8052**   So far as reasonably practicable, every part of a construction site must be kept in good order and every place of work in a reasonable state of cleanliness. Perimeters should be identified by suitable signs (see WORKPLACES – HEALTH, SAFETY AND WELFARE), and sites arranged so that their extent is readily identifiable. Moreover, no timber material with projecting nails must be used in work where nails might be dangerous or allowed to remain in a place where nails could be a source of danger. [*CHSW (SI 1996 No 1592), Reg 26*].

### Training

**C8053**   Any person who carries out construction work where training, technical knowledge or experience is necessary to reduce risk of injury, must either:

(*a*)    possess such training, knowledge or experience, or

(*b*)    be under the supervision of a person who so does.

[*CHSW (SI 1996 No 1592), Reg 28*].

### Inspection

**C8054**   The Regulations require that in the case of the following places of work:

(*a*)    working platforms or personal suspension equipment, (*b*)    excavations, and

(*c*)    cofferdams or caissons

work can only be carried out if such place has been inspected by a competent person as follows.

(1)    Working platforms and personal suspension equipment must be inspected by a competent person:

    (i)    before being taken into use for the first time,

    - (ii)    after substantial addition, dismantling or other alteration,

    (iii)    after any event likely to have affected their strength or stability, and

    (iv)    at regular intervals not exceeding 7 days following the last inspection.

(2)    Excavations must be inspected by a competent person:

    (i)    before a person carries out work at the start of every shift,

    (ii)    after any event likely to have affected the strength or stability of the excavation, and

    (iii)    after an accidental fall of rock/earth.

(3)    Cofferdams and caissons should be inspected by a competent person:

    (i)    before the start of every shift, and

    (ii)    after any event likely to have affected their strength or stability.

[*CHSW (SI 1996 No 1592), Reg 29(1), Sch 7*].

Where, following inspection, a place of work or plant and materials is not safe, this must be communicated to those in control and such place of work must not be used until defects have been remedied. [*CHSW (SI 1996 No 1592), Reg 29(3),(4)*].

In addition to the general duty to inspect places of work (above), in the case of scaffolds, excavations, cofferdams and caissons forming part of a place of work, employers must ensure that they are stable and of sound construction and that the requisite safeguards are in place before workers use such place of work for the first time. [*CHSW (SI 1996 No 1592), Reg 29(2)*].

*Reports*

**C8055**    Following inspection, a report must be prepared before the end of the working period in which the inspection was completed, and presented within 24 hours to the person on whose behalf it was carried out. [*CHSW (SI 1996 No 1592), Reg 30(1),(2)*]. The report (or a copy) must be kept at the site of such place of work and, after work there is completed, retained at the office of the person on whose behalf the inspection was made, for a minimum of three months. Such a report is available for inspection by an HSE inspector and, should he so require, extracts or copies must be sent to the inspector. [*CHSW (SI 1996 No 1592), Reg 30(3), (4)*].

Reports are not necessary in the following cases:

    (i)    working platforms where persons are not liable to fall more than 2 metres; and

    (ii)    mobile towers (unless remaining erect for 7 days or more).

[*CHSW (SI 1996 No 1592), Reg 30(5),(6)*].

### Enforcement

C8056 Penalties and defences in connection with the *Construction (Health, Safety and Welfare) Regulations 1996* are as for *HSWA 1974* (see ENFORCEMENT).

### Civil liability for breach of the regulations

C8057 Breach of these Regulations (and the *Work in Compressed Air Regulations 1996* and the *Construction (Head Protection) Regulations 1989* – see C8081 and C8097 below), resulting in injury to an employee, will give rise to civil liability, since safety regulations, even if silent regarding civil liability, are actionable (see further INTRODUCTION). A short guide to these Regulations, *'A guide to the Construction (Health, Safety and Welfare) Regulations 1996'* is available free from HSE. This lists the series of further guidance.

## Confined spaces and harmful atmospheres

C8058 The *Confined Spaces Regulations 1997 (SI 1997 No 1713)* apply in all premises and work situations in Great Britain subject to the *HSWA 1974*, with the exception of diving operations and below ground in a mine.

The Regulations are supported by an Approved Code of Practice and guidance – *Safe work in confined spaces (L101)* – providing practical guidance with respect to the requirements of:

— the *Confined Spaces Regulations 1997 (SI 1997 No 1713)* and the *HSWA 1974, ss 2, 4, 6* and *7*;

— the *Management of Health and Safety at Work Regulations 1999 (SI 1999 No 3242)*;

— the *Control of Substances Hazardous to Health Regulations 1999 (SI 1999 No 1657)*.

*Note:* the *COSHH Regulations* apply to all substances hazardous to health (other than lead or asbestos), such as toxic fume and injurious dust. The *Ionising Radiation Regulations 1999 (SI 1999 No 3232)* may apply where radon gas can accumulate in confined spaces, such as sewers, and where industrial radiography is used to look at, for example, the integrity of welds in vessels.

— the *Personal Protective Equipment at Work Regulations 1992 (SI 1992 No 2966)*;

— the *Provision and Use of Work Equipment Regulations 1998 (SI 1998 No 2306)*.

### Entry into confined spaces

C8059 A 'confined space' has two defining features. Firstly, it is a place which is substantially (though not always entirely) enclosed and, secondly, there will be a reasonably foreseeable risk of serious injury from hazardous substances or conditions within the space or nearby. [*SI 1997 No 1713, Reg 1(2)*].

Examples:

— ducts, vessels, culverts, tunnels, boreholes, bored piles, manholes, shafts, excavations, sumps, inspection pits, cofferdams, freight containers, building voids, some enclosed rooms (particularly plant rooms) and compartments within them, including some cellars, enclosures for the purpose of asbestos removal, and interiors of machines, plant or vehicles.

Some confined spaces are fairly easy to identify, for example closed tanks, vessels and sewers. Others are less obvious but may be equally dangerous, for example open-topped tanks and vats, closed and unventilated or inadequately ventilated rooms and silos, or constructions that become confined spaces during their manufacture. A confined space may not necessarily be enclosed on all sides.

*Respiratory protective equipment*

C8060    Where respiratory protective equipment (RPE) is provided or used in connection with confined space entry or for emergency or rescue, it should be suitable for the purpose for which it is intended, that is, correctly selected and matched both to the job and the wearer.

Where the intention is to provide emergency breathing apparatus to ensure safe egress or escape, or for self-rescue in case of emergency, the type commonly called an 'escape breathing apparatus' or 'self-rescuer' (escape set) may be suitable. These types are intended to allow time for the user to exit the hazard area. They are generally carried by the user or stationed inside the confined space, but are not used until needed. This equipment usually has a breathable supply of only short duration and provides limited protection to allow the user to move to a place of safety or refuge. This type of equipment is not suitable for normal work.

In some circumstances entry without the continuous wearing of breathing apparatus may be possible. Several conditions must be satisfied to allow such work including:

—    a risk assessment must be done and a safe system of work in place including all required controls, and continuous ventilation;

—    any airborne contamination must be of a generally non-toxic nature, or present in very low concentrations well below the relevant occupational exposure limits.

## Duties and responsibilities

C8061    There have been several court cases involving accidents and fatalities in sewers and other confined spaces (see for instance *Baker v Hopkins & Son [1959] AER 225).* More recently, in 1998 at Cardiff Crown Court, a record fine was imposed on Neath Port Talbot Council following the deaths of two employees (*R v Neath Port Talbot Council*). The judge, John Prosser, said that the accident should never have happened; the dangers of toxic gases associated with sewer work were well known. The case demonstrated the need for employers to carry out, with strict care, the undertaking of such work and that the difficulty and danger must not be underestimated.

Duties to comply with the *Confined Spaces Regulations (SI 1997 No 1713),* are placed on:

—    employers in respect of work carried out by their own employees and work carried out by any other person (for example, contractors) in so far as that work is to any extent under the employers' control [*SI 1997 No 1713, Reg 3(1)*]; and

—    the self-employed in respect of their own work and work carried out by any other person in so far as that work is to any extent under the control of the self-employed [*SI 1997 No 1713, Reg 3(2)*].

*Duty to prevent entry*

**C8062**     The principal duty imposed on employers is to prevent entering or working inside a confined space where it is reasonably practicable to undertake the work by other means [*SI 1997 No 1713, Reg 4*].

The duty extends to others who are to any extent within the employers' control (such as contractors) and in many cases it will be necessary to modify working practices following a risk assessment of each requirement to enter a confined space.

Examples:

—     modifying the confined space itself to avoid the need for entry, or to enable the work to be undertaken from outside;

—     testing the atmosphere or sampling the contents of confined spaces from outside using appropriate long tools and probes.

Another case where it may be necessary to modify working practices is where employers or the self-employed have duties in relation to people at work who are not their employees – then the duty is to do what is 'reasonably practicable' in the circumstances. In many cases, the employer or self-employed will need to liaise and co-operate with other employers to agree the respective responsibilities in terms of the regulations and duties. It is also necessary to take all reasonably practicable steps to engage competent contractors.

*Associated duties and responsibilities*

**C8063**     In addition to the requirements of the *HSWA 1974*, other legislation imposes duties with regard to the design, construction and operation within confined spaces.

Some duties extend to erectors and installers of equipment and would include situations where plant and equipment unavoidably involved confined spaces. Where it is not possible to eliminate a confined space completely, procedures must be drawn up to minimise the need to enter such spaces both during normal use or working, and for cleaning and maintenance.

Regarding the type of PPE to be provided, this will depend on the identified hazards and the type of confined space. It may be necessary, for example, to include safety lines and harnesses, and suitable breathing apparatus.

Examples:

—     the wearing of some respiratory protective equipment and personal protective equipment can contribute to heat stress;

—     footwear and clothing may require insulating properties, e.g. to prevent softening of plastics that could lead to distortion of components such as visors, air hoses and crimped connections.

## Risk assessment – the development of a safe system of work

**C8064**     The priority when carrying out a confined space risk assessment is to identify the measures needed so that entry into the confined space can be avoided. If it is not reasonably practicable to prevent work in a confined space the employer (or the self-employed) must assess the risks connected with persons entering or working in the space and also to others who could be affected by the work. The assessor(s) must understand the risks involved, be experienced and familiar with the relevant processes, plant and equipment and be competent to devise a safe system of working.

If, in the light of the risks identified, it cannot be considered reasonably practicable to carry out the work without entering the confined space, then it will be necessary to secure a safe system for working. The precautions required to create a safe system of work will depend on the nature of the confined space and the hazards identified during the risk assessment.

*Use of a permit-to-work procedure*

C8065   Not all work involving confined spaces requires the use of a permit-to-work system. For example, it is unlikely that a system would be needed where:

— the assessed risks are low and can be controlled easily; and

— the system of work is very simple; and

— it is known that other work activities being carried out cannot affect safe working in the confined space.

Although there is no set format for a permit system, it is often appropriate to include certain information relevant to all confined space working. In all cases, it is essential that a system is developed which ensures that:

(*a*)   the people working in the confined space are aware of the hazards involved and the identity, nature and extent of the work to be carried out;

(*b*)   there is a formal and methodological system of checks undertaken by competent people before the confined space is entered and which confirms that a safe system of work is in place;

(*c*)   other people and their activities are not affected by the work or conditions in the confined space.

Isolation requirements, that is, the need to isolate the confined space to prevent dangers arising from outside, should also be included in the permit system. Permits are particularly appropriate if essential supplies and emergency services such as sprinkler systems, communications etc., are to be disconnected. The most effective isolation technique is to disconnect the confined space completely by removing a section of pipe or duct and fitting blanks. Other methods include the use of spectacle blinds and lockable valves.

*Workforce involvement*

C8066   Employees and their representatives should be consulted when assessing the risks connected with entering or working in a confined space. Particular attention is required where the work circumstances change frequently such as at construction sites or steel fabrications.

*Model or generic risk assessments*

C8067   Where a number of confined spaces (for example, sewers or manholes) are broadly the same in terms of the conditions and the activities being carried out, model risk assessments are permitted provided that the risks and measures to deal with them are the same. Any differences in particular cases which would alter the conclusions of the model risk assessment must be identified.

## Planning an entry into a confined space

C8068   To satisfy the safe system requirement of the *Confined Spaces Regulations 1997 (SI 1997 No 1713), Reg 4*, it is necessary to plan the work thoroughly and to organise various facilities and arrangements. For a large confined space and multiple entries, a logging or tally system may be necessary in order to check everyone in and out and to control duration of entry.

### Competence for confined space working

C8069
The competent person carrying out the risk assessment for work in confined spaces will need to consider the suitability of individuals in view of the particular work to be done.

Examples:

—     suitable build of individuals for exceptional constraints in the physical layout of the space (this may be necessary to protect both the individual and others who could be affected by the work to be done);

—     medical fitness concerning claustrophobia or the wearing of breathing apparatus.

### Procedures and written instructions

C8070
To be effective a safe system of work needs to be in writing – in the form of written instructions setting out the work to be done and the precautions to be taken. Each procedure should contain all appropriate precautions to be taken and in the correct sequence.

In particular, procedures for confined space working should include instructions and guidance for:

(a)     *First aid* — the availability of appropriate first aid equipment for emergencies until professional medical help arrives.

(b)     First aiders — the strategic positioning of trained personnel to deal with foreseeable injuries.

(c)     Limiting working time — for example, when respiratory protective equipment is used, or when the work is to be carried out under extreme conditions of temperature and humidity.

(d)     Communications — that is, the system of adequate arrangements to enable efficient communication between those working inside the confined space and others to summon help in case of emergency.

(e)     Engine driven equipment — that is, the rules regarding the siting of such equipment which should be well away from the working area and downwind of any ventilator intakes.

(f)     Water surges — especially the anticipation that sewers can be affected over long distances by water surges, for example following sudden heavy rainfall upstream of where the work is being carried out.

(g)     Toxic gas, fume or vapour — procedures to ensure that work can be undertaken safely to include the availability of additional facilities and arrangements where residues may be trapped in sludge, scale or other deposits, brickwork, or behind loose linings, in liquid traps, joints in vessels, in pipe bends, or in other places where removal is difficult.

(h)     Testing/monitoring the atmosphere — procedures for the regular testing for hazardous gas, fume or vapour or to check the concentration of oxygen before entry or re-entry into the confined space.

*(i)*    Gas purging — the availability of suitable equipment to purge the gas or vapour from the confined space.

*(j)*    Ventilation requirements — the provision of suitable ventilation equipment to replace oxygen levels in the space, and to dilute and remove gas, fume or vapour produced by the work.

*(k)*    Lighting — procedures to ensure that the confined space is well lit by lighting equipment, including emergency lighting, which must be suitable for use in flammable or potentially explosive atmospheres.

(Generally all lighting to be used in confined spaces should be protected against knocks – for example, by a wire cage – and be waterproof. Where water is present in the space, suitable plug/socket connectors capable of withstanding wet or damp conditions should be used and protected by residual current devices (RCDs) suitable for protection against electric shock. The position of lighting may also be important, for example to give ample clearance for work or rescue to be carried out unobstructed.)

*Fire prevention and protection procedures*

C8071    The presence of flammable substances and oxygen enrichment in a confined space creates a serious hazard to workers inside the space. There is also a risk of explosion from the ignition of airborne flammable contaminants. In addition, a fire or explosion can be caused by leaks from adjoining plant or processes and the use of unsuitable equipment.

*Note:* in the case of *R v Associated Octel Co Ltd [1996] 4 AER 846* (see C8136 below) a contractor was badly burned when an explosion occurred in the confined space (a chemical storage tank) he was working in. The principal cause of the accident was unsuitable lighting which broke and ignited some acetone solvent contained in an old emulsion bucket.

There are many fire precautions necessary for safe working in confined spaces; some of the more important of these are outlined below:

*(a)*    *Fire prevention measures* — procedures to ensure that no flammable or combustible materials are stored in confined spaces that have not been specifically created or allocated for that purpose. In any event, the quantity of the material should be kept to a minimum and stored in suitable fire-resistant containers.

*(b)*    *Fire protection and fire-fighting equipment* — procedures to ensure the availability of appropriate fire-fighting equipment where the risk of fire has been identified. In some situations, a sprinkler system may be appropriate.

*(c)*    *Smoking* — procedures to ensure the prohibition of all smoking within and around all confined spaces.

*(d)*    *Static electricity* — procedures to ensure that the build-up of static in a confined space is minimised. It may be necessary to obtain specialist advice regarding insulating characteristics (for example, most plastics), steam or water jetting equipment, clothing containing cotton or wool, flowing liquids or solids such as sand.

## Supervision and training

C8072    It is likely that the risk assessment will identify a level of risk requiring the appointment of a competent person to supervise the work and ensure that the precautions are adhered to. Competence for safe working in confined spaces requires adequate training – in addition, experience in the particular work involved is essential. Training standards must be appropriate to the task, and to the individuals' roles and responsibilities as indicated during the risk assessment.

## Emergency arrangements and procedures

C8073    The arrangements for the rescue of persons in the event of an emergency must be suitable and sufficient and, where appropriate, include rescue and resuscitation equipment. The arrangements should be in place before any person enters or works in a confined space [*SI 1997 No 1713, Reg 5*].

The arrangements must cover any situation requiring the recovery of a person from a confined space, for example incapacitation following a fall.

### Size of openings to enable rescue from confined spaces

C8074    Experience has shown that the minimum size of an opening to allow access with full rescue facilities including self-contained breathing apparatus is 575 mm diameter. This size should normally be used for new plant, although the openings for some confined spaces may need to be larger depending on the circumstances, for example to take account of a fully equipped employee, or the nature of the opening.

### Public emergency services

C8075    In some circumstances, for example where there are prolonged operations in confined spaces and the risks justify it, there may be advantage in prior notification to the local emergency services before the work is undertaken. In all cases, however, arrangements must be in place for the rapid notification of the emergency services should an accident occur. On arrival, the emergency services should be given all known information about the conditions and risks of entering and/or leaving the confined space before a rescue is attempted.

### Training for emergencies and rescue

C8076    To be suitable and sufficient the arrangements for training site personnel for rescue and resuscitation should include consideration of:

—    rescue and resuscitation equipment;

—    raising the alarm and rescue;

—    safeguarding the rescuers;

—    fire safety;

—    control of plant;

—    first aid.

Regular refresher training in the emergency procedures is essential and practice drills including emergency rescues will help to check that the size of openings and entry procedures are satisfactory. The risk assessment may indicate that at least one person, dedicated to the rescue role, should be stationed outside the confined space to keep those inside in constant direct visual sight.

All members of rescue parties should be trained in the operation of appropriate fire extinguishers which should be strategically located at the confined space. In some situations, a sprinkler system may be appropriate. In all cases, in the event of a fire the local fire service should be called in case the fire cannot be contained or extinguished by first-aid measures.

The training syllabus should include the following, where appropriate:

— the likely causes of an emergency;

— rescue techniques and the use of rescue equipment, for example breathing apparatus, lifelines, and where necessary a knowledge of its construction and how it works;

— the checking procedures to be followed when donning and using breathing apparatus;

— the checking of correct functioning and/or testing of emergency equipment (for immediate use and to enable specific periodic maintenance checks);

— identifying defects and dealing with malfunctions and failures of equipment during use;

— works, site or other local emergency procedures including the initiation of an emergency response;

— instruction on how to shut down relevant plant as appropriate (this knowledge would be required by anyone likely to perform a rescue);

— resuscitation procedures and, where appropriate, the correct use of relevant ancillary equipment and any resuscitation equipment provided (if intended to be operated by those receiving emergency rescue training);

— emergency first aid and the use of the first aid equipment provided;

— liaison with local emergency services in the event of an incident, providing relevant information about conditions and risks, and providing appropriate space and facilities to enable the emergency services to carry out their tasks.

### *Rescue equipment*

**C8077**    When safety harness and lines are provided, it is essential that proper facilities to secure the free end of the line are available. In most cases the line should be secured outside the entry to the confined space. Lifting equipment may be necessary and the harness should be of suitable construction, and made of suitable material to recognised standards capable of withstanding both the strain likely to be imposed, and attack from chemicals.

## Maintenance of safety and rescue equipment

**C8078**    All equipment provided or intended to be used for the purposes of securing the health and safety of people in connection with confined space entry or for emergency or rescue, should be maintained in an efficient state, in efficient working order and in good repair. This should include periodic examination and testing as necessary. Some types of equipment, for example breathing apparatus, should be inspected each time before use.

Atmospheric monitoring equipment – and special ventilating or other equipment provided or used in connection with confined space entry – needs to be properly maintained by competent persons. It should be examined thoroughly, and where necessary calibrated and checked at intervals in accordance with recommendations accompanying the equipment or, if these are not specified, at such intervals determined from the risk assessment.

Records of the examination and tests of equipment should normally be kept for at least five years. The records may be in any suitable format and may consist of a suitable summary of the reports. Records need to be kept readily available for inspection by the employees, their representatives, or by inspectors appointed by the relevant enforcing authority or by employment medical advisers.

### Equipment for use in explosive atmospheres

C8079    When selecting equipment for use in confined spaces where an explosive atmosphere may be present, the requirements of the EU-originated Regulations – *Equipment and Protective Systems Intended for Use in Potentially Explosive Atmospheres Regulations (SI 1996 No 192)* – must be complied with. These Regulations apply to 'equipment' and 'protective systems' intended for use in potentially explosive atmospheres. Some of the terms used in the Regulations are defined below:

—    *equipment* means machines, apparatus, fixed or mobile devices, control components and instrumentation thereof and detection or prevention systems which, separately or jointly, are intended for the generation, transfer, storage, measurement, control and conversion of energy or the processing of material and which are capable of causing an explosion through their own potential sources of ignition;

—    *protective systems* means design units which are intended to halt incipient explosions immediately and/or to limit the effective range of explosion flames and explosion pressures; protective systems may be integrated into equipment or separately placed on the market for use as autonomous systems;

—    *devices* means safety devices, controlling devices and regulating devices intended for use outside potentially explosive atmospheres but required for or contributing to the safe functioning of equipment and protective systems with respect to the risks of explosion;

—    *explosive atmosphere* means the mixture with air, under atmospheric conditions, of flammable substances in the form of gases, vapours, mists or dusts in which, after ignition has occurred, combustion spreads to the entire unburned mixture.

### Selection and use of equipment

C8080    All equipment must bear the approved CE mark properly fixed in accordance with the requirements of the 1996 Regulations.

Any equipment provided for use in a confined space needs to be suitable for the purpose. Where there is a risk of a flammable gas seeping into a confined space, which could be ignited by electrical sources (for example a portable hand lamp), specially protected electrical equipment must be used.

To be suitable the equipment should be selected on the basis of its intended use – proper earthing is essential to prevent static charge build-up; mechanical equipment may need to be secured against free rotation, as people may tread or lean on it.

# Work in compressed air on construction sites – Work in Compressed Air Regulations 1996 (SI 1996 No 1656)

C8081    Replacing the *Work in Compressed Air Special Regulations 1958*, the *Work in Compressed Air Regulations 1996*, which came into effect on 16 September 1996, reflect more modern decompression criteria, being more concerned with the long-term effects of rapid return to atmospheric pressure than the short-term effects which were addressed by earlier regulations. The new Regulations require principal contractors to appoint competent compressed air contractors, and the compressed air contractors to appoint contract medical advisers. In addition, greater provision is required in connection with fire prevention and protection measures (including, in particular, emergency means of escape and rescue). Duties are laid on principal contractors, employers (including the self-employed – tunnellers to whom these Regulations are substantially addressed are generally self-employed), and employees.

## Principal contractor's duties

C8082  The principal contractor must appoint a compressed air contractor in respect of work in compressed air, who must be competent. A compressed air contractor may be the principal contractor himself, if competent. [*SI 1996 No 1656, Reg 5(1), (2)*].

## Compressed air contractor's duties – notification

C8083  The Regulations require that:

(*a*)  the compressed air contractor must not allow work in compressed air to be carried out unless written notice has been forwarded to the HSE at least 14 days before commencement of work. Where this is not practicable, owing to an emergency, notice must be given as soon as practicable after the necessity for such work becomes known to the compressed air contractor, and, anyway, before work commences. [*SI 1996 No 1656, Reg 6(1), (2)*];

(*b*)  no person must work in compressed air unless written notice is forwarded to:

(i)  the nearest suitably equipped hospital,

(ii)  the local ambulance service,

(iii)  the local fire service, and

(iv)  other establishments in the vicinity with an operable medical lock.

[*SI 1996 No 1656, Reg 6(3), (4)*];

(*c*)  notification should be in writing and contain the following information:

(i)  the fact that work in compressed air is being undertaken,

(ii)  the location of the site,

(iii)  date of commencement and anticipated completion of work,

(iv)  name of compressed air contractor and a 24 hour contact telephone number,

(v)  name, address and telephone number of the contract medical adviser,

(vi)  intended pressure at which the work is to be undertaken,

(vii)  anticipated pattern of work (e.g. shifts), and

(viii)  number of workers likely to be in each shift

[*SI 1996 No 1656, Reg 6(4), Sch 1*].

### Competent persons

C8084    The compressed air contractor must ensure that no person works in (or leaves) compressed air, except in accordance with a system of work which, so far as is reasonably practicable, is safe and without health risks. [*SI 1996 No 1656, Reg 7(1)*]. To this end, he must ensure that a sufficient number of 'competent persons' are immediately available on site to supervise execution of work in compressed air at all times and for up to 24 hours when work is being undertaken at or above a pressure of 0.7 bar. [*SI 1996 No 1656, Reg 7(2)*].

### Plant and equipment

C8085    The compressed air contractor must ensure that all plant and equipment is:

(*a*)    of a proper design and construction and of sufficient capacity;

(*b*)    safe and without health risks and safely maintained; and

(*c*)    where such plant and equipment is used for the purpose of containing air at a pressure greater than 0.15 bar, it is

   (i)    examined and tested by a competent person and any faults rectified prior to use, and

   (ii)    re-examined and re-tested after modification or alteration.

[*SI 1996 No 1656, Reg 8*].

### Compression and decompression procedures

C8086    The compressed air contractor must ensure that:

(*a*)    compression or decompression is only carried out as per procedures approved by the HSE;

(*b*)    no worker is subjected to a pressure greater than 3.5 bar (except in emergencies);

(*c*)    no worker is subjected to 'decanting' (i.e. rapid decompression in an airlock to atmospheric pressure followed promptly by rapid compression in an alternative airlock and subsequent decompression to atmospheric pressure – except in an emergency); and

(*d*)    an adequate record is made of exposure in respect of times and pressures at which work in compressed air is carried out, and kept for a minimum of 40 years (including individual exposure records). Such records must be made available to the worker himself and his employer, the latter being required to keep the record for at least 40 years.

[*SI 1996 No 1656, Reg 11*].

### Provision and maintenance of adequate medical facilities

C8087    The compressed air contractor must ensure provision and maintenance of adequate medical facilities (e.g. medical lock, recompression therapy) for the treatment of people working in compressed air and those who have worked in compressed air in the previous 24 hours. Where work is carried out at a pressure greater than 0.7 bar, facilities should include a medical lock; and where work is carried out at a pressure greater than 1.0 bar, a medical lock attendant should be present. [*SI 1996 No 1656, Reg 12*].

*Emergencies*

C8088    The compressed air contractor must ensure that no work in compressed air takes place in the absence of suitable and sufficient arrangements in the event of emergencies as follows:

(*a*)    provision and maintenance of a sufficient number of suitable means of access;

(*b*)    preparation of a suitable rescue plan which can be put into effect immediately (including the provision and maintenance of plant and equipment necessary to put the rescue plan into operation);

(*c*)    provision and maintenance of suitable lighting;

(*d*)    provision and maintenance of suitable means of raising the alarm; and

(*e*)    in cases where an airlock is required, maintenance of the airlock, so that it is fit to receive persons in the event of emergency (with particular regard to air supply and temperature of the airlock).

[*SI 1996 No 1656, Reg 13*].

*Fire precautions*

C8089    The compressed air contractor must ensure provision of suitable and sufficient means for fighting fire and that any airlock or working chamber is maintained and operated so as to minimise the risk of fire, and must ensure the enforcement of the prohibition against smoking. [*SI 1996 No 1656, Reg 14*].

*Information, instruction and training*

C8090    The compressed air contractor must ensure provision of adequate information, instruction and training to employees, including, particularly, information relating to the risks arising from the work and the precautions to be observed. [*SI 1996 No 1656, Reg 15*].

*Fitness for work*

C8091    The compressed air contractor must ensure that no one works in compressed air where he has reason to believe that the worker is subject to a medical or physical condition likely to make him unfit or unsuitable for such work. [*SI 1996 No 1656, Reg 16*].

*Prohibition against alcohol and drugs*

C8092    The compressed air contractor must prohibit anyone from working in compressed air where he believes such worker to be under the influence of drink and/or drugs. [*SI 1996 No 1656, Reg 17*].

## Employees' duties

C8093    Employees, including the self-employed, must:

(*a*)    when required to do so, and at the cost of the employer (see OCCUPATIONAL HEALTH AND DISEASES), submit to medical surveillance procedures during working hours [*SI 1996 No 1656, Reg 10(6)*];

(*b*)    avoid smoking or carrying smoking materials [*SI 1996 No 1656, Reg 14(2)*];

(*c*)    avoid consumption of alcohol or drugs [*SI 1996 No 1656, Reg 17(2)*]; and (*d*)  wear a badge or label for 24 hours after leaving work in compressed air [*SI 1996 No 1656, Reg 19(2)*].

### Contract medical adviser

**C8094**  Owing to the potentially serious dangers arising from pressure itself, or the construction work being done, appointment of a contract medical adviser is essential. Ideally, such person would be a doctor appointed by the HSE, who can carry out statutory medical examinations on compressed air workers on site. His principal role is to actively monitor incidence of decompression illness during work. In the event of decompression illness arising, the contract medical adviser should advise the medical lock attendant regarding appropriate treatment. Both the contract medical adviser and medical lock attendant are responsible for collation and maintenance of exposure records and completion of the worker's health and exposure record, and, on completion of the contract, assist the compressed air contractor in the preservation of formal health and exposure records for the statutory 40-year period.

### Competent persons

**C8095**  The phrase 'competent persons' can refer to:

(*a*)  the engineer in charge;

(*b*)  the compressor attendants;

(*c*)  the lock attendants;

(*d*)  the medical lock attendants (for work in compressed air over 1.0 bar); and

(*e*)  the contract medical adviser.

### Enforcement

**C8096**  In any proceedings for an offence consisting of a contravention of *Reg 14(3)* or *17(3)* (compressed air contractor's duty to ensure compliance with prohibitions against smoking, alcohol or drugs), it is a defence for any person to prove that he took all reasonable precautions and exercised all due diligence to avoid the commission of the offence. [*SI 1996 No 1656, Reg 20*].

## Construction (Head Protection) Regulations 1989 (SI 1989 No 2209)

**C8097**  Head injuries account for nearly one-third of all construction fatalities, but fell significantly after the introduction of the *Construction (Head Protection) Regulations 1989 (SI 1989 No 2209)*. These Regulations specify requirements for head protection during construction work, including offshore operations (see OFFSHORE OPERATIONS), but not diving operations at work. They place duties on employers, persons in control of construction sites, self-employed persons and employees regarding the wearing of head protection. The purpose of head protection is to prevent/mitigate head injury caused by: falling/swinging objects, e.g. materials and/or crane hooks; and striking the head against something, as where there is insufficient headroom. Circumstances where head injury is not reasonably foreseeable on construction sites are limited, but it probably would not be required on/in:

(*a*)  sites where buildings are completed and there is no risk of falling materials/ objects;

(*b*)    site offices, cabins, toilets, canteens or mess rooms;

(*c*)    cabs of vehicles, cranes etc.;

(*d*)    work at ground level, e.g. road works.

## Duties of employers

C8098    The following duties are laid on employers:

### (a) Provision/maintenance of head protection

Every employer (that is, main contractor, subcontractor etc.) must provide each employee, while at work on building/construction operations, with suitable head protection, and keep it maintained/replaced (as recommended by the manufacturer). [*SI 1989 No 2209, Reg 3(1), (2)*].

Moreover, head protection equipment must be kept in good condition and stored, when not in use, in a safe place, though not in direct sunlight or hot or humid conditions. It should be inspected regularly and have defective harness components replaced, and sweatbands regularly cleaned or replaced.

### (b) Ensuring head protection is worn

So far as reasonably practicable (for meaning, see E15039 ENFORCEMENT), every employer must ensure that each of his employees, whilst on construction work, wears suitable head protection, unless there is no foreseeable risk of injury to his head (other than by falling). [*SI 1989 No 2209, Reg 4(1)*].

Moreover, every employer (or employee) who has control (for meaning, see below) over any other person engaged in construction work, must ensure, so far as is reasonably practicable, that such persons wear suitable head protection, unless there is no foreseeable risk of injury to the head, other than by falling. [*SI 1989 No 2209, Reg 4(2)*].

## Persons in control of construction sites

C8099    For the purposes of these Regulations, the following persons may be deemed to be 'in control' of construction sites:

(*a*)    main contractor;

(*b*)    managing contractor;

(*c*)    contractor bringing in subcontractors;

(*d*)    contract manager;

(*e*)    site manager;

(*f*)    subcontractor;

(*g*)    managers, including foremen, supervisors;

(*h*)    engineers and surveyors;

(*i*)    (sometimes) clients and architects with control over persons at work.

### Procedures and rule making

C8100    Employers and others in control must:

(*a*)    identify when/where head protection should be worn;

(*b*)    inform site personnel procedurally when/where to wear head protection and post suitable safety signs to that effect;

(*c*)    provide adequate supervision;

(*d*)    check that head protection is, in fact, worn.

Supervision by those responsible for ensuring head protection is worn, is an on-going requirement, including monitoring helmet use at all times, starting early in the day and taking in arrivals on site.

Persons in control of construction works can (and should) make rules regulating the wearing of suitable head protection. Such rules must be in writing and be brought clearly to the attention of those involved. Such procedure is particularly useful to main/managing contractors on multi-contractor sites, and rules/regulations on head protection should form part of overall site safety procedures, such as construction phase safety plans in accordance with the *CDM Regulations* (see C8025 above).

## Wearing suitable head protection – duty of employees

C8101    Employees must also make full and proper use of head protection and return it to the accommodation provided for it after use. [*SI 1989 No 2209, Reg 6 as amended by the Personal Protective Equipment at Work Regulations 1992, Sch 2, para 24*]. They must also comply with the rules and regulations made for the wearing of head protection mentioned in C8098 above (see also PERSONAL PROTECTIVE EQUIPMENT). All employees, provided with suitable head protection, must take reasonable care of it and report any loss of it or obvious defect in it, to the employer etc. [*SI 1989 No 2209, Reg 7*].

## Suitable head protection

C8102    Suitable head protection refers to an industrial safety helmet conforming to British Standard BS EN 397: 1995 'Industrial Safety Helmets' – Specification for construction and performance (or an equivalent standard). For work in confined spaces, 'bump caps' to BS EN 812: 1998 are more suitable.

Suitability of head gear involves the following factors: (*a*) fit, (*b*) comfort, (*c*) compatibility with work to be done, and (*d*) user choice.

### (a) Fit

Head protection should be of an appropriate shell size for the person who is to wear it, and have an easily adjustable headband, nape and chin strap. The range of size adjustment should be sufficient to accommodate thermal liners in cold weather.

### (b) Comfort

Head gear should be as comfortable as possible, including:

(*a*)    a flexible headband of adequate width and contoured vertically and horizontally to fit the forehead;

(*b*)    an absorbent, easily cleanable or replaceable sweatband;

(*c*)    textile cradle straps;

(*d*)    chin straps (when fitted) which

(i)    fit round the ears,

(ii)  are compatible with any other personal protective equipment needed,

(iii)  are fitted with smooth, quick release buckles which do not dig into the skin,

(iv)  are made from non-irritant materials,

(v)  are capable of being stowed on the helmet when not in use.

*(c) Compatibility with work to be done*

Head gear should not impede work to be done. For instance, an industrial safety helmet with little or no peak is functional for a surveyor taking measurements, using a theodolite or to allow unrestricted upward vision for a scaffold erector. If a job involves work in windy conditions, at heights, or repeated bending or constantly looking upwards, a secure retention system is necessary. Flexible headbands and Y-shaped chin straps can help to secure the helmet on the head. If other personal protective equipment, such as ear defenders or eye protectors, are required, the design must allow them to be worn safely and in comfort.

*(d) User choice*

In order to avoid possibly unpleasant industrial relations consequences or a possible action for unfair dismissal (see further EMPLOYMENT PROTECTION), it is sensible and advisable to allow the user to participate in selection of head gear.

## Duties of self-employed personnel

C8103    Every self-employed person involved in construction/building operations, must:

(i)  provide himself with suitable head protection and maintain/replace it, whenever necessary [*SI 1989 No 2209, Reg 3(2)*];

(ii)  ensure that any person over whom he has control, wears suitable head gear, unless there is no foreseeable risk of injury [*SI 1989 No 2209, Reg 4(2)*];

(iii)  give directions to any other self-employed person regarding wearing of suitable head gear [*SI 1989 No 2209, Reg 5(4)*];

(iv)  wear properly suitable head protection, unless there is no foreseeable risk of injury to the head, and make full and proper use of it and return it to the accommodation provided for it after use [*SI 1989 No 2209, Reg 6(2)–(4)*];

(v)  where the presence of more than one risk to health or safety makes it necessary for him to wear or use simultaneously more than one item of personal protective equipment, see that such equipment is compatible and continues to be effective against the risk or risks in question [*Personal Protective Equipment at Work Regulations 1992 (SI 1992 No 2966), Reg 5(2)*].

## Exceptions

C8104    The following categories of workers on construction sites are exempt from the Regulations:

(a)  divers actually diving or preparing to dive;

(b)  Sikhs wearing turbans on construction sites [*Employment Act 1989, ss 11, 12*], though the Regulations do apply to Sikhs not normally wearing turbans at work. (The probability is that this exemption, under the *Employment Act 1989, s 11*, is now subordinate to the requirements of the *Construction (Head*

*Protection) Regulations 1989* and *HSWA 1974*, with the result that Sikhs working on construction sites will have to wear hard hats (*SS Dhanjal v British Steel plc (Case No 50740/91)*).)

### Visitors on site

C8105    It is not necessary that visitors are provided with or, even less, wear head protection, under these Regulations. Nevertheless, in order to satisfy their general duty under the *Health and Safety at Work etc. Act 1974 (HSWA 1974)*, *s 4* and additionally avoid any civil liability for injury at common law in an action for negligence (see further EMPLOYERS' DUTIES TO THEIR EMPLOYEES) and/or under the *Occupiers' Liability Act 1957* (see OCCUPIERS' LIABILITY), employers should provide visitors to the site with suitable head protection where there is a reasonably foreseeable likelihood of injury. This contention is further reinforced by the requirement for every employer to consider the risks inherent in his business which have the potential to harm his employees or any other persons who might be affected, and to take measures to remove or reduce such risks [*Management of Health and Safety at Work Regulations 1999 (SI 1999 No 3242), Reg 3*].

## Composition of construction products

C8106    Products must be suitable for construction works and works of civil engineering and can then carry the 'CE' mark. To that end, when incorporated into design and building, construction products should satisfy the following criteria, namely,

(*a*)    mechanical resistance and stability;

(*b*)    safety in case of fire;

(*c*)    hygiene, health and the environment;

(*d*)    safety in use;

(*e*)    protection against noise; and

(*f*)    energy economy and heat retention.

[*Construction Products Regulations 1991 (SI 1991 No 1620), Reg 3, Sch 2 as amended by SI 1994 No 3051*].

Manufacturers must show that their products conform to these specifications, if necessary, by submitting to third party testing (see also PERSONAL PROTECTIVE EQUIPMENT for products generally).

## Protecting visitors and the public

C8107    The HSE have issued revised guidance, HS(G)151 *Protecting the public – your next move* (June 1997), which provides practical advice on the measures to be taken to minimise risks to the public and others not directly involved in construction activities. The advice is aimed at preventing accidents and ill health and, to a limited extent, at reducing incidents of nuisance. The guidance does not cover deliberate illegal trespass or forced entry on to sites by protest groups or those intent on criminal activity.

In addition, reference should be made to the following related statutory provisions which have aspects relating to public safety during construction or building operations:

*(a) Roads and streets*

*Highways Act 1980:*

— *s 168* (building operations affecting public safety);

— *s 169* (the control of scaffolding on highways);

— *s 174* (the erection of barriers, signs and lighting etc.).

*New Roads and Street Works Act 1991:*

— *s 50* (lays down particular safety requirements for work in the street and, specifically, the measures to be taken to minimise inconvenience to the disabled).

*Environmental Protection Act 1990:*

— *s 79 as amended by the Noise and Statutory Nuisance Act 1993* (noise or vibration emitted from buildings and from or caused by a vehicle, machinery or equipment in a street).

*(b) Waste from building and demolition sites*

Waste produced on construction sites is classed as controlled waste and as such must be controlled to comply with EU-based Directives:

*Environmental Protection Act 1990:*

— *ss 33–46* (deal with waste management and licensing control).

*Controlled Waste (Registration of Carriers and Seizure of Vehicles) Regulations 1991 (SI 1991 No 1624 as amended)* (carriage of controlled waste by registered carriers only).

*Waste Management Licensing Regulations 1994 (SI 1994 No 1056 as amended)* (registers, applications and waste regulation authorities for the recovery and disposal of waste).

*Special Waste Regulations 1996 (SI 1996 No 972 as amended)* (hazardous properties of waste).

## Identifying hazards and evaluating risks

C8108

Construction work is by its nature carried out by workers away from the home base and may not be open to direct management and supervision. The employer's general duty of care to ensure that employees are not put at risk by their work activities (*HSWA 1974, s 2*) still applies. In addition, if the work activities impinge on others, such as another organisation or members of the public, a further duty of care (*HSWA 1974, s 3*) applies.

The *HSWA 1974, s 4* relates to the control of premises, rather than the control of undertakings. Persons who control premises used by people who are at work, but who are not their employees, need to ensure, so far as is reasonably practicable, that the premises, access to them and plant and substances used on them are safe and free from risks to health and safety. Site occupiers therefore share a duty of care with contractors (as both are employers) to ensure that all reasonably practicable precautions are taken to safeguard their own employees, other persons on site and the public.

Under the *Occupiers' Liability Act 1957* and the *Occupiers' Liability Act 1984* a duty of care is imposed on occupiers of existing premises regarding visitors. The duty of care extends to children – it should be noted that a child is regarded as being at greater risk than an adult (see O3010 OCCUPIERS' LIABILITY). The 1984 Act further extends the duty of an occupier to people other than lawful visitors, such as trespassers, to ensure that they are not injured whilst on the premises. This may involve making unauthorised access more difficult or putting up suitable warning signs regarding hazards on site.

### Safety policies and written arrangements

**C8109**      The *HSWA 1974, s 2(3)* requires written safety arrangements only with regard to employee safety. However, by virtue of the *MHSWR (SI 1999 No 3242), Reg 5* (health and safety arrangements) written arrangements are also required with regard to the protection of the public and other non-employees.

The *MHSWR* refer expressly to occupiers' responsibility to co-operate and co-ordinate arrangements *(SI 1999 No 3242), Regs 11* and *12*) and to provide information and training on risks and precautions *(SI 1999 No 3242, Regs 10* and *13)*. These duties apply whether or not payment is involved, for example free surveys, estimates, measurements, maintenance and servicing under warranty, etc.

Measures to ensure the safety of visitors and members of the public must be one result of the risk assessment task as required by *MHSWR (SI 1999 No 3242), Reg 3* (see R3004 RISK ASSESSMENT). Chemical installations or other high risk manufacturing or chemical storage premises are also subject to specific duties towards the general public under the *Control of Major Accident Hazards Regulations 1999* (see CONTROL OF MAJOR ACCIDENT HAZARDS).

Companies with cooling towers on site are also subject to specific controls ultimately designed to protect the public. In *R v Board of Trustees of the Science Museum [1993] The Times, March 15, CA* the prosecution had alleged that members of the public outside the Science Museum had been exposed to risks to their health from *legionella pneumophila*, because of inadequate maintenance of the museum's air conditioning system. The basis of their case had been that it is sufficient for the prosecution to show that there has been a risk to health.

The Court of Appeal decided that the word 'risks' in *HSWA 1974, s 3(1)* implied the idea of potential danger. There was nothing in the subsection which narrowed this meaning. *HSWA 1974* should be interpreted so as to make it effective in its role of protecting public health and safety. *Section 3(1)* was intended to be an absolute prohibition, subject to the defence of reasonable practicability.

### Insurance cover

**C8110**      The *Employers' Liability (Compulsory Insurance) Act 1969* states that an employer's legal liability for death, disease or bodily injury suffered by employees as a consequence of employment must be insured by the employer for their mutual protection under the duty of care owed by *HSWA 1974, s 2*. A copy of the current certificate of insurance (issued annually) must be displayed within all working premises. Other insurances, for example reflecting the risk of liability to non-employees under the duty of care imposed by *HSWA 1974, s 3*, are likely to be essential even if not compulsory.

### Site planning and layout

**C8111**      Risk assessment should decide how the site perimeters will be defined, what type of barriers and fencing will be most effective and where they should be placed.

For most sites the perimeter will be the geographical area within which the construction work will be carried out. Determining the perimeter is an important aspect of managing public risk. It must always be recognised that site perimeters need to be changed as the work progresses.

Under the *CDM Regulations (SI 1994 No 3140)*, the duties of the principal contractor are wide and varied. Importantly, *CDM* is excluded from use in civil proceedings, except for *Reg 10* which requires the client to ensure that an adequate health and safety plan has been prepared before the construction phase of the project commences, and *Reg 16(1)(c)* which requires the principal contractor to take appropriate steps to ensure that only authorised access is permitted to premises where construction work is continuing.

Similarly, where construction work is taking place on an occupied site, the client will impose existing security rules on everyone entering and leaving the site.

Under the *CDM Regulations*, other contractors involved in the construction work are required to co-operate with the principal contractor and comply with any directions or site rules. In addition, all contractors must provide appropriate information, including information relating to any injuries, diseases and dangerous occurrences.

## Employers' liability for the actions and safety of the public and non-employees

**C8112**   Under *HSWA 1974*, both employers and the self-employed have duties not only to their own workpeople but also to outside contractors, workers employed by them and to members of the public – whether within or outside the workplace – who may be affected by work activities. Undertakings must be conducted in such a way as to ensure, so far as is reasonably practicable, that they do not expose people who are not their employees to risks to their health and safety. The duty extends to, for example, risks to the public outside the workplace from fire or explosion, from falls of unsafely erected scaffolding or from the release of harmful substances into the atmosphere.

In general, the standard of protection required for visitors and others within a construction site will be similar to that given to employees. There may, however, be a need to apply different criteria to achieve these standards when assessing the risks to members of the public. For example, it will be necessary to consider that certain people, such as the very young or disabled, may be more vulnerable than others and that people visiting or passing a workplace may have less knowledge of the potential hazards and of how to avoid them.

The responsibilities of employers and the self-employed to non-employees will in certain circumstances extend to people entering workplaces without permission. This is apart from any liability under common law towards trespassers. The duty under *HSWA 1974* to conduct the business in such a way as not to expose people to risks to health and safety implies taking certain precautions to deter people from unlawfully entering the workplace, for example by the provision of fences, barriers and notices warning of the danger. The duty towards 'unauthorised' people is qualified 'so far as is reasonably practicable', and on construction sites and other open-air workplaces, which have particular dangers as far as children are concerned, simply locking or guarding main doors and gates may not be adequate.

*Duties of all people*

**C8113**   *HSWA 1974* imposes one duty on all people, both people at work and members of the public, including children: this is not intentionally to interfere with or misuse anything that has been provided in the interests of health, safety or welfare, whether it has been provided for the protection of employees or other people. The purpose of the provision is clearly to protect things intended to ensure people's safety, including fire escapes and fire extinguishers, perimeter fencing, warning notices for particular hazards, protective clothing, guards on machinery and special containers for dangerous substances.

### Control measures

C8114    The general duties of protection owed to visitors apply equally to the emergency services who should be given a plan or map of the premises together with information on specific high risk areas where high voltage or dangerous chemicals may be present. In addition, to comply with occupier's liability legislation the duty of care towards visitors includes contractors.

### (a) Visitors

C8115    In general, visitors to a construction site should not be left unaccompanied and they should not, if possible, be taken into any hazardous areas. All visitors should be made to sign in on arrival and sign out on departure and, ideally, be given basic instructions on what to do in the event of an emergency. The main element of looking after visitors is to ensure that they are accompanied at all times, so that the host can lead them to safety in the event of fire or other emergency. Constant accompaniment of visitors will, of course, also improve security arrangements.

### (b) Contractors

C8116    Under the *MHSWR* the occupier of the premises must ensure that contractors on site are provided with comprehensible information on:

—    the risks to health and safety arising out of the activities on site; and

—    the measures taken by the occupier to ensure compliance with statutory requirements.

[*SI 1999 No 3242, Reg 10*].

The ideal situation is where contractors can be provided with a completely separated area which can be designated as being under their control. Such an arrangement will normally only apply when the contractors are on site to undertake a major engineering or construction project; and it will only be successful if a contractor is actually given full control of the area – and the main site occupier and his or her employees only enter the area when authorised by the contractor. However, the main site occupier will retain the key responsibility for safety matters – as illustrated in the case of a south coast town council which employed contractors to remove part of a damaged pier. The council had accepted by far the lowest quote and did not discuss the system of work. During the demolition, there was a huge explosion which removed the derelict part of the pier but also caused considerable damage to cars and buildings on the seafront. The contractor and town council were held jointly responsible but the council suffered the larger fine because it failed to employ reputable contractors and did not request a method statement from them.

### (c) General public

C8117    Measures to ensure the safety of the general public are usually more difficult and must be one result of the risk assessment task as required by *MHSWR (SI 1999 No 3242), Reg 3*. Members of the public are owed a duty of care under *HSWA 1974, ss 3 and 4*, to ensure that they are not put at risk by the employer's undertaking. For example, an employer engaged in construction work near a public place must ensure that risks are assessed and adequately controlled. The Act also imposes a duty on employees to co-operate with their employer on health and safety matters and not to do anything which puts others at risk.

As far as protecting the public is concerned, adequate control measures must be determined which should not rely on the use of protective equipment.

## Risk assessments

C8118     Risk assessments are an integral part of the *CDM Regulations (SI 1994 No 3140)* and the *Confined Spaces Regulations 1997 (SI 1997 No 1713)*. Additionally, with respect to visitors and the general public, employers may be liable to pay compensation to people injured on their premises under the terms of the *Occupiers' Liability Act 1957*.

When carrying out a risk assessment to safeguard members of the public it is necessary to adopt a very wide approach and consider all the possible hazards and subsequent risks. This would include, but not be limited to, compiling data and control measures for:

(*a*)   *chemical hazards* — e.g., mist, vapour, gas, smoke, dust, aerosol, fumes;

(*b*)   *physical hazards* — e.g., noise, temperature, lighting, vibration, radiation (ionising and non-ionising), pressure;

(*c*)   *biological hazards* — e.g., bacteria, parasites.

## Public vulnerability

C8119     Experience has shown that members of the public are particularly vulnerable to those hazards and risks which are not readily identifiable by the normal senses of sight, smell or hearing. The problem may be exacerbated by disabilities and sensory impairments as well as by physical and mental conditions. These conditions would have been assessed for everyone inside the confines of the site but the employer must address the specific needs of all people who may be affected by the work when the hazards may extend outside the site boundaries. The needs of children and the elderly must always be given top priority.

### Cooling towers

C8120     The public is particularly vulnerable to cooling towers, and employers must therefore ensure, so far as is reasonably practicable, that no one is put at risk from legionellosis as a result of work activities. Plant of this type includes hot and cold water services, air conditioning and industrial cooling systems, spas and whirlpool baths, humidifiers and air washers.

Designers, manufacturers, importers, suppliers and installers of such plant or water systems – and water treatment contractors – have a duty to ensure, so far as is reasonably practicable, that the plant or system is so designed and constructed that it will be without risks to health. Appropriate information must be provided to users, and tests carried out if required [*HSWA 1974, s 6*].

The use of this type of plant must be notified to the local authority under the *Notification of Cooling Towers and Evaporative Condensers Regulations 1992 (SI 1992 No 2225)* and the requirements of the *COSHH Regulations (SI 1999 No 437)* must be complied with, particularly the provisions relating to:

—    *risk assessment* – to include breakdowns, abnormal operation and the possibility of exposure of susceptible people (for example in hospitals) [*SI 1999 No 437, Reg 6*]. The assessment must be reviewed at least once every five years or if there is a change in plant or operation;

—    *prevention or control of exposure* [*SI 1999 No 437, Regs 7, 8 and 9*]. Where potential exposure to infection cannot be prevented there must be a written control scheme to minimise exposure;

—    *health surveillance* where appropriate [*SI 1999 No 437, Reg 11*];

—    *information, instruction and training* [*SI 1999 No 437, Reg 12*].

(See further L8: *Legionnaires disease: The control of legionella bacteria in water systems* (ISBN 0 7176 1772 6), price £8.00, available from HSE books.

*Dusts and fibres*

C8121    Dust in the form of particulates suspended in air is generated from a number of construction work activities, including, but not limited to:

—    cutting bricks, blocks, tiles, slabs etc.;

—    sawing wood;

—    mixing cement, plasters etc.;

—    grinding operations;

—    blasting;

—    demolition operations.

Fibres from asbestos demolitions are particularly harmful and strict precautions must be taken in case of an uncontrolled release of asbestos fibres from the workplace.

## Environmental safety aspects during asbestos removal

C8022    Under the *Control of Asbestos at Work Regulations 1987 (SI 1987 No 2115), Reg 3*, employers have duties not only to their own employees but also to, for example:

(*a*)    visitors to the place where work with asbestos is being carried out;

(*b*)    the occupier's employees if the work is done in someone else's premises;

(*c*)    people in the neighbourhood who might be accidentally exposed to asbestos dust arising from the work.

Whenever two or more employers work with asbestos at the same time at one workplace they should co-operate in order to meet their separate responsibilities (for further detail see ASBESTOS).

Contractors undertaking work on materials containing asbestos were warned of the serious health hazards associated with such work when the *Control of Asbestos at Work Regulations 1987* came into force in 1988. The warning was reiterated in 1995 when a court case involving contractors cleaning an asbestos roof ruled that such contractors had a duty to take reasonable care and skill in the work including the taking of necessary precautions (*Barclays Bank plc v Fairclough Building Ltd (No 2) [1995] IRLR 605 CA*).

There have been numerous cases involving incidents during demolition and the removal of asbestos in the years following the above case and its warning. In a very significant case where the lives of children had been put at risk, HSE and the Environment Agency co-operated and raised a joint prosecution.

The case (*R v Rollco Screw and Rivet Co and Others [1998] HSE E198:98*) resulted in a defendant being jailed for nine months (the second custodial sentence for an asbestos offence). Five others and a company were ordered to pay fines and costs totalling £98,000. Birmingham Crown Court heard disturbing evidence of the casual attitude of the people carrying out the stripping of an asbestos roof and the subsequent disposal of blue, white and brown asbestos. The contractors were not licensed in accordance with the requirements of the *Asbestos (Licensing) Regulations 1983 (SI 1983 No 1649)*. The HSE inspector who conducted the investigation emphasised the importance of property owners and managers checking the qualifications of any person employed to carry out asbestos removal work. The inspector was especially critical of the clear attempt to gain financially from decisions taken which put the public at risk.

The QC for the Environment Agency gave evidence of nine contraventions of the *Environmental Protection Act 1990* (the keeping or disposal of controlled waste in such a way that pollution of the environment or harm to human health was likely) where approximately 300 bags of asbestos were dumped at different locations around the city. Some of the bags had been left open and others had burst, releasing asbestos fibres into the air. The court heard that children had been playing with loose asbestos material since it had been dumped recklessly and indiscriminately in a playground and in a supermarket car park as well as other locations.

Judge Charles Harris QC, in imposing the sentences, singled out one man for the custodial sentence and said that, unlike the others in the case, he knew the risks, he lied steadily and showed manifest dishonesty. He told him 'This was an act of the most astonishing criminal irresponsibility. You understood the nature of asbestos and yet you distributed it around Birmingham in places where people, including children, had easy access to it'. He described the co-defendants as being ignorant of the dangers of asbestos but their neglect had put others in serious danger.

*Fumes, mists and vapours*

C8123     Most dangers associated with fumes, mists and vapours from operations such as spreading adhesives, mixing and thinning paints and coatings and spraying are well known. In addition, care should be taken and appropriate precautions put in place for operations such as:

—     cleaning operations;

—     heat treatment processes;

—     disturbance of sludge and scale from vessels;

—     the release of gases from sewers and similar operations;

—     emissions from extraction equipment, LEV systems and the venting of relief valves etc.;

—     the use of aerosols;

—     the use of pesticides.

Fumes from cutting, welding, soldering and brazing operations are particularly dangerous and require a thorough assessment.

*Radiations and hazardous waves*

C8124     The dangers associated from the use of equipment emitting radiations, radio-frequency waves and micro-waves are well documented and the precautions to be observed during the use of such equipment must be strictly adhered to at all times. Some operations where the public may be at risk from uncontrolled releases or discharges from the equipment or, in some cases, from natural causes are:

— infra-red and ultraviolet radiations during cutting and welding;

— ionising radiation from radiography;

— laser rays (for example the use of lasers during accurate alignment operations of machinery or structures);

— X-rays from high voltage sources (for example non-destructive testing operations);

— the presence of radon on some soils and rocks.

*Fire and smoke inhalation*

C8125     In addition to the dangers of fire spreading to areas and premises occupied by members of the public, it is necessary to consider the effects of smoke from burning refuse and discarded materials. Advice should be sought from appropriate specialists and approval granted before commencing any burning operations.

*Noise control on construction sites*

C8126     In addition to the *Noise at Work Regulations 1989 (SI 1989 No 1790)* and HSE's supporting guidance to the Regulations (L108 – ISBN 0 7176 1511 1), there are other legislative requirements and codes designed to protect the public from noise on construction sites. Some of the most important are:

— *Control of Pollution Act 1974, s 71* – approval of codes and standards regarding noise control;

— the *Control of Noise (Codes of Practice for Construction and Open Sites) Orders 1984 (SI 1984 No 1992) and 1987 (SI 1987 No 1730)*; and

— the *Construction Plant and Equipment (Harmonisation of Noise Emission Standards) Regulations 1988 (SI 1988 No 361 as amended)* – noise from plant used in or about building or civil engineering operations.

*General construction operations*

C8127     The public are also at risk, but perhaps to a lesser degree, from normal construction work activities. Policies and procedures should be in place to cover contingencies and incidents arising from:

— electricity;

— excavations;

— explosives;

— flooding;

— lifting operations;

— materials handling;

— mechanical plant and general construction equipment;

— overhead working;

— piling;

— scaffolding;

— underground services;

— vehicles;

— vibration.

*References*

C8128    There are numerous publications available as reference documents which provide advice on the measures to be taken to protect visitors and members of the public during construction activities. In particular, the following HSE publications and Approved Codes of Practice (ACOPs) may be useful when formulating safety policies and procedures.

*Construction management*

**L111**    A guide to the Control of Major Accident Hazard Regulations (ISBN 0 7176 1604 5);

**HSR25**    Memorandum of Guidance on the Electricity at Work Regulations 1989 (ISBN 0 11 883963 2);

**L1**    A guide to the Health and Safety at Work etc Act 1974 (ISBN 0 7176 0441 1);

**L21**    Management of health and safety at work (ISBN 0 7176 2488 9);

**L24**    Workplace health, safety and welfare: ACOP to the 1992 Regulations (ISBN 0 7176 0413 6);

**L54**    Managing construction for health and safety: ACOP to the *CDM Regulations 1994* (ISBN 0 7176 0792 5);

**L55**    Preventing asthma at work (ISBN 0 7176 0661 9);

**L64**    Safety signs and signals – guidance to the Health and Safety (Safety Signs and Signals) Regulations 1996 (ISBN 0 7176 0870 0);

**L73**    A guide to the Reporting of Injuries, Diseases and Dangerous Occurrences Regulations 1995 (ISBN 0 7176 1012 8).

*Dangerous substances*

**COP2**    Control of lead at work: ACOP (ISBN 0 7176 1506 5);

**L5**    General COSHH ACOP, Carcinogens ACOP and Biological Agents ACOP, Control of Substances Hazardous to Health Regulations 1999 (ISBN 0 7176 1670 3);

**L27**    The control of asbestos at work: ACOP (ISBN 0 7176 1673 8);

**L28**    Work with asbestos insulation, asbestos coating and asbestos insulating board: ACOP (ISBN 0 1176 1674 6);

**L62**    Safety datasheets for substances and preparations dangerous for supply — guidance on regulation 6 of the Chemicals (Hazard Information and Packaging for Supply) Regulations 1994: ACOP (ISBN 0 7176 0859 X);

**L86**   Control of substances hazardous to health in fumigation operations: ACOP (ISBN 0 7176 1195 7).

*Explosives*

**L10**   A guide to the Control of Explosives Regulations 1991 (ISBN 0 11 885670 7).

*Gas*

**COP20**   Standards of training in safe gas installation: ACOP (ISBN 0 7176 0603 1);

**L56**   Safety in the installation and use of gas systems and appliances: The Gas Safety (Installations and Use) Regulations 1998 (ISBN 0 7176 1635 5);

**L80**   A guide to the Gas Safety (Management) Regulations 1996 (ISBN 0 7176 1159 0);

**L81**   Design, construction and installation of gas service pipes – ACOP to the Pipelines Safety Regulations 1996 (ISBN 0 7176 1172 8).

*LPG and petroleum spirit*

**COP6**   Plastic containers with nominal capacities up to 5 litres for petroleum spirit: Requirements for testing and marking or labelling (ISBN 0 11 883643 9).

*Pesticides*

**L9**   The safe use of pesticides for non-agricultural purposes. Control of Substances Hazardous to Health Regulations 1994: ACOP (ISBN 0 7176 0542 6).

*Pressure systems*

**L122**   Safety of pressure systems: Pressure Systems Safety Regulations 2000 (ISBN 0 7176 1767 X);

**L96**   A guide to the Work in Compressed Air Regulations 1996 (ISBN 0 7176 1120 5).

*Radiations*

**L121**   Work with ionising radiation: Ionising Radiations Regulations 1999 (ISBN 0 7176 1746 7).

*Site vehicles*

**L117**   Rider-operated lift trucks: Operator training (ISBN 0 7176 2455 2).

# Responsibility for contractors and subcontractors

C8129   Most industrial/commercial organisations delegate corporate functions and duties, placed on them by statute, regulation and common law, to contractors and subcontractors. This practice is particularly common in the construction industry, where a main contractor, in order the more competently and expeditiously to discharge his contractual obligations towards his employer (or builder owner), sublets performance of parts of the contract, e.g. steel erection, to specialists.

Significantly, this practice of subletting performance of parts of the entire contract is regarded as sufficiently important in the building industry to justify the existence of a Standard Form of Building Contract (the JCT Standard Form). This means that the rights/obligations of all interested parties, namely, the employer, main contractors and subcontractors, both nominated and domestic, are specified in a formal jointly witnessed contract, known as the Joint Contracts Tribunal (JCT). When a dispute arises between any of the interested parties, for example, who is liable for an injury to an employee of a subcontractor, reference is made to the Conditions of Contract (or Subcontract).

If necessary, such a dispute will be decided by arbitration, since the contract provides for independent arbitration machinery in the form of the RIBA (Royal Institute of British Architects). RIBA arbitration does not exclude jurisdiction of the courts but, in practice, that is often the result, since arbitration is quicker and cheaper. In other words, the building industry has its own quasi-judicial internal disputes machinery and procedures. This is preferable to no machinery at all, since all interested parties know where they stand – at least, that is the theory.

*Multiple occupation of construction sites – standard form work*

C8130    Where, as is normal on large construction sites, standard form (JCT) building work is being carried out, multiplicity of occupation (or control) is not uncommon. Here control will be shared among building owner(s), main contractor(s) and subcontractor(s). It has been decided that the legal nature of the relationship between a building owner and main contractor is that of licensor and licensee (*Hounslow London Borough Council v Twickenham Garden Developments Ltd [1970] 3 AER 326*).

This vests in the building owner some degree of control over the works e.g. if the contractor does not carry out and complete the works (in accordance with the requirements of Clause 2(1) of the JCT Standard Form Contract) the licence can, subject to certain exceptions, be terminated. Moreover, (given that some statutory duties can be modified) Clause 20(1) of the Conditions of Contract states that 'the contractor shall be liable for, and shall indemnify the employer against any expense, liability, loss or claim or proceedings whatsoever arising under any statute or at common law in respect of personal injury to or the death of any person whomsoever arising out of, or in the course of, or caused by the carrying out of the works, unless due to any act or neglect of the employer or of any person for whom the employer is responsible' (e.g. employee). The proviso to the clause 'unless due to any act or neglect of the employer' is limited solely to common law negligence and does not extend to statutory negligence.

In consequence, the building owner can insist that the main contractor(s) must take out insurance to meet that indemnity, and likewise the main contractor(s) can insist that the subcontractor(s) does the same (Clause 21.1 JCT Standard Form Contract). Thus, for the purposes of common law liability, based on occupation, persons injured on building sites can sue the building owner, main contractor and any subcontractor who may be responsible, the question of indemnity as between the liable parties being governed and determined by the terms of the JCT Contract.

# Liability of employer/occupier in connection with contract work

C8131    In practice, two sorts of situation give rise to liability:

(*a*)    injuries/diseases, or the risk of them, to employees of the contractor as a result of working on the occupier's premises; or, alternatively, injuries or the risk of them to the employer's own workforce as a result of the employer failing to acquaint the contractor's workforce with dangers, thereby endangering his own employees (see *R v Swan Hunter Shipbuilders Ltd* below);

(*b*)    injuries/damage to members of the public, or pollution or nuisance to neighbouring landowners.

Such liability can be both criminal and civil (often strict).

## Criminal liability

C8132    Criminal liability can arise under several statutes and at common law (e.g. where, owing to gross negligence, employers commit manslaughter – in practice, this is rare). Particularly relevant is the *HSWA 1974, ss 3(1), 4(2)*.

## Health and Safety at Work etc. Act 1974, s 3(1)

C8133    In particular, *HSWA 1974, s 3(1)* states: 'It shall be the duty of every employer to conduct his undertaking in such a way as to ensure, so far as is reasonably practicable, that persons not in his employment who may be affected thereby are not thereby exposed to risks to their health or safety'.

### The Swan Hunter case

C8134    An instructive case involving this section was *R v Swan Hunter Shipbuilders Ltd [1982] 1 AER 264*. During construction of a ship at a shipbuilder's yard, subcontractors, who had no contract with the shipbuilders, were working on the ship while it was being fitted out. The shipbuilders were aware that, because of use of oxygen hoses with fuel gases in welding, there was a risk of fire due to the atmosphere in confined and poorly ventilated spaces in the ship becoming oxygen enriched. In regard to that danger they had provided information and instruction for their own employees by way of a book of rules which stipulated that at the end of the day's work, all oxygen hoses should be returned from the lower decks to an open deck, or, where impracticable, the hoses should be disconnected at the cylinder or manifold. This rule book was *not* distributed to the subcontractor's employees working on the ship, and an employee of the subcontractor failed to disconnect the oxygen hose and oxygen was discharged during the night. In consequence, on the next morning, when a welder working in the lower deck lit his welding torch, a fierce fire escaped.

The shipbuilders were charged with failing to provide/maintain a safe system of work, contrary to *HSWA 1974, s 2(2)(a)*, and failing to provide such information/instruction as was necessary to ensure the health/safety of their employees, contrary to *HSWA 1974, s 2(2)(c)*.

The shipbuilders were also charged with failing to conduct their undertaking in such a way as to ensure that persons not in their employment, who might be affected thereby, were not exposed to risks to health and safety, contrary to *s 3(1)*.

On appeal against conviction on all three counts, it was held by the Court of Appeal that:

(i)    duties imposed on an employer by *HSWA 1974, ss 2 and 3* followed the common law duty of care of the main contractors to co-ordinate operations at a place of work so as to ensure not only the safety of his own employees but also that of the subcontractor's employees. The main contractor had to prove, on a balance of probabilities, that it was not reasonably practicable for him to carry out the duties under *HSWA 1974, ss 2* and *3*;

(ii) the shipbuilders were under a duty, under *HSWA 1974, s 2(2)(a)*, to provide/maintain a safe system of work for the subcontractor's employees, so far as was reasonably practicable, and provide them with information/ instruction so as to ensure their safety.

Accordingly, the main contractor, Swan Hunter Shipbuilders Ltd, was fined £3,000 and the subcontractor, Telemeters Ltd, £15,000 after eight men were trapped and killed on board HMS Glasgow.

Furthermore, if the main contractor fails, as in *Swan Hunter*, to comply with *HSWA 1974, s 3(1)*, in his duties towards subcontracted labour, it is likely that he would be in breach of his duty towards his own employees, under *s 2* of the 1974 Act. Thus, anyone who is responsible for co-ordinating work has to ensure that reasonable safety precautions are taken for the workmen of a contractor or subcontractor.

*The Rhone-Poulenc Rorer case*

**C8135**    Responsibility for contractors' work has been considered in several cases since the *Swan Hunter Shipbuilders* case resulting in further interpretation of *HSWA 1974, s 3* and the prosecution of employers. Decisions made in the courts have continued to emphasise the role of the main employer in organising and sharing responsibility for the safety of work carried out by contractors. One of these cases concerned a breach of the *Construction (Working Places) Regulations 1966, Reg 36(2)* (now revoked) in addition to *HSWA 1974, s 3* – the case of *R v Rhone-Poulenc Rorer Ltd [1996] ICR 1054* concerned the provision of suitable means for preventing a fall through fragile materials.

Counsel for the prosecution alleged that some sort of physical safety device is required to fulfil an employer's duty to prevent employees from falling through fragile material: neither a system of work based on instruction nor a Code of Practice will suffice.

The court heard that an employee of a subcontractor was instructed to repair a roof light at the company's factory in Dagenham. The company provided one of its own employees to supervise the work. The subcontractor was told not to climb on to the roof. He did so, and fell through the roof light on to a concrete floor 28 feet below and was killed. Rhone-Poulenc was charged under the 1974 Act and the 1966 Regulations. The company was fined £7,500 in respect of the former and £2,500 in respect of the latter, with £55,000 costs.

The company appealed and argued that the trial judge had misdirected the jury in telling them that it was necessary to prove that it had been impracticable to comply with the Regulations, not merely that it was not reasonable to do so.

The Court of Appeal rejected this argument. Wright J stated that the requirement under *Reg 36(2)* was absolute and that employers had a duty to provide such suitable means as might be necessary for preventing, so far as was reasonably practicable, persons from falling through fragile material. This meant that some sort of physical device, for example a safety harness, was required, where in the circumstances guard rails or covering could not be supplied. Falls through fragile material could not be prevented by the provision of a supervisor, a body of instructions, or a code of practice.

In relation to *HSWA 1974, s 3* it was held that because the occupier (Rhone-Poulenc Rorer Ltd) had been in breach of Regulations which applied to its own employees, it was also in breach of *s 3* so far as the contractor's employees were concerned.

*The Associated Octel case*

C8136    It was 1996 before the House of Lords had to deal with the interpretation of *HSWA 1974, s 3*. In *R v Associated Octel Co Ltd [1996] 4 AER 846* it was decided that the duty placed on the employer of contractors extended to persons not in his employment.

In 1990, during the course of an annual shutdown for planned maintenance, a specialist contractor, RGP, was called in for the purposes of cleaning and repairing a tank at Octel's chlorine plant at Ellesmere Port. Octel had effectively approved the system of work by virtue of having issued a permit-to-work that required the contractor's employee to enter the tank, taking lighting with him, and grind the internal surfaces of the tank and clean residues with an acetone solvent. In the event the light broke causing an explosion in which the contractor's employee was badly injured.

The HSE inspector who investigated the incident was critical of the system of work and identified aspects of the operations which were unsafe. The points raised included:

—    the acetone was carried in an old emulsion bucket;

—    Octel provided an unsuitable lamp from its own stores;

—    there was inadequate ventilation;

—    the precautions listed on the permit-to-work referred only to the grinding work and did not specify adequate precautions relating to work in a confined space.

The inspector referred to the fact that the site was a major hazard site and under the control of the *Control of Industrial Major Accident Hazard Regulations 1984 (CIMAH) (SI 1984 No 1902 as amended)* (now replaced by the *Control of Major Accident Hazards Regulations 1999*) which required a safety case to be submitted and complied with. RGP had employees at Octel's site on a regular basis and had worked for Octel over a number of years. Previously, Octel had exercised a degree of control over RGP's work performance and had a high level of understanding of the dangers involved in tank cleaning operations.

The case argued in the Crown Court and the Court of Appeal was a complex one where the central issue concerned 'control' of the work of the contractor. Octel's counsel referred to the Robens Report of 1972, and cited, *inter alia*, as precedents *R v Board of Trustees of the Science Museum [1993] 3 AER 853, R v Swan Hunter Shipbuilders Ltd [1982] 1 AER 264, Mailer v Austin Rover Group Ltd [1989] 2 AER 1087* and *RMC Roadstone Products Ltd v Jester [1994] 4 AER 1037*. Octel argued consistently that there was no case to answer because it could not be shown that it was the conduct of Octel's undertaking that endangered the RGP employee. RGP is a specialist contractor and Octel claimed that it had no right to control the manner in which its independent contractor did its work.

Octel lost its argument before the trial judge, as well as before the Court of Appeal for different and complicated legal reasons. However, it was decided that the chemical business was Octel's undertaking, and the undertaking included having the tank cleaned, whether by its own employees or by contractors.

Lord Hoffmann delivered the judgment of the House of Lords, upholding the decisions of the Crown Court and the Court of Appeal. *The Times* (15 November 1996) reported the following points made by Lord Hoffmann:

—   it was a question of fact in each case whether an activity which caused a risk to the health and safety of persons other than employees amounted to 'conduct of an undertaking';

—   *section 3* of the 1974 Act was not concerned with vicarious liability, but imposed a duty upon the employer himself;

—   if the employer engaged an independent contractor to do work forming part of the 'undertaking', then the employer had to stipulate whatever conditions were needed to avoid risks to health and safety;

—   the question was simply whether the activity in question could be described as part of the employer's undertaking. Octel's undertaking was running a chemical plant and it was part of the conduct of that undertaking to have the factory cleaned by contractors;

—   the tank was part of Octel's plant. The work formed part of a maintenance programme planned by the firm. The workers, although employed by an independent contractor, were almost permanently integrated into the firm's larger operations. In these circumstances, a properly instructed jury would undoubtedly have convicted.

*The Port Ramsgate ferry walkway case*

**C8137**   In this case a harbour operator, two foreign marine engineering companies (designers and builders) and Lloyd's Register of Shipping were all prosecuted and found guilty of failing to ensure the safety of passengers after the collapse of a walkway to a cross-channel ferry led to the deaths of six people and injured many more.

The case centred around the 'reasonably practicable' element of *HSWA 1974, s 3(1)* and concerned the design, construction, installation and the supervision and approval inspection of the walkway, contracted by the Port of Ramsgate Ltd. The accident occurred only four months after the walkway was commissioned because of the failure of a weld joining one of the feet to an axle. The walkway collapsed and fell some 30 feet on to a floating pontoon.

The QC who was prosecuting on behalf of the HSE gave evidence that the failure was the result of inaccurate stress calculations and also of inferior welding.

During the trial, many legal arguments took place as to who exactly was responsible. Port of Ramsgate Ltd was adamant that it had acted properly in placing contracts with appropriate, experienced contractors and that, by arranging for Lloyd's to manage the design, construction and installation, there was nothing else it could have done regarding the safety of its passengers. It argued strongly that there was no way of foreseeing the profound errors of judgment made by the various parties concerned.

The prosecution continued with its argument that there were measures that could have been taken to satisfy the 'reasonably practicable' element and that one of these might have been the inclusion of a simple fail-safe device such as safety chains.

The judge directed the jury to treat the question of the Port of Ramsgate's undertaking as a question of fact and left it for the jury to decide whether sufficient had been done to satisfy the grounds of 'reasonably practicability'. In the event, the jury found that all three companies were guilty of failing to satisfy the requirement. The judge imposed very high fines:

—   Port of Ramsgate Ltd: £200,000;

—   Lloyd's Register of Shipping: £500,000;

—    Fartygsentreprenader AB and Others (Sweden): £1 million.

It should be noted that this was a highly complex case and its implications for further cases will be considerable.

Although the case was brought before the implementation of the *CDM Regulations*, it should be noted that these Regulations do not expressly require quality assurance checks to be carried out.

If the same type of case occurred offshore, the *Offshore Installations and Wells (Design and Construction) Regulations 1996* would probably apply and in particular the requirement for 'verification' and the effect on the installation's safety case.

## Civil liability

C8138    Normally employers are only liable for the negligent acts/omissions of their own employees or agents but there are certain important exceptions, such as where an employee of an occupier is injured by the contractor's negligence but overall control rests with the occupier.

### The McDermid Nash case

C8139    An important case was heard in 1987 concerning a safe system of work, the delegation of the performance of that work and the competency of the person in charge of a situation where an individual, not being in the employ of that person, was injured.

During the case (*McDermid v Nash Dredging & Reclamation Co Ltd [1987] 2 AER 878*) several points were made regarding the legal responsibilities of the various people concerned when contracting an employee of another employer:

—    the employer's safety duties towards his employees are owed personally to those employees – they cannot be got rid of by delegation;

—    an employer who arranges for work to be done by another person, whether under contract or any other relationship, where that other will use employees of the employer, is vicariously liable for acts of negligence of the contractor or other person;

—    liability arises not because the contractor or other person is, for the time being, the employer of the employee in the legal sense but merely from the fact that the usual employer has entrusted the safety of his employee to that other person;

—    the employer still remains liable for the proper performance and the legal duties of his employee;

—    this continued liability does not rely on any contract between the employer and the other party. It arises whenever an employer entrusts the performance of safety duties to another by asking that other party to perform work on his behalf using his employees.

The UK subsidiary of a Dutch company secured a contract to dredge a fjord in Sweden. It was to be an enterprise where some 100 of the UK company's employees were to work on board Dutch vessels under the joint captaincy of a UK and a Dutch captain, each working alternate shifts. Mr McDermid's job was to keep the deck tidy and to tie up and untie the tug from its moorings when it went alongside the dredger.

While the Dutch captain was in charge, Mr McDermid's leg got caught in one of the ship's hawsers and was so badly injured it had to be amputated. The evidence showed that the Dutch captain had not set up a safe system to be sure that Mr McDermid was free of the ropes before applying power to move the tug away from its mooring.

Because of the difficulties of suing a Dutch company while operating in Swedish territorial waters, Mr McDermid sought damages from his UK employer, even though at the time he was working under the control of a foreign captain who was clearly not an employee of the UK company.

The court decided that there was no need to prove even a temporary relationship of employer and employee between the Dutch company and Mr McDermid. Under the common law of vicarious liability, the employer's safety duties are owed to the employee personally. They cannot be got rid of by delegation. Further, when an employer puts his employee into the hands of another he is entrusting the performance of his own safety duties to that other but the employer remains responsible.

Taking all the factors into account, the court ruled that Mr McDermid's employer was vicariously liable for the negligence of the Dutch tug captain and stated:

'It is clear therefore that if an employer delegates to another person, whether an employee or not, his personal duty to take reasonable care for the safety of his employees, the employer is liable for injury caused through the negligence of that person because it is in the eyes of the law his own negligence.'

The employer's appeal to the House of Lords was dismissed, and it was held that an employer's duty to his employee to exercise reasonable care to ensure that the system of work provided for him is safe, is 'personal' and 'non-delegable'. It is no defence for the employer to show that he delegated its performance to a person whom he reasonably believed to be competent to perform it.

It was also stated in court that the negligence of the Dutch captain was not casual but central. It involved abandoning a safe system and operating in its place a manifestly unsafe system.

*Hazards left on highways*

**C8140**  An occupier is not under a duty of care to check that a contractor removes hazards from a highway, and so is not liable for consequential injuries. In *Rowe v Herman and others, The Times, 9 June 1997*, the plaintiff (R) sought damages for injuries sustained by tripping over some metal plates left lying on the pavement by an independent contractor (L), which had been carrying out (and had finished) some building work for the occupier (H). H contended that he was not liable for L's negligence under the general principle that an employer is not liable for an independent contractor's negligence. There are two main exceptions to this basic principle – an employer is liable:

(i)   where the work commissioned involved extra hazardous acts; and

(ii)  where danger was created by work on a highway.

The county court held that although H was not liable for the hazard whilst work was being carried out, he became liable under the principle in (ii) once L had finished the work. H appealed.

The Court of Appeal allowed H's appeal. Previous cases, where the employer was held liable, concerned obstructions to the highway being caused as a result of work being carried out under statutory powers, such obstructions arising directly from the work which the employer was required to do (being integral to it). In this case H was not obliged to carry out the building work, and it was not an integral part of the work to obstruct the footway (the plates had merely been laid to prevent lorries from damaging the pavement). It was clear that if the accident had occurred whilst L was carrying out the work, H would not have been liable; it made no sense to suddenly place H under such a duty once L had left the site. Following the general principle that H had no control over the manner in which L carried out its work, so too H had no control over the way that L cleared up.

# Control of Major Accident Hazards

## Introduction

C10001    The *Control of Major Accident Hazards Regulations 1999 (SI 1999 No 743)* implement the requirements of the 'Seveso II' Directive (96/82/EC) on the control of major accident hazards involving dangerous substances. Seveso II replaced the original Seveso Directive (82/501/EEC) which was implemented in Great Britain by the *Control of Industrial Major Accident Hazards Regulations 1984 (CIMAH)* which in turn have been replaced by the *Control of Major Accident Hazards Regulations 1999 (COMAH)*. COMAH came into force on 1 April 1999. The provisions of Article 12 of Seveso II concerning land-use planning have been implemented in the *Planning (Control of Major Accident Hazards) Regulations 1999 (SI 1999 No 981)*.

## Control of Major Accident Hazards Regulations 1999 (SI 1999 No 743)

C10002    *COMAH* gives effect to a safety regime for the prevention and mitigation of major accidents resulting from ultra-hazardous industrial activities. The emphasis is on controlling risks to both people and the environment through demonstrable safety management systems, which are integrated into the routine of business rather than dealt with as an add-on.

An occurrence is regarded as a major accident if:

—    it results from uncontrolled developments (i.e. they are sudden, unexpected or unplanned) in the course of the operation of an establishment to which the Regulations apply; and

—    it leads to serious danger to people or to the environment, on or off-site; and

—    it involves one or more dangerous substances defined in the Regulations.

Major emissions, fires and explosions are the most typical major accidents.

The duties placed on operators by *COMAH* fall into two categories: 'lower tier' and 'top tier'. Lower tier duties fall upon all operators. Some operators are subject to additional, top-tier, duties.

An 'operator' is a person (including a company or partnership) who is in control of the operation of an establishment or installation. Where the establishment or installation is to be constructed or operated, the 'operator' is the person who proposes to control its operation – where that person is not known, then the operator is the person who has commissioned its design and construction.

The HSE and the Environment Agency (in England and Wales) or the Scottish Environment Protection Agency are jointly responsible as the competent authority (CA) for *COMAH*. A co-ordinated approach will be adopted with the HSE likely to act as the primary contact for operators. A charging regime has been introduced and fees are payable by the operator to the HSE for work carried out by the HSE and the

Environment Agency. Under *Reg 19*, the CA must organise an adequate system of inspections of all establishments, and then must prepare a report on the inspection.

## Application

C10003    The Regulations apply to an *establishment* where:

(*a*)    dangerous substances are present; or

(*b*)    their presence is anticipated; or

(*c*)    it is reasonable to believe that they may be generated during the loss of control of an industrial chemical process.

'Loss of control' excludes expected, planned or permitted discharges.

'Industrial chemical process' means that premises with no such chemical process do not fall within the scope of the Regulations solely because of dangerous substances generated during an accident.

An 'establishment' means the whole area under the control of the same person where dangerous substances are present in one or more installations. Two or more areas under the control of the same person and separated only by a road, railway or inland waterway are to be treated as one whole area.

'Dangerous substances' are those which:

(*a*)    are named at the appropriate threshold (see Table 1); or

(*b*)    fall within a generic category at the appropriate threshold (see Table 2).

There are two threshold levels: lower tier (Column 2 of the Tables) and top tier (Column 3).

## Table 1

| Column 1 | Column 2 | Column 3 |
|---|---|---|
| *Dangerous substances* | *Quantity in tonnes* | |
| Ammonium nitrate (see note below) | 350 | 2,500 |
| Ammonium nitrate (see note below) | 1,250 | 5,000 |
| Arsenic pentoxide, arsenic (V) acid and/or salts | 1 | 2 |
| Arsenic trioxide, arsenious (III) acid and/or salts | 0.1 | 0.1 |
| Bromine | 20 | 100 |
| Chlorine | 10 | 25 |
| Nickel compounds in inhalable powder form (nickel monoxide, nickel dioxide, nickel sulphide, trinickel disulphide, dinickel trioxide) | 1 | 1 |
| Ethyleneimine | 10 | 20 |
| Fluorine | 10 | 20 |
| Formaldehyde (concentration=90%) | 5 | 50 |

| | | |
|---|---|---|
| Hydrogen | 5 | 50 |
| Hydrogen chloride (liquefied gas) | 25 | 250 |
| Lead alkyls | 5 | 50 |
| Liquefied extremely flammable gases (including LPG) and natural gas (whether liquefied or not) | 50 | 200 |
| Acetylene | 5 | 50 |
| Ethylene oxide | 5 | 50 |
| Propylene oxide | 5 | 50 |
| Methanol | 500 | 5,000 |
| 4, 4-Methylenebis (2-chloraniline) and/or salts, in powder form | 0.01 | 0.01 |
| Methylisocyanate | 0.15 | 0.15 |
| Oxygen | 200 | 2,000 |
| Toluene diisocyanate | 10 | 100 |
| Carbonyl dichloride (phosgene) | 0.3 | 0.75 |
| Arsenic trihydride (arsine) | 0.2 | 1 |
| Phosphorus trihydride (phosphine) | 0.2 | 1 |
| Sulphur dichloride | 1 | 1 |
| Sulphur trioxide | 15 | 75 |
| Polychlorodibenzofurans and polychlorodibenzodioxins (including TCDD), calculated in TCDD equivalent | 0.001 | 0.001 |
| The following CARCINOGENS: | 0.001 | 0.001 |
| 4-Aminobiphenyl and/or its salts, Benzidine and/or salts, Bis(chloromethyl) ether, Chloromethyl methyl ether, Dimethylcarbamoyl chloride, Dimethylnitrosomine, Hexamethylphosphoric triamide, 2-Naphthylamine and/or salts, 1, 3 Propanesultone and 4-nitrodiphenyl | | |
| Automotive petrol and other petroleum spirit | 5,000 | 50,000 |

[*Schedule 1, Part 2*].

*Ammonium nitrate:*

(*a*)    The 350 / 2500 quantities apply to ammonium nitrate and ammonium nitrate compounds in which the nitrogen content as a result of the ammonium nitrate is more than 28 per cent by weight (except for those compounds referred to in (*b*) below) and to aqueous ammonium nitrate solutions in which the concentration of ammonium nitrate is more than 90 per cent by weight.

(*b*)    The 1250 / 5000 quantities apply to simple ammonium-nitrate based fertilisers which conform with the requirements of the *Fertilisers Regulations 1991* and to composite fertilisers in which the nitrogen content as a result of the ammonium nitrate is more than 28 per cent in weight (a composite fertiliser contains ammonium nitrate with phosphate or potash, or phosphate and potash).

[Notes 1 and 2 of *Part 2 of Schedule 1*].

Substances are classified according to *Regulation 5* of the *Chemicals (Hazard Information and Packaging for Supply) Regulations 1994.*

## Table 2

| Column 1 | Column 2 | Column 3 |
|---|---|---|
| Categories of dangerous substances | Quantity in tonnes | |
| 1.  VERY TOXIC | 5 | 20 |
| 2.  TOXIC | 50 | 200 |
| 3.  OXIDISING | 50 | 200 |
| 4.  EXPLOSIVE (see C10004 below) | 50 | 200 |
| 5.  EXPLOSIVE (see C10004 below) | 10 | 50 |
| 6.  FLAMMABLE (as defined in Sch 1 Part 3) | 5,000 | 50,000 |
| 7a. HIGHLY FLAMMABLE (as defined in Sch 1 Part 3) | 50 | 200 |
| 7b. HIGHLY FLAMMABLE liquids (as defined in Sch 1 Part 3) | 5,000 | 50,000 |
| 8.  EXTREMELY FLAMMABLE (as defined in Sch 1 Part 3) | 10 | 50 |
| 9.  DANGEROUS FOR THE ENVIRONMENT in combination with risk phrases: | | |
| R50: 'Very toxic to aquatic organisms' | 200 | 500 |
| R51: 'Toxic to aquatic organisms'; and R53: 'May cause long-term adverse effects in the aquatic environment' | 500 | 2,000 |
| 10. ANY CLASSIFICATION not covered by those given above in combination with risk phrases: | | |
| R14: 'Reacts violently with water' (including R14/15) | 100 | 500 |
| R29: 'in contact with water, liberates toxic gas' | 50 | 200 |

[*Schedule 1, Part 3*].

Where a substance or group of substances named in Table 1 also falls within a category in Table 2, the qualifying quantities set out in Table 1 must be used.

Dangerous substances present at an establishment only in quantities not exceeding 2 per cent of the relevant qualifying quantity are ignored for the purposes of calculating the total quantity present, provided that their location is such that they cannot initiate a major accident elsewhere on site.

### Explosives

C10004  Note 2 to *Part 3 of Schedule 1* defines an '*explosive*' as:

(*a*)  (i)  a substance or preparation which creates the risk of an explosion by shock, friction, fire or other sources of ignition;

(ii)  a pyrotechnic substance is a substance (or mixture of substances) designed to produce heat, light, sound, gas or smoke or a combination of such effects through non-detonating self-sustained exothermic chemical reactions; or

(iii)  an explosive or pyrotechnic substance or preparation contained in objects;

(*b*)  a substance or preparation which creates extreme risks of explosion by shock, friction, fire or other sources of ignition.

### Aggregation

C10005  There is a rule for aggregation of dangerous substances set out in Note 4 to *Part 3 of Schedule 1*. The rule will apply in the following circumstances:

(i)  for substances and preparations appearing in Table 1 at quantities less than their individual qualifying quantity present with substances having the same classification from Table 2, and the addition of substances and preparations with the same classification from Table 2;

(ii)  for the addition of categories 1, 2 and 9 present at an establishment together;

(iii)  for the addition of categories 3, 4, 5, 6, 7a, 7b and 8, present at an establishment together.

The sub-threshold quantities of named dangerous substances or categories of dangerous substances are expressed as partial fractions of the threshold quantities in column 3 of Table 1 or of Table 2, and added together. When the total exceeds 1, top-tier duties apply.

If the total is less than or equal to 1, the sub-threshold quantities of named dangerous substances or categories of dangerous substances are expressed as partial fractions of the threshold quantities in column 2 of Table 1 or of Table 2, and added together. If the total exceeds 1, lower tier duties apply.

Definitive guidance on aggregation can be found in HSE's '*Guide to the Control of Major Accident Hazards Regulations 1999*'.

### Exclusions

C10006  *COMAH* does not apply to:

—  Ministry of Defence establishments;

—  extractive industries exploring for, or exploiting, materials in mines and quarries;

—  waste land-fill sites;

—  transport related activities;

— substances at nuclear licensed sites which create a hazard from ionising radiation.

*COMAH does* apply to explosives and chemicals at nuclear installations.

## Lower tier duties

### General duty

C10007    Under *Reg 4*, every operator is under a general duty to take *all measures necessary* to prevent major accidents and limit their consequences to persons and the environment.

Although the best practice is to completely eliminate a risk, the Regulations recognise that this is not always possible. Prevention should be considered in a hierarchy based on the principle of reducing risk to a level as low as is reasonably practicable, taking account of what is technically feasible and the balance between the costs and benefits of the measures taken. Operators must be able to demonstrate that they have adopted control measures which are adequate for the risks identified. Where hazards are high, high standards will be expected by the enforcement agencies to ensure that risks are acceptably low.

### Major accident prevention policy (MAPP)

C10008    Under *Reg 5(1)*, every operator must prepare and keep a document (MAPP) setting out his policy with respect to the prevention of major accidents.

The requirement for a MAPP is new. The document must be in writing and must include sufficient particulars to demonstrate that the operator has established an appropriate safety management system. *Schedule 2* sets out the principles to be taken into account when preparing a MAPP document and at *para 4* lists the following specific issues to be addressed by the safety management system:

(*a*)   *organisation and personnel* – the roles and responsibilities of personnel involved in the management of major hazards at all levels in the organisation. The identification of training needs of such personnel and the provision of the training so identified. The involvement of employees and, where appropriate, sub-contractors;

(*b*)   *identification and evaluation of major hazards* – adoption and implementation of procedures for systematically identifying major hazards arising from normal and abnormal operation and the assessment of their likelihood and severity;

(*c*)   *operational control* – adoption and implementation of procedures and instructions for safe operation, including maintenance of plant, processes, equipment and temporary stoppages;

(*d*)   *management of change* – adoption and implementation of procedures for planning modifications to, or the design of, new installations, processes or storage facilities;

(*e*)   *planning for emergencies* – adoption and implementation of procedures to identify foreseeable emergencies by systematic analysis and to prepare, test and review emergency plans to respond to such emergencies;

(*f*)   *monitoring performance* – adoption and implementation of procedures for the on-going assessment of compliance with the objectives set by the operator's major accident prevention policy and safety management system, and the mechanisms for investigation and taking corrective action in the case of non-compliance. The procedures should cover the operator's system for reporting major accidents or near misses, particularly those involving failure of protective measures, and their investigation and follow-up on the basis of lessons learnt;

(g) *audit and review* – adoption and implementation of procedures for periodic systematic assessment of the major accident prevention policy and the effectiveness and suitability of the safety management system; the documented review of performance of the policy and safety management system and its updating by senior management.

The MAPP is a concise but key document for operators which sets out the framework within which adequate identification, prevention/control and mitigation of major accident hazards is achieved. Its purpose is to compel operators to provide a statement of commitment to achieving high standards of major hazard control, together with an indication that there is a management system covering all the issues set out in (*a*)–(*g*) above. The guidance to the Regulations suggests that the essential questions which operators must ask themselves are:

— does the MAPP meet the requirements of the Regulations?

— will it deliver a high level of protection for people and the environment?

— are there management systems in place which achieve the objectives set out in the policy?

— are the policy, management systems, risk control systems and workplace precautions kept under review to ensure that they are implemented and that they are relevant?

Not only must the MAPP be kept up to date (*Reg 5(4)*), but also the safety management system described in it must be put into operation (*Reg 5(5)*).

## *Notifications*

**C10009**    Notification requirements are set out in *Reg 6*. 'Notify' means notify in writing.

Within a reasonable period of time before the start of construction of an establishment and before the start of the operation of an establishment, the operator must send to the CA a notification containing the information which is specified in *Schedule 3*. There is no need for the notification sent before start-up to contain any information which has already been included in the notification sent before the start of construction, if that information is still valid.

The operator of an existing establishment must send a notification containing the specified information by 3 February 2000, unless a report has been sent to the HSE in accordance with *Reg 7 of the Control of Industrial Major Accident Hazards Regulations 1984*.

The following information is specified in *Schedule 3* for inclusion in a notification:

(*a*)    the name and address of the operator;

(*b*)    the address of the establishment concerned;

(*c*)    the name or position of the person in charge of the establishment;

(*d*)    information sufficient to identify the dangerous substances or category of dangerous substances present;

(*e*)    the quantity and physical form of the dangerous substances present;

(f)    a description of the activity or proposed activity of the installation concerned;

(g)    details of the elements of the immediate environment liable to cause a major accident or to aggravate the consequences thereof.

Notification is a continuing duty. *Regulation 6(4)* provides that an operator must notify the CA forthwith in the event of:

—    any significant increase in the quantity of dangerous substances previously notified;

—    any significant change in the nature or physical form of the dangerous substances previously notified, the processes employing them or any other information notified to the CA in respect of the establishment;

—    *Regulation 7* ceasing to apply to the establishment as a result of a change in the quantity of dangerous substances present there; or

—    permanent closure of an installation in the establishment.

Information that has been included in a safety report does not need to be notified.

*Duty to report a major accident*

C10010    Where a major accident has occurred at an establishment, the operator must immediately inform the CA of the accident [*Reg 15(3)*].

This duty will be satisfied when the operator notifies a major accident to the HSE in accordance with the requirements of the *Reporting of Injuries, Diseases and Dangerous Occurrences Regulations 1995*.

The CA must then conduct a thorough investigation into the accident [*Reg 19*].

## Top-tier duties

*Safety report*

C10011    Operators of top-tier sites are required to produce a safety report – its key requirement is that operators must show that they have taken all necessary measures for the prevention of major accidents and for limiting the consequences to people and the environment of any that do occur.

Safety reports are now required before construction as well as before start-up. *Regulation 7(1)* requires that within a reasonable period of time before the start of construction of an establishment the operator must send to the CA a report:

—    containing information which is sufficient for the purpose specified in *paragraph 3(a) of Part 1 of Schedule 4* (see below); and

—    comprising at least such of the information specified in *Part 2 of Schedule 4* (see below) as is relevant for that purpose.

Within a reasonable period of time before the start of the operation of an establishment the operator must send to the CA a report containing information which is sufficient for the purposes specified in *Part 1 of Schedule 4*, and comprising at least the information specified in *Part 2 of Schedule 4* [*Reg 7(5)*].

The report sent before start-up is not required to contain information already contained in the report sent before the start of construction.

An operator must ensure that neither construction of the establishment, nor its operation, is started until he has received the CA's conclusions on the report. The CA must communicate its conclusions within a reasonable period of time of receiving a safety report [*Reg 17(1)(a)*].

The operator of an existing establishment must send to the CA a report meeting the requirements of *Parts 1 and 2 of Schedule 4*. Current *CIMAH* top-tier sites that have submitted *CIMAH* safety reports in parts can continue to submit *COMAH* reports in parts. If a *CIMAH* report, or any part of it, is up for its three-yearly review before 3 February 2000, a *COMAH* report must be sent before that date or such later date (no later than 3 February 2001) as may be agreed by the CA. If the review would have fallen after that date a *COMAH* report must be sent by 3 February 2001. In any other case the safety report must be sent by 3 February 2002.

---

### PURPOSE OF SAFETY REPORTS

1.  Demonstrating that a major accident prevention policy and a safety management system for implementing it have been put into effect in accordance with the information set out in *Schedule 2;*

2.  Demonstrating that major accident hazards have been identified and that the necessary measures have been taken to prevent such accidents and to limit their consequences to persons and the environment;

3.  Demonstrating that adequate safety and reliability have been incorporated into the

    (a)   design and construction, and

    (b)   operation and maintenance,

    of any installation and equipment and infrastructure connected with its operation, and that they are linked to major accident hazards within the establishment;

4.  Demonstrating that on-site emergency plans have been drawn up and supplying information to enable the off-site plan to be drawn up in order to take the necessary measures in the event of a major accident;

5.  Providing sufficient information to the competent authority to enable decisions to be made in terms of the siting of new activities or developments around establishments.

    *[Schedule 4, Part 1]*

---

### MINIMUM INFORMATION TO BE INCLUDED IN SAFETY REPORT

1.  Information on the management system and on the organisation of the establishment with a view to major accident prevention.

    This information must contain the elements set out in *Schedule 2.*

2.  Presentation of the environment of the establishment:

    (a)   a description of the site and its environment including the geographical location, meteorological, geographical, hydrographic conditions and, if necessary, its history;

    (b)   identification of installations and other activities of the establishment which could present a major accident hazard;

    (c)   a description of areas where a major accident may occur.

3.  Description of installation:

    (a)  a description of the main activities and products of the parts of the establishment which are important from the point of view of safety, sources of major accident risks and conditions under which such a major accident could happen, together with a description of proposed preventive measures;

    (b)  description of processes, in particular the operating methods;

    (c)  description of dangerous substances:

         (i)   inventory of dangerous substances including –

               —   the identification of dangerous substances: chemical name, the number allocated to the substance by the Chemicals Abstract Service, name according to International Union of Pure and Applied Chemistry nomenclature;

               —   the maximum quantity of dangerous substances present;

         (ii)  physical, chemical, toxicological characteristics and indication of the hazards, both immediate and delayed, for people and the environment;

         (iii) physical and chemical behaviour under normal conditions of use or under foreseeable accidental conditions.

4.  Identification and accidental risks analysis and prevention methods:

    (a)  detailed description of the possible major accident scenarios and their probability or the conditions under which they occur including a summary of the events which may play a role in triggering each of these scenarios, the causes being internal or external to the installation;

    (b)  assessment of the extent and severity of the consequences of identified major accidents;

    (c)  description of technical parameters and equipment used for the safety of the installations.

5.  Measures of protection and intervention to limit the consequences of an accident:

    (a)  description of the equipment installed in the plant to limit the consequences of major accidents;

    (b)  organisation of alert and intervention;

    (c)  description of mobilisable resources, internal or external;

    (d)  summary of elements described in sub-paragraphs (a), (b) and (c) necessary for drawing up the on-site emergency plan.

    [*Schedule 4, Part 2*]

All or part of the information required to be included in a safety report can be so included by reference to information contained in another report or notification furnished by virtue of other statutory requirements. This should be done only where the information in the other document is up to date, and adequate in terms of scope and level of detail.

If an operator can demonstrate that particular dangerous substances are in a state incapable of creating a major accident hazard, the CA can limit the information required to be included in the safety report [*Reg 7(12)*].

An operator must provide the CA with such further information as it may reasonably request in writing following its examination of the safety report [*Reg 7(13)*].

*Review and revision of safety report*

C10012 Where a safety report has been sent to the CA, the operator must review it:

—   at least every five years;

—   whenever a review is necessary because of new facts or to take account of new technical knowledge about safety matters; and

—   whenever the operator makes a change to the safety management system, which could have significant repercussions.

Where it is necessary to revise the report as a result of the review, the operator must carry out the revision immediately and inform the CA of the details [*Reg 8(1)*].

An operator must inform the CA when he has reviewed the safety report but not revised it [*Reg 8(2)*].

Current *CIMAH* top-tier sites that have submitted *CIMAH* safety reports in parts must review each part within five years from the time when that part was sent to the CA.

When modifications which could have significant repercussions are proposed (to the establishment or an installation in it, to the process carried on there or the nature or quantity of dangerous substances present there), the operator must review the safety report and where necessary revise it, in advance of any such modification. Details of any revision must be notified to the CA.

*On-site emergency plan*

C10013 *Regulation 9(1)* requires operators of top-tier establishments to prepare an on-site emergency plan. The plan must be adequate to secure the objectives specified in *Part 1 of Schedule 5*, namely:

—   containing and controlling incidents so as to minimise the effects, and to limit damage to persons, the environment and property;

—   implementing the measures necessary to protect persons and the environment from the effects of major accidents;

—   communicating the necessary information to the public and to the emergency services and authorities concerned in the area;

—   providing for the restoration and clean-up of the environment following a major accident.

The plan must contain the following information:

—   names or positions of persons authorised to set emergency procedures in motion and the person in charge of and co-ordinating the on-site mitigatory action;

—   name or position of the person with responsibility for liaison with the local authority responsible for preparing the off-site emergency plan (see below);

—    for foreseeable conditions or events which could be significant in bringing about a major accident, a description of the action which should be taken to control the conditions or events and to limit their consequences, including a description of the safety equipment and the resources available;

—    arrangements for limiting the risks to persons on site including how warnings are to be given and the actions persons are expected to take on receipt of a warning;

—    arrangements for providing early warning of the incident to the local authority responsible for setting the off-site emergency plan in motion, the type of information which should be contained in an initial warning and the arrangements for the provision of more detailed information as it becomes available;

—    arrangements for training staff in the duties they will be expected to perform, and where necessary co-ordinating this with the emergency services;

—    arrangements for providing assistance with off-site mitigatory action.

[*Schedule 5, Part 2*].

Current *CIMAH* top-tier sites that were subject to *CIMAH* requirements for the preparation of an on-site emergency plan must prepare a *COMAH* emergency plan by 3 February 2001. Any other existing establishment must prepare an on-site emergency plan by 3 February 2002. New establishments must prepare such a plan before start-up.

When preparing an on-site emergency plan, the operator must consult:

—    employees at the establishment;

—    the Environment Agency (or the Scottish Environment Protection Agency);

—    the emergency services;

—    the health authority for the area where the establishment is situated; and

—    the local authority, unless it has been exempted from the requirement to prepare an off-site emergency plan.

### Off-site emergency plan

C10014    The local authority for the area where a top-tier establishment is located must prepare an adequate emergency plan for dealing with off-site consequences of possible major accidents. As with the on-site plan, it should be in writing.

The objectives set out in *Part 1 of Schedule 5* (see above) also apply to off-site emergency plans.

The plan must contain the following information:

—    names or positions of persons authorised to set emergency procedures in motion and of persons authorised to take charge of and co-ordinate off-site action;

—    arrangements for receiving early warning of incidents, and alert and call-out procedures;

—    arrangements for co-ordinating resources necessary to implement the off-site emergency plan;

—    arrangements for providing assistance with on-site mitigatory action;

— arrangements for off-site mitigatory action;

— arrangements for providing the public with specific information relating to the accident and the behaviour which it should adopt;

— arrangements for the provision of information to the emergency services of other Member States in the event of a major accident with possible transboundary consequences.

An operator must supply the local authority with the information necessary for the authority's purposes, plus any additional information reasonably requested in writing by the local authority.

In preparing the off-site emergency plan, the local authority must consult:

— the operator;

— the emergency services;

— the CA;

— each health authority for the area in the vicinity of the establishment; and

— such members of the public as it deems appropriate.

[*Reg 10(6)*].

In the light of the safety report, the CA may exempt a local authority from the requirement to prepare an off-site emergency plan in respect of an establishment [*Reg 10(7)*].


*Reviewing, testing and implementing emergency plans*

C10015 *Regulation 11* requires that emergency plans are reviewed and, where necessary, revised, at least every three years. Reviewing is a key process for addressing the adequacy and effectiveness of the components of the emergency plan – it should take into account:

— changes occurring in the establishment to which the plan relates;

— any changes in the emergency services relevant to the operation of the plan;

— advances in technical knowledge;

— knowledge gained as a result of major accidents either on-site or elsewhere; and

— lessons learned during the testing of emergency plans.

There is a new requirement to test emergency plans at least every three years. Such tests will assist in the assessment of the accuracy, completeness and practicability of the plan: if the test reveals any deficiencies, the relevant plan must be revised. Agreement should be reached beforehand between the operator, the emergency services and the local authority on the scale and nature of the emergency plan testing to be carried out.

Where there have been any modifications or significant changes to the establishment, operators should not wait for the three-year review before reviewing the adequacy and accuracy of the emergency planning arrangements.

When a major accident occurs, the operator and local authority are under a duty to implement the on-site and off-site emergency plans [*Reg 12*].

*Local authority charges*

C10016    A local authority may charge the operator a fee for performing its functions under *Regs 10 and 11*, i.e. for preparing, reviewing and testing off-site emergency plans.

The charges can only cover costs that have been reasonably incurred. If a local authority has contracted out some of the work to another organisation, the authority may recover the costs of the contract from the operator, provided that they are reasonable.

In presenting a fee to an operator, the local authority should provide an itemised, detailed statement of work done and costs incurred.

## Provision of information to the public

C10017    The operator must supply information on safety measures to people within an area without their having to request it. The area is notified to the operator by the CA as being one in which people are liable to be affected by a major accident occurring at the establishment. The minimum information to be supplied to the public is specified in *Schedule 6*:

---

### INFORMATION TO BE SUPPLIED TO THE PUBLIC

— name of operator and address of the establishment;

— identification, by position held, of the person giving the information;

— confirmation that the establishment is subject to these regulations and that the notification referred to in *Reg 6* or the safety report has been submitted to the competent authority;

— an explanation in simple terms of the activity or activities undertaken at the establishment;

— the common names or, in the case of dangerous substances covered by *Part 3 of Schedule 1*, the generic names or the general danger classification of the substances and preparations involved at the establishment which could give rise to a major accident, with an indication of their principal dangerous characteristics;

— general information relating to the nature of the major accident hazards, including their potential effects on the population and the environment;

— adequate information on how the population concerned will be warned and kept informed in the event of a major accident;

— adequate information on the actions the population concerned should take, and on the behaviour they should adopt, in the event of a major accident;

— confirmation that the operator is required to make adequate arrangements on site, in particular liaison with the emergency services, to deal with major accidents and to minimise their effects;

— a reference to the off-site emergency plan for the establishment. This should include advice to co-operate with any instructions or requests from the emergency services at the time of an accident;

---

> — details of where further relevant information can be obtained, unless making that information available would be contrary to the interests of national security or personal confidentiality or would prejudice to an unreasonable degree the commercial interests of any person.

Under *Sch 8*, the CA must maintain a public register which will include:

— the information included in the notifications submitted by the operators under *Reg 6*;

— top-tier operators' safety reports;

— the CA's conclusions of its examination of safety reports.

### Powers to prohibit use

**C10018**    The CA is required to prohibit the operation or bringing into operation of any establishment or installation or any part of it where the measures taken by the operator for the prevention and mitigation of major accidents are seriously deficient [*Reg 18(1)*].

The CA may prohibit the operation or bringing into operation of any establishment or installation or any part of it if the operator has failed to submit any notification, safety report or other information required under the Regulations within the required time. Where the CA proposes to exercise its prohibitory powers, it must serve on the operator a notice giving reasons for the prohibition and specifying the date when it is to take effect. A notice may specify measures to be taken. The CA may, in writing, withdraw any notice.

### Enforcement

**C10019**    The Regulations are treated as if they are health and safety regulations for the purpose of *HSWA 1974*. The provisions as to offences of the 1974 Act, *sections 33–42*, apply. A failure by the CA to discharge a duty under the Regulations is not an offence [*Reg 20(2)*], although the remedy of judicial review is available.

# Public Information for Radiation Emergencies Regulations 1992 (SI 1992 No 2997)

**C10020**    In the wake of Chernobyl, the *Public Information for Radiation Emergencies Regulations 1992* require employers in control of nuclear installations, from which radiation emergencies are reasonably foreseeable, to apprise the general public of the danger in tandem with local authorities. Ministry of Defence installations are exempt from these requirements if the interests of national security so dictate.

### Potential radiation emergency

**C10021**    An employer (or self-employed person) who conducts an undertaking, where a radiation emergency is reasonably foreseeable, must:

(*a*)    supply members of the public likely to be in an area in which they are liable to be affected by a radiation emergency arising from the undertaking with information, without their having to request it, concerning:

(i)    basic facts about radioactivity and its effects on persons/environment;

> (ii) the various types of radiation emergency covered and their consequences for people/environment;
>
> (iii) emergency measures to alert, protect and assist people in the event of a radiation emergency;
>
> (iv) action to be taken by people in the event of an emergency;
>
> (v) authority/authorities responsible for implementing emergency measures;
>
> (b) make the information publicly available; and
>
> (c) update the information at least every three years.

[*Reg 3 and Schedule 2*].

### Actual radiation emergency

**C10022**   It is incumbent on county councils to prepare and update information, including advice on appropriate health protection measures, relating to a radiation emergency. The information must be supplied at regular intervals to members of the public actually affected by the radiation emergency. The following information should be supplied:

(a) the type of emergency that has occurred and, where possible, its characteristics, for example, its origin, extent and probable development;

(b) advice on health protection measures which, depending on the type of emergency, might include:

> (i) restrictions on consumption of certain foodstuffs and water supply likely to be contaminated;
>
> (ii) hygiene and decontamination;
>
> (iii) recommendation to stay indoors;
>
> (iv) distribution/use of protective substances;
>
> (v) evacuation arrangements;
>
> (vi) special warnings for certain population groups;

(c) announcements concerning co-operation with instructions or compliance with competent authorities;

(d) if there has been no release of radioactivity/ionising radiations, but this is likely:

> (i) advice to listen to radio/television;
>
> (ii) preparatory advice to establishments with particular collective responsibilities;
>
> (iii) recommendations to occupational groups particularly affected;

(e) if time permits, information on the basic facts of radioactivity and its effects on persons/environment.

[*Reg 4 and Schedule 3*].

# Dangerous Substances I – at the Workplace

## Background and classification

D1001     Over the last hundred years the number of dangerous substances used at the workplace has multiplied enormously, as has the variety of processes, machinery and gadgetry generating dusts, fumes, gases and vapours. With technological development came a series of ad hoc regulations aimed at controlling the effects of dangerous substances in particular industries. Following the *Health and Safety at Work etc. Act 1974*, earlier legislation and regulations were replaced by regulations containing codes of practice, requiring employers to *assess* the health risks to employees and implement health-oriented and risk-preventive strategies – as shown by the *Control of Substances Hazardous to Health Regulations 1999* (see D1024 below).

The great majority of hazardous substances used in industry and commerce, as well as in research establishments, are chemical compounds, including several naturally occurring substances, such as asbestos (see ASBESTOS), heavy metals (such as zinc, chromium and lead), silica, mineral oils and compressed air. In addition, workers may be exposed to hazards from biological agents, such as bacteria, moulds and fungi, some of which are respiratory sensitisers (see D1049 below).

Exposure to a whole range of hazardous substances at work can lead to the onset of identifiable diseases and adverse health effects, including some diseases which are prescribed and for which disablement benefit is payable (see O1043 OCCUPATIONAL HEALTH AND DISEASES). This section examines:

(i)     notification of new substances (D1003);

(ii)    notification of sites handling hazardous substances (D1008);

(iii)   marking of hazardous sites (D1009);

(iv)    classification, packaging and labelling of dangerous substances for supply (D1013);

(v)     control of substances hazardous to health (including biological agents, carcinogens and respiratory sensitisers) (D1036, D1045, D1049);

(vi)    controls over lead (D1050);

(vii)   controls over radioactive substances (D1051);

(viii)  controls over explosives (D1070).


### New and existing substances

D1002     The European Inventory of Existing Commercial Chemical Substances (EINECS) lists all 100,000 substances marketed for commercial purposes between 1 January 1971 and 18 September 1981. These 'existing substances' are controlled by Council

Regulation 793/93/EEC, the *Existing Substances Regulations*, whilst *HSWA* enforcement powers regarding such substances are conferred by the *Notification of Existing Substances (Enforcement) Regulations 1994 (SI 1994 No 1806)*. By contrast, a new substance is one not listed in EINECS and controlled by the *Notification of New Substances Regulations 1993 (SI 1993 No 3050)*.

## Notification of new substances – Notification of New Substances Regulations 1993 (SI 1993 No 3050)

D1003    These regulations govern notification of new chemical substances scheduled for commercial circulation, and new substances, notified to the Secretary of State and HSE under these regulations, may appear in the European List of Notified Chemical Substances (ELINCS), subject to certain agreed information being kept confidential [*Reg 19*]. The regulations require:

(*a*)    *Full notification* – a person must not place a new substance on the market, in a total quantity of one tonne or more per year, unless he has sent to the 'competent authority' (i.e. the Secretary of State for the Environment, Transport and the Regions and the HSE acting together):

   (i)    a technical dossier evaluating foreseeable risks;

   (ii)    a written certificate to the effect that tests, in accordance with good laboratory practice, have been carried out on the new substance;

   (iii)    a declaration relating to the unfavourable effects of the substance; and

   (iv)    in the case of 'substances for supply' (see D1013 below), methods of proposed compliance with the *Chemicals (Hazard Information and Packaging for Supply) Regulations 1994 (CHIP 2)*.

[*Reg 4*].

(*b*)    *Follow-up information* – the competent authority must be notified of:

   (i)    changes in the annual or total quantity;

   (ii)    new knowledge of the effects on health or environment;

   (iii)    new uses for substances;

   (iv)    change in the composition of the substance;

   (v)    change in status of manufacturer/importer.

[*Reg 10*].

(*c*)    *Further testing* – in respect of substances already notified, the competent authority must be notified of:

   (i)    when the quantity of the substance placed on the market reaches 10 tonnes per year from a single manufacturer, or when the total quantity reaches 50 tonnes per manufacturer; the competent authority *may* then require some/all of the tests in *Schedule 3, level 1*, i.e. physico-chemical studies, toxicological and ecotoxicity studies;

   (ii)    when the quantity of the substance placed on the market reaches 100 tonnes per year from a single manufacturer, or when the total quantity reaches 500 tonnes per manufacturer; the competent authority *shall* then require the tests in *Schedule 3, level 1* (as in (*c*)(i) above), to be carried out;

(iii)    when the quantity of the substance placed on the market reaches 1,000 tonnes per year from a single manufacturer or when the total quantity of the substance reaches 5,000 tonnes per manufacturer; the competent authority *shall* then draw up a programme of tests at *Schedule 3, level 2*, i.e. toxicological and ecotoxicological studies.

[*Reg 5*].

The *Notification of New Substances Regulations 1993 (SI 1993 No 3050)* have been amended by the *Notification of New Substances (Amendment) Regulations 2001 (SI 2001 No 1055)* which came into force on 13 April 2001. They introduce the following changes: the exemption of new substances exclusively used in biocidal products; and a drafting change to clarify the existing exemption for active substances which are exclusively used in plant protection products.

The rationale behind the amendments is due to the Dangerous Substances Directive 67/548/EEC (on which the 1993 Regulations are based upon), which has recently been amended in order to avoid duplicate notification requirements following the introduction of the Biocidal Products Directive 98/8/EC – implemented in the UK by the *Biocidal Products Regulations 2001 (SI 2001 No 880)*.

The *Biocidal Products Regulations 2001 (SI 2001 No 880)* which came into force on 6 April 2001, introduce a new regulatory scheme which will ultimately require all biocidal products to be authorised before they can be placed on the market.

The new regulations implement the Biocidal Products Directive 98/8/EC which aims to harmonise the European market for biocidal products and their active substances, and to provide a high level of protection for humans and the environment.

Biocidal products containing an active substance new to the European market after 14 May 2000, must be authorised under the new regulations before they can be placed on the market. Biocidal products containing an active substance which was marketed prior to this date may continue to be produced and sold subject to current national controls, until the active substance has been reviewed.

An EC regulation will set out the review process which is expected to take 10 years to complete. The 2001 Regulations will eventually replace the current controls on non-agricultural pesticides under the *Control of Pesticides Regulations 1986 (SI 1986 No 1510)*.

The evaluation of active substances will be carried out by individual EU member states, and it will be for industry to supply the data required. The final decision as to whether an active substance can be used in biocidal products will be made by the European Commission acting on the advice of a European Committee, a body made up of representatives of all member states.

HSE has published a free new booklet *'A simple guide to the Biocidal Products Regulations'* which explains the provisions and is available from HSE Books.

## Reduced notification requirements – substances in small quantities

D1004    There are reduced notification requirements for substances placed on the market in a total quantity of less than one tonne per year by a single manufacturer and, indeed, some substances are deemed to have been notified, namely:

(*a*)    polymers (generally);

(*b*)   substances in quantities of less than 10 kg per manufacturer, accompanied by a technical dossier containing information necessary for the competent authority to assess risks to humans and the environment [*Sch 2, Part C*];

(*c*)   substances in quantities of less than 100 kg, intended for scientific research and development;

(*d*)   substances for process-oriented research and development with a limited number of registered customers in similarly limited quantities.

[*Reg 6*].

## Placing notified substances on the market

### (*a*) Full notification of substances

D1005   In the absence of objection by the competent authority, notified substances can be placed on the market after expiry of 60 days following receipt of notification.

### (*b*) Reduced notification of substances

In the absence of objection by the competent authority, reduced notification substances can be placed on the market after expiry of 30 days following receipt of notification.

[*Reg 8*].

In the case of both types of substances, the competent authority must carry out, and in certain circumstances review, a risk assessment to human health and the environment. [*Reg 16*].

## Enforcement

D1006   Enforcement of these regulations is by the HSE, and where breach of duty causes injury/damage, there is consequent civil liability. [*Reg 21*].

## Excluded substances

D1007   Some substances, when new, do not have to be notified, namely:

(*a*)   medicines;

(*b*)   food substances;

(*c*)   animal feeding stuffs;

(*d*)   plant protection products;

(*e*)   radioactive substances;

(*f*)   waste;

(*g*)   cosmetics;

(*h*)   substances in transit;

(*j*)   substances for export outside the EU; and

(*k*)   a new substance no longer polymer (i.e. placed on the market before 31 October 1993 and not notified under the *Notification of New Substances Regulations 1982 (SI 1982 No 1496)*).

[*Reg 3*].

## Notification of sites handling hazardous substances – Notification of Installations Handling Hazardous Substances Regulations 1982 (SI 1982 No 1357)

D1008    Activities involving a notifiable quantity (or more) of a 'hazardous substance' must not be carried on at any site or in (most) pipelines, unless the HSE has been notified in writing at least three months before such activity commences, or within such shorter time as the HSE specifies. [*Reg 3(1)*]. The notification should include all of the following matters:

(*a*)    *In the case of sites:*

   (i)    the name and address of the person making the notification;

   (ii)    the address of the site where the notifiable activity will take place (including ordnance survey grid reference);

   (iii)    the area of the site in question;

   (iv)    the date when it is anticipated that the notifiable activity will commence, or, if already commenced, a statement to that effect;

   (v)    a general description of the activities carried on or intended to be carried on;

   (vi)    the name and address of the planning authority; and

   (vii)    the name and maximum quantity of each hazardous substance liable to be on site.

[*Notification of Installations Handling Hazardous Substances Regulations, Reg 3(1), Sch 2 Pt I*].

(*b*)    *In the case of pipelines:*

   (i)    the name and address of the person making the notification;

   (ii)    the address of the place from which the pipeline activity is controlled and the addresses of the places where the pipeline starts and finishes, an ordnance survey grid reference of where the pipeline starts and finishes, and a map showing the pipeline route;

   (iii)    the date when it is anticipated that the notifiable activity will commence, or, if already commenced, a statement to that effect;

   (iv)    the name and address of the planning authorities in the area(s) where the pipeline lies; and

   (v)    the total length of the pipeline, its diameter and normal operating pressure, coupled with the name and maximum quantity of each hazardous substance liable to be in the pipeline.

[*Reg 3(1), Sch 2 Pt II*].

*Reg 3(1)* applies in the case of hazardous substances:

(i)    within 500 metres of the site of a pipeline and connected to it;

(ii)    any other site controlled by the same person within 500 metres of the site; and

(iii)    in any vehicle, vessel, aircraft or hovercraft under the control of the same person, used for storage purposes at the site, or within 500 metres of it, but *not* if used for transporting hazardous substances (for regulations and requirements relating to transportation of hazardous substances, see DANGEROUS SUBSTANCES II).

[*Reg 3(2)*].

Activities involving the following quantities of hazardous substances on sites or in pipelines must be notified to the HSE:

# Table 1

## Notifiable quantities of named hazardous substances in relation to sites

| 1<br>Substance | 2<br>Notifiable<br>quantity tonnes |
|---|---|
| Liquefied petroleum gas, such as commercial propane and commercial butane, and any mixture thereof held at a pressure greater than 1.4 bar absolute | 25 |
| Liquefied petroleum gas, such as commercial propane and commercial butane, and any mixture thereof held under refrigeration at a pressure of 1.4 bar absolute or less | 50 |
| Phosgene | 2 |
| Chlorine | 10 |
| Hydrogen fluoride | 10 |
| Sulphur trioxide | 15 |
| Acrylonitrile | 20 |
| Hydrogen cyanide | 20 |
| Carbon disulphide | 20 |
| Sulphur dioxide | 20 |
| Bromine | 40 |
| Ammonia (anhydrous or as solution containing more than 50% by weight of ammonia) | 100 |
| Hydrogen | 2 |
| Ethylene oxide | 5 |
| Propylene oxide | 5 |
| *tert*-Butyl peroxyacetate | 5 |
| *tert*-Butyl peroxyisobutyrate | 5 |
| *tert*-Butyl peroxymaleate | 5 |
| *tert*-Butyl peroxy isopropyl carbonate | 5 |
| Dibenzyl peroxydicarbonate | 5 |
| 2,2-Bis(*tert*-butylperoxy)butane | 5 |
| 1,1-Bis(*tert*-butylperoxy)cyclohexane | 5 |

| | |
|---|---|
| Di-sec-butyl peroxydicarbonate | 5 |
| 2,2-Dihydroperoxypropane | 5 |
| Di-*n*-propyl peroxydicarbonate | 5 |
| Methyl ethyl ketone peroxide | 5 |
| Sodium chlorate | 25 |
| Some cellulose nitrate | 50 |
| Some ammonium nitrate | 500 |
| Aqueous solutions containing more than 90 parts by weight of ammonium nitrate per 100 parts by weight of solution | 500 |
| Liquid oxygen | 500 |

[*Sch 1 Pt I*].

# Table 2

# Classes of substances not specifically named in Part I above

| | 1<br>Class of Substance | | 2<br>Notifiable quantity tonnes |
|---|---|---|---|
| 1. | Gas or any mixture of gases which is flammable in air and is held in the installation as a gas. | 15 | |
| 2. | A substance or any mixture of substances which is flammable in air and is normally held in the installation above its boiling-point (measured at 1 bar absolute) as a liquid or as a mixture of liquid and gas at a pressure of more than 1.4 bar absolute. | 25 | being the total quantity of substances above the boiling points whether held singly or in mixtures. |
| 3. | A liquefied gas or any mixture of liquefied gases, which is flammable in air, has a boiling point of less than 0°C (measured at 1 bar absolute) and is normally held in the installation under refrigeration or cooling at a pressure of 1.4 bar absolute or less. | 50 | being the total quantity of substances having boiling points below 0°C whether held singly or in mixtures. |
| 4. | A liquid or any mixture of liquids not included in items 1 to 3 above, which have a flash point of less than 21°C. | 10,000 | |

[*Sch 1 Pt II*].

# Marking of sites by signs – Dangerous Substances (Notification and Marking of Sites) Regulations 1990 (SI 1990 No 304)

**D1009**  These regulations are principally for the benefit of fire and emergency services attending the site. Where there is a total quantity of 25 tonnes (or more) of dangerous substances present on site, the *Dangerous Substances (Notification and Marking of Sites) Regulations 1990 (SI 1990 No 304)* require the *notification* and *marking* of such sites with appropriate safety signs. These regulations require that those in control of sites ensure that there are not more than 25 tonnes of 'dangerous substances' on site, unless there has first been notification to:

(*a*)  the local fire authority, and

(*b*)  HSE,

of

(i)  name and address of person notifying;

(ii)  full postal address of site;

(iii)  general description of nature of business;

(iv)  list of classifications of dangerous substances;

(v)  date when it is anticipated that total quantity of 25 tonnes (or more) of dangerous substances will be present.

[*Reg 4, Sch 2 Part I*].

A further notification is required when there is a cessation or reduction of dangerous substances already notified or if there is a change in the list of any classifications of dangerous substances. [*Reg 4, Sch 2 Part II*].

These requirements do not apply to:

(1)  radioactive substances (see D1051 below);

(2)  Class 1 explosives (see D1070–D1072 below);

(3)  substances in aerosol dispensers;

(4)  substances buried/deposited in the ground as waste.

[*Sch 1 para 1*].

Signs are to be kept clean and free from obstruction so far as reasonably practicable. [*Reg 7*].

### Exceptions to duty to notify

**D1010**  The following sites have their own notification procedure, namely,

(*a*)  sites notifiable to HSE, in accordance with the *Notification of Installations Handling Hazardous Substances Regulations 1982 (SI 1982 No 1357)* (see D1008 above);

(*b*)  sites controlled by *Reg 7* of the *Control of Major Accident Hazards Regulations 1999 (SI 1999 No 743)* (see CONTROL OF MAJOR ACCIDENT HAZARDS);

(*c*)  sites controlled by the *Petroleum Spirit (Consolidation) Act 1928*;

(*d*)   sites controlled by *Reg 27* of the *Dangerous Substances in Harbour Areas Regulations 1987 (SI 1987 No 37)*;

(*e*)   sites for which there exists a waste management licence under *s 35* of the *Environmental Protection Act 1990*; and

(*f*)   nuclear sites.

### Marking requirements

D1011   Where there are 25 tonnes (or more) of dangerous substances present on site, safety signs to BS 5378: 1980/1982 must be displayed, as specified in *Schedule 3*, so as to give adequate warning to firemen before entering a site in an emergency. Moreover, safety signs are required to be displayed at such locations on site as an inspector may direct, carrying the appropriate hazard warning symbol and text, e.g. skull and crossed bones – Toxic. In the case of substances with mixed classifications, the sign must carry the exclamation mark symbol (!) (see Table 3 below) plus the words 'DANGEROUS SUBSTANCE' (in capital letters). [*Reg 5*].

## Table 3

## Classifications and Hazard Warnings – Site markings (as per Marking of Sites Regulations 1990)

| 1 | 2 |
|---|---|
| *Classification* | *Hazard warning symbol and text* |
| Non-flammable compressed gas | COMPRESSED GAS |
| Toxic gas | TOXIC GAS |
| Flammable gas | FLAMMABLE GAS |

| Flammable liquid | **FLAMMABLE LIQUID** |
|---|---|
| Flammable solid | **FLAMMABLE SOLID** |
| Spontaneously combustible substance | **SPONTANEOUSLY COMBUSTIBLE** |
| Substance which in contact with water emits flammable gas | **DANGEROUS WHEN WET** |
| Oxidizing substance | **OXIDIZING AGENT** |
| Organic peroxide | **ORGANIC PEROXIDE** |

| | |
|---|---|
| Toxic substance | ⚠ TOXIC |
| Corrosive substance | ⚠ CORROSIVE |
| Harmful substance | |
| Other dangerous substance | ⚠ |
| Mixed hazards | DANGEROUS SUBSTANCE |

[*Sch 3*].

**Enforcement and penalties**

D1012

(*a*) Enforcement of notification requirements is by the HSE;

(*b*) enforcement of marking requirements is by the fire authority, except as follows:

(i) cessation of presence of dangerous substances on site,

(ii) reduction of quantity of dangerous substances below 25 tonnes, and

(iii) change in list of classifications notified

when notification must be to (*a*) the HSE and (*b*) the fire authority.

[*Reg 8, Sch 2 Part II*].

Penalties for breach are as in the case of a breach of *HSWA* (see E15032 ENFORCE-MENT).

# Classification, packaging and labelling of dangerous substances for supply – the Chemicals (Hazard Information and Packaging for Supply) Regulations 1994 (SI 1994 No 3247) (CHIP 2)

**Definitions**

D1013

Classification, packaging and labelling controls over substances dangerous for commercial/industrial supply are contained in the *Chemicals (Hazard Information* and Packaging for Supply) Regulations 1994 (SI 1994 No 3247), as amended by *SI 1996 No 1092*. Similar controls over chemicals conveyed by road are contained in the *Carriage of Dangerous Goods (Classification, Packaging and Labelling) and Use of Transportable Pressure Receptacles Regulations 1996 (SI 1996 No 2092)* (see D3005 DANGEROUS SUBSTANCES II).

These regulations apply to any substance/preparation except (mainly):

(*a*)   radioactive substances (see D1051 below);

(*b*)   animal feed stuffs;

(*c*)   cosmetics;

(*d*)   medicines;

(*e*)   drugs;

(*f*)   micro-organisms;

(*g*)   samples for enforcement purposes;

(*h*)   munitions;

(*j*)   foods;

(*k*)   products under Customs' control;

(*l*)   substances/preparations for export to non-EU states;

(*m*)   pesticides;

(*n*)   substances/preparations transferred from one workplace to another under common ownership and in the immediate vicinity; and

(*o*)   wastes.

[*Reg 3(1)*].

They impose classification, packaging and labelling duties on suppliers/importers into the EU of chemical substances/preparations classified as dangerous for supply.

## Classification of substances/preparations dangerous for supply

D1014       Suppliers are expected to know the classification of substances and provide up-to-date safety data sheets. In particular, suppliers must not supply substances/preparations dangerous for supply, unless:

(*a*)   they have first been classified;

(*b*)   (i)   a record of classification is kept for a minimum of three years, and

(ii)   made available for inspection (where necessary) to the enforcement authorities.

[*Regs 5(1)(4), 13 and 16(2)*].

The *Chemicals (Hazard Information and Packaging for Supply) (Amendment) Regulations 1997 (SI 1997 No 1460)* – 'CHIP 97' – ensure that users of dangerous chemicals are provided with adequate information about the hazards of those chemicals in order to protect people and the environment.

The *Chemicals (Hazard Information and Packaging for Supply) (Amendment) Regulations 1998 (SI 1998 No 3106)* – 'CHIP 98' – came into force on 6 January 1999 and introduce a fourth edition of the 'Approved Supply List' (which prescribes agreed

classification and labelling for many common chemical subs
mineral wools, refractory ceramic fibres and special purpose fib

The *Chemicals (Hazard Information and Packaging for Supply) (Ame
lations 1999 (SI 1999 No 197)* – 'CHIP 99' – came into force on 1 M
although suppliers of dangerous chemicals are allowed a transitional period
months in which to make the necessary changes to labels and safety data sh
They introduce a supplement to the 4th edition of the Approved Supply List b
amending about 60 substance entries and adding a similar number of new entries.

**Classification of substances and preparations dangerous for supply**

D1015

| **Table 4** | | | |
|---|---|---|---|
| **Classification of Substances and Preparations for Supply** | | | |
| CATEGORIES OF DANGER | | | |
| *Category of danger* | *Symbol letter* | *Indication of danger* | *Symbol (orange background)* |
| **Physico-chemical**  Explosive | E | Explosive | |
| Oxidising | O | Oxidising | |
| Extremely flammable | F+ | Extremely flammable | |
| Highly flammable | F | Highly flammable | |
| Flammable | | Flammable | |
| **Health**  Very toxic | T+ | Very toxic | |

| Category | Symbol letter | Indication of danger | Symbol |
|---|---|---|---|
| Toxic | T | Toxic | |
| Harmful | Xn | Harmful | |
| Corrosive | C | Corrosive | |
| Irritant | Xi | Irritant | |
| Sensitising | Xn | Harmful | |
|  | Xi | Irritant | |
| Carcinogenic *Categories 1 and 2* | T | Toxic | |
| *Category 3* | Xn | Harmful | |
| Mutagenic *Categories 1 and 2* | T | Toxic | |
| *Category 3* | Xn | Harmful | |
| Toxic for reproduction *Categories 1 and 2* | T | Toxic | |

| Category 3 | Xn | Harmful | |
|---|---|---|---|
| **Environmental** | Dangerous to the environment | N | Dangerous to the environment | |

*Source: HSE IND(G) 181 (L)*

## Provision of safety data sheets

D1016    Suppliers of dangerous substances/preparations must provide recipients with dated safety data sheets, updated as and when necessary, containing the following information:

(i)    identification of substance/preparation and company;

(ii)    composition/information on ingredients;

(iii)    hazards identification;

(iv)    first-aid measures;

(v)    fire-fighting measures;

(vi)    accidental release measures;

(vii)    handling and storage;

(viii)    exposure controls/personal protection;

(ix)    physical/chemical properties;

(x)    stability and reactivity;

(xi)    toxicological data;

(xii)    ecological data;

(xiii)    disposal considerations;

(xiv)    transport information;

(xv)    regulatory information;

(xvi)    other matters.

[*Reg 6, Sch 6*].

This is not necessary in cases where substances/preparations are sold to the general public from a shop (e.g. medicines), if sufficient information is given with the product to enable users to take the necessary health and safety measures but this exception does not apply if the product is to be used at work. [*Reg 6(5)*]. Safety sheets have to be supplied free of charge and with data in English except where the recipient is in another Member State, when it should be in that language. [*Reg 6(4), (6)*].

## Packaging requirements for substances dangerous for supply

D1017 Such substances must not be supplied/consigned, unless packaged suitably for the purpose. In particular,

(*a*)   the receptacle containing the substance/preparation must be designed/ constructed/maintained and closed, so as to prevent escape/spillage of contents – a requirement which can be satisfied by fitting a suitable safety device;

(*b*)   the receptacle, if likely to come into contact with the substance/preparation, must be made of materials which are not liable to be adversely affected nor, in combination, constitute a health and safety risk;

(*c*)   where the receptacle is fitted with a replaceable closure, the closure must be designed so that the receptacle can be repeatedly re-closed, without allowing escape of contents.

[*Reg 8*].

## Labelling requirements for substances/preparations dangerous for supply

### (*a*) Substances

D1018 With the exception of:

(i)   substances transferred from one workplace to another [*Reg 9(6)*];

(ii)   substances supplied in small quantities – except those which are (*a*) explosive, (*b*) very toxic and (*c*) toxic [*Reg 9(7)*],

suppliers must not supply substances, unless the following particulars are clearly shown:

(i)   name/full address/telephone number of supplier (whether manufacturer, importer, distributor);

(ii)   name of substance;

(iii)   (*a*)   indication(s) of danger and danger symbol(s),

(*b*)   risk phrases (as per Part III approved supply list – e.g. highly flammable, risk of serious damage to eyes, may cause cancer) [*Reg 9(8)*],

(*c*)   safety phrases (not necessary on packages containing fewer than 125 millilitres, unless (i) highly flammable, (ii) flammable, (iii) oxidising, (iv) irritant, and (v) (in the case of substances not intended for public sale) harmful) [*Reg 9(8)*],

(*d*)   the EEC number (if any) and if the substance is dangerous for supply in the 'Approved Supply List', the words 'EEC label'.

### (*b*) Preparations

Suppliers must not supply preparations unless the following particulars are clearly shown:

(i)   name/address/telephone number of supplier (whether manufacturer, importer, distributor);

(ii)   trade name or designation;

(iii)   (*a*)   identification of constituents,

(*b*)    indication(s) of danger and danger symbol(s),

(*c*)    risk phrases,

(*d*)    safety phrases,

(*e*)    if a pesticide,

   (i)    trade name,

   (ii)    name and concentration of active ingredients – to be expressed as percentage by weight (pesticides supplied as solids, in aerosol dispensers or as volatile/viscous liquids);

(*f*)    in the case of a preparation intended for sale to the general public, in a nominal quantity, risk phrases and safety phrases may be omitted so long as the substance is not classified as harmful and they may also be omitted in certain other cases involving less dangerous substances.

[*Reg 9(3)*].

Misleading phrases such as 'non-harmful', 'non-toxic' should be avoided in order to avoid possible expensive civil liability for injury/damage (*Vacwell Engineering Co Ltd v BDH Chemicals Ltd [1969] 3 AER 1681*) (see P9033 PRODUCT SAFETY).

## Particular labelling requirements for certain preparations

*Labelling requirements for certain preparations dangerous for supply*

D1019    Certain preparations carry particular labelling requirements as follows.

(*a*)    Preparations to be supplied to the general public:

'Keep locked up.
Keep out of reach of children.
In case of accident, seek medical advice.'.

If such preparations are very toxic, toxic or corrosive, and it is impossible to give information on the package itself, there must be precise and easily intelligible instructions relating to (*inter alia*) destruction of empty package.

(*b*)    Preparations intended for use by spraying:

'Do not breathe gas/fumes/vapour/spray.
In case of insufficient ventilation, wear suitable respiratory equipment.
Use only in well-ventilated areas.'.

(*c*)    Preparations containing risk of cumulative effects:

'Risk of cumulative effects.'.

(*d*)    Preparations that may cause harm to breastfed babies:

'May cause harm to breastfed babies.'.

[*Reg 10, Sch 6, Part IIA*].

*Labelling requirements for certain preparations whether or not dangerous for supply*

D1020    Certain preparations carry particular labelling requirements as follows.

(*a*)    Paints and varnishes containing lead:

(i)   labels of packages of paints and varnishes containing lead in quantities exceeding 0.15% expressed as weight of metal of the total weight of the preparation, as determined in accordance with ISO Standard 6503/1984, shall show the following particulars –

'Contains lead. Should not be used on surfaces that are liable to be chewed or sucked by children.';

(ii)   in the case of packages containing less than 125 millilitres of such preparations the particulars may be –

'Warning. Contains lead.'.

(*b*)   Cyanoacrylate based adhesives:

(i)   the immediate packages of glues based on cyanoacrylates shall bear the following inscription –

'Cyanoacrylate.
Danger.
Bonds skin and eyes in seconds.
Keep out of the reach of children.';

(ii)   appropriate safety advice shall accompany the package.

(*c*)   Preparations containing isocyanates:

the package labels of preparations containing isocyanates (whether as monomers, oligomers, prepolymers etc. or as mixtures thereof) shall bear the following inscriptions –

'Contains isocyanates.
See information supplied by the manufacturer.'.

(*d*)   Certain preparations containing epoxy constituents:

the package labels of preparations containing epoxy constituents with an average molecular weight LZ700 shall bear the following inscriptions –

'Contains epoxy constituents.
See information supplied by the manufacturer.'.

(*e*)   Preparations intended to be sold to the general public that contain active chlorine:

the package labels of preparations containing more than 1% of active chlorine which are intended to be sold to the general public shall bear the following inscription –

'Warning! Do not use with other products. May release dangerous gases (chlorine).'.

(*f*)   Preparations containing cadmium (alloys) intended to be used for brazing or soldering:

the package labels of preparations containing cadmium (alloys) intended to be used for brazing or soldering shall bear the following inscription –

'Warning. Contains cadmium.
Dangerous fumes are formed during use.
See information supplied by the manufacturer.
Comply with the safety instructions.'.

[*Reg 10, Sch 6, Part IIB*].

*Substances to be labelled 'Restricted to professional user'*

D1021   Certain Category 1 and 2 carcinogenic, mutagenic and toxic for reproduction substances require to be labelled 'Restricted to professional user', as follows:

| *Substance* | *CAS Number* |
| --- | --- |
| Carcinogenic substances of Category 1 | |
| 2-naphthylamine; ß-naphthylamine | 91-59-8 |
| biphenyl-4-ylamine; xenylamine; 4-aminobiphenyl | 92-67-1 |
| benzidine; 4,4'-diaminobiphenyl; biphenyl-4,4'-ylenediamine | 92-87-5 |
| chromium trioxide | 1333-82-0 |
| arsenic acid and its salts | — |
| arsenic pentoxide; arsenic oxide | 1303-28-2 |
| diarsenic trioxide; arsenic trioxide | 1327-52-3 |
| asbestos | 132207-33-1 |
| | 132207-32-0 |
| | 12172-73-5 |
| | 77536-66-4 |
| | 77536-68-6 |
| | 77536-67-5 |
| benzene | 71-43-2 |
| bis (chloromethyl) ether | 542-88-1 |
| chloromethyl methyl ether, chlorodimethyl ether | 107-30-2 |
| dinickel trioxide | 1314-06-3 |
| erionite | 12510-42-8 |
| nickel dioxide | 12035-36-8 |
| nickel monoxide | 1313-99-1 |
| nickel subsulphide | 12035-72-2 |
| nickel sulphide | 16812-54-7 |
| salts of 2-naphthylamine | — |
| salts of biphenyl-4-ylamine; salts of xenylamine; salts of 4-aminobiphenyl | — |
| salts of benzidine | — |
| vinyl chloride; chloroethylene | 75-01-4 |
| zinc chromates including zinc potassium chromate | — |
| *Carcinogenic substances of Category 2* | |
| 1-methyl-3-nitro-1-nitrosoguanidine | 70-25-7 |
| 1, 2–dibrimo-3'-chloropropane | 96-12-8 |

| Substance | CAS Number |
|---|---|
| 1,2-dimethylhydrazin | 540-73-8 |
| 1,3-butadiene, buta-1,3-diene | 106-99-0 |
| 1,3-dichloro-2-propanol | 96-23-1 |
| 1,3-propanesultone | 1120-71-4 |
| 3-propanolide; 1,3-propiolactone | 57-57-8 |
| 1,4-dichlorobut-2-ene | 764-41-0 |
| 2-nitronaphthalene | 581-89-5 |
| 2-nitropropane | 79-46-9 |
| 2,2'-dichloro-4,4'-methylenedianiline; 4,4'-methylene bis (2-chloroaniline) | 101-14-4 |
| 2-2'-(nitrosoimino) bisethanol | 1116-54-7 |
| 3,3'-dichlorobenzidine; 3,3'-dichlorobiphenyl-4,4'-ylenediamine | 91-94-1 |
| 3,3'-dimethoxybenzidine; o-dianisidine | 119-90-4 |
| 3,3'-dimethylbenzindine; o-toluidine | 119-93-7 |
| 4-aminoazobenzene | 60-09-3 |
| 4-amino-3-fluorophenol | 399-95-1 |
| 4-methyl-m-phenylenediamine | 95-80-7 |
| 4-nitrobiphenyl | 92-93-3 |
| 4,4'-methylenedi-o-toluidine | 838-88-0 |
| 4,4'-diaminodiphenylmethane; 4,4'-methylenedianiline | 101-77-9 |
| 5-nitroacenaphthene | 602-87-9 |
| 4-o-tolylazo-o-toluidine; 4-amino-2',3-dimethylazobenzene; fast garnet GBC base, AAT; o-aminoazotoluene | 97-56-3 |
| disodium-5[4'-((2,6-hydroxy-3-((2-hydroxy-5-sulphophenyl)azo) phenyl)azo)(1,1'-biphenyl)-4-yl)azo]salicylato(4-) cuprate(2-); Cl Direct Brown 95 | 16071-86-6 |
| cadmium oxide | 1306-19-0 |
| Extracts (petroleum), heavy naphthenic distillate solvent | 64742-11-6 |
| Extracts (petroleum), heavy paraffinic distillate solvent | 64742-04-7 |
| Extracts (petroleum), light naphthenic distillate solvent | 64742-03-6 |
| Extracts (petroleum), light paraffinic distillate solvent | 64742-05-8 |
| Extracts (petroleum), light vacuum gas oil solvent | 91995-78-7 |
| Hydrocarbons, C26-55, arom. rich | 97722-04-8 |
| N,N-dimethylhydrazine | 57-14-7 |
| acrylamide | 79-06-1 |
| acrylonitrile | 107-13-1 |

| Substance | CAS Number |
|---|---|
| ga, ga, ga–trichlorotoluene; benzotrichloride | 98-07-7 |
| benzo[a]anthracene | 56-55-3 |
| benzo[a]pyrene; benzo[d,e,f]chrysene | 50-32-8 |
| benzo[b]fluoranthene;benzo[e]acephenanthrylene | 205-99-2 |
| benzo[j]fluoranthene | 205-82-3 |
| benzo[k]fluoranthene | 207-08-9 |
| beryllium | 7440-41-7 |
| beryllium compounds with the exception of aluminium | |
| beryllium silicates | — |
| cadmium chloride | 10108-64-2 |
| cadmium sulphate | 10124-36-4 |
| calcium chromate | 13765-19-0 |
| captafol (ISO); 1,2,3,6-tetrahydro-N-(1,1,2,2-tetrachloroethylthio)phthalimide | 2425-06-1 |
| carbadox (INN); methyl-3-(quinoxalin-2-ylmethylene)carbazate 1,4-dioxide; 2-(methoxycarbonylhydrazonomethyl)quinoxaline 1,4-dioxide | 6804-07-5 |
| chromium III chromate; chromic chromate | 24613-89-6 |
| diazomethane | 334-88-3 |
| dibenz[a,h]anthracene | 53-70-3 |
| diethyl sulphate | 64-67-5 |
| dimethyl sulphate | 77-78-1 |
| dimethyl carbamoyl chloride | 79-44-7 |
| N-nitrosodimethylamine; dimethylnitrosamine | 62-75-9 |
| dimethylsulfamochloride | 13360-57-1 |
| 1-chloro-2,3-epoxypropane; epichlorohydrin | 106-89-8 |
| 1,2-dichloroethane; ethylene dichloride | 107-06-2 |
| ethylene oxide; oxirane | 75-21-8 |
| ethyleneimine; aziridine | 151-56-4 |
| hexachlorobenzene | 118-74-1 |
| hexamethylphosphoric triamide; hexamethylphosphoramide | 680-31-9 |
| hydrazine | 302-01-2 |
| hydrazobenzene; 1,2-diphenylhydrazine | 122-66-7 |
| methyl acrylamidomethoxyacetate (containing $\geqslant$ 0.1% acrylamide) | 77402-03-0 |

| Substance | CAS Number |
|---|---|
| methyl-ONN-azoxymethyl acetate; methyl azoxy methyl acetate | 592-62-1 |
| nitrofen (ISO); 2,4-dichlorophenyl 4-nitrophenyl ether | 1836-75-5 |
| nitrosodipropylamine | 621-64-7 |
| 2-methoxyaniline; o-anisidine | 90-04-0 |
| potassium bromate | 7758-01-2 |
| propylene oxide; 1,2-epoxypropane; methyloxirane | 75-56-9 |
| o-toluidine | 95-53-4 |
| 2-methylaziridine; propyleneimine | 75-55-8 |
| salts of 2,2'-dichloro-4,4'-methylenedianiline; salts of 4,4'-methylenebis (2-chloroaniline) | — |
| salts of 3,3'-dichlorobenzidine; salts of 3,3'-dichlorobiphenyl-4,4'-ylenediamine | — |
| salts of 3,3'-dimethoxybenzidine; salts of o-dianisidine | — |
| salts of 3,3'-dimethylbenzidine; salts of o-toluidine | — |
| strontium chromate | 7789-06-2 |
| styrene oxide; (epoxyethyl)benzene; phenyloxirane | 96-09-3 |
| sulfallate (ISO); 2-chlorallyl diethyldithiocarbamate | 95-06-7 |
| thioacetamide | 62-55-5 |
| urethane (INN); ethyl carbamate | 51-79-6 |
| *Mutagenic substances of Category 1* | |
| There are no substances classified in this category | |
| *Mutagenic substances of Category 2* | |
| 1,2-dibromo-3-chloropropane | 96-12-8 |
| acrylamide | 79-06-1 |
| benzo[a]pyrene; benzo[d,e,f]chrysene | 50-32-8 |
| diethyl sulphate | 64-67-5 |
| ethylene oxide; oxirane | 75-21-8 |
| ethyleneimine, aziridine | 151-56-4 |
| hexamethylphosphoric triamide; hexamethylphosphoramide | 680-31-9 |
| methyl acrylamidomethoxyacetate (containing $\geq$ 0.1% acrylamide) | 77402-03-0 |
| *Toxic for reproduction substances of Category 1* | |
| lead hexafluorosilicate | 25808-74-6 |
| lead acetate | 1335-32-6 |

| Substance | CAS Number |
|---|---|
| lead alkyls | — |
| lead azide | 13424-46-9 |
| lead chromate | 7758-97-6 |
| lead compounds, with the exception of those specified elsewhere in this Part of this Schedule | — |
| lead di(acetate) | 301-04-2 |
| lead 2,4,6-trinitroresorcinoxide; lead styphnate | 15245-44-0 |
| lead (II) methanesulfonate | 17570-76-2 |
| trilead bis(orthophosphate) | 7446-27-7 |
| warfarin; 4-hydroxy-3-(3-oxo-1-phenylbutyl)coumarin | 81-81-2 |
| *Toxic for reproduction substances of Category 2* | |
| 2-ethoxyethanol; ethylene glycol monoethyl ether | 110-80-5 |
| 2-ethylhexyl 3,5-bis(1,1-dimethylethyl)-4-hydroxyphenyl methyl thio acetate | 80387-97-9 |
| 2-methoxyethanol, ethylene glycol monoethyl ether | 109-86-4 |
| benzo[a]pyrene; benzo[d,e,f]chrysene | 50-32-8 |
| binapacryl (ISO); 2-sec butyl-4,6-dinitrophenyl-3-methylcrotonate | 485-31-4 |
| N,N-dimethylformamide; dimethyl formamide | 68-12-2 |
| dinoseb; 6-sec butyl-2,4-dinitrophenol | 88-85-7 |
| dinoterb; 2-tert-butyl-4,6-dinitrophenol | 1420-07-1 |
| ethylene thiourea; imidazolidine- 2-thione; 2-imidazoline-2-thiol | 96-45-7 |
| 2-ethoxyethyl acetate; ethylglycol acetate | 111-15-9 |
| methyl-ONN-azoxymethyl acetate; methyl azoxy methyl acetate | 592-62-1 |
| 2-methoxyethyl acetate; methylglycol acetate | 110-49-6 |
| nickel tetracarbonyl | 13463-39-3 |
| nitrofen (ISO); 2,4-dichlorophenyl 4-nitrophenyl ether | 1836-75-5 |
| salts and esters of dinoseb, with the exception of those specified elsewhere in this Part of this Schedule | — |
| salts and esters of dinoterb | — |
| *Chlorinated solvents requiring additional labelling phrase* | |
| chloroform | 67-66-3 |
| carbon tetrachloride | 56-23-5 |
| 1,1,2-trichloroethane | 79-00-5 |

| Substance | CAS Number |
|---|---|
| 1,1,2,2-tetrachloroethane | 79-34-5 |
| 1,1,1,2-tetrachloroethane | 630-20-6 |
| pentachloroethane | 76-01-7 |
| 1,1-dichloroethylene | 75-35-4 |
| 1,1,1-trichlororethane | 71-55-6 |

[*Reg 9(3A), (3B), Sch 6 Part III A, B, as inserted by SI 1996 No 1092*].

### Further labelling requirements

D1022   All labels for supply purposes must be indelibly marked and securely fixed to the package and the hazard warning sign must stand out from its background so that it is clearly noticeable. It must be possible to read the label horizontally when the package is set down normally and it must have a side length of 100 square millimetres. If it is not possible to comply with any of the requirements because of the shape of the package, it should be attached in some other appropriate manner.

The dimensions of the label for substances and preparations dangerous for supply are reproduced below.

| Capacity of package | Dimensions of label |
|---|---|
| (a) not exceeding 3 litres | if possible at least 52 × 74 millimetres |
| (b) exceeding 3 litres but not exceeding 50 litres | at least 74 × 105 millimetres |
| (c) exceeding 50 litres but not exceeding 500 litres | at least 105 × 148 millimetres |
| (d) exceeding 500 litres | at least 148 × 210 millimetres |

[*Reg 11*].

### Enforcement/penalties and civil liability

(*a*) *Enforcement*

D1023   The HSE is the enforcing authority for *CHIP Regulations*, except where the dangerous substance is supplied from a registered chemist, where the Royal Pharmaceutical Society is the enforcing authority. If the supply is from a shop, mobile vehicle or market stall, or to members of the public, the local Weights and Measures Authority is the enforcing authority. [*Reg 16(2)*].

(*b*) *Penalties*

Breach of the provisions of the *Chemicals (Hazard Information and Packaging for Supply) Regulations 1994* carries the same penalties as breach of the *HSWA* itself (see E15032 ENFORCEMENT).

## (c) Defence

It is a defence to a charge under these regulations that a person took all reasonable care and exercised all due diligence to avoid commission of that offence [*Reg 16(4)*] – a difficult test to satisfy (see *J H Dewhurst Ltd v Coventry Corporation [1969] 3 AER 1225*).

## (d) Civil liability

Where breach of duty causes damage/injury, this can give rise to civil liability. [*Reg 16(1)(b)*].

# Control of substances hazardous to health – Control of Substances Hazardous to Health Regulations 1999 (SI 1999 No 437) (COSHH)

**D1024**  The Control of Substances Hazardous to Health Regulations 1999 (SI 1999 No 437) came into force on 25 March 1999 and revoke and replace the following Regulations: the Control of Substances Hazardous to Health Regulations 1994 (SI 1994 No 3246), the Control of Substances Hazardous to Health (Amendment) Regulations 1996, the Control of Substances Hazardous to Health (Amendment) Regulations 1997, and the Control of Substances Hazardous to Health (Amendment) Regulations 1998. The new Regulations re-enact, with minor modifications, the 1994 Regulations as amended.

COSHH provides a comprehensive and systematic approach to the control of hazardous substances at work, where risk to health and the costs of failure are often substantial in both human and economic terms. The Regulations require employers to:

—   assess risks to health arising from exposure to hazardous substances;

—   prevent or adequately control exposure;

—   ensure control measures are used, maintained, examined and tested;

—   in some instances, monitor exposure and carry out appropriate health surveillance; and

—   inform, instruct and train employees.

In addition to minor and drafting amendments, the 1999 Regulations make the following changes of substance:

(a)   provide for the approval by the Health and Safety Commission of maximum exposure limits for substances in place of the provisions previously contained in *Schedule 1* to the *1994 Regulations*;

(b)   include certain further definitions, including:

•   expanding the definition of 'a substance hazardous to health' to include trigger limits for 'total inhalable dust' or 'respirable dust';

•   minor changes to the definitions of 'carcinogen' and 'Member State';

(c)   require personal protective equipment provided by an employer in pursuance of these Regulations to comply with the *Personal Protective Equipment (EC Directive) Regulations 1992 (SI 1992 No 3139)*;

(d)   give members of the armed forces an appeal against suspension from work on medical grounds; and (*e*)    revise the Schedule of *Other substances and processes to which the definition of 'carcinogen' relates* [*Sch 8*].

The 1999 Regulations thus see the removal of the schedule listing the substances assigned maximum exposure limits (MELs).

For maximum exposure limits and occupational exposure standards (OESs), see Appendix A at D1083 below.

More particularly, a 'substance hazardous to health' is a substance (or preparation):

(*a*)    listed in Part I of the 'Approved Supply List' as dangerous (see D1014 above);

(*b*)    for which the HSE has approved –

   (i)    a maximum exposure limit (MEL), or

   (ii)    an occupational exposure standard (OES)

(see Appendix A at D1083 below);

(*c*)    a biological agent (including micro-organisms, endoparasites, cell cultures);

(*d*)    a substantial concentration of airborne dust (see VENTILATION); or

(*e*)    any other substance creating a comparable health hazard.

[*Control of Substances Hazardous to Health Regulations 1999, Reg 2(1)*].

Although not specified above, these regulations also extend to (*a*) carcinogens (see D1045 below) and (*b*) respiratory sensitisers (see D1049 below).

However, the regulations do not cover:

   (i)    asbestos but may do so eventually (see ASBESTOS);

   (ii)    lead (see D1050 below);

   (iii)    ionising radiations (see D1052 below); and

   (iv)    highly flammable liquids and liquefied petroleum gases.

### Duties under COSHH

(*a*) *Employers*

D1025    Employers owe duties to employees, indirect workers and self-employed personnel, except as regards:

(*a*)    health surveillance (duty owed to employees only) [*Reg 11*]; and

(*b*)    monitoring information and training [*Regs 10, 12*] (duties owed to employees but also to others on premises where work is being carried on).

[*Reg 3(1)*].

The main duties are as follows:

(1)    to carry out (and review) a formal independent assessment of health risks to employees [*Reg 6*] (see D1026 below);

(2)    to prevent/control exposure of employees to health risks [*Reg 7*] (see D1027 below);

(3)    to institute proper use of controls and personal protective equipment [*Reg 8*] (see also PERSONAL PROTECTIVE EQUIPMENT);

(4)   to maintain, examine and test controls and keep records [*Reg 9*] (see D1029 below);

(5)   to monitor workplace exposure of employees [*Reg 10*] (see D1030 below);

(6)   provide health surveillance for employees, where necessary [*Reg 11*] (see D1031 below);

(7)   provide information, instruction and training regarding hazardous substances [*Reg 12*].

*(b) Employees*

(1)   to make full and proper use of control measures and personal protective equipment [*Reg 8(2)*];

(2)   at the cost of the employer, to present themselves for health surveillance [*Reg 11(9)*] (see D1042 below).

## Risk assessments (Regulation 6)

D1026   The object of a risk assessment is to enable decisions to be made regarding measures necessary to impose the requisite controls on 'substances hazardous to health'; in addition, a formal assessment system is proof that a particular organisation has taken cognisance of health hazards and has implemented, or is about to do so, steps to eliminate/minimise their incidence. More particularly, assessments should identify:

(i)   risks posed to the health of the workforce;

(ii)   steps necessary to control exposure to those hazards;

(iii)   other action necessary to achieve compliance with regulations relating to maintenance requirements and personal protective equipment; and

(iv)   the extent of exposure.

Merely following suppliers' product data is not necessarily sufficient for compliance purposes; HSE Guidance Notes and manufacturers' standards should also be consulted. Not to do so is to be left open to the charge that one has not done all that was 'reasonably practicable' – this statutory requirement implying that employers should keep up to date with the latest HSE, industrial and technical publications (*Stokes v Guest, Keen & Nettlefold (Bolts and Nuts) Ltd [1968] 1 WLR 1776*) (see E11006 EMPLOYERS' DUTIES TO THEIR EMPLOYEES).

## Controlling exposure (Regulation 7)

D1027   Employers must ensure that employees are not exposed to substances hazardous to health, where this can be prevented; if not possible, however, exposure must be adequately controlled. [*Reg 7(1)*]. So far as reasonably practicable, measures not requiring use of personal protective equipment should be used (except in the case of (*a*) carcinogens (see D1045 below) and (*b*) biological agents [*Reg 7(2)*]). Whilst maximum exposure must be below maximum exposure limits, control is only adequate if exposure is reduced to the lowest reasonably practicable. (Approved methods for averaging over specified reference periods appear year-on-year in updated form in Guidance Note EH 40 – 'Occupational exposure limits'.) There is no liability if exposure does not exceed the approved occupational standard, or if the employer acts quickly to remedy any excess, as soon as reasonably practicable.

Where measures do not prevent or adequately control exposure, employers must, in addition, supply employees with suitable personal protective equipment. [*Reg 7(4)*].

Such personal protective equipment/clothing must conform with statutory requirement and/or EU specification/standard; similarly, respiratory equipment (see PERSONAL PROTECTIVE EQUIPMENT). [*Reg 7(5)(8)*]. Moreover, employers must ensure that control measures and personal protective equipment/respiratory equipment are properly used and applied as well as regularly maintained in conjunction with systematic defects reporting. Records of tests/examinations, and any repairs consequent thereupon, should be kept for up to five years. [*Reg 9(4)*].

*Measures for preventing or controlling exposure*

**D1028**    These consist either exclusively or in combination of the following:

(*a*)    for preventing exposure;

   (i)    elimination of the use of the substance;

   (ii)   substitution by a less hazardous substance or by the same substance in a less hazardous form;

(*b*)    for controlling exposure:

   (i)    totally enclosed process and handling systems;

   (ii)   plant or processes or systems of work which minimise generation of, or suppress or contain, the hazardous dust, fume, micro-organisms etc. and which limit the area of contamination in the event of spills and leaks;

   (iii)  partial enclosure, with local exhaust ventilation;

   (iv)   local exhaust ventilation;

   (v)    sufficient general ventilation;

   (vi)   reduction of numbers of employees exposed and exclusion of non-essential access;

   (vii)  reduction in the period of exposure for employees;

   (viii) regular cleaning of contamination from, or disinfection of, walls, surfaces etc;

   (ix)   provision of means for safe storage and disposal of substances hazardous to health;

   (x)    suitable personal protective equipment;

   (xi)   prohibition of eating, drinking, smoking etc. in contaminated areas;

   (xii)  provision of adequate facilities for washing, changing and storage of clothing, including arrangements for laundering contaminated clothing.

In existing work situations, the present control measures should be carefully reviewed, and improved, extended or replaced as necessary to be capable of achieving, and sustaining, adequate control.

If, in spite of the above control measures, leaks, spills or uncontrolled releases of a hazardous substance could still occur, means should be available for limiting the extent of risks to health and for regaining adequate control as soon as possible. The means should include, where appropriate, established emergency procedures, safe disposal of the substance and sufficient suitable personal protective equipment to enable the source of the release to be safely identified and repairs to be made. All persons not concerned with the emergency action should be excluded from the area of contamination.

The Health & Safety Executive has published a free leaflet, '*Solvents and You*' – it advises people who work with solvents about the precautions they should be aware of. It specifically draws attention to the danger of working in confined spaces with solvents where particularly high exposures can occur.

The key aspects of emergency procedures in respect of chemical spillages or releases of corrosive, toxic or flammable materials, dust explosions and fires are detailed in another free HSE leaflet, '*Prepared for Emergency*' (ref: IND(G) 246L).

## Engineering controls – records of examination and test

D1029    Engineering controls should be subject to regular examination and test and records kept as follows:

| | | |
|---|---|---|
| (*a*) | local exhaust ventilation plant – every 14 months | |
| (*b*) | local exhaust ventilation plant in the following specific industries: | |
| | — blasting for the cleaning of metal castings | – every month |
| | — 12 hours in any week (not gold, platinum or iridium): | – every 6 months |
| | — non-ferrous metal castings | – every 6 months |
| | — jute cloth manufacture | – every month |
| (*c*) | any other case | – at suitable intervals |

[*Control of Substances Hazardous to Health Regulations 1999, Reg 9, Sch 4*].

## Monitoring exposure at the workplace

D1030    Where employees are exposed to substances hazardous to health, employers must ensure that there is adequate monitoring of exposure and records kept for 40 years. In particular, in the case of exposure to

(*a*)    vinyl chloride monomer – monitoring must be continuous;

(*b*)    vapour/spray emitted by electrolytic chromium processes (except trivalent chromium) – every 14 days.

[*Control of Substances Hazardous to Health Regulations 1999, Reg 10, Sch 5*].

## Provision of health surveillance

D1031    Health surveillance must be arranged by employers for employees following certain classifications as follows:

(A)    Schedule 6 employees;

(B)    where exposure is associated with either an identifiable disease (see OCCUPA-TIONAL HEALTH AND DISEASES) or adverse health effects (see, for instance, legionella at D1032 below).

### (A) Schedule 6 employees

*Schedule 6* requires that health surveillance of employees under an employment medical adviser or appointed doctor must be arranged by employers at intervals of not more than 12 months, i.e. employees exposed to:

(*a*)    vinyl chloride monomer (VCM) whilst engaged in

    (i)   manufacture,

    (ii)   production,

    (iii)   reclamation,

    (iv)   storage,

    (v)   discharge,

    (vi)   transport,

    (vii)   use,

    (viii)   polymerisation,

    (unless exposure is insignificant);

(*b*)    nitro/amino derivatives of phenol/benzene (or its homologues) whilst engaged in

    (i)    manufacture of nitro/amino derivatives of phenol/benzene, and

    (ii)    making of explosives with such substances;

(*c*)    potassium or sodium chromate or dichromate, whilst engaged in manufacture;

(*d*)    1-naphthylamine, orthotolidine, dianisidine, dichlorbenzidine, whilst engaged in manufacture;

(*e*)    auramine, magenta, whilst engaged in manufacture;

(*f*)    carbon disulphide, disulphur dichloride, benzene (and benzol), carbon tetrachloride, trichlorethylene, whilst engaged in processes in which these substances are

    (i)    used,

    (ii)    given off as vapour,

    in the manufacture of indiarubber or its articles or goods;

(*g*)    pitch, whilst engaged in manufacture of blocks of fuel consisting of

    (i)    coal,

    (ii)    coal dust,

    (iii)    coke/slurry,

    with pitch as a binding ambience.

### (B) Exposure-related identifiable diseases

Exposure to a whole range of substances at work can lead over a period of time to the onset of identifiable diseases and/or adverse health effects. Indeed, exposure to certain substances can lead to diseases which are prescribed, that is, for which disablement benefit is payable, without the employee having to establish negligence against his employer(s) (see OCCUPATIONAL HEALTH AND DISEASES); or to non-notifiable diseases (e.g. legionnaire's disease). Legionnaire's disease is neither notifiable (except in Scotland) (see Appendix B at A3030 ACCIDENT REPORTING) nor is it a prescribed occupational disease (see O1043 OCCUPATIONAL HEALTH AND DISEASES) though it is serious enough to have resulted in fatalities.

## Legionella

D1032      Between 100 and 200 cases of legionella are reported each year in England and Wales. *COSHH Regulations* extend to the prevention and control of risks from hazardous micro-organisms, including legionella. Occupiers of non-domestic premises must inform the local authority in writing where a 'notifiable device' exists on their premises. [*Notification of Cooling Towers and Evaporative Condensers Regulations 1992 (SI 1992 No 2225), Reg 3(1)*]. A 'notifiable device' is a cooling tower or an evaporative condenser, but not one

(*a*)    containing no water exposed to air; or

(*b*)    whose water/electricity supply is not connected.

[*Notification of Cooling Towers and Evaporative Condensers Regulations 1992, Reg 2*].

So far as reasonably practicable, employers (and occupiers), as regards factories, hospitals, laboratories, schools and construction sites with

(i)    water systems incorporating a cooling tower,

(ii)    water systems incorporating an evaporative condenser,

(iii)    hot water services (except where the volume of water does not exceed 300 litres),

(iv)    hot/cold water services (irrespective of size) in particularly susceptible premises (e.g. health care premises),

(v)    humidifiers/air washers, creating water droplets, where water temperature is likely to exceed 20°C,

(vi)    spa baths/pools where warm water is recirculated,

must

(1)    identify/assess sources of risk;

(2)    prepare schemes for preventing/controlling risk;

(3)    implement precautions;

(4)    keep records of precautions.

All systems (particularly those in nursing homes/hospitals) susceptible to colonisation by legionella should be assessed, with particular regard to

(A)    droplet formation potential;

(B)    water temperature;

(C)    risk to anyone inhaling water droplets;

(D)    means of preventing/controlling risk.

### Vulnerable areas of the workplace

D1033      The two most vulnerable areas of the workplace are (*a*) hot (and sometimes cold) water services and (*b*) air conditioning and industrial cooling systems.

### (a) Hot (and cold) water systems

Colonising typically storage tanks, calorifiers, pipework, dead legs, water softeners and filters, as well as taps and showers, legionella can proliferate in warm water temperatures. Cold water services normally are not so vulnerable, except in the case of large cold water systems where use is intermittent or where water temperatures can exceed 20°C.

### (b) Air conditioning/industrial cooling systems

Typically heated to 30°C, water from the cooling tower can become heavily contaminated by dust, slime and sludge, thereby providing ideal conditions for legionella to breed. Emanating from cooling towers, legionnaire's disease has resulted to date in a number of fatalities at work, and passers-by, as well as employees, are also at risk. Indeed, most industrial cooling systems operate at temperatures ideal for germination of legionella. Also, evaporative condensers have an industrial cooling function and are used for air conditioning purposes. Since the volume of water in such condensers is less than in a cooling tower, control of water quality is more difficult.

## Suitable precautions

D1034    (a) *Hot water systems*

Water services should be checked regularly and well maintained, particularly

(i)   water temperatures at calorifiers;

(ii)  water temperatures at taps after one minute's running (in any case, all taps should be inspected at least once a year);

(iii) tanks, for organic/bacteriological material (should be inspected at least annually);

(iv)  calorifiers, for organic/bacteriological material;

(v)   accessible pipework and insulation.

Where there is risk of legionnaire's disease, water systems should be disinfected, to BS 6700 'Specification for the design, installation, testing and maintenance of services supplying water for domestic use within buildings'. This can be achieved chemically, by chlorination, or thermally, by simply raising the temperature of the water to such level that legionella cannot survive.

In addition,

(vi)  avoid water temperatures between 20°C and 45°C;

(vii) avoid water stagnation;

(viii) avoid use of materials that harbour bacteria;

(ix)  keep system clear so as to avoid accumulation of sediment harbouring bacteria;

(x)   make use of water treatment systems and chemicals;

(xi)  ensure the whole system operates safely.

*(b)* *Cooling towers/air conditioning systems*

Precautions here include

(i)  designing cooling towers to ensure that aerosol release is minimised;

(ii)  locating towers away from ventilation inlets, opening windows and populated areas (in practice, cooling towers and air inlets are often situated together at roof level);

(iii)  maintaining the system in a clean and sound condition;

(iv)  controlling water quality.

### Prosecutions for legionella

D1035    Where an employer is prosecuted (under *Sec 3(1)* of the *Health and Safety at Work etc. Act 1974*) with exposing members of the public to health risks from legionella, it is not necessary to show that members of the public had actually inhaled bacterium, or that it had been there to be inhaled; it was enough that there had been a risk of its being there (*R v Board of Trustees of the Science Museum [1994] IRLR 25*).

## Protection against biological agents – COSHH 1999, Schedule 3

D1036    *COSHH 1999, Sch 3* contains special provisions relating to protection against biological agents, meaning micro-organisms, cell cultures, human endoparasites (including any genetically modified) which might cause infection, allergy, toxicity, or otherwise create a health hazard, including colonisation of a worker by tumour-derived cells, and listed pathogens. Most biological agents are micro-organisms (bacteria, fungi, viruses and microscopic parasites) classified, according to ascending propensity to cause infection, as follows:

*(a)*  Group 1 – unlikely to cause human disease;

*(b)*  Group 2 – can cause human disease;

*(c)*  Group 3 – can cause severe human disease; and

*(d)*  Group 4 – causes severe human disease.

(A comprehensive list of classified biological agents appears in Appendix B at D1084 below.)

### Particularly hazardous biological agents – Part V agents

D1037    Certain particularly hazardous biological agents are singled out, for notification purposes, by *Part V* of *Schedule 3*, as follows:

*(a)*  all Group 4 biological agents;

*(b)*  rabies virus;

*(c)*  simian herpes B virus;

*(d)*  Venezuelan equine encephalitis virus;

*(e)*  tick-borne encephalitis group viruses in Group 3;

*(f)*  monkeypox virus; and

*(g)*  mopeia virus.

## Duties of employers

D1038     The following are the main duties of employers regarding protection of employees (and others) against biological agents.

(*a*)     Risk assessment/control of exposure –

(i)     when making a risk assessment (for the purposes of *Reg 6* (see D1026 above)), taking account of the group classification of a biological agent [*para 4*];

(ii)     ensuring exposure of employees to biological agents is prevented by substitution if possible of a less hazardous agent [*para 5*];

(iii)     where (ii) is not reasonably practicable, exposure to an agent must be adequately controlled as follows:

—     keeping as low as practicable the number of employees likely to be exposed,

—     designing the work processes so as to minimise release of biological agents, or

—     displaying the biohazard sign (see D1040 below);

(iv)     preparing plans to deal with accidents involving biological agents;

(v)     specifying appropriate decontamination/disinfection procedures;

(vi)     instituting safe collection/storage/disposal of contaminated waste;

(vii)     specifying procedures for safe handling/transport of biological agents;

(viii)     specifying procedures for taking, handling and processing samples;

(ix)     providing collective/individual protection measures and supplying appropriate protective clothing (see below);

(x)     making available effective vaccines, where necessary;

(xi)     instituting hygiene measures to prevent/reduce accidental transfer/ release of biological agents, including in particular:

—     provision of appropriate/adequate washing/toilet facilities, and

—     prohibition of eating, drinking, smoking, cosmetics application, where there is risk of contamination.

[*para 6*].

(*b*)     Personal protective equipment/clothing – to ensure that personal protective equipment/ clothing is:

(i)     properly stored in a well–defined place;

(ii)     checked and cleaned regularly; and

(iii)     if defective, repaired or replaced.

Moreover, if personal protective equipment/clothing is contaminated by biological agents, it must be:

(i)     removed on leaving the work area;

(ii)     kept apart from uncontaminated clothing/equipment; or

(iii)     decontaminated and cleaned, or, failing that, destroyed.

[*para 9*].

(*c*)   Provision of information/display notices. In the event of:

   (i)   an accident/incident which has/may have resulted in a release of a biological agent that could cause human disease; or

   (ii)   handling of a Group 4 biological agent, to

   —   provide written instructions and (ideally) display notices relating to procedures to be followed,

   —   immediately inform employees/safety representatives of

   (1)   an accident/incident that could cause severe human disease, and

   (2)   as soon as practicable afterwards

   (A)   the cause(s) of such accident/incident, and

   (B)   the steps taken to rectify the situation.

[*para 10*].

(*d*)   List of employees exposed/retention of records – (except where work with biological agents is incidental or does not involve significant risk to health) to keep a list of all employees exposed to Group 3 and Group 4 biological agents for (normally) ten years, to which the employment medical adviser/safety representative has access, specifying:

   (i)   type of work done,

   (ii)   the biological agent in question (where known), and

   (iii)   records of exposures, accidents, incidents.

   Employees have right of access to their own personal records. [*para 11(1), (2), (4) and (5)*].

*Latent infections/retention of records*

In the case of exposures that may result in infections:

(1)   with agents capable of persistent or latent infections;

(2)   which are currently undiagnosable until illness later develops;

(3)   which have particularly long incubation periods;

(4)   which result in recurring illnesses at times over a long period, in spite of treatment; or

(5)   which have long-term consequences;

a record must be kept for forty years, to which the employment medical adviser/ safety representative similarly have access, along with employees themselves in the case of their own files. [*para 11(3)*].

(*e*)   Notification of authorities – the HSE must be notified of the use/storage of biological agents, in the case of:

   (i)   storage, or

   (ii)   use for the first time,

   of one or more biological agents in Groups 2, 3 or 4.

Employers must not (*a*) store or (*b*) use such biological agent, unless at least 30 days before they have notified HSE of the following details:

(1)    name/address of employer and address where biological agent will be stored/used;

(2)    name, qualifications, relevant experience of any employee with specific responsibility for health and safety;

(3)    results of risk assessment (see above);

(4)    group to which biological agent belongs; and

    —    if the agent is specified in Part V (see D1037 above), or

    —    is a Group 3 agent, not requiring approved classification,

the identity of the agent;

(5)    preventive/protective measures necessary;

(6)    each subsequent Part V biological agent (see D1037 above); and

(7)    each subsequent Group 3 biological agent not having an approved classification.

[*para 12(1)(2)*].

(This requirement does not apply if there has been compliance with the *Genetically Modified Organisms (Contained Use) Regulations 1992 (SI 1992 No 3217)*.)

## Consignment

D1039    Employers have a duty not to consign any biological agents in Part V (see D1037 above), or anything containing them, unless they have notified HSE at least 30 days in advance (except where consignment of the biological agent is for diagnosis, disposal or is present in a human being or animal being transported for medical purposes) of:

(*a*)    the identity of the biological agent and volume of the consignment;

(*b*)    name of consignor;

(*c*)    address of premises from which it will be transported;

(*d*)    name of consignee;

(*e*)    address to which it will be transported;

(*f*)    name of transport operator;

(*g*)    name of individual accompanying the consignment;

(*h*)    method of transportation;

(*j*)    packaging/containment precautions;

(*k*)    route; and

(*l*)    proposed date of transportation.

[*para 13*].

### Display of biohazard sign

D1040    Where there is risk of exposure to a biological agent, display the biohazard sign as follows:

[*para 6*].

*fig. 1*

### Duty of employee regarding biological agents

D1041    Every employee must report to his employer, or to the safety officer, any accident/ incident which has/may have resulted in release of a biological agent which could cause severe human disease. [*para 11(2)*].

### Medical examinations

D1042    Medical examination must be carried out by employment medical advisers or appointed doctors in the case of *Schedule 6* employees, e.g. exposure to VCM, and, preferably, in other (non-*Schedule 6*) cases as well. In the case of *Schedule 6* employees, medical examinations must take place annually. They must be paid for by employers and employees are entitled to see employment health records, on giving reasonable notice. Correspondingly, employees must submit to medical examination, when required to do so by the employer, during working hours. [*Reg 11(9)*]. If the employment medical adviser concludes that an employee should no longer be engaged in such work or only under specified conditions, the employer must not permit the employee to do such work or, alternatively, only under specified conditions. [*Reg 11(6)*]. In such circumstances, employees may be entitled to paid leave following suspension on medical grounds. Employers (or employees) who are dissatisfied with such suspension order, can apply to the HSE within 28 days for a review of the decision. [*Reg 11(11)*]. Medical records must be kept by the employer for at least 40 years [*Reg 11(3)*] and, on being given reasonable notice, employers must allow employees access to health records [*Reg 11(8)*].

### Disclosure of information to employees regarding hazardous substances

D1043    Given that prevention is better than cure, the regulations oblige employers to acquaint their employees with the dangers arising from working with substances hazardous to health, and, in consequence, the precautions that they should take.

Specifically, information must

(*a*)    include the results of monitoring exposure;

(*b*)    be given to the employees (or safety representative) where the maximum exposure (MEL) is exceeded in the case of *Schedule 1* substances, e.g. cadmium, carbon disulphide, isocyanates; and

(*c*)    be given about the collective results of health surveillance.

[*Reg 12*].

## Prohibition on use at work of certain hazardous substances

D1044    Certain substances are prohibited from importation which are also not to be used at work, namely:

(*a*)    2-napthylamine, benzidine, 4-aminodiphenyl, 4-nitrodiphenyl, their salts and any substance containing any of those compounds in a total concentration [equal to or greater than 0.1 per cent by mass];

(*b*)    matches filled with white phosphorus.

Benzene must not be supplied for use at work if its use is prohibited by Item 11 in the table below. [*Reg 4*].

In addition to specifying preventive measures, *COSHH* imposes prohibitions on the use at work of the following substances:

| PROHIBITION OF CERTAIN SUBSTANCES HAZARDOUS TO HEALTH FOR CERTAIN PURPOSES | |
|---|---|
| Column 1 | Column 2 |
| *Description of substance* | Purpose for which the substance is prohibited |
| 1.    2-naphthylamine; benzidine; 4-aminodiphenyl; 4-nitrodiphenyl; their salts and any substance containing any of those compounds, in a total concentration equal to or greater than 0.1 per cent by mass. | Manufacture and use for all purposes including any manufacturing process in which a substance described in column 1 of this item is formed. |
| 2.    Sand or other substance containing free silica. | Use as an abrasive for blasting articles in any blasting apparatus. |
| 3.    A substance– | Use as a parting material in connection with the making of metal castings. |
| (a)    containing compounds of silicon calculated as silica to the extent of more than 3% by weight of dry material other than natural sand, zirconium silicate (zircon), calcinated china clay, calcinated aluminous fireclay, sillimanite, calcinated or fused alumina olivine; or | |
| (b)    composed of or containing dust or other matter deposited from a fettling or blasting process. | |

| 4. | Carbon disulphide. | Use in the cold-cure process of vulcanising in the proofing of cloth with rubber. |
|---|---|---|
| 5. | Oils other than white oil, or oil of entirely animal or vegetable origin or entirely of mixed animal and vegetable origin. | Use for oiling the spindles of self-acting mules. |
| 6. | Ground or powdered flint or quartz other than natural sand. | Use in relation to the manufacture or decoration of pottery for the following purposes– |

|   | (a) | the placing of ware for the biscuit fire; |
|---|---|---|
|   | (b) | the polishing of ware; |
|   | (c) | as the ingredient of a wash for saggars, trucks, bats, cranks, or other articles used in supporting ware during firing; and |
|   | (d) | as dusting or supporting powder in potters' shops. |

| 7. | Ground or powdered flint or quartz other than– | | | Use in relation to the manufacture or decoration of pottery for any purpose except– | |
|---|---|---|---|---|---|
|   | (a) | natural sand; or | | (a) | use in a separate room or building for– |
|   | (b) | ground or powdered flint or quartz which forms part of a slop or paste. | | (i) | the manufacture of powdered flint or quartz; or |
|   |   |   |   | (ii) | the making of frits or glazes or the making of colours or coloured slips for the decoration of pottery; |
|   |   |   | (b) | | use for the incorporation of the substance into the body of ware in an enclosure in which no person is employed and which is constructed and ventilated to prevent the escape of dust. |

| 8. | Dust or powder of a refractory material containing not less than 80 per cent. of silica other than natural sand. | Use for sprinkling the moulds of silica bricks, namely bricks or other articles composed of refractory material and containing not less than 80 per cent. of silica. |
|---|---|---|
| 9. | White phosphorus. | Use in the manufacture of matches. |
| 10. | Hydrogen cyanide. | Use in fumigation except when– |

|   | (a) | released from an inert material in which hydrogen cyanide is absorbed; |
|---|---|---|
|   | (b) | generated from a gassing powder; or |

|  |  |  |
|---|---|---|
| (c) | applied from a cylinder through suitable piping and applicators other than for fumigations in the open air to control or kill mammal pests. | |
| 11. | Benzene and any substance containing benzene in a concentration equal to or greater than 0.1 per cent by mass, other than– | Use for all purposes except– <br><br> (a) use in industrial processes; and <br><br> (b) for the purposes of research and development or for the purpose of analysis. |
| | (a) motor fuels covered by Council Directive 85/210/EEC (OJ No L96, 3.4.85, p 25); | |
| | (b) waste covered by Council Directives 75/442/EEC (OJ No L194, 25.7.75, p 39), as amended by Council Directive 91/156/EEC (OJ No L78, 26.3.91, p 32), and 91/689/EEC (OJ No L377, 31.12.91, p 20). | |
| 12. | The following substances– <br><br> Chloroform CAS No 67-66-3; Carbon Tetrachloride CAS No 56-23-5; 1,1,2 Trichloroethane CAS No 79-00-5; 1,1,2,2 Tetrachloroethane CAS No 79-34-5; 1,1,1,2 Tetrachloroethane CAS No 630-20-6; Pentachloroethane CAS No 76-01-7; Vinylidene chloride (1,1 Dichloroethane) CAS No 75-35-4; 1,1,1 Trichloroethane CAS No 71-55-6; and any substance containing one or more of those substances in a concentration equal to or greater than 0.1 per cent by mass, other than– | Supply for use at work in diffusive applications such as in surface cleaning and the cleaning of fabrics except for the purposes of research and development or for the purpose of analysis. |
| | (a) medicinal products; | |
| | (b) cosmetic products. | |

## Carcinogens

D1045    Every employer must ensure that exposure of his employees to substances hazardous to their health is prevented, or if this is not reasonably practicable, is adequately controlled. If it is not reasonably practicable to prevent exposure of any employees to a *carcinogen* by using an alternative substance or process, then these measures must be taken:

(*a*)    the total enclosure of the process and handling systems unless this is not reasonably practicable;

(*b*)　plant, process and systems of work which minimise the generation of, or suppress and contain, spills, leaks, dust, fumes and vapours of carcinogens;

(*c*)　limitation of the quantities of a carcinogen at the place of work;

(*d*)　keeping the number of persons who might be exposed to a carcinogen to a minimum;

(*e*)　prohibiting eating, drinking and smoking in areas that may be contaminated by carcinogens;

(*f*)　the provision of hygiene measures including adequate washing facilities and regular cleaning of walls and surfaces;

(*g*)　the designation of those areas and installations which may be contaminated by carcinogens, and the use of suitable and sufficient warning signs; and

(*h*)　the safe storage, handling and disposal of carcinogens and use of closed and clearly labelled containers.

[*COSHH Regulations 1999, Reg 7(3)*].

If control measures fail and this results in the escape of carcinogens into the workplace, only persons charged with repairs must be allowed into the affected area and they must be provided with appropriate respiratory equipment. Employees must be informed immediately of the risk. [*COSHH Regulations 1999, Reg 7*].

## Definition of a carcinogen

D1046　A carcinogen is any substance/preparation classified as per the *Chemicals (Hazard Information and Packaging for Supply) Regulations 1994, Sch 3 para 15*, and requiring to be labelled with risk phrase R 45 'may cause cancer' or R 49 'may cause cancer by inhalation', whether or not the substance/preparation requires to be classified anyway under *COSHH 1999, Reg 2*, namely:

(*a*)　any of the carcinogenic substances which must be labelled R 45 or R 49, and

(*b*)　any of the following substances/processes, namely,

　　(i)　aflatoxins;

　　(ii)　arsenic;

　　(iii)　auramine manufacture;

　　(iv)　calcining, sintering or smelting of nickel copper matte or acid leaching or electro-refining of roasted matte;

　　(v)　coal soots, coal tar, pitch and coal tar fumes;

　　(vi)　hardwood dusts;

　　(vii)　isopropyl alcohol manufacture;

　　(viii)　leather dust in boot and shoe manufacture, arising during preparation and finishing;

　　(ix)　magenta manufacture;

　　(x)　mustard gas;

　　(xi)　rubber manufacturing and processing giving rise to rubber process dust and rubber fume;

　　(xii)　used engine oils.

[*COSHH 1999, Sch 1*].

Apart from specific requirements relating to the labelling of carcinogens, where it is not reasonably practicable to prevent exposure to a carcinogen employers should institute certain controls (see D1028 above).

### Prohibition on importation of carcinogens

D1047    Importation of the following substances/articles into the United Kingdom is forbidden as being carcinogenic, nor must any such substance/article be supplied for use at work:

(*a*)    2-naphthylamine,
benzidine,
4-aminodiphenyl,
4-nitrodiphenyl,
(and their salts and substances containing any of those compounds in a total concentration exceeding 0.1 per cent);

(*b*)    matches made with white phosphorus;

(*c*)    benzene (except in industrial processes or research).

[*Reg 4*].

### Penalties and defences under COSHH

D1048    Penalties for breach of *COSHH 1999* are as for those of *HSWA* (see E15032 ENFORCEMENT). It is a defence that an accused took all reasonable precautions and exercised all due diligence to avoid commission of the offence. [*Reg 16*].

## Respiratory sensitisers

D1049    A respiratory sensitiser is a substance which can cause the respiratory system to develop a condition liable to make it over-react – sensitisation – if the substance is inhaled again; as well as causing serious chronic diseases, such as asthma and farmer's lung (see OCCUPATIONAL HEALTH AND DISEASES). Symptoms can include rhinitis and mild asthma attacks. Significantly, since sensitisation affects only a minority of workers (or categories of workers), control can be difficult if not elusive, principally because employers may often not recognise the health hazard when present. Particular culprits are allergens and isocyanates, but not untypical are certain anhydrides, reactive dyes and platinum salts. Industries potentially at risk are polyurethane manufacture, food packaging, adhesives, plastics, resins, textile processes and platinum refining. Sensitisation can also occur from nickel in the plating industry, henna in hairdressing, hardwood dust in woodworking and furniture making, as well as in pharmaceutical manufacture, enzyme preparations and foodstuffs – such as egg proteins in food processing and crustaceans in sea-food processing. Flour being baked, grain milled and hay gathered can also have similar effects.

Once sensitised, an employee continually exposed to the sensitising agent will, in all probability, suffer severe symptoms and eventually, possibly, permanent lung damage. For instance, attacks of asthma can be brought on by inhalation of tobacco smoke and cold air, and can persist years after sensitisation. Employers should, therefore, establish a health surveillance programme, using skills of an occupational health doctor and nurse. Once done, such work can be continued by a trained responsible person who should, however, refer symptoms of sensitisation to a doctor.

In order to comply with *COSHH Regulations*, employers should prevent exposure of sensitive employees to respiratory sensitisers but, if this is not 'reasonably practicable', control it. This involves both formal assessment of risks and inventory of necessary control measures as well as provision of adequate information and training. Sensitised employees should be medically advised about the sort of work they can do without further risk to health.

## Control of lead at work – the Control of Lead at Work Regulations 1998 (SI 1998 No 543)

D1050     Many processes can lead to lead poisoning, most commonly lead smelting, melting and burning, vitreous enamelling on glass and metal, pottery glazing, manufacture of lead compounds and accumulators, painting, plumbing, soldering, and rubber production. The *Control of Lead at Work Regulations 1980 (SI 1980 No 1248)* have been revoked and re-enacted with modifications by the *Control of Lead at Work Regulations 1998 (SI 1998 No 543)* which came into force on 1 April 1998.

Employers must:

(i)    assess the health risks to employees created by work involving exposure to lead [*Reg 5*];

(ii)   provide employees with suitable and sufficient information, instruction and training so that the employees know not only the risks to health created by exposure to lead but also the precautions which should be taken [*Reg 11(1)*];

(iii)  ensure, where any employees are liable to receive significant exposure to lead, that a suitable procedure is in place to measure the concentration of lead in air to which the employees are exposed [*Reg 9(1)*], and that records of such air monitoring exercises are kept for at least five years [*Reg 9(5)*];

(iv)   ensure that the exposure of employees to lead is prevented by use of controls other than the mere provision of personal protective equipment – but where this is not reasonably practicable, such exposure to lead must be adequately controlled by way of appropriate control measures (other than the mere provision of personal protective equipment, so far as is reasonably practicable) [*Reg 6(1), (2)*];

(v)    provide personal protective equipment to employees, where necessary, and such equipment must comply with EU requirements or otherwise be approved by the Health and Safety Executive [*Reg 6(4), (6)*];

(vi)   take all reasonable steps to ensure that any control measure or personal protective equipment is properly used or applied, as the case may be [*Reg 6(7)*];

(vii)  ensure that at suitable intervals non-disposable respiratory protective equipment is thoroughly examined and tested [*Reg 8(3)*], and for at least five years employers must keep a record of such examinations and tests [*Reg 8(4)*];

(viii) take adequate steps to ensure, so far as is reasonably practicable, that employees do not eat, drink or smoke in any place which is contaminated by lead (or liable to be contaminated by lead) [*Reg 7(1)*].

In respect of employees who are, or are liable to be, exposed significantly to lead, employers must ensure that they are under surveillance by an appointed doctor or an employment medical adviser [*Reg 10(1)*]. Where medical surveillance is carried out on the premises of the employer, the employer must make sure that suitable facilities are made available [*Reg 10(6)*]. The medical surveillance should be begun, so far as is reasonably practicable, before an employee for the first time commences any work giving rise to exposure to lead, and in any event within fourteen working days of such commencement – and should subsequently be conducted at intervals of not more than twelve months or such shorter intervals as the doctor or employment medical adviser may require [*Sch 2*]. An adequate health record of the medical surveillance of employees should be kept for at least forty years from the date of the last entry made in it [*Reg 10(3)*].

Furthermore, the Regulations introduce various blood-lead action levels and blood-lead suspension levels and urinary lead suspension levels for (i) women of reproductive capacity and (ii) young persons and (iii) other employees, and specify the maximum intervals at which the biological monitoring of such categories of employees must be carried out. In addition, *Sched 1* provides that young persons or women of reproductive capacity may not be employed in any of the following activities:

(*a*)   in lead smelting and refining processes:

—   work involving the handling, treatment, sintering, smelting or refining of ores or materials containing not less than 5 per cent lead; and

—   the cleaning of any place where any of the above processes are carried out;

(*b*)   in lead-acid battery manufacturing processes:

—   the manipulation of lead oxides;

—   mixing or pasting in connection with the manufacture or repair of lead-acid batteries;

—   the melting or casting of lead;

—   the trimming, abrading or cutting of pasted plates in connection with the manufacture or repair of lead-acid batteries; and

—   the cleaning of any place where any of the above processes are carried out.

# Radioactive substances

D1051   Radiation is energy released variously as gamma rays, X-rays, visible light, infra-red and ultraviolet light and microwaves, in the form of waves or particles. The length and frequency of waves (the electromagnetic spectrum) is determined by the quantity of energy released by an atom. It is inherently harmful to people but has also been indispensable in the treatment of certain illnesses and has important industrial uses, such as lasers and welding. Radiation can be natural or of artificial origin; an example of the former is a gamma ray, of the latter an X-ray, such as is used in hospitals, clinics and dental practices. The main danger associated with exposure to radiation is cancer, with exposure to natural radiation being less controllable.

There are two main kinds of radiation, namely, (*a*) ionising radiations, and (*b*) non-ionising radiations, that is, sources lacking the energy to shatter or ionise atoms. Occupationally, the main source of ionising radiation is X-rays; whilst use of non-ionising radiations, in the form of visible, ultraviolet and infra-red light, microwave heat and radio frequency transmissions, is found in industries as various as textiles, furniture, paper, automotive, rubber, plastics, construction, communications and power. Legislation has grafted itself on to the distinction between ionising and non-ionising radiations, the former being controlled currently by the *Ionising Radiations Regulations 1999*, whilst the latter are the subject of a draft EU directive on Physical Agents.

### Effect of radiation exposure

*(a) Ionising radiations*

D1052 Ionising radiations cause tissue damage and the extent of tissue reaction depends on the density of ionisation in the path of radiation – a linear energy transfer (LET). Direct action of radiation on cells can cause cell death or induce mutation. Health effects of radiation can be genetic or somatic, the former affecting offspring, the latter the irradiated individual. Somatic effects take the form of early or late responses, the latter sometimes resulting in induction of malignant disease. Here there may be a latency of several decades between irradiation and tumour appearance.

Workers in hospitals, medical establishments, dental departments, laboratory staff and university researchers are vulnerable to hazards from ionising radiations. Radiation hazards can be emitted from two kinds of sources *(a)* a sealed source, and *(b)* an unsealed source. With the former, a sealed source, the source is contained so that the radioactive material cannot be released, e.g. an X-ray machine. Such radioactive material is usually solid, whereas unsealed sources take the form of gases, liquids or particulates and, because they are unsealed, entry into the body is more easy.

*(b) Non-ionising radiations*

Non-ionising radiations – such as lasers used in welding and cutting, ultraviolet radiation associated with arc welding and infra-red radiation emitted by radiant fires – particularly threaten the eye. Laser beams can cause blindness and exposure to ultraviolet radiation 'arc eye', if goggles or protective glasses are not worn.

## Ionising radiations – the Ionising Radiations Regulations 1999 (SI 1999 No 3232)

### Introduction

D1053 These Regulations replace the *Ionising Radiations Regulations 1985 (SI 1985 No. 1333)* and the *Ionising Radiations (Outside Workers) Regulations 1993 (SI 1993 No. 2379)*. They impose duties on employers to protect employees and other persons against ionising radiation arising from work with radioactive substances and other sources of ionising radiation. They also impose certain duties on employees.

The Regulations implement in part provisions of:

*(a)* Council Directive 96/29/EURATOM laying down basic safety standards for the protection of the health of workers and the general public against the dangers arising from ionising radiation;

*(b)* Council Directive 90/641/EURATOM on the operational protection of outside workers exposed to the risk of ionising radiation during their activities in controlled areas;

*(c)* Council Directive 97/43/EURATOM on health protection of individuals against the dangers of ionising radiation in relation to medical exposure.

The Regulations came into force on 1 January 2000 except *Reg 5* (requirement for prior authorisation of specified practices) which came into force on 13 May 2000.

### Application

D1054 Subject to certain exceptions the Regulations apply to:

*(a)* any practice, meaning work involving:

(i)   the production, processing, handling, use, holding, storage, transport or disposal of radioactive substances; or

(ii)  the operation of any electrical equipment emitting ionising radiation and containing components operating at a potential difference of more than 5kv,

which can increase the exposure of individuals to radiation from an artificial source, or from a radioactive substance containing naturally occurring radio-nuclides which are processed for their radioactive, fissile or fertile properties. [*Reg 2(1)*].

(*b*)   any work (other than a practice) carried out in an atmosphere containing radon 222 gas at a concentration in air, averaged over any 24 hour period, exceeding 400Bq m$^{-3}$ except where the concentration of the short-lived daughters of radon 222 in air averaged over any 8 hour working period does not exceed 6.24 x 10$^{-7}$ Jm$^{-3}$; and

(*c*)   any work (other than work referred to in sub-paragraphs (a) and (b) above) with any radioactive substance containing naturally occurring radionuclides. [*Reg 3(1)*].

## Authorisation of specified practices

D1055   A *'radiation employer'* (meaning one who carries out or intends to carry out work with ionising radiation) must not except in accordance with a *prior authorisation* granted by the HSE carry out any of the following practices:

(*a*)   the use of x-ray equipment for the purpose of:

(i)    industrial radiography;

(ii)   the processing of products;

(iii)  research; or

(iv)   the exposure of persons for medical treatment;

(*b*)   the use of accelerators, except electron microscopes unless the practice is of a type which is already subject to a general authorisation given by the HSE and the practice is or is to be carried out in accordance with the current conditions approved by the HSE in respect of that type of practice. [*Reg 5(1), (2)*].

An authorisation may be granted by the HSE subject to conditions and with a time limit and may be revoked at any time. [*Reg 5(3)*].

The radiation employer must notify the HSE of any material change to the circumstances relating to the authorisation. [*Reg 5(4)*].

A radiation employer may appeal to the Secretary of State against:

(*a*)   a decision of the HSE refusing, imposing a time limit on or revoking an authorisation; or

(*b*)   the terms of any conditions attached to the authorisation by the HSE. [*Reg 5(5)*].

## Duties of employers

D1056   (1)   Not to carry out for the first time work with ionising radiation unless at least 28 days prior to commencement of work, he

(*a*)   has notified HSE of the intention to carry out such work;

(*b*)    has supplied the following particulars:

    (i)    name/address of employer;

    (ii)    address of premises where work is to be carried out;

    (iii)    nature of business;

    (iv)    source of radiation, e.g. sealed source, unsealed radioactive substance, electrical equipment, atmosphere containing the short-lived daughters of radon 222;

    (v)    whether any source is to be used at other premises;

    (vi)    dates of notification and commencement of work.

*[Reg 6(2), Sch 2].*

The HSE may require additional particulars to be given of work that has been notified. *[Reg 6(3), Sch 3].*

There are certain exceptions to the general duty to notify, e.g. work at nuclear licensed sites, or involving radionuclides with concentrations of activity not exceeding specified levels (Bq/g). Material changes in work activity have to be notified, though not cessation, except where the site has been or is to be vacated. *[Reg 6(5), (6)].*

A person may provide a defence to the notification requirement if they can prove that:

(*a*)    he neither knew nor had reasonable cause to believe that he had carried out (or might be required to carry out) work with ionising radiation, and

(*b*)    where he had discovered that he had carried out (or was carrying out) work with ionising radiation, he had forthwith notified HSE of the necessary details.

*[Reg 36(1)].*

(2)    Not to commence a new activity involving work with ionising radiation unless he has carried out a *suitable and sufficient* assessment of the risk to any employee or other person in order to identify the measures he needs to take to restrict the exposure of that employee or other person to ionising radiation-.*[Reg 7(1)].* He must not carry out any work with ionising radiation unless he has made an assessment sufficient to demonstrate that:

(*a*)    all hazards that may cause a radiation accident have been identified; and

(*b*)    the risks to employees and other persons arising from those hazards have been evaluated. *[Reg 7(2)].*

Where the assessment shows that a radiation risk to employees or other persons exists from an identifiable radiation accident, the radiation employer must take all reasonable steps to:

    (i)    prevent any such accident;

    (ii)    limit the consequences of any such accident which does occur; and

    (iii)    provide employees with information, instruction, training and equipment necessary to restrict their exposure to ionising radiation. *[Reg 7(3)].*

The radiation employer must also prepare a *contingency plan* designed to ensure, so far as is reasonably practicable, the restriction of exposure to ionising radiation and the health and safety of persons who may be affected by such an accident. [*Reg 12(1)*].

(3)     To restrict, so far as is reasonably practicable (for the meaning of this expression, see E15039 ENFORCEMENT), the exposure of employees, and other persons to ionising radiation [*Reg 8(1)*]; this is to be done preferably by engineering controls and design features which include shielding, ventilation, and containment of radioactive substances. Warning devices and safe systems of work are also to be provided. [*Reg 8(2)(a) and (b)*].

(4)     To provide employees and others (e.g. outside maintenance workers) with adequate and suitable personal protective equipment. [*Reg 8(2)(c)*].

(5)     To ensure that:

(*a*)     where an employee notifies her employer that she is pregnant, the equivalent dose to the foetus is unlikely to exceed 1 mSv during the remainder of the pregnancy; and

(*b*)     where an employee is breastfeeding, the conditions of exposure are restricted so as to prevent significant bodily contamination of that employee. [*Reg 8(5)*].

(6)     To ensure that employees and others are not exposed to ionising radiation for the whole body greater than the following dose limits in any calendar year:

(*a*)     for employees of 18 or over 20 mSv;

(*b*)     for trainees under 18 6 mSv

(*c*)     for any other person (e.g. member of the public) 1 mSv

[*Reg 11, Sch 4*].

(7)     To appoint qualified persons as radiation protection advisers and provide them with adequate information and facilities. [*Reg 13*].

(8)     To ensure that employees who are engaged in work with ionising radiation are given appropriate training in the field of radiation protection and receive such information and instruction as is suitable and sufficient for them to know:

(*a*)     the risks to health created by exposure to ionising radiation;

(*b*)     the precautions which should be taken; and

(*c*)     the importance of complying with the medical, technical and administrative requirements of the Regulations,

and that female employees are informed of the possible risk arising from ionising radiation to the foetus and to a nursing infant and of the importance of those employees informing the employer in writing as soon as possible:

(i)     after becoming aware of their pregnancy; or

(ii)     if they are breast feeding.

[*Reg 14(a), (c)*].

(9)     To ensure that adequate information is given to other persons who are directly concerned with the work with ionising radiation carried on by the employer to ensure their health and safety so far as is reasonably practicable. [*Reg 14(b)*].

(10)  To designate as a *controlled area* any area where effective doses are likely to exceed 6 mSv a year or 30% of any dose limit for employees aged 18 or more [*Reg 16(1)*].

(11)  To designate as a *supervised area* any area (not being a controlled area) where effective doses are likely to exceed 1 mSv a year or 10% of any dose limit for employees aged 18 or more. [*Reg 16(3)*].

(12)  Not to permit employees (or others) to enter or remain in a controlled area, unless the employee (or other person)

  (*a*)  is a classified person (see (13) below);

  (*b*)  is an outside worker (i.e. a classified person employed by someone else); or

  (c)  enters or remains in the area under a written system of work for ensuring that:

    (i)  an employee of 18 or more does not receive a dose of ionising radiation more than would require that employee to be designated as a classified person,

    (ii)  any other person does not receive a dose of ionising radiation greater than the relevant dose limit.

  [*Reg 18(2)*].

(13)  In the case of employees of 18 or over, who are likely to receive an effective dose of ionising radiation greater than 6 mSv a year or 30% of any relevant dose limit, to designate them as '*classified persons*'. [*Reg 20(1)*].

  No such designation may be made, however, unless the medical adviser or appointed doctor has certified in the health record that in his professional opinion a person is fit to be classified. [*Reg 20(2)*].

(14)  In the case of classified persons, to ensure that all significant doses of ionising radiation received are assessed (preferably by use of personal dosemeters), and that health records of (*a*) classified persons and (*b*) employees who have been overexposed, are kept for at least 50 years and to send to the Executive within three months of the end of each calendar year or other agreed period summaries of all dose records for the year. [*Reg 21*].

(15)  In the case of:

  (*a*)  classified persons;

  (*b*)  employees who have received overexposure (but are not classified persons);

  (*c*)  employees engaged in work with ionising radiation on conditions imposed by an employment medical adviser (see above) or appointed doctor;

    (i)  to provide adequate medical surveillance, and

    (ii)  to have and maintain a health record (or copy) for at least fifty years from the date of the last entry and make it available to the employment medical adviser or appointed doctor.

  [*Reg 24(1)-(3)*].

(16)   To make an immediate investigation of any suspected overexposure of any person and, unless there are circumstances that show beyond reasonable doubt that no overexposure could have occurred, as soon as practicable to notify the suspected overexposure to:

(i)   HSE;

(ii)   in the case of an employee of another employer, that other employer;

(iii)   in the case of his own employee, the appointed doctor or employment medical adviser; and

(iv)   the person affected.

The circumstances of the exposure must be investigated and the relevant dose received must be assessed in order to determine, so far as is reasonably practicable, the measures, if any, required to prevent a recurrence of such overexposure. The results of the investigation and assessment must be notified to the persons mentioned above. [*Reg 25(1)*]. The report of the immediate investigation must be kept for at least 2 years and the report into the circumstances for at least 50 years. [*Reg 25(2)*].

## Ionising radiation information sheets (IRIS)

D1057   The HSE is in the process of producing a series of *Ionising Radiation Information Sheets (ISIS)* to provide advice on a range of matters covered by the 1999 Regulations. An Approved Code of Practice relating to the 1999 Regulations has also been published.

These are available from HSE Books.

## Control of radioactive substances

D1058   Control over radioactive substances must be exercised as follows:

(*a*)   so far as reasonably practicable, the substance should be in the form of a sealed source (see D1052 above); the design, construction and maintenance of articles containing and embodying radioactive substances must prevent leakage [*Reg 27(1)(2)*];

(*b*)   records relating to quantity and location of radioactive substances must be kept for at least two years [*Reg 28*];

(*c*)   radioactive substances must be kept in suitable receptacles in a suitable store [*Reg 29(1)*].

## Duties of employees

D1059   Employees are required:

(1)   not to expose themselves (or any other persons) to ionising radiation more than is reasonably necessary for carrying out the work [*Reg 34(1)*];

(2)   to make full and proper use of personal protective equipment [*Reg 34(2)*];

(3)   (in the case of women) to inform the employer as soon as they discover that they are pregnant [*Reg 12(d)*];

(4)   to present themselves for medical examination and tests during working hours (for medical surveillance purposes) (see above) [*Reg 34(5)*];

(5)   to notify their employer of any suspected overexposure [*Reg 34(6)*].

**Penalties**

D1060    Penalties under the *Ionising Radiations Regulations 1999* are as in *HSWA* (see further E15032 ENFORCEMENT).

**Persons undergoing medical exposure**

D1061    In the interest of persons (or patients) undergoing medical exposure, employers must ensure that their employees, carrying out such exposures are qualified and can produce a certificate to that effect. Employers must also retain a record of their training. [*Ionising Radiation (Medical Exposure) Regulations 2000 (SI 2000 No 1059)*].

# Non-ionising radiations – EU Directive on Physical Agents

D1062    In 1993, the European Commission made a proposal for a Council Directive on the minimum safety and health requirements regarding the exposure of workers to risks due to physical agents: (noise, physical vibration, optical radiation and magnetic fields and waves). The proposal as amended by the Commission is currently awaiting a statement of the formal position from the Council.

Regulation for both optical and non-optical radiation is proposed as follows:

(*a*)    *Optical radiation* (i.e. infra-red, visible and ultraviolet light) – threshold level to be *half* the ceiling value (the ceiling value equating with exposure limits recommended by the American Congress of Governmental Industrial Hygienists (ACGIH)). At threshold value, workers

   (i)    must be given adequate information and training;

   (ii)    must be supplied with personal protective equipment, on request;

   (iii)    are entitled to health surveillance.

At ceiling level

   (i)    employers would have to establish a regime of control strategies – copies being sent to safety representatives;

   (ii)    personal protective equipment would have to be used;

   (iii)    hazard areas would have to be designated; and

   (iv)    systematic health surveillance would have to be carried out.

(*b*)    *Non-optical radiation* (electric and magnetic fields with frequencies up to 300 GHz) – threshold level to be *one-fifth* of the ceiling level, ceiling values of electric currents and specific absorption rate of energy in the human body as well as contact current being tabulated. In addition, there are three action levels. At first action level, employers must

   (i)    carry out a risk assessment;

   (ii)    provide workers with information and training;

   (iii)    provide workers with personal protective equipment, on request (in the case of electric fields).

At second action level (1.6 times the value of fields serving as first action levels), employers will have to

   (i)    establish a regime of control strategies;

(ii)  designate hazard areas, restricting access;

(iii)  train operators and check their competence.

At third action level (three times the value of first action level) offending work activities must be notified to HSE. Equipment producing this level will have to be marked.

## Radioactive substances and the environment – Radioactive Substances Act 1993

D1063  Radioactive material – defined for the purposes of the *Radioactive Substances Act 1993* as actinium, lead, polonium, protoactinium, radium, radon, thorium, uranium and the products of nuclear fission – must not be kept on the premises of any undertaking, or caused or permitted to be kept or used on such premises, unless the premises are registered, following an application made to the appropriate Agency (EA or SEPA) [*Sec 6*]. The appropriate Agency can grant or refuse an application. Registration can be made subject to such limitations or conditions as the appropriate Agency thinks fit, including conditions:

—  relating to the premises or any apparatus, equipment or appliance to be used on the premises;

—  requiring the provision of information about removal of radioactive material from the premises; and

—  prohibiting the sale or supply of radioactive material from the premises unless it is labelled or marked as radioactive material.

There is an exemption from registration in respect of premises subject to a nuclear site licence and in respect of premises, undertakings and radioactive materials for which exemption orders have been made by the Secretary of State.

Following registration (or authorisation for waste disposal purposes – see D1067 below), copies of the certificate of registration or authorisation must be posted on the premises in a prominent position so that they can be conveniently read by persons having duties on those premises [*Sec 19*]. The appropriate Agency must send copies of applications and copies of any certificate of registration or authorisation to each local authority in whose area the premises are situated [*Sec 7*]. The appropriate Agency and each such local authority must make copies of registration and authorisation documents available for inspection by the public at all reasonable times and, on payment of a reasonable fee, provide copies [*Sec 39*]. The appropriate Agency may by notice require any person, to whom a registration or authorisation relates, to retain any site or disposal records for a specified period or to furnish the appropriate Agency with copies of records in the event of his registration or authorisation being cancelled or revoked or in the event of his ceasing to carry on the activities regulated by his registration or authorisation [*Sec 20*].

The unregistered keeping, using, lending, letting or hiring of mobile radioactive apparatus for testing, measuring or otherwise investigating any substances or articles, or releasing radioactive material into the environment or introducing it into organisms, is also prohibited [*Sec 9*]. The Secretary of State may by order exempt persons or types of mobile radioactive apparatus from registration [*Secs 10, 11*].

Appeal against refusal of an application for registration or authorisation, against any limitation or condition, against variation, cancellation or revocation of a registration or authorisation lies to the Secretary of State, as does an appeal against an enforcement notice or prohibition notice (see D1068 below) [*Sec 26*].

## Disposal of radioactive waste

D1064    The *Radioactive Substances Act 1993* prohibits disposal or accumulation (with a view to subsequent disposal) of any radioactive waste – other than radioactive waste arising from clocks or watches – except in accordance with an authorisation granted by the appropriate Agency [*Secs 13, 14*]. An authorisation may be granted subject to such limitations or conditions as the appropriate Agency thinks fit [*Sec 16*] and may be revoked or varied at any time [*Sec 17*]. In some cases, the Agency must consult relevant public or local authorities before granting the authorisation [*Sec 18*].

## Enforcement

D1065    The appropriate Agency may serve an *enforcement notice* if it is of the opinion that a person to whom a registration relates or an authorisation was granted is failing to comply with any limitation or condition subject to which the registration or authorisation has effect. A copy of the notice must be sent to any local or public authority to whom a copy of the registration or authorisation was sent [*Sec 21*]. If, however, the appropriate Agency is of the opinion that the keeping or use of radioactive material or of mobile radioactive apparatus, or the disposal or accumulation of radioactive waste, involves an imminent risk of pollution of the environment or of harm to human health, it may serve a *prohibition notice*, whether or not the manner of carrying on the activity complies with any limitations or conditions to which the registration or authorisation is subject [*Sec 22*]. The effect of a prohibition notice is to suspend the registration or authorisation in whole or in part and may specify limitations or conditions to which the registration or authorisation is to be subject until the notice is withdrawn. Again, a copy of the notice, and any further notice withdrawing a prohibition notice, must be sent to any public or local authority that received a copy of the registration or authorisation.

## Offences and penalties

D1066    It is an offence to:

(i)    contravene *sections 6* (use of radioactive material without registration), *9* (use of mobile radioactive apparatus without registration), *13* (disposal of radioactive waste except in accordance with authorisation) or *14* (accumulation of radioactive waste except in accordance with authorisation), or

(ii)    fail to comply with a limitation or condition subject to which a registration or exemption from registration has been granted, or

(iii)    fail to comply with a limitation or condition subject to which an authorisation has been granted, or

(iv)    fail to comply with any requirement of an enforcement or prohibition notice.

The maximum penalties are:

(*a*)    on summary conviction, a fine of up to £20,000 or imprisonment for up to six months, or both;

(*b*)    on conviction on indictment, an unlimited fine or to up to five years' imprisonment, or both.

Any requirement of an enforcement notice or prohibition notice may also be enforced by proceedings in the High Court for an injunction [*Sec 32*].

It is also an offence to contravene *section 19* (duty to display documents relating to registration or authorisation). The maximum penalties are:

(*a*)    on summary conviction, a fine of up to the statutory maximum;

(*b*)    on conviction on indictment, an unlimited fine [*Sec 33(1)*].

It is an offence to fail to comply with a requirement imposed under *section 20* (retention and production of site or disposal records). The maximum penalties are:

(*a*)    on summary conviction, a fine of up to the statutory maximum or up to three months' imprisonment, or both;

(*b*)    on conviction on indictment, an unlimited fine or up to two years' imprisonment, or both [*Sec 33(2)*].

Where a body corporate is guilty of an offence under the Act, and that offence is proved to have been committed with the consent or connivance of, or to be attributable to any neglect on the part of, any director, manager, secretary or other similar officer, or any person purporting to act in such capacity, he, as well as the body corporate, shall be guilty of that offence and liable to be proceeded against and punished accordingly [*Sec 36*].

# Classification and labelling of explosives – Classification and Labelling of Explosives Regulations 1983 (SI 1983 No 1140) as amended by the Carriage of Explosives by Road Regulations 1996 (SI 1996 No 2093)

D1067    Explosive articles and substances fall into one of the following categories, namely those with

|  |  | *Division* |
|---|---|---|
| (*a*) | mass explosion hazard | 1.1 |
| (*b*) | projection hazard (but not mass explosion hazard) | 1.2 |
| (*c*) | fire hazard and either: |  |
|  | (i)    minor blast hazard, or |  |
|  | (ii)   minor projection hazard, or | 1.3 |
|  | (iii)  both |  |
|  | (but not mass explosion hazard) |  |
| (*d*) | no significant hazard | 1.4 |
| (*e*) | very insensitive substances with mass explosion hazard | 1.5 |
| (*f*) | extremely insensitive articles which do not have a mass explosion hazard | 1.6 |

[*Classification and Labelling of Explosives Regulations 1983, Sch 1, as amended by SI 1996 No 2093*].

Explosive articles/substances must not be conveyed, kept or supplied, unless

(i)    they have been classified according to composition, and in the form and packaging necessary, and

(ii)   they and their packaging are correctly labelled.

[*Reg 3*].

*Exceptions*

(1)   explosives being manufactured/tested [*Reg 4(2)*];

(2)   explosives removed from their packaging for immediate use;

(3)   fireworks, small arms ammunition kept by a retailer, or so obtained [*Reg 4(3)*].

Moreover, both the explosives themselves and their inner and outer packagings must be correctly labelled.

## Labelling requirements of explosives

*Packaged explosives*

D1068   (*a*)   Packaged explosives in Class 1 Divisions 1.1, 1.2 and 1.3 must be labelled as in the following figure. (The number relates to the explosives Division Number i.e. 1.2, 1.4, and the letter to its Compatibility Group.)

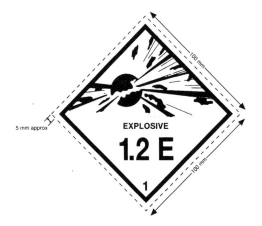

[*Sch 3 para 1*].

(*b*)   Packaged explosives of Divisions 1.4 and 1.5 as follows:

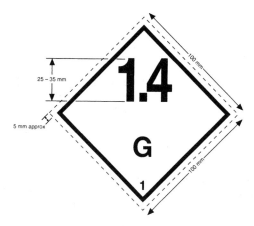

[*Sch 3 para 4*].

(*c*)    packaged explosives not within Class 1 as follows:

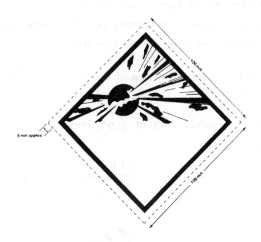

All the above labels are orange with black pictographs, numbers and letters. [*Sch 3 paras 10, 11*]. In addition to the above labels, a second label must be attached to packaged explosives in Class 1 [*Reg 6(1)*] showing:

(i)    its United Nations serial number;

(ii)    its name;

(iii)    if it has been imported, the name and address of the importer; and

(iv)    if it has not been imported, the name and address of the manufacturer.

[*Sch 3 para 12*].

Packaged fireworks in Class 1, Division 1.4 must be labelled 'FIREWORK' (in capital letters) on their outer packaging, with the appropriate hazard warning code i.e. (1.4 S). [*Sch 3 para 8*].

*Unpackaged explosives*

D1069    Unpackaged explosives are labelled in a similar fashion to packaged explosives above.

(*a*)    Unpackaged explosives in Class 1, Divisions 1.1, 1.2 and 1.3 shall be labelled as in D1071(*a*) (above) except that the hazard classification code shall be that for the article when not packaged.

(*b*)    Unpackaged articles (other than a firework) in Class 1, Division 1.4 shall be labelled as in D1071(*b*) (above) except that the hazard classification code shall be that for the article when it is not packaged, or

the word 'EXPLOSIVE' (in capital letters), followed by the hazard classification code (when not packaged) shall be displayed. If the article falls within Division 1.4, Compatibility Group 'S', then 1.4 S shall be displayed.

Unpackaged articles also require a second label to be used. [*Reg 6(2)(4)*]. This is the same as for packaged articles in D1071(i)-(iv) (above). [*Sch 3 para 13*].

## Labelling of packaging

*(a) Explosive articles in respect of which outer packaging must be labelled:*

explosive articles (not specified)

boosters without detonator

demolition charges

detonating cord

igniter cord

electric detonator

non-electric detonator

igniter fuse

safety fuse

detonating fuse

igniters

sounding devices

*[Reg 8(1), Sch 4]*.

*(b) Explosive substances in respect of which both inner and outer packaging must be labelled:*

barium azide

gunpowder

diazodinititrophenol (wetted)

blasting explosives

lead azide (wetted)

mercury fulminate

nitrocellulose

nitroglycerin

nitrostarch

pentolite

powder cake

explosive samples

explosive substances (not specified)

trinitrotoluene (TNT)

tritonal

*[Reg 8(1)(2), Sch 5]*.

In all cases, labelling should be durable and fixed on the packaging and article/ substance or on a piece of paper securely fixed to the packaging and article/ substance. *[Reg 10]*.

### Defence

D1071    It is a defence that a person charged took all reasonable precautions *and* exercised all due diligence to comply. [*Reg 12*]. Generally speaking, this 'due diligence' defence has not been invoked with much success.

## Control of explosives at work – Control of Explosives Regulations 1991 (SI 1991 No 1531)

### Duties of employers

D1072    With the exception of *Schedule 1* explosives, before an employer can acquire and keep explosives, he must

(*a*)    possess a valid explosives certificate to the effect that he is a fit person (i.e. free from criminal conviction);

(*b*)    acquire and keep

(i)    no more than the specified quantity, and

(ii)    only specified explosives

(*a*)    in a specified place, and

(*b*)    for specified purposes

[*Reg 7*].

(*c*)    keep up-to-date records of the explosives and their source for at least three years, which must be made available for inspection by a police officer [*Reg 12, Sch 3*];

(*d*)    report the loss of any explosive [*Reg 13*];

and he must not

(e)    transfer explosives, unless the transferee is in possession of a valid explosives licence and is a fit person [*Reg 8*].

### Enforcement

D1073    The enforcement agency for these regulations is the police. [*Reg 15*].

# Certificate for the purposes of acquiring/keeping explosives

D1074

FORM OF EXPLOSIVES CERTIFICATE

HEALTH AND SAFETY AT WORK ETC. ACT 1974

CONTROL OF EXPLOSIVES REGULATIONS 1991

*CERTIFICATE TO \*ACQUIRE/ACQUIRE AND KEEP EXPLOSIVES*

1. I the undersigned \*being/being duly authorised by the chief officer of police for ..................................police force, do hereby certify that (name) ..................................of (address) ..................................is a fit person to \*acquire/acquire and keep explosives in accordance with this certificate.

**Alternative A—acquisition only**

2. The maximum amount of explosives acquired on any one occasion shall not exceed ..................................

3. The only explosives which may be acquired are those of the following descriptions, namely ..................................................................................................................................

4. Explosives may only be acquired for the purpose(s) of ..................................................

5. This certificate shall be valid until..................................(maximum one year), unless notice of revocation by or on behalf of the chief officer of police has been served on the certificate holder at an earlier date.

*(Notes:*
(a) If this certificate relates to acquisition only, this section must be completed in accordance with these Notes and "alternative B" deleted.
(b) Each of paragraphs 2, 3 and 4 may be completed or deleted.
(c) Paragraph 5 must be completed.)

**Alternative B—acquisition and keeping**

2. The explosives may only be kept at the

\*licensed factory
\*licensed magazine
\*registered premises ⎫
\*store ⎬ at ..................................
\*premises occupied by the Secretary of State
\*premises used for keeping for private use ⎭

3. The only explosives which may be acquired or kept are those of the following descriptions, namely ..................................................................................................................................

4. The amount of explosives kept may not exceed the amount which may lawfully be kept at the said premises.

5. This certificate shall be valid until..................................(maximum three years), unless notice of revocation by or on behalf of the chief officer of police has been served on the certificate holder at an earlier date.

*(Notes:*
(a) If this certificate relates to acquisition and keeping, this section must be completed in accordance with these Notes and "alternative A" deleted.
(b) In paragraph 2 all but one of the alternatives marked with a \* must be deleted. No address should be inserted if the explosives are to be kept at premises used for keeping for private use. An address must be inserted in all other cases.
(c) If paragraph 2 allows explosives to be kept at a store, registered premises or premises used for keeping for private use paragraph 3 must be completed. If paragraph 2 refers to keeping explosives at premises used for keeping for private use, the description of explosives in paragraph 3 must not include any explosives other than one or more of those mentioned in regulation 10(1) of the Regulations.
(d) Paragraph 4 needs no change.
(e) Paragraph 5 must be completed.)

Signed..................................................................................................................................

Date ..................................................................................................................................

\* Delete as applicable                    *fig.2*

*fig.2*

# Marketing and transfer of explosives – Placing on the Market and Supervision of Transfers of Explosives Regulations 1993 (SI 1993 No 2714)

## Design/manufacture and marketing

D1075    With the exception of firearms, explosives for use by the police/armed forces, pyrotechnic articles, explosives used immediately at the place of manufacture, and for life saving purposes in a motor vehicle [*Reg 3(2)*], explosives must not be put into circulation unless:

(*a*)    they satisfy certain essential safety requirements [*Reg 4*], though there is sufficient compliance until 31 December 2002 if the explosives comply with statutory requirements existing on 31 December 1994 (see D1070 above, and DANGEROUS SUBSTANCES II);

(*b*)    their conformity with *SI 1993 No 2714* is attested [*Reg 5*]; and

(*c*)    CE marking has been affixed to the explosives [*Reg 7*].

*Safety criteria*

D1076    Design and manufacture of explosives must be such as to render minimal any risk to the safety of human life and health, property damage and to the environment. Explosives must be tested as to:

(i)    construction, including chemical composition;

(ii)    physical/chemical stability;

(iii)    sensitiveness to impact and friction;

(iv)    compatibility of all components;

(v)    chemical purity;

(vi)    resistance against influence of water;

(vii)    resistance to high/low temperatures;

(viii)    suitability for use in hazardous conditions;

(ix)    prevention of untimely or inadvertent ignition;

(x)    correct loading and functioning;

(xi)    suitable instructions/markings regarding safe handling, storage, use and disposal (in language of the recipient state);

(xii)    ability to withstand deterioration during storage; and

(xiii)    specification of all devices and accessories necessary for reliable and safe functioning.

[*Sch 1*].

*Conformity attestation*

D1077    Attestation of conformity with these regulations consists of:

(i)    EU type examination, and

(ii)    unit verification.

*CE marking*

D1078    CE marking must be visible, easily legible, indelible and, if durable, must remain so during transport/storage. It must be affixed either to the explosives themselves, or an identification plate which cannot be re-used, or to the packaging. [*Sch 3*].

## Transfer of explosives

D1079    Before any explosives are moved within Great Britain (except movement on the same site), the transferee must obtain transfer approval from the HSE, the document to be retained for three years. [*Reg 8*]. This is not applicable to the Crown, as regards explosives for defence purposes, or explosives transferred to or by the HSE. [*Reg 3(3)*].

In addition, as regards plastic explosives, it is proposed by the draft *Marketing of Plastic Explosives for Detection Regulations* that plastic explosives must contain a chemical detection agent before they can be manufactured, imported or possessed.

# Appendix A

## Maximum exposure limits and occupational exposure standards – COSHH Regulations

### (a) Maximum exposure limits

D1080      A maximum exposure limit (MEL) is the maximum concentration of an airborne substance, averaged over a reference period, to which employees may be exposed by inhalation in any circumstances, as specified by the HSC for use with the *Control of Substances Hazardous to Health Regulations 1999 (COSHH 1999)*. *Regulation 7* of *COSHH 1999* requires all employers to reduce the level of exposure to such a substance so far as is reasonably practicable and in any case below the MEL. An employer should carry out a monitoring programme (in accordance with *Reg 10*) to ensure that this requirement is met.

### LIST OF SUBSTANCES WITH APPROVED MAXIMUM EXPOSURE LIMITS

The maximum exposure limits of the dusts included in the list below refer to the total inhalable dust fraction, unless otherwise stated.

| Substance | Formula | Reference periods | | | |
| --- | --- | --- | --- | --- | --- |
| | | Long-term maximum exposure limit (8-hour TWA reference period) | | Short-term maximum exposure limit (15-minute reference period) | |
| | | ppm | mg m$^{-3}$ | ppm | mg m$^{-3}$ |
| Acrylamide | $CH_2=CHCONH_2$ | — | 0.3 | — | — |
| Acrylonitrile | $CH_2=CHCN$ | 2 | 4.4 | — | — |
| Aniline | $C_6H_5NH_2$ | 1 | 4 | — | — |
| Antimony & antimony compounds except stibine (as Sb) | Sb | — | 0.5 | — | — |
| Arsenic & compounds except arsine (as As) | As | — | 0.1 | — | — |
| Azodicarbonamide | $C_2H_4N_4O_2$ | — | 1.0 | — | 3.0 |
| Benzene | $C_6H_6$ | 5 | 16 | — | — |
| Beryllium and beryllium compounds (as Be) | Be | — | 0.002 | — | — |
| Bis (chloromethyl) ether | $ClCH_2OCH_2Cl$ | 0.001 | 0.005 | — | — |
| Buta-1, 3-diene | $CH_2=CHCH=CH_2$ | 10 | 22 | — | — |
| Cadmium & cadmium compounds, except cadmium oxide fume, cadmium sulphide and cadmium sulphide pigments (as Cd) | Cd | — | 0.025 | — | — |
| Cadmium oxide fume (as Cd) | CdO | — | 0.025 | — | 0.05 |

| | | Reference periods | | | |
|---|---|---|---|---|---|
| | | Long-term maximum exposure limit (8-hour TWA reference period) | | Short-term maximum exposure limit (15-minute reference period) | |
| Substance | Formula | ppm | mg m$^{-3}$ | ppm | mg m$^{-3}$ |
| Cadmium sulphide and cadmium sulphide pigments (respirable dust as Cd) | CdS | — | 0.03 | — | — |
| Carbon disulphide | CS$_2$ | 10 | 32 | — | — |
| 1-Chloro-2,3-epoxypropane (Epichlorohydrin) | OCH$_2$CHCH$_2$Cl | 0.5 | 1.9 | 1.5 | 5.8 |
| Chromium (VI) compounds (as Cr) | Cr | — | 0.05 | — | — |
| Cobalt and cobalt compounds (as Co) | Co | — | 0.1 | — | — |
| Cotton dust | | — | 2.5 | — | — |
| 1,2-Dibromoethane (Ethylene dibromide) | BrCH$_2$CH$_2$Br | 0.5 | 3.9 | — | — |
| 1,2-Dichloroethane (Ethylene dichloride) | ClCH$_2$CH$_2$Cl | 5 | 21 | — | — |
| Dichloromethane | CH$_2$Cl$_2$ | 100 | 350 | 300 | 1060 |
| 2,2'-Dichloro–4,4'-methylene dianiline (MbOCA) | CH$_2$(C$_6$H$_3$ClNH$_2$)$_2$ | — | 0.005 | — | — |
| Diethyl sulphate | C$_4$H$_{10}$O$_4$S | 0.05 | 0.32 | — | — |
| Dimethyl sulphate | C$_2$H$_6$O$_4$S | 0.05 | 0.26 | — | — |
| 2-Ethoxyethanol | C$_2$H$_5$OCH$_2$CH$_2$OH | 10 | 37 | — | — |
| 2-Ethoxyethyl acetate | C$_2$H$_5$OCH$_2$CH$_2$OOCCH$_3$ | 10 | 55 | — | — |
| Ethylene oxide | CH$_2$CH$_2$O | 5 | 9.2 | — | — |
| Ferrous foundry particulate | | | | | |
| total inhalable dust | | — | 10 | — | — |
| respirable dust | | — | 4 | — | — |
| Formaldehyde | HCHO | 2 | 2.5 | 2 | 2.5 |
| Glutaraldehyde | C$_5$H$_8$O$_2$ | 0.05 | 0.2 | 0.05 | 0.2 |
| Grain dust | | — | 10 | — | — |
| Halogeno-platinum compounds | | — | 0.002 | — | — |
| Hardwood dust | | — | 5 | — | — |
| Hydrazine | N$_2$H$_4$ | 0.02 | 0.03 | 0.1 | 0.13 |
| Hydrogen cyanide | HCN | — | — | 10 | 11 |
| Iodomethane | CH$_3$I | 2 | 12 | — | — |
| Isocyanates, all (as-NCO) | | — | 0.02 | — | 0.07 |
| Maleic anhydride | C$_4$H$_2$O$_3$ | — | 1 | — | 3 |
| Man-made mineral fibre | | — | 5 | — | — |
| 2-Methoxyethanol | CH$_3$OCH$_2$CH$_2$OH | 5 | 16 | — | — |

| | | Reference periods | | | |
|---|---|---|---|---|---|
| | | Long-term maximum exposure limit (8-hour TWA reference period) | | Short-term maximum exposure limit (15-minute reference period) | |
| Substance | Formula | ppm | mg m$^{-3}$ | ppm | mg m$^{-3}$ |
| 2-Methoxyethyl acetate | $CH_3COOCH_2CH_2OCH_3$ | 5 | 25 | — | — |
| 4,4'-Methylenedianiline | $CH_2(C_6H_4NH_2)_2$ | 0.01 | 0.08 | — | — |
| Nickel and its inorganic compounds (except nickel carbonyl): | Ni | | | | |
| water-soluble nickel compounds (as Ni) | | — | 0.1 | — | — |
| nickel and water- insoluble nickel compounds (as Ni) | | — | 0.5 | — | — |
| 2-Nitropropane | $CH_3CH(NO_2)CH_3$ | 5 | 19 | — | — |
| Phthalic anhydride | $C_8H_4O_3$ | — | 4 | — | 12 |
| Polychlorinated biphenyls (PCB) | $C_{12}H_{(10-X)}Cl_X$ | — | 0.1 | — | — |
| Propylene oxide | $C_3H_6O$ | 5 | 12 | — | — |
| Rosin-based solder flux fume | | — | 0.05 | — | 0.15 |
| Rubber fume | | — | 0.6 | — | — |
| Rubber process dust | | — | 6 | — | — |
| Silica, respirable crystalline | $SiO_2$ | — | 0.3 | — | — |
| Softwood dust | | — | 5 | — | — |
| Styrene | $C_6H_5CH=CH_2$ | 100 | 430 | 250 | 1080 |
| o-Toluidine | $CH_3C_6H_4NH_2$ | 0.2 | 0.89 | — | — |
| Trichloroethylene | $CCl_2=CHCl$ | 100 | 550 | 150 | 820 |
| Triglycidyl isocyanurate (TGIC) | $C_{12}H_{15}N_3O_6$ | — | 0.1 | — | — |
| Trimellitic anhydride | $C_9H_4O_5$ | — | 0.04 | — | 0.12 |
| Vinyl chloride | $CH_2=CHCl$ | 7 | — | — | — |
| Vinylidene chloride | $CH_2=CCl_2$ | 10 | 40 | — | — |
| Wool process dust | | — | 10 | — | — |

[*HSE (EH 40/99)*].

## (b) Occupational exposure standards

An occupational exposure standard (OES), as approved by the HSC, is the concentration of an airborne substance, averaged over a given period, at which, according to current knowledge, there is no evidence that it is likely to be injurious to employees if they are exposed by inhalation, day after day. Where a substance has been assigned an OES, the control of exposure by inhalation will be treated as adequate if that OES is not exceeded. Nevertheless, if exposure exceeds the OES, control is still treated as being adequate if the employer identifies the reason why the OES has been exceeded *and* takes appropriate action to remedy the situation as soon as is reasonably practicable.

HSE has now issued the latest edition of its list of such standards and limits *'EH40/2001 – Occupational Exposure Limits 2001'*. This differs from its predecessors in two respects. Firstly, it contains a new table containing the occupational exposure limits (OELs) derived from the European Commission's first list of Indicative Exposure Limit Values (IOELVs) as set out in Directive 2000/39/00. These limits were agreed by HSC on 19 December 2000 for implementation with effect from 31 December 2001. Although the table is for information only, it gives notice to duty holders of changes to OELs as a result of the implementation IOELVs on the relevant date.

The second way that EH40/2001 differs from previous versions is that HSE has agreed that it should be published in a shortened format – an update of the tables of EH40/2000 with the latter continuing to provide much of the supporting guidance. The reduced cover price of £5.00 reflects this.

The revisions to the lists of OESs and MELs approved by HSE include: one revised OES for ethyl acetate; seven deleted OESs for hydroquinone, manganese and its inorganic compounds, maganese fume, trimanganese tetroxide, chlorobenzene, chloroethane, and phenol – pending the development of MELs; and two new MELs for flour dust and vanadium pentoxide.

Copies of *EH40/2001 – Occupational Exposure Limits 2001* are available from, price £5.00 (£12.00 including a copy of EH40/2000).

# Appendix B

## Approved List of Classified Biological Agents

D1081  Classified biological agents, comprising bacteria, viruses, parasites and fungi, are listed below.

*Notes.*

A:  Possible allergic effects.

D:  List of workers exposed to this biological agent to be kept for 40 years after the end of the last known exposure.

T:  Toxin production.

V:  Effective vaccine available.

## BACTERIA

| Biological Agent | Classification | Notes |
|---|---|---|
| *Acinetobacter calcoaceticus* | 2 | |
| *Acinetobacter lwoffi* | 2 | |
| *Actinobacillus actinomycetemcomitans* | 2 | |
| *Actinomadura madurae* | 2 | |
| *Actinomadura pelletieri* | 2 | |
| *Actinomyces gerencseriae* | 2 | |
| *Actinomyces israelii* | 2 | |
| *Actinomyces pyogenes* | 2 | |
| *Actinomyces* spp | 2 | |
| *Aeromonas hydrophila* | 2 | |
| *Alcaligenes* spp | 2 | |
| *Arcanobacterium haemolyticum (Corynebacterium haemolyticum)* | 2 | |
| *Arizona* spp | 2 | |
| *Bacillus anthracis* | 3 | V |
| *Bacillus cereus* | 2 | |
| *Bacteroides fragilis* | 2 | |
| *Bacteroides* spp | 2 | |
| *Bartonella bacilliformis* | 2 | |
| *Bordetella bronchiseptica* | 2 | |
| *Bordetella parapertussis* | 2 | |
| *Bordetella pertussis* | 2 | V |
| *Borrelia burgdorferi* | 2 | |
| *Borrelia duttonii* | 2 | |

| Biological Agent | Classification | Notes |
|---|---|---|
| *Borrelia recurrentis* | 2 | |
| *Borrelia* spp | 2 | |
| *Brucella abortus* | 3 | |
| *Brucella canis* | 3 | |
| *Brucella melitensis* | 3 | |
| *Brucella suis* | 3 | |
| *Burkholderia cepacia* | 2 | |
| *Burkholderia mallei (Pseudomonas mallei)* | 3 | |
| *Burkolderia pseudomallei (Pseudomonas pseudomallei)* | 3 | |
| *Burkholderia* spp | 2 | |
| *Campylobacter fetus* | 2 | |
| *Campylobacter jejuni* | 2 | |
| *Campylobacter* spp | 2 | |
| *Cardiobacterium hominis* | 2 | |
| *Chlamydia pneumoniae* | 2 | |
| *Chlamydia psittaci* (non avian strains) | 2 | |
| *Chlamydia psittaci* (avian strains) | 3 | |
| *Chlamydia trachomatis* | 2 | |
| *Clostridium botulinum* | 2 | **T, V** |
| *Clostridium perfringens* | 2 | |
| *Clostridium tetani* | 2 | **T, V** |
| *Clostridium* spp | 2 | |
| *Corynebacterium diphtheriae* | 2 | **T, V** |
| *Corynebacterium minutissimum* | 2 | |
| *Corynebacterium pseudotuberculosis* | 2 | |
| *Corynebacterium* spp | 2 | |
| *Coxiella burnetti* | 3 | |
| *Edwardsiella tarda* | 2 | |
| *Ehrlichia sennetsu (Rickettsia sennetsu)* | 3 | |
| *Ehrlichia* spp | 3 | |
| *Eikenella corrodens* | 2 | |
| *Enterobacter aerogenes/cloacae* | 2 | |
| *Enterobacter* spp | 2 | |
| *Enterococcus* spp | 2 | |
| *Erysipelothrix rhusiopathiae* | 2 | |
| *Escherichia coli* (with the exception of non-pathogenic strains) | 2 | |
| *Flavobacterium meningosepticum* | 2 | |
| *Fluoribacter bozemanae (formerly Legionella)* | 2 | |
| *Francisella tularensis* (Type A) | 3 | |

| Biological Agent | Classification | Notes |
|---|:---:|:---:|
| *Francisella tularensis* (Type B) | 2 | V |
| *Fusobacterium necrophorum* | 2 | |
| *Fusobacterium* spp | 2 | |
| *Gardnerella vaginalis* | 2 | |
| *Haemophilus ducreyi* | 2 | |
| *Haemophilus influenzae* | 2 | |
| *Haemophilus* spp | 2 | |
| *Helicobacter pylori* | 2 | |
| *Klebsiella oxytoca* | 2 | |
| *Klebsiella pneumoniae* | 2 | |
| *Klebsiella* spp | 2 | |
| *Legionella pneumophila* | 2 | |
| *Legionella* spp | 2 | |
| *Leptospira interrogans* (all serovars) | 2 | |
| *Listeria ivanovii* | 2 | |
| *Listeria monocytogenes* | 2 | |
| *Moraxella catarrhalis* | 2 | |
| *Moraxella lacunata* | 2 | |
| *Morganella morganii* | 2 | |
| *Mycobacterium africanum* | 3 | V |
| *Mycobacterium avium/intracellulare* | 3 | |
| *Mycobacterium bovis* (BCG strain) | 2 | |
| *Mycobacterium bovis* | 3 | V |
| *Mycobacterium chelonae* | 2 | |
| *Mycobacterium fortuitum* | 2 | |
| *Mycobacterium kansasii* | 3 | |
| *Mycobacterium leprae* | 3 | V |
| *Mycobacterium malmoense* | 3 | |
| *Mycobacterium marinum* | 2 | |
| *Mycobacterium microti* | 3 | |
| *Mycobacterium paratuberculosis* | 2 | |
| *Mycobacterium scrofulaceum* | 3 | |
| *Mycobacterium simiae* | 3 | |
| *Mycobacterium szulgai* | 3 | |
| *Mycobacterium tuberculosis* | 3 | V |
| *Mycobacterium ulcerans* | 3 | |
| *Mycobacterium xenopi* | 3 | |
| *Mycoplasma hominis* | 2 | |
| *Mycoplasma pneumoniae* | 2 | |
| *Neisseria elongata* | 2 | |

| Biological Agent | Classification | Notes |
|---|---|---|
| *Neisseria gonorrhoeae* | 2 | |
| *Neisseria meningitidis* | 2 | V |
| *Nocardia asteroides* | 2 | |
| *Nocardia brasiliensis* | 2 | |
| *Nocardia farcinica* | 2 | |
| *Nocardia nova* | 2 | |
| *Nocardia otitidiscaviarum* | 2 | |
| *Nocardia* spp | 2 | |
| *Pasteurella multocida* | 2 | |
| *Pasteurella* spp | 2 | |
| *Peptostreptococcus anaerobius* | 2 | |
| *Peptostreptococcus* spp | 2 | |
| *Plesiomonas shigelloides* | 2 | |
| *Porphyromonas* spp | 2 | |
| *Prevotella* spp | 2 | |
| *Proteus mirabilis* | 2 | |
| *Proteus penneri* | 2 | |
| *Proteus vulgaris* | 2 | |
| *Providencia alcalifaciens* | 2 | |
| *Providencia rettgeri* | 2 | |
| *Providencia* spp | 2 | |
| *Pseudomonas aeruginosa* | 2 | |
| *Pseudomonas mallei – see Burkholderia mallei* | | |
| *Pseudomonas pseudomallei – see Burkolderia pseudomallei* | | |
| *Rhodococcus equi* | 2 | |
| *Rickettsia akari* | 3 | |
| *Rickettsia canada* | 3 | |
| *Rickettsia conorii* | 3 | |
| *Rickettsia montana* | 3 | |
| *Rickettsia prowazekii* | 3 | |
| *Rickettsia rickettsii* | 3 | |
| *Rickettsia tsutsugamushi* | 3 | |
| *Rickettsia typhi* | | |
| *(Rickettsia mooseri)* | 3 | |
| *Rickettsia* spp | 3 | |
| *Rochalimaea* spp *(formerly Bartonella)* | 2 | |
| *Rochalimaea quintana* | 2 | |
| *Salmonella arizonae* | 2 | |
| *Salmonella enteritidis* | 2 | |
| *Salmonella (other serovars)* | 2 | |

| Biological Agent | Classification | Notes |
|---|---|---|
| *Salmonella paratyphi* A,B,C | 3 | |
| *Salmonella typhi* | 3 | V |
| *Salmonella typhimurium* | 2 | |
| *Serpulina* spp | 2 | |
| *Serratia liquefaciens* | 2 | |
| *Serratia marcescens* | 2 | |
| *Shigella boydii* | 2 | |
| *Shigella dysenteriae* (Type 1) | 3 | T |
| *Shigella dysenteriae* (other than Type 1) | 2 | |
| *Shigella flexneri* | 2 | |
| *Shigella sonnei* | 2 | |
| *Staphylococcus aureus* | 2 | T |
| *Stenotrophomonas maltophilia* | 2 | |
| *Streptobacillus moniliformis* | 2 | |
| *Streptococcus pneumoniae* | 2 | |
| *Streptococcus pyogenes* | 2 | |
| *Streptococcus* spp | 2 | |
| *Treponema carateum* | 2 | |
| *Treponema pallidum* | 2 | |
| *Treponema pertenue* | 2 | |
| *Treponema* spp | 2 | |
| *Ureaplasma urealyticum* | 2 | |
| *Vibrio cholerae* (including El Tor) | 2 | T, V |
| *Vibrio parahaemolyticus* | 2 | |
| *Vibrio* spp | 2 | |
| *Yersinia enterocolitica* | 2 | |
| *Yersinia pestis* | 3 | V |
| *Yersinia pseudotuberculosis* | 2 | |
| *Yersinia* spp | 2 | |

# VIRUSES

| Biological Agent | Classification | Notes |
|---|---|---|
| **Adenoviridae** | 2 | |
| **Arenaviridae** | | |
| Amapari | 2 | |
| Flexal | 3 | |
| Guanarito | 4 | |
| Ippy | 2 | |
| Junin | 4 | |

| Biological Agent | Classification | Notes |
|---|---|---|
| Lassa Fever | 4 | |
| Latino | 2 | |
| Lymphocytic choriomeningitis | 3 | |
| Machupo | 4 | |
| Mobola | 2 | |
| Mopeia | 3 | |
| Parana | 2 | |
| Pichinde | 2 | |
| Sabia | 4 | |
| Tamiami | 2 | |
| **Astroviridae** | 2 | |
| **Bunyaviridae** | | |
| Akabane | 3 | |
| Bunyamwera | 2 | |
| California encephalitis | 2 | |
| Germiston | 3 | |
| Oropouche | 3 | |
| Hantaviruses: | | |
| Hantaan (Korean haemorrhagic fever) | 3 | |
| 'Muerto Canyon' | 3 | |
| Prospect Hill | 2 | |
| Puumala | 2 | |
| Seoul | 3 | |
| Other Hantaviruses | 2 | |
| Nairoviruses: | | |
| Bhanja | 3 | |
| Crimean/Congo haemorrhagic fever | 4 | |
| Hazara | 2 | |
| Phleboviruses: | | |
| Rift valley fever | 3 | V |
| Sandfly fever | 2 | |
| Toscana | 2 | |
| Uukuviruses | 2 | |
| Other Bunyaviridae known to be pathogenic | 2 | |
| **Caliciviridae:** | | |
| Hepatitis E | 3 | |
| Norwalk | 2 | |
| Other Caliciviridae | 2 | |
| **Coronaviridae** | 2 | |
| **Filoviridae** | | |

| Biological Agent | Classification | Notes |
|---|---|---|
| Ebola | 4 | |
| Marburg | 4 | |
| Reston | 4 | |
| **Flaviviridae:** | | |
| Flaviviruses | | |
| Dengue viruses Types 1-4 | 3 | |
| Israel turkey meningitis | 3 | |
| Japanese B encephalitis | 3 | V |
| Murray Valley encephalitis | 3 | |
| Rocio | 3 | |
| Sal Vieja | 3 | |
| San Perlita | 3 | |
| Spondweni | 3 | |
| St. Louis encephalitis | 3 | |
| Wesselsbron | 3 | |
| West Nile fever | 3 | |
| Yellow fever | 3 | V |
| Tick-borne virus group: | | |
| Absettarov | 3 | V |
| Hanzalova | 3 | V |
| Hypr | 3 | V |
| Kumlinge | 3 | |
| Kyasanur forest disease | 4 | V |
| Louping ill | 3 | V |
| Negishi | 3 | |
| Omsk haemorrhagic fever | 4 | V |
| Powassan | 3 | |
| Russian spring summer encephaltis | 4 | V |
| Hepatitis C group viruses: | | |
| Hepatitis C | 3 | D |
| Other Flaviviruses known to be pathogenic | 2 | |
| **Hepadnaviridae** | | |
| Hepatitis B | 3 | V, D |
| **Hepatitis D (delta)** | 3 | V, D |
| **Herpesviridae:** | | |
| Cytomegalovirus | 2 | |
| Epstein-Barr virus | 2 | |
| Herpesvirus simiae (B virus) | 3 | |
| Herpes simplex types 1 and 2 | 2 | |
| Herpesvirus varicella-zoster | 2 | |

| Biological Agent | Classification | Notes |
|---|---|---|
| Human B-cell lymphotropic virus 6 (HHV6) | 2 | |
| Human B-cell lymphyotropic virus 7 (HHV7) | 2 | |
| **Orthomyxoviridae:** | | |
| Influenza virus types A, B and C | 2 | V |
| Tick-borne orthomyxoviridae: Dhori and Thogoto | 2 | |
| **Papovaviridae:** | | |
| BK and JC viruses | 2 | D |
| Human papillomaviruses | 2 | D |
| **Paramyxoviridae** | | |
| Measles | 2 | V |
| Mumps | 2 | V |
| Newcastle disease | 2 | |
| Parainfluenza (Types 1 to 4) | 2 | |
| Respiratory syncytial virus | 2 | |
| **Parvoviridae** | | |
| Human parvovirus (B19) | 2 | |
| **Picornaviridae** | | |
| Acute haemorrhagic conjunctivitis virus (AHC) | 2 | |
| Coxsackieviruses | 2 | |
| Echoviruses | 2 | |
| Polioviruses | 2 | V |
| Rhinoviruses | 2 | |
| Hepatoviruses: Hepatitis A (human enterovirus type 72) | 2 | V |
| **Poxviridae** | | |
| Buffalopox | 2 | |
| Cowpox[1] | 2 | |
| Milker's nodes virus | 2 | |
| Molluscum contagiosum virus | 2 | |
| Monkeypox | 3 | V |
| Orf | 2 | |
| Vaccinia[2] | 2 | |
| Variola (major and minor)[3] | 4 | V |
| Yatapox (Tana & Yaba) | 2 | |
| **Reoviridae** | | |
| Coltivirus | 2 | |
| Human rotaviruses | 2 | |
| Orbiviruses | 2 | |
| Reoviruses | 2 | |
| **Retroviridae** | | |
| Human immunodeficiency viruses | 3 | D |

| Biological Agent | Classification | Notes |
|---|---|---|
| Human T-cell lymphotropic viruses (HTLV) types 1 and 2 | 3 | D |
| **Rhabdoviridae** | | |
| Duvenhage | 2 | V |
| Piry | 3 | |
| Rabies | 3 | V |
| Vesicular stomatitis | 2 | |
| **Togaviridae** | | |
| Alphaviuses: | | |
| Bebaru | 2 | |
| Chikungunya | 3 | |
| Eastern equine encephalomyelitis | 3 | V |
| Everglades | 3 | |
| Getah | 3 | |
| Mayaro | 3 | |
| Middleburg | 3 | |
| Mucambo | 3 | |
| Ndumu | 3 | |
| O'nyong-nyong | 3 | |
| Ross river | 2 | |
| Sagiyama | 3 | |
| Semliki forest | 2 | |
| Sindbis | 2 | |
| Tonate | 3 | |
| Venezuelan equine encephalomyelitis | 3 | V |
| Western equine encephalomyelitis | 3 | V |
| Other known alpha viruses | 2 | |
| Rubiviruses: Rubella | 2 | V |
| **Unclassified viruses** | | |
| Blood-borne hepatitis viruses not yet identified | 3 | D |
| **Unconventional agents** associated with: | | |
| Creutzfeldt-Jakob disease | 3 | D[4] |
| Gerstmann-Sträussler-Scheinker syndrome | 3 | D[4] |
| Kuru | 3 | D[4] |

[1] including strains isolated from cats and exotic species e.g. elephants, cheetahs.
[2] including strains originally classified as rabbitpox virus.
[3] all strains including 'whitepox virus'.
[4] long term record keeping is not required where the results of the assessment made under *Regulation 6* of the *COSHH Regulations 1999* indicate that the activity does not involve a deliberate intention to work with or use that biological agent; and there is no significant risk to the health of employees associated with that agent.

# PARASITES

| Biological Agent | Classification | Notes |
|---|:---:|:---:|
| *Acanthamoeba castellanii* | 2 | |
| *Acanthamoeba* spp | 2 | |
| *Ancylostoma duodenale* | 2 | |
| *Angiostrongylus cantonensis* | 2 | |
| *Angiostrongylus costaricensis* | 2 | |
| *Ascaris lumbricoides* | 2 | A |
| *Ascaris suum* | 2 | A |
| *Babesia divergens* | 2 | |
| *Babesia microti* | 2 | |
| *Balantidium coli* | 2 | |
| *Blastocystis hominis* | 2 | |
| *Brugia malayi* | 2 | |
| *Brugia pahangi* | 2 | |
| *Brugia timori* | 2 | |
| *Capillaria philippinensis* | 2 | |
| *Capillaria* spp | 2 | |
| *Clonorchis* – see *Opisthorchis* | | |
| *Cryptosporidium parvum* | 2 | |
| *Cryptosporidium* spp | 2 | |
| *Cyclospora cayetanensis* | 2 | |
| *Cyclospora app* | 2 | |
| *Dientamoeba fragilis* | 2 | |
| *Dipetalonema* – see *Mansonella* | | |
| *Diphyllobothrium latum* | 2 | |
| *Dracunculus medinensis* | 2 | |
| *Echinococcus granulosus* | 3 | |
| *Echinococcus multilocularis* | 3 | |
| *chinococcus vogeli* | 3 | |
| *Entamoeba histolytica* | 2 | |
| *Enterobius vermicularis* | 2 | |
| *Fasciola gigantica* | 2 | |
| *Fasciola hepatica* | 2 | |
| *Fasciolopsis buski* | 2 | |
| *Giardia lamblia (Giardia intestinalis)* | 2 | |
| *Hymenolepis diminuta* | 2 | |
| *Hymenolepis nana* | 2 | |
| *Isopora belli* | 2 | |
| *Leishmania aethiopica* | 2 | |

| Biological Agent | Classification | Notes |
|---|:---:|:---:|
| *Leishmania braziliensis* | 3 | |
| *Leishmania donovani* | 3 | |
| *Leishmania mexicana* | 2 | |
| *Leishmania peruviana* | 2 | |
| *Leishmania major* | 2 | |
| *Leishmania tropica* | 2 | |
| *Leishmania* spp | 2 | |
| *Loa loa* | 2 | |
| *Mansonella ozzardi* | 2 | |
| *Mansonella perstans* | 2 | |
| *Mansonella streptocerca* | 2 | |
| *Naegleria fowleri* | 3 | |
| *Necator americanus* | 2 | |
| *Onchocerca volvulus* | 2 | |
| *Opisthorchis sinensis (Clonorchis sinensis)* | 2 | |
| *Opisthorchis viverrini (Clonorchis viverrini)* | 2 | |
| *Opisthorchis felineus* | 2 | |
| *Opisthorchis* spp | 2 | |
| *Paragonimus westermani* | 2 | |
| *Paragonimus* spp | 2 | |
| *Plasmodium falciparum* | 3 | |
| *Plasmodium* spp (human & simian) | 2 | |
| *Sarcocystis suihominis* | 2 | |
| *Schistosoma haematobium* | 2 | |
| *Schistosoma intercalatum* | 2 | |
| *Schistosoma japonicum* | 2 | |
| *Schistosoma mansoni* | 2 | |
| *Schistosoma mekongi* | 2 | |
| *Schistosoma* spp | 2 | |
| *Strongyloides stercoralis* | 2 | |
| *Strongyloides* spp | 2 | |
| *Taenia saginata* | 2 | |
| *Taenia solium* | 3 | |
| *Toxocara canis* | 2 | |
| *Toxocara cati* | 2 | |
| *Toxoplasma gondii* | 2 | |
| *Trichinella nativa* | 2 | |
| *Trichinella nelsoni* | 2 | |
| *Trichinella pseudospiralis* | 2 | |
| *Trichinella spiralis* | 2 | |

| Biological Agent | Classification | Notes |
|---|---|---|
| *Trichomonas vaginalis* | 2 | |
| *Trichostrongylus orientalis* | 2 | |
| *Trichostrongylus* spp | 2 | |
| *Trichuris trichiura* | 2 | |
| *Trypanosoma brucei brucei* | 2 | |
| *Trypanosoma brucei gambiense* | 2 | |
| *Trypanosoma brucei rhodesiense* | 3 | |
| *Trypanosoma cruzi* | 3 | |
| *Trypanosoma rangeli* | 2 | |
| *Wuchereria bancrofti* | 2 | |

# FUNGI

| Biological Agent | Classification | Notes |
|---|---|---|
| *Aspergillus fumigatus* | 2 | A |
| *Blastomyces dermatitidis (Ajellomyces dermatitidis)* | 3 | |
| *Candida albicans* | 2 | A |
| *Candida* spp | 2 | |
| *Coccidioides immitis* | 3 | A |
| *Cryptococcus neoformans var neoformans (Filobasidiella neoformans var neoformans)* | 2 | A |
| *Cryptococcus neoformans var gattii (Filobasidiella bacillispora)* | 2 | A |
| *Emmonsia parva* var *parva* | 2 | |
| *Emmonsia parva* var *crescens* | 2 | |
| *Epidermophyton floccosum* | 2 | A |
| *Fonsecaea compacta* | 2 | |
| *Fonsecaea pedrosoi* | 2 | |
| *Histoplasma capsulatum* var *capsulatum (Ajellomyces capsulatus)* | 3 | |
| *Histoplasma capsulatum* var *duboisii* | 3 | |
| *Histoplama capsulatum* var *farcinimosum* | 3 | |
| *Madurella grisea* | 2 | |
| *Madurella mycetomatis* | 2 | |
| *Microsporum* spp | 2 | A |
| *Neotestudina rosatii* | 2 | |
| *Paracoccidioides brasiliensis* | 3 | |
| *Penicillium marneffei* | 3 | A |
| *Sporothrix schenckii* | 2 | |
| *Trichophyton rubrum* | 2 | |
| *Trichophyton* spp | 2 | |
| *Xylohypha bantiana* | 2 | |

# Dangerous Substances II – Transportation

## Introduction – transportation of dangerous substances by road and rail

D3001 In view of the risk of accidents and spillages in connection with transportation of dangerous goods and substances, and to harmonise EU law in relation to the transportation of dangerous goods by road and rail, considerable statutory duties are placed on consignors and operators of companies involved in the transportation of dangerous goods (including radioactive material) by both road and rail. Recent regulatory changes in this area are the result of the UK incorporating the international 'ADR' and 'RID' agreements into its domestic law.

The duties placed on consignors and operators essentially relate to:

(*a*)    classification, packaging and labelling;

(*b*)    physical transportation (or carriage) requirements relating to the dimensions and suitability of vehicles; and

(*c*)    the competence of drivers and attendants (where necessary).

The transportation of dangerous goods is covered in the following regulations:

(1)    the *Carriage of Dangerous Goods (Classification, Packaging and Labelling) and Use of Transportable Pressure Receptacles Regulations 1996 (SI 1996 No 2092)* (as amended by the *Pressure Systems Safety Regulations (SI 2000 No 128)*;

(2)    the *Carriage of Dangerous Goods by Road Regulations 1996 (SI 1996 No 2095)*;

(3)    the *Carriage of Dangerous Goods by Rail Regulations 1996 (SI 1996 No 2089)*;

(4)    the *Carriage of Explosives by Road Regulations 1996 (SI 1996 No 2093)*;

(5)    the *Carriage of Dangerous Goods by Road (Driver Training) Regulations 1996 (SI 1996 No 2094)*;

(6)    the *Transport of Dangerous Goods (Safety Advisers) Regulations 1999 (SI 1999 No 257)*;

(7)    the *Radioactive Material (Road Transport) (Great Britain) Regulations 1996 (SI 1996 No 1350)*; and

(8)    the *Packaging, Labelling and Carriage of Radioactive Material by Rail Regulations 1996 (SI 1996 No 2090)* (as amended by the *Ionising Radiation Regulations 1999 (SI 1999 No 3232)*.

The Health and Safety Executive has finalised the production of the series of six guidance documents which support the new regulations on the carriage of dangerous goods by road and rail.

The six guidance documents comprise a free introductory booklet and five priced publications which take the reader step by step through the new regulations. They are:

- Are you involved in the Carriage of Dangerous Goods by Road or Rail (Free Booklet);

- Carriage of Dangerous Goods Explained, Part 1 – Guidance for Consignors of Dangerous Goods by Road and Rail (Classification, Packaging, Labelling and Provision of Information) (Ref. HS(G)160), price £9.95 – provides guidance for consignors on classification, packaging and labelling requirements, as well as the use of transportable pressure receptacles;

- Carriage of Dangerous Goods Explained, Part 2 – Guidance for Road Vehicle Operators and others Involved in the Carriage of Dangerous Goods by Road, (Ref. HS(G)161), price £12.20 – provides guidance, principally for road vehicle operators and drivers,on requirements relating to the vehicle and its operation, such as design and construction, vehicle marking,transport documentation and the training of drivers. It also provides guidance on the design and construction of tankers, brought forward from the Approved Codes of Practice made under the 1992 tanker regulations;

- Carriage of Dangerous Goods Explained, Part 3 – Guidance for Rail Operators and Others Involved in the Carriage of Dangerous Goods by Rail, (Ref. HS(G)163), price £7.50 – covers areas similar to Part 2 but in relation to carriage by rail;

- Carriage of Dangerous Goods Explained, Part 4 – Guidance for Operators, Drivers and Others Involved in the Carriage of Explosives by Road, (Ref. HS(G)162), price £10.95 – provides guidance on the quantities of dangerous goods that may be carried (and mixing of loads), vehicle construction, driver training, loading and unloading, journey planning, provision of information, vehicle marking, ensuring safe carriage and handling emergencies; and

- Carriage of Dangerous Goods Explained, Part 5 – Guidance for Consignors, Rail Operators and Others Involved in the Carriage of Radioactive Material by Rail, (Ref. HS(G)164), price £8.95 – sets out guidance for consignors, rail operators and others involved in thepackaging, labelling and carriage of radioactive material by rail, including suitability of containers and wagons, loading, emergency arrangements, information and training.

All of the above publications are available from HSE Books.

This section concerns the regulations in (1)–(6) above.

*Dangerous goods*

D3002    'Dangerous goods' means any:

(*a*)    explosives;

(*b*)    radioactive material;

(*c*)    goods named individually in the Approved Carriage List (ACL);

(*d*)    any other goods having one or more hazardous properties; and

(*e*)    certain environmentally hazardous substances as stated in the *Health and Safety at Work etc. Act 1974 (Application to Environmentally Hazardous Substances) Regulations 1996 (SI 1996 No 2075)*.

[*The Carriage of Dangerous Goods (Classification, Packaging and Labelling) and Use of Transportable Pressure Receptacles Regulations 1996 (SI 1996 No 2092), Reg 2(1)*].

*Transit and carriage*

D3003    Dangerous goods are deemed to be carried from the time when they are placed on a vehicle for the purposes of carriage by road or on a railway, until either:

(*a*)    they are removed from the vehicle etc.; or

(*b*)    any receptacle containing the goods has been cleaned, so that any goods or their vapour which remain in the receptacle, are not sufficient to create or increase a significant risk to health and safety, whether or not the vehicle is actually on the road or railway.

'Carriage' or 'consignment' of dangerous goods includes where packages still contain sufficient dangerous goods (or their vapours) to create or increase risks to health and safety.

[*Carriage of Dangerous Goods (Classification, Packaging and Labelling) and Use of Transportable Pressure Receptacles Regulations 1996 (SI 1996 No 2092), Reg 3(2)(a)–(b)*].

### Defence under the regulations

D3004    The regulations detailed in (1)–(5) at D3001 above, all have a common defence, namely, that the person charged with an offence under those regulations can prove that:

(*a*)    the commission of the offence was due to the act or default of another person, not being an employee (see further ENFORCEMENT); and

(*b*)    he took all reasonable precautions and exercised all due diligence to avoid the commission of the offence (e.g. the *Carriage of Dangerous Goods (Classification, Packaging and Labelling) and Use of Transportable Pressure Receptacles Regulations 1996 (SI 1996 No 2092, Reg 19)*. The penalties applied for breaches of these regulations are the same as for breaches of *HSWA 1974* itself (see ENFORCEMENT).

## Classification, packaging and labelling of dangerous goods for carriage by road and rail – the Carriage of Dangerous Goods (Classification, Packaging and Labelling) and Use of Transportable Pressure Receptacles Regulations 1996 (SI 1996 No 2092) (as amended by the Pressure Systems Safety Regulations 2000 (SI 2000 No 128)

D3005    These Regulations, which came into force on 1 September 1996, specify requirements for the classification, packaging and labelling of dangerous goods (and substances) transported by road and rail. In any proceedings for an offence consisting of a contravention of the Regulations prior to 1 January 1999, compliance with the *Chemicals (Hazard Information and Packaging) Regulations 1993 (SI 1993 No 1746)* is a defence in the case of goods classified, packaged or labelled prior to 1 July 1995 in accordance with the *1993 Regulations*. [*Carriage of Dangerous Goods (Classification, Packaging and Labelling) and Use of Transportable Pressure Receptacles Regulations 1996 (SI 1996 No 2092), Reg 20(1)*].

## Classification requirements

D3006   Dangerous goods must not be conveyed by road or rail unless classified according to:

(a)   the Approved Carriage List (ACL);

(b)   the Approved Requirements and Test Methods for Classification and Packaging of Dangerous Goods for Carriage; and

(c)   the Approved Requirements for Transportable Pressure Receptacles (where applicable).

*Regulation 5* requires that, classification must refer to –

(i)   in the case of goods named individually in the Approved Carriage List:

—   classification code,

—   packaging group,

—   subsidiary hazard code,

—   proper shipping names,

—   UN number,

—   appropriate danger sign (see Table 1 below),

—   subsidiary hazard sign (if any); and

(ii)   in the case of all other goods:

—   classification code,

—   packing group,

—   subsidiary hazards,

—   proper shipping names,

—   UN number,

—   appropriate danger sign (see Table 1 below),

—   subsidiary hazard sign (if any).

[*Carriage of Dangerous Goods (Classification, Packaging and Labelling) and Use of Transportable Pressure Receptacles Regulations 1996 (SI 1996 No 2092), Reg 5, Sch 1 Parts I, II, Sch 2 Parts I, II*].

Optional lettering may be used as well, e.g. 'COMPRESSED GAS', 'TOXIC GAS', 'FLAMMABLE LIQUID', 'OXIDISING AGENT'. [*Carriage of Dangerous Goods (Classification, Packaging and Labelling) and Use of Transportable Pressure Receptacles Regulations 1996 (SI 1996 No 2092), Sch 1 Part I, column 7*]. In the case of 'TOXIC' substances, the word 'POISON' may be used, and, in the case of 'FLAMMABLE' substances, the word 'INFLAMMABLE'. [*Carriage of Dangerous Goods (Classification, Packaging and Labelling) and Use of Transportable Pressure Receptacles Regulations 1996 (SI 1996 No 2092), Sch 1 Part II, para 2(c)-(d)*].

*Exemptions from classification*

D3007   Certain viscous substances are exempt from classification as flammable liquids. These are:

(a)   substances not having properties of a toxic or corrosive substance;

(*b*) solutions which do not contain more than 20% nitro-cellulose, containing not more than 12.6% nitrogen by mass;

(*c*) substances where the flash point is equal to or greater than 23°C;

(*d*) solvents, where in solvent separation tests, the solvent which separates is not more than 3% of the volume of the substance;

(*e*) substances where the viscosity of the substance when determined at 23°C in a flow cup conforming to ISO 2431-1984 or ES EN 535-1991, and having a jet diameter of 6mm is

    (i) in a case where the substance contains not more than 60% of a flammable liquid with a flashpoint of 61°C or less, not less than 40 seconds, and

    (ii) in any other case, not less than 60 seconds.

[*Carriage of Dangerous Goods (Classification, Packaging and Labelling) and Use of Transportable Pressure Receptacles Regulations 1996 (SI 1996 No 2092), Sch 1, Part III*].

## Table 1

## Labelling requirements for dangerous substances carried by road and rail

SCHEDULE 1    CLASSIFICATION AND ASCERTAINMENT OF OTHER PARTICULARS OF DANGEROUS GOODS

PART I

TABLE OF CLASSIFICATIONS AND OTHER PARTICULARS

Regulation 5

| *(1)* | *(2)* | *(3)* | *(4)* | *(5)* | *(6)* | *(7)* |
|---|---|---|---|---|---|---|
| Classification | Hazardous properties | Relevant properties | Packing group | Class number | Danger sign | Optional lettering |
| Non-flammable, non-toxic gas | A substance which— (a) at 50°C has a vapour pressure greater than 300 kilopascals absolute or is completely gaseous at 20°C at a standard pressure of 101.3 kilopascals; and (b) is carried at an absolute pressure of not less than 280 kilopascals or in liquefied form. other than a toxic gas or a flammable gas. | — | — | 2.2 | | COMPRESSED GAS |
| Toxic gas | A substance which at 50°C has a vapour pressure greater than 300 kilopascals absolute or is completely gaseous at 20°C at a standard pressure of 101.3 kilopascals and which is toxic. | — | — | 2.3 | | TOXIC GAS |

SCHEDULE 1 *(continued)*

| *(1)* Classification | *(2)* Hazardous properties | *(3)* Relevant properties | *(4)* Packing group | *(5)* Class number | *(6)* Danger sign | *(7)* Optional lettering |
|---|---|---|---|---|---|---|
| Flammable gas | A substance which— <br><br>(a) at 50°C has a vapour pressure greater than 300 kilopascals absolute or is completely gaseous at 20°C at a standard pressure of 101.3 kilopascals and is flammable; or <br><br>(b) is packed in an aerosol dispenser where that dispenser contains either— <br><br>(i) more than 45 per cent by mass of a flammable substance, or <br><br>(ii) more than 250 grammes of a flammable substance, <br><br>and in this sub-paragraph flammable substance means a flammable gas or flammable liquid having a flash point less than or equal to 100°C | — | | 2.1 | FLAMMABLE GAS | |
| Flammable liquid | A liquid with a flash point— <br><br>(a) above 61°C, and which is carried at a temperature above its flashpoint; or <br><br>(b) of 61°C or below except- <br><br>(i) a liquid which has a flash-point equal to or more than 35°C, and when tested in accordance with the appropriate approved method does not support combustion. | (a) (in the case of any liquid having a flash point of less than 23°C and containing either not more than 5% of toxic or corrosive substances with a packing group of I or II or not more than 5% of flammable liquids with a packing group of I and a subsidiary hazard of toxic or corrosive)— | III | 3 | FLAMMABLE LIQUID | |

SCHEDULE 1 *(continued)*

| *(1)*<br>Classification | *(2)*<br>Hazardous properties | *(3)*<br>Relevant properties | *(4)*<br>Packing group | *(5)*<br>Class number | *(6)*<br>Danger sign | *(7)*<br>Optional lettering |
|---|---|---|---|---|---|---|
| | (ii) a viscous substance which complies with the provisions of Part III of this Schedule and is contained in a receptacle with a capacity of less than 450 litres, or | (i) less than 3% of it separates out into a clear solvent layer following a suitable solvent separation test, | | | | |
| | (iii) a substance which is classified as a flammable gas because it has the hazardous properties specified in sub-paragraph (b) of this column corresponding to the entry for a 'flammable gas' in column 1 of this Part. | (ii) the flash point of it is specified in column 1 of the table set out in Part IV of this Schedule, | | | | |
| | | (iii) the kinematic viscosity of it is within the range specified in column 2 of the table set out in Part IV of the Schedule which is opposite to the flash point of that liquid referred to in head (ii) of this sub-paragraph, and | | | | |
| | | (iv) is contained in a receptacle with a capacity of less than 450 litres; or | | | | |
| | | (b) (in the case of any other liquid) it has— | | | | |
| | | (i) an initial boiling point not greater than 35°C | | | | |
| | | (ii) an initial boiling point above 35°C and a flash point of less than 23°C, or | II | | | |
| | | (iii) an initial boiling point above 35°C and a flash point of 23°C or above. | III | | | |

SCHEDULE 1 *(continued)*

| (1) Classification | (2) Hazardous properties | (3) Relevant properties | (4) Packing group | (5) Class number | (6) Danger sign | (7) Optional lettering |
|---|---|---|---|---|---|---|
| Flammable solid | (a) a solid which, under conditions encountered in transport, is readily combustible or may cause or contribute to fire through friction; | A substance which is— | | | | FLAMMABLE SOLID |
| | (b) a self-reactive or related substance which is liable to undergo a strongly exothermic reaction; or | (a) water-wetted and (when in a dry state) required to be classified (as defined by regulation 2(1) of the Classification and Labelling of Explosives Regulations 1983) in pursuance of regulation 3(2)(a) of those Regulations; | I | | | |
| | (c) a desensitised explosive where the explosive properties have been suppressed. | (b) (i) a self-reactive substance, or | II | 4.1 | | |
| | | (ii) a readily combustible solid which, when ignited, burns very vigorously or intensely and is difficult to extinguish; or | | | | |
| | | (c) a readily combustible solid which when ignited, burns vigorously or intensely. | III | | | |
| Spontaneously combustible substance | A substance which is liable to spontaneous heating under conditions encountered in carriage or to heating in contact with air being then liable to catch fire. | A substance which is— | | | | |
| | | (a) a pyrophoric substance which ignites instantly on contact with air; | I | | | |
| | | (b) liable to ignite on contact with air within a short space of time, particularly under conditions of spillage; or | II | | | |

**SCHEDULE 1** *(continued)*

| *(1)* Classification | *(2)* Hazardous properties | *(3)* Relevant properties | *(4)* Packing group | *(5)* Class number | *(6)* Danger sign | *(7)* Optional lettering |
|---|---|---|---|---|---|---|
| | | (c) any other substance which is liable to ignite on contact with air. | III | 4.2 | | SPONTANE-OUSLY COMBUSTIBLE |
| Substance which in contact with water emits flammable gas | A substance which in contact with water is liable to become spontaneously combustible or to give off a flammable gas. | A substance which— | | | | |
| | | (a) either reacts vigorously with water at ambient temperatures and demonstrates generally a tendency for the gas produced to ignite spontaneously or reacts readily with water at ambient temperatures so that the rate of evolution of flammable gas is equal to or greater than 10 litres per kilogram of substance over any period of one minute; | I | | | |
| | | (b) reacts readily with water at ambient temperatures so that the maximum rate of evolution of flammable gas is equal to or greater than 20 litres per kilo gram of substance per hour; or | II | | | |
| | | (c) reacts slowly with water at ambient temperatures so that the maximum rate of evolution of flammable gas is greater than 1 litre per kilogram of substance per hour. | III | 4.3 | | DANGEROUS WHEN WET |

SCHEDULE 1 (continued)

| (1) Classification | (2) Hazardous properties | (3) Relevant properties | (4) Packing group | (5) Class number | (6) Danger sign | (7) Optional lettering |
|---|---|---|---|---|---|---|
| Oxidizing substance | A substance other than an organic peroxide which, although not necessarily combustible, may by yielding oxygen or by a similar process cause or contribute to the combustion of other material. | A solid substance which, when mixed with cellulose in a ratio of either 1:4 or 1:1 by mass, exhibits a burning rate at least as fast as that for a— | | 5.1 | | OXIDIZING AGENT |
| | | (a) 3:2 mixture by mass of potassium bromate and cellulose; | I | | | |
| | | (b) 2:3 mixture by mass of potassium bromate and cellulose; or | II | | | |
| | | (c) 3:7 mixture by mass of potassium bromate and cellulose. | III | | | |
| | | A liquid substance which, when mixed with cellulose in a ratio of 1:1 by mass, exhibits a pressure rise at least as fast as that of a 1:1 mixture by mass of— | | | | |
| | | (a) 50% perchloric acid and cellulose; | I | | | |
| | | (b) 40% aqueous sodium chlorate solution and cellulose; or | II | | | |
| | | (c) 65% aqueous nitric acid and cellulose. | III | | | |
| Organic peroxide | A substance which is— | Any substance classified as an organic peroxide | II | 5.2 | | ORGANIC PEROXIDE |
| | (a) an organic peroxide; and | | | | | |
| | (b) an unstable substance which may undergo exothermic self-accelerating decomposition. | | | | | |

SCHEDULE 1 *(continued)*

| (1) Classification | (2) Hazardous properties | (3) Relevant properties | (4) Packing group | (5) Class number | (6) Danger sign | (7) Optional lettering |
|---|---|---|---|---|---|---|
| Toxic substance | A substance which is liable either to cause death or serious injury or to harm human health if swallowed or inhaled or by skin contact. | A substance which has been allocated to– | | | | |
| | | (a) packing group I in accordance with the criteria set out in Part V of this Schedule; | I | | | |
| | | (b) packing group II in accordance with the criteria set out in Part V of this Schedule; or | II | | | |
| | | (c) packing group III in accordance with the criteria set out in Part V of this Schedule. | III | 6.1 | | TOXIC |
| Infectious substance | A substance which either contains viable micro-organisms that are known or reasonably believed to cause disease in animals or humans or genetically-modified micro-organisms and organisms which are infectious. | – | — | 6.2 | | INFECTIOUS SUBSTANCE |
| Corrosive substance | A substance which by chemical action will– | A substance which– | | | | |
| | (a) cause severe damage when in contact with living tissue; or | (a) causes full thickness destruction of skin tissue at the site of contact with an observation period of 60 minutes starting after testing on the intact skin of an animal for a period of 3 minutes or less, | I | | | |

**SCHEDULE 1** (*continued*)

| (1) Classification | (2) Hazardous properties | (3) Relevant properties | (4) Packing group | (5) Class number | (6) Danger sign | (7) Optional lettering |
|---|---|---|---|---|---|---|
| | (b) materially damage freight or equipment if leakage occurs. | (b) causes full thickness destruction of skin tissue at the site of contact with an observation period of 14 days starting after testing on the intact skin of an animal for a period of more than 3 minutes but not more than 60 minutes, or | II | | | |
| | | (c) (i) causes full thickness destruction of skin tissue at the site of contact with an observation period of 14 days starting after testing on the intact skin of an animal for a period of more than 60 minutes but not more than 4 hours; or | III | | | |
| | | (d) causes corrosion in steel or aluminium surfaces at a rate exceeding 6.25 mm a year at a test temperature of 55°C. | III | 8 | | CORROSIVE |
| Miscellaneous dangerous goods | A substance which– (a) is listed in the approved carriage list and which may create a risk to the health or safety of persons in the conditions encountered in carriage whether or not it has any of the hazardous properties of any other classification; or | – | – | 9 | | – |

SCHEDULE 1 *(continued)*

| (1) Classification | (2) Hazardous properties | (3) Relevant properties | (4) Packing group | (5) Class number | (6) Danger sign | (7) Optional lettering |
|---|---|---|---|---|---|---|
| | (b) contains a genetically-modified micro-organism which is capable of altering animals, plants or microbiological substances in a way which is not normally the result of natural reproduction but excluding any infectious substance; | | | | | |
| | (c) is hazardous to the environment but excluding any substance which– | | | | | |
| | | (i) is an explosive or radioactive material, | | | | |
| | | (ii) possesses any of the hazardous properties of any other classification, or | | | | |
| | | (iii) constitutes dangerous goods for any other reason. | | | | |

[*Carriage of Dangerous Goods (Classification, Packaging and Labelling) and Use of Transportable Pressure Receptacles Regulations 1996 (SI 1996 No 2092), Reg 5, Sch 1 Pt I*].

**Table 2**
**Subsidiary hazard signs for such substances and optional lettering**

| (1) | (2) | (3) |
|---|---|---|
| *Subsidiary hazard* | *Subsidiary hazard sign* | *Optional lettering* |
| Liable to explosion | | — |
| Danger of fire (flammable gas) | | FLAMMABLE GAS |
| Danger of fire (flammable liquid) | | FLAMMABLE LIQUID |
| Danger of fire (flammable solid) | | FLAMMABLE SOLID |
| Liable to spontaneous ignition | | SPONTANEOUSLY COMBUSTIBLE |
| Danger of emission of flammable gas on contact with water | | DANGEROUS WHEN WET |

| (1) Subsidiary hazard | (2) Subsidiary hazard sign | (3) Optional lettering |
|---|---|---|
| Fire intensifying hazard | | OXIDISING AGENT |
| Toxic | | TOXIC |
| Corrosive | | CORROSIVE |

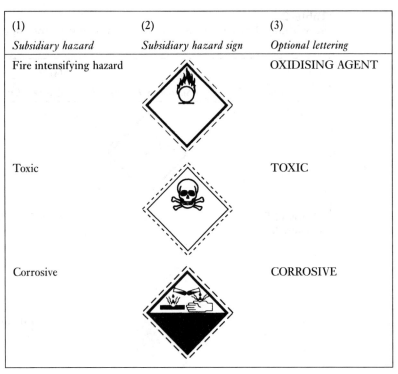

[*Reg 5, Sch 2 Pt I*].

### Packaging requirements

*Composition and design*

D3008 Consignors shall not consign any dangerous goods for carriage in packages unless those packages are suitable, and in particular unless:

(a) the packages, and any packaging or overpack associated with the packages are designed, constructed, maintained, filled and closed so as to prevent any of the contents of those packages from escaping when subjected to the stresses and strains of normal handling and conditions encountered in carriage;

(b) the packages, and any packagings or overpack associated with the packages, are made of materials which, if they come into contact with the contents of those packages, are not made of materials which are likely to be damaged by the contents so as to create a health and safety risk;

(c) (where fitted) receptacle closures must be able to be repeatedly re-closed without letting the contents escape;

(d) any conditions relating to packaging specified in the special provision code of the ACL are complied with; and

(e) packages have been tested and approved, a competent authority has approved the test, and the packagings allocated an ADR mark, RID mark, UN mark, or joint ADR/RID mark.

[*Carriage of Dangerous Goods (Classification, Packaging and Labelling) and Use of Transportable Pressure Receptacles Regulations 1996 (SI 1996 No 2092), Reg 6(1)*].

The requirements in (*e*) above do not apply if they:

  (i)  are transportable pressure receptacles or aerosols;

  (ii)  have a capacity of more than 3 cubic metres;

  (iii)  they contain certain goods specified in *Sch 3 column 1*, i.e.

    —   toxic gas 120 ml in aerosols

    —   non-flammable 120ml (or 1000 ml in metal/plastic aerosols)

    —   non-toxic gas

    —   provided that the total mass of the package does not exceed 30 kilograms;

  (iv)  are exempted in the Approved Carriage List;

  (v)  are exempted in the Approved Method; or

  (vi)

    —   have a nominal capacity of 25 litres or less,

    —   are uncleaned, empty, and

    —   are being consigned to a suitable place for cleaning or disposal.

[*Carriage of Dangerous Goods (Classification, Packaging and Labelling) and Use of Transportable Pressure Receptacles Regulations 1996 (SI 1996 No 2092), Reg 6(3), Sch 3*]. (See also Table 3 below.)


*Particulars to be shown on packages*

**D3009**   The following particulars must be shown, namely:

(*a*)    designation of the goods;

(*b*)    UN number;

(*c*)    danger sign; and

(*d*)    subsidiary hazard signs (if any);

and must

  (i)  be so displayed as to be easily read;

  (ii)  stand out from their background so as to be readily noticeable;

  (iii)  either be

    —   clearly and indelibly marked on the package, or

    —   clearly and indelibly printed on a label securely fixed to the package, or attached in some appropriate manner; and

  (iv)  be in English or the language of the recipient state.

[*Carriage of Dangerous Goods (Classification, Packaging and Labelling) and Use of Transportable Pressure Receptacles Regulations 1996 (SI 1996 No 2092), Regs 8, 11*].

## Table 3

## Packages/receptacles exempt from showing particulars under Regulation 8

| (1) Goods/Classification | (2) Packing group | (3) Maximum quantity per receptacle |
|---|---|---|
| Non-flammable, non-toxic, gas, except one with a fire intensifying subsidiary hazard | — | 120 ml (or 1.000 ml in metal or plastic aerosols). |
| Flammable gas or a non-flammable, non-toxic gas with a fire intensifying subsidiary hazard | — | 120 ml in glass aerosols. 1.000 ml in metal or plastic aerosols. |
| Toxic gas | — | 120 ml in aerosols. |
| Flammable liquid | II | 1 litre in metal packagings. 500 ml in glass or plastic packagings. |
| | III | 5 litres |
| Flammable solid | II | 500 g |
| | III | 3 kg |
| Substance (liquid or solid) which in contact with water emits flammable gas | II | 500 g |
| | III | 1 kg |
| Oxidizing substance (liquid or solid) | II | 500 g |
| | III | 1 kg |
| Organic peroxide (solid, of Type B or C as defined in the appropriate approved method, and not requiring temperature control) | II | 100 g |
| Organic peroxide (liquid, of Type B or C as defined in the appropriate approved method, and not requiring temperature control) | II | 25 ml |
| Organic peroxide (solid, of Type D, E or F as defined in the appropriate approved method, and not requiring temperature control) | II | 500 g |
| Organic peroxide (liquid, of Type D, E or F as defined in the appropriate approved method, and not requiring temperature control) | II | 125 ml |
| Toxic substance (solid) | II | 500 g |
| Toxic substance (liquid) | II | 100 ml |
| Toxic substance (solid) | III | 3 kg |
| Toxic substance (liquid) | III | 1 litre |
| Corrosive substance (solid) | II | 1 kg |
| Corrosive substance (liquid) | II | 500 ml. If glass, porcelain or stoneware receptacles are used they must be enclosed in compatible and rigid intermediate packagings. |
| Corrosive substance (solid) | III | 2 kg |
| Corrosive substance (liquid) | III | 1 litre |

| (1) | (2) | (3) |
|---|---|---|
| *Goods/Classification* | *Packing group* | *Maximum quantity per receptacle* |
| Diagnostic specimens in Group (b) (within the meaning of the approved methods) | — | 100 ml packed in accordance with the appropriate approved method. |
| Dibromodifluoromethane | — | 5 litres |
| Benzaldehyde | III | 5 litres |
| Environmentally hazardous substance (solid), NOS | III | 5 kg |
| Environmentally hazardous substance (liquid), NOS | III | 5 litres |

[*Carriage of Dangerous Goods (Classification, Packaging and Labelling) and Use of Transportable Pressure Receptacles Regulations 1996 (SI 1996 No 2092), Regs 6(3)(c), 8(4), Sch 3*].

## Exempted goods and substances

D3010    The following goods are exempted from the Regulations:

(*a*)    infectious substances affecting animals only (UN 2900);

(*b*)    environmentally hazardous substance (solid) (UN 3077);

(*c*)    environmentally hazardous substance (liquid) (UN 3082);

(*d*)    genetically modified micro-organisms (UN 3245);

carried in

(i)    an agricultural or forestry tractor;

(ii)    mobile machinery;

(iii)    a vehicle with less than 4 wheels;

(iv)    a vehicle with a maximum design speed of 25 km/h or less; or

(v)    armed forces vehicles.

[*Carriage of Dangerous Goods (Classification, Packaging and Labelling) and Use of Transportable Pressure Receptacles Regulations 1996 (SI 1996 No 2092), Reg 3(7)*].

## Main exempted operations

D3011    These include:

(*a*)    international transport operations within the meaning of COTIF (the Convention concerning international carriage by rail), where goods are classified, packaged and labelled in accordance with RID;

(*b*)    international transport operations within the meaning of ADR;

(*c*)    goods carried by sea and classified etc. in accordance with the International Maritime Dangerous Goods Code issued by the International Maritime Organisation;

(*d*)    goods carried by air and classified etc. in accordance with the Technical Instructions for the Safe Transport of Dangerous Goods by Air issued by the International Civil Aviation Organisation;

(*e*) goods carried in a vehicle which is not being used for, or in connection with, work;

(*f*) goods carried

(i) between private premises and another vehicle in the vicinity of those premises, or

(ii) between one part of the premises and another;

(*g*) goods carried in connection with the provision of emergency services, solely for the purpose of re-packaging or disposal at the destination (so long as they are clearly marked as dangerous and sealed to prevent them escaping);

(*h*) goods carried as a sample by an enforcement authority;

(*j*) goods carried on a railway from one part of a factory, mine, quarry or harbour area to another part;

(*k*) explosives;

(*l*) live animals;

(*m*) fuel, batteries or fire safety equipment used for the operation of the vehicle;

(*n*) petroleum spirit; and

(*o*) radioactive material (governed by the *Radioactive Material (Road Transport) (Great Britain) Regulations 1996 (SI 1996 No 1350)*).

[*Carriage of Dangerous Goods (Classification, Packaging and Labelling) and Use of Transportable Pressure Receptacles Regulations 1996 (SI 1996 No 2092), Reg 3(1)*].

## Importance of the approved information

D3012 Information relating to the classification, packaging and labelling criteria, for the purposes of transportation of dangerous goods by road and rail is contained in:

(*a*) the Approved Carriage List (ACL);

(*b*) the Approved Requirements and Test Methods for Classification and Packaging of Dangerous Goods for Carriage; and

(*c*) the Approved Requirements of Transportable Pressure Receptacles (formerly 'transportable gas containers').

The Health and Safety Commission has published a revision of the Approved Carriage List; Approved Requirements and Test Methods for the Classification and Packaging of Dangerous Goods for Carriage; and Approved Requirements for Transportable Pressure Receptacles. In addition to the classification of dangerous goods (as per *Schedule 1*), vehicles carrying dangerous goods or substances by road and rail must, where necessary, be labelled with subsidiary hazard signs (as per *Schedule 2*). [*Carriage of Dangerous Goods (Classification, Packaging and Labelling) and Use of Transportable Pressure Receptacles Regulations 1996 (SI 1996 No 2092), Regs 4, 5*]. (See Table 2 above.)

## Transitional defence

D3013 Apart from the general defence under these Regulations (see D3004 above), it is also a defence that goods were classified, packaged and labelled for carriage prior to 1 July 1995, in accordance with the previous regulations (the *Carriage of Dangerous Goods by Road and Rail (Classification, Packaging and Labelling) Regulations 1994*

*(SI 1994 No 669)).* [*Carriage of Dangerous Goods (Classification, Packaging and Labelling) and Use of Transportable Pressure Receptacles Regulations 1996 (SI 1996 No 2092), Reg 20*].

## Training of drivers of vehicles carrying dangerous goods – the Carriage of Dangerous Goods by Road (Driver Training) Regulations 1996 (SI 1996 No 2094)

D3014    These Regulations, which came into force on 1 September 1996, require that operators of vehicles engaged in the carriage of dangerous goods ensure that drivers are instructed and trained in the dangers associated with the carriage of dangerous goods and hold vocational training certificates. For the first time this instruction and training covers:

(*a*)    certain environmentally hazardous substances;

(*b*)    radioactive material; and

(*c*)    flammable liquids.

Under the Regulations, vehicles are considered to be engaged in the 'carriage' of dangerous substances from the commencement of loading until the vehicle has been unloaded and cleaned or purged of the goods to the extent that it no longer creates a significant health and safety risk to any person regardless of whether the vehicle is on the road at any time. [*Carriage of Dangerous Goods by Road (Driver Training) Regulations 1996 (SI 1996 No 2094), Reg 2(4)*].

In particular, drivers of the following vehicles carrying dangerous goods must receive adequate training and instruction:

(i)    road tankers with a capacity of 1,000 litres (or less);

(ii)    tank containers with a capacity greater than 3,000 litres (excluding the carriage of

—    explosives,

—    goods in transport category 4, and

—    radioactive material (generally))

[*Carriage of Dangerous Goods by Road (Driver Training) Regulations 1996 (SI 1996 No 2094), Reg 2(1)(a), (2)*];

(iii)    vehicles having a permissible maximum weight exceeding 3.5 tonnes

—    in bulk,

—    in a road tanker with a capacity of 1,000 litres (or less),

—    in a tank container with a capacity of 3,000 litres (or less),

—    where any of the goods are in transport category 0,

—    where goods carried are in packages, none of the goods is in transport category 0,

—    where goods carried are in packages, none of the goods is in transport category 0 and the total mass or volume is greater than 20,

—    where goods carried are in packages, none of the goods is in transport category 0 or 1, and the total mass or volume is greater than 200, or

—  where goods carried are in packages, none of the goods is in transport category 0, 1 or 2, and the total mass or volume is greater than 500.

[*Carriage of Dangerous Goods by Road (Driver Training) Regulations 1996 (SI 1996 No 2094), Reg 2(1)(a)*].

### Instruction and training requirements – (main) duties of operators

D3015   Operators of vehicles (other than those registered outside the United Kingdom), engaged in the carriage of dangerous goods, must ensure that drivers of such vehicles have received adequate instruction and training to enable them to understand:

(*a*)   the nature of dangers and risks involved, and action to be taken in emergencies;

(*b*)   their duties under the *HSWA 1974*; and

(*c*)   any regulations relevant to the operation, e.g. the *Carriage of Dangerous Goods by Road Regulations 1996 (SI 1996 No 2095)*.

[*Carriage of Dangerous Goods by Road (Driver Training) Regulations 1996 (SI 1996 No 2094), Reg 3(1)*].

The operator must keep a record of such training and, where necessary, make a copy available to the driver. [*Carriage of Dangerous Goods by Road (Driver Training) Regulations 1996 (SI 1996 No 2094), Reg 3(2)*]. More particularly, operators must ensure that drivers hold a valid 'vocational training certificate' issued by the Secretary of State. [*Carriage of Dangerous Goods by Road (Driver Training) Regulations 1996 (SI 1996 No 2094), Reg 4(1)*]. It is sufficient compliance if a driver holds a training certificate issued under the previous regulations (the *Road Traffic (Training of Drivers of Vehicles Carrying Dangerous Goods) Regulations 1992 (SI 1992 No 744)*). [*Carriage of Dangerous Goods by Road (Driver Training) Regulations 1996 (SI 1996 No 2094), Reg 5*]. Exceptions occur in the case of certain radioactive material. [*Carriage of Dangerous Goods by Road (Driver Training) Regulations 1996 (SI 1996 No 2094), Reg 4(9)*]. Drivers must keep such certificates for the whole of the period of carriage [*Carriage of Dangerous Goods by Road (Driver Training) Regulations 1996 (SI 1996 No 2094), Reg 6*], and may be required to produce them to a police constable or goods vehicle examiner [*Carriage of Dangerous Goods by Road (Driver Training) Regulations 1996 (SI 1996 No 2094), Reg 7*].

*Transitional defence*

D3016   Where there is a breach of training or vocational certificate requirements prior to 1 January 1997, it is a defence for an accused person to prove that he complied with *Regulation 4* or *5(1)* of the *Training of Drivers of Vehicles Carrying Dangerous Goods) Regulations 1992 (SI 1992 No 744)*. [*Carriage of Dangerous Goods by Road (Driver Training) Regulations 1996 (SI 1996 No 2094), Reg 11(1)*].

## Appointment of safety advisers for the transport of dangerous goods – the Transport of Dangerous Goods (Safety Advisers) Regulations 1999 (SI 1999 No 257)

D3017   The *Transport of Dangerous Goods (Safety Advisers) Regulations 1999 (SI 1999 No 257)* came into force on 1 March 1999 (except as regards its key requirement, *Reg 4*, for which the date is 31 December 1999). The Regulations implement Council Directive 96/35/EC on the appointment and vocational qualification of safety advisers for the transport of dangerous goods by road, rail and inland waterway. *Reg 3* provides that the Regulations are applicable to self-employed people in the same way as they are applicable to employers.

The Regulations provides that, before any employer transports dangerous goods by road, rail or inland waterway, he must have appointed an individual as a safety adviser for the purpose of advising him on health, safety and environmental matters relating to the transportation of those dangerous goods. [*Transport of Dangerous Goods (Safety Advisers) Regulations 1999 (SI 1999 No 257), Reg 4(1)*]. 'Dangerous goods' have the meaning given them by the *Carriage of Dangerous Goods (Classification, Packaging and Labelling) and Use of Transportable Pressure Receptacles Regulations 1996 (SI 1996 No 2092)* (see D3002 ABOVE). Under the Regulations, employers are required to provide adequate information, time and other resources to allow the safety advisers to fulfil their functions. Employers must ensure that a sufficient number of safety advisers have been appointed under *Reg 4(1)* to enable them to carry out their duties effectively. The exact number of advisers to appoint is a matter for each employer to determine – it depends upon what is appropriate, bearing in mind the scale of the operation, the number of sites involved, and how far duties are allocated to advisers themselves or to other staff. Crucially, where a number of employers frequently use the same site, such as a port or marshalling yard, they may co-operate and appoint the same person as their safety adviser.

The Regulations lists the functions of safety advisers as including:

— monitoring compliance with the rules relating to the transportation of dangerous goods;

— advising the employer on the transportation of dangerous goods;

— ensuring that an annual report to the employer is prepared on the activities of the employer concerning the transport of dangerous goods;

— monitoring the procedures for compliance with the rules governing the identification of dangerous goods being transported;

— monitoring the practice of the employer in taking into account, when buying means of transport, any special requirements in connection with the dangerous goods to be transported;

— monitoring the procedures for checking the equipment used in connection with the transport of dangerous goods;

— monitoring the training of the employer's employees and the maintenance of records of such training;

— implementing proper emergency procedures on the occurrence of any accident or incident which may affect safety during the transport of dangerous goods;

— investigating and preparing reports on serious accidents, incidents or infringements recorded during the transportation of dangerous goods;

— implementing measures to avoid the recurrence of serious accidents, incidents or infringements;

— verifying that employees involved in transporting dangerous goods have detailed operational procedures and instructions;

— implementing verification procedures to ensure that the documents and safety equipment which must accompany the transportation of the goods are indeed on board the vehicle and that they comply with health and safety regulations; and

— implementing verification procedures to ensure compliance with legislation governing the loading and unloading of dangerous goods.

[*Transport of Dangerous Goods (Safety Advisers) Regulations 1999 (SI 1999 No 257), Sch 2*].

If dangerous goods are being transported by the employer, and an accident occurs which affects the health or safety of any person or causes damage to the environment or to property, the safety adviser must ensure that a report on the accident is prepared and provided to the employer, who must keep the report for at least five years.

The Regulations provide that safety advisers must hold vocational training certificates, obtainable only after training has been completed and an examination passed. [*Transport of Dangerous Goods (Safety Advisers) Regulations 1999 (SI 1999 No 257), Reg 7*]. The safety adviser's certificate must be appropriate to the modes of transport used by the employer and to all dangerous goods specified and transported by the employer. Each certificate will be valid for five years: advisers will then need to pass a 'refresher' examination.

# Carriage of dangerous goods by road – the Carriage of Dangerous Goods by Road Regulations 1996 (SI 1996 No 2095)

D3018    These Regulations, which came into force on 1 September 1996, impose requirements on (mainly) operators in connection with the transportation of dangerous goods by road in containers, tanks and vehicles (other than radioactive material and explosives) as well as storage of petrol and its distribution from terminals to service stations. [*Carriage of Dangerous Goods by Road Regulations 1996 (SI 1996 No 2095), Sch 12*]. Additionally, designers, manufacturers, importers, suppliers and repairers of such vehicles as well as examiners and testers of tanks have duties. (For exempted operations see D3010, D3011 above.)

## Compliance with certification requirements

D3019    It is incumbent on:

(*a*)    operators of tanks and vehicles to comply with the Approved Carriage List (ACL);

(*b*)    designers, manufacturers, importers, suppliers and repairers of vehicles to comply with the Approved Vehicle Requirements; and

(*c*)    designers, manufacturers, importers, suppliers, repairers, examiners and testers to comply with the Approved Tank Requirements.

[*Carriage of Dangerous Goods by Road Regulations 1996 (SI 1996 No 2095), Reg 6*].

## Definitions

D3020    The relevant definitions relating to these regulations are as follows.

### (A) *Operator*

The operator of a 'container' or 'vehicle' is:

(*a*)    the person who, having a place of business in Great Britain, has the management of the container or vehicle for the time being, or, if there is no person falling within this definition;

(*b*)    the driver of the vehicle or, in the case of a container, the driver of the vehicle on which the container is carried.

The operator of a 'tank' (other than the carrying tank of a road tanker), shall be:

(i)    the person who, having a place of business in Great Britain owns the tank, or, if there is no person falling within this definition;

(ii)    the person who, having a place of business in Great Britain, has the management of that tank; or

(iii)    the person who, having a place of business in Great Britain, has the management of that tank for the time being; or

(iv)    if there is no person who satisfies the requirements of (i)-(iii) above, the driver of the vehicle on which the tank is carried.

[*Carriage of Dangerous Goods by Road Regulations 1996 (SI 1996 No 2095), Reg 4*].

## (B)  *Consignor*

'Consignor' is defined by the *Carriage of Dangerous Goods by Road Regulations 1996 (SI 1996 No 2095), Reg 2(1)* as:

(*a*)    a person who, having a place of business in Great Britain, consigns, whether as a principal or agent for another, dangerous goods for carriage; or

(*b*)    the consignee of the goods insofar as that person has control over the carriage of those goods in Great Britain.

## (C)  *Containers*

The definition of 'container' in the Regulations has the same meaning as in the *Carriage of Dangerous Goods (Classification, Packaging and Labelling) and Use of Transportable Pressure Receptacles Regulations 1996 (SI 1996 No 2092), Reg 2(1)*. This is an article of carriage equipment with an internal volume of not less than 1 cubic metre which is:

(*a*)    of a permanent character and strong enough for repeated use;

(*b*)    designed to facilitate the carriage of goods, by one or more modes of carriage, without intermediate reloading;

(*c*)    designed to be readily handled; and

(*d*)    designed to be easy to fill and empty,

but does not include

(i)    an intermediate bulk container;

(ii)    any packagings;

(iii)    a tank;

(iv)    a transportable pressure receptacle or vehicle.

**(D)** *Road tanker, tank, tank container, tank wagon*

The definitions of 'road tanker', 'tank', 'tank container', 'tank wagon' have the same meanings as in the *Carriage of Dangerous Goods (Classification, Packaging and Labelling) and Use of Transportable Pressure Receptacles Regulations 1996 (SI 1996 No 2092), Reg 2(1)*. These are as follows.

(*a*)     *Road tanker* – means a vehicle or trailer constructed or adapted for the carriage of goods which has a tank ('carrying tank') which is

    (i)     attached to the frame of the vehicle (whether structurally or otherwise) and (except when empty) is not intended to be removed from the vehicle;

    (ii)     an integral part of the vehicle; or

    (iii)     a demountable tank.

(*b*)     *Tank* – means a tank which is

    (i)     used for the carriage of a liquid, gaseous, powdery or granular material or a sludge; and

    (ii)     so constructed that it can be securely closed (except for the purpose of relieving excess pressure) during the course of carriage,

and includes an assembly of transportable pressure receptacles interconnected by a manifold and mounted on a frame where

    (iii)     the frame is permanently fixed to a vehicle; or

    (iv)     the receptacles have a total volume of 1,000 litres or more,

but does not include

    (v)     an intermediate bulk container;

    (vi)     a hopper with a loose-fitting lid;

    (vii)     a transportable pressure receptacle;

    (viii)     an aerosol; or

    (ix)     packagings which satisfy *Regulation 6* (see D3007 above) or are excluded from the Regulations.

(*c*)     *Tank container* – means a tank (other than the carrying tank of a road tanker or tank wagon), whether or not divided into separate compartments, having a total capacity of more than 450 litres (or 1,000 litres in the case of tanks used for the carriage of a gas).

(*d*)     *Tank wagon* – comprises of a superstructure of one or more tanks (including their openings and closures), their items of equipment, and an underframe fitted with its own items of equipment (including running gear, suspension, buffing, traction, braking gear and inscriptions).

## Main duties of consignors

D3021     Consignors who engage operators to carry dangerous substances have duties to ensure that any operator engaged by him to carry those goods is provided with certain information. [*Transport of Dangerous Goods (Safety Advisers) Regulations 1999 (SI 1999 No 257), Reg 13(1)*]. The duty is imposed to enable operators to comply with their duties (see below). Operators break the law if they undertake the carriage of dangerous goods without the receipt of such information. This does not apply to consignors who also act as the operator, provided that they carry the goods on their own behalf. [*Carriage of Dangerous Goods by Road Regulations 1996 (SI 1996 No 2095), Reg 13(3)*].

*Information to be provided by consignors*

D3022    Any consignor of dangerous goods must ensure that any operator engaged by him is provided with information in documentary form prior to the carriage of the goods. This includes:

(*a*)    the designation of the dangerous goods;

(*b*)    the classification code;

(*c*)    the UN number;

(*d*)    any extra information that may be required to determine the transport category of the dangerous goods;

(*e*)    the control and emergency temperatures (where appropriate);

(*f*)    where the dangerous goods are carried in packages, either:

    (i)    the mass or volume of each individual package and the number of packages consigned,

    (ii)    for each transport category, the sum of the mass or volume of the individual packages consigned;

(*g*)    where the dangerous goods are carried other than in packages, either:

    (i)    the mass or volume of the dangerous goods consigned in each container, tank or vehicle and the number of containers or tanks, or

    (ii)    for each transport category, the sum of the mass or volume of all the dangerous goods consigned in containers, tanks or vehicles;

(*h*)    the name and address of the consignor;

(*j*)    the name and address of the consignee (if known);

(*k*)    any other relevant information; and

(*l*)    a statement signed or authenticated by or on behalf of the consignor (a 'consignor's declaration') confirming that in accordance with the *Carriage of Dangerous Goods by Road Regulations 1996 (SI 1996 No 2095)* and the *Carriage of Dangerous Goods (Classification, Packaging and Labelling) and Use of Transportable Pressure Receptacles Regulations 1996 (SI 1996 No 2092)*:

    (i)    the dangerous goods as presented may be carried,

    (ii)    the dangerous goods and any packaging, intermediate bulk container or tank in which they are contained are in a fit condition for carriage and properly labelled (see D3027 below), and

    (iii)    where several packages are packed together in an overpack or in a single container, this mixed packing is not prohibited.

## Main duties of operators

D3023    Operators carrying dangerous goods are subject to the following duties, namely to ensure the following. (For the definition of 'operator' see D3020 above.)

(*a*)    The letter 'Y' appears in column 8 of the Approved Carriage List, where goods are carried in bulk in a container or vehicle. [*Carriage of Dangerous Goods by Road Regulations 1996 (SI 1996 No 2095), Reg 8*]. Operators of 'vehicles' carrying such dangerous goods in bulk also have to comply with the requirements of *Schedule 5*, and operators of 'containers' carrying dangerous goods in bulk with *Schedule 6*.

(*b*)    The letter 'Y' appears in column 7 of the Approved Carriage List, where goods are carried in a tank. [*Carriage of Dangerous Goods by Road Regulations 1996 (SI 1996 No 2095), Reg 9*].

(*c*)    A container, tank and vehicle being used for the carriage of dangerous goods is:

(i)    suitable for such carriage, having regard to the journey itself and the hazardous properties of the cargo, and

(ii)    has been adequately maintained.

[*Carriage of Dangerous Goods by Road Regulations 1996 (SI 1996 No 2095), Reg 10(1)*].

(*d*)    Any vehicle which is being used for the carriage of dangerous goods:

(i)    has only one trailer or semi-trailer;

(ii)    if used for carriage of packages, with packaging sensitive to moisture, is either

—    sheeted, or

—    closed; and

(iii)    has complied with the requirements of *Schedule 7* 'Types of vehicle to be used for the carriage of certain dangerous goods'.

[*Carriage of Dangerous Goods by Road Regulations 1996 (SI 1996 No 2095), Reg 10(2)*].

(*e*)    A certificate has been signed, dated and issued by a competent authority, in relation to a tank (before carrying dangerous goods), stating that the tank:

(i)    has been examined and tested in accordance with requirements which have been approved and published in the Approved Tank Requirements,

(ii)    conforms to the approved design, and

(iii)    is suitable for its intended purpose,

and is kept at the operators' principal place of business.

[*Carriage of Dangerous Goods by Road Regulations 1996 (SI 1996 No 2095), Reg 11(3),(7)*].

Where the operator is not the tank owner, it is sufficient compliance if:

(i)    an authenticated copy of the certificate is kept:

—    at the operator's principal place of business in Great Britain, or

—    if there is no place of business in Great Britain, on the vehicle; or

(ii)    the certificate is readily available from the owner of the tank.

[*Carriage of Dangerous Goods by Road Regulations 1996 (SI 1996 No 2095), Reg 11(8)*].

(*f*)     That he has:

(i)     obtained the consignor's declaration (if applicable), or an authenticated copy in relation to the dangerous goods carried; and

(ii)    he has taken reasonable steps to ensure that the goods are in a condition fit for carriage.

[*Carriage of Dangerous Goods by Road Regulations 1996 (SI 1996 No 2095), Reg 12(1)*].

(*g*)    In the case of vehicles:

(i)     used for the carriage of infectious substances or toxic goods; or

(ii)    which are empty but uncleaned after the carriage of such goods,

that the operator has ensured that no food is carried in the vehicle unless effectively separated from the infectious substance or toxic goods to avoid the risk of contamination by those goods.

[*Carriage of Dangerous Goods by Road Regulations 1996 (SI 1996 No 2095), Reg 12(7)*].

(*h*)    That any other operators engaged by them who are engaging in the carriage of dangerous goods are provided with the requisite transport documentation prior to the journey commencing. This includes:

(i)     name and address of the consignor;

(ii)    name and address of the consignee;

(iii)   designation of dangerous goods;

(iv)    classification code;

(v)     UN number;

(vi)    any other information required to determine the transport category of the goods;

(vii)   control and emergency temperatures;

(viii)  details of total mass of volume of dangerous goods;

(ix)    emergency action code (where appropriate);

(x)     prescribed temperature (where appropriate); and

(xi)    emergency information.

[*Carriage of Dangerous Goods by Road Regulations 1996 (SI 1996 No 2095), Regs 13(1),(2), 14(1)–(3)*].

(*j*)    That all steps as it is reasonable for them to take to ensure that nothing in the way that goods are loaded, stowed or unloaded from any container, tank or vehicle is liable to create a significant risk or significantly increase any existing risk to the health or safety of any person arising out of the presence of those dangerous goods. [*Carriage of Dangerous Goods by Road Regulations 1996 (SI 1996 No 2095), Reg 19(1), (2)(b), Sch 11*]. The same duties as are imposed on drivers (see (*g*)–(*q*) at D3026 below) apply to operators.

(*k*)    That any vehicle which is being used to convey dangerous goods is:

(i)     equipped so that the driver can take those measures detailed in the emergency information; and

(ii)    where toxic gases are being carried, that the vehicle crew are supplied with suitable respiratory protective equipment to enable them to escape safely in the event of any emergency.

[*Carriage of Dangerous Goods by Road Regulations 1996 (SI 1996 No 2095), Reg 21(1)*].

(*l*)    Ensure that the vehicle is equipped with:

(i)    at least one portable fire extinguisher with a minimum capacity of 2kg of dry powder (or other suitable extinguishant) suitable for fighting a fire in the engine or cab of the vehicle; and, if it is to be used to fight a fire involving the load, it does not aggravate the fire, and if possible, controls it; and

(ii)    at least one portable fire extinguisher with a minimum capacity of 6kg of dry powder (or other suitable extinguishant) suitable for fighting a tyre or brake fire or a fire involving the load, which does not aggravate the fire, and if possible, controls it,

and that the extinguishants contained therein, will not release toxic gases into the drivers cab when under the influence of the heat of a fire. [*Carriage of Dangerous Goods by Road Regulations 1996 (SI 1996 No 2095), Reg 23(2), (7)*].

The extinguisher must:

(1)    bear a mark of compliance with a standard issued by a recognised competent authority;

(2)    be fitted with a seal verifying that it has not been used; and

(3)    where it was manufactured after 31 December 1996, bear an inscription as to the date when it should next be inspected.

[*Carriage of Dangerous Goods by Road Regulations 1996 (SI 1996 No 2095), Reg 23(4)*].

If the load only comprises of infectious substances, the extinguisher in (ii) above need not be provided. [*Carriage of Dangerous Goods by Road Regulations 1996 (SI 1996 No 2095), Reg 23(3)(b)*].

(*m*)    Ensure that when the vehicle is parked it is parked to comply with certain requirements. The same duties that are imposed on drivers in this regard (see (*u*) at D3026 below) apply to operators.

(*n*)    No container, vehicle or tank shall carry any dangerous goods which are required by the *Carriage of Dangerous Goods (Classification, Packaging and Labelling) and Use of Transportable Pressure Receptacles Regulations 1996 (SI 1996 No 2092)* to be labelled with a subsidiary hazard sign 'liable to explosion' with any other dangerous goods unless effective measures are taken to ensure that carriage of the mixed load is no more dangerous than the total quantity of the unmixed load. [*Carriage of Dangerous Goods by Road Regulations 1996 (SI 1996 No 2095), Reg 18(1)*].

*Emergency information to be provided by operators*

**D3024**    The operator shall provide to other operators engaged by him details of measures to be taken by the driver in the event of an accident or emergency, and any other safety information concerning the goods. This includes:

(*a*)　the nature of the danger inherent in the dangerous goods being carried and the safety measures to be taken to avert such danger;

(*b*)　the measures to be taken and treatment to be given in the event of any person coming into contact with the dangerous goods being carried or with any substances which might evolve;

(*c*)　the measures to be taken in the case of fire, and, in particular, the fire-fighting appliances or equipment which must not be used;

(*d*)　the measures to be taken in the case of breakage or deterioration of packagings, especially where such breakage or deterioration can lead to the spillage of goods on to the road; and

(*e*)　any additional information required to be given in *Schedule 9* 'Additional emergency information relating to the carriage of certain dangerous goods'.

*Information to be kept by operators*

D3025　Operators of any vehicle which is used for the carriage of dangerous substances must also ensure that a record of information contained in the transport documentation (other than emergency information) is kept for at least three months after the completion of the journey. [*Carriage of Dangerous Goods by Road Regulations 1996 (SI 1996 No 2095), Reg 16*].

## Main duties of drivers

D3026　The following are the main duties of drivers:

(*a*)　Not to permit a person to be carried in the vehicle or tanker, other than a member of the vehicle crew, for the sole purpose of transporting that person. [*Carriage of Dangerous Goods by Road Regulations 1996 (SI 1996 No 2095), Reg 12(2)*].

(*b*)　Not to open a package containing dangerous goods, unless authorised by the operator of the vehicle. [*Carriage of Dangerous Goods by Road Regulations 1996 (SI 1996 No 2095), Reg 12(3)*].

(*c*)　Not to bring portable lighting apparatus onto a vehicle if such apparatus can produce a flame or has a metallic surface liable to produce sparks (except where only infectious substances are carried). [*Carriage of Dangerous Goods by Road Regulations 1996 (SI 1996 No 2095), Reg 12(4)–(5)*].

(*d*)　Not to enter a closed vehicle, which is being used for the carriage of liquids having a flash point of 61°C or below or flammable gases, carrying a lighting apparatus other than a portable lamp designed that it cannot ignite any flammable vapours or gases which may have penetrated into the interior of the vehicle. [*Carriage of Dangerous Goods by Road Regulations 1996 (SI 1996 No 2095), Reg 12(6)*].

(*e*)　In cases of a vehicle:

(i)　used for carriage of infectious substances/toxic goods, or

(ii)　which is empty and uncleaned after the carriage of such goods,

not to carry food therein, unless effectively separated from infectious substances and toxic goods. [*Carriage of Dangerous Goods by Road Regulations 1996 (SI 1996 No 2095), Reg 12(7)*].

(*f*)   To ensure transport documentation (see above) is:

(i)   readily available during carriage, and

(ii)   produced, on request, to a police constable or goods vehicle examiner.

[*Carriage of Dangerous Goods by Road Regulations 1996 (SI 1996 No 2095), Reg 15(1)*].

(*g*)   To ensure documentation relating to dangerous goods not being carried, is removed from the vehicle or placed in a securely closed container and clearly marked, indicating that it does not relate to any dangerous goods which are being carried. [*Carriage of Dangerous Goods by Road Regulations 1996 (SI 1996 No 2095), Reg 15(3)*].

(*h*)   To take such steps as is reasonably practicable to ensure that no dangerous goods are loaded, stowed or unloaded so as to create or increase significantly health and safety hazards associated with their presence. [*Carriage of Dangerous Goods by Road Regulations 1996 (SI 1996 No 2095), Reg 19(1), (2)(b), Sch 11*].

(*j*)   To load, stow, unload goods so as to prevent significant displacement in relation to each other and the sides of the vehicle. [*Carriage of Dangerous Goods by Road Regulations 1996 (SI 1996 No 2095), Reg 19(3)*].

(*k*)   Where dangerous goods have escaped from any package into a container or vehicle in which they are being carried, to ensure that the container or vehicle is cleaned as soon as possible, and definitely before re-loading. [*Carriage of Dangerous Goods by Road Regulations 1996 (SI 1996 No 2095), Reg 19(4)*].

(*l*)   To ensure that containers and vehicles which have been used for the carriage of dangerous goods in bulk, shall be properly cleaned before re-loading unless the new load consists of dangerous goods with the same designation as the preceding load. [*Carriage of Dangerous Goods by Road Regulations 1996 (SI 1996 No 2095), Reg 19(5)*].

(*m*)   Not to smoke in the vicinity of or inside the vehicle, during loading or unloading operations. [*Carriage of Dangerous Goods by Road Regulations 1996 (SI 1996 No 2095), Reg 19(6)*].

(*n*)   To ensure that where goods with a flash-point of 61°C or below are being carried in a tank that the chassis is earthed before the tank is filled or emptied, and the rate of filling is limited to avoid an electrostatic discharge which could cause ignition of any vapour present. [*Carriage of Dangerous Goods by Road Regulations 1996 (SI 1996 No 2095), Reg 19(7)*].

(*o*)   To shut off vehicle engines during loading and unloading operations. [*Carriage of Dangerous Goods by Road Regulations 1996 (SI 1996 No 2095), Reg 19(8)*].

(*p*)   Not to overfill tank or compartments with dangerous goods. [*Carriage of Dangerous Goods by Road Regulations 1996 (SI 1996 No 2095), Reg 19(9)*].

(*q*)   To ensure, so far as is practicable, that:

(i)   all openings in a tank, and

(ii)   valves and cap

are securely closed prior to the start of and throughout a journey. [*Carriage of Dangerous Goods by Road Regulations 1996 (SI 1996 No 2095), Reg 19(10)*].

(*r*)     In the event of accident or emergency, to take all reasonable steps to comply with instructions in the emergency information. [*Carriage of Dangerous Goods by Road Regulations 1996 (SI 1996 No 2095), Reg 22(1)*].

(*s*)     In the event of emergency, to notify emergency services by the quickest practical means. [*Carriage of Dangerous Goods by Road Regulations 1996 (SI 1996 No 2095), Reg 22(2)*].

(*t*)     Not to do anything liable to create or increase significantly the risk of fire or explosion. [*Carriage of Dangerous Goods by Road Regulations 1996 (SI 1996 No 2095), Reg 23(1)*].

(*u*)     When parked, that the vehicle (after being properly secured) is:

(i)     supervised by a competent person, either over 18 or a member of the armed forces; and

(ii)     is parked in an isolated position, either

— unsupervised in an open space in a secure depot or factory, or (failing that)

— in a vehicle park supervised by an appropriate person who has been notified of the nature of the load and the whereabouts of the driver, or (failing that)

— in a public/private vehicle park, where the vehicle is not likely to suffer damage, or (failing that)

— in a suitable open space separated from the public highway and dwellings, where the public does not normally pass or assemble

(except where the vehicle has been either damaged or has broken down and the driver has gone for assistance, and has taken all reasonable steps to secure the vehicle and its contents before leaving it). [*Carriage of Dangerous Goods by Road Regulations 1996 (SI 1996 No 2095), Reg 24(1)(2)*].

## Information to be displayed on containers, tanks and vehicles

**D3027**     In general, the following information must be displayed on the vehicle:

(*a*)     an orange-coloured panel, containing the UN number and emergency action code of the dangerous goods carried;

(*b*)     a telephone number where additional specialist information can be obtained concerning the load;

(*c*)     danger signs and subsidiary hazard signs; and

(*d*)     a hazard warning panel.

The requirements of the Regulations relating to information which must be displayed is contained in *Regulation 17* and *Schedule 10*.

The operator of any container, tank or vehicle which is being used for the carriage of dangerous goods has a duty to ensure that the information displayed on the container, tank or vehicle concerned is in accordance with *Schedule 10*. [*Carriage of Dangerous Goods by Road Regulations 1996 (SI 1996 No 2095), Reg 17(1)*]. No information, referred to in *Schedule 10* must remain on any container, tank or vehicle when it is not being used for the carriage of dangerous goods [*Carriage of Dangerous Goods by Road Regulations 1996 (SI 1996 No 2095), Reg 17(2)*], and no additional information which may cause confusion to the emergency services when read in conjunction with information required by *Schedule 10* should be attached

[*Reg 17(3)*]. The operator and the driver must ensure that any danger sign, hazard warning panel, orange-coloured panel or subsidiary hazard sign which is displayed is kept clean and free from obstruction [*Carriage of Dangerous Goods by Road Regulations 1996 (SI 1996 No 2095), Reg 17(4)*], and that when dangerous goods are no longer contained in the vehicle (e.g. after discharge or unloading) that the signs are covered, and that the material being used to cover them would withstand 15 minutes' engulfment in fire [*Carriage of Dangerous Goods by Road Regulations 1996 (SI 1996 No 2095), Reg 17(5)*].

*Schedule 10* contains detailed requirements as to the marking of vehicles.

### Orange-coloured panels, UN numbers and emergency action codes

**D3028**   Orange-coloured panels shall be displayed at the front and back of any vehicle carrying dangerous goods. [*Carriage of Dangerous Goods by Road Regulations 1996 (SI 1996 No 2095), Reg 17(1), Sch 10, Pt I*]. An example of an orange-coloured panel is illustrated as *Figure 1* below.

*Figure 1: Orange-coloured panel*

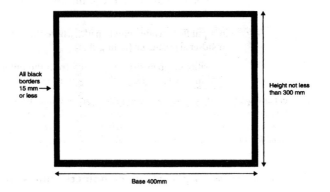

[*Sch 10 Pt II*].

Where a vehicle is carrying only one of the dangerous goods listed in the Approved Carriage List in a 'tank' the following information shall be displayed:

(*a*)   an orange-coloured panel at the rear of the vehicle bearing the appropriate UN number and the appropriate emergency action code (see *Figure 2* below); and

*Figure 2: Orange-coloured panel displaying the emergency action code and the UN number*

[*Sch 10, Pt II*].

(*b*)   an orange-coloured panel as in (*a*) above on both sides of

    (i)   the tank,

    (ii)   the frame of the tank, or

    (iii)   the vehicle, provided that the panel is positioned immediately below the tank.

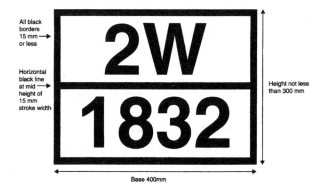

Where a vehicle is carrying a multi-load in tanks, the following information shall be displayed:

(*a*)     an orange-coloured panel at the rear of the vehicle bearing the appropriate emergency action code (see *Figure 3* below);

*Figure 3: Orange-coloured panel displaying the emergency action code*

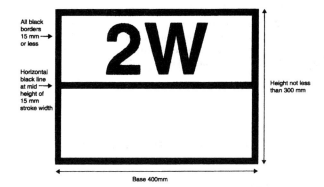

[*Sch 10, Pt II*].

(*b*)     an orange-coloured panel on the sides of each tank, or where the tank has more than one compartment, on each compartment, which are

    (i)     at least one on each side which conforms to that illustrated as *Figure 3* above, and

    (ii)     the remainder which bear the appropriate UN number (see *Figure 4* below); or

*Figure 4: Orange-coloured panel displaying the UN number*

[*Sch 10, Pt II*].

(*c*)    on both sides of the frame of each tank or on both sides of the vehicle provided they are positioned immediately below the tank or tank compartment concerned.

Where the vehicle is carrying only one of the dangerous goods listed in the Approved Carriage List in bulk, in the vehicle or container on the vehicle, it shall be labelled with:

(*a*)    an orange-coloured panel as in *Figure 2* above at the rear of the vehicle; and

(*b*)    an orange-coloured panel as in *Figure 2* above on each side of the vehicle.

Where a vehicle is carrying a multi-load in bulk, in separate compartments of the vehicle or in separate containers on the vehicle, it shall be labelled with:

(*a*)    an orange-coloured panel as in *Figure 3* above at the rear of the vehicle bearing the appropriate emergency action code; and

(*b*)    an orange-coloured panel displayed on each side of each compartment or on each container, of which

(i)    at least one conforms to *Figure 2* above, and

(ii)    the remainder conform to *Figure 4* above.

Any UN numbers or emergency action codes displayed need to be in black digits, measuring not less than 100mm in height and not less than 15mm stroke width. They also need to be able to be legible after 15 minutes engulfment in fire (unless the tank was constructed before 1 January 1999).

*Display of telephone number*

D3029    Where a vehicle is carrying only one dangerous good listed in the Approved Carriage List, the telephone number displayed shall be displayed:

(*a*)    at the rear of the vehicle;

(*b*)    on both sides of

(i)    the tank,

(ii)    the frame of the tank, or

(iii)    the vehicle; and

(*c*)    in the immediate vicinity of the orange-coloured panels.

Where a vehicle is carrying a multi-load in tanks, the telephone number shall be displayed:

(*a*)    at the rear of the vehicle;

(*b*)    on both sides of

(i)    the tank,

(ii)    the frame of the tank, or

(iii)    the vehicle; and

(*c*)    is in the immediate vicinity of the orange-coloured panels which conform to *Figures 2* or *3* (see D3028 above).

The telephone number shall consist of black digits of not less than 30mm in height and be displayed on an orange-coloured background. (See *Figure 5* below.) The telephone number may be substituted by the words 'consult local depot' or 'contact local depot'.

*Danger signs and subsidiary hazard signs*

D3030    The Regulations require that where a vehicle is carrying dangerous goods in packages in a container, any danger sign or subsidiary hazard sign which is required by the *Carriage of Dangerous Goods (Classification, Packaging and Labelling) and Use of Transportable Pressure Receptacles Regulations 1996 (SI 1996 No 2092)* shall be displayed on at least one side of the container.

Where the vehicle is carrying dangerous goods in a tank container or in bulk in a container, required danger signs or subsidiary hazard signs should be shown on each side of the container, and if not visible from the outside of the vehicle, the same signs should also be displayed on the rear of the vehicle.

These signs are required to be not less than 250mm in height, and have a line of the same colour as the symbol 12.5 mm inside the edge and running parallel to it.

*Hazard warning panels*

D3031    The labelling requirements in D3028–D3030 above may be displayed on a hazard warning panel as in *Figure 5* below.

*Figure 5: Hazard warning panel*

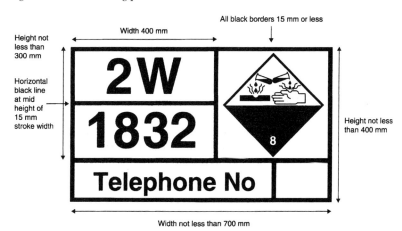

[*Sch 10, Pt II*].

## Petroleum deliveries at filling stations

D3032    The Regulations lay down requirements for the unloading of petrol at petroleum filling stations and other premises licensed for the unloading of petrol from the tank of a road tanker. [*Carriage of Dangerous Goods by Road Regulations 1996 (SI 1996 No 2095), Reg 20(1)*]. *Schedule 12* lays down detailed requirements. *Schedule 12, Part II* lays down detailed requirements for licensee-controlled deliveries, and *Schedule 12, Part III* for driver-controlled deliveries. A Part III Licence is required for driver-controlled deliveries.

*Schedule 12, para 20* lays down requirements to be met by licensees who intend to use driver-controlled deliveries under the Part III procedure.

### Defence

D3033    It is a defence to a charge under these Regulations for the person charged to prove:

(*a*)    that the commission of the offence was due to the act or default of another person not being one of his employees; and

(*b*)    that he took all reasonable precautions and excercised all due diligence to avoid the commission of the offence.

[*Carriage of Dangerous Goods by Road Regulations 1996 (SI 1996 No 2095), Reg 26(1)*].

### Transitional defence

D3034    In any proceedings for an offence under these Regulations prior to 1 January 1997, it is a defence for the accused to prove that the goods were carried:

(*a*)    in a road tanker in accordance with the *Road Traffic (Carriage of Dangerous Substances in Road Tankers and Tank Containers) Regulations 1992 (SI 1992 No 743)*; or

(*b*)    in bulk or in packages in accordance with the *Road Traffic (Carriage of Dangerous Substances in Packages etc.) Regulations 1992 (SI 1992 No 742)*.

[*Carriage of Dangerous Goods by Road Regulations 1996 (SI 1996 No 2095), Reg 28*].

## Transportation of explosives by road

D3035    Packaging of explosives is governed by the *Packaging of Explosives for Carriage Regulations 1991 (SI 1991 No 2097)*. Requirements concerning transportation are regulated by the *Carriage of Explosives by Road Regulations 1996 (SI 1996 No 2093)*. Labelling of explosives is governed by the *Classification and Labelling of Explosives Regulations 1983 (SI 1983 No 1140)* as amended by the *Carriage of Explosives by Road Regulations 1996 (SI 1996 No 2093), Sch 9* (see DANGEROUS SUBSTANCES I).

The *Carriage of Dangerous Goods (Amendment) Regulations 1998 (SI 1998 No 2885)* came into force on 30 December 1998. They amend the *Highly Flammable Liquids and Liquefied Petroleum Gases Regulations 1972 (SI 1972 No 917)*, the *Dangerous Substances in Harbour Areas Regulations 1987 (SI 1987 No 37)*, the *Carriage of Dangerous Goods by Rail Regulations 1996 (SI 1996 No 2089)*, the *Carriage of Dangerous Goods (Classification, Packaging and Labelling) and Use of Transportable Pressure Receptacles Regulations 1996 (SI 1996 No 2092)* and the *Carriage of Dangerous Goods by Road Regulations 1996 (SI 1996 No 2095)* to change the date for the application of certain provisions relating to tanks and transportable pressure receptacles from 1 January 1999 to 1 July 2001.

The *Carriage of Dangerous Goods (Amendment) Regulations 1999 (SI 1999 No 303)* came into force on 5 March 1999. They amend the following Regulations. They amend the following Regulations:

● the *Classification and Labelling of Explosives Regulations 1983 (SI 1983 No 1140)*;

● the *Pressure Systems and Transportable Gas Containers Regulations 1989 (SI 1989 No 2169)*;

● the *Packaging of Explosives for Carriage Regulations 1991 (SI 1991 No 2097)*;

- the *Carriage of Dangerous Goods by Rail Regulations 1996 (SI 1996 No 2089)*;

- the *Packaging, Labelling and Carriage of Radioactive Material by Rail Regulations 1996 (SI 1996 No 2090)*;

- the *Carriage of Dangerous Goods (Classification, Packaging and Labelling) and Use of Transportable Pressure Receptacles Regulations 1996 (SI 1996 No 2092)*;

- the *Carriage of Explosives by Road Regulations 1996 (SI 1996 No 2093)*;

- the *Carriage of Dangerous Goods by Road (Driver Training) Regulations 1996 (SI 1996 No 2094)*;

- the *Carriage of Dangerous Goods by Road Regulations 1996 (SI 1996 No 2095)*; and

- the *Health and Safety (Fees) Regulations 1999 (SI 1999 No 645)*.

The effect of the amendments is to align the above-mentioned Regulations with the latest versions of the ADR and RID agreements, as defined in the *Carriage of Dangerous Goods (Classification, Packaging and Labelling) and Use of Transportable Pressure Receptacles Regulations 1996, Reg 2(1)*.

The main changes are as follows:

(*a*)    a general disapplication:

— where goods are carried in an emergency for the purposes of saving life or protecting the environment;

— with regard to goods, except explosives, which are part of machinery or equipment;

— for certain pharmaceutical products packaged for retail sale and intended for personal or household use; and

— with regard to certain radioactive materials carried by rail;

(*b*)    a new requirement for large containers to meet international standards;

(*c*)    the carriage in bulk of used batteries to be allowed under certain conditions;

(*d*)    revisions to the content and format of emergency information for the carriage of dangerous goods by road;

(*e*)    a new training requirement for employees with responsibilities related to the carriage of dangerous goods by road;

(*f*)    training for the drivers of road vehicles which carry dangerous goods to be in the form of a theoretical course in specified subjects accompanied by practical exercises;

(*g*)    the introduction of additional arrangements for the carriage of certain oxidizing, toxic and corrosive substances in composite intermediate bulk containers;

(*h*)    the carriage in bulk of certain high temperature goods to be permitted in special vehicles, wagons and large containers;

(*i*)    greater flexibility in the carriage of mixed loads of explosives and other dangerous goods;

(*j*)    the requirement for an ADR (B3) certificate for Types II and III explosives vehicles constructed after 1 January 1997;

(*k*)    the introduction of transitional provisions in relation to the publication of a new edition of an Approved Document; and (*l*)   the substitution of fixed fees for applications for approvals of training or refresher courses under the *Carriage of Dangerous Goods by Road (Driver Training) Regulations 1996.*

## Carriage of explosives – The Carriage of Explosives by Road Regulations 1996 (SI 1996 No 2093)

D3036   These Regulations, which came into effect on 1 September 1996, specify requirements in relation to the carriage of explosives by road, placing duties mainly (but not exclusively) on the operators of vehicles carrying explosives. The Regulations do not apply to any explosive nuclear device or certain dangerous goods. [*Carriage of Explosives by Road Regulations 1996 (SI 1996 No 2093), Reg 3(5)–(6)*].

### Definitions

D3037   The relevant definitions contained in these Regulations are as follows.

(A) *Explosives*

These are explosive articles or substances which:

(i)    have been assigned on a classification to Class 1; or

(ii)   are unclassified.

(B) *Explosive substances*

These are:

(i)    a solid or liquid substance; or

(ii)   a mixture of solid or liquid substances or both,

which are capable by chemical reaction in itself of producing a gas at such a temperature and pressure and at such a speed as could cause damage to surroundings or which is designed to produce an effect by heat, light, sound, gas or smoke or a combination of these as a result of non-detonative self-sustaining exothermic chemical reactions.

(C) *Carriage*

Under the Regulations a vehicle or container shall be deemed to be engaged in the 'carriage' of explosives:

(i)    in the case of a vehicle, from the commencement of loading it with the explosives concerned for the purpose of carrying those explosives by road until that vehicle (or any compartment within it) has been unloaded, and, if necessary cleaned, so that any explosives which remain do not create a significant health or safety risk to any person;

(ii)   in the case of a container which is to be placed on a vehicle, from the commencement of loading, until the container is either

—    removed from the vehicle, or

—    unloaded, and where necessary cleaned, so that any explosives which remain are not significant to create a risk to the health and safety of any person.

It is immaterial in (i) and (ii) above, whether or not the vehicle or container is on a road at any material time.

## (D) *Operator*

Under the Regulations an 'operator' is defined as:

(i) a person who, having a place of business in Great Britain, has the management of a vehicle or container for the time being; or

(ii) the driver of the vehicle or, in the case of a container, the driver of the vehicle on which the container is carried.

However, a person is not to be regarded as being the operator of a vehicle or container solely because he has management of it during loading or unloading, or the vehicle or container is on premises which are under his control.

## (E) *Consignor*

This means:

(i) the person who, having a place of business in Great Britain, consigns, whether as a principal or agent for another, explosives for carriage; or

(ii) the person who has control over the carriage of explosives within Great Britain.

## (F) *Packaging, container, dangerous goods, trailer*

*Packaging* – has the same definition as in the *Carriage of Dangerous Goods (Classification, Packaging and Labelling) and Use of Transportable Pressure Receptacles Regulations 1996 (SI 1996 No 2092), Reg 2(1)*.

*Container* – has the same definition as in the *Carriage of Dangerous Goods (Classification, Packaging and Labelling) and Use of Transportable Pressure Receptacles Regulations 1996 (SI 1996 No 2092), Reg 2(1)*. (See D3020 above.)

*Dangerous goods* – has the same definition as in the *Carriage of Dangerous Goods (Classification, Packaging and Labelling) and Use of Transportable Pressure Receptacles Regulations 1996 (SI 1996 No 2092), Reg 2(1)*. (See D3002 above.)

*Trailer* – is defined in the *Road Vehicles (Construction and Use) Regulations 1986 (SI 1986 No 1078), Reg 3(2)*.

## Main duties of consignors

**D3038** Any consignor of explosives shall ensure that prior to carriage of any explosives by an operator engaged by him, that the operator is provided with information in documentary form as specified below. [*Carriage of Explosives by Road Regulations 1996 (SI 1996 No 2093), Reg 16(1), Sch 6*].

In relation to each type of explosive being carried this will be:

(*a*) the designation;

(*b*) the classification;

(*c*) the UN Number;

(*d*) the total net mass in tonnes or kilograms of explosives carried; and

(e)     whether, in the case of explosives in Compatibility Group C, D, or G, the explosives carried are explosive substances or explosive articles.

In relation to the consignment as a whole this will be:

(i)     the number of packages consigned;

(ii)    the name and address of the consignor;

(iii)   the name and address of the consignee;

(iv)    any other relevant information; and

(v)     a statement signed or authenticated by or on behalf of the consignor confirming that the explosives as presented to the operator are carried in conformity with the Regulations, and that the labelling and packaging conform with the *Packaging of Explosives for Carriage Regulations 1991 (SI 1991 No 2097)*, and the *Classification and Labelling of Explosives Regulations 1983 (SI 1983 No 1140)*.

*[Carriage of Explosives by Road Regulations 1996 (SI 1996 No 2093), Reg 16(1), Sch 6, Part I]*.


## Duties of operators

D3039     These are as follows.

(a)     Not to carry explosives of Compatibility Group K in a vehicle. *[Carriage of Explosives by Road Regulations 1996 (SI 1996 No 2093), Reg 7(1)]*.

(b)     Not to carry unclassified explosives in a vehicle (with certain exceptions). *[Carriage of Explosives by Road Regulations 1996 (SI 1996 No 2093), Reg 7(2)]*.

(c)     Not to carry explosives in a vehicle being used to carry passengers for hire (with certain exceptions). *[Carriage of Explosives by Road Regulations 1996 (SI 1996 No 2093), Reg 8(1)]*.

(d)     Not to carry in bulk explosives which are explosive substances. *[Carriage of Explosives by Road Regulations 1996 (SI 1996 No 2093), Reg 9]*.

(e)     To ensure that the vehicle and any container used for carriage is suitable for the safety and security of explosives. *[Carriage of Explosives by Road Regulations 1996 (SI 1996 No 2093), Reg 10]*.

(f)     To ensure that any vehicles used comply with any requirements entitled 'Approved Requirements for the Construction of Vehicles Intended for the Carriage of Explosives by Road' published by the Health and Safety Commission have been complied with. *[Carriage of Explosives by Road Regulations 1996 (SI 1996 No 2093), Reg 11]*.

(g)     Not to carry explosives which are in different compatibility groups together unless it is permitted by *Schedule 4* of the regulations or effective measures have been taken to ensure that the carriage of such a mixed load is no more dangerous than the carriage of the same quantity of explosives in any of the compatibility groups carried (with certain restrictions). *[Reg 14(1)(2)]*.

(h)     To display requisite information on the vehicle concerning explosives. *[Carriage of Explosives by Road Regulations 1996 (SI 1996 No 2093), Reg 15, Sch 5]*.

(*j*)   Not to display any information, orange-coloured panel, danger sign or subsidiary hazard sign when the vehicle or container is not being used for the carriage of explosives. [*Carriage of Explosives by Road Regulations 1996 (SI 1996 No 2093), Reg 15(5)*].

(*k*)   Not to allow any information to be displayed on a vehicle or container which is likely to confuse the emergency services when read in conjunction with any information displayed in accordance with *Schedule 5* 'Information to be displayed on vehicles and containers'. [*Carriage of Explosives by Road Regulations 1996 (SI 1996 No 2093), Reg 15(6)*].

(*l*)   To provide information to another operator engaged by him, with information provided by the consignors. [*Carriage of Explosives by Road Regulations 1996 (SI 1996 No 2093), Reg 17(1)*].

(*m*)   To provide information to any driver engaged by him, with information provided by the consignors, called the 'transport documentation'. [*Carriage of Explosives by Road Regulations 1996 (SI 1996 No 2093), Reg 17(2)*]. This transport documentation consists of the information provided by the consignors (see D3038 (*a*)-(*e*) and (i)-(v) above) together with:

   (i)    the total number of packages;

   (ii)   the name and address of the operator of the vehicle;

   (iii)  emergency information, consisting of details of measures to be taken by the driver in the event of an accident or emergency and other safety information concerning the explosives being carried. This includes

       —   the nature of the danger inherent in the explosives being carried and the safety measures to be taken to avert any such danger,

       —   the action to be taken and treatment to be given in the event of any person coming into contact with the explosives being carried or with any substances which might be evolved,

       —   the measures to be taken in the case of fire and, in particular, the fire-fighting appliances or equipment which must not be used,

       —   the measures to be taken in the case of breakage or deterioration of the packagings or of the explosives being carried, especially where such deterioration results in a spillage of the explosives onto the road, and

       —   the measures to be taken to avoid or minimise damage in the event of spillage of explosives which are pollutant to the aquatic environment.

(*n*)   To ensure that explosives are loaded, stowed, and unloaded so as not to create a significant health and safety risk. [*Carriage of Explosives by Road Regulations 1996 (SI 1996 No 2093), Reg 19(1)*].

(*o*)   To ensure that food is not carried with explosives, unless effectively separated and protected from the risk of contamination. [*Carriage of Explosives by Road Regulations 1996 (SI 1996 No 2093), Reg 19(3)*].

(*p*)   To ensure that when the vehicle:

   (i)    is not parked, an attendant accompanies the driver, and

   (ii)   is parked, and the driver is not present, a person competent to ensure security of explosives is constantly with the vehicle.

[*Carriage of Explosives by Road Regulations 1996 (SI 1996 No 2093), Reg 20(1)*].

(*q*)    To ensure that where more than 5 tonnes of explosives in Division 1 (see below) are being carried, to follow the route agreed with the police. [*Carriage of Explosives by Road Regulations 1996 (SI 1996 No 2093), Reg 21(1)*].

(*r*)    To take steps to

    (i)    prevent accidents and minimise the harmful effects of any which may occur; and

    (ii)    prevent unauthorised access to, or removal from, part of the load.

[*Carriage of Explosives by Road Regulations 1996 (SI 1996 No 2093), Reg 22*].

(*s*)    To ensure that people do not smoke whilst carrying explosives or during their unloading, or bring portable lighting equipment onto a vehicle if such equipment has any flame or is liable to produce sparks. [*Carriage of Explosives by Road Regulations 1996 (SI 1996 No 2093), Reg 23*].

(*t*)    To ensure that the vehicle is so equipped that the driver can take steps detailed in the emergency information. [*Carriage of Explosives by Road Regulations 1996 (SI 1996 No 2093), Reg 24*].

(*u*)    To ensure that there is not a significant risk of fire or explosion during the carriage of explosives. [*Carriage of Explosives by Road Regulations 1996 (SI 1996 No 2093), Reg 25*].

(*v*)    To ensure that in the event of accidents or emergencies, proper precautions are taken:

    (i)    for the safety of persons from ignition, and

    (ii)    for the security of explosives.

[*Carriage of Explosives by Road Regulations 1996 (SI 1996 No 2093), Reg 26(3)*].

(*w*)    Where an operator is informed of any emergency where the situation cannot be brought under immediate control, the operator shall inform the Health and Safety Executive by the quickest practicable means. [*Carriage of Explosives by Road Regulations 1996 (SI 1996 No 2093), Reg 26(2)*].

(*x*)    To ensure that not more than the specified quantity of explosives is carried. This is as follows:

| Division | Compatibility Group | Maximum quantity (kilograms) |
| --- | --- | --- |
| 1.1 | A | 50 |
| 1.1 | B, F, G or L | 5,000 |
| 1.1 | C, D, E or J | 16,000 |
| 1.2 | Any | 16,000 |
| 1.3 | Any | 16,000 |
| 1.4 | Any | 16,000 |
| 1.5 | Any | 16,000 |
| 1.6 | Any | 16,000 |

*[Carriage of Explosives by Road Regulations 1996 (SI 1996 No 2093), Reg 13, Sch 3, Part III].*

(y)    Where explosives have escaped from any package into a container or vehicle in which they are being carried, to ensure that the vehicle concerned is cleaned as soon as possible. *[Carriage of Explosives by Road Regulations 1996 (SI 1996 No 2093), Reg 19(2), Sch 7, para 2].*

(z)    To clean any surfaces onto which explosives will be loaded. *[Carriage of Explosives by Road Regulations 1996 (SI 1996 No 2093), Reg 19(2), Sch 7, para 3].*

(aa)    Except where the engine has to be used to drive pumps or other appliances for loading or unloading, to ensure that the vehicle's engine shall be shut off during loading and unloading operations. *[Carriage of Explosives by Road Regulations 1996 (SI 1996 No 2093), Reg 19(2), Sch 7, para 4].*

## Duties of drivers

**D3040**    These are as follows.

(a)    To ensure that the orange-coloured panel, danger sign or subsidiary hazard sign is affixed and displayed on the vehicle/container. *[Carriage of Explosives by Road Regulations 1996 (SI 1996 No 2093), Reg 15(5)].*

(b)    To ensure that Transport Documentation (e.g. designation, classification code, UN number etc.) is

    (i)    kept on the vehicle during carriage, and

    (ii)    produced, on request, to a police constable or goods vehicle examiner.

*[Carriage of Explosives by Road Regulations 1996 (SI 1996 No 2093), Reg 18(1)].*

(c)    To ensure that where a trailer which is being used for the carriage of explosives becomes detached from the motor vehicle, that:

    (i)    he gives the Transport Documentation to the occupier of any premises on which his trailer is parked, or

    (ii)    he attaches the Transport Documentation to the trailer in a readily visible position.

(d)    To ensure that any documentation relating to explosives not being carried in the vehicle is placed in a securely closed container, and clearly marked to show that it does not relate to any explosives being carried.

(e)    Not to load, stow, unload explosives, so as to create a significant health and safety risk. *[Carriage of Explosives by Road Regulations 1996 (SI 1996 No 2093), Reg 19(1)].*

(f)    Where explosives have escaped from any package into a container or vehicle in which they are being carried, to ensure that the vehicle concerned is cleaned as soon as possible. *[Carriage of Explosives by Road Regulations 1996 (SI 1996 No 2093), Reg 19(2), Sch 7, para 2].*

(g)    To clean any surfaces onto which explosives will be loaded. *[Carriage of Explosives by Road Regulations 1996 (SI 1996 No 2093), Reg 19(2), Sch 7, para 3].*

(h)    Except where the engine has to be used to drive pumps or other appliances for loading or unloading, to ensure that the vehicle's engine shall be shut off during loading and unloading operations. [*Carriage of Explosives by Road Regulations 1996 (SI 1996 No 2093), Reg 19(2), Sch 7, para 4*].

(*j*)   Not to carry food with explosives, unless the food is effectively separated. [*Carriage of Explosives by Road Regulations 1996 (SI 1996 No 2093), Reg 19(3)*].

(*k*)   Not to open a package containing explosives unless so authorised. [*Carriage of Explosives by Road Regulations 1996 (SI 1996 No 2093), Reg 19(4)*].

(*l*)   To ensure that when a vehicle:

   (i)   is not parked, an attendant accompanies the driver; and

   (ii)   when it is parked, and the driver is not present, a competent person constantly remains with the vehicle.

[*Carriage of Explosives by Road Regulations 1996 (SI 1996 No 2093), Reg 20(1)*].

(*m*)   Not to carry another person in a vehicle which is being used to carry explosives for the sole reason of transporting them. [*Carriage of Explosives by Road Regulations 1996 (SI 1996 No 2093), Reg 20(6)*].

(*n*)   If carriage is more than 5 tonnes of explosives in Division 1.1, to follow the route agreed with the police. [*Carriage of Explosives by Road Regulations 1996 (SI 1996 No 2093), Reg 21(1)*].

(*o*)   Where the driver's vehicle is part of a convoy carrying explosives, to keep a distance of at least 50 metres between each vehicle. [*Carriage of Explosives by Road Regulations 1996 (SI 1996 No 2093), Reg 21(2)*].

(*p*)   To apply the parking brake, when parking. [*Carriage of Explosives by Road Regulations 1996 (SI 1996 No 2093), Reg 21(3)*].

(*q*)   Where the driver is in control of the explosives during carriage, he shall take such steps as are reasonable to:

   (i)   prevent accidents and minimise the harmful effects of any accident which may occur; and

   (ii)   shall prevent unauthorised access to, or removal of, all or part of the load.

[*Carriage of Explosives by Road Regulations 1996 (SI 1996 No 2093), Reg 22*].

(*r*)   Not to smoke or produce an open flame where explosives are being carried or unloaded, or bring portable lighting apparatus which could produce a flame or spark near explosives. [*Carriage of Explosives by Road Regulations 1996 (SI 1996 No 2093), Reg 23(1), (2)*].

(*s*)   Not to cause or permit anything to be done which is liable to create a significant risk of explosion, or to increase any existing risk. [*Carriage of Explosives by Road Regulations 1996 (SI 1996 No 2093), Reg 25(1)*].

(*t*)   To ensure that at least one fire extinguisher is located in a trailer, located in such a way as to be easily accessible. [*Carriage of Explosives by Road Regulations 1996 (SI 1996 No 2093), Reg 25(2), Sch 8, paras 3, 7*].

(*u*)   In the event of an emergency or accident, to notify:

   (i)   the emergency services; and

   (ii)   the operator

by the quickest practical means.

[*Carriage of Explosives by Road Regulations 1996 (SI 1996 No 2093), Reg 26(1)*].

(v)    In the event of an emergency or accident, to ensure that precautions are taken for:

(i)    the safety of persons likely to be affected by ignition; and

(ii)    the security of explosives.

[*Carriage of Explosives by Road Regulations 1996 (SI 1996 No 2093), Reg 26(3)*].

Drivers and attendants, or persons responsible for the security of explosives must (generally) be over 18 years. [*Carriage of Explosives by Road Regulations 1996 (SI 1996 No 2093), Reg 28*].

## Marking of vehicles

D3041    Both operators and drivers of vehicles used for the carriage of explosives must ensure that such *vehicles* are marked with:

(*a*)    two black rectangular reflectorised orange-coloured panels at the front and back, having a black border not more than 15 millimetres wide. This panel should be clearly visible, and so far as is reasonably practicable be kept clean and free from obstruction at all times when explosives are being carried. Where explosives have been unloaded, the panel should be covered or removed, the covering being able to withstand engulfment in fire for 15 minutes.

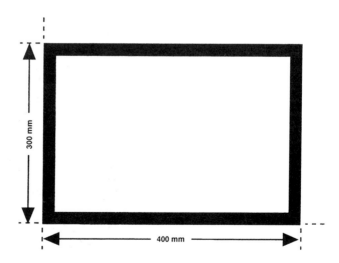

[*Sch 5 para 4*]

and in the case of explosives of divisions 1.1, 1.2 or 1.3 (i.e. more dangerous varieties);

(*b*)    two danger signs on each side of the *vehicle* or *container*, with orange-coloured background, having a black border (the Division Number 1.2 and the compatibility group letter 'E' are only examples)

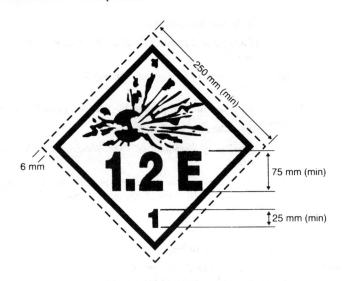

[*Sch 5 para 9*]

or, in the case of explosives of divisions 1.4, 1.5 or 1.6 (less powerful)

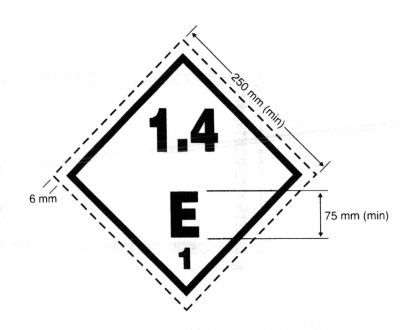

(The Division Number 1.4 and the compatibility group letter 'E' are only examples.)

[*Sch 5 para 10*]

Where explosives are carried in a *vehicle* or *container* solely in connection with an application for their classification, the following danger sign shall be displayed:

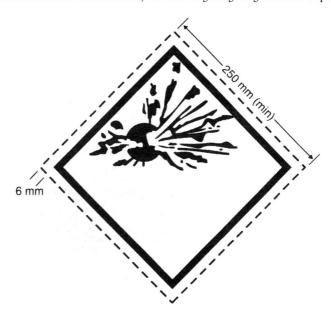

[*Sch 5 para 11*]

where explosives are allocated on classification UN Number 0018, 0019, 0020, 0021, 0076, 0077, 0143, 0224 or 03001 the *vehicle* or *container* shall be labelled with the subsidiary hazard sign:

[*Sch 5 para 12*]; and

where explosives are allocated on classification the UN number 0015, 0016, 0018, 0019, 0301 or 0303 the following subsidiary hazard sign shall be displayed:

[*Sch 5 para 13*]

In the case of a *vehicle* or *container* carrying explosives of different compatibility groups, no compatibility letter shall be written on any danger or subsidiary hazard sign required to be displayed. [*Sch 5 para 14*].

### Training for drivers carrying explosives

D3042    The *Carriage of Dangerous Goods by Road (Driver Training) Regulations 1996 (SI 1996 No 2094)* (see D3014 above) apply to drivers transporting explosives in or on a vehicle not being used to carry passengers for hire or reward [*Carriage of Explosives by Road Regulations 1996 (SI 1996 No 2093), Reg 2(1)(b)*] (with some exceptions [*Carriage of Explosives by Road Regulations 1996 (SI 1996 No 2093), Sch 1, Sch 2, Part II*]).

### Provision of information

D3043    Consignors must furnish operators with accurate and up-to-date information about explosives to be carried, so that operators can comply with their duties. [*Carriage of Explosives by Road Regulations 1996 (SI 1996 No 2093), Reg 16, Sch 6, Part I*]. (See D3038 above.)

In turn, operators must ensure that drivers (or their attendants) possess written information at the start of the journey. [*Carriage of Explosives by Road Regulations 1996 (SI 1996 No 2093), Reg 17(2), Sch 6, Part II*]. (See D3039(*m*) above.)

The requirement for written information does not apply to those explosives listed in *Schedule 1, Parts I-III* (see below). For explosives listed in *Schedule 1, Part II* the maximum amount of the explosives must not exceed 50 kilograms.

## PART I

| 1 | 2 |
|---|---|
| *Explosives* | UN Number |
| ARTICLES, PYROTECHNIC for technical purposes | 0432 |
| CARTRIDGES, POWER DEVICE | 0323 |
| CARTRIDGES, SIGNAL | 0405 |
| CARTRIDGES, SMALL ARMS | 0012 |
| CARTRIDGES SMALL ARMS, BLANK | 0014 |
| CASES CARTRIDGE, EMPTY, WITH PRIMER | 0055 |
| CUTTERS, CABLE EXPLOSIVE | 0070 |
| FIREWORKS | 0337 |
| FLARES, AERIAL | 0404 |
| FUSE, SAFETY | 0105 |
| IGNITERS | 0454 |
| LIGHTERS, FUSE | 0131 |
| PRIMERS, CAP TYPE | 0044 |
| SIGNAL DEVICES, HAND | 0373 |
| SIGNALS, RAILWAY TRACK, EXPLOSIVE | 0193 |

## PART II

| 1 | 2 |
|---|---|
| *Explosives* | UN Number |
| CARTRIDGES, SMALL ARMS* | 0328 |
| CARTRIDGES, SMALL ARMS | 0339 |
| CARTRIDGES, SMALL ARMS, BLANK* | 0327 |
| CARTRIDGES, SMALL ARMS, BLANK | 0338 |
| CASES, CARTRIDGE, EMPTY WITH PRIMER | 0379 |
| FIREWORKS* | 0333 |
| FIREWORKS* | 0334 |
| FIREWORKS* | 0335 |
| FIREWORKS | 0336 |
| SIGNAL DEVICES, HAND | 0191 |
| SIGNAL, DISTRESS, SHIP* | 0195 |

## PART III

| 1 | 2 |
|---|---|
| *Explosives* | UN Number |
| ARTICLES, PYROTECHNIC for technical purposes | 0428 |
| ARTICLES, PYROTECHNIC for technical purposes | 0429 |
| ARTICLES, PYROTECHNIC for technical purposes | 0430 |
| ARTICLES, PYROTECHNIC for technical purposes | 0431 |
| CARTRIDGES, OIL WELL | 0277 |
| CARTRIDGES, OIL WELL | 0278 |
| CARTRIDGES, POWER DEVICE | 0275 |
| CARTRIDGES, POWER DEVICE | 0276 |
| CARTRIDGES, POWER DEVICE | 0381 |
| CARTRIDGES, SIGNAL | 0054 |
| CARTRIDGES, SIGNAL | 0312 |
| CASES, COMBUSTIBLE EMPTY, WITHOUT PRIMER | 0446 |
| CASES, COMBUSTIBLE EMPTY, WITHOUT PRIMER | 0447 |
| CORD, IGNITER | 0066 |
| DINITROSOBENZENE | 0406 |
| FLARES, AERIAL | 0093 |
| FLARES, AERIAL | 0403 |
| FLARES, SURFACE | 0092 |
| FLASH POWDER | 0094 |
| FLASH POWDER | 0305 |
| FUSE, INSTANTANEOUS NON-DETONATING: (QUICKMATCH) | 0101 |
| IGNITERS | 0121 |
| IGNITERS | 0314 |
| IGNITERS | 0315 |
| IGNITERS | 0325 |
| 5-MERCAPTO-TETRAZOLE-1-ACETIC ACID | 0448 |
| POTASSIUM SALTS OF AROMATIC NITRO-DERIVATIVES, explosive | 0158 |
| PRIMERS, CAP TYPE | 0377 |
| PRIMERS, CAP TYPE | 0378 |
| ROCKETS, LINE THROWING | 0238 |

| 1 | 2 |
|---|---|
| *Explosives* | UN Number |
| ROCKETS, LINE THROWING | 0240 |
| ROCKETS, LINE THROWING | 0453 |
| SIGNALS, DISTRESS, ship | 0194 |
| SIGNALS, RAILWAY TRACK, EXPLOSIVE | 0192 |
| SIGNALS, SMOKE with explosive sound unit | 0196 |
| SIGNALS, SMOKE without explosive sound unit | 0197 |
| SODIUM DINITRO-o-CRESOLATE, dry or wetted with less than 15% water by mass | 0234 |
| SODIUM PICRAMATE, dry or wetted with less than 20% water by mass | 0235 |
| TETRAZOLE-1-ACETIC ACID | 0407 |
| ZIRCONIUM PICRAMATE, dry or wtted with less than 20% water by mass | 0236 |

### Enforcing authority

D3044    The enforcing authority for these Regulations is the Health and Safety Executive.

### Defence

D3045    It is a defence to a charge under these Regulations for the person charged to prove that:

(*a*)    the commission of the offence was due to the act or default of another person not being one of his employees; and

(*b*)    that he took all reasonable precautions and exercised all due diligence to avoid the commission of the offence.

[*Carriage of Explosives by Road Regulations 1996 (SI 1996 No 2093), Reg 31*].

*Transitional provisions*

D3046    Until 1 January 1997 it was sufficient compliance with the requirements of the Regulations to have complied with the requirements of the *Road Traffic (Carriage of Explosives) Regulations 1989 (SI 1989 No 615)*.

### Packaging of Explosives for Carriage Regulations 1991 (SI 1991 No 2097)

D3047    These Regulations cover the packaging of explosives, whereas the *Carriage of Explosives by Road Regulations 1996 (SI 1996 No 2093)* cover the labelling requirements of tankers and vehicles carrying those packaged explosives. The main requirements of these Regulations are:

(1)    explosives must not be transported unless they are in packaging which complies with the Regulations [*Packaging of Explosives for Carriage Regulations 1991 (SI 1991 No 2097), Reg 4*];

(2)     the packaging must be designed/constructed so that it will

(*a*)     protect the explosives,

(*b*)     prevent the escape of explosives,

(*c*)     avoid increased risk of ignition,

(*d*)     be able to be safely handled,

(*e*)     be able to withstand loading in the course of foreseeable stacking,

and so that

(*f*)     the inner packaging and interior of the outer packaging is free from grit or rust,

(*g*)     the explosives are not likely to come into contact with another substance or article that could cause an explosion.

[*Packaging of Explosives for Carriage Regulations 1991 (SI 1991 No 2097), Reg 5*].

## The export of dangerous chemicals outside the EU

D3048     The *Export of Dangerous Chemicals Regulations 1992 (SI 1992 No 2415)* relate to the EU common notification system for dangerous chemicals being imported from non-EU member states. These Regulations ban an exporter from providing false or misleading information relating to any requirement or prohibition relating to this form of export. The Health and Safety Executive is the enforcing authority and enforcement follows the *HSWA 1974* rules (see further ENFORCEMENT). It is proposed to add the following chemicals to the current list: pentachlorophenol, ugilec 121, ugilec 141, DBBT, ethylene oxide, dinoseb, binapacryl, captafol, dicofol, maleic hydrazide, choline/potassium and sodium salts of maleic hydrazide, quintozene, 2-Naphthylamine, benzedine, 4-Nitrobiphenyl, and 4-Aminobiphenyl.

## Carriage of dangerous goods by rail – The Carriage of Dangerous Goods by Rail Regulations 1996 (SI 1996 No 2089)

D3049     These Regulations which came into force on 1 September 1996, specify precautions in relation to the carriage of dangerous goods by train. As with the regulations concerning the carriage of dangerous goods by road, the classification and packaging requirements overlap with the *Carriage of Dangerous Goods (Classification, Packaging and Labelling) and Use of Transportable Pressure Receptacles Regulations 1996 (SI 1996 No 2092)*.

The Regulations apply to the carriage of any dangerous goods in a container, package, tank container, tank wagon or wagon, except where the carriage falls into one of the exceptions listed in *Regulation 2*. The exceptions include where:

(*a*)     the dangerous goods carried are carried for use solely in connection with the operation of the locomotive, container, tank container, tank wagon or wagon;

(*b*)     the carriage commences and terminates within the same factory, harbour area, military establishment, mine or quarry;

(*c*)     the goods are being carried solely for use in connection with the provision of train catering facilities; and (*d*)     the carriage forms part of an international transport operation which is subject to any bi-lateral or multilateral agreement and where the carriage is made under the Convention concerning International Carriage by Rail.

## Definitions

D3050     The relevant definitions relating to these Regulations are as follows.

### (A) *Operator*

The operator of a container, tank container, tank wagon or wagon is:

(*a*)     the person who, having a place of business in Great Britain, owns the container, tank container, tank wagon or wagon concerned; or

(*b*)     the person who, having a place of business in Great Britain, acts as agent for the owner of the container, tank container, tank wagon or wagon concerned; or

(*c*)     the operator of the train on which the container or tank container is carried or of which the tank wagon or wagon forms part.

The members of the crew includes the driver, guard and any other person on board who has responsibilities in relation to the carriage of dangerous substances on the train. [*Carriage of Dangerous Goods by Rail Regulations 1996 (SI 1996 No 2089), Reg 1(3)*].

A person to whom a container, tank container, tank wagon or wagon is leased or hired shall be deemed to be the owner, unless the lessor or hirer has made a written agreement with the person to whom he has leased or hired the container, to the effect that the lessor or hirer shall assume the responsibilities of the owner imposed by the Regulations. [*Carriage of Dangerous Goods by Rail Regulations 1996 (SI 1996 No 2089), Reg 1(4)*].

### (B) *Consignor*

The consignor has the same definition as in the *Carriage of Dangerous Goods (Classification, Packaging and Labelling) and Use of Transportable Pressure Receptacles Regulations 1996 (SI 1996 No 2092), Reg 2(1)*.

## Meaning of carriage

D3051     A container, package, tank container, tank wagon or wagon is deemed to be engaged in the carriage of dangerous goods throughout the period where such an item is:

(*a*)     loaded and brought on to the railway; or

(*b*)     where the item is brought on to the railway before loading, from the commencement of loading;

until

(*c*)     the item is removed from the railway; or

(*d*)     where any compartment of the item has been unloaded (and where necessary cleaned and decontaminated) that any of the vapours which remain are not sufficient to create a significant risk to the health and safety of any person.

[*Carriage of Dangerous Goods by Rail Regulations 1996 (SI 1996 No 2089), Reg 2(8)*].

## Duties/obligations imposed on all persons concerned with carriage

D3052    These include the following.

(*a*)    That no tank container or tank wagon, or any compartment is filled beyond its safe level with dangerous goods. [*Carriage of Dangerous Goods by Rail Regulations 1996 (SI 1996 No 2089), Reg 16*].

(*b*)    Not to carry any mixed loads specified in *Schedule 6* unless they are adequately segregated to prevent the creation of a mixture which is a greater risk than when the goods are carried separately. [*Carriage of Dangerous Goods by Rail Regulations 1996 (SI 1996 No 2089), Reg 17*].

(*c*)    Not to allow food to be carried in any container etc. unless the food is effectively separated from those goods or is otherwise adequately protected from the risk of contamination. [*Carriage of Dangerous Goods by Rail Regulations 1996 (SI 1996 No 2089), Reg 18(4)*].

(*d*)    To take all reasonable care to ensure that:

   (i)    nothing is done during carriage to create a significant risk or significantly increase any risk to health and safety; and

   (ii)    unauthorised access to dangerous goods is prevented.

[*Carriage of Dangerous Goods by Rail Regulations 1996 (SI 1996 No 2089), Reg 21*].

(*e*)    To ensure that no person shall cause or permit anything to be done which increases any existing risk of fire or explosion. [*Carriage of Dangerous Goods by Rail Regulations 1996 (SI 1996 No 2089), Reg 22*].

## Duties of consignors

D3053    Consignors of dangerous goods must ensure that any operator of a container, tank container, tank wagon or wagon engaged by him to carry the goods is provided with the following information in documentary form before carriage. The information as a whole is called the 'Carriage Information' and consists of:

(*a*)    in relation to each of the dangerous goods being carried –

   (i)    the designation,

   (ii)    the classification code,

   (iii)    the UN number,

   (iv)    the packaging group (where appropriate),

   (v)    in the case of explosives, the Compatibility Group and Division of each type of explosive being carried,

   (vi)    in the case of explosives within a Compatibility Group whose Compatibility Group letter is C, D or G, whether the explosives are explosive articles or explosive substances,

   (vii)    the mass or volume of the goods, and

   (viii)    the words 'salvage packaging' (if used); and

(*b*)    in relation to the consignment as a whole –

   (i)    the total mass or volume of the dangerous goods consigned,

(ii)   the name and address of the consignor,

(iii)  the name and address of the consignee (if known),

(iv)  the name and telephone number where specialist advice can be obtained in English at any time,

(v)   any other information relevant, and

(vi)  a statement dated and signed or authenticated by or on behalf of the consignor confirming that any of the following regulations have been complied with:

    — the *Classification and Labelling of Explosives Regulations 1983 (SI 1983 No 1140)*;

    — the *Packaging of Explosives for Carriage Regulations 1991 (SI 1991 No 2097)*; and

    — the *Carriage of Dangerous Goods (Classification, Packaging and Labelling) and Use of Transportable Pressure Receptacles Regulations 1996 (SI 1996 No 2092)*;

and that therefore

    — the dangerous goods as presented may be carried,

    — the dangerous goods and any packaging, intermediate bulk container, tank container or tank wagon in which they are contained are in a fit condition for carriage and properly labelled, and

    — where several packages are packed together in an overpack or single container, that this is not prohibited.

[*Carriage of Dangerous Goods by Rail Regulations 1996 (SI 1996 No 2089), Reg 11(2)*].

Consignors shall also ensure that any train operator engaged by him is supplied with the Carriage Information. [*Carriage of Dangerous Goods by Rail Regulations 1996 (SI 1996 No 2089), Reg 12(2)*].

### Duties of operators

D3054  Operators of containers, tank containers, tank wagons or wagons carrying dangerous goods must ensure the following.

(*a*)  That all reasonable steps are taken to ensure that the requirements specified in any of the approved documents relevant to the container, tank container, tank wagon or wagon are complied with. [*Carriage of Dangerous Goods by Rail Regulations 1996 (SI 1996 No 2089), Reg 4(a)*].

(*b*)  That a wagon or large container will not be permitted to carry dangerous substances in bulk unless:

(i)   the letter 'Y' appears in column 8 of the Approved Carriage List;

(ii)  any requirements specified in *Schedule 2* to the Regulations 'Requirements for the carriage in bulk of certain dangerous goods in wagons and large containers' is complied with;

(iii)  in the case of a wagon, it is:

    — closed,

— open and sheeted, or

— has a movable roof; and

(iv) in the case of a large container, it is:

— closed, or

— open and sheeted.

*[Carriage of Dangerous Goods by Rail Regulations 1996 (SI 1996 No 2089), Reg 5].*

(c) That small containers shall not carry dangerous goods unless the requirements in *Schedule 3* 'Requirements for the carriage in small containers of certain dangerous goods' are complied with. *[Carriage of Dangerous Goods by Rail Regulations 1996 (SI 1996 No 2089), Reg 6].*

(d) That no tank container or tank wagon shall carry dangerous goods unless the letter 'Y' appears in column 7 of the Approved Carriage List. *[Carriage of Dangerous Goods by Rail Regulations 1996 (SI 1996 No 2089), Reg 7(1)].*

(e) That no tank container or tank wagon shall carry dangerous goods unless the information relating to certification of tanks specified in the Approved Tank Requirements is indelibly marked on one or more corrosion-resistant plates which are securely fastened to the item concerned. *[Carriage of Dangerous Goods by Rail Regulations 1996 (SI 1996 No 2089), Reg 7(3)].*

(f) That any container, tank container, tank wagon or wagon shall not be used to carry dangerous goods unless:

(i) it is suitable for the purpose of such carriage; and

(ii) it has been adequately maintained.

*[Carriage of Dangerous Goods by Rail Regulations 1996 (SI 1996 No 2089), Reg 8(1)].*

'Suitable for such carriage' means that it is suitable with regard to:

(1) the nature and circumstances of the journey being undertaken; and

(2) the hazardous properties and quantities of dangerous goods and of all other goods to be carried with them.

(g) That no explosives are carried unless:

(i) he has taken all reasonable steps to ensure that those goods have been classified and labelled in accordance with the *Classification and Labelling of Explosives Regulations 1983 (SI 1983 No 1140)* as amended by the *Carriage of Explosives by Road Regulations 1996 (SI 1996 No 2093)* (see DANGEROUS SUBSTANCES I and D3036 above);

(ii) where the *Packaging of Explosives for Carriage Regulations 1991 (SI 1991 No 2097)* apply, he has taken all reasonable steps to comply with the Regulations; and

(iii) any requirements under the *Carriage of Dangerous Goods (Classification, Packaging and Labelling) and Use of Transportable Pressure Receptacles Regulations 1996 (SI 1996 No 2092)* have been complied with.

*[Carriage of Dangerous Goods by Rail Regulations 1996 (SI 1996 No 2089), Reg 10].*

*Part VII* of the Regulations 'Special requirements concerning the carriage of explosives' contains detailed requirements, including restrictions on the carriage of certain explosives, the carriage of explosives on passenger trains and the security measures to be taken.

(*h*)   That any train operator engaged by him is provided with the Carriage Information. [*Carriage of Dangerous Goods by Rail Regulations 1996 (SI 1996 No 2089), Reg 12(3)*].

(*j*)   To keep a record of information contained within the Carriage Information for at least three months following the completion of each journey. [*Carriage of Dangerous Goods by Rail Regulations 1996 (SI 1996 No 2089), Reg 13*].

(*k*)   To display information concerning the dangerous goods in the container, tank container, tank wagon or wagon. [*Carriage of Dangerous Goods by Rail Regulations 1996 (SI 1996 No 2089), Reg 14(1), Sch 5*]. These requirements as to the display of information are similar to those concerning the transport of dangerous substances by road (see D3027 above). Such information should not be displayed when the container etc. no longer contains the dangerous goods [*Carriage of Dangerous Goods by Rail Regulations 1996 (SI 1996 No 2089), Reg 14(2)*]; no information should be displayed which might confuse the emergency services if read in conjunction with the information displayed pursuant to *Schedule 5* [*Carriage of Dangerous Goods by Rail Regulations 1996 (SI 1996 No 2089), Reg 14(3)*]; the information displayed (i.e. danger sign, hazard warning panel, subsidiary hazard sign etc.) is free from obstruction when the container etc. is handed over to the train operator [*Carriage of Dangerous Goods by Rail Regulations 1996 (SI 1996 No 2089), Reg 14(5)*]; and he has taken all reasonable steps to ensure that the information displayed is in accordance with *Schedule 5* [*Carriage of Dangerous Goods by Rail Regulations 1996 (SI 1996 No 2089), Reg 14(6)*].

(*l*)   To ensure that dangerous goods are so loaded, stowed or unloaded as not to create a significant health and safety risk or increase one significantly. [*Carriage of Dangerous Goods by Rail Regulations 1996 (SI 1996 No 2089), Reg 18(1)*].

(*m*)   To ensure that any product remaining in a container etc. will not cause a significant risk to health, or increase an already existing risk if other dangerous goods are loaded. [*Carriage of Dangerous Goods by Rail Regulations 1996 (SI 1996 No 2089), Reg 18(3)*].

(*n*)   Ensure that all openings and discharge or filling openings are fitted with more than one valve or cap, and that all are closed prior to carriage. [*Carriage of Dangerous Goods by Rail Regulations 1996 (SI 1996 No 2089), Reg 19(1)*].

## Duties of train operators

**D3055**   Operators are under a duty to ensure the following.

(*a*)   That all reasonable steps are taken to ensure that the requirements specified in any of the approved documents relevant to the container, tank container, tank wagon or wagon are complied with. [*Carriage of Dangerous Goods by Rail Regulations 1996 (SI 1996 No 2089), Reg 4(b)*].

(*b*)   That any container, tank container, tank wagon or wagon shall not be used to carry dangerous goods unless:

(i)   it is suitable for the purpose of such carriage; and

(ii)   it has been adequately maintained.

[*Carriage of Dangerous Goods by Rail Regulations 1996 (SI 1996 No 2089), Reg 8(2)*].

(c)   That any other train operator engaged by him to carry dangerous goods is supplied with the Carriage Information. [*Carriage of Dangerous Goods by Rail Regulations 1996 (SI 1996 No 2089), Reg 12(4)*].

(d)   Where the train operator is considered to be the operator to keep a record of information contained within the Carriage Information for at least three months following the completion of each journey. [*Carriage of Dangerous Goods by Rail Regulations 1996 (SI 1996 No 2089), Reg 13*]. (See D3050(A) above for meaning of 'operator'.)

(e)   Shall take measures to ensure that any train being used for the carriage of dangerous goods during marshalling or formation does not create a significant increase in risk. [*Carriage of Dangerous Goods by Rail Regulations 1996 (SI 1996 No 2089), Reg 20*].

(f)   Shall, with facility operators and infrastructure controllers:

(i)   draw up, and where necessary give effect to, such safety systems and procedures that will adequately deal with any emergency involving dangerous goods; and

(ii)   co-operate with each other so as to ensure effective co-ordination of their respective safety systems and procedures.

[*Carriage of Dangerous Goods by Rail Regulations 1996 (SI 1996 No 2089), Reg 23*].

### Duties in relation to tanks

D3056   *Regulation 9* contains detailed requirements as to the examination, testing and certification of tanks. The provisions in *Regulation 9* only apply to tanks constructed after 31 December 1998.

No person shall manufacture, import or supply a tank intended for the use of the carriage of dangerous goods unless it is of an 'approved design' which has been certified by a competent authority. It must:

(a)   conform with requirements published in the Approved Tank Requirements; and

(b)   be suitable for the purpose for which it was intended.

Similarly, operators must comply with the above requirements and additionally:

(c)   ensure that it has been examined and tested in accordance with the Approved Tank Requirements.

[*Carriage of Dangerous Goods by Rail Regulations 1996 (SI 1996 No 2089), Reg 9(2),(3)*].

### Information to be displayed on containers, tank containers, tank wagons and wagons

D3057   In general, *Regulation 14* as supplemented by *Schedule 5* requires that the following information is displayed.

(a)   The UN number for the goods specified in the Approved Carriage List.

(*b*)    The emergency action code.

(*c*)    The danger sign for the goods ascertained in accordance with the *Carriage of Dangerous Goods (Classification, Packaging and Labelling) and Use of Transportable Pressure Receptacles Regulations 1996 (SI 1996 No 2092)*.

(*d*)    The subsidiary hazard sign.

(*e*)    A telephone number where specialist advice can be obtained in English at any time during the carriage of the goods.

The information is required to be displayed as follows.

(1)    The UN number and emergency action code in black letters of 100mm height and 15mm stroke thickness.

(2)    Where the emergency action code in column 5 of the Approved Carriage List indicates a white letter on a black background, that letter shall be displayed as an orange letter on a black rectangle, which has a height and a width at least 10mm greater than the height and width of the letter.

(3)    The danger and subsidiary hazard sign shall have sides which measure not less than 250mm.

(4)    The telephone number shall consist of black digits of 30mm height and shall be displayed on an orange-coloured background.

The orange-coloured panels and hazard warning panels shall be:

(i)    in the form of a plate;

(ii)    securely attached; and

(iii)   visible.

[*Carriage of Dangerous Goods by Rail Regulations 1996 (SI 1996 No 2089), Sch 5, para 2*].

(For examples of these panels see *Figures 1* and *5* at D3028 and D3031 above.)

Tank containers and tank wagons carrying dangerous goods shall display:

(A)    an orange-coloured panel on each side of the tank or tank container, bearing the UN Number and emergency action code;

(B)    the danger sign and subsidiary hazard sign, adjacent to the orange-coloured panel; and

(C)    the telephone number.

[*Carriage of Dangerous Goods by Rail Regulations 1996 (SI 1996 No 2089), Sch 5, para 5*].

For containers and wagons carrying dangerous goods in bulk,

(I)    an orange-coloured panel bearing the emergency action code and UN number shall be displayed on each side of the container or wagon; and

(II)   the danger sign or subsidiary hazard sign shall be displayed adjacent to the orange-coloured panel.

[*Carriage of Dangerous Goods by Rail Regulations 1996 (SI 1996 No 2089), Sch 5, para 4*].

## Defence

D3058    In any proceedings for an offence under the Regulations, it is a defence for the person charged to prove:

(*a*)    that the commission of the offence was due to the act or default of another person not being one of his employees; and

(*b*)    that he took all reasonable precautions and exercised all due diligence to avoid the commission of the offence.

[*Carriage of Dangerous Goods by Rail Regulations 1996 (SI 1996 No 2089), Reg 31*].

## Transitional defence

D3059    In any proceedings for an offence under the Regulations prior to 1 January 1997, it shall be a defence to prove that the goods were carried in accordance with the *Carriage of Dangerous Goods by Rail Regulations 1994 (SI 1994 No 670)*.

[*Carriage of Dangerous Goods by Rail Regulations 1996 (SI 1996 No 2089), Reg 33*].

# Disaster and Emergency Management Systems (DEMS)

## Historical Development of Disaster and Emergency Management

D6001    Disaster and Emergency Management (DEM) has evolved in three phases:

- **Phase 1**: pre-*CIMAH 1984* (*Control of Industrial Major Accident Hazards Regulations 1984 (SI 1984 No 1902)*

  DEM was largely confined to local government, the emergency services, large organisations and civil protection agencies (environmental, military etc.). This phase is marked by large scale macro plans and detailed, sequential procedures to be followed in the event of a 'disaster' or 'emergency'. It is exemplified in the guidance prevalent on 'incidents' involving radioactivity, available from central government, the United Nations, Red Cross and others.

- **Phase 2**: *Liberalisation Phase*

  With the advent of decentralisation of industry and the growth of privatisation, organisations (large or otherwise) began to focus on 'procedures' and 'business continuity planning'. British Telecom exemplified this with the establishment of its Disaster Recovery Unit and the offering of its expertise to customers at large. Incidents such as Chernobyl, Piper Alpha, Kings Cross, The Marchioness and Challenger to name a few, which hit the world headlines in the 1980s also focused planners minds on effective DEM not just isolated procedures.

- **Phase 3**: *Holistic Phase*

  This has two dimensions, first the role of Europe. The impact of the *Framework and Daughter Directives*, as transposed into the '*6 Pack Regulations*' of 1992, introduced for the first time explicit and strict duties on organisations in general to plan for 'serious and imminent dangers'. The European Commission also began to take the risks of trans-national 'disasters' more seriously, as highlighted by the greater role given to the Civil Protection Unit, in DGXI of the European Commission. Second, this phase sees domestic UK legislation becoming more cognisant of disaster and emergency issues (*Environment Act 1995* makes provisions for environmental emergencies; *Control of Major Accident Hazards Regulations 1999* (*COMAH*) (*SI 1999 No 743*) replaces *CIMAH 1984*; also the need for effective planning when carrying dangerous goods via road legislation, *Carriage of Dangerous Goods by Road Regulations 1996 (SI 1996 No 2095)*).

The most noticeable index of how DEM has changed is the availability of information and templates on 'disaster planning' and 'emergency planning' to organisations of all sizes. There is also a greater media focus on such issues, with the BBC for instance having a dedicated web page on disasters.

## Origin of Disaster and Emergency Management as a modern discipline

D6002   DEM owes its origin to four disciplines :

(a)   *Occupational Safety and Health (OSH)*

This concerns 'internal' or work-based causes of systems failures, with major impact on life and property. It has been exemplified by Heinrich in his publication *Unsafe Acts and Unsafe Conditions* in the early part of the 1900s, Bird and Loftus with their managerial failing explanations of accidents and incidents and Turner with his 'incubation' explanation of *Man-Made Disasters* in the 1970s. OSH academics have led the forefront in terms of analysing the branch and root causes of major industrial disasters.

(b)   *Security Management*

In the 1970s, security threats in the UK such as bomb explosions, terrorism and electronic surveillance failures have given insights to causation and the motivation behind man-made emergencies. Also, guidance from the Home Office as well as the emergency services has enabled a practical understanding of how to cope with emergency situations.

(c)   *Business Management*

The late 1980s saw a shift in the academic paradigm in economics and business management from 'static' or closed business planning – where businesses were told to make the assumption of *cetaris paribus*, that is assume all things are constant with the business acting as if it was the only one in the market place – to 'dynamic' or open planning. The latter sees uncertainty and risk being factored into decision making models. This influenced the development of 'business continuity planning', developing strategies when the business faces major corporate uncertainty and crises as well as 'contingency planning'.

(d)   *Insurance*

The fourth significant influence comes from insurance and loss control. The occurrence of disasters and accidents has involved loss adjusters and actuarial personnel. The former have developed methods of analysing the basic and underlying causes of an event, whilst the latter have been developing statistical methods for calculating the chance of failure and the risk premiums needed to indemnify that failure.

If one visualises these four subject areas as circles in a ven diagram, the area where all four intersect each other can be seen as DEM. DEM uses both quantitative (statistics, quantified risk assessments, hazard analysis techniques, questionnaires, computer simulation etc.) and qualitative methods (inspections, audits, case studies etc.).

## Definitions

D6003   Stan Kaplan (*The Words of Risk Analysis*, 1997, Risk Analysis, Vol 17, No 4) stated that 50 per cent of the problems with communication are due to individuals using the same words with different meanings. The remaining 50 per cent are due to individuals using different words with the same meaning. In DEM this is a basic problem. Some authors have argued distinguishing definitions has no practical value and can be '. . . highly undesirable to try to control how others use them . . .' (*Managing the Global Consequences of a Disaster,* Richard Read, Paper at the 2nd International Disaster and Emergency Readiness Conference, The Hague, October 1999, page 130 of IDER Papers). Nevertheless there is much confusion over the meaning given to core terms, so that basic definitions can assist in avoiding the Kaplan dilemma. Legislation or approved codes have not provided definitions of 'disaster' or 'emergency' for instance. *The New Oxford Dictionary of English*, OUP, (1999) provides the following primary meanings:

(*a*)     Catastrophe: 'an event causing great and often sudden damage or suffering: a disaster', page 287.

(*b*)     Crisis: 'a time of intense difficulty or danger', page 435.

(*c*)     Disaster: 'a sudden event, such as an accident or a natural catastrophe, that causes great damage or loss of life', page 524.

A catastrophe and a crisis are types of disaster, namely more severe.

(*d*)     Emergency: ' a serious, unexpected and often dangerous situation requiring immediate action', page 603.

Whilst both disasters and emergencies can be sudden, the former has a macro, large scale impact whilst the latter requires an immediate response.

(*e*)     Accident: '1. an unfortunate incident that happens unexpectedly and unin-tentionally, typically resulting in damage or injury, . . ..2. an event that happens by chance or that is without apparent or deliberate cause', page 10.

It can be noted that the *COMAH Regulations (SI 1999 No 743)* have introduced the term 'major accident'; this is due to:

(i)     unexpected, sudden, unplanned developments in the course of the operation;

(ii)     leads to serious danger to people and the environment both on site at the place of work and off site;

(iii)     the event involves at least one dangerous substance as defined by *COMAH.*

Given the potential for both human and property loss, and given the *COMAH* requirements for emergency on site and off site plans, there seems to be little practical difference between a major accident and an emergency. Both are response based concepts. However, if the legislators wished a major accident to be different from an emergency then they would have either said so or implied so. One can regard a major accident as a type of emergency situation.

(*f*)     Incident: ' an event or occurrence', page 923.

*Reporting of Injuries, Diseases and Dangerous Occurrences Regulations 1995 (RIDDOR) (SI 1995 No 3163)*, does not define an accident or incident, but gives a classification of the types. In *Dealing with Disaster* (Home Office, Third Edition), a 'major incident' is the only term explicitly defined by the Home Office: A major incident is any emergency that requires the implemen-tation of special arrangements by one or more of the emergency services, the NHS or the local authority for:

(i)     the initial treatment, rescue and transport of a large number of casualties;

(ii)  the involvement either directly or indirectly of large numbers of people;

(iii)  the handling of a large number of enquiries likely to be generated both from the public and the news media, usually to the police;

(iv)  the need for the large scale combined resources of two or more of the emergency services;

(v)  the mobilisation and organisation of the emergency services and supporting organisations, e.g. local authority, to cater for the threat of death, serious injury or homelessness to a large number of people, page 43.

This definition is accepted by the police, fire service, local government and broadly the NHS (they also have a specific definition of major incident).

Following on from this definition, one can regard a major accident, emergency, disaster, as well as the types of disasters (crisis and catastrophe) as referring to a major incident. Thus the term 'major incident' is a broad phrase encompassing an array of events. 'Accident' has not been included as a type of major incident given the definition of the latter requiring 'major' mobilisation of human and physical resources which in most accidents is not necessarily the case.

As an example:

(1)  two trains missing each other would be an 'incident' (near miss);

(2)  an employee or member of the public being injured on a train – this would be an 'accident', irrespective of the type of injury or fatality (following *RIDDOR*);

(3)  an event at a *COMAH* site where dangerous substances ignite causing damage to the plant, injury to personnel and emissions into the local community, would be a 'major accident' under *COMAH*;

(4)  the immediate event after the collision and the response needed to the chaos – this would be an 'emergency'. For example, the response by the emergency services to Ladbroke Grove;

(5)  if two trains collided causing multiple fatalities and immediate property and environmental damage, that would be referred to as a 'disaster'. For example Ladbroke Grove Rail Crash in 1999;

(6)  if the collision, with the multiple fatalities and property damage is difficult to access, manage and control, this would be a 'crisis'. Ladbroke Grove fell short from being a 'crisis' in contrast to the Clapham Junction in 1988 where a triple train crash caused major access and logistical problems;

(7)  if the event generated major environmental, public and social harm that has 'longer term' implications, over and above the immediate human and property loss, this would be a 'catastrophe' For example, Kings Cross Underground Fire (1987), Chernobyl (1986), Piper Alpha (1988) to name a few that had wider consequences over and above the immediate impact.

Events (1)–(7) would be major incidents.

Figure 1 summarises the essential differences between the above events.

# Figure 1: Classification of Incidents, Accidents and Major Incident types

| Characteristic | Event: | Incident | Accident | Major Accident | Emergency | Disaster | Crisis | Catastrophe |
|---|---|---|---|---|---|---|---|---|
| | | | Types of emegency | | | Types of disaster | | |
| | | | | | | 'MAJOR INCIDENTS' | | |
| 1. MPL | Low | | | | | | | Very High |
| 2. RISK: Severity | Near miss etc | | | | | | | Multiple Fatalities |
| Consequence | Minor | | | | | | | Major |
| 3. NUMBERS | 1-5 | | | | | | | 100 + |
| 4. SOCIO-LEGAL IMPACT | No change likely | | | | | | | New Laws or Guidance |
| 5. TIME | Short | | | | | | | Longer Impact |
| 6. COST: Individual | Short Term | | | | | | | Irreparable |
| Social | None Usually | | | | | | | Irreparable |
| Environment | None Usually | | | | | | | Irreparable |

Key:
MPL= Maximum Potential Loss (economic and property loss)
Risk= Severity x Consequence (Severity refers to the quantum of harm generated by the event whilst Consequence measures the scale of impact)
Numbers= The number of individuals affected
Socio-Legal Impact= The impact on social attitudes and legislation/guidance as a result of the event
Time= The length of the event
Cost= The loss suffered by the individual, society or nature

Such classifications are important , firstly from a philosophical perspective one needs to know how they differ. Secondly, from a planning perspective, as the resource allocation will accordingly differ. Thirdly, from a response perspective, the response to an incident differs from a disaster, with the organisation needing to define and clarify when an event is an incident and not a disaster.

# The Need for Effective Disaster and Emergency Management

D6004    There are several reasons why DEM is needed: legal reasons (see D6005); insurance reasons (see D6017); corporate reasons (see D6018); societal reasons (see D6019); environmental reasons (see D6020); and humanitarian reasons (see D6021).

### Legal reasons

D6005    There are important statutory legal reasons for DEM which are explained in the following paragraphs.

### The Health and Safety at Work etc. Act 1974

D6006    The intentions of *The Health and Safety at Work etc. Act 1974* are captured by *s 1(1)(a) – (d)* which states that the Act is concerned with 'securing the health, safety and welfare of persons at work', protecting the public, effective control over dangerous substances/explosives and the effective control of emission of noxious substances into the atmosphere. Implicit at least is the intention that this Act will influence actions that contribute to disaster and emergency situations, whether industrial, chemical or environmental. The Act does give expressed powers to the Health and Safety Commission to investigate and to hold inquiries in relation to '. . . any accident, occurrence, situation . . .'. [*s 14(1)*].

### The Management of Health and Safety at Work Regulations 1999 (MHSWR) (SI 1999 No 3242)

D6007    These Regulations provide the main detail applicable to all organisations, for providing 'procedures for serious and imminent danger and for danger areas' [*Reg* 8] and 'contacts with external services'. [*Reg* 9]. In relation to industrial and chemical based incidents, accidents and major incidents, the regulations require the existence and implementation of safety procedures (internal) as well as links with emergency and para-emergency services (external). This contrasts with the 1992 and 1994 amended version of the same Regulations. *Regulation 1* (Citation, commencement and interpretation) does not define 'procedure for serious and imminent danger', although the ACOP L21 to the MHSWR 1999 (SI 1999 No 3242) exemplifies such situtations, 'e.g. a fire, or for the police and emergency services an outbreak of public disorder' (page 20).

*Regulation 8(1)* says that a strict duty exists on all employers to:

(a)    'establish and where necessary give effect to appropriate procedures to be followed in the event of serious and imminent danger to persons at work in his undertaking'.

(b)    'nominate a sufficient number of competent persons to implement those procedures in so far as they relate to the evacuation from premises of persons at work in his undertaking'.

(*c*) 'ensure that none of his employees has access to any area occupied by him to which it is necessary to restrict access on grounds of health and safety unless the employee concerned has received adequate health and safety instruction'.

*Regulation 8(2)* says 'Without prejudice to the generality of paragraph (1)(a), the procedures referred to in that sub-paragraph shall:

(*a*) so far as is practicable, require any persons at work who are exposed to serious and imminent danger to be informed of the nature of the hazard and of the steps taken or to be taken to protect them from it;

(*b*) enable the persons concerned (if necessary by taking appropriate steps in the absence of guidance or instruction and in the light of their knowledge and the technical means at their disposal) to stop work and immediately proceed to a place of safety in the event of their being exposed to serious, imminent and unavoidable danger; and

(*c*) save in exceptional cases for reasons duly substantiated (which cases and reasons shall be specified in those procedures), require the persons concerned to be prevented from resuming work in any situation where there is still a serious and imminent danger'.

*Regulation 8(3)* says 'A person shall be regarded as competent for the purposes of paragraph (1)(b) where he has sufficient training and experience or knowledge and other qualities to enable him properly to implement the evacuation procedures referred to in that sub-paragraph'.

*Regulation 8* can be summarised:

(1) Procedures need to be sequential, logical, documented and clear (clarity of procedures).

(2) Justify and authorise the procedures (legitimise procedures).

(3) A 'hierarchy of procedural control' seems to be advocated:

— give information to those potentially affected by serious and imminent dangers;

— take actions or steps to protect such people;

— stop work activity if necessary to reduce danger;

— prevent the resuming of work if necessary until the danger has been reduced or eliminated.

(4) Appoint competent persons preferably from within the organisation who will assist in any evacuations. It is implied that the role and responsibility of such persons needs to be clearly demarcated.

(5) Generally prohibit access to dangerous areas (site management). If access to a 'danger area' is required i.e. a place which has an unacceptable level of risk but must be accessed by the employee, then appropriate measures must be taken as specified by other legislation (see below).

In addition, the regulations imply:

(6) Risk Assessments will identify foreseeable events that may need to be covered by procedures. Risk Assessments may also identify 'additional risks' that need additional procedures. Thus the Risk Assessment, as shall be discussed below, is a vital tool to keep procedures in tune with current generic and specific risks.

(7)    Procedures need to be dynamic – reflecting the fact that events can occur suddenly.

(8)    There may be a need to co-ordinate procedures where workplaces are shared.

(9)    Procedures should also reflect other legislative requirements (see below).

*Regulation 9* is a new addition to the *MHSWR (SI 1999 No 3242)*. *Regulation 9* reads ' Every employer shall ensure that any necessary contacts with external services are arranged, particularly as regards first aid, emergency medical care and rescue work'. It can be inferred that 'necessary contacts with external services' does not only relate to the emergency services but the organisation needs to identify both private sector and voluntary organisations that can be called on for assistance. The organisation needs to identify contact names, addresses and contact numbers of such bodies and develop relations with them.

*Control of Major Accident Hazards Regulations 1999 (COMAH) (SI 1999 No 743) (see C10002 for full details of COMAH 1999)*

D6008    In summary:

(*a*)    The General Rule

COMAH applies to those establishments that keep on site any substance that is specified in *Sch 1* of *COMAH (SI 1999 No 743)*. For example, keeping a certain amount of ammonium nitrate or oxygen on site. However, there are 'Top-Tier' and 'Lower-Tier' Threshold levels. If an establishment keeps an amount greater than or equal to an Upper Threshold Level, they are called Top-Tier. For instance, if an establishment keeps at least 2,500 tonnes of ammonium nitrate, then it is Top-Tier. If an establishment keeps a lower quantity than this, (greater than or equal to a lower threshold) then it is a Lower-Tier establishment. For example, the Lower-Tier for ammonium nitrate is 350 tonnes. Therefore, knowing the amount of substance being stocked is critical to knowing what tier the establishment falls under.

It can be noted, that even if the quantity of substance being held is below the Threshold Level, the establishment could be still subject to COMAH so long as the specified substance could be produced, assuming there is loss of control of the chemical process. This implies dangerous substances are produced through reaction with the establishment being unable to control the production of such amounts. This could happen if there is production failure or through unexpected chemical reactions.

(*b*)    Top-tier establishments :

(i)    Must produce both On-Site and Off-Site Emergency Plans. The former deals with risks that occur on the establishment and is produced by the operator. The latter deal with risks to the immediate social and physical environment due to the On-Site Emergency. It is prepared by the local authority. Both Plans should link together and be co-ordinated.

(ii)    Top-tier establishments that exceed Top-Tier Thresholds are required to provide information to the public of known and foreseeable risks, as well as the controls adopted. They would also have to provide a Safety Report, which shows the actions taken by the operator to prevent Accidents and mitigate harm to the environment. The establishment must be able to prove that they are operating the plant in accordance with the safety report.

(iii) Operators of existing *CIMAH* sites which became Top-Tier establishments on 1 April 1999 are given until February 2001 to prepare On-Site Emergency Plans and supply information to the local authority. Whilst other establishments that became Top-Tier sites on 1 April 1999 (e.g. those now encompassed by *COMAH* but not *CIMAH (SI 1984 No 1902)*), have until 3 February 2002 to prepare the On-Site Emergency Plan and supply the information to the local authority. However, for those establishments that became top-tier after 1 April 1999, they have a duty to prepare the On-Site Emergency Plan before starting any operation.

(iv) The local authority has six months to prepare an Off-Site Emergency Plan. The six months can start from the time they receive all necessary information to prepare the Plan. However, the period can be extended to nine months. It is recommended that arrangements are made nevertheless by the operator until the Off-Site Plan is available.

(v) Emergency plans should be reviewed and revised at least every three years.

(c) Lower-Tier establishments:

(i) Whilst under no duty to produce Emergency Plans, they are required however to develop Emergency Arrangements in the Major Accident Prevention Policy (MAPP).

(ii) The MAPP should specify safety and emergency management response systems in place in the event of a major accident and the procedures for identifying foreseeable emergency situations.

(d) *COMAH* does not apply to Ministry of Defence establishments, transport related activity, extractive industries exploiting/exploring in mines and quarries, waste land-fill sites nor to nuclear licensed sites that may have substances which generate ionising radiation. However, *COMAH* will apply to both chemicals and explosives at nuclear installations.

(e) A breach of *COMAH regulations* carries the same penalties as those under *ss 33 – 42* of the *Health and Safety at Work etc. Act 1974*, for example £20,000 fine per offence on summary conviction and unlimited fine and/or up to two years imprisonment on indictment.

## *Reporting of Injuries, Diseases and Dangerous Occurrences Regulations 1995 (RIDDOR) (SI 1995 No 3163)*

**D6009** *RIDDOR (SI 1995 No 3163)* will apply to 'accidents' through to 'major incidents'. *RIDDOR* is a reporting requirement that must be followed by the employer or 'responsible person' in notifying the enforcing authority by the quickest means practicable, when there is an event resulting in a reportable injury, reportable occupational disease, reportable dangerous occurrence, gas incidents, road incidents involving work and fatal or non-fatal injuries for example. In addition, work injuries lasting for three days or more are reported to the enforcing authority. (see A3001 Accident Reporting for further details).

## *The Health and Safety (First Aid) Regulations 1981 (SI 1981 No 917)*

**D6010** These regulations do not explicitly mention first aid Arrangements necessary in the event of an Emergency or Disaster. However, they will apply in all types of

Accidents and Major Incidents as defined above. The Regulations are a general statement of best practice, of ensuring the existence of adequate medical equipment, competent and trained first aiders or appointed persons and information on first aid facilities and equipment to staff/others. The Regulations should be read as best practice to be followed in the event of an Accident or Major Incident.

## The Construction (Health, Safety and Welfare) Regulations 1996 (SI 1996 No 1592)

**D6011**   *Regulation 20* requires employers to make emergency arrangements to cope with foreseeable emergency situations. It is primarily aimed at CDM sites where the Health and Safety Plans are operational. The plans should factor in emergency arrangements and procedures in the event of a Major Incident on site.   ·

## The Confined Spaces Regulations 1997 (SI 1997 No 1713)

**D6012**   *Regulation 5* imposes duties on employers and others to make arrangements for emergencies in 'confined spaces'. In summary:

(1)   'Suitable and sufficient arrangements' need to be made for rescue of persons working in confined spaces, with no person accessing a confined space until such arrangements have been developed. [*Reg 5(1)*].

(2)   So far as is reasonably practicable, the risks to persons required to put the arrangements into operation must also be considered as should resuscitation equipment in the event of it being required. [*Reg 5(2)*].

(3)   There is also a duty to act, to operationalise the arrangements when an emergency results. [*Reg 5(3)*].

Q. What are suitable and sufficient arrangements for rescue and resuscitation? This should include appropriate equipment, rescue procedures, warning systems that an emergency exists, fire safety systems, first aid, control of access and egress, liaison with the emergency services, training and competence of rescuers etc.

## Carriage of Dangerous Goods by Road Regulations 1996 (SI 1996 No 2095)

**D6013**   A duty is imposed on the operator of a 'container', 'vehicle' or 'tank' to provide information to other operators engaged/contracted, regarding the handling of emergencies or accident situations. Such information includes:

(*a*)   hazardness of the goods being carried and controls needed to make safe such hazards;

(*b*)   actions required if a person is exposed/makes contact with the goods being carried;

(*c*)   actions required to avert a fire and the equipment that should or should not be used to fight the fire;

(*d*)   the handling of a breakage/spillage; and

(*e*)   any additional information that should be given that can assist the operators or others.

## Carriage of Explosives by Road Regulations 1996 (SI 1996 No 2093)

D6014    *Regulation 26* says that the operator is under a duty to ensure that in the event of an Emergency or Accident, people are protected from ignition as well as the security of the explosives [*Reg 26(3)*]. The Regulation also requires the operator to inform the HSE by the quickest practicable means if the emergency cannot be immediately controlled. [*Reg 26(2)*].

Duties are also placed on the driver of the vehicle that in the event of an Emergency or Accident, the emergency services and the operator are notified by the quickest practicable means [*Reg 26(1)*]. The driver must also ensure that people are safe that could be affected by any ignition and that the explosives are made secure. [*Reg 26(3)*].

## The Environment Act 1995

D6015    Whilst the Act does not explicitly deal with DEM issues, its main objective is the mitigation or prevention of such events. For example, *ss 14 – 18* creates the flood defence committees to co-ordinate the prediction, consequence and response needed in the event of floods.

## 'Legislating the Criminal Code: Involuntary Manslaughter', Law Commission (Law Com No 237)

D6016    Disasters such as Piper Alpha, Kings Cross, Clapham Junction, Herald of Free Enterprise or Ladbroke Grove for example have seen multiple fatalities, allegations of managerial failure and negligence contributing to the Disasters. However, health and safety law has not permitted the successful prosecution and imprisonment of directors and senior managers because of the difficulty in establishing that the individuals in charge were 'the embodiment of the company'. All of the major disasters have involved large and complex organisations with many management layers, so who is the 'embodiment of the company' or the 'directing mind'? The Law Commission has drafted an *Involuntary Homocide Bill 1995*, which is still being considered by the UK Government. The main intention of the Bill is stated in the preamble, to ' Create new offences of reckless killing, killing by gross carelessness and corporate killing to replace the offence of manslaughter in cases where death is caused without the intention of causing death or serious injury'. The intention is to have a codified system of law as regards these three offences. Thus:

(a)    *Reckless killing*

This offence would be committed if the answers are 'yes' or 'affirmative' to all the following:

(i)    a person through their conduct causes the death of another;

(ii)    a person is aware that a risk exists and that their conduct whether causing that risk or acting on that risk will cause death or serious injury; and

(iii)    it is unreasonable for the person to take a risk, knowing the circumstances prevalent.

(b)    *Killing by gross carelessness*

This offence would arise if the answers are 'yes' or 'affirmative' to all the following:

(i)    a person by their conduct causes the death of another;

(ii)   a reasonable person in the position of the person under question realises that there is a risk that the person's conduct will cause death or serious injury;

(iii)   the person 'is capable of appreciating' the risk at that time in question; and

(iv)   either the person's conduct 'falls far below' what could be reasonably expected under those circumstances or, 'he or she intends by his conduct to cause some injury, or is aware of, and unreasonably takes, the risk that it may do so, *and* the conduct causing (or intended to cause) the injury constitutes an offence' (page 127/128). The former focuses on a breach of a duty whilst the second of this 'either or' option seems to require the elements of a crime, the *'action'* (action of 'unreasonably take' and 'conduct causing') and the *'intent'* ('intends by his conduct').

Both reckless killing and killing by gross carelessness are:

(1)   forms of 'individual manslaughter';

(2)   alternative verdicts to 'murder';

(3)   alternatives to each other for the court to consider;

(4)   both applicable to workplace and other situations, for example be available to the court in cases of road deaths or serious injury (although the Law Commission do not recommend a change to the existing offence of 'causing death by bad driving');

(5)   reckless killing would carry a maximum sentence of life imprisonment whilst the Commission do not recommend a maximum for killing by gross carelessness.

*(c)*   *Corporate killing*

This contrasts to the two proposed individual manslaughter offences above. The Law Commission says on page 128/129:

(i)   that there should be a special offence of corporate killing, broadly corresponding to the individual offence of killing by gross carelessness;

(ii)   that (like the individual offence) the corporate offence should be committed only where the defendant's conduct in causing the death falls far below what could reasonably be expected;

(iii)   that (unlike the individual offence) the corporate offence should not require that the risk be obvious, or that the defendant be capable of appreciating the risk; and

(iv)   that for the purposes of the corporate offence, a death should be regarded as having been caused by the conduct of a corporation if it is caused by a failure, in the way in which the corporation's activities are managed or organised, to ensure the health and safety of persons employed in or affected by those activities.

Therefore:

(1)   Corporate killing as an offence relies less on the 'intent' component and more on the actions/conduct and safety systems in place (or otherwise). There is also no reference to 'foreseeability of risk', with

the Commission arguing it is difficult to apply this concept to a corporation vis-à-vis an individual.

(2)     The Law Commission stress the role of 'management failure' by the corporation as a cause of death even though the 'immediate cause' could be the act or omission of some individual such as an employee.

(3)     Corporate killing applies to 'incorporated bodies' only e.g. limited and public limited companies and would not apply to 'sole traders'. Thus, the offence of corporate killing can only be by an incorporated body.

(4)     The Commission recommended that this offence should not require consent to bring a private prosecution for corporate killing.

(5)     That this offence be triable by indictment only.

(6)     The Commission is suggesting that on conviction of corporate killing the court should be empowered (upon the suggestion of the prosecution or the HSE) to recommend improvements to management systems to ensure death or serious injury at work does not arise again.

(7)     Assuming that the jury cannot convict under the proposed offences, it should be able to consider conviction under *s 2 or 3* of the *Health and Safety at Work etc. Act 1974.*

*(d)     Unlawful act manslaughter*

The Commission recommends the abolition of unlawful act manslaughter as it currently stands. This refers to where a person causes death whilst committing a criminal act, with this act carrying a risk of *some* harm to the other person. The Commission says '. . . we consider that it is wrong in principle that a person should be convicted for causing *death* when the gravest risk apparently inherent in his conduct was the risk of causing *some injury*'.

## Insurance reasons

D6017     There are also insurance based reasons for effective DEM:

(*a*)     given the positive correlation between risk and premium, the existence of DEM indicates hazard and risk control, consequently the premium ought to be less;

(*b*)     if insurers are not satisfied or dissatisfied with the DEM system in place then they may not insure the operation, in turn increasing corporate risk as well as reducing corporate credibility. It may also prohibit the operation from tendering for contracts.

## Corporate reasons

D6018     (*a*)     The corporate experience of companies like P & O European Ferries (Dover) Ltd, indicates that proactive DEM systems would have saved the company considerable money, publicity and reputation. In March 1987, the *Herald of Free Enterprise* the roll-on roll-off car ferry left Zeebrugge for Dover, thereafter it sunk resulting in 187 deaths. The case against the company and the five senior corporate officers collapsed for reasons cited above ('embodiment of the company' and 'controlling mind', see D6016).

(*b*)     Failures to have sound DEM systems can also have dire financial consequences as disasters as disparate as Piper Alpha to The Challenger Space-shuttle indicate. In the former case, Occidental Petroleum were generating 10 per cent of all the UK's North Sea output from Piper Alpha. Lord Cullen, who led the inquiry said 'The safety policy and procedures were in place: the practice was deficient'. Piper Alpha showed that the company had ineffective emergency response procedures resulting in persons being trapped, dying of smoke inhalation or jumping into the cold North Sea (something the procedures prohibited but a significant number of those that did jump into the sea survived). Such a disaster had consequences for Occidental's financial reputation, share value, ability to attract investment and growth potential. In contrast, in the case of The Challenger Disaster in January 1986, the o-rings that held the two segments of the rocket boosters, which carried the fuel to propel the Challenger into space, fell apart resulting in the Challenger exploding shortly after taking off. This shocked the USA public, resulting in delays and questions as to the viability of NASAs programmes. The failure of the o-rings was well known with the engineers down grading the risk from 'high to 'acceptable'.

### Societal reasons

D6019    Society expects its organisations to plan and prepare for the worst case scenarios and when this doesn't happen, society can seek the closure, forefeiture or expulsion of the organisation from society e.g. the legal and political costs to Union Carbide in India with its mis-management of its plant in Bhopal in India. The company has been banned from operating in India.

### Environmental reasons

D6020    Failure to prepare and plan for Disasters and Emergencies will also have environmental costs, no better illustrated than the Chernobyl Disaster in April 1986, with its impact not only on the population of Russia but as far as Wales in the United Kingdom. The aim was to test if the power reduction of a turbine generator would be sufficient given the use of some suitable voltage generator, to power an emergency core cooling system (ECCS) for a few minutes whilst the stand-by diesel generator became operational. The power fell to 7 per cent of full power with a benchmark of 20 per cent being critical for that make of RBMK reactor. Consequently, the reactor exploded with radioactive fall out polluting the physical environment.

### Humanitarian reasons

D6021    The human cost for not planning for worst case outcomes is the most significant. All the major Disasters documented in the media resulted in multiple fatalities – of all demographic and socio-economic groups. After the Ladbroke Grove Disaster in October 1999, when two trains collided resulting in 31 fatalities and 160 being critically injured, the public and the media made a significant outcry for change. This culminated in John Prescott, the Secretary of State for the Environment, Transport and the Regions establishing a Committee headed by Lord Cullen (of the Piper Alpha Inquiry), to investigate 'safety culture' on the railways.

## Disaster and Emergency Management Systems (DEMS)

D6022    A DEMS is outlined in Figure 2 below:

*Figure 2: Disaster and Emergency Management Systems (DEMS)*

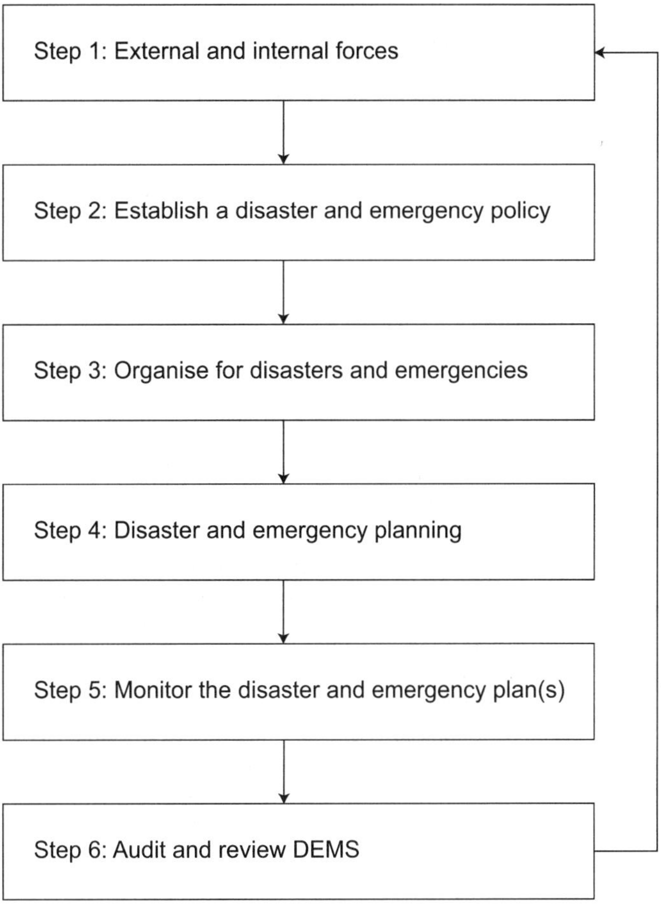

```
┌─────────────────────────────────────────────────────┐
│  Step 1: External and internal forces               │◄──┐
└─────────────────────────────────────────────────────┘   │
                          │                                │
                          ▼                                │
┌─────────────────────────────────────────────────────┐   │
│  Step 2: Establish a disaster and emergency policy  │   │
└─────────────────────────────────────────────────────┘   │
                          │                                │
                          ▼                                │
┌─────────────────────────────────────────────────────┐   │
│  Step 3: Organise for disasters and emergencies     │   │
└─────────────────────────────────────────────────────┘   │
                          │                                │
                          ▼                                │
┌─────────────────────────────────────────────────────┐   │
│  Step 4: Disaster and emergency planning            │   │
└─────────────────────────────────────────────────────┘   │
                          │                                │
                          ▼                                │
┌─────────────────────────────────────────────────────┐   │
│  Step 5: Monitor the disaster and emergency plan(s) │   │
└─────────────────────────────────────────────────────┘   │
                          │                                │
                          ▼                                │
┌─────────────────────────────────────────────────────┐   │
│  Step 6: Audit and review DEMS                      │───┘
└─────────────────────────────────────────────────────┘
```

# External and Internal Factors

D6023    The starting point with DEMS is understanding the variables that can influence or affect DEMS. These are both internal to the organisation and wider societal variables. It would be an erroneous assumption for the organisation to make, if it believed that DEMS can be made in isolation of wider societal variables; these variables need to be understood and factored into any DEMS. The larger the organisation and the more hazardous its operation, the more it needs to provide specific detail.

## External Factors influencing DEMS

D6024    (*a*)    The Natural Environment

The organisation needs to identify physical variables that can influence its reaction to a Disaster or Emergency. The organisation needs to identify:

(1)    Seasonal weather conditions – including weather type(s) and temperature range. Effective rescue can be hampered by failing to know, note

and record such variables. A simple chart, identifying in user-friendly terms on a monthly basis the weather conditions can assist the reader of any DEM plans.

(2) Geography around the site – a description of the physical environment such as terrain, rivers or sea, soil type, geology as well as longitude and latitude positioning of the site. These should be brief descriptions unless the site is remote and could have difficulty being accessed in an emergency.

(3) Time and distance – of the site from major emergency and accident centres, fire brigades, police etc. Both long and short routes need to be determined. Longitude and latitude co-ordinates should be identified.

(*b*) Societal Factors

These include:

(1) Demographics – the organisation needs to identify the age range, gender type, socio-economic structure of the immediate vicinity around the site. A major incident with impact on the local community requires the organisation to calculate risks to the community. *COMAH Off-Site Emergency Plans* indicates why planning is not just an on-site 'in these four walls' activity.

(2) Social attitudes – the organisation needs to investigate briefly and be aware of attitudes (reactions and responses) of the local town or city and the country to disasters and emergencies. Union Carbide made the assumption that the population and authorities in Madhya Pradesh, where Bhopal is located, would react like the communities in the USA. The response rates, awareness levels and information available to different communities differs.

(3) Perception of risk – how does the local community view the site or operation? Is the risk 'tolerable' and 'acceptable' to them for having the operation in their community? Both Chernobyl and Bhopal highlight that economic necessity can alter the perception of risk in contrast to the statistical level of risk.

(4) History of community response – in brief the organisation needs to determine how many Major Incidents there have been in the past and how effectively have the community assisted (emergency services and volunteers). Such support will be critical in a Disaster.

(5) The built environment – a brief description of the urban environment, namely the street layout, urban concentration level, population density, access/egress to railways, motorways are useful. These issues could be covered by the inclusion of a map of the area.

(*c*) Government and political factors

Relevant factors are:

(1) The policy of national government to Disasters and Emergencies. Are they proactive in advising organisations, what information and guidance do they give? The organisation needs to identify its local or regional office of the HSE, the Environment Agency or a similar body and make contact with officials and seek early input into any planning.

(2) Local government – their plans, information and guidance. DEM's need to be aware of any local government restrictions on managing

major incidents. In the case of *COMAH* sites, they will need to involve the local authority in preparing Off-Site Emergency Plans.

(3) Committees and agencies – there are many legal and quasi-legal bodies created by legislation which have guidance, information and templates on response. For example the flooding committees mentioned above under the *Environment Act 1995*.

(4) Emergency and medical services – making contact, obtaining addresses/contact numbers and knowing the efficiency of the emergency services/accident and emergency are critical actions.

(*d*) Legal factors

The organisation needs to know the legal constraints it has to operate within, not only to comply with the law but also to follow the best advice contained in legislation as a means of preventing disaster and emergency.

(*e*) Sources of information issues

These include:

(1) The local and national media – will not only report any Incidents but can be critical in relaying messages. Any planning requires the identification of local and national newspapers (their addresses/contact numbers), local/national radio details and any public sector media (through local government).

(2) Local library – they will in turn have considerable contact details and networks with other libraries so can be an efficient medium to relay urgent information. Making contact with the local librarian and identifying such contact details in any planing will be required.

(3) Business associations – Chambers of Commerce, Business Links, Training and Enterprise Councils need to be identified for the same reasons cited for local libraries. In the event of a Major Incident they can convey and provide information on a local rescue or occupational health organisation.

(4) Voluntary organisations – such as Red Cross, St. Johns Ambulance should be identified and noted.

The organisation needs to build information networks locally and nationally. The experience of major Disasters such as Chernobyl or Kings Cross indicate that letting others know of the Incident is not a shameful or embarrassing matter – rather it can warn others and halt others from attending the site.

(*f*) Technological factors

These concern what technology and equipment exists in the local community; what doesn't; lifting equipment, rescue, computers, monitoring equipment measuring equipment etc.

(*g*) Commercial factors

These include:

(1) Insurance – liaise with insurers from the beginning and ensure that all plans are drawn to their attention and if possible approved by them. This can avoid difficulties of any claim that may arise due to a Disaster or Emergency as well as ensure that best advice from the insurer has been factored into the plans.

(2)   Customer and supplier response – larger organisations need to identify the responses from customers and suppliers, their willingness to work with the organisation in the event of a worst case scenario and possible alternatives. Suppliers need to be identified. Issues of customer convenience and loyalty also need to be addressed.

(3)   Attitudes of the bank – liquidity issues will arise when a Major Incident strikes. Most organisations do not and cannot afford to make financial provisions for such eventualities. Therefore, if the operation is highly hazardous, establishing financial facilities before hand with the bank is necessary to ensure availability of liquid cash.

(4)   Strength of the economic sector and economy – larger organisations that are significant players in a sector or the economy need to be cognisant of the 'multiplier effect' that damage to their operation can do to the community and suppliers, employees and others.

## Internal Factors affecting DEMS

D6025   DEMS also need to be constructed after accounting for various internal or organisational variables.

(*a*)   Resource factors

Cash flow and budgetary planning whether annual or a longer period needs to account for resource availability for Major Incidents. This includes physical, human and financial resources. This is wider than banking facilities and encompasses equipment, trained personnel and contingency funds .

(*b*)   Design and architecture

Issues include – is the workplace physically/structurally capable of withholding a Major Incident? What are the main design and architectural risks? Also layout, access/egress, emergency routes, adequacy of space for vehicles etc.

(*c*)   Corporate culture and practice

The organisation needs to identify its own collective behaviour, attitude, strengths and weaknesses to cope with a Major Incident. Being a 'large organisation' does not mean it is a 'coping organisation'; there is also the delay in response that is associated with hierarchical structures. In this case, the organisation needs to consider small 'matrix' or project team cell in the hierarchy dedicated to incident response.

(*d*)   Individual's perceived behaviour

(1)   The *Hale and Hale Model* is an attempt to explain how individuals internalise and digest perceived information of danger; make decisions/choices according to the cost/benefit associated with each decision/choice; and the actual actions they take as well as any reactions that result from their actions. In short, these five variables need to be understood in the organisation setting and a picture built up of the behavioural response of an individual.

(2)   The *Glendon & Hale Model* is a macro model of how the organisation (behaving like a system), being dynamic and fluid, with objectives and indeed limitations (systems boundary) can shape behaviour and in turn influence Human Error. Following Rasmussen, Human Error can be Skill Based (failing to perform an action correctly), Rule Based (have not learned the sequences to avoid harm) or Knowledge Based

(breaching rules or best practice). If all three error types are committed then the danger level in the system is also greater. The model is a focus on how wider systems can contribute to Human Error and how that error can permeate into the organisation. The inference is the organisation needs to clearly define and communicate its intention and objectives and continuously monitor individual response.

(3)  *Reducing Error and Influencing Behaviour*, HSG 48, Health and Safety Executive, 1999 identifies the role of 'Human Error' and 'Human Factors' in Major Incident causation. The HSE says 'a human error is an action or decision which was *not intended*, which involved a deviation from an accepted standard, and which led to an undesirable outcome' (page 13). Following Rasmussen they classify four types:

   (i)  *slips* (unintended action);

   (ii)  *lapses* (short term memory failure) with slips and lapses being skill based;

   (iii)  *mistakes* (incorrect decision) which are rule based; and

   (iv)  *violations* (deliberate breach of rules) which are knowledge based.

Different types of Human Errors contribute in different ways to Major Incidents the HSE say and exemplify. Organisations need to identify from reported incidents the main types of Human Errors and why they are resulting and the negative harm generated. (Note that in the previous version of HSG 48 called *Human Factors in Industrial Safety*, five types of Human Errors were defined;

   (A)  *misperception* (tunnel vision, excluding wider factors from one's senses e.g. the belief that smoking is safe on the underground or that a 'smouldering' is not a significant fire as in the case of Kings Cross in 1987);

   (B)  *mistaken action* (doing something under the false belief it is correct e.g. the pilot switching off the good engine under the belief he was switching off the one with the fire, so both are off, hence the crash landing in the Kegworth Disaster);

   (C)  *mistaken priority* (a clash of objectives, such as safety and finance as implied in the Herald of Free Enterprise Disaster in 1987);

   (D)  *lapse of attention* (short term memory failure, not concentrating on a task e.g. turning on a valve under repair as in Piper Alpha in 1988); and

   (E)  *wilfulness* (intentionally breaching rules e.g Lyme Bay Disaster when the principal director received a two year imprisonment for the death of teenagers at a leisure centre under his control)).

The HSE says that understanding Human Factors is a means of reducing Human Error potential. Human Factors is a combination of understanding the Person's behaviour, the Job they do (ergonomics) and the wider Organisational system. Major incidents can result if the organisation does not analyse and understand these three variables.

(*e*)   Information systems at work

What types, how effective, and their accuracy needs to be identified. Thus telephone, fax, e-mail, cellular phone, telex etc. need to be assessed for performance and efficacy during a worst case scenario.

# Establish a Disaster & Emergency Policy

D6026   The DEM Policy is a document that highlights the corporate intent to cope with and manage a Major Incident. It will have three parts: Statement of Policy for managing Major Incidents (see D6027); Arrangements for Major Incident management (see D6028); and Command and Control charge of Arrangements (see D6029).

## Statement of policy for managing major incidents

D6027   This should be a short (maximum 1 page) missionary and visionary statement covering the following:

- Senior management commitment to be responsible for the co-ordination of Major Incident response.

- To comply with the Law, namely:

   — the protection of the health, safety and welfare of employees, visitors, the public and contractors;

   — to comply with the duties under *Regs 8 and 9* of the *Management of Health and Safety at Work Regulations 1999 (SI 1999 No 3242)* (see D6007);

   — to comply with any other legislation that may be applicable to the organisation.

- To make suitable arrangements to cope with a Major Incident and to be proactive and efficient in the implementation process.

- That this Statement applies to all levels of the organisation and all relevant sites in the country of jurisdiction.

- The commitment of human, physical and financial resources to prevent and manage Major Incidents.

- To consult with affected parties (employees, the local authority and others if needed).

- To review the Statement .

- To communicate the Statement.

- Signed and dated by the most senior corporate officer.

## The Arrangements for Major Incident management

D6028   (1)   This refers to what the organisation has done, is doing and will do in the event of a Major Incident and *how* it will react in those circumstances. The Arrangements are a legal requirement under *Regs 5, 8 and 9* of the *Management of Health and Safety at Work Regulations 1999 (SI 1999 No 3242)*.

(2)   Arrangements should be realistic and achievable. They should focus on major actions to be taken and issues to be addressed rather than being a 'shopping list'. The Arrangements will have to be verified (in particular for *COMAH* sites).

(3)     Arrangements could be under the following headings with explanations under each. To repeat, the larger the organisation and the more complex the hazard facing it, the more detailed the Arrangements need to be. For example:

- Medical assistance – including first aid availability, first aiders, links with accident and emergency at the medical centre, other specialists that could be called upon, rules on treating injured persons, specialised medical equipment and its availability etc.

- Facilities management – the location, site plans and accessibility to the main facilities (gas, electricity, water, substances etc.), rendering safe such facilities, availability of water supply in-house and within the perimeter of the site etc.

- Equipment to cope – identification of safety equipment available and/or accessible, location of such equipment, types (personal protective equipment, lifting, moving, working at height equipment etc.).

- Monitoring equipment – measuring, monitoring and recording devices needed, including basic items such as measuring tapes, paper, pens, tape recorders, intercom and loud-speakers.

- Safe systems – procedures to access site, working safely by employees and contractors under major incident conditions (what can and cannot be done), hazard/risk assessments of dangers being confronted etc., risks to certain groups and procedures needed for rescue (disabled, young persons, children, pregnant women, elderly persons).

- Public safety – ensuring non access to major incident site by the public (in particular children, trespassers, the media and those with criminal intent), warning systems to the public etc.

- Contractor safety – guidance and information to contractors at the major incident on working safely.

- Information arrangements – the supply of information to staff, the media and others (insurers, enforcers) to inform them of the events. Where will the information be supplied from, when will it be done and updates?

- The media – managing the media, confining them to an area, handling pressure from them, what to say and what not to say etc.

- Insurers/loss adjusters – notifying them and working with them at the earliest opportunity.

- Enforcers – notifying them of the major incident, working with them including several types e.g. HSE, Environment Agency (or Scottish equivalent) as well as local authority (environmental health, planning, building control for instance).

- Evidence and reporting arrangement – to cover strict rules on removal or evidence by employees or others, role and power of enforcers, incident reporting e.g under *RIDDOR (SI 1995 No 3163)* etc.

- The emergency services – working with the police, fire, ambulance/ NHS, and other specialists (Red Cross, Search & Rescue), rules of engagement, issues of information supply and communication with these services.

- Specialist arrangements for specific Major Incidents such as bomb explosions – issues of contacting the police, ordnance disposal, access and egress, rescue and search, economic and human impact to name a few issues were most evident during the London Dockland and Manchester Bombings in the 1990s.

- Human aspects – removing, storing and naming dead bodies or seriously injured persons during the incident. Informing the next-of-kin, issues of religious and cultural respect. Issues of counselling support and person-to-person support during the incident.

This is not an exhaustive list. The arrangements should not repeat those in the Safety Policy, rather the latter can be abbreviated and attached as a schedule to the above, so that the reader can have access succinctly to specific OSH arrangements such as fire safety, occupational health, safe systems at work, dangerous substances for instance.

## Command and Control Chart of Arrangements

D6029    This highlights who is responsible for the effective management of the Major Incident.

(1)    It should be a graphical representation preferably in a hierarchical format, clearly delineating the division of labour between personnel in the organisation and the emergency services/others.

(2)    The chart should display three broad levels of command and control, namely Strategic, Operational and Tactical. The first relates to the person(s) in overall charge of the Major Incident. Will this be the person who signed the Statement of Policy for Major Incidents or will it be another (disaster and emergency advisor, safety officer, others)? This person will make major decisions. The second relates to co-ordinators of teams. Operational level personnel need to have the above arrangements assigned to them in clear terms. The third refers to those at the front end of the major incident, for instance first aiders.

It is most important to note that internal Command and Control of Arrangements does not mean *overall* command and control of the Major Incident. This can (will be) vested with the appropriate emergency service, normally the police or the fire authority in the UK. In the event of any conflict of decisions, the external body such as the police will have the final veto. Therefore, the Chart and the Arrangements must reflect this variable.

(3)    The chart should list on a separate page names/addresses/emergency phone, fax, e-mail, cellular numbers of those identified on the chart. It should also list the numbers for the emergency services as well as others (Red Cross, specialist search and rescue, loss adjusters, enforcing body).

(4)    The chart should also clearly ratify a principle of command and control, as to who would be 'In-Charge 1', 'In-Charge 2', if the original person became unavailable.

(5)    The chart and the list of numbers should also be accompanied by a set of 'rules of engagement' in short 'bullet points' to remind personnel of the importance of command and control e.g. safety, obedience, communication, accuracy, humanity for instance.

## Summary

**D6030**

(1) The 3 parts of the DEM Policy need to be one document. Any detailed procedures can be separately documented ('disaster and emergency procedures') and indeed could be an extensive source of information. However, unlike the Safety Policy and any accompanying Safety Manual, the same volume of information cannot apply to the DEM Policy. For obvious reasons it must be concise, clearly written, very practical and without complex cross-referencing.

(2) The DEM Policy must 'fit' with the Safety Policy, there can be no conflict so the safety officer and the DEM officer need to cross check and liaise. The DEM Policy must also fit with the broader corporate/business policy of the organisation.

(3) The DEM Policy must be proactive and reactive. The former concerned with preventing/mitigating loss and the latter concerned with managing the Major Incident when it does arise in a swift and least harmful manner.

(4) The DEM Policy needs to be reviewed 'regularly'. This could be when there is 'significant change' to the organisation, or as a part of an audit (semi-annual or annual).

(5) It must be remembered that the DEM Policy is a 'live' document so that it must be accessible and up-to-date.

(6) Although accessibility is important, the Policy should also have controlled circulation to core personnel only (for example those identified in the chart, the legal department). If the Policy was to be accessed by individuals wishing to harm the organisations, this will enable such persons to pre-empt and reduce the efficacy of the Policy.

(7) Finally and most crucially, the core contents of the Policy need to be communicated to all staff and others (contractors, temporary employees, possibly local authority).

## Organise for Disasters & Emergencies

**D6031**

Once the establishment has accounted for External and Internal factors and has produced a DEM Policy taking account of such factors, it is then necessary to ensure personnel and others are aware of the issues raised in the DEM policy. The '4' C's approach of HSG 65 provides a logical framework to generate this *(Successful Health & Safety Management*, HSE): communication (see D6032); co-operation (see D6033); competence (see D6034); and control (see D6035).

### Establish effective communication

**D6032**

Communication is a process of transmission, reception and feedback of information, whether that information is verbal, written, pictorial or intimated. Effective communication of the DEM Policy therefore is not a matter of circulating copies but requires the following:

*(1) Transmission*

- The whole policy should not be circulated as it will mean little to employees and others. Rather an abridged version, possibly in booklet format or as an addition to any OSH documentation supplied will make more sense. Such copies must be clear, user friendly, non-technical as possible, be aware of the end user's capabilities to digest the information, be logical/sequential in explanation and use pictorial representation as much as possible.

- Being aware of the audience is central to the effective communication of the DEM Policy. The audience is not one entity but will consist of:

  — direct employees;

  — temporary employees;

  — contractors;

  — the media;

  — the enforcers (*COMAH* sites);

  — the local authority (*COMAH* sites);

  — insurers;

  — emergency services (*COMAH* sites);

  — the public (*COMAH* sites).

  This does not necessarily mean separate copies for each of these entities but the abridged copy will need to satisfy the needs of all such groups.

- Transmission should start from the board, through to departmental heads, and disseminated downwards and across.

*(2)  Reception*

- What format will the end-user receive the abridged copy in (hard copy, electronic on disc, via e-mail, etc)?

- When will the copy be circulated – upon induction, upon training, *ad hoc* ?

*(3)  Feedback*

- Will the end-user have the opportunity to raise questions, make suggestions, be critical if they spot inconsistencies in the DEM Policy?

- There should also be 'tool box talks' and other general awareness programmes to inform individuals of the DEM Policy. This could be combined with general OSH programmes or wider personnel programmes, so that a holistic approach is presented.

- The importance of feedback is that the policy becomes owned by all individuals, which in turn is the single most important factor in successful pre-planning to prevent Major Incidents.

In general it may be useful to retain copies of the abridged and the full policy with other safety documentation in an 'in-house' company library. For smaller organisations, this could be one or two folders on a shelf through to a dedicated room for larger organisations. Second, the abridged copy could be pasted onto an intranet site.

## Co-operation

D6033    Co-operation is concerned with collaborating, working together to achieve the shared goal and objectives:

- Firstly, co-operation between strategic, operational and tactical level management is critical. This reflects the chart in the DEM Policy, as discussed above. This could be consolidated as a part of a broader corporate meeting or preferably dedicated time to cover OSH and fatal incident issues. This could be a semi-annual event, with a dedicated day allotted for all grades of management to interface. This is not the same as a board level discussion or a management discussion.

- To give responsibility to either the Safety Committee or the safety group to co-ordinate review, debate and assessment of the DEM Policy or to fuse this function within a broader business/corporate review committee. The former has advantages as it is safety dedicated whilst the latter would integrate DEM Policy issues into the wider business debate.

- Involvement of Safety Representatives/Representatives of Employee Safety (ROES), is both a legal requirement as well as inclusive safety management. These persons can be central 'nodes' in linking 'management' and the 'workers' together. In the UK, there has been an increasing realisation that trained safety representatives are a knowledgeable resource with many being trained to IOSH/NEBOSH standard (as with the AEEU (electrical engineers) trade union, with their National Academy of Safety and Health, NASH).

- Co-operation also needs to extend to contractors. The person responsible for interfacing with contractors needs to up-date them and make them aware of the DEM Policy and seek their support and suggestions. It may also be valuable to invite contractors to OSH/fatal incident awareness days or the general committee meetings as observers.

- Co-operation is also needed between the organisation and external agencies such as the local authority, insurers, enforcers, media etc. This can be achieved through providing abridged copies of minutes or a 'newsletter' (1 – 2 sides of A4) distributed semi-annually informing such bodies of the DEM Policy and any changes as well as other OSH issues. *COMAH* sites will have to demonstrate as a legal requirement that plans and policies are up-to-date and effective.

## Competence

**D6034**     Competence is a process of acquiring knowledge, skill and experience to enhance both individual and corporate response. Thus, competence is about enhancing and achieving standards (set by the organisation or others).

- Competence is important, so that certain key persons are trained to understand the DEMS process. The above issues and their link to OSH in particular require personnel that can assimilate, digest and convey the above issues. Training does not necessarily mean formal or academic training but can be vocational or in-house. Neither does it mean the organisation expending vast sums but can be a part of a wider in-house OSH awareness programme (e.g. 1 day per quarter of a year).

- For larger organisations, they may be able to recruit 'competent persons' to advice on OSH and fatal incident matters.

- In short, all employees need to brought up to a minimal standard. Piper Alpha showed that whilst Occidental Petroleum had detailed procedures, the employees generally did not fully understand them nor had they the minimal understanding of major incident evacuation. The organisation had failed to impart knowledge, skill and experience sufficient to cope with fires and explosions on off-shore sites.

### Control

D6035  Control refers to establishing parameters, constraints and limits on the behaviour and action. This ensures that on the one hand an effective DEM policy exists and on the other, personnel will act and react in a co-ordinated and responsible manner. Controls can be achieved via for example:

- Contractual means – as a term of a contract of employment that instruction and direction on OSH and fatal incident matters must be followed by individuals.

- Corporate means – the organisation continuously makes individuals aware of following rules and best practice.

- Behavioural means – by establishing clear rules, training, supply of information, leading-through-example, showing top-level management commitment etc.

- Supervisory means – ensuring that supervisors monitor employee safety attitudes and risk perceptions.

The cumulative effect of the 4 C's should be a positive and proactive culture in which not only OSH issues but the DEM Policy issues are understood. .Factors that can mitigate or prevent a positive and proactive culture developing include lack of management commitment, lack of awareness of requirements, poor attitudes to work and life, misperception of the risk facing the organisation, lack of resources or the unwillingness to commit resources, fatalistic beliefs etc.

## Disaster & Emergency Planning

D6036  'Planning' is a process of identifying a clear goal and objectives and pursuing the best means to achieve that goal/objectives. Although 'Disaster' and 'Emergency' are two separate but related terms, in the case of planning the two need to be viewed together. This is because in practice one cannot divorce the serious event (the disaster) from the response to that serious event (emergency). There is no practical benefit from having a separate Disaster Plan and an Emergency Plan.

Disaster and Emergency Planning can be viewed in three broad stages:

—  stage 1: before the event; (see D6037)

—  stage 2: factors to consider during the event; (see D6044)

—  stage 3: after the event. (see D6045)

### Stage 1: before the event

D6037  Once the DEM Policy has been established and a culture created where the Policy has been understood and positively received, next one needs to be establish a 'state-of-preparedness', that is addressing issues, speculating on scenarios and developing support services when the major incident does strike. One can summarise this stage into three sections, with a special section on *COMAH* and the specific legal requirements for *COMAH* sites.

*The Risk Assessment of Major Incident potential and consequent Contingency Planning*

D6038     What is the probability of the Major Incident resulting? What would be the severity? What type of major incident would it be? Figure 3 depicts a 'major incident matrix':

*Figure 3: Major Incident Matrix*

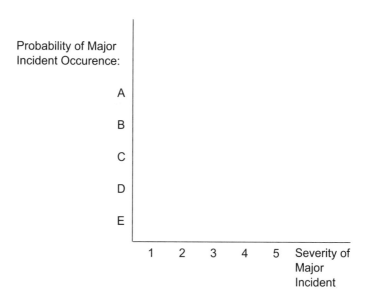

Where:

A=  Certainty of Occurrence (Probability = 1)
B=  Highly Probable
C=  0.5 Probability of Occurrence
D=  Low Probability
E=  Most Unlikely
And:
1=  Serious Injuries
2=  Multiple Fatalities
3=  Multiple Fatalities and Serious Economic/Property Damage
4=  FatalEnvironmental , Bio-Sphere and Social Harm
5=  Socio-Physical Catatstrophe

The planning responses therefore will differ according to the cell one finds oneself in. For example, cell 1E requires the least complex state of preparedness in terms of resources, detail of planning and urgency. Whilst 5A is a major societal event that requires macro and holistic responses, in which case the organisation's sole efforts at planning are futile. The organisation needs to assess in which cell the Major Incidents it will confront, will mainly fall in and accordingly develop plans. A conglomerate or an 'exposed operation' such as oil/gas refinery work may require planning at all 25 levels. This is *'Contingency Planning'* – an analysis of the alternative outcomes and providing adequate responses to those outcomes.

### Decisional Planning

D6039    Planning before the event also involves co-ordinating different levels of decision making. Figure 4 depicts a decisional matrix:

*Figure 4: Decisional Matrix*

| | Production Level | 1. INPUT | 2. PROCESS | 3. OUTPUT |
|---|---|---|---|---|
| **Management Level** | | | | |
| A. STRATEGIC | | | | |
| B. OPERATIONAL | | | | |
| C. TACTICAL | | | | |

Where:
A=    Strategic or Board/Shareholder/Controller Level (Gold Level)
B=    Operational or Departmental Level (Silver Level)
C=    Tactical or Factory/Office Level (Bronze Level)
And:
1=    Inputs or those resources that make production possible, thus raw materials, people, information, machinery and financial resources.
2=    Process or the manner in which the inputs are arranged or combined to enable production (method of production)
3=    Output or the product or service that is generated.

Decisional Planning requires Major Incident risks to be identified for each cell. Essentially this is assessing where in the production process and at which management level can problems arise that can lead to Major Incidents. This matrix is not 'closed' but is 'open' and 'dynamic', which means External Factors, which were discussed above as well as Internal Factors need to be accounted for. For example, in a commercial operation at board level, they need to consider:

(1)    INPUTS: purchasing policy of any raw materials used (safety etc.), recruitment of stable staff, adequacy of resources to enable safe production, known and foreseeable risks of inputs used, reliability of supply, commitment to environmental safety and protection etc.

(2)    PROCESS: external factors and their impact on production, production safety commitment, commitment to researching/investigating in the market for safer production processes etc.

(3)    OUTPUT: boardroom commitment to quality assurance, environmental safety of the service and/or product produced, customer care and social responsibility etc.

The end result should be, in each cell major risks to production and their impact on a major incident needs to be identified. This need not be a major, time consuming exercise, rather it can be determined through a 'brain-storming' session or each management level fills out the matrix during their regular meeting and then it is jointly co-ordinated in a short (2 – 5 page) document.

### Testing

D6040    This is considered to be a crucial aspect of pre-planning by all the emergency services in the UK. Testing is an objective rehearsal to examine the state of preparedness and to determine if the Policy and the Plan will perform as expected.

The Home Office guidance, *Dealing with Disaster* (1998, Third Edition) identifies Training and Exercising as types of Testing. Training is more personnel focused, aiming to assess how much the human resource knows about the Policy and Plan and means of enhancing the knowledge, skill and experience of that resource. Exercising is a broader approach, examining all aspects of the Policy and Plan, not just the human response but also physical and organisational capability to deal with the Major Incident.

*Training*

D6041    Carrying out a training needs analysis (TNA) to determine the quantity (in terms of time) and quality of training needed is essential. It may be that personnel and others adequately understand the Policy and Plan, therefore the training response should be proportionate. Excessive training is a motivational threat to the interest and enthusiasm of the person as is under-training. The HSE in HSG 65, *Successful Health & Safety Management* suggest that the TNA consists of issues such as:

—    Is the training 'necessary'? In other words, is there an alternative way of ensuring competence and awareness of the Policy and Plan, rather than just training? Could circulating the information be better? What about regular 'tool box talks'? It is important to weigh the costs and benefits of each option.

—    Is it 'needed'? Will the training meet Personal, Job or Organisational needs thereby enhancing awareness and appreciation of the policy and plan ?

—    What will be the intended learning objectives of the training? Will it be 'this is a course on the content of the DEM Policy and Plan'?

—    What type of training will be offered? Class-room, on-site or both? What are the costs and benefits associated with each?

—    Management of the training – where will the training be conducted? Who will deliver it? When will it be delivered – day or evening? What training aids will be provided – if any?

—    How does one measure the effectiveness of such training ?

*Exercising*

D6042    The Home Office cite three types of exercising:

●    Seminar Exercises

—    a broad, brain-storming session, assessing and analysing the efficacy of the Policy and Plan

—    seminars need to be 'inclusive', that is bring staff and others together in order to co-ordinate strategic, operational and tactical issues.

●    Table-Top Exercises

This is an attempt to identify visually using a model of the production or office site and surrounding areas, what types of problems could arise (access/ egress, crowd control, logistics etc.).

●    Live Exercises

This is a rehearsal of the Major Incident, actively and pro-actively testing the responses of the individual, organisation and possibly the community (emergency services, the media etc.). London Underground, the railway sector commonly, the civil aviation sector, tend to annually assume that a major incident has occurred and the consequential conditions are created.

- Synthetic Simulation

  Whilst this is not mentioned in Home Office or other emergency service guidance, this fourth approach is becoming a most popular option. It applies the techniques used in flight simulation and military simulation, to major incidents. Thus, using computers one can model the site and operation and in 3-D format move around the screen. This then enables various eye-points around the site, achieved by moving the mouse. Some advanced systems enable 'computer generated entities' to be included into the data-set. For example, a collision can be simulated outside the production plant or the rate of noxious substance release modelled and calculated across the local community.

  There are costs and benefits associated with each of the four approaches. The need is for developing exercise budgets which enable all four to be used in proportion and to compliment each other.

  Training and exercising are both necessary to ensure that human resources understand the policy and plan, as well as to ensuring that problems can be identified and competent responses developed.

  It can be noted that the guidance to the *COMAH Regulations (SI 1999 No 743)* do not distinguish between 'training' or 'exercising'. It identifies drills, which test a specific aspect of the Emergency Plan (e.g. fire drills), seminar exercises, walk through exercises, which involves visiting the site, table-top exercises, control post exercises, which assess the physical and geographical posting of the personnel and emergency services during a major incident and live exercises.

*COMAH sites*

D6043    *COMAH* sites, in addition to the above, also need to ensure that On-Site and Off-Site Emergency Plans are compliant with guidance and are realistic and achievable.

*(1)    On-Site Emergency Plan*

- A 'Site Main Controller' needs to be appointed. This is a strategic level person, who oversees the Major Incident (refer above to organisation chart under Policy). This person must:

  — oversee and take control over the event;

  — control the activities of site incident controller, that is operational and tactical level co-ordinators;

  — must contact and confirm that the emergency services have been contacted;

  — must confirm that on-site plan has been initiated;

  — mobilise key personnel, identified in the policy and pre-planning;

  — continuously review and assess the major incident;

  — authorise the evacuation process;

  — authorise closing down of plant and work equipment;

  — ensure casualties are being cared for and notify their relatives, as well as listing missing persons;

— monitor weather conditions;

— liaise with the HSE, local authority or the Environment Agency;

— account for all personnel and contractors;

— traffic management, site access/egress etc. must be strategically controlled;

— record keeping of all decisions made, for later assessment and inquiry;

— provide for welfare facilities (food, clothing etc.) of personnel;

— liaise with the media;

— compliance with the law – non-removing of evidence etc;

— control of affected areas after the major incident.

• On-Site Emergency Control Centre (ECC)

— This is a room or area near the major incident site, where the command and control decisions will be made.

— The ECC will also co-ordinate liaison with the media and the public.

— The ECC should contain: telecommunication equipment, cellular communication equipment, detailed site plans and maps, technical drawings of the operation and its shut-off points, list of critical/hazardous substances and waste on site, location of all safety equipment, location of fire safety equipment and access/egress points etc.

• The On-Site Emergency Plan must contain at least the following (*Sch 5, Part II* of *COMAH (SI 1999 No 743)*):

— name/position of person that can activate the Emergency Plan and that person (unless being the same person) who will co-ordinate/manage and mitigate the impact of the major incident;

— name/position of the person who will liaise with the local authority regarding the Off-Site Emergency Plan;

— description of the foreseeable factors that can increase (or mitigate) the severity and consequence of the event, thereby either classifying it as a Major Accident or worse;

— Arrangements for mitigating risks to persons on-site. Warning systems and rules that such persons must follow need to be listed;

— Arrangements for warning the local authority, so that they can activate the off-site emergency plan, as well as ensuring the local authority receives any other relevant information;

— Arrangements for training staff and effective liaison by them with the emergency services;

— Arrangements for providing assistance with 'off-site mitigatory action' such as special equipment that off-site personnel can use, media liaison etc.

(2)    Off-site emergency plan

- *Schedule 5, Part III* of *COMAH (SI 1999 No 743)* says that this Plan must contain at least:

    — name/position of person that can activate the Emergency Plan and the person (unless the same person), who will co-ordinate the off-site actions. This should be senior, strategic level management that will co-ordinate links with the local authority and the public;

    — Arrangements for receiving 'early warning of incident'. This can be via on-site team, technology etc. In addition, there must be Arrangements for alerting others of the event and procedures for call-out of the emergency services, specialist assistance, other search and rescue bodies;

    — Arrangements for co-ordinating resources so that the Off-Site Emergency Plan can be effectively implemented. This should identify those organisations that can assist in the Off-Site Emergency, how each of these organisations will be alerted, how personnel of the organisation affected will recognise and identify the emergency services and specialist services and vice-versa, channels of communication between personnel and those other emergency services, specialist organisations, meeting place, off-site needs to be identified, for direct communication between personnel and others, access to the operation to use equipment;

    — Arrangements for providing on-site assistance, such as from the fire brigade;

    — Arrangements for off-site occurrences and the mitigatory actions needed to protect the public and the environment;

    — Arrangements for providing information to the public and the appropriate behaviour expected from them. In addition, details of how the media could be utilised to disseminate information to the community and emergency organisations;

    — Arrangements for the provision of information to member states, when there is a 'reasonable likelihood' of impact on such neighbouring states.

- Off-Site Emergency Control Centre (ECC)

    — This parallels the on-site ECC and is at a safe distance from the site. It is a command and control centre for all off-site liaison.

    — It must also link up with the on-site ECC to ensure that plans are in unison.

Thus, under *COMAH*, the On-Site and Off-Site Emergency Plans are required to reflect, account for and provide details of the Arrangements and Command and Control variables identified in stage 2 of the DEMS process. The difference is that under Emergency Plans, these variables are specific and must be practical, whilst in the Disaster and Emergency Policy of DEMS, these variables will also include wider issues not necessarily a legal requirement under COMAH but significant to Major Incident management. However, not all sites (majority of sites) are *COMAH* regulated.

## Stage 2: during the event

D6044    *(1)    Activate Disaster and Emergency Policy and pre-planning*

Major Incident response and management ought to be clear and effective if one has followed the previous stages in the DEMS; accounted for External and Internal factors and uncertainties, developed a Chain of Command as well as Arrangements to cope, Organised the operation to cope with a Major Incident and finally pre-planned if the event actually arises. In the main, activating the Arrangements made is the central action (refer above).

*(2)    Co-ordination*

This is the central action to ensuring efforts are in unison. This includes both liasing with external bodies such as the emergency services, media and internally at strategic, operational and tactical levels (as discussed above). The police will normally have overall command and control, so their guidance must be followed.

*(3)    Code of conduct*

A code of conduct is a set of 'golden rules' that staff and contractors need to follow if the Major Incident arises. This includes:

- following instruction from those with command and control responsibilities;

- using self initiative;

- facilities management (gas, electricity, water) – making safe, when and when not to switch on or off;

- medical assistance – liaison with health service, first aiders, when not to administer and when to;

- rules of evacuation;

- site access and egress;

- site security;

- work and rescue equipment – its safe use and logistics of use;

- record keeping of the major incident (audio-visual, verbal and written);

- resources needed for effective major incident management;

- media and public relations management;

- issues of care and compassion of injured persons.

The code of conduct is a reflection of the Disaster and Emergency Policy and the pre-planning. It should be reinforced verbally and in writing (1 page of A4) and reiterated to the major incident team before and during the major incident. Whilst this seems bureaucratic, it must be noted that if the core team (internal and external) fail to follow best practice and safe-guard themselves, this increases the risk factor of the Major Incident and could even lead to a double tragedy. A five minute or so reiteration is a minor time cost.

*COMAH* sites will have to be aware of these issues also as well as activating the On-Site and Off-Site Emergency Plans.

## Stage 3: after the event

D6045    Major Incident Planning does not cease as soon as the Major incident is physically over. There are continuous issues over time that need to be addressed:

*Immediate term (immediately after the major incident and within a few days)*

D6046    • Statutory investigation

This will involve the HSE, local authority, Environment Agency/SEPA for instance. Under statute, these bodies have powers and a duty to investigate a Major Incident.

— The organisation must fully co-operate with these bodies and afford any assistance they require.

— There must be no removal or tampering with anything at the Major Incident site (or Off-Site in *COMAH* cases). There may be forensic or other data gathering required by these bodies.

— Provision of all documentation and information to these bodies.

• Business Continuity

This has to be planned for even whilst the investigation by authorised inspectors is being carried out.

'Business Continuity' is a planning exercise to ensure facilities are operational and available during and immediately after the major incident thereby enabling the organisation to function commercially and socially. *A forecasting process of recovery, assessment and ensuring the adequacy of resources for the organisation is relevant:*

(a)    *Recovery*

Recovery is a state of regaining or salvaging assets that otherwise would have been permanently lost. In the event of a major incident, recovery phase needs to focus on:

(i)    Human resource recovery

— ensuring personnel are safely evacuated;

— others such as lawful visitors and trespassers are evacuated;

— all persons in general are removed in the quickest and most practicable means.

(ii)    Information resource recovery

— essential documents and software;

— private and confidential documents.

(iii)    Physical resource recovery

— primary electrical and mechanical facilities such as power supply, water and gas services;

— essential work equipment, if possible and moveable.

(iv)    Financial resource recovery

If it is practicable then lastly, the recovery of any valuable assets.

The organisation needs to rate the recovery potential also – how possible is recovery? This could be rated from certain (1) through to not possible (5). This calculation requires different recovery responses; when the major incident strikes, those on the scene need to decide if the rating is 1 or say 5. Accordingly, the response will vary – if 5, then there is little purpose risking life and resources to salvage assets.

*(b)  Assessment*

Upon the immediate recovery, the organisation must ask, how much damage (deterioration, infliction of harm or erosion of value) has been inflicted to the operation by the major incident? Damage Assessment is a three stage activity:

(i)  Identify the type of damage

— human resource damage: physical and/or behavioural;

— informational resource damage: primary, secondary and tertiary documentation;

— physical resource damage: work equipment, property, facilities, environment;

— financial resource damage: cash, art, etc.

(ii)  Identify severity of damage

This can be a qualitative scale which says 'low' or 'high' to the age or a quantitative scale – the damage is rated on some scale e.g. from 0 – 5. The severity needs to be forecasted for human, informational, physical and financial resources.

— Human resources could be scaled from serious injury (1) through to fatality and multiple fatality (5).

— Informational: from minor harm (1) through to destroyed (5).

— Physical: from reparable (1) to unsalvageable (5).

— Financial: from no impact on cash flow (1) to financial ruin (5).

(iii)  Consequence of damage

How much does the damage affect the chance of the operation being resumed immediately or in the next few days? The longer it will take to resume, the worse has been the consequence. Consequence could be rated in quantitative terms also, such as a '1' for 'resume immediate' so the harm has been minimal through to say '5', or 'resumption will take months'. The consequence needs to be examined in each case:

— Human: how long will it take people to get back to work?

— Informational: how long will it take for manual and electronic systems to be operational?

— Physical:how long will it take for necessary facilities to be operational?

—    Financial: how long will it take for cash flow to become positive or to access financial facilities?

Severity x Consequence will give an index of forecasted potential Loss, which can then be assessed as a spreadsheet over time. Loss adjustors use various detailed statistical models based upon such generic principles.

*(c)    Adequacy of resources*

Once the organisation has forecasted the potential for recovery and hypothesised about damage assessment, next it needs to ensure that the organisation will have adequate resources to carry on operating, in light of the resource losses identified by the assessment. Adequacy needs to consider:

(i)    Human resources:

—    adequacy of competent and trained personnel at strategic, operational and tactical levels of the organisation;

—    availability of key advisory support services (lawyer, accountant, etc.);

—    if the Major Incident is classified as a 'Crisis', then there is a chance some of the key personnel are not available. Pre-planning therefore requires liaison with recruitment and selection specialists.

(ii)    Physical resources:

—    telephone, fax, e-mail, cellular connectivity and reliability;

—    furniture and fittings;

—    stationary;

—    work equipment (including computers/type-writers, filing cabinets);

—    working stock;

—    working space;

—    vehicles;

—    safety equipment (personal protective equipment);

—    etc.

(iii)    Informational resources:

—    legal documents (organisation's certificates of incorporation, insurance liability certificates etc.);

—    personnel documents (PAYE, NIC, personnel records);

—    financial documents (availability of bank books);

—    sales/marketing documents, this is at the heart of the operation and there will be a need to develop databases, contact potential customers and re-establish commercial functionality.

(iv)    Financial resources:

—    adequacy of working capital.

Also under the 'immediate term', in addition to the above, one needs to consider:

—    Insurers/ loss adjusters

Assuming that the insurance contract covers direct and consequential damage from a major incident (and not all will), the organisation needs to notify the insurer and ensure all paperwork is completed promptly. Most insurance contracts stipulate a time limit by which the paperwork has to be lodged with the insurer; the Major Incident will divert attention to other issues, so ensuring that a person is appointed to activate this insurance task is vital (this should be the organisation's lawyer).

The insurer in turn will notify their loss adjusters to investigate the basic and underlying causes of the event. Again, full disclosure and co-operation are implied insurance contractual requirements. Although, the organisation must check all documents that the loss adjusters completes, to ensure they are accurate and cover all aspects of the event.

—    The police

In the suspicion that criminal neglect played a role in the event, then the police will need to interview all core board members, senior management and others.

—    Building contractors

The organisation needs to plan for building contractors to visit the site and make it safe and secure. This may have to be done forthwith after the event, even if insurance issues have not been resolved. Therefore, adequacy of resources, as discussed above becomes vital.

—    Visitors

Major incidents also lead to the public and media making visits. The arrangements made to handle such groups must extend to after the event.

—    Counselling support

Counselling support to affected employees and possibly contractors is not just a personnel management requirement which shows 'caring management' but increasingly a legal duty of the organisation to provide such support. Issues of 'post traumatic stress', 'nervous shock' and 'bereavement' means that the organisation has common law obligations to offer medical and psychological support. This should involve a medical practitioner and an occupational nurse. The insurance policy can be extended before the event to cover the cost of such services.

*Short Term (a week onwards after the event)*

D6047    ●    Investigation and inquiry

This can be both a statutory inquiry (although most are called within days) and/or the in-house investigation of the event and lessons to be learnt. Issues to consider include:

—    Basic causes: was it a fire, bomb, an explosion or a natural peril?

—    Underlying causes: what led up to such a peril occurring? Examine the managerial, personnel, legal, technical, organisational and natural factors that could have caused the event.

—    Costs and losses involved.

—    Lessons for the future.

—    Did the Disaster and Emergency Plan operate as expected? Were there any failings? What improvements are required? There needs to be complete de-briefing and examination of the entire process involving internal personnel and external agencies.

The organisation should weigh up the possibility of external persons carrying out this exercise or whether in-house staff are objective and dispassionate enough to assess what went wrong.

●    Visit by enforcers

The organisation also needs to be prepared for further visits from the enforcers and the possibility of statutory enforcement notices being served to either regulate or prohibit the activity. Multiple notices are possible, from health and safety officers, fire authority, Environment Agency/SEPA, building control or planning officers. This will affect the operation, production process and have economic implications. This ought not to occur if the organisation has taken due care to pre-plan for the major incident and had continuous safety monitoring of the operation. Notices will be served if there is a failure to make safe the site.

●    Coping with speculation

The public, the media and employees will speculate about causation and there is the risk of adverse publicity. Public relations is a central activity. For legal and moral reasons, it is best practice to disclose all known facts unless the statutory investigation prohibits otherwise.

*Medium term (a month plus)*

D6048    The 'normalisation process' will begin. The organisation needs to carry on the operation, be prepared for further visits from enforcers, loss adjusters and re-assess its corporate/financial health.

*Long term (six month onwards)*

D6049    ●    Systems review

—    A review of the impact of the major incident and whether the organisation is recovering from it.

—    Impact on reputation .

—    Legal threats.

— Any positive outcomes – learning from mistakes, improving technical know-how, wider industrial benefits from knowing the chain reaction of events etc.

*Longer term (one year onwards)*

D6050    The organisation's memory and experience needs to be included in:

— in-house training programmes;

— factored into systems and procedures;

— review of entire *espirit de corps* and corporate philosophy.

Disaster and emergency planning is an extensive exercise, being dynamic and accounting for a diverse array of phenomena as industrial, man-made, environmental, socio-technical, radiological and natural events.

# Monitor the Disaster & Emergency Plan(s)

D6051    Monitoring is a process assessing and evaluating the value, efficiency and robustness of the Disaster and Emergency Plan(s). This involves looking at all three stages as discussed above (before, during and after the event stages) and not just the core document, 'the plan'. It is comprehensive and holistic in its questioning of the entire planning process.

Monitoring can be classified as proactive or reactive. The former attempts to identify problems with the plan(s) before the advent of a Major Incident. It is a case of continuously comparing the plan(s) with even minor incidents and loop-holes identified in any training/exercising sessions. Reactive monitoring occurs after a Major Incident or occurrences that could have led up-to a Major Incident, thereby reflecting back and assessing if the plan(s) need improvement. Both types are important.

*Figure 5: Monitoring Matrix*

| | Stages in Planning: | 1. Before the Major Incident | 2. During the Major Incident | 3. After the Major Incident |
|---|---|---|---|---|
| Monitoring Types: | | | | |
| A. PROACTIVE | | • Risk Assessments | • Inspections | • Inquiries |
| | | • Testing via Training or Exercises | • Live Interviews | • Systems Review |
| | | • Major Incident Assessment | • Feedback | • Counselling Reports |
| | | • Facilities Inspections | | |
| B. REACTIVE | | • Incident Statistics | • Critical Assessments | • Brainstorming |
| | | • Incident Reports | • Incident Levels | • Loss Assessments |
| | | • Warnings | • Audio-Visual Assessment | • Enforcement |
| | | • Notices | | |

The above cells are not strictly mutually exclusive; many techniques are both proactive and reactive. A third dimension is added in *COMAH* cases, that of, on-site and off-site emergency plans (types of planning).

- Cell A1 (proactive before the Major Incident)

  — Risk Assessments and Hazard Analysis techniques will identify significant hazards and their risk level. Monitoring such risk is an index of danger, which in turn is a variable in the type and potential of the major incident, outlined in Figure 1. The HSE's *Five Steps approach* or their *Quantified Risk Assessment* methodology provides outlines of assessing risk. Hazard techniques include Hazard and Operability Studies, HAZANS, Fault and Event Tree Analysis etc.

  — Testing will identify any problems or concerns with the disaster and emergency plan. For example, a live exercise or a synthetic simulation could identify factors the plan has not considered or which may not be practicable if the major incident was to arise. Thus, enabling questioning, critical appraisal and comments should not be perceived as a threat or being awkward with the plan(s) but can provide vital information.

  — Major Incident Assessment, which is a periodical overview of the plan(s), every quarter or semi-annual by both internal and external persons. This could identify areas of concern. This Assessment compares the plan(s) with the potential threat – can the former cope with the threat? Threats change as technology and know-how changes, so such Assessments become another vital source of information.

  — Facilities inspections of gas, electricity, water, building structure, equipment available/not available etc. can highlight issues of physical resourcing and adequacy of such resourcing.

- Cell B1 (reactive after the Major incident)

  — Incident statistics will show the type of incidences, the type of injury, when and where it occurred. This enables the organisation to hypothesise/build a picture of the potential and severity of a bigger incident. One cannot divorce occupational health and safety data from 'disaster and emergency management'.

  — Analysing incident reports should enable issues of causation to be assessed. What type of occurrence could trigger a major incident? Identifying and developing a pattern of causes will enable one to assess if the plan(s) account for such causes.

  — Warnings from employees, contractors, enforcers, public and others of possible and serious problems are to be treated with seriousness. All such warnings are to be analysed and a common pattern and trend spotted.

  — Any notices served by enforcers will identify failings in the operation and the remedial actions required. These can be factored into the plan(s).

- Cell A2 (proactive during the Major Incident)

  — Inspections will be made even as the event occurs. Inspections can range from the stability of the structure through to how personnel behaved and coped. As these inspections are made, the command and control team needs to evaluate if any aspect of the plan(s), which is a 'live document' need immediate changes.

— Live Interviews with internal personnel and emergency services' personnel will enable a continuous appraisal of any difficulty with procedures, arrangements and instructions that emanate from the plan(s). Again, these can lead to immediate changes to the plan(s).

— Feedback is a proactive technique of requesting regular, interval information on and off-site. This enables a picture to be constructed of what could happen next; trying to anticipate the next sequence and if the plan(s) can cope with it.

- Cell B2 (reactive during the Major Incident)

— Critical Assessments are carried out after some unexpected occurrence, which causes uncertainty and may even threaten the efficacy of the plan(s). The Critical Assessment is by the command and control team as a whole. Why did this happen? Why did we not account for it in the plan(s)?

— Incident levels – in particular if serious injury or fatalities are increasing, then at a moral or philosophical level one needs to ask if the plan(s) have been overwhelmed by reality. All forms of planning, including the statutory *COMAH* planning must not be viewed with rigidity. If the plan(s) are failing, it is better to re-appraise and re-plan. *COMAH (SI 1999 No 743)* does not overtly allow for this, although it stresses flexibility and continuous appraisal of the event. In such a case, there has to be quick and clear decision-making, with consequential command and control, as well as immediate communication of this 'alternative plan'. Training and exercising sessions need to factor in this dimension and equip people with decisional techniques.

— Audio-visual assessments can be a dramatic means of understanding the actual event. This can be video or photographic footage shot by the incident personnel or from the emergency services. This enables monitoring of the extent, potential and actual threat from the Major Incident.

- A3 (proactive after the Major Incident)

— Inquiries are proactive, even though the event has happened, the inquiry (whether internal or external) will identify strengths and weaknesses in the plan(s), which can lead to future improvements in planning.

— Systems review, is an overhaul of the entire reaction and holistic experience of the organisation to the trauma of a major incident. This involves developing future coping strategies for personnel and issues of how well did the organisation respond? Were there adequate resources in place to cope?

— Counselling reports will identify the experiences, perceptual and cognitive issues that affected personnel and others. This can provide probably the most significant information on behavioural response of the command and control team and those that were injured. Which in turn can be factored into training and exercise programmes, which itself will lead to personnel skill improvements.

- Cell B3 (reactive after the Major Incident)

— Brainstorming is an open-ended, participative and indeed critical analysis of what went wrong and what was right with the plan(s).

Brainstorming should also be inclusive, involving emergency services and possibly enforcers as well, so that their guidance is factored in.

— The loss adjusters report will be a vital document as to the chain reaction that lead to the event and the consequences that followed. For legal reasons, their findings may have to be applied before insurance cover is available.

— Enforcement notices and enforcers reports will contain recommendations, which need to be viewed as lessons for the future.

## Audit & Review

D6052
The final stage of the DEMS process is Audit and Review. An audit is a comprehensive and holistic examination of the entire DEMS process (Figure 2). An Audit will identify stages in this process that need improvement. A Review is an act of 'zooming in' into that particular stage and carrying out those improvements.

### Major Incident Auditing

D6053
(1) Major Incident Auditing can be qualitative or quantitative. The former adopts a 'yes' or 'no' response format to questions. The latter asks the auditor to rate the issue being examined from say 0 – 5.

(2) The Audit must be comprehensive, assessing every aspect of the DEMS process. This means that the Audit will take time to be completed. The Audit is not some 'inspection' which is more random focusing upon a hazard rather than the complete system.

(3) Audits essentially benchmark (compare and contrast) performance. This can be against the DEMS process identified above or against legislation (e.g. *COMAH (SI 1999 No 743)*). The benchmarking could also be against another site or wider industry standards.

(4) Should Audits be carried out in-house or rely on external consultants? There are costs and benefits associated with both, with no definitive answer. The *Management of Health and Safety at Work Regulations 1999 (SI 1999 No 3242)* in the UK, emphasises the need to develop and use in-house expertise in relation to general OSH issues, with a reliance on external specialists as a last resort. This may be interpreted as best practice for DEM.

(5) Audits can be annual or semi-annual. The more complex the operation and risk it poses, the greater the need for semi-annual audits.

(6) Audits should be proactive, that is learning from the weaknesses in the DEMS process and reducing or eliminating such weaknesses for the future.

(7) Finally, the results of the Audit need to be fed-back into the DEMS process and all affected persons informed of any changes and risk management issues arising.

(8) Audits are holistic (assess anything associated with major incidents), systemic (assess the entire DEMS process, i.e. the 'system') and systematic (that is logical and sequential in analysis).

### Review

D6054
(1) The Review of any specific problems needs to be actioned by the organisation. The consultant will identify the areas of concern and make recommendations

but the final discussion and implementation lies with the organisation. This needs to be led by senior officials in the organisation.

(2)   Reviews are by definition 'diagnostic', meaning the organisation needs to look at causation and cure of the failure in any part of the DEMS process.

(3)   Budgeting both in time and resource terms is critical in the Review, as it will require management and external agency involvement.

(4)   A Review can be carried out at the same time as an audit. A Review can also be a legal requirement, as with *Reg 11* of *COMAH (SI 1999 No 743)*, which requires a Review and where necessary a revision of the On-Site and Off-Site Emergency Plans for Top-Tier establishments.

# Case Studies

D6055    A summary of four Major Incidents follows (off-shore, rail underground, air aviation and land based chemical plant).

## Piper Alpha

D6032
- Offshore disaster in 1988. 167 workers died in North Sea.

- Major explosion and fire on offshore platform. Piper Alpha involved four rigs linked together. Gas, crude oil and compressed gases were drilled.

- Piper Alpha involved various levels of work along the platform – mining at a certain level, accommodation above that and the helicopter pad at the very top.

- At 22.00 hours whilst 62 worked night shifts and 226 were on the platform, an explosion occurred then a fireball swept the platform. Thereafter a number of small explosions occurred.

- The water systems and emergency systems failed to respond.

- Three may day calls were sent out and personnel assembled at deck d.

- The radio and lighting systems then failed.

- At 22.20 there was a rupture of the gas riser on another rig connected to Piper Alpha.

- This was followed by explosions and ignition of gas and crude.

- At 22.50 another explosion occurred followed by the structure collapsing.

- The formal inquiry found both technical and organisational failings. The maintenance error that led to the leak was due to lack of training and poor maintenance procedures.

- There was a breakdown in the communication systems and the permit to work system at shift changeover.

- There were inefficient safety procedures.

- Human error therefore existed at various levels.

## Moorgate

D6057
- Underground rail accident in 1974.

- A passenger train carrying 300, overshot the platform at a speed to be around 30 – 40 mph.

- The warning light was knocked down on the track and hit hydraulic buffers.

- The lead car and hit the tunnel roof with the second carriage hitting this.

- 42 people were killed plus the driver and 74 injured.

- Driver was inexperienced and guard had little training.

- Brakes had to be checked visually.

- Driver should have slowed train down via manual controls.

- Safety systems were criticised – poor use of modern technology to slow down the train and the design and layout of impact equipment.

### Kegworth

D6058
- A Boeing 737 had taken off to Belfast. A known fault to the right hand engine had been logged and corrected.

- The air conditioning on a 737 is driven from the right hand engine in most cases.

- During flight, the pilot spotted vibrations, excess of smoke and fumes; he throttles the right engine back. The left engine throttles back automatically at the same time.

- It is said that there was a warning light showing fire in the right engine.

- The pilot seeks to land at the East Midlands Airport near Derby.

- The signal was incorrect and really the problem was with the left engine. The correct functioning had been turned off. Thus, there was one faulty engine and one switched off. The plane could have landed with one engine.

- He landed on the M1 near Kegworth village.

- Kegworth demonstrates importance of cognitive factors and ergonomic design.

### Flixborough

D6059
- Chemical plant destroyed.

- A part (reaction vessel) is removed and in its place a bent pipe is inserted. The pipe is of inferior material and no problem assessment was carried out to assess the impact the pipe would have.

- The process was restarted and the pipe ruptured, releasing flammable vapour clouds that in turn ignited.

- Explosion resulted and other pipes were ruptured. Fires resulted in the complex.

- Poor maintenance and monitoring were prime factors in disaster.

## Conclusion

D6060
All organisations and societies need to prepare for worst case scenarios. DEMS provide a logical framework to understand the main stages in effective preparation.

The larger the organisation, the more detailed and analytical the preparation needs to be. Finally, DEMS is a live and open system requiring continuous monitoring.

## Sources of information

D6061    These include:

1.    Legislation

- *COMAH* sites and indeed non-*COMAH* sites will find it useful as regards to *COMAH (SI 1999 No 743)* as a legal or managerial benchmark.

2.    Guidance notes

- *Emergency Planning for Major Accidents: Control of Major Accident Hazards Regulations 1999* , HSG 191 is joint Guidance from the HSE, Environment Agency and the Scottish equivalent , SEPA. This interprets *COMAH* in a user-friendly manner and recommends implementation approaches.

- *Dealing with Disaster* by the Home Office (Third Edition) is a broad but useful outline of the managerial issues involved in planning. It is aimed at the Police, Fire Service and voluntary bodies.

- *Planning for Major Incidents: The NHS Guidance*, published by the Department of Health, NHS Executive (1998 Edition) is similar in approach to the Home Office Guidance. This is also available at http://www.open.gov.uk/doh/epcu/epcu/index.htm

- There are many other useful guidance documents that can be searched for at the following web sites:

    — http://www.open.gov.uk/hse

    This will enable one to search for specific guidance, case studies and documents.

    — epc.ho@gtnet.gov.uk

    The Home Office Emergency Planning College can be contacted at this web site where further assistance can be obtained.

    — http://www.environment-agency.gov.uk

    The Environment Agency will have details of specific natural environment or flood related guidance;

3.    The European Commission

    DG XI is the department responsible for environment, nuclear safety and civil protection. It can be accessed via the EC web site http://www.europa.eu.int

4.    International Agencies

    The United Nations web site is http://www.un.org and then search for 'humanitarian affairs'.

5.    Professional bodies such as the:

- International Institute of Risk & Safety Management, telephone 020 8741 0835.

- Institution of Occupational Safety & Health, telephone 0116 257 3100.

- Business Continuity Institute, telephone 0161 237 1007.

- Fire Protection Association, telephone 020 7902 5306.

- Loss Prevention Council, telephone 020 8207 2345.

- Society of Industrial and Emergency Safety Officers, telephone 01642 816281.

# Electricity

## Introduction

E3001 When used properly electricity is a safe, convenient and efficient source of energy for heat, light and power. However, between 1990 and 1995, 533 people were killed in electrical incidents in Great Britain. In 1995 alone there were 121 serious electrical fires costing more than £45 million in insurance claims. These are just two facts that can be gleaned from '*Electrical Incidents in Great Britain Statistical Summary*', published by the Health and Safety Executive (HSE) and available from HSE Books, PO Box 1999, Sudbury CO10 6FS. The publication also gives information on a wide range of electrical incidents, including examples of some of the most commonly recurring in a variety of locations, such as offices, farms, construction sites and the home. By recording the statistics and nature of the incidents occurring, the HSE aims to promote a greater awareness and understanding of the causes of electrical accidents so that those responsible for electrical safety are more fully aware of the risks involved and consequently, accidents and deaths can hopefully be prevented.

Further, another particular issue usually resulting in a serious injury or fatality is the inadvertent contact with overhead electric power lines. It is estimated that one-third of such contacts are fatal. The HSE has published guidance aimed at those working near overhead lines. The guidance contains separate sections dealing with agriculture and horticulture, arboriculture and forestry, construction, railways and other transport systems with overhead conductors and how the risks arise. See '*Guidance Note GS6*', revised in 1997, available from HSE Books.

Given that electrical accidents occurring at work often result in severe injuries or damage, high standards in relation to electrical installations and the use of electrical plant and apparatus are essential and adequate systems of control and maintenance are required. Further, there is a need for employers to ensure that those who work on or use such installations, plant and apparatus are sufficiently competent and that the workers are suitably trained, instructed and supervised.

## Electrical hazards

E3002 Electrical hazards may arise from bad design, construction or installation of relevant equipment, as a result of inadequate standards of protection or maintenance, or from inappropriate usage of the equipment or, indeed, its misuse. Such hazards can lead to electric shock or electric burns to the individual concerned, or can result in damaged equipment, an explosion or even a general fire.

An electric shock is the result of an electric current flowing through a part of the body. It can affect the nervous system and bodily organs and functions. The value of the current and the time it flows through the body are the two critical factors that determine the effect on the body. The heart is particularly susceptible to a condition known as ventricular fibrillation from currents as low as 50 milliamps flowing for a few seconds. No accidental current should be allowed to pass through the body but the risk of any effects, should it occur, should be kept to a minimum by ensuring that the current passing will be as small as possible and that it will pass for as short a time as possible.

One effect of a shock may be a rapid movement away from the source, which might lead to a further incident such as a severe knock or a fall. When an individual is working above ground level, a fall could be fatal. Additionally, extensive and deep burns, at both the point of entry and at the point of exit, can result from a current passing through the body.

To assist in ensuring that people respond safely and appropriately to an incident involving (or potentially involving) electricity, the HSE has issued a poster which should be displayed in relevant work environments. The poster 'Electricity Shock: First Aid Procedures' takes into account advice from the European Resuscitation Council and provides basic advice on how to break the contact between an electrical source and a casualty and how to implement resuscitation. Employers should ensure that such posters are placed in the appropriate work environment.

## Preventative action

E3003    Preventive action against shock and burns includes the following:

(*a*)    inspection of all electrical equipment, particularly portable hand-held tools;

(*b*)    checking suitable equipment is installed for circuit protection;

(*c*)    testing of equipment installed for circuit protection;

(*d*)    regular inspection of equipment to minimise the risks of shocks to personnel;

(*e*)    avoidance of work near live conductors;

(*f*)    the use of proper systems and methods of working;

(*g*)    ensuring that those using the equipment or involved with it are competent so to do.

Precautions against electrical dangers must be taken in the light of legal requirements, relevant standards and codes of practice. The HSE has published guidance relating to ensuring safe working practices when working with or near to electricity entitled '*Electricity at Work: Safe Working Practices*', ISBN 0 71760442X. In the event that the working environment exposes people to electrical dangers, the guidance should be considered and where appropriate, its recommendations implemented.

One additional point relating to prevention is ensuring the good design and construction of electrical equipment. In some instances, this may be assumed if the equipment complies with recognised standards and is marked in accordance with legal requirements. Further, it is important to note that good installation, protection and maintenance require competent staff or contractors to be employed and the correct operation and use of equipment will also depend on competence, achieved through adequate training, instruction and supervision.

## Legal requirements

E3004    Although electricity is not specifically mentioned in every case, the legal requirements relating to the safe working with electricity, the safety of electrical installations and the use of electricity are covered in the following:

(*a*)    the *Health and Safety at Work Act etc. 1974*;

(*b*)    the *Management of Health and Safety at Work Regulations 1999 (SI 1999 No 3242)*;

(*c*)    the *Construction (Design and Management) Regulations 1994 (SI 1994 No 3140)*;

(*d*)    the *Electricity at Work Regulations 1989 (SI 1989 No 635)*;

(*e*)    the *Provision and Use of Work Equipment Regulations 1998 (SI 1998 No 2306)*;

(*f*)    the *Electrical Equipment for Explosive Atmospheres (Certification) Regulations 1990 (SI 1990 No 13)*.

Each of the requirements impacts on how work with and near to electricity should be undertaken. Additionally, it is important to recall that the common law is also relevant when considering both the duties owed and the legal implications and consequences arising from an incident (see E11001). Where an incident occurs, an employer may well find itself on the wrong side of the law both in terms of a criminal offence and also a civil claim for damages or loss.

## General duties under the Health and Safety at Work etc. Act 1974

E3005    The *Health and Safety at Work etc Act 1974 (HSWA 1974)* provides a comprehensive legal framework for occupational health and safety. Although the Act does not expressly refer to electricity, many of its general requirements, for example, safe methods of working, training and supervision, are relevant to electricity and its use. The general obligations arising under the 1974 Act are discussed at E11017.

## The Management of Health and Safety at Work Regulations 1999

E3006    As with the *HSWA 1974*, the *Management of Health and Safety at Work Regulations 1999 (SI 1999 No 3242)* do not specifically refer to electricity. The assessment of risks required by these Regulations, however, certainly extends to working with electricity and importantly, the principle of prevention identified in the Regulations is also worth bearing in mind. The general requirements are echoed in the *Electricity at Work Regulations 1989 (SI 1989 No 635)*.

## The Construction (Design and Management) Regulations 1994 (as amended by the Construction (Design and Management) (Amendment) Regulations 2000

E3007    Although not expressly mentioned, the use of electricity and the installation of electrical equipment certainly come within the responsibilities of such persons as the designer, the client and the main contractor. The HSE specifies electricity in its guidance, '*Health and safety for small construction sites*', HS(G)130, and '*Health and Safety in Construction*', HS(G)150 and the guidance set out in these publications should be considered when construction works are being planned. Depending on the nature of the project there will be other issues to consider such as dangers from underground services, arc welding (see HSE publications '*Avoiding danger from underground services*', ISBN 0 7176 1744 0 and '*Electrical Safety in arc welding*', ISBN 0 7176 0704 6), and/or working with overhead cables (see *Guidance Note GS6*).

## The Electricity at Work Regulations 1989

E3008    The *Electricity at Work Regulations 1989 (SI 1989 No 635)* are aimed at the users rather than the suppliers or manufacturers of electrical equipment. The Regulations apply to all places of work, including factories, shops, offices, laboratories and educational establishments. In accordance with the *HSWA 1974*, they lay down the principles of electrical safety in general terms and also raise particular issues to be addressed. Further, it is necessary to bear these principles in mind prior to and during any work with electricity. Details of the design, selection, erection, inspection and testing of electrical installations have been published by the Institution of Electrical Engineers in '*IEE Wiring Regulations*' (currently 16th edition). This can be ordered from Publications Sales, IEE, PO Box 96, Stevenage, Hertfordshire SG1 2SD (tel: 01483 767 328).

The Regulations refer to the duties to prevent danger or injury i.e. the prevention of danger amounts to the avoidance of risk of injury. The Regulations also provide for different levels of duty, ranging from reasonably practicable to an absolute duty. In the case of an alleged breach of an absolute duty, it is a defence that reasonable measures have been taken and all due diligence observed. Importantly, the HSE has issued a '*Memorandum of Guidance on the Electricity at Work Regulations 1989*', ISBN 0 7176 1602 9). The Memorandum includes reference to the poster (referred to at E3002) and recommends that the poster is displayed in areas where workers are at a greater than average risk of electric shock, including supply industries, electricity generation, transmission and utilisation and also companies carrying out electrical testing.

### Safe system of work – general obligations

E3009    There is an overriding need to provide and maintain a proper safe system of work in connection with work on electrical systems, irrespective of whether they are alive or have been made dead. [*Electricity at Work Regulations 1989 (SI 1989 No 635), Regs 4, 13, 14*].

The HSE's leaflet, '*Electrical Safety and You*', IND(G)23(L), is especially aimed at small firms and is helpful in describing the main hazards, gives simple guidance on risk assessment and outlines the basic measures common to all industries required to assist in controlling the risks associated with using electricity at work. It also directs readers to more specific guidance produced by the HSE and other organisations.

In terms of one of the associated obligations, employers should use safety signs where there is a significant risk to health and safety that has not been avoided or controlled. This frequently involves the use of the 'Danger electricity' warning sign. These requirements are specified in the *Health and Safety (Safety Signs and Signals) Regulations (SI 1996 No 341)*.

### Design, construction and maintenance of electrical systems – general requirement

E3010    All systems must be constructed and maintained so as to prevent danger, so far as is reasonably practicable. Construction includes design of the system, selection of equipment used in it and installation.

Although the Regulations are user-orientated and do not impose duties on manufacturers and designers of electrical equipment, the *Provision and Use of Work Equipment Regulations 1998 (SI 1998 No 2306)* provide that every employer must ensure that work equipment is so constructed or adapted as to be suitable for the purpose for which it is used or provided. This means that the equipment supplied must be suitable for the work to be undertaken and that therefore any electrical use associated with the equipment must also be suitable for the purpose for which the equipment is supplied. Generally any system complying with the current *IEE Wiring Regulations* will go a long way to satisfying the *Electricity at Work Regulations 1989 (SI 1989 No 635)*.

## Portable electrical equipment

E3011    Since many accidents occur when portable tools are being used, the HSE has emphasised three stages of inspection and testing.

The first stage is a frequent visual inspection by the user which includes checking that the cable sheath is not damaged; the plug is not damaged; that there are no inadequate joints in the cable; that the sheath of the cable is securely attached to the plug and equipment on entry to both; that the equipment has not been used for work for which it is not suited, causing it, for example, to become wet or contaminated; that there is no damage to the external casing of the equipment and that there is no evidence of overheating or burns.

The second stage involves a more formal regular visual inspection by a competent person and might include the checking of connections within the plug and equipment; that the correct fuse is being used in the plug, and that there is no indication of any overheating or burning.

The third stage comprises a regular inspection and testing of the equipment by a competent person.

There are two levels of competency: (i) where the person is not skilled in electrical work and uses a simple pass/fail type of portable appliance tester (PAT); and (ii) where more sophisticated electrical skills are used and the readings on the instruments used need interpretation. (See HSE publication '*Maintaining portable and transportable electrical equipment*', HS(G) 107 (1994).)

## Strength and capability of electrical equipment

E3012    No electrical equipment should be used where the strength and capability of the particular piece of equipment may be exceeded in such a way as may give rise to danger. [*Electricity at Work Regulations 1989 (SI 1989 No 635), Reg 5*]. This is an absolute requirement and therefore must be complied with, irrespective of whether risk or injury is foreseeable. *Regulation 29* of the 1989 Regulations provides a defence if it can be shown that reasonable steps were taken and all due diligence was observed to avoid a breach. Before electrical equipment is put into use, it must therefore be properly selected and adequately rated for the work to be carried out.

In terms of more general duties, the *Electrical Equipment (Safety) Regulations (SI 1994 No 3260)* relate to laws concerning electrical equipment designed for use within certain voltage limits. The purpose behind the standard requirements (which arise from an EC Directive) is essentially directed to consumer protection. The Regulations require that electrical equipment is safe and that it is constructed in accordance with good engineering practice with the affixing of CE marking to electrical equipment and a written declaration of conformity being provided. Under the Regulations, the HSE may make arrangements for the enforcement of these Regulations in relation to equipment for use in the workplace under the *HSWA 1974*. It is a defence to proceedings brought under these Regulations to show that their requirements were satisfied in relation to the matter at hand.

## Siting of equipment in adverse or hazardous environments

E3013    The *Electricity at Work Regulations 1989 (SI 1989 No 635), Reg 6* provide that where it is reasonably foreseeable that electrical equipment is going to be exposed to:

(*a*)    mechanical damage;

(*b*)    the effects of weather, natural hazards, temperature or pressure;

(c)    the effects of wet, dirty, dusty or corrosive conditions; or

(d)    any flammable or explosive substances, including dusts, vapours and gases,

the equipment must be so constructed or protected so as to prevent, so far as reasonably practicable, danger from exposure of the equipment to the compromising situation.

This is aimed at conditions both indoors and outdoors, and includes the weather-proofing of switchboards housing electrical equipment.

### Insulation, protection and placement of conductors

E3014    The *Electricity at Work Regulations 1989 (SI 1989 No 635), Reg 7* provide that all conductors in a system giving rise to danger must either:

(a)    be suitably covered with insulating material and protected, so far as is reasonably practicable to prevent danger; or

(b)    have such precautions taken as will prevent danger, including being suitably placed.

The purpose of this requirement is to prevent danger from conductors in a system that can give rise to danger, such as an electric shock, by resorting to permanently safeguarding the live conductors. Where it is not possible to insulate fully, such as an electric overhead travelling crane, this requirement can be satisfied by live conductors being out of reach and therefore in a safe position. If the conductors intermittently come within reach, perhaps when a ladder is used, then a safe system of work should be used to limit or control such access e.g. a permit to work system may be of value in such situations.

### Earthing or other suitable precautions

E3015    Precautions must be taken, either by earthing or other suitable means, to prevent danger arising when it is reasonably foreseeable that any conductor (other than a circuit conductor) which may become charged, does become charged. This might occur when a system is misused or there is a fault in the system. The *Electricity at Work Regulations 1989 (SI 1989 No 635), Reg 29* provides a defence if it can be shown that reasonable steps have been taken and all due diligence observed to avoid a breach.

The usual precautionary measures include earthing any conductive parts that can be touched, i.e. the connection of such parts to the earth. This will include metal-cased equipment that can be touched. One way of earthing such equipment, along with pipes for water, gas or oil, is to connect all the equipment together. Such cross-bonding or equipotential bonding avoids the risk of dangerous voltages running through different exposed metal items. To be effective, the bonding conductors must be capable of carrying any fault current for the time it flows and the time will be dependent on the fuse or other protective system used. Another way of reducing the risks of danger when using electrical equipment is to use a residual current device (RCD) designed to operate rapidly if a small leakage current flows.

Reducing voltage will reduce the risk from a shock. 110-volt centre-tapped transformers are frequently used to do this on construction sites. Reduced voltage is particularly appropriate when working inside metal containers, such as boilers, with portable tools.

Removing the path to earth and working in an earth-free area, is another suitable precautionary measure. This approach means that even if the electricity source is earth-referenced, there can be no current path back to earth from the earth-free area and therefore no shock through an individual by a current to earth. This type of system is often used for testing electrical equipment.

### Integrity of referenced connectors

E3016   If a circuit conductor is connected to earth or to any other reference point, nothing which might reasonably be expected to give rise to danger, by breaking the electrical continuity or introducing high impedance, must be placed in that conductor unless suitable precautions are taken to prevent that danger. [*Electricity at Work Regulations 1989 (SI 1989 No 635), Regs 9 and 10*].

This requirement is especially important in the case of three-phase supplies, where the neutral conductor is connected to earth at source in the distribution system, so that phase voltages are not adversely affected by unbalanced loading. This does not mean that certain electrical devices, like joints or bolted links, cannot be connected in referential circuit conductors as long as suitable precautions have been taken to ensure that no danger is caused from their use or from their installation or removal. Fuses, thyristors, transistors and the like must not be installed in this way as they could give rise to danger if they become open circuit.

Every joint or connection in a system must be both mechanically and electrically suitable for use. [*Electricity at Work Regulations 1989 (SI 1989 No 635), Reg 10*]. This requirement includes the connections to plugs, sockets and other means of joining or connecting conductors, whether these connections are permanent or temporary. *Regulation 29* of the 1989 Regulations provides a defence if it can be shown that reasonable steps have been taken and all due diligence observed to avoid a breach.

### Excess current protection

E3017   There is also a requirement that efficient measures must be provided for protecting every part of a system from excess of current as may be necessary to prevent danger. [*Electricity at Work Regulations 1989 (SI 1989 No 635), Reg 11*]. This duty is absolute, but the defence of *Reg 29* is available. The provision recognises that faults may occur in electrical systems and requires that protective devices, such as fuses or circuit breakers, are installed to ensure that all parts of an electrical system are safeguarded from the consequences of fault conditions.

The main fault conditions are (i) overloads, (ii) short circuits, and (iii) earth faults. In all cases the protective device aims to detect the abnormal current flowing and then to interrupt the fault current before the danger causes damage or injury. The '*IEE Wiring Regulations*' give detailed guidance on selection and rating of protective devices.

### Cutting off supply and isolation of electrical equipment

E3018   Suitable means must exist for cutting off the electrical supply to any electrical equipment and for the isolation of any electrical equipment. [*Electricity at Work Regulations 1989 (SI 1989 No 635), Reg 12*]. This will include means of identifying circuits.

Isolation means the disconnection and separation of the electrical equipment from every source of electrical energy in such a way that this disconnection is secure.

*Precautions for work on equipment made dead*

E3019   Adequate precautions must be taken in respect of electrical equipment which has been made dead in order to ensure that, while work is being carried out on or near that equipment, there is no danger of the equipment becoming electrically charged during the work.

Several accidents occur each year because of work on a de-energised system which inadvertently is still live or becomes live whilst the work is being carried out. A safe system of work must therefore be used. This can include the following:

(a)   isolation from all points of supply;

(b)   securing each point of isolation, for example by locking off;

(c)   earthing the equipment that is being worked upon;

(d)   testing and thereby verifying that the equipment is dead before working on it;

(e)   creating a safe working zone only accessible to authorised persons;

(f)   safeguarding from other live conductors in proximity, for example by screening; and

(g)   issuing a permit to work.

*Work on or near live conductors*

E3020   The *Electricity at Work Regulations 1989 (SI 1989 No 635), Reg 14* provide that no person must carry out work on or so near to any live conductor (other than one suitably covered with insulating material to prevent danger) that danger may arise, unless:

(a)   it is unreasonable for it to be dead; and

(b)   it is reasonable for him to be at work on or near it, while it is live; and

(c)   suitable precautions, including provision of suitable protective equipment, are taken to prevent injury.

There are limited circumstances where live working is permitted, such as where it is not practicable to carry out work with the equipment dead, for example during testing; or where making the equipment dead might endanger other users of the equipment. This requirement imposes an absolute duty not to work on live electrical equipment unless the circumstances justify it. Such circumstances will need to be well documented together with the measures and precautions to be taken to prevent injury during the work. A written company policy specifying the criteria for live working and the precautions to be taken should be maintained.

*Precautions*

E3021   Live work should only be done by competent employees (see E3023 below) who are in possession of adequate information about the nature of the work and the system. Appropriate insulated tools, equipment and protective clothing, e.g. rubber gloves or rubber mats, should be used as well as screens. Such work should be done with another competent person present if this would minimise the risk of injury. In addition, access to the work area should be restricted and earth-free work areas established.

*Working space, access and lighting*

E3022    To prevent injury, adequate working space, adequate means of access and adequate lighting must be provided at all electrical equipment on which or near which work is being done in circumstances that might give rise to danger. [*Electricity at Work Regulations 1989 (SI 1989 No 635), Reg 15*]. (For access and lighting provisions, see ACCESS, TRAFFIC ROUTES AND VEHICLES and LIGHTING respectively.)

*Competent person*

E3023    No person shall be engaged in any work activity where technical knowledge or experience is necessary to prevent danger or injury, unless he possesses such knowledge or experience, or is under such degree of supervision, as may be appropriate having regard to the nature of the work.

Any supervision on electrical work, particularly live electrical work, must be by a suitably competent person.

## The Provision and Use of Work Equipment Regulations 1998

E3024    Electricity is not specifically mentioned in the *Provision and Use of Work Equipment Regulations (SI 1998 No 2306)*, but *Reg 4* provides that 'work equipment shall be so constructed or adapted as to be suitable for the purpose for which it is used or provided'.

## Use of electrical equipment in explosive atmospheres

E3025    The *Equipment and Protective Systems Intended for Use in Potentially Explosive Atmospheres Regulations 1996 (SI 1996 No 192)* now govern electrical equipment for use in potentially explosive atmospheres, e.g. mines, with the exception of equipment placed on the market before 30 June 2003 which complies with existing electrical safety requirements as indicated below in the *Electrical Equipment for Explosive Atmospheres (Certification) Regulations 1990 (SI 1990 No 13)*, which will be revoked as from 1 July 2003.

Certain equipment and systems are exempt, e.g. medical devices, equipment for domestic use and personal protective equipment. [*SI 1996 No 192, Sch 5*]. Manufacturers of such electrical equipment and components are under a duty to ensure that it complies with the necessary health and safety requirements (e.g. relating to potential ignition sources/hazards arising from external effects) [*SI 1996 No 192, Sch 3*], and appropriate conformity assessment procedures [*SI 1996 No 192, Regs 6 and 8*]. Suppliers of such equipment must also see that it is safe to put into circulation, though not in the case of products put into circulation before 1 March 1996 or previously supplied within the EU. [*SI 1996 No 192, Reg 7*].

Conformity assessment procedures (for which fees are payable) are to be determined by notified bodies, with personnel appointed, if necessary, by the Secretary of State. [*SI 1996 No 192, Regs 11 and 13*]. Breach of these Regulations is an offence, leading to a maximum period of imprisonment or a fine [*SI 1996 No 192, Regs 16 and 17*], but it is a defence that due diligence was taken to avoid the commission of the offence [*SI 1996 No 192, Reg 18*].

## Electrical Equipment for Explosive Atmospheres (Certification) Regulations 1990

E3026    Manufacturers of such equipment may apply to a certification body for a certificate which states that the electrical equipment conforms to the standards specified in the directive. The certification bodies are empowered to carry out checks. Manufacturers may also apply to the appropriate certification body for a certificate stating that the equipment offers a degree of safety equivalent to EC standards.

When issued with a certificate, the manufacturer can fix to the equipment the appropriate distinctive community mark, namely:

(*a*)   that specified in Annex II to the First Specific Directive – in the case of the Framework Directive;

(*b*)   that specified in Annex C – in the case of the Gassy Mines Directive.

[Electrical Equipment for Explosive Atmospheres (Certification) Regulations 1990 (SI 1990 No 13), Reg 11(1)].

Affixation of community marks, otherwise than in accordance with *reg 11(1)*, is punishable as a breach of health and safety regulations.

Where a certification body refuses to issue a certificate of conformity or inspection, or withdraws one already issued, the certification body must forthwith send a written notice of the decision to the manufacturer. [*Electrical Equipment for Explosive Atmospheres (Certification) Regulations 1990 (SI 1990 No 13), Reg 6*]. In such a case, a manufacturer can apply to the Secretary of State for a review of the decision of the certification body within 60 days of receipt of the written notice. [*Electrical Equipment for Explosive Atmospheres (Certification) Regulations 1990 (SI 1990 No 13), Reg 7*]. The application must be made in writing, stating the grounds on which it is made and copies of documents supplied by the manufacturer to the certification body and a copy of the notice of decision should be included with the application. The Secretary of State then has a discretion to direct the holding of an inquiry. [*Electrical Equipment for Explosive Atmospheres (Certification) Regulations 1990 (SI 1990 No 13), Reg 8*].

## Product liability

E3027   Electricity is a product for the purposes of the *Consumer Protection Act 1987*. Consequently, where a defect in an electrical installation or system results in an injury, damage and/or death, liability is strict (see PRODUCT SAFETY).

## Non-statutory standards and codes

E3028   The Institution of Electrical Engineers (IEE) has been producing the IEE Wiring Regulations since 1882 – they are now in their sixteenth edition. This edition includes requirements for design, installation, inspection, testing and maintenance of electrical installations in or about buildings generally. Although they have no statutory force, they provide a good indication of good industrial practice for the purposes of the *Electricity Regulations 1989*.

The National Inspection Council for Electrical Installations Contracting (NICEIC) enrols contractors whose work is of an approved standard. NICEIC surveys work to check that it complies with IEE Wiring Regulations.

The British Standards Institution, BSI, has issued many British Standards and codes of practice for electrical equipment and practice. Such standards and codes are subject to revision and supplementation. The standards range from insulation, earthing terminals and electrical connections of small equipment, to a complex set of precautions and specialised electrical equipment, based on the IEC concepts of flameproofing, intrinsic safety and other types of protection for electrical equipment in flammable atmospheres.

A few of the BSI codes are for earthing, street lighting, electrical equipment for industrial use and for office machines and the distribution of electricity on construction and building sites.

The British Approvals Service for Electrical Equipment in Flammable Atmospheres, BASEEFA, linked with the HSE, is the official UK body for testing and certificating electrical apparatus for use in hazardous atmospheres, to IEC standards as accepted by CENELEC and BSI.

The British Electrical and Allied Manufacturers' Association, BEAMA, issues a specialised range of standards and codes drawn up in consultation with users and others.

The British Electrical Approvals Board for Household Equipment, BEAB, gives its seal of approval to such domestic type equipment as satisfies design and safety standards.

The HSE has published a guidance note, PM 82, '*The selection, installation and maintenance of electrical equipment for use in and around buildings containing explosives*', to assist those responsible for design selection, installation, operation and maintenance of electrical equipment (including mobile mechanical handling equipment) used at premises where explosives are manufactured, handled or stored. It aims to prevent fires and explosions due to electrical causes. The main topics covered by the guidance note include:

(*a*)    site supplies;

(*b*)    area and building zoning and categorisation;

(*c*)    selection and siting of equipment;

(*d*)    lighting protection;

(*e*)    radio frequency ignition hazards;

(*f*)    portable equipment;

(*g*)    fork-lift trucks;

(*h*)    maintenance and testing of equipment and systems.

### Electricity (Standards of Performance) Regulations 1993

E3029    The *Electricity (Standards of Performance) Regulations 1993 (SI 1993 No 1193)* provide for compensation to be payable by electricity suppliers for interruptions to supply and breach of any other performance standards. These Regulations have been made under the *Competition and Service (Utilities) Act 1992* which itself introduced requirements for information on each public electricity supplier's performance standards and for each of them to establish a complaints procedure.

## Conclusion

E3030    As indicated by the above, there are a wide range of provisions, both general and specific, that relate to working with electricity and electrical installations and the use of electrical plant and apparatus. There are certain absolute duties which should be borne in mind when working with electricity, e.g. live working. Further, as noted there are particular situations which are recognised as giving rise to an increased risk such as overhead cables and/or construction work and in these situations, it would be prudent to ensure appropriate measures are taken to manage the risks.

# Emissions into the Atmosphere

## Introduction

E5001   Pollution of the atmosphere we breathe is a subject which encompasses the whole range of distance scales and can be important over minutes or lifetimes. Regulation of emissions, therefore, has to account for all of these effects and, as a consequence, has to take a variety of forms. The concept of the different distance scales is illustrated in Figure 1 below:

*Figure 1:*

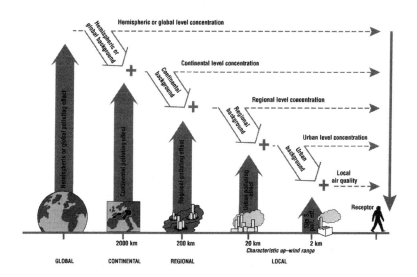

A 'receptor' (a human being, a population, an ecosystem) experiences air pollution as a sum of the contribution from sources which might be adjacent or at some other part of the planet. The extent to which the sources contribute might depend on the pollutant of concern. A pollutant such as sulphur dioxide is relatively short lived in the atmosphere and has the capacity to affect the lungs of people within tens of kilometres of the point of emission. At distances of hundreds of kilometres, however, the sulphur dioxide will have been transformed into sulphate, which may be absorbed into cloud water and be deposited on the ecosystems of another country. This is an example of trans-boundary pollution and popularly known as 'acid rain'.

Pollutants that are chemically more stable than sulphur dioxide have the potential to be dispersed throughout the globe. Some organic pollutants are an excellent example of this. Poly-chlorinated biphenyls were used widely in the middle of the twentieth century as a component part of electrical transformers. They are highly toxic and accumulate in body fats, so that animals (and humans) at the top of the food chain are most exposed. Hence, polar bears living in the Arctic Circle are far removed in distance and time from the original emission but still experience the impact.

Regulation of emissions from industry must recognise all these effects – from the large coal-fired power station with sulphur emissions to the small manufacturer using solvents. Where the potential exists for an air pollution impact, regulators will be seeking to restrict emissions. This chapter examines the means by which this goal is currently being achieved.

## Regulatory position

E5002   For air pollution, there are three main sources of legislation and regulation to which industry has to respond and which this chapter seeks to cover. These are the following:

- European Union directives on air quality and emissions;

- the Environment Agency and local authority implementation of Integrated Pollution Control (see E5059) and its successor, Integrated Pollution Prevention and Control (see E5027); and

- the Air Quality Strategy for England, Wales, Scotland and Northern Ireland, as prepared by the Department of the Environment, Transport and the Regions and the Scottish Executive.

In addition, emissions to atmosphere also encompass gases with the potential to contribute to global warming and stratospheric ozone depletion.

## Regulatory drivers

### Human health and toxicology

E5003   The effects of air pollution on human health have been recognised in the UK for more than 300 years. The often quoted example is the prohibition of coal burning in London in 1273, on the grounds that it was 'prejudicial to health'.

Coal burning has been the main cause of air pollution problems since then and has provoked most of the legislation aimed at improving air quality and human health. The infamous four day 'smog' of December 1952 was shown to have caused nearly 4,000 additional deaths through bronchitis and other diseases of the respiratory system. There was also an increase in heart disease.

It is less obvious now than in the 1950s that health is affected by exposure to air pollution, but epidemiologists can show statistically significant associations between high concentrations of certain pollutants and hospital admissions (and re-admissions), as well as mortality. Health effects include irritation and loss of organ functions (e.g. reduced lung capacity). The Committee on the Medical Effects of Air Pollutants estimates that 14,000-24,000 admissions a year are associated with short term air pollution, and that it causes between 12,000-24,000 premature deaths per year. The largest contribution to this total is made by inhalable particles, which, for example, may arise through combustion processes.

It is not only the 'classical' air pollutants that provoke concern with regard to their impact on human health through impairment of the respiratory and cardiovascular systems. Fears also exist about releases of substances with the potential for damage to other parts of the body through long term exposure at low levels. In particular, 'persistent organic pollutants' and heavy metals have the potential to cause human health effects through inhalation or entry into the food chain.

*The medical effects of air pollutants*

*Nitrogen dioxide (NO₂)*

E5004    This gas can cause the inflammation of the airways when in high concentrations, and long-term exposure can affect lung function. This exposure can enhance the response that people have to allergens and is particularly harmful to asthmatics.

*Particulate matter (PM₁₀)*

E5005    $PM_{10}$ are particles in the air that have an aerodynamic diameter of less than 10µm. Particulate air pollution is associated with a range of health effects including effects to the respiratory and cardiovascular systems. $PM_{10}$ is responsible for causing premature deaths to those with pre-existing heart and lung disease. The smaller the particle, the greater the likelihood that it can reach the furthest part of the lung where the delicate tissues are.

*Sulphur dioxide (SO₂)*

E5006    This gas constricts the airways by stimulating the nerves in the lining of the respiratory tissues. Asthmatics are particularly vulnerable to this.

*Carbon monoxide*

E5007    This gas causes the formation of carboxyhaemoglobin. This reduces the capacity of the blood to carry oxygen round the body. Those with an existing disease connected to the heart or brain are particularly vulnerable.

*Benzene*

E5008    This gas is a genotoxic human carcinogen, and there is no safe level that has been defined. There is a risk of leukaemia when people are exposed to high levels.

*1-3 butadiene*

E5009    This gas is also a genotoxic human carcinogen that can cause the induction of cancers of the lymphoid system, blood forming tissue, lymphomas and leukaemias.

*Ozone*

E5010    This gas can cause slight irritation to the eyes and nose and may exacerbate symptoms of those with respiratory conditions (e.g. asthma, pneumonia).

*Dioxins*

E5011    Short-term exposure may result in skin lesions and altered liver function. Long-term exposure may damage the immune system, the developing nervous system, the endocrine system and reproductive functions. One congener is a known human carcinogen, however it does not effect genetic material.

*Lead*

E5012    Lead causes problems in the synthesis of haemoglobin, it has effects on the kidneys, the gastrointestinal tract, joints and reproductive system, and the nervous system. The greatest cause for concern is the possible effect of lead on brain development in children. Food and water are the two main sources of ingestion for most people. Lead in air contributes to the lead levels in food through the deposition of dust and rain on crops and the soil.

*Polycyclic aromatic hydrocarbons ('PAHs')*

E5013    Some PAHs are genotoxic human carcinogens, suspected of causing lung cancers and leading to the induction of other cancers.

## Acid deposition and damage to ecosystems

E5014    When atmospheric pollutants such as sulphur dioxide ($SO_2$), nitrogen oxide ($NO_2$), and ammonia ($NH_3$) are deposited at the surface, this is referred to as acidification. This can occur through direct 'dry' deposition of the gases or through 'wet' deposition after transformation into sulphates and nitrates and absorption into rain and cloud water. This has been recognised as a threat to ecosystems, resulting in major international research projects and negotiations to reduce emissions. It is usually referred to by the more popular term of 'acid rain'.

Pollutants can be transported over considerable distance, affecting the air quality and ecosystems in adjacent or distant countries. Such effects can extend over several thousands of kilometres. Deposition of excess acid can result in changes to the chemical composition of soil and surface water, in turn interfering with ecosystems.

*Consequences of acidification*

E5015    Acidification has been a major problem in Europe with the highest deposition rates found in the highly populated and industrialised zone extending between Poland and the Netherlands. Within the next ten years, acid deposition in Europe is expected to decrease following the agreed reductions in European emissions of $SO_2$ and $NO_x$ (while ammonia emissions are not likely to change significantly).

Organisms in water are affected when the concentration of hydrogen ions increases (decreasing the pH of the water). As a result lake beds are covered in mosses, and there is an increase in the death of fish and other animals. Plants are affected by the changing chemistry and biology of the soil, altered by an increased amount of hydrogen ions. There has been a decline in the health of forests in central Europe because of acidification.

Modern forestry and agriculture can contribute to the pollution as well as suffer from it, through the use of fertilisers which release nitrogen and hydrogen ions into the air in the form of ammonia.

Deposition of excess nitrogen can lead to the eutrophication of fresh and marine waters.

Acidification in urban and industrial areas increases the deterioration of many buildings and construction materials. In sheltered positions, a black crust surface layer forms on calcareous materials, and the growth of lichen, mosses and algae is common. Historic monuments and buildings can be especially susceptible to damage.

Acidifying substances also contribute to climate change. Both $NO_2$ and $SO_2$ are radiatively active gases with a warming potential, although sulphate and nitrate aerosols result in cooling through reflection of sunlight in the upper part of the troposphere. Oxides of nitrogen are implicated strongly in the atmospheric chemistry of ozone formation, causing an excess of tropospheric ozone, and the depletion of stratospheric ozone.

## Nuisance

E5016    Air pollution can cause harm to the senses as well as harm to human health and the natural environment. Whilst not as damaging, odour and dust nuisance can result in costly disputes for industry and can be difficult to eliminate in many cases.

Another issue which can arise is the visual impact caused by plumes of water droplets, formed when a high moisture content plume enters the cool atmosphere and becomes visible through the condensation of its water vapour. The droplets then appear as a white plume, which may extend for some distance, depending on atmospheric conditions. Such a plume is harmless in terms of human health, but is disliked by regulatory authorities as it draws attention to the emission and can be a source of complaints.

At present, the UK regulatory climate discourages visible plumes, unlike Scandinavia and the USA for example, but the newer emphasis on energy efficiency may soon outweigh these concerns.

# Key pollutants and issues

## Introduction

E5017    The issues outlined above at E5003–E5016 are some of the main areas of concern which drive regulation aimed at reducing air pollution. The section below from E5018–E5024 provides background material on the main pollutants and their origin, as well as further material on the regional and global issues that result in industry being asked to emit less substances of a damaging nature to atmosphere.

## The UK priority pollutants

E5018    Emissions of pollutants have increased since the industrial revolution. Until quite recently, national air pollution control legislation was focussed on reducing air pollution from particular sectors of industry. Only since the late 1980s has this been added to by 'effects based' legislation. This approach takes as its start point an air quality standard or measure of harm in the environment and then policies are devised to enable this criterion to be attained.

This philosophy has reached its logical conclusion with the publication of the Air Quality Strategy (see below at E5064). This document targets eight priority pollutants and explains how the government will achieve air quality objectives relating to airborne concentrations of all of these eight pollutants.

*The priority pollutants*

| Pollutant | Origin | Comments |
|---|---|---|
| Sulphur dioxide ($SO_2$) | $SO_2$ dissolves in water to give an acidic solution (sulphuric acid). In the UK the main source of $SO_2$ is the combustion of fossil fuels which contain sulphur and the combustion of heavy oils. | At the beginning of the 20th century, $SO_2$ was emitted from the domestic sector, commercial and industrial premises, and power stations by the combustion of coal. The smogs of the 1950s prompted the *Clean Air Act 1956*. Cleaner fuels have since replaced coal in all sectors. However this use of coal is still significant in Northern Ireland and some other parts of the UK. |
| Nitrogen dioxide ($NO_2$) | All combustion processes in air produce oxides of nitrogen. $NO_2$ and nitric oxide are oxides of nitrogen and together they are referred to as $NO_x$. In the UK 50% of $NO_x$ emissions are from road transport, 20% from the electricity industry, and other industrial and commercial activities account for 17%. In London, it is thought that 75% of $NO_x$ emissions come from road transport. | There is evidence that $NO_2$ emissions from motor vehicles may continue to increase because of the growth in private car use in recent years. Reductions will be slow even if vehicle numbers and distances travelled were to stop increasing. The Air Quality Strategy estimates that $NO_2$ from road transport will gradually decrease, levelling off in 2015, and that petrol cars make the greatest contribution to $NO_2$ transport emissions in the UK. |
| Carbon monoxide (CO) | This gas is formed by the incomplete combustion of carbon containing fuels. The main source is road transport, particularly petrol-engined vehicles. | |

| Pollutant | Origin | Comments |
|---|---|---|
| Lead | Lead is the most widely used non-ferrous metal. The largest use is for the manufacture of batteries. | The sale of leaded petrol was banned from 1 January 2000 in the UK. Its use has been phased out gradually since 1985. This has led to significant decreases in emissions in urban areas. |
| Ozone | Ozone is not directly emitted from any man-made source in any significant quantities. Instead it arises from chemical reactions in the atmosphere caused by sunlight. $NO_x$ and volatile organic compounds ('VOCs') are the most important precursors of elevated levels of ozone. Its production can also be stimulated by CO, methane, and other VOCs which come from natural sources. | |
| Particles ($PM_{10}$) | $PM_{10}$ are particles with an aerodynamic diameter of less than 10mm. This is emitted from road transport, stationary combustion sources, and other industrial processes. | Diesel vehicles emit particles at a greater rate than petrol vehicles and nationally, road transport contributed approximately 25% of $PM_{10}$ emissions in 1996[1]. |
| Benzene | This gas is a VOC. In the UK the main sources are from the combustion and distribution of petrol. Diesel fuel is also a small source. | In recent years unleaded petrol consists of, on average, 2% by volume in the UK. |

| Pollutant | Origin | Comments |
|-----------|--------|----------|
| 1,3-Butadiene | There are trace amounts of this gas in the atmosphere from the combustion of petrol and other materials. It is used in industry for the production of rubber for tyres, however motor vehicles continue to be the dominant source. | |

(1)  Airborne Particles Expert Group ('APEG') 1999 Source Appointment of Airborne Particulate Matter in the UK Department of the Environment Transport and the Regions, the Welsh Office and the Department of the Environment (Northern Ireland).

*Other important pollutants*

E5020    The principal reason why the Air Quality Strategy is focussed on the eight priority pollutants is to protect the health of the population. It could be argued very easily that there are other pollutants which have the potential to harm health at sufficiently high concentrations. This might be especially true within the industrial sector where the possibility exists of localised 'hotspots' of concentrations of substances arising out of the particular industrial process in question. Examples are metals and individual organic compounds. For occupational hygiene and the indoor environment, the Health and Safety Executive publish safe limits for concentrations of several hundred substances. For the outdoor environment the same principles apply, but in most circumstances the concentrations are too low to cause a health effect.

In terms of the their abundance and toxicity, the following represents a list of pollutants which require regulation from industrial processes:

| | |
|---|---|
| • cadmium | • polycyclic aromatic hydrocarbons ('PAHs') |
| • mercury | • polychlorinated bipheyls |
| • nickel | • polychlorinated dibenzo-p-dioxins |
| • arsenic | • polychlorinated dibenzofurans |
| • vanadium | • hydrogen fluoride |
| • hydrogen chloride | |

## Trans-boundary pollution

E5021    In the 1970s and 1980s much of the air pollution control policy was aimed at reducing the long range transport of acidic pollution across national boundaries. The reported decline in the health of trees and the loss of life in lakes from Scandinavia to eastern Europe had provoked a strong response from the public and politicians. This issue is still very much alive, although much has been done to reduce national emissions of sulphur and nitrogen, especially from large power plants burning coal and oil. The UK was once perceived as being the 'dirty man' of Europe in the context of sulphur dioxide emissions, but can now reasonably claim to have reduced national emissions substantially. The United Nations Economic Commission for Europe ('UNECE') Convention on long-range trans-boundary air pollution ('CLRTAP') is an important framework for environmental assessment and policy in Europe.

## Climate change

E5022    The natural presence of 'radiatively-active' gases in the atmosphere is essential for life. These gases trap heat in the lower atmosphere, creating a greenhouse, and include the following:

●     carbon dioxide;

●     methane;

●     nitrous oxide ($N_2O$);

●     chlorofluorocarbons ('CFCs'); and

●     ozone.

Increasing concentrations of these greenhouse gases enables more infa-red radiation to be absorbed in the lower atmosphere, upsetting the earth's radiation balance. This increase allows the troposphere to be warmed more significantly, and the upper layers to be cooled. Without any greenhouse effect at all, the earth would be uninhabitable for humans. In previous periods of geological history, the earth has been warmer and colder than at present. The issue today is the rate at which the climate appears to be changing.

Emissions of these greenhouse gases come mainly from anthropogenic activity, especially combustion of fuel and are expected to rise, doubling by 2030. As a result, the atmosphere is being gradually heated up; the trend of global mean surface temperatures indicates an increase of 0.45°C over the past hundred years.

### *Consequences*

E5023    Vegetation will be in greater competition as optimum conditions become scarce. This may cause shifts of plant and animal life. Extra warmth can trigger insect plagues and plant diseases. Both of these consequences affect agriculture, which is also directly affected by an annual rainfall decrease. All these negative changes to the land can expose vulnerable areas to land degradation.

## The depletion of stratospheric ozone

E5024    The depletion of stratospheric ozone during the last few decades has been a global problem. Stratospheric ozone concentrations have been decreasing at an increasing rate over the last ten years. This trend is larger nearer the poles and is often referred to as the 'ozone hole'. The cause of this problem is the increase of industrially produced CFCs and halogens in the upper atmosphere, and these are expected to cause ozone depletion at least up to the year 2100.

### *Consequences*

E5025    The depletion of ozone means that certain wave lengths of ultra-violet solar radiation are able to penetrate through to the earth's surface, damaging human health and leading to an increase in the number of cases of skin cancer, as well as damaging ecosystems. This can also lead to a change in global circulation and climate, as the absorption of the radiation by ozone can lead to heat formation in the atmosphere.

# The European context

## The policy makers

E5026    In the world of air pollution, 'Europe' has several identities. There are two main bodies which drive legislation and protocols, namely the European Union and UNECE (see E5021 above). The latter body is composed of the EU member states, plus the countries of eastern Europe including Russia and the Ukraine. In all, it comprises 50 countries (and includes the USA and Canada.) Its chief role is to examine the consequences of trans-boundary pollution through CLRTAP (see E5021 above). The Convention states that all countries should;

*'endeavour to limit and, as far as possible, gradually reduce and prevent air pollution, including long range trans-boundary pollution.'*

In all, the Convention has been responsible for five protocols, as follows.

- *The 1985 Sulphur Protocol* required signatories to reduce national sulphur emissions by 30%, based on 1980 levels, on or before 1993. The UK was not a signatory to this Protocol. The Protocol was subsequently revised and signed in Oslo in June 1994 and came into force on 5 August 1998. This time the UK did ratify the Protocol (17 December 1996) and has agreed to reduce $SO_2$ emissions by 50% by 2000, 70% by 2005 and 80% by 2010, (again based on 1980 levels). This will require fuel switching and some advances in abatement technology. The government has drawn up a national plan to keep national emissions within these targets. In the main, these targets have most impact on the power generation and oil refining industries.

- *The 1988 Nitrogen Oxides Protocol,* signed in Sofia, came into effect in 1991 and sought to freeze emissions of $NO_x$ at their 1987 levels, with a target date of 1994. The UK ratified this Protocol in 1990. By 1996, UK emissions were 21% lower than in 1987.

- *The 1991 Volatile Organic Compounds Protocol* was signed in Geneva and came into force on 29 September 1997. The UK ratified the Protocol in June 1994. VOCs are defined as *'all organic compounds of anthropogenic nature, other than methane, that are capable of producing photochemical oxidants by reactions with nitrogen oxides in the presence of sunlight.'* The Protocol requires most parties to reduce overall VOC emissions by 30% on or before 1999, using a base year of 1988. Additionally, the protocol obliges signatories to control emissions from industries through new emission limits and to introduce abatement technologies as well as reduce solvent use and reduce VOC emissions through petrol distribution and refuelling.

- *The 1998 Heavy Metals Protocol* was signed in June 1998 at Aarhus. It requires emissions of cadmium, lead and mercury to be reduced below 1990 levels. Its aim is to reduce emissions through the use of stricter emissions limit values for industry and the use of best available technology (see E5027 below).

- *The Persistent Organic Pollutants Protocol* was also signed in June 1998 at Aarhus. It aims to phase out the production of and use of a defined list of substances, as well as imposing requirements to eliminate discharges, emissions and losses and to ensure safe disposal methods. The list covers 16 substances in three categories, (pesticides, industrial chemicals and by products or contaminants, e.g. dioxins.)

The effects of the Protocols on industry are not usually seen immediately or directly. Normally they take effect through the subsequent actions of national governments and regulatory agencies who propose action and legislation designed to achieve the aims of the Protocols. In this sense the European Commission is strongly interlinked with the CLRTAP Protocols. Not only is the Community a signatory in itself, but the Commission will frame directives so as to meet the aims of the Protocols.

The most active part of the Commission with regard to air quality legislation is Directorate General Environment ('DG Environment'). The units within this Directorate have direct responsibility for drafting new directives which set air quality standards and implement emissions reductions in key sectors. At present, their work has three main elements:

- The Auto-Oil II programme;

- National Emissions Ceilings;

- Daughter directives on air quality standards.

The DG Environment also has responsibility for some legislation relevant to industry and air pollution control, such as the implementation of Integrated Pollution Prevention and Control and the Waste Incineration Directive.

The work of the DG Environment in air pollution is characterised by a tension between the contribution from transport and from industry. The Auto-Oil programme of research and policy measures was established with the transport sector in mind. The feeling in the Commission now is that the transport 'problem' has been solved and more emphasis should return to the contribution from industry.

## Integrated pollution prevention and control ('IPPC') – an overview

E5027    The IPPC directive has been introduced into Europe (*Directive on Integrated Pollution Prevention Control 96/61/EC*), and is designed to prevent, reduce, and eliminate pollution at the source, through the careful use of natural resources. The directive is intended to help industries move towards greater environmental sustainability, and applies to the installation of the following activities:

- energy industries (power, oil and gas);

- the production and processing of metals (ferrous and non-ferrous);

- mineral industries (cement and glassworks);

- chemical industries (organic, inorganic, and pharmaceuticals);

- waste management (landfill sites and incinerators); and

- other (slaughter houses, food/milk processing, paper, tanneries, animal carcass disposal, pig/poultry units and organic solvent users).

IPPC covers emissions to air, land and water, as well as heat. IPPC goes further to cover noise, vibration, energy efficiency, environmental accidents, site protection, and many more processes.

The IPPC directive requires that applications must show that installations are run in a way that prevents emissions, and must use the following principles:

- must apply the best available techniques ('BAT') to control emissions. Account must be taken of the relative costs and advantages of the available techniques;

- waste is to be minimised and recycled where possible;

- energy is to be conserved;

- accidents are to be prevented, and their environmental consequences to be limited; and

- the site is to be returned to a satisfactory state after operations cease.

The overall objective for the directive is a high level of protection for the environment as a whole, and a system of permits has been set up to achieve this relating to:

- plant operating conditions;

- emission limits for certain substances to air, land and water; and

- annual reporting of pollutant releases.

When necessary, these permits will include conditions preventing emissions from crossing national boundaries. The emission limits and the operating conditions are based on BAT, taking into account the characteristics for installation, location, and local environmental conditions.

## BREF Notes

E5028    All permits for IPPC must be based on the concept of BAT, which is defined in Article 2 of the Directive. The licensing authorities need guidance as to which techniques are BAT. Consequently the European Commission is required to organise the exchange of information between industry, environmental organisations, and experts from the EU member states. This work is co-ordinated by the European IPPC Bureau. The Commission then publishes the results of the information exchange every three years in the form of BAT reference documents, known as BREF Notes. These are to be prepared for each industrial sector.

The BREF Notes form the basis of guidance issued in the UK. It has been proposed that the detailed guidance for a specific sector covering the full range of IPPC industries, which the information exchange intends to produce by 2001, will form a key input to the UK guidance. It has therefore been proposed that the UK guidance will not be produced until the appropriate BREF Note for the specific sector has been published. The BREFs are not guidance notes and so they need to be supplemented by domestic guidance.

The IPPC Bureau was set up in 1996 in Seville to control the information management system for the BREF Notes. There are four main bodies involved in the information exchange. These are the EC Directorate responsible for the environment (the DG Environment) which has overall control, the IPPC bureau, the information exchange forum (which is a committee of representatives from member states, industry and non-government organisations), and the technical working groups ('TWGs') which are made up of experts. The TWGs are where the information exchange really takes place. Information, BAT studies, and details on specific sectors and emission levels are provided by the experts, who meet at least twice for each industrial sector. The table below at E5029 shows the 'best guess' for the BREF Note completion for different industrial sectors.

*Best guess for BREF Note completion*

**E5029**

| BREF Note: | Date: |
|---|---|
| Primary/Secondary Steel | Feb 2000 |
| Cement & Lime | Feb 2000 |
| Paper/Pulp | Sept 2000 |
| Tanneries | Sept 2000 |
| Ferrous Metal Processing | Sept 2000 |
| Non Ferrous Metal Production and Processing | Sept 2000 |
| Glass | Sept 2000 |
| Chloralkali | Sept 2000 |
| Textiles | Feb 2001 |
| Foundaries | Feb 2001 |
| Large Volume Organic | Sept 2001 |
| Livestock: Poultry | Sept 2001 |
| Batch Organics in Multi-purpose Plants | Sept 2001 |
| Refineries | Sept 2001 |
| Food & Milk | Sept 2002 |
| Ceramics | Sept 2002 |
| Large Volume Solid Inorganic | Sept 2002 |
| Large Volume Gas & Liquid Inorganic | Sept 2002 |
| Large Combustion Plant | Sept 2002 |
| Polymers | Sept 2003 |
| Slaughterhouses/Carcasses | Sept 2003 |
| Surface Treatment of Metals | Sept 2003 |
| Hazardous Waste Incineration | Sept 2003 |
| Municipal waste Incineration | Sept 2003 |
| Coating activities etc using organic solvents | Sept 2003 |
| Landfill | Sept 2004 |
| Waste disposal and recovery (other than landfill, incineration) | Sept 2004 |
| Speciality Inorganics | Sept 2004 |
| Organic Fine Chemicals | Sept 2004 |

## The large combustion plant directive

E5030     *The Large Combustion Plant Directive 1988 (88/609/EEC)* commits member states to reductions in $SO_2$ and $NO_x$ from large fossil burning plants of $50MW_{th}$ or more. This Directive did not cover emissions from new solid fuel plants between 50-100MW. In 1994 an amendment *Directive (94/66)* was adopted to cover such a plant, setting an emission limit of 2000 mg m$^{-3}$ for $SO_2$. Proposals covering emissions for smaller plants are currently under discussion.

In 1998 the EU published proposals for amending its 1988 Directive to account for the technical developments since adoption. It proposes setting emission limit values for $NO_x$ and $SO_2$ based on BAT. For a solid and liquid fuel plant of less than 100MW, an emission limit of 850 mg m$^{-3}$ SO2 is proposed, and 200 mg m$^{-3}$ for those over 300MW. An emission limit of 400 mg m$^{-3}$ $NO_x$ is proposed for solid fuel plants with a capacity of less than 100MW-300MW. Large combustion plants over 50MW are required to comply with the IPPC Directive.

## Solvent emissions

E5031     In March 1999 *Directive 99/13* was adopted on the limitations of emissions of VOCs, to come into force in 2001. This was due to the use of organic solvents in certain activities and installations. It aims to reduce emissions by 50% by 2010 from various activities including printing, coating, dry cleaning and shoe manufacturing.

## Fuel directives

E5032     *Directive 93/12/EEC* limits the sulphur content of all gas oils (except aviation kerosene) to 0.2% by weight as from 1 October 1994, with a further reduction in the sulphur content of diesel fuel to 0.05% by weight as from 1 October 1996. The Directive also required member states to ensure that diesel fuel with a sulphur content of 0.05% or less becomes available from 1 October 1995. Thus enabling compliance with *EU Directive 91/542/EEC* on emissions from heavy duty vehicles. As part of its strategy to combat acidification, *Directive 99/32* adopted on 26 April 1999 amends *Directive 93/12/EC* to reduce the sulphur content of gas oil to 0.1% by weight from 1 January 2008.

## Framework directive on air quality assessment and management

E5033     *Directive 96/62/EC* on ambient air quality assessment, the Air Quality Framework directive, provides a framework for the EU to use to set limit values for pollutants. This directive identifies twelve pollutants for which limit or target values will be set in daughter directives. These are:

- sulphur dioxide ($SO_2$);

- nitrogen dioxide ($NO_2$);

- particulate matter ($PM_{10}$);

- lead;

- carbon monoxide;

- benzene;

- ozone;

- polyaromatic hydrocarbons;

- cadium;

- arsenic;

- nickel; and

- mercury.

This directive is particularly important, as it prepares the ground for a number of significant daughter directives on air quality standards and control measures, as set out below.

## Daughter directives

*Daughter directive for limit values of $SO_2$, oxides of nitrogen, particulate matter, and lead in ambient air*

E5034    The first Daughter Directive in 1998 established legally binding limit values for $SO_2$, $NO_2$ and $PM_{10}$, to be achieved by 1 January 2005 and 2010. This Directive was adopted in April 1999 and member states are required to implement it by July 2001.

*Daughter directive to reduce the sulphur content of liquid fuels*

E5035    This daughter directive aims to reduce further the emissions of $SO_2$ resulting from the combustion of liquid fuels. For heavy fuel oil member states have to ensure that from 1 July 2003 the sulphur content is not over 1% by mass. For gas oil limits are 0.2% by mass by July 2000 and 0.1% by mass from 1 January 2008. Certain classes of fuel used by ships are excluded.

*Daughter directive on limit values for benzene and carbon monoxide in ambient air*

E5036    In December of 1998 a proposal for a further daughter directive which sets limit values for benzene and carbon monoxide was published.

*Proposal for national emissions ceilings directive and ozone daughter directive*

E5037    In June 1999 proposals were put forward for two further daughter directives. One was to set target values for ozone and the other emission ceilings for various pollutants. The latter is referred to as the *national emissions ceilings directive* ('NECD'). This directive sets ceilings for national emissions of $SO_2$, $NO_2$, $NH_3$ and VOCs to be achieved by 2010. The NECD is the main instrument for attaining air quality targets for ambient ozone, which are also included in the proposal.

*Proposal for a daughter directive on the control of emissions from heavy goods vehicles*

E5038    This directive has been amended to introduce three stages of binding emission values.

*Other proposed daughter directives*

E5039    - proposal for a daughter directive on the control of emissions from tractors;

- proposal for a daughter directive on consumer information fuel economy for new cars;

- proposal for a daughter directive to set tighter emission limits for large combustion plants;

- proposal for a daughter directive on setting EU-wide air quality standards for benzene and CO;

- proposal for a daughter directive on the reduction targets for $SO_2$ and $NO_2$ emissions; and

- proposal for a daughter directive on setting new reduction target for ozone emissions.

The EU also awaits a proposal for tighter controls on the quality of diesel and petrol fuels.

## Summary of directives

E5040

| Directive | Comment |
|---|---|
| *Air Quality* | |
| Directive 96/62/EEC | Ambient air quality assessment. |
| Daughter directives | Directive for limit values of $SO_2$, oxides of nitrogen, particulate matter, and lead in ambient air. |
| | Directive to reduce the sulphur content of liquid fuels. |
| | Directive on limit values for benzene and carbon monoxide in ambient air. |
| *Fuel directives* | |
| Directive 93/12/EEC | Limits the sulphur content of all gas oils. |
| Directive 91/542/EEC | Emissions from heavy duty vehicles. |
| Directive 99/32/EEC | Amends Directive 93/12/EC. |
| *Solvent emissions* | |
| Directive 99/13/EEC | Limitations of emissions of volatile organic compounds ('VOCs'). |
| *The large combustion plant directive* | |
| Directive 88/609/EEC | Commits member states to reductions in SO2 and NOx |

# UK Regulations

## Introduction

E5041    Air pollution control for industry is dominated by the introduction of the IPPC Directive into UK law. This replaces the Integrated Pollution Control and Local Air Pollution Control ('LAPC') Regulations which have existed since 1991, which in turn replaced the old system of Best Practical Means Notes. Thus, the last decade has seen quite a transformation, overturning a system of controls and concepts which can be traced back to 1842.

*Definition of useful acronyms and terms*

**E5042**

| | |
|---|---|
| IPC · | Integrated Pollution Control |
| IPPC | Integrated Pollution Prevention Control |
| | IPPC is a regulatory system that employs an integrated approach to control the environmental impacts of certain industrial activities. It involves determining the appropriate controls for industry to protect the environment through a single permitting process. |
| LAPC | Local Air Pollution Control |
| BAT/BATNEEC | Best Available Technique /Best Available Technique Not Entailing Excessive Cost |
| | The Best Available Techniques are those that prevent or minimise pollution, and can be implemented effectively and are economically and technically viable while meeting the overall aims of the Directive. BATNEEC is a concept promoted by IPC and does not appear explicitly in IPPC legislation. |
| BPEO | Best Practical Environmental Option |
| Part A1 installations | The largest and most complex processes, regulated for releases to air, water and land by the Environment Agency in England and Wales. |
| Part A2 Installations | Processes with releases to air, water and land regulated by Local Authorities in England and Wales (but by SEPA in Scotland). |
| Part B installations | The smaller processes, with releases to air only regulated by Local Authorities in England and Wales (but by SEPA in Scotland). |

*Useful websites*

**E5043**

- *Environment Agency*: http://www.environment-agency.gov.uk

- *Department of the Environment Transport and the Regions (DETR):* http://www.detr.gov.uk

- *European Commission:* http://europa.eu.int/comm/index.htm

- *The UK National Air Quality Information Archive:* http://www.aeat.co.uk/netcen/airqual/

- *European Integrated Pollution Prevention and Control Bureau:* http://eippcb.jrc.es/

  N.B.: BREF notes can be downloaded from this site.

- *Scottish Executive:* http://www.scotland.gov.uk/consultations/environment

- *Scottish Executive:* http://www.scotland.gov.uk/environment/airquality

## The regulators

### The environment agencies

E5044    The agencies were established by the *Environment Act 1995*, and formally took over their pollution control and other functions on 1 April 1996.

In England and Wales the Agency's pollution control responsibilities are as follows:

- authorisations, licences and consents for emissions to air, water and land. Monitoring compliance and enforcement, including prosecution permitting of installations and enforcement of Regulations under IPPC; and

- advice and guidance to industry and others on best environmental practice.

### Scottish Environment Protection Agency

E5045    With regard to the Scottish Environment Protection Agency ('SEPA'), Scotland has been divided into the west, east and north for operational purposes. The roles for SEPA are similar for the Environment Agency for England and Wales. In addition it regulates Part B processes for air pollution under the *Environmental Protection Act 1990, Part I*. In other words in England and Wales this function has not been transferred to the Agency and remains with local authorities. SEPA also controls the installations regulated for IPPC.

### Northern Ireland

E5046    The Department of Environment ('DoE') (Northern Ireland) has overall responsibility for air pollution control in Northern Ireland. It is introducing a system similar to the IPC and air pollution control regimes operating in the rest of the UK prior to July 2000.

Part A processes are regulated for IPC by the Industrial Pollution and Radiochemical Inspectorate within the DoE (Northern Ireland). Part B processes are also regulated by the same Inspectorate.

### Local authorities

E5047    Local Authorities have a wide range of responsibilities covering the whole spectrum of pollution control and environmental protection. The local authority associations and the Environment Agency have signed a Memorandum of Understanding (1997) covering those areas of environmental protection for which they have responsibility.

## The end of IPC and LAPC

E5048    IPC should have been superseded by IPPC by 31 October 1999, as required by the Directive. In fact, it did not formally become part of legislation until August 2000. The consultation period was extended to April 2000 (with no less than five consultation papers being issued in all.) Implementation was delayed primarily because the regulatory structure was not in place to allow the environment agencies and local authorities to process applications for a permit. Whilst the transformation from IPC and LAPC to IPC is a straightforward one in principle, it has proved more difficult in practice to define the Regulations and to draft guidance to both industry and regulators on how they should be used.

In the UK the new system is known as Pollution Prevention Control ('PPC') as it includes provisions for both integrated (IPPC) and non-integrated (PPC) permits. In England, Wales and Scotland PPC has replaced the IPC and LAPC systems.

There are three main differences between IPC and IPPC:

(a)     IPC was concerned with releases of prescribed substances to air, water and land, whereas IPPC covers a wider range of environmental impacts.

(b)     IPPC covers many or more installations than IPC. The government estimates that 7,000 installations will be covered by IPPC, of which:

    (i)     2,000 were already covered by IPC;

    (ii)    2,500 were covered by LAPC;

    (iii)   1,000 are landfill sites;

    (iv)    1,000 are intensive pig and poultry farms;

    (v)     500 are food and drink factories.

(c)     IPC has approximately 400 processes which are not covered by the IPPC Directive but which will be covered by the UK implementation of the IPPC regime.

The new format of IPPC, as proposed, has been superimposed on the existing system. The approach is designed to give the power to make regulation which would set out one consistent regime.

## The Pollution Prevention and Control Act 1999

E5049     *The Pollution Prevention and Control Act 1999* received Royal Assent on 27 July 1999. It is an enabling Act, paving the way for Regulations to be made which implement the IPPC Directive. As such, it is not inherently revealing – the Regulations contain the detail which affects industry.

From a legal standpoint, it provides for the repeal of *Environmental Protection Act 1990, Part I* which covers IPC and LAPC. The Act also makes provision for waste licences issued under the *Control of Pollution Act 1974* and which had expired to be treated as though they were still in force. Another area which the Act covers is regulation of off-shore oil installations.

## PPC (England and Wales) Regulations and the Draft PPC (Scotland) Regulations 2000

*Application for permit*

E5050     A new installation cannot be brought into operation until an IPPC permit has been granted. Before the candidate makes an application they should check that they are actually required to make an application, and understand the requirements of the application. The application and associated Technical Guidance documents should also be consulted. It may be necessary to discuss the application with the Environment Agency before the application is prepared to help clarify important issues, and how to present the information that is required.

*Information on application*

E5051     To make an application the candidate should complete the Environment Agency's or SEPA's, standard application form which can be obtained from the local

Environment Agency or SEPA office, or from the Environment Agency website at http://www.environment-agency.gov.uk. (although the Scottish Draft Regulations state that an application for a permit to SEPA shall be acceptable in writing or in electronic format, they do not cite a web address to obtain the form.) The form should be submitted along with 10 copies (this requirement does not stand for SEPA applications) and all other additional information to the Environment Agency along with the appropriate fee. The application should include the following information:

(i)    full details of the operator, and the installation (address, national grid reference, map or plan of the installation), and the local authority in which the installation is situated;

(ii)    description of the installation and the activities that are to be carried out;

(iii)    the nature, quantities and sources of the likely emissions to the environment and their significant effects. (Part B installations release emissions to air only, and Part A installations release emissions to air, water and land);

(iv)    details of the technology that is to be used to prevent or reduce emissions; and

(v)    any proposals for monitoring emissions from the installation.

Applications for Part A installations must also include the following:

(i)    Measures that are to be taken for the prevention and recovery of waste that is generated by the installation when it is in operation.

(ii)    Details on the raw materials, any substances, and energy which is to be used or generated by the operation of the installation.

(iii)    A report on the current condition of the site, particularly identifying any substances that are around, in or under the site that may pose as a pollution risk in the future. The Agency is to produce guidance on the characterisation and the assessment of sites.

(iv)    Relevant information must be included that has been obtained as a result of carrying out an Environmental Assessment in accordance with *EU Directive 85/337.*

In addressing the BATs the applicant should ensure that in the application the following issues are included:

(i)    confirm compliance with any compulsory requirements e.g. other emission based Regulations/directives;

(ii)    where the indicative requirements are clearly stated, confirm compliance or justify proposals by describing how they will meet the BAT criteria. In particular confirm that all the measures described are utilised and if any are not used, give justification why;

(iii)    where there are no clear benchmarks or standards, describe how the proposals will meet the BAT criteria. In particular confirm that all the measures described are utilised and if any are not used, give justification why.

*Figure 2: The Application Process*

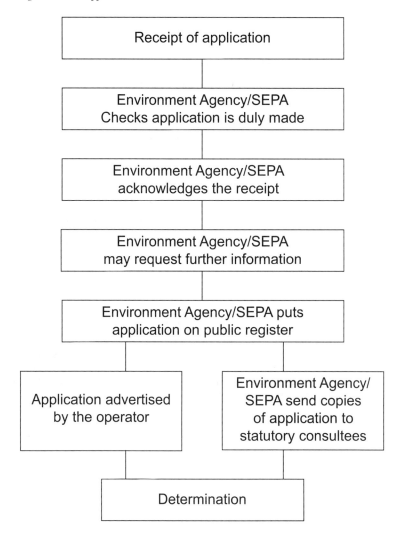

*Determination of an application*

E5052      Once the application has been submitted, the regulator then has four months from the date that it was received (or longer if agreed) in which to determine the application (see *figure 2 at* E5051 ABOVE). If the regulator requests additional information then the four months commences from when this is received. Commencing 14 days after submission, the applicant should publish details of the application made in one or more of the local newspapers in the area that the installation is located. Part A installations must also be published in the London Gazette. This advertisement must state where the site can be inspected and that any views on the application are to be sent to the Regulator within 28 days of the advertisement. Copies of all applications are put onto the public register. The applicant may request that certain information is excluded, the procedure for this is similar to the IPPC Application.

> Within 14 days of receiving the application, the regulator should distribute copies to all the statutory consultees:
>
> • The Health and Safety Executive;
>
> • The Health Authority in which the installation is situated;
>
> • The Nature Conservancy Council for England/Scottish Natural Heritage;
>
> • Any other persons at the Secretary of State; and
>
> • The local authority in which the application is situated;
>
> • In Scotland, the harbour authority.

Part A installation applications should also be distributed to:

• Minister of Agriculture, Fisheries and Food;

• Sewerage undertaker, Harbour Authority as appropriate;

• The relevant planning authority (for applications involving waste management activity); and

• The Environment Agency (for A2 applications) or the local authority (for A1 applications).

When the application includes off-site conditions then the Regulator should consult the owner, lessee, or occupier of the land and 28 days is allowed for representations.

The Secretary of State (or the Scottish Ministers) has (or have) the right to call upon any applications for determination. In these cases the regulator should inform the applicant of any representations that were received. Proceeding this the applicant and the regulator can request a hearing which should be made in writing within 21 days of being informed. These applications are then considered by the Secretary of State (or Scottish Ministers), who then directs the regulator as to whether a permit should be granted, and if so with what conditions.

When the Secretary of State (or the Scottish Ministers) is (or are) concerned that an installation will have significant negative effects on the environment of another Member State, then a copy of the permit application is sent to the Member State concerned to enable bi-lateral consultations to take place. Another Member State can also follow this procedure where they are likely to be significantly effected. This should be done as soon as the application is advertised. The four month period of determination does not begin until the consultations have been completed.

*Permits*

E5053    One permit can cover more than one installation, as long as these installations are on the same site, and are operated by the same operator. Therefore a single application can be used if the operator meets these requirements. If this is done then a single submission should be made comprising of separate completed application forms for each installation, with appropriate cross referencing on common elements (e.g. site management and condition).

When determining an application, it must be taken into account whether the applicant will operate the installation in accordance with the permit and any conditions that are attached. These all ensure that the installation will be operated so that there is no significant pollution, and that all preventative measures are taken. It is implied that operators should use the BATs to prevent or reduce the emissions. For Part A installations, the conditions should also ensure:

(i) energy is used efficiently;

(ii) waste production is avoided;

(iii) measures are taken to prevent accidents;

(iv) transboundary pollution is minimised;

(v) protection of soil and groundwater, and appropriate management of waste; and

(vi) suitable emissions monitoring equipment is in place.

The Scottish Draft Regulations also refer to the following condition:

(vii) setting out the steps to be taken prior to the operation of the installation and after the final cessation of operations.

If a permit is granted then suitable conditions like the size of the emission limit values will be included for the pollutants that are likely to be emitted in significant quantities. These are based on the BATs and, in the case of Part A installations, will take into account pollution to other environmental media. These should ensure that there is no breach of the environmental quality standards that are set by the EU. The Environment Agency may also require that the installation is operated in specific ways, for example by referring to the proposals that were made in the permit application on any subsequent occasions.

When setting a condition which regulates a discharge to water from an A2 installation, the local authority must have regard for any notice from the Environment Agency which specifies an emission limit value, and they may not include a less stringent value. They may however include a stricter one.

For the aspects of the installation that are not regulated by specific conditions, the PPC Regulations impose an implied permit condition requiring the operator to use BAT to prevent and reduce emissions (often referred to as 'residual BAT').

The operator must comply with the conditions of the permit, submitting monitoring data of appropriate quality to demonstrate this. The Environment Agency may also carry out inspections taking various actions to enforce compliance. These include serving enforcement notices, suspending operation, bringing prosecutions and, in rare cases, revoking the permit.

If the operator receives a permit then they are responsible for the obligations arising under it (including the payment of fees) until the Environment Agency or SEPA accepts the transfer of the permit to another operator, accepts the surrender of the permit, or revokes the permit.

Permits are to be periodically reviewed, especially when the BATs make further reductions feasible (with no extra cost) in a situation where, for instance:

*(a)*    there has been significant pollution from an installation and the emission limits need to be reviewed; or

*(b)*    a change in technique is needed to operate safely.

This may lead to a variation of the permit conditions. Guidance notes published by the Environment Agency set out the normal review periods that are appropriate for installations in each sector. Powers are granted to the Scottish Ministers to issue guidance to SEPA in respect of carrying out any of their functions under the Regulations.

*Fees*

E5054    The Environment Agency and SEPA recover the costs of granting and ensuring compliance with environmental licences by charging the applicant. Charges are in accordance with the number of components that the process contains, and these charges are reviewed each year.

At the time of publication, no scale of fees had been published by the Environment Agency. They are expected to be slightly greater than those in effect for IPC, but not substantially so.

*Compliance*

E5055    Within IPPC an effective system of management is the key to ensuring that all the appropriate pollution prevention and control techniques are delivered reliably and on an integrated basis.

The Environment Agency strongly supports the operation of environmental management systems which will encourage the operator to look for continuous improvement of environmental performance.

*Low impact installations*

E5056    Unlike IPC, IPPC does not exempt installations from requiring a permit even though their emissions as a result of a prescribed activity are 'trivial'. Therefore it has been proposed that low impact installations have a simplified permit procedure.

For this procedure to apply, the operator would have to demonstrate, and the regulator would have to be satisfied, that the installation has only a low impact on the environment. The normal application and determination procedure still apply with permits for such installations including simplified conditions, such as:

*(a)*    operating the installation in accordance with the application, and monitoring its operation to ensure compliance;

*(b)*    reporting any releases not in accordance with the application;

*(c)*    advising if the changes are proposed to the operation of or if it is closed down or ceases to operate.

The definition of a low impact installation has been set out by the Agency, according to a set of principles relating to the quantity of emissions to air, water and land.

*PPC implementation in Scotland*

E5057    In Scotland, *all* installations are to be regulated by SEPA. Schedule 1 attached to the Scottish Regulations lists Part A activities to be regulated for IPPC and Part B activities for air pollution control only.

Applications are advertised in the Edinburgh Gazette, as distinct from the London Gazette.

The draft states that the operation of the Regulations will be monitored on an ongoing basis. There will also be a formal review of the operations of the new arrangements after five years.

*Northern Ireland*

E5058    The introduction of IPPC to Northern Ireland has not yet been considered formally. It is only recently that IPC has been adopted, through the *Industrial Pollution Control (Northern Ireland) Order (SI 2777)* on 26 November 1997. There are three tiers of control in the Northern Ireland version of IPC:

1.    'integrated central control': Part A processes with high pollution potential are regulated for IPC by the Industrial Pollution and Radiochemical Inspectorate ('IPRI') within the DOE (Northern Ireland);

2.    'restricted central control': Part B processes with the potential to cause serious air pollution are be regulated for air pollution control, through the IPRI:

3.    'local control': Part C processes with significant but lesser potential for air pollution are regulated by district councils.

## IPC and its residual role

E5059    Although it is the clear intention that IPPC will replace IPC, there will be an inevitable period of transition (2000 – 2007), in which industrial processes will continue to be regulated by IPC (and LAPC in the case of Part B processes). The introduction of IPPC for existing processes will be accomplished through a timetable, conforming to the issue of BREF Notes. The Environment Agency and SEPA will seek to apply IPPC to industrial sectors one at a time, until all have an IPPC permit by 2007. So, for example, the cement and lime industry is the first to have to apply for IPPC permits, whereas organic fine chemicals are last on the timetable, as currently envisaged.

Until a permit for IPPC can be applied for and granted, it follows that industrial processes can only be regulated by IPC. The IPC Regulations and philosophy provides a good platform for the transition to IPPC, but there are differences. Not only does IPPC encompass more types of industrial activity, a greater number of processes overall and more environmental aspects than IPC, it also uses different terminology and has some important differences in approach. Some of these are listed below:

●    an IPC licence is referred to as an 'authorisation' to operate, as distinct from a permit. The process of obtaining and maintaining an authorisation is similar to that described above for an IPPC permit.

●    IPC applies to a site, typically. Its philosophy is one of preventing or minimising releases through an imaginary envelope at the site boundary to the external environment. IPPC relates to an installation, which could be an integral part of an overall industrial site, and takes a more holistic view of environmental issues.

●    IPC made use of the BATNEEC concept. This has disappeared from IPPC legislation, although the BAT concept does incorporate the economic component.

Obtaining a new authorisation to operate under IPC should be an unlikely requirement, as new processes will be brought into the IPPC regime immediately – although how this will work in practice, given the absence of some of the key BREF Notes, is unclear.

Current guidance from the DETR is that existing processes can still apply for a 'variation' to their current IPC authorisation, provided that the changes are positive with respect to environmental impact. Should the change be a negative one, however, then an IPPC permit will have to be applied for.

The fees which applied to IPC for 1999/2000 are set out in the Environment Act Charging Scheme 1999.

*Application for fees for IPC*

**E5060**

| Description | Fee | Notes |
|---|---|---|
| Application fee | £5,074 (per component) | |
| | (staged application £1,125 per day) | |
| Subsistence charge | £2,307 (per component) | This is payable annually, covering the cost of inspection, monitoring and enforcement. |
| Substantial variation fee | £1,699 | |

The cost of any routine monitoring is charged monthly in arrears to the operator, and reactive monitoring is covered by the subsistence charge. If the operator withdraws an application within 56 days of receipt from the Environment Agency then the fee will normally be refunded, however the Agency retains the right not to do so.

In August 1999 the Environment Agency published proposals for an interim charging scheme. This is to run from 31 October 1999 to 31 March 2001. During this time a new scheme will be developed for introduction from 1 April 2001. Installations with a low impact on the environment benefit from a reduction in charges. The final consultation of the Scottish regulations states that due to respondents making representations against the proposals issued separately by SEPA for an interim charging scheme for Part A installations, the Scottish Executive has asked SEPA to review the proposals. The interim charging scheme will need to have been approved by both the Treasury and the Scottish Ministers by the time the Regulations are in force.

*Public registers*

**E5061**    Registers of IPC have been established containing information to be maintained by the enforcing authorities. The following documentation is to be placed in the register:

- application for authorisation, and information relating to the application requested by the enforcing authority;

- a copy of the advertisement relating to the application and representations made on response to the advertisement;

- authorisations and their conditions;

- written notice of transfer authorisation to another person;

- any notices issued, or notification of withdrawal;

- any documentation relating to an appeal;

- details of convictions in relation to carrying on of a process with or without authorisation;

- monitoring data collected by the enforcing authority or data that has been submitted by an operator as a condition of the authorisation, where this information has been omitted because of commercial confidentiality, the enforcing authority should put a statement on the register which confirms the compliance or otherwise with the relevant condition of the authorisation;

- any information given to the enforcing authority after 1 April 1996 in compliance with a condition of authorisation, variation, enforcement or prohibition notice;

- reports by the enforcing authority which relate to the environmental consequences of a prescribed process in the locality of premises where the prescribed process is carried on under authorisation; and

- directions from the Secretary of State.

Exclusion of data on the grounds of commercial confidentiality lasts for four years, and after that it is added to the register unless a further four year exclusion is applied for and agreed. The Local Authorities in England and Wales have copies of entries relating to IPC processes in their areas in the registers, and they also maintain registers for air pollution processes – Part B processes – under their control. In Scotland SEPA will have information in respect of Part B processes.

Applications for an authorisation or variation which have been advertised in a paper should be put on the register within 14 days of receipt by the enforcing authority.

Information is removed from the register in the following circumstances:

- withdrawal of application for authorisation prior to determination. All documents are to be removed not less than two months, but within three months after the date of the withdrawal;

- if a process ceases to be a prescribed process, all documents are to be removed not less than two months but within three months of the date on which the process ceases to be prescribed;

- monitoring information relating to a process – four years after entering in the register; and

- information relating to a process that has been superseded – four years after the later information has been entered in the register.

Public registers have proved to be a powerful tool in enforcing the Regulations, as the operators are exposed to scrutiny.

## The Clean Air Act 1993

E5062    The IPPC legislation, and its predecessors IPC and LAPC, probably account for some 20,000 individual industrial processes. For those industrial processes which are not considered to be sufficiently polluting to warrant inclusion, it may be that other Regulations still apply to their activities. This is particularly true of processes which require the burning of fuel or waste. Historically, the *Clean Air Acts* of *1956* and

*1968* were concerned very much with the control and reduction of smoke, largely through the burning of coal. These Acts, and other clean air legislation such as the *Control of Pollution Act 1974* and the *Control of Pollution Act 1989* have been consolidated in the *Clean Air Act 1993*.

There are three parts to this Act which are relevant:

1.   *Part I: dark smoke*

   Prohibition of dark smoke from chimneys and from industrial or trade premises.

2.   *Part II: smoke, grit, dust and fumes*

   The Regulations control the emissions of particles emitted from furnaces and boilers. Direction is also given on the height of chimneys.

3.   *Part V: Information about air pollution*

   Regulations grant Local Authorities the power to provide information on emissions from specified premises, or to enter premises and make measurements.

### Statutory nuisance

E5063   Air pollution control legislation has been rooted historically in the concept of nuisance to humans, rather than harm to the environment. The causes of such nuisance have traditionally been the burning of fuel or waste materials, giving rise to 'fumes' and 'smoke'. Odour is another form of nuisance.

The main legislation relating to nuisance is now in the *Environment Protection Act 1990, Part III* as amended by the *Noise and Statutory Nuisance Act 1993*. It enables Local Authorities and individuals to secure the abatement of a statutory nuisance.

A nuisance is defined by the legislation, although only parts of the definition relate to air pollution. Others relate to noise and the state of premises which might be 'prejudicial to health'. In essence a nuisance can arise because of smoke or gases emitted from either private or business premises which are prejudicial to health or are a nuisance. A distinction is made between private dwellings and industrial premises in terms of the emissions. Private dwellings are exempt from causing a nuisance through emissions of 'dust, steam, smell or other effluvia'.

In effect, industrial premises currently regulated by IPC and LAPC are not likely to be prosecuted through the statutory nuisance legislation. Such action can only be taken with the consent of the Secretary of State. If a nuisance is reported, it is more likely that action will be taken by the appropriate regulatory authority.

The legislation also allows for exemption in the case of some specific cases, e.g. steam railway locomotives, recreational steam vessels and steam driven road vehicles.

### Air quality standards and guidelines

*Background*

E5064   For much of the twentieth century, UK air pollution control was exercised purely by reference to emissions, especially for industrial air pollution. Only in the 1990s did any concept of effects-based policies begin to emerge. This came about partly because European Community directives on air quality for pollutants such as $SO_2$ and $NO_2$ had been adopted, but also because the then Department of the Environment promoted such policies. In the acid rain debate, the effects were very much the start point for framing policies to reduce damage and the concept of a 'critical load' was used to define the extent of environmental damage. The trans-boundary issues were the dominant issue in air pollution policy debates in the 1980s, but subsequently interest in urban air quality and human health was re-awakened. No assessment of impacts in this topic can be made without reference to threshold concentrations at which health effects occur.

At present, it can be said with some justification that air quality standards are one of the primary regulatory influences on industry, transport and other emitters. For the UK, the main originators of air quality guidelines are the World Health Organisation and the DETR's Expert Panel on Air Quality Standards. These bodies are responsible for recommending guidelines on air quality that represent concentrations at which the most sensitive members of the population will be protected from the damaging effects of air pollutants. For most pollutants, it is possible to decide upon a threshold concentration below which no effects are discernible. For some pollutants, e.g. carcinogens, it is theoretically possible to see an effect right down to near zero concentrations.

A most important point to recognise is that air quality guidelines have no legal standing. They do provide the basis, however, for governments and the European Commission to develop standards. Usually, such standards reflect a degree of 'economic dilution' and the fact that it is rarely possible to achieve a target concentration for 100% of the time. It is more normal to permit a certain number of occasions on which a threshold value may be exceeded. For example, the UK Government in its 1997 version of the air quality strategy proposed that the 24 hour average value of inhalable particulate matter could be exceeded on several days in a year specifically to allow for national festivities, i.e. 'Bonfire Night'.

Different pollutants require different periods of time over which they should apply, depending on the health effect. Sulphur dioxide, for example, provokes a reaction in the human respiratory system over 10-15 minutes. Therefore, it is the short term peak fluctuations of $SO_2$ that need to be regulated. Lead, on the other hand, has an effect over a long period of time, as it accumulates in the human body. In this case, it is the annual average concentration of airborne lead which is the appropriate measure.

The multiplicity of ways in which air quality standards are expressed makes them rather confusing for those unfamiliar with the subject. In essence, however, they fall into two broad categories; those with averaging periods over a year and those with averaging periods over a short period of time, a day or less. The latter often have some expression of the number of occasions for which the threshold concentration may be exceeded. This is frequently described in terms of a 'percentile concentration'. For example, the most recent European Union Directive for $NO_2$ ambient concentrations specifies that the hourly concentration of 200 $\mu g\ m^{-3}$ should not be exceeded more than 18 times per year. A total of 18 hours represents 0.2% of the year. Hence, the standard can be expressed in an alternative manner as 200 $\mu g\ m^{-3}$, as the 99.8[th] percentile concentration.

### World Health Organisation

The World Health Organisation ('WHO') formally produced a set of air quality guidelines for Europe in 1987. This was a much referenced document, despite having no legal status. The WHO began to revise these guidelines in the early 1990's and has produced a revision in draft form in 1995. Unfortunately, a formal publication is still awaited.

The most recent WHO recommended air quality guidelines are used as a basis for setting standards in EU directives, and were also taken into account by the UK

Expert Panel on Air Quality Standard when making recommendations for UK air quality standards. The table below at E5066 shows WHO air quality guidelines. The table below at E5068 shows the standards and guidelines that the UK has adopted to meet with the Directive.

*WHO air quality guidelines*

E5066

| Substances | Time-weighted average | Averaging time |
|---|---|---|
| nitrogen dioxide | 200 μg m-3 | 1 hour |
| | 40 μg m-3 | annual |
| ozone | 120 μg m-3 | 8 hours |
| sulphur dioxide | 500 μg m-3 | 10 m10).ins |
| | 125 μg m-3 | 24 hour |
| | 50 μg m-3 | annual |
| carbon monoxide | 100 mg m-3 | 15 mins |
| | 60 mg m-3 | 30 mins |
| | 30 mg m-3 | 1 hour |
| | 10 mg m-3 | 8 hours |
| lead | 0.5 μg m-3 | annual |
| cadium | 5x10-3 μg m-3 | annual |
| mercury | 1.0 μg m-3 | annual |

In addition to the guidelines expressed as a threshold concentration, guidelines are also given as risk factors for exposure to carcinogens such as benzene and benzo(a)pyrene. The WHO also state that they are unable to set a threshold concentration as a guideline for exposure to inhalable particulate matter ($PM_{10}$).

*Air quality standards in the UK*

E5067

The most recent version of the Air Quality Strategy (see E5069 below), and the Regulations which have been passed subsequently, incorporate the EU directives on ambient air quality standards for the relevant pollutants.

These are summarised below at E5068.

*Summary of the objectives in the 2000 Air Quality Strategy*

E5068

| Pollutant | Concentration | Measured as | Date to be achieved by |
|---|---|---|---|
| Benzene | 16.25 μg m-3 | running annual mean | Dec 31, 2003 |
| 1,3-Butadiene | 2.25 μg m-3 | running annual mean | Dec 31, 2003 |
| Carbon monoxide | 11.6 mg m-3 | running 8 hour mean | Dec 31, 2003 |
| Lead | 0.5 μg m<br>30.25 μg m-3 | annual mean<br>annual mean | Dec 31, 2004<br>Dec 31, 2008 |

| Pollutant | Concentration | Measured as | Date to be achieved by |
|---|---|---|---|
| Nitrogen Oxide | 200 µg m-3 | 1 hour mean not to be exceeded more than 18 times a year. | Dec 31, 2005 |
| | 40 µg m-3 | annual mean | Dec 31, 2005 |
| Particles (PM10) | 50 µg m-3 | 24 hour mean not to be exceeded more than 35 times a year. | Dec 31, 2004 |
| | 40 µg m-3 | annual mean | Dec 31, 2004 |
| Sulphur dioxide | 350 µg m-3 | 1 hour mean not to be exceeded more than 24 times a year. | Dec 31, 2004 |
| | 125 µg m-3 | 24 hour mean not to be exceeded more than 3 times a year. | Dec 31, 2004 |
| | 266 µg m-3 | 15 minute mean not to be exceeded more than 35 times a year. | Dec 31, 2005 |

Notice that the UK standards have been expressed as 'objectives', with a target date by which these objectives are attained.

## The Air Quality Strategy ('AQS')

**E5069**    The AQS for England, Wales, Scotland and Northern Ireland describes the policies by which air quality will be improved. As noted above, it gives objectives for eight priority pollutants, in terms of achieving compliance with air quality standards. These are now based on the implementation of the EU directives. The strategy describes the current and future concentrations of the eight pollutants, providing a framework to help everyone to identify what they can do to help reduce emissions.

The AQS fulfils a requirement under the *Environment Act 1995*, setting out policies for managing ambient air quality. A national air quality strategy was first published in March 1997, with the first review taking place in 1998. The government consulted on its revised proposals in January 1999. It is an intentional feature of the strategy that it should be reviewed and revised at intervals.

The AQS identifies the need to work at international, national and local level to achieve the objectives. This strategy is essential to anybody interested in achieving the objectives of the directives, not just those who are responsible for them. The strategy has five guiding principles:

● the best practicable protection to human health and the environment;

● the expert panel on AQS recommendations should be the basis for objectives except where an objective derives from an air quality daughter directive limit value based on WHO guidelines;

● it should allow the UK to comply with EU daughter directives, but allow for stricter national objectives for some pollutants;

- objectives should reflect the practicability of the measures needed to reduce pollutants, their costs and benefits and other social and economic factors; and

- objectives should take into account EU legislation and scientific advances.

## Local air quality management

E5070    Local Authorities have a major role to play in delivering cleaner air. They are responsible for land-use planning and traffic management, and for controlling industrial pollution sources through the local air pollution control ('LAPC') regime, using action plans. Local Authorities have a long history of local environmental control. They have responsibilities in controlling:

- industrial pollution;

- local pollution hotspots under Local Air Quality Management ('LAQM'); and

- pollution from domestic sources.

In England and Wales the LAPC control certain industrial processes, in Scotland SEPA, and in Northern Ireland the Industrial Pollution and Radiochemical Inspectorate control the equivalent. Air quality has been given increased consideration more recently when they fulfil their strategic planning and transport roles. This has been a natural progression for Local Authorities.

Local Authorities are not obliged to prepare a local air quality strategy. The Environment Agency and other authorities are encouraged to work together by the government. All other authorities are encouraged to develop their own strategies, and are provided with advice. Under the new IPPC system most of the processes regulated under LAPC will be subject to control of emissions only, although some will be subject to integrated control. So Local Authorities will be responsible for some integrated permitting. The LAQM action plans are the major tool for tackling pollution hotspots often caused by road and transport.

*The Environment Act 1995, Part IV* requires Local Authorities in Scotland to conduct a review of the quality of air within their area. The *Air Quality (Scotland) Regulations 2000 (SI 2000 No 97)* prescribes the relevant period for the purpose of that review *(Regulation 3)* and sets out the air quality objectives to be achieved at the end of that period *(Regulation 4 and the Schedule)*. The objectives are the same as those set out in the Air Quality Strategy for England, Scotland, Wales and Northern Ireland (SE 2000/3, January 2000) published by the Scottish Executive. Guidance entitled *'Review and Assessment: Pollutant Specific Guidance LAQM TGU'* has been issued in respect of the appropriate methodology to be used by Local Authorities in undertaking their air quality review and assessment. The Strategy and Guidance are available from the Scottish Executive, Air, Climate and Engineering Unit (Air Quality Team), Victoria Quay, Edinburgh, EH6 6QQ.

# Employees' Duties to their Employers and others

## Introduction

E10001    Personal injury in the workplace is often caused by the negligence of employees. In the vast majority of cases, the insured employer is vicariously liable for the negligent acts and so the potential liability of the employee is not considered.

The reality is that the employee owes a duty of care to his work mates in how he behaves and carries out his work. The nature and extent of those duties and the sanctions for non-compliance will be considered in this chapter.

## Statutory duties of an employee

E10002    There are various statutory duties imposed on employees which are explained in the following paragraphs.

### Health and Safety at Work etc Act 1974

E10003    *Section 7* of the *Health and Safety at Work etc Act 1974* provides that it shall be the duty of every employee while at work:

(a)    to take reasonable care for the health and safety of himself and of other persons who may be affected by his acts or omissions at work; and

(b)    as regards any duty or requirement imposed on his employer or any other person by any of the relevant statutory provisions, to co-operate with him so far as is necessary to enable that duty or requirement to be performed or complied with.

In other words, an employee (defined under the *Health and Safety at Work etc Act 1974, s 53(1)* as an individual who works under a contract of employment), must give his employer every assistance in implementing the health and safety legislation. He cannot simply rely on others to do so.

The Scottish case of *Skinner v HM Advocate [1994] SCCR 316* is a useful illustration of this point. Skinner was a gas supervisor in charge of several sites, including one where a new mains pipe was being laid on a public roadway. Although a subordinate was responsible for failing to warn the motorists of the obstruction, Skinner was convicted under *s 7*. The Court of Session held that Skinner was not merely the colleague's superior, but a supervisor of the entire site and had been put on notice of the danger at this particular location.

The nature and scope of the duty depends on the foreseeability of risk. As *Skinner* illustrates, foreseeability of risk may extend the duty beyond fellow employees to third parties.

*Section 8* of the *Health and Safety at Work etc Act 1974* imposes a more specific duty on employees. They should not intentionally or recklessly interfere with or misuse anything provided in the interests of health, safety or welfare in pursuant to any of the relevant statutory provisions.

This section is designed to prevent employees from tampering with safety equipment such as fire extinguishers, fire escapes or guards on machinery and any personal protective equipment provided.

Breach of *ss 7 and 8* do not give rise to any civil liability. It is a criminal offence punishable on summary conviction to a fine not exceeding £20,000. There is no limit to the fine which may be imposed on conviction on indictment.

An employer cannot bring a private prosecution based on these sections. The Health and Safety Executive (HSE) (or a local authority if the Regulations so provide: see *Health and Safety at Work etc Act 1974, s 18(2)*) is the sole enforcing authority. It is rare for the HSE to prosecute employees.

## Management of Health and Safety at Work Regulations 1999 (SI 1999 No 3242)

E10004 The *Management of Health and Safety at Work Regulations 1999 (SI 1999 No 3242)* expand upon *s 7 of the Health and Safety at Work Act 1974* and impose a duty on employees to use the equipment their employer provides in accordance with their training.

*Regulation 14(1)* stipulates that every employee shall use any machinery, equipment, dangerous substance, transport equipment, means of production or safety device provided to him by his employer in accordance with any training and instructions given in its use by the employer. This must be in compliance with the requirements and prohibitions imposed upon that employer by the relevant statutory provisions.

The same Regulations impose a duty on employees to be proactive in assisting their employers in identifying risks to health and safety at work.

*Regulation 14(2)* states that every employee shall inform his employer or any other employee of that employer with specific responsibility for the health and safety of his fellow employees:

(a)     of any work situation which a person with the first mentioned employee's training and instruction would reasonably consider represented a serious and immediate danger to health and safety: and

(b)     of any matter which a person with the first mentioned employee's training and instruction would reasonably consider represented a shortcoming in the employer's protection arrangements for health and safety, insofar as that situation either affects the health and safety of that first – mentioned employee or arises in connection with his own activities at work, and has not previously been reported to his employer or to any other employee of that employer.

## Manual Handling Operations Regulations 1992 (SI 1992 No 2793)

E10005 *Regulation 5* of the *Manual Handling Operations Regulations 1992 (SI 1992 No 2793)* broadly mirrors *Regulation 14(1) of the Management of Health and Safety at Work Regulations 1999 (SI 1999 No 3242)*, in providing that each employee while at work shall make full and proper use of any system of work provided for his use by his employer.

### Control of Substances Hazardous to Health Regulations 1999 (SI 1999 No 437)

E10006    *Regulation 8(2)* of the *Control of Substances Hazardous to Health Regulations 1999 (SI 1999 No 437)* stipulates that every employee shall make full and proper use of any control measure, personal protective equipment or other thing or facility provided pursuant to the Regulations. Additionally, every employee shall take all reasonable steps to ensure it is returned after use to any accommodation provided for it and, if he discovers any defect therein, shall report it immediately to his employer.

The sanction for non-compliance with the duties set out in the Regulations is a fine of £5,000 on summary conviction. The fine is unlimited on conviction in the Crown Court. Again, the HSE rarely prosecute employees.

This is not an exhaustive list of an employee's statutory duties but it encapsulates the most important provisions.

## Additional duties

E10007    The law of negligence provides that an individual owes a duty of care to others to avoid causing them foreseeable injury. The contract of employment may expressly include additional duties and responsibilities to work mates. An employer is vicariously liable for any negligent acts carried out by its employees in the course of their employment.

Much publicity has been given to stress, bullying, substance abuse and smoking in the workplace. Damages may be claimed for personal injury caused by stressful working conditions, bullying and passive smoking. It is the employer who will be the defendant. In order to avoid such claims and also claims for unfair and constructive dismissal, it is advisable to have in place policy documents addressing each of these potential problem areas. The policies should incorporate the disciplinary procedure.

## Conclusion

E10008    The most effective sanctions against employees are contained in their contracts of employment and the employer's disciplinary procedure. However, reference to the criminal sanctions set out above should be made in the course of training programmes and in policy documents.

# Employers' Duties to their Employees

## Introduction

E11001     The purpose of this chapter is to provide a brief introduction to the common law duties and statutory duties of employers towards their employees, and the consequences of any breach of those duties.

## Common law duties

### Negligence

E11002     For there to be liability for negligence, the plaintiff must prove:

—     that the defendant owed him a duty of care;

—     that the defendant acted in breach of that duty; and

—     that the breach caused loss or injury of a kind which is recoverable at law.

### *The duty of care*

E11003     The question of whether a duty of care exists can be approached in two slightly different ways, one general and the other incremental. The general approach was summarised by Lord Wilberforce in *Anns v Merton London Borough Council [1978] AC 728* when he said:

> '. . . the position has now been reached that in order to establish that a duty of care arises in a particular situation, it is not necessary to bring the facts of that situation within those of previous situations in which a duty of care has been held to exist. Rather the question has to be approached in two stages. First one has to ask whether, as between the alleged wrongdoer and the person who has suffered damage there is a sufficient relationship of proximity or neighbourhood such that, in the reasonable contemplation of the former, carelessness on his part may be likely to cause damage to the latter, in which case a prima facie duty of care arises. Secondly, if the first question is answered affirmatively, it is necessary to consider whether there are any considerations which ought to negative, or to reduce or limit the scope of the duty or the class of person to whom it is owed or the damages to which a breach of it may give rise.'

The incremental approach was set out by Lord Roskill in *Caparo Industries v Dickman [1990] 2 AC 605* when he said:

> 'Phrases such as "foreseeability", "proximity", "neighbourhood", "just and reasonable", "fairness", "voluntary acceptance of risk" or "voluntary assumption of responsibility" will be found used from time to time in the different cases. But . . . such phrases are not precise definitions. At best they are but labels or phrases descriptive of the very different factual situations which can exist in particular cases and which must be carefully examined in each case before it can be pragmatically determined whether a duty of care exists and, if so, what is the scope

> *and extent of that duty. If this conclusion involves a return to the traditional categorisation of cases as pointing to the existence and scope of any duty of care . . . I think this is infinitely preferable to recourse to somewhat wide generalisations which leave their practical application matters of difficulty and uncertainty.'*

Either approach allows the duty of care placed upon an employer to develop over time so that as new risks to an employee's health and safety are recognised the scope of the duty of care expands to include them and impose liability.

## Vicarious liability

E11004    Employers are of course sometimes personally negligent. However, in a large number of cases an employee will be injured by the negligence of his fellow employees. The concept of vicarious liability renders the employer liable for the acts of his employees carried out in the course of their employment and when not 'off on a frolic' of their own. There will be responsibility even where an employee is carrying out an authorised act in an unauthorised way or in a manner prohibited by his employer – see *Rose v Plenty [1976] 1 AER 97* where a boy was injured on a milk float in circumstances where the driver, an employee, had been forbidden to 'employ' children to deliver milk and collect empties. Similarly, in *Kay v ITW Ltd [1967] 3 AER 22* a fork-lift truck driver, finding a lorry in his way, got in and moved it – although he was not authorised to drive lorries, this act was regarded to be in the course of his employment.

Liability arises even where an employee has been grossly negligent. In *Century Insurance Co Ltd v Northern Ireland Road Transport Board [1942] 1 AER 491*, an employee of the respondent was employed to deliver petrol in tankers to garages. Whilst delivering petrol at a garage forecourt, and whilst petrol was actually being transferred from the tanker to an underground tank at the garage, the employee decided to have a smoke. Having lit a match, he then threw it away while still alight, and it landed by the underground tank. There was an explosion which caused considerable damage. It was held that the employer was liable, since the employee was doing what he was employed to do, namely delivering petrol, even though he was acting in a grossly negligent way.

In addition, where an employee gives orders to a co-employee by way of a practical joke, he is still acting in the course of employment, and the employer is liable. In *Chapman v Oakleigh Animal Products (1970) 8 KIR 1063* the plaintiff employee was told to put his hand in the nozzle of a machine to clear an obstruction. Fellow employees wanted to spray him with crushed ice out of the machine. Another employee slipped and accidentally turned on the machine. The plaintiff's hand was injured in the machine. The employer was found to be liable.

An act or omission causing injury arises during the course of employment even if committed before work starts or after it finishes, so long as it is reasonably incidental to work. As regards travelling to and from work, the rule is that an employee is acting in the course of his employment only if he is going about his employer's business at the time. In *Vandyke v Fender [1970] 2 QB 292*, men travelling to work in a car provided by their employers and paid a travelling allowance (but no wages for travelling time) were not on duty and not in the course of their employment. By contrast, an employee required by his employer to travel from his home to a place away from his usual workplace to carry out work there, and who was paid wages for the travelling time, was acting in the course of his employment while travelling (*Smith v Stages and Another [1989] ICR 272 (HL)*).

There is a considerable body of case law on vicarious liability, establishing the following:

(*a*)    an employee is acting within the course of employment even if he performs his work or a task in contravention of a statute or regulation (*National Coal Board v England [1954] 1 AER 546*);

(*b*)    an employee who takes a lunch break during the course of a journey whilst at work, is acting within the course of employment (*Harvey v RG O'Dell Ltd [1958] 1 AER 657*);

(*c*)    an employee is acting within the course of employment if injured doing something incidental to work, e.g. having a cup of tea (*Davidson v Handley Page Ltd [1945] 1 AER 255*);

(*d*)    an employee may act within the course of employment if he stays in a dangerous workplace, contrary to instructions (*Stapley v Gypsum Mines Ltd [1953] 2 AER 478* – roof of gypsum mine);

(*e*)    an employee is acting within the course of employment if he uses an uninsured private car for company business (*Canadian Pacific Railway Co v Lockhart [1942] AC 591*);

(*f*)    an employee who uses a private car rather than a company lorry on a job, is acting within the course of employment (*McKean v Raynor Bros (Nottingham) Ltd [1942] 2 AER 650*);

(*g*)    by contrast, an employee who does an unauthorised act which is not so connected with an authorised act as to be a mode of doing it, but an independent act, is not acting within the course of his employment (*Aldred v Naconco [1987] IRLR 292* where an employee pushed an unsteady washbasin against another employee who suffered back injury from turning quickly and was unsuccessful in his action for damages);

(*h*)    an employer is vicariously liable for the negligence of an independent contractor, if the latter becomes part of his workforce and causes the death of an employee (*Marshall v Sharp & Sons 1991 SLT 114*).

There is Scottish authority that an employer is not vicariously liable for sexual harassment of an employee by another (*Ward v Scotrail Railways Ltd [1999] May CL*). In this case the male employee had sent the plaintiff a letter of a sexual nature, blocked her daily route to work and swapped shifts so as to work alongside her. It was held that the male employee had not been acting within the course of his employment and was motivated purely by personal emotions. It must be doubted whether the same result would have occurred in England. It should be noted that vicarious liability for sex and race discrimination under statute is wider than at common law (see *Jones v Tower Boot [1997] ICR 254*).

## Specific duties

E11005      The classic expression of the employer's duty of care towards his employee is that the employer must provide competent and safe fellow employees, safe equipment and place of work, and a safe system of work (*Wilson v Clyde Coal Co Ltd & English [1937] 3 AER 628*). All three are ultimately only manifestations of the duty of the employer to take reasonable care to carry out his operations so as not to subject those employed by him to unnecessary risk. However, the tripartite division is a convenient way of approaching the subject. The important points to note are:

(*a*)    *Competent and safe fellow employees.* This is generally important only where the employer has been negligent in selecting staff for particular work. Thus an untrained or inexperienced employee should not be put in charge of others in the carrying out of a task beyond his capacity. The duty also extends to cover the effects of persistent practical jokers who injure their fellow employees, where such behaviour was foreseeable. Obviously a failure to train employees will also result in their not being competent.

(b)   *Safe plant and machinery and a safe place of work.* The employer is responsible for defective equipment which he has purchased and which injures his employee. The *Employers' Liability (Defective Equipment) Act 1969, s 1(1)* provides:

'Where after the commencement of this Act–

(a)   an employee suffers personal injury in the course of his employment in consequence of a defect in equipment provided by his employer for the purposes of the employer's business; and

(b)   the defect is attributable wholly or in part to the fault of a third party (whether identified or not),

the injury shall be deemed to be also attributable to negligence on the part of the employer (whether or not he is liable in respect of the injury apart from this subsection), but without prejudice to the law relating to contributory negligence and to any remedy by way of contribution or in contract or otherwise which is available to the employer in respect of the injury.'

The employer's failure to comply with the duty can take the form of a failure to provide proper equipment for the job or failure to maintain it. It can also consist of a failure to supply proper personal protection equipment.

The duty is not absolute and the employer is not liable for a latent defect due to no-one's fault which cannot be detected by reasonable examination (*Pearce v Round Oak Steel Works [1969] 1 WLR 595*)

The duty to provide *a safe place of work* extends to entrance and egress and the general condition of premises.

(c)   *Safe system of work.* This is by far the most important aspect of the employer's duty. It is also the most difficult to describe in that there are as many systems of work as there are varieties of it. Illustrations of defective systems have sometimes been set out under the following headings:

—   faulty co-ordination of departments or branches of work;

—   faulty planning for a particular task or layout of plant;

—   unsafe method of using machinery or using machinery for the wrong process;

—   not enough men for the task;

—   insufficient supervision and instruction;

—   poor communication.

To these might be added the obligation to insist that safety aids and protective clothing etc. are used, the duty to warn where the employee is exposed to a risk against which it is not practicable to protect him (see below) and the obligation to assess the risks to employees of carrying out particular tasks and operations.

A system of work is not automatically unsafe because it is potentially hazardous. In *Nilsson v Redditch BC [1995] PIQR P199* a dustman was injured by a shard of glass poking from a refuse sack. The court held that although the 'black bag' system was potentially hazardous, it was not unsafe and so the local authority did not have to replace it with the wheelie bin system.

The duties apply even though an employee:

(i)    is working away on third party premises. Here the employer remains liable for any injuries arising in connection with the system of work on the third party premises, whilst in addition the occupier will (and the employer may) be responsible for defects in the structure of the premises or in respect of any defect in plant or substances provided by the occupier for use by persons not in his employment; or

(ii)   has been hired out to another employer, but control over the job he is performing remains with his permanent employer (*Mersey Docks and Harbour Board v Coggins and Griffith (Liverpool) Ltd [1947] AC 1* where the Board hired out the services of a skilled crane driver to a firm of stevedores, and the former was held liable for injury negligently caused by the crane driver whilst working for the stevedores).

There is doubt as to how far an employer is obliged to go in protecting his employees from the criminal acts of third parties. Any employee dealing with large numbers of members of the public, especially where money is involved, could be at foreseeable risk; it is probable, therefore, that an employer will be liable if he fails to take at least the standard sensible precautions where there is foreseeable risk to the employee.

Lastly, there are a few cases indicating that an employer will in certain circumstances have a duty to protect an employee against the consequences of his own drunkenness. Thus in *Barrett v Ministry of Defence [1995] 1 WLR 1217*, it was held that while the Ministry did not owe a duty to a soldier who became drunk while off duty with others, it did however assume a duty through the soldier's colleagues' actions. The colleagues had put the collapsed claimant to bed and provided him with inadequate care thereby failing to prevent him choking on his own vomit. Similarly, where a drunken soldier fell from a lorry supplied by the Ministry there was a breach of duty as a carrier for no reward, rather than directly as employer (see *Jebson v Ministry of Defence [2001] 1 WLR 2055*).

## The standard of the duty of care and the duty to warn

E11006   The standard of care which the employer must adopt is not absolute. In *Stokes v GKN (Bolts and Nuts) Ltd [1968] 1 WLR 1776*, Swanwick J stated the law as follows:

> '. . . *the overall test is still the conduct of the reasonable and prudent employer, taking positive thought for the safety of his workers in the light of what he knows or ought to know; where there is a recognised and general practice which has been followed for a substantial period in similar circumstances without mishap, he is entitled to follow it, unless in the light of common sense or newer knowledge, it is clearly bad; but, where there is developing knowledge, he must keep reasonably abreast of it and not be too slow to apply it; and where he has in fact greater than average knowledge of the risks, he may be thereby obliged to take more than the average or standard precautions. He must weigh up the risk in terms of the likelihood of injury occurring and the potential consequences if it does; and he must balance against this the probable effectiveness of the precautions that can be taken to meet it and the expense and inconvenience they involve. If he is found to have fallen below the standard to be properly expected of a reasonable and prudent employer in these respects, he is negligent.*'

Where an employer knows that employees will be injured as a consequence of, for instance, using a particular tool, then that does not mean that he is liable even though the injury is foreseeable. Thus Mustill J in *Thompson v Smiths Shiprepairers [1984] QB 405* (a deafness case) placed the following gloss on Swanwick J's words:

> *'In the passage just cited, Swanwick J drew a distinction between a recognised practice followed without mishap, and one which in the light of common sense or increased knowledge is clearly bad. The distinction is indeed valid and sufficient for many cases. The two categories are not, however, exhaustive as the present actions demonstrate. The practice of leaving employees unprotected against excessive noise had never been followed 'without mishap''. Yet even the plaintiffs have not suggested that it was 'clearly bad'', in the sense of creating a potential liability in negligence, at any time before the mid-1930s. Between the two extremes is a type of risk which is regarded at any given time (although not necessarily later) as an inescapable feature of the industry. The employer is not liable for the consequences of such risks, although subsequent changes in social awareness, or improvements in knowledge and technology, may transfer the risk into the category of those against which the employer can and should take care. It is unnecessary, and perhaps impossible, to give a comprehensive formula for identifying the line between the acceptable and the unacceptable.'*

When a practice shifts from acceptable to unacceptable, the first obligation on an employer to do something about a particular problem will frequently be to warn an employee of risks to which his work might expose him. Thus, in a case involving Vibration White Finger (VWF), Lawton LJ stated:

> *'Generally speaking, if a job has risks to health and safety which are not common knowledge, but of which an employer knows or ought to know and against which he cannot guard by taking precautions, then he should tell everyone to whom he is offering the job what those risks are if, on the material then available to him, knowledge of those risks would be likely to affect the decision of a sensible, level headed prospective employee about accepting the offer.' (White v Holbrook Precision Castings Ltd [1985] IRLR 215 (CA)).*

There are difficulties for a plaintiff in relying on such an argument because he would have to convince the court that having received the warning he would not have taken the employment, or, if the warning was given during the employment, that he would have left it.

In *Pickford v Imperial Chemical Industries plc [1998] 3 AER 462* the defendants avoided liability for a secretary's writer's cramp after appealing to the House of Lords. It was noted that the prescribed disease A4 (cramp of the hand or forearm due to repetitive movements) is not easily identifiable or understood and, in cases such as this, great caution should be exercised in imposing on the employer a duty to warn of the risks and of the need to take rest breaks. The trend has been for the courts to insist on the need for warnings where there is a risk of harm; the conclusion of the House of Lords in this case that no warning of the risks was necessary reverses this trend where symptoms of disease are diffuse and of uncertain origin.

## Liability for industrial diseases

E11007    The consequence of the court's approach that the standard of care is not absolute has meant that liability sometimes tends to lag some way behind scientific and medical knowledge.

Whilst it has been known for hundreds of years that exposure to loud noise caused deafness, it was only in the early 1970s that liability was recognised. Likewise the first common law liability for asbestosis and mesothelioma dates back to the same time. In *Smith v P&O Bulk Shipping Ltd [1998] 2 Lloyd's Rep 81*, an employee of the defendants died from mesothelioma as a result of asbestos exposure between 1954 and 1971. It was not until 1977 when the Department of Trade issued a circular to ship-owners warning of the dangers of asbestos that a reasonable ship-owner would have been aware of the risks. The employee had retired from work before then so the claim against P&O for negligence failed.

Unlike industrial accidents, diseases arise out of the working environment and system of work and are not referable to single identifiable incidents. In many conditions the damage or injury is cumulative, extending over decades, with long latent periods. Liability may commence only after significant injury has already been caused. In deafness cases it is not uncommon for proceedings to be issued in relation to working conditions which existed as long ago as the 1950s even though liability is unlikely to commence before 1963.

The most recent cases concerning the recognition of industrial diseases involve Repetitive Strain Injury and Vibration White Finger.

Repetitive Strain Injury (RSI) is an area bedevilled by disagreement between medical experts and by confusion of terminology. The phrase Repetitive Strain Injury has been called into question as failing to describe adequately the totality of the various illnesses, and has been replaced by Work Related Upper Limb Disorders (WRULDs).

Up until 1998 most of the reported cases have generally gone against claimants' favour. For example:

*Mughal v Reuters [1993] IRLR 571*: RSI claim

Judge Prosser rejected a claim for damages for generalised RSI. On the medical evidence in front of him he found that the diagnosis was meaningless.

*Land v Volex (January 1994) (unreported)*: RSI claim

No pathology and therefore no award of damages

*Astbury v Post Office (July 1994) (unreported)*: Occupational cramp

The medical evidence was divided, but there was no pathology. None the less, the judge found that the plaintiff was suffering from occupational cramp, but that there was no liability on the part of the employer because the employer could not have foreseen the onset of this injury.

*Ball v Post Office (June 1994) (unreported)*: Upper limb disorder

The plaintiff was diagnosed as having tenosynovitis. Although the judge accepted that this condition had been aggravated by the plaintiff's work as a sorter, the employer was found not liable as there had been no evidence of any significant history of upper limb disorders amongst sorters.

*Moran v South Wales Argus (1994) (unreported)*: RSI claim

The judge accepted the defendant's view that the plaintiff had suffered no physical injury. The workstation had been poorly designed, however, and in this regard the employer was in breach of its duty of care. Yet the employer was held not to be liable, because the plaintiff had suffered no physical injury.

*Amosu and Others v Financial Times (August 1998, unreported)*: Musculo–skeletal disorder

The Financial Times avoided liability for specific musculo–skeletal disorders which were familiar in everyday practice. The judge remained unpersuaded that the plaintiffs had established that they suffered from physical problems on the balance of probabilities. 'There was a long history of outbreaks of socially determined conditions which lacked any organic cause and went back to complaints about the replacement of the quill by steel nibbed pens' from clerks in the Civil Service in the last century.

However, liability may now be established in a number of ways. The House of Lords case of *Pickford v Imperial Chemical Industries plc [1998] 1 WLR 1189* is instructive. In that case it was held that it was forseeable that secretaries would suffer from RSI if they typed for excessive hours. However, whilst this particular claimant failed because she could not demonstrate this, it is difficult to see how it would be possible subsequently to hold that the condition did not exist. Thus the court held that where there was insufficient medical evidence to show pathology, a judge was entitled to consider other evidence and in essence whether a claimant was telling the truth about the symptoms. In addition, the Court of Appeal's judgement in the same case relied upon a breach of the duty to warn as a basis for liability although the House of Lords held that this was mistaken on the facts of the case because it was not forseeable that she would suffer from RSI in any event.

The House of Lords' approach has since been followed leading to successful claims for damages against a bank concerning encoders (*Alexander v Midland Bank [1999] IRLR 464* and a legal secretary (*Gallagher v Bond Pearce [2001] LTL 25/5/2001*).

With VWF there is less medical uncertainty. Unlike RSI, it is distinct from other upper limb disorders. Like RSI, it is not susceptible to objective clinical tests. In the case of *Armstrong & Others v British Coal Corporation (1996) (unreported)* the preliminary issues to be decided were:

'*From what date, if at all, ought the defendants to have recognised:*

(i)    *that the work with the tools complained of . . . gave rise to a foreseeable risk of VWF, and*

(ii)   *that effective precautions to guard against that risk could and ought to have been taken in respect of that work.'*

The plaintiffs contended for dates in the late 1960s and early 1970s, whilst the defendants argued for a date not earlier than the commencement of proceedings.

VWF has been known since the 1900s to have been produced by the use of vibrating hand tools. As already explained, where an employer knows that employees will be injured as a consequence of, for instance, using a particular tool, then that does not necessarily mean that he is liable even though the injury is foreseeable. He will only become liable when the risk becomes something which he should and indeed could guard against.

There had never been any obvious problem with VWF amongst miners. Virtually no cases were reported to the National Coal Board's very large in-house medical service. However, in 1967 the medical service carried out a small investigation into VWF at four collieries. The survey dealt with only a tiny sample of 22 miners, but identified VWF in some 18 per cent of those surveyed. It was held that this should have tilted the balance in favour of carrying out a full survey. It was held that such a survey would have disclosed a large incidence of VWF. The judge considered that a full survey would have taken several years and decided that it would have been completed by 1 January 1973. From that date the defendants should have recognised that there was a foreseeable risk of VWF.

This did not, however, mean that they were liable at that stage. It was the answer to the second question which determined when, in Mustill J's words, the defendants should have taken steps to prevent the injuries. The judge in fact decided that there was more than one date, and that a system of warnings and routine medical examinations should have been introduced by 1 January 1975, and a job rotation by 1 January 1976. On the adaptation of tools and eradication of the jobs, the judge could make no finding other than that the date would be after 1 January 1976. The date seems to have been based:

> '. . . *on general grounds of human experience and on the basis of the defendants' strength in the market and the agreed qualities of their own research department, not on any specific scientific engineering evidence.*'

The Court of Appeal has since broadly agreed with the approach adopted by the court.

Many of the plaintiffs had received substantial vibration doses before 1975 and damages were not reduced to reflect this non-negligent exposure where the plaintiffs' symptoms first began after 1975. Only nominal deductions of about £750 each were made to reflect latent damage already sustained at the beginning of 1975.

In *Allen and Others v BREL and RFS (1998, unreported)*, Smith J held that the defendants' engineering evidence provided an adequate basis on which to apportion the injury between the pre-negligent period (up to 1976 in most cases) and the negligent period (post-1976). She did not apportion the damage on a strictly straight-line basis but took into account varying vibration exposure labels and discounted somewhat those periods of exposure where damage was symptomless. This resulted in a significant reduction in damages.

In addition, she made a finding that it would have been impossible to eradicate vibration exposure completely. A further discount in damages was made to reflect non-negligent exposure post-1976. Smith J's decision was upheld by the Court of Appeal (*(2001) LTL 23/2/2001*)).

This 'discovery' of more and more occupational diseases, giving rise to liability at common law, is likely to be a continuing process.

### Industrial diseases and third parties

E11008    An employer can in certain circumstances, and especially with regard to industrial diseases, owe a duty of care to the family of an employee.

In the case of *Hewett v Alf Brown's Transport Ltd [1992] ICR 530* the plaintiff's husband worked as a lorry driver engaged in carrying lead-contaminated waste arising from the demolition of a gas works. In a nine-month period, six individuals suffered from lead poisoning although none were drivers. The plaintiff's husband wore overalls and a mask when involved in loading the lorry, and thus avoided poisoning. The plaintiff's wife suffered lead poisoning. The judge concluded, on the balance of probabilities, that her being poisoned was a consequence of her having washed her husband's overalls.

However, the plaintiff did not succeed. The court concluded that while the defendant would otherwise have owed a duty of care, the standard of care to be adopted by a reasonable employer was in effect codified by the *Control of Lead at Work Regulations 1980 (SI 1980 No 1248)*. These required certain precautions to be adopted, including the provision of washing and changing facilities where the exposure to lead of an employee was significant. Under the definition contained in the Regulations the exposure to lead of the plaintiff's husband was not significant, and accordingly he could have brought no claim himself. As he had no right of action, the court held that the plaintiff could not 'as a matter of law' succeed.

A very similar case, which involved asbestos, was *Gunn v Wallsend Slipway & Engineering Company, The Times, 23 January 1989*. Here the plaintiff's wife was exposed to asbestos dust from washing her husband's overalls before 1965. On occasions the plaintiff's husband would return from his employer's shipyard 'white with dust'. Waterhouse J concluded that until the publication of a paper in the *Journal of Industrial Medicine* in 1965 ('the Newhouse paper') no one engaged in shipbuilding or industry generally, or having responsibilities in that field, foresaw that there was a risk of injury to a person in the plaintiff's position. The judge rejected the plaintiff's argument that it was known that those living in the vicinity of asbestos mines could develop asbestos-related diseases, or that under *Smith v Leech Brain [1962] 2 QB 405* the defendants owed a duty of care because it could be foreseen that the plaintiff would suffer some lung injury, even if it was not mesothelioma.

He said:

> *'The reality of the matter is that, on the evidence before me, no one in the industrial world before October 1965 directed his or her mind to the risk of physical injury from domestic exposure to asbestos dust, except in what I will call 'the asbestos neighbourhood cases''. In particular, no one directed his or her mind to the risk to another from an asbestos worker's person or working clothes. There was no medical literature on the subject, no warnings or guidance in industrial or official publications even hinting at the problem, and no approved practice in relation to the storage and washing of working clothes. Even if the defendants had employed appropriate medical and safety personnel, it is most unlikely that they would have become aware of the risk from domestic exposure to asbestos dust before about the end of 1965.'*

The plaintiff's claim accordingly failed.

It might therefore be expected that a date of guilty knowledge for mesothelioma caused to those who suffered heavy exposure to dust through living near an asbestos factory could be no earlier than 1960.

That is not, however, what Holland J decided in the case of *Hancock and Margereson v Turner & Newall (1995) (unreported)*.

Mrs Margereson claimed as widow and administratrix of her deceased husband. Mr Margereson had lived in the immediate vicinity of Turner & Newall's factory from his birth in 1925 until 1943, and thereafter between 1948 and 1957. He died of mesothelioma. Mrs Hancock had spent her childhood living adjacent to the factory between 1938 and 1951.

Within the factory the whole process of producing asbestos materials was carried out and inevitably produced a great deal of dust. The staple asbestos produced for much of the period was blue.

Witnesses described how children played on bales of blue asbestos at the factory loading bay, and how the dust got everywhere in the immediately adjacent houses and streets. One witness stated:

> *'I also remember that on occasions my bedroom would change colour overnight with the dust. The walls of my bedroom were supposed to be pink, but overnight it would change to blue or white depending on the dust . . . I remember dry dust and fibre all round on the streets near the factory. A lot of the time it would look like candy floss or cotton wool . . . I have seen it blow around like a snow storm.'*

The judge found that this and similar evidence was unexaggerated.

The judge also concluded that from around 1930 the defendants very well knew that exposure to asbestos within the factory was such as to injure their employees. The factory had an inadequate dust control system.

On the basis of the medical evidence the judge found that:

'1. *Neither at any material time nor now would any of the medical witnesses have foreseen asbestosis as likely to be caused by environmental exposure, that is, by exposure to asbestos dust other than within the confines of a factory workroom.*

2. *At no material time was there established a level of exposure to dust that was safe, nor one that was not dangerous.*

3. *There was then a perceived relationship between tuberculosis and asbestosis so that it was thought that anyone suffering or likely to suffer from the former condition was more at risk of contracting the latter.*

4. *As the material period progresses, the notion of a potential association between asbestosis and lung cancer developed.*

5. *At no material time was mesothelioma a concept known to medicine, neither was the potential for such being caused by lesser levels of exposure to asbestos such as could be available in the vicinity of the defendant's factory.*

6. *There is no evidence that anyone has ever contracted asbestosis by reason of environmental exposure in this country.'*

The judge then went on to consider the *Asbestos Industry Regulations 1931 (SI 1931 No 1140)*. These were absolute in their terms and effectively prohibited the exposure of workers to visible asbestos dust. They also prohibited the employment of young persons within the factory because of the perceived connection between exposure and tuberculosis and to minimise the length of exposure of employees.

The test adopted by Holland J to decide liability was:

'*Ought the defendants at any material time to have reasonably foreseen that their conduct would expose the plaintiffs to the risk of personal injury so as to come under a duty of care to them?'*

He concluded that there was no doubt that the defendants owed a duty of care to their employees. He went on:

'*If the evidence shows with respect to a person outside the factory that he or she was exposed to the knowledge of the defendants, actual or constructive, to conditions in terms of dust emissions not materially different to those giving rise within the factory to duty of care then I see no reason not to extend to that extramural 'neighbour" a comparable duty of care.'*

There were no material differences between exposure in the offices of the factory, and in the adjacent houses, between the factory yard and the outside street and this gave rise to the same foresight of potential injury to those exposed for prolonged periods.

In the light of the facts concerning the exposure of children, the judge considered that:

'. . . *no responsible contemporaneous medical opinion could have discounted the risk of injury to such children through inhalation as 'a mere possibility which would not occur to the mind of a reasonable man".'*

The injury to the plaintiffs was therefore foreseeable. Holland J was thus following the approach of Lord Ackner in *Page v Smith [1995] 2 WLR 644* where it was said in an entirely different context (a very minor road traffic accident giving rise to myalgic encephalomyelitis) that:

> *'Assuming in favour of the respondent that the circumstances of the accident were such that (1) the risk of injury by nervous shock was remote and (2) such a risk, although a possibility, would become an actuality only in very exceptional circumstances, nevertheless the risk could not be said to be so far-fetched or fantastic as to be 'a mere possibility which would never occur to the mind of a reasonable man" (per Lord Dunedin in Fardon v Harcourt-Rivington (1932) 146 LT 391 at 392). The risk was a real risk in the sense that it was justifiable not to take steps to eliminate it only if the circumstances were such that a reasonable man, careful of the safety of his neighbours, would think it right to neglect it.'*

Accordingly in the *Hancock and Margereson* case the defendants were liable because they had exposed the plaintiffs as children to asbestos dust.

The judge did not find liability on the basis that the defendants owed a duty of care to the whole area because neither of the plaintiffs fell within that category and because he envisaged:

> *'... real difficulty in holding that the defendants as factory occupiers should have anticipated such a level of inhalation at such a remove from their premises as then (that is, before knowledge of mesothelioma and the level of exposure capable of inducing such) would raise foresight of personal injury. Introduce the fact of distance and the balance of probabilities favours the defendants. The inhalation that was condemned in the 1930 Report and that founded the 1931 Regulations is a concept that was then to be readily associated with the immediate environs of this factory, but not elsewhere.'*

The Court of Appeal upheld the judge's decision in robust terms and it would appear to be only a matter of time, depending on the particular circumstances, before a spouse case succeeds.

## Liability for psychological injury

E11009     The law concerning psychological injury can be distilled into seven propositions (*per* Law Commission Consultation Paper 137, *Liability for Psychiatric Illness*). These are:

(*a*)     The plaintiff must have suffered from a recognised psychiatric illness that, at least where the plaintiff is a secondary victim, must be shock induced. The primary victim is the person who is injured as a direct result of the defendant's negligence. The secondary victim is the person who witnesses the primary victim's injury and suffers from psychiatric injury himself as a consequence.

(*b*)     It must have been reasonably foreseeable that the plaintiff might suffer a physical or psychiatric illness as a result of the defendant's negligence.

It was initially thought that the psychiatric injury itself must be foreseeable.

In *Page v Smith [1995] 2 WLR 644* the plaintiff was driving a car involved in a minor collision. No one suffered any physical injury in the accident. The plaintiff had suffered from chronic fatigue syndrome ('CFS') on an intermittent basis for some 20 years. It was alleged that his condition had become chronic and permanent as a result of the collision. Understandably, perhaps, the defendants seem to have been most reluctant to pay the plaintiff any compensation.

Otton J at first instance found that it was foreseeable that such an accident could cause CFS. The Court of Appeal, however, held that it was not foreseeable that a person of ordinary fortitude would have suffered any psychiatric illness as a result of the accident.

In the House of Lords, Lord Lloyd stated the majority view that, where the plaintiff was the primary victim, foreseeability of physical injury was enough to enable the plaintiff to recover damages for psychiatric injury. He said:

'It could not be right that a negligent defendant should escape liability for psychiatric injury just because, although serious physical injury was foreseeable, it did not in fact transpire.'

'Since liability depends on foreseeability of physical injury, there could be no question of the defendant finding himself liable to all the world.'

'Nor in the case of a primary victim is it appropriate to ask whether he is a person of "ordinary phlegm". In the case of physical injury there is no such requirement. The negligent defendant, or more usually his insurer, takes his victim as he finds him.'

'In claims by secondary victims the law insists on certain control mechanisms, in order as a matter of policy to limit the number of potential claimants. Thus, the defendant will not be liable unless psychiatric injury is foreseeable in a person of normal fortitude.'

'In an age when medical knowledge is expanding fast, and psychiatric knowledge with it, it would not be sensible to commit the law to a distinction between physical and psychiatric injury, which may already seem somewhat artificial, and may soon be altogether outmoded.'

*Page v Smith* has since been followed in *Giblett v P & NE Murray Ltd [1999] The Times 21 May*. There the trial judge had erred in holding that cessation of sexual activity as a consequence of a car accident which caused whiplash was not foreseeable. The Court of Appeal held that the correct test was to determine whether, on balance of probabilities, the accident caused or materially contributed to the development, or increased the duration, of a pre-existing psychiatric illness. The plaintiff had only to show that her physical or psychiatric injury was reasonably foreseeable and that negligence had caused her injury. On the facts she failed because there was no proved causal link between the accident and the cessation of sexual activity.

Thus with the primary victim there is need only to foresee the risk of personal injury in order to be able to claim damages for psychiatric injury. Only in the case of the secondary victim is there any requirement that it must be reasonably foreseeable that mental injury will result.

(*c*)     The plaintiff can recover damages if the foreseeable psychiatric illness arose from a reasonable fear of immediate physical injury to himself. An employee who is put in fear for his own physical safety but escapes with only mental injury will be able to recover damages. Psychiatric harm suffered by an employee as a result of witnessing the electrocution of a fellow employee who was working close by so that he was lucky not to have been electrocuted himself may fall within the ambit of this proposition (see *Young v Charles Church (Southern) Ltd (unreported, May 1997, Court of Appeal)*.

(*d*)   Where the defendant has negligently injured or imperilled someone other than the plaintiff, and the plaintiff, as a result, has foreseeably suffered a shock-induced psychiatric illness, the plaintiff can recover if he can establish the requisite degree of proximity in terms of:

   (i)   the class of persons whose claims should be recognised, and

   (ii)   the closeness of the plaintiff to the accident in time and space, and

   (iii)   the means by which the shock is caused.

In respect of the class of persons, those with a tie of love and affection to the primary victim are included. This will normally include parents and their children, but not, it seems, siblings. Rescuers and those who are involuntary participants are included, but mere bystanders are not.

There is no special category for professional rescuers such as the emergency services. Where such employees are secondary victims they will be able to claim only if they otherwise satisfy the tripartite test (*Frost v Chief Constable of South Yorkshire Police [1997] 1 WLR 1194*).

The requirement for closeness as to time and space includes coming on the immediate aftermath. The perception must be through one's own unaided senses. This was broadly confirmed in *Alcock v Chief Constable of South Yorkshire Police [1992] 1 AC 310*. There it was held by the House of Lords that the Chief Constable was entitled to rely on the television companies complying with their own codes of practice and not broadcasting pictures which contemporaneously showed the suffering of recognisable individuals. Leading counsel for some of the plaintiffs indeed accepted that had such pictures been shown there would have been a *novus actus interveniens*.

Lord Nolan and Lord Ackner, however, both foresaw circumstances in which it would be possible to claim on the basis of television pictures transmitted live. It can only be a matter of time before such claims are successfully made.

(*e*)   Where the defendant has negligently damaged or imperilled property belonging to the plaintiff, and the plaintiff as a result has suffered a psychiatric illness, it would appear that in certain circumstances the plaintiff can recover.

(*f*)   It is unclear whether there can be liability for the negligent communication of news to the plaintiff which has foreseeably caused him to suffer psychiatric illness.

(*g*)   There are miscellaneous cases where the primary victim can recover, particularly involving employees who have suffered stress at work as in *Walker v Northumberland County Council [1995] 1 AER 737*.

The first English case indicating an expansion of the previously perceived boundaries of the employer's duty of care to his employee came in *Johnstone v Bloomsbury Health Authority [1992] QB 333*.

In that case a junior hospital doctor alleged that he had suffered from depression because he had been required to work excessive hours. His contract of employment enabled his employers to require him to work 48 hours per week on average. In fact he worked for up to 100 hours per week, and on at least one occasion worked for 36 hours with only 30 minutes' sleep.

Although the doctor's contract of employment would have ostensibly enabled his employer to require him to work such hours, so long as on some kind of average calculation he did not work more than 48 hours per week, the Court of Appeal held that the employer's ability to require him to work overtime must be exercised reasonably and hence with proper regard to the employee's health. The claim was settled, before its merits could be decided one way or another, for a sum in the region of £5,000.

The case of *Walker* re-emphasised the existence of an employer's duty of care to his employees not to cause them psychiatric injury through stress. Mr Walker was employed by the defendants as an area social services officer which was a middle manager position. In that role he had to deal with an increasing number of child care problems which were by their very nature extremely stressful. There was plainly too much work and in November 1986 Mr Walker suffered a nervous breakdown.

He was away from work until March 1987. When he returned he was promised additional support which did not materialise. Indeed the amount of work had increased while he had been away and perhaps inevitably he suffered a second nervous breakdown in September 1987. He was unable to return to work again.

Colman J commented:

> 'There has been little judicial authority on the extent to which an employer owes to his employees a duty not to cause them psychiatric damage by the volume or character of the work which the employees are required to perform. It is clear law that an employer has a duty to provide his employee with a reasonably safe system of work and to take reasonable steps to protect him from risks which are reasonably foreseeable. Whereas the law on the extent of this duty has developed almost exclusively in cases involving physical injury to the employer as distinct from injury to his mental health, there is no logical reason why risk of psychiatric damage should be excluded from the scope of an employer's duty of care or from the co-extensive implied term in the contract of employment. That said, there can be no doubt that the circumstances in which claims based on such damage are likely to arise will often give rise to extremely difficult evidential problems of foreseeability and causation. This is particularly so in the environment of the professions, where the plaintiff may be ambitious and dedicated, determined to succeed in his career in which he knows the work to be demanding, and may have a measure of discretion as to how and when and for how long he works, but where the character or volume of the work given to him eventually drives him to breaking point. Given that the professional work is intrinsically demanding and stressful, at what point is the employer's duty to take protective steps engaged? What assumption is he entitled to make about the employee's resilience, mental toughness and stability of character, given that people of clinically normal personality may have a widely differing ability to absorb stress attributable to their work?'

The judge held that in assessing an employer's conduct the law calls for no more than a reasonable response to the danger which is being guarded against. He stated that what is reasonable depends on the nature of the relationship, the magnitude of the risk of injury which was reasonably foreseeable, the seriousness of the consequences for the person owed the duty, and the cost and practicability of preventing the risk.

Colman J decided that the case turned on the question of:

> '. . . whether it ought to have been foreseen that Mr Walker was exposed to a risk of mental illness materially higher than that which would ordinarily affect a social services middle manager in his position

with a really heavy workload. For if the foreseeable risk were not materially greater than that, there would not, as a matter of reasonable conduct, be any basis upon which the council's duty to act arose.'

He decided that as there was no prior indication that the stress Mr Walker underwent before his first illness would cause such an illness there was no liability for it. However, the first illness made the second entirely foreseeable and hence the council was found to be liable.

Since then, there have been several out-of-court settlements by local authorities (see *Ratcliff v Pembrokeshire County Council (1998) (unreported)*, where a deputy teacher in a primary school who alleged he had suffered two nervous breakdowns after being bullied by the headmistress received a £100,000)

In many ways *Walker* raises more questions than it answers. The employer could presumably have dismissed Mr Walker after the first illness and avoided any possibility of paying damages beyond wages for the period of notice.

### Contributory negligence and causation

E11010    The employee is under a duty of care not to injure himself. The defence of *volenti non fit injuria* is generally unavailable, that is the employer cannot say he is not liable because the employee has voluntarily accepted a risk of injury in carrying out a particular task.

An employee's damages will be reduced to the extent that he can be shown to have been contributorily negligent. However, what would otherwise be the effect of such negligence is mitigated by the attitude of the law which excuses an employee's inadvertence. Thus Lord Wright said in *Caswell v Powell Duffryn Associated Collieries [1940] AC 152*:

> 'The jury have to draw the line where mere thoughtlessness or inadvertence ceases, and where negligence begins. What is all important is to adapt the standard of negligence to the facts and to give due regard to the actual conditions under which men work in a factory or mine, to the long hours and the fatigue, to the slackening of attention which naturally comes from constant repetition of the same operation, to the noise and confusion in which the man works, to his preoccupation in what he is actually doing at the cost of some inattention to his own safety.'

This approach developed as a means of preventing contributory negligence vitiating the strict civil liability placed on employers in respect of their statutory duties under the *Factories Acts*. It has, however, been of fairly general application. Mere inadvertence is therefore unlikely to be penalised although when an experienced worker chooses to step into a situation of danger he can properly be found guilty of contributory negligence (*Clemisnon v Ashley (1999) LTL 6/8/99*).

When considering contributory negligence, it is important not to confuse it with questions of causation. In *Chapman v Tangmere Airfield Nurseries Ltd (1998)* the plaintiff fell while reaching for a tomato after attempting to steady himself on a trolley which he thought was there but which had in fact run ahead on its rails. At first instance the judge held that while the defendant had been negligent in failing to ensure that the trolley did not move, there was no liability because 'but for' the plaintiff's failure to look first for the trolley there would have been no accident. The Court of Appeal held that this was an incorrect approach, and that a defendant should be held liable if the consequence of his negligence was 'a' cause of an accident, even if it was not 'the' cause of it. The only question was as to the degree of the plaintiff's contributory negligence.

# Breach of statutory duties

E11011     Various statutes impose duties on employers to look after the health and welfare of their employees. Duties are also imposed on employees to look after their work-mates' and their own health and safety.

The principal legislation is contained in the *Health and Safety at Work etc. Act 1974 (HSWA 1974)*, the *Management of Health and Safety at Work Regulations 1999 (SI 1999 No 3242)* and the *Workplace (Health, Safety and Welfare) Regulations 1992 (SI 1992 No 3004)*. These statutes and regulations set out both general duties and duties specific to particular circumstances and processes.

The *Workplace Regulations* are not examined here as they are dealt with in WORKPLACES – HEALTH, SAFETY AND WELFARE.

## Statutory duty and negligence compared

E11012     Statutory duties are distinct from common law duties but they tend to be broadly similar. Statutes and regulations generally describe the nature and scope of an employer's duty in more detail than is provided by the law of negligence. They constitute a clearer framework of what the law requires in specific circumstances.

Nevertheless, an action for breach of statutory duty involves different principles from those applicable in a negligence action. Foreseeability of injury, for example, will often be irrelevant to an action for breach of statutory duty. A person may establish liability in negligence but fail to prove a breach of statutory duty, because statutory duties tend to be strictly defined. The statutory duty may or may not require the same actions by an employer as the common law of negligence.

## Criminal sanctions

E11013     The general duties set out in *HSWA 1974* and in the *Management of Health and Safety at Work Regulations 1999 (SI 1999 No 3242)* do not confer a civil right of action for damages on an injured individual except where the person is a new or expectant mother. It is likely that an injured baby would also have a right of action.

Instead, breach of the provisions is a criminal offence rendering an employer or employee liable to prosecution. The case may be heard in the magistrates' court or the Crown Court. The penalty is a fine. The maximum fine that the magistrates can impose is £20,000. The Crown Court has unlimited powers to fine.

A statutory duty may not be delegated. An employer remains responsible for the safety of employees (and of independent contractors where they are engaged in work which forms part of the employer's undertaking – see *R v Associated Octel Co Ltd [1996] 1 WLR 1543 (HL)*) even where, for instance, outside consultants have been employed to devise and implement safety standards. If they perform their brief so that there is a breach of statutory duty, and injury results, a prosecution against the employer remains a possibility.

The employer may attempt to argue, in mitigation, that he himself was not at fault and that any fine should be reduced accordingly.

However, this approach might prove counter-productive. In *R v Mersey Docks and Harbour Company (1995) 16 Cr App R (S) 806* the Court of Appeal held that it was no mitigation to say that matters of safety were left to other people. The court should impose fines which left people in no doubt that it was their duty and they had to discharge it. In this case the employers had wholly disregarded the risk, and the steps taken to carry out its duty were superficial and inadequate.

The employer is generally a legal entity and not an individual. It has been settled since the middle of the last century that a corporate employer may be convicted for a breach of statutory duty.

Corporate criminal liability arises in respect of breaches of statutory duty because the duty imposed on the employer is non-delegable and the statute provides that breach is a criminal offence.

Under *HSWA 1974, s 37* a director, manager or other similar member of a corporation may be prosecuted personally in addition to the corporation. He will be convicted if it is proved that he consented to the commission of the offence by the corporation or if the offence is attributable to his neglect.

### Corporate manslaughter

E11014    The commission of a criminal offence generally involves two elements: a particular state of mind accompanied by a particular act.

It was formerly thought that a corporation could not commit a criminal offence because, although it was a legal entity, it had no mind or body. It is now settled that a corporation can commit a criminal offence.

In every corporation there is a mind and body in the form of its controlling or directing officers. Their acts and decisions are the company's acts and decisions.

It is a question for both the judge and the jury to decide whether an employee in a given case exercises a sufficient degree of control as to become part of the corporation. If not, he is merely the company's servant or agent as opposed to the company, and the company is unlikely to be vicariously liable for his criminal acts.

Until *P&O European Ferries (Dover) Ltd (1991) 93 Cr App R 72* it was thought that a corporation could not be convicted of an offence involving personal violence. It was argued that since 1601 authoritative books had described manslaughter as 'the killing of a human being by a human being'. The argument was rejected and it was held that an indictment for manslaughter would lie against the company allegedly responsible for the Zeebrugge disaster.

Similarly, a manslaughter prosecution against an employer might arise out of a fatal accident at work.

There are two types of manslaughter, voluntary and involuntary. Voluntary manslaughter involves an intent to kill or do serious injury with mitigating circumstances which include provocation or diminished responsibility.

Involuntary manslaughter comprises all other unlawful killings. These are divided into two categories: (i) manslaughter by an unlawful and dangerous act, and (ii) manslaughter by reckless or possibly gross negligence.

The *P&O* case fell into category (ii). At the time the test was largely one of subjective recklessness involving appreciation of an obvious and serious risk by the directing mind of the company (i.e. its directors and senior managers). One of the reasons why the prosecution failed was that there was insufficient evidence to prove that any of the individuals making up the directing mind had sufficient knowledge of the risk that a ferry might sail with its bow doors open to make them reckless. None of them knew that there had been five earlier instances of P&O ferries putting to sea with the bow doors open.

The situation was altered to an extent by the introduction of a new test in *R v Adomako [1995] AC 171*:

*'The jury will have to decide whether the extent to which the defendant's conduct departed from the proper standard of care incumbent upon him . . .was such that it should be judged criminal.'*

This injected an element of objectivity. On this test it might have been open to the jury to conclude that one of the causes of the disaster was the failure of the company to provide a safe system for the operation of ferries; and that failure fell far below what could reasonably have been expected.

However, that would not necessarily have overcome the difficulty of proving that an individual forming part of the directing mind had sufficient knowledge to mean the company was guilty. The trial judge specifically declined to adopt the aggregation principle which would have allowed the faults of a number of individuals, none whose faults were sufficient to make them guilty of manslaughter, to be aggregated so that in their totality there was such a high degree of fault that the company was guilty. The aqgregation principle was specifically rejected by the Court of Appeal in *Attorney General's Reference (No 2 of 2000) [2000] AER (D) 1717* arising out of the failed prosecution of Great Western Train Ltd for the Southall train accident.

This has meant that smaller companies with basic management structures are more likely to be convicted of an offence. Thus in *R v Kite and OLL Ltd (1994)*, both OLL Ltd and its managing director were convicted of manslaughter following the death of four youths in a canoeing accident at Lyme Regis. Given the simplicity of OLL's management structure, it was relatively straightforward to establish liability because the managing director had personal knowledge of the inadequacies of the safety systems and the consequent risks which were said by the prosecution to be 'obvious and serious'.

Since *OLL* there has been only one other successful prosecution for corporate manslaughter. This was in 1996 when Jackson Transport (Ossett) Ltd was convicted with its managing director. Whilst Jackson Transport was a larger company than OLL with approximately 40 employees, the prosecution succeeded against the company because it had a basic management structure and it was possible to identify a guilty directing mind.

In 1996, the Law Commission's Report on Involuntary Manslaughter considered the specific problems associated with corporate manslaughter. The report commented, 'the problems that confront a prosecution for corporate manslaughter explain why there has only been one successful prosecution [the report was published before the *Jackson Transport* case], . . . we have welcomed the opportunity to consider the principles of corporate liability in the light of great obstacles now confronting those wishing to bring a prosecution'.

The report's central recommendation was that there should be a new offence of corporate killing, committed where a company's conduct in causing death falls far below what could reasonably be expected. Unlike common law manslaughter it would not require the risk of death to be obvious or that the company be capable of appreciating the risk. The requirement would be for a death to have been caused by a company's failure in the way in which its activities are managed and organised.

No legislation has yet resulted although the government's white paper *Reforming the Law on Involuntary Manslaughter* (May 2000) broadly follows the Law Commission's recommendations.

## Civil liability for breach of statutory duty

E11015    A person injured in the course of employment is likely to assert that the employer was both negligent and in breach of its statutory duty. Breach of the subsidiary regulations under *HSWA 1974* and a wide variety of other regulations give rise to civil liability.

In a successful action for breach of statutory duty, the following issues will be proved.

(*a*)    The statute imposes a duty on the defendant. Occupational health and safety legislation is generally directed at the employer with a view to reducing injuries at work.

(*b*)    The defendant has failed to perform the duty. Statutory duties incorporating the word 'shall' are absolute duties unless qualified. Anything which an Act specifies shall be done must be done irrespective of any constraints imposed by particular circumstances.

If, for instance, a flywheel is insecurely fenced and injury ensues, the employer is liable even if he did everything in his power to ensure that the fencing was safe under *s 12* of the *Factories Act 1961*. It is irrelevant that fencing might make the machine unusable. A finding of negligence would be unlikely in similar circumstances.

Occupational health and safety legislation generally qualifies the absolute nature of the duty with the words 'practicable' or 'as far as is reasonably practicable.' New and recent legislation tends to use the word 'practicable'.

To do what is 'practicable' means to do what is feasible or what is capable of being done, given current knowledge, irrespective of inconvenience or difficulty. Financial considerations do not enter the equation. It may be practicable or feasible to remove an obstruction from a gangway while the duty of reasonable care in negligence requires no more than that a warning be given.

To do what is 'reasonably practicable' often involves something more than the negligence test of reasonable care. Inconvenience and expense may be taken into account and a view may be formed on whether or not the necessary time and money are proportionate to the result to be achieved. Any such computation should be made before any accident occurs and with the benefit of all available current knowledge on the level of risk and the steps possible to reduce it.

The onus of establishing that something was not practicable or reasonably practicable lies on the defence in both civil and criminal actions.

There is a substantial body of case law on the application of the practicability and reasonable practicability tests in particular circumstances.

Employers are expected to be aware of official HSE publications, including Codes of Practice. They should also keep abreast of relevant recent legislation and statutory instruments published by the Stationery Office. They should also keep abreast of current technical publications and developments potentially affecting their product and/or business.

(*c*)    The breach of duty has caused the plaintiff injury. The same principle applies as in the law of negligence: an injured person will not recover damages from the employer unless he shows that it was the employer's wrongdoing which caused or contributed to his injuries. Where an employer has been at fault but that fault has not caused any injuries, no compensation is payable.

(*d*)    The injury was of the kind envisaged by the statute. There may be difficulties in proving that the nature of the injury was of the kind envisaged by the statute if the injury occurs in an unusual way which the provision was not designed to prevent. There are a variety of cases on this point dealing with particular circumstances. The tendency of the courts is to lean in favour of compensation for injured employees.

## Defences

E11016    Contributory negligence may reduce the extent of the employer's liability in a civil action but it is rarely a complete defence. Where there is a breach of a duty imposed on the injured party personally, it is equivalent to contributory negligence.

The defence of *volenti non fit injuria* is not available in an action for breach of statutory duty.

In exceptional circumstances where the breach has occurred solely as a result of the plaintiff's conduct without any fault on the part of the defendant or anyone for whom he is responsible, the defendant will not be liable.

## Duties under the Health and Safety at Work etc. Act 1974

E11017    *Duty owed by employer to his employees.* An employer owes a general duty to his employees to ensure their health, safety and welfare at work [*HSWA 1974, s 2*].

An employer or self-employed person, save where it is an educational establishment, owes a duty to his trainees even where there is no contract of employment with the trainee (see the *Health and Safety (Training for Employment) Regulations 1990 (SI 1990 No 1380)*).

The following aspects of the duty are highlighted [*HSWA 1974, s 2(2)(a)–(e)*]:

(*a*)    the provision and maintenance of safe plant and systems of work;

(*b*)    adequate arrangements for the safe use, handling, storage and transport of articles and substances;

(*c*)    the provision of information, instruction, training and supervision necessary to ensure health and safety;

(*d*)    the maintenance in a safe condition of the place of work and access to it and egress from it; and

(*e*)    the provision and maintenance of a working environment that is safe and without health risks, including adequate arrangements for the welfare of employees while at work.

There is a duty on every employer who employs five employees or more to prepare and revise as appropriate a written statement of his general policy on the health and safety at work of his employees and the arrangements in force for carrying out that policy. The statement and any revisions should be brought to the notice of the employees. Reference may be made to any no smoking policy. [*HSWA 1974, s 2(3)*].

There is a duty to consult any safety representatives appointed by a recognised trade union on safety matters. [*HSWA 1974, 2(4)*]. This duty has recently been extended to any employees who are not members of a group covered by trade union safety representatives (see the *Health and Safety (Consultation with Employees) Regulations 1996 (SI 1996 No 1513)*).

*Duty owed by employer and self-employed to those who are not employees.* An employer owes a duty not only to his employees but also to those others who may be affected by the way he conducts his undertaking. The duty extends to members of the general public. He must ensure that their health and safety is not at risk. A self employed person owes the same duty. [*HSWA 1974, s 3(1) and (2)*].

Proof of harm is not necessary to prove a breach of this section. A risk or possibility of danger is sufficient.

*Duty owed by those with control of premises to non-employees using the premises as a place of work.* Where a person has a degree of control over premises, he owes a duty to those who use the premises as a place of work or for the use of machinery or substances to ensure that the premises and any machinery or substances in the premises are safe and without risks to health.

The duties set out above are not absolute but are qualified by the words 'so far as is reasonably practicable'.

*Duty owed by employee.* An employee owes a duty while at work to take reasonable care for the health and safety of himself and those who may be affected by his acts or omissions. He must co-operate with his employer so far as is necessary to enable him to comply with his duties. [*HSWA 1974, s 7*].

## Management of Health and Safety at Work Regulations 1999 (SI 1999 No 3242)

E11018    The regulations are a new departure in the law relating to both statutory duty and negligence. They impose a positive duty on employers to investigate the existence of possible risks to health, irrespective of whether an employer has been put on notice of any risks. The assumption is that there may be risks even if there is no evidence of any.

A failure to implement the regulations is likely to be persuasive evidence of negligence.

### Risk assessments

E11019    The purpose of the employer's assessment is to identify any measures necessary to keep his employees safe. [*Management of Health and Safety at Work Regulations 1999 (SI 1999 No 3242), Reg 3*]. The duty is likely to extend to temporary workers.

Assessments must not be confined to employees but must extend to the health and safety of any person likely to be affected by the employer's undertaking.

Self-employed persons have identical duties which encompass the assessment of any risk to which they themselves might be exposed as well as the assessment of any risk to those affected by their undertakings or businesses.

Employers who share the same workplace should co-operate with each other in assessing risks and implementing preventative measures.

An employer of five or more employees must record in writing the significant findings of any assessment. The record should identify the risk, specify the group affected and set out preventative measures taken.

The Approved Code of Practice accompanying the regulations sets out the assessment required. This is a systematic examination of the workplace, examining the hazards present and the likelihood of their arising.

A Health and Safety Executive guide sets out a simple and practical approach which every employer should take.

The assessment should address the risk of stress.

The regulations have been amended to impose a specific duty towards new and expectant mothers. Where risks to the mother or her baby cannot be avoided, the employer should alter the working conditions or hours worked 'if it is reasonable to do so'. If such an alteration is not possible, the pregnant employee should be suspended.

## Information

E11020 The employer should supply his employees with information on the risks identified. The same information should be provided to any other employer who shares the workplace. Information on risks should be provided to anyone working in the undertaking; that this duty extends to temporary workers. Employers of employees working in a host employer's undertaking must be informed of any risks and preventative measures adopted by the host employer.

An employer owes a duty to temporary workers, who are working under a fixed term contract or are employed by an agency, to provide them with comprehensible information on the qualifications or skills required to carry out the work safely and any health surveillance required to be provided [*Management of Health and Safety at Work Regulations 1999 (SI 1999 No 2051), Reg 15*]. Where temporary workers are provided by an agency, the necessary health and safety information must be provided to the agency for passing to the temporary staff. The employment agency must take all necessary steps to acquaint itself with the risks its employees will face, wherever they work, and to ensure their protection accordingly.

## Control, monitoring and review

E11021 Where preventative measures are implemented, arrangements must be made for their control, monitoring and review. The arrangements must be recorded in writing where more than five persons are employed.

## Competent assistance

E11022 Every employer, with certain limited exceptions, must appoint one or more competent persons to assist in undertaking the health and safety measures required. A competent person will have sufficient training and experience or knowledge to enable him properly to assist [*Management of Health and Safety at Work Regulations 1999 (SI 1999 No 3242), Reg 7*].

## Health surveillance

E11023 Appropriate health surveillance must be provided where risks to health and safety have been identified by the assessment [*Management of Health and Safety at Work Regulations 1999 (SI 1999 No 3242), Reg 6*].

## Duty to train employees in safe working practices

E11024 The *Management of Health and Safety at Work Regulations 1999 (SI 1999 No 3242), Regulation 13* imposes a duty on an employer to ensure that his employees are provided with adequate health and safety training. This applies both to when they are recruited and on their being exposed to any new or increased risks. Training should also be provided when new working practices are introduced.

Employers using subcontracted labour are under a duty to train and instruct subcontract personnel where there is a risk to their safety. This is part of the general duty imposed by *HSWA 1974, s 3*.

In entrusting an employee with a task the employer must take into account the person's capabilities as regards health and safety.

Employees are under a corresponding duty to act in accordance with the training given. Failure to do so can lead to prosecution and/or, more often, dismissal.

Arrangements for the provision of safety training should be included in a company's health and safety policy.

*Procedures for serious and imminent danger*

**E11025**   The employer must keep under review procedures to deal with serious and imminent danger, to appoint staff to take charge of evacuating buildings in emergencies (such as fire marshals), to take measures to prevent untrained staff from having access to places where particular hazards exist, and to permit employees to take action to save themselves (if necessary, without managerial approval) [*Management of Health and Safety at Work Regulations 1999 (SI 1999 No 3242), Reg 7*]. These procedures must be communicated to all employees [*Management of Health and Safety at Work Regulations 1999 (SI 1999 No 3242), Reg 8*].

# Damages and limitation of actions

## Egg-shell skull

**E11026**   Generally a defendant is only liable for the foreseeable loss and damage which will be caused by his negligence. However, an employer may well be liable for 'most' direct consequences, whether foreseeable or not, on the principle that a 'wrongdoer takes his victim as he finds him' (and that if he happens to have an egg-shell skull, so much the worse).

In *Smith v Leech Brain & Co Ltd [1961] 3 AER 1159* the plaintiff's husband had been a galvaniser at the defendant's factory. He suffered a burn on the lip from a splash of molten metal. The injury would not have happened if the employer had taken adequate statutory precautions. The burn led to terminal cancer, to which the deceased had a predisposition, as he had earlier worked in a gasworks. It was held that the employer was liable for the cancer. 'It has always been the law of this country that a tortfeasor takes his victim as he finds him . . . The test is not whether these defendants could reasonably have foreseen that a burn would cause cancer and that Mr Smith would die. The question is whether these defendants could reasonably foresee the type of injury which he suffered, namely, the burn' (*per* Lord Parker).

Moreover, when the act of a third person intervenes between the original act or omission (i.e. original act of negligence) and the damage, the original act or omission is still the direct cause of damage, if the intervention of the third person might reasonably have been expected: *Robinson v Post Office [1974] 2 AER 737* in which the appellant suffered a minor wound at work when he slipped on a ladder with an oily rung. He was given anti-tetanus serum and later developed encephalitis. The doctor had not followed the correct procedure for giving a test dose before administering a full dose. However, even if the test dose had been correctly given, the appellant would have shown no reaction. It was held that although the doctor had been negligent, his negligence had not caused encephalitis. The Post Office were liable for the encephalitis suffered by the plaintiff – they were bound to take the plaintiff as they found him, i.e. with an allergy to the serum.

## General and special damages

E11027    It would not be appropriate to discuss in any detail how damages for personal injury are assessed, save to say that damages are paid for pain and suffering as well as for economic losses. In the case of death the dependants are able to claim for the value of their lost dependency.

## Limitation

E11028    The standard limitation period for personal injuries is three years from when the cause of action arose. There are a variety of complicated exceptions the effect of which, *inter alia*, that claims for industrial diseases can frequently be made many years after the exposure to the substance or thing which caused the injury.

# Employers' Liability Insurance

## Introduction

E13001 Most employers carrying on business in Great Britain are under a statutory duty to take out insurance against claims for injuries/diseases brought against them by employees. When such a compulsory insurance policy is taken out the insurance company issues the employer with a certificate of insurance, and the employer must keep a copy of this displayed in a prominent position at his workplace, so that employees can see it. It is a criminal offence to fail to take out such insurance and/or to fail to display a certificate (see E13013-E13015 below); however, such a failure does not give rise to any civil liability on the part of a company director (*Richardson v Pitt-Stanley [1995] 1 AER 460*. Here the plaintiff suffered a serious injury to his hand in an accident at work, and obtained judgment against his employer, a limited liability company, for breach of the *Factories Act 1961, s 14(1)* (failure to fence dangerous parts of machinery). Before damages were assessed, the company went into liquidation and there were no assets remaining to satisfy the plaintiff's judgment. The company had also failed to insure against liability for injury sustained by employees in the course of their employment, as required by the *Employers' Liability (Compulsory Insurance) Act 1969, s 1. Sec 5* of that Act makes failure to insure a criminal offence. The plaintiff then sued the directors and secretary of the company who, he alleged, had committed an offence under *Sec 5*, claiming as damages a sum equal to the sum which he would have recovered against the company, had it been properly insured. His action failed. It was held that the *Employers' Liability (Compulsory Insurance) Act 1969* did not create a civil as well as criminal liability). These duties are contained in the *Employers' Liability (Compulsory Insurance) Act 1969* (referred to hereafter as the '*1969 Act*') and in the *Employers' Liability (Compulsory Insurance) Regulations 1998 (SI 1998 No 2573)* (referred to hereafter as the '*1998 Regulations*'). In addition, the requirements of the *1969 Act* extend to offshore installations but do not extend to injuries suffered by employees when carried on or in a vehicle, or entering or getting onto or alighting from a vehicle, where such injury is caused by, or arises out of use, by the employer, of a vehicle on the road. [*1998 Regulations, Reg 9 and Schedule 2 para 14*]. Such employees would normally be covered under the *Road Traffic Act 1988, s 145* as amended by the *Motor Vehicles (Compulsory Insurance) Regulations 1992 (SI 1992 No 3036)*. As from 1 July 1994, liability for injury to an employee whilst in a motor vehicle has been that of the employer's motor insurers.

## Purpose of compulsory employers' liability insurance

E13002 The purpose of compulsory employers' liability insurance is to ensure that employers are covered for any legal liability to pay damages to employees who suffer bodily injury and/or disease during the course of employment and as a result of employment. It is the liability of the employer towards his employees which has to be covered; there is no question of compulsory insurance extending to employees, since employers are under no statutory or common law duty to insure employees against risk of injury, or even to advise on the desirability of insurance; it is their potential legal liability to employees which must be insured against (see E13008 below). Such liability is normally based on negligence, though not necessarily personal negligence on the part of the employer. Moreover, case law suggests that employers' liability is becoming stricter. The rule that employers must 'take their victims as they find them' underlines the need for long-tail cover because the employer may find himself liable for injuries/diseases which 'trigger off' or exacerbate existing conditions. (See further E11025 EMPLOYERS' DUTIES TO THEIR EMPLOYEES.)

An employers' liability policy is a legal liability policy. Hence, if there is no legal liability on the part of an employer, no insurance moneys will be paid out. Moreover, if the employee's action against the employer cannot succeed, the action for damages cannot be brought against an employer's insurer (*Bradley v Eagle Star Insurance Co Ltd [1989] 1 AER 961* where the employer company had been wound up and dissolved before the employer's liability to the injured employee had been established) (see below for the transfer of an employer's indemnity policy to an employee). The effect of this decision has been reversed by the *Companies Act 1989, s 141*, amending the *Companies Act 1985, s 651* which allows the revival of a dissolved company within two years of its dissolution for the purpose of legal claims and, in personal injuries cases, the revival can take place at any time subject to the existing limitation of action rules contained in the *Limitation Act 1980*. For example, in the case of *Re Workvale Ltd (No 2) [1992] 2 AER 627*, the court exercised its discretion under *Sec 33* of the *Limitation Act 1980* to allow a personal injuries claim to proceed after the three-year limitation period had expired. This meant that the company could also be revived under the provisions of *CA 1985, s 651(5) and (6)* (as amended). Thus, proceedings under the *Third Parties (Rights against Insurers) Act 1930, s 1, 1(b)* may be brought in this manner.

If the employer becomes bankrupt or if a company becomes insolvent, the employer's right to an indemnity from his insurers is transferred to the employee who may then keep the sums recovered with priority to his employer's creditors. This is only so if the employer has made his claim to this indemnity by trial, arbitration or agreement before he is made bankrupt or insolvent (*Bradley v Eagle Star Insurance Co Ltd [1989] 1 AER 961*). The employee must also claim within the statutory limitation period from the date of his injury (see E13007 below for subrogation rights generally).

The policy protects an employer from third party claims; an employee as such is not covered since he normally incurs no liability. Although offering wide cover an employers' liability policy does not give cover to third party non-employees (e.g. independent contractors and members of the public). Such liability is covered by a public liability policy which, though advisable, is not compulsory.

This section examines:

—    the general law relating to contracts of insurance (see E13003–E13006 below);

—    the insurer's right of recovery (i.e. subrogation) (see E13007 below);

—    the duty to take out employers' liability insurance (see E13008–E13012 below);

—    issue and display of certificates of insurance (see E13013 below);

—    penalties (see E13014, E13015 below);

—    scope and cover of policy (see E13016–E13019 below);

—    'prohibition' of certain terms (see E13020 below);

—    trade endorsement for certain types of work (see E13021, E13022 below).

# General law relating to insurance contracts

E13003 Insurance is a contract. When a person wishes to insure, for example, himself, his house, his liability towards his employees, valuable personal property or even loss of profits, he (the proposer) fills in a proposal form for insurance, at the same time making certain facts known to the insurer about what is to be insured. On the basis of the information disclosed in the proposal form, the insurer will decide whether to accept the risk or at what rate to fix the premium. If the insurer elects to accept the risk, a contract of insurance is then drawn up in the form of an insurance policy. (Incidentally, it seems to matter little whether the negotiations leading up to contract took place between the insured (proposer) and the insurance company or between the insured and a broker, since the broker is often regarded as the agent of one or the other, generally of the proposer (*Newsholme Brothers v Road Transport & General Insurance Co Ltd [1929] 2 KB 356).*) However, a lot depends on the facts. If he is authorised to complete blank proposal forms, he may well be the agent of the insurer.

## Extent of duty of disclosure

E13004 A proposer must disclose to the insurer all material facts within his actual knowledge. This does not extend to disclosure of facts which he could not reasonably be expected to know. 'The duty is a duty to disclose, and you cannot disclose what you do not know. The obligation to disclose, therefore, necessarily depends on the knowledge you possess. This, however, must not be misunderstood. The proposer's opinion of the materiality of that knowledge is of no moment. If a reasonable man would have recognised that the knowledge in question was material to disclose, it is no excuse that you did not recognise it. But the question always is – Was the knowledge you possessed such that you ought to have disclosed it?' (*Joel v Law Union and Crown Insurance Co [1908] 2 KB 863* per Fletcher Moulton LJ).

The knowledge of those who represent the directing mind and will of a company and who control what it does, e.g. directors and officers, is likely to be identified as the company's knowledge whether or not those individuals are responsible for arranging the insurance cover in question (*PCW Syndicates v TCW Reinsurers [1996] 1 Lloyd's Rep 241*).

An element of consumer protection, in favour of insureds, was introduced into insurance contracts by the Statement of General Insurance Practice 1986, a form of self-regulation applicable to many but not to all insurers. This has consequences for the duty of disclosure, proposal forms (E13005 below), renewals and claims. In particular, with regard to the last element (claims), an insurer should not refuse to indemnify on the grounds of:

(*a*)  non-disclosure of a material fact which a policyholder could not reasonably be expected to have disclosed; or

(*b*)  misrepresentation (unless it is a deliberate non-disclosure of, or negligence regarding a material fact). Innocent misrepresentation is not a ground for avoidance of payment.

The trend towards greater consumer protection in (*inter alia*) insurance contracts is reflected in the *Unfair Terms in Consumer Contracts Regulations 1994 (SI 1994 No 3159)*. These regulations which came into force on 1 July 1995 apply in the case of 'standard form' (or non-individually negotiated) contracts. [*Reg 3*]. They:

(i)  invalidate any 'unfair terms' therein, in favour of the insured [*Reg 5*] – an 'unfair term' being one which, contrary to the requirement of 'good faith'

[*Reg 4(3), 2 Sch*], 'causes a significant imbalance in the parties' rights and obligations, to the insured's detriment' [*Reg 3, 3 Sch*];

(ii) require a written contract term to be expressed in plain, intelligible language, if there is doubt about the meaning of terminology, a construction in favour of the insured will prevail [*Reg 6*]; and

(iii) where the seller/supplier claims that a term was individually negotiated, he must prove it [*Reg 3(5)*].

Complaints (other than frivolous or vexatious ones) relating to 'unfair terms' in standard form contracts, are addressable by the Director General of Fair Trading, who may prevent their continued use. [*Reg 8*]. See also P9056 PRODUCT SAFETY.

### Filling in proposal form

E13005    Generally only failure to make disclosure of relevant facts will allow an insurer subsequently to invalidate the policy and refuse to compensate for the loss. The test of whether a fact was or was not relevant is whether its omission would have influenced a prudent insurer in deciding whether to accept the risk, or at what rate to fix the premium.

The arm of *uberrima fides* (i.e. the utmost good faith) is a long one. If, when filling in a proposal form, a statement made by the proposer is at that time true, but is false in relation to other facts which are not stated, or becomes false before issue of the insurance policy, this entitles the insurer to refuse to indemnify. In *Condogianis v Guardian Assurance Co Ltd [1921] 2 AC 125* a proposal form for fire cover contained the following question: 'Has proponent ever been a claimant on a fire insurance company in respect of the property now proposed, or any other property? If so, state when and name of company'. The proposer answered 'Yes', '1917', 'Ocean'. This answer was literally true, since he had claimed against the Ocean Insurance Co in respect of a burning car. However, he had failed to say that in 1912 he had made another claim against another insurance company in respect of another burning car. It was held that the answer was not a true one and the policy was, therefore, invalidated.

### Loss mitigation

E13006    There is an implied term in most insurance contracts that the insured will take all reasonable steps to mitigate loss caused by one or more of the insured perils. Thus, in the case of burglary cover of commercial premises, this could extend to provision of security patrols, the fitting of burglar alarm devices and guard dogs. In the case of employers' liability, it will extend to appointment or use of services of an accredited safety officer and/or occupational hygienist, either permanently or temporarily. Again, in the case of fire cover, steps to mitigate the extent of the loss on the part of the insured, might well extend to regular visits by the local fire authority and/or advice on storage of products and materials by reputable risk management consultants. Indeed, it is compliance with this implied duty in insurance contracts that accounts for the growth of the practice of risk management, and good housekeeping on the part of more and more companies.

## Subrogation

E13007    Subrogation enables an insurer to make certain that the insured recovers no more than exact replacement of loss (i.e. indemnity). 'It (the doctrine of subrogation) was introduced in favour of the underwriters, in order to prevent their having to pay more than a full indemnity, not on the ground that the underwriters were sureties, for they are not so always, although their rights are sometimes similar to those of sureties, but in order to prevent the assured recovering more than a full indemnity' (*Castellain v Preston (1883) 11 QBD 380* per Brett LJ). *Subrogation does not extend to accident insurance moneys, whereby the insured (normally self-employed) is promised a fixed sum in the event of injury or illness (Bradburn v Great Western Railway Co (1874) LR 10 Exch 1* where the appellant was injured whilst travelling on a train, owing to the negligence of the respondent. He had earlier bought personal accident insurance to cover him for the possibility of injury on the train. It was held that he was entitled to both damages for negligence *and* insurance moneys payable under the policy (see further COMPENSATION FOR WORK INJURIES/DISEASES)). The right of subrogation does not arise until the insurer has paid the insured in respect of his loss, and has been invoked infrequently in employers' liability cases. In *Morris v Ford Motor Co Ltd [1973] 2 AER 1084* the Ford Motor Co had subcontracted cleaning at one of their plants to the X company, for which the appellant worked. Whilst engaged on this work at the plant, the appellant was injured owing to the negligence of an employee whilst driving a forklift truck. The appellant claimed damages from the respondent company for the negligence of their employee, on the grounds of vicarious liability. X company had, however, entered into a contract of indemnity with the respondent company, agreeing to indemnify the company for all losses or claims for injury arising out of the cleaning operations. Although accepting that they were bound by the terms of this contract of indemnity, the X company argued that they should be subrogated against the negligent Ford employee, on the ground that the employee had carried out his work negligently. It was held that the agreement by the British Insurance Association that they would not sue an employee of an insured employer in respect of injury caused to a co-employee, unless there was either (*a*) collusion and/or (*b*) wilful misconduct on the part of the employee, was binding and that the X company could not recoup its loss from the negligent employee.

# Duty of employer to take out and maintain insurance

**E13008**  'Every employer carrying on business in Great Britain shall insure, and maintain insurance against liability for bodily injury or disease sustained by his employees, and arising out of and in the course of their employment in Great Britain in that business.' [*Employers' Liability (Compulsory Insurance) Act 1969, s 1(1)*].

Such insurance must be provided under one or more 'approved policies'. An 'approved policy' is a policy of insurance not subject to any conditions or exceptions prohibited by regulations (see E13020 below). [*Sec 1(3)*]. This now includes insurance with an approved EU insurer. [*Insurance Companies (Amendment) Regulations 1992 (SI 1992 No 2890)*].

There is no duty under the *1969 Act* to warn or insure the employee against risks of employment outside Great Britain (*Reid v Rush Tompkins Group plc [1989] 3 AER 228*) although the *1998 Regulations* require the employer to insure employees employed on or from offshore installations or associated structures – see E13009 below.

### Employees covered by the Act

**E13009**  Cover is required in respect of liability to employees who:

(*a*)   are ordinarily resident in Great Britain; or

(*b*)   though not ordinarily resident in Great Britain, are present in Great Britain in the course of employment here for a continuous period of not less than 14 days; or

(c)    though not ordinarily resident in the United Kingdom, have been employed on or from an offshore installation or associated structure for a continuous period of not less than seven days.

[*Employers' Liability (Compulsory Insurance) Regulations 1998, Reg 1(2)*].

## Employees not covered by the Act

**E13010**    An employer is not required to insure against liability to an employee who is (*a*) a spouse, (*b*) father, (*c*) mother, (*d*) son, (*e*) daughter, (*f*) other close relative. [*Sec 2(2)(a)*]. Those who are not ordinarily resident in the UK are not covered by the Act except as above. Nor are employees working abroad covered. Such employees can sue under English law in limited circumstances (*Johnson v Coventry Churchill International Ltd [1992] 3 AER 14* where an employee, working in Germany for an English manpower leasing company, was injured when he fell through a rotten plank. He was unable to sue his employer under German law; although he was working in Germany, it was held that England was the country with the most significant relationship with the claim because he had made the contract in England, his employers had covered him with personal liability insurance and he therefore expected them to compensate him through these insurers for any personal injury sustained in Germany).

## Degree of cover necessary

**E13011**    The amount for which an employer is required to insure and maintain insurance is £5 million in respect of claims relating to any one or more of his employees, arising out of any one occurrence. [*Employers' Liability (Compulsory Insurance) Regulations 1998, Reg 3(1)*].

Between 1 January 1972 (when the *Employer's Liability (Compulsory Insurance) Act 1969* came into force) and 1994, insurers, in practice, provided unlimited cover under employers' liability policies. As from 1 January 1995, as a result of payments made in respect of claims exceeding the amount of premiums received during the period 1989–1993, unlimited liability was withdrawn, but most insurers continued to offer a minimum of £10 million indemnity for onshore work. A consultative document issued by the Department of the Environment, Transport and the Regions entitled *The Draft Employers' Liability (Compulsory Insurance) General Regulations [C4857 September 1997]* (hereafter referred to as 'the 1997 consultative document') which preceded the *1998 Regulations* assumed that this practice would continue.

Where a company has subsidiaries, there will be sufficient compliance if a company insures/maintains insurance for itself *and* on behalf of its subsidiaries for £5 million in respect of claims affecting any one or more of its own employees and any one or more employees of its subsidiaries arising out of any one occurrence. [*Employers' Liability (Compulsory Insurance) Regulations 1998, Reg 3*].

Insurers and the courts have interpreted the legislation to mean that all injuries resulting from one incident (e.g. an explosion) are treated as one occurrence, and each individual case of gradually occurring injury or disease is treated as an individual occurrence – the only exception being a situation where a sudden and immediate outbreak of a disease amongst the workforce is clearly attributable to an identifiable incident (e.g. the escape of a biological agent). The introduction to the 1997 consultative document suggested that this interpretation might be challenged and set out a possible alternative regulation to be used instead of what is now *Reg 3* of the *1998 Regulations* if clarification was felt necessary. This was not adopted so presumably the Government are now satisfied that the position is clear.

**Exempted employers**

E13012 The following employers are exempt from the duty to take out and maintain insurance:

(*a*)  nationalised industries;

(*b*)  any body holding a Government department certificate that any claim which it cannot pay itself will be paid out of moneys provided by Parliament;

(*c*)  any Passenger Transport Executive and its subsidiaries, London Regional Transport and its subsidiaries;

(*d*)  statutory water undertakers and certain water boards;

(*e*)  the Commission for the New Towns;

(*f*)  health service bodies, National Health Service Trusts;

(*g*)  probation and after-care committees, magistrates' court committees, and any voluntary management committee of an approved bail or approved probation hostel;

(*h*)  governments of foreign states or commonwealth countries and some other specialised employers;

(*j*)  Railtrack Group plc and its subsidiaries (the exemption ceasing when it is no longer owned by the Crown);

(*k*)  the Qualifications & Curriculum Authority.

There are other types of employer specified in the regulations, but these are the main exceptions. [*Employers' Liability Compulsory Insurance Act 1969, s 3; Employers' Liability (Compulsory Insurance) Regulations 1998, Schedule 2*].

# Issue, display and retention of certificates of insurance

E13013 The insurer must issue the employer with a certificate of insurance, which must be issued not later than 30 days after the date on which insurance was commenced or renewed. [*Employers' Liability (Compulsory Insurance) Act 1969, s 4(1); Employers' Liability (Compulsory Insurance) Regulations 1998, Reg 4*]. Where there are one or more contracts of insurance which jointly provide insurance cover of not less than £5 million, the certificate issued by any individual insurer must specify both the amount in excess of which insurance cover is provided by the individual policy, and the maximum amount of that cover. [*Employers' Liability (Compulsory Insurance) Regulations 1998, Reg 4(3)*].

A copy or copies of the certificate must be displayed at each place of business where there are any employees entitled to be covered by the insurance policy and the copy certificate(s) must be placed where employees can easily see and read it and be reasonably protected from being defaced or damaged. [*Employers' Liability (Compulsory Insurance) Regulations 1998, Reg 5*]. The exception is where an employee is employed on or from an offshore installation or associated structure, when the employer must produce, at the request of that employee and within ten days from such request, a copy of the certificate. [*Employers' Liability (Compulsory Insurance) Regulations 1998, Reg 5(4)*].

An employee must, if a notice has been served on him by the Health and Safety Executive, produce a copy of the policy to the officers specified in the notice and he must permit inspection of the policy by an inspector authorised by the Secretary of State to inspect the policy. [*Employers' Liability (Compulsory Insurance) Regulations 1998, Regs 7, 8*].

A change introduced by the *1998 Regulations* is that employers are now required by law to retain any certificate of employers' liability insurance (or a copy) for a period of 40 years beginning on the date on which the insurance to which it relates commences or is renewed [*Employers' Liability (Compulsory Insurance) Regulations 1998, Reg 4(4)*]. Companies may retain the copy in any eye-readable form in any one of the ways authorised by the *Companies Act 1985, ss 722 and 723* [*Employers' Liability (Compulsory Insurance) Regulations 1998, Reg 4(5)*].

# Penalties

## Failure to insure or maintain insurance

E13014    Failure by an employer to effect and maintain insurance for any day on which it is required is a criminal offence, carrying a maximum penalty on conviction of £2,500. [*Criminal Justice Act 1991, s 17(1)*].

## Failure to display a certificate of insurance

E13015    Failure on the part of an employer to display a certificate of insurance in a prominent position in the workplace is a criminal offence, carrying a maximum penalty on conviction of £2,500. [*Criminal Justice Act 1991, s 17(1)*].

In the 1997 consultative document, the Government suggests that penalties should be increased to become the same as those under the *Health and Safety at Work etc Act 1974*, i.e. fines of £20,000 in a magistrates' court and unlimited in the Crown Court. To implement this change will require primary legislation, and the Government says that it will be 'looking for opportunities in a Criminal Justice Bill'.

# Cover provided by a typical policy

## Persons

E13016    Cover is limited to protection of employees. Independent contractors are not covered; liability to them should be covered by a public liability policy. Directors who are employed under a contract of employment are covered, but directors paid by fees who do not work full-time in the business are generally not regarded as 'employees'. Liability to them would normally be covered by a public liability policy. Similarly, since the judicial tendency is to construe 'labour-only' subcontractors in the construction industry as 'employees' (see CONSTRUCTION AND BUILDING OPERATIONS), employers' liability policies often contain the following endorsement: 'An employee shall also mean any labour master, and persons supplied by him, any person employed by labour-only subcontractors, any self-employed person, or any person hired from any public authority, company, firm or individual, while working for the insured in connection with the business'. The public liability policy should then be amended to exclude the insured's liability to 'employees' so designated.

In the 1997 consultative document, the Government points out that the issue as to what constitutes 'an employee' cannot be completely resolved without primary legislation, but proposes to issue guidance on interpretation.

## Scope of cover

E13017    The policy provides for payment of:

(*a*)    costs and expenses of litigation, incurred with the insurer's consent, in defence of a claim against the insured (i.e. civil liability);

(*b*)    solicitor's fees, incurred with the insurer's consent, for representation of the insured at proceedings in any court of summary jurisdiction (e.g. magistrates' court or Crown Court), coroner's inquest, or a fatal accident inquiry (i.e. criminal proceedings), arising out of an accident resulting in injury to an employee. It does *not* cover payment of a fine imposed by a criminal court.

The policy will often contain an excess negotiated between the insurer and employer, i.e. a provision that the employer pay the first £x of any claim. For the purposes of the *1969 Act*, any condition in a contract of insurance which requires a relevant employee to pay, or an insured employer to pay the relevant employee, the first amount of any claim or any aggregation of claims, is prohibited. Agreements will still be permitted which provide that the insurer will pay the claim in full and may then seek some reimbursement from the employer. [*Employers' Liability (Compulsory Insurance) Regulations 1998, Reg 2*].

## Geographical limits

E13018    Cover is normally limited to Great Britain, Northern Ireland, the Channel Islands and the Isle of Man, in respect of employees normally resident in any of the above, who sustain injury whilst working in those areas. Cover is also provided for such employees who are injured whilst temporarily working abroad, so long as the action for damages is brought in a court of law of Great Britain, Northern Ireland, the Channel Islands or the Isle of Man – though even this proviso is omitted from some policies.

Employers must also have employers' liability insurance in respect of employees who, though not ordinarily resident in the United Kingdom, have been employed on or from an offshore installation or associated structure for a continuous period of not less than seven days; or who, though not ordinarily resident in Great Britain, are present in Great Britain in the course of employment for not less than fourteen days. [*Employers' Liability (Compulsory Insurance) Regulations 1998, Reg 1(2)*].

## Conditions which must be satisfied

E13019    (*a*)    Cover only relates to bodily injury or disease; it does not extend to employee's property. This latter cover is provided by an employers' public liability policy.

(*b*)    Injury must arise out of and during the course of employment (see E11004 EMPLOYERS' DUTIES TO THEIR EMPLOYEES). If injury does not so arise, cover is normally provided by a public liability policy.

(*c*)    Bodily injury must be caused during the period of insurance. Normally with injury-causing accidents there is no problem, since injury follows on from the accident almost immediately. Certain occupational diseases, however, may not manifest themselves until much later, e.g. asbestosis, mesothelioma, pneumoconiosis, deafness. Here legal liability takes place when the disease manifests itself, or is 'discovered'. Moreover, at least as far as occupational deafness is concerned, liability between employers can be apportioned, giving rise to contribution between insurers (see further NOISE AND VIBRATION).

(*d*)    Claims must be notified by the insured to the insurer as soon as possible, or as stipulated by the policy.

Regulation 2 does not fetter the freedom of underwriters to apply certain conditions in connection with intrinsically hazardous work; for instance, exclusion of liability for accidents arising out of demolition work, or in connection with use of explosives.

## 'Prohibition' of certain conditions

E13020    All liability policies contain conditions with which the insured must comply if the insurer is to 'progress' his claim, e.g. notification of claims. Failure to comply with such condition(s) could jeopardise cover under the policy: the insured would be legally liable but without insurance protection. In the case of an employers' liability policy, an insurer might seek to avoid liability under the policy if the condition requiring the insured to take reasonable care to prevent injuries to employees, and/or comply with the provisions of any relevant statutes/statutory instruments (e.g. *HSWA; Ionising Radiations Regulations 1985*), or to keep records, was not complied with.

The object of the *1969 Act* was to ensure that an employer who had a claim brought against him would be able to pay the employee any damages awarded. Regulations made under the Act, therefore, seek to prevent insurers from avoiding their liability by relying on breach of a policy condition, by way of 'prohibiting' certain conditions in policies taken out under the Act. More particularly, insurers cannot avoid liability in the following circumstances:

(*a*)    some specified thing being done or being omitted to be done after the happening of the event giving rise to a claim (e.g. omission to notify the insurer of a claim within a stipulated time) [*Employers' Liability (Compulsory Insurance) Regulations 1998, Reg 2(1)(a)*];

(*b*)    failure on the part of the policy-holder to take reasonable care to protect his employees against the risk of bodily injury or disease in the course of employment [*Employers' Liability (Compulsory Insurance) Regulations 1998, Reg 2(1)(b)*]. As to the meaning of 'reasonable care' or 'reasonable precaution' here, 'It is eminently reasonable for employers to entrust . . . tasks to a skilled and trusted foreman on whose competence they have every reason to rely'. (*Woolfall and Rimmer Ltd v Moyle and Another [1941] 3 AER 304*). The prohibition is therefore, not broken by a negligent act on the part of a competent foreman selected by the employer. Where, however, an employer acted wilfully (in causing injury) and not merely negligently (though this would be rare), the insurer could presumably refuse to pay (*Hartley v Provincial Insurance Co Ltd [1957] Lloyd's Rep 121* where the insured employer had not taken steps to ensure that a stockbar was securely fenced for the purposes of the *Factories Act 1937, s 14(3)* in spite of repeated warnings from the factory inspector, with the result that an employee was scalped whilst working at a lathe. It was held that the insurer was justified in refusing to indemnify the employer who was in breach of statutory duty and so liable for damages). This was confirmed in *Aluminium Wire and Cable Co Ltd v Allstate Insurance Co Ltd [1985] 2 Lloyd's Rep 280*;

(*c*)    failure on the part of the policy-holder to comply with statutory requirements for the protection of employees against the risk of injury [*Employers' Liability (Compulsory Insurance) Regulations 1998, Reg 2(1)(c)*] – the reasoning in *Hartley v Provincial Insurance Co Ltd* (see (*b*) above), that wilful breach may not be covered, probably applies here too;

(*d*)    failure on the part of the policy-holder to keep specified records and make such information available to the insurer [*Employers' Liability (Compulsory*

*Insurance) Regulations 1998, Reg 2(1)(d)]* (e.g. accident book or accounts relating to employees' wages and salaries (see ACCIDENT REPORTING));

(e)    by means of the use of an excess in policies [*Employers' Liability (Compulsory Insurance) Regulations 1998, Reg 2(2)]* – see E13017 above

## Trade endorsements for certain types of work

E13021    There are no policy exceptions to the standard employers' liability cover. Trade endorsements, however, are used frequently in underwriting employers' liability risks, and there is nothing in the *1969 Act* to prevent insurers from applying their normal underwriting principles and applying trade endorsements where they consider it necessary, i.e. they will amend their standard policy form to exclude certain risks. Thus, there may be specific exclusions of liability arising out of types of work, such as demolition, or the use of mechanically driven woodworking machinery, or work above certain heights, unless the appropriate rate of premium is paid. This does mean that there are still circumstances where an employee will not obtain compensation from his employer based on the employer's insurance cover.

## Measure of risk and assessment of premium

E13022    Certain trades or businesses are known to be more dangerous than others. For most trades or businesses insurers have their own rate for the risk, expressed as a rate per cent on wages (other than for clerical, managerial or non-manual employees for whom a very low rate applies). This rate is used as a guide and is altered upwards or downwards depending upon:

(a)    previous history of claims and cost of settlement;

(b)    size of wage roll;

(c)    whether certain risks are not to be covered, e.g. the premium will be lower if the insured elects to exclude from the policy certain risks, such as the use of power driven woodworking machinery;

(d)    the insured's attitude towards safety.

Many insurers survey premises with the object of improving the risk and minimising the incidence of accidents and diseases. This is an essential part of their service, and they often work in conjunction with the insured's own safety staff.

## Extension of cover

E13023    In addition to employers' liability insurance, it is becoming increasingly common for companies to buy insurance in respect of directors' personal liability. Indeed, in the United States, some directors refuse to take up appointments in the absence of such insurance being forthcoming.

# Employment Protection

## Introduction

E14001  Legislative changes introduced by the Labour government have had a significant impact on the characterisation of the employment relationship. Government policy has been to promote a flexible labour market based on effective partnership at work. This policy extends certain employment protection rights to workers as well as employees. For example, the *Public Interest Disclosure Act 1998* applies to 'workers' and defines this term broadly, and the *Working Time Regulations 1998 (SI 1998 No 1833)* apply to 'workers' which is a wider category than persons categorised as employees under traditional English employment law analysis.

As a result, this is a period of some change in terms of the approach taken by Parliament to employment protection and to employment law in general. The *Employment Relations Act 1999* received Royal Assent on 27 July 1999. The vast majority of the provisions of this Act have already been brought into force. The 1999 Act introduces some important changes to the treatment of the employment relationship – including the relative roles of trade unions and individuals. Topics such as recognition of unions and consultation with employee representatives in various fields may take on a more significant role than has been the case in the last ten or fifteen years.

The relationship between an employer and an employee is a contractual one and as such must have all the elements of a legally binding contract to render it enforceable. In strict contractual terms an offer is made by the employer which is then accepted by the employee. As in the case of the offer, the acceptance may be oral, in writing, or by conduct, for example by the employee turning up for work. The consideration on the employer's part is the promise to pay wages and on the employee's part to provide his services for the employer. Once the employer's offer has been accepted, the contract comes into existence and both parties are bound by any terms contained within it (*Taylor v Furness, Withy & Co Ltd (1969) 6 KIR 488*).

The contractual analysis of the employment relationship is not entirely satisfactory in explaining the relationship between employee and employer. To fit the contract model, various elements comprising the reality of the employment relationship become part of the contract by implication.

An employment contract is unlike many other contracts, because many of the terms will not have been individually negotiated by the parties. The contract will contain the express terms that the parties have agreed – most commonly hours, pay, job description – and there will be a variety of other terms which will be implied into the contract from other sources and which the parties have not agreed. Many of these are relevant to health and safety. If any of the express or implied terms in the contract are breached, the innocent party will have certain remedies. The fact that various employee rights, particularly in relation to health and safety, are implied into the contractual terms and conditions is important for this reason.

In addition to terms implied into the contract by the common law, statute (such as the *Employment Rights Act 1996*) has created additional employment protection rights for employees, including some specific rights in relation to health and safety. These are in addition to detailed rights and duties arising from health and safety legislation and regulations which are discussed elsewhere. An employer will often lay down health and safety rules and procedures. While the law allows an employer the ultimate sanction of dismissal as a method of ensuring that safety rules are observed, such dismissals should be lawful, that is generally with notice, and should be fair. Furthermore, statute has created specific protection from victimisation for employees who are protecting themselves or others against perceived health and safety risks. All of these provisions are the subject of this section.

As a specific health and safety protection measure, the *Health and Safety at Work etc. Act 1974, s 2 (HSWA 1974)* lays a general duty on all employers to ensure, so far as is reasonably practicable (for the meaning of this expression, see E15039 ENFORCE-MENT), the health, safety and welfare of all their employees. An employer is also under a duty to consult about health and safety matters. In addition, a number of codes of practice have been issued under the *HSWA 1974* by the Health and Safety Executive, for example relating to safety representatives and allowing them time off to train.

## Sources of contractual terms

### Express terms

E14002    These are the terms agreed by the parties themselves and may be oral or in writing. Normally the courts will uphold the express terms in the contract because these are what the parties have agreed. However, if the term is ambiguous the court may be called upon to interpret the ambiguity, for example what the parties meant by 'reasonable overtime'.

Generally the express terms cause no legal problems and the parties can insert such terms into the contract as they wish, subject to the following:

(*a*)    An employer cannot restrict his liability for the death or personal injury of his employees caused by his negligence. Further, he can only restrict liability for damage to his employee's property if such a restriction is reasonable (*Unfair Contract Terms Act 1977, s 2*).

(*b*)    The terms in the contract cannot infringe the *Equal Pay Act 1970*, and the *Sex Discrimination Acts 1975* and *1986*.

(*c*)    The terms in the contract cannot infringe the *Part-time Workers (Prevention of Less Favourable Treatment) Regulations 2000 (SI 2000 No 1551)*. The Regulations provide that unless justified on objective grounds, a part-time worker has the right not to be treated less favourably than a comparable full-time worker on the ground that the worker is a part-timer in relation to the terms of the contract.

(*d*)    The terms in the contract cannot infringe the *Race Relations Act 1976*.

(*e*)    The terms cannot infringe the *Disability Discrimination Act 1995*.

(*f*)    The employer cannot have a notice provision which gives the employee less than the statutory minimum notice guaranteed by the *Employment Rights Act 1996, s 86*.

(*g*)    Prior to the *Employment Relations Act 1999*, there was provision for an employee under a fixed term contract of one year or more to agree to waive the right to unfair dismissal. This kind of waiver is no longer possible. Any term which prevents the employee from suing for unfair dismissal is void. A term preventing the employee from pursuing a claim for a redundancy payment is void unless it is contained in a fixed term contract of two years or more (*Employment Rights Act 1996, s 203*).

(*h*)   Some judges have suggested that any express terms regarding hours are subject to the employer's duty to ensure his employee's safety and must be read subject to this, so that a term requiring an employee to work 100 hours a week will not be enforceable (see for example Stuart-Smith LJ in *Johnstone v Bloomsbury Health Authority [1991] IRLR 118*). More specifically, the provisions of the *Working Time Regulations 1998 (SI 1998 No 1833)* affect the contractual term in relation to working hours. The 1998 Regulations and the *Working Time Regulations 1999 (SI 1999 No 3372)* implement the European Working Time Directive and, save in the case of specified exemptions, set a maximum working week of 48 hours averaged over a 17 week reference period. In addition, the Regulations provide for an obligatory daily rest period, weekly rest, rest breaks, limits on night work and minimum annual leave and otherwise regulate working time. In *Barber v RJB Mining UK Ltd [1999] IRLR 308*, the court decided that the maximum imposed on weekly working time by the Regulations was part of the employees' contract. This decision gives some protection to employees who refuse to work beyond the statutorily stated maximum. It is possible under the 1998 Regulations for a worker to agree with his or her employer in writing to opt-out of the 48 hour working week, subject to complying with certain requirements.

(*i*)   The terms in the contract cannot infringe the *Maternity and Parental Leave etc Regulations 1999 (SI 1999 No 3312)*, which entitle employees with one year's continuous service who have responsibility for a child born after 15 December 1999, to be absent from work for up to 13 weeks parental leave.

(*j*)   The terms cannot infringe the *Regulation of Investigatory Powers Act 2000*. The Act and the associated Regulations, the *Telecommunications (Lawful Business Practice) (Interception of Communications) Regulations 2000 (SI 2000 No 2699)*, came into force in October 2000. Under the new legislation, any interception of a communication via an employer's communication system carried out by or with the consent of the employer, will be actionable (by the sender, recipient or intended recipient) if it is without lawful authority. Broadly, in order for an interception to have lawful authority, an employer will have to show either that he has reasonable grounds for believing that both the sender and recipient consented to the interception, or that the interception falls within the statutory exemptions relating to monitoring or keeping a record of 'business communications' for prescribed purposes.

(*k*)   Confidentiality provisions should be subject to an employee's right to make a protected disclosure in accordance with the provisions set out in the *Employment Rights Act 1996*.

As well as preventing unlawful discrimination, the effect of the *Sex Discrimination Acts 1975* and *1986* has been to remove some of the restrictions on women and their employment generally and health and safety specifically. In particular, the *Sex Discrimination Act 1975* allowed machine attendants, for the purposes of the *Operations at Unfenced Machinery Regulations 1938 (SR & O 1938 No 641)* (which remained in force until 1 January 1997), to be women. Moreover, restrictions on the employment of women by night imposed in the *Hours of Employment (Conventions) Act 1936* were removed by the *Sex Discrimination Act 1986, s 7(1)*. The further restrictions on employment of women as regards hours of employment, holidays etc. specified in the *Factories Act 1961, ss 86-94* (and the corresponding restrictions of the *Mines and Quarries Act 1954*) have also been repealed by *s 7*.

However, some restrictions/prohibitions on certain types of employment by women, in the interests of health and safety at work, still remain.

Under the *Control of Lead at Work Regulations 1998 (SI 1998 No 543)*, which came into force on 1 April 1998, an employer is prohibited from employing women of reproductive capacity or young people in particular activities relating to lead processes as follows:

(*a*)   In the lead smelting and refining process:

    (i)   handling, treating, sintering, smelting or refining any material containing 5 per cent or more of lead; or

    (ii)   cleaning where any of the above activities have taken place.

(*b*)   In the lead acid manufacturing process:

    (i)   manipulating lead oxides;

    (ii)   mixing or pasting;

    (iii)   melting or casting;

    (iv)   trimming, abrading or cutting of pasted plates; or

    (v)   cleaning where any of the above activities have taken place.

## Common law implied terms

E14003   The court may imply terms into the contract when a situation arises which was not anticipated by the parties at the time they negotiated the express terms. As such, the court is 'filling in the gaps' left by the parties' own negotiations. The courts use two tests to see if a term should be implied, (i) the 'business efficacy' test (*The Moorcock (1889) 14 PD 64*) or (ii) the 'officious bystander' or 'oh of course' test (*Shirlaw v Southern Foundries Ltd [1939] 2 KB 206*). Once the court has decided, by virtue of one of these tests, that a term should be implied, it will use the concept of reasonableness to decide the content of the term. Often this will involve looking at how the parties have worked the contract in the past. For example, if the contract does not contain a mobility clause, but the employee has always worked on different sites, the court will normally imply a mobility clause into the contract (*Courtaulds Northern Spinning Ltd v Sibson [1988] IRLR 305*). (See also *Aparau v Iceland Frozen Foods plc [1996] IRLR 119*, where the Employment Appeal Tribunal refused to imply a mobility clause on the basis that there were other ways of achieving the necessary flexibility.) In relation to dismissal, a term has been implied that, except in the case of summary dismissal, the employer will not terminate the employment contract while the employee is incapacitated where the effect would be to deprive the employee of permanent health insurance benefits (*Aspden v Webbs Poultry and Meat Group (Holdings) Ltd [1996] IRLR 521*). Terms can also be implied by the conduct of the parties or by custom and practice in a particular industry or area. The test for this is relatively difficult to fulfil – the term must be notorious and certain and, in effect, everyone in the industry/enterprise must know that it is part of the contract. Arguments based on custom and practice come into play in relation to issues such as statutory holidays and redundancy policies.

## Collective agreements

E14004   Collective agreements are negotiated between an employer or employer's association and a trade union or unions. This means that they are not contracts between an employer and his individual employees because the employee was not one of the negotiating parties. Some terms of the collective agreement will be procedural and will govern the relationship between the employer and the union; some, on the other hand, will impact on the relationship between the employer and each individual employee, for example a collectively bargained pay increase. As the employee is not a party to the collective agreement, the only way he can enforce a term which is relevant to him is if the particular term from the collective agreement has become a term of his individual employment contract. Procedural provisions, policy and more general aspirations are not suitable for incorporation into an individual contract of employment. Incorporation is important because the collective agreement is not a legally binding contract between the employer and the union (*Trade Union and Labour Relations (Consolidation) Act 1992, s 179(1)*) and thus needs to be a term of an employment contract to make it legally enforceable.

The two main ways that a term from a collective agreement becomes a term of an employment contract is by express or implied incorporation. Until recently, implied incorporation was the most common and was complex. It generally required the employee to be a member of the union which negotiated the agreement, to have knowledge of the agreement and of the existence of the term, and to have conducted himself in such a way as to indicate that he accepted the term from the collective agreement as a term of his contract. A recent Employment Appeal Tribunal case, *Healy & Others v Corporation of London (24 June 1999) (unreported)*, illustrates that habitual acceptance of the benefits of a collective agreement does not, in itself, lead to the conclusion that the terms of that collective agreement have become contractually binding on an individual employee. There can be many reasons for an individual to accept the benefits of collective bargaining which do not amount to an acceptance that the underlying agreement forms part of his or her contract.

Express incorporation meant that the employee had expressly agreed (normally in his contract) that any term collectively agreed would become part of his contract. This used to be unusual, but with the change made to the statutory statement which must be given to all employees (see below) employees must be told of collective agreements which apply to them, and this has been held as expressly incorporating those agreements into the contract.

## Statutory statement of terms and conditions

E14005 By the *Employment Rights Act 1996, s 1* every employee no later than two months after starting employment, must receive a statement of his basic terms and conditions. The statement must contain:

(*a*)   the names of the employer and employee;

(*b*)   the date the employment began;

(*c*)   the date the employee's continuous employment began;

(*d*)   the scale or rate of remuneration and how it is calculated;

(*e*)   the intervals when remuneration is paid;

(*f*)   terms and conditions relating to hours;

(*g*)   terms and conditions relating to holidays;

(*h*)   terms relating to sick pay (if any);

(*i*)   terms and conditions relating to pensions;

(*j*)   notice requirements;

(*k*)   job description;

(*l*)   title of the job;

(*m*)   if the job is not permanent, the period of employment;

(*n*)   place of work, or if various the address of the employer;

(*o*)   any collective agreements which affect terms and conditions and, if the employer is not a party to the agreements, the persons with whom they were made;

(*p*)   if the employee is required to work outside the UK for more than one month, the period he will be required to work, the currency in which he will be paid, any additional benefits paid to him and any terms and conditions relating to his return to the UK.

The terms in (*a*), (*b*), (*c*), (*d*), (*e*), (*f*), (*g*), (*k*), (*l*) and (*n*) must all be contained in a single document. In relation to pensions and sick pay the employer may refer the employee to a reasonably accessible document, and in respect of notice the employer can refer the employee to a reasonably accessible collective agreement or to the *Employment Rights Act 1996, s 86* which contains provisions relating to minimum notice periods.

In addition, if the employer employs more than twenty employees, he must give them written details of any disciplinary and grievance procedures which apply to them. If the employer employs fewer than twenty employees, he must let them know to which person they can take a grievance to– there is no requirement for him to give details of the disciplinary procedures. There is also no duty on an employer to give details of any disciplinary or grievance procedures relating to health and safety. Given the employer's duties under the *HSWA 1974, s 2*, however, and given the law relating to unfair dismissal, it is good industrial relations practice to ensure that all employees know of all the disciplinary procedures which could be invoked against them. The written statement must also provide (either by instalments or in one single document) details of whether the employment is contracted out of the State Earnings Related Pension Scheme.

## Works rules

E14006    Works rules may or may not be part of the contract. If they are part of the contract and thus contractual terms, they can be altered only by mutual agreement, that is the employee must agree to any change. It is unusual, however, for such rules to be contractual – to be so, there would have to be some reference to them within the contract and an intention that they are terms of the contract. The more usual position with regard to the employer's rules was stated in *Secretary of State for Employment v ASLEF (No 2) [1972] 2 QB 455* where Lord Denning said that they were merely instructions from an employer to an employee. This means that they are non-contractual and the employer can alter the rules without the consent of the employees. The fact that they are not contractual does not mean that they cannot be enforced against an employee. All employees have a duty to obey lawful, reasonable orders (see E14008 below) and thus failing to comply with the rules will be a breach of this duty and therefore a breach of contract. The only requirement that the law stipulates is that the order must be lawful and reasonable and it is unlikely that an order to comply with any health and safety rules would infringe these requirements.

## Disciplinary and grievance procedures

E14007    It has already been noted that the employer must give details of grievance procedures to all employees. Failing to do so could lead to the employee resigning and claiming constructive dismissal (*W A Goold (Pearmak) Ltd v McConnell [1995] IRLR 516 and below*). In addition, if the employer employs more than 20 employees he must give details of the disciplinary grievance procedures to those employees. Many employers adopt the ACAS Code of Practice on Disciplinary Procedures (as amended). This gives guidelines as to the sanctions which can be employed for breaches of the employer's rules. The code was recently updated to incorporate the new statutory right to be accompanied by a fellow employee or by a trade union representative of the employee's choice during certain grievance and disciplinary proceedings under the *Employment Relations Act 1999, ss 10–15,* which came into force on 4 September 2000. This right is enforceable in the Employment Tribunal and compensation is payable for any failure. It is worth noting that fellow employees are under no duty to perform the role of accompanying individual.

Subject to the above, employers may establish their own disciplinary procedures. Such procedures may become part of the contract. If, for example, the employer gives the employee a copy of the procedures with the contract, and the contract refers to the procedures and the employee signs for receipt of the contract and the procedures, it is likely that they will be contractual. Employers may prefer their disciplinary procedures not to be contractual. If the procedures are contractual, any employee will be able to claim that his or her contract has been breached if they are not followed. This possibility also applies to those employees who have been employed for less than the one year qualifying period required to bring a claim for unfair dismissal. In response to a claim of breach of contract, a court may award damages against the employer. These damages are based on an assessment of the time for which, if the procedure had been followed, the employee's employment would have continued.

## Common law implied duties

E14008    Both the employer and employee owe duties towards each other. These are duties implied into every contract of employment and should be distinguished from the implied terms discussed above which are implied into a particular individual contract. Although there are a number of different duties, three are of major importance for the purposes of this work: the duty on the part of the employee to obey lawful reasonable orders and to perform his work with reasonable care and skill, and the duty on the part of the employer to ensure his employee's safety. The duty to obey lawful reasonable orders ensures that the employer's safety rules can be enforced and, as it is a contractual duty, breach will allow the employer to invoke certain sanctions against the employee, the ultimate of which may be dismissal. The same is true of the duty to perform his work with reasonable care and skill. Should the employee be in breach of this duty and place his or others' safety at risk, the employer may impose sanctions against him including dismissal. The imposition of the employer's duty is to complement the statutory provisions. Statutes such as the *HSWA 1974* provide sanctions against the employer should he fail to comply with the legislation or any regulations made thereunder. The common law duty provides the employee with a remedy should the duty be broken, either in the form of compensation if he is injured, or, potentially, with a claim of unfair dismissal. The employer's duty to ensure his employees' safety is one of the most important aspects of the employment relationship. At least one judge has argued that it is so important that any express term must be read subject to it (see *Johnstone v Bloomsbury Health Authority [1991] IRLR 118* at E14002 above). Breach of this duty can lead to the employee resigning and claiming constructive dismissal (see below). In *Walton & Morse v Dorrington [1997] IRLR 488,* an employee claimed that she had been constructively dismissed (unfairly) because her employer had breached the implied term of her contract of employment that it would provide, so far as reasonably practicable, a suitable working environment. The employee had been forced to work in a smoke-filled environment for a prolonged period of time and her employer did not take appropriate steps to redress the problem when she raised the issue. The Employment Appeal Tribunal agreed that she had been constructively dismissed because the employer had breached its duty to her. Further, the employer's duty to ensure his employee's safety has been held to cover stressful environments resulting in injury to the employee. In *Walker v Northumberland County Council [1995] IRLR 35*, the High Court held that an employer was liable for damages on the basis that they owed their employee a duty not to cause him psychiatric damage by the volume and/or character of work that he was required to undertake. In *Fraser v The State Hospitals Board for Scotland (11 January 2000) (2000 Rep LR 94)*, the Court of Session held that there was no reason to qualify an employer's duty to take reasonable care for the safety of employees so as to restrict the nature of the injury suffered to a physical one in circumstances where the employee claimed damages for psychological damage as a result of disciplinary measures. The claim failed on the basis of lack of foreseeability.

# Employee employment protection rights

## Right not to suffer a detriment in health and safety cases

E14009    By the *Employment Rights Act 1996, s 44* every employee has the right not to be subjected to a detriment, by any act or any failure to act, by his employer on the grounds that:

(a) having been designated by the employer to carry out activities in connection with preventing or reducing risks to health and safety at work, the employee carried out (or proposed to carry out) any such activities;

(b) being a representative of workers on matters of health and safety at work or a member of a safety committee –

(i) in accordance with arrangements established under or by virtue of any enactment; or

(ii) by reason of being acknowledged as such by the employer;

the employee performed (or proposed to perform) any functions as such a representative or a member of such committee;

(ba) the employee took part (or proposed to take part) in consultation with the employer pursuant to the *Health and Safety (Consultation with Employees) Regulations 1996 (SI 1996 No 1513)* or in an election of representatives of employee safety within the meaning of those Regulations (whether as a candidate or otherwise);

(c) being an employee at a place where –

(i) there was no such representative or safety committee; or

(ii) there was such a representative or safety committee but it was not reasonably practicable for the employee to raise the matter by those means;

he brought to his employer's attention, by reasonable means, circumstances connected with his work which he reasonably believed were harmful or potentially harmful to health or safety;

(d) in circumstances of danger which the employee reasonably believed to be serious and imminent and which he could not reasonably have been expected to avert, he left (or proposed to leave) or (while the danger persisted) refused to return to his place of work or any dangerous part of his place of work; or (*e*)  in circumstances of danger which the employee reasonably believed to be serious and imminent, he took (or proposed to take) appropriate steps to protect himself or other persons from the danger.

In considering whether the steps the employee took or proposed to take under (*e*) were reasonable, the court must have regard to all the circumstances including the employee's knowledge and the facilities and advice available to him (*Employment Rights Act 1996, s 44(2)*). In *Kerr v Nathan's Wastesavers Ltd (1995) IDS Brief 548*, however, the Employment Appeal Tribunal stressed that tribunals should not place too onerous a duty on the employee to make enquiries to determine if his belief is reasonable. Danger under *(d)* does not necessarily have to arise from the circumstances of the workplace, but can include the risk of attack by a fellow employee (*Harvest Press Ltd v McCaffrey [1999] IRLR 778*). Danger under *(e)* can include danger to others as well as the employee himself (*Mosiak v City Restaurants (UK) Ltd [1999] IRLR 180*). Various actions by the employer can constitute a detriment to the employee (such as disciplining the employee). Likewise, a failure to act on the part of the employer can also constitute a detriment (for example not sending the employee on a training course). Furthermore, the section is not restricted to the health and safety of the employee or his colleagues. In *Barton v Wandsworth Council (1995) IDS Brief 549* a tribunal ruled that an employee had been unlawfully disciplined when he voiced concerns over the safety of patients due to what he considered to be the lack of ability of newly introduced escorts. This shows that the legal protection is triggered in relation to any health and safety issue and includes cases where the employee voices concerns, and is not limited to only those circumstances where the employee commits more positive action. The *Employment Rights Act 1996, s 44(3)*, however, provides that an employee is not to be regarded as subjected to a detriment if the employer can show that the steps the employee took or proposed to take were so negligent that any reasonable employer would have treated him in the same manner. Furthermore, if the detriment suffered by the employee is dismissal, there is special protection under *s 100* (see below).

If the employee should suffer a detriment within the terms of *s 44* he may present a complaint to an Employment Tribunal (*Employment Rights Act 1996, s 48*). The complaint must be presented within three months of the act (or failure to act) complained of, or, if there is a series of acts, within three months of the date of the last act. The tribunal has a discretion to waive this time limit if it was not reasonably practicable for the employee to present his complaint in time. If the tribunal finds the complaint well founded, it must make a declaration to that effect and may make an award of compensation to the employee, the amount of compensation being what the tribunal regards as just and equitable in all the circumstances (*Employment Rights Act 1996, s 49(2)*). The amount of compensation shall take into account any expenses reasonably incurred by the employee in consequence of the employer's action and any loss of benefit caused by the employer's action. Compensation can be reduced because of the employee's contributory conduct.

The protection from being dismissed or subjected to a detriment on the health and safety grounds specified in *s 44* and *s 100* of the *Employment Rights Act 1996* has been reinforced by a new, more general protection for whistleblowers.

*The Public Interest Disclosure Act 1998* came in to force on 2 July 1999. It provides protection to workers who make disqualifying disclosures about health and safety matters, as well as about criminal acts, failure to comply with legal obligations, miscarriages of justice, damage to the environment and deliberate concealment of any of these matters. Under the Act, which inserts new sections into the *Employment Rights Act 1996*, a worker who makes a 'qualifying disclosure' which he reasonably believes shows one of these matters, may be protected against dismissal or being subjected to a detriment (*Fernandes v Netcom Consultants (UK) Ltd (2000) (unreported)*).

Disclosures are only protected if they are made to appropriate persons – which often means that the employer must to be approached in the first instance. There are other possibilities available under the Act: disclosure to a legal adviser, disclosure to a prescribed person (e.g. the FSA or the Inland Revenue), and a more general category for disclosures made provided that certain specified conditions are met. The *Public Interest Disclosure (Prescribed Persons) Order 1999 (SI 1999 No 1549)* deals with 'prescribed persons', i.e. organisations to whom a worker may 'blow the whistle'.

In terms of health and safety risks, protection under the 1998 Act for qualifying disclosures is not limited to cases of imminent or serious danger – it can apply where the health and safety of any individual has been, is being or is likely to be, endangered. In all cases the worker must have a reasonable belief and make the disclosure in good faith (except in the case of disclosure to a legal adviser).

If a disclosure is protected, and an employee is subjected to any detriment or dismissed as a result, it is unlawful. A dismissal in these circumstances is deemed to be automatically unfair, and there is no minimum qualifying period for entitlement to make an unfair dismissal claim for this reason. This means that if the dismissal was in relation to the employee making a protected disclosure, the dismissal is automatically unfair and the tribunal is not required to consider whether or not the employer's actions were reasonable. The *Employment Rights Act 1996, s 124(1A)* provides that there are no limits on the compensation available to whistleblowers who are unfairly dismissed because they have made a protected disclosure.

## Dismissal on health and safety grounds

E14010    In addition to the normal protection against dismissal (see below), where an employee is dismissed (or selected for redundancy) and the reason or principal reason for the dismissal is one of the grounds listed in the *Employment Rights Act 1996, s 44*, the dismissal will be automatically unfair. The only defence available to an employer applies to a dismissal taken by the employee to protect himself or others from danger that the employee reasonably believed was serious and imminent (*Employment Rights Act 1996, ss 44(1)(e) and 100(1)(e)*). The employer can escape a finding of unfair dismissal if he can show that the actions taken or proposed by the employee were so negligent that any reasonable employer would have dismissed the individual concerned. In respect of a dismissal falling within *s 100*, the normal qualifying period of employment does not apply nor does the upper age limit (*Employment Rights Act 1996, ss 108(3)(c) and 109(2)(c)*). Thus an employee who has only been employed for a few weeks or who is over the normal retirement age for the job can claim unfair dismissal for a breach of *s 100*. A dismissal which is not automatically unfair under *s 100* may nevertheless be unfair under the general reasonableness test under *s 98*.

The *Employment Relations Act 1999, s 124(1A)* removes any limit on compensation for any unfair dismissal on health and safety grounds.

## Dismissal for assertion of a statutory right

E14011    By the *Employment Rights Act 1996, s 104*, an employee is deemed to be unfairly dismissed where the reason or principal reason for that dismissal was that the employee –

(*a*)    brought proceedings against an employer to enforce a right of his which is a relevant statutory right, or (*b*)    alleged that the employer had infringed a right of his which is a relevant statutory right.

It is immaterial whether or not the employee has the right or whether or not the right has been infringed, as long as the employee made it clear to the employer what the right claimed to have been infringed was and the employee's claim is made in good faith. A statutory right for the purposes of the section is any right under the *Employment Rights Act 1996* in respect of which remedy for infringement is by way of complaint to an Employment Tribunal, a right under *s 86* of the 1996 Act (minimum notice requirements), or rights in relation to trade union activities under the *Trade Union and Labour Relations (Consolidation) Act 1992*.

This is an important right for employees. If, for example, after the employee has successfully claimed compensation from his employer for a breach of s *44* he is dismissed, the dismissal will be automatically unfair under *s 104*. Again, if the employer unlawfully demotes or suspends without pay as a disciplinary sanction for breach of health and safety rules, and after proceedings against him for an unlawful deduction from wages the employer dismisses the employee, this will be unfair under *s 104*. As with dismissal in health and safety cases under *s 100*, the normal qualifying period of employment does not apply – neither does the upper age limit.

# Enforcement of safety rules by the employer

## The rules

E14012    Given the statutory duty on the employer, under the *HSWA 1974, s 2*, to have a written statement of health and safety policy, and the common law duty on the employer to ensure his employees' safety, the employer should lay down contractual health and safety rules, breach of which will lead to disciplinary action against the employee. These rules must be communicated to the employee and be clear and unambiguous so that the employee knows exactly what he can and cannot do.

The employer's disciplinary rules will often classify misconduct, e.g. as minor misconduct, serious misconduct and gross misconduct. It is unlikely that a tribunal would uphold as fair a dismissal for minor misconduct. It will underline the importance of health and safety rules if their breach is deemed to be serious or gross misconduct. The tribunal will, however, look at all the circumstances of the case – it does not automatically follow, therefore, if an employer has stated that a breach of a particular rule will be gross misconduct, that a tribunal will find a resultant dismissal fair.

## The procedures

E14013    Once an employer has laid down his rules, he must ensure that he has adequate procedures (which should be non-contractual) to deal with a breach. The procedures used by an employer are scrutinised by a tribunal in any unfair dismissal claim and past cases indicate that many employers have lost such claims due to inadequate procedures. As discussed below, an employer in an unfair dismissal claim must show the tribunal that he acted reasonably. This concentrates on the fairness of the employer's actions and not on the fairness to the individual employee (*Polkey v A E Dayton Services Ltd [1987] IRLR 503*). This means that an employer cannot argue that a breach of procedures has made no difference to the final outcome and that he would have dismissed the employee even if he had adhered to his procedure. Breach of procedures themselves by an employer is likely to render a dismissal unfair regardless of which rule was broken. Following the introduction of the statutory rule in relation to the conduct of disciplinary proceedings, (the right under the

*Employment Relations Act 1999* to be accompanied – see E14007 above), the employer must be particularly careful that proper procedures are followed.

Many employers adopt the ACAS procedures. Essentially any disciplinary procedure should contain three elements: an investigation, a hearing and an appeal and should observe the principles of natural justice.

### (a) Investigation

The law requires that the employer has a genuine belief in the employee's 'guilt', and that the belief is based on reasonable grounds after a reasonable investigation (*British Home Stores v Burchell [1978] IRLR 379*). If the employer suspends the employee during the investigation, this suspension should be with pay and in accordance with the disciplinary procedure. An investigation is important because it may reveal defects in the training of the employee, or reveal that the employee was not told of the rules, or that another employee was responsible for the breach. In all of these cases, disciplinary action against the suspended employee will be unfair. Any investigation should be as thorough as possible and documented. It should also take place as soon as possible since memories fade quickly and this is particularly important if other employees are to be questioned as witnesses. Likewise, taking too long to start an investigation may lead the employee to think that no action will be taken and to then discipline him may itself be unfair. No disciplinary action should be taken until a careful investigation has been concluded.

### (b) Hearing

Once the employer has investigated, he must conduct a hearing to make a decision as to the sanction, if any, he will impose. To act fairly, the employer must comply with the rules of a fair hearing. These are:

(i) The employee must know the case against him to enable him to answer the complaint. This also means that the employee should be given sufficient time before the hearing with copies of relevant documents to enable him to prepare his case.

(ii) The employee should have an opportunity to put his side of the case, i.e. the employer should listen to the employee's side of the story and allow the employee to put forward any mitigating circumstances.

(iii) The employee must be allowed to be accompanied at the hearing by a fellow employee or a trade union representative of his choice (*Employment Relations Act 1999*).

(iv) The hearing should be unbiased, i.e. the person chairing the hearing should come to it with an open mind and not have prejudged the issue.

(v) The employee should be provided with an explanation as to why any sanctions are imposed.

(vi) The employee should be informed of his right to appeal (and the way in which he should go about it) to a higher level of management which has not been involved in the first hearing. If the employee fails to exercise his right of appeal, however, he will not have failed to mitigate his loss, if ultimately a tribunal finds that he has been unfairly dismissed and thus his compensation will not be reduced (*William Muir (Bond 9) Ltd v Lamb [1985] IRLR 95*). Failing to allow an employee to exercise a right of appeal will almost certainly render any dismissal unfair (*West Midlands Co-operative Society Ltd v Tipton [1986] IRLR 112*).

(*c*) *Appeal*

In an unfair dismissal case a tribunal is required to consider the reasonableness of the employer's action taking into account the resources of the employer and the size of the employer's undertaking. This means that in the case of all but very small undertakings, the tribunal will expect the employer to have provided an appeal for the employee. All the rules of a fair hearing equally apply to an appeal. Only an appeal which is a complete rehearing of the case (rather than merely a review of the written notes of the disciplinary hearing) can rectify procedural flaws committed earlier on in the procedure (*Jones v Sainsbury's Supermarkets Ltd (2000) (unreported)*. An appeal, however, cannot endorse the sanction imposed by the earlier hearing for a different reason, unless the employee has had notice of the new reason and has been given an opportunity to put forward his argument in respect of it.

## Sanctions other than dismissal

**E14014**  There are a variety of sanctions apart from dismissal that an employer may impose. It is important however that the 'punishment fits the crime'. The imposition of too harsh a sanction may entitle the employee to resign and claim constructive dismissal (see below).

(*a*) *Warnings*

The ACAS Code recommends three warnings in cases of normal misconduct before dismissing: the first oral, the second written and a final written warning stating that a repetition will result in dismissal. These are only guidelines, however, and it clearly depends on the circumstances of the case. A minor breach of a health and safety rule, for example, may justify a final written warning given the potential seriousness and consequences of breaches of such rules. The ACAS Code urges that, apart from gross misconduct, no employee should be dismissed for a first breach of discipline, although, again, breaches of health and safety rules have been held to be gross misconduct. The Code also recommends that warnings should remain on the employee's record for a definite period of time (six to twelve months). Once this time has expired, the warnings will be ignored when looking to see if the procedure has been followed in later cases of misconduct, but can be considered when the employer is looking at the employee's work record to decide what sanction to impose.

(*b*) *Fines or deductions*

The employer must have contractual authority or the written permission of the employee before he can make a deduction from the employee's wages as a disciplinary sanction. Deducting without such authority is a breach of the *Employment Rights Act 1996, s 13* and gives the employee the right to sue for recovery in the Employment Tribunal. It will also lead to a potential constructive dismissal claim.

(*c*) *Suspension without pay*

Any suspension without pay will have the same consequences as a fine or deduction if there is no contractual authority or written authorisation from the employee to impose such a sanction.

### (*d*) Demotion

Most demotions will involve a reduction in pay, and thus without written or contractual authority to demote the employer will be in breach of the *Employment Rights Act 1996, s 13* and liable to a constructive dismissal claim.

### Suitable alternative work

E14015  Where an employee is suspended from work on maternity grounds, the employer must offer available suitable alternative work. Alternative work will only be suitable if:

(*a*)  the work is of a kind which is both suitable in relation to the employee and appropriate for the employee to do in the circumstances; and

(*b*)  the terms and conditions applicable for performing the work are not substantially less favourable than corresponding terms and conditions applicable for performing the employee's usual work (*Employment Rights Act 1996, s 67*).

If an employer fails to offer suitable alternative work, the employee may bring a claim before an Employment Tribunal which can award 'just and equitable' compensation. Such complaint must normally be lodged within three months of the first day of the suspension (*Employment Rights Act 1996, s 70(4)*).

### Remuneration on suspension from work

E14016  An employee who is suspended on medical grounds is entitled to normal remuneration for up to 26 weeks. An employee who is suspended on maternity grounds, if no suitable alternative work is available, is entitled to normal remuneration for the duration of the suspension. However, in either case, if the employee unreasonably refuses an offer of suitable alternative work, no remuneration is payable for the period during which the offer applies. An employee may bring a complaint to an Employment Tribunal if an employer fails to pay the whole or any part of the remuneration to which the employee is entitled (*Employment Rights Act 1996, ss 64, 68, 70(1)*). (See *British Airways Ltd v Moore [2000] IRLR 296*, in which the Employment Appeal Tribunal upheld a purser's claim to a flying allowance on the basis that suitable work must be on terms and conditions not substantially less favourable.)

# Dismissal

E14017  Dismissal is the ultimate sanction that an employer can impose for breach of health and safety rules. All employees are protected against wrongful dismissal at common law, but, in addition, some employees have protection against unfair dismissal. The protection against unfair dismissal comes from statute (the *Employment Rights Act 1996*) and therefore the employee must satisfy any qualifying criteria laid down by the statute before he can claim. Given that the protection against wrongful and unfair dismissal rest alongside each other, an employee may claim for both, although he will not be compensated twice. Wrongful dismissal is based on a breach of contract by the employer and compensation will be in the form of damages for that breach – that is, the damage the employee has suffered because the employer did not comply with the contract. Unfair dismissal, on the other hand, is statute based and is not dependent on a breach of contract by the employer. Compensation for such dismissal is based on a formula within the statute.

## Wrongful dismissal

**E14018**   A dismissal at common law is where the employer unilaterally terminates the employment relationship with or without notice. A wrongful dismissal is where the employer terminates the contract in breach, for example, by giving no notice or shorter notice than is required by the employee's contract and the employee's conduct does not justify this. An employer is entitled to dismiss without notice only if the employee has committed gross misconduct. In all other circumstances the employer must give contractual notice to end the relationship, or pay wages in lieu of notice. However, this does require qualification. Firstly, the law decides what is gross misconduct and not the employer. Just because the employer has stated that certain actions are gross misconduct does not mean that the law will regard it as such. Only very serious misconduct is regarded by the law as gross, such as refusing to obey lawful and reasonable orders, gross neglect, theft. Secondly, contractual notice periods are subject to the statutory minimum notice provisions contained in the *Employment Rights Act 1996, s 86*. Any attempt by the contract to give less than the statutory minimum notice is void. These periods apply to all employees who have been employed for one month or more and are:

(*a*)    not less than one week if the employee has been employed for less than two years;

(*b*)    after the employee has been employed for two years, one week for each year of service, up to a statutory maximum of 12 weeks.

Where an employer terminates the contract and pays the employee in lieu of notice, in the absence of an express right to do so, this will be a technical breach of contract. The employee can waive his right to notice or accept wages in lieu of notice. If the contract gives notice periods which are greater than the statutory minimum, the contractual notice prevails. Therefore, if the employer has an employee who has been employed for six years, and the employer sacks him with four weeks' notice, the employee can sue for a further two weeks' wages in the Employment Tribunal. Finally, if the employer fundamentally alters the terms of the employee's contract, without his consent, in reality the employer is terminating (repudiating) the original contract and substituting a new one. The employee should therefore be given the correct notice before the change comes into effect. A unilateral change by the employer to a fundamental term of the contract (followed by resignation by the employee) will amount to constructive dismissal (i.e. repudiation) and compensation in the form of damages for breach of contract. The employee must take all reasonable steps to mitigate his loss by seeking other employment.

## Unfair dismissal

### Dismissal

**E14019**   While all employees are protected against wrongful dismissal, generally employees must be employed for one year or more before they gain protection against unfair dismissal. In certain circumstances, however, an employee is protected immediately and does not need a year of employment. One of these is dismissal on certain health and safety grounds discussed above. The qualifying period was reduced from two years by way of statutory instrument with effect from June 1999 (in respect of termination dates falling on or after 1 June 1999).

The two year qualifying period rule was challenged as being discriminatory against women and the House of Lords referred the issue to the European Court of Justice (*R v Secretary of State for Employment ex parte Seymour-Smith and Perez, The Times 13 March 1997*). The ECJ did not decide whether the two year qualifying period was discriminatory but remitted this particular question to the House of Lords for determination on the facts in the United Kingdom – i.e. whether a significantly smaller proportion of women than of men could comply with the two year qualifying period. The majority of the House of Lords held that the two year qualifying period was indirectly discriminatory during the period from 1985 to 1991, because the statistics for that period indicated that it had a considerably greater adverse impact on women than men. However, the two year requirement was objectively justified during that period on the basis that it rejected a legitimate aim of social policy to encourage employers to engage employees, which was unrelated to sex and that it was unreasonable to believe that such a measure was a suitable means for attaining that aim (*R v Secretary of State for Employment ex parte Seymour-Smith (No.2) [2000] IRLR 263*).

As a consequence, the position is uncertain for cases relating to the period after 1991 (at which time is unclear whether the objective justification argument submitted by the Government would still apply), but before 1 June 1999, when the qualifying period was reduced to one year.

Once an employee is protected against unfair dismissal the *Employment Rights Act 1996, s 95* recognises three situations which the law regards as dismissal. These are:

(*a*)   the employer terminating the contract (with or without notice);

(*b*)   a fixed term contract which expires and is not renewed;

(*c*)   the employee resigning in circumstances in which he is entitled to do so without notice because of the employer's conduct – a constructive dismissal.

In the first situation the employer is unilaterally ending the relationship. Even if the employer gives the correct amount of notice so that the dismissal is lawful, it does not necessarily follow that the dismissal will be fair.

The second situation needs no explanation. If a fixed term contract has come to an end and is not renewed, this is, in effect, the employer deciding to end the relationship. As from 25 October 1999, it is no longer possible for employees to validly waive unfair dismissal rights in fixed term contracts (*Employment Relations Act 1999*).

In the third situation, the constructive dismissal, is much more complex. On the face of it the employee has resigned. However if the reason for his resignation is the employer's conduct, then the law treats the resignation as an employer termination. The action on the part of the employer which entitles the employee to resign and claim constructive dismissal is a repudiatory breach of contract. In other words, the employer has committed a breach which goes to the root of the contract and has, therefore, repudiated it. This means that not all breaches by the employer are constructive dismissals but that serious breaches may be. It is also important to recognise that, as discussed above, the terms of the contract may include those which have not been expressly agreed by the parties and therefore rules, disciplinary procedures, terms collectively bargained, and all the implied duties discussed in E14008 above, may all be contractual terms. Breach of the health and safety duties owed to all employees is likely to give rise to a constructive dismissal claim (*Day v T Pickles Farms Ltd [1999] IRLR 217*). In addition, the law requires as an implied term of the contract that both the employer and employee treat each other with mutual respect and do nothing to destroy the trust and confidence each has in the other. Breach of this duty may give rise to a constructive dismissal claim. In one case, a demotion imposed as a disciplinary sanction was held to be excessive by the Employment Appeal Tribunal. Its very excessiveness was a breach of the duty of mutual respect which entitled the employee to resign and claim constructive dismissal. It has also been held that an employer's disclosure in a reference on behalf of an employee of complaints against the employee, before first giving the individual an opportunity to explain, was a fundamental breach of the implied term of mutual trust and confidence when amounted to constructive (since the employee resigned) and unfair dismissal (*TSB Bank v Harris [2000] IRLR 157*). In *Reed v Stedman [1999] IRLR 299*, the Employment Appeal Tribunal held that in a case where the employer was aware of an employee's deteriorating health, and the employee concerned had complained to colleagues at work about harassment, it was encumbent on the employer to investigate and their failure to do so was enough to justify a finding of breach of trust and confidence and thus constructive dismissal.

Where an employee with one or more year's continuous service is constructively dismissed, he or she will also have the right to claim unfair dismissal (unless one of the specified reasons apply which render a dismissal automatically unfair). Obviously, the employee must resign before he can make a claim for unfair dismissal. In the majority of cases the repudiatory breach by the employer is a fundamental alteration of the contractual terms (for example hours). In this situation, the employer still wishes to continue the relationship, albeit on different terms. The employee has two choices: he can resign or he can continue to work under the new terms. If the employee continues to work and accepts the changed terms, the contract is mutually varied and no action will lie, provided that the employee was given the correct notice before the change was implemented. If the employee resigns, however, he will have been dismissed. In *Walton & Morse v Dorrington [1997] IRLR 488*, the employee waited to find alternative employment before she resigned. The Employment Appeal Tribunal decided that, in her circumstances, this was a reasonable thing to have done and agreed that she had not accepted her employer's breach of its duty to her and had been constructively dismissed (see E14008 above).

*Reasons for dismissal*

E14020     *Section 98* of the *Employment Rights Act 1996* gives five potentially fair reasons for dismissal. These are:

(*a*)     capability or qualifications;

(*b*)     conduct;

(*c*)     redundancy;

(*d*)     contravention of statute;

(*e*)     some other substantial reason.

Dismissal on health and safety grounds could potentially fall within most of these reasons. It should, however, be remembered that, where an employee is dismissed in circumstances where continued employment involves a risk to the employee's health and safety, the employer may nevertheless face claims of unfair dismissal. Before terminating employment, an employer should consider all the circumstances of the case and assess the risk involved and take measures which are reasonably necessary to eliminate the risk.

Illness may make it unsafe to employ the employee; breach of health and safety rules will normally fall under misconduct; to continue to employ the employee may contravene health and safety legislation or it may be that the employer has had to reorganise his business on health and safety grounds and the employee is refusing to accept the change. This latter situation could be potentially fair under 'some other substantial reason'. (However, an employer may be liable under the *Disability Discrimination Act 1995*.)

*Reasonableness*

E14021   Merely having a fair reason to dismiss does not mean that the dismissal is fair. *Section 98(4)* of the *Employment Rights Act 1996* requires the tribunal in any unfair dismissal case to consider whether the employer acted reasonably in all the circumstances (including the size and administrative resources of the employer's undertaking). This means that the tribunal will look at two things – (i) was the treatment of the employee procedurally fair, and (ii) was dismissal a reasonable sanction in relation to the employee's actions and all the circumstances of the case.

Procedures have already been discussed at E14013 above. If the employer has complied with his procedures, he will not be found to have acted procedurally unfairly unless the procedures themselves are unfair. This is unlikely if the employer is following the ACAS Code.

In respect of the fairness of the decision, the tribunal should consider whether the employer's decision to dismiss fell within the band of reasonable responses to the employee's conduct which a reasonable employer could adopt. The tribunal will look at three things – (i) has the employer acted consistently, (ii) has he taken the employee's past work record into account, and (iii) has the employer looked for alternative employment. The latter aspect is of major importance in relation to redundancy, incapability due to illness or dismissal because of a contravention of legislation, but will not usually be relevant in dismissals for misconduct. It is important to note in addition that special obligations apply to an employer in the case of a disabled employee within the meaning of the *Disability Discrimination Act 1995.*

When looking at consistency, the tribunal will look for evidence that the employer has treated the same misconduct the same way in the past. If the employer has treated past breaches of health and safety rules leniently it will be unfair to suddenly dismiss for the same breach, unless he has made it clear to the employees that his attitude has changed and breaches will be dealt with more severely in the future. Employees have to know the potential disciplinary consequences for breaches of the rules, and if the employer has never dismissed in the past he is misleading employees unless he tells them that things have changed. The law, however, only requires an employer to be consistent between cases which are the same. This is where a consideration of the employee's past work record is important. It is not inconsistent to give a long-standing employee with a clean record a final warning for a breach of health and safety rules and to dismiss another shorter-serving employee with a series of warnings behind him, as long as both employees know that the penalty for breach of the rules could be dismissal. The cases are not the same. It would, however, be unfair if both the employees had the same type of work record and length of service and only one was dismissed, and dismissal had never been imposed as a sanction for that type of breach in the past. In order for a misconduct dismissal to be fair, the employer must have had a reasonable belief in the guilt of the employee of the misconduct in question on the basis of a reasonable investigation.

*Remedies for unfair dismissal*

*(a) Reinstatement*

E14022   The first remedy that the tribunal is required to consider is reinstatement of the employee. When doing so the tribunal must take into account whether the employee wishes to be reinstated, whether it is practicable for the employer to reinstate him and, if the employee's conduct contributed to or caused his dismissal, whether it is just to reinstate him. In order to resist an order for reinstatement, an employer must provide evidence to show that it is not practicable because the implied term of mutual trust and confidence between employer and employee has broken down (*IPC Magazines Ltd v Clements, EAT/456/99; Gentle & Ors v Perkins Group Ltd, EAT/670/99*). Reinstatement means that the employee must return to his old job with no loss of benefits. If reinstatement is ordered and the employer refuses to comply with the order, or only partially complies, compensation will be increased. Reinstatement, however, is rarely ordered by tribunals.

*(b) Re-engagement*

If the tribunal does not consider that reinstatement is practicable, it must consider whether to order the employer to re-engage the employee. In making its decision the tribunal looks at the same factors as when it considers reinstatement. Re-engagement is an order requiring the employer to re-employ the employee on terms which are as favourable as those he enjoyed before his dismissal, but it does not require the employer to give the employee the same job back. Failure on the part of the employer to comply with an order of re-engagement will lead to increased compensation, although tribunals rarely make re-engagement orders.

*(c) Compensation*

Compensation falls under a variety of different heads. In an unfair dismissal case the employee will receive:

**Basic award**: This is based on his age, years of service and salary –

(i)    one and a half weeks' pay for each year of service over the age of 41;

(ii)   one week's pay for each year of service between 41 and 22;

(iii)  half a week's pay for each year of service below the age of 22.

This is subject to a statutory maximum of £230 a week, (£240 if the effective date of the termination falls on or after 1 February 2001), and a maximum of twenty years' service. Compensation is reduced by one-twelfth for each month the employee works during his 64th year. Where the employee is unfairly dismissed for health and safety reasons under the *Employment Rights Act 1996, s 100*, the minimum basic award is £3,100 (at present) (£3,3000 if the effective date of termination falls on or after 1 February 2001).

**Compensatory award**: This is payable in addition to the basic award to compensate the employee for loss of future earnings, benefits etc, which are in excess of the basic award. As with the basic award the compensatory award can be reduced for contributory conduct. The present maximum compensatory award is £50,000 (£51,700 if the effective date of termination falls on or after 1 February 2001).

**Additional award**: If the employer fails to comply with a reinstatement or re-engagement order, the tribunal may make an additional award. This will be between 26 and 52 weeks' pay (at a maximum of £230 per week or £240 if the effective date of termination falls on or after 1 February 2001).

The old system of additional and special awards of compensation for unfair dismissal was consolidated in to a single additional award in respect of dismissals where the effective date of termination falls on or after 25 October 1999 (*Employment Relations Act 1999, s 33*). With effect from that date, special awards available in cases of automatically unfair dismissal relating to (*inter alia*) the activities of safety representatives, were abolished.

**Note**: The *Employment Relations Act 1999* also removes the limit on the compensatory award for employees who are dismissed for health and safety reasons (see E14010).

The *Sex Discrimination and Equal Pay (Remedies) Regulations 1993 (SI 1993 No 2798)* abolished the limit on awards of compensation in sex discrimination and equal pay cases and made provision for interest to be included in such awards. Employers could therefore be faced with claims leading to the award of large amounts of compensation in cases of unlawful sex discrimination.

There is also no upper limit on the amount of the compensation that a tribunal may award in a case of discrimination under the *Disability Discrimination Act 1995*. In cases of sex and disability discrimination, compensation may include compensation for injury to feelings.

# Health and safety duties in relation to women at work

## Sex discrimination

E14023    Since health and safety issues may give rise to sex discrimination claims under the *Sex Discrimination Act 1975 (SDA 1975)*, it is appropriate to examine what particular considerations an employer needs to bear in mind in its relations with female employees.

The steps necessary to be taken by an employer, in order to comply with his duties under *HSWA 1974, s 2*, may differ for women.

New or expectant mothers are particularly vulnerable to adverse or indifferent working conditions. Indeed, most employers have probably taken measures to guard against risks to new and expectant mothers, in accordance with their general duties under *HSWA 1974, s 2*, and the *Management of Health and Safety at Work Regulations 1999 (SI 1999 No 3242)* (see EMPLOYERS' DUTIES TO THEIR EMPLOYEES). In addition, employers are required to protect new and expectant mothers in their employment from certain specified risks if it is reasonable to do so, and to carry out a risk assessment of such hazards. If the employer cannot avoid the risk(s), he must alter the working conditions of the employee concerned or the hours of work, offer suitable alternative work and, if no suitable alternative work is available, suspend the employee on full pay (see E14024 below).

Although *SDA 1975* prohibits discrimination on grounds of sex, *s 51(1)* provides that any action taken to comply with certain existing health and safety legislation (e.g. *HSWA 1974*) will *not* amount to unlawful discrimination. In *Page v Freight Hire (Tank Haulage) Ltd [1981] IRLR 13*, the complainant was an HGV driver. The employer, acting on the instructions of the manufacturer of the chemical dimethyl-formamide (DMF), refused to allow her to transport the chemical which was potentially harmful to women of child bearing age. She brought a complaint of sex discrimination. It was held that the fact that the discriminatory action was taken in the interests of safety did not of itself provide a defence to a complaint of unlawful discrimination. However, the employer was protected by *s 51(1)* of *SDA 1975* because the action taken was necessary to comply with the employer's duty under *HSWA 1974*.

## Pregnant workers, new and breastfeeding mothers

E14024    The *Management of Health and Safety at Work Regulations 1999 (SI 1999 No 3242)* re-enact the 1992 Regulations *(SI 1992 No 2051)*, as amended by *Management of Health and Safety at Work (Amendment) Regulations 1994 (SI 1994 No 2865)*. *Regulations 16 to 18* of the 1999 Regulations provide for a duty of employers to protect new or expectant mothers from any process or working conditions or certain physical, chemical and biological risks at work (see E14025 below). The phrase 'new or expectant mother' is defined as a worker who is pregnant, who has given birth within the previous six months, or who is breastfeeding. 'Given birth' is defined as having delivered a living child or, after 24 weeks of pregnancy, a stillborn child.

*Risk assessment*

**E14025**    The 1999 Regulations require employers to carry out an assessment of the specific risks posed to the health and safety of pregnant women and new mothers in the workplace and then to take steps to ensure that those risks are avoided. Risks include those to the unborn child or child of a woman who is still breastfeeding – not just risks to the mother.

An interesting development in relation to this requirement is the case of *Day v T Pickles Farms Ltd [1999] IRLR 217*, where the employee suffered nausea when pregnant as a result of the smell of food at her workplace. As a result of the nausea, she was unable to work and was eventually dismissed after a prolonged absence.

The Employment Appeal Tribunal found that she had not been constructively dismissed, but decided that her employers should have carried out a risk assessment when employing her, a woman of childbearing age. The question of whether the applicant had been subjected to a detriment was remitted to the Employment Tribunal.

The Employment Appeal Tribunal's interpretation of the *Management of Health and Safety at Work Regulations 1992*, was that the obligation to carry out a risk assessment which considers possible risks to the health and safety of a pregnant female employee is relevant from the moment an employer employs a woman of childbearing age.

The Health and Safety Executive has published a booklet entitled *'New and expectant mothers at work – A guide for employers'*. The booklet provides guidance on what employers need to do to comply with the legislation. The booklet includes a list of the known risks to new and expectant mothers and suggests methods of avoidance.

The main risks to be avoided are as follows:

(*a*)    Physical agents:

— shocks/vibrations/movement (including travelling and other physical burdens),

— handling of loads entailing risks,

— noise,

— non-ionising radiation,

— extremes of heat and cold.

(*b*)    Biological agents:

— such as listeria, rubella and chicken pox virus, toxoplasma, cytomegalovirus, hepatitis B and HIV.

(*c*)    Chemical agents:

— such as mercury, antimiotic drugs, carbon monoxide, chemical agents of known and percutaneous absorption and chemicals listed under various Directives.

(*d*)    Working conditions:

— such as mining work and work with display screen equipment (VDUs).

Where a risk has been identified following the assessment, affected employees or their representatives should be informed of the risk and the preventive measures to be adopted. The assessment should be kept under review.

In particular, employers must consider removing the hazard or seek to prevent exposure to it. If a risk remains after preventive action has been taken, the employer must take the following course of action:

(i) temporarily adjust her working conditions or hours of work (*Management of Health and Safety at Work Regulations 1999 (SI 1999 No 3242), Reg 16(2)*).

If it is not reasonable to do so or would not avoid the risk:

(ii) offer suitable alternative work (*Employment Rights Act 1996, s 67*).

If neither of the above options is viable:

(iii) suspend her on full pay for as long as necessary to protect her health and safety or that of her child (*Management of Health and Safety at Work Regulations 1999 (SI 1999 No 3242), Regs 16(2) and 16(3); Employment Rights Act 1996, s 67*).

Appendix 1 of the booklet lists aspects of pregnancy such as morning sickness, varicose veins, increasing size etc. that may affect work and which employers may take into account in considering working arrangements for pregnant and breastfeeding workers. These are merely suggestions and not requirements of the law.

### Night work by new or expectant mother

E14026    Where a new or expectant mother works at night and has been issued with a certificate from a registered doctor or midwife stating that night work would affect her health and safety, the employer must first offer her suitable alternative daytime work, and suspend her as detailed at E14015 above if no suitable alternative employment can be found (*Management of Health and Safety at Work Regulations 1999 (SI 1999 No 3242), Reg 17*).

### Notification

E14027    An employer is not required to alter a woman's working conditions or hours of work or suspend her from work under *Management of Health and Safety at Work Regulations 1999 (SI 1999 No 3242), Reg 16(2)* or *(3)* until she notifies him in writing that she is pregnant, has given birth within the previous six months or is breastfeeding. Additionally, the suspension or amended working conditions do not have to be maintained if the employee fails to produce a medical certificate confirming her pregnancy in writing within a reasonable time if the employer requests her to do so. The same applies once the employer knows that the employee is no longer a new or expectant mother or if the employer cannot establish whether she remains so (*Management of Health and Safety at Work Regulations 1999 (SI 1999 No 3242), Reg 18*). However, an employer has a general duty under *HSWA 1974* and the *Management of Health and Safety at Work Regulations 1999* to take steps to protect the health and safety of a new or expectant mother, even if she has not given written notification of her condition.

### Maternity leave

E14028    All pregnant workers have a right to 18 weeks' maternity leave, regardless of length of service and number of hours worked. The maternity leave period starts from:

(*a*) the notified date of commencement; or

(*b*)    the first day of absence because of pregnancy or childbirth after the beginning of the sixth week before the expected week of confinement; or

(*c*)    the date of childbirth;

which ever is the earlier, and continues for eighteen weeks or until the end of the compulsory leave period if later.

If an employee is prohibited from working for a specified period after childbirth by virtue of a legislative requirement (e.g. under the *Public Health Act 1936, s 205*), her maternity leave period must continue until the expiry of that later period. The *Employment Rights Act 1996, s 72(1)*, provide that an employee entitled to maternity leave should not work or be permitted to work by her employer during the period of two weeks beginning with the date of childbirth.

# Enforcement

## Introduction

E15001    In the last decade there has been a movement away from a purely legalistic approach towards health and safety at work to one concerned with loss prevention, asset protection, accountability and consultation with the workforce, a situation without parallel under previous protective legislation. An effective system of enforcement is still, however, essential if workplaces are to be kept safe and accidents prevented. Prior to the *Health and Safety at Work etc. Act 1974* (*HSWA*), the principal sanction against breach of a statutory requirement was prosecution. This preoccupation with criminal proceedings was criticised by the Robens Committee (para 142) as being largely ineffective in securing the most important end result, namely that the breach should be remedied as soon as possible. The *HSWA*, therefore, has given HSE inspectors a range of enforcement powers which do not necessarily depend on prosecution for their efficacy. Most important of these are the powers to serve improvement and prohibition notices. Contravention of an improvement/prohibition notice carries with it, on summary conviction, a maximum fine of £20,000 or, alternatively, six months' imprisonment and on conviction on indictment an unlimited fine or two years' imprisonment (see E15036 below). In particular, a prohibition notice may be served by an inspector where he believes there to be a risk of serious personal injury, regardless of whether any offence has actually been committed. Equally important, though less obvious perhaps, HSE inspectors and environmental health officers, the two principal enforcement authorities, can use powers given to them by *HSWA*, i.e. serve improvement and prohibition notices, in order to enforce remaining pre-*HSWA* statutory requirements, e.g. duties under the *Factories Act 1961* and *Offices, Shops and Railway Premises Act 1963* (*OSRPA*), since these qualify as 'relevant statutory provisions' (see E15012 below).

More recently, the *Environmental Protection Act 1990* and the *Environment Act 1995* have conferred similar notice-serving powers on the Environment Agency. The *Radioactive Material (Road Transport) Act 1991* has given transport inspectors powers to detain, search and generally 'quarantine' vehicles carrying radioactive packages in breach of that Act and the *Radioactive Substances Act 1993* similarly empowers inspectors in respect of premises containing radioactive substances and mobile radioactive apparatus (see D1068–D1071 DANGEROUS SUBSTANCES I).

Such enforcement powers apart, breach of a statutory requirement is still a criminal offence. Prosecution, albeit a 'reserve weapon', is an important one; in 1997/98 there were 1,627 prosecutions for health and safety offences. Persons committing a breach, or permitting one to occur, should be in no doubt that they stand to be prosecuted. It is not just the employer who is liable to prosecution: employees' and junior and middle management and even visitors to the workplace can also be prosecuted, either in tandem with the employer or alone. If the employer is a company or local authority, the company, its directors and/or officers, as well as councillors may be charged with an offence (see E15040 below).

Prosecutions and other enforcement procedures are the responsibility of the appropriate 'enforcing authority' (see E15007–E15011 below). In addition, where an employee is injured or killed as a result of negligence or breach of a statutory requirement, a civil action may be brought against the employer for damages.

(Although possibly an additional form of enforcement, civil liability is mainly discussed in EMPLOYERS' DUTIES TO THEIR EMPLOYEES at E11001.)

This section deals with the following aspects of enforcement:

— The role of the Health and Safety Commission and the Health and Safety Executive (see E15002–E15006).

— The 'enforcing authorities' (see E15007–E15011 below).

— The 'relevant statutory provisions' which can be enforced under *HSWA* (see E15012 below).

*Part A: Enforcement Powers of Inspectors*

— Improvement and prohibition notices (see E15013–E15018 below).

— Appeals against improvement and prohibition notices (see E15019, E15020 below).

— Grounds for appeal against a notice (see E15021–E15025 below).

— Inspectors' investigation powers (see E15026 below).

— Inspectors' powers of search and seizure (see E15027 below).

— Indemnification by enforcing authority (see E15028 below).

— Public register of notices (see E15029 below).

*Part B: Offences and Penalties*

— Prosecution for contravention of the relevant statutory provisions (see E15030, E15031 below).

— Main offences and penalties (see E15032–E15038 below).

— Offences committed by particular types of persons, including the Crown (see E15039–E15045 below).

— Sentencing guidelines.(see E15043 below).

(For offences under the *Environmental Protection Act 1990* and the *Environment Act 1995*, see E5020–E5025 EMISSIONS INTO THE ATMOSPHERE.)

# The role of the Health and Safety Commision and Executive

E15002    Under the *HSWA* the administration and enforcement of health and safety law is carried out by the Health and Safety Commission (HSC) and its executive arm the Health and Safety Executive (HSE). The HSC consists of a chairman and not fewer than six, nor more than nine, other members. Of those members three represent employers, three employees and the remainder are from bodies such as local authorities and professional organisations [*HSWA s 10(2), (3)*]. The HSE is the executive arm of the HSC and consists of a director general appointed by the HSE, a deputy director general and head of operations. Both the HSC and HSE are independent of any government department, but owe direct responsibilities to the relevant Secretary of State (the Secretary of State for the Environment).

## The functions of the HSC

E15003    The functions of the HSC include promoting the general aims of the *HSWA* and other health and safety legislation generally, drawing up proposals for regulations, replacing/updating existing law and regulations, preparing approved codes of practice and ensuring arrangements are in place for research and training [*HSWA s 11(2); Employment Protection Act 1975, s 116, Sch 15 para 4*].

The HSC is given consequential powers to make agreements with other government departments, established advisory committees, etc. for the purpose of discharging its functions. [*HSWA s 13*]. It may also delegate the exercise of certain of its functions to the HSE [*HSWA s 11(4)(a)*], for example, it may ask the HSE to carry out research or provide publicity or educational materials.

The HSC can also ask the HSE to conduct a special investigation and to report to them on their findings or, with the consent of the Secretary of State, direct that an inquiry be held into any accident, occurrence or matter [*HSWA s 14*].

## Preparation by the HSE of draft regulations and issue of approved codes of practice

E15004    One of the most important functions of the HSC is to prepare draft regulations for the Secretary of State, including new regulations seeking to implement EU directives relating to health and safety at work. This normally involves preparation of a consultative document and draft regulations which are considered by industry and employee bodies, trade associations and other interested bodies, such as local authorities and educational establishments. Draft regulations are submitted to the Secretary of State for approval after consultation. Although the power to make regulations rests with the Secretary of State, he has a duty to consult the HSC before doing so.

Such regulations can:

(*a*)    repeal or modify any of the 'relevant statutory provisions' (see E15012 for the definition of this term);

(*b*)    exclude or modify any of the 'existing statutory provisions' e.g. the *Employers' Health and Safety Policy Statements (Exception) Regulations 1975 (SI 1975 No 1584)*, exempt employers employing fewer than *five* employees from issuing a written company safety policy, as required by *HSWA s 2(3)*;

(*c*)    make a specified authority responsible for the enforcement of any of the relevant statutory provisions.

[*HSWA s 15(3)(c)*].

Although the HSC does not have power to make regulations, it can approve and issue of codes of practice providing practical guidance on the requirements imposed by health and safety legislation or regulations [*HSWA s 16*]. In all cases the HSC must consult with any appropriate government departments and obtain the consent of the Secretary of State before the issue of Approved Codes of Practice ('ACOP's').

## Functions of the Health and Safety Executive

E15005    The main function of the HSE is to enforce health and safety legislation unless responsibility lies with another enforcing body, such as a local authority [*HSWA s 18(1)*]. The HSE's functions are principally performed by its inspectors and include carrying out routine inspections of premises, investigating workplace accidents, dangerous occurrences or cases of ill health and providing advice to companies and individuals on the legal requirements under health and safety legislation. The HSE also publish guidance documents (see E15006 below), provide an information service, carry out research and license or approve certain hazardous operations, such as nuclear site licensing and accepting offshore installation safety cases.

The *Health and Safety (Fees) Regulations 1999 (SI 1999 No. 645)*, as amended (by *SI 1999 No. 2597*) also provide that the HSE may, in certain limited circumstances, charge for their services. In particular, fees are payable for (*inter alia*):

(*a*) assessment of all safety cases prepared under gas transportation, offshore installation and railways legislation. Providing advice on such applications, including applications for an exemption, and carrying out inspections to ensure compliance with the safety cases;

(*b*) an approval under mines and quarries legislation;

(*c*) an approval of certain respiratory protective equipment;

(*d*) examination or surveillance by an employment medical adviser;

(*e*) an approval of a scheme or programme under the *Freight Containers (Safety Convention) Regulations 1984 (SI 1984 No 1890)*;

(*f*) a licence under the *Asbestos (Licensing) Regulations 1983 (SI 1983 No 1649)*;

(*g*) an approval of dosimetry services and type approval of radiation generators or apparatus containing radioactive substances under the *Ionising Radiations Regulations 1985 (SI 1985 No 1333)*;

(*h*) a licence or approval under explosives legislation;

(*i*) an approval under the *Carriage of Dangerous Goods by Road (Driver Training) Regulations 1996 (SI 1996 No 2094)*;

(*j*) a vocational training certificate under the *Carriage of Dangerous Goods by Road (Driver Training) Regulations 1996 (SI 1996 No 2094)*;

(*k*) a vocational training certificate under the *Transport of Dangerous Goods (Safety Advisers) Regulations 1999 (SI 1999 No 257)*; and

(*l*) notification of new substances under the *Notification of New Substances Regulations 1993 (SI 1993 No 3050)*.

## HSE publications

E15006  The HSE (through HSE Books) also publish a series of guidance notes/advisory literature for employers, local authorities, trade unions etc. on most aspects of health and safety of concern to industry. These are divided into five main areas i.e. Chemical Safety (CS), Environmental Hygiene (EH), General Series (GS), Medical Series (MS), and Plant or Machinery (PM).

In addition there are the Health and Safety (Guidance) Series (HS(G)); the Health and Safety (Regulations) Series (HS(R)); Legal Series (L); Best Practicable Means Leaflets (BPM); Emission Test Methods (ETM); Health and Safety Commission Leaflets (HSC); Health and Safety Executive Leaflets (HSE); Industry General Leaflets (IND(G)); Industry Safety Leaflets (IND(S)); similarly, Methods for the Determination of Hazardous Substances (MDHS); Toxicity Reviews (TR); Occasional Papers; and Agricultural Safety Leaflets (AS).

# Enforcing authorities

E15007     Whilst the HSE is the central body entrusted with the enforcement of health and safety legislation, in any given case enforcement powers rest with the body which is expressed by statute to be the 'enforcing authority'. Here the general rule is that the 'enforcing authority', in the case of industrial premises, is the HSE and, in the case of commercial premises within its area, the local authority (the enforcing authority in over a million premises), except that the HSE cannot enforce provisions in respect of its own premises, and similarly, local authorities' premises are inspected by the HSE. Each 'enforcing authority' is empowered to appoint suitably qualified persons as inspectors for the purpose of carrying into effect the 'relevant statutory provisions' within the authority's field of responsibility. [*HSWA s 19(1)*]. Inspectors so appointed can exercise any of the enforcement powers conferred by *HSWA* (see E15013–E15018 below) and bring prosecutions (see E15030, E15031 below).

## The appropriate 'enforcing authority'

E15008     The general rule is that the HSE is the enforcing authority, except to the extent that:

(*a*)     regulations specify that the local authority is the enforcing authority instead; the regulations that so specify are the *Health and Safety (Enforcing Authority) Regulations 1998 (SI 1998 No 494)*; or;

(*b*)     one of the 'relevant statutory provisions' specifies that some other body is responsible for the enforcement of a particular requirement.

[HSWA s 18(1), (7)(a)].

*Activities for which the HSE is the enforcing authority*

E15009

The HSE is specifically the enforcing authority in respect of the following activities (even though the main activity on the premises is one for which a local authority is usually the enforcing authority in accordance with the *Health and Safety (Enforcing Authority) Regulations 1998(SI 1998 No 494)*, *1 Sch* (see E15010 below):

1.     Any activity in a mine or quarry;

2.     Fairground activity;

3.     Broadcasting, recording, filming, or video recording and any activity in premises occupied by a radio, television or film undertaking where such work is carried on;

4.     The following work carried out by independent contractors:

  *(a)*     certain construction work;

  *(b)*     installation, maintenance or repair of gas systems or work in connection with a gas fitting;

  *(c)*     installation, maintenance or repair of electricity systems;

  *(d)*     most work with ionising radiations;

5.     Use of ionising radiations for medical exposure;

6.     Any activity in radiography premises where work with ionising radiations is carried out;

7. Agricultural activities, including agricultural shows (but excluding garden centres);

8. Any activity on board a sea-going ship;

9. Ski slope, ski lift, ski tow or cable car activities;

10. Fish, maggot and game breeding (but not in a zoo);

11. The operation of a railway;

12. Any activity in relation to a pipeline;

13. Enforcement of *HSWA s 6* (duties of manufacturers/suppliers of industrial products).

[*Health and Safety (Enforcing Authority) Regulations 1998, Reg 4(4)(b) and 2 Sch*]

---

The HSE is the enforcing authority against the following, and for any premises they occupy, including parts of the premises occupied by others providing services for them. (This is so even though the main activity is listed in *1 Sch* of the 1998 regulations, see E15010 below):

14. County councils;

15. Local authorities;

16. Parish or community councils;

17. Police authorities;

18. Fire authorities;

19. International HQ's and defence organisations and visiting forces;

20. United Kingdom Atomic Energy Authority (UKAEA);

21. The Crown (except where premises are occupied by the HSE itself).

[*Health and Safety (Enforcing Authority) Regulations 1998, Reg 4(1)–(3)*].

---

The HSE is also the enforcing authority for the premises set out below, even if occupied by more than one occupier:

22. Airport land;

23. The Channel Tunnel system;

24. Offshore installations;

25. Building/construction sites;

26. University, polytechnic, college, school etc. campuses;

27. Hospitals;

[*Health and Safety at Work (Enforcing Authority)Regulations 1998, Reg 3(5)*]

and for the following:

28.  Common parts of domestic premises *(Reg 3(1))*;

29.  Certain areas within an airport *(Reg 3(4)(b))*;

30.  Common parts of railway stations/termini/goods yards *(Reg 3(6))*.

*Activities for which local authorities are the enforcing authorities*

**E15010**

Where the main activity carried on in non-domestic premises is one of the following, the local authority is the enforcing authority (i.e. the relevant county, district or borough council):

1.  Sale or storage of goods for retail/wholesale distribution (including sale and fitting of motor car tyres, exhausts, windscreens or sunroofs), except:

    (*a*)  at container depots where the main activity is the storage of goods which are of transit to or from dock premises, an airport or railway;

    (*b*)  where the main activity is the sale or storage for wholesale distribution of dangerous substances;

    (*c*)  where the main activity is the sale or storage of water or sewage or their by-products or natural or town gas.

2.  Display or demonstration of goods at an exhibition, being offered or advertised for sale.

3.  Office activities.

4.  Catering services.

5.  Provision of permanent or temporary residential accommodation, including sites for caravans or campers.

6.  Consumer services provided in a shop, except:

    (*a*)  dry cleaning;

    (*b*)  radio/television repairs.

7.  Cleaning (wet or dry) in coin-operated units in laundrettes etc.

8.  Baths, saunas, solariums, massage parlours, premises for hair transplant, skin piercing, manicuring or other cosmetic services and therapeutic treatments, except where supervised by a doctor, dentist, physiotherapist, osteopath or chiropractor.

9.  Practice or presentation of arts, sports, games, entertainment or other cultural/recreational activities, save where the main activity is the exhibition of a cave to the public.

10.  Hiring out of pleasure craft for use on inland waters.

11.  Care, treatment, accommodation or exhibition of animals, birds or other creatures, except where the main activity is:

    (*a*)  horse breeding/horse training at stables;

    (*b*)  agricultural activity;

    (*c*)  veterinary surgery.

> 12.    Undertaking, but not embalming or coffin making.
>
> 13.    Church worship/religious meetings.
>
> 14.    Provision of care parking facilities within an airport.
>
> 15.    Childcare, playgroup or nursery facilities.
>
> [*Health and Safety (Enforcing Authority) Regulations 1998, Reg 3(1) and 1 Sch*].

### Transfer of responsibility between the HSE and local authorities

E15011    Enforcement can be transferred (though not in the case of Crown premises), by prior agreement, from the HSE to the local authority and vice versa. The Health and Safety Commission is also empowered to effect such a transfer, without the necessity of such agreement. In either case, parties who are affected by such transfer must be notified. [*Health and Safety (Enforcing Authority) Regulations 1998, Reg 5*]. Transfer is effective even though the above procedure is not followed (i.e. the authority changes when the main activity changes) (*Hadley v Hancox (1987) 85 LGR 402*, decided under the previous Regulations).

Where there is uncertainty, these Regulations also allow responsibility to be assigned by the HSE and the local authority jointly to either body. [*Reg 6(1)*].

## 'Relevant statutory provisions' covered by the Health and Safety at Work etc. Act 1974

E15012    The enforcement powers conferred by *HSWA* extend to any of the 'relevant statutory provisions'. These comprise:

(*a*)    the provisions of *HSWA Part I* (i.e. *Secs 1-53*); and

(*b*)    any health and safety regulations passed under *HSWA*, e.g. the *Ionising Radiations Regulations 1985 (SI 1985 No 1333)*, the *Management of Health and Safety at Work Regulations 1999 (SI 1999 No 3242)* and the *Workplace (Health, Safety and Welfare) Regulations 1992 (SI 1992 No 3004)*; and

(*c*)    the 'existing statutory provisions', i.e. all enactments specified in *HSWA 1 Sch*, including any regulations etc. made under them, so long as they continue to have effect; that is, the *Explosives Acts 1875-1923*, the *Mines and Quarries Act 1954*, the *Factories Act 1961*, the *Public Health Act 1961*, the *Offices, Shops and Railway Premises Act 1963* and (by dint of the *Offshore Safety Act 1992*) the *Mineral Workings (Offshore Installations) Act 1971* [*HSWA s 53(1)*].

## Part A: Enforcement Powers of Inspectors

### Improvement and prohibition notices

E15013    It was recommended by the Robens Committee that 'Inspectors' should have the power, without reference to the courts, to issue a formal improvement notice to an employer requiring him to remedy particular faults or to institute a specified programme of work within a stated time limit.' (Cmnd 5034, para 269). 'The improvement notice would be the inspector's main sanction. In addition, an alternative and stronger power should be available to the inspector for use where he considers the case for remedial action to be particularly serious. In such cases he should be able to issue a prohibition notice.' (Cmnd 5034, para 276). *HSWA* put these recommendations into effect.

## Improvement notices

E15014    An inspector may serve an improvement notice if he is of the opinion that a person:

(*a*)    is contravening one or more of the 'relevant statutory provisions' (see E15012 above); or

(*b*)    has contravened one or more of those provisions in circumstances that make it likely that the contravention will continue or be repeated.

[*HSWA s 21*].

In the improvement notice the inspector must:

(i)    state that he is of the opinion in (*a*) and (*b*) above; and

(ii)    specify the provision(s) in his opinion contravened; and

(iii)    give particulars of the reasons for his opinion; and

(iv)    specify a period of time within which the person is required to remedy the contravention (or the matters occasioning such contravention).

[*HSWA s 21*].

The period specified in the notice within which the requirement must be carried out (see (iv) above) must be at least 21 days – this being the period within which an appeal may be lodged with an industrial tribunal (see E15019 below) [*HSWA s 21*]. In order to be validly served on a company, an improvement notice relating to the company's actions as an employer must be served at the registered office of the company, not elsewhere. Service at premises occupied by the company will only be valid if the notice relates to a contravention by the company in the capacity of occupier (*HSE v George Tancocks Garage (Exeter) [1993] COD 284*).

Although formal procedures requiring inspectors to give written notice of their intention to serve an improvement notice have been withdrawn, the HSC has announced (*Press Release C11:98, 31 March 1998*) that informal consultation between inspectors and employers regarding the issue of such notices will continue. Inspectors are expected to discuss with the employer concerned the alleged breaches of the law and any remedial action required in an attempt to resolve any points of difference before issuing a notice.

Failure to comply with an improvement notice can have serious penal consequences (see E15036 below).

## Prohibition notices

E15015    If an inspector is of the opinion that, with regard to any activities to which *Sec 22(1)* applies (see below), the activities involve or will involve a risk of serious personal injury, he may serve on that person a notice (a prohibition notice). [*HSWA s 22(2)*].

It is incumbent on an inspector to show, on a balance of probabilities, that there is a risk to health and safety (*Readmans Ltd v Leeds CC [1992] COD 419* where an environmental health officer served a prohibition notice on the appellant regarding shopping trolleys with child seats on them, following an accident involving an eleven-month-old child. The appellant alleged that the industrial tribunal had wrongly placed the burden of proof on them, to show that the trolleys were not dangerous. It was held by the High Court (allowing the appeal), that it was for the inspector to prove that there was a health and/or safety risk).

Prohibition notices differ from improvement notices in two important ways:

(*a*)   with prohibition notices, it is not necessary that an inspector believes that a provision of *HSWA* or any other statutory provision is being or has been contravened;

(*b*)   prohibition notices are served in *anticipation* of danger.

*Sec 22* applies where, in the inspector's opinion, there is a hazardous activity or state of affairs generally. It is irrelevant that the hazard or danger is not mentioned in *HSWA*; it can exist by virtue of other legislation, or even in the absence of any relevant statutory duty. In this way notices are used to enforce the later statutory requirements of *HSWA* and the earlier requirements of the *Factories Act 1961* and other protective occupational legislation.

A prohibition notice must:

(*a*)   state that the inspector is of the opinion stated immediately above;

(*b*)   specify the matters which create the risk in question;

(*c*)   where there is actual or anticipatory breach of provisions and regulations, state that the inspector is of the opinion that this is so and give reasons;

(*d*)   direct that the activities referred to in the notice must not be carried out on, by or under the control of the person on whom the notice is served, unless the matters referred to in (*b*) above have been remedied.

[*HSWA s 22(3)*].

Failure to comply with a prohibition notice can have serious penal consequences (see E15028 below).

## Differences between improvement and prohibition notices

E15016   Unlike an improvement notice, where time is allowed in which to correct a defect or offending state of affairs, a prohibition notice can take effect immediately.

A direction contained in a prohibition notice shall take effect:

(*a*)   at the end of the period specified in the notice; or

(*b*)   if the notice so declares, immediately.

[*HSWA s 22(4) as substituted by Consumer Protection Act 1987, 3 Sch*].

Risk of injury need not be imminent, even if the notice is to take immediate effect (*Tesco Stores Ltd v Kippax COIT No 7605-6/90*).

An improvement notice gives a person upon whom it is served time to correct the defect or offending situation. A prohibition notice, which is a direction to stop the work activity in question rather than put it right, can take effect immediately on issue; alternatively, it may allow time for certain modifications to take place (i.e. deferred prohibition notice). Both types of notice will generally contain a schedule of work which the inspector will require to be carried out. If the nature of the work to be carried out is vague, the validity of the notice is not affected. If there is an appeal, an industrial tribunal may, within its powers to modify a notice, rephrase the schedule in more specific terms (*Chrysler (UK) Ltd v McCarthy [1978] ICR 939*).

## Effect of non-compliance with notice

E15017    If, after expiry of the period specified in the notice, or in the event of an appeal, expiry of any additional time allowed for compliance by the tribunal, an applicant does not comply with the notice or modified notice, he can be prosecuted. If convicted of contravening a prohibition notice, he may be imprisoned. [*HSWA s 33(1)(g), (3)(b)(i)*]. In *R v Kerr; R v Barker (1996) unreported* the directors of a company were each jailed for four months after allowing a machine which was subject to a prohibition notice – following an accident in which an employee lost an arm – to continue to be operated.

## Service of notice coupled with prosecution

E15018    Where an inspector serves a notice, he may at the same time decide to prosecute for the substantive offence specified in the notice. The fact that a notice has been served is not relevant to the prosecution. Nevertheless, an inspector will not normally commence proceedings until after the expiry of 21 days, i.e. until he is satisfied that there is to be no appeal against the notice or until the tribunal has heard the appeal and affirmed the notice, since it would be inconsistent if conviction by the magistrates were followed by cancellation of the notice by the tribunal. The fact that an industrial tribunal has upheld a notice is not binding on a magistrates' court hearing a prosecution under the statutory provision of which the notice alleged a contravention; it is necessary for the prosecution to prove all the elements in the offence (see E15031 below).

Industrial tribunals are mainly concerned with hearing unfair dismissal claims by employees'; only a tiny proportion of cases heard by them relate specifically to health and safety. Moreover, they are not empowered to determine breaches of criminal legislation.

## Appeals against improvement and prohibition notices

E15019    A person on whom either type of notice is served may appeal to an industrial tribunal within 21 days from the date of service of the notice. The tribunal may extend this time where it is satisfied, on application made in writing (either before or after expiry of the 21-day period), that it was not reasonably practicable for the appeal to be brought within the 21-day period. On appeal the tribunal may either affirm or cancel the notice and, if it affirms it, may do so with modifications in the form of additions, omissions or amendments. [*HSWA ss 24(2), 82(1)(c); Industrial Tribunals (Constitution and Rules of Procedure) Regulations 1993 (SI 1993 No 2687), Reg 8(4) and 4 Sch*].

### *Effect of appeal*

E15020    Where an appeal is brought against a notice, the lodging of an appeal automatically suspends operation of an improvement notice, but a prohibition notice will continue to apply unless there is a direction to the contrary from the tribunal. Thus:

(*a*)    in the case of an improvement notice, the appeal has the effect of suspending the operation of the notice;

(*b*)    in the case of a prohibition notice, the appeal only suspends the operation of the notice in the following circumstances:

(i)    if the tribunal so directs, on the application of the appellant; and

(ii)    the suspension is then effective from the time when the tribunal so directs.

[*HSWA s 24(3)*].

## Grounds for appeal

E15021    The main grounds for appeal are:

(*a*)    the inspector wrongly interpreted the law (see E15022 below);

(*b*)    the inspector exceeded his powers, though not necessarily intentionally, under an Act or regulation (see E15023 below);

(*c*)    breach of law is admitted but the proposed solution is not 'practicable' or not 'reasonably practicable', or that there was no 'best practicable means' other than that used where 'best practicable means' is also a defence to a charge of statutory nuisance (depending on the terminology of the particular statute) (see E15024 below);

(*d*)    breach of law is admitted but the breach is so insignificant that the notice should be cancelled (see E15025 below).

The merits of appealing the issue or terms of an enforcement notice should always be considered carefully as, in practice, this may be the employer's only opportunity to dispute the reasonableness of the requirements imposed. Failure to comply with a notice is a strict liability offence and if a prosecution is brought it is not open to the employer to argue that he did everything 'reasonably practicable' to comply with the notice (*Deary v Mansion Hide Upholstery Ltd [1983] ICR 610*, see E15031 below).

The delay involved in lodging an appeal can have important practical consequences. It is not uncommon for up to four months to elapse before an appeal against an improvement notice can be heard by the tribunal (in the case of prohibition notices it is about one month). For this reason particularly, and in view of the fact that notice of appeal suspends operation of an improvement notice, many companies opt for appealing, since at the time of service of notice they may not be in a position to meet the requirements of the notice; whereas, three or four months later, the position may have changed. If, however, the sole reason for appealing is to gain time and nothing else, the tribunal is unlikely to be sympathetic and costs could be awarded against the unsuccessful appellant, though this is rare. [*Industrial Tribunals (Constitution and Rules of Procedure) Regulations 1993, Reg 8(4), 4 Sch* which states that: 'a tribunal may make an Order that a party shall pay to another party either a specified sum in respect of the costs of or in connection with an appeal incurred by that other party or, in default of agreement, the taxed amount of those costs'.]

*Inspector's wrong interpretation of the law*

E15022    It is doubtful whether many cases have, or indeed would, succeed on this ground. Where regulations impose a strict duty (for example the duty under *Reg 6(1)* of the *Provision and Use of Work Equipment Regulations 1992 (SI 1992 No 2932)* to provide work equipment in good repair) there is no scope for argument by the employer. However, where the statute provides a defence, for example, it requires the duty to be carried out 'so far as reasonably practicable' (discussed more fully at E15031 below) or it provides for a due diligence defence, there is some scope to argue that the inspectors' interpretation of the law is incorrect. For example, in *Canterbury City Council v Howletts and Port Lympne Estates Limited (The Times, 13 December 1996)*, a prohibition notice was served on Howletts Zoo following the death of a keeper while he was cleaning the tigers' enclosure. It was Howletts' policy to allow their animals to roam freely; the local authority argued that the zoo's keepers could have carried out their tasks in the tigers' enclosure with the animals secured. The High Court affirmed the industrial tribunal's decision to set aside the notice, holding that *HSWA s 2* was not intended to render illegal certain working practices simply because they were dangerous.

Employers should note that contesting a prohibition notice on the ground that there has been no legal contravention is pointless, since valid service of a prohibition notice does not depend on legal contravention (*Roberts v Day, COIT No 1/133, Case No 3053/77*). In addition, inspectors can use their powers under *HSWA ss 21, 22* and *25* ('search and destroy dangerous articles and substances') in respect of one or more of the 'relevant statutory provisions' (see E15012 above).

*Inspector exceeded powers under statute*

E15023     It can happen that an inspector exceeds his powers under statute by reason of misinterpretation of the statute or regulation (*Deeley v Effer, COIT No 1/72, Case No 25354/77*). This case involved the requirement that 'all floors, steps, stairs, passages and gangways must, so far as is reasonably practicable, be kept free from obstruction and from any substance likely to cause persons to slip'. [*OSRPA s 16(1)*] (now replaced by equivalent duties under the *Workplace (Health, Safety and Welfare) Regulations 1992*). The inspector considered that employees were endangered by baskets of wares in the shop entrance. The tribunal ruled that the notice had to be cancelled, since the only persons endangered were members of the public, and *OSRPA* is concerned with dangers to employees.

*Proposed solution not practicable*

E15024     The position in a case where, although breach of the law is admitted, the proposed solution is not considered practicable, depends upon the nature of the obligation. The duty may be strict, or have to be carried out so far as practicable or, alternatively, so far as reasonably practicable. In the first two situations cost of compliance is irrelevant; in the latter case, where a requirement has to be carried out 'so far as reasonably practicable', cost effectiveness is an important factor but has to be weighed against the risks to health and safety involved in failing to implement the remedial measures identified in the enforcement notice. Where there is a real danger of serious injury the cost of complying with the notice is unlikely to be decisive. Thus in a leading case, the appellant was served with an improvement notice requiring secure fencing on transmission machinery. An appeal was lodged on the ground that the proposed modifications were too costly (£1,900). It was argued that because of the intelligence and integrity of the operators a safety screen costing £200 would be adequate. The tribunal dismissed the appeal: the risk justified the cost (*Belhaven Brewery Co Ltd v McLean [1975] IRLR 370*).

The cost of complying with a notice is likely to carry less weight in the case of a prohibition notice than an improvement notice, as there must be 'a risk of serious personal injury' for a prohibition notice to be served (*Nico Manufacturing Co Ltd v Hendry [1975] IRLR 225*, where the company argued that a prohibition notice in respect of the worn state of their power presses should be cancelled on the ground that it would result in a 'serious loss of production' and endanger the jobs of several employees'. The tribunal dismissed this argument, having decided that using the machinery in its worn condition could cause serious danger to operators). Similarly, an undertaking by a company to take additional safety precautions against the risk of injury from unsafe plant until new equipment was installed was not sufficient (*Grovehurst Energy Ltd v Strawson (HM Inspector) COIT No 5035/90*).

Where cost is a factor this is not to be confused with the current financial position of the company. A company's financial position is irrelevant to the question whether a tribunal should affirm an enforcement notice. Thus in *Harrison (Newcastle-under-Lyme) Ltd v Ramsay (HM Inspector) [1976] IRLR 135*, a notice requiring cleaning, preparation and painting of walls had to be complied with even though the company was on an economy drive.

Tribunals have power under *HSWA s 24* to alter or extend time limits attaching to improvement and prohibition notices (*D J M and AJ Campion v Hughes (HM Inspector of Factories) [1975] IRLR 291*, where even though there was an imminent risk of serious personal injury, a further four months were allowed for the erection of fire escapes as it was not practicable to carry out the remedial works within the time limits set). Extensions of time in which to comply with notices are most commonly granted where the costs of the improvements and modifications required by the notice are significant.

*Breach of law is insignificant*

E15025    Tribunals will rarely cancel a notice which concerns breach of an absolute duty where the breach is admitted but the appellant argues that the breach is trivial: *South Surbiton Co-operative Society Ltd v Wilcox [1975] IRLR 292*, where a notice had been issued in respect of a cracked wash-hand basin, being a breach of an absolute duty under the *Offices, Shops and Railway Premises Act 1963*. It was argued by the appellant that, in view of their excellent record of cleanliness, there was no need for officials to visit the premises. The appeal was dismissed.

## Inspectors investigation powers

E15026    Inspectors have wide ranging powers under *HSWA* to investigate suspected health and safety offences. These include powers to:

(*a*)    enter and search premises;

(*b*)    direct that the premises or anything on them be left undisturbed for so long as is reasonably necessary for the purpose of the investigation;

(*c*)    take measurements, photographs and recordings;

(*d*)    take samples of articles or substances found in the premises and of the atmosphere in or in the vicinity of the premises;

(*e*)    dismantle or test any article which appears to have caused or be likely to cause danger;

(*f*)    detain items for testing or for use as evidence;

(*g*)    interview any person;

(*h*)    require the production and inspection of any documents and to take copies; and

(*i*)    require the provision of facilities and assistance for the purpose of carrying out the investigation.

[*HSWA s 20*]

Under these powers inspectors may require interviewees to answer such questions as they think fit and sign a declaration that those answers are true. [*HSWA s 20(1)(j)*]. However, evidence given in this way is inadmissible in any proceedings subsequently taken against the person giving the statement or his or her spouse. [*HSWA s 20(7)*]. Where prosecution of an individual is contemplated the inspector will, therefore, usually exercise his evidence-gathering powers under the *Police and Criminal Evidence Act 1984 (PACE)*. Evidence given in this way is admissible against that person in later proceedings. Interviews conducted under *PACE* are subject to strict legal controls, for example, interviewees must be cautioned before the interview takes place, they have certain 'rights to silence' (although these were qualified by the *Criminal Justice and Public Order Act 1994*), and there are rules relating to the recording of the interview.

In practice, the enforcing authorities usually only investigate the most serious workplace accidents: in 1998/9 approximately 6 per cent of all reported accidents were investigated. The HSE aim to investigate all fatalities and a substantial number of major injuries. The Environment, Transport and Regional Affairs Committee has described this level of investigation as disappointingly low (*Fourth Report, 15 February 2000*) and urged the HSE to meet their proposed target of a 3 per cent increase in the investigation of reported injuries over the next 3 years.

## Inspectors' powers of search and seizure in case of imminent danger

E15027　Where an inspector has reasonable cause to believe that there are on premises 'articles or substances ('substance' includes solids, liquids and gases – *HSWA s 53(1)*) which give rise to imminent risk of serious personal injury', he can:

(*a*)　seize them; and

(*b*)　cause them to be rendered harmless (by destruction or otherwise).

[*HSWA s 25(1)*].

Enforcing authorities are given similar powers regarding environmental pollution, under the *Environment Act 1995, ss 108, 109*. (See E5004 EMISSIONS INTO THE ATMOSPHERE.)

Before an article forming 'part of a batch of similar articles', or a substance is rendered harmless, an inspector must, if practicable, take a sample and give to a responsible person, at the premises where the article or substance was found, a portion which has been marked in such a way as to be identifiable. [*HSWA s 25(2)*]. After the article or substance has been rendered harmless, the inspector must sign a prepared report and give a copy of the report to:

(i)　a responsible person (e.g. safety officer); and

(ii)　the owner of the premises, unless he happens to be the 'responsible person'. (See A3005 ACCIDENT REPORTING for the meaning of this term.)

[*HSWA s 25(3)*].

Analogous powers are given to transport inspectors under the *Radioactive Material (Road Transport) Act 1991, s 5* in respect of vehicles carrying radioactive packages.

A customs officer may assist the enforcing authority or the inspector in his enforcement duties under the *Health and Safety at Work etc Act 1974* by seizing any imported article or substance. He may then detain it for not more than 2 working days and may disclose information about it to the enforcing authorities or inspectors. [*HSWA ss 25A, 27A.inserted by Consumer Protection Act 1987, Sch 3*].

## Indemnification by enforcing authorities

E15028　Where an inspector has an action brought against him in respect of an act done in the execution or purported execution of any of the 'relevant statutory provisions' (see E15012 above), and is ordered to pay damages and costs (or expenses) in circumstances where he is not legally entitled to require the enforcing authority which appointed him to indemnify him, he may be able to take advantage of *HSWA s 26*. By virtue of that provision, the authority nevertheless has the power to indemnify the inspector against all or part of such damages where the authority is satisfied that the inspector honestly believed:

(*a*)    that the act complained of was within his powers; and

(*b*)    that his duty as an inspector required or entitled him to do it.

In practice there will be very few circumstances where an inspector is held liable for advice given or enforcement action taken as part of his statutory duties. The Court of Appeal has ruled (in *Harris v Evans and Another [1998] 3 All ER 522*) that an enforcing authority giving advice which leads to the issue of enforcement notices does not owe a duty of care to the owner of the premises affected by the notice and a claim for economic loss arising from such allegedly negligent advice cannot therefore arise. The court said that if enforcing authorities were to be exposed to liability in negligence at the suit of owners whose businesses are adversely affected by their decisions it would have a detrimental effect on the performance by inspectors of their statutory duties. The *HSWA* contains its own statutory remedies against errors by inspectors and the court was not prepared to add to those measures. The court did, however, suggest that a possible exception might arise if a requirement imposed by the inspector introduced a new risk or danger which resulted in physical damage or economic loss.

## Public register of improvement and prohibition notices

E15029    Improvement (though not in the case of the *Fire Precautions Act 1971*) and prohibition notices relating to public safety matters have to be entered in a public register as follows:

(*a*)    within 14 days following the date on which notice is served in cases where there is no right of appeal;

(*b*)    within 14 days following the day on which the time limit expired, in cases where there is a right of appeal but no appeal has been lodged within the statutory 21 days.

(*c*)    within 14 days following the day when the appeal is disposed of, in cases where an appeal is brought.

[*Environment and Safety Information Act 1988, s 3*].

Notices which impose requirements or prohibitions solely for the protection of persons at work are not included in the register. [*Environment and Safety Information Act 1988, s 3(3)*].

In addition, registers must be kept of notices served by:

(i)    fire authorities, under the *Schedule* to the *Environment and Safety Information Act 1988* for the purpose of *Sec 10* of the *Fire Precautions Act 1971* (not improvement notices);

(ii)    local authorities, under the *Schedule* to the *Environment and Safety Information Act 1988* for the purpose of *Sec 10* of the *Safety of Sports Grounds Act 1975*;

(iii)    responsible authorities (as defined by the *Environment and Safety Information Act 1988, s 2(2)*) and the Minister of Agriculture, Fisheries and Food under *Sec 2* of the *Environment and Safety Information Act 1988* for the purpose of *Sec 19* of the *Food and Environment Protection Act 1985*;

(iv)    enforcing authorities, under *Sec 20* of the *Environmental Protection Act 1990*; and

(v)    enforcing authorities, under the *Radioactive Substances Act 1993* (see D1068 DANGEROUS SUBSTANCES I).

These registers are open to inspection by the public free of charge at reasonable hours and, on request and payment of a reasonable fee, copies can be obtained from the relevant authority. [*Environment and Safety Information Act 1988, s 1*]. Such records can also be kept on computer.

# Part B: Offences and Penalties

## Prosecution for breach of the 'relevant statutory provisions'

E15030    Prosecutions can follow non-compliance with an improvement or prohibition notice, but equally inspectors' will sometimes prosecute without serving a notice. Service of notices remains the most usual method of enforcement. In 1997/98 approximately 8,900 enforcement notices were issued by the HSE compared with about 1,600 prosecutions for health and safety offences. Prosecutions are most commonly brought after a workplace accident or dangerous incident (such as a fire or explosion). Investigations by the enforcing authorities may take many months to complete and, in complex cases, it is not unusual for prosecutions to be commenced up to a year after the original incident. Prosecutions normally take place before the magistrates but there is increasing pressure for more serious cases, involving work related fatalities or major injuries, to be prosecuted on indictment in the Crown Court, where increased penalties are available. The determining factor behind prosecution on indictment is the gravity of the offence. Whilst the decision whether to prosecute, issue an enforcement notice, or simply to give advice lies within the discretion of the inspector concerned, the enforcing authorities aim to pursue a policy which is open, consistent and proportionate to the risks in deciding what enforcement action to take (see the HSC's *Enforcement Policy Statement* of *October 1995*, and the *Enforcement Concordat* published by the Better Regulation Taskforce in April 1999 which has been adopted by the HSE and most local authorities).

HSE recently published its first ever enforcement report naming hundreds of companies, organisations and individuals convicted of health and safety crimes during 1999/2000. The report *'Health and safety offences and penalties'*, lists around 1,600 individual offences. Full details of each conviction are available on a special website database, www.hse-databases.co.uk/prosecutions/. Users can access this information in a number of ways, including by geographical location, type of industry, size of fine and type of work activity.

## Burden of proof

E15031    Throughout criminal law, the burden of proof of guilt is on the prosecution to show that the accused committed the particular offence (*Woolmington v DPP [1935] AC 463*). The burden is a great deal heavier than in civil law, requiring proof of guilt beyond a reasonable doubt as distinct from on a balance of probabilities. While not eliminating the need for the prosecution to establish general proof of guilt, *HSWA s 40* makes the task of the prosecution easier by transferring the onus of proof to the accused for one element of certain offences. *Sec 40* states that in any proceedings for an offence consisting of a failure to comply with a duty or requirement to do something so far as is practicable, or so far as reasonably practicable, or to use the best practicable means to do something, the onus is on the accused to prove (as the case may be) that it was not practicable, or not reasonably practicable to do more than was in fact done to satisfy the duty or requirement, or that there was no better practicable means than was in fact used to satisfy the duty or requirement. However, *Sec 40* does not apply to an offence created by *Sec 33(1)(g)* of the *HSWA* – failing to comply with an improvement notice.

In *Deary v Mansion Hide Upholstery Ltd [1983] ICR 610*, an improvement notice was served on the defendant company requiring it to provide the fire resistant storage for polyurethane foam. The company did not comply, nor did it appeal. It was irrelevant that the company had complied with the notice so far as 'reasonably practicable' as that was not a requirement of the offence charged. A similar burden of proof exists under the *Environmental Protection Act 1990* (see E5015 EMISSIONS INTO THE ATMOSPHERE).

## Main offences and penalties

E15032    Health and safety offences are either (a) triable summarily (i.e. without jury before the magistrates), or (b) triable summarily and on indictment (i.e. triable either way), or (c) triable only on indictment. Most health and safety offences, however, fall into categories (*a*) and (*b*). The main offences falling into these two categories are set out below.

### Summary only offences

E15033    (*a*)    contravening a requirement imposed under *HSWA s 14* (power of the HSC to order an investigation);

(*b*)    contravening a requirement imposed by an inspector under *HSWA s 20*;

(*c*)    preventing or attempting to prevent a person from appearing before an inspector, or from answering his questions;

(*d*)    intentionally obstructing an inspector or customs officer in the exercise of his powers;

(*e*)    falsely pretending to be an inspector.

### 'Either way' offences

E15034    (*a*)    failure to carry out one or more of the general duties of *HSWA ss 2–7*;

(*b*)    contravening either:

(i)    *HSWA s 8* – intentionally or recklessly interfering with anything provided for safety;

(ii)    *HSWA s 9* – levying payment for anything that an employer must by law provide in the interests of health and safety (e.g. personal protective clothing);

(*c*)    contravening any health and safety regulations;

(*d*)    contravening a requirement imposed by an inspector under *HSWA s 25* (power to seize and destroy articles and substances);

(*e*)    contravening a requirement of a prohibition or improvement notice;

(*f*)    intentionally or recklessly making false statements, where the statement is made:

(i)    to comply with a requirement to furnish information; or

(ii)    to obtain the issue of a document;

(*g*)  intentionally making a false entry in a register book, notice etc. which is required to be kept;

(*h*)  failing to comply with a remedial court order made under *HSWA s 42*.

[*HSWA s 33(1)*].

In England and Wales there is no time limit for bringing prosecutions for offences, except for offences tried summarily in the magistrates' courts – where the time limit is 6 months from the date the complaint was laid. [*Magistrates' Courts Act 1980, s 127(1)*]. In Scotland the 6 month time limit extends to 'either way' offences tried summarily. The period may be extended in the case of special reports, coroners' court hearings or in cases of death generally. [*HSWA s 34(1)*] There is no time limit for commencing hearings in the Crown Court.

*Summary trial or trial on indictment*

E15035    Most offences triable either way are tried summarily. However an increasing number of serious offences are being referred to the Crown Court, which has increased sentencing powers, for trial on indictment. The Court of Appeal has advised magistrates to exercise caution in accepting jurisdiction in health and safety cases where the offence may require a penalty greater than they can impose or where death or serious injury has resulted from the offence (see *R v F Howe & Son (Engineers) Ltd* at E15043 below). The defendant may also refuse to consent to summary trial and opt for trial on indictment.

*Penalties for health and safety offences*

E15036    Penalties tend to relate to the three main categories of offences characterising breach of health and safety legislation, namely:

(*a*)  breaches of *Secs 2–6* of the *HSWA* – serious offences:

   (i)  summary conviction – a maximum £20,000 fine;

   (ii)  conviction on indictment – an unlimited fine (but no imprisonment);

(*b*)  breaches of improvement or prohibition orders, or orders under *Sec 42* of the *HSWA* to remedy the cause of the offence – serious offences:

   (i)  summary conviction – a maximum £20,000 fine, or imprisonment for up to six months or both;

   (ii)  conviction on indictment – an unlimited fine or imprisonment for up to two years or both;

(*c*)  most other offences, including breaches of health and safety regulations:

   (i)  summary conviction – a maximum fine of £5,000;

   (ii)  conviction on indictment – an unlimited fine. For licence breaches and explosives offences, the court may also order up to two years imprisonment (see, for example, *R v Hill (1996) unreported*, where a demolition contractor was jailed for three months for breach of asbestos licensing regulations).

[*HSWA s 33(1A), (2) and (2A)* as inserted by the *Offshore Safety Act 1992*, and *HSWA s 33(3)*].

These penalties may soon be increased. In December 1999, the Lord Chancellor announced that the Government intends to legislate to increase the penalties available for health and safety offences as soon as parliamentary time allows. A private members bill, the *Health and Safety at Work (Offences) Bill*, was introduced in December, but it is uncertain if sufficient parliamentary time is available to allow it to progress. The Bill, if enacted, would raise the maximum fine which can be imposed in the Magistrates Court to £20,000 for most offences, including breach of health and safety regulations, and make imprisonment an option for most health and safety offences in both the higher and lower courts.

### Defences

E15037    Although no general defences are specified in the *Health and Safety at Work etc Act 1974*, some regulations passed under the Act carry the defence of 'due diligence' (for example, the *Control of Substances Hazardous to Health Regulations 1999 (SI 1999 No 437)*).

### Manslaughter

E15038    In cases of workplace death, manslaughter charges may also be brought if there is sufficient evidence. The decision to prosecute rests with the Crown Prosecution Service, not the enforcing authorities under health and safety legislation. Manslaughter convictions linked to breaches of safety legislation are rare but are becoming more common. There have been a series of individual prosecutions for manslaughter of directors or managers responsible for workplace deaths and, in 1994, the first successful prosecution for corporate manslaughter involved OLL Ltd, the activity centre responsible for organising the Lyme Bay canoeing trip in which four teenagers died. (See EMPLOYERS' DUTIES TO THEIR EMPLOYEES at E11014.)

## Offences committed by particular types of persons

*Corporate offences – delegation of duties to junior staff*

E15039    Companies cannot avoid liability for breach of general duties under Secs. 2-6 *HSWA* by arguing that the senior management and 'directing mind' of the company had taken all reasonable precautions, and that responsibility for the offence lay with a more junior employee or agent who was at fault. The *HSWA* generally imposes strict criminal liabilities on employers and others (subject to the employer being able to establish that all reasonably practicable precautions had been taken) and it is not open to corporate employers to seek to avoid liability by arguing that their general duties have been delegated to someone lower down the corporate tree. In *R v British Steel plc [1995] IRLR 310*, British Steel were prosecuted under *HSWA s 3* after a fatal accident to a subcontractor who was carrying out construction work under the supervision of a British Steel engineer. British Steel argued that it was not responsible under *Sec 3* for the actions of the supervising engineer as the engineer was not part of the 'directing mind' of the company and all reasonable precautions to ensure the safety of the work had been taken by senior management. The Court of Appeal dismissed this argument. A similar decision was reached in *R v Gateway Foodmarkets Ltd, [1997] IRLR 189*, which concerned a breach of *HSWA s 2* arising out of a fatal accident to an employee who fell through a trap door in the floor of a lift control room. The accident occurred while the store manager was manually attempting to rectify an electrical fault in the lift in accordance with a local practice which was not authorised by Gateway's head office. The Court of Appeal held that the failure at store manager level was attributable to the employer.

However, it does not follow that an employer will automatically be held criminally responsible for an isolated act of negligence by an employee performing work on its behalf. This is because it may still be possible for the employer to establish that it has done everything reasonably practicable in the conduct of its undertaking to ensure that employees and third parties are not exposed to risks to their health and safety by virtue of the way it has conducted its business (see *R v Nelson Group Services (Maintenance) Limited [1999] IRLR 646, Court of Appeal*).

The definition of 'reasonably practicable' was authoritatively laid down in *Edwards v National Coal Board [1949] 1 All ER 743* where it was said that: 'Reasonably practicable' is a narrower term than 'physically possible', and seems to imply that a computation must be made by the owner in which the quantum of risk is placed on one scale and the sacrifice involved in the measures necessary for averting the risk (whether in money, time or trouble) is placed in the other, and that, if it be known that there is a gross disproportion between them – the risk being insignificant in relation to the sacrifice – the defendants discharge the onus on them.'

In a series of decisions the Court of Appeal have concluded that the words 'so far as reasonably practicable' provide a limited defence to what are otherwise absolute obligations on employers and other duty holders (*R v British Steel Plc [1995] IRLR 310*, approved by the House of Lords in *R v Associated Octel Co Ltd [1996] 1WLR 1543*). Although the circumstances where such a defence may be established are likely to be rare – it involves doing more than simply exercising reasonable care – the Court of Appeal in *R v Nelson Group Services (Maintenance) Limited* made clear that an isolated act of negligence by an employee performing work on behalf of the company does not preclude that employer from establishing a defence that it has done everything reasonably practicable. The court said: '*It is not necessary for the adequate protection of the public that the employer should be held criminally liable even for an isolated act of negligence by the employee performing the work. Such persons are themselves liable to criminal sanctions under the Act and under the Regulations. Moreover it is a sufficient obligation to place on the employer in order to protect the public to require the employer to show that everything reasonably practicable has been done to see that a person doing the work has the appropriate skill and instruction, has had laid down for him safe systems of doing the work, has been subject to adequate supervision, and has been provided with safe plant equipment for the proper performance of the work.*'

The question of what is reasonably practicable is a question of fact which must be determined in the light of the circumstances of each case. The burden of proving, on the balance of probabilities, that all reasonably practicable steps have been taken rests with the employer (see also E15024).

Similarly, where there is a defence of due diligence to the legislation allegedly breached, the company may be able to avoid liability if the members of senior management responsible for actual control of the company's operations have exercised due diligence and the failure occurs because of the actions of a junior member of staff: *Tesco Supermarkets Ltd v Nattrass [1972] AC 153*, a House of Lords decision on the wording of the *Trade Descriptions Act 1968*. The case was considered by the Court of Appeal in *R v British Steel plc [1994] IRLR 540* who distinguished it from the factual circumstances before them on the basis that the *Tesco* decision involved application of a due diligence defence which was not part of *HSWA s 3*.

### Offences of directors or other officers of a company

E15040    Where an offence is committed by a body corporate, senior persons in the hierarchy of the company may also be individually liable. Thus, where the offence was committed with the consent or connivance of, or was attributable to any neglect on the part of a director or officer of the company, that person is himself guilty of an offence and liable to be punished accordingly. Those who may be so liable are:

(*a*)  any functional director;

(*b*)  a manager (which does not include an *employee* in charge of a shop while the manager is away on a week's holiday (*R v Boal [1992] 1 QB 591*, concerning *Sec 23* of the *Fire Precautions Act 1971* – identical terminology to *HSWA s 37*));

(*c*)  a company secretary;

(*d*)  another similar officer of the company;

(*e*)  anyone purporting to act as any of the above.

[HSWA s 37(1)].

It is not sufficient that the company through its 'directing mind' (its board of directors) has committed an offence – there must be some degree of personal culpability in the form of proof of consent, connivance or neglect by the individual concerned. Evidence of this sort can be difficult to obtain and prosecutions under *Sec 37(1)* have, in the past, been rarely compared with prosecutions of companies (although they are increasing in number).

Directors, managers and company secretaries can be personally liable for ensuring that corporate safety duties are performed throughout the company (for example, a failure to maintain a safe system of work can give rise to personal liability). Liability may also arise as a result of a failure to perform an obligation placed on individuals by their employment contracts and job descriptions – for example, obligations imposed under a safety policy – not just in relation to duties imposed by law. In the case of *Armour v Skeen (Procurator Fiscal, Glasgow) [1977] IRLR 310*, an employee fell to his death whilst repairing a road bridge over the River Clyde. The appellant, who was the Director of Roads, was held to be under a duty to supervise the safety of council workmen. He had not prepared a written safety policy for roadwork, despite a written request that he do so, and was found to have breached *HSWA s 37(1)*.

Similar duties exist under the *Environmental Protection Act 1990* and the *Environment Act 1995, s 95(2)–(4)*. (See E5023 EMISSIONS INTO THE ATMOSPHERE.) Directors convicted of a breach of *HSWA s 37* may also be disqualified, for up to two years, from being a director of a company, under the provisions of the *Company Directors Disqualification Act 1986, s 2(1)* as having committed an indictable offence connected with (*inter alia*) the management of a company. In *R v Chapman (1992)*, *unreported*, a director of a quarrying company was disqualified and fined £5,000 for contravening a prohibition notice on an unsafe quarry where there had been several fatalities and major injuries.

### Directors' insurance

**E15041**  Companies can now buy insurance in order to protect directors. [*Companies Act 1985, s 310(3)*]. Moreover, directors need not contribute towards premiums, as they had to previously. Such insurance, which must be mentioned in the Annual Report and Accounts, may (subject to the terms of the policy), protect directors against:

(*a*)  civil liability for claims made against them in breach of directorial duties, e.g. by shareholders when directors acted in breach of their duty of care to the company, as well as legal costs and expenses incurred in defence or settlement of such claims;

(*b*)    legal costs and expenses involved in defending criminal actions (e.g. breach of *HSWA s 37*), but not the fine or other penalty incurred, it being illegal to insure against payment of penalties (see further E13017 EMPLOYERS LIABILITY INSURANCE).

Companies can also indemnify directors against such costs and damages, but only where judgement is ultimately given in the individual's favour or he is acquitted.

*Offences due to the act of another person*

E15042    *Section 36(1)* of *HSWA* makes clear that although provision is separately made for the prosecution of less senior corporate staff, e.g. safety officers, works managers, this does not prevent a further prosecution against the company itself. The section states that where an offence under *HSWA* is due to the act or default of some other person, then:

(*a*)    that other person is guilty of an offence; and

(*b*)    a second person can be charged and convicted, whether or not proceedings are taken against the first-mentioned person.

Where the enforcing authorities rely on *HSWA s 36*, this must be made clear to the defendant. In *West Cumberland By Products Ltd v DPP, The Times, 12 November 1987*, the conviction of a company operating a road haulage business for breach of regulations relating to the transport of dangerous substances was set aside as the offence charged related to the obligations of the driver of the vehicle and, in prosecuting the operating company, reliance was not placed on *HSWA s 36*.

## Sentencing Guidelines

E15043    The level of fine imposed for health and safety offences will ultimately depend on the facts and circumstances of the case, including the gravity of the offence, whether the breach resulted in death or serious injury, and any mitigating evidence the defendant is able to put forward (including details of its means and ability to pay any fine imposed). In the past there have been wide variations in the sentences handed down by different courts for similar breaches of the legislation and there has also been concern at the general low level of fines imposed for health and safety offences. In *R v F Howe & Son (Engineers) Limited [1999] 2 All ER 249*, the Court of Appeal sought to address these concerns by laying down guidelines to assist magistrates and judges in sentencing health and safety offences. The case concerned an appeal by the company against fines totalling £48,000 and an order for costs of £7,500 imposed in respect of four health and safety offences arising from a fatal accident to one of the company's employees who was electrocuted while using an electric vacuum machine to clean a floor at the company's premises. In reducing the level of fine imposed to reflect the company's limited financial resources, the Court of Appeal laid down the following general guidelines:

---

*Sentencing Guidelines*

*General Principles*

The level of fine should reflect:

● the gravity of the offence and the standard of the defendant's conduct;

● the degree of risk and extent of danger;

● the extent of the breach – an isolated incident may attract a lower fine than a continuing unsafe state of affairs;

---

> ●     the defendant's resources and the effect of the fine on its business.
>
> *Aggravating Factors*
>
> ●     failure to heed warnings;
>
> ●     if the defendant deliberately flouts safety legislation for financial reasons;
>
> ●     if the offence results in a fatality.
>
> *Mitigating factors*
>
> ●     prompt admission of liability and guilty plea;
>
> ●     steps taken to remedy deficiencies;
>
> ●     a good safety record.

In applying these factors, the Court of Appeal made clear that every case needs to be considered on its own facts. It declined to lay down a tariff for particular offences or to link the level of fine directly to the defendant's turnover or net profit. However, it emphasised the importance of the defendant's means, as well as the gravity of the offence, in determining the appropriate level of fine, stating that this should be large enough to impress on both the management and shareholders of the defendant company the importance of providing a safe working environment. Although there might be cases where the offences are so serious that the defendant company ought not to be in business, in general the fine 'should not be so large as to emperil the earnings of employees or create a risk of bankruptcy'. In essence, the courts must answer two questions in determining the appropriate level of fine:

1.     What financial penalty does the offence merit?

2.     What penalty can the defendant reasonably be ordered to pay?

The Court of Appeal specifically made clear that the size and resources of the defendant company and its ability to provide safety measures or to employ in-house safety advisers are not a mitigating factor: the legislation imposes the same standard of care irrespective of the size of the organisation.

It also emphasised that if the offence results in a fatality that is a serious aggravating factor: 'the penalty should reflect public disquiet at the unnecessary loss of life.' In general, cases involving death or serious injury should be dealt with by the Crown Court, which has increased sentencing powers: the judgement in *Howe* made clear that 'magistrates should always think carefully before accepting jurisdiction' in such cases.

In *R v Rollco Screw & Rivet Co Ltd [1999] IRLR 439*, the Court of Appeal approved the principles laid down in *Howe* and indicated that the fine imposed should make clear that there is a personal responsibility on directors for their company's health and safety arrangements. It did, however, acknowledge that caution was necessary in the case of smaller companies, where the directors were also shareholders, to avoid imposing a fine which amounted to double punishment of the individuals concerned.

The court went on to suggest that, in appropriate circumstances, corporate defendants may be ordered to pay fines and costs by instalments over many years. In reducing Rollco's total payment period to 5 years and 7 months, the court held that there was no maximum period for payment of fines and costs. Although there might be good reason to limit the period of payment of fines and costs by a personal defendant, who may suffer anxiety because of his continuing financial obligations, the same considerations do not apply to a corporate defendant. The Court of Appeal indicated that, in proper circumstances, it might be appropriate to order payment of fines and costs by a corporate defendant over a 'substantially longer period' than would be appropriate in the case of an individual.

## Publication of convictions for health and safety offences

E15044    In an attempt to improve compliance with health and safety legislation, the HSE are also pursuing an active policy of naming companies that breach the legislation. Details of firms and individuals convicted of health and safety offences are published in an annual report and the HSE have indicated that they intend to publicise impending prosecutions and convictions as these take place (*HSE Press Release E233:99, 22 November 1999*).

## Position of the Crown

E15045    The general duties of *HSWA* bind the Crown. [*HSWA s 48(1)*]. (For the position under the *Factories Act 1961*, see W11031 WORKPLACES – HEALTH, SAFETY AND WELFARE.) However, improvement and prohibition notices cannot be served on the Crown, nor can the Crown be prosecuted. [*HSWA s 48(1)*]. Crown employees', however, can be prosecuted for breaches of *HSWA*. [*HSWA s 48(2)*]. Crown immunity is no longer enjoyed by health authorities, nor premises used by health authorities (defined as Crown premises) including hospitals (whether NHS hospitals or NHS trusts or private hospitals). [*National Health Service and Community Care Act 1990, s 60*]. Health authorities are also subject to the *Food Safety Act 1990*. Most Crown premises can be inspected by authorised officers in the same way as privately run concerns, though prosecution against the Crown is not possible. [*Food Safety Act 1990, s 54(2)*].

# Environmental Management

## Introduction

E16001 The management of environmental performance is now well-accepted as a critical issue for organisations in both the public and private sectors.

Broadly speaking, environmental management refers to the controls implemented by an organisation to minimise the adverse environmental impacts of its operations; in many cases this leads to opportunities to improve business performance in general.

Historically, environmental management tends to have been driven by a complex and interacting array of external pressures, to which business somewhat reluctantly responded.

However, business is becoming more proactive in its approach to environmental management, as the benefits of it become more apparent. External pressures are still important influences, but increasingly they tend to shape the nature and scope of business' environmental management practices, rather than triggering them in the first place. The emergence of co-operative and constructive stakeholder dialogue as an element of corporate environmental management is an encouraging indication that business recognises the value of effective and proactive environmental management. Furthermore, the ongoing development of new and increasingly innovative approaches to environmental management reflects the fact that there is commercial value to be gained from continuous improvement.

Examples of sources of pressure on business to adopt more sustainable management practices include:

- changing corporate governance expectations;
- management information needs;
- employees;
- legislation;
- market mechanisms;
- the financial community;
- the supply chain;
- community and environmental groups;
- environmental crises;
- the business community;
- customers; and
- competitor initiatives.

## Internal drivers

### Corporate governance

E16002 The concept of corporate governance has changed substantially during the last decade, reflecting the changed conditions in which business operates. The removal of trade barriers, the subsequent growth and political influence of trans-national companies, the opening of previously restricted markets and a general reduction in corporate taxation rates have contributed to radical changes in the way business operates, including increasing the extent to which it controls its own performance. Consequently, the notion of corporate responsibility has also changed. Society is looking less to government to control the social and environmental impacts of business activity, and instead is seeing business as being accountable for those impacts. Good corporate governance is no longer merely a reflection of responsible fiscal performance. As a result, the mandate of corporate directors and managers is expanding and they are recognising the need to operate in a more transparent and inclusive manner. Proactive environmental management is a key aspect of that.

## Management information needs

E16003    Effective business management relies on timely and reliable information on the multitude of factors that influence it. As managers' understanding of the relationship between environmental performance and business performance increases, so too does their requirement for information pertaining to environmental performance. Such information assists to increase their control over those factors.

This reflects the growing acceptance of the sustainability concept, which recognises that long-term business success requires environmental, social and economic factors to be balanced. While there is no clear guidance or agreement on how such a balance should be achieved, it is clear that it must be based on appropriate information on all three primary elements. Thus the recognition of the relevance of environmental performance to business performance, the value of controlling it and the need for expanded management information is an increasingly important driver of environmental management practices. Structured environmental management systems not only provide a means of controlling environmental performance *per se*, but also allow more informed strategic and operational decisions to be made by management.

## Employees

E16004    Employees have a potentially strong influence over the environmental management practices of an organisation. The desire to minimise staff turnover means that companies are becoming more responsive to employee enquiries and suggestions regarding corporate environmental performance. Conversely, companies wishing to attract high calibre recruits are increasingly realising the importance of maintaining a strong and positive corporate image, which is often dependent on environmental performance, amongst a number of other things.

# External drivers

## Legislation

E16005    UK companies are influenced by a range of international treaties, conventions and protocols; European regulations and directives; and domestic legislation. The latter may be a tool for implementing European directives, or they may have been enacted independently of any requirement of the European Union.

Enforcement of the various legal instruments within England and Wales is primarily the responsibility of the Environment Agency, although local authorities also play a role. In Scotland, responsibility lies with the Scottish Environment Protection Agency.

Good corporate environmental management requires a thorough understanding of the legal requirements imposed on a company, in addition to evidence that the company has made reasonable attempts to ensure ongoing compliance with them, either through technological, procedural and/or administrative mechanisms.

It is interesting that a large number of published corporate environmental policies now commit to going 'beyond compliance'. That is, legislative compliance is increasingly being seen as a minimum standard.

Other initiatives are forcing companies that have not voluntarily responded, to give more systematic consideration to environmental management and performance in making strategic and operational business decisions.

The Company Law Review, launched by the Department of Trade and Industry (DTI) in March 1998, and due to make its final recommendations for new legislation in 2001, has produced a number of consultation papers. The last of these was published in November 2000 and this included a refinement of proposals in earlier documents on broader accountability for directors, that included environmental issues. Among the proposals in the Company Law Review is the institution of a Companies Commission. One of the Commission's roles would be to monitor the operation of the Combined Code and determine how or whether it should be amended or extended to unlisted companies.

*The Combined Code Principles of Good Governance and Code of Best Practice*, published in June 1998, lays out a set of principles with detailed code provisions on implementation. The listing rules require the annual report and accounts of each listed company incorporated in the UK to include a narrative statement as to how it has applied the principles and whether or not the company has complied with the provisions. Principle D.2 states that the company should maintain a sound system of internal controls to safeguard shareholders' investment and the company's assets. Such controls could include environmental issues. Under the provisions, the directors are required, at least annually, to conduct a review of the effectiveness of internal controls and to report to shareholders that they have done so. If the company does not have an internal audit function it should periodically review the need for one.

## Market mechanisms

E16006    While the command and control approach embodied in environmental legislation and regulations represents a significant pressure on business, policy makers have begun to examine new tools to encourage better management of environmental performance.

A range of measures is beginning to emerge designed to influence the economics of polluting activities. These so-called market-based instruments impose costs on pollution-causing activities and provide incentives for companies to look for ways of minimising environmental damage. Such instruments being discussed or implemented include:

(*a*)    a carbon tax aimed at raising the cost of all fossil fuels, and those with a high carbon content becoming more expensive than others. This is designed to encourage energy conservation and a switch to cleaner fuels. In the UK, the climate change levy, which came into effect in April 2001, introduced a tax on most non-domestic uses of energy derived from fossil fuels. All revenues are recycled back to business through a 0.3% cut in employers' National Insurance contributions and additional support for energy-efficiency measures and energy-saving technologies.

(*b*)    tradable emissions permits which set pollution quotas. Companies that reduce their emissions below the quota can sell the unused part of their quota to other firms. Businesses thus have the incentive to improve their emissions performance. Such a scheme is included in the Kyoto Protocol, adopted in 1997 but not yet ratified, which sets out formal targets for cuts in greenhouse gas emissions by developed countries. Article 17 of the Protocol allows developed countries that reduce their emissions by more than their assigned target to gain credits which can be sold to other developed countries. In the UK, the Government has published draft proposals for a voluntary domestic emissions trading scheme, scheduled to start in April 2002. This would be one of the first national greenhouse gases trading schemes in the world;

(c)     taxes and credits. A number of initiatives within the UK suggest that taxes and credits will increasingly be used as a mechanism for controlling environmental performance. For example, the UK introduced a Landfill Tax in October 1996 to encourage companies to reduce their waste streams. In 1999, the Government made a commitment to increase this by £1 per tonne a year for five years until 2004. The tax is payable by landfill operators at a standard rate, which was set at £12 per tonne. From April 2001 a lower charge of £2 per tonne applies to inactive waste.

In the UK, other environmental tax reforms have been announced over the past few years. Changes to company car taxation and vehicle excise duty favour those vehicles with lower CO2 emission rates. An aggregates levy of £1.60 per tonne is due to start in April 2002, with the revenues raised returned to business and the local communities affected by quarrying, through a 0.1% cut in employers' National Insurance contributions and a new sustainability fund. It is intended that the levy will help to ensure that the environmental impact of aggregate extraction is reflected in the price. This is aimed at encouraging more efficient use of aggregates and the development of alternatives including waste glass, tyres and recycled construction and demolition waste.

## The financial community

E16007     The emerging realisation of the link between environmental performance and business performance has encouraged investors, shareholders and insurers to develop a direct interest in the environmental performance of companies. The financial community is therefore increasingly seeking information on how environmental issues will potentially impact on the long term viability of the companies in which they have a commercial interest. In particular, they are concerned about the extent to which environmental risks are being controlled. They want reassurance that companies are not in breach of legal requirements with the consequent threats of fines, reputational damage and the need for unanticipated expenditure. They need to be sure that assets, in the form of plant, equipment, property and brand value, against which they have lent money, are correctly valued. Raw materials, by-products and end products may need to be replaced, modified and/or discontinued, which may require provisions or contingent liabilities to be included in the corporate accounts. Such a situation may arise as a result of substances being phased out (for example, legal controls on CFC production), or it may reflect changing market attitudes such that the demand for less environmentally damaging products begins to decline. Additional research and development costs are likely to be associated with such changes.

Institutional investors are increasingly demanding reassurances that companies are aware of their environmental risks and that such factors should be included in annual environmental reports. For example, Morley Fund Management has recently stated publicly that it requires FTSE 100 companies to disclose environmental information. The Association of British Insurers ('ABI') is expected to adopt guidelines in 2002 setting out what institutional investors expect to see in the annual reports of the companies in which they invest. The guidelines will ask companies to disclose whether the Board takes account of environmental, social and ethical policies and procedures and the related risks to the company's value. The ABI also plan to monitor reports for the quality of information supplied.

Consideration of environmental risks is now an established component of acquisitions, mergers, flotations, buyouts or divestments. Management of companies involved in any of these deals must be able to demonstrate that environmental liabilities do not constitute an unacceptable risk for investors or insurers.

In March 2001 FTSE, the leading equity index manager announced the launch of the FTSE4Good Index Series to include companies with the strongest records of corporate social and environmental performance. They provide a basis for launching investment funds or performance benchmarking and set a global standard for socially responsible investment. The indicies use globally recognised standards to define best practice in corporate responsibility and sets a global agenda for engagement between companies and their investors.

## Supply chain

E16008　Most businesses are both purchasers and suppliers of a range of goods and services. Introducing environmental criteria into procurement decision-making processes emphasises the importance of issues other than price and quality in purchasing goods or services. Examples of environmental criteria are selecting materials, components or products that were manufactured using relatively less energy than alternatives, or that require relatively less energy in operations. Another approach is to use environmental criteria as specifications for a particular material, component or product, such as conforming to an eco-label. The UK Government has recently introduced procedures for procurement under its *Greening Government* initiative which outlines how environmental issues can be taken into account for all buying decisions. As part of a plan to ban hazardous chemicals from all their products in the next few years, B & Q and Homebase are pressing suppliers to start substituting chemical substances of concern with safer alternatives. This means that one company can directly influence the environmental performance of another. As a result, many companies are taking active steps to control their environmental performance throughout the supply chain. For example, it is quite common for purchasing companies to require their suppliers to demonstrate ongoing compliance with formal environmental management standards such as ISO 14001 or EMAS, and to provide information on the environmental performance of the supplier and the products and services it provides. Regardless of the approach that is used, the criteria should be relevant to each procurement decision and should be designed to enable a business to directly influence the attributes and performance of its products at other stages of their life cycles.

## Community and environment group pressure

E16009　The majority of public pressure on companies to improve their environmental performance is initiated by local communities which experience the direct effects of pollution. Most companies recognise the importance and value of working co-operatively with local communities. In fact many have established community liaison panels, which comprise representatives of the local community. Such panels interact with the company on a regular basis and provide input on environmental and other community issues.

Environmental pressure groups, often supported by a high level of legal and technical expertise, are also influential. Previously the relationship between environmental pressure groups and business was characterised by mutual mistrust and reactive criticism. The emergence of the concept of 'stakeholder engagement', whereby companies take a more inclusive approach to business management, means that environmental pressure groups can be expected to have more direct access to companies and management in the future. In fact their opinions are already actively sought by many organisations, which recognise the importance of constructive dialogue. While companies will not necessarily implement all suggestions made by external pressure groups, the trend towards more timely and constructive dialogue is likely to continue.

The evolution of the Internet and other sophisticated communication media has significantly increased public awareness of and access to information about corporate environmental performance, as well as increasing the speed with which such information can be transferred and responded to. The result of this is that sources of pressure on companies to improve environmental performance have broadened into the international arena. Companies are finding it necessary to develop and adopt consistent environmental and social performance standards in all markets in which they operate, since their performance is increasingly subject to international scrutiny.

## Environmental crises

E16010   High profile environmental crises are, unfortunately, often a trigger for improved environmental management. There are two main types:

(*a*)   crises that are generated as a result of the actions of an individual company, the effects of which are generally experienced at a local scale;

(*b*)   crises that are generated by collective action or by natural forces, the effects of which are often experienced at the national or international scale.

Individual companies that have been associated with environmentally damaging events such as oil spills generally find themselves exposed to intense pressure to improve their environmental management practices in the immediate future. The need to correct the reputational damage caused by environmental crises is a further incentive to respond quickly. Obviously the costs of responding to pressures arising from catastrophic environmental incidents can be extremely high, and most companies seek to avoid those by incorporating environmental issues into their corporate risk management programmes.

Global or national environmental crises tend to emerge more gradually, and with considerably more debate about accountability and appropriate responses. Nevertheless, there are a number of examples of global environmental issues that have facilitated more systematic and intensive environmental management practices than may otherwise have occurred in the same time period. The most obvious examples are the depletion of the ozone layer and the greenhouse effect. At a national level, issues such as water shortages, topsoil losses and regional air pollution have triggered the adoption of improved environmental management practices on an extensive scale.

## Business community

E16011   Trade associations and business groups such as the Confederation of British Industry (CBI) and the International Chamber of Commerce (ICC) have played a leading and effective role in encouraging businesses to adopt environmental management practices. Increasingly the importance of doing this within a sustainable development framework is being accepted. Sustainable development is generally recognised as the inter-relationship and inter-dependence of the three core elements of economic, environmental and social consideration, although it is a concept that is open to wide interpretation. However, it is generally understood to mean achieving a better quality of life with effective environmental protection. The most widely used definition is contained in the 1987 United Nations Brundtland report to the World Commission on Environment and Development. This definition states that it is 'development which meets the needs of the present without compromising the ability of future generations to meet their own needs.'

The ICC *Business Charter for Sustainable Development*, launched in 1991, is a set of 16 principles to guide company strategies and operations towards sustainable development. The principles have been adopted widely by companies throughout the world. The principles require adherents to make environmental management a high priority, with detailed programmes and practices for its implementation integrated with existing management systems and procedures. The charter highlights such areas as employee and customer education, research facilities and operations, contractors and suppliers and emergency preparedness. It requires organisations to support the transfer of technology, be open to concerns expressed by the public and employees and carry out regular environmental reviews and report progress.

In 1995 the World Industry Council on the Environment (WICE) and the Business Council for Sustainable Development (BCSD) merged to become the World Business Council for Sustainable Development (WBCSD). In 2001, it consisted of a coalition of some 150 international companies from 30 countries committed to the principles of sustainable development. WBCSD seeks to promote the effective implementation of these principles through a combination of advocacy, research, education, knowledge-sharing and policy development.

The Responsible Care programme is an example of an international initiative from a specific industry sector. The programme has been adopted by around 41 national chemical industry associations, including the Chemical Industries Association (CIA) in the UK. All of those associations have made acceptance of Responsible Care requirements compulsory for individual member companies. Responsible Care is designed to promote continuous improvement, not only in environmental management, but also health and safety. The companies must also adopt a policy of openness by releasing information about their activities. Adherence to the principles and objectives of Responsible Care is a condition of membership of CIA.

In the UK, the Prince of Wales Business Leaders Forum (PWBLF), which incorporates Business in the Environment (BiE), was formed in 1990 and currently has 50 international member companies. It has played a major role in raising awareness of the relevance of environmental management and sustainable development to business, and promoting practical tools for improving performance.

Individual companies have also contributed to the development of improved environmental performance standards. As the relevance of good environmental management to overall business performance has become more apparent, progressive companies have voluntarily adopted a number of innovative and unique approaches to corporate environmental management. This has had the effect of constantly moving the frontiers of 'acceptable' environmental management practices and created substantial peer pressure which in turn has encouraged other companies to adopt similar or even more effective practices.

# Environmental management guidelines

## Standards for environmental management

E16012    Various guidelines exist for responding to those many pressures to minimise damage to the environment and health. Effective environmental management, like quality management or financial management, requires *inter alia*:

(*a*)    the setting of objectives and performance measures;

(*b*)    the definition and allocation of responsibilities for implementing the various components of environmental management;

(*c*)    the measurement, monitoring and reporting of information on performance;

(*d*)    a process for ensuring feedback on systems and procedures so that the necessary changes can be actioned.

There are two main instruments which influence current approaches to environmental management. The first is the EU Eco-Management and Audit Scheme (EMAS) Regulation. The second is the International Standards Organisation Series of Environmental Management Standards.

## The Eco-Management and Audit Scheme (EMAS) Regulation

E16013    This voluntary scheme came into force in July 1993 and has been open for participation by companies in all member States since April 1995. By March 2001, 77 industrial sites were registered in the UK and a total of 3,122 industrial sites registered throughout Europe, the majority of which were in Germany. EMAS has two main aims:

(*a*)    to encourage better environmental management at individual production sites within particular industries; and

(*b*)    to improve the disclosure of information on the impacts of those sites on the environment.

The Regulation sets out a number of elements of systematic environmental management. Sites that can demonstrate ongoing compliance with those requirements to an independent assessor have the right to be registered under EMAS.

Following the adoption of a company policy, an initial environmental review is made to identify the potential impacts of a site's operations, and an internal environmental protection system must be established. The system must include specific objectives for environmental performance and procedures for implementing them. The system, and the results of the initial environmental review, must be described in an initial environmental statement. The statement must be validated by an accredited external organisation before being submitted to nominated national authorities in individual States for registration of the site under the scheme.

There are a number of key points here:

(*a*)    the first stage in developing environmental management is to carry out a thorough review of impacts on the environment;

(*b*)    setting up an environmental management system is a prerequisite of registration under the scheme;

(*c*)    external validation of the environmental statement is intended to ensure consistency in environmental management systems;

(*d*)    the description of the environmental management system within the statement will be on the public record.

Once a site has been registered under the scheme, it will require regular audits to review the effectiveness of the environmental management system as well as giving information on environmental impacts of the site. Here it is sufficient to note that development of procedures for internal auditing is a crucial part of an environmental management system. In addition to the audit, the preparation and external validation of an environmental statement, submitted to the competent authority for continued registration and made public, are elements of an on-going procedure.

In order to attract more registrations and make the scheme more competitive, EMAS was revised by Regulation (EC) No 761/2001, with the revisions taking effect in April 2001. The scheme is now open to all sectors of the economy, including financial companies, transport and local and public bodies. In addition, registered organisations can use an official logo to publicise their participation in EMAS as well as gaining regulatory benefits. The new scheme also encourages more involvement by employees in implementation and strengthens the role of the environmental statement to improve the transparency of organisations and their stakeholders.

## International standards on environmental management (the ISO 14000 series)

**E16014**    The International Standards Organisation is continuing to develop a series of standards for various aspects of environmental management. All are designed to assist organisations with implementing more effective environmental management systems. Table 1 outlines the various standards and guidelines within the series.

The most high profile of these standards is ISO 14001, published in June 1996, which sets out the characteristics for a certifiable environmental management system (EMS). ISO 14001 was based on the British Standard on Environmental Management Systems (BS 7750), although the latter has been superseded by the international standard.

The format of ISO 14001 reflects the procedures and manuals approach of the ISO 9000 quality management systems series. In practice this means that organisations which operate to the requirements of ISO 9000 can extend their management systems to incorporate the environmental management standard, although the existence of a certified quality management system is not a prerequisite for ISO 14001.

ISO 14001 requires an organisation to develop an environmental policy which provides the foundation for the rest of the system. The standard includes guidance on the development and implementation of other elements of an EMS, which is ultimately designed to allow an organisation to manage those environmental aspects over which it has control, and over which it can be expected to have an influence. ISO 14001 does not itself stipulate environmental performance criteria.

At the end of 1999, 14,106 ISO 14000 certificates had been issued to organisations in 84 countries. The majority of these were issued in Europe and the Far East, where a total of 11,715 certificates were issued. Both Germany and Britain had over 1,000 certifications each.

## Table 1: The ISO 14000 series

| | |
|---|---|
| ISO 14001: 1996 | Environmental management systems – Specifications with guidance for use |
| ISO 14004: 1996 | Environmental management systems – General guidelines on principles, systems and supporting techniques |
| ISO 14010: 1996 | Guidelines for environmental auditing – General principles |
| ISO 14011: 1996 | Guidelines for environmental auditing – Audit procedures – Auditing of environmental management systems |
| ISO 14012: 1996 | Guidelines for environmental auditing – Qualification criteria for environmental auditors |
| ISO 14040: 1997 | Environmental management – Life cycle assessment – Principles and framework |
| ISO 14041: 1998 | Environmental management – Life cycle assessment – Goal and scope definition and inventory analysis |
| ISO 14050: 1998 | Environmental management – Vocabulary |
| ISO/FDIS 14020 | Environmental labels and declarations – General principles |
| ISO/DIS 14021 | Environmental labels and declarations – Environmental labelling – Self-declared environmental claims – Terms and definitions |
| ISO/DIS 14024 | Environmental labels and declarations – Environmental labelling TYPE 1 – Guiding principles and procedures |
| ISO/FDIS 14031 | Environmental performance evaluation – Guidelines |
| ISO/DIS 14042 | Environmental management – Life cycle assessment – Impact assessment |

### Differences between ISO 14001 and EMAS

E16015    The key differences between ISO 14001 and EMAS are:

(*a*)    ISO 14001 can be applied on a company-wide basis, whereas EMAS registration is only granted at individual site level or for particular services;

(*b*)    ISO 14001 does not currently include a requirement for public reporting of environmental performance information, whereas sites registered under EMAS must produce an independently validated, publicly available environmental statement;

(*c*)    ISO 14001 does not require a register of environmental effects or legislation;

(*d*)    the level of control of contractors and suppliers required in EMAS is not matched in ISO 14001, which stipulates only that required procedures are communicated to them.

The new revised EMAS allows integration of an existing ISO 14001 certification, to allow a smoother transition and avoid duplication when upgrading from ISO 14001 to EMAS.

# Implementing environmental management

## Practical requirements

E16016    Both EMAS and ISO 14001 set a pattern for companies wishing to develop environmental management systems. The key steps in implementing such systems involve:

(*a*)    conducting an initial review, designed to establish the current situation with respect to legislative requirements, potential environmental impacts and existing environmental management controls;

(*b*)    developing an environmental policy which will provide the basis of environmental management practices as well as informing day to day operational decisions;

(*c*)    establishing specific objectives and performance improvement targets;

(*d*)    developing a programme to implement the objectives and establish operational control over environmental performance;

(*e*)    ensuring information systems are adequate to provide management with complete, reliable and timely information; and

(*f*)    auditing the system to compare intended performance with actual performance.

## Review

E16017    In order to be able to actively manage its interactions with the environment, an organisation needs to understand the relationship between its business processes and its environmental performance. An environmental review should therefore be conducted, which clarifies how various business activities could potentially affect (or be affected by) the quality of different components of the environment (air, land, water, natural resources). This will allow an organisation to understand which of its activities have the greatest potential impact on the environment (usually, but not always, these will relate to procurement and/or manufacturing processes), and also which elements of environmental management and performance have the greatest potential impact on business performance (for example, high profile environmental prosecutions can have a significant impact on corporate reputation and brand value).

The initial (and subsequent) review should also consider the current and likely future legislative requirements that the company must comply with. It should also consider the overall organisational strategy, any other relevant corporate policies, customer specifications and community expectations which could influence environmental management practices. The review also offers the opportunity to establish a baseline of actual management organisation, systems and procedures, its compliance record and the range of initiatives already in place to improve performance.

Ideally, an environmental review should involve input from a range of stakeholders, both internal and external to the organisation. This promotes a wider perspective on potential environmental impacts, and ensures that the resulting policies and programmes to be developed by the organisation will reflect a comprehensive range of issues and risks. Consequently, the chances of unidentified and therefore uncontrolled risks emerging will be minimised.

## Policy

E16018   The results of the initial review should inform the development of a written environmental policy. The policy directs and underpins the remainder of the EMS, and represents a statement of intent with regard to environmental performance standards and priorities.

The policy should be endorsed by the highest level of management in the company, and should be communicated to all stakeholders.

## Objectives

E16019   It is important that the policy be supported by objectives that are both measurable and achievable. They should be cascaded throughout an organisation, so that at each level there are defined targets for each function to assist in the achievement of the objectives. A key part of ensuring continuous improvement in environmental performance is to review and update objectives in the light of progress and changing regulations and standards.

Objectives should be developed in conjunction with the groups and individuals who will have responsibility for achieving them. They should also be clearly linked to the overall business strategy and as far as possible with operational objectives. This ensures that environmental management is viewed as relevant and integral to business performance, rather than being seen as an isolated initiative.

The process of objective setting also needs to consider the most appropriate performance measures for tracking progress towards the ultimate objective. For example, if an objective is to reduce waste by 20 per cent over five years, a number of parameters could be used to reflect different aspects of the organisation's waste reduction efforts towards that, including volumes of waste recycled, efficiency with which raw materials are converted to product, and proportion of production staff that have received waste management training.

ISO 14031 provides useful guidance on the principles to be applied in the selection of appropriate environmental performance indicators. Performance in whichever parameters are selected should be measured regularly to enable corrective actions to be taken in a timely manner. As far as possible, performance measures and the achievement of quantified targets should be linked to existing appraisal systems for business units or individuals.

## Responsibilities

E16020   Allocation of responsibilities is vital for successful environmental management. Its implementation will typically involve changes in management systems and operations, training and awareness of personnel at all levels and in marketing and public relations.

A wide range of business functions will therefore need to be involved in developing and implementing environmental management systems. The commitment of senior personnel to introduce sound environmental management throughout the organisation, and to communicate it to all staff is vital.

Companies have adopted a range of organisational approaches as part of their environmental management systems. In some cases there is a single specialist function with responsibility for monitoring and auditing the system. An alternative is to have a central environmental function with only an advisory role which can also undertake verification of the internal audits carried out by other divisions or departments. The approach needs to be adapted to the culture and structure of the organisation, but whatever system is adopted, there are a number of crucial elements:

(*a*)    access to expertise in assessing environmental impacts and developing solutions;

(*b*)    a degree of independence in the auditing function;

(*c*)    a clear accountability for meeting environmental management objectives;

(*d*)    adequate information systems to help those responsible for evaluating performance against objectives, to identify problem areas and to ensure that action is taken to solve them.

## Training and communications

E16021     Both ISO 14001 and EMAS include training and communications as a key requirement of the EMS. In particular, they focus on ensuring that employees at all levels, in addition to contractors and other business partners, are aware of company policy and objectives; of how their own work activities impact on the environment and the benefits of improved performance; what they need to do in their jobs to help meet the company's environmental objectives; and the risks to the organisation of failing to carry out standard operating procedures.

This can involve a significant investment for companies, but if integrated with existing training modules and reinforced regularly, many hours of essential training can be achieved. An important benefit of training is that it can be a fertile ground for new ideas to minimise adverse environmental impacts.

Communication with, for example, regulators, investors, public bodies and local communities is an important part of good environment management and requires a preparedness to be open, honest and informative. It also requires clear procedures for liaising with external groups.

## Operational controls

E16022     The operational control elements of an EMS define its scope and essentially set out a basis for effective day-to-day management of environmental performance. Typically, such controls would include:

(*a*)    a register of relevant legislation and corporate policies that must be complied with;

(*b*)    a plan of action for ensuring that the policy is met, objectives are achieved and environmental management is continuously improved. This sets out the various initiatives to be proactively implemented and milestones to be achieved, and could be considered a 'road map' for guiding environmental performance;

(*c*)    a compilation of operating procedures which define the limits of acceptable and unacceptable practices within a company and which incorporate consideration of the environmental interactions identified in the review and the objectives and targets that were defined subsequently;

(*d*)    an emergency response plan to be implemented in the event of a sudden, unexpected and potentially catastrophic event which could potentially influence a company's environmental performance in an adverse manner;

(*e*)    a programme for monitoring, measuring, recording and reviewing environmental performance. This should incorporate a mechanism for regularly reporting back to senior management, since they are the key enablers of the EMS and because they retain ultimate responsibility of business performance.

These operational controls, and indeed all elements of an EMS, should be documented.

## Information management and public reporting

E16023    The critical factor in an EMS is the quality and timeliness of information to internal and external users. The importance of providing performance information to external users is increasing as expectations of greater transparency and corporate accountability continue to grow. Such expectations have been supported in the UK by strong encouragement from Government for companies to voluntarily and publicly report on their environmental performance. It has challenged all businesses in the FTSE top 350 to voluntarily and publicly report on their environmental performance by the end of 2001 and is encouraging other businesses to do likewise. However, at the beginning of 2001, less than 100 of the FTSE 350 companies were reporting on environmental performance. At present the Government is pursuing a policy of naming and shaming the UK's largest companies for failing to report on environmental performance, rather than drawing up plans for compulsory reporting.

Public environmental reporting is encouraged, but not mandated, by ISO 14001, although EMAS has always included a requirement for the preparation of an environmental statement as a condition of registration under the scheme.

Regardless of whether they have adopted EMAS, ISO 14001, or neither, many companies have a statutory duty to report on some aspects of their environmental performance to demonstrate legislative compliance. Some of that information is publicly available. An increasing number of companies are choosing to provide information on their environmental performance, either in their annual report and accounts, or in a stand-alone document. In most cases, the information provided extends well beyond a demonstration of legislative compliance, and tends towards a general overview of all significant aspects of environmental management and performance. Furthermore, many companies, recognising the importance of sustainability, are beginning to measure and report on their performance in terms of social impact.

As stakeholders and communication media become more sophisticated, and our understanding of environmental interactions increases, so information requirements become more complex. This means that management information systems must incorporate database management, modelling, measuring, monitoring and flexible reporting. The trend also means that environmental reports that have been produced solely as a means of improving public relations and to defuse external pressures are becoming less acceptable to many stakeholders. The main reasons for this appear to be that they are seldom generated in response to internal management information needs, which in turn means that they tend to focus on statements of management intent, qualitative claims and descriptive anecdotes rather than actual performance. They are therefore less likely to include detailed and verifiable information.

Instead, companies are recognising the value of maintaining a constructive and open dialogue with stakeholders, and published reports are being used as part of those efforts. The Association of Chartered Certified Accountants ('ACCA') has held annual awards for environmental reporting for the last decade, over which time it has identified a steady increase in both the quantity and quality of environmental reports. Furthermore the initial tendency of large manufacturing companies to report has spread to small and medium sized enterprises, the public sector and service industries such as financial services.

Institutional investors needing reassurance that companies are aware of their environmental risks, are also driving companies into providing more environmental information. Morley Fund Management stated in April 2001 that unless FTSE 100 companies publish an annual environmental report, it will vote against the adoption of annual reports and accounts. The introduction in July 2000 of a requirement for occupational pension funds to state the extent to which they consider environmental, social and ethical factors in investment decisions, has also increased the pressure for environmental reporting amongst companies.

While no standards on environmental reporting currently exist, a number of sources of guidance are available. Current 'best practice' environmental reporting in the UK is dictated by the United Nations Environment Program (UNEP)/SustainAbility benchmark study into corporate environmental reporting, the results of which have been published annually since 1996. The Global Reporting Initiative (GRI) was established in 1997 in an attempt to develop globally applicable guidelines for reporting on the economic, environmental and social performance of business, governments and non-government organisations. It incorporates the participation of corporations, NGOs, accountancy organisations, business associations and other stakeholders from around the world. The GRI's Sustainability Reporting Guidelines were released for consultation in March 1999 and revised guidelines issued in June 2000. They represent an expanded model for non-financial reporting and reflect the move towards broader sustainability reporting.

The Association of British Insurers ('ABI') is expected to adopt guidelines in 2002 setting out what institutional investors expect to see in the annual reports of the companies in which they invest. The guidelines were developed by the Socially Responsible Investment ('SRI') Forum, a grouping of institutional investors that collectively hold 15 per cent of the UK stock market. The guidelines will ask companies to disclose in their annual reports whether the Board takes account of environmental, social and ethical policies and procedures and the related risks to the company's value. The ABI also plan to monitor reports for the quality of information supplied.

Draft guidelines issued for consultation by the UK Government in March 2001 outline the main elements required in an effective environmental report. The guidance draws on existing reporting schemes, including the GRI, and outlines ten basic elements that should feature in a report. It also states that the report should cover all environmental impacts of a company's performance and that it should be readily accessible to the intended audience. However, it leaves reporters free to decide where and how to publish environmental information.

The European Commission has recently adopted a draft Recommendation providing guidelines on the information relating to environmental expenditures, liabilities and risks that companies should publish in their annual accounts and reports. Among those proposed is experience in implementing environment protection measures. It also advocates that where relevant, this should contain quantitative measures in areas such as emissions and consumption of water, energy and materials. Unlike a Directive, the recommendation will not be binding.

In an attempt to increase the credibility of published reports and identify opportunities for improving management information systems, a number of companies are seeking independent assurance on the reliability, completeness and likely accuracy of information contained in their reports. Although there are no standards for providing an independent opinion on corporate environmental reports, the long-established financial audit model provides a useful framework. Contemporary financial audit practice does not require reconciling and cross-checking every individual figure included in a report. Instead it relies on a review of the effectiveness of the systems, procedures and controls that have been used to generate the information included in the report. That review is supplemented by testing, on a sample basis, of the application of a number of the procedures, and correlation of resulting information with that included in the report.

### Auditing and review

E16024    Auditing of environmental management systems, whether conducted by internal or external parties, is a means of identifying potential risk areas and can assist in identifying actions and system improvements required to facilitate ongoing system and performance improvement.

## Benefits of environmental management

### Effective environmental management

E16025    Effective environmental management will involve changes across all business functions. It requires commitment from senior management and is likely to need additional human and financial resources initially. However, it can also offer significant benefits to businesses. These include:

(*a*)    avoidance of liability and risk. Good environmental management allows businesses to choose when and how to invest in better environmental performance, rather than reacting at the last minute to new legislation or consumer pressures. Unforeseen problems will be minimised, prosecution and litigation avoided;

(*b*)    gaining competitive advantage. A business with sound environmental management is more likely to make a good impact on its customers. The business will be better placed to identify and respond rapidly to opportunities for new products and services, to take advantage of 'green' markets and also respond to the increasing demand for information on supplier environmental performance;

(*c*)    achievement of a better profile with investors, employees and the public. Increasingly investors and their advisers are avoiding companies with a poor environmental record. The environmental performance of businesses is an increasing concern for existing staff and potential recruits. Some businesses are finding that a good environmental record helps to boost their public image;

(*d*)    cost savings from better management of resources and reduction of wastes through attention to recovering, reusing and recycling; and reduced bills from more careful use of energy;

(*e*)    an improved basis for corporate decision-making. Effective environmental management can provide valuable information to corporate decision-makers by expanding the basis of such decisions beyond financial considerations. Companies that understand the interactions between their business activities and environmental performance are in a strong position for integrating environmental management into their business, thereby incorporating key elements of the principles of sustainable development.

Effective environmental management can turn environmental issues from an area of threat and cost to one of profit and opportunity. As standards for environmental management systems are adopted and are widely applied, the question will increasingly become, as with quality management, can a company afford not to adopt environmental management? The external pressures on organisations to improve environmental performance are unlikely to abate. Environmental management systems can help companies respond to the pressures in a timely and cost-effective way.

# The future

E16026
Environmental management is now well-established as an essential component of effective business management. Environmental management systems have been widely adopted and in most cases these have facilitated demonstrable and ongoing improvements in environmental performance. The involvement of a range of stakeholders in corporate environmental management is no longer the exception; the constructive contribution that they make is actively sought. The publication of environmental reports has also come to be relatively common among leading companies; most include a mechanism for obtaining feedback from external stakeholders, and an increasing number are independently assured in a similar way to annual financial reports and accounts.

However, there is already a noticeable trend towards sustainability management, whereby companies are attempting to systematically balance economic, environmental and social considerations in business strategies and operations. The strong inter-relationships and inter-dependence between these three elements of sustainable development make it imperative for companies to move towards a more integrated approach to managing them.

In late 1998, the UK Government announced a number of national 'sustainability indicators' to be used to assess the effectiveness of Government policies and initiatives. Pressures on business to do likewise will increase, and the efforts of a number of organisations including WBCSD, UNEP, the GRI consortium and organisations seeking to implement their guidelines will help to respond to those pressures.

The UK Government launched its updated national strategy for sustainable development in 1999, entitled *A Better Quality of Life*, which clearly acknowledges the role that business must play in facilitating sustainable development. Several companies have responded to this to this by producing public sustainability reports.

Model reports such as *Sooner, Sharper, Simpler* by the Centre for Tomorrow's Company and *Prototype plc* by the Institute of Chartered Accountants of England and Wales (ICAEW) provide useful guidance on the direction in which corporate performance reporting is likely to go. Initiatives such as the GRI are expected to further facilitate a change in approach and foster a more sustainable approach to business management.

Continued development of this approach will be greatly influenced by shareholders, market analysts and financial institutions recognising the value of non-financial performance information as a basis for evaluating management competence and predicting business performance. Consequently they can increasingly be expected to insist on changes to the information presented to them by companies, thereby generating a radical shift in the traditional business paradigm.

Therefore, while environmental management will remain a critical issue for business to address, it will increasingly become integrated with other aspects of business management, reflecting a growing acceptance of the importance of sustainability.

# Fire and Fire Precautions

## Introduction – the parameters of fire safety legislation

F5001    Fire safety legislation is dually but separately concerned with (*a*) the imposition of controls on the design and construction of buildings (building control law, applying to all *new* buildings, including private individual dwellings), and (*b*) the safe management of *existing* buildings (i.e. premises) by way of imposition of specified precautionary measures, e.g. regular inspection to ensure in particular that occupants are able to leave safely in the event of fire.

'Existing buildings' are:

(*a*)    some workplaces (mainly factories, offices and shops), and

(*b*)    places to which the public has access (shops, libraries, swimming pools, theatres, hotels, boarding houses), but not private dwellings.

The precautionary measures are of two types:

(i)    general fire precautions (e.g. alarms, drills), and

(ii)    process fire precautions (e.g. control of hazardous work activities and substances).

This section deals, almost exclusively, with the safe management of the workplace.

In this connection, the current *Fire Precautions Act 1971* introduced a series of controls, by way of regulations passed thereunder, for the protection of workers in factories, offices and shops as well as various sections of the general public. The basis of this protection is 'certification', this being dependent on 'designation'. Moreover, the *Fire Precautions (Workplace) Regulations 1997 (SI 1997 No 1840)* as amended by the *Fire Precautions (Workplace) (Amendment) Regulations 1999 (SI 1999 No 1877)* extend protection to nearly all other workplaces. Fire safety signs must be provided and maintained where indicated by risk assessment to ensure that occupants leave safely in event of fire (*Health and Safety (Safety Signs and Signals) Regulations 1996 (SI 1996 No 341), Reg 4*).

## The current position – overview

F5002    Statute law relating to fire and fire precautions is extensive and located mainly in the *Fire Precautions Act 1971 (FPA)* (and regulations and orders made thereunder), the *Fire Safety and Safety of Places of Sport Act 1987*, the *Fire Precautions (Workplace) Regulations 1997* as amended by the *Fire Precautions (Workplace) (Amendment) Regulations 1999*, the *Health and Safety at Work etc. Act 1974 (HSWA)* (in the form of the *Fire Certificates (Special Premises) Regulations 1976 (SI 1976 No 2003)* (see F5033 below)), the *Petroleum Acts* (and regulations made thereunder), the *Public Health Acts 1936-1961*, the *Building Act 1984* (and the *Building Regulations 1991* made thereunder), the *Fire Services Act 1947* and the *Fires Prevention (Metropolis) Act 1774* as well as certain regulations, made under the *Factories Act 1961*, such as the *Highly Flammable Liquids and Liquefied Petroleum Gases Regulations 1972*.

The *Fire Precautions Act 1971* imposes requirements relating to fire precautions upon occupiers of premises (whether or not employers) where there is a fire risk; whilst the *Fire Safety and Safety of Places of Sport Act 1987* is a deregulating measure modifying some of the duties of the *Fire Precautions Act 1971* (see F5012-F5023 below). Meanwhile, *HSWA* is concerned specifically with premises containing dangerous materials and/or where hazardous processes are carried on. The *Petroleum Spirit (Consolidation) Act 1928* imposes requirements on storage and transportation of petroleum spirit, whilst the *Public Health Acts* and, more particularly, the *Building Act 1984* (and *Building Regulations 1991*) apply health, safety and welfare requirements to *new* buildings (industrial, commercial and private) and buildings under construction and altered buildings, in the interests of occupants, both present and future. The *Fire Services Act 1947* specifies the duties of local fire authorities and the *Fires Prevention (Metropolis) Act 1774*, *inter alia*, regulates liability of occupiers of premises to adjoining occupiers for damage caused by fire spread. The *Fire Precautions (Workplace) Regulations 1997* and the 1999 Amendment Regulations impose a requirement on the employer to conduct a fire risk assessment.

The first four Acts, the *Fire Precautions Act 1971*, the *Fire Safety and Safety of Places of Sport Act 1987*, *HSWA 1974* and the *Public Health Acts 1936* and *1961* are predominantly penal measures, whilst the *Fires Prevention (Metropolis) Act 1774* concerns civil liability. More particularly, the *Fire Precautions Act 1971* (as amended by the *Fire Safety and Safety of Places of Sport Act 1987*) and *HSWA* specify fire precautions in relation to commercial and industrial (and a limited number of other) buildings already in existence (see F5006 below), whilst the *Public Health Acts* and the *Building Regulations* apply mainly to *new* buildings – industrial, commercial and private, and *buildings under construction as well as altered buildings*.

The Government has recently reviewed fire safety legislation and some consolidation of legislation is expected in the near future. The form in which this is to be implemented has not been decided. A *Fire Safety Bill* was considered but deregulation may be used instead.

The Health and Safety Executive is reviewing the *Petroleum Spirit (Consolidation) Act 1928* and it is expected that many of the provisions in this Act will be incorporated into current regulations dealing with dangerous substances. No date has been published for the completion of this work.

## Specific fire precautions regulations

F5003     The main legislation relating to fire safety in workplaces is the *Fire Precautions Act 1971* (as amended by the *Fire Safety and Safety of Places of Sport Act 1987*), the effect of which latter Act was to deregulate, to a limited extent, fire precautions law. The key to operation of the *Fire Precautions Act 1971* was (and still is) *certification* – that is, if premises were to be put to certain uses, they would require a valid fire certificate. The *Fire Precautions (Workplace) Regulations 1997* ('the Workplace Regulations') and the recent *Fire Precautions (Workplace) (Amendment) Regulations 1999 (SI 1999 No 1877)* require all employers to conduct a fire risk assessment of the workplaces for which they are responsible. However, application must still be made for a fire certificate for premises designated under the *Fire Precautions Act 1971*, i.e. hotels and boarding houses, offices, factories and railway premises. Fire certificates are also required for 'special premises' (see below.)

The 1997 Workplace Regulations originally allowed designated premises, i.e. those with fire certificates or with certificate applications pending, to be excepted from the requirement to carry out a risk assessment, but the exception was removed by the *Fire Precautions (Workplace) (Amendment) Regulations 1999* (see F5024 and F5025). Thus virtually all places of employment are now caught by the Workplace Regulations.

The Workplace Regulations do not allow the contents of a fire certificate to be such that people complying with the certificate will contravene these regulations. The Workplace Regulations allow fire authorities to modify certificates accordingly.

Similarly, safety certificates issued under the *Safety of Sports Grounds Act 1975* or the *Fire Safety and Safety of Places of Sport Act 1987* are not allowed to require anyone to do anything that would cause them to contravene the Workplace Regulations.

The principal regulations made under the *Fire Precautions Act 1971, s 12* (the regulation-enabling section) are:

(*a*)    the *Fire Precautions (Factories, Offices, Shops and Railway Premises) Order 1989 (SI 1989 No 76)*;

(*b*)    the *Fire Precautions (Hotels and Boarding Houses) Order 1972 (SIs 1972 Nos 238, 382)*;

(*c*)    the *Fire Certificates (Special Premises) Regulations 1976 (SI 1976 No 2003)* (the *'Special Premises' Regulations*); and

(*d*)    the *Fire Precautions (Workplace) Regulations 1997 (SI 1997 No 1840)*.

((*a*) to (*d*) above are collectively known as the 'fire regulations'). (For offences and penalties in connection with the 'fire regulations', see F5012 below.)

## Fire certification – anchor of the Fire Precautions Act 1971

F5004    The anchor of the *Fire Precautions Act 1971* was the requirement for 'designated' premises to be 'fire-certificated' – normally by the local fire authority, though in the case of exceptionally hazardous industrial premises (i.e. special premises) by the HSE. To date, two designation orders have been made affecting factories, offices and shops *and* hotels and boarding houses (see further F5005 below). A fire certificate must be produced on demand to a fire officer, for inspection purposes, or a copy of it (*Fire Precautions Act 1971, s 19(1)(c)*). (For offences/penalties, see F5012 below.)

Fire certificates specify:

(*a*)    use/uses of premises;

(*b*)    means of escape in case of fire;

(*c*)    how means of escape can be safely and effectively used;

(*d*)    alarms and fire warning systems; and

(*e*)    fire-fighting apparatus to be provided in the building.

Moreover, at its discretion, the fire authority can, additionally, impose requirements relating to:

(i)     maintenance of means of escape and fire-fighting equipment;

(ii)    staff training; and

(iii)   restrictions on the number of people within the building.

Prior to the issue of a fire certificate, premises must be inspected by the fire authority, though failure to do so or inadequate inspection or advice cannot involve the fire authority in liability for negligence (see F5007 below).

### Fire-certificated (or designated premises)

F5005    The *Fire Precautions Act 1971* allowed the Secretary of State responsible to issue designation orders from time to time whereby premises put to certain designated uses would be required to have fire certificates. Although a range of uses was provided for in the Act, to date only two such orders have been issued. These have designated hotels and boarding houses (see F5003(*b*)) and factories, offices, shops and railway premises (see F5003(*a*)).

### Work premises requiring a fire certificate

F5006    Under the *Fire Precautions (Factories, Offices, Shops and Railway Premises) Order 1989 (SI 1989 No 76)* a certificate must be applied for in the following situations:

(*a*)    (i)    where more than 20 people are at work, or

(ii)    more than 10 are at work elsewhere than on the ground floor

(in shops, factories, offices and railway premises);

(*b*)    in buildings in multiple occupation containing two or more individual factory, office, shop or railway premises, when the aggregate of people at work exceeds the same totals;

(*c*)    in factories where explosive or highly flammable materials are stored, or used in or under the premises, unless, in the opinion of the fire authority, there is no serious risk to employees.

[*Fire Precautions (Factories, Offices, Shops and Railway Premises) Order 1989 (SI 1989 No 76), Reg 5*].

In light of the amendment of the *Fire Precautions Act 1971* by the *Fire Safety and Safety of Places of Sport Act 1987*, some relaxation of earlier requirements is now possible (see F5013 below).

### Applications for local authority fire certificate

F5007    Where a fire certificate is required in respect of premises, that is premises which have not been granted exemption, as low risk (see F5013 below), from certification under the *Fire Safety and Safety of Places of Sport Act 1987*, applications for a fire certificate relating to appropriate premises (see F5006 above) must be made to the local fire authority on the correct form (see F5008 below), obtainable from each fire authority. Plans may be required and the premises will be inspected before issue of a certificate. If the fire authority is not satisfied as to existing arrangements, it will specify the steps to be taken before a certificate is issued, and notify the occupier or owner that they will not issue a certificate until such steps are taken within the specified time (*Fire Precautions Act 1971, s 5*). (Hospitals, NHS trusts and private hospitals must conform to the requirements of FIRECODE. For the position of hospitals, see generally E15035 ENFORCEMENT and F5021 below.)

Despite the fact that the *Fire Precautions Act 1971, s 5(3)* lays a duty on a fire authority to carry out an inspection of premises in respect of which an occupier has applied for a fire certificate, it seems that if the fire authority fails to do so it cannot be sued for negligence, as this would amount to provision of 'gratuitous insurance' for damage (see further F5055 below). Nor is the fire authority under a duty to advise hoteliers not to reopen (see F5010 and F5058 below, *Hallett v Nicholson*).

## Form for application for fire certificate

F5008 Applications for a fire certificate must be made on the form prescribed by the *Fire Precautions (Application for Certificate) Regulations 1989 (SI 1989 No 77).*

### FIRE PRECAUTIONS ACT 1971, s.5

#### APPLICATION FOR A FIRE CERTIFICATE

For Official Use Only

* In the case of Crown premises, substitute H.M. Inspector of Fire Services.

To the Chief Executive of the Fire Authority*

I hereby apply for a fire certificate in respect of the premises of which details are given below. I make the application as, or on behalf of, the occupier/owner of the premises.

Signature ...........................................................................

Name: Mr/Mrs/Miss.............................................................
(in block capitals)

If signing on behalf of a company or some other person, state the capacity in which

signing.............................................................................................

Address.............................................................................................

Telephone number........................................... Date.........................................

To be completed by the Applicant:–
1. Postal address of the premises ...............................................................
....................................................................................................
....................................................................................................
....................................................................................................

2. Name and address of the owner of the premises

Name ...............................................................................................

Address ...........................................................................................
....................................................................................................
....................................................................................................

(In the case of premises in plural ownership the names and addresses of all owners should be given.)

3. Details of the premises
(If the fire certificate is to cover the use of two or more sets of premises in the same building, details of each set of premises should be given on a separate sheet.)

(a) Name of occupier .......................................................................

(and any trading name, if different) ...............................................

....................................................................................................

F50/5

(b)  Use(s) to which premises put .................................................................................................

(c)  Floor(s) in building on which premises situated (e.g. basement(s), ground floor, first floor etc.) ..................................................................................................................................

..................................................................................................................................

(d)  Number of persons employed to work in the premises .................................................

(e)  Maximum number of persons at work or it is proposed will work in the premises at any one time (including employees, self-employed persons and trainees)–

(i)  below the ground floor of the building ...................................................................

(ii)  on the ground floor of the building .......................................................................

(iii)  on the first floor of the building ..........................................................................

(iv)  in the whole of the premises ................................................................................

(f)  Maximum number of persons other than persons at work likely to be in the premises at any one time ............................................................................................................

(g)  Number of persons (including staff, guests and other residents) for whom sleeping accommodation is provided in the premises–

(i)  below the ground floor of the building ...................................................................

(ii)  above the first floor of the building .......................................................................

(iii)  in the whole of the premises ................................................................................

---

**4.**  If the premises consist of part only of a building, the uses to which the other parts of the building are put (on a floor by floor basis):

..................................................................................................................................

..................................................................................................................................

..................................................................................................................................

---

**5.**  (a)  Total number of floors (excluding basements) in the building in which the premises are situated .................................................................................................................

(b)  Total number of basements in that building ..................................................................

---

**6.**  Approximate date of construction of the premises .................................................................

---

**7.**  Nature and quantity of any explosive or highly flammable materials stored or used in or under the premises

| Materials | Maximum quantity stored | Method of storage | Maximum quantity liable to be exposed at any one time |
|---|---|---|---|
|  |  |  |  |

(Continue on a separate sheet if necessary)

**8.** Details of fire-fighting equipment available for use in the premises

| Nature of equipment | Number Provided | Where installed | Is the equipment regularly maintained? |
|---|---|---|---|
| (a) Hosereels | | | Yes/No |
| (b) Portable fire extinguishers | | | Yes/No |
| (c) Others | | | Yes/No |
| (specify types e.g. sand/water buckets. fire blanket) | | | |

(Continue on a separate sheet if necessary)

## Who should apply?

F5009    Application should normally be made by the occupier in the case of factories, offices and shops. In the following cases it must be made by the owner or owners:

(*a*)    premises consisting of part of a building, all parts of which are owned by the same person (i.e. multi-occupancy/single ownership situations);

(*b*)    premises consisting of part of a building, the different parts being owned by different persons (i.e. multi-occupancy/plural ownership situations).

[*Fire Precautions Act 1971, s 5, Sch 2 Part II*].

## Categories of fire risk premises

F5010    Where there is in the opinion of the fire authority a serious risk to persons from fire on premises, unless steps are taken to minimise that risk, and the fire authority thinks that a particular use of premises should be either prohibited or restricted, it may apply to the court for an order prohibiting or restricting that use of premises until remedial steps are taken (*Fire Precautions Act 1971, s 10(2)*). This requirement does not impose a duty on a fire authority to advise an occupier not to reopen; hence, if he reopens and suffers loss from fire, the fire authority will not be liable (*Hallett v Nicholson*, see F5058 below).

The 1997 Workplace Regulations amend the *Fire Precautions Act 1971, ss 10* to *10B*, to include tents and other movable structures and places of work in the open air.

## Contents of a fire certificate

F5011    A fire certificate specifies:

(*a*)    the particular use or uses of premises which it covers;

(*b*)    the means of escape in the case of fire (as per plan);

(*c*)    the means for securing that the means of escape can be safely and effectively used at all relevant times (e.g. direction signs/emergency lighting/fire or smoke stop doors);

(*d*)    the means for fighting fire for use by persons in the building;

(*e*)    the means for giving warnings in the case of fire;

(f)    in the case of any factory, particulars as to any explosives or highly flammable materials stored or used on the premises.

[*Fire Precautions Act 1971, s 6(1)*].

In addition, a fire certificate may require:

(i)    maintenance of the means of escape and their freedom from obstruction;

(ii)   maintenance of other fire precautions set out in the certificate;

(iii)  training of employees on the premises as to what to do in the event of fire and keeping of suitable records of such training;

(iv)   limitation of number of persons who at any one time may be on the premises;

(v)    any other relevant fire precautions.

[*Fire Precautions Act 1971, s 6(2)*].

## Offences/penalties for breach of the Fire Precautions Act 1971

F5012    Failure to have/exhibit a valid fire certificate, or breach of any condition(s) in such certificate is an offence, committed by the holder, carrying:

(a)    on summary conviction, a maximum fine of £5,000; and

(b)    on conviction on indictment, an indefinite fine or up to two years' imprisonment (or both).

[*Fire Precautions Act 1971, s 7(1)(5) as amended by the Criminal Justice Act 1991, s 17(1)*].

An occupier also commits an offence if the fire authority or inspectorate is not informed of a proposed structural or material alteration (*Fire Precautions Act 1971, s 8*). Breach carries the same penalties as for breach of *s 7* (above). Other offences include obstructing a fire inspector (*s 19(6)*) and forging/falsifying a fire certificate (*s 22(1)*).

## Waiver of certification for designated premises

F5013    Under the insertions in the *Fire Safety and Safety of Places of Sport Act 1987*, a fire authority can grant exemption from certification requirements in the case of 'designated use' premises (*Fire Precautions Act 1971, s 1(3A)*). The powers to grant exemption are given to the local fire authority by the amended *Fire Precautions Act 1971, s 5A*. Exemption from certification requirements can be granted, either on application for a fire certificate, or at any time during the currency of a fire certificate. Fire certificates are not necessary, in the case of factory, office, shop and railway premises, where either

(a)    a fire authority has granted exemption (under the *Fire Precautions Act 1971, s 5A* (as amended)) in the case of 'low-risk' premises, or

(b)    there are fewer than

(i)    20 employees in buildings containing two or more factory and/or office premises at any one time, or

(ii)   10 employees in buildings containing two or more factory and/or office premises at any one time, elsewhere than on the ground floor.

(1989 Code of Practice for fire precautions in factories, offices, shops and railway premises not required to have a fire certificate, operational as from 1 April 1989.)

It is not necessary formally to apply for exemption (*Fire Precautions Act 1971 (as amended), s 5A(2)*). Normally, however, exemption would not be granted unless the fire authority had first carried out an inspection within the previous twelve months. Hence, if exemption is granted on application for a fire certificate, the grant disposes of the application; alternatively, if the grant is made during the currency of a fire certificate, the certificate ceases to have effect. Any exemption certificate must specify the greatest number of persons who can safely be in the premises at any one time. Such exemptions can be withdrawn by the fire authority without an inspection/inquiry as to the degree of seriousness of risk from fire to persons on the premises etc., in which case notice of withdrawal must be given.

## Change of conditions affecting premises for which exemption is granted

F5014    If, while an exemption is in force an occupier proposes to carry out material changes in the premises, the occupier must inform the fire authority of the proposed changes. Not to do so is to commit an offence (*Fire Precautions Act 1971, s 8A(1)*). This applies where it is proposed:

(*a*)    to make an extension of, or structural alteration to the premises which would affect the means of escape from the premises; or

(*b*)    to make an alteration in the internal arrangement of the premises, or in the furniture or equipment, which would affect the means of escape from the premises; or

(*c*)    to keep explosive or highly flammable materials under, in or on the premises, in a quantity or aggregate quantity greater than the prescribed maximum; or

(*d*)    (where an exemption grant depends on a specified number of persons being on the premises) to make use of the premises which involves there being a greater number of persons on the premises.

[*Fire Precautions Act 1971, s 8A(2)*].

## Offences/penalties – exempted premises

F5015    Any person found guilty of any of these offences is liable:

(*a*)    on summary conviction to a maximum fine of £5,000,

(*b*)    on conviction on indictment, to an indefinite fine or imprisonment for up to two years (or both).

[*Fire Precautions Act 1971, s 8A(3)*].

## Duty to provide/maintain means of escape – exempted premises

F5016    Premises which are exempt from fire certification must be provided with:

(*a*)    means of escape in the case of fire; and

(*b*)    means of fighting fire;

as may reasonably be required by the fire authority (*Fire Precautions Act 1971, s 9A(1)*, but this section does not apply where *Part II* of the *Fire Precautions (Workplace) Regulations 1997* applies. *Part II* of the *1997 Regulations* is entitled 'Fire Precautions in the Workplace' and comprises *Regs 3–6*).

Breach of this duty carries with it a maximum fine of £5,000 (*Fire Precautions Act 1971, s 9A(3)*). However, it is important to note that there is no breach of duty to provide means of escape/fire-fighting equipment where the fire authority has served an *improvement notice* in respect of the premises (see F5018 below). A code of practice has been issued (*'Code of practice for fire precautions in factories, offices, shops and railway premises not required to have a fire certificate'* ISBN 0 11 340904 4). This means that an occupier who failed to follow a provision of a code of practice would have non-compliance taken into account under proceedings for breach of the Act. Compliance with such codes of practice will be admissible as a defence.

### Definition of 'escape'

F5017    In relation to premises 'escape' means 'escape from them to some place of safety beyond the building, which constitutes or comprises the premises, and any area enclosed by it or within it; accordingly, conditions or requirements can be imposed as respects any place or thing by means of which a person escapes from premises to a place of safety' (*Fire Precautions Act 1971, s 5(5) as amended by FSSPSA 1987, s 4(2)*).

# Improvement notices

F5018    Use of improvement notices, which have proved effective in general health and safety law for upgrading standards of health and safety at the workplace, has been duplicated in fire precautions law. Thus, where a fire authority is of the opinion that the duty to provide:

(*a*)    means of escape; and

(*b*)    means of fire-fighting;

has been breached, they can serve on the occupier an improvement notice, specifying, particularly by reference to a code of practice (see F5016 above), what measures are necessary to remedy the breach and requiring the occupier to carry out this remedial work within three weeks, or alternatively appeal (*Fire Precautions Act 1971, s 9D*). Service of such notice need not be recorded in a public register (see further E15022 ENFORCEMENT).

### Relevance of Building Regulations

F5019    Where premises are those to which, during erection, the *Building Regulations 1991(SI 1991 No 2768)* as amended by the *Building Regulations (Amendment) (No 2 Regulations 1999 (SI 1999 No 3410)* impose requirements as to means of escape in case of fire, and in consequence plans were deposited with the local authority, the fire authority cannot serve an improvement notice requiring structural or other alterations, unless the fire authority is satisfied that the means of escape in case of fire are inadequate, by reason of matters/circumstances of which particulars were not required by the *Building Regulations*. (*Fire Precautions Act 1971, s 9D(3)*).

The Amendment Regulations 1999 make changes to the 1991 Regulations requiring, among others, 'appropriate' provisions for the early warning of fire and 'reasonable facilities to assist fire fighters in the protection of life'. This brings these Regulations into line with the 1997 Workplace Regulations.The amendments came into force in July 2000 and are reflected in the accompanying approved document (*'Approved Document B, Fire Safety', 2000 edition* available from the Stationary Office or the Department of the Environment, Transport and the Regions (DETR)).

More particularly, the following requirements are specified in respect of new premises:

(1)     The building must be designed/constructed so that there are *means of escape* in case of fire, to a place of safety outside.

*Internal fire spread*

(2)     To inhibit internal fire spread, internal linings must:

(*a*)     adequately resist flame spread over surfaces;

(*b*)     if ignited, have a reasonable rate of heat release.

(3)     The building must be designed and constructed so that, in the event of fire, its stability will be maintained for a reasonable period; and a common wall should be able to resist fire spread between the buildings.

(4)     The building must be designed and constructed so that unseen fire/smoke spread within concealed spaces in its fabric and structure, is inhibited.

*External fire spread*

(5)     External walls shall adequately resist fire spread over walls and from one building to another.

(6)     A roof should be able to resist fire spread over the roof and from one building to another.

Finally:

(7)     The building must be designed and constructed to provide facilities to firefighters and enable fire appliances to gain access.

[*Building Regulations 1991 (SI 1991 No 2768), Sch 1*].

*Means of warning and escape*

(8)     The building shall be designed and constructed so that there are appropriate provisions for the early warning of fire, and appropriate means of escape in case of fire from the building to a place of safety outside the building capable of being safely and effectively used at all material times.

*Access and facilities for the fire service*

(9)     The building shall be designed and constructed so as to provide reasonable facilities to assist fire fighters in the protection of life and reasonable provision made within the site of the building to enable fire appliances to gain access.

Practical guidance is given in '*Approved Document B*' 2000 edition to the *Building Regulations 1991*, published by the Stationery Office and the DETR.

## Appeals against improvement notices

**F5020**     An appeal must be lodged against an improvement notice within 21 days from the date of service. Moreover, unlike prohibition notices, the effect of an appeal is to suspend operation of the improvement notice. Presumably, a ground of appeal would be that occupiers of 'low risk' premises have achieved satisfactory fire safety standards by means other than those specified in a code of practice.

If the appeal fails, the occupier must carry out the remedial work specified in the notice. Failure to do so carries with it:

(*a*)    on summary conviction a maximum fine of £5,000;

(*b*)    on conviction on indictment, an indefinite fine or imprisonment for up to two years (or both).

[*Fire Precautions Act 1971, ss 9E, 9F*].

## Premises involving serious risk of injury to persons – prohibition notices

F5021    In places of work generally, health and safety inspectors can serve prohibition notices requiring a hazardous activity to cease in cases where there is thought to be a serious risk of personal injury. Now, in the case of fire hazards where there is thought to be a serious risk of injury to persons from fire, the fire authority is in a similar way empowered to serve on the occupier a prohibition notice. The effect of such notice (which need not affect all the premises) will be to prohibit use of the premises or activity until the risk is removed. The original *s 10* of the *Fire Precautions Act 1971* was replaced by a new *s 10*, empowering fire authorities to issue prohibition notices. This replacement section applies to the following premises, in respect of which prohibition notices can be served, i.e. premises:

(*a*)    providing sleeping accommodation;

(*b*)    providing treatment/care;

(*c*)    for the purposes of entertainment, recreation or instruction, or for a club, society or association;

(*d*)    for teaching, training or research;

(*e*)    providing access to members of the public, whether for payment or otherwise;

(*f*)    places of work.

(This includes hospitals, factories and places of public worship, but not private dwellings (*Fire Safety and Safety of Places of Sport Act 1987, s 13*). Thus, a fire authority could restrict/prohibit the use of any part of a hospital, factory or place of religious worship, presenting a serious fire risk to persons – premises which are also subject to the *Building Act 1984* and *Building Regulations 1991* (see W11042 WORKPLACES – HEALTH, SAFETY AND WELFARE). In particular, after consultation with the fire authority, if a local authority is not satisfied with the means of escape in case of fire, it can serve a notice requiring the owner to carry out remedial work in residential premises of all kinds, including inns, hotels and nursing homes and certain commercial premises with sleeping accommodation above them, whether a fire certificate is in force or not (*Building Act 1984, s 72*).)

The fire authority is most likely to serve prohibition notices in cases where it considers that means of escape are inadequate or could be improved. As with prohibition notices served generally in respect of workplaces, it can be immediate or deferred. Occupiers must lodge an appeal within 21 days; moreover, the appeal does not, as with improvement notices (above), suspend operation of the notice which remains in force.

Entry of such notices must appear in a public register (*Environment and Safety Information Act 1988, ss 1, 3 and Sch*).

## Offences/penalties

F5022    A person found guilty of contravening a prohibition notice is liable to:

(*a*)    a maximum fine of £5,000 on summary conviction; and

(*b*)    on conviction on indictment, an indefinite fine or up to two years' imprisonment (or both).

[*Fire Precautions Act 1971, s 10B(3) as inserted by Fire Safety and Safety of Places of Sport Act 1987, s 9*].

It is, however, a defence that the person did not know *and* had no reason to believe that the prohibition notice had been served (*Fire Precautions Act 1971, s 10B(2) as inserted by Fire Safety and Safety of Places of Sport Act 1987, s 9*).

## Civil liability/actionability

F5023    Any person suffering injury/damage as a result of breach of or failure to comply with the provisions of the *Fire Precautions Act 1971*, must in most cases prove negligence at common law if he wishes to secure compensation. There is an action for breach of statutory duty in the case of *s 9A* (duty as to means of escape and for fighting fire) but otherwise the Act excludes civil proceedings. The regulations made under the Act also exclude civil proceedings unless they provide otherwise. [*Fire Precautions Act 1971, s 27A (as amended)*]. This means that the effect of the decision in *Hallett v Nicholson* (F5058 below), which was concerned with fire certificate requirements, exempts fire authorities from civil liability (but see further F5055 below).

# The Fire Precautions (Workplace) Regulations 1997 as amended by the Fire Precautions (Workplace) (Amendment) Regulations 1999

### Extension of statutory requirements to 'non-designated' workplaces

F5024    By way of implementation of the Framework and Workplace Directives in relation to fire safety, the *Fire Precautions (Workplace) Regulations 1997 (SI 1997 No 1840)* pursuant to the *Fire Precautions Act 1971, s 12*, extend fire precautions requirements to most places of work. This includes some workplaces currently designated and certificated under the *Factories Act 1961* and the *Offices, Shops and Railway Premises Act 1963*.

The *Management of Health and Safety at Work Regulations 1999 (SI 1999 No 3242)* amend some aspects of the Workplace Regulations, mostly where references to the 1992 Management Regulations have been changed. Also *Regulation 3* of the 1999 Management Regulations requires employers, among other things, to carry out a fire risk assessment to identify measures needed to comply with the provisions of the *Fire Precautions (Workplace) Regulations 1997* (as amended).

Where there are five or more employees, the fire risk assessment must be recorded and retained.

The *Fire Precautions (Workplace) (Amendment) Regulations 1999 (SI 1999 No 1877)* make amendments to the 1997 Workplace Regulations. The main changes are to extend the scope of the Regulations by removing some of the excepted categories of workplace that appeared in the 1997 Workplace Regulations. These amendments have been brought in to address concerns expressed by the European Union that the

1997 Regulations did not fully implement the Framework and Workplace Directives (see above) and to resolve the resulting legislative overlaps.

## Workplaces to which the Regulations do not apply

**F5025**   These include the following:

- Workplaces used only by the self-employed.

- Private dwellings.

- Mine shafts and mine galleries, other than surface buildings.

- Construction sites (any workplace to which the *Construction (Health, Safety and Welfare) Regulations 1996* apply).

- Ships within the meaning of the *Docks Regulations 1988* (including those under construction or repair by persons other than the crew).

- Means of transport used outside the workplace and workplaces which are in or on a means of transport.

- Agricultural or forestry land situated away from the undertaking's main buildings.

- Offshore installations (workplaces to which the *Offshore Installations and Pipelines Works (Management and Administration) Regulations 1995* apply).

[*Fire Precautions (Workplace) Regulations 1997, Reg 3(5)* as amended by *Fire Precautions (Workplace) (Amendment) Regulations 1999, Reg 5(c)*].

All other workplaces, including those subject to certification under the *Fire Precautions Act 1971* are covered by the 1999 Workplace Amendment Regulations.

## Fire risk assessment

**F5026**   The fire risk assessment may involve six stages:

*Stage 1* – identifying the fire hazards;

*Stage 2* – identifying the people at risk;

*Stage 3* – removing or reducing the hazards;

*Stage 4* – assigning a risk category;

*Stage 5* – deciding if existing arrangements are satisfactory or need improvement;

*Stage 6* – recording the findings. This is a statutory requirement if more than five people are employed.

Further, detailed guidance is available in '*The Fire Protection Association Library of Fire Safety, Volume 5 – Fire Risk Management in the Workplace*' published by the Fire Protection Association and in '*Fire Safety. An employer's guide*' published by the Stationary Office and HSE books.

## Fire-fighting and fire detection

**F5027**   Where necessary (whether due to the features of a workplace, the activity carried on there, any hazard present there or any other relevant circumstances i.e. as a result of a fire risk assessment) in order to safeguard the safety of employees in case of fire:

(*a*)   a workplace must, to the extent that is appropriate, be equipped with appropriate fire-fighting equipment and with fire detectors and alarms; and (*b*)   any non-automatic fire-fighting equipment so provided must be easily accessible, simple to use and indicated by signs,

and for the purposes of sub-paragraph (*a*) what is appropriate is to be determined by the dimensions and use of the building housing the workplace, the equipment it contains, the physical and chemical properties of the substances likely to be present and the maximum number of people that may be present at any one time i.e. as a result of a fire risk assessment (*Reg 4(1)*).

Where necessary in order to safeguard the safety of his employees in case of fire, an employer must:

(*a*)   take measures for fire-fighting in the workplace, adapted to the nature of the activities carried on there and the size of his undertaking and of the workplace concerned and taking into account persons other than his employees who may be present;

(*b*)   nominate employees to implement those measures and ensure that the number of such employees, their training and the equipment available to them are adequate, taking into account the size of, and the specific hazards involved in, the workplace concerned; and

(*c*)   arrange any necessary contacts with external emergency services, particularly as regards rescue work and fire-fighting (*Reg 4(2)*).

### Emergency routes and exits

F5028    Routes to emergency exits from a workplace and the exits themselves must be kept clear at all times, where this is necessary for safeguarding the safety of employees in case of fire (*Reg 5(1)*).

The following requirements must be complied with in respect of a workplace where necessary (whether due to the features of the workplace, the activity carried on there, any hazard present there or any other relevant circumstances) in order to safeguard the safety of employees in case of fire:

(*a*)   emergency routes and exits must lead as directly as possible to a place of safety;

(*b*)   in the event of danger, it must be possible for employees to evacuate the workplace quickly and as safely as possible;

(*c*)   the number, distribution and dimensions of emergency routes and exits must be adequate having regard to the use, equipment and dimensions of the workplace and the maximum number of persons that may be present there at any one time;

(*d*)   emergency doors must open in the direction of escape;

(*e*)   sliding or revolving doors must not be used for exits specifically intended as emergency exits;

(*f*)   emergency doors must not be so locked or fastened that they cannot be easily and immediately opened by any person who may require to use them in an emergency;

(*g*)   emergency routes and exits must be indicated by signs; and

(*h*)   emergency routes and exits requiring illumination must be provided with emergency lighting of adequate intensity in the case of failure of their normal lighting (*Reg 5(2)*).

## Maintenance

F5029   The workplace and any equipment and devices provided in respect of the workplace under *Regs 4 and 5* must be subject to a suitable system of maintenance and be maintained in an efficient state, in efficient working order and in good repair, where this is necessary for safeguarding the safety of employees in case of fire (*Reg 6*).

## Enforcement

F5030   The duty of enforcing the workplace fire precautions legislation falls on fire authorities, who may appoint inspectors for this purpose (*Reg 10*).

A fire authority can issue an enforcement notice in respect of a serious breach. The enforcement notice must notify the person who is served with it that the fire authority is of the opinion that he is in breach of the workplace fire precautions legislation and that such breach is putting one or more employees at serious risk. The notice must also:

—   specify the steps required to remedy the breach;

—   require those steps to be taken within a given time; and

—   provide details of the appeals procedure relating to enforcement notices.

[*Reg 13*].

## Offences and penalties

F5031   A person is guilty of an offence if:

(*a*)   being under a requirement to do so, he fails to comply with any provision of the workplace fire precautions legislation;

(*b*)   that failure places one or more employees at serious risk (i.e. subject to a risk of death or serious injury which is likely to materialise) in case of fire; and

(*c*)   that failure is intentional or is due to his being reckless as to whether he complies or not.

[*Reg 11(1)*].

Any person guilty of an offence under *Reg 11(1)* is liable:

(*a*)   on summary conviction, to a fine; or

(*b*)   on conviction on indictment, to a fine, or to imprisonment for a term not exceeding two years, or both.

[*Reg 11(2)*].

A person is not guilty of an offence under *Reg 11(1)* in respect of any failure to comply with the workplace fire precautions legislation which is subject to an enforcement notice (*Reg 11(3)*).

## Application to the Crown

F5032   These regulations do not extend to premises used solely by the armed forces, but otherwise apply to premises which are Crown occupied and Crown owned. *Section 10* of the *Fire Precautions Act 1971* only binds the Crown in so far as it applies to premises and workplaces owned by the Crown but not occupied by the Crown (*Reg 18*).

# Ultra-hazardous premises – (special premises) – the Fire Certificates (Special Premises) Regulations 1976 (SI 1976 No 2003)

F5033   In the case of premises containing hazardous materials or processes (i.e. special premises), a fire certificate must be obtained from HSE. This applies even if only a small number of persons is employed there. Exemption from this requirement may be granted where the regulations are inappropriate or not reasonably practicable of implementation.

When a certificate has been issued by the HSE the occupier of those premises must post a notice in those premises, stating:

(*a*)   that the certificate has been issued; and

(*b*)   the places where it (or a copy) can be inspected easily by any person who might be affected by its provisions; and

(*c*)   the date of the posting of the notice.

[*Fire Certificates (Special Premises) Regulations 1976, Reg 5(5)(6)*].

These conditions do not override those applicable to a licence for the storage of petroleum spirit under the *Petroleum Spirit (Consolidation) Act 1928*.

### 'Special premises' for which a fire certificate is required from the HSE

F5034   The 'special premises' for which a fire certificate is required from the HSE are set out for reference in Table 1 below.

---

### Table 1

### 'Special premises' for which a fire certificate is required by HSE

| 1 | Any premises at which are carried on any manufacturing processes in which the total quantity of any highly flammable liquid under pressure greater than atmospheric pressure and above its boiling point at atmospheric pressure may exceed 50 tonnes. |
|---|---|
| 2 | Any premises at which is carried on the manufacturing of expanded cellular plastics and at which the quantities manufactured are normally of, or in excess of, 50 tonnes per week. |
| 3 | Any premises at which there is stored, or there are facilities provided for the storage of, liquefied petroleum gas in quantities of, or in excess of, 100 tonnes except where the liquefied petroleum gas is kept for use at the premises either as a fuel, or for the production of an atmosphere for the heat-treatment of metals. |
| 4 | Any premises at which there is stored, or there are facilities provided for the storage of, liquefied natural gas in quantities of, or in excess of, 100 tonnes except where the liquefied natural gas is kept solely for use at the premises as a fuel. |

5   Any premises at which there is stored, or there are facilities provided for the storage of, any liquefied flammable gas consisting predominantly of methyl acetylene in quantities of, or in excess of, 100 tonnes except where the liquefied flammable gas is kept solely for use at the premises as a fuel.

6   Any premises at which oxygen is manufactured and at which there are stored, or there are facilities provided for the storage of, quantities of liquid oxygen of, or in excess of, 135 tonnes.

7   Any premises at which there are stored, or there are facilities provided for the storage of, quantities of chlorine of, or in excess of, 50 tonnes except when the chlorine is kept solely for the purpose of water purification.

8   Any premises at which artificial fertilizers are manufactured and at which there are stored, or there are facilities provided for the storage of, quantities of ammonia of, or in excess of, 250 tonnes.

9   Any premises at which there are in process, manufacture, use or storage at any one time, or there are facilities provided for such processing, manufacture, use or storage of, quantities of any of the materials listed below in, or in excess of, the quantities specified —

| | |
|---|---|
| Phosgene | 5 tonnes |
| Ethylene oxide | 20 tonnes |
| Carbon disulphide | 50 tonnes |
| Acrylonitrile | 50 tonnes |
| Hydrogen cyanide | 50 tonnes |
| Ethylene | 100 tonnes |
| Propylene | 100 tonnes |
| Any highly flammable liquid not otherwise specified | 4,000 tonnes |

10   Explosives, factories or magazines which are required to be licensed under the Explosives Act 1875.

11   Any building on the surface at any mine within the meaning of the Mines and Quarries Act 1954.

12   Any premises in which there is comprised —

(a)   any undertaking on a site for which a licence is required in accordance with section 1 of the Nuclear Installations Act 1965 or for which a permit is required in accordance with section 2 of that Act; or

(b)   any undertaking which would, except for the fact that it is carried on by the United Kingdom Atomic Energy Authority, or by, or on behalf of, the Crown, be required to have a licence or permit in accordance with the provisions mentioned in sub-paragraph (a) above.

13   Any premises containing any machine or apparatus in which charged particles can be accelerated by the equivalent of a voltage of not less than 50 megavolts except where the premises are used as a hospital.

14   Premises to which Regulation 26 of the Ionising Radiations Regulations 1985 (SI 1985 No 1333) applies.

15   Any building, or part of a building, which either —

(a)   is constructed for temporary occupation for the purposes of building operations or works of engineering construction; or

(b)   is in existence at the first commencement there of any further such operations or works

and which is used for any process of work ancillary to any such operations or works (but see F5035 below).

[*Fire Certificates (Special Premises) Regulations 1976, Sch 1 Part I*].

## Temporary buildings used for building operations or construction work – exempted

**F5035**   By virtue of the *Special Premises Regulations 1976, Sch 1 para 15* a fire certificate is required in the case of buildings constructed for temporary occupation for the purposes of building operations or works of engineering construction (see CONSTRUCTION AND BUILDING OPERATIONS), and buildings already in existence for such purposes when such operations or works begin. An exemption is available, however, if:

(*a*)   fewer than 20 persons are employed at any one time, or fewer than 10 elsewhere than on the ground floor; and

(*b*)   the nine conditions set out in *Sch 1 Pt II* are satisfied.

[*Special Premises Regulations, Reg 3(1), Sch 1 para 15*].

There must, however, be provided suitable means of escape in case of fire, adequate fire-fighting equipment, exit doorways that can be easily and immediately opened from inside, unobstructed passageways as well as distinctive and conspicuous marking of fire exits.

## Other dangerous processes

**F5036**   Certain particularly dangerous processes are controlled, as far as fire prevention measures are concerned, by specific regulations. These are:

(*a*)   the *Celluloid (Manufacture, etc.) Regulations 1921 (SR & O 1921 No 1825)* – applying to the manufacture, manipulation and storage of celluloid and the disposal of celluloid waste;

(*b*)   the *Manufacture of Cinematograph Film Regulations 1928 (SR & O 1928 No 82)* – applicable to the manufacture, repair, manipulation or use of cinematograph film;

(*c*)   the *Cinematograph Film Stripping Regulations 1939 (SR & O 1939 No 571)* – applicable to the stripping, drying or storing of cinematograph film;

(*d*)   the *Highly Flammable Liquids and Liquefied Petroleum Gases Regulations 1972 (SI 1972 No 917)* – applicable to premises containing highly flammable liquids and liquefied petroleum gases;

(*e*)   the *Magnesium (Grinding of Castings and Other Articles) Special Regulations 1946 (SR & O 1946 No 2017)* – prohibition on smoking, open lights and fires;

(*f*)   the *Factories (Testing of Aircraft Engines & Accessories) Special Regulations 1952 (SI 1952 No 1689)* – applicable to the leakage or escape of petroleum spirit;

(*g*)   the *Electricity at Work Regulations 1989 (SI 1989 No 635), Reg 6(d)* – electrical equipment which may reasonably foreseeably be exposed to any flammable or explosive substance, must be constructed or protected so as to prevent danger from exposure;

(*h*)   the *Dangerous Substances in Harbour Areas Regulations 1987 (SI 1987 No 37)* – applicable to risks of fire and explosion in harbour areas. A fire certificate is not required for these premises [*Special Premises Regulations, Reg 3A, as amended*];

(*j*)   the *Gas Safety (Installation and Use) Regulations 1994 (SI 1994 No 1886)* (as amended by *SI 1996 No 550*) – to avoid explosion/fire as a result of gas fitting of appliances/pipes/tanks;

(*k*)   the *Offshore Installations (Prevention of Fire and Explosion, and Emergency Response) Regulations 1995 (SI 1995 No 743)* – to prevent and minimise the effects of fire and explosion on offshore installation;

(*l*)   the *Construction (Health, Safety and Welfare) Regulations 1996 (SI 1996 No 1592), Reg 21*; and

(*m*)   the *Work in Compressed Air Regulations 1996 (SI 1996 No 1656), Reg 14.*

### Application for fire certificate for 'special premises'

F5037   In order to obtain a fire certificate for 'special premises' (see F5034 above for definition), the occupier or owner (see F5009 above) must apply to the relevant HSE inspectorate, e.g. the factory inspectorate in respect of factory premises. No form is prescribed but certain particulars must be provided, including:

(*a*)   the address and description of the premises;

(*b*)   the nature of the processes carried on or to be carried on there;

(*c*)   nature and approximate quantities of any explosive or highly flammable substance kept or to be kept on the premises;

(*d*)   the maximum number of persons likely to be present on the premises;

(*e*)   the name and address of the occupier.

Plans may be required to be deposited and premises will be inspected, and the occupier may well have to make improvements to the fire precautions before a certificate is issued (*Special Premises Regulations, Reg 4*).

# Appeals relating to the issue of a fire certificate

F5038   An appeal may be made to the magistrates' court by an applicant for a fire certificate in relation to:

(*a*)   a requirement specified by a fire authority or the HSE; or

(*b*)   the fire authority or the HSE refusing to issue a certificate; or

(*c*)   the contents of a certificate.

An appeal must be lodged within 21 days of the date of notice from the fire authority (*Special Premises Regulations, Reg 12*).

# Duty to keep fire certificate on the premises

F5039    Every fire certificate must be kept on the premises to which it relates (and preferably displayed), as long as it is in force (*Fire Precautions Act 1971, s 6(8)*). Failure to comply with this subsection is an offence (*Fire Precautions Act 1971, s 7(6)*).

# Notification of alteration to premises

F5040    Any proposed structural alterations or material internal alteration to premises for which a fire certificate has been issued, must first be notified to the local fire authority or inspectorate (as appropriate). Similarly, any proposed material alteration to equipment in the premises must be so notified. Not to do so is to commit an offence (see F5012 above). The premises may be inspected by staff from the relevant enforcement agency at any reasonable time while the certificate is in force (*Fire Precautions Act 1971, s 8(1)(2)*).

## Penalties

F5041    A person found guilty of an offence under the *Fire Precautions Act 1971, s 7(1)* is liable to:

(*a*)    a fine not exceeding £5,000 (on summary conviction); or

(*b*)    an unlimited fine or imprisonment for not more than two years, *or both* (on indictment).

[*Fire Precautions Act 1971, s 7(1) as amended by the Criminal Justice Act 1991, s 17(1)*].

# Licensed premises and fire safety

F5042    Some premises, other than work premises, which must have a current licence in order to operate, will have a licence refused or not renewed by the local magistrates if the local fire authority is not satisfied as to the fire precautions necessary in the premises. (As far as these premises are places of work, the *Fire Precautions (Workplace) Regulations 1997* will apply.) The premises are as follows:

*Cinemas*

F5043    Safety in cinemas is controlled by the *Cinematograph (Safety) Regulations 1955 (SI 1955 No 1129)* (as subsequently amended). Cinemas must be provided with:

(*a*)    adequate, clearly marked exits, so placed as to afford safe means of exit;

(*b*)    doors which are easily and fully openable outwards;

(*c*)    passages and stairways kept free from obstruction

[*Reg 2*];

(*d*)    suitable and properly maintained fire appliances;

(*e*)    proper instruction of licensee and staff on fire precautions;

(*f*)    treatment of curtains so that they will not readily catch fire;

(*g*)    use of non-flammable substances for cleaning film or projectors

[*Reg 5*];

(*h*)    prohibition on smoking in certain parts of the premises (*Reg 6*);

(*j*)    appropriate siting of heating appliances (*Reg 24*).

### Theatres

F5044    Under *s 12(1)* of the *Theatres Act 1968* premises used for the public performance of a play must be licensed. The conditions for obtaining or having renewed a licence include compliance with rules relating to safety of persons in the theatre, and particularly, staff fire drills, provision of fire-fighting equipment, maintenance of a safety curtain and communication with the fire service; gangways and seating correctly arranged and free from obstruction, doors and exits, marking and method of opening, lighting arrangements; also scenery and draperies must be non-flammable and there are controls over smoking and overcrowding.

### Gaming houses (casinos, bingo halls etc.)

F5045    Issue or retention of a licence to operate depends *inter alia* on compliance with fire requirements (*Gaming Act 1968*).

### Premises for music, dancing etc.

F5046    Issue or retention of a licence to operate premises for public music or entertainment depends on compliance with the fire requirements (*Local Government (Miscellaneous Provisions) Act 1982, Sch 1*).

Similarly, in the case of premises used for private music/dancing, e.g. dancing schools, there must be compliance with the fire requirements (*Private Places of Entertainment (Licensing) Act 1967*).

### Schools

F5047    In the case of local authority controlled schools, including special schools, the 'health and safety of their occupants, and in particular, their safe escape in the event of fire, must be reasonably assured', with particular reference to the design, construction, limitation of surface flame spread and fire resistance of structure and materials therein (*Standards for School Premises Regulations 1972 (SI 1972 No 2051)*).

As far as a school is a place of work, the *Fire Precautions (Workplace) Regulations 1997* also apply.

### Children's and community homes

F5048    Both these local authority controlled establishments must carry out fire drills and practices and, in addition, consult with the fire authorities (*Children's Homes Regulations 1991 (SI 1991 No 1506)*; *Community Homes Regulations 1972 (SI 1972 No 319)*).

As far as a children's or community home is a place of work, the *Fire Precautions (Workplace) Regulations 1997* also apply.

## Residential and nursing homes

F5049    Similar requirements apply in the case of:

(*a*)   residential homes (*National Assistance (Conduct of Homes) Regulations 1962 (SI 1962 No 2000)*); and

(*b*)   nursing homes (*Nursing Homes and Mental Nursing Homes Regulations 1981 (SI 1981 No 932) as amended*).

In particular, satisfactory arrangements must be made for the evacuation of patients and staff in the event of fire.

As far as a residential or nursing home is a place of work, the *Fire Precautions (Workplace) Regulations 1997* also apply.

## Crown premises

F5050   As with other health and safety duties and regulations, generally speaking, statutory fire duties and fire regulations apply to the Crown (*Fire Precautions Act 1971, s 40*; *Fire Precautions (Workplace) Regulations 1997, Reg 18*) but, owing to Crown immunity in law – itself referable to the fiction that the king can do no wrong – proceedings cannot be enforced against the Crown (see further E15035 ENFORCE-MENT). This has the effect that Crown premises, that is, government buildings such as the Treasury and the Foreign Office as well as royal palaces, are required to be fire-certificated but, if they fail to apply for certification, they cannot, like other occupiers, be prosecuted. Secondly, failure to acquire fire-certificate status could prejudice the safety of fire-fighters called upon to combat fires in Crown premises (see further F5056 below). Moreover, fire certificates are not required in (*a*) prisons, (*b*) special hospitals for the mentally incapacitated and (*c*) premises occupied exclusively by the armed forces (*Fire Precautions Act 1971, s 40(2)*).

## Civil liability at common law and under the Fires Prevention (Metropolis) Act 1774 for fire damage

F5051   Civil liability, in respect of fire damage, can arise in one of several ways: an occupier of premises from which fire escapes and does damage can be liable to adjoining occupiers and/or fire-fighters, or even members of the public injured or killed whilst fighting the fire on the premises; conversely, the occupier of premises may be injured as a consequence of damage negligently caused to his property by the fire authority whilst fighting a fire on his premises. Again, a fire fighter may be injured whilst fighting a fire owing to the negligence of his superior officers in failing to ascertain the dangerous state of the premises where the fire is to be fought, or a member of the public, assisting the fire authority to fight a fire on his premises, because he has not been given suitable equipment or proper fire-fighting instruc-tions or protective clothing, may be injured. In addition, a fire fighter or third party, whether pedestrian or motorist, may be injured as a result of a fire appliance being driven dangerously on the way to a fire or as a result of crossing adverse traffic lights. All these situations are potential 'candidates' for the imposition of civil liability. Moreover, liability for damage done by fire spread is not necessarily confined to negligence; such liability can be strict if fire spread is within the rule in *Rylands v Fletcher* (see F5054 below). In order to ensure therefore that occupiers and others involved may minimise their liability, insurance cover, though not compul-sory, is highly desirable. The basic principles relating to fire cover are considered below (see F5060 below).

### Liability of occupier

F5052   An occupier of premises where fire breaks out can be liable to (*a*) lawful visitors to the premises injured by the fire or falling debris (and is also liable to unlawful visitors, i.e. trespassers, as the principle of 'common humanity', enunciated in *Herrington v British Railways Board* applies as does the *Occupiers' Liability Act 1984*, see OCCUPIERS' LIABILITY); (*b*) firemen injured during fire-fighting operations; and (*c*) adjoining occupiers.

## Fire-fighters

F5053    The main principles established by case law are as follows:

(*a*)    The occupier owes a duty to a fire-fighter not to expose him to unexpected hazards (i.e. hazards over and above that of fire – *Hartley v British Railways Board, The Times, 2 February 1981* where a fireman was injured whilst searching the roof space of the respondent's premises which had caught fire. He had been told that the station building was occupied when in fact it was not. The respondents were held liable for the confusion as to whether the station was occupied or not, the confusion having led to the hazardous situation causing injury).

(*b*)    The occupier is liable to a fire-fighter for any hazard for which he is responsible, if the hazard is over and above the normal fire-fighting hazard (*Hartley v Mayoh [1953] 2 AER 525* where a fireman was killed whilst fighting a fire at a pickle manufacturing factory. The attempt to cut off electricity supply failed, owing to the novel construction of the switches, with the result that unknown to him power continued to flow. It was held that the occupier was liable because he should have known how the switches worked; the fact that he did not constituted an additional hazard for the fireman). In *Salmon v Seafarer Restaurants [1983] 1 WLR 1264*, the proprietor of a fish and chip shop failed to extinguish a light under a chip fryer and was held liable for a fireman's injury.

(*c*)    Decisions and conduct resulting from them which, in other circumstances, could well be regarded as negligent, may well not be negligent in an emergency (*Bull v London County Council, The Times, 29 January 1953* where an experienced fireman fell from the extension ladder at the height of a fire and was seriously injured. It was held that climbing the extension ladder in a fire emergency was not negligence on the part of the fireman).

(*d*)    More recently, occupiers, in the form of householders, were held liable to a fireman who was injured, on normal grounds of foreseeability and causation. The respondent, when burning off paint on his house, negligently set fire to roof timbers. The appellant, a fireman, sprayed water on the fire and the resulting steam caused him injuries. It was held that the appellant was so closely and directly affected by the respondent's act that the respondent ought reasonably to have had him in contemplation when directing his mind to the acts or omissions in question, namely, using the blowlamp without taking care to avoid setting the rafters alight (*Ogwo v Taylor [1987] 3 AER 961*). This includes the reasonably foreseeable *consequences* of an occupier's negligence, e.g. post-traumatic stress (*Hale v London Underground Ltd, The Times, 5 November 1992* concerning £147,000 damages awarded to a fireman injured going to the rescue of another fireman at the King's Cross fire in 1987).

## Adjoining occupier

F5054    Originally liability for fire spread causing damage to adjoining property was strict (and in certain limited circumstances, still is (see below *Rylands v Fletcher*)). Current law, however, is traceable back to the *Fires Prevention (Metropolis) Act 1774, s 86* which provides that unless an occupier has been negligent he will not be liable for damage to adjoining property caused by fire spread. This extends to failure on the part of an occupier to take effective measures to prevent fire spread once a fire has started (*Goldman v Hargrave [1967] 1 AC 645*).

If, however, fire spreads and does damage in circumstances within the rule in *Rylands v Fletcher [1861-73] AER Rep 1*, liability is strict. The point here is that fire in itself is not regarded as ultra-hazardous and hence not governed by strict liability criteria; if however fire is caused by some activity/operation on land, or container capable of self-propulsion or explosion (e.g. petrol in storage), and it escapes and causes injury and/or damage to adjoining property, there will be liability irrespective of negligence. The main purpose of the rule in *Rylands v Fletcher* is to ensure that those putting land to ultra-hazardous use, e.g. electrical supply, water storage in bulk, petrol storage, keep the danger in 'at their peril'. Thus, 'Where a person for his own purposes brings and keeps on land in his occupation anything likely to do mischief if it escapes, (he) must keep it in at his peril, and if he fails to do so, he is liable for all damage naturally accruing from the escape' (Blackburn J). This applies to fire (*Emanuel v Greater London Council (1970) 114 SJ 653* where a contractor, who was an employee of the Ministry of Public Building and Works, removed prefabricated bungalows from the council's land. He then lit a fire and the sparks spread to the plaintiff's land, where buildings and products belonging to the plaintiff were damaged. It was held that, although the council had not been negligent, they were still liable). In fairness, however, it should be emphasised that the rule in *Rylands v Fletcher* has been interpreted restrictively. Thus, 'I should hesitate to hold that in these days and in an industrial community it was a non-natural use of land to build a factory on it and conduct there the manufacture of explosives' (per Lord Macmillan in *Read v J Lyons & Co Ltd [1947] AC 156*). Indeed, given the dominance of planning decisions in land development over the past forty years, presumptively, if planning permission has been obtained by an operator for a particular use(s) of land (as will be normal), it is impossible to say that use of said land is 'non-natural'; hence in most cases potentially dangerous activities are outside the scope of the rule of strict liability.

## Liability of fire authority

### General

F5055     Civil liability of fire brigades and fire authorities for injury or damage to members of the public and their property must be regarded as an unsettled area of law. Such uncertainty arises because

(*a*)     neither the *Fire Services Act 1947* nor the *Fire Precautions Act 1971* make express provision for civil liability in connection with their operational activities;

(*b*)     the leading case on civil liability of statutory authorities/undertakers generally (*East Suffolk Rivers Catchment Board v Kent [1941] AC 74*) was concerned with damage caused in exercise of a statutory *discretion* (or power), whereas fire brigades/fire authorities are under a statutory *duty* to attend fires. Thus, the *Fire Services Act 1947, s 1* imposes a general duty on every fire authority to make provision for firefighting purposes. In particular, the services of a fire brigade and equipment necessary to meet all normal requirements should be secured, as well as arrangements for dealing with calls for fire brigade assistance in cases of fire; and

(*c*)     *Atkinson v Newcastle & Gateshead Waterworks Co (1877) LR 2 Ex D 441* had established that statutory utility authorities (e.g. water, fire) were not indiscriminate providers of gratuitous insurance to beleaguered property owners/ occupiers, with the consequence that there was no liability upon such authorities at common law for negligence. Property owners/occupiers had to provide their own insurance against risks such as fire/water damage. In *Atkinson's* case the plaintiff's timber yard was gutted by fire, there being insufficient water in the mains to extinguish it. The defendants were required by statute to maintain a certain pressure of water in their pipes, with a daily penalty for failure to do so. The plaintiff sued the defendants for loss caused by fire on the ground that they were in breach of a statutory duty to maintain a specified water pressure in the pipes. It was held that the statute did not disclose a cause of action, since it was not the intention of Parliament to make water authorities indiscriminate providers of gratuitous insurance. A rash of recent cases illustrates the uncertainty.

In *Duff v Highland and Islands Fire Board 1995 SLT 1362* Lord Macfadyen stated that, should injury befall a fire-fighter or member of the public whilst attending or going to a fire, or damage occur to attended property or adjoining ones, as a general principle, in such operational matters, the fire brigade/fire authority did not enjoy immunity from civil action analogous with that enjoyed by the police in the investigation of crime. This view was recently confirmed in *Capital and Counties plc v Hampshire CC, The Times, 26 April 1996,* where a fire brigade was held liable in negligence when a fireman ordered a sprinkler system to be turned off in a burning building; the brigade was not immune from liability to the owner of the building on the ground of public policy. Similarly, in *Crown River Cruises Ltd v Kimbolton Fireworks Ltd and the London Fire and Civil Defence Authority (Queen's Bench), 27 February 1996,* during the course of a fireworks display a small fire started on a dumb barge, caused by hot and burning debris falling during the display, and was attended by the London Fire and Civil Defence Authority. Subsequently, a passenger vessel moored alongside the barge as usual. Later that night fire broke out on that vessel with substantial damage being caused to the barge as well. The fire on board the passenger vessel was the result of the fire authority's negligent failure to extinguish the original fire properly. It was held that both the firework display organiser and the London Fire Authority were liable 25% and 75% to the plaintiff.

A different view prevailed, however, in *Church of Jesus Christ of Latter-Day Saints (Great Britain) v Yorkshire Fire and Civil Defence Authority, The Times, 9 May 1996.* Here an entire chapel as well as a classroom were gutted by fire because hydrants did not work and water had to be obtained from a dam half a mile away. An action for negligence brought against the fire brigade because (*a*) hydrants had not been regularly inspected, and (*b*) defects had not been observed and repaired, failed because the *Fire Services Act 1947* did not confer a private right of action, and this was the outcome in the slightly later case of *John Munroe (Acrylics) Ltd v London Fire and Civil Defence Authority, The Times, 22 May 1996.* Here four fire engines arrived in response to emergency calls, by which time most of the burning debris and fires on wasteland had (apparently) been put out. Firemen, however, did not inspect one unit, which abutted the wasteland, where there was combustible material visible. It was held that neither the fire brigade directly nor the fire authority vicariously was liable for damage ensuing. In particular, there was not sufficient proximity between a fire brigade and an owner/occupier of premises which might be on fire so as to impose upon the fire brigade directly, and upon the fire authority vicariously, a duty at common law to respond to a call for assistance. On the contrary, imposition of a duty at common law might well lead to defensive fire-fighting. If the efficiency of the emergency services were to be tested, this should be done, not by way of private litigation, but by national and/or local inquiries instituted by local authorities.

*Injury to fire-fighters*

**F5056**   Just as any other employer, a fire authority can be vicariously liable when a fire-fighter is injured whilst being driven negligently to a fire; or when he suffers injuries fighting a fire, though in practice such cases are likely to be rare. Moreover, as an employer a fire authority has duties to its employees under *HSWA*, and particularly under *s 2*, to provide a safe system of work and adequate information/ training in connection with fire-fighting. Thus, if a fire authority sent an insufficient number of men to fight a large fire this could be regarded as a defective system of work for the purposes of *HSWA, s 2(2)(a)*; similarly, where a fireman was injured or killed whilst fire-fighting and it was shown that he had received inadequate training, there might well be breach of *HSWA, s 2(2)(c)*.

Of course, a fire-fighter can only be instructed and trained in fire-fighting and its hazards within the 'state of the art'. If the hazards of a particular type of fire are not known or not documented, the fire authority would not be liable for the fire-fighter's injury (*Biggerstaff v Glasgow Corporation (1962) (unreported)* where a huge fire broke out in a bonded warehouse containing millions of gallons of whisky. Whilst the fire was being fought an explosion ripped out the walls, killing some firemen and injuring the plaintiff, the driver of a turntable ladder. He sued his employer, the fire authority, on two grounds: (*a*) that they had not removed non-essential personnel from the immediate area of the explosion, and (*b*) that training given to fire officers to fight hazards associated with whisky vapour fires was inadequate. The action failed, principally because this type of accident was (then) unique and the true hazards of whisky vapour were not appreciated).

*Injury to members of the public fighting a fire*

**F5057**   A fire authority could be liable to other persons legitimately and foreseeably (i.e. invited and/or allowed to participate by fire-fighters at the incident) fighting a fire who are injured or killed, e.g. ambulance staff, staff on the premises where a fire breaks out or spreads to, the in-house fire brigade (if any), or the owner or occupier of premises which have caught fire and who assists in fire-fighting. In such cases the fire authority can be liable if it fails to take similar precautions as it would take in respect of its own members (*Burrough v Berkshire & Reading Joint Fire Authority (1972) (unreported)* where the plaintiff suffered head injuries whilst helping to fight a fire at his barn. He had not been provided with a protective helmet. The fire authority was held to be liable).

*Injury to visitors of the occupier's premises*

**F5058**   Where a fire causes injury or death to visitors of an occupier, e.g. a hotelier, it is doubtful whether the fire authority can be sued for negligence for breach of the *Fire Precautions Act 1971, s 5(3)* (granting of a fire certificate to premises for particular use, following inspection) (*Hallett v Nicholson 1979 SC 1* where hoteliers were sued by children whose parents had died in a fire at the hotel. The hoteliers had applied for a certificate under *FPA 1971, s 1* and they argued that the fire authority was under a duty under *s 5(3)* to inspect the hotel; and, in addition, that the fire authority had failed to advise the hotelier not to reopen, under *s 10(2)*. It was held that the fire authority was not liable because (*a*) acts/omissions on the part of a statutory authority in the proper exercise of its statutory duties were not actionable; (*b*) the failure of the fire authority to advise the hoteliers not to reopen under *s 10(2)* was not obligatory but discretionary; (*c*) the *Fire Precautions Act 1971* did not empower, even less impose, a duty on a fire authority to recommend interim measures; and (*d*) in the absence of a request on the part of the hoteliers for advice on interim measures, the fire authority was under no duty to give such advice).

Moreover, a fire authority was not liable when a fireman deliberately drove very slowly during an industrial dispute and the plaintiff's premises were destroyed by a fire. Their manner of driving was not merely a wrongful and unauthorised mode of doing an act authorised by their employers, but was so unconnected with what they were authorised to do that it was not a mode of performing an authorised act at all (*General Engineering Services Ltd v Kingston and Saint Andrew Corp [1988] 3 AER 867*).

*Injury to third party road user, whilst speeding to scene of fire*

F5059    An innocent third party road user is entitled to assume that a fire engine will stop at adverse traffic signals, and so, if he suffered injury or death as a result of its not stopping, the fire authority would be liable (*Ward v London County Council [1938] 2 AER 341*). The contrary is the position where, however, a fire engine stops and proceeds with caution at adverse traffic signals (*Buckoke v Greater London Council [1971] Ch 655* where the chief London Fire Brigade officer issued an order that adverse traffic lights could and should be passed through with caution; this order laid the onus of avoiding accidents on the driver of the fire engine. Some firemen went to court to test the order's legality. It was held by the Court of Appeal that the order was lawful).

# Fire insurance

F5060    There is no statutory definition of fire, as there is of certain other insurable risks, e.g. theft, burglary. What is insured is loss or damage caused by fire. Hence, fire must be the proximate cause of loss/damage. This is not always easy to determine where there are several vying causes. For example, a shopkeeper insured his plateglass against loss/damage arising from any cause except fire. Fire broke out in a neighbour's property, in consequence of which a mob gathered. The mob rioted and broke the plateglass. It was held that the riot not the fire was the cause of the loss and so the insured was entitled to recover (*Marsden v City and County Insurance (1865) LR 1 CP 232*).

Where the fire insured against is imminent, loss caused to property by action taken to avert the risk, is covered. A cargo of cork insured against loss by fire and stored on a pier, was thrown into the sea in order to prevent an existing fire spreading. It was held that the damage by water loss was covered, since the dominant (or proximate) cause of the cork loss was the fire, itself an insured peril (*Symington v Union Insurance of Canton (1928) 97 LJKB 646*).

In order for there to be a fire, actual ignition is necessary. In *Austin v Drewe (1816) 6 Taunt 436*, stock in a sugar refinery was insured against loss by fire. A flue went up through all the floors of the refinery from a stove situated on the ground floor. There was a register, which was closed at night to retain heat, but opened when a fresh fire was lit in the morning. One morning an employee of the insured forgot to open the register. Intense heat in the flue damaged sugar on the top floor. There were smoke and sparks but the sugar did not ignite. It was held that there was no loss by fire.

In order to qualify for compensation for loss/damage caused by fire:

(*a*)    there must be actual ignition;

(*b*)    the outbreak of fire (from the insured's point of view) was accidental; and (*c*)   something must be on fire which should not be on fire. Thus, a fire lit for a particular purpose would not qualify, e.g. fire to burn rubbish. But if such fire escaped, doing damage, the insurer would be liable (*Upjohn v Hitchens [1918] 2 KB 18*).

# Fire prevention and control

## Elements of fire

F5061   There are three prerequisites for fire:

(*a*)   oxygen;

(*b*)   fuel (or combustible substance);

(*c*)   source of energy;

the so-called 'fire triangle'.

Fire is a mixture in gaseous form of a combustible substance and oxygen, given sufficient energy to start a fire. Once a fire is under way, energy output guarantees a continuous source of sustainable energy, with excess taking the form of sensible heat. Fire takes place in a gaseous state, though it may be convenient to label fires as solids (e.g. wood), liquid (e.g. petrol) and gas (e.g. gas flame). In the former two cases, close inspection reveals that the flame burns a little way away from the wood or liquid.

This part of the chapter considers generally the practical aspects of fire prevention and control. It should be borne in mind that *special risks* involving flammable or toxic liquids, metal fires or other hazards should be separately evaluated for loss prevention and as regards control techniques. (For precautions against fire hazards from flammable liquids, see the *Highly Flammable Liquids and Liquefied Petroleum Gases Regulations 1972 (SI 1972 No 917)*, and HSE Guidance documents HS(G) 51 and HS(G) 176).

It is the responsibility of management to consider how safe is safe: that is, to balance the costs of improvement against the financial consequences of fire. Considerable improvement can often be made immediately at little or no cost. Other recommendations which may require a financial appraisal must be related to loss effect values. In certain cases, however, due to high loss effect, special protection may be needed almost regardless of cost.

Modern developments in fire prevention and protection can now provide a solution to most risk management problems within economic acceptability. It must be pointed out, however, that it is a waste of time and money installing protective equipment unless it is designed to be functional and the purpose of such equipment is understood and accepted by all personnel. The reasons for providing such equipment should, therefore, be fully covered in any fire training course. Fire routines should also be amended as necessary to ensure that full advantage is taken of any new measures implemented.

## Common causes of fires

F5062   The following, in no particular order of significance, are the commonest causes of fires in industrial and non-industrial premises:

(*a*)   wilful fire raising and arson;

(*b*)   careless disposal of cigarettes, matches;

(*c*)   combustible material left near to sources of heat;

(*d*)    accumulation of easily ignitable rubbish or paper;

(*e*)    inadvertence on the part of contractors, maintenance workers 'usually involving hot work';

(*f*)    electrical equipment left on inadvertently when not in use;

(*g*)    misuse of portable heaters;

(*h*)    obstructing ventilation of heaters, machinery or office equipment;

(*j*)    inadequate cleaning of work areas;

(*k*)    inadequate supervision of cooking activities.

## Fire classification

F5063    There are five categories of fire which are related to the fuel involved and the method of extinction, as follows.

(*a*)    *Class A.* Fires generally involving solid organic materials, such as coal, wood, paper and natural fibres, in which the combustion takes place with the formation of glowing embers. Extinction is achieved through the application of water in jet or spray form.

(*b*)    *Class B.* Fires involving:

(i)    liquids, which can be separated into those liquids which mix with water e.g. acetone, acetic acid and methanol; and those which do not mix with water e.g. waxes, fats, petrol and solvents; and

(ii)    liquefiable solids e.g. animal fats, solid waxes, certain plastics.

Foam, carbon dioxide and dry powder can be used on all these types of fire. However, some types of foam break down on contact with water-miscible liquids – special alcohol-resistant foam is needed for large volumes of such liquids. Water spray can be used on liquids that mix with water. Water must not be used on fats, petrol, etc. With foam, carbon dioxide and dry powder, extinction is principally achieved by smothering, with a certain degree of cooling in some cases. Water acts primarily by cooling.

(*c*)    *Class C.* Fires involving gases should only be controlled by stopping the gas supply if safe to do so. Burning gas should not be extinguished as a build-up of unburnt gas may explode.

(*d*)    *Class D.* Fires involving certain flammable metals, such as aluminium or magnesium. These fires burn with very high temperatures, and their extinction is achieved by the use of special powders.

(*e*)    *Class F.* Fires involving cooking oils and fats. Extinguishers using special wet chemical extinguishants, foam or dry powder can be assessed for their effectiveness for this type of fire using test fires defined in BS 7937: 2000.

### Electrical fires

F5064    Fires involving electrical apparatus must always be tackled by first isolating the electricity supply and then by the use of carbon dioxide or dry powder. EU Regulations are expected to be in force by late 2000 banning the use of halon as an extinguishant in most applications by the end of 2003.

Table 2 below classifies fires which can be controlled by portable fire appliances (see also BS EN 3 and BS 6643).

## Table 2

| Class of fire | Description | Appropriate extinguisher |
|---|---|---|
| A | Solid materials, usually organic, with glowing embers | Water (foam, dry powder or $CO_2$ will work but may be less effective than water) |
| B | Liquids and liquefiable solids: | Foam, $CO_2$, dry powder |
|  | miscible with water e.g. acetone, methanol | Alcohol-resistant foam, $CO_2$, dry powder, skilled use of water spray |
|  | immiscible with water e.g. petrol, benzene, fats, waxes | Foam, dry powder, $CO_2$ |

## Fire extinction – active fire protection measures

F5065    Extinction of a fire is achieved by one or more of the following:

(*a*)    *starvation* – this is achieved through a reduction in the concentration of the fuel. It can be effected by:

   (i)    removing the fuel from the fire;

   (ii)    isolating the fire from the fuel source; and

   (iii)    reducing the bulk or quantity of fuel present;

(*b*)    *smothering* – this brings about a reduction in the concentration of oxygen available to support combustion. It is achieved by preventing the inward flow of more oxygen to the fire, or by adding an inert gas to the burning mixture;

(*c*)    *cooling* – this is the most common means of fire-fighting, using water. The addition of water to a fire results in vaporisation of some of the water to steam, which means that a substantial proportion of the heat is not being returned to the fuel to maintain combustion. Eventually, insufficient heat is added to the fuel and continuous ignition ceases. Water in spray form is more efficient for this purpose as the spray droplets absorb heat more rapidly than water in the form of a jet.

## Property risk

F5066    Fire safety precautions needed for the protection of life are dealt with by legislation, as detailed in F5001–F5050 ABOVE.

In order to ensure the survival of a business in the event of fire, property protection must be considered and a business risk assessment carried out. The involvement of a company's insurer is essential as insurers have considerable experience in this field. The business risk assessment follows similar stages to the life risk assessment (see F5024 ABOVE) but assesses the importance of each area to the function of the business and how vulnerable they are to fire.

For example, an area where essential records or documents are stored is likely to have a serious effect should a fire occur; essential equipment, plant or stock which, if destroyed or severely damaged by fire, might be difficult to replace or have a serious effect on production would require special consideration, and often high fire protection requirements to minimise such an effect.

These risks should be determined by management; they need to be identified, considered and evaluated. A report should be produced by each departmental head, outlining areas which may require special consideration. Such a report should also include protection of essential drawings, records and other essential documents.

A typical area of high loss effect would be the telephone equipment room. The loss of this equipment could have a serious and immediate effect upon communications generally. Fire separation (to keep a fire out) is therefore considered essential, and automatic fire suppression by self-contained extinguishing units should be strongly recommended.

Essential data, usually on computer magnetic media, should be duplicated and the copy stored in a safe area which preferably is off-site. Paper records can be copied and reduced photographically and similarly stored.

## Passive and active fire protection

F5067 Passive fire protection is where part of the structure of a building is inherently fire resistant. Most buildings are divided into fire-resisting compartments. These serve two functions. One is to limit the spread of fire and can be a property protection measure as well as life safety. The other is to protect escape routes by making the escape route a fire-resisting compartment. All fire escape stairways are fire-resisting compartments. In day-to-day work these compartments are most obvious where doorways pass through the compartment walls. The doors in these openings are nearly always self-closing fire resisting door sets. It is essential that these doors are not obstructed and are allowed to self-close freely at all times. Any glazing in such doors must also be fire resisting and if damaged must be repaired to the appropriate standard. (Guidance on the most common types of fire door is given in BS 8214: 1990. *Code of practice for fire door assemblies with non-metallic leaves.*)

Active fire protection involves systems that are activated when a fire occurs, for example automatic fire detection or automatic sprinkler systems. As such systems are only required in an emergency it is essential that they are routinely tested and maintained.

## Fire procedures and portable equipment

### Fire procedures

F5068 The need for effective and easily understood fire procedures cannot be over-emphasised. It may be necessary to provide a fire procedure manual, so arranged that it can be used for overall fire defence arrangements, and sectioned for use in individual departments or for special risks.

It is essential that three separate procedures are considered:

(*a*)    procedure during normal working hours;

(*b*)    procedure during restricted manning on shifts;

(*c*)    procedure when only security staff are on the premises.

All procedures should take into consideration absence of personnel due to sickness, leave, etc. The fire brigade should be called immediately any fire occurs, irrespective of the size of the fire. Any delay in calling the fire brigade must be added to the delay before the fire brigade's actual arrival, which will be related to the traffic conditions or the local appliances already attending another fire.

A person should be given the responsibility for ensuring that pre-planned action is carried out when a fire occurs. Large fires often result from a delayed call, which may be due not to delayed discovery but to wrong action being taken in the early stages following discovery of a fire. A pre-planned fire routine is essential for fire safety. The fire brigade, when called, should be met on arrival by a designated person available to guide them directly to the area of the fire. It is essential that all fire routines, when finalised, be made known to the fire brigade.

## Fire equipment

F5069    There has been a number of cases where a person using an extinguisher has been seriously injured. Investigations have shown that either the wrong type of extinguisher was supplied or the operator had no training in the correct use of the extinguisher. The latter should not need to be over-emphasised, especially in areas of special risk, oil dipping tanks, furnace areas, highly flammable liquids, gas or cylinder fires etc.

The following recommendations are given in order to allow an evaluation of an existing problem and may need to be related to process risks:

(*a*)    it is essential that persons be trained in the use of extinguishers, especially in areas where special risks require a specific type of extinguisher to be provided;

(*b*)    any person employed to work, who is requested to deal with a fire, should be clearly instructed that at no time should that person jeopardise his own safety or the safety of others;

(*c*)    persons who may be wearing overalls contaminated with oil, grease, paint or solvents should not be instructed to attack a fire. Such contaminated materials may vaporise due to heat from the fire, and ignite.

## Types of fire extinguisher

F5070    The type of extinguisher provided should be suitable for the risk involved, adequately maintained and appropriate records kept of all inspections, tests etc. All fire extinguishers should be fitted on wall brackets. It has been found that if this is not done, extinguishers are removed or knocked over and damaged. Extinguishers should be sited near exits or on the line of exit.

### Water extinguishers

F5071    This type of extinguisher is suitable for ordinary combustible fires, for example wood and paper, but are not suitable for flammable liquid fires. Such extinguishers should also be labelled 'not to be used on fires involving live electricity'. Water spray extinguishers are recommended.

### Foam extinguishers

F5072    These are suitable for small liquid spill fires or small oil tank fires where it is possible for the foam to form a blanket over the surface of the flammable liquids involved. Foam extinguishers may not extinguish a flammable liquid fire on a vertical plane. Alcohols miscible with water, when on fire, will break down ordinary foam and should be considered a special risk. Alcohol resistant foams are available.

### Dry powder extinguishers

**F5073**   This type will deal effectively with flammable liquid fires and is recommended, as it is capable of quick knock-down of a fire. The size of the extinguisher is important and it must be capable of dealing effectively with the possible size of the spill fire which may occur, with some extinguishant in reserve. The recommended minimum size is a 9 kg trigger-controlled extinguisher. (Dry powder extinguishers are also safe on fires involving electrical equipment.)

### Bcf extinguishers

**F5074**   The extinguishing medium in these is a halon. Manufacture of this class of chemicals is no longer permitted due to their adverse effect on the environment. New extinguishers of this type are no longer available although some old ones may still be in service. Recharging of existing extinguishers is no longer practised and replacement by dry powder or carbon dioxide extinguishers is recommended. EU Regulations are expected to be in force in late 2000 prohibiting the use of halon as an extinguishant in most applications (aircraft and military applications will be exempt) by the end of 2003. Any halon extinguishers in normal service should be decommissioned and disposed of safely by 31 December 2003 This type of extinguisher is suitable for fires where electrical or electronic equipment may be involved. This type of extinguisher can also be used on flammable liquid fires; such use may, however, produce large quantities of toxic irritant gases. The hotter the fire, the more toxic the vapours produced. Therefore, a quick knock-down is essential. Bcf extinguishers should not be used on high temperature, metal or deep fat fires, especially in confined areas.

### Carbon dioxide extinguishers

**F5075**   For fires involving electrical equipment, carbon dioxide extinguishers are recommended. Carbon dioxide ($CO_2$) extinguishers are quite heavy and may be at high pressure. A minimum size of 2 kg is recommended. $CO_2$ is not recommended for flammable liquid fires, except for small fires. Training in the use of $CO_2$ extinguishers is essential.

Dry powder or $CO_2$ extinguishers which are too small can be hazardous due to the danger of re-ignition or flash-back.

## Colour coding of portable fire extinguishers

**F5076**   All new certified fire extinguishers for use throughout the EU are to be coloured red, as from 1 January 1997, following the introduction of BS EN 3 and the removal of the current British Standard BS 5423. Manufacturers will be allowed, under BS 7863 (new), to affix different coloured panels on or above the operation instructions label. Existing extinguishers need not be replaced until they have served their useful life.

## Fire alarms in 'certificated' premises

**F5077**   A manually operated fire alarm system is required in any 'certificated' premises (see F5005 above), and will be indicated on the fire certificate. The system should comply with the British Standard Code of Practice for the installation of fire alarms, and any equipment used should comply with the appropriate British Standard specification. The system should be tested weekly.

## Good 'housekeeping'

F5078    The need for good 'housekeeping' cannot be over-emphasised. Poor housekeeping is the greatest single cause of fire. A carelessly discarded cigarette end, especially into a container of combustible waste or amongst combustible storage, often results in fire. The risk is higher in an area which is infrequently used. The following are essential guidelines:

(*a*)    where smoking is permitted, suitable deep metal ashtrays should be provided. Ashtrays should not be emptied into combustible waste unless the waste is to be removed from the building immediately. It is recommended that smoking ceases before close of work so that if smouldering occurs this will be detected before staff leave the premises;

(*b*)    combustible waste and contaminated rags should be kept in separate metal bins with close fitting metal lids;

(*c*)    cleaners should, preferably, be employed in the evenings when work ceases. This will ensure that combustible rubbish is removed from the building to a place of safety before the premises are left unoccupied;

(*d*)    rubbish should not be kept in the building overnight, or stored in close proximity to the building;

(*e*)    'no smoking' areas should be strictly enforced, especially in places which are infrequently used, e.g. stationery stores, oil stores, or telecommunications intake room. Suitable 'smoking prohibited' notices should be displayed throughout such areas – notices should comply with BS 5499 and the *Health and Safety (Safety Signs and Signals) Regulations 1996 (SI 1996 No 341)*;

(*f*)    where 'no smoking' is enforced due to legal requirements (for example, areas where flammable liquids are used or stored) or in areas of high risk or high loss effect, it is recommended that the notice read 'Smoking prohibited – dismissal offence';

(*g*)    materials should not be stored on cupboard tops, and all filing cabinets should be properly closed, and locked if possible, at the end of the day.

## Pre-planning of fire prevention

F5079    A pre-planned approach to fire prevention and control is essential. Fire spreads extremely fast, the temperature can rise to 1,000°C in only one minute. Smoke can be flammable and toxic. The essential factor is to re-evaluate the risk, identify areas of high loss effect or high risk, and plan accordingly to meet requirements and legal responsibilities.

### Means of escape

F5080    Means of escape should be designed and constructed around fire travel. This consists of three stages as follows:

(*a*)    travel within rooms;

(*b*)    travel from rooms to a stairway or exit;

(*c*)    travel within stairways to a final exit.

In particular, for offices:

(i)    total travel distance between any point in a building and the nearest final exit should not exceed

> — 25m, if there is only one exit, or
>
> — 45m, if more than one exit;

(ii) two or more exits are necessary

> — from a room in which more than 60 people work, or
>
> — if any point in the room is more than 12m from the nearest exit;

(iii) minimum width of exit should be 750mm;

(iv) — corridors should be at least 1m wide;

> — office corridors should be divided by fire-resisting doors if they are longer than 45m;

(v) stairways should be at least 800mm wide and in a fire-resistant enclosure; so, too, should doors connecting them;

(vi) one stairway is adequate in a building of up to four storeys only;

(vii) escape doors should never be locked. If, for security reasons, they have to be secured against external entry, panic bolts or similar fastenings (complying with BS EN 1125) should be fitted;

(viii) fire exit notices should be affixed to or above fire escape doors;

(ix) corridors and stairways, which are a means of escape, should have half-hour fire resistance and preferably be constructed from brick or concrete with a non-combustible surface;

(x) fire alarms should be audible all through the building. In multi-storey buildings such alarms will normally be electrically operated, whereas in smaller buildings a bell or gong is sufficient;

(xi) it should not normally be necessary for a person to travel more than 30m to the nearest alarm point.

In any certificated premises the means of escape certificate or fire certificate must be available on demand. The following are essential:

(*a*) all doors affording means of escape in case of fire should be maintained easily and readily available for use at all times that persons are on the premises;

(*b*) all doors not in continuous use, affording a means of escape in case of fire, should be clearly indicated;

(*c*) sliding doors should also clearly indicate the direction of opening and, where possible, not be used on escape routes;

(*d*) doors should be adequately maintained and should not be locked or fastened in such a way that they cannot be easily and immediately opened by persons leaving the premises. Moreover, all gangways and escape routes should be kept clear at all times.

## Unsatisfactory means of escape

**F5081**  The following are unsatisfactory means of escape in case of fire:

(*a*) lifts;

(*b*) portable ladders;

(*c*) spiral staircases;

(*d*)    escalators;

(*e*)    lowering lines.

## Fire drill

F5082 As well as being a statutory requirement in procedures relating to 'events of serious and imminent danger' (*Management of Health and Safety at Work Regulations 1999 (SI 1999 No 3242), Reg 8(1)*), as a matter of good housekeeping (in addition to being probably required as well by the fire certificate (see F5011 above, 'Contents of a fire certificate')), employers should acquaint the workforce with the arrangements for fire drill. This consists of putting up a notice in a prominent place stating the action employees should take on

(*a*)    hearing the alarm, or

(*b*)    discovering the fire.

Ideally, employees should receive regular fire drill, even though normal working is interrupted. Indeed, fire alarms should be sounded weekly so that employees may familiarise themselves with the sound, and evacuation drills should be carried out at least annually. Trained employees should be designated as fire wardens and carry out head counts on evacuation, as well as acting as last man out and generally advising and shepherding the public. In addition, selected employees should be trained in the proper use of fire extinguishers. Moreover, periodical visits by the local fire authority should be encouraged by employers, since this provides a valuable source of practical information on fire fighting, fire protection and training.

### Typical fire drill notice

F5083 When the fire alarm sounds:

1.    Switch off electrical equipment and leave room, closing doors behind you.

2.    Walk quickly along escape route to open air.

3.    Do not use lifts.

4.    Report to fire warden at assembly point.

5.    Do not re-enter building.

When you discover a fire:

1.    Raise alarm (normally by operating a break glass call point).

2.    Leave the room, closing doors behind you.

3.    Leave the building by escape route.

4.    Report to fire warden at assembly point.

5.    Do not re-enter building.

## Fires on construction sites

F5084 Each year there are numerous fires, of a major kind, on construction sites and in buildings undergoing refurbishment. For that reason the '*Joint Code of Practice on the Protection from Fire of Construction Sites and Buildings Undergoing Renovation*' (published by the Fire Protection Association, Bastille Court, 2 Paris Garden, London SE1 8ND) proposes that the main contractor should appoint a *site fire safety co-ordinator*, responsible for assessing the degree of fire risk and for formulating and regularly updating the *site fire safety plan*; he should liaise with the co-ordinator for the design phase (see F5087 below). The site fire safety plan should detail:

(*a*)    organisation of and responsibilities for fire safety;

(*b*)    general site precautions, fire detection and warning alarms;

(*c*)    requirements for a Hot Work Permit system;

(*d*)    site accommodation;

(*e*)    fire escape and communications system (including evacuation plan and procedures for raising the fire brigade);

(*f*)    fire brigade access, facilities and co-ordination;

(*g*)    fire drill and training;

(*h*)    effective security measures to minimise the risk of arson;

(*j*)    materials storage and waste control system.

### Role of site fire safety co-ordinator

F5085    The site fire safety co-ordinator must:

(*a*)    ensure that all procedures, precautionary measures and safety standards (as specified in the site fire safety plan) are clearly understood and complied with by all those on the project site;

(*b*)    ensure establishment of Hot Work Permit systems;

(*c*)    carry out weekly checks of firefighting equipment and test all alarm and detection devices;

(*d*)    conduct weekly inspections of escape routes, fire brigade access, firefighting facilities and work areas;

(*e*)    liaise with local fire brigade for site inspections;

(*f*)    liaise with security personnel;

(*g*)    keep a written record of all checks, inspections, tests and fire drill procedures;

(*h*)    monitor arrangements/procedures for calling the fire brigade;

(*j*)    during the alarm, oversee safe evacuation of site, ensuring that all staff/visitors report to assembly points;

(*k*)    promote a safe working environment.

### Emergency procedures

F5086    The following emergency procedures should be implemented, where necessary,

(*a*)    establish a means of warning of fire, e.g. handbells, whistles etc.;

(*b*)    display written emergency procedures in prominent locations and give copies to all employees;

(*c*)    maintain clear access to site and buildings;

(*d*)    alert security personnel to unlock gates/doors in the event of an alarm;

(*e*)    install clear signs in prominent positions, indicating locations of fire access routes, escape routes and positions of dry riser inlets and fire extinguishers.

## Designing out fire

F5087 Construction works should be designed and sequenced to accommodate

(*a*)    permanent fire escape stairs, including compartment walls;

(*b*)    fire compartments in buildings under construction, including installation of fire doors;

(*c*)    fire protective materials to structural steelwork;

(*d*)    planned firefighting shafts duly commissioned and maintained;

(*e*)    lightning conductors;

(*f*)    automatic fire detection systems;

(*g*)    automatic sprinkler and other fixed fire fighting installations.

Moreover, adequate water supplies should be available and hydrants suitably marked and kept clear of obstruction.

## Other fire precautions on site

F5088 Portable fire extinguishers can represent the difference between a conflagration and a fire kept under control. Therefore, personnel must be trained in the use of portable firefighting equipment and adequate numbers of suitable types of portable extinguishers should be available. They should be located in conspicuous positions near exits on each floor. In the open, they should be 500 mm above ground bearing the sign 'Fire Point' and be protected from both work activities and adverse weather conditions. In addition, all mechanically-propelled site plant should carry an appropriate fire extinguisher, and extinguishers, hydrants and fire protection equipment should be maintained and regularly inspected by the site fire safety co-ordinator.

Plant on construction sites also constitutes a potential danger. All internal combustion engines of powered equipment, therefore, should be positioned in the open air or in a well-ventilated non-combustible enclosure. They should be separated from working areas and sited so that exhaust pipes/gases are kept clear of combustible materials. Moreover, fuel tanks should not be filled whilst engines are running and compressors should be housed singly away from other plant in separate enclosures.

## Consequences of failure to comply with code

F5089 Non-compliance with the provisions of this code could well result in insurance ceasing to be available or being withdrawn, thereby constituting a breach of a Standard Form contract (see C8127 CONSTRUCTION AND BUILDING OPERA-TIONS). Where fire damage is caused to property by the negligence of employees of a subcontractor, then, in accordance with Clause 6.2 of the JCT Contract, to the effect that the contractor is liable for 'injury or damage to property', the contractor is liable and not the employer (or building owner); even though, under Clause 6.3B, the employer is required to insure against loss or damage to existing structures, to the work in progress, and to all unfixed materials and goods intended for, delivered to or placed on the works (*National Trust v Haden Young Ltd, The Times, 11 August 1994*). The practical implementation of fire precautions on construction sites forms part of the overall construction health and safety plan (see C8024 CONSTRUCTION AND BUILDING OPERATIONS).

# First-Aid

## Introduction

F7001 People can and do suffer injury or fall ill at work. This may or may not be as a result of work related activity. However, it is important that they receive immediate attention.

The *Health and Safety (First-Aid) Regulations 1981 (SI 1981 No 917)*, which came into operation on 1 July 1982, require employers to have facilities for the provision of first-aid in their place of work.

Medical treatment should be provided at the scene promptly, efficiently and effectively before the arrival of any medical teams that may have been called. First-aid can save lives and can prevent minor injuries from becoming major ones. Employers are responsible for making arrangements for the immediate management of any illness or injury suffered by a person at work. First-aid at work covers the management of first-aid in the workplace – it does not include treating ill or injured people at work with medicines.

However, the Regulations do not prevent specially trained staff taking action beyond the initial management of the injured or ill at work.

## The employer's duty to make provision for first-aid

F7002 Employers must provide or ensure that there is equipment and facilities provided that are adequate and appropriate for rendering first-aid if any of their employees are injured or become ill at work. Employers must also ensure that there are an adequate and appropriate number of suitable persons who:

(*a*) are trained and have such qualifications as the Health and Safety Executive may approve for the time being; and

(*b*) have additional training, if any, as may be appropriate in the circumstances.

Where such a suitable person is absent in temporary and exceptional circumstances, an employer can appoint a person, or ensure that a person is appointed:

(*a*) to take responsibility for first-aid in situations relating to an injured or ill employee who needs help from a medical practitioner or nurse;

(*b*) to ensure that equipment and facilities are adequate and appropriate in the circumstances.

With regard to any period of absence of the first-aider, consideration must be given to:

(*a*) the nature of the undertaking;

(*b*) the number of employees at work; and

(*c*) the location of the establishment.

# The assessment of first-aid needs

F7003    The employer should assess his first-aid needs and requirements as appropriate to the circumstances of his workplace. The employer's principal aim must be the reduction of the effects of injury and illness at the place of work. Adequate and appropriate first-aid personnel and facilities should be available for rendering assistance to persons with common injuries or illnesses and those likely to arise from specific hazards at work. Similarly, there must be adequate facilities for summoning an ambulance or other professional medical help.

The extent of first-aid provision in a particular workplace that an employer must make depends upon the circumstances of that workplace. There are no fixed levels of first-aid – the employer must assess what personnel and facilities are appropriate and adequate. Employers with access to advice from occupational health services may wish to use these resources for the purposes of conducting such assessment, and then take the advice given as to what first-aid provision would be deemed appropriate.

In workplaces that employ:

- qualified medical doctors registered with the General Medical Council; or

- nurses whose names are registered in Part 1, 2, 10 or 11 of the Single Professional Register maintained by the United Kingdom Central Council for Nursing, Midwifery and Health Visiting,

the employer may consider that there is no need to appoint first-aiders.

There is no requirement for the results of the first-aid risk assessment to be recorded in writing, although it may nevertheless be a useful exercise for the employer – for he may subsequently be asked to demonstrate that the first-aid provision is adequate and appropriate for the workplace.

When assessing first-aid needs, employers must consider the following:

— the hazards and risks in the workplace;

— the size of the organisation;

— the history of accidents in the organisation;

— the nature and distribution of the workforce;

— the distance from the workplace to emergency medical services;

— travelling, distant and lone workers' needs and requirements;

— employees working on shared or multi-occupied sites;

— annual leave and other absences of first-aiders and appointed persons.

## The hazards and risks in the workplace

F7004    *The Management of Health and Safety at Work Regulations 1999 (SI 1999 No 3242)* require employers to make a suitable and sufficient assessment of the risks to health and safety at work of their employees. The assessment must be designed to identify the measures required for controlling or preventing any risks to the workforce: highlighting what types of accidents or injuries are most likely to occur will help employers address such key questions as the appropriate nature, quantity and location of first-aid personnel and facilities.

Where the risk assessment conducted by an employer identifies a low risk to health and safety, employers may only need to provide (i) a first-aid container clearly identified and suitably stocked, and (ii) an appointed person to look after first-aid arrangements and resources and to take control in emergencies.

Where risks to health and safety are greater, employers may need to ensure the following:

- the provision of an adequate number of first-aiders so that first-aid can be given immediately;

- the training of first-aiders to deal with specific risks or hazards;

- informing the local emergency services in writing of the risks and hazards on the site where hazardous substances or processes are in use;

- the provision of a first-aid room(s).

Employers will need to consider the different risks in each part of their company or organisation. Where an organisation occupies a large building with different processes being performed in different parts of the premises, each area's risks must be assessed separately. It would not be appropriate to conduct a generic assessment of needs to cover a variety of activities – the parts of the building with higher risks will need greater first-aid provision than those with lower risk.

## The size of the company

F7005
In general, the amount of first-aid provision that is required will increase according to the number of employees involved. Employers should be aware, however, that in some organisations there may be few employees but the risks to their health and safety might be high – and, as a result, their first-aid needs will also be high.

## The history of incidents and accidents

F7006
When assessing first-aid needs, employers might find it useful to collate data on accidents that have occurred in the past, and then analyse, for example, the numbers and types of accidents, their frequency and consequences. Organisations with large premises should refer to such information when determining the first-aid equipment, facilities and personnel that are required to cover specific areas.

## The character and dispersion of the workforce

F7007
The employer should bear in mind that the size of the premises can affect the time it might take a first-aider to reach an incident. If there are a number of buildings on the site, or the building in question comprises several storeys, the most suitable arrangement might be for each building or floor to be provided with its own first-aiders. Where employees work in shifts or in self-contained areas, first-aid arrangements may need to be tailored to reflect that fact.

Employees who are potentially at higher risk, such as trainees, young workers or people with disabilities, will need to be given special consideration.

## The distance from the workplace to emergency medical services

F7008
Where a workplace is far from emergency medical services, it may be necessary to make special arrangements for ensuring that appropriate transport can be provided for taking an injured person to the emergency medical services.

In every case where the place of work is remote, the very least that an employer should do is to give written details to the local emergency services of the layout of the workplace, plus any other relevant information, such as information on specific hazards.

## The needs and requirements of travelling, distant and lone workers

**F7009** Employers are responsible for meeting the needs of their employees whilst they are working away from the main company premises.

When assessing the needs of staff who travel long distances or who are constantly mobile, consideration should be given to the question of whether they ought to be provided with a personal first-aid kit.

Organisations with staff working in remote areas must make special arrangements for those employees in respect of communications, special training and emergency transport.

## Personnel on sites that are shared or multi-occupied

**F7010** Employers with personnel working on shared or multi-occupied sites can agree to have one employer on the site who is solely responsible for providing first-aid cover for all the workers. It is strongly recommended that this agreement is written to avoid confusion and misunderstandings between the employers. It will highlight the risks and hazards of each company on the site, and will make sure that the shared provision is suitable and sufficient. After the employers have agreed the arrangement, the personnel must be informed accordingly.

When employees are contracted out to other companies their employer must ensure they have access to first-aid facilities and equipment. The user employer bears the responsibility for providing such facilities and equipment.

## First-aiders on annual leave or absent from the workplace

**F7011** Adequate provision of first-aid must be available at all times. Employers should therefore ensure that the arrangements they make for the provision of first-aid at the workplace are adequate to cover for any annual leave of their first-aiders or appointed persons. Such arrangements must also be able to cover for any unplanned or unusual absences from the workplace of first-aiders or appointed persons.

## Other important points

**F7012** Employers are not obliged by these regulations to provide first-aid facilities for members of the public. Although the regulations are aimed at employees, including trainees, many organisations like health authorities, schools and colleges, places of entertainment, fairgrounds and shops do make first-aid provision for persons other than their employees. Other legislation deals with public safety and first-aid facilities for the public – for example, the *Road Traffic Act 1960* regulates first-aid provision on buses and coaches.

Where employers extend their first-aid provision to cover more than merely their employees, the provision for the employees must not be diminished and should not fall below the standard required by these regulations.

The compulsory element of employers' liability insurance does not cover litigation resulting from first-aid given to non-employees. It is advised that employers check their public liability insurance policy on this issue.

### Reassessing first-aid needs

F7013   In order to ensure that first-aid provision continues to be adequate and appropriate, employers should from time to time review the first-aid needs in the workplace, particularly when changes have been made to working practices.

## Duty of the employer to inform employees of first-aid arrangements

F7014   Employers are under a duty to inform employees of the arrangements that have been made for first-aid in their workplace. This may be achieved by:

- Distributing guidance to all employees which highlights the key issues in the first-aid arrangements, such as listing the names of all first-aiders and describing where first-aid resources are located.

- Nominating key employees to ensure that the guidance is kept up to date and is distributed to all staff, and to act also as information officers for first-aid in the workplace.

- Internal memos can be used as a method of keeping the personnel informed of any changes in the first-aid arrangements.

- Displaying announcements up on notice boards informing employees of the first-aid arrangements and of any changes to those arrangements.

- Providing new employees with the information as part of their induction package.

  Any person with a reading or language problem must be given the information in a way that they can understand.

## First-aid and the self-employed

F7015   The self-employed should provide, or ensure that there is provided, such equipment, if any, as is appropriate in the circumstances to enable them to render first-aid to themselves whilst at work. The self-employed who work in low-risk areas, for example at home, are required merely to make first-aid provision appropriate to a domestic environment.

When self-employed people work together on the same site, they are each responsible for their own first-aid arrangements. If they wish to collaborate on first-aid provision, they may agree a joint arrangement to cover all personnel on that particular site.

## Number of first-aiders

F7016   Sufficient numbers of first-aiders should be located strategically on the premises to allow for the administration of first-aid quickly when the occasion arises. The assessment of first-aid needs may have helped to highlight the extent to which there is a need for first-aiders. The table below gives suggested numbers of first-aiders or appointed persons who should be available at the workplace. The suggested numbers are not a legal requirement – they are merely for guidance.

There are no hard and fast rules on numbers – employers will have to make a judgement, taking into account all the circumstances of their organisation. If the company is a long way from a medical facility or there are shift workers on site or the premises cover a large area, the numbers of first-aid personnel set out below may not be sufficient – the employer may have to make provision for a greater number of first-aiders to be on site.

### Selection of first-aiders

F7017      First-aiders must be reliable and of good disposition. Not only should they have good communication skills, but they must also possess the ability and aptitude for acquiring new knowledge and skills and must be able to handle physical and stressful emergency incidents and procedures. Their position in the company should be such that they are able to leave their place of work immediately to respond to an emergency.

## Table 1
## First-aid personnel

| Category of risk | Numbers employed at any location | Suggested number of first-aid personnel |
|---|---|---|
| **Lower risk** – e.g. shops, offices, libraries | Fewer than 50 | At least one appointed person |
| | 50–100 | At least one first-aider |
| | More than 100 | One additional first-aider for every 100 employed |
| **Medium risk** – e.g. light engineering and assembly work, food processing, warehousing | Fewer than 20 | At least one appointed person |
| | 20–100 | At least one first-aider for every 50 employed (or part thereof) |
| | More than 100 | One additional first-aider for every 100 employed |
| **Higher risk** – e.g. most construction, slaughterhouse, chemical manufacturer, extensive work with dangerous machinery or sharp instruments | Fewer than 5 | At least one appointed person |
| | 5–50 | At least one first-aider |
| | More than 50 | One additional first-aider for every 50 employed |
| | Where there are hazards for which additional first-aid skills are necessary | In addition, at least one first-aider trained in the specific emergency action |

### The training and qualifications of first-aid personnel

F7018      Individuals nominated to be first-aiders must complete a programme of competence-based training in first-aid at work run by an organisation approved by the HSE. See APPENDIX B for a range of first-aid competencies which make up a basic curriculum. Organisations that are contracted to train first-aid personnel may be notified of any particular risks or hazards in a workplace so that the first-aid course that is provided can be tailored to include the risks specific to that workplace.

Additional special training may be undertaken to deal with unusual risks and hazards. This will enable the first-aider to be competent in dealing with such risks. Such special training may be separate from the basic course or an extension to it but does not need approval by the HSE. The first-aid certificate awarded may be endorsed to verify that special training has been received.

It is important for employers to understand that first-aid at work certificates are valid for three years. Employers wishing to arrange for re-testing of competence training must do so before the original first-aid certificate expires. If the certificate of any first-aider expires, he or she will have to attend a full course of training to regain their first-aid at work certificate. Employers can arrange for re-testing of competence training up to three months before the expiry date of the certificate – the new first-aid at work certificate will then run from the date of the expiry of the old certificate. It is advisable for employers to keep a record of first-aiders in the company, together with their certification dates, in order to assist them in organising refresher training. Employers should develop a programme of knowledge and skills training for their first-aiders to enable them to be updated on new skills and to make them aware of suitable sources of first-aid information, such as occupational health services and training organisations qualified by the HSE to conduct first-aid at work training.

## Appointed persons

**F7019**    An appointed person is an individual who takes charge of first-aid arrangements for the company including looking after the facilities and equipment and calling the emergency services when required. The appointed person is allocated these duties when it is found through the first-aid needs assessment that a first-aider is not necessary. The appointed person is the minimum requirement an employer can have in the workplace. Clearly, even if the company is considered a low health and safety risk and, in the opinion of the employer, a first-aider is unnecessary, an accident or illness still may occur – therefore somebody should be nominated to call the emergency services, if required.

Appointed persons are not first-aiders – and therefore they should not be called upon to administer first-aid if they have not received the relevant training. However, employers may consider it prudent to send appointed persons on first-aid training courses. Such a course normally last for four hours and includes the following topics:

●     action necessary in an emergency;

●     cardio-pulmonary resuscitation;

●     first-aid treatment for the unconscious casualty;

●     first-aid treatment for the bleeding or the wounded.

●     HSE approval is not required for this training.

The only time an appointed person can replace a first-aider is when the first-aider is absent, due to circumstances which are temporary, unforeseen and exceptional. Appointed persons cannot replace first-aiders who are on annual leave. If the first-aid assessment has identified a requirement for first-aiders, they should be available whenever there is a need for them in the place of work.

# Records and record keeping

F7020    It is considered good practice to keep records of incidents which required the attendance of a first-aider and treatment of an injured person. It is advisable for smaller companies to have one record book but for larger organisations this may not be practicable.

The data entered in the record book should include the following:

- the date, time and place of the incident;

- the injured person's name and job title;

- a description of the injury or illness and of the first-aid treatment administered;

- details of where the injured person went after the incident, i.e. hospital, home or back to work;

- the name and signature of the first-aider or person who dealt with the incident.

This information may be collated, to help the employer improve the environment with regard to health and safety in the workplace. It could be used to help determine future first-aid needs assessment and will be helpful for insurance and investigative purposes. The statutory accident book is not the same as the record book, but they may be combined.

## First-aid resources

F7021    Having completed the first-aid needs requirements assessment, the employer must provide the resources, i.e. the equipment, facilities and materials, that will be needed to ensure that an appropriate level of cover is available to the employees at all relevant times. First-aid equipment, suitably marked and obtainable, must be made available at specific sites in the workplace.

### First-aid containers

F7022    First-aid equipment must be suitably stocked and contained in a properly identifiable container. One first-aid container with sufficient quantity of first-aid materials must be made available for each worksite – this is the minimum level of first-aid equipment. Larger premises, for example, will require the provision of more than one container.

First-aid containers should be easily accessible and, where possible, near handwashing facilities. The containers should be used only for first-aid equipment. Tablets and medications should not be kept in them. The first-aid materials within the containers should be protected from damp and dust.

Having completed the first-aid needs assessment, the employer will have a good idea as to what first-aid materials should be stocked in the first-aid containers. If there is no specific risk in the workplace, a minimum stock of first-aid materials would normally comprise the following (there is no mandatory list):

- a leaflet giving guidance on first-aid (for example, HSE leaflet *Basic advice on first aid at work*);

- 20 individually wrapped sterile adhesive dressings (assorted sizes), appropriate to the type of work;

- two sterile eye pads;

- four individually wrapped triangular bandages (preferably sterile);

- six safety pins;

- six medium-sized individually wrapped sterile unmedicated wound dressings – approximately 12cm x 12cm;

- two large sterile individually wrapped unmedicated wound dressings – approximately 18cm x 18cm;

- one pair of disposable gloves.

This list is a suggestion only – other equivalent materials will be deemed acceptable.

An examination of the first-aid kits should be conducted frequently. Stocks should be replenished as soon as possible after use, and ample back-up supplies should be kept on the company premises. Any first-aid materials found to be out of date should be carefully discarded.

All first-aid containers should have a white cross on a green background as identification.

## Additional first-aid resources

F7023
If the results of the assessment suggest a need for additional resources such as scissors, adhesive tape, disposable aprons, or individually wrapped moist wipes, they can be kept in the first-aid container if space allows. Otherwise they may be kept in a different container as long as they are ready for use if required.

If the assessment highlights the need for such items as protective equipment, they must be securely stored next to first-aid containers or in first-aid rooms or in the hazard area itself. Only persons who have been trained to use these items may be allowed to use them.

If there is a need for eye irrigation, and mains tap water is unavailable, at least a litre of sterile water or sterile normal saline solution (0.9%) in sealed, disposable containers should be provided. If the seal is broken, the containers should be disposed of and not reused. Such containers should also be disposed of when their expiry date has been passed.

## First-aid kits for travelling

F7024
First-aid kits for travelling may contain the following items:

- a leaflet giving general guidance on first-aid (for example, HSE leaflet *Basic advice on first aid at work*);

- six individually wrapped sterile adhesive dressings;

- one large sterile unmedicated dressing – approximately 18cm x 18cm;

- two triangular bandages;

- two safety pins;

- individually wrapped moist cleansing wipes;

- one pair of disposable gloves.

This list is a suggestion only – it is not mandatory. However, the kit must be regularly inspected and topped up from a back-up store at the home site.

## Rooms designated as first-aid areas

F7025    A suitable room should be made available for first-aid purposes where the first-aid needs assessment found such a room to be necessary. Such room(s) should have sufficient first-aid resources, be easily accessible to stretchers and be easily identifiable, and where possible should be used only for administering first-aid.

First-aid rooms are normally necessary in organisations operating within high-risk industries. Therefore they would be deemed to be necessary on, chemical, ship building and large construction sites or on large sites remote from medical services. A person should be made responsible for the first-aid room.

On the door of the first-aid room a list of the names and telephone extensions of all the first-aiders should be displayed, together with details as to how and where they may be contacted on site.

First-aid rooms should:

- have enough space to hold a couch with space in the room for people to work, a desk, a chair and any other resources found necessary (see below);

- where possible, be near an access point in the event that a person needs to be taken to hospital;

- have heating, lighting, and ventilation;

- have surfaces that can be easily washed;

- be kept clean and tidy; and

- be available and ready for use whenever employees are in the workplace.

The following is a list of resources that may be found in a first-aid room:

- a record book for logging incidents where first-aid has been administered;

- a telephone;

- a storage area for storing first-aid materials;

- a bed/couch with waterproof protection and clean pillows and blankets;

- a chair;

- a foot operated refuse bin with disposable yellow clinical waste bags or some receptacle suitable for the safe disposal of clinical waste;

- a sink that has hot and cold running water – also drinking water and disposable cups;

- soap and some form of disposable paper towel.

If the designated first-aid room has to be shared with the working processes of the company, the employer must consider the implications of the room being needed in an emergency and whether the working processes in that room could be stopped immediately. Can the equipment in the room be removed in an emergency so as not to interfere with any administration of first-aid? Can the first-aid resources and equipment be stored in such a place as to be available quickly when necessary? Lastly, the room must be appropriately identified and, where necessary, be signposted by white lettering or symbols on a green background.

# *Appendix A*

## Assessment of first-aid needs – checklist

The minimum first-aid provision for each worksite is:

- a suitably stocked first-aid container;

- an appointed person to take charge of first-aid arrangements;

- information for employees on first-aid arrangements.

*This checklist will help you assess whether you need to make any additional provisions.*

| | Aspects to consider | Impact on first-aid provision |
|---|---|---|
| 1. | What are the risks of injury and ill health arising from the work as identified in your risk assessment? | If the risks are significant you may need to employ first-aiders. |
| 2. | Are there any specific risks, such as:<br>• hazardous substances;<br>• dangerous tools;<br>• dangerous machinery;<br>• dangerous loads or animals? | You will need to consider:<br>• specific training for first-aiders;<br>• extra first-aid equipment;<br>• precise siting of first-aid equipment;<br>• informing emergency services;<br>• a first-aid room. |
| 3. | Are there parts of your establishment where different levels of risk can be identified (e.g. a university with research labs)? | You will probably need to make different levels of provision in different parts of the establishment. |
| 4. | Are large numbers of people employed on site? | You may need to employ first-aiders to deal with the higher probability of an accident. |
| 5. | What is your record of accidents and cases of ill-health? What type are they and where did they happen? | You may need to:<br>• locate your provision in certain areas;<br>• review the contents of the first-aid box. |
| 6. | Are there inexperienced workers on site, or employees with disabilities or special health problems? | You will need to consider:<br>• special equipment;<br>• local siting of equipment. |
| 7. | Are the premises spread out, e.g. are there several buildings on the site or multi-floor buildings? | You will need to consider provision in each building or on several floors. |
| 8. | Is there shiftwork or out-of-hours working? | Remember that there needs to be first-aid provision at all times people are at work. |

| 9. | Is your workplace remote from emergency medical services? | You will need to: <br> • inform local medical services of your location; <br> • consider special arrangements with the emergency services. |
|----|----|----|
| 10. | Do you have employees who travel a lot or work alone? | You will need to: <br> • consider issuing personal first-aid kits and training staff in their use; <br> • consider issuing personal communicators to employees. |
| 11. | Do any of your employees work at sites occupied by other employers? | You will need to make arrangements with the other site occupiers. |
| 12. | Do you have any work experience trainees? | Remember that your first-aid provision must cover them. |
| 13. | Do members of the public visit your premises? | You have no legal responsibilities for non-employees, but HSE strongly recommends that you include them in your first-aid provision. |
| 14. | Do you have employees with reading or language difficulties? | You will need to make special arrangements to give them first-aid information. |

Do not forget to allow for leave or absences of first-aiders and appointed persons. First-aid personnel must be available at all times when people are at work.

## *Appendix B*

### First-aid competencies

Employees who have successfully completed first-aid training must be able to apply the following competencies:

(*a*)   to act safely, promptly and effectively when an incident occurs at work;

(*b*)   to administer cardio-pulmonary resuscitation (CPR) promptly and effectively;

(*c*)   to administer first-aid safely, promptly and effectively to a casualty who is unconscious;

(*d*)   to administer first-aid safely, promptly and effectively to a casualty who is wounded or bleeding;

(*e*)   to administer first-aid safely, promptly and effectively to a casualty who:

— is burnt or scalded;

— has an injury to bones, muscles or joints;

— is in shock;

— has an eye injury;

— is suffering from poisoning;

— has been overcome by gas or fumes;

(*f*)   the transportation of the casualty safely in the workplace;

(*g*)   the recognition and management of common major illnesses;

(*h*)   the recognition and management of minor illnesses;

(*i*)   the management of records and the provision of written information to medical staff if required.

First-aiders must also know and understand the following elements of first-aid at work:

(*a*)   the legal requirements relating to the provision of first-aid at work;

(*b*)   first-aider responsibilities and procedures in an emergency;

(*c*)   safety and hygiene in first-aid procedures;

(*d*)   how to use first-aid equipment provided in the workplace.

# Food Safety and Standards

## Introduction

F9001 Legislation has governed the sale of food for centuries. In Europe we can trace it back at least to the Middle Ages, and the ancient Hebrew food laws, found notably in the Book of Deuteronomy, show that it goes back even further. Two themes have existed from the start:

- *Food Safety* – the protection of the health and well being of anyone eating food; and

- *Food Standards* – the control of composition and adulteration of food for the prevention of fraud.

UK legislation is structured principally around the *Food Safety Act 1990* supported by a whole raft of more detailed regulations. Increasingly over the past thirty years directives and regulations from the European Union have determined UK legislation. More recently, devolution within the UK has seen the responsibility for food policy shifted to the Scottish parliament and regional assemblies. This may allow greater diversity of regulation to develop within the UK as far as this is possible within the EU framework.

## Food safety

F9002 The principal legislation is the *Food Safety Act 1990*. Since the inception of the European Economic Community (EEC), now the European Union (EU), European 'hygiene' regulations have developed on the basis of specific measures for specific food sectors, the so-called 'vertical' regulations. A full complement of these was in place by the 1990s covering the processing of most foods of animal origin including meat, fish, eggs and dairy products. The vertical regulations do not in general cover businesses selling food direct to the ultimate consumer, for example catering or retail businesses.

Only in 1993 did the EU publish the 'horizontal' Food Hygiene Directive 93/43. This establishes general principles for food hygiene and sets hygiene standards for those businesses not covered by 'vertical' legislation. These include food factories processing non-animal products and also retail or catering outlets. This directive passed into UK law as the *Food Safety (General Food Hygiene) Regulations 1995 (SI 1995 No 1763)* ('the General Food Hygiene Regulations'). These Regulations were supplemented by the *Food Safety (Temperature Control) Regulations 1995 (SI 1995 No 2200)* ('the Temperature Control Regulations').

The EU is now planning a radical overhaul of the 'vertical' directives and regulations, which will be consolidated around the framework of a revised version of Directive 93/43. The following account will be largely restricted to the provisions of the Food Safety Act, the General Food Hygiene Regulations and the Temperature Control Regulations. Food processors who may be covered by the 'vertical' legislation will need to take more specific advice.

## Food standards

F9003 Food standards is governed by a complex range of regulations. Despite its name, the *Food Safety Act 1990* is also the primary legislation covering most aspects of food standards and a number of regulations have been made under it. Over the recent past there has been a significant change in emphasis. Previously there was a tendency to prescribed compositional standards for foods. For example, the meat content of certain products, the fruit content of drinks and so on. A little of this legacy remains, but the approach proved inflexible especially in a climate of rapid innovation and product development. The emphasis has now shifted to allow more diversity of composition, but supported by informative labelling. The *Food Labelling Regulations 1996 (SI 1996 No 1499)* play an important role. The *Food Labelling (Amendment) Regulations 1998 (SI 1998 No 1398)* took this even further with a specific requirement that pre-packed foods must carry a 'quantitative ingredient declaration' or 'Quid'. This dictates that the label must carry a declaration of the percentage quantity of the main ingredient or ingredients of any food. Food standards and labelling may also be enforced through the more general *Trades Descriptions Act 1968.*

## Administrative regulations

F9004     Finally, there are more general regulations made under the *Food Safety Act 1990.* These may regulate the law enforcement process, setting criteria for inspectors, food analysts or examiners. Or they may be more general requirements for food businesses such as the *Food Premises (Registration) Regulations 1991 (SI 1991 No 2825).* Under these Regulations all food premises must register with the local authority. The Regulations have been amended twice (by *SI 1993 No 2022* and *SI 1997 No 723*).

Of course many other pieces of consumer protection legislation can apply; notably the *Weights and Measures Act 1985*, which controls the way in which food is sold by weight or other measures, and the *Prices Act 1974.* The *Price Indications (Food and Drink on Premises) Order 1079* requires prices for food and drinks to be displayed by catering premises following a particular format.

## Policy and enforcement

F9005     Until the year 2000, government policy on food came largely from the Ministry of Agriculture, Fisheries and Food (MAFF) and the Department of Health (DH). MAFF had particular responsibility for the 'upstream' parts of the food chain and for food standards. DH was naturally more involved in questions of food safety, and they took a role in liaison with enforcement authorities.

April 2000 saw the establishment of the Food Standards Agency (FSA). This is a non-ministerial government department designed to take all of the policy functions from MAFF and DH into an organisation at arms length from the government. This should allow it to act more independently and primarily in the consumers' interest. The FSA is controlled by a board of directors and operates through a chief executive and officials, the majority of whom joined the FSA from similar roles in MAFF or DH. Complementary FSA structures exist in Scotland, Wales and Northern Ireland. The FSA is created and empowered by the *Food Standards Act 1999.*

Complex arrangements are in place for the enforcement of food legislation. Traditionally local authorities have had the responsibility although central government officials have particular responsibilities in 'upstream' parts of the food chain. This is particularly true of 'meat hygiene' in abattoirs and cutting plants. This role was taken away from local authorities to a central Meat Hygiene Service (MHS) with the MHS itself becoming a branch of the FSA from April 2000. The FSA has also developed a new role of local authority monitoring.

Most food enforcement at the production and retail level falls to two groups of local government officers:

- Environmental Health Officers (EHOs) have responsibility for food safety legislation. They are generally employed at district council (town hall) level.

- Trading Standards Officers (TSOs) take control of food standards issues, including weights and measures. Generally they are employed at county council level.

The distinction between district and county councils has become increasingly blurred with much local government organised on a unitary basis. This includes most English metropolitan areas and all authorities in Scotland. In these cases TSO and EHO functions are usually combined in the same department.

# Food Safety Act 1990

F9006    The *Food Safety Act 1990* describes the offences that may be committed if food legislation is contravened and also explains the defences that may be used if charges are instigated. It sets up the mechanisms to enforce the laws and fixes penalties that may be levied. The Act also enables the government to make regulations that include more detailed food safety and consumer protection measures.

The Act is divided into four principle sections:

(i)     Part I: Definitions and responsibilities for enforcement;

(ii)    Part II: Main provisions;

(iii)   Part III: Administrative and enforcement issues such as powers of entry; and

(iv)    Part IV: Miscellaneous arrangements notably the power to issue codes of practice.

The following is a brief summary of the main provisions contained within the Act.

## Section 1: definitions

F9007    Under the *Food Safety Act 1990* 'food' has a wide meaning and includes:

- drink;

- articles and substances of no nutritional value which are used for human consumption;

- chewing gum and similar products;

- articles and substances used as ingredients in any of the above foods.

Food does not include live animals, birds or fish (although shellfish that are eaten raw and alive such as oysters and similar are classed as 'food'). Neither does 'food' include animal feed, nor controlled drugs that might be taken orally.

The scope of the Act is very wide ranging and covers all commercial businesses. A business may be a canteen, club, school, hospital, care home and so on, whether or not it is run for profit. Government establishments that once had 'crown immunity' are treated no differently to other food businesses. Charity events that sell food are also subject to the Act.

The Act covers any premises from abattoir to retail superstore, from street vendor to a five star hotel. It includes any place (including premises used only occasionally for a food business such as a village hall), any vehicle, mobile stall and temporary structure.

The *Food Safety Act 1990, s 2* provides an extended meaning to the word 'sale' of food, and *s 3* establishes a presumption that food is intended for human consumption. The meaning of 'sale' of food is very wide. The Act does not apply only to sales where money changes hands and the business is run for profit. It also covers food given as a prize or as a reward by way of business promotion or entertainment. Entertainment includes social gatherings, exhibitions, games, sport and so on. Thus, if food, which turns out to be unfit is given as a prize for a darts competition, it could be subject to an action under the 1990 Act. If someone has food in their possession the Act presumes that the intention is to sell it unless it can be proved otherwise. For example, food past its 'use by' date must be segregated from food that is for sale and should be marked clearly otherwise an EHO or TSO could presume that it was for sale.

The Food Safety Act 1990, ss 4–6 describe who does what under food law and defines the various responsibilities of local and central government.

## Part II: main provisions of the Act

F9008     The main provisions of the *Food Safety Act 1990* fall within *ss 7* to *22*. The offences are divided into two types: food safety and consumer protection which each breakdown into two separate offences:

    (i)   *Food Safety*

- *Section 7*: Rendering food injurious to health.

- *Section 8*: Selling food not complying with food safety requirements.

    (ii)   *Consumer Protection*

- *Section 14*: Food not of the nature, substance or quality demanded.

- *Section 15*: Falsely presenting or describing food.

### Section 7: rendering food injurious to health

F9009     It is an offence to do anything intentional that would make food harmful to anyone that eats it. Even if one did not know that it would have that effect, an offence would still have been committed. For example subjecting food to poor temperature control that allows bacteria to multiply could render food injurious to health.

Food is considered injurious to health if it would harm most people who ate it. It would not be considered 'injurious to health' if it contained an ingredient (like peanuts) that may only affect a small proportion of people who have a specific allergy. It would be injurious to health if it were likely to cause immediate harm to anyone that ate it, for example botulism in yoghurt. It would also be injurious to health if the harm were cumulative over a long period, for example fungal toxins in cereal products.

### Section 8: selling food not complying with food safety requirements

F9010     Whilst *s 7* deals with the person who renders food injurious to health, the *Food Safety Act 1990, s 8* goes on to prevent him or anyone else from selling the food. This can apply to anyone in the food chain. The predecessor to the 1990 Act only intercepted food as it was sold to the consumer. The 1990 Act allows action to be taken at any stage in the chain.

Food would fail to comply with food safety requirements if:

(*a*)   it has been rendered injurious to health as described above;

(*b*)   it is unfit for human consumption;

(*c*)   it is so contaminated that it would be unreasonable to expect it to be eaten.

Food would be unfit for consumption if it was putrid or toxic or it contained serious foreign material, for example a dead mouse.

The third part of *s 8* was a new provision in 1990 and gave wide scope to prosecute someone for selling food that fails to meet a customer's expectations. For example the food is mouldy or contains a rusty nail or there are excessive antibiotic residues in meat.

(The *Food Safety Act 1990, ss 9–13* provide enforcement procedures for food safety offences.) (These sections are dealt with from F9014–F9019.)

## Section 14: selling food not of the nature, substance or quality demanded

F9011   It is an offence to supply to the prejudice of the purchaser food which is not of the nature, substance or quality demanded. The purchaser in this case does not have to be a customer in a retail store or catering outlet. One company, large or small may purchase from another and an offence is committed if the food is inferior in nature or substance or quality to that which they demanded. Once again this allows the law to be applied at any point of the food chain.

The purchaser does not have to buy the food for his or her own use to be prejudiced. They may intend to give it to someone else, for example members of their family.

The three parts of the offence are separate and a charge will be brought under one of the three according to the circumstances.

If a purchaser asks for cod and gets coley, or beef mince contains a mixture of lamb or chicken, it would be not of the 'nature' demanded.

If a purchaser asked for diet cola and was served regular cola, or expected a sheep's milk cheese and it was made from cow's milk, it would be not of the 'quality' demanded.

Food that was not of the quality or substance demanded often formed the basis for complaints of mouldy food or foreign material. Such complaints are likely to be taken under the *Food Safety Act 1990, s 8(2)(c)* (i.e. that the food is so contaminated that it would be unreasonable to expect it to be eaten).

More recently, the above provision has been used when a susceptible customer has requested information about peanuts or similar ingredients to which they may have a severe allergic reaction. If, notwithstanding such a request, the consumer is sold food that triggers a reaction, cases have been brought on the grounds that the food was not of the 'substance' demanded.

## Section 15: falsely presenting or describing food

F9012   It would be an offence to make a statement on the food label that was untrue, or even if there was a misleading pictorial representation. It is also an offence if material that is technically accurate is presented in such a way as to mislead the consumer.

The *Food Safety Act 1990, s 15* is backed up with very detailed requirements on labelling in the *Food Labelling Regulations 1996 (SI 1996 No 1499)*. For some offences, especially labelling by caterers on menus or chalkboards, TSOs may invoke the more general requirements under the *Trades Descriptions Act 1968.*

### Enforcement

F9013    The *Food Safety Act 1990* gives enforcement officers strong powers, namely:

- To enter food premises to investigate possible offences.

- To inspect food.

- To detain or seize suspect food.

- To take action that requires a business to put things right.

- If all else fails:

  — to prosecute,

  — to prohibit the use of premises or equipment,

  — to bar an individual from working in a food business.

Under the *Food Safety Act 1990, ss 32* and *33,* enforcement officers have rights of access at any reasonable time and an offence will be committed if they are obstructed. They must be given reasonable information and assistance. They can inspect premises, processes and records. If records are kept on a computer, they are entitled to have access to them. They can copy records, take samples, take photographs and even videos. If they are refused access to any of these, they can apply to a magistrate for a warrant. They must give 24 hours notice to enter private houses used in connection with a food business.

Of course none of these requirements to co-operate with officers and give them access to information cancel the basic right to avoid self-incrimination. In the extreme situation one has the right to remain silent and to consult a solicitor.

Officers themselves commit an offence if they reveal any trade secrets learned in the course of official duties.

The *Food Safety Act 1990, ss 29–31* allow officers to procure samples and control the sampling and testing procedures. A section 40 code of practice (no. 7) covers 'Sampling for Analysis or Examination'. Samples that are taken carelessly may give unreliable results and may be not be acceptable as evidence in court.

The *Food Safety Act 1990,* ss *9–13* provide enforcement officers with a series of enforcement measures to control food or food businesses that present a health risk.

### Section 9: detention and seizure of food

F9014    If an officer suspects that food is unfit or fails to meet food safety requirements, he can issue a detention notice. This requires the person in charge of the food to keep it in a specified place and not to use it for human consumption pending investigation. The detention notice must be written on a prescribed form. It is an offence to ignore or contravene a detention notice even if you may believe that it is unjustified. The officer has 21 days to complete his investigations. If he concludes that the food was actually safe, he must withdraw the notice (using another prescribed form) and restore the food to the person in charge.

Authority                                                                FORM 1

**Food Safety Act 1990 - Section 9**

## DETENTION OF FOOD NOTICE

Reference Number:

1. To: ......................................................................................................
   Of: ......................................................................................................

2. Food to which this notice applies:
   Description: ...............................................................................
   Quantity: ...............................................................................
   Identification marks: ...............................................................................

3. *THIS FOOD IS NOT TO BE USED FOR HUMAN CONSUMPTION.*
   In my opinion, the food does not comply with food safety requirements because: ......................
   ......................................................................................................
   ......................................................................................................

4. The food must not be removed from:
   ......................................................................................................
   ......................................................................................................
   *unless it is moved to:
   ......................................................................................................
   ......................................................................................................
   (*Officer to delete if not applicable)

5. Within 21 days, either this notice will be withdrawn and the food released, or the food will be seized to be dealt with by a justice of the peace, or in Scotland a sheriff or magistrate, who may condemn it.

   Signed: ...................................................................... Authorised Officer
   Name in capitals: ...............................................................................
   Date: ...............................................................................
   Address: ...............................................................................
   ......................................................................................................
   ......................................................................................................
   Tel: ........................... Fax:.............................................................

> *Please read the notes overleaf carefully. If you are not sure of your rights or the implications of this notice, you may want to seek legal advice.*

Authority: _____    FORM 2

Food Safety Act 1990--Section 9

# WITHDRAWAL OF DETENTION OF FOOD NOTICE

1. To: .........................................................................................................
   Of: ......................................................................................................
   .............................................................................................................

2. Detention Notice Number ........................ dated ............................... and served on you on
   ..................................... (date) is now withdrawn. The food described in paragraph 3 below can
   now be used for human consumption.

3. Food released for human consumption:
   Description: .............................................................................................
   Quantity: ................................................................................................
   Identification marks: ................................................................................

   Signed: .......................................................................... Authorised Officer
   Name in capitals: .......................................................................................
   Date: .......................................................................................................
   Address: ...................................................................................................
   ..............................................................................................................
   ..............................................................................................................
   Tel: ............................... Fax ................................................................

> *Please read the notes overleaf carefully. If you are not sure of your rights or the implications of this notice, you may want to seek legal advice.*

Authority:_____     FORM 3

**Food Safety Act 1990--Section 9**

# FOOD CONDEMNATION WARNING NOTICE

Reference Number:

1.  To: ------------------------------------------------------------------------------
    Of: ------------------------------------------------------------------------------
    --------------------------------------------------------------------------------

2.  This Notice applies to the following food which has been seized by an officer of this authority:
    Description         ------------------------------------------------------------
    Quantity            ------------------------------------------------------------
    Identification marks ------------------------------------------------------------

3.  *IT IS MY INTENTION TO APPLY TO A JUSTICE OF THE PEACE,*
    *OR IN SCOTLAND A SHERIFF OR MAGISTRATE, AT*
    --------------------------------------------------------------------------------
    *ON ----------------------- (DATE) AT -------------- AM/PM FOR THE ABOVE*
    *FOOD TO BE CONDEMNED.*
    because ------------------------------------------------------------------------

4.  As the person in charge of the food, you are entitled to attend and to bring witnesses.

5.  A copy of this notice has also been given to:
    --------------------------------------------------------------------------------
    --------------------------------------------------------------------------------
    who may also attend and bring witnesses.

    Signed:          ------------------------------------------------------------- Authorised Officer
    Name in capitals: --------------------------------------------------------------
    Date:            --------------------------------------------------------------
    Address:         --------------------------------------------------------------
                     --------------------------------------------------------------
                     --------------------------------------------------------------
    Tel:             --------------------------- Fax: -------------------------------

> *Please read the notes overleaf carefully. If*
> *you are not sure of your rights or the*
> *implications of this notice, you may want to*
> *seek legal advice.*

On the other hand, the EHO may conclude that the food is unsafe. He can seize it and take it before a justice of the peace (JP). The EHO may reach this conclusion as a result of tests performed during the 21 days after serving the detention notice. But in some circumstances, he may be confident that it is unsafe from the beginning and seize the food immediately without using a detention notice. Once again there is a form that must be used and the EHO must state exactly what is happening and when. After seizure the matter should be taken before the JP within 2 days, quicker in the case of perishable food.

The hearing before the JP may not only decide the fate of the batch of food but may also be a forerunner to other legal proceedings. One is allowed to make representations at this hearing and to call witnesses. It is probably advisable to take specific legal advice from a solicitor when the first detention notice is issued. It is wise to have legal representation at a hearing following seizure.

If the JP decides that the food is unsafe he can order it to be destroyed and he may order the offender to cover the costs of its disposal. If the seized food is only part of a larger batch the court will presume that the whole batch fails unless evidence is provided to the contrary.

If it turns out that the EHO was wrong, the offender may be entitled to compensation. If the food has deteriorated as a result they may be entitled to compensation equal to the loss in value. If a reasonable sum cannot be agreed with the authority there is an arbitration procedure.

*Section 10: improvement notices*

F9015     EHOs have a range of powers to deal with unsatisfactory premises from informal advice through to prosecution and emergency prohibition. If an authorised officer believes that a business does not comply with hygiene or processing regulations, he can issue a formal improvement notice demanding that it puts matters right. This provides a quicker and cheaper remedy than taking the business to court. An improvement notice should not be ignored. It is an offence to fail to comply with a notice and either matters must be put right as indicated on the notice or an appeal lodged against it.

An improvement notice must contain four elements:

(i)     the reasons for believing that the requirements are not being complied with;

(ii)    the ways in which regulations are being breached;

(iii)   the measure which should be taken to put things right;

(iv)   the time allowed for putting things right (this cannot be less than 14 days).

One can choose to put things right in a different way to that suggested by the EHO provided that the EHO is satisfied that it will have the required effect.

If a party does not agree with an improvement notice the *Food Safety Act 1990, s 37* gives the right to appeal to a magistrate within one month of its issue or within the time specified on the notice if shorter than one month. The EHO must inform the party about their rights to appeal and provide the name and address of the court when he serves the notice.

The notice may contain a number of points but the whole notice does not have to be appealed. One may appeal just one point or simply ask for a time extension. The notice is effectively suspended during the appeal, but it is best to let the EHO, as well as the court, know about the appeal. The *Food Safety Act 1990, s 39* allows the magistrate to modify or cancel any part of the notice.

Authority: ...........................................................................   FORM 1

**Food Safety Act 1990–Section 10**
**IMPROVEMENT NOTICE**

Reference Number:

1.   To: .................................................................. (Proprietor of the food business)

     At: ...............................................................................................................

     ...............................................................................................................

     ........................................................................................ (Address of proprietor)

2.   In my opinion the:

     ...............................................................................................................

     ...............................................................................................................

     [Office to insert matters which do not comply with the Regulations]

     in connection with your food business ...............................................................

     ........................................................................................ (Name of business)

     at ...............................................................................................................

     ........................................................................................ (Address of business)

     do/does* not meet the requirements of ...............................................................

     of the ........................................... Regulations

     because:

     ...............................................................................................................

     [* Officer to delete as appropriate]

3.   In my opinion, the following measures are needed for you to comply with these
     Regulations: ...............................................................................................

     ...............................................................................................................

     ...............................................................................................................

4.   These measures or measures that will achieve the same effect must be taken
     by: ............................ (date)

5.   *It is an offence not to comply with this improvement notice by the date stated.*

     Signed: ................................................................... Authorised Officer

     Name in capitals: .......................................................................................

     Date: .........................................................................................................

     Address: .....................................................................................................

     ...............................................................................................................

     Tel: ....................................... Fax: .......................................................

> *Please read the notes overleaf carefully.*
> *If you are not sure of your rights or the*
> *implications of this notice, you may want to*
> *seek legal advice.*

(Until April 2001 there was an additional procedure involved in the issue of improvement notices. Any improvement notice had to be preceded with a 'minded to' notice. This was an informal notification from the EHO that he or she intended to issue an improvement notice. It gave the opportunity to put things right without a formal improvement notice. The 'minded to' procedure was ended by the *Regulatory Reform Act 2001*.)

*Section 11: prohibition orders*

F9016    If one is successfully prosecuted for food safety offences, the EHO can also apply for a prohibition order. He or she must establish that there is a danger to the public.

The first step the authority must take is to get a successful prosecution for a breach of food hygiene or food safety regulations. The offence may be failing to comply with an improvement notice. If the court decides that there is an ongoing risk to public health it must issue a prohibition order. The order can deal with any of one three issues depending upon the actual risk:

- to prohibit a process or treatment,

- to deal with the *structure* of the premises or the use of equipment,

- to deal with a problem that relates to the *condition* of the premises or equipment.

In either of the last two cases, the order may prohibit the use of the equipment or the premises.

Any prohibition order must be served on the proprietor of the business. If it relates to equipment it will also be fixed to the equipment and if it relates to the premises it will be fixed prominently to the premises. It is automatically an offence if one knowingly breaches a prohibition order.

As soon as a party believes that they have put matters right and that the health risk no longer exists they can apply to the EHO to have the prohibition lifted. The EHO must respond by reaching a decision within a fortnight and if they believe that things are satisfactory, issue a certificate within another three days. The certificate will state that enough has been done to ensure that there is no longer an unacceptable risk to public health. If the authority disagrees and refuses to issue a certificate they must give their reasons and one can appeal to a magistrate to have the order lifted. The authority must give information on the right to appeal, and who to contact as well as the time scale (in this case one must appeal within one month).

*Personal prohibition under section 11*

F9017    The court can also prohibit a person from running or managing a food business. One can apply to the court to lift a personal prohibition but cannot do so within 6 months of its imposition and if an appeal is unsuccessful it cannot be appealed again for three months.

*Section 12: emergency prohibition*

F9018    *Section 11* prohibitions are imposed only by a court following conviction. But in an emergency, an EHO can act on his or her own authority and with immediate effect. They must be satisfied that a business presents an imminent risk to health. In such circumstances they can serve an emergency prohibition notice without prior reference to a court. Emergency prohibition can apply to the whole premises or a specific

# PROHIBITION ORDER

(Food Safety Act 1990, s. 11)

### Magistrates' Court

(Code)

Date            :

Accused         :        WHEREAS

of              :

being the proprietor of a food business carried on at premises at

has today been convicted by this court of an offence under regulations to which section 11 of the Food Safety Act 1990 applies [by virtue of section 10(3)(b) of the said Act], namely:-

Decision        :        AND WHEREAS the Court is satisfied that there exists a risk of injury to health by reason of

[the use for the purposes of the said food business of a certain [process] [treatment], namely

                                                                          ]

[the [construction] [state or condition] of the premises at

used for the purposes of the said food business]

[the [use for the purposes of the said food business] the [state or condition] of certain equipment [used for the purposes of the said food business], namely

                                                                          ]

and it is ORDERED that

Order           :        [the use of the said [process][treatment] for the purposes of the business] [the use of the said [premises] [equipment] for the purposes of [the business] [any other food business of the same class or description, namely

                                                                          ]

[any food business]]
[and that the participation by the accused in the management of any food business [of the said class or description]
is prohibited.

[By Order of the Court]

*[Justice of the Peace ] [Justices' Clerk ]*

Delete any words within square brackets which do not apply.

**FS 46**            Copyright forms are reproduced by permission of the publishers, Shaw & Sons Ltd., Shaway House, Crayford, Kent, DA1 4BZ, from whom copies may be purchased.

part. The notice will be fixed in a prominent place and anyone removing it or deliberately ignoring it is guilty of an offence.

The officer must take the matter before a magistrates' court within three days of serving the notice. At least one day before it goes to court the EHO must serve a notice on the proprietor of the business telling him of the court hearing. Once again, if one finds themself faced with action of this kind it is advisable to seek specific legal advice.

If the court agrees that the EHO's actions were justified it will make an emergency prohibition order which replaces the emergency prohibition notice. The arrangements for lifting the order are the same as a *section 11* order. If the court does not uphold an emergency prohibition, the proprietor may seek compensation for loss or damages. An emergency prohibition order cannot be made against an individual. Prohibition of a person can only be made under *section 11* following a conviction.

### Section 13: emergency control orders

F9019    This power would normally be exercised by the government. It may be that an unsafe batch of food has already been distributed around the country. Emergency prohibition of the manufacturing site would stop further production but it would not control the risk from food already in the system. The *Food Safety Act 1990, s 13* allows an emergency control order to require all steps to be taken that will remove the threat. This is a wide-ranging power that will only be used in exceptional circumstances. Of course in most cases, any business told that it has received unsafe food from a supplier would stop selling it simply to protect their own reputation. If an emergency control order is invoked, there is no right of appeal and no compensation arrangements.

Voluntary arrangements are in place to co-ordinate food hazards and issue warnings and organise recalls when food is distributed more widely than the local area in which it is produced. These warnings are circulated by electronic mail to EHOs around the country. Where possible, trade organisations and the media are also informed. The Food Standards Agency is demonstrating a greater commitment to freedom of information than previous departments. Nowadays food hazard warnings and recalls are better publicised, not least through the FSA website at: www.foodstandards.gov.uk

### Sections 16 to 18: power to make regulations

F9020    The *Food Safety Act 1990, ss 16–18*, include wide-ranging enabling powers that allow ministers to make regulations. For example:

- To prohibit specified substances in foods.

- To prohibit a certain food process.

- To require hygienic conditions in commercial food premises.

- To dictate microbiological standards for foods.

- To make standards on food composition.

- To specify requirements for food labelling.

- To restrict and control claims made in the advertising of food.

They also provide the power to ban from sale food originating from potentially diseased sources. For example these powers were used to prohibit the sale of certain

Authority: ...................................................................................    FORM 2

**Food Safety Act 1990–Section 12**

**EMERGENCY PROHIBITION NOTICE**

Reference Number:

1.  To: ................................................................ (Proprietor of the food business)

    At: ............................................................................................................................

    ............................................................................................................................

    .................................................................................... (Address of proprietor)

2*  I am satisfied that: ................................................................................................

    ............................................................................................................................

    ............................................................................................................................

    at ......................................................................................................................

    .................................................................................... (Address of business)

*POSES AN IMMINENT RISK OF INJURY TO HEALTH because:*

    ............................................................................................................................

    ............................................................................................................................

    ............................................................................................................................

*(\*See Note 1 overleaf)*

3.  *YOU MUST NOT USE IT FOR THE PURPOSE OF THIS/ANY/THIS OR ANY SIMILAR\* FOOD BUSINESS.*

[\* Officer to delete as appropriate]

    Signed: ................................................................ Authorised Officer

    Name in capitals: ...............................................................................................

    Date: ..................................................................................................................

    Address: .............................................................................................................

    ............................................................................................................................

    Tel: ...................................................... Fax: ...........................................................

> *Please read the notes overleaf carefully.*
> *If you are not sure of your rights or the*
> *implications of this notice, you may want to*
> *seek legal advice.*

parts of beef cattle for human food on the basis that they may have been suffering from BSE. Much of the detail of food law is in the regulations made under *s 16*.

*Section 17* allows the government to bring EU provisions into UK law. *Section 18* regulations will cover very particular circumstances such as genetically modified foods.

### Section 19: registration and licensing

**F9021**     The *Food Safety Act 1990, s 19* permits the government to bring in regulations demanding licensing or registration of certain food businesses.

Registration and licensing confer significantly different powers on enforcement authorities. Registration is simply an administrative exercise. It is designed primarily to let enforcement agencies know what food businesses are operating in their area. It also provides some basic information on the size of the business and the type of food that they produce. No conditions are attached to registration, the local authority cannot refuse to register a business, there is no charge, and it does not have to be renewed periodically.

Licensing (or 'prior approval') is quite different. It is a control measure. Precise licensing criteria will be specified and there would normally be prior inspection and approval before a new business is allowed to open. There is often a charge for a licence, which must be renewed periodically. The enforcement authority will usually have the right to withdraw a licence if standards fall. The business would have to close.

Amongst enforcement officers there is generally a preference for licensing rather than registration. But at present, licensing only applies to a handful of different types of food business mostly meat or dairy operations. More recently, licensing was imposed on retail butchers' shops following the recommendation of the Pennington Group after the North Lanarkshire E coli outbreak. Shops selling both raw and cooked meat must be licensed. The licensing conditions include compliance with the General Food Hygiene Regulations supplemented by enhanced requirements for Hazard Analysis Critical Control Points ('HACCP') and staff training. At the outset the annual licence fee was £100.

Most other types of food businesses are subject only to registration. The *Food Premises (Registration) Regulations 1991 (SI 1991 No 2828)* (as amended by *SI 1993 No 2022* and *SI 1997 No 723*) were enacted under *s 19* and described later.

### Defences against charges under the Food Safety Act 1990

**F9022**     The following paragraphs explain the defences available under the *Food Safety Act 1990*.

### Section 21: defence of due diligence

**F9023**     The so called 'due diligence' defence first appeared within food safety legislation when the *Food Safety Act 1990* was passed. Previously, the provision had been tried and tested within a number of other pieces of legislation after it first appeared just over 100 years before in the *Merchandise Marks Act 1887*. Indeed legislation that included a due diligence defence, such as the *Trades Descriptions Act 1968*, already overlapped with food legislation. So although the defence was new to food law there were numerous precedents to signal the implications of the due diligence provision.

The *Food Safety Act 1990* creates offences of strict liability. The prosecution is not required to show that the offence was committed intentionally. However the due diligence defence is intended to balance the protection of the consumer against the right of traders not to be convicted for an offence that they have taken all reasonable care to avoid committing. The intention of the due diligence defence is to encourage traders to take proper responsibility for their products and processes.

The *Food Safety Act 1990, s 21* states: 'in any proceedings for an offence under any of the preceding paragraphs of this Part . . . it shall be . . . a defence for the person charged to prove that he took all reasonable precautions and exercised all due diligence to avoid the commission of the offence by him or any person under his control.'

The onus is on the business to establish its defence on the balance of probabilities. Part of the due diligence defence may be to establish that someone else was at fault. If that is what is intended, the prosecutor must be informed at least seven days before the hearing, or if one has been in court already, within one month of their appearance. Under the 1990 Act, one can no longer rely upon a supplier's warranty alone, although a warranty may be part of due diligence defence.

It is impossible to give precise advice on what any business would need to do to have a due diligence defence. Cases that have been decided by the courts serve only to demonstrate that each case is decided on its own facts. What is certain is that doing nothing will never provide a due diligence defence. One must take some positive steps.

The defence has two distinct parts:

- Taking *reasonable precautions* involves setting up a system of control. One must consider the risks that threaten their operation and take *all reasonable precautions* that may be expected of a business of the size and type.

- Exercising *due diligence* means that one continues to take those precautions on a continuous basis.

*All* reasonable precautions and *all* due diligence are needed. The courts have decided consistently that if a precaution could reasonably have been taken but was not taken then the defence would not succeed.

The test is 'what is reasonable?' One will be expected to take greater precautions with high risk ready to eat foods than are needed for boiled sweets or biscuits. What is reasonable for a large-scale food business may not be reasonable for a smaller enterprise.

One must be careful that the scope of 'due diligence' covers all aspects of food law requirements. It is no good having excellent control of food safety hazards if there are no precautions in place to ensure that the composition and labelling of food complies with the regulations.

Documentation is important. Unless the precautions are written down, it will be difficult to persuade the EHO or the court that a proper system is in place. The same is true of records of any checks made to demonstrate that the system is followed diligently. The burden of proof lies with you to establish that the defence is satisfied.

A good 'HACCP' plan (see below) may be helpful in showing that a systematic approach to identifying the food safety precautions needed in the operation has been adopted. Cross-reference to industry guidelines or codes of practice may show that the system has a sound basis. Documentation from the hazard analysis will add to the evidence that precautions have been taken. Records such as specifications, cleaning schedules, training programmes and correspondence with suppliers or customers may all play a part in establishing the defence. An organisation chart and job descriptions that identify roles and responsibilities will also be useful evidence of the precautions taken.

Not all food businesses have the same defence. Some traders within the retail and catering end of the food supply chain may use a simpler defence of 'deemed due diligence' from the *Food Safety Act 1990, s 21 (3), (4)*. Even then 'deemed due diligence ' is not available against the *s 7* offence of rendering food injurious to health. Manufacturers and importers must satisfy the full defence. Larger businesses may be expected to take more precautions than smaller businesses. Those selling 'own label' packs may have greater responsibility for upstream activity than those selling manufacturers' 'branded' products.

*Section 35: penalties under the Food Safety Act 1990*

F9024     The courts decide penalties on the merits of individual cases but they are limited by maximum figures included in the *Food Safety Act 1990, s 35*. For most offences the crown court can send offenders to prison for up to 2 years and/or impose an unlimited fine. Even the magistrates' court, where most cases are heard, can set fines of up to £5,000 per offence and up to 6 months imprisonment. For the two food safety offences in sections *7* and *8* and the first of the consumer protection offences (*s 14*), the fine may be up to £20,000. In Scotland the sheriff may impose equivalent penalties.

Each set of regulations made under the Act will have its own level of penalties that will not exceed the levels mentioned here.

*Section 40: codes of practice*

F9025     The *Food Safety Act 1990, s 40* allows for the development of codes of practice. Section 40 codes of practice are primarily intended to instruct and inform enforcement officers and related bodies or personnel, for example food analysts or examiners. In carrying out their duties, enforcement professionals must have regard for section 40 codes of practice. Any failure to follow a code requirement might seriously jeopardise their ability to bring a successful prosecution. By the middle of the year 2001 there were eighteen codes made under section 40. Some had already undergone several revisions. The subjects of early codes are general matters, such as the demarcation of responsibility for enforcing different parts of the Act or general inspection procedures. Later ones provide more specific information on the enforcement of particular regulations, for example the Dairy Hygiene Regulations.

The most significant of the general codes is CoP number 9 on food hygiene inspections. It contains detailed advice to environmental health officers on how to conduct such inspections. It includes a 'risk rating' system whereby inspectors can prioritise different food businesses and determine the necessary inspection frequency. Codes also give guidance on such issues as the powers of inspecting officers and the communication of findings to the business. The FSA has indicated its intention to radically revise the section 40 codes and probably to consolidate them in fewer separate codes.

Section 40 codes should not be confused with 'industry guides' that are promoted by the EU General Food Hygiene Directive and the General Food Hygiene Regulations. These 'guides' provide more detailed practical explanation of the implications of the particular regulations in a food business sector. There are also numerous other guides and codes of practice published by industry, government, and other organisations.

# Food premises regulations

F9026    The following paragraphs deal with the main Regulation that covers food premises.

## The Food Premises (Registration) Regulations 1991 (as amended by SI 1993 No 2022) and SI 1997 No 723)

F9027    All food premises including retail and catering premises must register with the local authority unless they are already required by other legislation to be licensed. The Regulations demand the registration of individual food *premises* and not food businesses. So premises that are used only occasionally by food businesses, and maybe even by different food businesses, must be registered by the owner of the premises. For example a church hall, village hall or scout hut used from time to time for the sale of food must be registered. The criterion is that they are used by commercial food businesses for five or more days (which do not have to be consecutive) in any period of five weeks.

Similarly, markets or other premises used by more than one food business must also be registered. The market operator or the person in charge of the premises is responsible. Staff restaurants must be registered. Contractors and clients should have a clear agreement as to who will action this. All premises should have been registered by May 1992. New premises must apply to be registered at least 28 days before opening. This is designed to allow an EHO the opportunity to look at a business before it opens. However, if the EHO does not take that opportunity, one does not have to wait for a visit or for permission from the EHO before opening provided that the necessary registration form has been sent off.

If mobile food premises are used they may have to be registered. These can range from a handcart in a market to a forty-foot trailer used for hospitality. If one uses their own moveable premises in a market, they must be registered even though the market is registered by the operator. (If stalls provided by the market are used, registration is not necessary). If mobile food premises are operated, the premises at which they are normally kept must be registered, with the food authority local to the base.

To register, one must supply a range of information on a registration form obtained from the local EHO department, which is normally contacted via the Town Hall. The local authority may prefer for their version of the form to be used instead. Registration must take place 28 days before the business opens. In case of doubt, it is best to keep a note of when the form was sent. If possible check that it has been received. Sending the form by fax may be helpful in establishing the transmission date.

Of course, some of the information may change over time. The Regulations only demand that the authorities are notified about certain fundamental points. If the proprietor or the nature of the business changes they should be notified of this, e.g. changing from selling fruit and vegetables only to become a deli. The authority must be notified of the change within 28 days. Many of the other pieces of information on the application form may also change, for example the name of the manager, the phone number, the number of employees and so on but these changes do not need to be notified. By failing to register, giving false or incomplete information or failing to notify any of the changes mentioned above, can trigger prosecution proceedings.

Food premises exempted from registration fall into a number of categories as follows.

FORM OF APPLICATION FOR REGISTRATION OF FOOD PREMISES

1. Address of premises ..................................................................................................
   (or address at which movable                    Post code ....................................
   premises are kept)

2. Name of food business..........................................    Telephone no: ...............................
   (trading name)

3. Type of premises Please tick ALL the boxes that apply

   | | | | |
   |---|---|---|---|
   | Farm/smallholding | ☐ | Staff restaurant/canteen/kitchen | ☐ |
   | Food/manufacturing/processing | ☐ | Catering | ☐ |
   | Slaughterer | ☐ | Hospital/residential home/school | ☐ |
   | Packer | ☐ | Hotel/pub/guest house | ☐ |
   | Importer | ☐ | Private house used for a food business | ☐ |
   | wholesale/cash and carry | ☐ | Premises used by a number of | |
   | | | businesses | ☐ |
   | Distribution/warehousing | ☐ | Moveable premises | |
   | Retailer | ☐ | | |
   | Market | ☐ | Other: please give details ......................... | |
   | Restaurant/cafe/snack bar | ☐ | ............................................................ | |

4. Does your business handle or involve any of the following? Please tick ALL the boxes that apply

   | | | | |
   |---|---|---|---|
   | Chilled foods | ☐ | Alcoholic drinks | |
   | Frozen foods | ☐ | Canning | ☐ |
   | Fruit and vegetables | ☐ | Vacuum packing | ☐ |
   | Fish/fish products | ☐ | Bottling and other packing | ☐ |
   | Fresh/frozen meat | ☐ | Table meals/snacks | ☐ |
   | Fresh/frozen poultry | ☐ | Takeaway food | ☐ |
   | Meat products or delicatessen | ☐ | Accommodation | ☐ |
   | Dairy products | ☐ | Delivery service | ☐ |
   | Eggs | ☐ | Chilled food storage | ☐ |
   | Bakery | ☐ | Bulk storage | |
   | Sandwiches | ☐ | Use of private water supply | ☐ |
   | Confectionery | ☐ | Other: please give details ..................... | |
   | Ice cream | ☐ | ............................................................ | |

5. Are vehicles or ships        Are vehicles, stalls or ships        Number of
   used for transporting        used for preparing or selling        vehicles/stalls/ships kept at or
   food kept at or used          food, kept at or used from          used from the premises, and
   from the premises?            the premises?          Yes/No        used for preparing, selling or
                    Yes/No                                            transporting food.
                                                                      5 or less ☐    6–10 ☐
                                                                      11-50 ☐    51 plus ☐

6. Name(s) of proprietor(s) of food business .....................................................................
   Address of business head office or registered office ......................................................
   if different from address of premises
   ..........................................................    Post code .....................................

7. Name of manager if different from proprietor ................................................................

8. If this is a new business......................    9. If this is a seasonal business .......................
   Date you intend to open                              Period during which you intend to be open
                                                        each year

10. Number of people engaged in food business         0–10   11–50   51 plus (Please tick one box)
    Count part-timer(s) (25 hrs per week or less)       ☐       ☐       ☐
    as one-half

    **It is an offence to give false or incomplete
    information**

    *The completed form should be sent to:*

    [                              ]        Signature  ........................................
                                            Date  ............................................
                                            Name  ...........................................
    [                              ]        (BLOCK CAPITALS)
                                            Position in company/business......................

*Already licensed or registered under other measures*

F9028
- Slaughterhouses.
- Poultry slaughterhouses and cutting premises.
- Meat export cutting premises and stores.
- Meat product plants.
- Butchers' shops selling both raw and ready to eat meat.
- Dairies or farm dairies.
- Milk distribution premises.

*Premises used only occasionally*

F9029
- Premises used for less than five days (not necessarily consecutive) in five consecutive weeks.

*Low risk activities exempt unless used for retail sales*

F9030
- Where game is killed in sport (grouse moors).
- Where fish is taken for food (but not processed).
- Where crops are harvested, cleaned, stored or packed. However, if the crops are put into the final consumer pack they must register.
- Where honey is harvested.
- Where eggs are produced or packed.
- Livestock farms and markets.
- Shellfish harvesting areas.
- Places where no food is kept, for example an administrative office or head quarters of a food business.

*Some domestic premises*

F9031
Some domestic premises that might technically be deemed to be food premises are also exempt in the following situations:
- Childminders caring for no more than six children (*SI 1993 No 2022*).
- People preparing foods for sale in WI Country Markets Ltd. (*SI 1997 No 723*).
- Where the resident is not the owner of the food business (for example a mobile food vehicle is sometimes kept at the premises of the driver) If the premises are used for the purpose of for example peeling shrimps or prawns they must be registered.
- Premises used for the production and sale of honey.
- Where crops are produced, cleaned, packed and sold whether wholesale or retail.
- Premises which provide bed and breakfast accommodation in not more than three bedrooms.

*Some vehicles*

F9032
- Private cars.
- Aircraft.
- Ships unless permanently moored or used for pleasure excursions in inland or coastal waters.
- Food vehicles normally based outside the UK.
- Vehicles or stalls kept at premises that are themselves registered or exempt.
- Market stalls owned by the market controller.
- Tents, marquees and awnings.

*Other exemptions*

F9033
- Places where the main activity has nothing to do with food but where light refreshments such as biscuits and drinks are served to customers without charge (for example hairdressers salons).
- Where food is sold only through vending machines.
- Places run by voluntary or charitable organisations and used only by those organisations provided that no food is stored on the premises except tea, coffee, dry biscuits etc. For example some village or church halls, but not if they are used more than five days in five weeks by commercial caterers.
- Crown premises exempted for security reasons.
- Places supplying food and drink in religious ceremonies.
- Stores of food kept for an emergency or national disaster.

# Food hygiene regulations

F9034
The following account will concentrate on the *Food Safety (General Food Hygiene) Regulations 1995 (SI 1995 No 1763)* that stem from the 'horizontal' food hygiene Directive 93/43. It will also cover the *Food Safety (Temperature Control) Regulations 1995 (SI 1995 No 2200)*. Both of these Regulations apply to the retail and catering sale of all types of food and also to the production and preparation of non-animal products at earlier points of the food supply chain. More specific 'vertical' regulations apply to manufacture and processing of animal products including fish and dairy products. A detailed account of the vertical regulations is beyond the scope of this publication.

## Food Safety (General Food Hygiene) Regulations 1995

F9035
The structure of the *Food Safety (General Food Hygiene) Regulations 1995 (SI 1995 No 1763)* is closely aligned to the principles established by the Codex Alimentarius of the World Health Organisation. Food safety controls must be based on a HACCP system, supported by a range of hygiene pre-requisites. The only difference is that the hazard analysis requirement within the 1995 Regulations is not quite so full and formal as HACCP. Opinions differ as to exactly how far short it is of full HACCP, but the most obvious omission is that there is no overt requirement for documentation or records.

Hygiene has a wider meaning than just the safety of food. It is defined in the Regulations as 'all measures necessary to ensure the safety and wholesomeness of food during preparation, processing, manufacturing, packaging, storing, transportation, distribution, handling and offering for sale or supply to the consumer.' Wholesomeness means 'fitness for human consumption as far as hygiene is concerned.'

Early parts of the Regulations, specify some broad hygiene objectives. Latter parts specify some particular goals that must be achieved to help meet those objectives.

*Regulation 4(1)* demands that 'A proprietor of a food business shall ensure that any of the following operations, namely, the preparation, processing, manufacturing, packaging, storing, transportation, distribution, handling and offering for sale or supply, of food are carried out in a hygienic way'.

The so-called 'hazard analysis' provision is contained within *Reg 4(3)*. This effectively demands a systematic approach to food safety controls appropriate to the business. The historical tendency towards very prescriptive hygiene regulations is seen to be inflexible with the very wide diversity of the food industry. HACCP is a formalised system that allows effective controls to be developed that suit the products and production methods of the individual business.

## Hazard analysis

F9036

The *Food Safety (General Food Hygiene) Regulations 1995 (SI 1995 No 1763)* specify five elements that must be included in the process of identifying steps in the activities of the business that are 'critical' to ensuring that food is safe:

- Analyse the food hazards that may be encountered.

- Identify the points in the process where these may occur.

- Decide which of these points may be 'critical' to the safety of the food.

- Identify effective controls that can be applied at critical points. In every case, identify a system of monitoring those controls, and implement both control and monitoring into the process.

- Review the system periodically and make changes if necessary.

HACCP is a powerful and sophisticated management tool that can be used by businesses to develop a food control plan. Full and formal HACCP requires quite detailed expert knowledge and training. A significant amount of literature has built up over the years. It serves well those larger businesses that employ staff with technical training. Smaller food businesses tend to find HACCP literature to be too full of jargon and inaccessible.

Clear guidance has been developed by central government for some specific food sectors. The most notable recent example was a guide for butchers' shops in England that was drafted in preparation for the introduction of licensing. Other guidance aimed at the catering industry was published much earlier at the start of the 1990s, notably *Assured Safe Catering*. Although serving a useful purpose at the time, this document is now seriously in need of updating. Without up to date central guidance, ideally from the FSA, interpretation and implementation of hazard analysis is likely to remain confused and inconsistent.

Critical control points (CCP) for microbiological food poisoning hazards will tend to focus on a small number of areas.

COOKING: In most processes there is likely to be a risk of pathogens in raw ingredients, so cooking is frequently a CCP. Adequate cooking temperatures will be the control measure, and target temperatures should be established. These can be monitored either by checking the food temperature directly or monitoring the process. For example using a cooking time and temperature that you know will achieve a satisfactory temperature.

CONTAMINATION: Process steps at which ready to eat food may become contaminated are also likely to be CCPs. Contamination could come from contact with raw food ('cross contamination'), or from contact with contaminated equipment or personnel. Separation of raw and ready to eat foods, and cleaning and disinfection routines will be appropriate control measures. In a good hazard analysis system these procedures will be specified objectively to allow them to be monitored. Written cleaning schedules will help. Nowadays there are also rapid test systems that will assess effectiveness of cleaning.

TIME AND TEMPERATURE CONTROLS: Cooling of food after cooking is often a CCP, as are storage times and temperatures of ready to eat foods. In most cases, controls will be expressed as a combination of time and temperature. The critical limits may be just a few hours if the food is kept at warm room temperature, or many days if it is kept in good refrigeration. In this area technology is providing increasingly sophisticated monitoring options include automatic alarms and real-time data monitoring. The temperature control regulations also intervene by prescribing certain targets.

### Documentation and records

F9037     A proper HACCP system would be fully documented. Any monitoring or verification procedures would be recorded and records kept. There is no explicit requirement for either of these in the *Food Safety (General Food Hygiene) Regulations 1995 (SI 1995 No 1763)* except in butchers' shops covered by the licensing amendment. Most businesses would be advised to keep some concise and succinct documentation. Without it, it may not be easy to demonstrate compliance with the legislation. It will certainly be difficulty to muster a convincing due diligence defence if that should become necessary.

### Hygiene 'pre-requisites'

F9038     Codex Alimentarius, the definitive guide to HACCP, says that any HACCP system must be supported by basic hygiene controls. These have become known as the pre-requisites to HACCP. The *Food Safety (General Food Hygiene) Regulations 1995 (SI 1995 No 1763), Sch 1 ('The Rules of Hygiene')* take a similar approach by establishing certain requirements for structures and services. They cover the following subjects within ten chapters:

   (i)    Chapter I: General requirements.

   (ii)    Chapter II: Rooms where food is prepared.

   (iii)    Chapter III: Movable or temporary premises, etc.

   (iv)    Chapter IV:Transport.

   (v)    Chapter V: Equipment.

   (vi)    Chapter VI: Food waste.

   (vii)    Chapter VII: Water Supply.

   (viii)    Chapter VIII: Personal hygiene.

   (ix)    Chapter IX: Protection of food from contamination.

   (x)    Chapter X: Training

*Chapter I: General requirements for food premises, equipment and facilities*

F9039     Food premises must be kept clean, and in good repair and condition. The layout, design, construction, and size must permit good hygiene practice and be easy to clean and/or disinfect and should protect food against external sources of contamination such as pests.

Adequate sanitary and handwashing facilities must be available and lavatories must not lead directly into food handling rooms. Washbasins must have hot and cold (or better still mixed) running water and materials for cleaning and drying hands. Where necessary there must be separate facilities for washing food and hands. Drainage must be suitable and there must be adequate changing facilities.

Premises must have suitable natural or mechanical ventilation. Ventilation systems must be accessible for cleaning, for example to give easy access to filters, and adequate natural and/or artificial lighting.

*Chapter II: Specific requirements in food rooms*

F9040     Food rooms should have surface finishes that are in good repair, easy to clean and, where necessary, disinfected. This would, for instance, apply to wall, floor and equipment finishes. The rooms should also have adequate facilities for the storage and removal of food waste. Of course, every food premises must be kept clean. How they are cleaned and how often, will vary. For example it will be different for a manufacturer of ready-to-eat meals than for a bakery selling bread.

There must be facilities, including hot and cold water, for cleaning and where necessary disinfecting tools and equipment. There must also be facilities for washing food wherever this is needed.

*Chapter III: Temporary and occasional food businesses and vending machines*

F9041     Most of the requirements apply equally to food businesses trading from temporary or occasional locations like marquees or stalls. For reasons of practicability, some requirements are slightly modified in this chapter.

*Chapter IV: Transport of food*

F9042     The design of containers and vehicles must allow cleaning and disinfection. Businesses must keep them clean and in good order to prevent contamination and place food in them so as to minimise risk of contamination. Precautions must be taken if containers or vehicles are used for different foods or for both food and non-food products. You should also separate different products to protect against the risk of contamination, and clean vehicles or containers effectively between loads.

*Chapter V: Equipment*

F9043     All equipment and surfaces that come into contact with food must be well constructed and kept clean. One interpretation of this requirement is that wooden cutting boards are not deemed suitable for use with ready to eat foods.

*Chapter VI: Food waste*

F9044     Food and other waste must not accumulate in food rooms any more than is necessary for the proper functioning of the food business. Containers for waste must be kept in good condition and easy to clean and disinfect. Waste storage containers should be lidded to keep out pests. The waste storage area must be designed so that it can be easily cleaned and prevent pests gaining access. There should be arrangements for the frequent removal of refuse and the area should be kept clean.

*Chapter VII: Water supply*

**F9045**   There must be an adequate supply of potable (drinking) water. Ice must be made from potable water.

*Chapter VIII: Personal hygiene*

**F9046**   Anyone who works in a food handling area must maintain a high degree of personal cleanliness. The way in which they work must also be clean and hygienic. Food handlers must wear clean and, where appropriate, protective clothes. Anyone whose work involves handling food should:

- follow good personal hygiene practices;

- wash their hands routinely when handling food;

- never smoke in food handling areas;

- be excluded from food handling if carrying an infection that may be transmitted through food if there is a risk of contamination of the food.

In this case, the obligation on the business proprietor to take action is supplemented by an obligation on every employee contained within the *Food Safety (General Food Hygiene) Regulations 1995 (SI 1995 No 1763), Reg 5*. Personnel working in food handling areas are obliged to report any illness (like diarrhoea or vomiting, infected wounds, skin infections) immediately to the proprietor of the business. If a manager receives such notification he or she may have to exclude them from food handling areas. Such action should be taken urgently. If there is any doubt about the need to exclude, it is best to seek urgent medical advice or consult the local council EHO.

These personal hygiene provisions are wide ranging. They apply not only to food handlers, but anyone working in food handling areas. There have been well-documented cases of cleaners contaminating working surfaces or equipment with pathogens that are later transmitted to food.

*Chapter IX: Preventing food contamination*

**F9047**   Food and ingredients must be protected against contamination that may make them unfit for human consumption or a health hazard. For example, raw poultry must not be allowed to contaminate ready-to-eat foods.

*Chapter X: Training and supervising food handlers*

**F9048**   Whereas nine of the chapters deal with structural and physical pre-requisites, the final chapter deals with the higher-level issue of competence of personnel to do their job. This provision is more subtle than it is often given credit for. Prior to the publication of the Regulations, many training providers hoped that the legislation would simply prescribe certain levels of food hygiene training, ideally with a requirement for regular refresher courses. The provision is still subject to occasional criticism that it is too lenient on training requirements. In fact the provision recognises that there is more to it than that. It refers to three complementary elements, instruction, training and supervision.

Food handlers must receive proper supervision, instruction and/or training in food hygiene that is commensurate with their work. Of course they may need training in the principles of food hygiene. They must also be instructed on how to do their particular jobs properly and supervised to make sure that they follow instructions. The requirements will differ according to the nature of the business and the job of the individual staff member.

*Industry guides to good hygiene practice*

F9049    The *Food Safety (General Food Hygiene) Regulations 1995 (SI 1995 No 1763)* introduce a new concept of voluntary industry guides to good hygiene practice. These provide more detailed guidance on complying with the Regulations as they relate to specific industry sectors. They are usually produced by trade associations and recognised by the government (formerly the Department of Health latterly the FSA). Importantly, enforcement officers are obliged to have regard for them when examining how businesses are operating. The publication of a guide for the vending industry in 2001 brought the total number of guides published in the UK to eight since the publication of the Catering Guide in 1995. Sectors covered are:

- Vending.

- Catering.

- Retail.

- Baking.

- Wholesale.

- Markets and Fairs.

- Fresh Produce.

- Flour Milling.

## Food Safety (Temperature Control) Regulations 1995

F9050    Growth of pathogenic bacteria in food will significantly increase the risk of food poisoning. Indeed growth of any micro-organisms in food will compromise its wholesomeness. Temperature controls at certain food holding or processing steps will be CCPs in most HACCP plans. The importance of good control of food temperatures is emphasised by the fact that some controls are prescribed in regulations.

The *Food Safety (Temperature Control) Regulations 1995 (SI 1995 No 2200)* require food business proprietors to observe certain temperatures during the holding of food if this is necessary to prevent a risk to health. The Regulations only cover safety issues. For example hard cheese that may go mouldy if kept at room temperature is not covered because it would not support the growth of pathogens. These Regulations impact on similar businesses to those covered by the General Food Hygiene Regulations. Again, the vertical regulations set more specific rules, including temperature controls, for most foods of animal origin during processing and handling prior to the retail or catering outlet.

The Temperature Control Regulations make a fairly simple issue extraordinarily complex. We do not even have the same regulations in Scotland as the rest of the UK. (The EU Directive 93/43 does not recommend specific temperature controls and for the time being, decisions are made nationally.)

The following table contains a very brief summary of the requirements. The Regulations prescribe temperatures for some but not all steps. The Regulations in

Scotland also have similar gaps but not always at the same step. The industry guides, particularly the catering guide, fill in the gaps with recommendations of good practice.

|  | *Rest of the UK* | *Scotland* | *Recommended good practice targets* |
|---|---|---|---|
| Chill store | 8°C maximum | Not specified | 5°C |
| Cook | Not specified | Not specified | 70°C for 2 minutes or 75°C minimum |
| Hot hold | 63°C | 63°C | 63°C min |
| Cool | Not specified | Not specified | Below 10°C in 4 hours |
| Reheat | Not specified | 82°C | 70°C for 2 minutes or 75°C minimum |

Frozen storage is not covered by the General Food Hygiene Regulations and will not be a food safety CCP. Other legislation and best practice indicate a frozen storage temperature of –18°C

*Relationship between time and temperature*

F9051    Almost invariably the control of micro-organisms in food depends upon a combination of time and temperature. Temperature alone does not have an absolute effect. For example, destruction of micro-organisms can be effected in a very short time (seconds) at temperatures above 100°C or in a couple of minutes at around 70°C. A similar thermal destruction can be achieved even at temperatures as low as 60°C but exposure for around 45 minutes will be necessary. Similarly in chilled storage, food can remain safe and wholesome for many days if the temperature can be kept close to freezing point at around –1°C. However, it will have a much shorter life at higher storage temperatures around 10°C.

Of course one should note that the above remarks are generalisations and not all micro-organisms will react in the same way. Some organisms show greater resistance to heating; some are able to grow at storage temperatures as low as 3°C whereas others will show little growth a temperatures cooler than 15°C. But the general point that control is a function of time and temperature remains true.

Broadly speaking, this relationship is recognised in the Regulations. In some instances, time is actually prescribed in the temperature control regulations. An example is the so called 'four hour rule' for display of food at a temperature warmer than 8°C. In other cases times are implicit in the temperature control regulations, such as the necessity to cool food rapidly after heating. Actual parameters for compliance are outlined in the industry guides. For other situations there is an inter-relationship with other regulations. For example the storage life of pre-packed, microbiologically perishable food must be controlled under requirements of the Food Labelling Regulations. It must be labelled with an indication of its 'minimum durability' that takes the form of a 'use by' date. There is an onus on the producer to ascertain a safe shelf life having regard for the nature of the food and its likely storage conditions and to use this as the basis of the date mark.

*Temperature controls – England and Wales*

F9052    The regulations governing temperature controls were largely new provisions introduced in the early 1990s and refined during the first half of the decade culminating
in the *Food Safety (Temperature Control) Regulations 1995 (SI 1995 No 2200)*. The
structure of the Regulations in England and Wales has the main requirement that
chilled storage should be at 8°C or cooler, followed by a series of exemptions for
particular circumstances. The general requirement under *Reg 10* of these Regulations comes from the EU directive and it is generally assumed that compliance with
the other more specific regulations will deliver compliance with *Reg 10*. The
requirements are outlined in the table below.

| Provision within the Temperature Control Regulations | Requirement | Comment |
| --- | --- | --- |
| Reg 10 | A general requirement for all food to be kept under temperature control if that is needed to keep it safe. | Applies to raw materials and foods in preparation. Limited periods outside temperature control are permitted for certain practicalities. No temperature is specified. A combination of time and temperature will be important. |
| *Reg 4* | Chilled food must be kept at 8°C or cooler. | Applies only to foods that would become unsafe. |
| *Reg 5* | Various cold foods are exempt: shelf stable, canned foods, raw materials, cheeses during ripening, and others where there is no risk to health. | Soft cheeses once ripe, and perishable food from opened cans must be kept below 8°C. |
| *Reg 6* | Manufacturers may recommend higher storage temperature/shorter storage life (provided that safety is verified). | Caterers must use the food within the 'use by' date indicated. |
| *Reg 7(1)* | Cold food on display or for service can be warmer than 8°C. A maximum of 4 hours is allowed. | Any item of food can be displayed outside temperature control only once. The burden of proof is on the caterer. |

| Provision within the Temperature Control Regulations | Requirement | Comment |
|---|---|---|
| *Reg 7(2)* | Tolerances outside of temperature control are also allowed during transfer or preparation of food, and defrost or breakdown of equipment. | No time/temperature limits specified. Both should be minimized consistently with food safety. |
| *Regs 8, 9* | Hot food should be kept at 63°C or hotter. | Food may be kept at a temperature cooler than 63°C for maximum 2 hours if it is for service or on display. |
| *Reg 11* | Food must be cooled quickly after heating or preparation. | No limits are specified – must be consistent with food safety. |

Note that all temperatures specified are food temperatures not the air temperature of refrigerators, vehicles or hot cabinets.

*Chilled storage and foods included in the scope of the regulations*

**F9053**     The principal rule for chilled storage is contained within the *Food Safety (Temperature Control) Regulations 1995 (SI 1995 No 2200), Reg 4(1)*: 'Subject to paragraph (2) and regulation 5, no person shall keep any food — (a) which is likely to support the growth of pathogenic micro-organisms or the formation of toxins; and (b) with respect to which any commercial operation is being carried out, at or in food premises at a temperature above 8 degrees C.'

*Regulation 4(1)* only applies to food that will support the growth of pathogenic micro-organisms. Such foods must be kept at 8°C or cooler. The types of food that will be subject to temperature control are indicated in the following table.

It is often good practice to keep foods at temperatures cooler than 8°C either to preserve quality or to allow longer-term storage and to allow a margin of error below the legal standard. Industry guides suggest that one should aim for a target food temperature of 5°C. This is especially important in cabinet fridges. There can be significant temperature rises during frequent door opening.

| Food type | Comment |
|---|---|
| Cooked meats and fish, meat and fish products. | Includes prepared meals, meat pies, pates, potted meats, quiches and similar dishes based on fish. |
| Cooked meats in cans that have been pasteurised rather than fully sterilised. | Typically large catering packs of ham or cured shoulder. |

| *Food type* | *Comment* |
|---|---|
| Cooked vegetable dishes. | Includes cereals, rice and pulses. Some cooked vegetables or dessert recipes may have sufficiently high sugar content* (possibly combined with other factors like acidity) to prevent the growth of pathogenic bacteria. These will not be subject to mandatory temperature control. |
| Any cooked dish containing egg or cheese. | Includes flans, pastries etc. |
| Prepared salads and dressings. | Includes mayonnaise and prepared salads with mayonnaise or any other style of dressing. Some salads or dressings may have a formulation (especially the level of acidity**) that is adequate to prevent growth of pathogens. |
| Soft cheeses/mould ripened cheeses (after ripening). | Cheeses will include Camembert, Brie, Stilton, Roquefort, Danish Blue and any similar style of cheese. |
| Smoked or cured fish, and raw scombroid fish. | For example smoked salmon, smoked trout, smoked mackerel etc. Also raw tuna, mackerel and other scombroid fish. |
| Any sandwiches whose fillings include any of the foods listed in this Table. | |
| Low acid** desserts and cream products. | Includes dairy desserts, fromage frais and cream cakes. Some artificial cream may be 'ambient stable' due to low water activity and/or high sugar. Any product that does not support the growth of pathogenic micro-organisms does not have to be kept below 8°C. It may be necessary to get clarification from suppliers. |
| Fresh pasta and uncooked or partly cooked pasta and dough products. | Includes unbaked pies and sausage rolls, unbaked pizzas and fresh pasta. |
| Smoked or cured meats which are not ambient stable. | Salami, parma hams and other fermented meats will not be subject to temperature controls if they are ambient shelf stable. |

*Technically Aw (water activity) is the key criterion.

**Technically, pH 4.5 (or more acid) is the critical limit.

*Mail order foods*

**F9054**  There is a controversial exemption from the specific 8°C requirement if the food is being conveyed by post or by a private or common carrier to the ultimate consumer.

The sender still has a responsibility for the safety of the food but the specific 8°C temperature does not apply. This exemption for mail order foods cannot apply to supplies to caterers or retailers neither of whom meet the definition of 'ultimate consumers'.

*Short 'shelf life' products*

F9055   Some perishable foods are allowed to be kept at ambient temperatures for the duration of their shelf life with no risk to health. This may be because they are intended to be kept for only very short periods (sandwiches). Bakery products like fresh pies, pasties, custard tarts can also be kept without refrigeration for limited periods.

*Canned foods and similar*

F9056   One does not have to keep sterilised cans or similar packs under temperature control until the hermetically sealed pack is opened. After that perishable food must be kept chilled (for example corned beef, beans, canned fish, and dairy products). Some canned meats are not fully sterilised (e.g. large catering packs of ham or pork shoulder). They must be kept chilled even before the can is opened.

High acid canned or preserved foods (some fruit, tomatoes, etc.) do not have to be kept chilled after opening for safety reasons. However it is advisable to remove these from the can for chilled storage after opening. It will inhibit mould growth and avoid any chemical reaction with the metal can body.

*Raw food for further processing*

F9057   Raw food for further processing does not have to be kept at 8°C or cooler. Thus it is not against the Regulations to keep raw meat, poultry and fish out of the fridge. Of course for quality reasons it is best kept in the fridge. Processed foods must be kept at 8°C or cooler even if they are to be heated again.

Raw meat or fish that is intended to be eaten without further processing (for example beef for steak tartare, or fish for sushi) will not be exempted by this provision. It must be kept chilled. Raw scombroid fish (tuna, mackerel, etc.) will also not be exempted by this provision. The 'scombrotoxin' is heat stable and processing will not render contaminated food fit for consumption. Scombroid fish must be kept at 8°C or cooler.

*Variations from 8°C storage*

F9058   The *Food Safety (Temperature Control) Regulations 1995 (SI 1995 No 2200), Reg 4(1)*, allow the producer of a food to recommend that it can be kept safely at a temperature above 8°C. He must label the food clearly with the recommended storage temperature and the safe shelf life at that temperature. He must also have good scientific evidence that the food is safe at that temperature. Little use has been made of this provision.

*The 4-hour rule*

F9059   The '4-hour rule' allows cold food to be kept above 8°C when it is on display. This is crucial. Without it you could not serve food on a buffet without refrigeration. The time that the food is on display must be controlled. The maximum time allowed is four hours. Most catering operations and many retailers depend upon this exemption for at least some of their operation.

Only one such period of display is allowed no matter how short. For example, if you put a dish of food on display for 1 hour at the end of a service period, you cannot have another 3 hours above 8°C at the next service. Food uneaten at the end of a display period does not have to be discarded provided that it is still fit for consumption. The food must be cooled to 8°C or cooler and kept at that temperature until it can be used safely.

The burden of proof is on the business. One must be able to demonstrate that the time limit is observed. Good management of food displays will be important. The amount of food on display must be kept to a minimum consistent with the pattern of trade.

There needs to be systems to help keep to the time limit and to demonstrate that they are being adhered to. These may include the labelling of dishes to indicate when they went onto display. Avoid topping-up of bulk displays of food. Food at the bottom of the dish will remain on display for much longer than 4 hours if topping-up is allowed.

*Exemptions for other contingencies*

F9060   The Regulations allow for the fact that food may rise above 8°C for limited periods of time in unavoidable circumstances such as:

● transfers to or from vehicles;

● during handling or preparation;

● during defrost of equipment;

● during temporary breakdown of equipment.

The Regulations do not put specific figures on the length of time allowed or how warm the food might become. This tolerance is allowed as a defence and the burden of proof will be on the business to show that:

● the food was unavoidably above 8°C for one of the reasons allowed;

● that it was above 8°C for only a limited period;

● that the break in temperature control was consistent with food safety.

The acceptable limits will obviously depend upon the combination of time and temperature. Under normal circumstances, a single period of up to two hours is unlikely to be questioned.

All transfers of food must be organised so that exposure to warm ambient temperatures is reduced and that rises in food temperature are kept to a minimum. For example, put deliveries away quickly and move chilled food first, then frozen, then grocery

If food from a cash and carry warehouse is being collected, insulated bags or boxes should be used for any chilled foods to which the Regulations apply. The chilled food should be taken straight back to the outlet and quickly put them into chilled storage.

Equipment breakdown should be avoided by ensuring planned and regular maintenance.

*Hot food*

F9061    Hot food must be kept at 63°C or hotter if this is necessary for safety. This will apply to the same types of food described in the earlier table (see F9053 above). For example the rule does not apply to hot bread or doughnuts.

Food must be kept at 63°C or hotter, whether:

● it is in the kitchen or bakery awaiting service or dispatch;

● or in transit to a serving point, no matter how near or far;

● or actually on display in the serving area.

Some tolerance or limited exemptions are allowed for practical handling reasons. As similar to the 4-hour rule for chilled food, hot food can be kept for service or display at less than 63°C for one period of up to 2 hours.

Again one must be able to show that:

● the food was for service or on display for sale;

● it had not been kept for more than 2 hours;

● it had only had one such period.

Generally there should be less problems with meeting the 63°C target in hot display equipment than encountered in achieving 8°C in 'chilled' display units. Hot display units are not designed to heat or cook foods from cold. They should be used for holding only not heating.

*Cooling*

F9062    Food that becomes warmer than 8°C during processing must be cooled again to 8°C 'as quickly as possible'. In another of the more controversial aspects of the Regulations, no time and temperatures are specified. Over the years a wide variety of cooling times have been recommended by different sources. Cooling times as short as 1.5 hours are specified in UK Department of Health guidelines on cooking chilled foods and published in the early 1980s. Many EHOs have regarded this figure as definitive. More recent literature from the USA recommends a cooling time of exactly ten times that long. The UK industry guides recommend that cooling between 60°C and 10°C should be accomplished in a maximum of 4 hours. Recent UK research suggests that this may be conservative.

Note that rapid cooling is not only necessary for food that has been heated. Food that has become warm during processing must also be returned to chilled storage below 8°C as quickly as possible after the process is completed.

*Temperature controls – Scotland*

F9063    The Scottish Regulations include at *Reg 16* of the *Food Safety (Temperature Control Regulations) 1995 (SI 1995 No 2200)* the same general requirement from the EU directive found at *Reg 10*. Otherwise the Scottish Regulations have remained largely unchanged for many years. Some would say that they are now anachronistic. No chilled storage temperature is specified, yet the 82°C requirement for re-heating pre-cooked food appears unnecessarily high, unsupported by the science and potentially detrimental to the quality of many foods.

| Provision within the Temperature Control Regulations | Requirement | Comment |
|---|---|---|
| Reg 16 | A general requirement similar to that which applies to England and Wales under Reg 10 for all food to be kept under temperature control if that is needed to keep it safe. Additionally it includes the need for rapid cooling. | Applies to raw materials and foods in preparation. Limited periods outside temperature control are permitted for certain practicalities. No temperature is specified. A combination of time and temperature will be important. |
| *Reg 13* | Cold food must be kept in a cool place or refrigerator. | No temperature is specified. |
| *Reg 13* | Hot food must be kept at 63°C or hotter. | There are exemptions for food on display, during preparation, etc. |
| *Reg 14* | Food that is reheated must reach 82°C. | Exemption in place if 82°C is detrimental to food quality. |
| *Reg 15* | Gelatin must be boiled, or held at 71°C for at least 30 minutes. | Unused glaze must be chilled quickly and kept in a refrigerator. |

Again, note that all temperatures specified are food temperatures not the air temperature of refrigerators, vehicles or hot cabinets.

*Cool storage*

F9064    The *Food Safety (Temperature Control Regulations) 1995 (SI 1995 No 2200), Reg 13* will apply to any food that may support the growth of food poisoning organisms within the 'shelf life' for which the food will be kept.

The types of food that will be subject to the provision are the same as those that fall under *Reg 4* of the Regulations (applicable to England and Wales).

If cold, this food must be kept either in a refrigerator or a cool well-ventilated place. The Scottish Regulations do not specify a temperature but in practice, it is advisable to follow the same rules and recommendations that apply in the rest of the UK. In any case, the hazard analysis requirement of the General Food Hygiene Regulations does apply in Scotland, and one is obliged to establish controls at CCPs.

*Hot food*

F9065    The target for hot food is the same as England and Wales, 63°C or hotter.

*Cooling*

F9066    The Scottish Regulations demand rapid cooling and the requirement is considered to be identical to *Reg 11* of the Regulations (applicable to England and Wales).

*Exemptions during practical handling*

**F9067**    In certain circumstances food does not have to be kept cold or above 63°C:

- if it is undergoing preparation for sale;

- if it is exposed for sale or it has already been sold;

- if it is being cooled;

- if it is available to consumers for sale;

- if it is shelf stable.

Again these Regulations have remained unchanged for many years and are less detailed than those that apply in the rest of the UK.

*Reheating of food*

**F9068**    In Scotland only, food that has been heated and is being reheated must be raised to a temperature of 82°C or hotter. Fortunately this is qualified by a clause to say that this is not necessary if it is detrimental to the quality of the food. This should provide the opportunity for most businesses to reheat food to the more sensible, perfectly adequate and scientifically verified temperature of around 70°C.

*Gelatine*

**F9069**    Scotland also has specific rules about the use of gelatine:

1.    Immediately before it must be boiled it or held at at 71°C or hotter for at least 30 minutes

2.    Any left over gelatine must be discarded or cooled quickly and stored in a refrigerator or cool larder.

3.    Leftover gelatine must be pasteurised again before re-use, using either of the treatments described in point 1 above.

# Food Safety Manual – food safety policy and procedures

**F9070**    Both the *Food Safety Act 1990* and the Regulations made under it provide an obligation on proprietors of food businesses to operate within the law. In addition, the *Food Safety Act 1990, s 21* provides the defence of 'due diligence'. One way for a business to demonstrate its commitment to operating safely and within the law is to document its management system, including the relevant policies and procedures. This documentation may form a significant part of a due diligence defence. The policy and procedures will illustrate the precautions that should be taken by the business and its staff in their day-to-day operations. The procedures will normally require the keeping of various records, and these will in turn help to demonstrate that the '*reasonable precautions*' are being followed '*with all due diligence*'.

It is often convenient to keep these policies and procedures together in a 'Food Safety Manual'. The following provides a brief outline of the contents of a Food Safety Manual for a typical food business.

## Policy and procedures

**F9071**    The 'policy' will be a statement of intent by the business. A Food Safety Manual may begin with a fairly broad statement of policy. Later there may be more specific policy statements linked to particular outcomes, for example a policy to take all reasonable precautions to minimise the contamination of food with foreign material.

Procedures will detail the ways in which the business intends to put the policies into effect. A typical layout of any 'Quality Manual' is to begin each section or subject heading with a statement of policy, and to follow that with the procedures intended to deliver it. Procedures are often referred to by the acronym SOPs – 'Standard Operating Procedures'.

### General policy and organisation

**F9072**    A Food Safety Manual would normally begin with a top-level statement of the business's policy with regard to food safety. Recognising the wider scope of 'food safety' within the meaning of the 1990 Act, it may be advisable to add a statement about commitment to true and accurate labelling of food and adherence to compositional requirements.

The statement should be signed by the proprietor of the business, who is the person with ultimate legal responsibility. In a large group this may be the group chief executive.

The early part of the manual should also illustrate the organisational structures and management hierarchy that has responsibility for implementing the policy and procedures. There may be technical support services, (e.g. pest control, testing laboratories) either from inside or outside the business. Their roles and responsibilities can also be identified within the organisational structures in this part of the manual.

### Hazard Analysis (HACCP)

**F9073**    Today, any food safety policy must be centred on a hazard analysis approach. The Food Safety Manual should include a policy statement to that effect. This will be followed by procedures to describe how you will go about the hazard analysis and record its outcomes and implementation.

#### Pre-requisites to Hazard Analysis

**F9074**    A modern approach to HACCP will focus on a very small number of process steps that are truly critical to the safety of the food. These are the steps that *must* be controlled (and monitored) to ensure that the food is safe. But this control must operate against a background of good hygiene practice. The so-called 'pre-requisites' to HACCP must all be in place. The Food Safety Manual should include policies and procedures for all of these.

- Design – structures and layout

  The Food Safety Manual should include a policy that the design, structure and layout will promote hygienic operation. The procedures should detail specific arrangements to achieve that. This section should also cover points such as the services, especially water and ventilation; provision for washing of hands, equipment and food; and removal of waste.

- Equipment specification

  The policy should be that the business will only acquire and use equipment that is fit for its purpose. The focus is often on cleanability alone. However in many cases, the ability of equipment to do the job can be even more important. For example, can refrigeration equipment keep food at a specified temperature in operational conditions?

- Maintenance

  A policy for maintenance should address both the premises in general and the equipment. Procedures should detail the arrangements for routine and emergency maintenance. There should be a record of any maintenance whether routine or emergency.

- Cleaning and disinfection

  Detailed cleaning schedules for sections of the building or particular pieces of equipment should be available. Cleaning should be recorded.

- Pest Control

  Employing a pest control contractor is only one small part of the pest control procedures. The prevention of pest access, the integrity of pest proofing, cleaning and the need for vigilance should also be included in the procedures. Records would normally include any sightings of or evidence of pests, positions of bait stations, visits by the contractor together with observations and action taken, and even details such as the changing of UV tubes on Electronic Flying Insect Killers.

- Personal hygiene

  The business should have a very clear policy on personal hygiene. The arrangements will include a very clear statement of the dress code and personal hygiene requirements for all staff working in or passing through food areas. There must also be very particular policies and procedures to deal with staff suffering illness that may potentially be foodborne.

- Food purchasing

  It may be easy to state a policy that the business should purchase only from reputable suppliers. It may be more difficult to deliver such a policy, especially for smaller businesses that do not have the resources to inspect their suppliers. One may be able to rely on third party inspection systems that have developed during the late 1990s; especially those operated by accredited inspection or certification bodies.

  Supply specifications may also be drafted. Such specifications will usually cover food 'quality' in its broadest sense. They are the ideal route through which to state your food safety conditions such as delivery temperature, shelf life remaining after delivery, packaging and so on.

- Storage

  Most businesses will have documented procedures for the storage of various categories of food as well as for stock checks to ensure proper storage temperature and stock rotation.

- Food handling and preparation

  The general policy should be to manage all steps in food handling and preparation so as to minimise contamination with any hazardous material or pathogenic micro-organisms. And there should be precautions to minimise the opportunities for growth of any bugs that might get into the food. The procedures will be unique to the business, its particular range of foods and preparation methods.

- Foreign material

  You should have a policy to take all precautions to minimise the risk of foreign material contamination including chemical hazards such as cleaning materials. In general terms, procedures will cover three points:

  (*a*)   Excluding or controlling potential sources of contamination.

  (*b*)   Protecting food from contamination.

  (*c*)   Taking any complaints seriously, tracking down what caused them and stopping them from happening again.

### *Allergy (Anaphylaxis)*

F9075   A responsible business will have a policy to protect susceptible customers from exposure to foods to which they may be allergic. In general terms procedures will rely upon:

(*a*)   Awareness amongst staff of the types of food that may cause reaction.

(*b*)   Labelling of the foods that include such ingredients.

(*c*)   Careful use of these ingredients in the kitchen to avoid 'cross-contamination' to other dishes.

(*d*)   An ability to supply reliable information about all ingredients on request from guests.

### *Vegetarians and other dietary preferences*

F9076   Similarly, most food businesses today recognise the need to cater for guests with particular dietary preferences, notably vegetarians. You should have a policy to be able to supply vegetarian dishes properly formulated and accurately labelled.

### *Consumer concerns*

F9077   From time to time particular issues will come to the forefront of consumer consciousness. For example, the irradiation of food, genetically modified ingredients or animal welfare issues such as veal production, foie gras and intensive rearing of poultry. The Food Safety Manual could include a statement of the policy on whichever of these issues that one thinks might be relevant. One would also need procedures to deliver them.

### *Labelling and composition of foods and 'fair-trading'*

F9078   In view of the fact that the *Food Safety Act 1990* deals not only with health and hygiene one may also wish to include policies and procedures on fair-trade topics such as food composition and labelling.

### *Product recall*

F9079   Businesses involved in central production and distribution of food that will have several days 'shelf life' if not more should have contingency plans for product recall. Do you label the product in such a way that you can identify batches? Do you have records of where it might have been delivered?

*Complaints*

F9080     Complaints are an important source of information. A business should have a policy and procedures to deal with them. These will normally include keeping a record of every complaint and making every attempt to track down its cause.

*Training, instruction and supervision*

F9081     Cutting across all of the other policies and procedures will be a policy on staff training, instruction and supervision. Typically a business will keep a personal training record for all members of staff.

**Summary**

F9082     Modern businesses recognise the value of a properly documented management system. A Food Safety Manual can provide the focus of such a system. The design of a Food Safety Manual must be a fine balance between conflicting objectives. On the one hand, it must be reasonably comprehensive if it is to stand up as part of a 'due diligence' defence. On the other hand, it must be sufficiently concise to be usable as an effective working tool within the business.

# Gas Safety

## Introduction

G1001 Not surprisingly, explosions caused by escaping gas have been responsible for large-scale damage to property and considerable personal injury, including death. Although escape of metered gas or gas in bulk holders might possibly have attracted civil liability under the rule in *Rylands v Fletcher* (see further F5054 FIRE AND FIRE PRECAUTIONS), statutory authority to perform a public utility (i.e. supply gas) used to constitute a defence in such proceedings, coupled with the fact that negligence had to be proved in order to establish liability for personal injury (*Read v J Lyons & Co Ltd [1947] AC 156*). This situation has now changed in favour of imposition of strict product liability for injury/damage caused by escape of gas and incomplete or inefficient combustion causing carbon monoxide poisoning.

According to research undertaken by the Consumer's Association, over half of the appliances surveyed in dwellings had not been serviced in accordance with the requirements of the Gas Safety Regulations. As some well-publicised court cases have demonstrated, landlords and those they employ to deal with gas installations face heavy fines and possibly imprisonment for breach of the regulations (see G1026 BELOW).

Changes have also been made to the gas industry itself, stemming from the Government's policy of creating competition in the gas supply field. These changes have resulted in the introduction of new and revised legislation, namely:

- *Gas Act 1986*

  This has been considerably modified and extended by the *Gas Act 1995*.

- *Gas Safety (Installation and Use) Regulations 1998 (SI 1998 No 2451)*

  These Regulations were made under the authority of the *Health and Safety at Work etc. Act 1974*.

- *Gas Safety (Management) Regulations 1996 (SI 1996 No 551)*

  These Regulations were made under the authority of the *Health and Safety at Work etc. Act 1974*.

- *Pipelines Safety Regulations 1996 (SI 1996 No 825)*

  These Regulations were made under the authority of the *Health and Safety at Work etc. Act 1974*.

- *Gas Safety (Rights of Entry) Regulations 1996 (SI 1996 No 2535)*

  These Regulations were made under the authority of the *Gas Act 1986* (as amended).

In practice, many of the legislative changes were introduced for the purposes of increasing responsibilities for safety of gas processors, gas transporters and gas suppliers and are therefore outside the scope of this handbook. This chapter concentrates on the legislation which deals with the knowledge required by landlords, managing agents, health and safety managers, employers and other responsible persons who must ensure that gas appliances and fittings are installed safely and checked by a competent person every twelve months.

It should be noted that although the legislation discussed in this chapter is current at the date of publication, the Health and Safety Executive (HSE) is at present considering changes that could affect the *Gas Act 1986 (as amended)* and some of the regulations referred to in this section. The proposed changes are outlined in a HSE document entitled '*Fundamental Review of Gas Safety Regime Proposals for Change*', which is the result of consultation with interested parties throughout the gas industry.

Gas is defined in the *Gas Act 1986* (as amended) and the *Gas Safety (Installation and Use) Regulations 1998 (SI 1998 No 2451)* to include methane, ethane, propane, butane, hydrogen and carbon monoxide mixtures of any two or more of these gases together with inert gases or other non-flammable gases; or combustible mixtures of one or more of these gases and air. However, the definition does not include gas consisting wholly or mainly of hydrogen when used in non-domestic premises.

# Gas supply – the Gas Act 1986, as amended

G1002    The *Gas Act 1986* (as amended) requires the Secretary of State for the Environment to establish a Gas Consumers' Council and appoint an officer – the Director General of Gas Supply – to perform the functions relating to the supply of gas as set out in Part I of the Act.

As far as safety in the supply of gas is concerned, the Secretary of State and the Director each have a principal duty to exercise the functions assigned to them under Part I for the protection of the public from dangers arising from the conveyance or from the use of gas conveyed through pipes.

The following persons are defined in the *Gas Act 1986* as having duties and responsibilities in respect of the safe supply of gas:

### (a) *Domestic customer*

A domestic customer is a person who is supplied by a gas supplier with gas conveyed to particular premises at a rate which is reasonably expected not to exceed 2,500 therms a year.

### (b) *Owner*

In relation to any premises or other property, 'owner' includes a lessee, and cognate expressions are construed accordingly.

### (c) *Relevant authority*

— in relation to dangers arising from the conveyance of gas by a public gas transporter, or from the use of gas conveyed by such a transporter, 'relevant authority' means that transporter; and

— in relation to dangers arising from the conveyance of gas by a person other than a public gas transporter, or from the use of gas conveyed by such a person, 'relevant authority' means the Secretary of State for the Environment.

With regard to safety, the *Gas Act 1986* (as amended) provides for:

— licensing and general duties [*Gas Act 1986, ss 4A, 7–10 and 23*];

— security [*Gas Act 1986, s 11*];

— safety regulations regarding rights of entry for inspection of connected systems and equipment and the making safe and investigation of gas escapes [*Gas Act 1986, ss 18 and 18A*];

— pipeline capacity [*Gas Act 1986, ss 21, 22, 22A*];

— standards of performance [*Gas Act 1986, s 33* as amended by the *Competition and Service (Utilities) Act 1992*].

# Gas supply management – the Gas Safety (Management) Regulations 1996 (SI 1996 No 551)

G1003    Principally, the *Gas Safety (Management) Regulations 1996 (SI 1996 No 551)* require an appointed person – the 'network emergency co-ordinator' – to prepare a safety case for submission to and acceptance by HSE before a gas supplier can convey gas in a specified gas network [*SI 1996 No 551, Reg 3*].

## The safety case

G1004    The safety case document must contain:

— the name and address of the person preparing the safety case (the duty holder);

— a description of the operation intended to be undertaken by the duty holder;

— a general description of the plant, premises and interconnecting pipes;

— technical specifications;

— operation and maintenance procedures;

— a statement of the significant findings of the risk assessment carried out pursuant to the *Management of Health and Safety at Work Regulations 1999 (SI 1999 No 3242), Reg 3*;

— particulars to demonstrate the adequacy of the duty holder's management system to ensure the health and safety of his employees and of others (in respect of matters within his control);

— particulars to demonstrate adequacy in the dissemination of safety information;

— particulars to demonstrate the adequacy of audit and reporting arrangements;

— particulars to demonstrate the adequacy of arrangements for compliance with the duty of co-operation [*Gas Safety (Management) Regulations 1996 (SI 1996 No 551), Reg 6*];

— particulars to demonstrate the adequacy of arrangements for dealing with gas escapes and investigation [*Gas Safety (Management) Regulations 1996 (SI 1996 No 551), Reg 7*];

— particulars to demonstrate compliance with the content and characteristics of the gas to be conveyed in the network [*Gas Safety (Management) Regulations 1996 (SI 1996 No 551), Reg 8*];

— particulars to demonstrate the adequacy of the arrangements to minimise the risk of supply emergency;

— particulars of the emergency procedures [*Gas Safety (Management) Regulations 1996 (SI 1996 No 551), Reg 3(1) and Sch 1*].

*Duties of compliance and co-operation*

G1005    The duty holder must ensure that the procedures and arrangements described in the safety case and any revision of it are followed. In addition, a duty of co-operation is placed upon specified persons including:

—    a person conveying gas in the network;

—    an emergency service provider;

—    the network emergency co-ordinator in relation to a person conveying gas;

—    a person conveying gas in pipes which are not part of a network;

—    the holder of a licence issued under the *Gas Act 1986, s 7*;

—    the person in control of a gas production or processing facility [*Gas Safety (Management) Regulations 1996 (SI 1996 No 551), Regs 5 and 6*].

The *Gas Safety (Management) Regulations 1996 (SI 1996 No 551), Reg 7* deals with the duties and responsibilities of gas suppliers, gas transporters and 'responsible persons' regarding actions to be taken in the event of gas escape incidents. All incidents must be investigated including those resulting in an accumulation of carbon monoxide gas from incomplete combustion of a gas fitting.

Anyone discovering or suspecting a gas leak must notify British Gas plc immediately by telephone. British Gas are obliged to provide a continuously manned telephone service in Great Britain. The person appointed 'responsible person' for the premises must take all reasonable steps to shut off the gas supply.

The reporting of gas incidents to the HSE is laid down in the *Reporting of Injuries, Diseases and Dangerous Occurrences Regulations 1995 (SI 1995 No 3163) (RIDDOR)* in conjunction with HSE Form F2508G.

For further information regarding compliance with these Regulations see the HSE publication L80: '*A guide to the Gas Safety (Management) Regulations 1996*' (ISBN 0 7176 1159 0).

# Rights of entry – the Gas Safety (Rights of Entry) Regulations 1996 (SI 1996 No 2535)

G1006    Where an officer authorised by a public gas transporter has reasonable cause to suspect an escape of gas into or from premises supplied with gas, he is empowered to enter the premises and to take any steps necessary to avert danger to life or property. [*Gas Safety (Rights of Entry) Regulations (SI 1996 No 2535), Reg 4*].

### Inspection, testing and disconnection

G1007    On production of an authenticated document, an authorised person must be allowed to enter premises in which there is a service pipe connected to a gas main for the purpose of inspecting any gas fitting, flue or means of ventilation. Fittings and any part of a gas system may be disconnected and sealed off when it is necessary to do so for the purpose of averting danger to life or property.

It is incumbent on the authorised officer carrying out any disconnection or sealing off activities to give a written statement to the consumer within five days. The notice must contain:

—    the nature of the defect;

—    the nature of the danger in question;

— the grounds and the manner regarding the appeal procedure available to the consumer.

Prominent and conspicuous notices must also be affixed at appropriate points of the gas system regarding the consequences of any unauthorised reconnection to the gas supply. [*Gas Safety (Rights of Entry) Regulations (SI 1996 No 2535), Regs 5–8*].

*Prohibition of reconnection*

G1008    It is an offence for any person, except with the consent of the relevant authority, to reconnect any fitting or part of a gas system. This provision is qualified by the term 'knows or has reason to believe that it has been so disconnected'. [*Gas Safety (Rights of Entry) Regulations (SI 1996 No 2535, Reg 9*].

# Pipelines – the Pipelines Safety Regulations 1996 (SI 1996 No 825)

G1009    The *Pipelines Safety Regulations 1996 (SI 1996 No 825)* apply to all pipelines in Great Britain, both on and offshore, with the following exceptions:

— pipelines wholly within premises;

— pipelines contained wholly within caravan sites;

— pipelines used as part of a railway infrastructure;

— pipelines which convey water.

For the purposes of the Regulations, a pipeline for supplying gas to premises is deemed not to include anything downstream of an emergency control valve, that is, a valve for shutting off the supply of gas in an emergency, being a valve intended for use by a consumer of gas. [*SI 1996 No 825, Reg 3(4)*].

The Regulations complement the *Gas Safety (Management) Regulations 1996 (SI 1996 No 551)* and include:

— the definition of a pipeline [*SI 1996 No 825, Reg 3*];

— the general duties for all pipelines [*SI 1996 No 825, Regs 5–14*];

— the need for co-operation among pipeline operators [*SI 1996 No 825, Reg 17*];

— arrangements to prevent damage to pipelines [*SI 1996 No 825, Reg 16*];

— the description of a dangerous fluid [*SI 1996 No 825, Reg 18*];

— notification requirements [*SI 1996 No 825, Regs 20–22*];

— the major accident prevention document [*SI 1996 No 825, Reg 23*];

— the arrangements for emergency plans and procedures [*SI 1996 No 825, Regs 24–26*].

Generally, the Regulations place emphasis on 'major accidents' and the preparation of emergency plans by local authorities. As with the *Gas Safety (Management) Regulations 1996 (SI 1996 No 551)*, the detail relates to the specification and characteristics of gas and the design of the pipes to convey it. The design of gas service pipelines is specifically addressed in the HSE Approved Code of Practice, L81: '*Design, construction and installation of gas service pipes*' (1996) (ISBN 0 7176 1172 8). For further information on and guidance to the *Pipelines Safety Regulations 1996*, see the HSE Publication L82: '*A guide to the Pipelines Safety Regulations 1996*' (ISBN 0 7176 1182 5).

## Gas systems and appliances – the Gas Safety (Installation and Use) Regulations 1998 (SI 1998 No 2451)

G1010    The *Gas Safety (Installation and Use) Regulations 1998 (SI 1998 No 2451)* are supported by the HSE Approved Code of Practice and Guide, L56: '*The Gas Safety (Installation and Use) Regulations 1998*'.

The Regulations aim at protecting the gas-consuming public and cover natural gas, liquefied petroleum gas (LPG), landfill gas, coke, oven gas, and methane from coal mines when these products are 'used' by means of a gas appliance. Such appliances must be designed for use by a gas-consumer for heating, lighting and cooking. However, a gas appliance does not include a portable or mobile appliance supplied with gas from a cylinder except when such an appliance is under the control of an employer or self-employed person at a place of work. Similarly, the Regulations do not cover gas appliances in domestic premises where a tenant is entitled to remove such appliances from the premises.

In addition to the general provisions governing the safe installation of gas appliances and associated equipment by HSE approved and competent persons, the 1998 Regulations lay down specific duties for landlords.

Except in the case of 'escape of gas' (*SI 1998 No 2451, Reg 37*), and certain types of valves to control pressure fluctuations, the Regulations do not apply to the supply of gas when used in connection with:

—    bunsen burners in an educational establishment [*SI 1998 No 2451, Reg 2*];

—    mines or quarries [see *Mines and Quarries Act 1954*];

—    factories [see *Factories Act 1961 (FA61), s 175*] or electrical stations [*FA61, s 123*], institutions [*FA61, s 124*], docks [*FA61, s 125*] or ships [*FA61, s 126*];

—    agricultural premises;

—    temporary installations used in connection with any construction work within the meaning of the *Construction (Design and Management) Regulations 1994 (SI 1994 No 3140)*;

—    premises used for the testing of gas fittings; or

—    premises used for the treatment of sewage.

*Note*: The Regulations would apply in relation to the above premises (or parts of those premises) if used for domestic or residential purposes or as sleeping accommodation, but not to hired touring caravans. [*SI 1998 No 2451, Reg 2*].

Generally, gas must be used in order to come within the scope of the Regulations. Therefore, the venting of waste gas from coal mines and landfill sites is excepted unless the gas is collected and intended for use. Gas used as motive power or from grain drying is also not covered by the Regulations. Service pipes (that is, the pipes for distributing gas to premises from a distribution main and the outlet of the first emergency control downstream of the main) remain the property of the gas supplier or gas transporter. At least 24 hours' notice should be given to the relevant organisation before any work can be performed on a service pipe. [*L56, paras 2–11*].

'Work' in relation to a gas fitting is defined in the Regulations as including any of the following activities carried out by any person, whether an employee or not, that is to say:

(*a*)    installing or reconnecting the fitting;

(*b*)    maintaining, servicing, permanently adjusting, disconnecting, repairing, altering or renewing the fitting or purging it of air or gas;

(*c*)    where the fitting is not readily movable, changing its position; and

(*d*)    removing the fitting.

The Approved Code of Practice, L56: '*The Gas Safety (Installation and Use) Regulations 1998*', provides further guidance on the meaning of work and states that 'work' for the purposes of these Regulations also includes do-it-yourself activities, work undertaken for friends and work for which there is no expectation of reward or gain, such as charitable work. [*L56, para 12*].

## Duties and responsibilities

G1011    Duties are placed on a wide range of persons associated with domestic premises and on persons concerned with the supply of gas to those premises and to industrial premises which have accommodation facilities.

Most of the legal requirements are 'absolute', i.e. they are not qualified by 'as far as is practicable' or 'so far as is reasonably practicable'; in all cases the duty must be satisfied to avoid committing an offence. Persons affected by the Regulations include:

—    *individuals.* These include householders and other members of the general public;

—    *responsible person.* This is the occupier of the premises or, where there is no occupier or the occupier is away, the owner of the premises or any person with authority for the time being to take appropriate action in relation to any gas fittings;

—    *landlord.* In England and Wales the landlord is defined as follows:

(i)    where the relevant premises are occupied under a lease, the person for the time being entitled to the reversion expectant on that lease or who, apart from any statutory tenancy, would be entitled to possession of the premises; and

(ii)    where the relevant premises are occupied under a licence, the licensor, save where the licensor is himself a tenant in respect of those premises.

In Scotland, the landlord is the person for the time being entitled to the landlord's interest under a lease;

—    *tenant.* In England and Wales the tenant is defined as follows:

(i)    where the relevant premises are so occupied under a lease, the person for the time being entitled to the term of that lease; and

(ii)    where the relevant premises are so occupied under a licence, the licensee.

In Scotland, the tenant is the person for the time being entitled to the tenant's interest under a lease.

Duties are imposed on employers and the self-employed to ensure that all persons carrying out work in relation to gas fittings are competent to do so and are members of HSE approved organisations. [*Gas Safety (Installation and Use) Regulations 1998 (SI 1998 No 2451), Reg 3*].

Persons connected with work activities include:

— *supplier.* In relation to gas, a 'supplier' means:

  (i) a person who supplies gas to any premises through a primary meter; or

  (ii) a person who provides a supply of gas to a consumer by means of the filling or refilling of a storage container designed to be filled with gas at the place where it is connected for use, whether or not such container is or remains the property of the supplier; or

  (iii) a person who provides gas in refillable cylinders for use by a consumer whether or not such cylinders are filled, or refilled, directly by that person and whether or not such cylinders are or remain the property of that person.

  *Note:* A retailer is not a supplier when he sells a brand of gas other than his own.

— *transporter.* This is defined as meaning a person, other than a supplier, who conveys gas through a distribution main.

— *gas installer.* This is any person who installs, services, maintains, removes or repairs gas fittings whether he is an employee, self-employed or working on his own behalf (for example, a do-it-yourself activity).

## Escape of gas

**G1012**    It is the duty of the responsible person for the premises to take immediate action to shut off the gas supply to the affected appliance or fitting and notify the gas supplier (or the nominated gas emergency call-out office if different from the supplier). All reasonable steps must be taken to prevent further escapes of gas, and the gas supplier must stop the leak within twelve hours from the time of notification. This may entail cutting off the gas supply to the premises. [*Gas Safety (Installation and Use) Regulations 1998 (SI 1998 No 2451), Reg 37(1)–(3)*].

An escape of gas also includes an emission of carbon monoxide resulting from incomplete combustion in a gas fitting. However, the legal duties regarding the action to be taken by the gas supplier are limited to making safe and advising of the need for immediate action by a competent person to examine, and if necessary carry out repairs, to the faulty fitting or appliance. [*Gas Safety (Installation and Use) Regulations 1998 (SI 1998 No 2451), Reg 37(8)*].

## Competent persons and quality control

**G1013**    No work is permitted to be carried out on a gas fitting or a gas storage vessel except by a competent person. [*Gas Safety (Installation and Use) Regulations 1998 (SI 1998 No 2451), Reg 3(1)*].

Where work to a gas fitting is to any extent under their control – or is to be carried out at any place of work under their control – employers (and self-employed persons) must ensure that the person undertaking such work is registered with an HSE-approved body such as the Council of Registered Gas Installers (CORGI). [*Gas Safety (Installation and Use) Regulations 1998 (SI 1998 No 2451), Reg 4*].

A gas fitting must not be installed unless every part of it is of good construction and sound material, of adequate strength and size to secure safety and of a type appropriate for the gas with which it is to be used. [*Gas Safety (Installation and Use) Regulations 1998 (SI 1998 No 2451), Reg 5(1)*].

### Competent persons – qualifications and supervision

G1014   To achieve competence in safe installation, a person's training must include knowledge of purging, commissioning, testing, servicing, maintenance, repair, disconnection, modification and dismantling of gas systems, fittings and appliances. In addition, a sound knowledge of combustion and its technology is essential, including:

— properties of fuel gases,

— combustion,

— flame characteristics,

— control and measurement of fuel gases,

— gas pressure and flow,

— construction and operation of burners, and

— operation of flues and ventilation.

To reach the approval standard required by *Gas Safety (Installation and Use) Regulations 1998 (SI 1998 No 2451), Reg 3*, gas installers and gas fitters should know:

(*a*)   where/how gas pipes/fittings (including valves, meters, governors and gas appliances) should be safely installed;

(*b*)   how to site/install a gas system safely, with reference to safe ventilation and flues;

(*c*)   associated electrical work (e.g. appropriate electrical power supply circuits, that is, overcurrent and shock protection from electrical circuits, earthing and bonding);

(*d*)   electrical controls appropriate to the system being installed/maintained/repaired;

(*e*)   when/how to check the whole system adequately before it is commissioned;

(*f*)   how to commission the system, leaving it safe for use.

In addition, they should know how to recognise and test for conditions that might cause danger and what remedial action to take, as well as being able to show consumers how to use any equipment they have installed or modified, including how to shut off the gas supply in an emergency. They should also alert customers to the significance of inadequate ventilation and gas leaks and the need for regular maintenance/servicing.

To meet the criteria for HSE approval, individual gas fitting operatives must be assessed (or reassessed) by a certification body accredited by the United Kingdom Accreditation Service. The scheme requires every registered gas fitter or gas installer to possess a certificate, which consumers can ask to see.

### Materials and workmanship

G1015   It is incumbent on gas installers to acquaint themselves with the appropriate standards about gas fittings and to ensure that the fittings they use meet those standards. Most gas appliances are subject to the *Gas Appliances (Safety) Regulations 1992 (SI 1992 No 711)* and therefore should carry the CE mark or an appropriate European/British Standard.

It is an offence to carry out any work in relation to a gas fitting or gas storage vessel other than in accordance with the appropriate standards and in such a way as to prevent danger to any person. [*Gas Safety (Installation and Use) Regulations 1998 (SI 1998 No 2451), Reg 5(3)*]. Gas pipes and pipe fittings installed in a building must be metallic or of a type constructed in an encased metallic sheath and installed, so far as is reasonably practicable, to prevent the escape of gas into the building if the pipe should fail. Pipes or pipe fittings made from lead or lead alloy must not be used. [*Gas Safety (Installation and Use) Regulations 1998 (SI 1998 No 2451), Reg 5(2)*].

## General safety precautions

G1016    A general duty is imposed on all persons in connection with work associated with gas fittings to prevent a release of gas unless steps are taken which ensure the safety of any person [*SI 1998 No 2451, Reg 6(1)*].

The *Gas Safety (Installation and Use) Regulations 1998 (SI 1998 No 2451), Regs 6(2)–(6)* provide that the following precautions must be observed when carrying out work activities:

—    a gas fitting must not be left unattended unless every complete gasway has been sealed with an appropriate fitting;

—    a disconnected gas fitting must be sealed at every outlet;

—    smoking or the use of any source of ignition is prohibited near exposed gasways;

—    it is prohibited to use any source of ignition when searching for escapes of gas;

—    any work in relation to a gas fitting which might affect the tightness of the installation must be tested immediately for gas tightness.

With regard to gas storage vessels it is an offence for any person intentionally or recklessly to interfere with a vessel, or otherwise do anything which might affect it so that the subsequent use of that vessel might cause a danger to any person. [*SI 1998 No 2451), Reg 6(9)*]. In addition:

—    gas storage vessels must only be installed where they can be used, filled or refilled without causing danger to any person [*SI 1998 No 2451, Reg 6(7)*];

—    gas storage vessels, or appliances fuelled by LPG which have an automatic ignition device or a pilot light, must not be installed in cellars or basements [*SI 1998 No 2451, Reg 6(8)*];

—    methane gas must not be stored in domestic premises [*SI 1998 No 2451, Reg 6(10)*].

## Gas appliances

G1017    Precautions to be observed regarding gas appliances apply to everyone, not just gas installers. Generally, it is an offence for the occupier, owner or other responsible person to permit a gas appliance to be used if at any time he knows, or has reason to suspect, that the appliance is unsafe or that it cannot be used without constituting a danger to any person. [*SI 1998 No 2451, Reg 34*]. It is also an offence for anyone to carry out work in relation to a gas appliance which indicates that it no longer complies with approved safety standards. [*SI 1998 No 2451, Reg 26(7), (8)*]. The

*Gas Safety (Installation and Use) Regulations 1998 (SI 1998 No 2451), Reg 27* imposes similar safety requirements on persons who install or connect gas appliances to flues (see G1019 BELOW).

All gas appliances must be installed in a manner which permits ready access for operation, inspection and maintenance. [*SI 1998 No 2451, Reg 28*]. Manufacturer's instructions regarding the appliance must be left with the owner or occupier of the premises after its installation. [*SI 1998 No 2451, Reg 29*]. If the appliance is of the type where it is designed to operate in a suspended position, the installation pipework and other associated fittings must be constructed and installed as to be able to support the weight of the appliance safely. [*SI 1998 No 2451, Reg 31*].

During installation it is essential to ensure that all gas appliances are:

— connected (in the case of a flued domestic gas appliance) to a gas supply system by a permanently fixed rigid pipe [*SI 1998 No 2451, Reg 26(2)*];

— installed with a means of shutting off the supply of gas to the appliance unless it is not reasonably practicable to do so [*SI 1998 No 2451, Reg 26(6)*].

With the exception of the direct disconnection of the gas supply from a gas appliance, or the purging of gas or air which does not adversely affect the safety of that appliance, all commissioning operations and any other work performed on a gas appliance must be immediately examined to ensure the effectiveness of flues, and checks must be made with regard to:

— the supply of combustion air;

— the operating pressure or heat input; and

— the operation of the appliance to ensure its safe functioning.

[*SI 1998 No 2451, Reg 26(9)*].

Any defects must be rectified and reported to the appropriate responsible person as soon as is practicable; the defect must be reported to the appropriate gas supply organisation if a responsible person or the owner is not available. [*SI 1998 No 2451, Reg 26(9)*].

## Room-sealed appliances

G1018
A room-sealed appliance is an appliance whose combustion system is sealed from the room in which the appliance is located and which obtains air for combustion from a ventilated uninhabited space within the premises or directly from the open air outside the premises. The products of combustion must be vented safely to open air outside the premises.

A room-sealed appliance must be used in the following rooms:

— a bathroom or a shower room [*SI 1998 No 2451, Reg 30(1)*];

— in respect of a gas fire, gas space heater or gas water heater (including instantaneous water heaters) of more than 14 kilowatt gross heat input, in a room used or intended to be used as sleeping accommodation [*SI 1998 No 2451, Reg 30(2)*].

Gas heating appliances which have a gross heat input rating of less than 14 kilowatt or an instantaneous water heater may incorporate an alternative arrangement, i.e. an approved safety control designed to shut down the appliance before a build-up of dangerous combustion products can occur [*Reg 30(3)*].

For the purposes of the *Gas Safety (Installation and Use) Regulations 1998* (*SI 1998 No 2451*), *Reg 30(1)–(3)*, a room also includes:

— a cupboard or compartment within such a room; or

— a cupboard, compartment or space adjacent to such a room if there is an air vent from the cupboard, compartment or space into such a room [*SI 1998 No 2451, Reg 30(4)*].

### Flues and dampers

G1019   A flue is a passage for conveying the products of combustion from a gas appliance to the external atmosphere and includes the internal ducts of the appliance. Generally, it is prohibited to install a flue other than in a safe position, and, in the case of a power-operated flue, it must prevent the operation of the appliance should the draught fail [*Gas Safety (Installation and Use) Regulations 1998* (*SI 1998 No 2451*), *Reg 27(4), (5)*].

A flue must be suitable and in a proper condition for the operation of the appliance to which it is fitted. It is prohibited to install a flue pipe so that it enters a brick or masonry chimney in such a manner that the seal cannot be inspected. Similarly, an appliance must not be connected to a flue surrounded by an enclosure, unless the enclosure is sealed to prevent spillage into any room or internal space other than where the appliance is installed. [*Gas Safety (Installation and Use) Regulations 1998* (*SI 1998 No 2451*), *SI 1998 No 2451, Reg 27(1)–(3)*].

Manually operated flue dampers must not be fitted to serve a domestic gas appliance, and, similarly, it is prohibited to install a domestic gas appliance to a flue which incorporates a manually operated damper unless the damper is permanently fixed in the open position.

In the case of automatic dampers, the damper must be interlocked with the gas supply so that the appliance cannot be operated unless the damper is open. A check must be carried out immediately after installation to verify that the appliance and the damper can be operated safely together and without danger to any person.

### Gas fittings

G1020   Gas fittings are those parts of apparatus and appliances designed for domestic consumers of gas for heating, lighting, cooking or other approved purposes for which gas can be used (but not for the purpose of an industrial process occurring on industrial premises), namely:

— pipework;

— valves; and

— regulators, meters and associated fittings.

[*Gas Safety (Installation and Use) Regulations 1998* (*SI 1998 No 2451*), *SI 1998 No 2451, Reg 2*].

### Emergency controls

G1021   An emergency control is a valve for use by a consumer of gas for shutting off the supply of gas in an emergency. Emergency controls must be appropriately positioned with adequate access, and there must be a prominent notice or other indicator showing whether the control is open or shut. A notice must also be posted either next or near the emergency control indicating the procedure to be followed in the event of an escape of gas. [*Gas Safety (Installation and Use) Regulations 1998 (SI 1998 No 2451), SI 1998 No 2451, Reg 9*].

## Meters and regulators

G1022    The *Gas Safety (Installation and Use) Regulations 1998 (SI 1998 No 2451), Reg 12* provides that gas meters must be installed where they are readily accessible for inspection and maintenance. A meter must not be so placed as to adversely affect a means of escape or where there is a risk of damage to it from electrical apparatus. After installation, meters and other other associated fittings should be tested for gastightness and then purged so as to remove safely all air and gas other than the gas to be supplied. [*SI 1998 No 2451, Reg 12(6)*].

Meters must be of sound construction so that, in the event of fire, gas cannot escape from them and, where a meter is housed in an outdoor meter box, the box must be so designed as to prevent gas entering the premises or any cavity wall, i.e. any escaping gas must disperse to the air outside. Combustible materials must not be kept inside meter boxes. Where a meter is housed in a box or compound that includes a lock, a suitably labelled key must be provided to the consumer. [*SI 1998 No 2451, Reg 13*].

The *Gas Safety (Installation and Use) Regulations 1998 (SI 1998 No 2451), Regs 14–17* prescribe detailed precautions to be observed during the installation of the various types of meters. Most of these are for compliance by gas installers and should be included in work procedures. In essence, a meter must not be installed in service pipework unless:

(a)    there is a regulator to control the gas pressure [*SI 1998 No 2451, Reg 14(1)(a),(b)*];

(b)    a relief valve or seal is fitted which is capable of venting safely [*SI 1998 No 2451, Reg 14(1)(c)*]; and

(c)    the meter contains a prominent notice (in permanent form) specifying the procedure in the event of an escape of gas [*SI 1998 No 2451, Reg 15*].

Similar requirements are imposed regarding gas supplies from storage vessels and re-fillable cylinders. [*SI 1998 No 2451, Reg 14(2)–(4)*].

Where gas is supplied from a primary meter to a secondary meter, a line diagram must be provided and prominently displayed showing the configuration of all meters, installation pipework and emergency controls. It is incumbent on any person who changes the configuration to amend the diagram accordingly. [*SI 1998 No 2451, Reg 17*].

## Installation pipework

G1023    For the purposes of this chapter, 'installation pipework' covers any pipework for conveying gas to the premises from a distribution main, including pipework which connects meters or emergency control valves to a gas appliance, and any shut-off devices at the inlet to the appliance. The term 'service pipe' is used to describe any pipe connecting the distribution main with the outlet of the first emergency control downstream from the distribution main. Similarly, 'service pipework' are those pipes which supply gas from a gas storage vessel. All service pipes normally remain the property of the gas supplier or transporter and their permission must be obtained before any work associated with such pipes can be performed.

Installation pipework must not be installed:

—    where it cannot safely be used, having regard to other pipes, pipe supports, drains, sewers, cables, conduits and electrical apparatus;

—    in or through any floor or wall, or under any building, unless adequate protection is provided against failure caused by the movement of these structures;

—    in any shaft, duct or void, unless adequately ventilated;

—    in a way which would impair the structure of a building or impair the fire resistance of any part of its structure;

—    where deposit of liquid or solid matter is likely to occur, unless a suitable vessel for the reception and removal of the deposit is provided. (It should be noted that such clogging precautions do not normally need to be taken in respect of natural gas or LPG as these are 'dry' gases.)

[*Gas Safety (Installation and Use) Regulations 1998 (SI 1998 No 2451), Regs 18–21*].

Following work on installation pipework, the pipes must immediately be tested for gastightness and, if necessary, a protective coating applied; followed, where gas is being supplied, by satisfactory purging to remove all unnecessary air and gas. Except in the case of domestic premises, the parts of installation pipework which are accessible to inspection must be permanently marked as being gas pipes. [*Gas Safety (Installation and Use) Regulations 1998 (SI 1998 No 2451), Regs 22, 23*].

## Testing and maintenance requirements

G1024    According to the *Gas Safety (Installation and Use) Regulations 1998 (SI 1998 No 2451), Reg 33(1)*, a gas appliance must be tested when gas is supplied to premises to verify that it is gastight and to ensure that:

(*a*)    the appliance has been installed in accordance with the requirements of the 1998 Regulations;

(*b*)    the operating pressure is as recommended by the manufacturer;

(*c*)    the appliance has been installed with due regard to any manufacturer's instructions accompanying the appliance; and

(*d*)    all gas safety controls are in proper working order.

If adjustments are necessary in order to comply with (*a*) to (*d*) above, but cannot be carried out, the appliance must be disconnected or sealed off with an appropriate fitting. [*SI 1998 No 2451, Reg 33(2)*].

A general duty is imposed on employers and self-employed persons to ensure that any gas appliance, installation pipework or flue in places of work under their control is maintained in a safe condition so as to prevent risk of injury to any person. [*SI 1998 No 2451, Reg 35*].

A similar duty is imposed on landlords of premises occupied under a lease or a licence to ensure that relevant gas fittings and associated flues are maintained in a safe condition. [*SI 1998 No 2451, Reg 36(2)*]. A relevant gas fitting includes any gas appliance (other than an appliance which the tenant is entitled to remove from the premises) or installation (not service) pipework installed in such premises.

It is the responsibility of landlords to ensure that each gas appliance and flue is checked by a competent person (HSE approved person) at least every 12 months. [*SI 1998 No 2451, Reg 36(3)*]. Such safety checks shall include, but not be limited to, the following:

(*a*)    the effectiveness of any flue;

(*b*)    the supply of combustion air;

(*c*)    the operating pressure and/or heat input of the appliance;

(*d*)    the operation of the appliance to ensure its safe functioning.

Nothing done or agreed to be done by a tenant can be considered as discharging the duties of a landlord in respect of maintenance except in so far as it relates to access to the appliance or flue for the purposes of carrying out such maintenance or checking activities. [*SI 1998 No 2451, Reg 36(10)*].

In addition, it is the duty of landlords to ensure that appliances and relevant fittings are not installed in any room occupied as sleeping accommodation such as to cause a contravention of *Reg 30(2)* or *(3)* (see G1018 above).

## *Inspection and maintenance records*

**G1025**    The *Gas Safety (Installation and Use) Regulations 1998 (SI 1998 No 2451)* mark a significant increase in the obligations now placed upon landlords.

A landlord is under a duty to retain a record of each inspection of any gas appliance or flue for a period of two years from the date of the inspection. The record must include:

—    the date on which the appliance or flue is checked;

—    the address of the premises at which the appliance or flue is installed;

—    the name and address of the landlord of the premises at which the appliance or flue is installed;

—    a description of, and the location of, each appliance and flue that has been checked together with details of defects and any remedial action taken.

The person who carries out the safety check must enter on the record his name and his particulars of registration. Then he should sign the record confirming that he has examined the following:

—    the effectiveness of any flue;

—    the supply of combustion air;

—    the operating pressure and/or heat input of the appliance;

—    the operation of the appliance to ensure its safe functioning.

[*SI 1998 No 2451, Reg 36(3)*].

Within 28 days of the date of the check, the landlord must ensure that a copy of the record is given to each tenant of the premises to which the record relates. [*SI 1998 No 2451, Reg 36(6)(a)*]. In addition, before any new tenant moves in, the landlord must provide any such tenant with a copy of the record – however, where the tenant's right to occupation is for a period not exceeding 28 days, a copy of the record may instead be prominently displayed within the premises. [*SI 1998 No 2451, Reg 36(6)(b)*]. A copy of the inspection record given to a tenant under *Reg 36(6)(b)* need not include a copy of the signature of the person who carried out the inspection, provided that it includes a statement that the tenant is entitled to have another copy, containing a copy of such signature, on request to the landlord at an address specified in the statement. Where the tenant makes such a request, the landlord must provide the tenant with such a copy of the record as soon as is practicable. [*SI 1998 No 2451, Reg 36(8)*].

The *Gas Safety (Installation and Use) Regulations 1998* (*SI 1998 No 2451*), *Reg 36(7)* provides that where any room occupied, or about to be occupied, by a tenant does not contain any gas appliance, the landlord may – instead of giving the tenant a copy of the inspection record in accordance with *Reg 36(6)* (see above) – prominently display a copy of the record within the premises, together with a statement endorsed upon it that the tenant is entitled to have his own copy of the record on request to the landlord at an address specified in the statement. Where the tenant makes such a request, the landlord must provide the tenant with a copy of the record as soon as is practicable.

# Summaries of relevant court cases

G1026    The importance of the provisions relating to the correct installation and regular maintenance aspects of gas appliances, even in the earlier Gas Safety Regulations, is demonstrated in the following summaries of recent court cases.

## Unsafe gas fittings

G1027    A Nottingham landlord narrowly escaped a charge of manslaughter when he was tried and convicted of carrying out unsafe work practices which resulted in the deaths of two people.

The court heard of makeshift repairs to a gas boiler which then leaked carbon monoxide into an adjacent flat. The gas supplier (British Gas) gave evidence of having previously made the boiler inoperable because of its unsafe condition but it was reconnected by the landlord without any authority to do so, in December 1992. The landlord was charged under the *Gas Safety (Installation and Use) Regulations 1984* and the *Health and Safety at Work etc. Act 1974, s 3(2)*. He was accused of failing in his duty as a self-employed person to conduct his undertaking so as not to put himself or others at risk and of failing to carry out work in relation to a gas fitting in a proper and workmanlike manner.

The judge made it clear that if the legislation had carried a penalty of imprisonment, he would have imposed it. The seriousness of the case could only be reflected by a heavy fine and he sentenced the landlord with a fine of £32,000 with £24,800 costs.

[*Leicester Crown Court, June 1996*].

*Note:* The *Gas Safety (Installation and Use) Regulations 1994* introduced a wider scope of control and increased the penalties for contravention to an unlimited fine and a maximum of two years' imprisonment.

## Local authority (as landlord) guilty of bad gas safety management

G1028    A local authority found itself in court for nine breaches of the *Gas Safety (Installation and Use) Regulations 1994* (failing to carry out safety checks and to keep records) and for failing to ensure the safety of tenants, contrary to the *Health and Safety at Work etc. Act 1974, s 3(1)*. The case was brought after the discovery of more than 150 flues which were left disconnected after refurbishment work on a London council estate; and on other estates, annual safety checks had not been carried out.

The magistrate commented that there had been serious risk to hundreds of householders and imposed fines on the council of £27,000 for the breaches of the *Gas Safety (Installation and Use) Regulations 1994* and £17,000 for the offences which contravened the *Health and Safety at Work etc. Act 1974.*

[*Clerkenwell Magistrates' Court, January 1997*].

*Note:* The HSE pointed out that local authorities were the largest landlords in the country and that failure to manage in this case had put many tenants at risk of carbon monoxide poisoning and fire and explosion.

## Gas explosion results in three separate prosecutions

**G1029**  A major gas explosion at a twenty two-storey tower block resulted in the prosecution of a borough council, an installation company and a self employed electrician. The explosion blew off the roof of a boiler house, only minor injuries were sustained but there was considerable property damage from flying debris. There had been serious risk to hundreds of householders.

An investigation revealed that new gas burners and gas pressure booster pumps had been inadequately installed and not commissioned correctly.

The borough council was fined £75,000.00 for failing to manage the project.

The installation company was fined £10,200.00 for responsibility for the inadequate installation and management of the project.

The electrician was fined £3,000.00 for failing to install and commission the boilers correctly, not being competent, and not registered with CORGI.

[*Middlesex Guildhall Crown Court, September 1999*].

## Student death – landlord and gas fitter imprisoned

**G1030**  A landlord and an unregistered gas fitter were charged and convicted of manslaughter following the death of a student who inhaled carbon monoxide fumes from an inappropriate type of gas boiler which was not correctly ventilated.

The investigation into the incident by the HSE originated with the *Gas Safety (Installation and Use) Regulations 1994* which required gas fitters to be registered with the Council of Registered Gas Installers (CORGI). The charge of manslaughter was brought because of the seriousness of the offence: it had resulted in the death of one student and the hospitalisation of four other tenants who had been affected by poisonous fumes.

Both the landlord and the gas fitter pleaded guilty to manslaughter: the landlord was judged to be most responsible and was imprisoned for two years. The gas fitter was imprisoned for fifteen months.

[*Stafford Crown Court, December 1997*].

*Note:* Broadly, the law of manslaughter is part of the law of homicide. It is less serious than murder with the sentence at the discretion of the court. For health and safety purposes, manslaughter may be tentatively defined as killing without the intention to kill or to cause serious bodily harm. This case was the second health and safety manslaughter charge to result in imprisonment.

**Gas fitter jailed – chimney flue capped with concrete caused death**

G1031    This case involved an unregistered gas fitter who failed to notice that the flue into which he had connected a gas fire was capped with a concrete slab.

The fitter, the landlord and the landlord's son were charged with manslaughter following the death of a tenant in a bedsit. The prosecuting counsel told the court that the landlord of the bedsit, and his son who was looking after the property on behalf of his father, were also responsible for the death. He gave evidence of negligence in 20 other properties where failure to maintain gas appliances properly could have had similar tragic consequences.

In the case in question the judge said that the landlord and his son had been lulled into a false sense of security by a gas safety certificate provided by the fitter. He imposed the following sentences:

Gas fitter: 12 months' imprisonment, six of which were suspended;

Landlord and his son: 9 months' imprisonment suspended for 18 months – the landlord's son was also ordered to pay £16,000 costs.

[*Norwich Crown Court, April 1998*].

**Unsafe gas appliance – landlord guilty**

G1032    A landlord was charged with:

—    failing to maintain gas appliances in a safe condition, contrary to the *Gas Safety (Installation and Use) Regulations 1994, Reg 35A*; and with

—    providing false information in connection with his failure to comply with an improvement notice, contrary to the *Health and Safety at Work etc. Act 1974, ss 20 and 21*.

Two tenants who suffered dizziness and headaches informed the gas emergency company which then inspected the gas boiler and declared it unsafe. The boiler was switched off and a label was attached, warning that it should not be used.

The landlord instructed an unregistered gas fitter to repair the boiler; he failed to check for carbon monoxide leaks after switching the boiler back on. Two days later the two tenants collapsed after inhaling poisonous fumes and were hospitalised.

The HSE found that both the boiler and a gas cooker in the same property were leaking dangerously high levels of carbon monoxide gas. The landlord gave false information about the identity of the fitter who had carried out the work and switched the boiler back on.

The Crown Court judge said that the landlord was very lucky not to be facing manslaughter charges and imposed fines and costs totalling £24,000.

[*Cardiff Crown Court, May 1998*].

# Gas safety requirements in factories

G1033    Where part of plant contains explosive/flammable gas under pressure greater than atmospheric, that part must not be opened unless:

(*a*)    before the fastening of any joint of any pipe, connected with that part of the plant, any flow of gas has been stopped by a stop-valve;

(*b*)     before such fastening is removed, all practicable steps have been taken to reduce the gas pressure in the pipe or part of the plant, to atmospheric pressure; and

(*c*)     if such fastening is loosened or removed, inflammable gas is prevented from entering the pipe/part of the plant, until the fastening has been secured or securely replaced.

No hot work must be permitted on any plant or vessel which has contained gas until all practicable steps have been taken to remove the gas and any fumes arising from it, or to render it non-explosive or non-flammable. Similarly, and if any plant or vessel has been heated, no gas shall be allowed to enter it until the metal has cooled sufficiently to prevent any risk of ignition.

[*Factories Act 1961, s 31(3), (4)*].

## Pressure fluctuations

G1034     The *Gas Safety (Installation and Use) Regulations 1998 (SI 1998 No 2451), Reg 38,* provides that where gas is used in plant which is liable to produce pressure fluctuations in the gas supply, such as may cause danger to other consumers, the person responsible for the plant must ensure that any directions given to him by the gas transporter to prevent such danger are complied with.

If it is intended to use compressed air or any gaseous substance in connection with the consumption of gas, at least 14 days' written notice must be given to the gas transporter.

Any device fitted to prevent pressure fluctuations or to prevent the admission of a gaseous substance into the gas supply must be adequately maintained.

# Harassment in the Workplace

## Introduction

H1701 It is a common misconception that there exists in English law a particular cause of action for sexual harassment in the workplace. However, the law relating to sexual (and indeed racial) harassment is but a specific example of the general law relating to discrimination in the workplace and, as such, the main legislation dealing with the subject of sexual harassment is the *Sex Discrimination Act 1975 (SDA 1975)*. This said, although harassment is a particular example of discrimination, the area is of such significant importance that the European Commission has been moved to publish a Recommendation (O.J.1992, L49/1) and annexed Code of Practice on the protection of the dignity of men and women at work (see H1703 below). Reference will also be made during the course of this chapter to the similar provisions in the *Race Relations Act 1976 (RRA 1976)* where relevant examples under that legislation need to be discussed.

## History

H1702 The first significant decision on the issue of whether sexual harassment amounted to discrimination for the purposes of the *SDA 1975* was *Porcelli v Strathclyde Regional Council [1986] IRLR 134*. Here, the applicant was a female laboratory assistant working at a school alongside two male colleagues. The male assistants did not like the employee and they subjected her to a campaign of harassment in the form of brushing against her in the workplace and making sexually suggestive remarks to her in order to make her leave her job. The campaign was a 'success' in that it did indeed force the applicant to apply for a transfer to another school. Having done so, the applicant then brought a claim against her employer claiming that the actions of her former colleagues amounted to direct sex discrimination for the purposes of the *SDA 1975, s 1(1)(a)* in that she had been subjected to a detriment. The employer tried to defend the claim by calling in evidence the male employees responsible for the course of harassment. During their evidence they ventured to suggest that the conduct that had been meted out to the applicant would also have been displayed towards a hypothetical male comparator employee that they did not like and, consequently, the employer could not have committed sex discrimination against the applicant since the treatment was gender neutral.

The Scottish Court of Session refused to accept the defence. Lord Emslie stated of sexual harassment that it is:

> '... a particularly degrading and unacceptable form of treatment which it must be taken to have been the intention of Parliament to restrain'.

The Court likened the use of sexual harassment as a 'sexual sword' which had been 'unsheathed and used because the victim was a woman'. It added that, although an equally disliked male employee may well have been subjected to a campaign of harassment, the harassment would not have had as its cutting edge the gender of the victim. The Court then went on to give general guidance as to what harassment is. It stated that sexual harassment amounted to:

'. . . *[u]nwelcome acts which involve physical contact which, if proved, would also amount to offences at common law, such as assault or indecent assault; and also conduct falling short of such physical acts which can be fairly described as sexual harassment'.*

The law has moved on since the *Porcelli* decision, most notably in the re-statement by the EAT in the case of *(1) Reed (2) Bull Information Systems Ltd v Stedman [1999] IRLR 299* (see below at H1710). As will be seen in the course of this chapter, various defences to such claims have been developed, and, as stated above, the European Commission was moved to set down the Recommendation and Code of Practice following a report commissioned by it from Michael Rubenstein in 1988.

# The European Commission Recommendation and Code of Practice

H1703    As stated at H1701 above, the European Commission was prompted into drafting a Recommendation and Code of Practice dealing with the issue of sexual harassment following a report undertaken for it in 1988 (*The Dignity of Women at work: A report on the problem of sexual harassment in the Member States of the European Communities, 1988*). The Recommendation was made on 27 November 1991 and the Code was published in the Official Journal of the European Communities, 4 February 1992.

## Content of the Recommendation

H1704    *Art 1* of the Recommendation is its key element, requiring Member States to:

'. . . *take action to promote awareness that conduct of a sexual nature, or other conduct based on sex affecting the dignity of women and men at work, including conduct of superiors and colleagues, is unacceptable if:*

*(a)*    such conducted is unwanted, unreasonable and offensive to the recipient;

*(b)*    a person's rejection of or submission to, such conduct on the part of employers or workers (including superiors or colleagues) is used explicitly or implicitly as a basis for a decision which affects that person's access to vocational training, access to employment, continued employment, promotion, salary or any other employment decisions; and/or

*(c)*    such conduct creates an intimidating, hostile or humiliating working environment for the recipient,

*and that such conduct may, in certain circumstances, be contrary to the principle of equal treatment within the meaning of Articles, 3,4 and 5 of Directive 76/207/ EEC [the Equal Treatment Directive]'.*

The Recommendation is designed to draw to the attention of employers the nature of sexual harassment and to give broad outlines as to the ways in which it occurs together with an indication of the effect of such conduct (i.e. to highlight that it may be actionable as a form of discrimination).

## Content of the Code of Practice

H1705    The Code of Practice goes on to provide clear guidance to employers as to:

(*a*)    the nature of sexual harassment including the effect of harassment on victims;

(*b*)     a definition of harassment. This amounts to: '. . . unwanted conduct of a sexual nature, or other conduct based on sex affecting the dignity of women and men at work. This can include unwelcome physical, verbal or non-verbal conduct';

(*c*)     the legal implications for employers; and

(*d*)     the steps employers should take to prevent the spread of harassment in the workplace.

The Code goes beyond the position as it currently stands at English law. For example, it expressly states that sexual harassment is capable of occurring to homosexuals who are harassed in the workplace on account of their sexual orientation. Yet, the Court of Appeal in this country has stated that harassment of a person on account of their sexual orientation is not *per se* discriminatory within the meaning of the *SDA 1975* (per *Smith v Gardner Merchant Limited [1998] IRLR 520*, below at H1709).

There is no denying that employers should familiarise themselves with the contents of the Code. It amounts to a sensible extension to good human resources practice and, even though it may go beyond the requirements of English sex discrimination law, it should be remembered that harassment which is not currently actionable in terms of sex discrimination may in any event amount to conduct which could allow employees to claim that their contracts of employment have been repudiated by their employer thereby allowing them to claim unfair dismissal.

*Legal effect of the Recommendation and Code of Practice*

H1706     The Recommendation and Code are not law in this country and it still remains to be seen what the Government will do to adopt the Code on a formal basis. As regards employers, they should be aware that the Code is readily accepted by employment tribunals as evidence of good practice.

# Definition

## The Sex Discrimination Act 1975

H1707     The starting point in connection with sexual harassment is the *SDA 1975*. Sexual harassment is direct discrimination, i.e. it is treatment meted out to the recipient simply because that person is a woman or a man.

The provision of the *SDA 1975* dealing with sexual harassment is *SDA 1975, s 6(2)(b)* which states that:

'*It is unlawful for a person, in the case of a woman employed by him at an establishment in Great Britain, to discriminate against her —*

*(b)     by . . . subjecting her to any other detriment*'.

Effectively, sexual harassment requires a three stage test to be satisfied, this being that:

(*a*)     'less favourable treatment' has been shown to an applicant;

(*b*)     the proximate cause of the differential treatment is the applicant's gender; and

(*c*)     the differential treatment has subjected the victim to a detriment.

*The case of Waters v Commissioner of Police of the Metropolis [2000] IRLR 720* heard by the House of Lords involved claims of sex discrimination and negligence/ harassment.

Eileen Waters, a woman police constable, alleged that she was sexually assaulted whilst off duty by a male police constable. She reported the assault to her superiors, but following an internal inquiry, no action was taken. Following her complaint, she alleged that from that time on she was subjected to harassment, unfair treatment and victimisation by other police officers. She argued that this lead to ill health, including mental illness and post-traumatic stress disorder.

Miss Waters brought two separate proceedings: a complaint of sex discrimination and a negligence claim.

The sex discrimination claim arose from the removal of Miss Waters' name from the 'POLSA' list of specially trained officers used in relation to important police searches. She complained to an industrial tribunal that this was an act of victimisation contrary to the *Sex Discrimination Act 1975, s 4(1)(d)*.

The sex discrimination complaint was dismissed by the employment tribunal, the EAT *[1995] IRLR 531* and the Court of Appeal *[1997] IRLR 589* on the grounds that the alleged perpetrator was not acting in the course of his employment.

The civil action pursued was for negligence and/or harassment, seeking damages against the Commissioner. The High Court struck out the claim.

The Court of Appeal *[1997] IRLR 589,* heard the appeal against both claims and dismissed them. It held that the Commissioner was not under a personal duty of care to a police officer under his direction and control, equivalent to an employer's duty to provide a safe system of work, not to cause foreseeable injury to her. The court stated that there are well established policy reasons which prevent any duty of care between a chief officer of police and the officers under his direction and control from having such scope.

Miss Waters appealed against this finding but did not appeal the sex discrimination complaint.

The House of Lords allowed the appeal. The Lords held that the appellant's claim alleging that the Commissioner of Police has acted negligently in failing to deal with her complaint that she had been sexually assaulted by a male colleague, and had caused or permitted other police officers to harass her, should not have been struck out. It was not obvious that no duty of care could be owed to the appellant by the Commissioner on the facts, or that if there was such a duty that the facts could not amount to a breach.

If an employer is aware that other employees during the course of their employment may be causing physical or mental harm to another employee, and does nothing to prevent such behaviour, it is arguable that he may be in breach of his duty to that employee. In the instance of a complaint of alleged sexual assault by another colleague, it is arguable that it is foreseeable that some retaliatory steps may be taken against the complainant and that she may suffer harm as a result. In this instance, protective steps should be taken.

The House of Lords did not agree with the Court of Appeal's view that as a matter of public policy, the Commissioner did not owe a duty of care to the claimant to protect her from victimisation and harassment by her fellow officers.

Per Lord Hutton: 'A person employed under an ordinary contract of employment can have a valid cause of action in negligence against her employer if the employer fails to protect her against victimisation and harassment which causes physical or psychiatric injury. This duty arises under the common law principles of negligence, although an employer will not be liable unless he knows or ought to know that harassment is taking place and fails to take reasonable steps to prevent it'.

*Less favourable treatment*

**H1708**    In dealing with the question of whether or not sexual harassment amounted to less favourable treatment, the Court of Session in *Porcelli v Strathclyde Regional Council [1986] IRLR 134* stated that:

> '*In a case of alleged sexual harassment, the correct primary question is not 'was there sexual harassment?'', a phrase which is not found in the statute, but 'was the applicant less favourably treated on the ground of her sex than a man would have been treated?'' If that question is answered in the affirmative, there is discrimination within the meaning of the Sex Discrimination Act*'.

The Act does, however, have its limitations. In the first instance, it is entirely conceivable that situations could arise where although an employer treats an employee in a manner that seems to amount to a *prima facie* case of harassment, it may do so in circumstances that would not amount to 'less favourable treatment' for the purposes of the *SDA 1975*. For example, there can be circumstances arising from conduct which could equally affront a male employee. A good illustration is the case of *Stewart v Cleveland Guest (Engineering) Ltd [1994] IRLR 440*. Here, the applicant was a female engineer who frequently had to make visits to the factory floor in order to carry out her duties. She was upset at the display of posters of nude women that adorned the factory floor area and complained to the employer's management. She asked for the posters to be removed. Her requests were ignored and the employee resigned and claimed that she had been constructively dismissed. She alleged that she had been subjected to less favourable treatment on the grounds of her sex which had ultimately led to her constructive dismissal. An employment tribunal and, on appeal, the EAT, found that the display of such posters was gender neutral since a male employee might also have been equally upset at the posters. In the circumstances, it was not possible to say that the employee had been treated less favourably than a male comparator.

Another example is the case of *Balgobin v London Borough of Tower Hamlets [1987] IRLR 401*. This case concerned complaints by female employees who claimed that they had been subjected to the detriment of being required to work with their alleged harasser after an investigation into the allegations of harassment was found to be inconclusive. Again, the EAT refused to accept that the employee had been treated less favourably since it was possible that if a male employee had been harassed, the employer would have treated the male in a similar way.

Finally, it is conceivable that a harasser may be bi-sexual and therefore a defence could exist to the effect that the harasser would indeed treat a man in a similar fashion.

This is not to say that employers can use these lines of defence to totally escape liability. It needs to be remembered that although the treatment might not be less favourable for the purposes of sex discrimination, it may still amount to a breach of the implied duty to maintain the trust and confidence of employees and may therefore be a precursor to an unfair dismissal claim.

In any event, in spite of the above, it seems that an argument does still exist to the effect that sexual harassment, since it is gender specific (in much the same way as pregnancy), does not require a comparison to be made as to whether a male employee would have been treated in the same way. Indeed, the EAT accepted as much in *British Telecommunications Ltd v Williams [1997] IRLR 668*. The EAT in this case even went on to specifically add that it would be no defence for an employer to state that a male employee would have been treated in a similar fashion. Unfortunately, some of the credibility in the *Williams* case is lost in that it made no reference to the decision in *Stewart*. There must also be some doubt as to whether the argument can survive following the decision of the European Court of Justice in *Grant v South-West Trains Ltd [1998] CMLR 993* (dealing with an employer's policy of not providing travel concessions to partners in same sex relationships) which held that, provided a policy or treatment is applied equally to men and women, there can be no discrimination.

*Differential treatment is on grounds of sex*

H1709      In order for sex discrimination to occur, it is necessary that a woman is treated less favourably than an actual or hypothetical male comparator. To this end, one of the defences that has been raised is to argue that harassment against a female employee would have occurred equally to a male employee. The case of *Porcelli v Strathclyde Regional Council [1986] IRLR 134* (above) shows the limits of this line of defence. The Court of Session stated of the comparison between male and female employees:

> 'If any material part of unfavourable treatment to which a woman is subjected includes a significant element of a sexual character to which a man would not be vulnerable, the treatment is on grounds of the woman's sex within the meaning of s 1(1)(a)'.

It will be recalled that the defence raised by the employer in this case was that a hypothetical male employee would have been treated in a similar fashion. The defence failed and the Court of Session commented upon the nature of the treatment that had been received by the applicant in the following terms.

> 'The [employment] tribunal . . . concentrated on the unpleasantness of the treatment meted out to the respondent and compared it with the unpleasantness of the treatment which they considered would have been meted out to a man whom his colleagues had disliked as much as her colleagues had disliked the respondent. That was a question of fact; but the question which had to be asked after that conclusion had been reached was 'Was the treatment, or any part of it, which was meted out to the respondent less favourable, than that which would have been meted out to the notional man because the respondent was a woman?"'.

An example of a decision that was resolved in a contrary fashion was the case of *Smith v Gardner Merchant Limited [1998] IRLR 520*. The facts of this case were that the applicant was a male homosexual who had been dismissed for gross misconduct. He brought a claim for sex discrimination, one of the limbs of which was an allegation that he had been harassed by a female employee who had asked a series of offensive questions about his sexuality, made various accusations to him along the lines that gay people had all sorts of diseases and stated to him that gay people who spread the HIV virus should be put on an island. Mr Smith claimed that he had been treated less favourably on account of his gender. The Court of Appeal took the view that although there may have been less favourable treatment, it was on account of Mr Smith's sexual orientation rather than his gender. Accordingly, the relevant grounds of comparison that would need to be made were whether a female homosexual with the same personal characteristics of Mr Smith would have been subjected to similar or differential treatment. Whether or not such a decision is consistent with the provisions of the *Human Rights Act 1998, Arts 8 and 14, Sch 1* (which recognises a right to respect for a person's private life and prohibits discrimination in relation to that right on any ground) remains to be seen. Indeed, from a commonsense point of view, there does seem to be some contradiction in the law to the extent that it does not protect homosexuals from harassment as to their sexuality and yet does protect transsexuals against treatment meted out to them on the grounds of gender reassignment (as occurred in *Chessington World of Adventures Ltd v Reed [1997] IRLR 556* — see also now the *Sex Discrimination (Gender Reassignment) Regulations 1999 (SI 1999 No 1102)* outlawing discrimination on the grounds of gender reassignment). It remains to be seen whether the Government will pass similar legislation in relation to homosexuals following its defeat in the European Court of Human Rights in the case of *Smith & Grady v UK [1999] IRLR 734* (involving the right of homosexuals to serve in the UK armed forces).

## Detriment

H1710   The final hurdle to be crossed in order to bring a successful claim is to show that the employee has suffered a detriment. As to what is capable of amounting to a detriment, the starting point is again the decision in *Porcelli v Strathclyde Regional Council [1986] IRLR 134*. Here, the Court of Session stated that a detriment, in its statutory context, simply means a disadvantage.

The matter has been re-examined in the case of *Reed and Bull Information Systems v Stedman [1999] IRLR 299*. The facts of the case were that the claimant had resigned claiming that the behaviour of her manager amounted to sexual harassment and therefore discrimination. The employee cited a list of fifteen alleged incidents that she considered amounted to a course of harassment. The employment tribunal concentrated on four of the allegations, these being such matters as telling the employee that sex was a beneficial form of exercise, telling dirty jokes to colleagues in her presence, making a pretence of looking up the employee's skirt and then laughing when she angrily left the room and stating to her when she was listening to a trial presentation that 'You're going to love me so much for my presentation so that when I finish you will be screaming out for more and you will want to rip my clothes off'. The tribunal added that, of themselves, each of the allegations was insufficient to amount to sexual harassment. However, if the claimant was able to prove the incidents, they would amount to a course of conduct that would itself be sufficient to amount to harassment. The employment tribunal went on to find that the acts had occurred and that the employer and the manager had therefore discriminated against the applicant. The employer and manager appealed to the EAT. The EAT dismissed the appeal agreeing that the actions by the manager, although not meant to be sexually harassing, were indeed discriminatory. It added:

> '*It seems to us important to stress at the outset that 'sexual harassment' is not defined by the [SDA 1975]. It is a colloquial expression which describes one form of discrimination in the workplace made unlawful by s 6 of the Sex Discrimination Act 1975. Because it is not a precise or defined phrase, its use, without regard to s 6, can lead to confusion. Under s 6 it is unlawful to subject a person to a 'detriment' on the grounds of their sex. Sexual harassment is a shorthand for describing a type of detriment. The word detriment is not further defined and its scope is to be defined by the fact-finding tribunal on a common-sense basis by reference to the facts of the particular case. The question in each case is whether the alleged victim has been subjected to a detriment and, second, was it on the grounds of sex'.*

Consequently, in order to determine whether or not conduct of a sexual nature is sexual harassment and therefore a 'detriment' within the meaning of the *SDA 1975*, it is necessary to consider whether it is a disadvantage which is itself determined from the particular circumstances of the case.

### Detriment — subjective or objective determination?

H1711   The EAT in *Reed and Bull Information Systems* (see above at H1710) also discussed the question as to whether a 'detriment' was something that was to be determined subjectively from the perspective of an applicant to a tribunal or objectively by the tribunal. The EAT dealt with the issue by posing a series of questions that would typically be asked in harassment cases, these being as follows.

(*a*)   If a woman regards as harassment of a sexual nature words or conduct to which many women would not take exception or regard as harassment, has her claim been made out?

(*b*)   If a man does not appreciate that his words or conduct are unwelcome, has her claim been proved?

(*c*)   Is a 'one-off' act (words or conduct) sufficient to constitute harassment?

The tribunal answered the questions that it posed by stating as to the first of the questions that it is up to the victim of harassment to determine what she finds unwelcome or offensive. Simply because a tribunal does not necessarily find the words or conduct offensive will not lead to a complaint being dismissed. Indeed, the EAT stated that there is a range of factual situations that are capable of amounting to harassment. Inevitably, once a victim of harassment has received unwelcome attention from a person it is possible that further attention that would not ordinarily attract comment may take on a different context in the light of previous unwelcome attentions. Consequently, it is up to the victim to determine what words or conduct she is unhappy with and for a tribunal to determine in the totality of the facts whether those words or conduct could reasonably be viewed as offensive and unwelcome.

As to the second question, the EAT acknowledged that it is trite law that the motive and intention of the discriminator are irrelevant to the question of whether or not discrimination has occurred.

Finally, as to the third question, the EAT stated that the fundamental question to be addressed by a tribunal was whether the applicant was subjected to a detriment on account of her sex. It went on to add that this was not a question that was answered by counting up the number of incidents that had occurred, rather it was answered by looking at whether an incident or series of them damaged the working environment and constituted a barrier to sexual equality in the workplace which constituted a detriment.

Ultimately, the view of the EAT is that the test as to whether a detriment has been suffered focuses upon an applicant's subjective determination of whether conduct to which she is subjected is unwelcome and that determination has then to be judged by a tribunal which must ask itself whether that is a reasonable position for the applicant to take.

## Examples of sexual harassment

H1712   As was stated in the case of *Reed and Bull Information Systems v Stedman [1999] IRLR 299*, sexual harassment is a shorthand way of expressing the legal requirement in *SDA 1975, s 6(2)* of a 'detriment'. The case also recognises that the type of situations in which sexual harassment can occur are legion. However, of the cases that have been reported to date they can broadly be categorised as:

(*a*)   course of conduct cases;

(*b*)   single incident cases; and

(*c*)   failure to investigate or protect cases.

*Course of conduct cases*

H1713    As the heading suggests, the hallmark of this genus of cases is that an employee is subjected to repeated harassment in the course of her employment. The following are reported examples of such cases.

(*a*)    *Porcelli v Strathclyde Regional Council [1986] IRLR 134.* The applicant was a female laboratory assistant and was the victim of a campaign of harassment by fellow male employees to make her leave her job. The male employees would frequently brush past the applicant in a sexually suggestive manner and direct comments of a sexual nature at her. The Court of Session held that the applicant had suffered a detriment in having to put up with the conduct which had clear sexual overtones and to which a similarly disliked hypothetical male comparator would not have been subjected.

(*b*)    *Reed and Bull Information Systems v Stedman [1999] IRLR 299.* The applicant was a junior secretary responsible to the marketing manager of the employer. The applicant catalogued fifteen separate incidents ranging from the telling of dirty jokes by the manager to other colleagues in her presence to the pretence of looking up her skirt in the office smoking room. The EAT upheld the findings of the employment tribunal that, although the incidents by themselves would have been insufficient to amount to a detriment, collectively they amounted to a course of conduct of innuendo and general sexist behaviour amounting to harassment and therefore a detriment for the purposes of the *SDA 1975.*

(*c*)    *Chessington World of Adventures Ltd v Reed [1997] IRLR 556.* The applicant was a biological male and was undergoing gender reassignment from male to female. The applicant was subjected to a prolonged campaign of ostracism and harassment (which the employer was found to have done nothing to investigate or curb) having as its proximate cause the therapy that the applicant was undertaking. In the circumstances, the employer was held to have subjected the applicant to a detriment.

(*d*)    *R v Wakefield; R v Lancashire, The Times, 12 January 2001.* Wakefield, Lancashire and the female victim were work colleagues. Lancashire, had often, and over several months, carried out actions at the workplace and in front of others, such as pushing the victim against a filing cabinet and stimulating intercourse with her, and grabbing her between the legs. The victim had complained to Wakefield, the manager, but soon after, he too had assaulted her indecently. She ultimately left her employment and became severely depressed. Both Wakefield and Lancashire were subsequently charged with indecent assault and were convicted at Nottingham Crown Court. They appealed the conviction. In the Court of Appeal Mr Justice Goldring, dismissing their appeals, said that this was a serious case of sexual bullying involving a prolonged period of conduct which was both humiliating and degrading. In such situations, custodial sentences were accepted as 'inevitable'. In the instant case their length was unimpeachable. Women were fully entitled to be protected from such treatment.

*Single incident cases*

H1714    The hallmark of 'single incident' cases is that they are effectively a 'bolt from the blue', yet comply with the requirements in *Reed and Bull Information Systems v Stedman [1999] IRLR 299* in that they provide a barrier to sexual equality in the workplace.

(*a*)   *Bracebridge Engineering Ltd v Darby [1990] IRLR 3.* The applicant was physically manhandled into the office of the works manager by both a chargehand and the works manager and then indecently assaulted. She was warned not to complain because no-one would believe her. The applicant did subsequently complain but the complaint was then not properly investigated by the employer. It was held by the EAT that the assault was sufficiently serious to amount to a detriment.

(*b*)   *Insitu Cleaning Co Ltd v Heads [1995] IRLR 4.* The applicant was a cleaning supervisor who attended at a company meeting. Also present was the son of one of the directors of the company who greeted her by saying 'Hiya, big tits'. The applicant found the remarks particularly distressing as the director's son was approximately half her age. The EAT held that the remark was capable of subjecting the applicant to a detriment and rejected the employer's contention that the remark was of the same effect as a statement made to a bald male employee about his head.

(*c*)   *Chief Constable of the Lincolnshire Police v Stubbs [1999] IRLR 81.* The applicant was a Detective Constable in the Lincolnshire Constabulary. She attended an off duty drink with some colleagues in a public house one evening after work. During the course of the evening a male colleague pulled up a stool next to her, flicked her hair and re-arranged her collar so as to give the impression that there was a relationship between himself and the applicant. The applicant found this attention to be distressing and moved away from him. On another occasion at a colleagues leaving party that she had attended with her boyfriend, she was accosted on her way to the toilet by the same officer who stated to her 'Fucking hell, you look worth one. Maybe I shouldn't say that it would be worth some money'. The applicant found the remark to be humiliating and brought proceedings for sex discrimination. The EAT upheld the decision of the employment tribunal that the statement amounted to a detriment.

*Failures to investigate or protect*

**H1715**   Where an allegation of sexual harassment is brought by an employee, an employer has a duty to carry out a proper investigation into the complaint and to take such further steps as are necessary in the light of the findings of the investigation. A failure to carry out such a proper investigation is capable of amounting to a detriment in its own right. The following cases are examples of alleged failures to investigate or protect employees.

(*a*)   *Balgobin v London Borough of Tower Hamlets [1987] IRLR 401.* The employees were female cleaners working in a local authority hostel. They alleged that they had been sexually harassed by a male cook at the hostel. The employer suspended the cook and carried out a full investigation into the allegations which resulted in a failure to find that the complaints of the applicants had been proved. Consequently, the cook was allowed to return to work and the cleaners were required to carry on working with him. The employees complained that they were subjected to the detriment of having to work with the cook. The EAT held that there had been no discrimination since it was possible that a male cleaner to whom homosexual advances had been made could have been treated in a similar fashion by the employer.

(*b*)   *Bracebridge Engineering Ltd v Darby [1990] IRLR 3.* (See H1714 above for the facts.) The assault that took place on the employee was coupled with a failure to properly investigate the incident on the part of the employer who, through its personnel manager, simply accepted that it was the word of two employees against one and that there was insufficient evidence to warrant further investigation. The EAT held that where serious allegations of sexual harassment are made, employers have a duty to properly investigate them.

(c)   *Burton v De Vere Hotels [1996] IRLR 596.* The case took place under the provisions of both the *SDA 1975* and the identical provisions of the *Race Relations Act 1976.* The case was brought by a waitress at a hotel and concerned the detriment of suffering sexual and racial harassment from a third party not connected to the employer but whom over the employer was able to exercise control (the case concerned the applicant being subjected to sexist and racial abuse masquerading as comedy from a well known comedian at a hotel function. The applicant was humiliated in front of the audience by the comedian). Although the employer apologised to the employee for the actions of the comedian, the employee lodged proceedings for sexual and racial harassment and succeeded in the claim. The EAT held that, where an employer was in a position to exercise control over a third party so that discrimination would either not occur, or the extent of it would be reduced, the employer would be subjecting an applicant to a detriment by failing to take the steps necessary to control the employee.

(d)   *Chessington World of Adventures Ltd v Reed [1997] IRLR 556.* (See above at H1713.) Added to the campaign of harassment that was suffered by the employee was a failure to curb the harassment when complaints were made by the applicant. This was held to be capable of amounting to a detriment since the employer was plainly able to stop the harassment.

## Victimisation

H1716     Victimisation is the third category of sex discrimination that exists under the *SDA 1975* after straightforward discrimination (whether direct or indirect) (*SDA 1975, s 1*) and marital discrimination (*SDA 1975, s 3*). Victimisation exists under the *SDA 1975, s 4.*

Victimisation is defined by the *SDA 1975, s 4.* This provides that somebody discriminates against another person where he treats that person less favourably that he treats or would treat other persons and does so because the victimised person has:

(a)   brought proceedings against the discriminator or any other person under the *SDA 1975,* the *Equal Pay Act 1970* or *ss 62 to 65* of the *Pensions Act 1995;*

(b)   given evidence or information in connection with proceedings brought by any person against the discriminator or any other person under the aforementioned Acts;

(c)   otherwise done anything under or by reference to these Acts; or

(d)   alleged that the discriminator or any other person has committed an act which (whether or not the allegation so states) would amount to a contravention of the *SDA 1975* or give rise to a claim under the *Equal Pay Act 1970* or *ss 62 to 65* of the *Pensions Act 1995,*

or because the discriminator knows the person victimised intends to do any of those things, or suspects the person victimised has done, or intends to do, any of them.

The above does not apply to treatment of a person by reason of any allegation made by him if the allegation was false and not made in good faith.

As will be seen, the protection provided by the Act is far reaching and covers not just the victims of the abuse of a right under the *SDA 1975,* the *Equal Pay Act 1970* or the relevant provisions of the *Pensions Act 1995,* but also those who honestly but erroneously believe themselves to be such victims and those who go to the aid of such people by providing assistance to them for the purposes of tribunal applications.

The victimisation provisions are aimed at preventing an employer from curtailing the right of an employee to legitimately protect his position opposite the employer. The leading case is the House of Lords decision in *Nagarajan v London Regional Transport [1999] IRLR 572* (decided under the similar provisions in the *Race Relations Act 1976*). Their Lordships held, by a majority (and in the face of a powerful dissenting speech by Lord Browne-Wilkinson), that victimisation occurs where less favourable treatment is meted out to a complainant because the victimised person had done an act protected under the provisions of the Act. Their Lordships went on to add that whether the discriminator intended to engage in an act of discrimination towards the victim was irrelevant. Accordingly, it is sufficient for a victimisation claim to arise that an employer is aware of the existence of the fact that an employee has a protected right under the *SDA 1975* and then unconsciously treats the employee less favourably than he would treat another not having a protected right.

### Remedies

H1717   The remedies that are available to an applicant successfully bringing a victimisation complaint are the same as those arising in relation to sex discrimination — see H1725 below.

# Employers' liability

## Vicarious liability

H1718   The legal problem that occurs in connection with sexual harassment is that, often, it is not the employer that directly subjects a victim of harassment to the course of conduct, rather it is a fellow employee who is responsible. The employer may then be held responsible for the employee's actions on the grounds of vicarious liability.

The problem that arises in legal theory with vicarious liability is that employers do not employ staff to harass other members of the workforce. Therefore, it is necessary to determine what amounts to 'the course of employment' in order to see when an employer will be liable for the harassment of its employees by other members of staff.

### *The course of employment*

H1719   The first case to take as a line of defence the fact that a harasser was not acting in the course of his employment was *Tower Boot Co Ltd v Jones [1997] IRLR 168*. The case concerned proceedings brought under the provisions of the *Race Relations Act 1976* in respect of racial harassment. The applicant had been subjected to a particularly vicious campaign of name calling and physical assaults. An employment tribunal found that this constituted racial harassment and that the employer was vicariously liable for the acts of the employees engaged in the course of conduct. The employer appealed to the EAT which found for the employer on the ground that the common law test for vicarious liability had not been satisfied. The EAT took the view that for this test to be met the aggressor employees had to be engaged in doing the business of the employer, albeit in an improper manner, i.e. the act had to be a different mode of doing what the aggressor employees were employed to do. The EAT then held that on the facts, the actions of the aggressor employees could not 'by any stretch of the imagination' be found to be an improper method of doing what the aggressors were properly employed to do.

The EAT decision was widely condemned on the grounds that the more serious that harassment was, the less likely that an employer would be found to be vicariously liable for it. Indeed, the logical conclusion to the EAT's decision was that, since people were not employed to harass other members of staff, employers would never be liable, a surprising result indeed. Unsurprisingly, the decision was appealed to the Court of Appeal which readily found for the employee. In doing so, the Court held that the words, 'in the course of his employment' in *s 32(1)* of the *RRA 1976* were not subject to the common law rules in the Salmond test which would artificially restrict the natural everyday sense that every layman would understand of the wording in *s 32(1)* of the 1976 Act (*SDA 1975, s42(1)*). Consequently, harassment by an aggressor employee did not have to be connected with acts authorised to be done as part of his work. In so deciding, the Court of Appeal attacked the reasoning of the EAT, stating that its interpretation of the section creating liability:

'. . . *cut across the whole legislative scheme and underlying policy which was to deter racial and sexual harassment through a widening of the net of responsibility beyond the guilty employees themselves by making all employers additionally liable for such harassment'.*

*Requirement of causal link with employment*

H1720

It is not every act of harassment that is committed by an employee that will create a liability on the part of the employer. There must still be a causal link with employment. A good example of this point is the case of *Waters v Commissioner of Police of the Metropolis [1997] IRLR 589*. In this case, the complaint was one of sexual harassment in the form of an alleged sexual assault by a male police officer on a female police officer in her section house room after they had returned from a late night walk together. Given that the attack took place outside the normal working hours of the applicant, the employment tribunal refused to follow the decision in the *Tower Boot* case and held that the applicant was in the same position as if the alleged assailant had been a total stranger to the employer. The alleged assailant did not live in the section house, both officers were both off duty and there was nothing linking the alleged assailant to the employer other than the fact that he was a police officer. The decision of the tribunal was ultimately upheld on appeal by the Court of Appeal.

This said, the decision in *Waters* does not provide an absolute defence to harassment undertaken after employees leave work for the day. Whether there is a causal link between the harassment and the employment, thereby attaching liability to the employer, will be a question of fact in each particular situation. An example of this point is *Chief Constable of the Lincolnshire Police v Stubbs [1999] IRLR 81*. The complainant had been the subject of distressing personal comments of a sexual nature from a fellow police officer made at a colleague's leaving party (see above at H1714). The employment tribunal at first instance held that since the party was an organised leaving party, the incidents was 'connected' to work and the workplace. It stated that the incident:

'. . . *would not have happened but for [WPC Stubbs'] work. Work-related social functions are an extension of employment and we can see no reason to restrict the course of employment to purely what goes on in the workplace'.*

The EAT emphasised, however, that it would have been different 'had the discriminatory acts occurred during a chance meeting' between the employee and the harasser outside of the workplace.

The decisions give a wide degree of discretion to tribunals on the facts of a particular case to decide whether harassment is committed in the course of employment. If a tribunal finds that it is not committed in such circumstances, the effect is that whilst an employee may be able to sue the harasser in tort, the remedy that is provided may well be empty if the harasser does not have the means to pay for his wrongdoing.

### Employer's defence

H1721 A defence is provided to employers under the *SDA 1975, s 41(3)*. This provides that:

> '*In proceedings brought under this Act against any person in respect of an act alleged to have been done by an employee of his it shall be a defence for that person to prove that he took such steps as were reasonably practicable to prevent the employee from doing that act, or from doing in the course of his employment acts of that description*'.

The problem for employers with this defence is that whilst it will provide a defence in a situation where an employer has a full procedure dealing with harassment (including such matters as monitoring, complaints handling and disciplinary proceedings), the provision requires that the employer must pay more than mere lip service to the existence of these matters and must also be able to show that its employees were aware of the procedures and, where relevant, that the employer had fully implemented the procedures in practice. A good example of a case where the defence succeeded was *Balgobin v London Borough of Tower Hamlets [1987] IRLR 401* (see H1715 above). Here, the alleged harasser was suspended following the initial allegations, his conduct was fully investigated and it was found that there was insufficient evidence against the cook to justify the claims. The EAT was moved to comment that it was difficult to see what further steps the employer could have taken to avoid the alleged discrimination.

Ultimately, if an employer has gone to the expense of having policies and procedures drafted then they should not be kept in the office safe. Employees should be left under no illusions as to what will happen in cases of harassment.

### Liability of employees

H1722 Although an employer may be vicariously liable for acts of harassment, it needs to be remembered that primary responsibility for such action should remain with the employee who has committed the discrimination and, to this end the *SDA 1975, s 42* provides as follows.

> '*(1)   A person who knowingly aids another person to do an act made unlawful by this Act shall be treated for the purposes of this Act as himself doing an unlawful act of the like description.*
>
> *(2)   For the purposes of subsection (1) an employee or agent for whose act the employer or principal is liable under section 41 (or would be so liable but for section 41(3)) shall be deemed to aid the doing of the act by the employer or principal.*'

The scope of the provision was given a liberal interpretation in *AM v WC & SPV [1999] IRLR 410*. Here, the EAT held that an employment tribunal had erred in not allowing a police officer to bring a complaint of harassment against another individual officer. The EAT considered that the construction of *ss 41(1), (3)* and *s 42, SDA 1975* was to make an employer vicariously liable for acts of discrimination committed by staff (*s 41(1)*), to provide conscientious employers with a defence for the actions of staff where the actions are effectively a 'bolt from the blue' (*s 41(3)*) and to allow an employee who has committed acts of discrimination against another to be joined as a 'partner' to proceedings commenced against an employer (*s 42*).

The EAT added that even where a defence did exist for an employer under s 41(3), there was nothing in the *SDA 1975* that prevented the victim of discrimination from launching proceedings against a discriminator employee alone.

## Narrowing the extent of employers' liability

H1723   Where an employee is able to establish that she has been the victim of sexual harassment, there can be circumstances where the damages that would otherwise be awarded to a victim of such discrimination will be dramatically reduced. This will be where the victim's conduct shows that she would not have suffered a serious detriment as a consequence of the harassment. For example, in *Snowball v Gardner Merchant Ltd [1987] IRLR 397*, the applicant complained that she had been sexually harassed by her manager. The allegations were denied and the applicant was subjected to questioning at the tribunal hearing as to her attitude to matters of sexual behaviour so as to show that even if she had been harassed, her feelings had not been injured. In particular, evidence was called as to the fact that she referred to her bed as her 'play pen' and that she had stated that she slept between black satin sheets. On appeal, the EAT held that the evidence had been correctly admitted so as to show that the applicant was not likely to be offended by a degree of familiarity having a sexual connotation.

Likewise, in *Wileman v Minilec Engineering Ltd [1988] IRLR 144*, the EAT refused to overturn an award of damages in the sum of £50 that had been made for injury to feelings. In this case, the applicant had made a complaint of sexual harassment against one of the directors of her employer. The award had been set at this figure on account of the fact that the victim had worn revealing clothes and it made it inevitable that comment would be passed.

With respect to the EAT, these cases, whilst reflecting that harassment can still occur in cases where a complainant has a high degree of confidence in sexual banter, unfortunately appear to send out the wrong message in that they can be construed as being as a 'harasser's charter' and do not seem to recognise that a person may be particularly upset by the unwelcome attentions of a specific person. It is worth noting that both of the decisions pre-date the EC Code of Practice and the enactment of the *Human Rights Act 1998* and it will be interesting to see if the effect of the decisions is in any way curbed at a future date by these matters.

# Legal action and remedies

H1724   Where a person sexually harasses another, the consequences of such action can be extremely far reaching and potentially spread across the full range of actions in both civil and criminal law.

## Sex discrimination

*Elements of the tort*

H1725   The most obvious form of action that a victim of sexual harassment may consider is direct sex discrimination under the *SDA 1975, s 1(1)(a)*. Liability arises because a person engaged in harassing another subjects that other to a detriment (*SDA 1975, s 6(2)(c)*). This head of liability is fully covered at H1703 ET SEQ above.

*Remedies*

H1726   The remedies that are open to a victim of sexual harassment are:

(*a*)   a declaration;

(*b*)    recommendation; or

(*c*)    compensation.

A declaration is a formal acknowledgement from an employment tribunal that discrimination in the form of harassment has occurred. It will be granted in every successful case brought before a tribunal.

Recommendations are used where an applicant to an employment tribunal remains in the employment of her employer. The purpose of a recommendation is for a tribunal to give guidance to an employer relating to its business for the purposes of eliminating discrimination.

However, the main remedy that victims of harassment will seek is compensation for the loss that has been suffered as a result of the harassment including, particularly, injury to feelings.

## Unfair dismissal

H1727    Unfair dismissal can arise as a claim where an employer fails to control sexual harassment in the workplace or fails to properly investigate complaints of sexual harassment. Such failures may and probably will also act to undermine the employee's trust and confidence in the employer. The result of such actions is that an employee may be able to claim that the employer has constructively dismissed the employee, thereby amounting to a dismissal for the purposes of the *Employment Rights Act 1996, s 95(1)(c)*. Indeed, where a sexual harassment claim has been brought on the back of an employee's departure from her employment, most cases will also include a claim for unfair dismissal as well.

### Proving constructive dismissal

H1728    The first hurdle that an employee has to overcome is to prove that she has been dismissed for the purposes of the *Employment Rights Act 1996, s 95(1)(c)*. It is trite law that for an employee to show that she has been constructively dismissed the acts of her employer must show that the employer, by its conduct, evinced an intention not to be bound by the terms and conditions of the contract of employment (see, to this effect, *Western Excavating (ECC) Limited v Sharp [1978] IRLR 27*). The problem that an employee may face in this regard is that if an employer has in place a full anti-harassment policy that is properly implemented, the employee may fail to establish that the employer has acted in breach. For an example of this occurring in practice see *Balgobin v London Borough of Tower Hamlets [1987] IRLR 401* (see above at H1715).

Likewise, an employee may also fail to show that an employer has breached the implied term of trust and confidence where the act is a serious one off act of harassment that the employer was unable to predict would happen and where the employer properly deals with the matter immediately upon a complaint being made. To the extent that the employer does not properly investigate a complaint in such circumstances it is almost inevitable that the employer will breach the contract. For a good example of this principle, see *Bracebridge Engineering Ltd v Darby [1990] IRLR 3*.

Finally, it will be recalled, that, following, *Smith v Gardner Merchant Limited [1998] IRLR 520*, sexual harassment on the grounds of sexual orientation is difficult prove since the applicant will have to show that the person subjecting her to harassment would also treat a homosexual man in like fashion. This does not release an employer from an obligation to investigate since such conduct on the part of fellow employees, if left unchecked by the employer, can clearly breach the implied duty of the employer to maintain the employee's trust and confidence.

*Remedies*

H1729    The remedies that can be provided for unfair dismissal are those set out in the *Employment Rights Act 1996, ss 113–118* namely:

(*a*)    an order for reinstatement;

(*b*)    an order for re-engagement; or

(*c*)    an order for compensation.

The practical consequence of the employee claiming that she has been constructively dismissed as a result of an employer's breach of the implied duty of trust and confidence is that a tribunal will be unwillingly to make an order of reinstatement or re-engagement and therefore the reality is that most cases will provide for compensation to be awarded. The downside to claiming unfair dismissal as opposed to sex discrimination is that, whereas, the compensation for sex discrimination is both unlimited as regards the amount that can be awarded (following *Southampton and South West Hampshire AHA v Marshall [1993] IRLR 445*) and can contain an award for injury to feelings, the compensation that is available for unfair dismissal is subject to a cap of £50,000 and cannot include an award for injury to feelings.

## Actions in tort

H1730    Broadly speaking, torts are the category of actionable civil wrongs not including claims for breach of contract or those arising in equity. Acts of sexual harassment, depending upon the particular characteristics of the harassment, are capable of amounting to a variety of different torts.

*Assault and battery*

H1731    Assault and battery are forms of trespass to the person. They are separate torts and occur where a person fears that either she will receive or has been the subject of unlawful physical contact. As was stated of the torts in *Collins v Wilcock [1984] 3 All ER 374*:

> '*An assault is an act which causes another person to apprehend the infliction of immediate, unlawful, force on his person; a battery is the actual infliction of unlawful force on another person*'.

For the tort of assault to be committed it is irrelevant that the victim is not in fear of harm. Consequently, it is possible for an assault to occur where a victim of harassment is threatened with the possibility that she will receive unwanted physical contact. All that must exist for the tort to be committed is that the victim must have a reasonable apprehension that she will imminently receive unwanted contact.

Further, for either tort, the use of the word 'force' in the formulation of the tort does not mean physical violence. It is not necessary that the victim is subjected to a full scale attack (as occurred for example in *Bracebridge Engineering Ltd v Darby [1990] IRLR 3*). It is perfectly possible for the torts to be committed where a person brushes past another suggestively (as in *Porcelli v Strathclyde Regional Council [1986] IRLR 134*) or even kisses another without her consent. The torts therefore cover the full range of possible forms of contact related harassment from physical injury to unwanted molestation and are capable of providing a cause of action even though no actual physical harm has been occasioned to the victim of the particular tort.

*Negligence*

H1732    While negligence may imply to the layman that an act committed against a person has been committed carelessly, it is perfectly possible for the tort to be committed intentionally by a person. The classic phrasing of the tort is derived from the case of *Donoghue v Stevenson [1932] AC 562*, where Lord Atkin stated of the elements of the tort:

> '*You must take reasonable care to avoid acts or omissions which you can reasonably foresee would be likely to injure your neighbour . . . [who are] persons who are so closely and directly affected by my act that I ought reasonably to have them in contemplation as being so affected when I am directing my mind to the acts or omissions which are called in question*'.

The test thus framed ensures that liability will be created where there is reasonable foresight of harm being inflicted upon persons foreseeably affected by an actor's conduct. Consequently, the conduct can be intentional or reckless as well as careless.

Where it is the case that an employee harasses a fellow employee, the harasser and victim will be within the relationship of proximity required by the law (it being recognised that fellow employees owe a duty of care to each other).

Once it has been established that a duty is owed, three other factors become relevant these being whether harm has been sustained by a victim, whether the magnitude of the harm suffered by the victim is far greater than the actor intended and whether an employer has a defence if an action is brought for vicarious liability.

(*a*)    *Requirement for loss.* For the tort of negligence to be committed, the victim must suffer loss or damage flowing from the negligent act. An obvious form that is likely to be sustained in the case of harassment is in the form of stress related illnesses that can occur from prolonged harassment (nervous shock). It is well recognised in law that where a person suffers from medically treatable stress related illnesses that are caused by the negligence of an employer, it is possible to recover damages for the injuries so inflicted (see to this end the non-harassment case of *Walker v Northumberland County Council [1995] ICR 702*).

(*b*)    '*Eggshell-skulls*'. The extent of the injury suffered, provided that a victim could foreseeably have suffered a particular form of harm (e.g. distress) from the commission of the unlawful act, it is irrelevant that the final extent of the harm would not necessarily have been foreseen. This principle is known as the 'eggshell-skull' rule. The law recognises that it is possible for 'eggshell-personalities' to exist (see, for example, *Malcolm v Broadbent [1970] 3 All ER 508*). It is irrelevant that another female would not have suffered nervous shock as a consequence of harassment being meted out to her provided that the hypothetical female would have been distressed by it.

(*c*)    *Vicarious liability*. Finally, there is the question as to whether it is possible for an employer to be sued for harm that is occasioned in negligence from an act of harassment. Whilst the case of *Chief Constable of the Lincolnshire Police v Stubbs [1999] IRLR 81* recognised that employers could become vicariously liable for the acts of employees for the tort of sex discrimination (due to the provisions of s 41(1), SDA 1975), it will also be recalled that in the earlier case of *Tower Boot Co Ltd v Jones [1997] IRLR 168* (dealing with racial harassment), it had been recognised by the EAT that, since, at common law, employers can only be liable for the misperformance of an act that an employee is performed to do, and, since an employer does not employ people to harass others, it should not be possible at common law for an employer to be vicariously liable for the harassment of an employee. Whilst the decision was overturned on appeal, the appeal only dealt with the creation of vicarious liability under the anti-discrimination legislation. In the circumstances, it is conceivable that an employer would still have a defence to a claim for negligence. However, where the claim is framed on the grounds that the employer was aware of the harassment yet failed to act when called upon to do so and harm was occasioned by the employer's failure to act, vicarious liability is not an issue since what is being complained of is the employer's primary failure.

Given that it is possible to recover damages for injury to feelings occasioned as a consequence of sex discrimination, it may well be the case that an employee will not want to pursue a claim for negligence. This said, it is not possible to obtain an injunction in respect of sexual harassment under the *SDA 1975*.

### Remedies in tort

H1733    Where an employee commits an actionable tort (outside of harassment, the remedies for which are provided under the *Protection from Harassment Act 1997* — see below at H1734), two remedies will commonly be available to the victim. These will be:

(*a*)    damages (which is available as of right for a tort); and

(*b*)    an injunction (where damages are not adequate).

In tort, the correct measure of damages is that the victim should be given such a sum by way of compensation as would put her in the position as if the tort had not been committed (*Livingstone v Rawyards Coal Co (1880) 5 App Cas 25*). As to how much this will be is a question of fact in each case and, potentially, in the case of a course of harassment that induces nervous shock preventing an employee from working, could run into hundreds of thousands of pounds.

However, the problem incurred with the common law solution of awarding damages to the victim of a tort in the context of sexual harassment is that the victim may not be properly compensated for on-going acts. In the circumstances, damages may not be adequate in such a situation and the better remedy may be to sue for an injunction.

Further, the use of an injunction to stop on-going harassment may be of more practical benefit to a currently distressed employee than would a future award of damages. This is because injunctions can be applied for and obtained relatively speedily as an intermediate remedy pending a full liability trial.

The problem with pursuing this remedy is that, assuming that the injunction is applied for whilst both the harasser and the victim are still in the employment of their employer, the victim's faith in her employer may well have become exhausted (by the employer's failure to take action in relation to the employee). Indeed, it would be surprising if this were not the case. Consequently, in many cases, the better course of action may well be to leave employment on the grounds of constructive dismissal and sue for compensation under the *SDA 1975*.

### Protection from Harassment Act

H1734    An offence and tort of harassment was created by the *Protection From Harassment Act 1997*. The legislation was passed to protect victims of 'stalking' but there is no reason why its provisions cannot be used to protect victims of sexual harassment in the workplace. Harassment is not specifically defined by the 1997 Act, although *s 7* provides that it must amount to a course of conduct causing alarm or distress to a person.

The phrase 'a course of conduct' is defined to be conduct on two or more occasions and 'conduct' includes words. [*s 7(4)*)].

It is possible to injunct a harasser under s 3 of the Act and also to claim damages.

## Breach of contract

H1735 Where an employee harasses a fellow employee, the harasser will almost certainly breach one or more of the terms of his employment contract. In the first instance, most disciplinary procedures provide that harassment of fellow employees on grounds of sex, race or disability amounts to gross misconduct. Given that many contracts of employment provide that a disciplinary procedure is contractual, harassment per se may provide grounds for summary dismissal.

Even if an employer fails to provide a contractual disciplinary procedure, an employee may well be in breach of various of the implied terms under his contract of employment if he is engaged in sexually harassing a fellow employee. This is because the employee will owe a duty of care to the employer which requires him to take reasonable care for fellow employees. Deliberate sexual harassment will breach this term.

Further, employees must maintain the trust and confidence of the employer during their employment. Sexual harassment of fellow employee's will undermine an employer's confidence and would provide grounds for a conduct related dismissal.

### Remedies

H1736 As with remedies provided for torts, the remedies for breach of contract will be either damages or an injunction.

The law places a different emphasis on the method of computing damages for breach of contract to that provided in relation to torts. Practically though, in the context of a contract of employment, the final outcome will usually be the same. In the law of contract, the victim is to be placed so far as possible in the position as if the contract had been properly performed by the employer (*Robinson v Harman (1848) 1 Exch 850*). The amount payable will vary according to the loss that has been suffered by a victim. Ordinarily, if the employee leaves her employment claiming constructive dismissal, the employee will be able to claim damages for loss of contractual benefits during her notice period (subject to her duty to mitigate). However, it seems that in spite of the decision of the House of Lords in *Malik v BCCI [1997] IRLR 462*, following the subsequent decision of the Court of Appeal in *Johnson v Unisys Ltd [1999] IRLR 90*, it is not possible to recover damages for injury to feelings occasioned as a result of the humiliating manner of a dismissal.

This said, if the claim is framed by an employee as one going to the employer's duty of care to the employee (due to stress related illness being induced by harassment and the employer's unreasonable failure to prevent the cause of the stress) it is well established that an employee will be able to claim damages for the illness so caused (see, to this effect, *Walker v Northumberland County Council [1995] ICR 702*).

## Criminal action

H1737 The conduct of a person who sexually harasses another may also amount to one or more of the following crimes:

(a) battery;

(b) harassment under the *Protection from Harassment Act 1997* (see above at H1734); or

(c) sexual harassment under the *Public Order Act 1986*.

*Battery*

H1738    Battery is a common law offence. The elements of the offences are that the harasser intentionally and unlawfully inflicts personal violence upon the victim. In *Collins v Wilcock [1984] 3 All ER 374* the Court of Appeal held that there was a general exception to the crime which embraced all forms of physical contact generally acceptable. However, it is clear from this that if the victim makes known to her harasser the fact that she does not welcome physical contact from him, the harasser will commit the offence simply by touching her.

The offence can only be tried summarily.

*Harassment under the Protection from Harassment Act 1997*

H1739    The tortious aspects of this Act are considered at H1734 above. The 1997 Act also criminalises a course of conduct pursued by a person who 'knows or ought to know' that the conduct amounts to harassment. *Section 1(2)* of the Act provides that a person will be deemed to have knowledge where a reasonable person in possession of the same information as the harasser would think that the course of conduct amounted to harassment.

The offence is one that is triable either way. If the offence is tried on indictment, the maximum penalty is five years imprisonment or a fine or both. If tried summarily, the maximum penalty is a term of imprisonment not exceeding six months, a fine subject to the statutory maximum or both.

*Sexual harassment under the Public Order Act 1986*

H1740    The offence exists under *s 4A* of the *POA 1986* and criminalises threatening, abusive or insulting words of behaviour thereby causing harassment, alarm or distress. The offence can be committed in a public or private place (other than a dwelling). Consequently, sexual harassment in the workplace is capable of being covered by the Act.

The offence can only be tried summarily and a fine on level 3 of the standard scale can be levied upon conviction.

## Preventing and handling claims

### Harassment policy

H1741    The Equal Opportunities Commission (EOC) recommends the creation and use an of equal opportunity policy by employers. In particular, the EOC's Code of Practice states:

> *'The primary responsibility at law rests with each employer to ensure that there is no unlawful discrimination. It is important, however, that measures to eliminate discrimination or promote equality of opportunity should be understood and supported by all employees. Employers are therefore recommended to involve their employees in each opportunity policies (para 4).*

> *An equal opportunities policy will ensure the effective use of human resources in the best interests of both the organisation and its employees. It is a commitment by an employer to the development and use of employment procedures and practices which do not discriminate on grounds of sex or marriage and which provide genuine equality of opportunity for all employees. The detail of the policy will vary according to size of the organisation (para 34)'.*

In order for the policy to be effective and properly used, it must have the full support of senior managers within the business and must be used fairly and properly on each occasion that its provisions become relevant. So as to achieve this, it is important that the policy is clear and made known to all employees (para 35). A harassment policy is an essential feature of a proper equal opportunities policy and should exhibit the following characteristics:

(*a*)     a complaints procedure;

(*b*)     confidentiality;

(*c*)     a method for informal action to be taken; and

(*d*)     a method for formal action to be taken.

### Complaints procedure

H1742     The hallmark of an effective policy is that provision is made for a complaints procedure that both encourages justifiable complaints of harassment to be made and protects the maker of the complaint. The EC Code of Practice states in this regard (at section B paragraph (iii)) that a formal complaints procedure is needed so as to:

'*. . . give employees confidence that the organisation will take allegations of sexual harassment seriously*'.

The Code also states that such a procedure should be used where employees feel that informal resolution of a dispute is inappropriate or has not worked.

In order for the complaints procedure to be effective, the Code recommends that employees should know clearly whom to make a complaint to and should also be provided with an alternative source of person to make the complaint to in the event that the primary source is inappropriate (e.g. because that person is the alleged harasser).

The Code adds that it is good practice to allow complaints to be made to a person of the same sex as the victim.

### Confidentiality

H1743     In order for complaints to be made effectively, it is necessary that some measure of confidentiality is maintained in the complaint making procedure. The problem that arises here is that there is an inevitable trade-off between the right of the victim of sexual harassment to be protected against recrimination and the right of an alleged harasser to know the case that he is meeting for disciplinary purposes. Indeed, to the extent that complaints are made against a person who is not told where, when and whom he is alleged to have harassed and the alleged harasser is then disciplined as a result of the complaint, there is a chance that the employer will be acting in breach of the duty to maintain the alleged harasser's trust and confidence.

To this end, the requirement for confidentiality exists to the extent that although a harasser may have the right to know the full nature of the complaint that he has to meet, the victim should be protected from recrimination in the workplace by the employer ensuring that all details surrounding the complaint are suppressed from other employees in the workplace save to the extent that it is necessary to involve them to either prove or disprove the allegations of harassment.

Further, the requirement of confidentiality also extends to ensuring that the allegations, to the extent that they are made in good faith, are not subsequently used against the complainant for any other purposes connected with the complainant's employment (thereby tying in with the duty of the employer to ensure that there is no victimisation occasioned to the complainant — see *Nagarajan v London Regional Transport [1999] IRLR 572* dealing with the issue of victimisation).

*Informal action*

H1744    As the EOC Code points out, most victims of harassment simply want the unwanted attention or conduct towards them to stop. Whilst the employer's policy should leave employees in no doubt as to the fact that deliberate harassment will amount to a case of gross misconduct being brought against an employee, it may be the case that the form of the harassment is innocent in nature and can be remedied by informal action. As the EOC Code points out, it may be the case that the victim of harassment can simply explain to the harasser that the conduct that she is receiving is unwelcome and makes the victim feel uncomfortable in the workplace. The Code goes on to state that where the victim finds it embarrassing or uncomfortable to address the harasser, it may be possible for a fellow employee (in the case of a larger organisation possibly a confidential counsellor) to make the requests to the harasser.

This said, in some cases it simply will not be possible or appropriate for the matter to be dealt with informally and where this is the case, the only possible resolution will be through formal channels.

*Formal action*

H1745    In the event that formal action is required to end harassment, both harassers and their victims should be made fully aware as to the procedures that an employer will adopt in relation to a claim of harassment. The EOC Code provides an illustration as to the type of features that should be included in a policy. This will include providing details as to:

(*a*)    how investigations are to be carried out;

(*b*)    the time frame for investigations (which should be as short as possible for the benefit of both the victim of actual harassment and the alleged harasser);

(*c*)    whether there is to be a period of suspension whilst a claim is investigated; and

(*d*)    the penalty for an employee who is found to have engaged in harassment

The Code concludes that it may be necessary to require employees to be transferred to different duties or sites (in some cases even where a case is not proven against an alleged harasser so as to prevent the employees being forced to work with each other against their will). Indeed, where they are required to do so in the face of an unproved allegation, unless the matter has been thoroughly investigated by the employer, it may be a recipe for litigation as the case of *Balgobin v London Borough of Tower Hamlets [1987] IRLR 401* illustrates.

## Training

H1746    Another of the statements made by the EOC Code is that training of the workforce is essential in order to ensure that harassment does not occur in the first place. The Code specifically focuses on training for supervisory staff and managers. The recommendations for training include:

(*a*)    identifying the factors contributing to a working environment free of sexual harassment;

(*b*)    familiarisation of employees with the employer's harassment policy;

(*c*)    specialist training of those employees required to implement the harassment policy; and

(*d*)    training at induction days for new employees as to the employers policy on harassment.

### Monitoring and review

H1747   The acid test of a company's equal opportunity policy is not how it looks on paper but whether and how it is implemented and monitored in practice. The EOC stresses this point. As to monitoring, much will depend upon the facts relating to particular employers. In the case of smaller employers, it may simply require the employer to be aware of any recommendations that are proposed by bodies such as the EOC or the Institute of Personnel and Development. However, where employers are larger, the monitoring function may require a full comparative analysis of complaints made in order to determine what matters need to be implemented with regard to training and whether any changes need to be made to the employer's policy for the purposes of such matters as investigating complaints and tightening up the policy generally.

In short, once the policy is adopted, it must be kept up to date with regard to what is acceptable within the workplace.

## Future developments

### The EOC white paper — 'Equality in the 21st Century: A New Approach'

H1748   The White Paper *Equality in the 21st Century: A New Approach* 'sets out what needs to be done by legislation to promote equal opportunities for men and women'. It provides a full review of the current legislation under the SDA 1975 and the Equal Pay Act 1970 and also examines the impact of the EOC Code of Practice in relation to harassment. The White Paper ultimately concludes that a new, unifying Act dealing with all forms of sex discrimination needs to be enacted in order for the Government to fully tackle sex discrimination.

### *Recommendations in relation to sexual harassment*

H1749   Paragraph 22 of the White Paper specifically deals with the issue of sexual harassment. It recommends that the proposed new single Act should specifically prohibit sexual harassment and adopt the EOC Code definition of harassment for these purposes.

The White Paper goes on to add that the sexual harassment should be extended to cover all areas covered by the Act and not just employment.

It remains to be seen whether the White Paper will be adopted especially in the light of the fact that the Government has announced that it does not propose to enact any further changes to employment law in the lifetime of this current Parliament.

# Joint Consultation in Safety – Safety Representatives, Safety Committees, Collective Agreements and Works Councils

## Introduction

The provision of 'information, consultation and participation' and of 'health protection and safety at the workplace' are outlined as two of the 'fundamental social rights of workers' in accordance with the Community Charter of Fundamental Rights of 1989. Combined with Art 138 of the Treaty of Rome 1957 (as amended by the Treaty of Amsterdam 1997), the Health and Safety Directive 1989 (resulting in 'the Six Pack' collection of regulations) and the United Kingdom's signing of the Social Chapter in 1998, the EU has provided great stimuli for the introduction of extensive obligations to consult on health and safety issues.

At national level, there has already been change to the obligations owed by employers to their workers. The *Working Time Regulations 1998* were introduced in October 1998 (and have subsequently been amended by the *Working Time Regulations 1999 (SI 1999 No 3372)*). Most recently, the obligations owed under the European Works Councils Directive 1994 have been transposed into national law under the *Transnational Information and Consultation of Employees Regulations 1999 (SI 1999 No 3323)*. There is also a European Council proposal for European Works Councils to be introduced into all workplaces with 50 or more workers (albeit that the progress of this proposed Directive is currently stalled). Consultation with the workforce is likely to become a central issue for industrial relations and health and safety over the next few years.

The Health and Safety Commission is also currently seeking to promote change. It has recently published the consultative document '*Employee consultation and involvement in health and safety*', which has made a number of recommendations in relation to health and safety consultation. In particular, it recommends:

(*a*) giving trade union safety representatives the legal power to issue their employer with provisional improvement notices requiring the employer to rectify stated defects within a fixed period of time;

(*b*) extending the unfair dismissal protection provided to 'whistleblowers' to health and safety representatives where the representatives recommend that workers leave their place of work due to circumstances giving rise to a serious, imminent and unavoidable danger at the workplace;

(*c*) extending access to specific information to all employees of an employer;

(*d*) the introduction of specially trained union safety representatives whose function is to undertake workplace inspections at the workplaces of different employers where their members work; and (*e*)   extending protection against victimisation to safety representatives.

This chapter looks at the existing domestic legislation that places an employer under an obligation to consult with its workforce.

## Regulatory framework

J3002   The legal requirements for consultation are more convoluted than might be expected, principally because there are two groups of workers who are treated as distinct for consultation purposes. Until 1996 only those employers who recognised a trade union for any collective bargaining purpose were obliged to consult the workforce through safety representatives. The *Safety Representatives and Safety Committees Regulations 1977 (SI 1977 No 500) (as amended)* ('the *Safety Representatives Regulations*'), which were made under the provisions of the *Health and Safety at Work etc. Act 1974 (HSWA 1974)*, *s 2(6)*, came into effect in 1978 and introduced the right for recognised trade unions to appoint safety representatives. The *Safety Representatives Regulations* were amended in 1993 – by the *Management of Health and Safety at Work Regulations 1992 (SI 1992 No 2051)* now superseded by *SI 1999 No 3242* – to extend employers' duties to consult and provide facilities for safety representatives.

The duty to consult was extended on 1 October 1996 by virtue of the *Health and Safety (Consultation with Employees) Regulations 1996 (SI 1996 No 1513) ('HSCER 1996')*. These regulations were introduced as a 'top up' to the *Safety Representatives Regulations*, extending the obligation upon employers to consult all of their employees about health and safety measures. The 1996 Regulations expanded the obligation beyond just trade union appointed representatives. When introduced, the 1996 Regulations addressed the general reduction of union recognition over the preceding five years. However, the more recent trend in workforces, driven by the twin forces of Europe and the current Labour Government, is for greater worker participation in the employer's undertaking and the current framework facilitates this whether or not a union is the conduit for worker consultation.

The obligation of consultation, its enforcement and the details of the role and functions of safety representatives and representatives of employee safety, whether under the *Safety Representatives Regulations* or the *Health and Safety (Consultation with Employees) Regulations 1996*, are almost identical but, for the sake of clarity, are dealt with separately below. The primary distinction is that different obligations apply depending upon whether the affected workers are unionised or not. The respective regulations also cover persons working in host employers' undertakings.

There are specific supplemental provisions which apply for offshore installations, which are governed by the *Offshore Installations (Safety Representatives and Safety Committees) Regulations 1989 (SI 1989 No 971)*.

Although the *Health and Safety (Consultation with Employees) Regulations 1996* (as amended) and the *Safety Representatives Regulations* are based upon good industrial relations practice, there is still the possibility of a prosecution by the Health and Safety Executive (HSE) inspectors of employers who fail to consult their workforce on health and safety issues. There is substantial overlap, however, with employment protection legislation and the obligations in respect of consultation – as can be seen from the protective rights which are conferred upon safety representatives, such as the right not to be victimised or subjected to detriment for health and safety activities, together with the consequential right to present a complaint to an employment tribunal if they are dismissed or suffer a detriment as a result of carrying out their duties.

The *Health and Safety (Consultation with Employees) Regulations 1996* (as amended) also extend these rights to the armed forces. However, armed forces representatives are to be appointed rather than elected, and no paid time off is available. The *Health and Safety (Consultation with Employees) Regulations 1996* (as amended) do not apply to sea-going ships.

The Working Time Directive 1994 has resulted in the *Working Time Regulations 1998 and 1999 (SIs 1998 No 1833 and 1999 No 3372)* under national law. These regulations allow collective modification of the night working requirements in *Reg 6*, the daily rest provisions in *Reg 10*, the weekly rest provisions in *Reg 11*, the rest break provisions in *Reg 12* and also allow modification of the averaging period for calculating weekly working time under *Reg 4* where the same is either for objective, technical or organisational reasons. The method of modification is either by collective agreement in the case of a unionised workforce or by workforce agreement (as defined in the 1998 Regulations, *Sch 1*) in the case of non-unionised employees.

Finally, in relation to pan-European employers, obligations are owed to workers under the European Works Councils Directive 1994. The United Kingdom adopted the Directive on 15 December 1997 and provisions were enacted into national law by the *Transnational Information and Consultation of Employees Regulations 1999 (SI 1999 No 3323)* and came into force on 15 January 2000. Whilst the 1999 Regulations do not specifically encompass health and safety obligations, these issues are within the remit of a European Works Council.

## Consultation obligations for unionised employers

J3003     Under the *Safety Representatives Regulations*, a trade union has the right to appoint an individual to represent the workforce in consultations with the employer on all matters concerning health and safety at work, and to carry out periodic inspections of the workplace for hazards. Every employer has a duty to consult such union-appointed safety representatives on health and safety arrangements (and, if they so request him, to establish a safety committee to review the arrangements – see J3017 below). [*HSWA 1974, s 2I*].

### General duty

J3004     The general duty of the employer under the *Safety Representatives Regulations* is to 'consult with safety representatives with regard to both the making and maintaining of arrangements that will enable the employer and its workforce to co-operate in promoting and developing health and safety at work, and monitoring its effectiveness'. General guidance has been issued by the Health and Safety Commission in the form of the Codes of Practice '*Safety Representatives and Safety Committees*' and '*Time Off for the Training of Safety Representatives*' to which regard should be had generally.

### Appointment of safety representatives

J3005     The right of appointment of safety representatives was, until 1 October 1996, restricted to independent trade unions who are recognised by employers for collective bargaining purposes. The *HSCER 1996* extended this to duly elected representatives of employee safety, as detailed above.

The terms 'independent' and 'recognised' are defined in the *Safety Representatives Regulations* and follow the definitions laid down in the *Trade Union and Labour Relations (Consolidation) Act 1992, ss 5* and *178(3)* respectively. The regulations make no provision for dealing with disputes which may arise over questions of independence or recognition (this is dealt with in the *Trade Union and Labour*

*Relations (Consolidation) Act 1992, ss 6* and *8* – the amendments that have been made to the *Trade Union and Labour Relations (Consolidation) Act 1992* by the *Employment Relations Act 1999* in relation to recognition of unions do not help as the new *Sch A1* is confined to recognition disputes concerning pay, hours and holiday). Safety representatives must be representatives of recognised independent trade unions, and it is up to each union to decide on its arrangements for the appointment or election of its safety representatives [*Reg 3*]. Employers are not involved in this matter, except that they must be informed in writing of the names of the safety representatives appointed and of the group(s) of employees they represent [*Reg 3(2)*].

The *Safety Representatives Regulations, Reg 8*, state that safety representatives must be employees except in the cases of members of the Musicians' Union and actors' Equity. In addition, where reasonably practicable, safety representatives should have at least two years' employment with their present employer or two years' experience in similar employment. The HSC guidance notes advise that it is not reasonably practicable for safety representatives to have two years' experience, or employment elsewhere, where:

(*a*)     the employer is newly established,

(*b*)     the workplace is newly established,

(*c*)     the work is of short duration, or

(*d*)     there is high labour turnover.

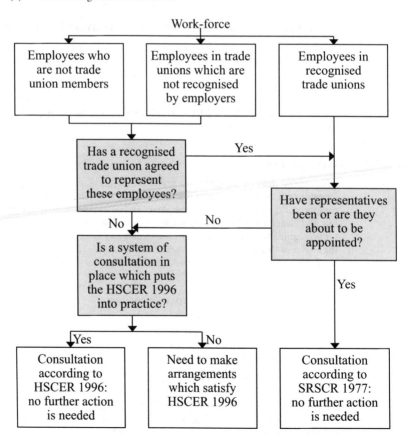

The same general guidance is followed for employee safety representatives under the *HSCER 1996*.

## Number of representatives for workforce

J3006   The *Safety Representatives Regulations* do not lay down the number of safety representatives that unions are permitted to appoint for each workplace. This is a matter for unions themselves to decide, having regard to the number of workers involved and the hazards to which they are exposed. The HSE's view is that each safety representative should be regarded as responsible for the interests of a defined group of workers. This approach has not been found to conflict with existing workplace trade union organisation based on defined groups of workers. The size of these groups does vary from union to union and from workplace to workplace. While normally each workplace area or constituency would need only one safety representative, additional safety representatives are sometimes required where workers are exposed to numerous or particularly severe hazards; where workers are distributed over a wide geographical area or over a variety of workplace locations; and where workers are employed on shiftwork.

## Role of safety representatives

J3007   The *Safety Representatives Regulations, Reg 4(1)* (as amended by the *Management of Health and Safety at Work Regulations 1992 (SI 1992 No 2051)* – now superseded by the *Management of Health and Safety at Work Regulations 1999 (SI 1999 No 3242)*) lists a number of detailed functions for safety representatives:

(*a*)   to investigate potential hazards and causes of accidents at the workplace;

(*b*)   to investigate employee complaints concerning health etc. at work;

(*c*)   to make representations to the employer on matters arising out of (*a*) and (*b*) and on general matters affecting the health etc. of the employees at the workplace;

(*d*)   to carry out the following inspections (and see J3008 below):

— of the workplace (after giving reasonable written notice to the employer – see *Reg 5*);

— of the relevant area after a reportable accident or dangerous occurrence (see accident reporting) or if a reportable disease is contracted, if it is safe to do so and in the interests of the employees represented (see *Reg 6*);

— of documents relevant to the workplace or the employees represented which the employer is required to keep (see *Reg 7*) – reasonable notice must be given to the employer;

(*e*)   to represent the employees they were appointed to represent in consultations with the HSE inspectors, and to receive information from them (see J3016 below);

(*f*)   to attend meetings of safety committees.

These functions are interrelated and are to be implemented proactively rather than reactively. Safety representatives should not just represent their members' interests when accidents or near-misses occur or at the time of periodic inspections, but should carry out their obligations on a continuing day-to-day basis. The *Safety Representatives Regulations* make this obligation clear by stating that safety representatives have the functions of investigating potential hazards and members' complaints *before* accidents, as well as investigating dangerous occurrences and the causes of accidents *after* they have occurred. These functions are only assumed when the employer has been notified in writing by the trade union or workforce of the identity of the representative.

Thus safety representatives may possibly be closely involved not only in the technical aspects of health, safety and welfare matters at work, but also in those areas which could be described as quasi-legal. In other words, they may become involved in the interpretation and clarification of terminology in the *Safety Representatives Regulations*, as well as in discussion and negotiation with employers as to how and when the regulations may be applied. This would often happen in committee meetings.

By *Reg 4A(1) Safety Representatives Regulations* (introduced by the *Management of Health and Safety at Work Regulations 1992*), the subjects on which consultation 'in good time' between employers and safety representatives should take place are:

(*a*)    the introduction of any new measure at a workplace which may substantially affect health and safety;

(*b*)    arrangements for appointing competent persons to assist the employer with health and safety and implementing procedures for serious and imminent risk;

(*c*)    any health and safety information the employer is required to provide; and

(*d*)    the planning and organisation of health and safety training and health and safety implications of the introduction (or planning) of new technology.

The safety representative's terms of reference are, therefore, broad, and exceed the traditional 'accident prevention' area. For example, *Reg 4(1)* empowers safety representatives to investigate 'potential hazards' and to take up issues which affect standards of health, safety and welfare at work. In practice it is becoming clear that four broad areas are now engaging the attention of safety representatives and safety committees:

—    health;

—    safety;

—    environment;

—    welfare.

These four broad areas effectively mean that safety representatives can, and indeed often do, examine standards relating, for example, to noise, dust, heating, lighting, cleanliness, lifting and carrying, machine guarding, toxic substances, radiation, cloakrooms, toilets and canteens. The protective standards that are operating in the workplace, or the lack of them, are now coming under much closer scrutiny than hitherto.

## Workplace inspections

J3008    Arrangements for three-monthly and other more frequent inspections and reinspections should be by joint arrangement. The TUC advises that the issues to be discussed with the employer can include:

—    more frequent inspections of high risk or rapidly changing areas of work activity;

—    the precise timing and notice to be given for formal inspections by safety representatives;

— the number of representatives taking part in any one formal inspection;

— the breaking-up of plant-wide formal inspections into smaller, more manageable inspections;

— provision for different groups of safety representatives to carry out inspections of different parts of the workplace;

— the kind of inspections to be carried out, e.g. safety tours, safety sampling or safety surveys;

— the calling in of independent technical advisers by the safety representatives.

Although formal inspections are not intended to be a substitute for day-to-day observation, they have on a number of occasions provided an opportunity to carry out a full-scale examination of all or part of the workplace and for discussion with employers' representatives about remedial action. They can also provide an opportunity to inspect documents required under health and safety legislation, e.g. certificates concerning the testing of equipment. It should be emphasised that, during inspections following reportable accidents or dangerous occurrences, employers are not required to be present when the safety representative talks with his members. In workplaces where more than one union is recognised, agreements with employers about inspections should involve all the unions concerned. It is generally agreed that safety representatives are also allowed under the regulations to investigate the following:

— potential hazards;

— dangerous occurrences;

— the causes of accidents;

— complaints from their members.

This means that imminent risks, or hazards which may affect their members, can be investigated right away by safety representatives without waiting for formal joint inspections. Following an investigation of a serious mishap, safety representatives are advised to complete a hazard report form, one copy being sent to the employer and one copy retained by the safety representative.

## Rights and duties of safety representatives

*Legal immunity*

J3009

Ever since the *Trade Disputes Act 1906*, trade unions (and employers' associations) have enjoyed immunity from liability in tort for industrial action, taken or threatened, in contemplation or furtherance of a trade dispute (although such freedom of action was subsequently curtailed by the *Trade Union and Labour Relations (Consolidation) Act 1992, s 20*). Not surprisingly, perhaps, this immunity extends to their representatives acting in a lawful capacity. Thus, the *Safety Representatives Regulations* state that none of the functions of a safety representative confers legal duties or responsibilities [*Reg 4(1)*]. As safety representatives are not legally responsible for health, safety or welfare at work, they cannot be liable under either the criminal or civil law for anything they may do, or fail to do, as a safety representative under these Regulations. This protection against criminal or civil liability does not, however, remove a safety representative's legal responsibility as an employee. Safety representatives must carry out their responsibilities under *HSWA 1974, s 7* if they are not to be liable for criminal prosecution by an HSE inspector. These duties as an employee are to take reasonable care for the health and safety of one's self and others, and to co-operate with one's employer as far as is necessary to enable him to carry out his statutory duties on health and safety.

### Time off with pay

*General right*

J3010    Under the *Safety Representatives Regulations* safety representatives are entitled to take such paid time off during working hours as is necessary to perform their statutory functions, and reasonable time to undergo training in accordance with a Code of Practice approved by the Health and Safety Commission.

*Definition of 'time off'*

J3011    The *Safety Representatives Regulations, Reg 4(2)* provides that the employer must provide the safety representative with such time off with pay during the employee's working hours as shall be necessary for the purposes of:

(*a*)    performing his statutory functions; and

(*b*)    undergoing such training in aspects of those functions as may be reasonable in all the circumstances.

Further details of these requirements are outlined in the Code of Practice attached to the *Safety Representatives Regulations* and the HSC Approved Code of Practice on time off for training. The Code of Practice is for guidance purposes only – its contents are recommendations rather than requirements. However, it is guidance that an employment tribunal can and will take into account if a complaint is lodged in relation to an employer's unreasonable failure to allow time off.

The combined effect of the ACAS Code No 3: '*Time Off for Trade Union Duties and Activities*' (1991) carried over into the *Trade Union and Labour Relations (Consolidation) Act 1992* and the HSC Approved Code of Practice on time off is that shop stewards who have also been appointed as safety representatives are to be given time off by their employers to carry out both their industrial relations duties and their safety functions, and also paid leave to attend separate training courses on industrial relations and on health and safety at work – this includes a TUC course on *COSHH* (*Gallagher v The Drum Engineering Co Ltd, COIT 1330/89*).

An employee is not entitled to be paid for time taken off in lieu of the time he had spent on a course. This was held in *Huirsine v Hull City Council [1992] IRLR 211* when a shift worker, whose shift ran from 3 pm to 11 pm, attended a trade union course from 9 am to 4 pm and then carried out his duties until 7 pm. He was paid from 3 pm to 7 pm and he could claim no more. However, where more safety representatives have been appointed than there are sections of the workforce for which safety representatives could be responsible, it is not unreasonable for an employer to deny some safety representatives time off for fulfilling safety functions (*Howard and Peet v Volex plc (HSIB 181)*).

A decision of the EAT *seems* to FAVOUR JOINTLY sponsored in-house courses, except as regards the representational aspects of the functions of safety representatives, where the training is to be provided exclusively by the union (*White v Pressed Steel Fisher [1980] IRLR 176*). Moreover, one course per union per year is too rigid an approach (*Waugh v London Borough of Sutton (1983) HSIB 86*).

*Definition of 'pay'*

J3012    The amount of pay to which the safety representative is entitled is contained in the Schedule to the Regulations.

*Recourse for the safety representative*

J3013    Where the employer's refusal to allow paid time off is unreasonable, he must reimburse the employee for the time taken to attend [*Reg 4(2), Schedule*]. *Scarth v East Herts DC (HSIB 181)*: the test of reasonableness is to be judged at the time of the decision to refuse training.

Safety representatives who are refused time off to perform their functions or who are not paid for such time off are able to make a complaint to an employment tribunal [*Reg 11*].

## Facilities to be provided by employer

J3014    The type and number of facilities that employers are obliged to provide for safety representatives are not spelled out in the regulations, Code of Practice or guidance notes, other than a general requirement in the *Safety Representatives Regulations, Reg 5(3)* which states, *inter alia*, that 'the employer shall provide such facilities and assistance as the safety representatives shall require for the purposes of carrying out their functions'. Formerly, the requirement to provide facilities and assistance related only to inspections.

Trade unions consider that the phrase 'facilities and assistance' includes the right to request the presence of an independent technical adviser or trade union official during an inspection, and for safety representatives to take samples of substances used at work for analysis outside the workplace. The TUC has recommended that the following facilities be made available to safety representatives:

(*a*)    a room and desk at the workplace;

(*b*)    facilities for storing correspondence;

(*c*)    inspection reports and other papers;

(*d*)    ready access to internal and external telephones;

(*e*)    access to typing and duplicating facilities;

(*f*)    provision of notice-boards;

(*g*)    use of a suitable room for reporting back to and consulting with members;

(*h*)    other facilities should include copies of all relevant statutes, regulations, Approved Codes of Practice and HSC guidance notes; and copies of all legal or international standards which are relevant to the workplace.

## Disclosure of information

J3015    Employers are required by the *Safety Representatives Regulations* to disclose information to safety representatives which is necessary for them to carry out their functions [*Reg 7(1)*]. A parallel provision exists under the *Management of Health and Safety at Work Regulations 1999, Reg 10(2)* in relation to the information that is to be provided to the parents of a child to be employed by an employer (see CHILDREN AND YOUNG PERSONS C3005).

*Regulation 7* is consolidated by paragraph 6 of the Code of Practice which details the health and safety information 'within the employer's knowledge' that should be made available to safety representatives. This should include:

(*a*)    plans and performance and any changes proposed which may affect health and safety;

(b)   technical information about hazards and precautions necessary, including information provided by manufacturers, suppliers and so on;

(c)   information and statistical records on accidents, dangerous occurrences and notifiable industrial diseases; and

(d)   other information such as measures to check the effectiveness of health and safety arrangements and information on articles and substances issued to homeworkers.

The exceptions to this requirement are where disclosure of such information would be 'against the interests of national security'; where it would contravene a prohibition imposed by law; any information relating to an individual (unless consent has been given); information that would damage the employer's undertaking; and information obtained for the sole purpose of bringing, prosecuting or defending legal proceedings [*Safety Representatives Regulations, Reg 7(2)*].

However, the decision in *Waugh v British Railways Board [1979] 2 AER 1169* established that where an employer seeks, on grounds of privilege, to withhold a report made following an accident, he can only do so if its dominant purpose is related to actual or potential hostile legal proceedings. In this particular case, a report was commissioned for two purposes following the death of an employee: (a) to recommend improvements in safety measures, and (b) to gather material for the employer's defence. It was held that the report was not privileged.

This was followed in *Lask v Gloucester Health Authority [1986] HSIB 123* where a circular *'Reporting Accidents in Hospitals'* had to be discovered by order after an injury to an employee whilst he was walking along a path.

Where differences of opinion arise as to the evaluation or interpretation of technical aspects of safety information or health data, unions are advised to contact the local offices of the HSE, because of the HSE expertise and access to research.

### Technical information

J3016   HSE inspectors are also obliged under *HSWA 1974, s 28(8)*, to supply safety representatives with technical information – factual information obtained during their visits (i.e. any measurements, testing the results of sampling and monitoring), notices of prosecution, copies of correspondence and copies of any improvement or prohibition notices issued to their employer. The latter places an absolute duty on an inspector to disclose specific kinds of information to workers or their representatives concerning health, safety and welfare at work. This can also involve personal discussions between the HSE inspector and the safety representative. The inspector must also tell the representative what action he proposes to take as a result of his visit. Where local authority health inspectors are acting under powers granted by *HSWA 1974* (see ENFORCEMENT), they are also required to provide appropriate information to safety representatives.

### Safety committees

J3017   There is a duty on every employer, in cases where it is prescribed (see below), to establish a safety committee if requested to do so by safety representatives. The committee's purpose is to monitor health and safety measures at work [*HSWA 1974, s 2(7)*]. Such cases are prescribed by the *Safety Representatives Regulations* and limit the duty to appoint a committee to requests made by trade union safety representatives.

### Establishment of a safety committee

**J3018**  If requested by at least two safety representatives in writing, the employer must establish a safety committee [*Safety Representatives Regulations (as amended), Reg 9(1)*].

When setting up a safety committee, the employer must:

(*a*)  consult with both:

—  the safety representatives who make the request; and

—  the representatives of recognised trade unions whose members work in any workplace where it is proposed that the committee will function;

(*b*)  post a notice, stating the composition of the committee and the workplace(s) to be covered by it, in a place where it can easily be read by employees;

(*c*)  establish the committee within three months after the request for it was made.

[*Reg 9(2)*].

### Function of safety committees

**J3019**  In practical terms, trade union appointed safety representatives are now using the medium of safety committees to examine the implications of hazard report forms arising from inspections, and the results of investigations into accidents and dangerous occurrences, together with the remedial action required. A similar procedure exists with respect to representatives for tests and measurements of noise, toxic substances or other harmful effects on the working environment.

Trade unions regard the function of safety committees as a forum for the discussion and resolution of problems that have failed to be solved initially through the intervention of the safety representative in discussion with line management. There is, therefore, from the trade unions' viewpoint, a large measure of negotiation with its consequent effect on collective bargaining agreements.

If safety representatives are unable to resolve a problem with management through the safety committee, or with the HSE, they can approach their own union for assistance – a number of unions have their own health and safety officers who can, and do, provide an extensive range of information on occupational health and safety matters. The unions, in turn, can refer to the TUC for further advice.

The 'Brown Book', which contains the *Safety Representatives Regulations*, Code of Practice and guidance, was revised in 1996 to include the amendments made in 1993 by the *Management of Health and Safety at Work Regulations 1992* (as amended) (see above) and the *Health and Safety (Consultation with Employees) Regulations 1996* (see below).

## Non-unionised workforce – consultation obligations

**J3020**  A representative of employee safety is an elected representative of a non-unionised workforce who is assigned with broadly the same rights and obligations as a safety representative in a unionised workforce.

### General duty

**J3021**  The *Health and Safety (Consultation with Employees) Regulations 1996* introduced a new duty to consult any employees who are not members of a group covered by safety representatives (appointed under the *Safety Representatives Regulations*).

Employers therefore have the choice of consulting their employees either directly or by way of an appointed representative of employee safety. The obligation is to consult those employees in good time on matters relating to their health and safety at work.

## Number of representatives for workforce

J3022   Guidance notes on the *Health and Safety (Consultation with Employees) Regulations 1996* state that the number of safety representatives who can be appointed depends on the size of the workforce and workplace, whether there are different sites, the variety of different occupations, the operation of shift systems and the type and risks of work activity. A DTI Workplace Survey has concluded that in a non-unionised workplace which has appointed worker representatives, it is usual for there to be several representatives, with the median being three. The survey estimated that there are approximately 218,000 representatives across all British workplaces with 25 or more employees.

## Role of safety representatives

J3023   The functions of representatives of employee safety are:

(*a*)   to make representations to the employer of potential hazards and dangerous occurrences at the workplace which affect or could affect the group of employees he represents;

(*b*)   to make representations to the employer on general matters affecting the health and safety at work of the group of employees he represents, and in particular on such matters as he has been consulted about by the employer under the 1996 Regulations; and

(*c*)   to represent that group of employees in consultations at the workplace with inspectors appointed under *HSWA 1974*.

## Rights and duties of representatives of employee safety

*Time off with pay*

J3024   Under the *Health and Safety (Consultation with Employees) Regulations 1996, Reg 7(1)(b)*, the right that a representative of employee safety has to take time off with pay is generally the same as that for safety representatives.

*Definition of 'time off'*

J3025   An employer is under an obligation to permit a representative of employee safety to take such time off with pay during working hours as shall be necessary for:

(*a*)   performing his functions; and

(*b*)   undergoing such training as is reasonable in all the circumstances.

A candidate standing for election as a representative of employee safety is also allowed reasonable time off with pay during working hours in order to perform his functions as a candidate [*Reg 7(2)*].

*Definition of 'pay'*

J3026   *Schedule 1* to the 1996 Regulations deals with the definition of pay, and generally the definition is the same as that for union safety representatives.

*Provision of information*

J3027 The employer must provide such information as is necessary to enable the employees or representatives of employee safety to participate fully and effectively in the consultation. In the case of representatives of employee safety, the information must also be sufficient to enable them to carry out their functions under the Regulations.

Information provided to representatives must also include information which is contained in any record which the employer is required to keep under *RIDDOR 1995* and which relates to the workplace or the group of employees represented by the representatives. Note that there are exceptions to the requirement to disclose information similar to those under the *Safety Representatives Regulations, Reg 7* (see J3015 above).

*Relevant training*

J3028 Representatives of employee safety must be provided with reasonable training in respect of their functions under the *Health and Safety (Consultation with Employees) Regulations 1996*, for which the employer must pay.

*Remedies for failure to provide time off or pay for time off*

J3029 A representative of employee safety, or candidate standing for election as such, who is denied time off or who fails to receive payment for time off, may make an application to an employment tribunal for a declaration and/or compensation. As in the case of safety representatives, the remedies obtainable (set out in *Schedule 2* to the 1996 Regulations) are similar to those granted to complainants under the *Trade Union and Labour Relations (Consolidation) Act 1992, s 168* (time off for union duties).

## Recourse for safety representatives

J3030 Safety representatives (whether they are appointed under the *Safety Representatives Regulations* or the *Health and Safety (Consultation with Employees) Regulations 1996*) are provided with statutory protection for the proper execution of their duties.

An employee who is:

(*a*)  designated by his employer to carry out a health and safety related function,

(*b*)  a representative of employee safety, or

(*c*)  a candidate standing for election as such,

has the right not to be subjected to any detriment or unfairly dismissed on the grounds that:

—  having been designated by the employer to carry out a health and safety related function, he carried out, or proposed to carry out, the function;

—  he undertook, or proposed to undertake, any function(s) consistent with being a safety representative or member of a safety committee;

—  he took part in, or proposed to take part in, consultation with the employer; or

—  he took part in an election of representatives of employee safety.

In relation to a detriment claim, where the employer infringes any of these rights, the employee has the right to make a complaint to an employment tribunal under the *Employment Rights Act 1996, s 44(1)* (as amended by the *Health and Safety*

*(Consultation with Employees) Regulations 1996, Reg 8)*. A tribunal can make a declaration and also award compensation (*Employment Rights Act 1996, ss 48, 49*). There is no minimum qualifying period of service nor upper age limit for bringing such a claim.

If the employer unfairly dismisses such an employee for one of the above reasons, or where it is the principal reason for the dismissal, that dismissal shall be deemed automatically unfair (*Employment Rights Act 1996, s 100*, as amended by the *Health and Safety (Consultation with Employees) Regulations 1996, Reg 8*). It will also be an automatically unfair dismissal to select a representative or candidate for redundancy for such a reason (*Employment Rights Act 1996, s 105*). The normal minimum qualifying period of service, the normal upper age limit and the cap on the compensatory award for unfair dismissal claims do not apply (*Employment Rights Act 1996, ss 108, 109 and 124(1A)* (as amended by the *Employment Relations Act 1999, s 37(1)*).

# European developments in health and safety

## Introduction

J3031    Health and safety law will continue to be subject to change in the future with the implementation of further European directives and the HSC programme of modifying and simplifying health and safety law. At a European level the most important legislation is the directives made under Art 138 of the Treaty of Rome (as amended). The Framework Directive, from which the *Health and Safety (Consultation with Employees) Regulations 1996* were derived, will continue to drive forward developments in UK health and safety law.

Further developments have occurred under European law which are having an impact at national level these being in the form of the Working Time Directive (93/104) and the European Works Councils Directive (94/45). These Directives have been implemented into national law under the *Working Time Regulations 1998 and 1999 (SIs 1998 No 1833 and 1999 No 3372)* and the *Transnational Information and Consultation of Employees Regulations 1999 (SI 1999 No 3323)* respectively.

## The Working Time Regulations 1998 and 1999

J3032    A full discussion of the impact of the Regulations is beyond the scope of this chapter – readers are referred to WORKING TIME for a discussion of the impact of the *Working Time Regulations* generally.

That said, the *Working Time Regulations* have introduced a joint consultation function into the operation of the Regulations by use of collective, workforce and relevant agreements. The Regulations provide that it is possible to vary the extent to which the Regulations must be strictly complied with through the use of these devices. The various types of agreements can be described as follows:

(a)    Collective agreements – these are defined by *s 178 of the Trade Union and Labour Relations (Consolidation) Act 1992* as being agreements between independent trade unions and employers;

(b)    Workforce agreements – these were created by the Regulations and are defined in *the Working Time Regulations 1998, Reg 2 and Sch 1*. They amount to agreements between an employer and either duly elected worker representatives of the employer or, in the case of an employer employing less than 20 workers, a majority of the individual workers themselves, where the agreement concluded:

    —    is in writing;

—   has effect for a specified period not exceeding five years;

—   applies to either:

   (i)   all of the relevant members of the workforce, or

   (ii)   all of the relevant members of the workforce who belong to a particular sub-group;

—   is signed:

   (i)   by the worker representatives or by the particular group of workers, or

   (ii)   in the case of an employer having less than 20 employees on the date on which the agreement is first concluded, either by appropriate representatives or by a majority of the workers working for the employer; and

—   before being made available for signature, copies of the agreement were provided to all of the workers to whom the agreement was intended to apply, together with such guidance as the workers might reasonably require in order to understand the draft agreement;

(*c*)   Relevant agreements – these are workforce agreements that cover a worker, any provision of a collective agreement that is individually incorporated into the contract of employment of a worker, or any other agreement in writing between a worker and his employer that is legally enforceable (e.g. a staff handbook).

By *Reg 23(a) of the Working Time Regulations 1998*, it is possible to modify the provisions relating to:

(*a*)   the length of night work (see *Reg 6*); and

(*b*)   the minimum daily and weekly rest periods and rest breaks (see *Regs 10-12* respectively).

Modification must be by way of a collective or workforce agreement and such an agreement must make provision for a compensatory rest period of equivalent length (*Reg 24*).

Further, by *Reg 23(b)*, it is possible for an employer and its workers to agree by collective or workforce agreement to vary the reference period for calculating the maximum working week from the usual 17 weeks to a 52 week period if there are objective or technical reasons relating to the organisation which justify such a change.

The variation provisions allow a degree of flexibility where it is necessary for the interests of an employer's business to effect such change for operational reasons whilst still ensuring the protection of the health and safety of the workforce. The provisions also ensure that any change that is to be made must survive collective scrutiny of the employer's workforce.

## European Works Councils and Information and Consultation Procedures

J3033   The provisions relating to European Works Councils are at present confined to large pan-European entities. However, as stated at J3001, a draft directive has been proposed that would make works councils obligatory for any employer employing more than 50 workers.

The European Work Council Directive (94/45) was incorporated into national law by the *Transnational Information and Consultation of Employees Regulations 1999 (SI 1999 No 3323)* ('the *Works Councils Regulations*'). A full discussion of the operation of the *Works Councils Regulations* is beyond the scope of this chapter, which instead focuses upon the health and safety aspect of the Regulations.

The *Works Councils Regulations* govern employers employing a total of 1,000 or more workers where at least 150 workers are so employed in each of two or more member states.

Their main purpose is procedural. Part IV of the Regulations creates machinery between workers and their employer for the purpose of establishing either a European Works Council ('EWC') or an Information and Consultation Procedure ('ICP'). *Regulation 17(1)* provides that the central management of the employer and a special negotiating body (defined in *Part III of the Works Councils Regulations*) are bound to:

'. . . negotiate in a spirit of co-operation with a view to reaching a written agreement on the detailed arrangements for the information and consultation of employees in a Community-scale undertaking or Community-scale group of undertakings'.

*Regulation 17(3)* leaves the choice of whether to proceed with an EWC or an ICP to the parties.

The parties are free to include in the agreement reference to whatever matters are likely to affect the workers of the employer at a trans-national level. Health and safety is clearly such an issue.

If:

(*a*)    the parties fail to agree the content of the agreement; or

(*b*)    within six months of a valid request being made to the central management of an employer the employer fails to negotiate so as to create either an EWC or ICP; or

(*c*)    after three years of negotiation to produce an agreement for an EWC or ICP the parties cannot agree as to the constitution,

default machinery is provided by the *Schedule to the Works Councils Regulations [Reg 18(1)]*. *Paragraph 6 of the Schedule* provides in relation to EWCs that:

'The competence of the European Works Council shall be limited to information and consultation on the matters which concern the Community-scale undertaking or Community-scale group of undertakings as a whole or at least two of its establishments or group undertakings situated in different Member States'.

In relation to ICPs, *para 7(3)* provides that meetings of ICPs:

'. . . shall relate in particular to the structure, economic and financial situation, the probable development of the business and of production and sales, the situation and probable trend of employment, investments, and substantial changes concerning organisation, [and] introduction of new working methods or production processes . . .'

Although not expressly providing for discussion of health and safety issues, the provisions relating to both EWCs and ICPs will, by implication, include debate of health and safety matters.

# Lifting Machinery and Equipment

## Introduction

There are several distinct categories or groups of machinery which relate to lifting. Each group is dealt with within the regulatory framework in a slightly different way.

The legislation separates lifting machinery from lifts which are permanently installed in buildings. The latter are covered by the EU's Lifts Directive which is implemented into UK law by the *Lifts Regulations 1997 (SI 1997 No 831)*. The *Lifts Regulations 1997* make reference to the Machinery Directive and the Construction Products Directive.

The lifting machinery which is not covered by the Lifts Directive is covered by the Machinery Directive which is implemented into UK law by the *Supply of Machinery (Safety) Regulations 1992 (SI 1992 No 3073* as amended by *SI 1994 No 2063)*. The Machinery Directive deals directly with safety for suppliers of lifting machines and lifting accessories.

There are specific requirements for lifting machinery in addition to the common requirements for all machinery. These extra requirements deal with matters such as lifting coefficients for tests, whether machines lift goods and/or people, and what control systems are appropriate (see the *Supply of Machinery (Safety) Regulations 1992, Schedule 3 para 4* 'Essential health and safety requirements to offset the particular hazards due to a lifting operation').

In addition, specific types of lifting equipment including lifting devices which raise people to a height of more than three metres, and vehicle servicing lifts, are within the *Supply of Machinery (Safety) Regulations 1992, Schedule 4*, and require the conformity to be subject to scrutiny by a notified body within the Machinery Directive. 'State-of-the-art' for safety is established in some cases in the relevant transposed harmonised standards, e.g. BS EN 1443: 1999 – Vehicle lifts.

Lifts controlled by electrical equipment are also subject to the relevant parts of the *Electrical Equipment (Safety) Regulations 1994 (SI 1994 No 3260)* implementing the Low Voltage Directive, and the *Electromagnetic Compatibility Regulations 1992 (SI 1992 No 2372* as amended by *SI 1994 No 3080)*. Lifts installed in buildings are also subject to the IEE Wiring Regulations (BS 7671: 1992 – Requirements for electrical installations).

These above rules and regulations apply to the supply of lift equipment. In addition the *Lifting Operations and Lifting Equipment Regulations 1998 (SI 1998 No 2307)* apply to their use and upkeep.

This chapter examines:

(i)   hoists and lifts;

(ii)   forklift trucks;

(iii)   lifting machinery other than hoists and lifts – particularly cranes and the safe use of mobile cranes;

(iv)   lifting tackle (ropes, rings, hooks and slings);

(v)   lifting operations on construction sites; and

(vi) statutory requirements relating to lifting equipment, namely:

    (i) the *Lifts Regulations 1997 (SI 1997 No 831)*;

    (ii) the *Lifting Operations and Lifting Equipment Regulations 1998 (SI 1998 No 2307)*.

## Hoists and lifts

**L3002**      The safe use and maintenance of hoists and lifts is governed primarily by the *Lifting Operations and Lifting Equipment Regulations 1998 (SI 1998 No 2307)*.

Examples include: goods lifts; man hoists (for example those found in flour mills), paternoster lifts (for transporting passengers vertically – usually up to six); scissors lifts and passenger lifts.

Powered working platforms are commonly used for fast and safe access to overhead machinery/plant, stored products, lighting equipment and electrical installations as well as for enabling maintenance operations to be carried out on high-rise buildings. Their height, reach and mobility give them distinct advantages over scaffolding, boatswain's chairs and platforms attached to fork lift trucks. Typical operations are characterised by self-propelled hydraulic booms, semi-mechanised articulated booms and self-propelled scissors lifts.

Platforms should always be sited on firm level working surfaces and their presence indicated by traffic cones and barriers. Location should be away from overhead power lines – but, if this is not practicable, a permit to work system should be instituted. A key danger arises from overturning as a consequence of overloading the platform. Maximum lifting capacity should, therefore, be clearly indicated on the platform as well as in the manufacturer's instructions, and it is inadvisable to use working platforms in high winds (i.e. above Force 4 or 16 mph). Powered working platforms should be regularly maintained and only operated by trained personnel.

A simple guide on the thorough examination and testing of hoists and lifts aimed at helping small businesses has been published by HSE Books. *'A thorough examination and testing of lifts: simple guidance for lift owners'* explains in a free leaflet what duty holders need to do to comply with the law. It includes a summary of the legal requirements, an explanation of the purpose of thorough examination and what it should include and advice on how to select a competent person to carry out the examination.

## Fork lift trucks

**L3003**      Fork lift trucks are the most widely used item of mobile mechanical handling equipment. There are several varieties which are as follows:

(1) *Pedestrian-operated stackers – manually-operated and power-operated*

    Manually-operated stackers are usually limited in operation, for example, for moving post pallets, and cannot pick up directly from the floor. Whereas power-operated stackers are pedestrian-operated or rider-controlled, operate vertically and horizontally and can lift pallets directly from the floor.

(2) *Reach trucks*

    Reach trucks enable loads to be retracted within their wheel base. There are two kinds, namely, (*a*) moving mast reach trucks, and (*b*) pantograph reach trucks. Moving mast reach trucks are rider-operated, with forward-mounted load wheels enabling carriage to move within the wheel base – mast, forks and load moving together. Pantograph reach trucks are also rider-operated, reach movement being by pantograph mechanism, with forks and load moving away from static mast.

(3)    *Counterbalance trucks*

Counterbalance trucks carry loads in front counterbalanced to the weight of the vehicle over the rear wheels. Such trucks are lightweight pedestrian-controlled, lightweight rider-controlled or heavyweight rider-controlled.

(4)    *Narrow aisle trucks*

With narrow aisle trucks the base of the truck does not turn within the aisle in order to deposit/retrieve load. There are two types, namely, side loaders for use on long runs down narrow aisles, and counterbalance rotating load turret trucks, having a rigid mast with telescopic sections, which can move sideways in order to collect/deposit loads.

(5)    *Order pickers*

Order pickers have a protected working platform attached to the lift forks, enabling the driver to deposit/retrieve objects in or from a racking system. Conventional or purpose-designed, they are commonly used in racked storage areas and operate well in narrow aisles.

# Lifting machinery (other than hoists/lifts)

L3004    All lifting equipment is covered by the *Lifting Operations and Lifting Equipment Regulations 1998 (SI 1998 No 2307)* which includes cranes, lifts as well as components such as chains, ropes, slings, shackles and eyebolts.

## Cranes

L3005    Cranes are widely used in lifting/lowering operations in construction, dock and shipbuilding works. The main hazard, generally associated with overloading or incorrect slewing, is collapse or overturning, the latter in consequence of the crane driver exceeding the 'maximum permitted moment' (mpm). Contact with overhead power lines is also a danger. In such cases, the operator should normally remain inside the cab and not allow anyone to touch the crane or load; the superintending engineer should immediately be informed. (For reportable dangerous occurrences in connection with cranes etc., see ACCIDENT REPORTING at A3027.)

There are several varieties of crane in frequent use, namely, fixed cranes used at docks and railway sidings; tower cranes on construction sites; mobile cranes used for lifting/lowering loads onto particular locations; overhead travelling cranes – these last operating along a fixed railtrack; in addition, on construction sites there are rough-terrain cranes as well as crawler and wheeled cranes all carrying suspended loads. Persons in the foreseeable impact area of an overhead travelling crane are especially at risk. In order to avoid accidents, electrical supply to the crane should be isolated and a permit to work system instituted. Trained signallers (or banksmen) should be on hand to direct movement of the crane and in a position to see the load clearly and be clearly seen by the driver.

## Safe lifting operations by mobile cranes

L3006    A mobile crane is a crane which is capable of travelling under its own power.

Safe lifting operations – as per BS 7121 'Safe use of cranes' – depend on co-operation between supervisor (or appointed person), slinger (and/or signaller) and crane driver.

(*a*)    *Appointed person*

Overall control of lifting operations rests with an 'appointed person', who can, where necessary, stop the operation. Failing this, control of operations will be in the hands of the supervisor (who, in some cases, may be the slinger). The appointed (and competent) person must ensure that:

    (i)    lifting operations are carefully planned and executed;

    (ii)    weights and heights are accurate;

    (iii)    suitable cranes are provided;

    (iv)    the ground is suitable;

    (v)    suitable precautions are taken, if necessary, regarding gas, water and electricity either above or below ground;

    (vi)    personnel involved in lifting/lowering are trained and competent.

    (vii)    access within the vicinity at where the lifting operation is undertaking is minimised.

(*b*)    *Supervisor*

Supervisors must:

    (i)    direct the crane driver where to position the crane;

    (ii)    provide sufficient personnel to carry out the operation;

    (iii)    check the site conditions;

    (iv)    report back to the appointed person in the event of problems;

    (v)    supervise and direct the slinger, signaller and crane driver;

    (vi)    stop the operation if there is a safety risk.

(*c*)    *Crane driver*

Crane drivers must:

    (i)    erect/dismantle and operate the crane as per manufacturer's instructions;

    (ii)    set the crane level before lifting and ensure that it remains level;

    (iii)    decide which signalling system is to apply;

    (iv)    inform the superviser in the event of problems;

    (v)    carry out inspections/weekly maintenance relating to

       —    defects in crane structure, fittings, jibs, ropes, hooks, shackles,

       —    correct functioning of automatic safe load indicator, over hoist and derrick limit switches.

Drivers should always carry out operations as per speeds, weights, heights and wind speeds specified by the manufacturer, mindful that the weight of slings/lifting gear is part of the load. Such information should be clearly displayed in the cab and not obscured or removed. Windows and windscreens should be kept clear and free from stickers containing operational data. Any handrails, stops, machinery guards fitted to the crane for safe access should always be replaced following removal for maintenance; and tools, jib sections and lifting tackle properly secured when not in use.

After a load has been attached to the crane hook by the lifting hook, tension should be taken up slowly, as per the slinger's instructions, the latter being in continuous communication with the driver. In the case of unbalanced loads, drivers/slingers should be familiar with a load's centre of gravity – particularly if the load is irregularly shaped. Once in operation, crane hooks should be positioned directly over the load, the latter not remaining suspended for longer than necessary. Moreover, suspended loads should not be directed over people or occupied buildings.

(*d*)   *Slingers*

Slingers must:

(i)    attach/detach a load to/from the crane;

(ii)   use correct lifting appliances;

(iii)  direct movement of a load by correct signals. Any part of a load likely to shift during lifting/lowering must be adequately secured by the slinger beforehand. Spillage or discharge of loose loads (e.g. scaffolding) can be a problem, and such loads must be properly secured/fastened. Nets are useful for covering palletised loads (e.g. bricks).

(*e*)   *Signallers*

Quite frequently, signallers are responsible for signalling in lieu of slingers. Failing this, their remit is to transmit instructions from slinger to crane driver, when the former cannot see the load.

# Lifting tackle

L3007   Lifting tackle refers to:

(*a*)   chain slings;

(*b*)   rope slings;

(*c*)   rings;

(*d*)   hooks;

(*e*)   shackles;

(*f*)   swivels.

[*Factories Act 1961, s 26(3)*].

## Materials used for the manufacture of lifting equipment

L3008   All materials have unique physical properties and will behave in different ways depending on the conditions to which they are exposed. For example some materials are more likely to suffer the effects of exposure to high temperatures whilst others are more vulnerable to low temperatures.

## Chains

L3009   A chain is a classic example of lifting tackle, in spite of an increase in use of wire ropes. There are several varieties, including mild high-tensile, and alloy steel. The principal risk is breakage, usually occurring in consequence of a production defect in a link, or through application of excessive loads.

### Ropes

L3010    Ropes are used quite widely throughout industry in lifting/lowering operations, the main hazard being breakage through overloading and/or natural wear and tear. Ropes are either of natural (e.g. cotton, hemp) or man-made fibre (e.g. nylon, terylene). Natural fibre ropes, if they become wet or damp, should be allowed to dry naturally and kept in a well-ventilated room. They do not require certification prior to service but six months' examination thereafter is compulsory (all lifting equipment accessories require a six monthly examination to meet the requirements under the *Lifting Operations and Lifting Equipment Regulations 1998*). If the specified safe working load (SWL) cannot be maintained by a rope, it should forthwith be withdrawn from service. Of the two, man-made fibre ropes have greater tensile strength, are not subject so much to risk from wear and tear, are more acid/corrosion-resistant and can absorb shock loading better.

Wire ropes are much in use in cranes, lifts, hoists, elevators etc. and are normally lubricant-impregnated to minimise corrosion and reduce wear and tear.

### Slings, hooks, eyebolts, pulley blocks etc.

L3011    Slings are chains or ropes (either fibre or wire) and should be of adequate strength. Wire rope slings should always be well lubricated and, where multiple slings are in use, the load should be evenly distributed. Hooks are of forged steel and should be fitted with a safety catch to ensure that the load does not slip off. Eyebolts are mainly for lifting heavy concentrated loads; there being several types, namely, dynamo, collar and eyebolt incorporating link. Pulley blocks, ideally made from shock-resistant metal, are also widely used in lifting and lowering operations. In particular, however, blocks designed for use with fibre rope should not be operated with wire rope.

## Lifting operations on construction sites

L3012    Lifting/lowering activities are typical on construction sites. Hazards peculiar to this environment, which crane drivers should beware of, are:

(*a*)    uneven floor surface;

(*b*)    adverse weather, e.g. heavy rain, causing ground sinkage, thereby necessitating levelling checks or mat packing;

(*c*)    underground services, e.g. drains, sewers, mains;

(*d*)    overhead wires and obstructions;

(*e*)    uncompacted landfill;

(*f*)    movement and circulation of other heavy mobile vehicles;

(*g*)    excavations. Crane operators should always check with supervisors before travelling close to excavations, and, in any case, regularly check the excavation face, especially after heavy rainfall. Moreover, crane travel, whether with or without loads on site, should proceed only when accompanied by a slinger to keep an eye open for obstructions and hazards and warn other people in the vicinity. When travelling minus load, chains/slings should be detached from the hook and the hookblock secured. Similarly, cranes should not be left unattended unless:

(i)     loads have been detached,

(ii)    the lifting device has been secured,

(iii)   the engine has been turned off,

(iv)   brakes and locks have been applied,

(v)    the ignition key has been removed.

Cranes travelling on public highways are governed by the same rules and regulations as apply to other road users; drivers must be in possession of a valid current driving licence and over 21. They should be aware of the crane's overall clearance height and see that slings, shackles etc. are either removed or secured.

## Statutory requirements relating to lifting equipment

L3013    The *Lifts Regulations 1997 (SI 1997 No 831)* came into force on 1 July 1997 and the *Lifting Operations and Lifting Equipment Regulations 1998 (SI 1998 No 2307)* came into force on 5 December 1998. These two regulations replaced the previous provisions contained in the *Factories Act 1961*, the *Offices, Shops and Railway Premises (Hoists and Lifts) Regulations 1968*, the *Construction (Lifting Operations) Regulations 1961* and the *Lifting Plant and Equipment (Records of Test and Examination etc.) Regulations 1992*.

This section examines:

(*a*)    the *Lifts Regulations 1997 (SI 1997 No 831)*; and

(*b*)    the *Lifting Operations and Lifting Equipment Regulations (SI 1998 No 2307)*.

In this context certain words need explanation:

'Lift' – this means an appliance serving specific levels, having a car moving along guides which are rigid – or along a fixed course even where it does not move along guides which are rigid (for example, a scissor lift) – and inclined at an angle of more than 15 degrees to the horizontal and intended for the transport of:

—     persons,

—     persons and goods, or

—     goods alone if the car is accessible, that is to say, a person may enter it without difficulty, and fitted with controls situated inside the car or within reach of a person inside;

'Accessory for lifting' – this means 'work equipment for attaching loads to machinery for lifting';

'Lifting equipment' – this means 'work equipment for lifting or lowering loads and includes its attachments used for anchoring, fixing or supporting it'.

### The Lifts Regulations 1997

L3014    These Regulations apply to lifts permanently serving buildings or constructions; and safety components for use in such lifts. [*Reg 3*].

These Regulations do not apply to:

(*a*)    the following lifts – and safety components for such lifts:

—     cableways, including funicular railways, for the public or private transportation of persons,

—   lifts specially designed and constructed for military or police purposes,

—   mine winding gear,

—   theatre elevators,

—   lifts fitted in means of transport,

—   lifts connected to machinery and intended exclusively for access to the workplace,

—   rack and pinion trains,

—   construction–site hoists intended for lifting persons or persons and goods.

[*Reg 4, Schedule 14*].

(*b*)   any lift or safety component which is placed on the market (i.e. when the installer first makes the lift available to the user, but see L3019 below) and put into service before 1 July 1997 [*Reg 5*].

(*c*)   any lift or safety component placed on the market and put into service on or before 30 June 1999 which complies with any health and safety provisions with which it would have been required to comply if it was to have been placed on the market and put into service in the United Kingdom on 29 June 1995.

This exclusion does not apply in the case of a lift or a safety component which;

—   unless required to bear the CE marking pursuant to any other Community obligation, bears the CE marking or an inscription liable to be confused with it; or

—   bears or is accompanied by any other indication, howsoever expressed, that it complies with the Lifts Directive.

[*Reg 6*].

(*d*)   any lift insofar as and to the extent that the relevant essential health and safety requirements relate to risks wholly or partly covered by other Community directives applicable to that lift [*Reg 7*].

### General requirements

*General duty relating to the placing on the market and putting into service of lifts*

L3015   (i)   Subject to *Reg 12* (see L3019 BELOW), no person who is a responsible person shall place on the market and put into service any lift unless the requirements of paragraph (ii) below have been complied with in relation to it [*Reg 8(1)*].

(ii)   *Regulation 8(2)* provides that the requirements in respect of any lift are that:

—   it satisfies the relevant essential health and safety requirements and, for the purpose of satisfying those requirements:

—   where a transposed harmonised standard covers one or more of the relevant essential health and safety requirements, any lift constructed in accordance with that transposed harmonised standard shall be presumed to comply with that (or those) essential health and safety requirement(s); and

— by calculation, or on the basis of design plans, it is permitted to demonstrate the similarity of a range of equipment to satisfy the essential safety requirements;

— the appropriate conformity assessment procedure in respect of the lift has been carried out in accordance with *Reg 13(1)* (see L3020 below);

— the CE marking has been affixed to it by the installer of the lift in accordance with *Schedule 3*;

— a declaration of conformity has been drawn up in respect of it by the installer of the lift; and

— it is in fact safe.

*Note: Reg 18(1)* provides that a lift which bears the CE marking, and is accompanied by an EC declaration of conformity in accordance with *Reg 8(2)*, is taken to conform with all the requirements of the *Lifts Regulations 1997*, including *Reg 13* (see L3020 below), unless reasonable grounds exist for suspecting that it does not so conform.

(iii) Any technical documentation or other information in relation to a lift required to be retained under the conformity assessment procedure used must be retained by the person specified in that respect in that conformity assessment procedure for any period specified in that procedure [*Reg 8(3)*].

In these Regulations, 'responsible person' means:

— in the case of a lift, the installer of the lift;

— in the case of a safety component, the manufacturer of the component or his authorised representative established in the Community; or

— where neither the installer of the lift nor the manufacturer of the safety component nor the latter's authorised representative established in the Community, as the case may be, have fulfilled the requirements of *Reg 8(2)* (see above) or *Reg 9(2)* (see L3016 below), the person who places the lift or safety component on the market.

*General duty relating to the placing on the market and putting into service of safety components*

L3016    Safety components include devices for locking landing doors; devices to prevent falls; overspeed limitation devices; and electric safety switches.

(i) Subject to *Reg 12* (see L3020 below), no person who is a responsible person shall place on the market and put into service any safety component unless the requirements of paragraph (ii) below have been complied with in relation to it [*Reg 9(1)*].

(ii) *Regulation 9(2)* provides that the requirements in respect of any safety component are that:

— it satisfies the relevant essential health and safety requirements and for the purpose of satisfying those requirements where a transposed harmonised standard covers one or more of the relevant essential health and safety requirements, any safety component constructed in accordance with that transposed harmonised standard shall be presumed to be suitable to enable a lift on which it is correctly installed to comply with that (or those) essential health and safety requirement(s);

> — the appropriate conformity assessment procedure in respect of the safety component has been carried out in accordance with *Reg 13(1)* (see L3021 below);
>
> — the CE marking has been affixed to it, or on a label inseparably attached to the safety component, by the manufacturer of that safety component, or his authorised representative established in the Community, in accordance with *Schedule 3* (which specifies the requirements for CE marking);
>
> — a declaration of conformity has been drawn up in respect of it by the manufacturer of the safety component or his authorised representative established in the Community; and
>
> — it is in fact safe.

*Note: Reg 18(1)* provides that a safety component – or its label – which bears the CE marking, and is accompanied by an EC declaration of conformity in accordance with *Reg 9(2)*, is taken to conform with all the requirements of the *Lifts Regulations 1997*, including *Reg 13* (see L3021 below), unless reasonable grounds exist for suspecting that it does not so conform.

(iii) Any technical documentation or other information in relation to a safety component required to be retained under the conformity assessment procedure used must be retained by the person specified in that respect in that conformity assessment procedure for any period specified in that procedure [*Reg 9(3)*].

*General duty relating to the supply of a lift or safety component*

L3017    Subject to *Reg 12* (see L3020 below) any person who supplies any lift or safety component but who is not a person to whom *Reg 8* or *9* applies (see L3015 and L3016 above) must ensure that that lift or safety component is safe [*Reg 10*].

*Penalties for breach of Regs 8, 9 or 10*

L3018    A person who is convicted of an offence under *Reg 8, 9* or *10* above is liable to imprisonment (not exceeding three months) or to a fine not exceeding level 5 on the standard scale, or both. *Reg 22*, however, provides a defence of due diligence: i.e. the defendant must show that he took all reasonable steps and exercised all due diligence to avoid committing the offence.

*Specific duties relating to the supply of information, freedom from obstruction of lift shafts and retention of documents*

L3019    (i) The person responsible for work on the building or construction where a lift is to be installed and the installer of the lift must keep each other informed of the facts necessary for, and take the appropriate steps to ensure, the proper operation and safe use of the lift. Shafts intended for lifts must not contain any piping or wiring or fittings other than that which is necessary for the operation and safety of that lift.

(ii) Where, in the case of a lift, for the purposes of *Reg 8(2)* (see L3015 above) the appropriate conformity assessment procedure is one of the procedures set out in *Reg 13(2)(a), (b) or (c)* (see L3021 below), the person responsible for the design of the lift must supply to the person responsible for the construction, installation and testing all necessary documents and information for the latter person to be able to operate in absolute security.

A person who is convicted of an offence under (i) or (ii) above is liable to imprisonment (not exceeding three months) or to a fine not exceeding level 5 on the standard scale, or both. *Reg 22*, however, provides a defence of due diligence: i.e. the defendant must show that he took all reasonable steps and exercised all due diligence to avoid committing the offence.

(iii) A copy of the declaration of conformity mentioned in *Reg 8(2)* or *9(2)* must:

— in the case of a lift, be supplied to the EC Commission, the member states and any other notified bodies, on request, by the installer of the lift together with a copy of the reports of the tests involved in the final inspection to be carried out as part of the appropriate conformity assessment procedure referred to in *Reg 8(2)*; and

— be retained, by the person who draws up that declaration, for a period of ten years – in the case of a lift, from the date on which the lift was placed on the market; and in the case of a safety component, from the date on which safety components of that type were last manufactured by that person.

A person who fails to supply or keep a copy of the declaration of conformity, as required above, is liable on summary conviction to a fine not exceeding level 5 on the standard scale. *Reg 22*, however, provides a defence of due diligence: i.e. the defendant must show that he took all reasonable steps and exercised all due diligence to avoid committing the offence.

[*Reg 11*].

*Exceptions to placing on the market or supply in respect of certain lifts and safety components*

L3020  For the purposes of *Reg 8, 9* or *10*, a lift or a safety component is not regarded as being placed on the market or supplied:

(i) where that lift or safety component will be put into service in a country outside the Community; or is imported into the Community for re-export to a country outside the Community – but this paragraph does not apply if the CE marking, or any inscription liable to be confused with such a marking, is affixed to the lift or safety component or, in the case of a safety component, to its label; or

(ii) by the exhibition at trade fairs and exhibitions of that lift or safety component, in respect of which the provisions of these Regulations are not satisfied, if:

— a notice is displayed in relation to the lift or safety component in question to the effect that it does not satisfy those provisions; and that it may not be placed on the market or supplied until those provisions are satisfied; and

— adequate safety measures are taken to ensure the safety of persons.

[*Reg 12*].

*Conformity assessment procedures*

L3021  For the purposes of *Reg 8(2)* or *9(2)* (see L3015 and L3016 above), the appropriate conformity assessment procedure is as follows:

*For lifts – one of the following procedures:*

—  if the lift was designed in accordance with a lift having undergone an EC type-examination as referred to in *Schedule 5*, it must be constructed, installed and tested by implementing:

—  the final inspection referred to in *Schedule 6*; or

—  the quality assurance system referred to in *Schedule 11* or *Schedule 13*; and

the procedures for the design and construction stages, on the one hand, and the installation and testing stages, on the other, may be carried out on the same lift;

—  if the lift was designed in accordance with a model lift having undergone an EC type-examination as referred to in *Schedule 5*, it must be constructed, installed and tested by implementing:

—  the final inspection referred to in *Schedule 6*; or

—  one of the quality assurance systems referred to in *Schedule 11* or *Schedule 13*; and

all permitted variations between a model lift and the lifts forming part of the lifts derived from that model lift must be clearly specified (with maximum and minimum values) in the technical dossier required as part of the appropriate conformity assessment procedure;

—  if the lift was designed in accordance with a lift for which a quality assurance system pursuant to *Schedule 12* was implemented, supplemented by an examination of the design if the latter is not wholly in accordance with the harmonised standards, it must be installed and constructed and tested by implementing, in addition, the final inspection referred to in *Schedule 6* or one of the quality assurance systems referred to in *Schedule 11* or *Schedule 13*;

—  the unit verification procedure, referred to in *Schedule 9*, by a notified body (see L3023 below); or

—  the quality assurance system in accordance with *Schedule 12*, supplemented by an examination of the design if the latter is not wholly in accordance with the transposed harmonised standards.

*For safety components – one of the following procedures:*

—  submit the model of the safety component for EC type-examination in accordance with *Schedule 5* and for production checks by a notified body (see L3023 below) in accordance with *Schedule 10*;

—  submit the model of the safety component for EC type-examination in accordance with *Schedule 5* and operate a quality assurance system in accordance with *Schedule 7* for checking production; or

—  operate a full quality assurance system in accordance with *Schedule 8*.

[*Reg 13*].

*Requirements fulfilled by the person who places a lift or safety component on the market*

L3022  Where in the case of a lift or a safety component, any of the requirements of *Regs 8, 9, 11* and *13* to be fulfilled by the installer of the lift or the manufacturer of the safety component or, in the case of the latter, his authorised representative established in the

Community, have not been so fulfilled such requirements may be fulfilled by the person who places that lift or safety component on the market [*Reg 14*].

This provision, however, does not affect the power of an enforcement authority to take action in respect of the installer of the lift, the manufacturer of the safety component or, in the case of the latter, his authorised representative established in the Community in respect of a contravention of or a failure to comply with any of those requirements.

*Notified bodies*

L3023    For the purposes of these Regulations, a notified body is a body which has been appointed to carry out one or more of the conformity assessment procedures referred to in *Reg 13* which has been appointed as a notified body by the Secretary of State in the United Kingdom or by a member State.

[*Reg 15*].

## The Lifting Operations and Lifting Equipment Regulations 1998

L3024    The requirements imposed by these Regulations on an employer in relation to lifting equipment apply in respect of lifting equipment provided for use or used by an employee of his at work. They also apply to a self-employed person, with regard to lifting equipment he uses at work, and to anyone with control, to any extent, of:

—    lifting equipment;

—    a person at work who uses or supervises or manages the use of lifting equipment; or

—    the way in which lifting equipment is used,

and to the extent of his control.

*General requirements*

*Strength and stability*

L3025    Every employer must ensure that lifting equipment is of adequate strength and stability for each load, having regard in particular to the stress induced at its mounting or fixing point – and that every part of a load and anything attached to it and used in lifting it is of adequate strength [*Reg 4*].

*Lifting equipment for lifting persons*

L3026    Every employer must ensure that lifting equipment for lifting persons:

(i)    is such as to prevent a person using it being crushed, trapped or struck or falling from the carrier;

(ii)    is such as to prevent so far as is reasonably practicable a person using it, while carrying out activities from the carrier, being crushed, trapped or struck or falling from the carrier;

(iii)    has suitable devices to prevent the risk of a carrier falling, and, if the risk cannot be prevented for reasons inherent in the site and height differences, the employer must ensure that the carrier has an enhanced safety coefficient suspension rope or chain which is inspected by a competent person every working day;

(iv)    is such that a person trapped in any carrier is not thereby exposed to danger and can be freed.

[*Reg 5*].

*Positioning and installation*

L3027    Employers must ensure that lifting equipment is positioned or installed in such a way as to reduce to as low as is reasonably practicable the risk of the lifting equipment or a load striking a person, or the risk from a load:

—    drifting;

—    falling freely; or

—    being released unintentionally,

and that otherwise it is safe.

Employers must also ensure that there are suitable devices for preventing anyone from falling down a shaft or hoistway [*Reg 6*].

*Marking of lifting equipment*

L3028    Employers must ensure that:

(i)    machinery and accessories for lifting loads are clearly marked to indicate their safe working loads;

(ii)    where the safe working load of machinery for lifting loads depends on its configuration, either the machinery is clearly marked to indicate its safe working load for each configuration, or information which clearly indicates its safe working load for each configuration is kept with the machinery;

(iii)    accessories for lifting are also marked in such a way that it is possible to identify the characteristics necessary for their safe use;

(iv)    lifting equipment which is designed for lifting persons is appropriately and clearly marked to this effect; and

(v)    lifting equipment which is not designed for lifting persons but which might be mistakenly so used is appropriately and clearly marked to the effect that it is not designed for lifting persons.

[*Reg 7*].

*Organisation of lifting operations*

L3029    Every employer must ensure that any lifting or lowering of a load which involves lifting equipment is properly planned by a competent person, appropriately supervised and carried out in a safe manner [*Reg 8*].

*Thorough examination and inspection*

L3030    An employer is under a duty to ensure:

(i)    before lifting equipment is put into service for the first time by him, that it is thoroughly examined for any defect unless:

—    the lifting equipment has not been used before; and

—    in the case of lifting equipment for which an EC declaration of conformity could or (in the case of a declaration under the *Lifts*

*Regulations 1997)* should have been drawn up, the employer has received such declaration made not more than twelve months before the lifting equipment is put into service; or

— if obtained from the undertaking of another person, it is accompanied by physical evidence referred to in (iv) below;

[*Reg 9(1)*].

(ii) where the safety of lifting equipment depends on the installation conditions, that it is thoroughly examined – after installation and before being put into service for the first time and after assembly and before being put into service at a new site or in a new location, to ensure that it has been correctly installed and is safe to operate [*Reg 9(2)*];

(iii) that lifting equipment which is exposed to conditions causing deterioration which is liable to result in dangerous situations is:

thoroughly examined;

— at least every six months, in the case of lifting equipment for lifting persons or an accessory for lifting;

— at least every twelve months, in the case of other lifting equipment; or

— in either case, in accordance with an examination scheme; and

— whenever exceptional circumstances which are liable to jeopardise the safety of the lifting equipment have occurred, and

if appropriate for the purpose, is inspected by a competent person at suitable intervals between thorough examinations,

to ensure that health and safety conditions are maintained and that any deterioration can be detected and remedied in good time;

[*Reg 9(3)*].

(iv) that no lifting equipment leaves his undertaking; or, if obtained from the undertaking of another person, is used in his undertaking, unless it is accompanied by physical evidence that the last thorough examination required to be carried out under this regulation has been carried out.

[*Reg 9(4)*].

*Reports and defects*

L3031  (i)  A person making a thorough examination for an employer under *reg 9* must:

— immediately notify the employer of any defect in the lifting equipment which in his opinion is or could become a danger to anyone;

— write a report of the thorough examination (see L3031 below) to the employer and any person from whom the lifting equipment has been hired or leased;

— where there is in his opinion a defect in the lifting equipment involving an existing or imminent risk of serious personal injury send a copy of the report to the relevant enforcing authority ('relevant enforcing authority' means, where the defective lifting equipment has been hired or leased by the employer, the Health and Safety Executive – and otherwise, the enforcing authority for the premises in which the defective lifting equipment was thoroughly examined).

(ii)    A person making an inspection for an employer under *Reg 9* must immediately notify the employer of any defect in the lifting equipment which in his opinion is or could become a danger to anyone, and make a written record of the inspection.

(iii)    Every employer who has been notified under (i) above must ensure that the lifting equipment is not used before the defect is rectified; or, in the case of a defect which is not yet but could become a danger to persons, after it could become such a danger.

[*Reg 10*].

*Prescribed information*

L3032    *Schedule 1* specifies the information that must be contained in a report of a thorough examination, made under *Reg 10* (see L3031 above). The information must include the following:

(i)    The name and address of the employer for whom the thorough examination was made.

(ii)    The address of the premises at which the thorough examination was made.

(iii)    Particulars sufficient to identify the lifting equipment including its date of manufacture, if known.

(iv)    The date of the last thorough examination.

(v)    The safe working load of the lifting equipment or, where its safe working load depends on the configuration of the lifting equipment, its safe working load for the last configuration in which it was thoroughly examined.

(vi)    In respect of the first thorough examination of lifting equipment after installation or after assembly at a new site or in a new location:

—    that it is such thorough examination; and

—    if in fact this is so, that it has been installed correctly and would be safe to operate.

(vii)    In respect of all thorough examinations of lifting equipment which do not fall within (vi) above:

(*a*)    whether it is a thorough examination under *Reg 9(3)*:

—    within an interval of six months;

—    within an interval of twelve months;

—    in accordance with an examination scheme; or

—    after the occurrence of exceptional circumstances;

(*b*)    if in fact this is so, that the lifting equipment would be safe to operate.

(viii)    In respect of every thorough examination of lifting equipment:

(*a*)    identification of any part found to have a defect which is or could become a danger to anyone, and a description of the defect;

(*b*)    particulars of any repair, renewal or alteration required to remedy a defect found to be a danger to anyone;

(*c*)    in the case of a defect which is not yet but could become a danger to anyone:

— the time by which it could become such a danger;

— particulars of any repair, renewal or alteration required to remedy the defect;

(*d*) the latest date by which the next thorough examination must be carried out;

(*e*) particulars of any test, if applicable;

(*f*) the date of the thorough examination.

(ix) The name, address and qualifications of the person making the report; that he is self-employed or, if employed, the name and address of his employer.

(x) The name and address of a person signing or authenticating the report on behalf of its author.

(xi) The date of the report.

*Keeping of information*

L3033      An employer who obtains lifting equipment to which the 1998 Regulations apply, and who receives an EC declaration of conformity relating to it, must keep the declaration for so long as he operates the lifting equipment [*Reg 11(1)*].

*Regulation 11(2)(a)* provides that the employer must ensure that the information contained in every report made to him under *Reg 10(1)* (see L3031 above) is kept available for inspection:

— in the case of a thorough examination under *Reg 9(1)* (see L3030 above) of lifting equipment other than an accessory for lifting, until he stops using the lifting equipment;

— in the case of a thorough examination under *Reg 9(1)* (see L3030 above) of an accessory for lifting, for two years after the report is made;

— in the case of a thorough examination under *Reg 9(2)* (see L3030 above), until he stops using the lifting equipment at the place it was installed or assembled;

— in the case of a thorough examination under *Reg 9(3)* (see L3030 above), until the next report is made under that paragraph or the expiration of two years, whichever is later.

The employer must ensure that every record made under *Reg 10(2)* (see L3031 above) is kept available until the next such record is made [*Reg 11(2)(b)*].

# Cranes, hoists and lifting equipment – common causes of failure

## General

L3034      The principal cause of failure in all forms of lifting equipment is that of overloading, i.e. exceeding the specified safe working load (SWL) of the crane, forklift truck, hoist, chain, etc. in use for a specific lifting job. Every year there are numerous accidents and scheduled dangerous occurrences reported which are caused as a result of overloading. A second common cause of failure, and one which is inexcusable, is associated with neglect of the equipment while not in use. Neglect may be associated with poor or inadequate maintenance of the fabric of a crane or its safety devices, or simply a failure to store rope slings properly while not in use. One of the results of neglect is corrosion of metal surfaces resulting in weakened crane structures, wire ropes and slings. This is why lifting equipment is subject to statutory inspection.

Examples of specific causes of failure are outlined below.

## Cranes

L3035   (*a*)   Failure to lift vertically, e.g. dragging a load sideways along the ground before lifting.

(*b*)   'Snatching' loads, i.e. not lifting slowly and smoothly.

(*c*)   Exceeding the maximum permitted moment, i.e. the product of the load and the radius of operation.

(*d*)   Excessive wind loading, resulting in crane instability.

(*e*)   Defects in the fabrication of the crane, e.g. badly welded joints.

(*f*)   Incorrect crane assembly in the case of tower cranes.

(*g*)   Brake failure (rail-mounted cranes).

(*h*)   In the case of mobile cranes:

　　(i)   failure to use outriggers;

　　(ii)   lifting on soft or uneven ground; and

　　(iii)   incorrect tyre pressures.

## Hoists and lifts

L3036   (*a*)   Excessive wear in wire ropes.

(*b*)   Excessive broken wires in ropes.

(*c*)   Failure of the overload protection device.

(*d*)   Failure of the overrun device.

## Ropes

*Fibre ropes*

L3037   (*a*)   Bad storage in wet or damp conditions resulting in rot and mildew.

(*b*)   Inadequate protection of the rope when lifting loads with sharp edges.

(*c*)   Exposure to direct heat to dry, as opposed to gradual drying in air.

(*d*)   Chemical reaction.

*Wire ropes*

L3038   (*a*)   Excessive broken wires.

(*b*)   Failure to lubricate regularly.

(*c*)   Frequent knotting or kinking of the rope.

(*d*)   Bad storage in wet or damp conditions which promotes rust.

### Chains

L3039   (*a*)   Mechanical defects in individual links.

   (*b*)   Application of a static in excess of the breaking load.

   (*c*)   Snatch loading.

### Slings

L3040   Slings are manufactured in natural or man-made fibre or chain. The safe working load of any sling varies according to the angle formed between the legs of the sling.

The relationship between sling angle and the distance between the legs of the sling is also important. (See Table 1 below.)

---

**Table 1**

**Safe working load for slings**

| *Sling Angle* | *Distance between legs* |
|---|---|
| 30° | ½ leg length |
| 60° | 1 leg length |
| 90° | 1⅓ leg length |
| 120° | 1⅔ leg length |

---

For a one tonne load, the tension in the leg increases as shown in Table 2 below.

---

**Table 2**

**Safe working load for slings – increased tension**

| *Sling leg angle* | *Tension in leg (tonnes)* |
|---|---|
| 90° | 0.7 |
| 120° | 1.0 |
| 151° | 2.0 |
| 171° | 6.0 |

---

Other causes of failure in slings are:

(*a*)   Cuts, excessive wear, kinking and general distortion of the sling legs.

(*b*)   Failure to lubricate wire slings.

(*c*)   Failure to pack sharp corners of a load, resulting in sharp bends in the sling and the possibility of cuts or damage to it.

(*d*)   Unequal distribution of the load between the legs of a multi-leg sling.

### Hooks

L3041   (*a*)   Distortion of the hook due to overloading.

   (*b*)   Use of a hook without a safety catch.

   (*c*)   Stripping of the thread connecting the hook to the chain fixture.

### Forklift trucks

L3042   (*a*)   Uneven floors, steeply inclined ramps or gradients, i.e. in excess of 1:10 gradient.

(*b*)   Inadequate room to manoeuvre.

(*c*)   Inadequate or poor maintenance of lifting gear.

(*d*)   The practice of driving forwards down a gradient with the load preceding the truck.

(*e*)   Load movement in transit.

(*f*)   Sudden or fast braking.

(*g*)   Poor stacking of goods being moved.

(*h*)   Speeding.

(*i*)   Turning corners too sharply.

(*j*)   Not securing load sufficiently e.g. pallets stacked poorly.

(*k*)   Hidden obstructions in the path of the truck.

(*l*)   Use of the forward tilt mechanism with a raised load.

(*m*)   Generally bad driving, including driving too fast, taking corners too fast, striking overhead obstructions, particularly when reversing and excessive use of the brakes.

## Mobile lifting equipment

L3043   Mobile work equipment is any equipment which carries out work whilst travelling. It may be self-propelled, towed or remotely controlled and it may incorporate attachments. An example of mobile lifting equipment is an excavator involved in digging tasks.

The risk of mobile lifting equipment overturning is another cause for concern, and the problem was addressed by the additional requirements introduced in the *Provision and Use of Work Equipment Regulations 1998 (SI 1998 No 2306)*. These implement into UK legislation the amending directive to the *Use of Work Equipment Directive (AUWED)*. Under this legislation, workers must be protected from falling out of the equipment and from unexpected movement e.g. overturning.

To prevent such equipment overturning, the following action should be taken:

—   fit stabilisers (e.g. outriggers or counterbalance weights);

—   have in place a structure which ensures that it does no more than fall on its side;

—   ensure the structure gives sufficient clearance to anyone being carried if it overturns more than on its side;

—   installation of roll-over protective structure;

—   provision of harnesses or a suitable restraining system to protect against being crushed;

—   use only on firm ground;

—   avoid excessive gradients.

HSE has published guidance on the fitting and use of restraining systems on lift trucks. The guidance explains when operator restraint should be fitted to a lift truck, when it should be used, and what to do if it cannot be fitted. It also describes the type of lift trucks most at risk of overturning and gives advice on how to prevent overturning accidents. The guidance is aimed at employers, drivers and others with a responsibility for managing the safe operation of lift trucks. Copies of *'Fitting and use of restraining systems on lift trucks'*, MISC 241, can be ordered free of charge from HSE Books.

# Lighting

## Introduction

L5001  Increasingly, over the last decade or so, employers have come to appreciate that indifferent lighting is both bad economics and bad ergonomics, not to mention potentially bad industrial relations; and conversely, good lighting uses energy efficiently and contributes to general workforce morale and profitability – that is, operating costs fall whilst productivity and quality improve. Alternatively, poor lighting reduces efficiency, thereby increasing the risk of stress, denting workforce morale, promoting absenteeism and leading to accidents, injuries and even deaths at work.

Ideally, good lighting should 'guarantee' (*a*) employee safety, (*b*) acceptable job performance and (*c*) good workplace atmosphere, comfort and appearance. This is not just a matter of maintenance of correct lighting levels. Ergonomically relevant are:

(*a*)  horizontal illuminance;

(*b*)  uniformity of illuminance over the job area;

(*c*)  colour appearance;

(*d*)  colour rendering;

(*e*)  glare and discomfort;

(*f*)  ceiling, wall, floor reflectances;

(*g*)  job/environment illuminance ratios;

(*h*)  job and environment reflectances;

(*j*)  vertical illuminance.

## Statutory lighting requirements

### General

L5002  Adequate standards of lighting in all workplaces can be enforced under the general duties of the *Health and Safety at Work etc. Act 1974*, which require provision by an employer of a safe and healthy working environment (see EMPLOYERS' DUTIES TO THEIR EMPLOYEES). *Regulation 8* of the *Workplace (Health, Safety and Welfare)Regulations 1992 (SI 1992 No 3004, req*uires that all workplaces have suitable and sufficient lighting and that, so far is reasonably practicable, the lighting should be natural light.

More particularly, however, people should be able to work and move about without suffering eye strain and having to avoid shadows. Local lighting may be necessary at individual workstations and places of particular risk. Outdoor traffic routes used by pedestrians should be adequately lit after dark. Lights and light fittings should avoid dazzle and glare and be so positioned that they do not cause hazards, whether fire, radiation or electrical. Switches should be easily accessible and lights should be replaced, repaired or cleaned before lighting becomes insufficient. Moreover, where persons are particularly exposed to danger in the event of failure of artificial lighting, emergency lighting must be provided. [*Workplace (Health, Safety and Welfare) Regulations 1992 (SI 1992 No 3004), Reg 8(3)*] (and ACOP).

To accommodate these 'requirements', refresh rates (flickering), a combination of general and localised lighting (not to be confused with 'local' lighting, e.g. desk light) is often necessary. Moreover, state of the art visual display units have thrown up some occupational health problems addressed by the *Health and Safety (Display Screen Equipment) Regulations 1992 (SI 1992 No 2792)* (see O5005 *et seq.* OFFICES AND SHOPS).

## Specific processes

*Lighting and VDUs*

L5003     Annex A to BS EN 9241–6–1999, provides guidance on illuminance levels, specifically in relation to use with display screen equipment (BS EN 9241 – Ergonomic requirements for office work with visual display terminals (VDTs); Part 6 – Guidance on work environment).

*Machinery and work equipment – Provision and Use of Work Equipment Regulations 1998 (SI 1998 No 2306)*

L5004     Lighting requirements, applicable to woodworking machines in the *Woodworking Machines Regulations 1974 (SI 1974 No 903), Reg 43* have now been revoked. This now comes under the *Provision and Use of Work Equipment Regulations 1998 (SI 1998 No 2306), Reg 21*. This Regulation is very broad and merely requires that suitable and sufficient lighting is provided, taking into account the operations to be carried out. To ascertain what is required to meet this duty the HSE guidance has been produced. This refers to occasions when additional or localised lighting may be needed such as:

—    when the task requires a high perception of detail;

—    when there is a dangerous process;

—    to reduce visual fatigue;

—    during maintenance operations.

Additional guidance is provided in the HSE Guidance Note HS(G) 38. '*Lighting at Work*'

*Lighting requirements on construction sites – Construction (Health, Safety and Welfare) Regulations 1996 (SI 1996 No 1592)*

L5005     Every workplace; approach to the workplace; and traffic route in and around the workplace, shall have suitable and sufficient lighting. Where reasonably practicable, this lighting shall be by natural light. The colour of every artificial light must not adversely affect or change the perception of any sign or signal provided for health and safety reasons. Suitable and sufficient secondary lighting must be provided in places where there is risk to health and safety in the event of the failure of the primary lighting. [*SI 1996 No 1592, Reg 25*]

*Lighting requirements for electrical equipment – Electricity at Work Regulations 1989 (SI 1989 No 635)*

L5006  So as to prevent injury, adequate lighting must be provided at all electrical equipment on which or near which work is being done in circumstances that may give rise to danger. [*Electricity at Work Regulations 1989 (SI 1989 No 635), Reg 15.*]

# Sources of light

## Natural lighting

L5007  Daylight is the natural, and cheapest, form of lighting, but it has only limited application to places of work where production is required beyond the hours of daylight, at all seasons, and where day-time visibility is restricted by climatic conditions. But, however good the outside daylight, windows can rarely provide adequate lighting alone for the interior of large floor areas. Single storey buildings can, of course, make use of insulated opaque roofing materials, but the most common provision of daylight is by side windows. There is also the fact that the larger the glazing area of the building, the more other factors such as noise, heat loss in winter, and unsatisfactory thermal conditions in summer must be considered.

Modern conditions, where the creation of pleasant building interior environment requires the balanced integration of lighting, heating, air conditioning, acoustic treatment, etc., are such that lighting cannot be considered in isolation. At the very least, natural lighting will have to be supplemented for most of the time with artificial lighting, the most common source for which is electric lighting.

## Electric lighting

L5008  Capital costs, running costs and replacement costs of various types of electric lighting have a direct bearing on the selection of the sources of electric lighting for particular application. Such costs are as important considerations as the size, heat and colour effects required of the lighting. The efficiency of any type of lamp used for lighting is measured as light output, in lumens, per watt of electricity. Typical values for various types of lamp are as follows (the term 'lumen' is explained in the discussion of standards of illuminance in L5007 below).

| *Type of lamp* | *Lumens per watt* |
|---|---|
| Incandescent lamps | 10 to 18 |
| Tungsten halogen | 22 |
| High pressure mercury | 25 to 55 |
| Tubular fluorescent | 30 to 80 (depending on colour) |
| Mercury halide | 60 to 80 |
| High pressure sodium | 100 |

In general, the common incandescent lamps (coiled filament lamps, the temperature of which is raised to white heat by the passage of current, thus giving out light) are relatively cheap to install but have relatively expensive running costs. A discharge or fluorescent lighting scheme (which works on the principle of electric current passing through certain gases and thereby producing an emission of light) has higher capital costs but higher running efficiency, lower running costs and longer lamp life. In larger places of work the choice is often between discharge and fluorescent lamps. The normal mercury discharge lamp and the low pressure sodium discharge lamp have restricted colour performance, although newly developed high pressure sodium discharge lamps and colour corrected mercury lamps do not suffer from this disadvantage.

# Standards of lighting or illuminance

## The technical measurement of illuminance

L5009 The standard of illuminance (i.e. the amount of light) required for a given location or activity depends on a number of variables, including general comfort considerations and the visual efficiency required. The unit of illuminance is the 'lux' which equals one lumen per square metre: this unit has now replaced the 'foot candle' which was the number of lumens per square foot. The term 'lumen' is the unit of luminous flux, describing the quantity of light received by a surface or emitted by a source of light.

## Light measuring instruments

L5010 For accurate measurement of the degree of illuminance at a particular working point, a reliable instrument is required. Such an instrument, suitable for most measurements, is a pocket lightmeter which incorporates the principle of the photo-electric cell, which generates a tiny electric current in proportion to the light at the point of measurement. This current deflects a pointer on a graduated scale measured in lux. Manufacturers' instructions should, of course, be followed in the care and use of such instruments.

## Average illuminance and minimum measured illuminance

L5011 HSE Guidance Note HS(G) 38 'Lighting at work' (1997) relates illuminance levels to the degree or extent of detail which needs to be seen in a particular task or situation. Recommended illuminances are shown in Table 1 at L5010 below.

This guidance note makes recommendations both for average illuminance for the work area as a whole and for minimum measured illuminance at any position within it. As the illuminance produced by any lighting installation is rarely uniform, the use of the average illuminance figure alone could result in the presence of a few positions with much lower illuminance which pose a threat to health and safety. The minimum measured illuminance is therefore the lowest illuminance permitted in the work area taking health and safety requirements into account.

The planes on which the illuminances should be provided depend on the layout of the task. If predominantly on one plane, e.g. horizontal, as with an office desk, or vertical, as in a warehouse, the recommended illuminances are recommended for that plane. Where there is either no well defined plane or more than one, the recommended illuminances should be provided on the horizontal plane and care taken to ensure that the reflectances of surfaces in working areas are high.

## Illuminance ratios

L5012 The relationship between the lighting of the work area and adjacent areas is significant. Large differences in illuminance between these areas may cause visual discomfort or even affect safety levels where there is frequent movement, e.g. forklift trucks. This problem arises most often where local or localised lighting in an interior exposes a person to a range of illuminance for a long period, or where there is movement between interior and exterior working areas exposing a person to a sudden change of illuminance. To reduce hazards and possible discomfort specific recommendations shown in Table 1 below should be followed.

Where there is conflict between the recommended average illuminances shown in Table 1 and maximum illuminance ratios shown in Table 2, the higher value should be taken.

## Table 1

### Average illuminances and minimum measured illuminances for different types of work

| General activity | Typical locations/types of work | Average illuminance (Lx) | Minimum measured illuminance (Lx) |
|---|---|---|---|
| Movement of people, machines and vehicles1 | Lorry parks, corridors, circulation routes | 20 | 5 |
| Movement of people, machines and vehicles in hazardous areas; rough work not requiring any perception of detail | Construction site clearance, excavation and soil work, docks, loading bays, bottling and canning plants | 50 | 20 |
| Work requiring limited perception of detail2 | Kitchens, factories, assembling large components, potteries | 100 | 50 |
| Work requiring perception of detail | Offices, sheet metal work, bookbinding | 200 | 100 |
| Work requiring perception of fine detail | Drawing offices, factories assembling electronic components, textile production | 500 | 200 |

*Notes*

1. Only safety has been considered, because no perception of detail is needed and visual fatigue is unlikely. However, where it is necessary to see detail to recognise a hazard or where error in performing the task could put someone else at risk, for safety purposes as well as to avoid visual fatigue, the figure should be increased to that for work requiring the perception of detail.

2. The purpose is to avoid visual fatigue: the illuminances will be adequate for safety purposes.

## Table 2

## Maximum ratios of illuminance for adjacent areas

| Situations to which recommendation applies | Typical location | Maximum ratio of illuminances | |
|---|---|---|---|
| | | Working area | Adjacent area |
| Where each task is individually lit and the area around the task is lit to a lower illuminance | Local lighting in an office | 5  :  | 1 |
| Where two working areas are adjacent, but one is lit to a lower illuminance than the other | Localised lighting in a works store | 5  :  | 1 |
| Where two working areas are lit to different illuminances and are separated by a barrier but there is frequent movement between them | A storage area inside a factory and a loading bay outside | 10  :  | 1 |

### Maintenance of light fitments

L5013   The lighting output of a given lamp will reduce gradually in the course of its life but an improvement can be obtained by regular cleaning and maintenance, not only of the lamp itself but also of the reflectors, diffusers and other parts of the luminaire. A sensible and economic lamp replacement policy is called for (e.g. it may be more economical, in labour cost terms to change a batch of lamps than deal with them singly as they wear out).

# Qualitative aspects of lighting and lighting design

L5014   While the quantity of lighting afforded to a particular location or task in terms of standard service illuminance is an important feature of lighting design, it is also necessary to consider the qualitative aspects of lighting, which have both direct and indirect effects on the way people perceive their work activities and dangers that may be present. The quality of lighting is affected by the presence or absence of glare, the distribution of the light, brightness, diffusion and colour rendition.

### Glare

L5015   This is the effect of light which causes impaired vision or discomfort experienced when parts of the visual field are excessively bright compared with the general surroundings. It may be experienced in three different forms:

(a)   disability glare – the visually disabling effect caused by bright bare lamps directly in the line of vision;

(b)   discomfort glare – caused by too much contrast of brightness between an object and its background, and frequently associated with poor lighting design. It can cause discomfort without necessarily impairing the ability to see detail. Over a period it can cause visual fatigue, headaches and general fatigue;

(c)  reflected glare – is the reflection of bright light sources on shiny or wet work surfaces, such as plated metal or glass, which can almost entirely conceal the detail in or behind the object which is glinting.

N.B.  The Illuminating Engineering Society (IES) publishes a Limiting Glare Index for each of the effects in (a) and (b) above. This is an index representing the degree of discomfort glare which will be just tolerable in the process or location under consideration. If exceeded, occupants may suffer eye strain or headaches or both.

## Distribution

L5016   Distribution is concerned with the way light is spread. The British Zonal Method classifies luminaires (light-fittings) according to the way they distribute light from BZ1 (all light downwards in a narrow column) to BZ10 (light in all directions). A fitting with a low BZ number does not necessarily imply less glare, however. Its positioning, the shape of the room and the reflective surfaces present are also significant.

The actual spacing of luminaires is also important when considering good lighting distribution. To ensure evenness of illuminance at operating positions, the ratio between the height of the luminaire and the spacing of it must be considered. The IES spacing: height ratio provides a basic guide to such arrangements. Under normal circumstances, e.g. offices, workshops and stores, this ratio should be between 1½:1 and 1:1 according to the type of luminaire.

## Brightness

L5017   Brightness or 'luminosity' is very much a subjective sensation and, therefore, cannot be measured. However, it is possible to consider a brightness ratio, which is the ratio of apparent luminosity between a task object and its surroundings. To ensure the correct brightness ratio, the reflectance (i.e. the ability of a surface to reflect light) of all surfaces in the working area should be well maintained and consideration given to reflectance values in the design of interiors. Given a task illuminance factor (i.e. the recommended illuminance level for a particular task) of 1, the effective reflectance values should be ceilings – 0.6, walls – 0.3 to 0.8, and floors – 0.2 to 0.3.

## Diffusion

L5018   This is the projection of light in all directions with no predominant direction. The directional flow of light can often determine the density of shadows, which may prejudice safety standards or reduce lighting efficiency. Diffused lighting will reduce the amount of glare experienced from bare luminaires.

## Colour rendition

L5019   Colour rendition refers to the appearance of an object under a specific light source, compared to its colour under a reference illuminant, e.g. natural light. Good standards of colour rendition allow the colour appearance of an object to be properly perceived. Generally, the colour rendering properties of luminaires should not clash with those of natural light, and should be just as effective at night when there is no daylight contribution to the total illumination of the working area.

### Stroboscopic effect

L5020   One aspect of lighting quality that formerly gave trouble was the stroboscopic effect of fluorescent tubes which gave the illusion of motion or even the illusion that a rotating part of machinery was stationary. With modern designs of fluorescent tubes, this effect has largely been eliminated.

# Machinery Safety

## Introduction

M1001 Several people are seriously injured on a daily basis whilst using work equipment – whether a power press, lawn mower or photocopier – resulting possibly in limb amputation, disfigurement or even death. It is not surprising, therefore, that traditionally machinery safety has always been in the vanguard of safety at work, being a fertile source of case law – case law under the (now defunct) *Factories Act 1961, s14*, for instance, achieving almost biblical significance. More particularly, a substantial part of the *Factories Act 1961, Part II* was devoted to specifying requirements relating to safe operation of machinery in factories, and a succession of regulations passed thereunder (ranging from the *Horizontal Milling Machines Regulations 1928*, through to the *Operations at Unfenced Machinery Regulations 1938* and the *Power Presses Regulations 1965* to the *Abrasive Wheels Regulations 1970* and the *Woodworking Machines Regulations 1974*) were equally concerned with imposition of maximum safety standards and training of operators. Such regulations sometimes set standards more draconian than those of the *Factories Act 1961* itself, e.g. the *Woodworking Machines Regulations 1974*. Some machinery was regarded as dangerous *per se* (e.g. prime movers and transmission machinery), where breach of fencing requirement causing injury entitled an operator to damages automatically, without having to establish negligence; other machinery had to be demonstrably dangerous, that is, the cause of reasonably foreseeable injury – often by reference to past track accident record (e.g. parts of machinery other than prime movers and transmission machinery).

The above mentioned regulations are now incorporated into the *Provision and Use of Work Equipment Regulations 1998 (PUWER) (SI 1998 No 2306)*.

'A part of machinery is dangerous if it is a possible cause of injury to anybody acting in a way in which a human being may be reasonably expected to act in circumstances which may be reasonably expected to occur' (*Walker v Bletchley-Flettons [1937] 1 AER 170* per *du Parcq J*).

Because design of accident-free machinery was regarded as idealistic, statutory requirement tended to underline the importance of fencing and guarding, with the corollary that duties were laid on employers, as distinct from designers and manufacturers of industrial machinery. In more recent times, however, legislation increasingly reflects a change of emphasis, with equal (if not more) responsibility being allocated to designers and manufacturers, a trend initially sign-posted by the *HSWA 1974, s 6* (see P9012 PRODUCT SAFETY) and later compounded by the *Supply of Machinery (Safety) Regulations 1992* and *1994*. Moreover, earlier law (i.e. the *Factories Act 1961*) was anachronistic and reflected the absence of a general statutory requirement or criterion throughout industry to machinery safety. Thus, the fencing requirements of the *Factories Act 1961* applied only to factories, safety requirements relating to agricultural machinery were out of date and the *Operations at Unfenced Machinery Regulations* did not extend to robots.

Currently, statutory duties are dually (but separately) laid on both manufacturers of machinery for use at work and employers and users of such machinery and equipment, prior compliance, on the part of manufacturers leading to compliance on the part of employers/users. General and specific duties are imposed on manufacturers by the *Supply of Machinery (Safety) Regulations 1992 (SI 1992 No 3073)* as amended by the *Supply of Machinery (Safety) (Amendment) Regulations 1994 (SI 1994 No 2063)*. Correspondingly, general and specific duties (of a parallel nature) are laid on employers and users of work machinery by *PUWER*. These two sets of regulations interface as follows: designers and manufacturers are required to design and manufacture machinery and equipment suitable for specified work purposes (that is, equipment accommodating reasonably foreseeable injury precautions) in alignment with BS 5304 (1988 'Code of Practice for Safety of Machinery', as updated by BS EN 292 'Basic Concepts, General Principles for Design' (1991)). Employers and users, on the other hand, are required, by inspection, to identify foreseeable hazards (if any) during risk assessment.

## The importance of design as regards machine safety

M1002    A machine is defined as an assembly of linked parts or components, at least one of which moves, with the appropriate machine actuators, control and power circuits, joined together for a specific application, in particular for the processing, treatment, moving or packaging of a material. More particularly, machines embrace:

(*a*)    operational parts, performing the principal output function of the machine (i.e. manufacture) (e.g. chuck, drill bit of a vertical drill); and

(*b*)    non-operational parts, conveying power/motion to the operational parts (e.g. motor drives).

An operator is liable to injury from machinery in a variety of ways, such as:

(i)    coming into contact with it;

(ii)    being trapped between machinery and material in it;

(iii)    being struck by machinery or becoming entangled in its motion;

(iv)    being struck by parts of machinery ejected from it; or

(v)    being struck by material ejected from machinery.

These dangers sought to be addressed previously by the fencing/guarding requirements of the *Factories Act 1961* and are currently the remit of *PUWER 1998 (SI 1998 No 2306)* and the *Supply of Machinery (Safety) Regulations (as amended by SI 1994 No 2063)* (see M1019 below). Because the legal requirements are generally stringent, Great Britain has a good accident record by international standards. Engineering design of safeguards, however, is often poor, indicating that the law is honoured in the breach rather than in the observance. The HSE states that about three-quarters of all moving machinery accidents are preventable with reasonably practicable precautions. Half the number of preventable accidents arise as a consequence of a failure on the part of employers to provide proper safeguards. The other half are largely caused by workmen removing safety devices.

Design of machine guards to date has not been particularly successful, though design standards, were set in 1975 by BS 5304: 'Code of Practice for safe guarding of machinery'. Progress was made on certain machines, partly as a result of innovative guard design and partly as a result of operative training, thus minimising the level of serious injuries. Design of machine guards is covered by BS EN 953; this is complemented by several other BS EN standards for machinery safety (see APPEN-DIX 3), replacing the old BS 5304: 1975 and its later version BS 5304: 1988. These standards, together with the General Product Safety Directive (see P9001 PRODUCT SAFETY) and the regulations on the safety of machinery (see M1011 and M1016 below) are expected to succeed in further reducing operator injuries.

Responsibility for poor guard design rests predominantly with the fact that the law has laid emphasis on the user's obligations in respect of factory machinery, rather than considering the measure of involvement which designers and manufacturers of factory machinery should carry. It seems true to say that in some cases injured workmen have been blamed, or lost all or part of their compensation, for what amounts to lack of commitment on the part of design engineers. To some extent this regressive state of affairs was ameliorated by the introduction of *HSWA 1974, s 6*, placing for the first time, general duties regarding product safety upon designers, manufacturers, importers and suppliers, and by the *Consumer Protection Act 1987* (see PRODUCT SAFETY). The stricter safeguards in recent legislation should make further improvements.

# Practical control methods to prevent accidents

M1003 There are two main reasons why accidents happen: either because of a failure to identify danger or acknowledge the possibility of harm, or because control measures are inadequate. Historically three control methods have prevailed:

(*a*) motivation of personnel at risk in an effort to make them cope better with danger;

(*b*) provision of protective clothing (which complies with legal requirements but does not embrace machine operation and unpredictable behaviour);

(*c*) provision and maintenance of physical safeguards to meet the needs of those at risk and to cope with unpredictable behaviour.

The success of (*a*) and (*b*) depends on changing people's attitudes and skills regarding safety, or on employing people with the requisite attitudes and skills. Evidence shows overwhelmingly that the benefits here are likely to be short term. Conversely, adoption of the approach in (*c*) has proved highly successful, especially where it is written into legal requirement.

# Machinery hazards

M1004 Hazards associated with machinery can be classified as follows.

*(a) Traps*

Traps created by machinery are of three basic types:

(i) *In-running nips*: a common feature of conveyorised systems, traps are created where a moving chain meets a toothed wheel, where a moving belt meets a roller, or at the point where two revolving drums, rollers or toothed wheels meet. See *fig. 1* below:

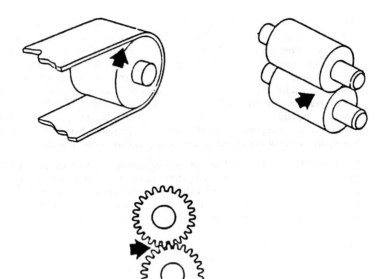

(ii)    *Reciprocating traps*: these are a feature particularly of presses operating under vertical or horizontal motion. See *fig. 2* below:

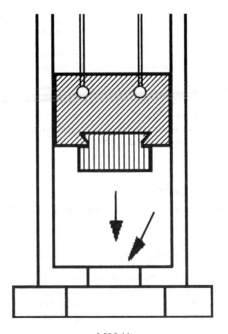

(iii)    *Shearing traps*: where a moving part of machinery traverses a fixed part, or where two moving parts traverse each other, as with a pair of garden shears, and a guillotine effect is produced. See *fig. 3* below:

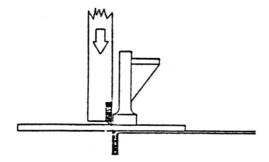

*(b) Entanglement*

The risk of entanglement of clothing, hair and limbs is associated with unfenced revolving shafts, pulleys, drills or chucks to drills. See *fig. 4* below:

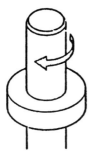

*(c) Contact*

Contact with machinery may cause injury, for instance abrasions due to contact with a grinding wheel, burns from hot surfaces, or amputations through contact with a circular saw.

*(d) Ejection*

Machines may frequently eject particles of wood or metal during a processing operation, or parts of the machine may be thrown out of it.

*(e) Impact*

Certain fast-moving machines could cause injury if an individual gets in the way during the cycle of the machine, e.g. certain types of meat slicing machine.

## Classified dangerous parts of machinery

M1005    The HSE has classified the following parts of machinery as inherently dangerous and, as such, access to them must be protected in accordance with *PUWER 1998 (SI 1998 No 2306)* using the hierarchy of controls specified in the Guidance to the Regulations:

(*a*)   revolving shafts, spindles, mandrels and bars, e.g. line and counter shafts, machine shafts, drill spindles, chucks and drills, etc., boring bars, stock bars, traverse shafts;

(*b*)   in-running nips between pairs of rotating parts, e.g. gear wheels, friction wheels, calendar bowls, mangle rolls, metal manufacturing rolls, rubber washing, breaking and mixing rolls, dough brakes, printing machines, paper-making machines;

(*c*)   in-running nips of the belt and pulley type, e.g. belts and pulleys, plain, flanged or grooved, chain and sprocket gears, conveyor belts and pulleys, metal coiling and the like;

(*d*)   projections on revolving parts, e.g. key heads, set screws, cotter pins, coupling bolts;

(*e*)   discontinuous rotating parts, e.g. open arm pulleys, fan blades, spoked gear wheels and spoked flywheels;

(*f*)   revolving beaters, spiked cylinders and revolving drums, e.g. scutchers, rag flock teasers, cotton openers, carding engines, laundry washing machines;

(*g*)   revolving mixer arms in casing, e.g. dough mixers, rubber solution mixers;

(*h*)   revolving worms and spirals in casings, e.g. meat mincers, rubber extruders, spiral conveyors;

(*i*)   revolving high speed cages in casings, e.g. hydro-extractors, centrifuges;

(*j*)   abrasive wheels, e.g. manufactured wheels, natural sandstone wheels;

(*k*)   revolving cutting tools, e.g. circular saws, milling cutters, circular shears, wood slicers, routers, chaff cutters, woodworking machines such as spindle moulders, planing machines and tenoning machines;

(*l*)   reciprocating tools and dies, e.g. power presses, drop stamps, relief stamps, hydraulic and pneumatic presses, bending presses, hand presses, revolution presses;

(*m*)   reciprocating knives and saws, e.g. guillotines for metal, rubber and paper, trimmers, corner cutters, perforators;

(*n*)   closing nips between platen motions, e.g. letter press platen printing machines, paper and cardboard platen machine cutters, some power presses, foundry moulding machines;

(*o*)   projecting belt fasteners and fast-running belts, e.g. bolt and nut fasteners, wire pin fasteners and the like, woodworking machinery belts, textile machinery side belting, centrifuge belts;

(*p*)   nips between connecting rods or links, and rotating wheels, cranks or discs, e.g. side motion of certain flat-bed printing machines, jacquard motions or looms;

(*q*)   traps arising from the traversing carriages of self-acting machines, e.g. metal planing machines.

## Machinery guards

M1006    A guard is part of a machine used to provide protection by means of a physical barrier. Depending on its construction, a guard may be called casing, cover, screen, door or enclosing guard. A guard may act alone: it is then effective only when it is closed. Alternatively a guard may be used in conjunction with an interlocking device (with or without guard locking – see below): in this case, protection is certain whatever the position of the guard. A wide range of guards or guarding systems is available.

(*a*)    *Fixed guard*

BS EN 953: 1998 'Safety of machinery – Guards – General requirements for the design and construction of fixed and movable guards' defines a fixed guard as 'a guard kept in place (i.e. closed)', either permanently or by means of fasteners (screws, nuts) making removal/opening impossible without using tools.

There are two kinds of fixed guards:

—    an enclosing guard which prevents access to the danger zone from all sides;

—    a distance guard which does not completely enclose a danger zone, but which prevents or reduces access because of its dimensions and its distance from the danger zone, e.g. a perimeter fence or tunnel guard. A tunnel guard is commonly used with metal cutting machinery: the strip metal can only be fed through the tunnel to the cutters, thereby ensuring that users have no access to the cutting mechanism.

(*b*)    *Movable guard*

According to BS EN 953: 1998, this is a guard which is connected by mechanical means (e.g. hinges or slides) to the machine frame or an attached element and which can be opened without the use of tools.

There are three basic kinds of movable guards:

—    a power operated guard: this is operated with the assistance of power from a source other than manual effort or gravity;

—    a self-closing guard: this works by means of gravity, a spring or other external power;

—    a control guard: this is a guard associated with an interlocking device so that the hazardous machine functions 'covered' by the guard cannot operate until the guard is closed, and the closing of the guard initiates the operation of these functions.

(*c*)    *Adjustable guard*

This is defined by BS EN 953: 1998 as a fixed or movable guard which is adjustable as a whole or which incorporates an adjustable part or parts. The adjustment remains fixed during a particular operation. Such guards are appropriate for many band saws, drilling machines and circular saws.

(*d*)    *Interlocking guard*

EN 953: 1998 defines this form of guard as one associated with an interlocking device so that:

—    the hazardous machine functions 'covered' by the guard cannot operate until the guard is closed;

—    if the guard is opened while hazardous machine functions are operating, a stop instruction is given;

—    when the guard is closed, the hazardous machine functions 'covered' by the guard can operate, but the closure of the guard does not itself initiate their operation.

(*e*)   *Interlocking guard with guard locking*

This is a guard associated with an interlocking device and a guard locking device so that:

— the hazardous machine functions 'covered' by the guard cannot operate until the guard is closed and locked;

— the guard remains closed and locked until the risk of injury from the hazardous machine functions has passed;

— when the guard is closed and locked, the hazardous machine functions 'covered' by the guard can operate, but the closure and locking of the guard do not by themselves initiate their operation.

## Safety devices

M1007   A safety device is a protective appliance, other than a guard, which eliminates or reduces risk, alone or associated with a guard. There are many forms of safety device available.

(*a*)   *Trip device*

A trip device is one which causes a machine or machine elements to stop (or ensures an otherwise safe condition) when a person or a part of his body goes beyond a safe limit (EN 292-1: 1991). Trip devices take a number of forms – for example, mechanical, electro-sensitive safety systems and pressure-sensitive mat systems.

Trip devices may be:

— mechanically actuated – e.g. trip wires, telescopic probes, pressure-sensitive devices; or

— non-mechanically actuated – e.g. photo-electric devices, or devices using capacitive or ultrasonic means to achieve detection.

(*b*)   *Mechanical restraint device*

Such a device introduces into a mechanism a mechanical obstacle (for example, a wedge, spindle, strut or scotch) which, by virtue of its own strength, can prevent any hazardous movement, such as the fall of a ram, due to the failure of the normal retaining system.

(*c*)   *Interlocking device (interlock)*

The purpose of this sort of device, which may be mechanical, electrical or some other type, is to prevent the operation of machine elements under specified conditions (generally as long as a guard is not closed).

(*d*)   *Enabling (control) device*

This is an additional manually operated control device used in conjunction with a start control and which, when continuously actuated, allows a machine to function.

(*e*)   *Hold-to-run control device*

This device initiates and maintains the operation of machine elements for only as long as the manual control (actuator) is actuated. The manual control returns automatically to the stop position when released.

(*f*)   *Two-hand control device*

A hold-to-run control device which requires at least simultaneous actuation by the use of both hands in order to initiate and to maintain, whilst hazardous condition exists, any operation of a machine thus affording a measure of protection only for the person who actuates it. EN 574:1996 lays down specific recommendations relating to the design of such devices.

(*g*)   *Limiting device*

Such a device prevents a machine or machine elements from exceeding a designed limit (e.g. space limit, pressure limit).

(*h*)   *Limited movement control device*

The actuation of this sort of device permits only a limited amount of travel of a machine element, thus minimising risk as much as possible; further movement is precluded until there is a subsequent and separate actuation of the control.

(*i*)   *Deterring/impeding device*

This comprises any physical obstacle which, without totally preventing access to a danger zone, reduces the probability of access to this zone by preventing free access.

## Other aspects of machinery safety

M1008   Consideration should also be given to the following matters.

(*a*)   *Position of controls*

Control should be so positioned and spaced as to provide safe and easy operation with ample clearance between each control. Two-hand control devices should not be used as an alternative to guarding, but as an extra safeguard. Actuators which are used to initiate a start function or the movement of machine elements ought to be constructed and mounted so as to minimise inadvertent operation. Push button start controls should be shrouded and pedal-operated controls should be protected to prevent accidental operation. Controls should be clearly identifiable and readily distinguishable from each other. (BS 3641: 1990 and EN 60204-1: 1998).

(*b*)   *Emergency stops*

Each machine must be fitted with one or more emergency stop devices to enable actual or impending danger to be averted. The following exceptions apply:

—   machines in which an emergency stop device would not lessen the risk, either because it would not reduce the stopping time or because it would not enable the special measures required to deal with the risk to be taken;

—   hand-held portable machines and hand-guided machines.

An emergency stop device must stop the dangerous process as quickly as possible, without creating additional hazards. The emergency stop control must remain engaged; it must be possible to disengage it only by an appropriate operation on the control device itself. Disengaging the control must not restart the machinery, but only permit restarting. The stop control function must not trigger the stopping function before being in the latched position. (Essential Health and Safety Requirements, and EN 418: 1992).

(*c*)    *Colour*

It may be necessary to paint certain parts of machines a distinguishing colour which will only be visible when a danger exists, e.g. the insides of hinged or sliding covers which, when open, expose dangerous machine parts or a part of the machine which remains with the source of danger.

(*d*)    *Spindles*

Spindles should be able to be brought to rest quickly and consistently. Spindle brakes which are activated by mechanical, hydraulic, pneumatic or electrical means should bring the spindle to rest, or retain their capability of bringing the spindle to rest, in the event of a power failure. The braking system should be such that the spindle will not automatically rotate when power is resumed after a power failure. Rotating parts and equipment fastened to rotating parts should be so secured as to prevent dislodgement in consequence of the brake action.

(*e*)    *Handles and handwheels*

Cranked handles or handwheels used to operate a mechanism, which can also be operated under power at a peripheral speed of the handwheel of more than 20 metres per minute, should be designed to prevent rotation under power, be solid and be provided with a device that stalls rotation if obstructed. (Machine Tool Traders Association Standards Instruction Sheet No 11.)

(*f*)    *Power-operated workholding devices*

These devices should be designed so that a dangerous situation is prevented in the event of failure of the power supply. On automatic machines the control system should be interlocked to prevent the machine from being operated until power is supplied to the workholding device and the workpiece is clamped. The control system should be such that the power-operating system for the workholding device cannot be operated to unclamp the workpiece whilst the machine is in operation.

(*g*)    *Equipment*

—    Electrical equipment should comply with EN 60204-1: 1998;

—    Hydraulic equipment should comply with EN 982: 1996;

—    Pneumatic equipment should comply with EN 983: 1996.

(*h*)    *Coolants*

Where a coolant is used, machines should be designed to contain the coolant at least during the more usual operations. It may also be necessary to add a bactericide to the coolant to prevent bacterial growth. Coolant reservoirs should be covered where possible. The coolant system should be designed so that coolant troughs, reservoirs, etc. can be easily cleaned. Nozzles should be designed so that they will stay firmly in position when set and not require adjustment by the operator during the machining process. On-off volume controls should not be adjacent to the nozzle and should be positioned so as to ensure operator safety when adjustments are made. Additional splash guards should be used where necessary. Means should be provided for the safe removal of swarf from the work area.

(*i*)    *Lubrication*

Lubrication points should be easily accessible. Care should be taken to avoid any accidental mixing of coolant, cutting fluids and lubricants. Excess lubricants should be prevented from reaching the surrounding floor area. On machines in which the failure of an automatic lubrication system could cause a hazard to the operator, such a lubrication system should incorporate a suitable indication of its correct functioning.

(*j*)    *Counterweights and enclosures*

Counterweights, related machine elements and their movements which constitute a hazard, should be safeguarded.

Enclosures used within the machine to house mechanical, electrical, hydraulic equipment, etc. which constitute a hazard should be provided with fixed covers and guards.

(*k*)    *Lifting gear*

All fixtures used on the machine and other externally-mounted devices should be provided with means for their safe loading and unloading. When a machine is provided with lifting gear and appliances, the supplier should provide details of the safe working load and notify the user of the need to obtain a certificate of test and examination. [*Supply of Machinery (Safety) (Amendment) Regulations 1994 (SI 1994 No 2063)*]. Eyebolts and eyebolt holes should be identified to prevent mismatching. (HSE Guidance Note PM 16; BS 4278: 1998). (See LIFTING MACHINERY AND EQUIPMENT.)

# Non-mechanical machinery hazards

M1009    Other hazards associated with machinery operation, which can be a contributory factor in accidents and/or occupational ill-health, include:

(*a*)    inadequate temperature, lighting and ventilation control of the machine area, frequently resulting in steep temperature gradients, shadows, glare and general discomfort;

(*b*)    noise from machinery, which reduces the chance of operators hearing warning signals, such as the fire alarm or a forklift truck horn, and can result in operators going deaf over a period of time;

(*c*)    chemical substances used in machinery-operated processes, which can cause dermatitis or even result in a gassing accident;

(*d*)    ergonomic design faults, leading to postural fatigue, visual fatigue, back and other body strains, and an increased risk of operator error;

(*e*)    ionising radiation, due to inadequate containment of sealed and unsealed sources of radiation; and resulting in various occupational cancers; and

(*f*)    dust and fume emission, resulting in certain conditions of the respiratory tract, such as silicosis, and the potential for dust explosions.

All these factors should be considered in the assessment of machinery hazards.

# Legal requirements in connection with machinery

## Definition of machinery for use at work

M1010    'Machinery for use at work' (for manufacturing purposes) means machinery:

(*a*)  designed for use/operation, whether exclusively or not, by persons at work, or

(*b*)  designed for use/operation, otherwise than at work, in non-domestic premises made available to persons at a place where they may use the machinery provided for their use there.

[*Supply of Machinery (Safety) (Amendment) Regulations 1994 (SI 1994 No 2063)*].

'Work equipment' (for employer/user purposes) means:

'*any machinery, appliance, apparatus, tool or installation for use at work (whether exclusively or not)*'.

[*PUWER 1998 (SI 1998 No 2306), Reg 2(1)*].

## Duties of employers – Provision and Use of Work Equipment Regulations 1998 (SI 1998 No 2306) (PUWER)

M1011  Statutory duties of employers regarding machinery used, were concerned almost exclusively with fencing and guarding – witness the *Factories Act 1961, ss 12–16*. Now, in the light of *PUWER*, employers are required to select suitably safe new or second-hand equipment for use at work, maintain it properly and inform operators of foreseeable dangers, in the interests of the general safety of legitimate users of such machinery.

'Use' of machinery refers to any activity involving work equipment, including 'starting, stopping, programming, setting, transporting, repairing, modifying, maintaining, servicing and cleaning'. [*PUWER 1998 (SI 1998 No 2306), Reg 2(1)*].

The main aim of *PUWER* is to protect workers against dangerous machinery and parts (that is, machinery and parts that could foreseeably cause operators injury when properly used). In this connection, there is an overriding strict duty (*a*) to prevent access to dangerous parts and (*b*) to stop movement of dangerous parts before a person (or any part of him/her) enters a danger zone. Guarding and the establishment of safe work systems should be the objective of all employers, whenever reasonably practicable. (Alternatively, if dangerous parts cannot be completely guarded, instructions and training courses coupled with safe work systems represent a fall-back position.) The regulations, applicable to all workplaces, including factories, offices, service industries, construction sites and offshore installations, and covering employees, self-employed personnel and members of the public using work equipment in public places, specify both general and specific requirements in relation to machinery, its installation and use.

The case of *Stark v The Post Office (2000) (unreported)* provides the first clear decision on the scope of *PUWER*.

Mr Stark was employed as a postman and was provided with a bicycle to make his deliveries. On 29 July 1994, in the course of his employment, he was riding his bicycle when without warning his front wheel locked and he was propelled over the handlebars and he suffered a serious injury. The accident was caused by the stirrup which was part of the front brake which broke into two, with one part becoming lodged in the front wheel. The evidence given and accepted was that the cause of the stirrup breaking was either metal fatigue or some manufacturing defect. The judge at first instance found that the '*defect would not and could not have been discoverable on any routine inspection*' and '*a perfectly rigorous examination would not have revealed this defect*'. He rejected the claimant's case for compensation both at common law and under *PUWER 1992*.

Lord Justice Walker allowing the appeal and giving the only judgement in *Stark* stated:

'In the circumstances, it seems to me that reg 6(1) does impose an absolute obligation, and that accordingly, since the bicycle was not in an efficient state or in efficient working order when the stirrup broke, the Post Office were in breach of their statutory duty'.

This approach is also consistent with the view taken by the Court of Appeal in another recent case *Hawkes v London Borough of Southwark (1998) (unreported)*. It was made clear by the Court of Appeal in *Hawkes* that a traditional interpretation should be given to the concept of reasonable practicability:

'I believe it is proper to conclude that Parliament had in mind, when they enacted the Regulations, the construction of the words "reasonably practicable" which had been accepted by court since 1938', per Aldous LJ.

## General requirements

M1012   Every employer must ensure:

(*a*)   *Selection of equipment* – that he has regard to the working conditions and to the risks, existing on the premises, to the health and safety of persons and to any additional risk posed by use of that work equipment. [*PUWER 1998 (SI 1998 No 2306), Reg 4*].

(*b*)   *Suitability of work equipment* – that work equipment is:

    (i)   constructed or adapted so as to be suitable for the purpose for which it is provided;

    (ii)   used only for operations for which, and under conditions for which, it is suitable (i.e. will not affect the health or safety of any person).

[*PUWER 1998 (SI 1998 No 2306), Reg 4*].

(*c*)   *Maintenance* – that work equipment is maintained in an efficient state and working order, and in good repair, and, where there is a maintenance log for machinery, that the log is kept up to date. [*PUWER 1998 (SI 1998 No 2306), Reg 5*].

(*d*)   *Inspection* – that work equipment is inspected and that the result of an inspection is recorded and kept until the next inspection is recorded. Inspection should be carried out:

    (i)   where the safety of work equipment depends on the installation conditions – after installation and before being put into service for the first time, or after assembly at a new site/location;

    (ii)   where work equipment exposed to conditions causing deterioration is liable to result in dangerous situations – at suitable intervals, and each time that exceptional circumstances which are liable to jeopardise the safety of the work equipment have occurred.

[*PUWER 1998 (SI 1998 No 2306), Reg 6*].

It must be clear who is responsible for the inspection of the equipment – it is not acceptable to disown the equipment.

(*e*)   *Specific risks* – that where any use of work equipment is likely to involve a specific risk to the health or safety of any person

(i)    use of that work equipment must be restricted to those persons given the task of using it, and

(ii)    repairs, modifications, maintenance or servicing be restricted to persons specifically designated to carry out such operations (whether or not also authorised to carry out other operations) who must have received adequate training.

[*PUWER 1998 (SI 1998 No 2306), Reg 7*].

(*f*)    *Information/instructions* – that all persons who use equipment or who supervise or manage the use of work equipment must have available to them adequate health and safety information and, where appropriate, written instructions readily comprehensible to the workers concerned, including instructions relating to:

(i)    the conditions in which, and the methods by which, the work equipment is to be used;

(ii)    foreseeable abnormal situations and the action to be taken in such circumstances;

(iii)    any conclusions to be drawn from experience in using the equipment.

[*PUWER 1998 (SI 1998 No 2306), Reg 8*].

(*g*)    *Training* – that all persons using work equipment or who supervise or manage same must have adequate training. [*PUWER 1998 (SI 1998 No 2306), Reg 9*].

(*h*)    *Conformity with EU requirements* – that work equipment has been designed and constructed in compliance with any statutory instruments, listed in *Sch 1*, which give effect to EU directives concerning product safety [*PUWER 1998 (SI 1998 No 2306), Reg 10*].

## Specific requirements – dangerous parts of machinery

M1013    Every employer must ensure that effective measures are taken:

1.    *Dangerous parts of machinery* – in order

(a)    to prevent access to dangerous parts of machinery or any rotating stock-bar, or

(*b*)    to stop movement of any dangerous parts of machinery or rotating stock-bar before any part of a person enters a danger zone (i.e. a zone where a person is exposed to risk from dangerous parts of machinery),

guards/protection devices must be provided, so far as practicable.

A hierarchy of such measures consists of:

(i)    fixed guards enclosing every dangerous part; if not practicable then –

(ii)    other guards or protection devices where fixed guards are not possible; if not practicable then –

(iii)    provision of jigs, holders, push-sticks or similar protection if practicable; if not practicable then –

(iv)    information, instruction, training and supervision must be provided.

Guards must:

(1)    be suitable for their purpose;

(2) be of good construction, sound material and adequate strength;

(3) be properly maintained;

(4) not create additional risks to health or safety;

(5) not be easily bypassed or rendered inoperative;

(6) be situated at sufficient distance from a danger zone;

(7) not restrict more than necessary any view of the operation of work equipment; and

(8) allow for fitting, replacing of parts, and maintenance work, without having to remove the guard or protective device.

[*PUWER 1998 (SI 1998 No 2306), Reg 11*].

2. *Protection against failure* – so far as is reasonably practicable (see E15039 ENFORCEMENT), that work equipment is protected or, if it is not reasonably practicable, adequately controlled without the use of PPE against risks to health or safety from:

— ejected/falling objects;

— rupture/disintegration;

— overheating/catching fire;

— unintended/premature discharge or ejection of any article, gas, dust, liquid or vapour;

— unintended/premature explosion of work equipment or material produced, used or stored in it.

[*PUWER 1998 (SI 1998 No 2306), Reg 12*].

3. *High/low temperature* – that parts of work equipment and material produced or used in it, which might burn, scald or sear, be protected to prevent persons being so injured. [*PUWER 1998 (SI 1998 No 2306), Reg 13*].

4. *Controls for starting equipment* – that work equipment is provided with one or more controls to:

(*a*) start equipment (as well as re-start); and

(*b*) change speed, pressure or operating conditions,

and it must not be possible to perform any of the above operations except by deliberate action (other than in the case of an automatic device). [*PUWER 1998 (SI 1998 No 2306), Reg 14*].

5. *Stop controls* – that work equipment is provided with readily accessible stop controls (including emergency stop controls [*PUWER 1998 (SI 1998 No 2306), Reg 16*]), which:

(*a*) must bring equipment to a complete stop safely, and

(*b*) if necessary, disconnect all energy sources, and

(*c*) must operate in priority to controls which start or change the work equipment's operating conditions.

[*PUWER 1998 (SI 1998 No 2306), Reg 15*].

6. *Position of controls* – that controls of work equipment are clearly visible and identifiable, have appropriate marking where necessary and are not in a

danger zone (except where necessary). In particular, no one should be in a danger zone *vis-à-vis* the position of any control affecting a danger zone hazard; but, if not reasonably practicable, no one should be in a danger zone when work equipment is about to start; but, if the latter is not reasonably practicable, audible/visible warning should be given when work equipment is about to start. [*PUWER 1998 (SI 1998 No 2306), Reg 17*].

7.    *Control systems* – must be safe so far as practicable and chosen – making due allowance for the failures, faults and constraints to be expected in the planned circumstances of use – so that:

(*a*)    their operation does not create increased risk to health or safety;

(*b*)    no fault in them can result in increased risk to health or safety; and

(*c*)    they do not hinder the operation of stop or emergency stop controls.

[*PUWER 1998 (SI 1998 No 2306), Reg 18*].

8.    *Isolation from energy sources* – that equipment must be provided with appropriate means to isolate it from its sources of energy; such means must be clearly identifiable and accessible. Reconnection of energy sources to work equipment must not expose operatives to risk. [*PUWER 1998 (SI 1998 No 2306), Reg 19*].

9.    *Stability* – that work equipment is stabilised by clamping, etc. [*PUWER 1998 (SI 1998 No 2306), Reg 20*].

10.    *Lighting* – that any place where work equipment is used, be adequately lit. [*PUWER 1998 (SI 1998 No 2306), Reg 21*].

11.    *Maintenance operations* – that, so far as is reasonably practicable, maintenance operations which involve a risk to health or safety can be carried out while the equipment is shut down, or otherwise without exposing anyone carrying them out to such risk, or, alternatively, appropriate protective measures can be taken. [*PUWER 1998 (SI 1998 No 2306), Reg 22*].

12.    *Markings* – that equipment be appropriately marked (i.e. CE markings). [*PUWER 1998 (SI 1998 No 2306), Reg 23*].

13.    *Warnings* – that equipment incorporate clear and unambiguous warnings or warning devices. [*PUWER 1998 (SI 1998 No 2306), Reg 24*].

(These requirements are applicable also to offshore operations (see OFFSHORE OPERATIONS).)

## Mobile work equipment

Every employer must ensure:

(*a*)    *Employees carried on mobile work equipment* – that no employee is carried by mobile work equipment unless:

(i)    it is suitable for carrying persons; and

(ii)    it incorporates features – for reducing risks to their safety – to as low as is reasonably practicable.

[*PUWER 1998 (SI 1998 No 2306), Reg 25*].

(*b*)    *Rolling over of mobile work equipment* – that where there is a risk to an employee riding on mobile work equipment from its rolling over, it is minimised by:

(i)    stabilising the work equipment;

(ii)    a structure which ensures that the work equipment does no more than fall on its side;

(iii)    a structure giving sufficient clearance to anyone being carried if it overturns further than that; or

(iv)    a device giving comparable protection.

This regulation does not apply to a fork-lift truck having a structure as described in (*b*)(ii) and (*b*)(iii) above.

The employer must ensure that the mobile work equipment has a suitable restraining system where there is a risk of anyone on it being crushed if it rolls over.

Compliance with this regulation is not required where:

—    it would increase the overall risk to safety;

—    it would not be reasonably practicable to operate the mobile work equipment in consequence; or

—    in relation to an item of work equipment provided for use in the undertaking or establishment before 5 December 1998 it would not be reasonably practicable.

[*PUWER 1998 (SI 1998 No 2306), Reg 26*].

(*c*)    *Overturning of fork-lift trucks* – that a fork-lift truck having a structure as described in (*b*)(ii) and (*b*)(iii) above and which carries an employee is adapted or equipped to reduce the risk to safety from its overturning to as low as is reasonably practicable. [*PUWER 1998 (SI 1998 No 2306), Reg 27*].

(*d*)    *Self-propelled work equipment* – that where it may, while in motion, involve risk to the safety of persons:

(i)    it has facilities for preventing its being started by an unauthorised person;

(ii)    it has appropriate facilities for minimising the consequences of a collision where there is more than one item of rail-mounted work equipment in motion at the same time;

(iii)    it has a device for braking and stopping;

(iv)    where safety constraints so require, emergency facilities operated by readily accessible controls or automatic systems are available for braking and stopping the work equipment in the event of failure of the main facility;

(v)    where the driver's direct field of vision is inadequate to ensure safety, there are adequate devices for improving his vision so far as is reasonably practicable;

(vi)    if provided for use at night or in dark places – it is equipped with lighting appropriate to the work to be carried out, and is otherwise sufficiently safe for such use;

(vii)    if it, or anything carried or towed by it, constitutes a fire hazard, appropriate fire-fighting equipment should be carried or kept close to it.

[*PUWER 1998 (SI 1998 No 2306), Reg 28*].

(e)   *Remote-controlled self-propelled work equipment* – that where it involves a risk to safety while in motion, it stops automatically once it leaves its control range; and, where the risk is of crushing or impact, it has features to guard against such risk unless other appropriate devices are able to do so.

[*PUWER 1998 (SI 1998 No 2306), Reg 29*].

(f)   *Drive shafts* – that where the seizure of the drive shaft between mobile work equipment and its accessories or anything towed is likely to involve a risk:

(i)   the work equipment has a means of preventing such seizure; or

(ii)   where such seizure cannot be avoided, take every possible measure to avoid an adverse effect on the safety of an employee.

The employer must also ensure that the work equipment has a system for safeguarding the shaft, where:

(i)   the mobile work equipment has a shaft for the transmission of energy between it and other mobile work equipment; and

(ii)   the shaft could become soiled or damaged by contact with the ground while uncoupled.

[*PUWER 1998 (SI 1998 No 2306), Reg 30*].

## Power presses

M1015   'Power press means a press or press brake for the working of metal by means of tools, or for die proving, which is power driven and which embodies a flywheel and clutch'. [*PUWER 1998 (SI 1998 No 2306), Reg 2(1)*].

(a)   *Power presses to which regulations 32–35 do not apply:*

(i)   a power press for the working of hot metal;

(ii)   a power press not capable of a stroke greater than 6 mm;

(iii)   a guillotine;

(iv)   a combination punching and shearing machine, turret punch press or similar machine for punching, shearing or cropping;

(v)   a machine, other than press brake, for bending steel sections;

(vi)   a power press for the compacting of metal powders;

(vii)   machines for straightening, upsetting, heading, riveting, eyeletting, press-stud attaching, zip fastener bottom stop attaching, stapling or wire stitching.

[*PUWER 1998 (SI 1998 No 2306), Reg 31*].

(b)   *Thorough examination of power presses, guards and protection devices* – every employer shall ensure that:

(i)   a power press is not put into service for the first time after installation, or after assembly at a new site or in a new location, unless it has been thoroughly examined to ensure that:

—   it has been installed correctly;

—   it is safe to operate; and

—   any defect has been remedied;

(ii)     a guard, other than one to which paragraph (iii) relates – or protection device – is not put into service for the first time on a power press unless it has been thoroughly examined when in position on that power press to ensure that it is effective for its purpose, and any defect has been remedied;

(iii)     part of a closed tool which acts as a fixed guard is not used on a power press unless it has been thoroughly examined when in position on any power press in the premises to ensure that it is effective for its purpose, and any defect has been remedied;

(iv)     for the purposes of ensuring that health and safety conditions are maintained, and that any deterioration can be detected and remedied in good time: every power press must be thoroughly examined – if it only has fixed guards at least every twelve months; otherwise at least every six months – and whenever exceptional circumstances have occurred which are liable to jeopardise the safety of the power press or its guards or protection devices. Any defects must be remedied before reusing the power press.

[*PUWER 1998 (SI 1998 No 2306), Reg 32*].

(*c*)    *Inspection of guards and protection devices*

(i)     every employer must ensure that a power press is not used after the setting, re-setting or adjustment of its tools, except in trying out its tools or die proving, unless its every guard and protection device has been inspected and tested while in position on the power press by a person appointed in writing by the employer who is:

    —   competent; or

    —   undergoing training for that purpose and acting under the immediate supervision of a competent person,

and who has signed a certificate which complies with paragraph (iii) below; or

    —   the guards and protection devices have not been altered or disturbed in the course of the adjustment of its tools;

(ii)     every employer must ensure that a power press is not used after the expiration of the fourth hour of a working period unless its every guard and protection device has been inspected and tested while in position on the power press by a person appointed in writing by the employer who is:

    —   competent; or

    —   undergoing training for that purpose and acting under the immediate supervision of a competent person,

and who has signed a certificate which complies with paragraph (iii) below;

(iii)     a certificate referred to in (i) and (ii) above:

    —   must contain sufficient particulars to identify every guard and protection device inspected and tested and the power press on which it was positioned at the time of the inspection and test;

    —   must state the date and time of the inspection and test;

— must state that every guard and protection device on the power press is in position and effective for its purpose.

[*PUWER 1998 (SI 1998 No 2306), Reg 33*].

(*d*)   *Reports*

(i)   a person making a thorough examination for an employer under *Reg 32* must:

— immediately notify the employer of any defect in a power press (or its guard or protection device) which in his opinion is or could become a danger to persons;

— write a report of the thorough examination to the employer;

— where there is in his opinion a defect in a power press (or its guard or protection device) which is or could become a danger to persons, send a copy of the report to the enforcing authority for the premises in which the power press is situated;

[PUWER 1998 (SI 1998 No 2306), Reg 34(1)]

(ii)   a person making an inspection and test for an employer under *Reg 33* must immediately notify the employer of any defect in a guard or protection device which in his opinion is or could become a danger to persons and the reason for his opinion.

[PUWER 1998 (SI 1998 No 2306), Reg 34(2)].

(*e*)   *Keeping of information* – every employer must ensure that reports that comply with *Reg 34(1)* are kept available for inspection for two years, and that certificates belonging to supervising persons under *Reg 33* are kept available for inspection – at or near the power press to which they relate until superseded by a later certificate – and, after that, until six months have elapsed since it was signed.

[*PUWER 1998 (SI 1998 No 2306), Reg 35*].

# Duties on designers and manufacturers – Supply of Machinery (Safety) Regulations 1992 (SI 1992 No 3073), as amended

M1016   General and specific duties relating to machinery safety are laid on designers and manufacturers of machinery for use at work by the *Supply of Machinery (Safety) Regulations 1992*, as amended by the *Supply of Machinery (Safety) (Amendment) Regulations 1994 (SI 1994 No 2063)*.

Supply of safe machinery (including safety components, roll-over protective structures and industrial trucks) is governed by these regulations. The 1994 Regulations extend to machinery for lifting people [*SI 1994 No 2063, Reg 4, Sch 2, para 10* (e.g. elevating work platforms). The combined effect of the two sets of regulations requires that, when machinery or components are properly installed, maintained and used for their intended purposes, there is no risk (except a minimal one) of their being a cause or occasion of death or injury to persons, or damage to property [*SI 1992 No 3073, Reg 2(2)*, as amended by *SI 1994 No 2063, Reg 4, Sch 2, para 5*.

## Relevant machinery

M1017    The *Supply of Machinery (Safety) Regulations 1992 (as amended by SI 1994 No 2063)* do not apply to:

(*a*)    specific machinery or safety components supplied before 1 January 1995 [*SI 1992 No 3073, Reg 7A, as inserted by SI 1994 No 2063, Reg 4, Sch 2, para 8*;

(*b*)    machinery complying with health and safety requirements as at 31 December 1992, which has been put into service before 31 December 1994;

(*c*)    machinery covered by other directives (see P9001 PRODUCT SAFETY); and

(*d*)    electrical equipment.

The regulations cover:

(i)    safety components [*SI 1992 No 3073, Reg 3 as amended by SI 1994 No 2063, Reg 4, Sch 2, para 6*;

(ii)    machinery/components for lifting or moving persons [*SI 1992 No 3073, Reg 5, Sch 5 as amended by SI 1994 No 2063, Reg 4, Sch 2, para 10*;

(iii)    roll-over protective structures; and

(iv)    industrial trucks.


## Excluded machinery

M1018    Certain machinery is outside the ambit of these regulations namely:

(*a*)    machinery whose only power source is directly applied manual effort unless it is a machine used for lifting or lowering loads;

(*b*)    machinery for medical use used in direct contact with patients;

(*c*)    special equipment for use in fairgrounds and/or amusement parks;

(*d*)    steam boilers, tanks and pressure vessels;

(*e*)    machinery specially designed or put into service for nuclear purposes which, in the event of failure, may result in an emission of radioactivity;

(*f*)    radioactive sources forming part of a machine;

(*g*)    firearms;

(*h*)    storage tanks and pipelines for petrol, diesel fuel, flammable liquids and dangerous substances;

(*i*)    means of transport, that is vehicles and their trailers intended solely for transporting passengers by air or on road, rail or water networks, as well as means of transport in so far as such means are designed for transporting goods by air, on public road or rail networks or on water. Vehicles used in the mineral extraction industry shall not be excluded;

(*j*)    seagoing vessels and mobile offshore units together with equipment on board such vessels or units;

(*k*)    cableways, including funicular railways, for the public or private transportation of persons;

(*l*)    agricultural and forestry tractors;

(*m*)    machines specifically designed and constructed for military or police purposes;

(*n*)  lifts which permanently serve specific levels of buildings and constructions, having a car moving between guides which are rigid and inclined at an angle of more than 15 degrees to the horizontal and designed for the transport of:

— persons,

— persons and goods,

— goods alone if the car is accessible, that is to say, a person may enter it without difficulty, and fitted with controls situated inside the car or within reach of a person inside;

(*o*)  means of transport of persons using rack and pinion rail mounted vehicles;

(*p*)  mine winding gear;

(*q*)  theatre elevators; and

(*r*)  construction site hoists for lifting persons or persons and goods.

*[Supply of Machinery (Safety) Regulations 1992 (SI 1992 No 3073), Sch 5 as amended by the Supply of Machinery (Safety) (Amendment) Regulations 1994 (SI 1994 No 2063), Reg 4, Sch 2, para 23.*

### General machinery and machinery posing special hazards

M1019  The regulations draw a distinction between general machinery and machinery posing special hazards, in that the latter's – machinery posing special hazards – technical file, which must be prepared in either case for relevant machinery, must be sent to

(i)  an approved body for retention/verification – in the case of machinery manufactured according to transposed harmonised standards [*SI 1992 No 3073 as amended, Reg 14*], and

(ii)  an approved body, coupled with an example of machinery for EU-type-examination – in the case of machinery not manufactured according to transposed harmonised standards.

[*SI 1992 No 3073 as amended, Regs 13, 15*].

### Machinery posing special hazards – Schedule 4 machinery

M1020  Such machinery includes:

*(A) Machinery:*

(1)  circular saws (single or multi-blade) for working with wood and analogous materials or for working with meat and analogous materials;

(2)  sawing machines with fixed tool during operation, having a fixed bed with manual feed of the workpiece or with a demountable power feed;

(3)  sawing machines with fixed tool during operation, having a manually operated reciprocating saw-bench or carriage;

(4)  sawing machines with fixed tool during operation, having a built-in mechanical feed device for the workpieces, with manual loading and/or unloading;

(5)  sawing machines with movable tool during operation, with a mechanical feed device and manual loading and/or unloading;

(6)  hand-fed surface planing machines for woodworking;

(7) thicknessers for one-side dressing with manual loading and/or unloading for woodworking;

(8) band-saws with a fixed or mobile bed and band-saws with a mobile carriage, with manual loading and/or unloading, for working with wood and analogous materials or for working with meat and analogous materials;

(9) combined machines of the types referred to in (1) to (8) and (11) for working with wood and analogous materials;

(10) hand-fed tenoning machines with several tool holders for woodworking;

(11) hand-fed vertical spindle moulding machines for working with wood and analogous materials;

(12) portable chain saws for woodworking;

(13) presses, including press-brakes, for the cold working of metals, with manual loading and/or unloading, whose movable working parts may have a travel exceeding 6 mm and a speed exceeding 30 mm/s;

(14) injection or compression plastics-moulding machines with manual loading or unloading;

(15) injection or compression rubber-moulding machines with manual loading or unloading;

(16) machinery for underground working of the following types:

— machinery on rails, locomotives and brake-vans,

— hydraulic-powered roof supports,

— internal combustion engines to be fitted to machinery for underground working;

(17) manually-loaded trucks for the collection of household refuse incorporating a compression mechanism;

(18) guards and detachable transmission shafts with universal joints;

(19) vehicles servicing lifts;

[*Supply of Machinery (Safety) Regulations 1992 (SI 1992 No 3073), Sch 4* as amended by the *Supply of Machinery (Safety) (Amendment) Regulations 1994 (SI 1994 No 2063), Reg 3, Sch 1, para 4*]

and

(20) devices for the lifting of persons involving a risk of falling from a vertical height of more than three metres;

(21) machines for the manufacture of pyrotechnics.

[*Supply of Machinery (Safety) Regulations 1992 (SI 1992 No 3073), Sch 4* as amended by the *Supply of Machinery (Safety) (Amendment) Regulations 1994 (SI 1994 No 2063), Reg 4, Sch 2, para 22*].

*(B) Safety components:*

(1) electro-sensitive devices designed specifically to detect persons in order to ensure their safety (non-material barriers, sensor mats, electromagnetic detectors, etc.);

(2)    logic units which ensure the safety functions of bi-manual controls;

(3)    automatic movable screens to protect presses;

(4)    roll-over protective structures (ROPS); and

(5)    falling object protective structures (FOPS).

[*Supply of Machinery (Safety) Regulations 1992 (SI 1992 No 3073), Sch 4* as amended by the *Supply of Machinery (Safety) (Amendment) Regulations 1994 (SI 1994 No 2063), Reg 4, Sch 2, para 22*].


### Technical file

*Machinery posing special hazards*

M1021    In respect of relevant machinery that is Schedule 4 machinery manufactured in accordance with transposed harmonised standards, the responsible person must select one of the following paths:

—    draw up a technical file and forward it to an approved body for retention by that body;

—    submit the technical file to an approved body requesting (i) verification by that body that the transposed harmonised standards have been correctly applied, and (ii) that the body draw up a certificate of adequacy for the file; or

—    submit the technical file to an approved body together with an example of the relevant machinery for EC type-examination or, where appropriate, a statement as to where such an example might be EC type-examined.

In the case of relevant machinery which is Schedule 4 machinery and which is not or only partly manufactured in accordance with transposed harmonised standards, or in respect of which there are no transposed harmonised standards, the responsible person must submit a technical file to an approved body together with an example of the machinery for EC type-examination or, where appropriate, a statement as to where such an example might be EC type-examined.

The technical file must include:

(*a*)    an overall drawing of the machinery together with drawings of the control circuits;

(*b*)    full, detailed drawings, accompanied by any calculation notes, test results and such other data as may be required to check the conformity of the machinery with the essential health and safety requirements;

(*c*)    a description of methods adopted to eliminate hazards presented by the machinery, a list of transposed harmonised standards used or, alternatively, a list of standards used;

(*d*)    a copy of the instructions for the machinery drawn up; and

(*e*)    for series manufacture, the internal measures that will be implemented to ensure that all the items of machinery so produced are in conformity with the provisions of the Machinery Directive.

The technical file must be drawn up in an official language of the member state in which the approved body is established or in such other language as is acceptable to the approved body, always provided that the instructions for the machinery are in one of the EU languages. On being put into service, the machinery must be accompanied not only by the instructions in the original language, but also by a translation of the instructions in the language(s) of the country in which the machinery is used.

*General machinery*

M1022    In the case of relevant machinery which is not Schedule 4 machinery, the responsible person must draw up a technical file which consists of:

(*a*)    an overall drawing of the machinery together with drawings of the control circuits;

(*b*)    full, detailed drawings, accompanied by any calculation notes, test results and such other data as may be required to check the conformity of the machinery with the essential health and safety requirements;

(*c*)    a list of the essential health and safety requirements, transposed harmonised standards, relevant standards and other technical specifications which were used when the machinery was designed;

(*d*)    a description of the methods adopted to eliminate the hazards presented by the machinery;

(*e*)    if he so desires, any technical report or certificate obtained from a competent body or laboratory;

(*f*)    if he declares conformity with a transposed harmonised standard which provides therefor, any technical report giving the results of tests carried out at his choice either by himself or by a competent body or laboratory; and

(*g*)    a copy of the instructions for the machinery.

For series manufacture, the responsible person must also have available documentation in respect of the internal measures that will be implemented to ensure that all the items of machinery so produced are in conformity with the provisions of the Machinery Directive.

Where the technical file is drawn up in the United Kingdom, it must be in English – always provided that the instructions for the machinery referred to above at (*g*) are in one of the EU languages. On being put into service, the machinery must be accompanied not only by the instructions in the original language, but also by a translation of the instructions in the language(s) of the country in which the machinery is used.

# Essential health and safety requirements for general machinery and machinery posing special hazards

M1023    Essential health and safety features relate to:

(1)    general design features;

(2)    controls;

(3)    mechanical hazards;

(4)    non-mechanical hazards;

(5)    maintenance;

(6)    indicators.

The key objective of the regulations is to integrate safety into workplace machinery throughout the process which begins with the design and development stage of the machinery and ends with its distribution.

## (1) General design features

M1024   To that end the following general design features should be incorporated:

(*a*)   machinery must be constructed so as to be fit for function, and adjustable/ maintainable without endangering operators;

(*b*)   in order to do this, manufacturers should

  (i)   eliminate and/or reduce inherent risks as far as possible,

  (ii)   take necessary protection measures in relation to risks that cannot be eliminated,

  (iii)   inform users of residual risks owing to shortcomings in protection measures,

  (iv)   specify training needs,

  (v)   specify personal protection needs;

(*c*)   design of machinery should envisage not just normal use but also reasonably foreseeable use, and machinery should be designed to prevent reasonably foreseeable abnormal use;

(*d*)   discomfort, fatigue and psychological stress faced by an operator must be reduced to a minimum;

(*e*)   constraints upon operators must be accommodated, including requisite and foreseeable use of personal protective equipment;

(*f*)   supply of machinery must be accompanied by special equipment and accessories for use, adjustment and maintenance purposes;

(*g*)   machinery should not endanger the operator when being filled or used with or drained of fluids;

(*h*)   integral lighting should be supplied where there is a risk from lack of it, in spite of normal ambient lighting;

(*i*)   machinery must be capable of being handled and stored safely.

[*SI 1992 No 3073 as amended, Sch 3*].

## (2) Controls – starting and stopping

M1025   Control systems must be safe and reliable, in a way that they can withstand the rigours of normal use and external factors and that errors in logic do not lead to dangerous situations. Control devices must be:

(*a*)   clearly visible and appropriately marked;

(*b*)   positioned for safe operation;

(*c*)   located outside a danger zone, except for emergency stops or consoles;

(*d*)   positioned so that their operation cannot cause additional risk;

(*e*)   designed so that risk cannot occur without intentional operation;

(*f*)    made to withstand foreseeable strain, especially as regards emergency stop devices;

(*g*)    in the case of a multi-action control, the action to be performed, must be clearly displayed;

(*h*)    fitted with indicators which the operator can read;

(*i*)    prevented from exposing persons in danger zones – and the operator must be able to ensure this from the main control position; failing this, an acoustic and/or visual warning signal must be given whenever machinery is about to start.

## Starting and stopping

(*a*) *Starting*

M1026    It must be possible to

(i)    start machinery, only by deliberate intended action;

(ii)    re-start machinery after stoppage;

(iii)    effect change in speed pressure only by voluntary action of control (though not from the normal sequence of the automatic cycle).

(*b*) *Stopping*

M1027    Stopping devices must accommodate both normal and emergency stopping.

(i)    *Normal stop.* Machinery must be fitted with a control to bring it safely to a complete stop and each workstation, too, to stop some or all of the moving parts, so that it is made safe. Stop controls must have priority over start controls, and, once machinery is stopped, energy supply must be cut off.

(ii)    *Emergency stop.* Emergency stops/devices must be easily identifiable, clearly visible and quickly accessible, and able to stop a dangerous process as quickly as possible. The emergency stop must remain engaged, and disengagement must not reactivate machinery. Further, stop controls must not trigger the stopping function before being in the engaged position. Once active operation of the emergency stop control has ceased following stop command, that command must be sustained by engagement of the emergency stop device until that engagement is specifically overridden. It must not be possible to engage the device without triggering a stop command. Disengaging the stop device must not reactivate machinery but only permit restarting.

(iii)    *Mode selection.* Control mode selected must override all other control systems, except the emergency stop. If, for certain operations, machinery has to operate with protection devices neutralised, the mode selector must simultaneously

(*a*)    disable automatic control mode;

(*b*)    permit movements only by controls requiring sustained action;

(*c*)    permit operation of dangerous moving parts only in enhanced safety conditions (e.g. reduced speed);

(*d*)    prevent any movement liable to pose a danger by acting voluntarily or involuntarily on a machine's internal sensors.

(iv)    *Failure of power supply/failure of control circuit.* Neither failure of power supply or of control circuit must lead to:

(*a*)    machinery starting unexpectedly;

(*b*)    machinery being prevented from stopping if the command has been given;

(*c*)    any moving part/piece falling out or being ejected;

(*d*)    impeding of automatic or manual stopping of moving parts;

(*e*)    protection devices becoming ineffective.

[*SI 1992 No 3073 as amended, Sch 3*].

### (3) Protection against mechanical hazards

M1028    Machinery must:

(*a*)    be stable enough for use without risk of overturning, falling or unexpected movement. If necessary, anchorage must be incorporated (and indicated);

(*b*)    be able to withstand workplace stresses and not be likely to break up, including fatigue, ageing, corrosion and abrasion. In particular, manufacturers must indicate the type and frequency of inspection and maintenance and specify the parts likely to need replacement. Where a workpiece comes into contact with a tool, the tool must be operating normally; when the tool starts or stops, intentionally or accidentally, feed and tool movement must be co-ordinated;

(*c*)    prevent objects, such as tools/workpieces, being ejected;

(*d*)    not have sharp edges/angles/rough surfaces;

(*e*)    where intended to carry out various operations, be able to be used separately, and it must be possible to start and stop separately;

(*f*)    where designed to perform under different conditions or speeds, selection and adjustment must be able to be completed safely;

(*g*)    prevent hazards arising from moving parts of machinery, or if hazards are not avoidable, moving parts must be fixed with guards. In particular, manufacturers should indicate how, if necessary, equipment can be safely unblocked.

[*SI 1992 No 3073 as amended, Sch 3*].

*Guards*

M1029    In order to ensure maximum safety with machinery, guards (or safety devices) should be used (see M1006, M1007 above for varieties) to protect the operator against the risk from:

(*a*)    moving transmission parts; and/or

(*b*)    moving parts directly involved in the work process.

In principle, machinery with moving transmission parts (e.g. belts/pulleys) can have fixed or movable guards – the latter being preferable where frequent access is foreseeable; but, whichever is used, it should always:

(i)    be of robust construction;

(ii)    not give rise to any additional risk;

(iii)   not be easily by-passable or rendered non-operational;

(iv)   be located at an adequate distance from a danger zone;

(v)   cause minimum obstruction to the view of those involved in the production process; and

(vi)   enable installation, replacement or maintenance work to be carried out, if possible, without the guard having to be dismantled.

However, where moving parts cannot be made wholly or even partially inaccessible during operation, requiring operator intervention, either (*a*) fixed or (*b*) adjustable guards (i.e. incorporating an adjustable element which, once adjusted, remains *in situ* during operation) should be used.

### *Fixed guards – special requirements*

M1030    Fixed guards should be:

(*a*)   securely held in place;

(*b*)   fixed by systems that can be opened with tools; and

(*c*)   where possible, unable to remain in place without their fixings.

### *Movable guards – special requirements*

M1031

(*a*) *Movable guards offering protection against moving transmission parts*

These should

(i)   remain fixed to machinery when open, as far as possible;

(ii)   be interlocking

—    to prevent activation of moving parts, and

—    give stop command when they are no longer closed.

(*b*) *Movable guards offering protection against moving parts directly involved in work process*

These should ensure that:

(i)   moving parts cannot start up while within the operator's reach;

(ii)   the exposed person cannot reach the moving parts once activated;

(iii)   they can be adjusted only by means of an intentional action, such as the use of a tool or key;

(iv)   the absence or failure of one of the component parts prevents starting, or stops moving parts;

(v)   the protection against any risk of ejection is proved by means of an appropriate barrier.

### *Adjustable guards (resisting access to parts involved)*

M1032    These should:

(*a*)   be adjustable manually or automatically;

(*b*)    be readily adjustable without use of tools;

(*c*)    reduce as far as possible the likelihood of ejection.

Interlocking systems may be mechanical, electrical (e.g. control interlocking, power interlocking), hydraulic, pneumatic (or any permutation) and should be 'fail-safe'. Guards can also be automatic, in which case, they are activated by the mechanism of the machinery (see further M1006 above). These are frequently used on power presses.

[*SI 1992 No 3073 as amended, Sch 3*].

### (4) Protection against non-mechanical hazards

M1033    Additionally, machinery must protect against:

(*a*)    electrical hazards – voltage limits must be observed;

(*b*)    a build-up of electrostatic charges and/or be fitted with a discharging system;

(*c*)    all potential hazards from energy supplies other than electricity (e.g. hydraulic, pneumatic or thermal energy);

(*d*)    fitting errors – in particular, incorrect fluid connections, electrical conductors, via information on pipes, cables etc.;

(*e*)    hazards of extreme temperatures, either high or low;

(*f*)    fire, either through overheating of machinery or caused by gases, liquids, dusts, vapours;

(*g*)    explosion;

(*h*)    noise – airborne noise must be reduced to the lowest practicable level;

(*i*)    vibration – must be reduced to the lowest practicable level;

(*j*)    radiation – the effects on exposed persons must be eliminated or reduced to safe levels, and external radiation must not interfere with its operation;

(*k*)    accidental radiation, in the case of laser equipment; as for optical equipment, this must not create health risks from laser rays; and laser equipment on machinery must not create health risks through reflection or diffusion;

(*l*)    emissions of dust, gases, liquids and vapours. If such hazard exists, machinery must be able to contain or evacuate it; and if not enclosed during normal operation, containment/evacuation devices must be as close as possible to emission source;

(*m*)    the risk of being trapped – a person should be able to summon help;

(*n*)    the risk of slipping or tripping or falling.

[*SI 1992 No 3073 as amended, Sch 3*].

### (5) Maintenance

M1034    (*a*)    Adjustment, maintenance, repair, cleaning and servicing must be able to be carried out while machinery is at a standstill; but if for technical reasons these operations cannot be undertaken while the machinery is at a standstill, at least it must be possible to carry them out without risk. In case of automated machinery and, where necessary, other machinery, the manufacturer must make provision for a connecting device for mounting diagnostic fault-finding equipment. Automated machine components, which have to be changed frequently, must be easily and safely removable and replaceable.

(*b*)     Safe means of access to areas of production, adjustment and maintenance should be provided and designed to prevent falls.

(*c*)     The machinery must be fitted with means of isolating it from all energy sources, clearly identifiable and capable of being locked where an operator cannot check whether energy is still cut off.

(*d*)     If operator intervention cannot be avoided, it must be possible to carry out maintenance easily and in safety.

(*e*)     Cleaning of internal parts with dangerous substances or preparations must be possible without entry; and unblocking should take place from outside. If cleaning by entry is necessary, this should be able to be done with a minimum of danger.

[*SI 1992 No 3073 as amended, Sch 3*].

## (6) Indicators

M1035     Machinery must be fitted with indicators and the necessary unambiguous and intelligible information to control it easily. Indicators can consist of:

(*a*)     *Information devices.* Information given must not be excessive to the extent of overloading the operator. Where the health and safety of exposed persons may be endangered by a fault in the operation of unsupervised machinery, the machinery must be equipped to give an appropriate acoustic or light signal as a warning.

(*b*)     *Warning devices.* The operator must have facilities which enable him to check the operation of warning devices at all times. Any warning of residual risks should preferably be given in readily understandable pictograms and/or be given in one of the languages of the country in which the machinery is to be used.

(*c*)     *Markings.* All machinery (including interchangeable equipment and safety components) must be marked legibly and indelibly as follows:

(i)     name/address of manufacturer;

(ii)     CE mark, including year of construction;

(iii)     designation of series or type;

(iv)     use in an explosive atmosphere;

(v)     safe use specifications (e.g. maximum speed of rotating parts);

(vi)     its mass, if machinery is to be handled.

(*d*)     *Instructions.* Machinery must be accompanied by the following instructions:

(i)     marking information;

(ii)     maintenance information (e.g. address of importer);

(iii)     foreseeable use;

(iv)     likely workstation of operator;

(v)     instructions for

—     safe putting into service,

—    safe use,

—    safe handling,

—    safe assembly and dismantling,

—    safe maintenance, servicing, repair,

—    safe adjustment,

—    training instructions, if necessary,

—    properties of tools to be fitted,

—    incorrect use of machinery.

*Instructions*

M1036    (*a*)    The instructions for the machinery must be in one of the EU languages. On being put into service, the machinery must be accompanied by a translation of the instructions in the language or languages of the country in which the machinery is used and by the instructions in the original language.

(*b*)    They must contain drawings and diagrams for putting into service, maintenance, inspection and repair as well as for safety purposes.

(*c*)    Installation and assembly requirements for reducing noise and vibration.

(*d*)    (With reference to airborne noise emissions):

—    equivalent continuous A-weighted sound pressure (see N3005 NOISE AND VIBRATION) at workstations where this exceeds 70 dB(A); if not in excess of 70 dB(A), this must be shown;

—    peak C-weighted instantaneous sound pressure value at workstations, where this exceeds 63Pa (130 dB in relation to 20 μ Pa);

—    sound power level emitted by machinery where equivalent continuous A-weighted sound pressure level at workstations exceeds 85 dB(A).

(*e*)    If necessary, precautions relating to use in explosive atmospheres.

(*f*)    In case of machinery which may also be intended for use by non-professional operators, the wording and layout of the instructions for use must take into account the general level of education and ability that can reasonably be expected from such operators.

[*SI 1992 No 3073 as amended, Sch 3*].

## Health and safety requirements applicable to machinery for lifting/moving persons

M1037    The devices must be located so that:

(*a*)    the floor of the lifting/moving device must be designed and constructed so as to offer space and strength according to the maximum number of persons and the maximum working load specified by the manufacturer;

(*b*)    persons inside the device must be able to control movements upwards and downwards or move it horizontally;

(*c*)    excess speeds must not cause hazards;

(*d*)   if necessary, devices must be fitted with a sufficient number of anchorage points for persons possibly using it, which are strong enough for attachment of personal protective equipment against the danger of falling;

(*e*)   trapdoors in floors/ceilings/side doors must open in a direction that prevents the risk of falling, if they open unexpectedly;

(*f*)   when the device is moving, floors must not tilt to an extent that occupants are in danger of falling, and must be slip-resistant;

(*g*)   the device must be designed/constructed so as to prevent its falling or overturning;

(*h*)   acceleration/braking of the device must not endanger persons; and

(*i*)   essential safety information must be provided to occupants.

[*Supply of Machinery (Safety) (Amendment) Regulations 1994 (SI 1994 No 2063), Reg 4, Sch 2, para 21*].

# Enforcement

**M1038**   Enforcement is by HSE, since the regulations qualify as 'relevant statutory provisions' (see ENFORCEMENT). [*Supply of Machinery (Safety) Regulations 1992 (SI 1992 No 3073 as amended), Sch 6*].

## (*a*) Offences/Defences

**M1039**   Breach of the regulations, as well as failing to comply with the necessary marking requirements, is an offence under *HSWA 1974, s 29* and the *Supply of Machinery (Safety) Regulations 1992 (SI 1992 No 3073 as amended), Sch 6.*

## (*b*) Defences

**M1040**   It is a defence that a person charged took all reasonable steps *and* exercised all due diligence to avoid committing the offence. [*Supply of Machinery (Safety) Regulations 1992 (SI 1992 No 3073 as amended), Reg 31(1)*]. Where the substance of the defence is that commission of the offence was due either to

(*a*)   act or default of another, or

(*b*)   reliance on information given by another,

the accused cannot rely on this defence, unless

(i)    he served notice of this on the prosecutor at least seven days before the hearing,

(ii)   the notice sufficiently identifies the other person,

(iii)  it was reasonable for him to have relied on the information.

[*Supply of Machinery (Safety) Regulations 1992 (SI 1992 No 3073 as amended), Reg 31(2)(3)(4)*].

In such circumstances the 'other person' may be proceeded against, though this is no bar to prosecution against the original accused [*Supply of Machinery (Safety) Regulations 1992 (SI 1992 No 3073 as amended), Reg 31(1)*] (see further E15031 ENFORCEMENT). Similarly, offences may be committed by bodies corporate, companies and directors under these regulations (see E15039 ENFORCEMENT).

### (c) Penalties

**M1041**    Breach of an offence under *Supply of Machinery (Safety) Regulations 1992 (SI 1992 No 3073 as amended), Reg 11* – duty to supply safe machinery – carries a maximum penalty:

(a)    on summary conviction, of a fine of £5,000; or

(b)    on conviction on indictment, an indefinite fine, except for:

(i)    breach of an improvement/prohibition notice, or

(ii)    failure to disclose information to the HSC or an enforcement officer

which can invoke imprisonment for up to two years, or a fine (or both).

[*Supply of Machinery (Safety) Regulations 1992 (SI 1992 No 3073 as amended), Sch 6, para 3*].

### Civil liability

**M1042**    Breach of the regulations causing injury/damage will give rise to civil liability, even though the regulations, as here, are silent on the point, since they do not state otherwise [*HSWA 1974, s 47(2)*] (see 20, INTRODUCTION).

## Checklist for machinery safeguards

**M1043**    The following is a list of safeguards for machine accident prevention:

(a)    Does the safeguard totally prevent dangerous access (or otherwise eliminate danger) when in its correct position and when working properly?

(b)    Is the guard reasonably convenient to use (i.e. does it interfere with either the speed or quality of the work); are there foreseeable reasons why it should be defeated?

(c)    How easy is it to defeat or misuse the safeguard? (The 'cost' of defeating a safeguard should always outweigh the benefits. It is wise never to underestimate the ingenuity of the man who spends all day, every day, working with what he believes is a perverse and unnecessary safety device.)

(d)    Are the components of the safeguard:

(i)    reliable;

(ii)    fail-safe?

(e)    Does the safeguard cope with foreseeable machine failures?

(f)    Is the safeguard straightforward to inspect and maintain?

(g)    Are all controls to the machine safely located, correctly designed and clearly identified?

(h)    Is there an efficient emergency stopping device? Is it clearly identified? (NB: There is a sign specified for this purpose in the *Health and Safety (Safety Signs and Signals) Regulations 1996 (SI 1996 No 341)*.

(i)    Does all electrical equipment comply with EN 60204–1? Is there an effective system for checking and maintaining such equipment?

(j)    Are coolant systems effective and easy to maintain?

(k)    Is access for lubrication readily and safely available? Are all lubrication points clearly identified?

(*l*)   Is the machine safely located so that other workers are not exposed to danger? Does the current layout of the machining area permit easy movement between machines, workbenches and other items?

(*m*)   What is the sound pressure level emitted by the machine? Is it in excess of 90 dBA? If so, what modifications must be made to control noise at source, or should the machine be installed in a soundproof enclosure? If hearing protection is provided for operators and other workers in the immediate vicinity, are they appropriate to the noise risks and are they being worn all the time during machine operation?

(*n*)   What is the procedure to ensure effective preventive maintenance? Is the procedure documented, including allocation of responsibilities? What are the mechanical and other hazards which may arise during routine maintenance of the machine?

(*o*)   What chemical substances are used in the machine process? Have they been checked for toxicity, flammability and other dangerous properties? Have operators been trained to recognise these hazards and to take suitable precautions?

(*p*)   Does the machine emit:

   (i)   dust;

   (ii)   fumes;

   (iii)   gases; or

   (iv)   other airborne contaminants?

   What is the system for removing these contaminants at the point of emission? How frequently is the efficiency of the system checked to ensure it is operating effectively?

(*q*)   Is the general lighting in the machine area adequate? Is lighting at specific danger points adequate?

(*r*)   Does the machine emit heat? Are there hot surfaces which could cause burns on contact?

(*s*)   Is the level of ventilation in the machine area satisfactory?

# Manual Handling

## Introduction

More than one-third (36.5%) of accidents reported to the Health and Safety Executive (HSE) and local authority environmental health departments result from manual handling. It is the single most common cause of workplace injury and research suggests that over 600,000 people in Britain consider that they have a health problem caused by manual handling at work.

Many of these accidents relate to back injuries, but injuries to the feet, hands, arms and legs, including fractures and lacerations, also occur. The three main risks are accidental injury, over-exertion and cumulative damage. Many manual handling injuries build up over a long period of time rather than being caused by a single incident.

Such injuries are not restricted to areas seen as traditionally heavy industries, but occur across the range of industry and service sectors, in offices, shops and warehouses, hospitals, banks, laboratories, factories, farms and building sites, and while making deliveries.

On average, each injury results in 20 days being taken off work, and in some cases, workers are unable to return to work as a result of becoming permanently disabled. For example, many nurses are invalided out of the health service as a result of back injuries caused by manual handling. And back injuries represent the biggest single group of claims for incapacity benefit.

It is estimated that back injuries, many caused by manual handling, cost British employers in the region of £6 billion every year in lost production. In addition, there have been a number of large compensation awards for damages paid out to workers who have been injured through manual handling as a result of their employer's negligence.

For example, in 1998, nursery nurse Jenny Bentley received £78,000 in compensation from Stockport City Council after a lifting injury damaged her back so severely that she was unable to work in the four years it took for her case to be settled. She had been asked to move a locker weighing up to 75 pounds across a busy main road, a distance of up to 600 yards.

Public services union, Unison, which backed her claim for compensation, said that employers should be more aware of the risks of back injury before they ask staff to lift heavy or awkward loads. Most accidents resulting in injury are prevented by taking very simple steps.

HSE has issued a revised version of its free leaflet, '*Getting to Grips with Manual Handling*'. The aim of the publication continues to be to provide free and simple advice to employers on the seriousness of manual handling risks to health and on how to tackle them. The guidance in the leaflet has been slightly revised to agree with changes made to more detailed guidance on compliance with the *Manual Handling Operations Regulations 1992* (this more detailed guidance is '*Manual Handling: Guidance on Regulations*', ref L23, price £8.00, available from HSE Books).

# Employers' legal duties to prevent injury

## Health and Safety at Work etc. Act 1974

M3002    Under the *Health and Safety at Work etc. Act 1974 (HSWA)*, employers have a general duty to ensure the health, safety and welfare at work of their employees. In particular, they have a duty to ensure the safe use, handling, storage and transport of articles and substances so far as is reasonably practicable [*HSWA, s 2(2)a*].

The term 'reasonably practicable' is used throughout health and safety legislation and means that the costs of carrying out a measure must be weighed up against the risks if it is not carried out.

## Management of Health and Safety at Work Regulations 1999 (SI 1999 No 3242)

M3003    *Regulation 3(1)* of the *Management of Health and Safety at Work Regulations 1999* requires employers to assess the risks to health and safety arising from their work activities. This general risk assessment should identify whether there is a risk of injury from manual handling operations in the workplace. If this is the case, the employer should comply with the more specific requirements of the *Manual Handling Operations Regulations 1992*.

## Manual Handling Operations Regulations 1992 (SI 1992 No 2793)

M3004    These regulations are based on an ergonomic approach to preventing manual handling injuries. This involves fitting the job to the worker, taking into account anatomy, physiology and psychology. Whereas previous legislation set limits on the weight of loads that could be lifted, these regulations require a number of relevant factors to be taken into consideration, including the nature of the task, the load, the working environment and the individual capability of workers.

The Regulations define manual handling operations as: 'any transporting or supporting of a load (including lifting, putting down, pushing, pulling, carrying or moving thereof) by hand or by bodily force'.

A load is a discrete movable object, and includes people and animals. However, the definition of an injury excludes those caused by corrosive or toxic spillages, which are covered instead by the *Control of Substances Hazardous to Health Regulations 1999 (COSHH) (SI 1999 No 437)*.

The Regulations set out a hierarchy of measures employers should work through in order to prevent or reduce the risk of injury to their employees from the manual handling of loads:

(i)    Avoid hazardous manual handling operations so far as is reasonably practicable (*Reg 4(1)(a)*). This maybe done by redesigning the task to avoid moving the load or by automating or mechanising the process;

(ii)    Make a suitable and sufficient assessment of any hazardous manual handling tasks that cannot be avoided (*Reg 4(1)(b)(i)*);

(iii)    Reduce the risk of injury from those operations to the lowest level reasonably practicable (*Reg 4(1)(b)(ii)*).

In *Swain v Denso Martin, the Times 24 April 2000*, an employee (S) sought damages from his employer for a crushing injury he sustained to his hand while undertaking a manual handling operation in the course of his employment. Under *Reg 4(1)(b)(I)* of the *Manual Handling Operations Regulations 1992 (MOHR)*, employers are under a duty to carry out a 'suitable and sufficient assessment' of their manual handling operations. Under *Reg 4(1)(b)(iii)* of *MOHR 1992*, employers have a responsibility to take appropriate steps to provide any of those employees who are undertaking any such manual handling operations with general indications and, 'where it is reasonably practicable to do so, precise information on' the weight of the load.

The county court judge had held that *Reg 4(1)(b)(i)–(iii)* had to be read conjunctively, and since the employers had not carried out a risk assessment under *Reg 4(1)(b)(i)* they were not under an obligation to comply with the requirements of *Reg 4(1)(b)(iii)*. The Court of Appeal allowed S's appeal. The fact that *Reg 4(1)(b)* imposed three separate obligations did not mean that an employer's breach of one exonerated it from the other two. Thus, regardless of whether a risk assessment had been carried out in respect of manual handling operations which involved a risk of injury to employees, the employer was required to take appropriate steps to give general indications and, where practicable, precise information on the weight of the load.

People working under the control and direction of others, even if they are treated as being self-employed for tax and National Insurance purposes, are classed as employees for health and safety purposes and are therefore covered by these regulations.

The HSE published revised guidance to support the Regulations in 1998. The new guidance includes a revised Appendix 1, which sets out a detailed assessment guidelines filter. It also has an example of an assessment checklist with notes on its completion and a worked example of a pallet process operation in Appendix 2. The guidance also contains expanded advice on:

(*a*)   duties of the self-employed working under the direction of other people;

(*b*)   the increased risk to pregnant workers and the advantages of having a well-defined plan to respond to a worker becoming pregnant;

(*c*)   the *Disability Discrimination Act 1995* and advice on the needs of disabled people;

(*d*)   the risk associated with lifting loads from floor level;

(*e*)   the duties of manufacturers and suppliers;

(*f*)   how the risk may be affected if reducing the weight of the load means increasing the frequency of handling; and

(*g*)   the use of abdominal and back support belts.

## Avoiding manual handling operations

**M3005**   Employers should firstly look at how manual handling operations can be avoided or minimised, either by redesigning the workplace or work organisation, or automating or mechanising tasks. Automation includes palletisation, vacuum handling, lift trucks and conveyors.

If the operations are automated or mechanised, an assessment of the new risks involved will be necessary since, for example, conveyors can present trapping hazards, while forklift trucks have caused crush injuries and may lead to the build up of diesel fumes in the workplace. There also needs to be consideration as to whether additional manual handling problems are caused, particularly at loading or off-loading points.

Some handling aids need to be maintained and the *Lifting Operations and Lifting Equipment Regulations 1998 (SI 1998 No 2307)* may apply. These require certain pieces of equipment to be regularly examined and tested. If vehicles are used, such as forklift trucks, the *Workplace (Health, Safety and Welfare) Regulations* 1992 (SI 1992 No 3004) require that traffic routes are organised so that vehicles and people can circulate safely in the workplace, and are kept apart where practicable.

### HSE guidance

**M3006**     In the HSE publication, *Manual handling – solutions you can handle*, the HSE advises that avoiding manual handling operations can be very simple, and gives the example of fitting a hosepipe to a tap to avoid having to lift a bucket into a sink to fill it. It gives an intermediate solution – palletising operations so that loads can be lifted with a forklift truck rather than manually – and says that a more complicated solution could involve redesigning the workplace to minimise the amount of handling.

The guidance gives the following examples of steps to avoid or reduce manual handling:

(*a*)     Where powders, granules or liquids have to be transferred, these can be fed into a machine from a bulk container by suction or using a pump, rather than workers carrying loads up steps.

(*b*)     Where loads are transferred between conveyor belts and weighing machines, ensuring that these are in line can reduce manual handling.

(*c*)     Where patients are liable to fall out of bed, fitting side guards prevents this, reducing the amount of manual handling because staff do not have to lift them back into bed, and reducing injuries to patients.

Another HSE publication, *A pain in your workplace? Ergonomic problems and solutions*, gives some examples of how manual handling operations have been reduced or eliminated in particular types of workplaces.

In one example, longer retractable handles and a vertical handle were fitted into a hospital toilet used by geriatric and infirm patients. They had needed manual assistance from hospital staff in order to be able to use the toilet, but with the new handles, most were able to support themselves with little or no assistance. This gave the patients increased independence as well as reducing the amount of handling, and therefore the risk of injury to staff.

In another example at a wine merchants, changing the way customers collected cases of beer reduced the amount of manual handling required. The cases had been delivered to a garage at the back of the shop, brought into the shop by the shop assistant, and then the customer would carry the cases out to the car park after purchasing them. The system was changed so that the cases were left in the garage; customers paid in the shop and received a voucher. The cases were then collected from the garage by customers in their cars, meaning less manual handling for the customer as well as the shop assistant.

## Carrying out the risk assessment

**M3007**     In some situations it may not be reasonably practicable to avoid the need for employees to carry out manual handling tasks. The Regulations require that where this is the case, a 'suitable and sufficient' assessment of manual handling operations should be carried out.

### HSE guideline figures

M3008 Where the general assessment under the *Management of Health and Safety at Work Regulations 1999 (SI 1999 No 3242)* has indicated the possibility of injury, but manual handling operations cannot be avoided, an appendix to the HSE's Guidance on the *Manual Handling Operations Regulations 1992 (SI 1992 No 2793)* provides guideline figures.

*Lifting and lowering:* The basic guideline figures for identifying when manual lifting and lowering operations may not need a detailed assessment are set out in Figure 1. If the handler's hands enter more than one of the box zones during the operation, the smallest weight figures apply. It is important to remember, however, that the transition from one box zone to another is not abrupt; an intermediate figure may be chosen where the handler's hands are close to a boundary. Where lifting or lowering with the hands beyond the box zones is unavoidable, a more detailed assessment should always be made.

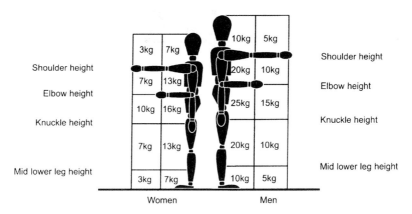

*Fig. 1: Lifting and lowering*

These basic guideline figures for lifting and lowering are for relatively infrequent operations – up to approximately 30 operations per hour. The guideline figures will have to be reduced if the operation is repeated more often. As a rough guide, the figures should be reduced by 30% where the operation is repeated once or twice per minute, by 50% where the operation is repeated around five to eight times per minute and by 80% where the operation is repeated more than about 12 times per minute.

Even if the operations are within the guidelines, a more detailed assessment should still be made where the pace of work is not under the control of the worker, there is no change of activity providing the opportunity for other muscles to be used, there are inadequate rest periods, or where the handler must support the load for any length of time.

*Carrying:* The guideline figures can be used where loads are held against the body and carried up to about ten metres before resting. If loads are carried greater distances without a rest, or the hands are below knuckle height, a more detailed assessment will be needed.

*Pushing and pulling:* The guideline figures can also be used where pushing and pulling operations are being carried out and the hands are between knuckle and shoulder height. The guideline figure for starting or stopping a load is a force of about 25kg for men and 16kg for women, and for keeping it in motion, 10kg and 7kg respectively. There is no specific limit to the distance over which the load may be pushed or pulled, provided that there are adequate opportunities for rest or recovery.

*Handling while seated:* The basic guideline figure for handling operations carried out while seated, shown in Figure 2, is 5kg for men and 3kg for women. These guidelines only apply when the hands are within the box zone indicated. If handling beyond the box zone is unavoidable, a more detailed assessment should be made.

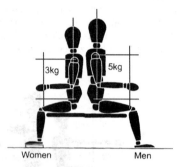

*Fig. 2: Handling while seated*

The HSE advises that where twisting or turning is involved, a detailed risk assessment should normally be made as there is an increased risk of injury, unless the operation is fairly infrequent (up to about 30 operations an hour), and there are no other posture problems. The guideline figures should be reduced by about 10% where the worker twists through 45 degrees, and 20% where the worker twists through 90 degrees.

## Carrying out a detailed risk assessment

M3009

Where an initial assessment shows that a more detailed assessment is necessary, this must take into account the factors listed in *Schedule 1* to the *Manual Handling Operations Regulations 1992* which are summarised below.

Do the tasks involve:

(*a*)   holding or manipulating loads at a distance from the trunk;

(*b*)   unsatisfactory bodily movement or posture, particularly twisting the trunk, stooping, reaching upwards;

(*c*)   excessive movement of loads, especially lifting, lowering or carrying distances;

(*d*)   excessive pushing or pulling of loads;

(*e*)   risk of sudden movement of loads;

(*f*)   frequent or prolonged physical effort;

(*g*)   insufficient rest or recovery periods; or

(*h*)   a rate of work imposed by a process?

Are the loads:

(*a*)   heavy;

(*b*)     bulky or unwieldy;

(*c*)     difficult to grasp;

(*d*)     unstable or with contents likely to shift; or

(*e*)     sharp, hot or otherwise potentially damaging?

In the working environment, are there:

(*a*)     space constraints preventing good posture;

(*b*)     uneven, slippery or unstable floors;

(*c*)     variations in the level of floors or work surfaces;

(*d*)     extremes of temperature or humidity;

(*e*)     conditions causing ventilation problems or gusts of wind; or

(*f*)     poor lighting conditions?

Does the job:

(*a*)     require unusual strength, height etc;

(*b*)     create a hazard to those who may reasonably be considered to be pregnant or have a health problem; or

(*c*)     require special information or training for its safe performance?

Is movement or posture hindered by personal protective equipment or clothing?

### Pregnant workers

M3010     Although the HSE advises that variations in individual capability are generally less important than the nature of the manual handling operations in causing injury, there are nevertheless, particular issues around manual handling and pregnancy which employers need to consider. The health of pregnant women and the foetus can be affected by manual handling, particularly if it involves prolonged standing or walking, and as size increases, it can be difficult to achieve and maintain correct postures. In addition, hormonal changes during pregnancy can affect the ligaments and joints, increasing the risk of injury, and women returning to work after maternity leave may still be vulnerable to injury.

In addition to the duties set out under the *Manual Handling Operations Regulations 1992*, the *Management of Health and Safety at Work Regulations 1999 (SI 1999 No 3242)*, *Reg 16* require that when a woman has informed her employer that she is pregnant, the employer must assess the risks to her health and safety to which she is exposed.

The HSE advises that it is good practice for the following measures to be considered when assessing the risks to the health and safety of pregnant workers from manual handling tasks:

(*a*)     a reassessment of manual handling tasks to look at what improvements can be made;

(*b*)     provision of training in how work may be altered to accommodate changes in posture and physical capability, including taking breaks;

(*c*)     job rotation, relocation or suspension on full pay;

(*d*)     liaison with the GP to ensure capability; and

(*e*)    monitoring following a return to work after maternity leave to assess the need for any changes.

### Disabled workers

M3011    Under the *Disability Discrimination Act 1995* employers must make reasonable adjustments to the workplace or employment arrangements so that a disabled person is not at a substantial disadvantage compared to other workers or job applicants. With regard to manual handling operations, this could include limiting the size, weight or number of loads, or providing suitable manual handling aids.

### HSE guidance

M3012    The HSE guidance to the *Manual Handling Operations Regulations 1992* says that assessments should be based on a thorough practical understanding of manual handling tasks, the loads and the working environment, and points out that employers or managers should be better placed to know about manual handling operations in their own organisations than someone from outside. However, it says that there may be a place for outside organisations to provide training for in-house assessors.

It advises that setting up teams of people with different specialisms, for example in legal requirements, the operations being carried out, human capabilities, high-risk activities and the measures necessary to reduce the risks, can be effective.

The guidance also says that safety representatives and employees should play a positive part in the assessment, since they will have practical experience of carrying out the tasks and will know about any problems in the working environment. Analysing accident and ill-health records can also be useful in identifying problem areas.

## Reducing the risk of injury

M3013    *Regulation 4(1)(b)(iii)* of the *Manual Handling Operations Regulations 1992* requires that where manual handling operations that involve a risk of injury cannot be avoided, appropriate steps must be taken to reduce the risk of injury to as low a level as reasonably practicable. This will involve an examination of the task, load, working environment and individual capability.

### HSE guidance

M3014    Again, the HSE publication, *A pain in your workplace? Ergonomic problems and solutions*, gives some examples of how the risk of manual handling injury can be reduced in different types of workplaces.

For example, a woman working in radio equipment assembly carried out a job involving lifting and moving heavy pieces of radio equipment from one workbench to another several times an hour. She developed pain in her shoulder and was diagnosed as having a frozen shoulder. The safety manager moved the two workbenches together so that she did not have to lift the equipment, only push it on to the other bench. This very simple modification improved the work routine and the pain stopped.

In another example, there were high levels of sickness absence due to back pain among airport baggage handlers. A number of improvements were implemented, including labelling baggage over 25kg with its weight, to enable workers to prepare for a lift, standardising the height of conveyors to 650 millimetres in order to reduce stooping, and improving the spread of work between teams of staff more evenly.

The HSE guidance to the *Manual Handling Operations Regulations*, and the HSE publication *Manual handling – solutions you can handle* give a number of examples of how manual handling injuries can be reduced, by making improvements to various aspects of the work.

The HSE has also published a leaflet on how to reduce injuries caused by manual handling in the woodworking industry. *'Manual handling solutions in woodworking'* summarises the legal requirements that apply to manual handling activities in the workplace. It also contains a series of case studies describing how real solutions can be applied to high risk handling activities, showing effective ways in which risks can be reduced in practice.

### Making alterations to the load

M3015　　Loads can be made lighter, smaller or provided with handles to make them easier to hold. However, where loads are made smaller or lighter, if this means that handling is more frequent, this must be taken into account as it could make the situation worse.

Containers with liquids or loose powder should be filled almost full so that the contents are not liable to shift suddenly. Sharp corners and rough surfaces should be avoided, as should corrosive or oily deposits.

Metal containers can be drilled with holes to make them lighter, smaller containers can be used for filling, with these being continually refilled from a supply tank, or the load can be put on wheels. For example, a bucket used for cleaning purposes can be fitted with castors so it can be pushed along with the mop rather than being carried.

### Improvement to the task

M3016　　This means reducing the amount of bending, stooping, stretching, pushing and pulling required. For example, storage heights can be changed to waist level, obstacles that have to be reached over or into can be removed, and lifting can be replaced with controlled pulling or pushing. Job rotation can allow one group of muscles to rest while another group is being used, or heavy work can be interspersed with lighter work.

Height and angle adjustable worktables can be adjusted to suit particular jobs and reduce bending, platforms can be provided to avoid lifts above shoulder height for shorter workers, and containers with removable sides which allow access to the bottom can reduce stooping.

In addition, changes can be made to allow the body to be used more efficiently. In general, any change that allows loads to be held closer to the body will be an improvement. When lifting of loads at or near floor level is unavoidable, handling techniques which allow the use of the legs rather than the back are preferable, as long as the load is small enough to be held close to the trunk.

### Mechanical assistance

M3017　　Handling aids can be provided so that although there is still some manual handling, there is less risk of injury. These include levers, hoists, roller conveyors, trucks, trolleys, chutes and handling devices, such as hand-held hooks and suction pads.

For example, lifting hooks can help lift large awkward loads, and paving slab handlers are available. Platform trucks that can be raised and lowered further reduce handling by avoiding the need for bending. Tracks and chutes allow heavy and bulky loads to be moved manually or by gravity under their own weight. If portable conveyors are used to reduce manual handling, they should be at a height of around 0.9m where loads are light enough to be lifted with one hand; around 0.75m height where heavier loads such as cases and cartons are loaded, and at around floor level for heavy loads like drums.

Workers who will be using handling aids should be able to express their preference. The moving and handling co-ordinator at Wigan and Leigh Health Service NHS Trust told the 1998 NHS workforce conference that allowing nurses to choose new lifting equipment resulted in a six-fold reduction in sickness absence due to manual handling injuries. She estimated the trust had saved £2 million over a four-year period.

*The working environment*

M3018 Having a workplace with adequate space to manoeuvre, clear floor spaces and adequate headroom can reduce the risk of injury. The ground should be stable and level, spillages should be dealt with promptly, and there should be a comfortable working environment with adequate lighting.

Where there are space constraints, it may be necessary to increase the width of openings to ease manoeuvring of loads. If there are uneven, slippery or unstable floors which mean there is a risk that workers could lose their balance, improvements may include good housekeeping, special floor surfaces and coatings, and as a temporary measure, large boards over an uneven area may help. Where there are variations in floor levels, ramps instead of stairs can allow wheeled handling aids to be used.

*Individual capability*

M3019 Particular consideration should be given to those who are pregnant (see above) or who have a history of back, knee or hip trouble or hernia problems, but in general medical screening is not recommended as a way of reducing the risk of injury.

Safety representatives and employees should be involved in redesigning work in order to minimise injuries.

## Abdominal and back support belts

M3020 The merits of abdominal and back support belts is controversial, since although manufacturers and suppliers claim that they can reduce manual handling injuries, some research has shown they have no effect, and there are concerns that they may put some people at additional risk of injury. In addition, there is some concern that muscles could be weakened in the long term and this has yet to be studied.

The HSE advice is that although the decision as to whether to use them or not rests with employers, it is normally possible to reduce risks more effectively with safe systems of work, providing protection to all workers not just particular individuals. It also says that relying solely on support belts will not meet the employer's duties under the regulations.

In general, health and safety legislation always prioritises the control or prevention of hazards at source, with the provision of personal protective clothing and equipment as a last resort to control risks where they cannot be controlled by other means.

## Providing additional information about the load

**M3021**   *Regulation 4(1)(b)(iii)* requires that where it is not reasonably practicable to avoid the need for employees to undertake manual handling operations which involve a risk of injury, employees should be provided with general indications, and where reasonably practicable to do so, precise information on the weight of each load and the heaviest side where the centre of gravity is not positioned centrally.

General indications should generally be given during basic training on manual handling. Where employers originate loads, the best way of giving precise information is to mark it on the loads. Suppliers should also be asked to do this.

## Information and training

**M3022**   Training should be seen as complementing safe systems of work, and not as an alternative to such systems. Safety representatives and employees should be involved in the development of manual handling training. This should cover:

(*a*)   avoiding hazards;

(*b*)   dealing with unavoidable or unfamiliar manual handling operations;

(*c*)   proper use of handling aids and personal protective equipment;

(*d*)   features of the working environment contributing to safety;

(*e*)   the importance of good housekeeping;

(*f*)   factors affecting capability; and

(*g*)   good handling technique.

It should include recognition of loads whose weight or shape could cause injury, and assessing weight before attempting to lift a load. It is important that the practices taught on training courses can actually be used in the workplace.

## Good handling techniques

**M3023**   Again, training in good handling techniques is not a substitute for other measures to reduce injury, but it can be valuable alongside other risk reduction measures, as long as it can actually be put into practice at the workplace. It should also be tailored to the particular handling operations being undertaken.

The HSE guidance to the *Manual Handling Operations Regulations* provides an example of a lifting task to illustrate the following advice:

(*a*)   plan the lift, asking whether help or handling aids are required;

(*b*)   place the feet apart to give a balanced and stable base for lifting;

(*c*)   adopt a good posture with the knees bent and the hands level with the waist when grasping the load, the back straight, maintaining its natural curve and the chin tucked in;

(*d*)   get a firm grip with the arms within the boundary formed by the legs;

(*e*)   carry out the lifting movement smoothly, raising the chin as the lift begins and keeping control of the load;

(*f*)   move the feet rather than twisting the trunk when turning to the side;

(*g*)   keep close to the load for as long as possible, keeping the heaviest side of the load next to the trunk; and

(*h*)   put down the load, then adjust the positioning afterwards.

## Reviewing the assessment

M3024

*Regulation 4(2)* of the *Manual Handling Operations Regulations 1992* requires that assessments are kept up to date and reviewed where there has been a significant change in manual handling operations, there is reason to suspect that the assessment is no longer valid, or where a reportable injury occurs. (See *Reporting of Injuries, Diseases and Dangerous Occurrences Regulations 1995 (RIDDOR)* in ACCIDENT REPORTING).

## Employees' duties

M3025

*Regulation 5* of the *Manual Handling Operations Regulations 1992* requires employees to make full and proper use of any system of work for handling of loads laid down by the employer.

# Noise and Vibration

## PART A: Noise at Work

### Introduction

N3001      Although detailed advice on the risks of occupational noise exposure has been widely available since 1974, the Health and Safety Executive estimates that over 1.3 million workers are still exposed to over 85 dB(A), the first action level prescribed in the *Noise At Work Regulations 1989 (SI 1989 No 1790)*. It also states that there are over 170,000 cases of work-related deafness, tinnitus and other ear conditions.

The Department of Social Security (DSS) pays disablement benefit to people who suffer at least 50 decibels (dB) of noise-induced hearing loss in both ears. This level of hearing loss is roughly equivalent to listening to the television or a conversation through a substantial brick wall. Moreover, claimants must have been employed for at least ten years in a specified noisy occupation. Despite these restrictions, the number of new awards remains significant: 413 in 1996/97, 258 in 1997/98 and 316 in 1998/99. There are currently 14,200 people, 99 per cent of them men, receiving disablement benefit from the DSS.

The number of claimants with between 35 and 49 decibels of hearing loss (still a severe disability, equivalent to listening through a substantial partition wall in a house shows an improving trend. According to statistics from audiological examinations, the number of claimants has fallen from 1,200 in 1995 to 710 in 1999.

### Hearing damage

N3002      We all lose hearing acuity with age, and this loss is accelerated and worsened by exposure to excessive noise. Fortunately, in early life, we have much greater hearing acuity than modern life demands, and a small loss is readily compensated by turning up the volume of the radio or TV.

Loud noises cause permanent damage to the nerve cells of the inner ear in such a way that a hearing aid is ineffective. At first, the damage occurs at frequencies above normal speech range, so that the sufferer may have no inkling of the problem, although it could be identified easily by an audiogram, which measures the sensitivity of the ear at a number of frequencies across its normal range. As exposure continues, the region of damage progresses to higher and lower frequencies. Damage starts to extend into the speech range, making it difficult to distinguish consonants, so that words start to sound the same. Eventually, speech becomes a muffled jumble of sounds.

Some people are much more susceptible to hearing damage than others. A temporary dullness of hearing, or tinnitus (a ringing or whistling sound in the ears) when emerging from a noisy place are both indicative of damage to the nerve cells of the inner ear. Because these symptoms tend to disappear with continued exposure, they are often misinterpreted as the ear becoming 'hardened', whereas in fact it is losing its ability to respond to the noise. Even when hearing has apparently returned to normal, a little of the sensitivity is likely to have been lost. Therefore, anyone who experiences dullness of hearing or tinnitus after noise exposure must take special care to avoid further exposure. They may also be advised to seek medical advice and an audiogram.

Apart from catastrophic exposures (usually to explosive sounds), the risk of hearing loss is closely dependent on the 'noise dose' received, and especially on the cumulative effect over a period of time. British Standard BS 5330 gives a procedure for estimating the risk of 'hearing handicap' due to noise exposure. Handicap is there defined as a hearing loss of 30 dB, which is sufficiently severe to impair the understanding of conversational speech or the appreciation of music. This may be compared with the loss of 50 dB required for DSS disability benefit.

## The perception of sound

N3003 Sound is caused by a rapid fluctuation in air pressure. The human ear can hear a sensation of sound when the fluctuations occur between 20 times a second and 20,000 times a second. The rate at which the air pressure fluctuates is called the frequency of the sound and is measured in Hertz (Hz). The loudness of the sound depends on the amount of fluctuation in the air pressure. Typically, the quietest sound that can be heard (the threshold of hearing) is zero decibels (0 dB) and the sound becomes painful at 120 dB. Surprisingly perhaps, zero decibels is not zero sound. The sensitivity and frequency range of the ear vary somewhat from person to person and deteriorate with age and exposure to loud sounds.

The human ear is not equally sensitive to sounds of different frequencies (i.e. pitch): it tends to be more sensitive in the frequency range of the human voice than at higher or lower frequencies (peaking at about 4 kHz). When measuring sound, compensation for these effects can be made by applying a frequency weighting, usually the so-called 'A' weighting, although other weightings are sometimes used for special purposes.

The ear has an approximately logarithmic response to sound: for example, every doubling or halving in sound pressure gives an apparently equal step increase or decrease in loudness. In measuring environmental noise, sound pressure levels are therefore usually quoted in terms of a logarithmic unit known as a decibel (dB). To signify that the 'A' weighting has been applied, the symbol of dB(A) is often used. However, current practice tends to prefer the weighting letter to be included in the name of the measurement index, see below. For example, dB(A) $L_{eq}$ and dB $L_{Aeq}$ both refer to the 'A' weighted equivalent sound level in decibels.

Depending upon the method of presentation of two sounds, the human ear may detect differences as small as 0.5 dB(A). However, for general environmental noise the detectable difference is usually taken to be between 1 and 3 dB(A), depending on how quickly the change occurs. A 10 dB(A) change in sound pressure level corresponds, subjectively, to an approximate doubling or halving in loudness. Similarly, a subjective quadrupling of loudness corresponds to a 20 dB(A) increase in sound pressure level (SPL). When two sounds of the same SPL are added together, the resultant SPL is approximately 3 dB(A) higher than each of the individual sounds. It would require approximately *nine* equal sources to be added to an original source before the subjective loudness is doubled.

## Noise indices

N3004 The sound pressure level of industrial and environmental sound fluctuates continuously. A number of measurement indices have been proposed to describe the human response to these varying sounds. It is possible to measure the physical characteristics of sound with considerable accuracy and to predict the physical human response to characteristics such as loudness, pitch and audibility. However, it is not possible to predict *subjective* characteristics such as annoyance with certainty. This should not be surprising: one would not expect the light meter on a camera to be able to indicate whether one was taking a good or a bad photograph, although one would expect it to get the physical exposure correct. Strictly speaking, therefore, a meter can only measure sound and not noise (which is often defined as sound unwanted by the recipient): nevertheless, in practice, the terms are usually interchangeable.

### Equivalent continuous 'A' weighted sound pressure level, $LA_{eq}$

N3005    This unit takes into account fluctuations in sound pressure levels. It can be applied to all types of noise, whether continuous, intermittent or impulsive. $L_{Aeq}$ is defined as the steady, continuous sound pressure level which contains the same energy as the actual, fluctuating sound pressure level. In effect, it is the energy-average of the sound pressure level over a period which must be stated, e.g. $L_{Aeq}$, (18-hour).

This unit is now being put forward as a universal noise index, because it can be used to measure all types of noise, although it has yet to supplant older units in certain cases, particularly for the assessment of road traffic noise where calculation techniques and regulatory criteria have not been updated.

Levels measured in $L_{Aeq}$ can be added using the rules mentioned earlier. There is also a time trade-off: if a sound is made for half the measurement period, followed by silence, the $L_{Aeq}$ over the whole measurement period will be 3 dB less than during the noisy half of the period. If the sound is present for one-tenth of the measurement period, the $L_{Aeq}$ over the whole measurement period will be 10 dB less than during the noisy one-tenth of the measurement period. This is a cause of some criticism of $L_{Aeq}$: for discontinuous noise, such as may arise in industry, it does not limit the maximum noise level, so it may be necessary to specify this as well.

### Daily personal noise exposure, $L_{EP,d}$

N3006    This is used in the *Noise at Work Regulations 1989 (SI 1989 No 1790)* as a measure of the total sound exposure a person receives during the day. It is formally defined in a Schedule to the regulations.

$L_{EP,d}$ is the energy-average sound level ($L_{Aeq}$) to which a person is exposed over a working day, disregarding the effect of any ear protection which may be worn, adjusted to an 8-hour period. Thus, if a person is exposed to 90 dB $L_{Aeq}$ for a 4-hour working day, their $L_{EP,d}$ is 87 dB, but if they work a 12-hour shift, the same sound level would give them an $L_{EP,d}$ of 91.8 dB.

### Maximum 'A' weighted sound pressure level, $L_{Amax,T}$

N3007    The maximum 'A'-weighted root-mean-square (rms) sound pressure level during the measurement period is designated $L_{Amax}$. Sound level meters indicate the rms sound pressure level averaged over a finite period of time. Two averaging periods *(T)* are defined, S (slow) and F (fast), having averaging times of 1 second and 1/8th second. It is necessary to state the averaging period. Maximum SPL should not be confused with Peak SPL which is a measure of the instantaneous peak pressure.

*Peak sound pressure*

N3008    Instantaneous peak sound pressure can only be measured with specialist instruments. It is used in the assessment of explosive sounds, such as from gunshots and blasting, and in hearing damage assessments of this type of sound. Where the maximum sound level exceeds 125 dB $L_{Amax,F}$, then an accurate measurement of peak pressure is advisable to check for compliance with the peak action level of the *Noise at Work Regulations 1989 (SI 1989 No 1790)*.

*Background noise level, $L_{A90}$*

N3009    $L_{A90}$ is the level of sound exceeded for 90 per cent of the measurement period. It is therefore a measure of the background noise level – in other words, the sound drops below this level only infrequently. (The term 'background' should not be confused with 'ambient', which refers to *all* the sound present in a given situation at a given time.)

*Sound power level, $L_{WA}$*

N3010    The sound output of an item of plant or equipment is frequently specified in terms of its sound power level. This is measured in decibels relative to a reference power of 1 pico-Watt (dB re $10^{-12}$ W), but it must not be confused with sound pressure level. The sound pressure level at a particular position can be calculated from a knowledge of the sound power level of the source, provided the acoustical characteristics of the surrounding and intervening space are known. As a crude analogy, the power of a lamp bulb gives an indication of its light output, but the illumination of a surface depends on its distance and orientation from the source, and the presence of reflecting and obstructing objects in the surroundings.

To give a rough idea of the relationship between sound power level and sound pressure level, for a noise source which is emitting sound uniformly in all directions close above a hard surface in an open space, the sound pressure level 10 metres from the source would be 28 dB below its sound power level.

# General legal requirements

N3011    Statutory requirements relating to noise at work *generally* are contained in the *Noise at Work Regulations 1989 (SI 1989 No 1790)*. Replacing the previous Department of Employment (voluntary) Code of Practice on Noise (1972), these regulations require employers to take reasonably practicable measures, on a long-term on-going basis, to reduce employees' exposure to noise at work to the lowest possible level, and to lower noise exposure where employees are exposed to levels of 90 dB(A) or above, or to peak action level or above (200 Pascals). In addition, ear protectors must be provided and worn and ear protection zones designated. Estimates throughout industry overall suggest that about 1.3 million workers may be exposed above 85 dB(A), the first action level.

At present, there are no specific provisions relating to *vibration* other than those contained in the *Social Security (Industrial Injuries) (Prescribed Diseases) Regulations 1985 (SI 1985 No 967)* and the *Reporting of Injuries, Diseases and Dangerous Occurrences Regulations 1985 (SI 1985 No 2023)*. Occupational deafness and certain forms of vibration-induced conditions, i.e. vibration-induced white finger, are prescribed industrial diseases for which disablement benefit is payable (though the 14 per cent disablement rule will obviously limit the number of successful claimants. Damages may also be awarded against the employer (see further N3021 below).

**Noise At Work Regulations 1989 (SI 1989 No 1790)**

N3012     The following duties are laid on employers.

1.     To make (and update where necessary) a formal noise assessment, where employees are likely to be exposed to:

   (*a*)     first action level or above (85 dB(A)),

   (*b*)     peak action level or above (200 Pascals).

   [*Regs 2(1), 4(1)*].

   Such assessment should be made by a competent person and adequately:

   (i)     identify which employees are exposed, and

   (ii)     provide the employer with such information as will enable him to carry out his statutory duties, and

   (iii)     when there is reason to suppose that the assessment is no longer valid, or when there has been a significant change in the work to which the assessment relates, review noise levels and make any changes recommended by the review.

   [*Reg 4(2)*].

2.     To keep an adequate record of such assessment until a further assessment is made. [*Reg 5*].

3.     (As a long-term strategy, and on an on-going basis), to reduce the risk of damage to the hearing of their employees from exposure to noise to the lowest level reasonably practicable. [*Reg 6*].

4.     To reduce, so far as is reasonably practicable, the exposure to noise of employees (other than by provision of personal ear protectors), where employees are likely to be exposed to (*a*) 90 dB(A) or above or (*b*) peak action level (200 Pascals) or above. [*Reg 7*].

5.     To provide, at the request of an employee, suitable and efficient personal ear protectors where employees are likely to be exposed to 85 dB(A) or above but less than 90 dB(A). [*Reg 8(1)*].

6.     To designate ear protection zones, indicating:

   (*a*)     that it is an ear protection zone, and

   (*b*)     the need for employees to wear personal ear protectors whilst in such zone where any employee is likely to be exposed to 90 dB(A) or above, or to peak action level or above. Moreover, no employee should enter such zone unless he is wearing personal ear protectors.

   [*Reg 9*].

   Ear protection so provided must be maintained in an efficient state and employees must report any defects in it to the employer and see that it is fully and properly used. [*Reg 10*].

7.     To provide employees, likely to be exposed to 85 dB(A) or above, or to peak action level or above, with adequate information, instruction and training with regard to:

   (*a*)     risk of damage to that employee's hearing,

   (*b*)     steps the employee can take to minimise the risk,

(*c*)    the requirement on employees to obtain personal ear protectors from the employer, and

(*d*)    the employee's duties under the regulations.

[*Reg 11*].

In addition, there are specific legal requirements applying to tractor cabs and offshore installations and construction sites (see below).

*Fig. 1 Sign for informing that ear protectors must be worn (white on a circular blue background)*

*From the Health and Safety (Safety Signs and Signals) Regulations 1996 (SI 1996 No 341)*

### Legal obligations of designers, manufacturers, importers and suppliers of plant and machinery

N3013    The *Supply of Machinery (Safety) Regulations 1992 (SI 1992 No 3073)* require manufacturers and suppliers of noisy machinery to design and construct such machinery so that the risks from noise emissions are reduced to the lowest level taking account of technical progress. Information on noise emissions must be provided when specified levels are reached.

If a machine is likely to cause people at work to receive a daily personal noise exposure exceeding the first or peak action levels, adequate information on noise must be provided. If the second or peak action levels are likely to be exceeded, this should include a permanent sign or label, or if the machine may be noisy in certain types of use, an instruction label which could be removed following noise testing.

# Specific legal requirements

## Agriculture

N3014    The *Agriculture (Tractor Cabs) Regulations 1974 (SI 1974 No 2034)* (as amended by *SI 1990 No 1075*) provide that noise levels in tractor cabs must not exceed 90 dB(A) or 86 dB depending on which annex is relevant in the certificate under Directive 77/311/EEC. [*Reg 3(3)*].

## Construction sites

N3015    There are 23 EC directives relating to the noise emission of construction plant and equipment. These govern the maximum permissible levels of noise from a wide range of construction plant, and the way in which the emitted level is to be determined and marked. The directives are implemented in the UK via a series of statutory instruments, with titles of the form *Construction Plant and Equipment (Harmonisation of Noise Emission Standards) Regulations (SI 1985 No 1968; SI 1988 No 361; SI 1989 No 1127; SI 1992 No 488; SI 1995 No 2357); Lawnmowers (Harmonisation of Noise Emission Standards) Regulations (SI 1986 No 1795; SI 1987 No 876; SI 1992 No 168).*

A new EC directive relating to noise emission in the environment by equipment for use outdoors (Directive 2000/14/EC) consolidates and updates the earlier directives and has been implemented into UK legislation by the *Noise Emission in the Environment by Equipment for use Outdoors Regulations 2001 (SI 2001 No 1701).* The earlier statutory instruments will be revoked from 3 January 2002 and replaced by the provisions within the new 2001 Regulations.

*The Supply of Machinery (Safety) Regulations, 1992 (SI 1992 No 3073) (as amended by SI 1994 No 2063)* are also relevant to noise emissions from machinery.

## Noise and vibration control on construction and open sites, BS 5228: Parts 1 to 5

N3016    This code of practice gives detailed guidance on the assessment of noise and vibration from construction sites, open-cast coal extraction, piling operations, and surface mineral extraction. Part 1, revised in 1997, gives detailed noise calculation and assessment procedures. Its predecessor (published in 1984) was an approved code of practice under the *Control of Pollution Act 1974.* Part 1 of the code of practice is principally concerned with environmental noise and vibration, but also briefly recites the *Noise at Work Regulations 1989.*

# Compensation for occupational deafness

## Social security

N3017    The most common condition associated with exposure to noise is occupational deafness. Deafness is prescribed occupational disease A 10 (see OCCUPATIONAL HEALTH AND DISEASES). Prescription rules for occupational deafness have been extended three times, in 1980, 1983 and 1994. It is defined as: 'sensorineural hearing loss amounting to at least 50 dB in each ear being the average of hearing losses are 1, 2 and 3 kHz frequencies, and being due, in the case of at least one ear, to occupational noise'. [*Social Security (Industrial Injuries) (Prescribed Diseases) Amendment Regulations 1989 (SI 1989 No 1207), Reg 4(5)*]. Thus, the former requirement for hearing loss to be measured by pure tone audiometry no longer applies. Extensions of benefit criteria relating to occupational deafness are contained in the *Social Security (Industrial Injuries) (Prescribed Diseases) Regulations*

1985 (SI 1985 No 967), which are amended, as regards assessment of disablement for benefit purposes, by the *Social Security (Industrial Injuries) (Prescribed Diseases) Amendment Regulations 1994 (SI 1994 No 2343)*.

## Conditions for which deafness is prescribed

N3018    Any occupation involving:

(*a*)    the use of powered (but not hand-powered) grinding tools on metal (other than sheet metal or plate metal), or work wholly or mainly in the immediate vicinity of those tools whilst they are being so used; or

(*b*)    the use of pneumatic percussive tools on metal, or work wholly or mainly in the immediate vicinity of those tools whilst they are being so used; or

(*c*)    the use of pneumatic percussive tools for drilling rock in quarries or underground or in mining coal, or in sinking shafts or for tunnelling in civil engineering works, or work wholly or mainly in the immediate vicinity of those tools whilst they are being so used; or

(*d*)    the use of pneumatic percussive tools on stone in quarry works, or work wholly or mainly in the immediate vicinity of those tools whilst they are being so used; or

(*e*)    work wholly or mainly in the immediate vicinity of plant (excluding power press plant) engaged in the forging (including drop stamping) of metal by means of closed or open dies or drop hammers; or

(*f*)    work in textile manufacturing where the work is undertaken wholly or mainly in rooms or sheds in which there are machines engaged in weaving man-made or natural (including mineral) fibres or in the high speed false twisting of fibres; or

(*g*)    the use of, or work wholly or mainly in the immediate vicinity of, machines engaged in cutting, shaping or cleaning metal nails; or

(*h*)    the use of, or work wholly or mainly in the immediate vicinity of, plasma spray guns engaged in the deposition of metal; or

(*j*)    the use of, or work wholly or mainly in the immediate vicinity of, any of the following machines engaged in the working of wood or material composed partly of wood, that is to say: multi-cutter moulding machines. This does not extend to multi-cross cutting machines used for cutting newsprint (R(I)2/92), planing machines, automatic or semi-automatic lathes, multiple cross-cut machines, automatic shaping machines, double-end tenoning machines, vertical spindle moulding machines (including high speed routing machines), edge banding machines, bandsawing machines with a blade width of not less than 75 millimetres and circular sawing machines in the operation of which the blade is moved towards the material being cut; or

(*k*)    the use of chain saws in forestry; or

(*l*)    air arc gouging or work wholly or mainly in the immediate vicinity of air arc gouging; or

(*m*)    the use of band saws, circular saws or cutting discs for cutting metal in the metal founding or forging industries, or work wholly or mainly in the immediate vicinity of those tools whilst they are being so used; or (*n*)   the use of circular saws for cutting products in the manufacture of steel, or work wholly or mainly in the immediate vicinity of those tools whilst they are being so used; or

(*o*)   the use of burners or torches for cutting or dressing steel based products, or work wholly or mainly in the immediate vicinity of those tools whilst they are being so used; or

(*p*)   work wholly or mainly in the immediate vicinity of skid transfer banks; or

(*q*)   work wholly or mainly in the immediate vicinity of knock out and shake out grids in foundries; or

(*r*)   mechanical bobbin cleaning or work wholly or mainly in the immediate vicinity of mechanical bobbin cleaning; or

(*s*)   the use of, or work wholly or mainly in the immediate vicinity of, vibrating metal moulding boxes in the concrete products industry; or

(*t*)   the use of, or work wholly or mainly in the immediate vicinity of, high pressure jets of water or a mixture of water and abrasive material in the water jetting industry (including work under water); or

(*u*)   work in ships' engine rooms; or

(*v*)   the use of circular saws for cutting concrete masonry blocks during manufacture, or work wholly or mainly in the immediate vicinity of those tools whilst they are being so used; or

(*w*)   burning stone in quarries by jet channelling processes, or work wholly or mainly in the immediate vicinity of such processes; or

(*x*)   work on gas turbines in connection with:

    (i)   performance testing on test bed,

    (ii)   installation testing of replacement engines in aircraft, and

    (iii)   acceptance testing of Armed Service fixed wing combat planes; or

(*y*)   the use of, or work wholly or mainly in the immediate vicinity of:

    (i)   machines for automatic moulding, automatic blow moulding or automatic glass pressing and forming machines used in the manufacture of glass containers or hollow ware,

    (ii)   spinning machines using compressed air to produce glass wool or mineral wool,

    (iii)   continuous glass toughening furnaces.

[*Social Security (Industrial Injuries) (Prescribed Diseases) Regulations 1985 (SI 1985 No 967); Social Security (Industrial Injuries) (Prescribed Diseases) Amendment No 2 Regulations 1987 (SI 1987 No 2112); Social Security (Industrial Injuries) (Prescribed Diseases) Amendment Regulations 1994 (SI 1994 No 2343); Social Security (Industrial Injuries and Diseases) (Miscellaneous Amendments) Regulations 1996 (SI 1996 No 425)*].

'Any occupation' covers activities in which an employee is engaged under his contract of employment. The fact that the workforce is designated, classified or graded by reference to function, training or skills (e.g. labourer, hot examiner, salvage and forge examiner) does not of itself justify a conclusion that each separate designation, classification or grading involves a separate occupation (*Decision of the Commissioner No R(I) 3/78*).

'Assistance in the use' of tools qualifies the actual *use* of tools, not the process in the course of which tools are employed. Thus, a crane driver who positions bogies to enable riveters to do work on them and then goes away, assists in the process of getting bogies repaired, which requires use of pneumatic tools, but this is not assistance in the actual use of tools, for the purposes of disablement benefit. The position is otherwise when a crane holds a bogie in suspension to enable riveters to work *safely* on them. Here the crane driver assists in the actual *use* of pneumatic percussive tools (*Decision of the Commissioner No R(I) 4/82*).

## Conditions under which benefit is payable — Social Security (Industrial Injuries) (Prescribed Diseases) Regulations 1985 (SI 1985 No 967)

N3019    For a claimant to be entitled to disablement benefit for occupational deafness, the following conditions currently apply:

(*a*)    he must have been employed:

(i)    at any time on or after 5 July 1948, and

(ii)    for a period or periods amounting (in the aggregate) to at least ten years.

(*b*)    there must be permanent sensorineural hearing loss, and loss in each ear must be at least 50 dB; and

(*c*)    at least loss of 50 dB in one ear must be attributable to noise at work. [*Sch 1, Pt I*].

(There is a presumption that occupational deafness is due to the nature of employment [*Reg 4(5)*]);

(*d*)    the claim must be made within five years of the last date when the claimant worked in an occupation prescribed for deafness [*Reg 25(2)*];

(*e*)    any assessment of disablement at less than 20% is final [*Reg 33*].

A person, whose claim for benefit is turned down because he/she had not worked during the five years before the claim in one of the listed occupations, may claim if he/she continued to work and later met the time conditions. If a claim is turned down as the disability is less than 20 per cent, the claimant must wait three years before re-applying. If, by waiting three years, it would be more than five years since the applicant worked in one of the listed occupations, the three-year limit is waived.

## Assessment of disablement benefit for social security purposes

N3020    The extent of disablement is the percentage calculated by:

(*a*)    determining the average total hearing loss due to all causes for each ear at 1, 2 and 3 kHz frequencies; and

(*b*)    determining the percentage degree of disablement for each ear; and then

(*c*)    determining the average percentage degree of binaural disablement.

[*Social Security (Industrial Injuries) (Prescribed Diseases) Amendment Regulations 1989, Reg 4(2)*].

The following chart (Table 1 below) shows the scale for all claims made on/after 3 September 1979.

## Table 1
## Percentage degree of disablement in relation to hearing loss

| Hearing loss | Percentage degree of disablement |
|---|---|
| 50–53 dB | 20 |
| 54–60 dB | 30 |
| 61–66 dB | 40 |
| 67–72 dB | 50 |
| 73–79 dB | 60 |
| 80–86 dB | 70 |
| 87–95 dB | 80 |
| 96–105 dB | 90 |
| 106 dB or more | 100 |

[*Social Security (Industrial Injuries) (Prescribed Diseases) Regulations 1985, Reg 34, Sch 3 Pt II, as amended*].

Any degree of disablement, due to deafness at work, assessed at less than 20 per cent, must be disregarded for benefit purposes. [*Social Security (Industrial Injuries) (Prescribed Diseases) Amendment Regulations 1990 (SI 1990 No 2269)*].

## Action against employer at common law

N3021    There is no separate action for noise at common law; liability comes under the general heading of negligence (see EMPLOYERS' DUTIES TO THEIR EMPLOYEES). Indeed, it was not until as late as 1972 that employers were made liable for deafness negligently caused to employees (*Berry v Stone Manganese Marine Ltd [1972] 1 Lloyd's Rep 182*). Absence of a previous general statutory requirement on employers regarding exposure of employees to noise sometimes led to the law being strained to meet the facts *(Carragher v Singer Manufacturing Co Ltd 1974 SLT (Notes) 28 relating to the Factories Act 1961, s 29*: 'every place of work must, so far as is reasonably practicable, be made and kept safe for any person working there', to the effect that this is wide enough to provide protection against noise). Admittedly, it is proper to regard noise as an aspect of the working environment (*McCafferty v Metropolitan Police District Receiver [1977] 2 AER 756* where an employee, the plaintiff, who was a ballistics expert, suffered ringing in the ears as a result of the sounds of ammunition being fired from different guns in the course of his work. When he complained about ringing in the ears – the ballistics room had no sound-absorbent material on the walls and he had not been supplied with ear protectors – he was advised to use cotton wool, which was useless. It was held that his employer was liable since it was highly foreseeable that the employee would suffer hearing injury if no steps were taken to protect his ears, cotton wool being useless). Moreover, although there are specific statutory requirements to minimise exposure to noise (in agriculture and offshore operations and construction operations, see N3014, N3015 above), these have generated little or no case law.

The main points established at common law are as follows.

(*a*)    As from 1963, the publication date by the (then) Factory Inspectorate of 'Noise and the Worker', employers have been 'on notice' of the dangers to hearing of their employees arising from over-exposure to noise (*McGuinness v Kirkstall Forge Engineering Ltd 1979, unreported*). Hence, consistent with their common law duty to take reasonable care for the health and safety of their employees, employers should 'provide and maintain' a sufficient stock of ear muffs.

This was confirmed in *Thompson v Smiths, etc.* (see (*d*) below). However, more recently, an employer was held liable for an employee's noise-induced deafness, even though the latter's exposure to noise, working in shipbuilding, had occurred *entirely before* 1963. The grounds were that the employer had done virtually nothing to combat the *known* noise hazard from 1954–1963 (apart from making earplugs available) (*Baxter v Harland & Wolff plc, Northern Ireland Court of Appeal 1990 (unreported)*).

This means that, as far as Northern Ireland is concerned, employers are liable at common law for noise-induced deafness as from 1 January 1954 – the earliest actionable date. Limitation statutes preclude employees suing prior to that date (*Arnold v Central Electricity Generating Board [1988] AC 228*).

(*b*)    Because the true nature of deafness as a disability has not always been appreciated, damages have traditionally not been high (*Berry v Stone Manganese Marine Ltd [1972]* – £2,500 (halved because of time limitation obstacles); *Heslop v Metalock (Great Britain) Ltd (1981)* – £7,750; *O'Shea v Kimberley-Clark Ltd (1982)* – £7,490 (tinnitus); *Tripp v Ministry of Defence [1982] CLY 1017* – £7,500).

(*c*)    Damages will be awarded for exposure to noise, even though the resultant deafness is not great, as in tinnitus (*O'Shea v Kimberley-Clark Ltd, The Guardian, 8 October 1982*).

(*d*)    Originally the last employer of a succession of employers (for whom an employee had worked in noisy occupations) was exclusively liable for damages for deafness, even though damage (i.e. actual hearing loss) occurs in the early years of exposure (for which earlier employers would have been responsible) (*Heslop v Metalock (Great Britain) Ltd, The Observer, 29 November 1981*). More recently, however, the tendency is to *apportion* liability between offending employers (*Thompson, Gray, Nicholson v Smiths Ship Repairers (North Shields) Ltd; Blacklock, Waggott v Swan Hunter Shipbuilders Ltd; Mitchell v Vickers Armstrong Ltd [1984] IRLR 93*). This is patently fairer because some blame is then shared by the original employer(s), whose negligence would have been responsible for the actual hearing loss.

(*e*)    Because of the current tendency to apportion liability, even in the case of pre-1963 employers (see *McGuinness v Kirkstall Forge Engineering Ltd* above), contribution will take place between earlier and later insurers.

(*f*)    Although judges are generally reluctant to be swayed by scientific/statistical evidence, the trio of shipbuilding cases (see (*d*) above) demonstrates, at least in the case of occupational deafness, that this trend is being reversed (see Table 2 below, the 'Coles-Worgan classification'); in particular, it is relevant to consider the 'dose response' relationship published by the National Physical Laboratory (NPL), which relates long-term continuous noise exposure to expected resultant hearing loss. This graph always shows a rapid increase in the early years of noise exposure, followed by a trailing off (see N3022 below, 'Relevance of Coles-Worgan scale').

(*g*)    Current judicial wisdom identifies three separate evolutionary aspects of deafness, i.e. (i) hearing loss (measured in decibels at various frequencies); (ii) disability (i.e. difficulty/inability to receive everyday sounds); (iii) social handicap (attending musical concerts/meetings etc.). That social handicap is a genuine basis on which damages can be (*inter alia*) awarded, was reaffirmed in the case of *Bixby, Case, Fry and Elliott v Ford Motor Group (1990, unreported)*.


## Relevance of Coles-Worgan scale

N3022     The Coles-Worgan scale (see Table 2 below) was used to assess disability in the trio of shipbuilding cases; this gives a better assessment of disability than reference to hearing loss alone. This scale takes account of hearing loss at 0.5, 1.0, 2.0 and 4.0 kHz and also clinical symptoms, the subject being assigned to one of ten classes or 'groups' of increasing severity, e.g. 'slight', 'moderate' etc. (0.5, 1.0, 2.0 and 4.0 kHz are the denoted 'frequencies of interest' from a hearing loss point of view. These cover the range of frequencies of principal importance to speech intelligibility and are, therefore, significant in any assessment by audiometry of hearing loss).

## Table 2

## The Coles-Worgan classification for occupational deafness

| | | |
|---|---|---|
| Group O | — | No significant auditory handicap. |
| Group I | — | The hearing is not sufficiently impaired to affect the perception of speech, except for a slight (additional to normal) difficulty in noisy backgrounds. |
| Groups II & III | — | Slight (II) and moderate (III) difficulty whenever listening to faint speech, but would usually understand normal speech. The subject would also have distinctly greater difficulty when trying to understand speech against a background of noise. |
| Groups IV & V | — | Frequent difficulty with normal speech and would sometimes (IV) or often (V) have to ask people to 'speak up' in order to hear them, even in face-to-face conversation. Great (IV) or very great (V) difficulty in a background of noise. |
| Group VI | — | Marked difficulties in communication since he would sometimes be unable to clearly understand even loud speech. In noise the subject would find it impossible to distinguish speech. |
| Groups VII & VIII | — | Would only understand shouted or amplified speech, and then only moderately well (VII) or poorly (VIII). |
| Group IX | — | Minimal speech intelligibility even with well-amplified speech. |
| Group X | — | Virtually totally deaf with respect to the understanding of speech. |

# General guidance on noise at work

## Guidance on the Noise at Work Regulations 1989

N3023    The Health and Safety Executive has revised and updated its noise guides which are regarded as providing authoritative and detailed guidance on the *Noise at Work Regulations 1989*. These are now published in a single volume called '*Reducing Noise at Work Guidance on the Noise at Work Regulations 1989*', ISBN 0 7176 1511 1, which covers the following areas:

(*a*)    legal duties of employers to prevent damage to hearing;

(*b*)    duties of designers, manufacturers, importers and suppliers;

(*c*)    how to choose a competent person – advice for employers;

(*d*)    how to carry out a noise assessment – advice for the competent person;

(*e*)    control of noise exposure – advice for employers and engineers;

(*f*)    selection and use of personal ear protection – advice for employers.

## Guidance on specific working environments

N3024    Certain working environments carry particular difficulties in the assessment and control of noise exposure, mainly because of the variability of the noise levels and the length of exposure.

The following specific guidance may be of assistance:

—    *A Guide to Reducing the Exposure of Construction Workers to Noise*. R A Waller, Construction Industry Research and Information Association. CIRIA Report 120, 1990.

—    *Offshore Installations: Guidance on design and construction, Part II, Section 5*. Department of Energy, 1977.

—    *Guide to Health, Safety and Welfare at Pop Concerts and Similar Events*. Health and Safety Commission, Home Office and the Scottish Office. HMSO, 1993.

## Ear protection

N3025    There are many types of ear protection, falling into two main categories: (i) ear muffs which fit over and surround the ears, and which seal to the head by cushions filled with soft plastic foam or a viscous liquid; and (ii) ear plugs, which fit into the ear canal. Ear protectors will only be effective if they are in good condition, suit the individual and are worn properly. All ear protectors can be uncomfortable, especially if they press too firmly on the head or ear canal, or cause too much sweating. Individuals differ greatly in their preference, and wherever possible the employer should select more than one type of suitable protector and offer the user a personal choice. British Standard BS EN 458: 1994 gives guidance and recommendations for the selection, use, care and maintenance of hearing protectors.

## Sound systems for emergency purposes

N3026    Voice messages can be superior to bells or sirens to convey warnings and instructions in emergencies. However, these must be properly audible in noisy places. British Standard BS 7443: 1991 gives specifications for sound systems for emergency purposes.

# PART B: Effects of Vibration on People

## Introduction

N3027    The effects of vibration on people can be divided into three broad classes:

—    people in buildings;

—    people in vehicles, etc., and industrial situations;

—    hand-arm vibration on people operating certain tools or machines.

## Vibration white finger

N3028    The effects of industrial vibration on people received little attention until an award of damages to seven ex-British Coal miners in July 1998, in a landmark Court of Appeal decision (*Armstrong and Others v British Coal Corporation (1998) (unreported)*. The miners received compensation ranging from £5,000 to £50,000 for the effects of vibration white finger (VWF), a form of hand-arm vibration syndrome characterised by the fingers becoming numb and turning white. In its early stages, the disease is reversible, but continued exposure leads to permanent damage and even gangrene, resulting in the loss of fingers or even a complete hand. The decision was important not only for the size of the awards, but also in setting out the terms in which British Coal were negligent and the standards of exposure that would be reasonable.

The Government set up a compensation scheme for miners (now closed to new claimants) to avoid the need for individual litigation, which is eventually expected to award 40,000 miners a total of £500 million. However, by January 2001, only £212 million had been paid.

This landmark award is inevitably being followed by many others. For example, in August 2000, eight workers of North-West Water received a £1.2 million settlement. They contracted VWF whilst using jackhammers and whackers when breaking and re-instating concrete surfaces.

More detail on the assessment criteria is given later in this chapter.

## Whole-body vibration

N3029    The four principal effects of whole-body vibration are considered to be:

(*a*)    degraded health;

(*b*)    impaired ability to perform activities;

(*c*)    impaired comfort;

(*d*)    motion sickness;

Exposure to whole-body vibration causes a complex distribution of oscillatory motions and forces within the body. These may cause unpleasant sensations giving rise to discomfort or annoyance, result in impaired performance (e.g. loss of balance, degraded vision) or present a health risk (e.g. tissue damage or deleterious physiological change). However, there is little evidence that vibration directly affects thought processes. Many factors influence human response to vibration, including the type and direction of vibration and the type of person involved. The present state of knowledge does not permit a definitive dose-effect relationship between whole-body vibration and injury or health.

People can overcome moderate effects of vibration on task performance by making greater effort, and this may initially improve performance, although at the cost of greater fatigue, with ultimate degradation of performance.

Effects on comfort depend greatly on the circumstances, for example whether the person expects to be able to read or write in the prevailing conditions.

Low frequency oscillation of the body can cause the motion sickness syndrome (kinetosis) characterised principally by pallor, sweating, nausea and vomiting.

## Buildings and structures

N3030    Vibration can affect buildings and structures, but a detailed treatment of this is beyond the scope of the present chapter. People are more sensitive to vibration than buildings or structures, so vibration within a building is likely to become unacceptable to the occupants at values well below those which pose a threat to a structurally sound building. For detailed technical guidance on the measurement and evaluation of the effects of vibration on buildings, British Standard BS 7385: Part 1: 1990 [ISO 4866: 1990] and BS 7385: Part 2: 1993 may be consulted.

### Vibration measurement

*Measurement units*

N3031    Vibration is the oscillatory motion of an object about a given position. The rate at which the object vibrates (i.e. the number of complete oscillations per second) is called the frequency of the vibration and is measured in Hertz (Hz). The frequency range of principal interest in vibration is from about 0.5 Hz to 100 Hz, i.e. below the range of principal interest in noise control.

The magnitude of the vibration is now generally measured in terms of the acceleration of the object, in metres per second squared (i.e. metres per second, per second) denoted $m.s^{-2}$ or $m/s^2$. However, vibration magnitude can also be measured in terms of peak particle velocity, in metres per second (denoted $m.s^{-1}$ or $m/s$), or in terms of maximum displacement (in metres or millimetres).

For simple vibratory motion, it is possible to convert a measurement made in any one of these terms to either of the other terms, provided the frequency of the vibration is known, so the choice of measurement term is to some extent arbitrary. However, *acceleration* is now the preferred measurement term because modern electronic instruments generally employ an *accelerometer* to detect the vibration. As the name suggests, this responds to the acceleration of the vibrating object and hence this characteristic can be measured directly.

*Direction and frequency*

N3032    The human body has different sensitivity to vibration in the head to foot direction, the side to side direction, and in the front to back direction, and this sensitivity varies according to whether the person is standing, sitting or lying down. In order to assess the effect of vibration, it is necessary to measure its characteristics in each of the three directions and to take account of the recipient's posture. The sensitivity to vibration is also highly frequency-dependent. BS 6841: 1987 'Measurement and evaluation of human exposure to whole-body mechanical vibration and repeated shock' provides a set of six frequency-weighting curves for use in a variety of situations. The curves may be considered analogous to the 'A'-weighting used for noise measurement. However, few instruments have these weightings built into them.

*Vibration dose value*

N3033    In most situations, vibration magnitudes do not remain constant, and the concept of vibration dose value (VDV) has been developed to deal with such cases. This is analogous to the concept of noise dose used in the *Noise at Work Regulations 1989 (SI 1989 No 1790)*. Again, few instruments are capable of measuring VDV. Taken with the frequency-weighting system, it is possible to introduce a single-number vibration rating, but the present state of research falls short of providing limit values in definitive terms. However, vibration dose values in the region of 15 m.s-1.75 will usually cause severe discomfort, and increased exposure to vibration can be expected to increase the risk of injury.

Structural vibration of buildings can be felt by the occupants at low vibration magnitudes. It can affect their comfort, quality of life and working efficiency. Low levels of vibration may provoke adverse comments, but certain types of highly sensitive equipment (e.g. electron microscopes) or delicate tasks may require even more stringent criteria.

Adverse comment regarding vibration is likely when the vibration magnitude is only slightly in excess of the threshold of perception and, in general, criteria for the acceptability of vibration in buildings are dependent on the degree of adverse comment rather than other considerations such as short-term health hazard or working efficiency.

Vibration levels greater than the usual threshold may be tolerable for temporary or infrequent events of short duration, especially when the risk of a startle effect is reduced by a warning signal and a proper programme of public information.

Detailed guidance on this subject may be found in British Standard BS 6472: 1992 'Evaluation of human exposure to vibration in buildings (1 Hz to 80 Hz)'.

## Hand-arm vibration

N3034    Intensive vibration can be transmitted to the hands and arms of operators from vibrating tools, machinery or workpieces. Examples include the use of pneumatic, electric, hydraulic or engine-driven chain-saws, percussive tools or grinders. The vibration may affect one or both arms, and may be transmitted through the hand and arm to the shoulder.

The vibration may be a source of discomfort, and possibly reduced proficiency. Habitual exposure to hand-arm vibration has been found to be linked with various diseases affecting the blood vessels, nerves, bones, joints, muscles and connective tissues of the hand and forearm.

## Vibration-induced white finger (VWF)

N3035    Extensive and prolonged exposure to hand-arm vibration can give rise to the condition known as 'vibration white finger' (VWF), which arises from progressive loss of blood circulation in the hand and fingers, sometimes resulting in necrosis (death of tissue) and gangrene for which the only solution may be amputation of the affected areas or complete hand. Initial signs are mild tingling and numbness of the fingers. Further exposure results in blanching of the fingers, particularly in cold weather and early in the morning. The condition is progressive to the base of the fingers, sensitivity to attacks is reduced and the fingers take on a blue-black appearance. The development of the condition may take up to five years according to the degree of exposure to vibration and the duration of such exposure.

VWF is prescribed occupational disease A11. It is described as: 'episodic blanching, occurring throughout the year, affecting the middle or proximate phalanges or in the case of a thumb the proximal phalanx, of:

(*a*)    in the case of a person with five fingers (including thumb) on one hand, any three of those fingers;

(*b*)    in the case of a person with only four such fingers, any two of those fingers; or

(*c*)    in the case of a person with less than four such fingers, any one of those fingers or . . . the remaining one finger.'

[*Social Security (Industrial Injuries) (Prescribed Diseases) Regulations 1985 (SI 1985 No 967]*.

### Action at common law

N3036        In July 1998, the Court of Appeal upheld an award of damages to seven employees of British Coal claiming damages for vibration white finger (VWF). The court determined that after January 1976, British Coal should have implemented a range of precautions, including training, warnings, surveillance and job rotation where exposure to vibration was significant.

The court went on to consider what degree of exposure would be reasonable. They supported the standards set out in the HSE Guidance booklet *'Hand-arm vibration'* published in 1994, which establishes limits for vibration dose measured as an eight-hour average or A8. The court considered that an exposure of 2.8 m/sec2 A8 would be an appropriate level for prudent employers to use. This level of exposure would lead to a 10 per cent risk of developing finger blanching (the first reversible stage of VWF) within eight years.

The court also suggested a form of wording to warn employees: 'If you are working with vibrating tools and you notice that you are getting some whitening or discolouration of any of your fingers then, in your own interests, you should report this as quickly as possible. If you do nothing, you could end up with some very nasty problems in both hands.'

### Stages of vibration white finger

N3037        Damages are awarded according to the stage of the disease at the time of the action from the date the employer should have known of the risk. The Taylor-Pelmear Scale is usually used to describe these stages as follows.

| Taylor-Pelmear Scale System | | |
| --- | --- | --- |
| *Stage* | Grade | Description |
| 0 | — | No attacks |
| 1 | Mild | Occasional attacks affecting the tips of one or more fingers |
| 2 | Moderate | Occasional attacks affecting the tips and the middle of the fingers (rarely the base of the fingers) on one or more fingers |
| 3 | Severe | Frequent attacks affecting the entire length of most fingers |

| 4 | Very severe | As in stage 3, with damaged skin and possible gangrene in finger tips |
|---|---|---|

*Prescription of hand-arm vibration syndrome*

N3038 Foreseeably, prescription may extend to hand arm vibration syndrome (HAVS) instead of vibration white finger (VWF). The former would cover recognised neurological effects as well as the currently recognised vascular effects of vibration. Neurological effects will include numbness, tingling in the fingers and reduced sensibility. Moreover, the current list of occupations, for which VWF is prescribed, may be replaced by a comprehensive list of tools/rigid materials against which such tools are held, including:

(*a*) percussive metal-working tools (e.g. fettling tools, riveting tools, drilling tools, pneumatic hammers, impact screwdrivers);

(*b*) grinders/rotary tools;

(*c*) stone working, mining, road construction and road repair tools;

(*d*) forest, garden and wood-working machinery (e.g. chain saws, electrical screwdrivers, mowers/shears, hedge trimmers, circular saws); and

(*e*) miscellaneous process tools (e.g. drain suction machines, jigsaws, pounding-up machines, vibratory rollers, concrete levelling vibratibles).

(Cm 2844).

## Vibratory hand tools

N3039 The energy level of the hand tool is significant. Percussive action tools, such as compressed air pneumatic hammers, operate within a frequency range of 33-50 Hz. These cause considerable damage whereas rotary hand tools, which operate within the frequency range 40-125 Hz, are less dangerous.

Use, either frequent or intermittent, of hand-held vibratory tools, can result in injury to the wrist. Carpal tunnel syndrome arising in this way is now prescribed occupational disease A12. [*Social Security (Industrial Injuries) (Prescribed Diseases) Amendment Regulations 1993 (SI 1993 No 862), Reg 6(2)*].

## Personal protection against hand-arm vibration

N3040 There is no adequate personal protective equipment presently available against hand-arm vibration. Wearing gloves may help, but mainly by keeping hands warm and protecting against injury. 'Anti-vibration' gloves are not generally effective in reducing vibration exposure, and can even increase it. Their bulk may also reduce the ability of workers to control the equipment.

Workers can reduce the risk by keeping the blood flowing while working, for example by keeping warm whilst working, not smoking especially whilst working, and exercising hands and fingers. Tools should be designed for the job, both to lessen vibration and to reduce the strength of grip and amount of force needed. The equipment should be used in short bursts rather than long sessions. Symptoms should not be ignored. Vibration white finger is reportable under the *Reporting of Injuries, Diseases and Dangerous Occurrences Regulations 1995 (RIDDOR) (SI 1995 No 3163)*. The Health and Safety Executive publishes a full guide on *Hand-arm vibration*, HS(G)88, (1994), together with leaflets for employers and employees.

### HSE guidance on hand-arm vibration

N3041    The Health and Safety Executive publishes a full guide on *'Hand-arm vibration'*, HS(G)88, ISBN 0 7176 0743 7. It also publishes a book of 51 case studies dealing with vibration, titled *'Vibration solutions: Practical ways to reduce the risk of hand-arm vibration injury'*, ISBN 0 7176 0954 5. An HSE video pack *'Hard to handle'* includes the book and a leaflet, along with a 15-minute video giving an introduction to the risks of hand-arm vibration and how to manage them. A CD-ROM *'The successful management of hand-arm vibration'* (1999), for managers and safety specialists, has also been published by HSE.

In addition to the above, HSE publishes a number of leaflets, including:

*'Hand-arm vibration: Advice for employees and the self-employed'* (1999), ISBN 0 7176 1554 5;

*'Health risks from hand-arm vibration: Advice for employers'* (1998), ISBN 0 7176 1553 7;

*'Reducing the risk of hand arm vibration injury among Stonemasons'* (1998), MISC 112.

### Proposed EC directive physical agents at work

N3042    In early 1993, the European Commission published its proposal for a Directive (ref 93/077/02) on the protection of workers from exposure to physical agents, covering noise, vibration and non-ionising radiation, which would replace the current EC directive on worker noise exposure. Following comments from member states and the European parliament, revised proposals were published in April 1994 (ref 94/C230/03).

For *noise*, this would set 75 dB(A) daily personal exposure as the threshold at which workers should be informed of risks, 80 dB(A) as the level at which personal ear defenders would need to be provided, and 85 dB(A) as the level at which a programme of noise control would need to be established. 90 dB(A) would be the level at which ear defenders must be used, and 105 dB(A) the level at which noisy activities must be declared to the responsible authority.

For *hand-arm vibration*, the threshold would be a daily personal exposure of 1 m/s$^2$, at which workers are to be told of the risks; at 2.5 m/s$^2$, assessments become mandatory; at 5 m/s$^2$ systematic health surveillance would be required; 10 m/s$^2$ is permissible 'for a few minutes', but efforts must be made to reduce the level of vibration, and sufficient work breaks introduced to bring down the average level. Where the daily personal dose would exceed 20 m/s2, the offending equipment must be marked and the activities declared to the responsible authority.

For *whole-body vibration*, the threshold would be a daily personal exposure of 0.25 m/s$^2$, at which workers are to be told of the risks; at 0.5 m/s$^2$ (or at 1.25 m/s$^2$ for a one-hour average), a regime of vibration control strategies would be required; at 0.7 m/s$^2$, health surveillance would be required, and at 1.25 m/s$^2$ daily personal exposure, offending work activities must be notified.

The proposals are accompanied by a number of new administrative requirements. The revised proposals have been resisted as unnecessarily bureaucratic and have not yet progressed further.

# Occupational Health and Diseases

## Introduction

O1001 'Occupational disease' is a label commonly used, but one which tends to hide the more complex causes of disease. There are about 70 prescribed occupational diseases or conditions recognised under the *Social Security (Industrial Injuries) (Prescribed Diseases) Regulations 1985 (SI 1985 No 967)* (as amended) for which benefit may be claimed, subject to certain qualifications (see O1045). There are also many other conditions which may have an occupational cause and which are not on the prescribed list. Some conditions may have more than one cause: for example, hearing loss in the inner ear may be due to prolonged exposure to excessive noise, but may additionally be due to the effects of ageing (presbyacusis). Some conditions may have a non-occupational origin which is then exacerbated by work. Establishing occupational causation is therefore a complicated exercise that involves the careful elimination of other possible causes.

The compensation factor cannot be overlooked as the confirmation of an occupational cause often opens the door to a possible claim for benefit from the Department of Social Security or for civil liability for an employer or other negligent party (usually through an insurer). Those who suffer from a non-occupational condition will usually visit their GP or hospital in the first instance, but those who believe there is an occupational cause will usually first consult their trade union or a solicitor before seeking medical advice. This different emphasis is important as those who examine the compensation seeker should always have regard to the motive behind the consultation.

Diagnosis of some occupational diseases is difficult: in some cases there are no universally recognised clinical tests and the examiner must rely on the subjective history provided by the patient. For example, in the early stages of vibration white finger, the symptoms may be transient and not present at the time of the examination.

The extent of occupational disease in the United Kingdom is unknown. It certainly runs into millions of sufferers but numbers depend on the extent of reporting, the gathering of this information and in some cases, the accuracy of the diagnosis. Department of Social Security statistics suggest that there are at least 60,000 new claims each year, but this is only the tip of the iceberg as many do not qualify for benefit. Insurance statistics of civil claims made may be a more reliable indicator but reporting is spasmodic and there may be overlap where one person is claiming damages from several parties.

Occupational disease has a clear impact, not just in terms of sickness absence but also in relation to the additional costs associated with managing lost time/ productivity/human resources at employer level and paying/administering benefits at state level.

Occupational diseases are widespread amongst those who have worked in hazardous industries such as mining, construction and certain heavy industries. But there is now an increasing occurrence of 'white collar' disease: the widespread use of visual display units has brought potential risks of musculo-skeletal disorders and eyesight problems. Increasing work pressures may lead to stress-related conditions. This shift is reflected by the changing emphasis of health and safety legislation. Most of the previous legislation based on the *Factories Act 1961* and the *Offices, Shops and Railway Premises Act 1963*, together with detailed regulations applying to specific trades and processes, has been replaced by new legislation which is more widely based and which applies generally to people 'at work'. The first radical change was the *Health and Safety at Work etc. Act 1974 (HSWA 1974)*, but subsequent legislation has largely been due to the implementation of various EU health and safety at work directives.

It is likely that occupational disease will be more common in areas of former heavy industry although it is difficult to generalise. Some national companies carrying out similar operations at different locations may find that one location has a much higher incidence of occupational disease reporting than the others. This may be due partly to the culture within the local community or in the workplace itself but the desire for compensation, and the extent to which it is encouraged should not be overlooked. Employers often find a greater incidence of disease reporting by workers who are being made redundant or where a factory is to close completely.

Some conditions, like dermatitis, are known as short-tail diseases because the symptoms often become manifest within a short period of time from the relevant exposure. Others, like asbestos-related diseases, are long-tail as the symptoms may not arise for many years after the relevant exposure; one particular asbestos disease, mesothelioma, may not become manifest until 40 or 50 years later. This means that there could be generations of workers whose exposure ceased in the 1960s and 1970s but whose symptoms may not appear until the first part of the 21st century. When such conditions do arise, investigation of exposure will be exceedingly difficult with the passage of time. One should also remember that some diseases are suffered by those who do not have direct contact. This so-called 'neighbourhood exposure' could affect others working nearby, those washing a worker's dusty overalls or, in one case, even children playing in a dusty factory yard. Noise exposure may also cause neighbourhood problems as it may affect not only the user of the noisy equipment but others in the vicinity, or perhaps those who are unfortunate enough to live close to a noisy workplace.

Many diseases are incurable although there may be treatment that alleviates the symptoms. The progression of some diseases may be halted by prompt intervention, but the removal of the worker from the harmful exposure is often necessary and this may mean the loss of a job or the transfer to lower-paid work. Regrettably, some diseases, especially lung conditions, are often fatal. Most long-tail diseases are caused by past neglect of proper preventative action, even when viewed in the light of knowledge at the time. Strict observance of current legislation and codes of practice should go a long way to ensure that the present epidemic of occupational disease does not continue.

## Long-tail diseases

O1002    Most of these diseases originate from the former manufacturing industries and, because of the latent period between the first exposure and the onset of the condition, we are now faced with the legacy of those workers who are suffering because of past neglect. Many of these workers are no longer in the jobs where their exposure occurred and many of their former workplaces have either closed or have been drastically changed. This makes investigation into the cause of the disease somewhat difficult.

Health and safety legislation in the 1990s should help to eradicate many of the old problems that were the root cause of these conditions but it would be naïve to think that no-one remains at risk from long-tail hazards. There are also those working today who are already suffering from one or more of these diseases due to past exposures, so it is essential that any present employer is made aware of their pre-existing problems and takes adequate steps to prevent further harm.

Three typical long-tail diseases have been selected for detailed comment:

—    Asbestos-related diseases;

—    Noise-induced hearing loss (NIHL); and

—    Hand arm vibration syndrome (HAVS).

## Asbestos-related diseases

**O1003**    Asbestos is a name given to a group of minerals whose common feature is their fibrous nature. It is found in rock fissures in certain parts of the world, including Canada and Southern Africa. It is a very versatile mineral which, when broken down into fibres, may be spun, woven and incorporated into many compounds. There are three main kinds of asbestos:

(*a*)    *Chrysotile (white)*. This is the most commonly used, and has strong, silky, flexible fibres which are easily used in the making of asbestos textiles.

(*b*)    *Crocidolite (blue)*. This has brittle fibres with high tensile strength which are highly resistant to chemicals and sea water.

(*c*)    *Amosite (brown)*. This has long, fairly strong fibres with good insulation properties.

It is commonly believed that blue asbestos is the most dangerous of the three types because of its fibre length and diameter, but all three types should be regarded as being dangerous to health because of their indestructible nature. The fibres have the propensity to penetrate all the body's natural defence mechanisms and to lodge permanently in the lungs.

The use of asbestos grew considerably through the first part of the 20th century and probably reached a peak in the 1960s and early 1970s. Its uses are many and varied and include:

(*a*)    manufacture of asbestos textiles;

(*b*)    thermal insulation (lagging), especially in shipyards and power stations;

(*c*)    electrical insulation;

(*d*)    clutch and brake linings;

(*e*)    asbestos cement products (like roofing sheets and pipework).

Dockers who unloaded sacks of raw asbestos may also have been exposed, and exposure may be an ongoing problem where asbestos lagging has to be removed.

From the early part of the 20th century, some of the health problems associated with asbestos were beginning to become apparent. The first statutory controls were contained in the *Asbestos Industry Regulations 1931* but this legislation was limited to the asbestos manufacturing processes. After World War II it was suspected that certain groups of shipyard workers may have been at risk and some asbestos controls were incorporated in the *Shipbuilding and Ship-repairing Regulations 1960 (SI 1960 No 1932)*. There were also more general requirements in the *Factories Acts of 1937 and 1961* relating to ventilation and the removal of dust. It is probably fair to say that most of these statutory requirements went unheeded by the majority of employers until the mid-to late 1960s, when the extent of the asbestos problem began to be fully realised.

Firstly, an investigation into conditions in a mining area of South Africa, published in 1960 found a high incidence of a rare cancer, mesothelioma, amongst those who lived and worked there. Secondly, an investigation in 1965 discovered a high incidence of this disease in the London area. Public concern grew and the *Asbestos Regulations 1970* (of much wider application than the 1931 Regulations), were introduced. Further stringent measures have since been taken, culminating in the *Control of Asbestos at Work Regulations 1987 (SI 1987 No 2115)* and the *Asbestos (Licensing) Regulations 1983 (SI 1983 No 1649)* (amendments to both regulations have been made which came into force in 1999) and the *Asbestos (Prohibitions) Regulations 1992 (SI 1992 No 3067)*.

The conditions which may arise from asbestos exposure are:

(*a*)    mesothelioma;

(*b*)    asbestosis;

(*c*)    bronchial carcinoma (lung cancer);

(*d*)    diffuse pleural thickening; and

(*e*)    pleural plaques.

## Mesothelioma

O1004    This is a cancer of the pleura, a thin lining which surrounds the lungs. Sometimes it may also affect the peritoneum, the lining of the abdominal cavity. It is believed that only a relatively small degree of exposure is necessary for the disease to be initiated. Blue asbestos is thought to be the culprit but other types cannot be excluded.

There is usually an extremely long latent period between exposure and onset during which time the cells are slowly multiplying but remain undetected. Patients may first suffer chest pains and breathlessness and begin to lose weight, but by the time the condition is diagnosed, it is too late. Progression is rapid, the cancer invades the lungs and the condition becomes extremely painful and distressing. This type of cancer does not respond to treatment or surgical intervention and most patients die within 12 to 18 months of the initial diagnosis. Mesothelioma is quite rare in the normal population, so where there is a history of asbestos exposure, causation is seldom in dispute. The condition may be detected on X-ray or CT scan.

Because the uses of asbestos peaked in the 1960s and 1970s and because the latency period is typically 40 to 50 years, the incidence of mesothelioma is likely to peak in the first quarter of the 21st century.

## Asbestosis

O1005    This is a type of scarring or fibrosis of the lungs which is caused by asbestos bodies penetrating through to the alveoli – the tiny vessels at the end of the airways where oxygen is taken into the bloodstream and carbon dioxide removed. The lung's defences cause the fibrosis to occur and this gradually spreads so as to block the actions of the alveoli. Unlike mesothelioma, asbestosis is a dose-related condition: it is believed that causation depends upon a significant degree of exposure over several year for it to take hold, and the severity of the disease may be related to the extent of the exposure and the period of time over which the exposure takes place. The latency period is thought to be at least ten years from first exposure.

Symptoms may include breathlessness on exertion, crackling sounds in the base of the lungs and finger clubbing. The fibrosis may sometimes be seen on X-ray or CT scan and a lung function test may reveal reduced gas transfer. Asbestosis is not invariably fatal but may cause severe respiratory disability. Complications, particularly lung cancer, may arise which will have a significant effect on life expectancy.

## Lung cancer

O1006    This disease is of course widely associated with cigarette smoking but it is believed that it can arise directly as a result of asbestos exposure in non-smokers. However, where there is a combination of cigarette smoking and asbestos exposure, the likelihood of lung cancer developing is extremely high.

## Diffuse pleural thickening

O1007    This is a fairly uncommon condition where asbestos bodies cause a thickening of the lining of the pleura, resulting in breathlessness. Unlike mesothelioma, it is a benign condition but those suffering from it could develop the malignant condition at a later stage.

## Pleural plaques

O1008    These are small areas of fibrous thickening on the walls of the pleura which usually cause no respiratory disability but which may be detected on X-ray examination. They are probably an indication that the individual has had asbestos exposure.

Although there is no disability, the patient who is told about the finding may be understandably anxious about the future. In a small percentage of cases the condition may progress into one of the disabling conditions listed above. For this reason, those who have been advised that they have pleural plaques may seek an award of provisional damages, with a proviso that they may return to the court for a more substantial award at a later date if they succumb to one of the more serious conditions.

## Civil liability

O1009    There are seldom many disputes about the issues of liability to the individual claimant. If there has been exposure and if the *Factories Acts* applied, the stringent requirements of the sections relating to ventilation and the removal of dust would be difficult for most employers to defend. The greater problem arises where there is more than one defendant and in trying to establish how much each is going to pay. Some insurers are parties to sharing arrangements that help to resolve this issue speedily. Because of the latent period it is usually accepted that any exposure that took place within the last ten years before the disease was diagnosed is not relevant.

In the last few years there have been two particularly important decisions on causation in this field. *Holtby v Brigham & Cowan (Hull) Ltd [2000] 3 AER 421* concerned the liability of one employer in an asbestos-related claim involving asbestosis, where the claimant had been potentially exposed to asbestos during other periods of employment. The Court of Appeal made a distinction between 'divisible' (i.e. dose related conditions like asbestosis/pleural thickening) and 'non-divisible' conditions (like mesothelioma). Where the condition is divisible, the court will do its best to apportion the damages to reflect the defendant's responsibility for the injury suffered in the course of that employment. Where the condition is not divisible, the claimant will recover in full. The court was split 2–1 on the question of burden of proof . The majority said that the burden stayed with claimant throughout, but the dissenting opinion of Clarke LJ has great force.

In *Fairchild v Glenhaven Funeral Services Ltd and others [2001] AER (D) 12 (Feb)* the court was concerned with a mesothelioma claim against three defendants. The medical evidence indicated that one or more asbestos fibres caused this condition but it was not possible to say which defendant was responsible on the balance of probabilities for the guilty fibre(s). In circumstances where it is impossible to say that guilty exposure is more likely by one defendant than another, the claim must fail against all defendants. A material increase in risk is not enough to establish legal causation. This decision is unsurprisingly unpopular with claimants.

# Noise-induced hearing loss (NIHL)

O1010    The condition is more commonly called 'occupational deafness' but NIHL is now a more acceptable term because the word 'deafness' implies almost total loss of hearing whereas noise exposure at work often causes only a partial hearing loss.

The general view is that NIHL is the most common occupational disease, although work-related stress conditions are on the increase. Although no reliable figures are available, it is believed that at least 2 million workers in the UK may have been exposed to excessive noise for at least a significant period of their employment. The DSS statistics are of little assistance because benefit is not paid until the claimant has a high level of hearing loss. Although the disease was extremely common in the traditional heavy industries, like shipbuilding, boilermaking, steel manufacture and mining, most factories have some noisy areas and there are many parts of the service industry where workers are at risk.

## Noise

O1011    Noise is simply unwanted sound. This is sometimes subjective: a rock band may give one person much pleasure but cause annoyance to another. However, it is generally accepted that excessive noise at work is not only unwanted but potentially harmful.

There are three important factors when considering the effects of noise:

— intensity (or loudness);

— frequency (or pitch); and

— daily dose (or duration of exposure).

### Intensity

The louder the sound, the greater the likelihood of hearing damage. The range of intensity levels which may be heard by the human ear varies enormously from the slightest whisper to the sound of a jet engine on take-off. The latter may be 100 million, million (1014) times as loud as the former so a logarithmic scale, known as the decibel (dB) scale, is used to simplify the numbering of the ratios. 0 dB is the threshold of normal hearing, 140 dB would be the sound of a jet engine, whereas factory noise or a heavy goods vehicle would be typically in the 80 to 90 dB range. As the scale is logarithmic, the following examples should be noted:

— 90dB is 10 times as loud as 80dB.

— ± 1dB represents an increase/decrease of 1.26 (100.1) in the intensity level.

— 93 dB is twice as loud as 90dB (3dB = 1.263).

— 96 dB is four times as loud as 90dB.

— 87dB is half as loud as 90dB.

Noise intensity levels may be measured in the workplace by a noise level meter. Personal dose meters may also be used to assess an individual's noise dose over a period of time.

*Frequency*

Sounds may occur at various frequencies which range from a low rumble to a high-pitched whine or whistle. The human ear responds differently to sounds of the same intensity but at different frequencies – some high frequency sounds will appear to be louder. Frequencies are banded together in octaves (like the notes on a piano) but when measuring the effects of noise at work, it is usual to average out the bands and to apply a weighting factor which allows for the differing responses of the ear. This is known as the A-weighted scale and a measurement of intensity would be expressed as 90 dB(A), for example.

Frequencies are usually measured at their octave band centres. The unit of measurement is the Hertz (Hz). 1 Hz = 1 cycle per second; 1000Hz = 1 kiloHertz (1 kHz). The range of hearing in a normal healthy young adult is between about 20 Hz and 20 kHz but the range for the understanding of most speech is between about 1 and 3 kHz.

*Daily dose*

The risk of hearing damage from noise at work is dose related. The unprotected ear may be exposed to a moderately loud noise for a short period of time without harm but if the exposure continues for several hours, there may be a risk of temporary hearing loss. If this daily pattern of exposure continues over a number of years, the temporary hearing loss will inevitably become permanent. The UK control standard is based on daily personal exposure to noise over an 8 hour working day (LEP,d.).

## Control measures

O1012     The first official attempt at assessing the risk to hearing from noise at work and advising on preventative steps was a booklet called '*Noise and the Worker*', published by the Ministry of Labour in 1963. The booklet advised employers to measure noise levels and, if they exceeded a level which would now be expressed at approximately 89 dB(A), to take preventative measures. This would include the issue of personal hearing protection, which by that time was reasonably effective in attenuating high noise levels. '*Noise and the Worker*' was followed by more detailed and updated guidance in a Code of Practice, published in 1972 by the Department of Employment.

With a few minor exceptions, there was no specific legislation aimed at noise control at work until the *Noise at Work Regulations 1989 (SI 1989 No 1790)* (implementing an EU Noise at Work Directive) were introduced. These regulations had the following main objectives:

(*a*)     General duty to reduce the risk of hearing damage to the lowest level reasonably practicable.

(*b*)     Assessments of noise exposure to be made.

(*c*)     Reduce noise exposure as far as reasonably practicable.

(*d*)     Provision of information to workers.

(*e*)     Two main action levels at or above 85 dB(A) and 90 dB(A):

   (i)     At the first level (85dBa) and above, ear protection must be provided to workers on request;

(ii)    At the second level (90dBa), the protection must be issued to all those exposed and ear protection zones established where all those entering must wear protection.

HSE has published updated guidance on ear protection for employers to refer to entitled '*Ear protection: Employers' duties explained*', and for employees '*Protect your hearing*'. These update and compliment an earlier HSE guidance '*Reducing noise at work: Guidance on the Noise at Work Regulations 1989*'.

The HSE like to emphasize that ear protection should be a last resort and that reduction of noise at source is always preferable.

## Damage to hearing by noise

O1013    The human ear is divided into three sections:

(*a*)    The outer ear, which extends along the ear canal to the ear drum;

(*b*)    The middle ear, containing a set of three bones, the ossicles, which link the ear drum to the inner ear; and

(*c*)    The inner ear which contains the cochlea, the organ of hearing.

The cochlea is connected to the brain by the auditory nerve. Inside the cochlea are receptor cells which have hair-like tufts and groups of these cells respond to different frequency ranges. Continuous exposure to loud noise will tend to permanently damage these cells so that the efficiency of the hearing organ is gradually diminished.

The cells which respond to the high frequency ranges are situated close to the oval window in the cochlea, a membrane which connects the cochlea to the ossicles in the middle ear. These cells tend to suffer from the greatest damage by noise and those exposed typically have their greatest hearing loss at or about the 4 kHz frequency. The effect of this is that they have difficulty in distinguishing the high-pitched consonant sounds like sh, th, p etc., especially in crowded places where there others are talking. They may also have problems hearing the doorbell or telephone ringing.

Other typical indicators of NIHL are:

(*a*)    It causes damage only to the inner ear (sensori-neural loss);

(*b*)    It is in both ears (bilateral);

(*c*)    The extent of the loss is about the same in each ear (symmetrical); and

(*d*)    It develops gradually over a period of years of exposure to high noise levels.

There are many other causes of hearing loss, some of which, like presbyacusis (senile deafness) also affect the inner ear. Correct diagnosis will involve the consideration of all the other possible causes. The most common method of measuring hearing loss is by pure tone audiometry, whereby tones are delivered to the subject through an earphone and responses are recorded on a graph. The object is to establish the threshold of hearing for a given frequency, this threshold being measured in dB (i.e. the intensity level at which the subject begins to hear the sound). An audiogram of a typical NIHL subject will show that the hearing threshold is greatest at or around the 4 kHz frequency and this will be shown by a dip or notch in the graph.

## Tinnitus

O1014    This is a symptom which consists of a sensation of noises in the ear without external stimulus. Typically, it consists of ringing noises but whistling, buzzing, roaring or clicking sounds are reported by some. Its cause is not well established but it can arise in connection with several conditions of the inner ear, including NIHL but also with presbyacusis and Meni's Disease, for example.

The effect of tinnitus varies enormously from mild to very severe. Most people have experienced a ringing sensation from time to time, for example after visiting a disco or perhaps during a respiratory infection. These transient symptoms cause few problems, but there are some who suffer from continuous, loud noises in the ear which often disturb sleep, and in rare cases, may even cause them to become suicidal.

### Civil liability

O1015    As with asbestos claims, the investigation of noise exposure is often difficult to investigate because of the passage of time. Some employers may have done noise surveys in the past, but these frequently provide only a snapshot of conditions at a particular time, and it is often argued by claimants that these surveys are unrepresentative. Defendants also have the problem of co-ordinating the claim where there are multiple defendants.

Because specific statutory control only started in 1990, many NIHL claims are based on common law. In this context, the actions of a reasonable and prudent employer in the light of current knowledge and invention is relevant (following *Stokes v GKN [1968] 1 WLR 1776*). The so-called guilty knowledge began, for most defendants, only in 1963 when *'Noise and the Worker'* was first published, so, where there was pre-1963 exposure, liability and damages should be apportioned between the 'innocent' and 'guilty' periods (see *Thompson v Smiths Shiprepairers [1984] 1 All ER 881*).

There are a number of NIHL claims held to have been statute barred because of excessive delay in bringing the proceedings. Although *s 33* of the *Limitation Act 1980* provides courts with a discretion to override the three-year time limit for bringing claims, this discretion will not be exercised where there has been inexcusable delay which has caused prejudice to the defendant (see for example *Barrand v British Cellophane, The Times, 16 February 1995*).

# Hand arm vibration syndrome (HAVS)

O1016    This is the name given to a group of diseases relating to vibration induced conditions in the upper limbs. The most common and widely known condition is vibration white finger (VWF). This is an occupationally-induced form of a condition known as Raynaud's Phenomenon and arises after prolonged and excessive use of vibration hand tools.

Recent HSE funded research suggests that over a million workers are potentially exposed to harmful levels of hand arm vibration. The construction industry was particularly affected with around 460,000 individuals affected.

### Vibration

O1017    Like NIHL, VWF is dose related and many who suffer from an occupational hearing loss may also have this condition as hand-held tools which are noisy may also vibrate excessively, but VWF is confined to those who actually use the equipment. The measurement factors are:

—    magnitude of vibration;

—    frequency of the vibration; and

—    the daily dose.

### Magnitude

Measurement of magnitude is complex and needs to be done by a skilled person. The aim is to measure the acceleration of the tool, the unit of measurement being in meters per second squared (m/s2). An accelerometer is fixed to the handle of the tool and measurements are taken along three axes (x, y and z). Variations in results are likely due to the condition of the tool, the material being worked upon and the way in which the operator grips the tool.

### Frequency

As with noise measurement, the frequency range is an important factor, but with vibration exposure the harmful effects are most likely to be in the low frequency range from about 2 Hz to 1250 Hz. A weighted average is normally used.

### Daily dose

The current action level is contained in British Standard BS 6842:1987 and applies when the daily dose reaches 2.8 m/s2 over 8 hours. Because of the problems with variable measurement it is suggested that the following guidelines may be appropriate:

(*a*)    any tool causing tingling and numbness after 10 minutes' use should be suspect;

(*b*)    almost any exposure which exceeds 2 hours a day is likely to cause harm; and

(*c*)    exposure which exceeds 30 minutes a day with tools like caulking or chipping hammers, rock drills, pneumatic road breakers, or heavy duty portable grinders is likely to cause harm.

## Effects of exposure to excessive vibration

O1018    There are two main symptoms of the VWF condition:

(*a*)    *Vascular*: blanching of one or more parts of the fingers; and

(*b*)    *Neurological*: tingling and (sometimes) numbness in the fingers.

In the early stages, the attacks are transient, perhaps lasting up to one hour. As the patient recovers from the attack, there is aching and redness. Initial attacks occur in cold conditions, usually in winter. It is believed that early vascular damage may be subject to spontaneous recovery but by the time the neurological damage occurs the condition will be permanent.

It should be emphasised that these symptoms are the same whether the subject suffers from the non-occupational Raynaud's Phenomenon or from VWF. The former is a naturally occurring condition in the general population and is particularly common in women where it is believed that about 10 per cent suffer from it. Raynaud's Phenomenon may arise as a complication of various conditions, including rheumatoid arthritis, frostbite, and vascular disease, and may also arise as a result of cigarette smoking or from trauma or surgery to the hands.

Where the condition is work-related, continuous exposure may cause damage to the blood supply to the fingers and to the nerve endings. With time, the attacks become more prolonged and the effects more serious and in a very few cases, gangrene may occur. The condition starts at the tips of the fingers, but as it progresses, more parts of the fingers are affected. It is rare for the thumbs to be involved. As cold conditions may bring on attacks, workers may be advised to wear gloves and perhaps avoid working in exposed locations.

If the disease is diagnosed at an early stage, the worker may be advised to cease work with vibratory tools. If this is done, it is unlikely that the condition will progress and in some cases, a complete recovery may be possible.

## Classification of symptoms

O1019    There are two recognised scales for assessing the severity of symptoms. The Taylor-Pelmear scale is the oldest and uses four stages of severity but is perhaps too crude a measure for medico-legal purposes and may rely on some non-clinical factors, such as a change of job. The later Stockholm scale grades symptoms separately for vascular and sensori-neural components and for the number of affected fingers on each hand. This more detailed approach is now favoured by many examiners although they will often refer to both scales in a medico-legal context.

## Preventative steps

O1020    These may be summarised as follows:

(*a*)    Risk assessment – identifying the processes and individuals at risk.

(*b*)    Warnings – advising those at risk of the hazards and action to be taken.

(*c*)    Training and adequate supervision.

(*d*)    Minimising daily exposure time.

(*e*)    Proper tool control and maintenance.

(*f*)    Medical surveillance to ensure that symptoms are reported promptly and that harmful exposure does not continue.

It is questionable whether the wearing of gloves will reduce the magnitude of vibration and their use should be confined to the role of keeping the hands warm and/or protection from sharp edges etc.

## Civil liability

O1021    There is no specific statutory requirement relating to VWF so most of the claims are based on duty at common law. As with deafness claims, there is a date when guilty knowledge commences and, in most cases, this will be 1976 or thereabouts. This date is used following the publication of a book – *Vibration white finger in industry* by Taylor and Pelmear (1975) – and by the introduction of a draft British Standard (DD 43) in the same year. (See *Armstrong v British Coal, 30 September 1997*, Kemp & Kemp at H6A-002 and *White v Holbrook Castings [1985] IRLR 215*.)

The Court of Appeal has recently confirmed that an employer in a VWF claim will only be liable for the excess damage which can be attributed to that employer's negligence or breach of duty – thus confirming the dose related nature of the condition (See *Allen and others v British Rail Engineering Ltd and another [2001] AER (D) 291 (Feb)*. Defendant's can use this decision to argue for broad brush reductions to reflect inevitable VWF that can be proved during any period of negligence.

In the *Armstrong case*, the court made reference to HSE Booklet '*Hand Arm Vibration*' (1994) which provides a useful starting point when looking at current standards.

In the future we should expect further European guidance in this area probably in the form of an EU Directive.

# The changing pattern of occupational diseases

O1022    Technological and socio-economic changes have continued to alter the pattern and nature of occupational health problems in the UK and abroad. The gradual shift from manufacturing to service-related employment has resulted in the development of many so-called 'white collar' diseases. Obviously, there is a geographic pattern to the development of these new diseases.

The 1992 'Six Pack' Regulations reflect a partial response to these changes and a move away from the factory based legislation of yesteryear.

### Stress

O1023    Two growth areas include:

(*a*)    Work-related stress.

(*b*)    Work-related upper limb disorders (WRULDs).

## Work-related stress

O1024    Stress is hardly a new problem restricted to modern man. People have suffered from stress-related conditions, one suspects back to our very earliest stages of evolution. We all suffer stress in one form or another during our lifetime whether it be due to work pressures or difficult life events related to personal tragedy.

### What is stress?

O1025    The word 'stress' has many connotations and meanings but is frequently used to describe the psychological, physiological and behavioural responses to external stimuli. Not all stimuli causes excessive stress levels and not all stress is bad.

The HSE's definition of stress ascribes a negative connotation:

*'the reaction people have to excessive pressures or the types of demands placed upon them.'*

*'It arises when they worry that they cannot cope.'*

The late 20th Century saw the development of a new breed of claim – work-related stress. These claims stem not only from a changed perception of what is now acceptable in the workplace but also the courts, or perhaps more importantly, lawyers' willingness to expand the sphere of employers' liability.

It is important to emphasise that stress is not a separate diagnosable illness nor a discrete medical condition – the word is commonly used to describe symptomology including depression, anxiety, guilt, apathy, sleeplessness, behavioural changes (psychological) and tension, high blood pressure, weight loss, loss of appetite (physical). Media presentation of work-related stress concentrates very much on the psychological aspects of work-related stress.

We should not underestimate the socio-economic impact of work-related stress. Research undertaken by the International Stress Management Association UK and Royal Sun Alliance revealed that 70 per cent of UK adults had experienced stress at work – 49 per cent indicating that stress levels had increased over the last twelve months.

Health and Safety Commission (HSC) concluded following an extensive public consultation exercise (which included the publication *'Managing Stress at Work'*) that work-related stress was a serious health and safety problem which could only be tackled in part by the existing health and safety legislation. At present an approved code of practice in the field is deemed unenforceable but HSE has this under review.

## What causes stress?

O1026 When looking for work-related trends there are a number of factors or 'stressors' which can contribute towards an individuals level of stress:

(*a*)    Time pressures.

(*b*)    Overload/underload.

(*c*)    Interpersonal relationships.

(*d*)    Working hours.

(*e*)    Working environment – physical and systemic.

(*f*)    Personality.

(*g*)    Changes – technological, procedural and systemic.

Stress-related illness often arises as a result of a combination of the above as well as contribution from external stressors (e.g. death, family problems or physical illness). It is the multi-factorial nature of stress-related illness that makes it difficult to identify the cause and to prevent occurrence. It is often impossible to unravel the occupational causes from the non-occupational elements and this creates particular difficulties in the medico-legal context.

Although it is dangerous to generalise in this area, research has shown that some employees especially nurses, professionals, education/welfare/security workers and senior management are particularly affected by work-related stress. See HSE report *'The scale of occupational stress: A further analysis of the impact of demographic factors and type of job'*. Men and women appear to be similarly afflicted although this report suggests a higher incidence within non-white ethnic groups.

## Civil liability

O1027    *(a)    Statutory*

The Government has sought to address the number of hours worked by any one individual through the enactment of the *Working Time Regulations 1998 (SI 1998 1833) (as amended by SI 1999 No 3372)*. These Regulations implement Council Directive 93/104 (1992 OJL 307/18) and Council Directive 94/93 (1994 OJL 216/12). Obligations are imposed on employers concerning the maximum average weekly working time of workers, the average normal hours of night workers, the provision of health assessments for night workers, rest breaks to be given to workers engaged in certain kinds of work and keeping records of workers' hours of work. Whilst these Regulations do not confer a civil right of action they may be relevant in 'overload' claims.

Under the *Management of Health and Safety at Work Regulations 1999 (SI 1999 No 3242)* employers are required to make a suitable and sufficient assessment of the risks to the health and safety of their employees to which they are exposed whilst at work. This includes excessive stress levels whether it be caused by difficult time pressures or bullying by co-workers.

## (b)    Common law

We are seeing a growing number of first instance decisions but little by way of higher court authority.

*Walker v Northumberland County Council [1995] 1 AER 737* is often cited as the watershed decision in this area but many argue that it followed well established principles. Mr Walker managed four teams of social service field workers in a depressed area of Northumberland. He found the strain of the job too much and at the end of November 1986 suffered a nervous breakdown. His symptoms included anxiety, headaches, sleeplessness and an inability to cope with any levels of stress. On medical advice he was absent from work for three months. He returned to work but in September 1987 stress induced symptoms returned and he was subsequently diagnosed as suffering from stress-related anxiety and was advised to take sick leave. In February 1988 he had a second mental breakdown and was later dismissed on the grounds of permanent ill health. The local authority was held liable. It was found that an employer does owe a duty of care to an employee not to cause him psychiatric injury as a result of the volume or character of work which the employees is required to do. Although the first breakdown was found not to be reasonably foreseeable to the defendant, the second one was. It was reasonably foreseeable that there was a real risk of repetition of his illness if he was exposed to the same workload and if his duties were not alleviated by effective additional assistance. In continuing to employ him but providing no effective help the council had acted unreasonably and was in breach of it's duty of care.

The House of Lords in *Page v Smith [1995] 2 AER 736* confirmed that there was no distinction between foreseeable physical and psychiatric injury arising from a breach of duty.

One important point made by Colman J in *Walker* was:

> 'The question is whether it ought to have foreseen that Mr Walker was exposed to a risk of mental illness materially higher than that which would ordinarily affect (an employee) in his position with a really heavy workload.
>
> For if the foreseeable risk were not materially greater than that, there would not, as a matter of reasonable conduct, be any basis upon which the council's duty to act arose.'

He clearly acknowledges that not all work stress can be removed nor would it be reasonable to impose such a duty on employers.

The *Walker* approach on duty has not been seriously challenged in the higher courts and indeed received support in some of their Lordships' judgements in *Frost v Chief Constable of South Yorkshire (1999) 2 AC 455.*

What about the standard of care? In *Walker*, Colman J said:

> 'It is clear law that an employer has a duty to provide his employee with a reasonably safe system of work or to take reasonable steps to protect him from risks which are reasonably foreseeable ... the standard of care required for the performance of that duty must be measured against a yardstick of reasonable conduct on the part of a person in the position of that person who owes the duty. ... It calls for no more than a reasonable response, what is reasonable being measured by the nature of the employer–employee relationship, the magnitude of the risk of injury which was reasonably foreseeable, the seriousness of the consequence for the person to whom the duty is owed of a risk of eventuating and the cost in practicality of preventing the risk ... the practicality of remedial measures must clearly take into account the resources and facilities at the disposal of the personal body owing the duty of care ... and the purpose of the activity which has given rise to the risk of injury.'

Practitioners should have regard to the following HSE guidance when considering the standard of care in this area – *'Stress at work: Guide for employers'* (1995), HSG 116, *'Help on work-related stress: A short guide'* (1998), INDG281 and *'Managing occupational stress: A guide for managers and teachers in the schools sector'*.

*Causation* and the nature of injury are important features of these claims. The claimant must establish that he or she has suffered a definable psychiatric illness (see *Page v Smith* (above) and *Fraser v State Hospital Board of Scotland, The Times, 11 September 2000)*. The illness must have been materially contributed to by the breach of duty and there will be no compensatable claim if the same extent of psychiatric illness would have occurred in any event and but for the work stressors.

Overload claims continue to feature prominently in this field but harassment/ victimisation is a significant strand to many of the claims coming through. In *Ratcliffe – v-Pembrokeshire County Council (1998) (unreported)* it was claimed that Mr Ratcliffe, a teacher, had suffered a nervous breakdown which he attributed to a systematic period of bullying by his headmistress. Although the defendants in that case maintained a total denial of liability throughout, the action was subsequently compromised upon terms that resulted in Mr Ratcliffe receiving damages of £101,028. In *Ingrams v Worcester CC (unreported)* the claimant was a warden managing traveller's sites and it was alleged that he and his family were subjected to abuse and on at least one occasion, violence. He alleged that his employer actively undermined his position. Liability was admitted and settled at £203,432. In *Waters v Metropolitan Police [2000] IRLR 720* the House of Lords refused to strike out a claim against the metropolitan police where a police officer alleged that her employer had breached their duty of care to prevent assaults by other officers.

### Preventative steps

O1028    These can be summarised as follows:

(*a*)    Risk assessment.

(*b*)    Recognition of tell tale signs of excess stress e.g absences, lateness, staff turnover, poor quality or quantity of work.

(*c*)    Act on identified stressors/ reports of excess stress.

(*d*)    Monitor stress-related absences, ensure any return is monitored and refer to medical profession for clarification of capacity to work.

# Work-related upper limb disorders (WRULDs)

## Definition

O1029    Such disorders were previously referred to as RSI (this terminology as a separate form of injury was rejected by Prosser J in *Mughal v Reuters [1993] IRLR 571*.)

Claims arise out of a wide variety of jobs. In relation to white-collar workers, claims are commonly made by VDU operators and typists and data processors. A recent IOM study funded by HSE found that secretarial staff and temps were significantly over-represented amongst female workers reporting upper limb disorders(ULD's). As regards blue-collar workers, claims can be seen from heavy repetitive manual or routine repetitive line workers (for example assembly work).

Upper limb disorders (ULDs) include a wide range of conditions affecting the fingers, hands, wrists and forearms. Some are prescribed diseases, some are not. Some are known to be work-related, some not. Medical opinion remains fairly divided.

See Table 1 below for a list of common upper limb disorders.

## Table 1
## Common upper limb disorders

| Medical condition | Description | Clinical signs and symptoms |
|---|---|---|
| Peritendonitis Crepitans PD A8 | Inflammation of tendon of hand or forearm. | Swelling, heat, redness, pain and crepitus (creaking) of wrist. Can be caused by rapid repeated movement and thus caused by work. |
| Carpal Tunnel Syndrome | Compression of the medial nerve of the wrist as it passes through the carpal tunnel. | Pain, numbness in palm and fingers on the lateral side of the hand and wrist, difficulty in moving fingers, decreased hand strength. Electro-conductivity diagnostic tests. It is a prescribed disease where associated with vibration. |
| Tendonitis PD A8 | Inflammation of tendons. | Pain and swelling. Tendons can become locked in their sheaths so that the fingers become locked in flexion. Repeated extension and flexion of fingers thought to be causative. |
| Tenosynovitis (trigger digit/trigger thumb) PD A8 | Inflammation of the tendon sheath. | Swelling, tenderness and pain in the tendon sheath of fingers or thumbs, accompanied by a characteristic 'locking'. Can be caused by repetitive motions of the digits. |
| De Quervains Syndrome (De Quervains Stenosing Tenovaginitis) PD A8 | Thickening of the tendon sheath over the radial borders of the wrist at the junction of the thumb/wrist. | Reduction in the grip strength, tenderness and swelling, pain on radial side of wrist. Caused by repeated pinching and gripping with thumb or repeated ulnar deviation of wrist. Can develop spontaneously. |

| Tennis Elbow (Lateral Epicondylitis) | Inflammation of the tendons that attach the forearm muscles to the bony knob on the outer elbow. | Tenderness of outer or inner aspect of the elbow, extending into the forearm along a palpable band in line with the extensor muscles. Accompanied by pain and swelling. No clear medical evidence that the conditions are related to work although they are exacerbated by heavy repetitive manual labour. |
|---|---|---|
| Golfer's Elbow (Medial Epicondylitis) | Inflammation of the tendons of the forearm muscles that attach to the inner aspect of the bony knob of the elbow. | |
| PDA4 (Writer's cramp) | Cramp of the hand or forearm. | Can be caused by prolonged periods of handwriting, typing or other repetitive movements of the fingers, hand or arms. |
| Ganglions | Cysts containing viscous, mucinous fluid found in vicinity of joints and tendons in various parts of the body, although the majority are on the wrist. | Not believed to be work-related but can be exacerbated by work. |

## Civil liability

O1030    To bring a successful WRULD claim the claimant will need to establish:

(*a*)    That it was foreseeable to a reasonable and prudent employer that the work engaged in could give rise to an upper limb disorder.

(*b*)    That he or she has suffered an injury (but see *Alexander v Midland Bank plc* below).

(*c*)    That this injury has been caused or exacerbated by his work and as a result of any breach of duty owed to him either in common law or pursuant to statute by his employers.

Problems arise because a claimant has difficulty in satisfying one of the definable medical conditions listed in Table 1 above. In *Mughal v Reuters [1993] IRLR 571* the plaintiff was unable to establish one of the specific upper limb conditions and was suffering from a diffuse range of symptoms. Prosser J could not accept RSI as a separate form of injury and in the absence of a specific organic condition rejected the claim.

It is not enough for a claimant to say that he or she has suffered 'passing minimal discomfort' (see *Griffiths v British Coal Corporation (unreported)*).

Many of the recent cases have turned on the establishment of an organic condition. Following *Mughal, some claimants suffering from diffuse symptoms attempted to identify their problem as a specific upper limb condition (see for example Pickford)*. Alternatively, a number of alternative labels such as fibro-myalgia or reflex sympathetic dystrophy were adopted on their behalf by the treating or expert medical practitioner.

In *Alexander and Others v Midland Bank [1999] IRLR 723* five female bank employees claimed that they were suffering from regional fibro-myalgia arising from their work as data processor operators. The claimants all worked in the nine district centres set up by Midland Bank to process cheques and vouchers. Their job involved rapid repetitive keying in work on encoding machines over long periods of time, often one-handed. By 1991 some of the claimants began to report symptoms in the upper limbs. The pain and discomfort became more persistent and intense. It was held at first instance that the plaintiffs' symptoms were more than passing minimal discomfort and were sufficient to form an actionable claim for personal injury notwithstanding the lack of precision in the description of the pathology of their pain. HH Byrt QC found that the pressure of the decoders' work contributed towards their injuries, and the bank knew or ought to have reasonably foreseen that these factors invited the risk of injury and were held in breach of their duty.

The bank appealed. The Court of Appeal found that the lack of precise pathological/physiological explanation for the claimants' symptoms did not rule out recovery providing there was medical evidence that those symptoms were caused by the work/breach of duty.

In *Amosu and Others v The Financial Times, 31 July 1998 (unreported)* the court considered a claim by five journalists at the *Financial Times* who each claimed to have suffered specific musculo-skeletal disorders following the introduction of a computerised system for the writing, editing and printing of the paper. The allegations included the provision of bad and poorly ergonomically designed work stations and the exposure to excessive pressures of work with inadequate rest breaks. On this occasion the court held that each of the claimants had failed to demonstrate or prove on the balance of probabilities that they had suffered from the various physical problems as alleged.

In the majority decision by the House Lords in *Pickford v Imperial Chemical Industries plc (1998) 1 WLR 1189* the claimant failed to satisfy the court that her symptoms were organic and caused by typing work. Mrs Pickford alleged that she had developed prescribed disease PD A4 commonly known as writer's cramp because of the large amount of typing work carried out at speed for long periods without breaks. The House of Lords found that it was not reasonably foreseeable that a secretary working in the same work regime as the plaintiff would be likely to suffer from the condition. There was no specific duty on ICI to provide rest breaks as her work was sufficiently varied to allow rotation between typing and other known repetitive work. Further there was no specific duty to warn of the specific risks of developing PD A4 as this was not practice in the industry at the time and such warnings would have been counter productive precipitating the very condition it was intended to avoid.

### Employers' duties and prevention

O1031 The primary source is the *Health and Safety (Display Screen Equipment) Regulations 1992 (SI 1992 No 2792)*, but see also the *Management of Health and Safety At Work Regulations 1999 (SI 1999 No 3242)* and the *Workplace (Health, Safety and Welfare) Regulations 1992 (SI 1992 No 3004)*.

Further guidance can be found in HSE publication *'Work-related upper limb disorders: A guide to prevention'* (1990).

Prudent employers should look to:

(*a*)    Provide suitable and adequate health and safety training/information relating to the use of equipment, posture and breaks;

(*b*)    Provide a suitable work station;

(*c*)    Provide suitable rotation and breaks. Employers should carry out risk assessments looking at the necessary application of force, the speed of work, the repetition and the awkwardness of any specific task;

(*d*)    Provide warnings where appropriate; and

(*e*)    Cover health surveillance.

# Preventative management

### Safety policy

O1032 *Section 2(3)* of *HSWA 1974* requires those employing five or more people to have a written statement of general policy on matters of health and safety and to revise it as necessary. The document should detail the organisation and arrangements for carrying out the policy and it should be brought to the notice of all employees.

This is an important document which should be signed by a senior person within the organisation (usually the chief executive). It should clearly set out the obligations of line managers in carrying out the objectives of the organisation. Where there are specific hazards (e.g. asbestos) the policy should deal with the measures to be taken. This may be in the form of an internal code of practice.

### Risk assessment

O1033 This is the cornerstone of modern occupational health and safety management and stems from EU Directives on health and safety which have been subsequently implemented by UK legislation.

Regulations which contain the requirement to carry out risk assessments include:

(*a*)    *Control of Asbestos at Work Regulations 1987 (SI 1987 No 2115);*

(*b*)    *Control of Lead at Work Regulations 1998 (SI 1998 No 543);*

(*c*)    *Control of Substances Hazardous to Health Regulations 1994 (COSHH) (SI 1994 No 3246);*

(*d*)    *Health and Safety (Display Screen Equipment) Regulations 1992 (SI 1992 No 2792);*

(*e*)    *Management of Health and Safety at Work Regulations 1999 (SI 1999 No 3242);*

(*f*)    *Manual Handling Operations Regulations 1992 (SI 1992 No 2793) ;*

(*g*)    *Noise at Work Regulations 1989 (SI 1989 No 1790);*

(*h*)    *Personal Protective Equipment at Work Regulations 1992 (SI 1992 No 2966);*

(*i*)    *Workplace (Health, Safety and Welfare) Regulations 1992 (SI 1992 No 3004).*

An employer is required to carry out a suitable and sufficient risk assessment where there may be a risk of injury or disease. Having identified the areas of risk, protective measures which either eliminate or minimise the risk must be indicated.

The assessments may be carried out by outside agencies, but are often best done internally where there are staff familiar with the processes and potential hazards. Management should consider seeking the help and advice of employees in this task, particularly where there are employee health and safety representatives. Assessments are not necessarily confined to the risks to employees, but others who may be affected by their undertaking: this may include contractors, customers, delivery drivers and others likely to visit the premises. Where employees are working away from the normal workplace, they need to be given special consideration.

Risk assessments are not static: they must be reviewed constantly in the light of changing circumstances. They will normally be in writing and these records should be retained for as long as they are relevant. It is particularly important that where there is a risk of occupational disease, assessments should deal specifically with the problem. For example, where there is a problem with excessive noise, there should be a detailed survey of noisy areas and risks to individuals, but this may also need to be supported by health surveillance in the form of audiometry to test the effectiveness of the control measures. Regular safety audits are also an effective way of checking the effectiveness of the risk assessments.

## Ceasing exposure

O1034    In some cases, the risk of harm from a substance or process is so great that consideration should be given to ceasing the exposure entirely. This may mean closing the workplace or discontinuing the hazardous process. Such radical steps may be necessary where the process carries a risk of serious injury and the employer is not satisfied that control measures will eliminate the risk. An example of this might be the total ban on the use or handling of asbestos and the substitution by another insulating material.

## Minimising exposure

O1035    A less radical solution may be to reduce the level of exposure to the lowest level that is reasonably practicable. The aim should be to reduce the exposure not only to the occupational exposure standard (which should be regarded as the maximum allowable in any event), but to aim for the lowest level that is reasonably achievable. For example, in a noisy workplace, an employer may aim to reduce exposure to the first action level of 85 dB(A) but cannot be confident that this level may always be achieved. Further engineering measures could bring the level to well below 85 dB(A), ensuring that none of the workforce is at risk and avoiding the necessity to have hearing protection available.

## Enclosing the process

O1036    Risks arising from a hazardous process may be substantially reduced if it is enclosed to ensure that there is no escape of the substance. However, there must be provision for access by personnel to carry out essential maintenance and the employer must ensure that such persons are adequately trained and are provided with the necessary personal protection when working in the enclosure.

### Enclosing the operator

O1037 This is the reverse of the above system of control. It is especially suitable where the process is on a scale that makes enclosure uneconomic (e.g. a noisy bottling plant). The operator and the plant controls are situated in a sealed control room and access on to the floor of the plant is carefully controlled with the necessary personal protection worn.

### Automating or mechanising the process

O1038 The aim of this system is to remove the human element from some or all of the process. Where there is a high incidence of musculo-skeletal problems in the workplace, this may be an appropriate measure to consider. However, the different risks involved with the introduction of new machinery may need to be assessed.

### Minimising exposure time

O1039 Many occupational diseases are dose-related so every effort should be made to ensure that workers are exposed to hazards for as little time as possible during their working day. In theory, this is a very effective control measure and should be cost-effective, but it does need proper supervision and worker co-operation to ensure that it is effective. A simple example is where VDU operators are given adequate rest breaks coupled with other tasks (e.g. filing) which are performed away from the display screen.

### Monitoring exposure

O1040 Monitoring is an important part of the process for ensuring that exposure is maintained at or below the maximum safe level. For example, dust levels may be monitored by regular environmental samples and supplemented by personal dose sampling on workers who are at risk. Continuous automatic sampling may be necessary in some cases. Monitoring should be done regularly and proper records maintained.

### Personal protective equipment (PPE)

O1041 The use of PPE is now governed by the *Personal Protective Equipment at Work Regulations 1992 (SI 1992 No 2966)*. In the guidance notes to the Regulations it is stressed that in the hierarchy of control measures, PPE must be regarded as a last resort: engineering controls and safe systems of work should come first although there may be a need for personal protection whilst such measures are being implemented. The reason for the 'last resort' status is because there are so many problems involved in the reliance upon PPE as a safe method of prevention, and in some workplaces there is reluctance by the workforce to wear the protection provided.

There are however circumstances where the employer has no alternative but to use PPE. If this is so, there are many points to consider to ensure that the protection is effective, including:

(*a*) risk assessment to ensure that if PPE is the only means of controlling exposure, the equipment is suitable and effective;

(*b*) ensuring that the necessary equipment is issued to all workers who may be at risk;

(c)     ensuring that the equipment fits correctly and is compatible with other PPE that may be worn;

(d)     arrangements for the maintenance and replacement of the equipment;

(e)     suitable accommodation for the equipment (e.g. lockers);

(f)     information, instruction and training to advise workers about the risks of exposure, the need for the protection, the manner of its use, and how to maintain the equipment;

(g)     information given needs to be comprehensible to the worker – a point to consider where there may be language difficulties.

If a control system relies on PPE, it is essential that there is adequate supervision to ensure that equipment is being properly worn at all relevant times. Having regard to all the problems, an employer may well be advised to look again at other control measures.

## Information, instruction, training and supervision

O1042    These have been discussed in relation to PPE but they are essential ingredients of the total programme of preventative management.

(a)     *Information.* Those who are at risk must be told the precise nature of the risks that they face and what they need to do to avoid or minimise these risks. For example, if there is a problem with noise, they should be told how noise can damage hearing, what areas of the workplace are hazardous, and where they must wear hearing protection. Instructional videos are often available for this sort of education.

(b)     *Instruction.* In addition to giving advice on the health risks, a worker should also receive clear instructions as to any steps which need to be taken. This instruction may be verbal but is best supplemented by an instruction booklet and perhaps warning notices. Instructions may need to be in foreign languages where appropriate.

(c)     *Training.* Following instruction there must be adequate training to ensure that the worker understands what needs to be done. This may include, for example, a demonstration on the correct method of wearing PPE.

(d)     *Supervision.* Adequate supervision is the key to effective preventative management. If this does not exist then all the assessments, plans and procedures are so much waste paper. First line supervisors are on the spot and can immediately see what is right or wrong. They can ensure for example that protection is being worn or that hazardous dust is not allowed to escape. Employers should ensure that health and safety is an essential part of the supervisor's role and that they are given the time and resources to perform that function.

## Medical surveillance

O1043    The purpose of medical surveillance is to identify at an early stage health risks and control measures. There are certain statutory requirements for this (eg. in the COSHH Regulations) but in addition, employers may choose to implement their own programme. The surveillance may take several forms:

(a)     pre-employment questionnaire and/or examination to ensure that new entrants are screened for suitability;

(*b*)   new starters may have initial tests, such as audiometry, which will establish a benchmark against which further progress can be checked;

(*c*)   regular examinations, say every year, to ensure that health is maintained;

(*d*)   providing a service where workers with symptoms may report them immediately (this is particularly beneficial with work-related upper limb disorders, for example); and

(*e*)   a referral procedure where those returning from sickness absence may be examined as to their continuing suitability for certain work.

### Future trends

O1044   Increasing technological development will undoubtedly change the risks to which workers are exposed and as a consequence the nature of occupational health problems.

Asthma and other environmental conditions are likely to be at the forefront of new claims along with WRULDs and stress.

As individuals become ever more litigious we can expect lawyers to attempt to push open new causes of action founded on new occupational diseases.

Although law and practice change to reflect each new risk there is inevitably a time gap and whilst the incidence of many traditional industrial diseases have been halted or reduced we should not expect an eradication of all occupational health diseases. The very technological advancements which have reduced many of the traditional risks in industry have brought a whole new set of occupational health issues and problems.

# Current list of prescribed occupational diseases

O1045   The current list of prescribed occupational diseases is contained in the *Social Security (Industrial Injuries) (Prescribed Diseases) Regulations 1985 (SI 1985 No 967)* (the main regulations), the *Social Security (Industrial Injuries) (Prescribed Diseases) Amendment Regulations 1987 (SI 1987 No 335)*, the *Social Security (Industrial Injuries) (Prescribed Diseases) (Amendment No 2) Regulations 1987 (SI 1987 No 2112)*, the *Social Security (Industrial Injuries) (Prescribed Diseases) Amendment Regulations 1989 (SI 1989 No 1207)*, the *Social Security (Industrial Injuries) (Prescribed Diseases) Amendment Regulations 1990 (SI 1990 No 2269)*, the *Social Security (Industrial Injuries) (Prescribed Diseases) Amendment Regulations 1991 (SI 1991 No 1938)*, the *Social Security (Industrial Injuries) (Prescribed Diseases) Amendment Regulations 1993 (SI 1993 No 862)*, the *Social Security (Industrial Injuries) (Prescribed Diseases) Amendment (No 2) Regulations 1993 (SI 1993 No 1985)*, the *Social Security (Industrial Injuries) (Prescribed Diseases) Amendment Regulations 1994 (SI 1994 No 2343)* and the *Social Security (Industrial Injuries and Diseases) (Miscellaneous Amendments) Regulations 1996 (SI 1996 No 425)*. *Schedule 1* to the main regulations and occupations for which they are prescribed are reproduced in Table 2 below. Pneumoconiosis and the occupations for which it is prescribed are set out in *Schedule 2* to the main regulations and is also reproduced below. Compensation for pneumoconiosis etc. is dealt with in COMPENSATION FOR WORK INJURIES AND DISEASES and O1048 below.

The question whether a claimant is suffering from a prescribed disease is a diagnosis one, falling within the remit of the Medical Appeal Tribunal; the question whether a disease is prescribed is for the Adjudicating Officer, the Social Security Appeal Tribunal and the Commissioner. Where a claimant is suffering from a prescribed disease, it is open to the Adjudicating Officer to seek to show that the particular disease was not due to the nature of the claimant's employment (R(I) 4/91 – primary neoplasm C 23, invoking *Reg 4* of the *Social Security (Industrial Injuries) (Prescribed Diseases) Regulations 1985*). In addition, a Medical Appeal Tribunal can decide disablement issues (R(I) 2/91 – disablement assessed at 7% in respect of vibration white finger, A 11).

Moreover, medical practitioners and specially qualified medical practitioners can now adjudicate upon matters relating to industrial injuries and prescribed diseases (hitherto the exclusive province of medical boards or special medical boards). [*Social Security (Industrial Injuries and Adjudication) Regulations 1993 (SI 1993 No 861); Social Security (Industrial Injuries) (Prescribed Diseases) Amendment (No 2) Regulations 1993 (SI 1993 No 1985)*].

## Table 2
## Current list of prescribed occupational diseases

| Prescribed disease or injury | Occupation |
|---|---|
| A. *Conditions due to physical agents* | *Any occupation involving:* |
| 1. Inflammation, ulceration or malignant disease of the skin or subcutaneous tissues or of the bones, or blood dyscrasia, or cataract, due to electro-magnetic radiations (other than radiant heat), or to ionising particles. | Exposure to electro-magnetic radiations (other than radiant heat) or to ionising particles. |
| 2. Heat cataract. | Frequent or prolonged exposure to rays from molten or red-hot material. |
| 3. Dysbarism, including decompression sickness, barotrauma and osteonecrosis. | Subjection to compressed or rarified air or other respirable gases or gaseous mixtures. |
| 4. Cramp of the hand or forearm due to repetitive movements. | Prolonged periods of handwriting, typing or other repetitive movements of the fingers, hand or arm. |
| 5. Subcutaneous cellulitis of the hand (Beat hand). | Manual labour causing severe or prolonged friction or pressure on the hand. |
| 6. Bursitis or subcutaneous cellulitis arising at or about the knee due to severe or prolonged external friction or pressure at or about the knee (Beat knee). | Manual labour causing severe or prolonged external friction or pressure at or about the knee. |
| 7. Bursitis or subcutaneous cellulitis arising at or about the elbow due to severe or prolonged external friction or pressure at or about the elbow (Beat elbow). | Manual labour causing severe or prolonged external friction or pressure at or about the elbow. |

| | | | |
|---|---|---|---|
| 8. | Traumatic inflammation of the tendons of the hand or forearm, or of the associated tendon sheaths. | | Manual labour, or frequent or repeated movements of the hand or wrist. |
| 9. | Miner's nystagmus. | | Work in or about a mine. |
| 10. | Substantial sensorineural hearing loss amounting to at least 50dB in each ear, being due in the case of at least one ear to occupational noise, and being the average of pure tone loss measured by audiometry over the 1, 2 and 3 kHz frequencies (occupational deafness). | (*a*) | The use of, or work wholly or mainly in the immediate vicinity of, pneumatic percussive tools or high-speed grinding tools, in the cleaning, dressing or finishing of cast *metal* or of ingots, billets or blooms (but not stone/concrete used in road/railway construction; or |

Any occupation involving:

(*b*)   the use of, or work wholly or mainly in the immediate vicinity of, pneumatic percussive tools on metal in the shipbuilding or ship repairing industries; or

(*c*)   the use of, or work in the immediate vicinity of, pneumatic percussive tools on metal, or for drilling rock in quarries or underground, or in mining coal, for at least an average of one hour per working day; or

(*d*)   work wholly or mainly in the immediate vicinity of drop-forging plant (including plant for drop-stamping or drop-hammering) or forging press plant engaged in the shaping of metal; or

(*e*)   work wholly or mainly in rooms or sheds where there are machines engaged in weaving man-made or natural (including mineral) fibres or in the bulking up of fibres in textile manufacturing; or

(*f*)   the use of, or work wholly or mainly in the immediate vicinity of, machines engaged in cutting, shaping or cleaning metal nails; or

(g)   the use of, or work wholly or mainly in the immediate vicinity of, plasma spray guns engaged in the deposition of metal; or

(h)   the use of, or work wholly or mainly in the immediate vicinity of, any of the following machines engaged in the working of wood or material composed partly of wood, that is to say; multi-cutter moulding machines, planing machines, automatic or semi-automatic lathes, multiple cross-cut machines, automatic shaping machines, double-end tenoning machines, vertical spindle moulding machines (including high-speed routing machines), edge banding machines, bandsawing machines with a blade width of not less than 73 millimetres and circular sawing machines in the operation of which the blade is moved towards the material being cut; or

(j)   the use of chain saws in forestry; or

(k)   air arc gouging or work wholly or mainly in the immediate vicinity of air arc gouging; or

(l)   the use of band saws, circular saws or cutting discs for cutting metal in the metal founding or forging industries, or work wholly or mainly in the immediate vicinity of those tools whilst they are being so used; or

(m)   the use of circular saws for cutting products in the manufacture of steel, or work wholly or mainly in the immediate vicinity of those tools whilst they are being so used; or (*n*)   the use of burners or torches for cutting or dressing steel based products, or work wholly or mainly in the immediate vicinity of those tools whilst they are being so used; or

(*o*)   work wholly or mainly in the immediate vicinity of skid transfer banks; or

(*p*)   work wholly or mainly in the immediate vicinity of knock out and shake out grids in foundries; or

(*q*)   mechanical bobbin cleaning or work wholly or mainly in the immediate vicinity of mechanical bobbin cleaning; or

(*r*)   the use of, or work wholly or mainly in the immediate vicinity of, vibrating metal moulding boxes in the concrete products industry; or

(*s*)   the use of, or work wholly or mainly in the immediate vicinity of, high pressure jets of water or a mixture of water and abrasive material in the water jetting industry (including work under water); or

(*t*)   work in ships' engine rooms; or

(*u*)   the use of circular saws for cutting concrete masonry blocks during manufacture, or work wholly or mainly in the immediate vicinity of those tools whilst they are being so used; or

(*v*)   burning stone in quarries by jet channelling processes, or work wholly or mainly in the immediate vicinity of such processes; or

(*w*)   work on gas turbines in connection with:

    (i)   performance testing on test bed,

|  |  |  |  |
|--|--|--|--|
|  |  | (ii) | installation testing of replacement engines in aircraft, |
|  |  | (iii) | acceptance testing of Armed Service fixed wing combat planes; or |
|  | (*x*) | the use of, or work wholly or mainly in the immediate vicinity of: | |
|  |  | (i) | machines for automatic moulding, automatic blow moulding or automatic glass pressing and forming machines used in the manufacture of glass containers or hollow ware; |
|  |  | (ii) | spinning machines using compressed air to produce glass wool or mineral wool; |
|  |  | (iii) | continuous glass toughening furnaces. |

Any occupation involving:

| | | | |
|--|--|--|--|
| 11. | Episodic blanching, occurring through out the year, affecting the middle or proximal phalanges or in the case of a thumb the proximal phalanx, of – | (*a*) | The use of hand-held chain saws in forestry; or |
| | (*a*) in the case of a person with 5 fingers (including thumb) on one hand, any 3 of those fingers, or | (*b*) | the use of hand-held rotary tools in grinding or in the sanding or polishing of metal, or the holding of material being ground, or metal being sanded or polished, by rotary tools; or |
| | (*b*) in the case of a person with only 4 such fingers, any 2 of those fingers, or | (*c*) | the use of percussive metal-working tools, or the holding of metal being worked upon by percussive tools, in riveting, caulking, chipping, hammering, fettling or swaging; or |

(c)   in the case of a person with less than 4 such fingers, any one of those fingers or, as the case may be, the one remaining finger (vibration white finger).

(d)   the use of hand-held powered percussive drills or hand-held powered percussive hammers in mining, quarrying, demolition, or on roads or footpaths, including road construction; or

(e)   the holding of material being worked upon by pounding machines in shoe manufacture.

12.   Carpal tunnel syndrome.

Use of hand-held vibrating tools whose internal parts vibrate so as to transmit that vibration to the hand, but excluding those which are solely powered by hand

B.   *Conditions due to biological agents*

*Any occupation involving:*

1.   Anthrax.

Contact with animals infected with anthrax or the handling (including the loading or unloading or transport) of animal products or residues.

2.   Glanders.

Contact with equine animals or their carcases.

3.   Infection by leptospira. (See below*)

(a)   Work in places which are, or are liable to be, infested by rats, field mice or voles, or other small mammals; or

(b)   work at dog kennels or the care or handling of dogs; or

(c)   contact with bovine animals or their meat products or pigs or their meat products.

*Any occupation involving:*

4.   Ankylostomiasis.

Work in or about a mine.

5.   Tuberculosis.

Contact with a source of tuberculosis infection.

6.   Extrinsic allergic alveolitis (including farmer's lung).

Exposure to moulds or fungal spores or heterologous proteins by reason of employment in:

(a)   agriculture, horticulture, forestry, cultivation of edible fungi or malt-working; or

(b)   loading or unloading or handling in storage mouldy vegetable matter or edible fungi; or

|     |     |     |                                                                      |
| --- | --- | --- | -------------------------------------------------------------------- |
|     |     | (c) | caring for or handling birds; or                                     |
|     |     | (d) | handling bagasse.                                                    |

| 7. | Infection by organisms of the genus brucella. | Contact with – |
| --- | --- | --- |

|     |     |     |                                                                                                          |
| --- | --- | --- | -------------------------------------------------------------------------------------------------------- |
|     |     | (a) | animals infected by brucella, or their carcases or parts thereof, or their untreated products; or        |
|     |     | (b) | laboratory specimens or vaccines of, or containing, brucella.                                             |

| 8. | Viral hepatitis. | Close and frequent contact with – |
| --- | --- | --- |

|     |     |     |                                        |
| --- | --- | --- | -------------------------------------- |
|     |     | (a) | human blood or human blood products; or |
|     |     | (b) | a source of viral hepatitis.           |

| 9. | Infection by *Streptococcus suis*. | Contact with pigs infected by *Streptococcus* suis, or with the carcases, products or residues of pigs so infected. |
| --- | --- | --- |

| 10. | (a) | Avian chlamydiosis | Contact with birds infected with chlamydia psittaci, or with the remains or untreated products of such birds. |
| --- | --- | --- | --- |

|     | (b) | Ovine chlamydiosis. | Contact with sheep infected with chlamydia psittaci, or with the remains or untreated products of such sheep. |
| --- | --- | --- | --- |

| 11. | Q fever. | | Contact with animals, their remains or their untreated products. |
| --- | --- | --- | --- |

| 12. | Orf. | | Contact with sheep, goats or with the carcases of sheep or goats. |
| --- | --- | --- | --- |

| 13. | Hydatidosis. | | Contact with dogs. |
| --- | --- | --- | --- |

\* (This can also give rise to liability at common law, where an employer fails to set up a system for killing off rats, or, alternatively fails to instruct employees to take proper precautions by washing their hands frequently (*Campbell v Percy Bilton Ltd (1988) (unreported)*). Previously, common law liability for Weil's disease, carried by rats, was unlikely (*Tremain v Pike [1969] 3 AER 1303* where a farmer was held not liable to an employee who contracted Weil's disease on a rat-infested farm, as no warnings had been issued by the local health authority). Today, however, with greater awareness and knowledge of health and hygiene hazards, liability is more likely. Even so, the likelihood of injury, magnitude of risk and cost of an exterminating operation would all be relevant to liability (see further *Paris v Stepney Borough Council [1951] 1 AER 42*).)

| C. | *Conditions due to chemical agents* | *Any occupation involving:* |
|---|---|---|
| 1. | Poisoning by lead or a compound of lead. | The use or handling of, or exposure to the fumes, dust or vapour of, lead or a compound of lead, or a substance containing lead. |
| 2. | Poisoning by manganese or a compound of manganese. | The use or handling of, or exposure to the fumes, dust or vapour of, manganese or a compound of manganese, or a substance containing manganese. |
| 3. | Poisoning by phosphorus or an inorganic compound or phosphorus or poisoning due to the anti-cholinesterase or pseudo anti-cholinesterase action of organic phosphorus compounds. | The use or handling of, or exposure to the fumes, dust or vapour of, phosphorus or a compound of phosphorus, or a substance containing phosphorus. |
| 4. | Poisoning by arsenic or a compound of arsenic. | The use or handling of, or exposure to the fumes, dust or vapour of, arsenic or a compound of arsenic, or a substance containing arsenic. |
| 5. | Poisoning by mercury or a compound of mercury. | The use or handling of, or exposure to the fumes, dust or vapour of, mercury or a compound of mercury, or a substance containing mercury. |
| 6. | Poisoning by carbon bisulphide. | The use or handling of, or exposure to the fumes or vapour of, carbon bisulphide or a compound of carbon bisulphide, or a substance containing carbon bisulphide. |
| 7. | Poisoning by benzene or a homologue of benzene. | The use or handling of, or exposure to the fumes of, or vapour containing benzene or any of its homologues. |
| 8. | Poisoning by nitro-or amino-or chloro-derivative of benzene or of a homologue of benzene, or poisoning by nitrochlorbenzene. | The use or handling of, or exposure to the fumes of, or vapour containing a nitro-or amino-or chloro-derivative of benzene, or of a homologue of benzene, or nitrochlorbenzene. |
| 9. | Poisoning by dinitrophenol or a homologue of dinitrophenol or by substituted dinitrophenols or by the salts of such substances. | The use or handling of, or exposure to the fumes of, or vapour containing, dinitrophenol or a homologue or substituted dinitrophenols or the salts of such substances. |
| 10. | Poisoning by tetrachloroethane. | The use or handling of, or exposure to the fumes of, or vapour containing, tetrachloroethane. |

| 11. | Poisoning by diethylene dioxide (dioxan). | | The use or handling of, or exposure to the fumes of, or vapour containing, diethylene dioxide (dioxan). |
|-----|-------------------------------------------|---|----|
| 12. | Poisoning by methyl bromide. | | The use or handling of, or exposure to the fumes of, or vapour containing, methyl bromide. |

Any occupation involving:

| 13. | Poisoning by chlorinated naphthalene. | | The use or handling of, or exposure to the fumes of, or dust or vapour containing, chlorinated naphthalene. |
|-----|------|---|----|
| 14. | Poisoning by nickel carbonyl. | | Exposure to nickel carbonyl gas. |
| 15. | Poisoning by oxides of nitrogen. | | Exposure to oxides of nitrogen. |
| 16. | Poisoning by gonioma kamassi (African boxwood). | | The manipulation of gonioma kamassi or any process in or incidental to the manufacture of articles therefrom. |
| 17. | Poisoning by beryllium or a compound of beryllium. | | The use or handling of, or exposure to the fumes of, or dust or vapour of, beryllium or a compound of beryllium, or a substance containing beryllium. |
| 18. | Poisoning by cadmium. | | Exposure to cadmium dust or fumes. |
| 19. | Poisoning by acrylamide monomer. | | The use or handling of, or exposure to, acrylamide monomer. |
| 20. | Dystrophy of the cornea (including ulceration of the corneal surface) of the eye. | (*a*) | The use or handling of, or exposure to, arsenic, tar, pitch, bitumen, mineral oil (including paraffin), soot or any compound, product or residue of any of these substances, except quinone or hydroquinone; or |
| | | (*b*) | exposure to quinone or hydroquinone during their manufacture. |
| 21. | (*a*) Localised new growth of the skin, papillomatous or keratotic; | | The use or handling of, or exposure to, arsenic, tar, pitch, bitumen, mineral oil (including paraffin), soot or any compound, product or residue of any of these substances, except quinone or hydroquinone. |
| | (*b*) squamous-celled carcinoma of the skin. | | |

22.  (*a*)  Carcinoma of the mucous membrane of the nose or associated air sinuses;

     (*b*)  primary carcinoma of a bronchus or of a lung.

Work in a factory where nickel is produced by decomposition of a gaseous nickel compound which necessitates working in or about a building or buildings where that process or any other industrial process ancillary or incidental thereto is carried on.

23.  Primary neoplasm (including papilloma, carcinoma-in-situ and invasive carcinoma) of the epithelial lining of the urinary tract (renal pelvis, ureter, bladder and urethra).

(*a*)  Work in a building in which any of the following substances is produced for commercial purposes:

    (i)  alpha-naphthylamine, beta-naphthylamine or methylene-bis-orthochloroaniline;

    (ii)  diphenyl substituted by at least one nitro or primary amino group or by at least one nitro and primary amino group (including benzidine);

    (iii)  any of the substances mentioned in sub-paragraph (ii) above if further ring substituted by halogeno, methyl or methoxy groups, but not by other groups;

    (iv)  the salts of any of the substances mentioned in sub-paragraphs (i) to (iii) above;

    (v)  auramine or magenta; or

Any occupation involving:

(*b*)  the use or handling of any of the substances mentioned in sub-paragraph (a) (i) to (iv), or work in a process in which any such substance is used, handled or liberated; or

|  |  |  |  | (c) | the maintenance or cleaning of any plant or machinery used in any such process as is mentioned in sub-paragraph (*b*), or the cleaning of clothing used in any such building as is mentioned in sub-paragraph (*a*) if such clothing is cleaned within the works of which the building forms a part or in a laundry maintained and used solely in connection with such works; or |
|---|---|---|---|---|---|
|  |  |  |  | (d) | Soderberg aluminium smelting process. [*SI 1993 No 862*]. |
| 24. | (a) | Angiosarcoma of the liver; |  | (a) | Work in or about machinery or apparatus used for the polymerization of vinyl chloride monomer, a process which, for the purposes of this provision, comprises all operations up to and including the drying of the slurry produced by the polymerization and the packaging of the dried product; or |
|  | (b) | osteolysis of the terminal phalanges of the fingers; |  |  |  |
|  | (c) | non-cirrhotic portal fibrosis. |  |  |  |
|  |  |  |  | (b) | work in a building or structure in which any part of that process takes place. |
| 25. |  | Occupational vitiligo. |  |  | The use or handling of, or exposure to, para-tertiary-butylphenol, para-tertiarybutylcatechol, para-amyl-phenol, hydroquinone or the monobenzyl or monobutyl ether of hydroquinone. |
| 26. |  | Damage to the liver or kidneys due to exposure to carbon tetrachloride. |  |  | Use of or handling of or exposure to the fumes of, or vapour containing carbon tetrachloride. |
| 27. |  | Damage to the liver or kidneys due to exposure to trichloromethane (chloroform). |  |  | Use of or handling of or exposure to fumes of or vapour containing trichloromethane (chloroform). |
| 28. |  | Central nervous system dysfunction and associated gastro-intestinal disorders due to exposure to chloromethane (methyl chloride). |  |  | Use of or handling of or exposure to fumes or vapours containing chloromethane (methyl chloride). |

Any occupation involving:

| | | |
|---|---|---|
| 29. | Peripheral neuropathy due to exposure to n-hexane or methyl n-butyl ketone. | Use of or handling of or exposure to the fumes of or vapours containing n-hexane or methyl n-butyl ketone. |
| 30. | (As from 24 March 1996) chrome dermatitis, or ulceration of the mucous membranes or epidermis, resulting from exposure to chromic acid, chromates or bi-chromates. | Use or handling of, or exposure to, chromic acid, chromates or bi-chromates. |

D. *Miscellaneous Conditions*

1. Pneumoconiosis.     Any occupation involving –

(*a*)   the mining, quarrying or working of silica rock or the working of dried quartzose sand or any dry deposit or dry residue of silica or any dry admixture containing such materials (including any occupation in which any of the aforesaid operations are carried out incidentally to the mining or quarrying of other minerals or to the manufacture of articles containing crushed or ground silica rock);

(*b*)   the handling of any of the materials specified in the foregoing sub-paragraph in or incidental to any of the operations mentioned therein, or substantial exposure to the dust arising from such operations.

Any occupation involving the breaking, crushing or grinding of flint or the working or handling of broken, crushed or ground flint or materials containing such flint, or substantial exposure to the dust arising from any of such operations.

Any occupation involving sand blasting by means of compressed air with the use of quartzose sand or crushed silica rock or flint, or substantial exposure to the dust arising from sand and blasting.

Any occupation involving work in a foundry or the performance of, or substantial exposure to the dust arising from, any of the following operations:

(*a*)    the freeing of steel castings from adherent siliceous substance;

(*b*)    the freeing of metal castings from adherent siliceous substance–

    (i)    by blasting with an abrasive propelled by compressed air, by steam or by a wheel; or

    (ii)    by the use of power-driven tools.

Any occupation in or incidental to the manufacture of china or earthenware (including sanitary earthenware, electrical earthenware and earthenware tiles), and any occupation involving substantial exposure to the dust arising therefrom.

Any occupation involving the grinding of mineral graphite, or substantial exposure to the dust arising from such grinding.

Any occupation involving the dressing of granite or any igneous rock by masons or the crushing of such materials, or substantial exposure to the dust arising from such operations.

Any occupation involving the use, or preparation for use, of a grindstone, or substantial exposure to the dust arising therefrom.

Any occupation involving–

(*a*)    the working or handling of asbestos or any admixture of asbestos;

(*b*)    the manufacture or repair of asbestos textiles or other articles containing or composed of asbestos;

|  |  | (c) | the cleaning of any machinery or plant used in any foregoing operations and of any chambers, fixtures and appliances for the collection of asbestos dust; |
|---|---|---|---|

(d)  substantial exposure to the dust arising from any of the foregoing operations.

Any occupation involving–

(a)  work underground in any mine in which one of the objects of the mining operations is the getting of any mineral;

(b)  the working or handling above ground at any coal or tin mine of any minerals extracted therefrom, or any operation incidental thereto;

(c)  the trimming of coal in any ship, barge, or lighter, or in any dock or harbour or at any wharf or quay;

(d)  the sawing, splitting or dressing of slate, or any operation incidental thereto.

Any occupation in or incidental to the manufacture of carbon electrodes by an industrial undertaking for use in the electrolytic extraction of aluminium from aluminium oxide, and any occupation involving substantial exposure to the dust arising therefrom.

Any occupation involving boiler scaling or substantial exposure to the dust arising therefrom.

[*Social Security (Industrial Injuries) (Prescribed Diseases) Regulations 1985 (SI 1985 No 967), Sch 1, Part II*].

Any occupation involving:

2.    Byssinosis.

Work in any room where any process up to and including the weaving process is performed in a factory in which the spinning or manipulation of raw or waste cotton or of flax, or the weaving of cotton or flax, is carried on.

| 3. | Diffuse mesothelioma (primary neoplasm of the mesothelium of the pleura or of the pericardium or of the peritoneum). | (a) | The working or handling of asbestos or any admixture of asbestos; or |
|----|----|----|----|
| | | (b) | the manufacture or repair of asbestos textiles or other articles containing or composed of asbestos; or |
| | | (c) | the cleaning of any machinery or plant used in any of the foregoing operations and of any chambers, fixtures and appliances for the collection of asbestos dust; or |
| | | (d) | substantial exposure to the dust arising from any of the foregoing operations. |
| 4. | (As from 24 March 1996) allergic rhinitis | | Exposure to any of the following agents: |
| | | (a) | isocyanates; |
| | | (b) | platinum salts; |
| | | (c) | fumes or dusts arising from the manufacture, transport or use of hardening agents (including epoxy resin curing agents) based on phthalic anhydride, tetrachlorophthalic anhydride, trimellitic anhydride or triethylene-tetramine; |
| | | (d) | fumes arising from the use of rosin as a soldering flux; |
| | | (e) | proteolytic enzymes; |
| | | (f) | animals including insects and other arthropods used for the purposes of research or education or in laboratories; |
| | | (g) | dusts arising from the sowing, cultivation, harvesting, drying, handling, milling, transport or storage of barley, oats, rye, wheat or maize, or the handling, milling, transport or storage of meal or flour made therefrom; |
| | | (h) | antibiotics; |
| | | (i) | cimetidine; |
| | | (j) | wood dust; |

| | |
|---|---|
| | (*k*) ispaghula; |
| | (*l*) castor bean dust; |
| | (*m*) ipecacuanha |
| | (*n*) azodicarbonamide; |
| | (*o*) animals including insects and other arthropods or their larval forms, used for the purposes of pest control or fruit cultivation, or the larval forms of animals used for the purposes of research or education or in laboratories; |
| | (*p*) glutaraldehyde; |
| | (*q*) persulphate salts or henna; |
| | (*r*) crustaceans or fish or products arising from these in the food processing industry; |
| | (*s*) reactive dyes; |
| | (*t*) soya bean; |
| | (*u*) tea dust; |
| | (*v*) green coffee bean dust; |
| | (*w*) fumes from stainless steel welding. |
| 5. Non-infective dermatitis of external origin (but excluding dermatitis due to ionising particles or electromagnetic radiations other than radiant heat). | Exposure to dust, liquid or vapour or any other external agent (except chromic acid, chromates or bi-chromates – as from 24 March 1996) capable of irritating the skin (including friction or heat but excluding ionising particles or electro-magnetic radiations other than radiant heat). |
| 6. Carcinoma of the nasal cavity or associated air sinuses (nasal carcinoma). | (*a*) Attendance for work in, on or about a building where wooden goods are manufactured or repaired; or |
| | (*b*) attendance for work in a building used for the manufacture of footwear or components of footwear made wholly or partly of leather or fibre board; or |

|  |  |  |
|---|---|---|
|  |  | (c)  attendance for work at a place used wholly or mainly for the repair of footwear made wholly or partly of leather or fibre board. |

Any occupation involving:

7.  Asthma which is due to exposure to any of the following agents:

Exposure to any of the agents set out in column 1 of this paragraph.

(a)  isocyanates;

(b)  platinum salts;

(c)  fumes or dusts arising from the manufacture, transport or use of hardening agents (including epoxy resin curing agents) based on phthalic anhydride, tetrachlorophthalic anhydride, trimellitic anhydride or triethylene-tetramine;

(d)  fumes arising from the use of rosin as a soldering flux;

(e)  proteolytic enzymes;

(f)  animals including insects and other anthropods used for the purposes of research or education or in laboratories;

(g)  dusts arising from the sowing, cultivation, harvesting, drying, handling, milling, transport or storage of barley, oats, rye, wheat or maize, or the handling, milling, transport or storage of meal or flour made therefrom;

(h)  antibiotics;

(i)  cimetidine;

(j)  wood dust;

(k)  ispaghula;

(*l*)    castor bean dust;

(*m*)    ipecacuanha;

(*n*)    azodicarbonamide;

(*o*)    animals including insects and other arthropods or their larval forms, used for the purposes of pest control or fruit cultivation, or the larval forms of animals used for the purposes of research, education or in laboratories;

(*p*)    glutaraldehyde;

(*q*)    persulphate salts or henna;

(*r*)    crustaceans or fish or products arising from these in the food processing industry;

(*s*)    reactive dyes;

(*t*)    soya bean;

(*u*)    tea dust;

(*v*)    green coffee bean dust;

(*w*)    fumes from stainless steel welding;

(*x*)    any other sensitising agent; (occupational asthma).

Moreover, the time at which a person shall be treated as having developed prescribed diseases B 12 and B 13, or occupational asthma due to exposure to agents specified in D 7 (o) to (x), is the first day on which that person is incapable of work, or suffering from a loss of faculty as a result of those diseases after 25 September 1991.

Any occupation involving:

8.    Primary carcinoma of the lung where there is accompanying evidence of one or both of the following:

(*a*)    The working or handling of asbestos or any admixture of asbestos; or

(*a*)    asbestosis;

(*b*)    the manufacture or repair of asbestos textiles or other articles containing or composed of asbestos; or

|  |  |  |  |
|---|---|---|---|
| | (*b*) bilateral diffuse pleural thickening. | (*c*) | the cleaning of any machinery or plant used in any of the foregoing operations and of any chambers, fixtures and appliances for the collection of asbestos dust; or |
| | | (*d*) | substantial exposure to the dust arising from any of the foregoing operations. |
| 9. | Bilateral diffuse pleural thickening. | (*a*) | The working or handling of asbestos or any admixture of asbestos; or |
| | | (*b*) | the manufacture or repair of asbestos textiles or other articles containing or composed of asbestos; or |
| | | (*c*) | the cleaning of any machinery or plant used in any of the foregoing operations and of any chambers, fixtures and appliances for the collection of asbestos dust; or |
| | | (*d*) | substantial exposure to the dust arising from any of the foregoing operations. |
| 10. | Primary carcinoma of the lung. | (*a*) | Work underground in a tin mine; or |
| | | (*b*) | exposure to bis (chloromethyl) ether produced during the manufacture of chloromethyl methyl ether; or |
| | | (*c*) | exposure to pure zinc chromate, calcium chromate or strontium chromate. |
| 11. | Primary carcinoma of the lung with silicosis. (Presumed not to be recrudescent.) [*SI 1993 No 862, Reg 5*]. | | Any occupation involving exposure to silica dust in the course of |
| | | (*a*) | manufacture of glass or pottery; |
| | | (*b*) | tunnelling in or quarrying sandstone or granite; |
| | | (*c*) | mining metal ores; |
| | | (*d*) | slate quarrying; |
| | | (*e*) | mining clay; |

| | |
|---|---|
| | (*f*)  use of siliceous materials as abrasives; |
| | (*g*)  cutting stone; |
| | (*h*)  stonemasonry; |
| | (*j*)  work in a factory. |
| | Any occupation involving: |
| 12.  Chronic bronchitis or emphysema (or both) (except where claimant is entitled to disablement benefit for pneumoconiosis, under Reg 22(1) – 'where a person is disabled by pneumoconiosis, or pneumoconiosis accompanied by tuberculosis – assessed at, at least, 50%, the effects of any emphysema and chronic bronchitis are to be treated as pneumoconiosis'). | Exposure to coal dust by reason of working underground in a coal mine for a period of, or periods amounting in the aggregate to, at least, 20 years (whether before or after 5 July 1948). |
| (In order to qualify for benefit a claimant must show | |
| (*a*)  by means of a chest radiograph that he has coal dust retention to at least the level of Category 1 in the ILO's publication 'The Classification of Radiographs of Pneumoconioses' (Revised Edition 1980, 8th Impression 1992); | |
| (*b*)  a forced expiratory volume in one second at least one litre below the mean value predicted in accordance with 'Lung function: Assessment and Application in Medicine' (Cotes, 4th Edition 1979) for a person of the claimant's age, height and sex, measured from the position of maximum inspiration with the claimant making maximum effort.) | |

[*Social Security (Industrial Injuries) (Prescribed Diseases) Regulations 1985 (SI 1985 No 967), Sch 1; Social Security (Industrial Injuries) (Prescribed Diseases) Amendment Regulations 1987 (SI 1987 No 335); Social Security (Industrial Injuries) (Prescribed Diseases) (Amendment No 2) Regulations 1987 (SI 1987 No 2112), Reg 2, Sch; Social Security (Industrial Injuries) (Prescribed Diseases) Amendment Regulations 1989 (SI 1989 No 1207), Reg 6, Sch; Social Security (Industrial Injuries) (Prescribed Diseases) Amendment Regulations 1990 (SI 1990 No 2269); Social Security (Industrial Injuries) (Prescribed Diseases) Amendment Regulations 1991 (SI 1991 No 1938); Social Security (Industrial Injuries) (Prescribed Diseases) Amendment Regulations 1993 (SI 1993 No 862); Social Security (Industrial Injuries) (Prescribed Diseases) Amendment (No 2) Regulations 1993 (SI 1993 No 1985); Social Security (Industrial Injuries) (Prescribed Diseases) Amendment Regulations 1994 (SI 1994 No 2343); Social Security (Industrial Injuries and Diseases) (Miscellaneous Amendments) Regulations 1996 (SI 1996 No 425)*].

# Occupiers' Liability

## Introduction

O3001      Inevitably, by far the greater part of this work details the duties of employers (and employees) both at common law, and by virtue of the *Health and Safety at Work etc. Act 1974* (*HSWA 1974*) and other kindred legislation. This notwithstanding, duties are additionally laid on persons (including companies and local authorities) who merely *occupy* premises which other persons either visit or carry out work activities upon, e.g. repair work or servicing. More particularly, persons in control of premises (see O3004 below for meaning of 'control'), that is, occupiers of premises and employers, where others work (*although not their employees*), have a duty under *HSWA 1974*, s 4 to take reasonable care towards such persons working on the premises. Failure to comply with this duty can lead to prosecution and a fine on conviction (see further ENFORCEMENT). This duty applies to premises not *exclusively* used for private residence, e.g. lifts/electrical installations in the *common parts* of a block of flats, and exists for the benefit of workmen repairing/servicing them (*Westminster City Council v Select Managements Ltd [1985] 1 AER 897*). Moreover, a person who is injured while working on or visiting premises, may be able to sue the occupier for damages, even though the injured person is not an employee. Statute law relating to this branch of civil liability (i.e. occupiers' liability) is to be found in the *Occupiers' Liability Act 1957* (*OLA 1957*) and, as far as trespassers are concerned, in the *Occupiers' Liability Act 1984* (*OLA 1984*). (In Scotland, the law is to be found in the *Occupiers' Liability (Scotland) Act 1960*.)

## Duties owed under the Occupiers' Liability Act 1957

O3002      An occupier of premises owes the same duty, the 'common duty of care', to all his lawful visitors. [*OLA 1957*, s 2(1)]. 'The common duty of care is a duty to take such care as in all the circumstances of the case is reasonable to see that the visitor will be reasonably safe in using the premises for the purposes for which he is invited or permitted by the occupier to be there.' [*OLA 1957*, s 2(2)]. Thus, a local authority which failed, in severe winter weather, to see that a path in school grounds was swept free of snow and treated with salt and was not in a slippery condition, was in breach of s 2, when a schoolteacher fell at 8.30 am and was injured (*Murphy v Bradford Metropolitan Council [1992] 2 AER 908*).

The duty extends only to requiring the occupier to do what is 'reasonable' in all the circumstances to ensure that the visitor will be safe. Some injuries occur where no one is obviously to blame. For example, in *Graney v Liverpool County Council (1995) (unreported)* an employee who slipped on icy paving slabs could not recover damages against his employer. The Court of Appeal held that many people slip on icy surfaces in cold weather – it did not follow that in this particular case the employer was to blame.

## Nature of the duty

O3003    *OLA 1957* is concerned only with civil liability. 'The rules so enacted in relation to an occupier of premises and his visitors shall also apply, in like manner and to like extent as the principles applicable at common law to an occupier of premises and his invitees or licensees would apply. . .' [*OLA 1957, s 1(3)*]. This contrasts with *HSWA 1974*, in which the obligations are predominantly penal measures enforced by the HSE (or some other 'enforcing authority'). *OLA 1957* cannot be enforced by a state agency – nor does it give rise to criminal liability. Action under *OLA 1957* must be brought in a private suit between parties.

The liability of an occupier towards lawful visitors at common law was generally based on negligence; so, too, is the liability under *OLA 1957*. It is never strict. In *Neame v Johnson [1993] PIQR 100*, a case concerning an ambulance man who was injured in the defendant's house when carrying him unconscious in a chair in poor lighting conditions, the ambulance man knocked over a pile of books stacked by a wall on a landing, and consequently slipped on a book, injuring himself. It was held that the pile of books did not create a 'reasonably foreseeable risk of injury', and so there was no liability. Nor does the duty of the occupier extend to replacing glass panels in an ageing building. In *McGivney v Golderslea Ltd (1997) (unreported)* the defendant owned a block of flats which had been built in 1955 – the glass in the door at the foot of the communal stairs had been installed at the same time. When the plaintiff, who was visiting a friend on the third floor, came down the stairs, he slipped and his hand went through the glass panel on the front door resulting in personal injuries. The plaintiff claimed that the defendant was in breach of *OLA 1957, s 2(2)*. However, at the time the flats were built the glass satisfied the building regulations then in force. Since 1955 building regulations have been updated and, in such a building being constructed today, stronger glass must be used such that on the balance of probabilities the plaintiff's accident would not have occurred. The Court of Appeal found that there was no duty on the defendant to replace the glass and the plaintiff's claim therefore failed.

The relationship of occupier and visitor is less immediate than that of employer and employee, and is not, as far as occupiers' liability is concerned, underwritten by compulsory insurance (but by public liability insurance, which is not obligatory but advisable).

## Who is an 'occupier'?

O3004    'Occupation' is not defined in the Act, which merely states that the 'rules regulate the nature of the duty imposed by law in consequence of a person's occupation or control of premises . . . but they (shall) not alter the rules of the common law as to the persons on whom a duty is so imposed or to whom it is owed . . .'. [*OLA 1957, s 1(2)*]. The meaning of 'occupation' must, therefore, be gleaned from the rules of common law. Where premises, including factory premises, are leased or subleased, control may be shared by lessor and lessee or by sublessor and sublessee. 'Wherever a person has a sufficient degree of control over premises that he ought to realise that any failure on his part to use care may result in injury to a person coming lawfully there, then he is an "occupier" and the person coming lawfully there is his "visitor" and the "occupier" is under a duty to his "visitor" to use reasonable care. In order to be an occupier it is not necessary for a person to have entire control over the premises. He need not have exclusive occupation. Suffice it that he has some degree of control with others' (per Lord Denning in *Wheat v E Lacon & Co Ltd [1965] 2 AER 700*). However, the 'degree of control' must be sufficient to give rise to a duty of care (*Bailey v Armes and another [1999] PLSCS 34*). In *Jordan v Achara (1988) 20 HLR 607*, the plaintiff, who was a meter reader, was injured when he fell down stairs in a basement of a house. The defendant landlord, who was the owner of the house, had divided it into flats. Because of arrears of payment, the electricity supply had been disconnected. The local authority, having arranged for it to be reconnected for the tenants, recovered payment by way of rents paid directly to the authority. It was held that the landlord was liable for the injury, under *OLA 1957*, since he was the occupier of the staircase and the passageway (where the injury occurred) and his duties continued in spite of the local authority being in receipt of rents.

Liability associated with dangers arising from maintenance and repair of premises will be that of the person responsible, under the lease or sublease, for maintenance and/or repair. 'The duty of the defendants here arose not out of contract, but because they, as the requisitioning authority, were in law in possession of the house and were in practice responsible for repairs . . . and this control imposed upon them a duty to every person lawfully on the premises to take reasonable care to prevent damage through want of repair' (per Denning LJ in *Greene v Chelsea BC [1954] 2 AER 318*, concerning a defective ceiling which collapsed, injuring the appellant, a licensee). Significantly also, managerial control constitutes 'occupation' (*Wheat v Lacon*, see above, concerning an injury to a customer at a public house owned by a brewery and managed by a manager – both were held to be 'in control'). Moreover, if a landlord leases part of a building but retains other parts, e.g. roof, common staircase, lifts, he remains liable for that part of the premises (*Moloney v Lambeth BC (1966) 64 LGR 440*, concerning a guest injured on a defective common staircase in a block of council flats). In *Ribee v Norrie, The Times, 22 November 2000*, it was held that a hostel owner, who did not live at the hostel, was liable as the occupier of the communal area for damage caused to a neighbouring property by a fire started from a smouldering cigarette left by an unidentified hostel resident. The Court of Appeal found that the hostel owner had retained exclusive possession of the common parts and had full control over those parts. He could have imposed rules preventing smoking in common areas. In this case, the court found that it was reasonable to anticipate that, in the absence of 'no smoking' rules, persons in the communal area might smoke and inadvertently discard lit cigarettes, eventually setting the area on fire and causing injury.

However, it is not the occupier's duty to make sure that the visitor is *completely safe*, but only reasonably so. For example, in *Berryman v London Borough of Hounslow, The Times, 18 December 1996*, the plaintiff injured her back when she was forced to carry heavy shopping up several flights of stairs because the lift in the block of flats maintained by the landlord was broken. The landlord's obligation to take care to ensure that the lift he provided was reasonably safe was discharged by employing competent contractors. There was no causal connection between the plaintiff's injury on the stairs and the absence of a lift service. In other words, the injury to the plaintiff was not a 'foreseeable consequence' of the broken lift.

## Premises

**O3005**    *OLA* regulates the nature of the duty imposed by law in consequence of a person's occupation of premises. [*OLA 1957, s 1(2)*]. This means that the duties are not *personal* duties but depend on occupation of *premises*; and extend to a 'person occupying, or having control over, any fixed or movable structure, including any vessel, vehicle or aircraft' [*OLA 1957, s 1(3)(a)*] (e.g. a car, *Houweling v Wesseler [1963] 40 DLR(2d) 956-Canada* or, more recently, a sea wall in *Staples v West Dorset District Council (1995) 93 LGR 536* (see O3006 below)). In *Bunker v Charles Brand & Son Ltd [1969] 2 AER 59* the defendants were contractors digging a tunnel for the construction of the Victoria Line of London Underground. To this end they used a large digging machine which moved forward on rollers. The plaintiff was injured when he slipped on the rollers. The defendants were held to be occupiers of the tunnel, even though it was owned by London Transport.

## To whom is the duty owed?

*Visitors*

O3006    Visitors to premises entitled to protection under the Act are both (*a*) invitees and (*b*) licensees. This means that protection is afforded to all lawful visitors, whether the visitors enter for the occupier's benefit (clients or customers) or for their own benefit (factory inspectors, policemen), though not to persons exercising a public or private way over premises. [*OLA 1957, s 2(6)*]. The House of Lords in *McGeown v Northern Ireland Housing Executive [1995] 1 AC 233* found that no duty of care was owed by an occupier of land over which a public right of way existed to persons lawfully exercising that right of way. They were not visitors for the purposes of *OLA 1957*, because use of a public right of way was incompatible with the concept of a visitor as defined in *OLA 1957*. This was clear because the defendant housing executive was found to have no power to exclude anyone from using the pathway. The concept of 'visitor' under the Act suggests the person in question has permission to be in a particular place at a particular time. Once a public right of way has been established, the question of permission being granted by the owner to those who choose to use the public right of way is irrelevant. They do so as of right and not by virtue of any licence or invitation.

Nevertheless, occupiers are under a duty to erect a notice warning visitors of the immediacy of a danger (*Rae (Geoffrey) v Mars (UK) [1990] 3 EG 80* where a deep pit was situated very close to the entrance of a dark shed, in which there was no artificial lighting, into which a visiting surveyor fell, sustaining injury. It was held that the occupier should have erected a warning). In some instances it may be necessary not only to provide proper warning notices but also to arrange for the supervision of visitors at the occupier's premises (*Farrant v Thanet District Council (1996) (unreported)*). Much will depend upon the facts of each case. For example, there was no duty on an employer to light premises at night, which were infrequently used by day and not occupied at night. It was sufficient to provide a torch (*Capitano v Leeds Eastern Health Authority, Current Law, October 1989* where a security officer was injured when he fell down a flight of stairs at night, while checking the premises following the sounding of a burglar alarm. The steps were formerly part of a fire escape route but were now infrequently used). In *Staples v West Dorset (1995) 93 LGR 536*, the court held that a council, as owners of the sea wall at Lyme Regis, owed no duty of care to warn a visitor of the obvious dangers of slipping on algae on the sea wall. The visitor was well able to evaluate the danger himself. Even if a warning sign had been erected, the court held that, in all probability, the visitor would have ignored it. In a more recent case, no warning sign was needed for an obvious danger of drowning in a National Trust pond, where the warning sign would have told the adult swimmer no more than he already knew (*Darby v National Trust, NLD, 29 January 2001*). This case appears to take a small step towards re-establishing a common sense view of the need for adults to take proper responsibility for their own actions.

*Trespassers*

O3007    '. . . a trespasser is not necessarily a bad man. A burglar is a trespasser; but so too is a law-abiding citizen who unhindered strolls across an open field. The statement that a trespasser comes upon land at his own risk has been treated as applying to all who trespass, to those who come for nefarious purposes and those who merely bruise the grass, to those who know their presence is resented and those who have no reason to think so.' (*Commissioner for Railways (NSW) v Cardy [1960] 34 ALJR 134*).

Common law defines a trespasser as a person who:

(*a*)    goes onto premises without invitation or permission; or

(*b*)    although invited or permitted to be on premises, goes to a part of the premises to which the invitation or permission does not extend; or

(*c*)    remains on premises after the invitation or permission to be there has expired; or

(*d*)    deposits goods on premises when not authorised to do so.

# Duty owed to trespassers, at common law and under the Occupiers' Liability Act 1984

## Common law

O3008    The position under common law used to be that an occupier was not liable for injury caused to a trespasser, unless the injury was either intentional or done with reckless disregard for the trespasser's presence (*R Addie & Sons (Collieries) Ltd v Dumbreck [1929] AC 358*). In more recent times, however, the common law has adopted an attitude of humane conscientiousness towards simple (as distinct from aggravated) trespassers. '. . . the question whether an occupier is liable in respect of an accident to a trespasser on his land would depend on whether a conscientious, humane man with his knowledge, skill and resources could reasonably have been expected to have done, or refrained from doing, before the accident, something which would have avoided it. If he knew before the accident that there was a substantial probability that trespassers would come I think that most people would regard as culpable failure to give any thought to their safety.' (*Herrington v British Railways Board [1972] 1 AER 749*). The effect of this House of Lords case was that it became possible for a trespasser to bring a successful action in negligence under the common law. However, the precise nature of the occupier's duty to the trespasser remained unclear, leading to Parliamentary intervention culminating in *OLA 1984*.

## Occupiers' Liability Act 1984

O3009    *OLA 1984* introduced a duty on an occupier in respect of trespassers, that is persons whether they have 'lawful authority to be in the vicinity or not' who may be at risk of injury on his premises. [*OLA 1984, s 1*]. Thus, an occupier owes a duty of care to a trespasser in respect of any injury suffered on the premises (either because of any danger due to the state of the premises, or things done or omitted to be done) [*OLA 1984, s 1(3)(a)*], in the following circumstances:

(*a*)    if he was aware of the danger or had reasonable grounds to believe that it exists;

(*b*)    if he knows or has reasonable grounds to believe that a trespasser is in the vicinity of the danger concerned, or that he may come into the vicinity of the danger; and

(*c*)    if the risk is one against which, in all the circumstances of the case, he may reasonably be expected to offer some protection.

Where under *OLA 1984*, the occupier is under a duty of care to the trespasser in respect of the risk, the standard of care is 'to take such care as is reasonable in all the circumstances of the case to see that he does not suffer injury on the premises by reason of the danger concerned'. [*OLA 1984, s 1(4)*]. The duty can be discharged by issuing a warning, e.g. posting notices warning of hazards; these, however, must be explicit and not merely vague. Thus, 'Danger' might not be sufficient whereas 'Highly Flammable Liquid Vapours – No Smoking' would be [*OLA 1984, s 1(5)*] (see O3015 below). Moreover, under *OLA 1984* there is no duty to persons who willingly accept risks (see O3016 below). However, the fact that an occupier has taken precautions to prevent persons going on to his land, where there is a danger, does not mean that the occupier has reason to believe that someone would be likely to come into the vicinity of the danger, thereby owing a duty to the trespasser, under *OLA 1984, s 1(4)* (*White v St Albans City and District Council, The Times, 12 March 1990*). In *Revil v Newbury, The Times, 3 November 1995*, the court considered the duty of an occupier to an intruder. It found that the intruder could recover damages despite being engaged in unlawful activities at the time the injury occurred. The defendant was held to have injured the intruder by using greater force than was justified (by shooting the intruder through a locked door) in protecting himself and his property. The doctrine of *ex turpi causa non oritur actio* (i.e. no cause of action may be founded on an immoral or illegal act) cannot, without more, be relied upon by the defendant to escape liability. Violence may be returned with necessary violence, but the force used must not exceed the limits of what is reasonable in all the circumstances. For the extent of the intruder's contributory negligence, see O3011 below.

## Children

O3010    In proper cases, 'an occupier must be prepared for children to be less careful than adults.' [*OLA 1957, s 2(3)(a)*]. Where an adult would be regarded as a trespasser, a child is likely to qualify as an implied licensee, and this in spite of the stricture that 'it is hard to see how infantile temptations can give rights however much they excuse peccadilloes' (per Hamilton LJ in *Latham v Johnson & Nephew Ltd [1913] 1 KB 398*). If there is something or some state of affairs on the premises (e.g. machinery, a boat, a pond, bright berries, a motor car, forklift truck, scaffolding), this may constitute a 'trap' to a child. If the child is then injured by the 'trap', the occupier will often be liable. Though sometimes the presence of a parent may be treated as an implied condition of the permission to enter premises (e.g. when children go on to premises at dusk – *Phipps v Rochester Corporation [1955] 1 AER 129*). Perhaps the current common law position regarding 'child-trespass' was best put as follows: 'The doctrine that a trespasser, however innocent, enters land at his own risk, that in no circumstances is he owed a duty of reasonable or any care by the owners or occupiers of the land, however conscious they may be of the likelihood of his presence and of the grave risk of terrible injury to which he will probably be exposed, may have been all very well when rights of property, particularly in land, were regarded as more sacrosanct than any other human right. . . It is difficult to see why today this doctrine should not be buried' (per Salmon LJ in *Herrington v British Railways Board*, concerning a six-year-old boy electrocuted on the defendant's electrified line) (but see O3017 below, *Titchener v British Railways Board*). Even though the children had been warned of the danger, the defendant company was still held liable in *Southern Portland Cement v Cooper [1974] AC 623*.

In *Jolley v London Borough of Sutton [2000] 1 WLR 1082*, a 14 year old schoolboy was awarded damages (reduced by 25 per cent for contributory negligence) for severe injuries sustained when he and a friend were attempting to restore an abandoned cabin cruiser on council land. In order to carry out repairs to the hull, the boys used a car jack to lift the front of the boat off the ground. However, the boat was rotten and no amount of work would have rendered the boat seaworthy. The plaintiff was underneath the boat when it fell on him. It was accepted that the council owed the child a duty of care under *OLA 1957, s 2(3)(a)*, and was negligent in failing to remove the boat, but the Court of Appeal held that the immediate cause of the accident was the propping up of the boat by the boys. The court criticised the approach traditionally taken in previous cases to accidents involving children: 'There was . . . a tendency to proceed from the proposition that once meddling by children was foreseeable then, whatever form it might take none of its manifestations could be regarded as unexpected. That approach was flawed.' Despite owing them a duty of care, it was the boys' actions which actually caused the accident and not the council's negligence in failing to remove the boat. However, allowing the plaintiff's appeal, the House of Lords found the council liable for the plaintiff's injuries, on the ground that an accident of the type which in fact occurred was reasonably foreseeable. The key factors leading to the decision were that since the council had conceded that it should have removed the boat because of the risk that children might suffer minor injury, the wider risk of more serious injury being caused by the condition of the boat, which could have been eliminated without the council incurring additional expense, also fell within the scope of the council's duty of care to children. Failure to remove the boat rendered the council liable for the plaintiff's injuries. As Lord Hoffman concluded: 'it has been repeatedly been said in cases about children that their ingenuity in finding unexpected ways of doing mischief to themselves and others should never be underestimated'.

### Contributory negligence

**O3011**  In a number of cases brought under *OLA 1957*, the question of contributory negligence is often considered and impacts considerably on the amount of damages eventually awarded. This may be because the duty on the occupier is only to take such care as is reasonable to see that the visitor will be reasonably safe in using his premises. Therefore, it is possible to imagine that, even where an occupier is found to have breached his duty of care, the injured party may also, by his own conduct, have contributed to the circumstances giving rise to the injury and may have exacerbated the severity of the injuries sustained. The *Law Reform (Contributory Negligence) Act 1945, s 1(1)* provides that 'where any person suffers damage as the result partly of his own fault and partly of the fault of another person, a claim in respect of that damage shall not be defeated by reason of the fault of the person suffering the damage, but the damage recoverable in respect thereof shall be reduced to such extent as the court thinks just having regard to the claimant's share in the responsibility of the damage'. In *Revil v Newbury* (see O3009 above), although the defendant's conduct was not reasonable, the adult intruder was found to be two-thirds to blame for the injuries he suffered and his damages were reduced accordingly. There is nothing to suggest that the above provision does not apply to children or trespassers. Lord *Denning in Gaugh v Thorn [1966] 3 AER 398*, held that '. . . a very young child cannot be guilty of contributory negligence. An older child may be. But it depends on the circumstances'. For example, in *Adams v Southern Electricity Board, The Times, 21 October 1993*, the Court of Appeal found that the electricity board owed a duty of care to an intelligent teenage boy to ensure that he was prevented from climbing up a pole in a high voltage electrical installation. The Board was found liable in part for the injuries that the boy suffered as a result of going up the pole, climbing over a defective anti-climbing device and onto a transformer.

## Dangers to guard against

**O3012**  The duty owed by an occupier to his lawful visitors is a 'common duty of care', so called since the duty is owed to both invitees and licensees, i.e. those having an interest in common with the occupier (e.g. business associates, customers, clients, salesmen) and those permitted by regulation/statute to be on the premises, e.g. factory inspectors/policemen. That duty requires that the dangers against which the occupier must guard are twofold: (*a*) structural defects in the premises; and (*b*) dangers associated with works/operations carried out for the occupier on the premises.

## Structural defects

O3013    As regards structural defects in premises, the occupier will only be liable if either he actually knew of a defect or foreseeably had reason to believe that there was a defect in the premises. Simply put, the occupier would not incur liability for the existence of latent defects causing injury or damage, unless he had *special* knowledge in that regard, e.g. a faulty electrical circuit, unless he were an electrician; whereas, he would be liable for patent (i.e. obvious) structural defects, e.g. an unlit hole in the road. This duty now extends to 'uninvited entrants', e.g. trespassers, under *OLA 1984, s 1*.

## Workmen on occupier's premises

O3014    'An occupier may expect that a person, in the exercise of his calling, will appreciate and guard against any special risks ordinarily incident to it, so far as the occupier leaves him free to do so.' [*OLA 1957, s 2(3)(b)*]. This has generally been taken to imply that risks associated with system or method of work on customer premises are the exclusive responsibility of the employer (not the customer or occupier) (*General Cleaning Contractors Ltd v Christmas* (see W9035 WORK AT HEIGHTS)), though how far this rule now applies specifically to window cleaners themselves is doubtful (see *King v Smith* at W9035 WORK AT HEIGHTS). This means that risks associated with the system or method of work on third party premises are the responsibility of the employer not the occupier (*General Cleaning Contractors Ltd v Christmas [1952] 2 AER 1110*, concerning a window cleaner who failed to take proper precautions in respect of a defective sash window: it was held that there was no liability on the part of the occupier, but liability on the part of the employer (see EMPLOYERS' DUTIES TO THEIR EMPLOYEES)). This has been confirmed more recently in the unreported case of *Makepeace v Evans Brothers (Reading) (A firm) (1) Alfred Macalpine Construction Ltd (2)*, in which an employee sued his employer and the main contractor for injuries suffered when a scaffold tower provided by the main contractor collapsed. The employer was found liable but it was held that an occupier would not usually be liable to an employee of a contractor employed to carry out work at the occupier's premises if the employee was injured as a result of any unsafe system of work used by the employee and the contractor. The occupier will only incur liability for a structural defect in premises which the oncoming workman would not normally guard against as part of a safe system of doing his job, i.e. against 'unusual' dangers. 'And with respect to such a visitor at least, we consider it settled law that he, using reasonable care on his part for his own safety, is entitled to expect that the occupier shall on his part use reasonable care to prevent damage from unusual danger, which he knows or ought to know' (per Willes J in *Indermaur v Dames [1866] LR 1 CP 274*, concerning a gasfitter testing gas burners in a sugar refinery who fell into an unfenced shaft and was injured).

Case law has highlighted some liability on the part of occupiers to particular classes of employees, namely firemen and, more recently, window cleaners (*King v Smith [1995] ICR 339*).

The law is not entirely settled in the case of firemen (*Sibbald v Sher Bros, The Times, 1 February 1981*): '(It (is) . . . very unlikely that the duty of care owed by the occupier to workers was the same as that owed to firemen,' (per Lord Fraser of Tullybelton), (but) it is arguable that a 'fireman (is) a "neighbour" of the occupier in the sense of Lord Atkin's famous dictum in *Donoghue v Stevenson [1932] AC 562*, so that the occupier owes him some duty of care, as for instance, to warn firemen of an unexpected danger or trap of which he knew or ought to know' (per Waller LJ in *Hartley v British Railways Board (1981) SJ 125*). This was confirmed in the case of *Simpson v A L Dairies Farm Ltd [2001] AER (D) 31*, when it was held that an occupier was liable for failing to warn a fireman of the danger of a concealed concrete ledge which had been temporarily covered by standing water.

One's neighbour was defined in law as follows: 'persons who are so closely and directly affected by my act that I ought reasonably to have them in contemplation as being so affected when I am directing my mind to the acts or omissions which are called in question' (per Lord Atkin in *Donoghue v Stevenson [1932] AC 562*).

In summary, an occupier will be liable:

(*a*)   if he exposes a fireman to the risk of injury/death over and above the normal risks (see further F5053 (*a*) and (*b*) FIRE AND FIRE PRECAUTIONS); and

(*b*)   in accordance with the general principles of negligence, in non-emergency situations (as per *Ogwo v Taylor [1987] 3 AER 961*, applying the 'neighbour' principle of *Donoghue v Stevenson*).

In both cases, the basis of action is negligence, either at common law or under *OLA 1957* or both.

### Dangers associated with works being done on premises

O3015   Where work is being done on premises by a contractor, the occupier is not liable if he:

(*a*)   took care in selecting a competent contractor; and

(*b*)   satisfied himself that the work was being properly done by the contractor.

*[OLA 1957, s 2(4)(b)]*.

As regards (*b*) it may be highly desirable (indeed necessary) for an occupier to delegate the 'duty of satisfaction', especially where complicated building/ engineering operations are being carried out, to a specialist, e.g. an architect, geotechnical engineer. Not to do so, in the interests of safety of visitors, is probably negligent. 'In the case of the construction of a substantial building, or of a ship, I should have thought that the building owner, if he is to escape subsequent tortious liability for faulty construction, should not only take care to contract with a competent contractor . . . but also cause that work to be supervised by a properly qualified professional . . . such as an architect or surveyor . . . I cannot think that different principles can apply to precautions during the course of construction, if the building owner is going to invite a third party to bring valuable property on to the site during construction' (per Mocatta J in *AMF International Ltd v Magnet Bowling Ltd [1968] 2 AER 789*).

# Waiver of duty and the Unfair Contract Terms Act 1977 (UCTA)

O3016   Where damage was caused to a visitor by a danger of which he had been warned by the occupier (e.g. by notice), an explicit notice, e.g. 'Highly Flammable Liquid Vapours – No Smoking' (as distinct from a vague notice such as 'Fire Hazards') used to absolve an occupier from liability. Now, however, such notices are ineffective (except in the case of trespassers, see O3008 above) and do not exonerate occupiers. Thus: 'a person cannot by reference to any contract term or to a notice given to persons generally or to particular persons exclude or restrict his liability for death or personal injury resulting from negligence'. [*UCTA 1977, s 2*]. Such explicit notices are, however, a defence to an occupier when sued for negligent injury by a simple trespasser under *OLA 1984*. As regards negligent damage to property, a person can restrict or exclude his liability by a notice or contract term, but such notice or contract term must be 'reasonable', and it is incumbent on the occupier to prove that it is in fact reasonable. [*UCTA 1977, ss 2(2), 11*].

The question of whether the defendant did what was reasonable fairly to bring to the notice of the plaintiff the existence of a particularly onerous condition, regarding his statutory rights, was considered in *Interfoto Picture Library Ltd v Stiletto Visual Programmes Ltd [1989] QB 433*. It was held that for a condition seeking to restrict statutory rights (e.g. under *OLA 1957*) to be effective it must have been fairly brought to the attention of a party to the contract by way of some clear indication which would lead an ordinary sensible person to realise, at or before the time of making the contract, that such a term relating to personal injury was to be included in the contract.

## Risks willingly accepted – 'volenti non fit injuria'

O3017    'The common duty of care does not impose on an occupier any obligation to a visitor in respect of risks willingly accepted as his by the visitor'. [*OLA 1957, s 2(5)*]. However, this 'defence' has generally not succeeded in industrial injuries claims. This is similarly the case with occupiers' liability claims (*Burnett v British Waterways Board [1973] 2 AER 631* where a lighterman was held not to be bound by the terms of a notice erected by the respondent, even though he had seen it many times and understood it). This decision has since been reinforced by the *Unfair Contract Terms Act 1977*. 'Where a contract term or notice purports to exclude or restrict liability for negligence a person's agreement to or awareness of it is not of itself to be taken as indicating his voluntary acceptance of any risk.' [*UCTA 1977, s 2(3)*]. *OLA 1957* makes clear that there may be circumstances in which even an explicit warning will not absolve the occupier from liability. Nevertheless, the occupier is entitled to expect a reasonable person to appreciate certain obvious dangers and take appropriate action to ensure his safety. In those circumstances no warning would appear to be required. It was not necessary, for example, to warn an adult of sound mind that it was dangerous to go near the edge of a cliff in *Cotton v Derbyshire Dales District Council, The Times, 20 June 1994*. This is not, however, the position with respect to trespassers. *OLA 1984, s 1(6)* states, 'No duty is owed . . . to any person in respect of risks willingly accepted as his by that person . . .'. This applies even if the trespasser is a child (see O3010 above) (*Titchener v British Railways Board 1984 SLT 192* where a 15 year old girl and her boyfriend aged 16 had been struck by a train. The boy was killed and the girl suffered serious injuries. They had squeezed through a gap in a fence to cross the line as a short-cut to a disused brickworks which was regularly used. It was held by the House of Lords that the respondent did not owe a duty to the girl to do more than they had done to maintain the fence. It would have been 'quite unreasonable' for the respondent to maintain an impenetrable and unclimbable fence. But the 'duty (to maintain fences) will tend to be higher with a very young or a very old person than with a normally active and intelligent adult or adolescent' (per Lord Fraser)). In *Adams v Southern Electricity Board, The Times, 21 October 1993*, the electricity board was held to be liable to a teenage trespasser for injuries sustained when he climbed on to apparatus by means of a defective anti-climbing device.

In the curious case of *Arthur v Anka [1996] 2 WLR 602* a car was parked without permission in a private car park. It was clamped but the driver removed his vehicle with the clamp still attached. The owner of the car park sued the driver for the return of the wheel clamp and payment of the fine for illegal parking. The question of *volenti* was considered in detail. The judge held that the owner parked his car in full knowledge that he was not entitled to do so and that he was therefore consenting to the consequences of his action (payment of the fine); he could not complain after the event. The effect of this consent was to render conduct lawful which would otherwise have been tortious. By voluntarily accepting the risk that his car might be clamped, the driver accepted the risk that the car would remain clamped until he paid the reasonable cost of clamping and de-clamping.

# Actions against factory occupiers

O3018    The *Workplace (Health, Safety and Welfare) Regulations 1992 (SI 1992 No 3004)* which came into force, in so far as existing workplaces are concerned, on 1 January 1996 now apply with respect to the health, safety and welfare of persons in a defined workplace. The application of the Regulations is not confined to factories and offices – they also affect public buildings such as hospitals and schools, but they do not apply to, for example, construction sites and quarries. Employers, persons who have control of the workplace and occupiers are all subject to the Regulations, the provisions of which address the environmental management and condition of buildings, such as the day-to-day considerations of ventilation, temperature control and lighting and potentially dangerous activities such as window cleaning. In many ways the Regulations reflect the obligations imposed by the old *Factories Act 1961*. For example, *Regulation 12(3)* requires floors and traffic routes, 'so far as is reasonably practicable', to be kept free from obstacles or substances which may cause a person to 'slip, trip or fall'. These Regulations also closely mirror the general obligation placed on employers by *HSWA 1974, s 2* to ensure so far as is reasonably practicable, the health, safety and welfare of their employees whilst at work. Breach of these Regulations gives rise to civil liability by virtue of *HSWA 1974, s 47(2)* (for criminal liability, see O3019 below and ENFORCEMENT).

An approved Code of Practice and Guidance to the Regulations is available from the Health and Safety Commission.

# Occupier's duties under HSWA 1974

O3019    In addition to civil liabilities under *OLA 1957* and at common law, occupiers of buildings also have duties, the failure of which to carry out can lead to criminal liability under *HSWA 1974*. More particularly, 'each person who has, to any extent, control of premises (i.e. "non-domestic" premises) or the means of access thereto or egress therefrom or of any plant or substance in such premises' must do what is reasonably practicable to see that the premises, means of access and egress and plant/substances on the premises, are safe and without health risks. [*HSWA 1974, s 4(2)*]. This section applies in the case of (*a*) non-employees and (*b*) non-domestic premises. [*HSWA 1974, s 4(1)*]. In other words, it places health and safety duties on persons and companies letting or sub-letting premises for work purposes, even though the persons working in those premises are not employees of the lessor/ sublessor. The duty also extends to non-working persons, e.g. children at a play centre (*Moualem v Carlisle City Council (1994) 158 JPN 786*). As with most other forms of leasehold tenure, the person who is responsible for maintenance and repairs of the leased premises is the person who has 'control' (see, by way of analogy, O3004 above). [*HSWA 1974, s 4(3)*]. Included as 'premises' are common parts of a block of flats. These are 'non-domestic' premises (*Westminster City Council v Select Manage-*

*ments Ltd [1985] 1 AER 897* which held that being a 'place' or 'installation on land', such areas are 'premises'; and they are not 'domestic', since they are in common use by the occupants of more than one private dwelling).

Moreover, the reasonableness of the measures which a person is required to take to ensure the safety of those premises is to be determined in the light of his knowledge of the expected use for which the premises have been made available and of the extent of his control and knowledge, if any, of the use thereafter. More particularly, if premises were not a reasonably foreseeable cause of danger to anyone acting in a way a person might reasonably be expected to act, in circumstances that might reasonably be expected to occur during the carrying out of the work, further measures would not be required against unknown and unexpected events (*Mailer v Austin Rover Group [1989] 2 AER 1087* where an employee of a firm of cleaning contractors, whilst cleaning one of the appellant's paint spray booths and the sump underneath it, was killed by escaping fumes. The contractors had been instructed by the appellants not to use paint thinners from a pipe in the booth (which the appellants had turned off but not capped) and only to enter the sump (where the ventilator would have been turned off) with an approved safety lamp and when no one was working above. Contrary to those instructions, an employee used thinners from the pipe, which had then entered the sump below, where the deceased was working with a non-approved lamp, and an explosion occurred. It was held that the appellant was not liable for breach of *HSWA 1974, s 4(2)*).

When considering criminal liability of an occupier under *HSWA 1974* in relation to risks to outside contractors, *s 4* is likely to be of less significance in the future because of the decision of the House of Lords in *R v Associated Octel [1994] ICR 281*, a decision which in effect enables *HSWA 1974, s 3* to be used against occupiers. *Section 3(1)* provides that 'It shall be the duty of every employer to conduct his undertaking in such a way as to ensure, so far as is reasonably practicable, that persons not in his employment who may be affected thereby are not thereby exposed to risks to their health or safety'. The decision establishes that an occupier can still be conducting his undertaking by engaging contractors to do work, even where the activities of the contractor are separate and not under the occupier's control. *Section 3* therefore requires the occupier to take steps to ensure the protection of contractors' employees from risks not merely arising from the physical state of the premises but also from the process of carrying out the work itself.

# Offices and Shops

## Introduction

O5001    The principal health, safety and welfare requirements in offices and shops are contained in the *Workplace (Health, Safety and Welfare) Regulations 1992 (SI 1992 No 3004)* (see W11001 WORKPLACES – HEALTH, SAFETY AND WELFARE). There are only a few remaining provisions of the *Offices, Shops and Railway Premises Act 1963* still in force (although much of the old Act has been preserved in so far as it applies to registrars of births, deaths and marriages and to the police). Although not so intrinsically or potentially hazardous as factories and other workshops, offices and shops can still pose dangers to employees, visitors and members of the public. This chapter considers the main hazards in offices and shops along with recommended remedial action as well as the topical issue of VDUs. Moreover, since shops are workplaces visited daily by members of the public, civil liability relating to injuries suffered by customers has tended to be strict.

## Hazards in offices

O5002    The average office would appear to be a relatively safe place compared with, say, a typical factory or workshop. Nevertheless, injuries do occur to office staff by way of slips, trips and falls, often when moving equipment or carrying loads or passing along blocked corridors or passageways. Electricity transmission can also pose dangers as a result of defective plugs or sockets, or of inappropriate loads, and, more topically, VDUs have attracted (and continue to do so) a considerable volume of litigation. In addition, photocopying equipment requires particular precautions. There are certain specified machines which cannot be operated in offices unless the operator has been adequately trained and is under supervision.

Fire is probably the main office hazard. This may be simply associated with human carelessness, such as the inadvertent disposal of cigarette ends. A wide range of flammable materials can be found in offices: spirit-based cleaning fluids, floor polishes, paper and many forms of packaging materials. All these substances are fire hazards if not controlled. Equally important in combating risk of fire is the maintenance of high safety standards in respect of electricity. It is important to bear in mind the following:

(*a*)    the provision of sufficient socket outlets and the minimal use of adaptors;

(*b*)    sockets should not be overloaded;

(*c*)    electrical equipment should be regularly tested;

(*d*)    taped joints for connecting cables should be prohibited;

(*e*)    plugs and leads should be regularly inspected in order to identify damage to cables and signs of overheating;

(*f*)    equipment should be switched off before it is unplugged or cleaned;

(*g*)    faulty switches should be identified;

(*h*)    malfunctioning electrical equipment should be reported.

The introduction of computerised equipment and word processors can create electrical hazards. The fact is that many of the older offices were not designed for so much electrical equipment, with the result that there is overloading with frequent use of multi-point adaptors, extension leads, wiring of more than one appliance into a 13 amp plug and overfilling of riser shafts. In older offices without central heating, there are freestanding heating appliances which can lead to further overloading of the electricity supply. There is also the risk of such appliances falling or being knocked over, leading to the danger of fire on the premises.

# Visual display units and lighting

## Health factors

O5003    The introduction of new technology, in the form of VDUs, has incurred, over the last decade, a vast amount of complaints from operators, the principal complaint being eye strain or visual fatigue. It is thought that 1 in 3 VDU operators suffers from eye strain, back pain or general lethargy, and 1 in 4 from headaches attributable to glare discomfort and terminal reflections. Moreover, incidence of ocular discomfort among VDU operators, such as secretaries, journalists, finance dealers and graphic designers, has been reported as being twice that of the rest of the national workforce.

Visual fatigue is common to many tasks requiring a high degree of concentration and visual perception. Common symptoms are eye irritation, aggravated by rubbing; redness and soreness, together with temporary blurring and visual confusion. Spots, shapes in front of the eyes and chromatic effects (i.e. the sensation of coloured shapes before the eyes) surrounding viewed objects, also occur. Some people experience a fear or dislike of light or bright lights (photophobia), resulting in the need to wear dark glasses. Headaches are the most common symptom.

Generally, visual fatigue has a varied and complex pattern of symptoms, a component generally being anxiety. It is a temporary and reversible phenomenon, current optical wisdom arguing that it is impossible to damage eyes through the use of VDUs. Age, visual sharpness and performance are all significant in assessing whether an operator is likely to be affected by visual fatigue (see O5004 below). VDU operators can also suffer from musculo-skeletal strain – stiffness and tenderness of the neck, shoulders and forearms as well as Repetitive Strain Injury (RSI) now referred to as work related upper limb disorder (WRULD) (see further OCCUPATIONAL HEALTH AND DISEASES) caused by repeated finger, hand/arm movements emanating from use of a keyboard, and also stress. More rarely, they may suffer from photogenic epilepsy. Compensation has been awarded to employees on the ground of RSI (see *McSherry and Lodge v British Telecom Ltd [1992] 3 Med LR 129*), sometimes in excess of £200,000.

Methods of combating visual fatigue include investment in the installation of a non-reflective, protective VDU glare filter screen varying employees' visual tasks, with only a specified percentage (say 50 per cent) of a working day devoted to VDU work, and a specified maximum continuous period of work (say 1 hour), followed by a break (say of 15 minutes), location of the display screen to minimise glare, correct specification and use of window coverings, etc.

## Operational considerations

O5004    Visual fatigue can be associated with:

(*a*)  poor legibility, due to factors in the VDU such as 'flicker', 'shimmer' and 'jitter', which are directly related to the 'refresh rate' (i.e. the rate at which the phosphors return to luminosity after they have faded) of the display system;

(*b*)  poor definition of the screen characters against the background field;

(*c*)  glare;

(*d*)  unsuitable background lighting;

(*e*)  poor quality source material; and

(*f*)  visual defects on the part of the operator.

Items (*a*) to (*d*) above can be corrected through good VDU and workplace design. Very few people, however, have perfect vision, the ability to see varying with age, and the presence or absence of visual defects, e.g. myopia (short-sightedness) and hypermetropia (long-sightedness). On this basis, it is recommended that vision screening should be a standard feature of any pre-employment health examination for VDU operators, followed by further vision screening at intervals. Operators may need modifications to their prescription lenses to undertake such work. They should consult their optician whenever discomfort or visual fatigue is experienced, informing the optician of the type of work they perform (see O5005, O5006 below for statutory eyetest rights).

## Statutory requirements relating to VDUs – the Health and Safety (Display Screen Equipment) Regulations 1992

O5005     The *Health and Safety (Display Screen Equipment) Regulations 1992 (SI 1992 No 2792)* impose the following duties on employers:

(1)  To assess (and review) health and safety risks to persons exposed at VDU workstations, whether or not provided by the employer, and reduce risks so identified. [*Health and Safety (Display Screen Equipment) Regulations 1992 (SI 1992 No 2792), Reg 2*].

Given the health risks involved (see O5003 above) and the possibility of liability being incurred by an employer for musculo-skeletal disorders, employers will have to assess the extent of such risks in the case of display screen workers who are:

(*a*)  employees, including home-workers;

(*b*)  employees of other employers ('temps'); or

(*c*)  self-employed (e.g. self-employed temps, journalists).

Workstations used at home will also have to be assessed.

The risk assessment should be:

(i)  systematic, with investigation of non-obvious causes, e.g. poor posture may be a response to glare rather than poor furniture;

(ii)  appropriate to the foreseeable degree of risk – itself depending on duration, intensity or difficulty of work; and

(iii)  comprehensive, covering organisational, job, workplace and individual factors.

Probably the best form of assessment is an ergonomic checklist and employees must have received the necessary training (see O5007 below) before completing such checklist. Once done, the assessment must be recorded, if necessary electronically, and kept readily accessible. Assessments should be reviewed in the following cases:

(A)    major change to software;

(B)    major change to hardware;

(C)    major change to workstation furniture;

(D)    relocation of workstation;

(E)    significant modification of lighting; and

(F)    change in the user's VDU related workload, either in terms of quantity or complexity.

(2)    To ensure that display screen equipment (DSE) work is periodically interrupted by breaks or changes of activity so as to reduce the workload of employees. [*Health and Safety (Display Screen Equipment) Regulations 1992 (SI 1992 No 2792), Reg 4*].

(3)    Provide employees with:

(*a*)    initial eye/eyesight tests on request;

(*b*)    subsequent eye/eyesight tests at regular intervals, with consent of the operator;

(*c*)    additional eye/eyesight tests on request, where users are encountering visual difficulties;

(*d*)    special corrective appliances where tests show that normal corrective appliances cannot be used

[*Health and Safety (Display Screen Equipment) Regulations 1992 (SI 1992 No 2792), Reg 5*]

(employees cannot, however, be required to take eyesight tests against their will [*Reg 5(6)*]);

(*e*)    adequate health and safety training in use of the workstation and whenever the workstation is substantially modified [*Health and Safety (Display Screen Equipment) Regulations 1992 (SI 1992 No 2792), Reg 6*] (see further O5007 below); and

(*f*)    adequate health and safety information in connection with the workstation and in order to enable them to comply with *Regs 2–6* [*Health and Safety (Display Screen Equipment) Regulations 1992 (SI 1992 No 2792), Reg 7*].

Penalties for breach of these regulations coincide with those for breach of *HSWA 1974* (see ENFORCEMENT).

## Employee eye care

**O5006**    Employers can arrange with individual opticians to provide care and examination on site or at an optician's practice; the employee cannot elect which. Sometimes, however, an employer may wish to offer 'vision screening'; if an employee does not want to be screened he can opt for full eye examination; similarly, if he is vision-screened but still has visual symptoms when using the screen. For this reason, many opticians provide a 'vision-work' service, offering on-site facilities for screening and full eyesight testing.

## Training and health and safety information

O5007    (*a*)    *Information* should be provided to all operators of VDUs or to employees and/or agency workers and should relate to:

(i)    risks from display screen equipment    – employees

(ii)    risk assessments (see O5005 above) and    – employees of others
measures to reduce risks and any risks    (e.g. agency workers or
resulting from changes to the workstation    temps)

– self-employed opera-
tors

(iii)    breaks/activity changes    – employees

(iv)    eye/eyesight tests    – employees

(v)    initial training    – employees

(vi)    training following modification of workstation – employees

(*b*)    *Training* (which is only required to be given to employees) should relate to:

(i)    comfort of posture and importance of postural change;

(ii)    use of adjustment mechanisms, especially furniture;

(iii)    use and arrangement of components for good posture and to prevent overreaching and avoid glare and reflections;

(iv)    need for regular cleaning of screens and other equipment;

(v)    need for breaks and activity changes.

## Workstation equipment

O5008    (*a*)    *Display screens* must have

(i)    well-defined, clean characters,

(ii)    stable, flicker-free image,

(iii)    adjustable brightness/contrast,

(iv)    easy swivel/tilt, and

(v)    be free of glare/reflections.

(*b*)    *Keyboards* must

(i)    be tiltable and separate from display,

(ii)    have space in front to support arms/hands,

(iii)    have matt, non-reflective surfaces,

(iv)    have adequately contrasted symbols.

(*c*)    *Work desks* must have

(i)    a large, low reflectance surface,

(ii)    a document holder, if necessary,

| | | | |
|---|---|---|---|
| ① | SCREEN: READABLE AND STABLE IMAGE, ADJUSTABLE, GLARE FREE | ⑥ | LIGHTING: PROVISION OF ADEQUATE CONTRAST, NO DIRECT OR INDIRECT GLARE OR REFLECTIONS |
| ② | KEYBOARD: USABLE, ADJUSTABLE, KEY TOPS LEGIBLE | ⑦ | DISTRACTING NOISE MINIMISED |
| ③ | WORK SURFACE: ALLOW FLEXIBLE ARRANGEMENT, SPACIOUS, GLARE FREE, DOCUMENT HOLDER AS APPROPRIATE | ⑧ | NO EXCESSIVE HEAT, ADEQUATE HUMIDITY |
| ④ | WORK CHAIR: APPROPRIATE ADJUSTABILITY PLUS FOOT REST | ⑨ | SOFTWARE: APPROPRIATE TO THE TASK AND ADAPTED TO USER CAPABILITIES, PROVIDE FEEDBACK ON SYSTEM STATUS, NO CLANDESTINE MONITORING |
| ⑤ | LEG ROOM AND CLEARANCES: TO FACILITATE POSTURAL CHANGE | | |

*VDUs – User/Equipment Interface*

    (iii)    adequate space for comfortable position.

  (*d*)    *Work chairs* must

    (i)    be stable but allow worker easy freedom of movement,

    (ii)    be adjustable in backrest height/tilt and seat height,

    (iii)    have a footrest available, if necessary.

## Workstation environment

O5009    The following environmental conditions should be satisfied.

  (*a*)    *Space* – it should be designed to allow for change of posture.

  (*b*)    *Lighting* – there should be satisfactory lighting conditions, secondary adjustable lighting, and glare should be avoided by layout and design of light fittings.

  (*c*)    *Heat* – equipment heat should not cause discomfort.

(d)   *Radiation* – all electromagnetic radiation (except visible light) should be reduced to negligible levels.

(e)   *Humidity* – an adequate level of humidity should be maintained.

(f)   *Operator/computer interface* – the workstation should:

   (i)   be easy to use,

   (ii)   be adapted to user's level of knowledge,

   (iii)   have a system to provide feedback to user,

   (iv)   have information displayed in a format and at a pace adapted to operator,

   (v)   accommodate the principles of software ergonomics.

Clandestine monitoring of an operator's performance is not permitted.


## Workstation design

O5010   In terms of workstation design, reference should be made to the guidelines contained in BS EN ISO 9241: Ergonomic Requirements for Work with Visual Display Terminals, and in particular to Part 5 of this Standard.

Document holders should be used whenever appropriate, to reduce the head and body movements when transferring gaze from documents to screen and back again.


## Lighting

O5011   The VDU should, wherever possible, be positioned so that office lights or windows do not reflect directly on the face of the screen.

Office lighting should be adequate but not too bright to interfere with the screen image. Harsh lighting contrasts should be avoided. (See L5009 LIGHTING FOR GUIDANCE ON ILLUMINATION LEVELS.)

Glare can be reduced by:

(a)   changing the position of the VDU screen to eliminate reflections from the screen or other surfaces, e.g. by siting the VDU parallel to fluorescent light fittings, or so that the VDU does not pick up reflections from windows;

(b)   using a non-reflective VDU screen or filter over the screen;

(c)   reducing the brightness of the light source;

(d)   fitting lights with suitable diffusers; and

(e)   as a last resort, changing the position of troublesome lights.

In certain cases, the provision of window blinds may be necessary where there is reflection from the screen face. Generally, any sort of light used by one operator whether emanating from the screen or otherwise, should be screened from other operators. [*Health and Safety (Display Screen Equipment) Regulations 1992 (SI 1992 No 3004), Sch 1*].

## Equipment maintenance

O5012    Regular maintenance and servicing of equipment should be undertaken in accordance with the manufacturer's instructions. Where there is evidence of screen flicker, poor contrast adjustment or other faults, the maintenance contractor or supplier should be contacted.

## Display screens and the working environment

O5013    As regards *display screens*:

(*a*)    characters on screen must be well-defined and clearly formed, of adequate size with adequate spacing between characters and lines;

(*b*)    the image on the screen must be stable, with no flickering;

(*c*)    brightness and contrast between characters must be easily adjustable;

(*d*)    the screen must swivel and tilt easily;

(*e*)    it must be possible to use a separate base for the screen or an adjustable table;

(*f*)    the screen must be free of reflective glare and discomfort-causing reflections.

As regards the *keyboard*:

(*a*)    it must be tiltable and separate from the screen so as to allow the user to find a comfortable working position;

(*b*)    the space in front of the keyboard must provide support for the hands/arms of the user;

(*c*)    it must have a matt surface and avoid reflective glare;

(*d*)    arrangement of keyboard/characteristics of keys must facilitate the use of the keyboard;

(*e*)    symbols on keys must be adequately contrasted and legible from the design working position.

As regards the *work desk or work surface*:

(*a*)    it must have a sufficiently large, low-reflectance surface and allow flexible arrangement of screen, keyboard, documents etc.;

(*b*)    the document holder must be stable and adjustable so as to minimise the need for uncomfortable head/eye movements;

(*c*)    there must be adequate space for users to find a comfortable position.

As regards the *work chair*:

(*a*)    it must be stable and allow the user freedom of movement and a comfortable position;

(*b*)    the seat must be adjustable in height;

(*c*)    the seat back must be adjustable in height and tilt;

(*d*)    a footrest must be available, if needed.

As regards the *working environment*:

(*a*)    the workstation must be dimensioned and designed so as to allow sufficient space for the user to change position/vary movements;

(*b*) room lighting/spot lighting must ensure satisfactory lighting conditions and appropriate contrast between screen and background environment. Disturbing glare/reflections on the screen must be prevented by co-ordinating the workplace and the workstation layout with positioning of artificial light sources;

(*c*) workstations must be so designed as to avoid glare from windows, transparent or translucid walls, as well as distracting reflections on screen;

(*d*) equipment should not be too noisy or produce excess heat, and radiation, with the exception of the visible part of the electro-magnetic spectrum, must be reduced to negligible levels, and an adequate humidity level must be maintained.

As regards the *user/computer interface*:

(*a*) software must be suitable;

(*b*) software must be easy to use and adaptable to the user's level of knowledge or experience;

(*c*) systems must provide feedback on the system's performance;

(*d*) systems must display information in a format and at a pace adapted to users;

(*e*) principles of software ergonomics must be applied, in particular to human data processing.

[*Health and Safety (Display Screen Equipment) Regulations 1992 (SI 1992 No 2792), Sch 1*].

## Repetitive strain injury (RSI)

O5014    The most common affliction of regular keyboard users is repetitive strain injury (RSI) now more commonly described as work related upper limb disorder (WRULD) (see further M3023 GOOD HANDLING TECHNIQUES and OCCUPATIONAL HEALTH AND DISEASES) and, in future, it would seem, it is going to become increasingly more difficult for employers to avoid liability for this condition – at least, if they cannot show that they have provided reasonable safeguards against keyboard-related injuries. More significantly, the developing practices of computer manufacturers of providing explicit warnings about conditions associated with keyboards and other equipment when supplying personal computers will have the following consequences:

(*a*) employers will no longer be able to rely on the absence of manufacturers' warnings (in order to avoid liability) but will have to show that they have complied with the requirements of the *Health and Safety (Display Screen Equipment) Regulations 1992 (SI 1992 No 3004)* (O5005–O5007 above); and

(*b*) employees/users will have responsibilities themselves to use equipment in a way consistent with the safety and comfort guides provided to them; failure to do so, after being made aware of the health risks in the warning, may well amount to assumption of risk of injury on their part, thereby invalidating a claim for damages (see further E11010 EMPLOYERS' DUTIES TO THEIR EMPLOYEES).

# Photocopying equipment

O5015    A number of hazards have been identified with photocopiers, including risks of:

(*a*)    inhalation of fumes from aqueous solutions of ammonia (in the case of dyeline copiers only); and

(*b*)    ozone emission created by electrical discharge.

The following precautions should be adopted, particularly where photocopying equipment is located in well-populated office locations:

(i)    the photocopier should be serviced in accordance with the manufacturer's instructions;

(ii)    staff servicing the copier should be adequately trained, especially regarding the cleaning of the drum;

(iii)    the photocopier should be sited in accordance with the manufacturer's guidelines on minimum siting requirements – otherwise additional ventilation may be needed to control heat, humidity and gaseous emissions; and

(iv)    in the case of dyeline copiers only, staff engaged in cleaning and maintenance should be provided with eye protection.

The HSE has issued updated advice on how best to control the possible health risks that could result from exposure at work to ozone*. It is aimed particularly at employers and managers as well as employees and health and safety professionals. The guidance emphasises what needs to be done and what does not.

Significant additions to the guidance include:

(*a*)    practical advice to employers on controlling exposure to ozone in accordance with the requirements of the *Control of Substances Hazardous to Health Regulations 1999 (SI 1999 No 437) (COSHH)*, and on how best to keep any exposure at or below the new Occupational Exposure Standard (OES). The OES for ozone is 0.2ppm in air averaged over an 8 hour reference period and 0.4ppm in air averaged over a 15 minute reference period; and

(*b*)    advice to many work situations that involve exposure only to small amounts of ozone with no significant risk to health (for example, in the use of office equipment such as photocopiers, printers and X-ray machines). The document stresses that where this type of equipment is the only source of ozone in a particular workplace, and if the guidance is followed, then an employer need only keep the risk assessment and control measures under review.

The guidance is intended to be read in conjunction with the Health and Safety Commission's ACoP *'General COSHH ACoP (Control of Substances Hazardous to Health)'* (L5), 3rd edition, ISBN 0717616703, price £8.50, available from HSE Books.

* *'Ozone: Health Hazards and Precautionary Measures'* (EH38 (revised)), price £4, and Guidance Note EH40/2000 *'Occupational Exposure Limits'* (2001 supplement available, price £5.00), price £9.50, are both available from HSE Books. (The package price when ordering both publications together is £12.00.)

## Dangerous machines in offices

O5016    It is an offence to allow any person employed to work in an office or shop to work at a dangerous machine, unless:

(*a*)    he has been adequately informed as to dangers (including written instructions, if appropriate, provided in a readily comprehensible form); and

(*b*)    he is adequately trained to use the machine and to take necessary precautions against risks which its use may entail.

[*Provision and Use of Work Equipment Regulations 1998 (SI 1998 No 2306), Regs 8 and 9*].

Specific rules applying to office machinery contained in the *Prescribed Dangerous Machines Order 1964* have been repealed (along with the *Offices, Shops and Railway Premises Act 1963, s 19*) and replaced by the generally applicable machinery safety requirements of the *Provision and Use of Work Equipment Regulations 1998 (SI 1998 No 2306)* – see MACHINERY SAFETY.

### Slips, trips and falls

O5017   Slips, trips and falls tend to happen to office workers when they are moving equipment about or carrying loads. In order to avoid risk of such injuries, trailing leads should not be allowed to create tripping hazards; where necessary, torn floor coverings should be replaced; spillages should always be quickly cleaned up; passageways, doorways and corridors as well as entrances should not become or be left blocked; also handrails should be provided on stairways – stairs and stairwells should be well lit – see the *Workplace (Health, Safety and Welfare) Regulations 1992 (SI 1992 No 3004)* and W11009 WORKPLACES – HEALTH, SAFETY AND WELFARE);

### Overall responsibilities of office management

O5018   Office managers should ensure compliance with accident rules and procedures (see ACCIDENT REPORTING). Employers should make sure that there are written safety policies and that these are revised when necessary. All employers should ensure that:

(*a*)   new office premises are duly notified to the local authority pursuant to the *Offices, Shops and Railway Premises Act 1963, s 49*;

(*b*)   workstations are comfortable with seating and footrests (if appropriate) (see W11008 WORKPLACES – HEALTH, SAFETY AND WELFARE);

(*c*)   first-aid boxes are always fully stocked, with someone appointed to take charge in an emergency and call an ambulance (see FIRST-AID);

(*d*)   adequate rest areas are provided for staff;

(*e*)   air conditioning systems with a water cooling tower are notified to the local authority (see D1034 DANGEROUS SUBSTANCES I);

(*f*)   where VDUs are in continuous or intensive use, adequate breaks are arranged and staff taught how to arrange the workstation so as to avoid awkward movements, reflections and general aches and pains;

(*g*)   trolleys and/or castors are provided for moving cabinets, desks and other bulky items so as to minimise risk of back injury (see M3023);

(*h*)   staff are instructed and provided with necessary protective equipment, to deal with risk of personal violence, particularly when carrying cash or valuables.

## Shops

O5019   Although not obviously so hazardous and accident-prone as factories and manufacturing establishments, shops need to maintain high health and safety standards in the interests of both employees and the general public. Special considerations include the need to take into account the risks associated with large numbers of persons visiting shop premises and the potential dangers to children, the elderly and those with disabilities.

Shop management should also consider, for example, the dangers associated with continual use of escalators between floors and lifts, and inform customers accordingly with boldly worded notices. Similarly, entrance and exit points, as well as means of escape in case of fire, should be clearly identified. Shop entrances and exits to and from, in many cases, a main street or busy thoroughfare, should at all times be kept clear from obstructions as well as delivery points, often at the rear of commercial premises, and members of the public should be prohibited from parking in such restricted areas. Special care is needed to ensure that trolleys and other equipment for moving stock (such as ladders) do not block access and are not left accessible to children. Where necessary, staff should see that wandering trolleys are returned to ranks and spillages eliminated as soon as possible (see O5021 below).

Out of bounds areas, such as lift motor rooms and staff offices, should be clearly signposted and marked 'Private. No admittance except for staff'. Latent structural hazards should be clearly identified, e.g. a dark or unlit staircase, and even patent dangers should be drawn to the attention of unattended children (see O3010 OCCUPIERS' LIABILITY). Where repairs are being carried out or remedial or decorative work is going on above, customers and visitors should be alerted to this. Wherever possible, particularly in large multi-storey stores, lighting should be evenly distributed.

Staff should be made aware, as part of induction training, of their health and safety duties to the general public and the possibility of liability, both criminal and civil, if potentially dangerous situations arise or someone is accidentally injured.

More so than with factories and offices, shop staff – in constant contact with the general public – should be au fait with risks to the public (and especially children) and, where necessary, briefed as to first-aid location and provision. Moreover, since fire hazard and risk of fire spread is one of the deadliest dangers in shops, staff should be briefed in fire hazards and routine fire fighting techniques (see also FIRE AND FIRE PRECAUTIONS). A knowledge of the location of fire extinguishers and how to operate them is essential, as well as any dangerous cutting machines at food counters.

Employees operating bacon slicers and similar food processing machines should be instructed in the inherent dangers of such machines and management should make failure to comply with guarding requirements a dismissible offence. Prominent signs should prohibit smoking (by staff on duty as well as customers).

Maintenance of high health and safety and public hygiene standards in shops (as well as restaurants and hotels) is required by a variety of overlapping statutes and regulations. Apart from the *Health and Safety at Work etc. Act 1974*, which applies in a general way to shops, the principal legislation applicable to shops, hotels and restaurants is the *Workplace (Health, Safety and Welfare) Regulations 1992 (SI 1992 No 3004)*, the *Food Safety Act 1990* and subsequent regulations (see further FOOD AND FOOD HYGIENE) and the *General Product Safety Regulations 1994 (SI 1994 No 2328)* (see further PRODUCT SAFETY).

Law in shops is enforced by environmental health officers, except for the fire regulations which are enforced by the local fire authority, with whom on-going consultation and co-operation by shop management is strongly advised. Since much of the liability associated with shops legislation is criminal and depends on either 'sale' having taken place or with 'offering for sale' products, case law has instructively established that display of products in a supermarket, hypermarket or shop for self-service purposes is not an 'offer for sale' (*Pharmaceutical Society of Great Britain v Boots Cash Chemists Ltd [1953] 1 QB 401*) (see also *Fisher v Bell [1960] 3 AER 731* relating to the display of a flick knife). Actual sale takes place when money is handed over at the check-out in return for goods.

### Loading bays and warehousing

O5020    A particular problem with wholesale and commercial premises is the safety of loading bays as everything coming into or leaving a warehouse has to pass the loading dock. With increased efficiency in the distribution industry, loading docks have become very busy areas, in continual use by the likes of heavy forklift trucks and juggernaut road vehicles. Not atypically, where lorries move off unexpectedly or trailers creep away from loading docks, coupled with constant movement from forklift trucks unloading loads, a forklift truck can career off the loading dock or cause an operator to become trapped between handling equipment and a lorry trailer. Together with the often generally low appreciation of the risks involved (given that many trucks are driven by employees of foreign companies with little knowledge of English) this makes for a growing hazard, resulting increasingly in the voluntary installation of vehicle restraints. All parties involved have obligations to ensure adequate safety in such situations under the general duties of the *Health and Safety at Work etc. Act 1974* (*BOC Distribution Services v HSE [1995] JPIL 128*). (See also ACCESS, TRAFFIC ROUTES AND VEHICLES.)

## Civil liability for injuries in shops

O5021    A shop, supermarket or hypermarket qualifies as 'premises' for the purposes of the *Occupiers' Liability Act 1957*, and customers visiting shops are 'lawful visitors'. They are therefore entitled to protection under that Act, unless they go or stray to places or parts of the premises (e.g. staff rooms) to which they are not invited/permitted, or from which they are specifically excluded. In particular, an enormous variety of gadgetry in shops and supermarkets is a fertile source of attraction to children. These range from sweets to medicines, and from coat hangers to lifts and escalators. These can constitute 'traps' which the 'common duty of care' under the Act requires to be dealt with by reasonable measures to protect children.

### Res ipsa loquitur – unusual dangers

O5022    Where a customer on shop premises is injured as a result of an accident which, in the ordinary course of things, should not happen if the management is exercising proper care, liability may be established easily without detailed proof of negligence. Thus, 'the duty of the shopkeeper in this class of case is well established. It may be said to be a duty to use reasonable care to see that the shop floor, on which people are invited, is kept reasonably safe, and if an unusual danger is present, of which the injured person is unaware, and the danger is one which would not be expected and ought not to be present, the onus of proof is on the defendants to explain how it was that the accident happened' (per Lord Goddard CJ in *Turner v Arding & Hobbs Ltd [1949] 2 AER 911*).

In *Ward v Tesco Stores Ltd [1976] 1 AER 219* the appellant slipped, while shopping, on some yoghurt which had spilled on to the floor, was injured and sued the respondent for negligence. It was held that it was the duty of the respondents, through their employees, to see that floors were kept clean and free from spillages. Since the appellant's injury was not one which, in the ordinary course of things, would have happened if the floor had been kept clean and spillages dealt with as soon as they occurred, it was for the respondents to demonstrate that the accident had not arisen from lack of reasonable care on their part. In the absence, therefore, of a satisfactory explanation as to how yoghurt got on to the floor, the inference was that the spillage had occurred because the respondents had failed to exercise reasonable care.

However, in *Furness v Midland Bank plc (unreported)*, Court of Appeal, 10 November 2000 (Simon Brown LJ, Sir Christopher Slade), which referred to *Ward v Tesco Stores*, showed that reasonable forseeability and care were adequate defences where the public were not involved.

In *Furness* the appellant fell on a staircase landing used only by employees of the bank, and a few droplets of water were found to be present on the landing after the fall. It was held that the risk of such an accident was minimal and *Ward v Tesco Stores* was distinguished. In the latter case it had been necessary to keep a constant lookout and to instruct staff accordingly over spillages as it was the public who were put at risk in a supermarket. In the present case it was held that such precautions would not have served any useful purpose and would not have been a reasonably practicable way of keeping the staircase free from it's few drops of water. All practicable measures had been taken and the accident was therefore found not to be the employer's responsibility.

The law on the maxim *res ipsa loquitur* was authoritatively laid down by Erle CJ in *Scott v London and St Katharine Docks Co (1865) 3 H & C 596*: 'But where the thing is shewn to be under the management of the defendant or his servants, and the accident is such as in the ordinary course of things does not happen if those who have the management use proper care, it affords reasonable evidence, in the absence of explanation by the defendants, that the accident arose from want of care'. Thus, there are four circumstances in which *res ipsa loquitur* applies:

(a)    the 'thing' causing the accident must be under the control of the employer, or under his management;

(b)    the injury-causing accident must be one which does not happen in the ordinary course of things;

(c)    the accident would not have happened if management had been exercising reasonable care;

(d)    absence of explanation, on the part of the defendant, to show that they used reasonable care.

Lately the courts have declined to adopt overly formulistic approaches to the maxim, stressing that it is to be applied with common sense, as it is no more than a phrase 'to describe the proof of facts which are sufficient to support an inference that a defendant was negligent and therefore to establish a *prima facie* case against him' (per Hobhouse LJ in *Ratcliffe v Plymouth & Torbay Health Authority and Exeter and North Devon Health Authority [1998] PIQR 170*). This approach was adopted in a more recent case, *Gray v Southampton and South West Hampshire Health Authority (2001) 57 BMLR 148*, QBD, 13 June 2000 (Toulson J), in which the possibility of negligence was decided by reference to the *balance of probabilities* of different circumstances being the causal factor for brain damage after an operation.

## Office and shop units and common parts

O5023     The remaining provisions of the *Offices, Shops and Railway Premises Act 1963* impose requirements for the safety, cleanliness and adequate lighting of common parts such as lobbies, stairs and storage areas shared between tenants or other businesses occupying shop or office units. Responsibility lies with the owner of the building (as opposed to the occupiers of the units) or the owner of the common parts in situations of divided ownership. [*Offices, Shops and Railway Premises Act 1963, ss 42 and 43*].

# Personal Protective Equipment

## Introduction

P3001    Conventional wisdom suggests that 'safe place strategies' are more effective in combating health and safety risks than 'safe person strategies'. Safe systems of work, and control/prevention measures serve to protect everyone at work, whilst the advantages of personal protective equipment are limited to the individual(s) concerned. Given, however, the fallibility of any state of the art technology in endeavouring to achieve total protection, some level of personal protective equipment is inevitable in view of the obvious (and not so obvious) risks to head, face, neck, eyes, ears, lungs, skin, arms, hands and feet.

Current statutory requirements for employers to provide and maintain suitable personal protective equipment are contained in the *Personal Protective Equipment at Work Regulations 1992 (SI 1992 No 2966)*, enjoining them to carry out an assessment to determine what personal protective equipment is needed and to consider employee needs in the selection process. Adjunct to this, common law insists, not only that employers have requisite safety equipment at hand, or available in an accessible place, but also that management ensure that operators use it (see *Bux v Slough Metals Ltd*). That the hallowed duty to 'provide and maintain' has been getting progressively stricter is evidenced by *Crouch v British Rail Engineering Ltd [1988] IRLR 404* to the extent that employers could be in breach of either statutory or common law duty (or both) in the case of injury/disease to a member of the employee's immediate family involved, say, in cleaning protective clothing – but the injury/disease must have been foreseeable (*Hewett v Alf Brown's Transport Ltd [1992] ICR 530*).

This section deals with the requirements of the *Personal Protective Equipment at Work Regulations 1992*, the *Personal Protective Equipment (EC Directive) Regulations 1992 (SI 1992 No 3139)* as amended by the *Personal Protective Equipment (EC Directive) (Amendment) Regulations 1994 (SI 1994 No 2326)*, the duties imposed on manufacturers and suppliers of personal protective equipment, the common law duty on employers to provide suitable personal protective equipment, and the main types of personal protective equipment and clothing and some relevant British Standards.

## The Personal Protective Equipment at Work Regulations 1992 (SI 1992 No 2966)

P3002    With the advent of the *Personal Protective Equipment at Work Regulations 1992*, all employers must make a formal assessment of the personal protective equipment needs of employees and provide ergonomically suitable equipment in relation to foreseeable risks at work (see further P3006 below). However, employers cannot be expected to comply with their new statutory duties, unless manufacturers of personal protective equipment have complied with theirs under the requirements of the *Personal Protective Equipment (EC Directive) Regulations 1992 (SI 1992 No 3139)* and *SI 1994 No 2326* – that is, had their products independently certified for

EU accreditation purposes. Although imposing a considerable remit on manufacturers, EU accreditation is an indispensable condition precedent to sale and commercial circulation (see P3012 below).

It is important that personal protective clothing and equipment should be seen as 'last resort' protection – its use should only be prescribed when engineering and management solutions and other safe systems of work do not effectively protect the worker from the danger.

Employees must be made aware of the purpose of personal protective equipment, its limitations and the need for on-going maintenance. Thus, when assessing the need for, say, eye protection, employers should first identify the existence of workplace hazards (e.g. airborne dust, projectiles, liquid splashes, slippery floors, inclement weather in the case of outside work) and then the extent of danger (e.g. frequency/velocity of projectiles, frequency/severity of splashes). Selection can (and, indeed, should) then be made from the variety of CE-marked equipment available, in respect of which manufacturers must ensure that such equipment provides protection, and suppliers ascertain that it meets such requirements/standards [*HSWA s 6*] (see further PRODUCT SAFETY). Typically, most of the risks will have already been logged, located and quantified in a routine risk/safety audit (see R3020 RISK ANALYSIS AND SAFETY MONITORING), and classified according to whether they are physical/chemical/biological in relation to the part(s) of the body affected (e.g. eyes, ears, skin).

Selection of personal protective equipment is a first stage in an on-going routine, followed by proper use and maintenance of equipment (on the part of both employers and employees) as well as training and supervision in personal protection techniques. Maintenance presupposes a stock of renewable spare parts coupled with regular inspection, testing, examination, repair, cleaning and disinfection schedules as well as keeping appropriate records. Depending on the particular equipment, some will require regular testing and examination (e.g. respiratory equipment), whilst others merely inspection (e.g. gloves, goggles). Generally, manufacturers' maintenance schedules should be followed.

Suitable accommodation must be provided for protective equipment in order to minimise loss or damage and prevent exposure to cold, damp or bright sunlight, e.g. pegs for helmets, pegs and lockers for clothing, spectacle cases for safety glasses.

On-going safety training, often carried out by manufacturers for the benefit of users should combine both theory and practice.

## Work activities/processes requiring personal protective equipment

**P3003**   Examples abound of processes/activities of which personal protective equipment is a prerequisite, from construction work and mining, through work with ionising radiations, to work with lifting plant, cranes, as well as handling chemicals, tree felling and working from heights. Similarly, blasting operations, work in furnaces and drop forging all require a degree of personal protection.

## Statutory requirements in connection with personal protective equipment

**P3004**   General statutory requirements relating to personal protective equipment are contained in of the *Health and Safety at Work etc. Act 1974, ss 2, 9* (see further E11017 EMPLOYERS' DUTIES TO THEIR EMPLOYEES), and in the *Personal Protective Equipment at Work Regulations 1992*, 'Every employer shall ensure that suitable personal protective equipment is provided to his employees who may be exposed to a risk to their health or safety at work except where, and to the extent that such risk has been adequately controlled by other means which are equally or more effective'. [*Reg 4(1)*]. More specific statutory requirements concerning personal protective equipment exist in the *Personal Protective Equipment at Work Regulations 1992* (in tandem with the *Personal Protective Equipment (EC Directive) Regulations 1992 (SI 1992 No 3139)* and *SI 1994 No 2326)*), and sundry other recent regulations applicable to particular industries/processes, e.g. asbestos, noise, construction (see P3008 below). Where personal protective equipment is a necessary control measure to meet a specific statutory requirement or following a risk assessment, this must be provided free of charge [*HWSA* s 9]. However, where it is optional or non essential, there is nothing to stop the employer from seeking a financial contribution.

## General statutory duties – HSWA 1974

P3005    Employers are under a general duty to ensure, so far as reasonably practicable, the health, safety and welfare at work of their employees – a duty which clearly implies provision/maintenance of personal protective equipment. [*HSWA s 2(1)*].

## Specific statutory duties – Personal Protective Equipment at Work Regulations 1992 (SI 1992 No 2966)

*Duties of employers*

P3006    Employers – and self-employed persons in cases (*a*), (*b*), (*c*), (*d*) and (*e*) below, must undertake the following:

(*a*)    Formally assess (and review periodically) provision and suitability of personal protective equipment. [*Reg 6(1)(3)*].

The assessment should include:

(i)    risks to health and safety not avoided by other means;

(ii)    reference to characteristics which personal protective equipment must have in relation to risks identified in (i); and

(iii)    a comparison of the characteristics of personal protective equipment having the characteristics identified in (ii).

[*Reg 6(2)*].

The aim of the assessment is to ensure that an employer knows which personal protective equipment to choose; it constitutes the first stage in a continuing programme, concerned also with proper use and maintenance of personal protective equipment and training and supervision of employees.

(*b*)    Provide suitable personal protective equipment to his employees, who may be exposed to health and safety risks while at work, except where the risk has either been adequately controlled by other equally or more effective means. [*Reg 4(1)*].

Personal protective equipment is not suitable unless:

(i)    it is appropriate for risks involved and conditions at the place of exposure;

(ii)    it takes account of ergonomic requirements and the state of health of the person who wears it;

(iii)    it is capable of fitting the wearer correctly; and

(iv) so far as reasonably practicable (for meaning, see ENFORCEMENT), it is effective to prevent or adequately control risks involved without increasing the overall risk.

[*Reg 4(3)*].

(*c*) Provide compatible personal protective equipment – that is, that the use of more than one item of personal protective equipment is compatible with other personal protective equipment. [*Reg 5*].

(*d*) Maintain (as well as replace and clean) any personal protective equipment in an efficient state, efficient working order and in good repair. [*Reg 7*].

(*e*) Provide suitable accommodation for personal protective equipment when not being used. [*Reg 8*].

(*f*) Provide employees with information, instruction and training to enable them to know

(i) the risks which personal protective equipment will avoid or minimise;

(ii) the purpose for which and manner in which personal protective equipment is to be used;

(iii) any action which the employee might take to ensure that personal protective equipment remains efficient.

[*Reg 9*].

(*g*) Ensure, taking all reasonable steps, that personal protective equipment is properly used. [*Reg 10*].

*Summary of employer's duties*

(1) duty of assessment

(2) duty to provide suitable PPE

(3) duty to provide compatible PPE

(4) duty to maintain and replace PPE

(5) duty to provide suitable accommodation for PPE

(6) duty to provide information and training

(7) duty to see that PPE is correctly used.

*Duties of employees*

P3007     Every employee must:

(*a*) use personal protective equipment in accordance with training and instructions [*Reg 10(2)*];

(*b*) return all personal protective equipment to the appropriate accommodation provided after use [*Reg 10(4)*]; and

(*c*) report forthwith any defect or loss in the equipment to the employer [*Reg 11*].

### Specific requirements for particular industries and processes

P3008   In addition to the general remit of the *Personal Protective Equipment at Work Regulations 1992*, the following regulations impose specific requirements on employers to provide personal protective equipment up to the EU standard.

(1)   *Control of Lead at Work Regulations 1998 (SI 1998 No 543), Regs 6, 8* – supply of suitable respiratory equipment and where exposure is significant, suitable protective clothing and equipment (see APPENDIX 4);

(2)   *Control of Asbestos at Work Regulations 1987 (SI 1987 No 2115), Regs 8, 17-28* – supply of respiratory protective equipment/suitable protective clothing (see APPENDIX 4);

(3)   *Control of Substances Hazardous to Health Regulations 1999 (SI 1999 No 437) (COSHH), Regs 7, 8, 9* – supply of suitable protective equipment where employees are foreseeably exposed to substances hazardous to health;

(4)   *Noise at Work Regulations 1989 (SI 1989 No 1790), Reg 8* – personal ear protectors;

(5)   *Construction (Head Protection) Regulations 1989 (SI 1989 No 2209), Reg 3* – suitable head protection (for the position of Sikhs, see C8047 CONSTRUCTION AND BUILDING OPERATIONS);

(6)   *Ionising Radiations Regulations 1999 (SI 1999 No 3232), Reg 9* – supply of suitable personal protective equipment and respiratory protective equipment;

(7)   *Shipbuilding and Ship-repairing Regulations 1960 (SI 1960 No 1932), Regs 50, 51* – supply of suitable breathing apparatus, belts, eye protectors, gloves and gauntlets (see APPENDIX 4).

[*Miscellaneous Factories (Transitional Provisions) Regulations 1993 (SI 1993 No 2482)*].

## Increased importance of uniform European standards

P3009   To date, manufacturers of products, including personal protective equipment (PPE), have sought endorsement or approval for products, prior to commercial circulation, through reference to British Standards (BS), HSE or European standards, an example of the former being Kitemark and an example of the latter being CEN or CENELEC. Both are examples of *voluntary* national and international schemes that can be entered into by manufacturers and customers, under which both sides are 'advantaged' by conformity with such standards. Conformity is normally achieved following a level of testing appropriate to the level of protection offered by the product. With the introduction of the *Personal Protective Equipment (EC Directive) Regulations 1992* as amended by *SI 1994 No 2326* (see P3012 below), this voluntary system of approval was replaced by a statutory certification procedure.

### Towards certification

P3010   Certification as a condition of sale is probably some time away. Transition from adherence based on a wide range of voluntary national (and international) standards to a compulsory universal EU standard takes time and specialist expertise. Already, however, British Standards Institution (BSI) has adopted the form BS EN as a British version of a uniform European standard. But, generally speaking, uniformity of approach to design and testing, on the part of manufacturers, represents a considerable remit and so statutory compliance with tougher new European standards is probably not likely to happen immediately. Here, too, however, there is evidence of some progress, e.g. the EN 45000 series of standards on how test houses and certification bodies are to be established and independently accredited. In addition, a range of European standards on PPE have been implemented in BS EN format, for example, on eye protection, fall arrest systems and safety footwear.

### Interim measures

P3011    Most manufacturers have elected to comply with the current CEN standard when seeking product certification. Alternatively, should a manufacturer so wish, the inspection body can verify by way of another route to certification – this latter might well be the case with an innovative product where standards did not exist. Generally, however, compliance with current CEN (European Standardisation Committee) or, alternatively, ISO 9000: Quality Assurance has been the well-trodden route to certification. To date, several UK organisations, including manufacturers and independent bodies, have established PPE test houses, which are independently accredited by the National Measurement Accreditation Service (NAMAS). Such test houses will be open to all comers for verification of performance levels.

### Personal Protective Equipment (EC Directive) Regulations 1992 (SI 1992 No 3139) as amended by SI 1994 No 2326

P3012    The *Personal Protective Equipment (EC Directive) Regulations 1992* as amended by *SI 1994 No 2326* require most types of PPE (for exceptions, see P3019 below) to satisfy specified certification procedures, pass EU type-examination (i.e. official inspection by an approved inspection body) and carry a 'CE' mark both on the product itself and its packaging before being put into commercial circulation. Indeed, failure on the part of a manufacturer to obtain affixation of a 'CE' mark on his product before putting it into circulation, is a criminal offence under the *Health and Safety at Work etc. Act 1974*, s 6 carrying a maximum fine, on summary conviction, of £20,000 (see ENFORCEMENT). Enforcement is through trading standards officers. [*The Personal Protective Equipment (EC Directive) (Amendment) Regulations 1993 (SI 1993 No 3074)*].

### *CE mark of conformity*

P3013    The *Personal Protective Equipment (EC Directive) Regulations 1992* as amended by the *Personal Protective Equipment (EC Directive) (Amendment) Regulations 1994 (SI 1994 No 2326)* specify procedures and criteria with which manufacturers must comply in order to be able to obtain certification. Essentially this involves incorporation into design and production basic health and safety requirements. Hence, by compliance with health and safety criteria, affixation of the 'CE' mark becomes a condition of sale and approval (see *fig. 1* below). Moreover, compliance, on the part of manufacturers, with these regulations, will enable employers to comply with their duties under the *Personal Protective Equipment at Work Regulations 1992*. *Reg 4(3)(e)* of the *Personal Protective Equipment at Work Regulations 1992* requires the PPE provided by the employer to comply with this and any later EU directive requirements.

CE accreditation is not a synonym for compliance with the CEN standard, since a manufacturer could opt for certification via an alternative route. Neither is it an approvals mark. It is rather a quality mark, since all products covered by the regulations are required to meet formal quality control or quality of production criteria in their certification procedures. [*Arts 8.4, 11, 89/686/EEC*].

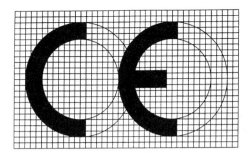

## Certification procedures

The *Personal Protective Equipment (EC Directive) Regulations 1992* as amended by *SI 1994 No 2326*, identify three categories of PPE:

— PPE of simple design;

— PPE of non-simple design;

— PPE of complex design.

Each of these have different requirements for manufacturers to follow.

In order to obtain certification, manufacturers must submit to an approved body the following documentation (except in the case of PPE of simple design, where risks are minimal).

(1)  PPE – simple design

This includes use of PPE where risks are minimal e.g. gardening gloves, helmets, aprons, thimbles. This type of equipment must be subject to a manufacturers declaration of conformity.

(2)  PPE – non-simple design

In order to obtain certification, manufacturers must submit to an approved body the following documentation:

(*a*)  Technical file, i.e.

(i)  overall and detailed plans, accompanied by calculation notes/ results of prototype tests; and

(ii)  an exhaustive list of basic health and safety requirements and harmonised standards taken into account in the model's design.

(*b*)  Description of control and test facilities used to check compliance with harmonised standards.

(*c*)  Copy of information relating to:

(i)  storage, use, cleaning, maintenance, servicing and disinfection;

(ii)  performance recorded during technical tests to monitor levels of protection;

(iii)  suitable PPE accessories;

(iv)  classes of protection appropriate to different levels of risk and limits of use;

(v)  obsolescence deadline;

(vi)   type of packaging suitable for transport;

(vii)   significance of markings.

[Art 1.4, Annex II; Art 8.1, Annex III].

This must be provided in the official language of the member state of destination.

(3)    PPE – complex design

This includes use of PPE for protection against mortal/serious dangers and requires compliance with a quality control system.

This category of PPE, including:

(*a*)    filtering, respiratory devices for protection against solid and liquid aerosols/ irritant, dangerous, toxic or radiotoxic gases;

(*b*)    respiratory protection devices providing full insulation from the atmosphere, and for use in diving;

(*c*)    protection against chemical attack or ionising radiation;

(*d*)    emergency equipment for use in high temperatures, whether with or without infrared radiation, flames or large amounts of molten metal (100°C or more);

(*e*)    emergency equipment for use in low temperatures (–50°C or less);

(*f*)    protection against falls from heights;

(*g*)    protection against electrical risks; and

(*h*)    motor cycle helmets and visors;

must satisfy either

(i)    —    an EU quality control system for the final product, or

   —    a system for ensuring EU quality of production by means of monitoring;

and in either case,

(ii)   an EU declaration of conformity.

[*Art 8.4*].


## Basic health and safety requirements applicable to all PPE

P3015    All PPE must:

(*a*)    be ergonomically suitable, that is, be able to perform a risk-related activity whilst providing the user with the highest possible level of protection;

(*b*)    preclude risks and inherent nuisance factors, such as roughness, sharp edges and projections and must not cause movements endangering the user;

(*c*)    provide comfort and efficiency by facilitating correct positioning on the user and remaining in place for the foreseeable period of use; and by being as light as possible without undermining design strength and efficiency; and

(*d*)    be accompanied by necessary information – that is, the name and address of the manufacturer and technical file (see P3014 above).

[*Annex II*].

## General purpose PPE – specific to several types of PPE

P3016  (*a*)  PPE incorporating adjustment systems must not become incorrectly adjusted without the user's knowledge;

(*b*)  PPE enclosing parts of the body must be sufficiently ventilated to limit perspiration or to absorb perspiration;

(*c*)  PPE for the face, eyes and respiratory tracts must minimise risks to same and, if necessary, contain facilities to prevent moisture formation and be compatible with wearing spectacles or contact lenses;

(*d*)  PPE subject to ageing must contain date of manufacture, the date of obsolescence and be indelibly inscribed if possible. If the useful life of a product is not known, accompanying information must enable the user to establish a reasonable obsolescence date. In addition, the number of times it can be cleaned before being inspected or discarded must (if possible) be affixed to the product; or, failing this, be indicated in accompanying literature;

(*e*)  PPE which may be caught up during use by a moving object must have a suitable resistance threshold above which a constituent part will break and eliminate danger;

(*f*)  PPE for use in explosive atmospheres must not be likely to cause an explosive mixture to ignite;

(*g*)  PPE for emergency use or rapid installation/removal must minimise the time required for attachment and/or removal;

(*h*)  PPE for use in very dangerous situations (see P3015 above) must be accompanied with data for exclusive use of competent trained individuals, and describe procedure to be followed to ensure that it is correctly adjusted and functional when worn;

(*j*)  PPE incorporating components which are adjustable or removable by user, must facilitate adjustment, attachment and removal without tools;

(*k*)  PPE for connection to an external complementary device must be mountable only on appropriate equipment;

(*l*)  PPE incorporating a fluid circulation system must permit adequate fluid renewal in the vicinity of the entire part of the body to be protected;

(*m*)  PPE bearing one or more identification or recognition marks relating to health and safety must preferably carry harmonised pictograms/ideograms which remain perfectly legible throughout the foreseeable useful life of the product;

(*n*)  PPE in the form of clothing capable of signalling the user's presence visually must have one or more means of emitting direct or reflected visible radiation;

(*o*)  multi-risk PPE must satisfy basic requirements specific to each risk.

[*Art 2, Annex II*].

## Additional requirements for specific PPE for particular risks

P3017  There are additional requirements for PPE designed for certain particular risks as follows:

PPE protection against

(1)   *Mechanical impact risks*

    (i)   impact caused by falling/projecting objects must be sufficiently shock-absorbent to prevent injury from crushing or penetration of the protected part of the body;

    (ii)   falls. In the case of falls due to slipping, outsoles for footwear must ensure satisfactory adhesion by grip and friction, given the state and nature of the surface. In the case of falls from a height, PPE must incorporate a body harness and attachment system connectable to a reliable anchorage point. The vertical drop of the user must be minimised to prevent collision with obstacles and the braking force injuring, tearing or causing the operator to fall;

    (iii)   mechanical vibration. PPE must be capable of ensuring adequate attenuation of harmful vibration components for the part of the body at risk.

(2)   *(Static) compression of part of the body* – must be able to attenuate its effects so as to prevent serious injury of chronic complaints.

(3)   *Physical injury* – must be able to protect all or part of the body against superficial injury by machinery, e.g. abrasion, perforation, cuts or bites.

(4)   *Prevention of drowning* – (lifejackets, armbands etc.) must be capable of returning to the surface a user who is exhausted or unconscious, without danger to his health. Such PPE can be wholly or partially inherently buoyant or inflatable either by gas or orally. It should be able to withstand impact with liquid, and, if inflatable, able to inflate rapidly and fully.

(5)   *Harmful effects of noise* – must protect against exposure levels of the *Noise at Work Regulations 1989* (i.e. 85 and 90 dB(A)) and must indicate noise attenuation level.

(6)   *Heat and/or fire* – must possess sufficient thermal insulation capacity to retain most of the stored heat until after the user has left the danger area and removed PPE. Moreover, constituent materials which could be splashed by large amounts of hot product must possess sufficient mechanical-impact absorbency. In addition, materials which might accidentally come into contact with flame as well as being used in the manufacture of fire-fighting equipment, must possess a degree of non-flammability proportionate to the risk foreseeably arising during use and must not melt when exposed to flame or contribute to flame spread. When ready for use, PPE must be such that the quantity of heat transmitted by PPE to the user must not cause pain or health impairment. Second, ready-to-use PPE must prevent liquid or steam penetration and not cause burns. If PPE incorporates a breathing device, it must adequately protect the user. Accompanying manufacturers' notes must provide all relevant data for determination of maximum permissible user exposure to heat transmitted by equipment.

(7)   *Cold* – must possess sufficient thermal insulating capacity and retain the necessary flexibility for gestures and postures. In particular, PPE must protect tips of fingers and toes from pain or health impairment and prevent penetration by rain water. Manufacturers' accompanying notes must provide all relevant data concerning maximum permissible user exposure to cold transmitted by equipment.

(8)   *Electric shock* – must be sufficiently insulated against voltages to which the user is likely to be exposed under the most foreseeably adverse conditions. In particular, PPE for use during work with electrical installations (together with packaging), which may be under tension, must carry markings indicating either protection class and/or corresponding operating voltage, serial number and date of manufacture; in addition, date of entry into service must be inscribed as well as of periodic tests or inspections.

(9)   *Radiation*

(*a*)   Non-ionising radiation – must prevent acute or chronic eye damage from non-ionising radiation and be able to absorb/reflect the majority of energy radiated in harmful wavelengths without unduly affecting transmission of the innocuous part of the visible spectrum, perception of contrasts and distinguishment of colours. Thus, protective glasses must possess a spectral transmission factor so as to minimise radiant-energy illumination density capable of reaching the user's eye through the filter and ensure that it does not exceed permissible exposure value. Accompanying notes must indicate transmission curves, making selection of the most suitable PPE possible. The relevant protection-factor number must be marked on all specimens of filtering glasses.

(*b*)   Ionising radiation – must protect against external radioactive contamination. Thus, PPE should prevent penetration of radioactive dust, gases, liquids or mixtures under foreseeable use conditions. Moreover, PPE designed to provide complete user protection against external irradiation must be able to counter only weak electron or weak photon radiation.

(10)   *Dangerous substances and infective agents*

(*a*)   respiratory protection – must be able to supply the user with breathable air when exposed to polluted atmosphere or an atmosphere with inadequate oxygen concentration. Leak-tightness of the facepiece and pressure drop on inspiration (breath intake), as well as in the case of filtering devices purification capacity, must keep the contaminant penetration from the polluted atmosphere sufficiently low to avoid endangering health of the user. Instructions for use must enable a trained user to use the equipment correctly;

(*b*)   cutaneous and ocular contact (skin and eyes) – must be able to prevent penetration or diffusion of dangerous substances and infective agents. Therefore, PPE must be completely leak-tight but allow prolonged daily use or, failing that, of limited leak-tightness restricting the period of wear. In the case of certain dangerous substances/infective agents possessing high penetrative power and which limit duration of protection, such PPE must be tested for classification on the basis of efficiency. PPE conforming with test specifications must carry a mark indicating names or codes of substances used in tests and standard period of protection. Manufacturers' notes must contain an explanation of codes, detailed description of standard tests and refer to the maximum permissible period of wear under different foreseeable conditions of use.

(11)   *Safety devices for diving equipment* – must be able to supply the user with a breathable gaseous mixture, taking into account the maximum depth of immersion. If necessary, equipment must consist of

(*a*)   a suit to protect the user against pressure;

(*b*)  an alarm to give the user prompt warning of approaching failure in supply of breathable gaseous mixture;

(*c*)  life-saving suit to enable the user to return to the surface.

[*Art 3, Annex II*].

### Excluded PPE

P3018  (*a*)  PPE designed and manufactured for use specifically by the armed forces or in the maintenance of law and order (helmets, shields);

(*b*)  PPE for self-defence (aerosol canisters, personal deterrent weapons);

(*c*)  PPE designed and manufactured for private use against

(i)  adverse weather (headgear, seasonal clothing, footwear, umbrellas),

(ii)  damp and water (dish-washing gloves),

(iii)  heat (e.g. gloves);

(*d*)  PPE intended for the protection or rescue of persons on vessels or aircraft, not worn all the time.

[*Annex I*].

# Main types of personal protection

The main types of personal protection covered by the *Personal Protective Equipment at Work Regulations 1992* are (*a*) head protection, (*b*) eye protection, (*c*) hand/arm protection, (*d*) foot protection and (*e*) whole body protection.

In particular, these regulations do not cover ear protectors and most respiratory protective equipment – these areas are covered by other existing regulations and guidance, for example the *Noise at Work Regulations 1989* and HSE's guidance booklet HS(G) 53, 'Respiratory protective equipment: a practical guide for users'.

### Head protection

P3019  This takes the form of:

(*a*)  crash, cycling, riding and climbing helmets;

(*b*)  industrial safety helmets – to protect against falling objects;

(*c*)  scalp protectors (bump caps) – to protect against striking fixed obstacles;

(*d*)  caps/hairnets – to protect against scalping,

and is particularly suitable for the following activities:

(i)  building work – particularly on scaffolds;

(ii)  civil engineering projects;

(iii)  blasting operations;

(iv)  work in pits and trenches;

(v)  work near hoists/lifting plant;

(vi)  work in blast furnaces;

(vii)  work in industrial furnaces;

(viii)  ship-repairing;

(ix)  railway shunting;

(x)  slaughterhouses;

(xi)  tree-felling;

(xii)  suspended access work, e.g. window cleaning.

## Eye protection

P3020    This takes the following forms:

(*a*)  safety spectacles – these are the same as prescription spectacles but incorporating optional sideshields; lenses are made from tough plastic, such as polycarbonate – provide lateral protection;

(*b*)  eyeshields – these are heavier than safety spectacles and designed with a frameless one-piece moulded lens; can be worn over prescription spectacles;

(*c*)  safety goggles – these are heavier than spectacles or eye shields; they are made with flexible plastic frames and one-piece lens and have an elastic headband – they afford total eye protection; and

(*d*)  faceshields – these are heavier than other eye protectors but comfortable if fitted with an adjustable head harness – faceshields protect the face but not fully the eyes and so are no protection against dusts, mist or gases.

Eye protectors are suitable for working with:

(i)  chemicals;

(ii)  power driven tools;

(iii)  molten metal;

(iv)  welding;

(v)  radiation;

(vi)  gases/vapours under pressure;

(vii)  woodworking.

## Hand/arm protection

P3021    Gloves provide protection against:

(*a*)  cuts and abrasions;

(*b*)  extremes of temperature;

(*c*)  skin irritation/dermatitis;

(*d*)  contact with toxic/corrosive liquids,

and are particularly useful in connection with the following activities/processes:

(i)  manual handling;

(ii)  vibration;

(iii)  construction;

(iv)  hot and cold materials;

(v)  electricity;

(vi)   chemicals;

(vii)  radioactivity.

### Foot protection

P3022

This takes the form of:

(*a*)   safety shoes/boots;

(*b*)   foundry boots;

(*c*)   clogs;

(*d*)   wellington boots;

(*e*)   anti-static footwear;

(*f*)   conductive footwear,

and is particularly useful for the following activities:

(i)    construction;

(ii)   mechanical/manual handling;

(iii)  electrical processes;

(iv)   working in cold conditions (thermal footwear);

(v)    chemical processes;

(vi)   forestry;

(vii)  molten substances.

### Respiratory Protective Equipment

P3023

This takes the form of:

(*a*)   half-face respirators,

(*b*)   full-face respirators,

(*c*)   air-supply respirators,

(*d*)   self-contained breathing apparatus,

and is particularly useful for protecting against harmful

(i)    gases;

(ii)   vapours;

(iii)  dusts;

(iv)   fumes;

(v)    smoke;

(vi)   aerosols.

### Whole body protection

P3024

This takes the form of:

(*a*)   coveralls, overalls, aprons;

(*b*)   outfits to protect against cold and heat;

(c)    protection against machinery and chainsaws;

(d)    high visibility clothing;

(e)    life-jackets,

and is particularly useful in connection with the following activities:

(i)    laboratory work;

(ii)    construction;

(iii)    forestry;

(iv)    work in cold-stores;

(v)    highway and road works;

(vi)    food processing;

(vii)    welding;

(viii)    fire-fighting;

(ix)    foundry work;

(x)    spraying pesticides.

**Some relevant British Standards for protective clothing and equipment**

P3025    Although not, strictly speaking, a condition of sale or approval, for the purposes of the *Personal Protective Equipment (EC Directive) (Amendment) Regulations 1994 (SI 1994 No 2326)*, compliance with British Standards (e.g. ISO 9000: 'Quality Assurance') may well become one of the well-tried verification routes to obtaining a 'CE' mark. For that reason, if for no other, the following non-exhaustive list of British Standards on protective clothing and equipment should be of practical value to both manufacturers and users.

| **Table 1** | |
|---|---|
| **Protective clothing** | |
| BSEN 60903: 1986 | Specification for rubber gloves for electrical purposes |
| BS 3314: (1998) | Specification for protective aprons for wet work |
| BS 5426: 1993 | Specification for workwear and career wear |
| BS 5438: 1976 | Methods of test for flammability of vertically oriented textile fabrics and fabric assemblies subjected to a small igniting flame |
| 1989 (1995) | Methods of test for flammability of textile fabrics when subjected to a small igniting flame applied to the face or bottom edge of vertically oriented specimens |
| BS 6408: (1990) | Specification for clothing made from coated fabrics for protection against wet weather |
| BS EN 340: 1993 | Protective clothing. General Requirements |

| | |
|---|---|
| BS EN 341: (1999) | Personal Protective Equipment against falls from a height. Descender devices |
| BS EN 348: 1992 | Protective clothing. Determination of behaviour of materials on impact of small splashes of molten metal |
| BS EN 353: 1993 | Personal protective equipment against falls from a height. Guided type of fall arresters |
| BS EN 354: 1993 | Personal protective equipment against falls from a height. Lanyards |
| BS EN 355: 1993 | Personal protective equipment against falls from a height. Energy Absorbers |
| BS EN 360: 1993 | Personal protective equipment against falls from a height. Retractable type fall arresters |
| BS EN 361: 1993 | Personal protective equipment against falls from a height. Full body harnesses |
| BS EN 362: 1993 | Personal protective equipment against falls from a height. Connectors |
| BS EN 363: 1993 | Personal protective equipment against falls from a height. Fall arrest systems |
| BS EN 364: 1993(1999) | Personal protective equipment against falls from a height. Test methods |
| BS EN 365: 1993 | Personal protective equipment against falls from a height. General Requirements for instructions for use and for marking |
| BS EN 366: 1993 | Protective clothing. Protection against heat and fire |
| BS EN 367: 1992 | Protective clothing. Protection against heat and fires |
| BS EN 368: 1993 | Protective clothing. Protection against liquid chemicals |
| BS EN 369: 1993 | Protective clothing. Protection against liquid chemicals |
| BS EN 373: 1993 | Protective clothing: Assessment of resistance of materials to molten metal splash |
| BS EN 381 Part 1: 1993 | Protective clothing for users of hand-held chain saws |
| BS EN 463: 1995 | Protective clothing. Protection against liquid chemicals. Test method |
| BS EN 464: 1994 | Protective clothing. Protection against liquid and gaseous chemicals including liquid aerosols and solid particles. Test method |
| BS EN 465: 1995 | Protective clothing: Protection against liquid chemicals. Performance requirements for chemical protective clothing |

| | |
|---|---|
| BS EN 4661: 1995 | Protective clothing: Protection against liquid chemicals. Performance requirements for chemical protective clothing |
| BS EN 467: 1995 | Protective Clothing: protection against liquid chemicals. |
| BS EN 468: 1995 | Protective clothing for use against liquid chemicals. Test method |
| BS EN 469: 1995 | Protective clothing for firefighters |
| BS EN 470 | Protective clothing for use in welding and allied processes |
| Part 1: 1995 | General requirements |
| BS EN 471: 1994 | Specification for high visibility warning clothing |
| BS EN 510: 1993 | Specification for protective clothing for use where there is a risk of entanglement with moving parts |
| BS EN 530: 1995 | Abrasion resistance of protective clothing material |
| BS EN 531: 1995 | Protective clothing for workers exposed to heat |
| BS EN 532: 1995 | Protective clothing. Protection against heat and flame |
| BS EN 533: 1997 | Clothing for protection against heat or flame |
| **Protective footwear** | |
| BS 2723: 1956 (1995) | Specification for fireman's leather boots |
| BS 4676: 1983 (1996) | Specification for gaiters and footwear for protection against burns and impact risks in foundries |
| BS 5145: 1989 | Specification for lined industrial vulcanized rubber boots |
| BS 6159: | Polyvinyl chloride boots |
| Part 1: 1987 | Specification for general and industrial lined or unlined boots |
| BS EN | Safety, protective and occupational footwear for professional use |
| BS EN 345 | Safety footwear for professional use |
| BS EN 346 | Protective footwear for professional use |
| BS EN 347 | Occupational footwear for professional use |
| BS EN 381 | Protective clothing for users of hand-held chain saws |
| **Head protection** | |
| BS 6658: 1985(1995) | Specification for protective helmets for vehicle users |
| BS 6473: 1984 | Specification for protective hats for horse and pony riders |
| BS 3864: 1989 | Specification for protective helmets for firefighters |

| BS 4033: 1978 | Specification for industrial scalp protectors (light duty) |
| BS 4423: 1969 | Specification for climbers helmets |
| BS 4472: 1988 | Specification for protective skull caps for jockeys |

**Face and eye protection**

| BS 679 : 1989 | Specification for filters, cover lenses and backing lenses for use during welding and similar industrial operations |
| BS 1542: 1982 (1995) | Specification for eye, face and neck protection against non-ionising radiation arising during welding and similar operations |
| BS 2092: 1987 | Specification for eye protectors for industrial and non-industrial users |
| BS 2724: 1987 (1995) | Specification for sunglare eye protectors for general use |
| BS 4110: 1999 | Specification for eye-protectors for vehicle users |
| BS 7028: 1999 | |
| BS EN 167: 1995 | Personal eye protection. Optical test methods |
| BS EN 168: 1995 | Personal eye protection. Non-optical test methods |
| BS EN 169: 1992 | Specification for filters for personal eye-protection equipment used in welding and similar operations |
| BS EN 170: 1992 | Specification for filters for ultraviolet filters used in personal eye-protection equipment |
| BS EN 171: 1992 | Specification for infra-red filters used in personal eye protective equipment |
| BS EN 172: (2000) | Specification for sunglare filters used in personal eye-protectors equipment for industrial sue |

**Respiratory protection**

| BS 4001 | Care and maintenance of underwater breathing apparatus |
| Part 1 (1998) | |
| Part 2 (1995) | Standard diving equipment |
| BS 4275: 1997 | Guide to implementing an effective respiratory protective device programmme |
| BS 4400: 1969 (1995) | Method for sodium chloride particulate test for respirator filters |
| BS EN 132: 1999 | Respiratory protective devices. Definitions of terms and pictograms |
| BS EN 133: 1991 | Respiratory protective devices. Classification |
| BS EN 134: 1998 | Respiratory protective devices. Nomenclature of compounds |

| | |
|---|---|
| BS EN 135: 1999 | Respiratory protective devices. List of equivalent terms |
| BS EN 136: 1998 | Respiratory protective devices. Full face mask requirements for testing and marking |
| BS EN 137: 1993 | Specification for respiratory protective devices self-contained open-circuit compressed air breathing apparatus |
| BS EN 138: 2000 | Respiratory protective devices. Specification for fresh air hose breathing apparatus for use with full face mask, half mask or mouthpiece assembly |
| BS EN 139: 1995 | Respiratory protective devices. Compressed air line breathing apparatus for use with a full face mask, half mask or a mouthpiece assembly. Requirements, testing, marking |
| BS EN 141: 1991 | Specification for gas filters and combined filters used in respiratory protective equipment |
| BS EN 143: 1991 | Specification for particle filters used in respiratory protective equipment |
| BS EN 144 | Respiratory protective devices. Gas cylinder valves |
| BS EN 145: 1998 | Respiratory protective devices. Self-contained closed-circuit compressed oxygen breathing apparatus |
| BS EN 146: 1992 | Respiratory protection devices. Specification for powered particle filtering devices incorporating helmets or hoods |
| BS EN 147: 1992 | Respiratory protection devices. Specification for power assisted particle filtering devices incorporating full face masks, half masks or quarter masks |
| BS EN 148 | Specification for thread connection |
| BS EN 149: 1992 | Specification for filtering half masks to protect against particles |
| BS EN 371: 1992 | Specification for AX gas filters and combined filters against low boiling organic compounds used in respiratory protective equipment |
| BS EN 372: 1992 | Specification for SX gas filters and combined filters against specific named compounds used in respiratory protective equipment |
| **Radiation protection** | |
| BS 1542: 1982 (1995) | Specification for equipment for eye, face and neck protection against non-ionising radiation arising during welding and similar operations |
| BS 3664: 1963 | Specification for film badges for personnel radiation monitoring |

| BS EN 269: 1995(2000) | Respiratory protective devices. Specification for powered fresh air hose breathing apparatus incorporating a hood. |
|---|---|
| BS EN 270: 1995 | Respiratory protective devices. Compressed air line breathing apparatus incorporating a hood. Requirements, testing, marking |
| **Hearing protection** | |
| BS EN 352: | Hearing protectors. Safety requirements and testing |
| Part 1 1993 | Ear muffs |
| Part 2 1993 | Ear plugs |
| Part 3 1997 | Ear muffs attached to an industrial safety helmet |
| **Hand protection** | |
| BS EN 374: | Protective gloves against chemicals and microorganisms |
| Part 1: 1994 | Terminology and performance requirements |
| Part 2: 1994 | Determination of resistance to penetration |
| Part 3: 1994 | Determination of resistance to permeation by chemicals |
| BS EN 511: 1994 | Specification for protective gloves against cold |
| BS EN 421: 1994 | Protective gloves against ionising radiation and radioactive contamination |
| BS EN 407: 1994 | Protective gloves against thermal risks (heat and/or fire) |
| BS EN 388: 1994 | Protective gloves against mechanical risks |

## Common law requirements

P3026    In addition to general and/or specific statutory requirements, the residual combined duty, on employers at common law, to provide and maintain a safe system of work, including appropriate supervision of safety duties, still obtains, extending, where necessary, to protection against foreseeable risk of eye injury (*Bux v Slough Metals Ltd*) and dermatitis/facial eczema (*Pape v Cumbria County Council [1991] IRLR 463*). *Pape* concerned an office cleaner who developed dermatitis and facial eczema after using Vim, Flash and polish. The employer was held liable for damages at common law, since he had not instructed her in the dangers of using chemical materials with unprotected hands and had not made her wear rubber gloves.

## Consequences of breach

P3027    Employers who fail to provide suitable personal protective equipment, commit a criminal offence, under the *Health and Safety at Work etc. Act 1974* and the *Personal Protective Equipment at Work Regulations 1994* and sundry other regulations (see P3006–P3008 above). In addition, if, as a result of failure to provide suitable equipment, an employee suffers foreseeable injury and/or disease, the employer will be liable to the employee for damages for negligence. Conversely, if, after instruction and, where necessary, training, an employee fails or refuses to wear and maintain suitable personal protective equipment, he too can be prosecuted and/or dismissed and, if he is injured or suffers a disease in consequence, will probably lose all or, certainly, part of his damages.

# Product Safety

## Introduction

With the expansion of EU Directives and other legislation aimed at manufacturers, designers, importers and suppliers, product safety emerges as a fast growth area – a development expedited by the introduction of the *General Product Safety Regulations 1994 (SI 1994 No 2328)*. Indeed, there is an identifiable trend towards placing responsibilities on producers and those involved in commercial circulation as well as on employers and occupiers (see MACHINERY SAFETY and PERSONAL PROTECTIVE EQUIPMENT). Although there is no question of removal of duties from employers and occupiers and users of industrial plant, machinery and products, there is a realisation that the *sine qua non* of compliance on the part of employers and users with their safety duties is compliance with essential health and safety requirements on the part of designers and manufacturers. This trend is likely to continue with more products being brought within the scope of the EU's 'new approach' regime which promotes supply of products throughout the single market provided they meet essential requirements which can be demonstrated by compliance with harmonised European standards. As far as civil liability is concerned, this trend may well result in a long-term shift in the balance of liability for injury away from employers and occupiers towards designers, manufacturers and other suppliers.

It was thalidomide that first focused serious attention on the legal control of product safety, leading to the Medicinal Products Directive (65/65/EEC) and the *Medicines Act 1968*, the first comprehensive regulatory system of product testing, licensing and vigilance. Since then a host of regulations has appeared, covering areas as diverse as pencils, aerosols, cosmetics and electrical products. More recently the General Product Safety Directive (92/59/EEC), implemented by the *General Product Safety Regulations 1994 (SI 1994 No 2328)*, requires in a general way that producers of consumer goods place only safe products on the market and undertake appropriate post-marketing surveillance. The significance of these Regulations lies not in their substantive requirements (which are not at all detailed or especially onerous). Their importance lies more in the completion of an all-embracing consumer product safety regime across the European Union. Whilst specific regulatory requirements will take precedence (e.g. duties specified in sectoral directives or directives dealing with particular risks such as the Electromagnetic Compatibility Directive (89/336/EEC)) aspects of the *General Product Safety Regulations 1994* are meant to cover any gaps in the consumer protection network left by existing regulatory requirements.

The regulation of products for use in the workplace has developed along separate lines (although there is an increasing overlap by virtue of the 'new approach' Directives, such as those for machinery or electromagnetic compatibility, which apply uniform requirements for consumer and workplace products albeit with separate enforcement regimes). Under the *Health and Safety at Work etc. Act 1974 (HSWA 1974)*, s 6 all articles and substances for use at work are required to be as safe as is reasonably practicable, and manufacturers and other suppliers are under obligation to provide information and warnings for safety in use. Various product-specific regulations have also been made under *HSWA 1974*, for example the *Chemicals (Hazard Information and Packaging for Supply) Regulations 1994 (SI 1994 No 3247)* (as amended) and the *Asbestos (Prohibitions) Regulations 1992 (SI 1992 No 3067)* (as amended).

As far as commercial considerations are concerned, quality and fitness for purpose of products has been an implied statutory term in contracts for sale of goods in legislation stemming from the late nineteenth century and which is now found in the *Sale of Goods Act 1979*, as amended by the *Sale and Supply of Goods Act 1994* and the *Sale of Goods (Amendment) Act 1995*. These 1994 amendments included a more focused definition of the standard of *satisfactory quality* which a supplier is obliged by contract to provide, the criteria for which now explicitly includes safety, durability, and freedom from minor defects. The ability to exclude these statutory terms, or insist that buyers waive the rights they have, is now strictly curtailed by the *Unfair Contract Terms Act 1977* (banning exclusion of the most significant rights in consumer contracts, and subjecting exclusions in standard form commercial contracts to a statutory test of 'reasonableness'). In addition, and based on the Directive on Unfair Terms and Consumer Contracts (93/13/EEC), there are now other restrictions contained in the *Unfair Terms in Consumer Contracts Regulations 1999 (SI 1999 No 2083)* imposing a requirement of fairness on most terms in consumer contracts which are not individually negotiated. These Regulations also lay down a requirement for suppliers to ensure that terms are expressed in plain, intelligible language. The most important restriction of all for present purposes in these two sets of Regulations is the effective ban on notices and contract terms seeking to exclude liability for death or personal injury resulting from negligence, a prohibition which is reinforced in relation to defective products by the *Consumer Protection Act 1987, s 7*.

This section deals with criminal and civil liabilities for unsafe products for consumer and industrial use as well as the duties imposed on sellers and suppliers of consumer products and after-sales personnel as far as contract law is concerned.

## Consumer products

### General Product Safety Regulations 1994

*Duties of producers and distributors*

P9002    The *General Product Safety Regulations 1994 (SI 1994 No 2328)* lay down general requirements concerning the safety of products intended for or likely to be used by consumers. Products used solely in the workplace are not covered, but the fact that a product has a wider industrial application will not prevent it being a consumer product for the purposes of these Regulations if it is supplied to consumers. All manner of products are potentially caught, including clothing, primary agricultural products, DIY equipment and motor vehicles.

The Regulations do not apply to:

—    second-hand products which are antiques;

—    products supplied for repair or reconditioning before use, provided that the purchaser is clearly informed accordingly;

—    products exported direct by the UK manufacturer to a country outside the European Union.

Furthermore, the Regulations are disapplied in relation to any product where there are specific provisions in European law governing *all aspects* of the safety of a product. Where there are product-specific provisions in European law which do not cover all aspects, the 1994 Regulations apply to the extent that specific provision is not made by European law. [*General Product Safety Regulations 1994 (SI 1994 No 2328), Reg 3(c) and Reg 4*].

The main requirements of the Regulations are that:

(*a*)   no producer may place a product on the market unless it is safe [*General Product Safety Regulations 1994 (SI 1994 No 2328), Reg 7*];

(*b*)   producers provide consumers with relevant information, so as to enable them (i.e. consumers) to assess risks inherent in products throughout the normal or foreseeable period of use, where such risks are not immediately obvious without adequate warnings, and to take precautions against those risks [*General Product Safety Regulations 1994 (SI 1994 No 2328), Reg 8(1)(a)*];

(*c*)   producers update themselves regarding risks presented by their products and take appropriate action (if necessary recall and withdrawal), for example by:

(i)   identifying products/batches of products by marking,

(ii)   sample testing,

(iii)   investigating and following up *bona fide* complaints,

(iv)   keeping distributors informed accordingly

[*General Product Safety Regulations 1994 (SI 1994 No 2328), Reg 8(1)(b), (2)*];

(*d*)   in order to enable producers to comply with their duties, distributors must act with due care and in particular:

(i)   must not supply products to any person which are known or presumed (on the basis of information in their possession and as professionals) to be dangerous products, and

(ii)   must participate in monitoring safety of products placed on the market – in particular, by passing on information on product risks and co-operating in action to avoid risks.

[*General Product Safety Regulations 1994 (SI 1994 No 2328), Reg 9(a)(b)*].

## *Presumption of conformity with safety requirements*

P9003   A 'safe' product is a product which, under normal or reasonably foreseeable conditions of use (as well as duration), does not present any risk (or only minimal risks) compatible with the product's use, considered as acceptable and consistent with a high level of protection for the safety and health of consumers, with reference to:

(*a*)   product characteristics (e.g. composition, packaging, assembly and maintenance instructions);

(*b*)   the effect on other products, where use with other products is reasonably foreseeable;

(*c*)   product presentation (i.e. labelling, instructions for use and disposal); and

(*d*)   categories of consumers at serious risk – in particular, children.

[*General Product Safety Regulations 1994 (SI 1994 No 2328), Reg 2(1)*].

In this connection, where a product conforms with specific UK safety requirements (e.g. the *Plugs and Sockets etc (Safety) Regulations 1994 (SI 1994 No 1768)*) there is a presumption that the product is safe, until the contrary is proved. In the absence of specific regulations governing the health and safety aspects of a product, the assessment of safety is to be made by taking into account:

(i)    voluntary national standards implementing European standards;

(ii)    EU technical specifications, or, failing these,

—    standards drawn up in the UK, or

—    codes of practice relating to the product, or

—    state of the art and technology

and the safety that consumers may reasonably expect.

[*General Product Safety Regulations 1994 (SI 1994 No 2328), Reg 10*].

### Offences, penalties and defences

**P9004**    Contravention of *Regs 7–9(a)* (above) is an offence, carrying, on summary conviction, a maximum penalty of:

(*a*)    imprisonment for up to three months, or

(*b*)    a fine of £5,000, or

(*c*)    both.

[*General Product Safety Regulations 1994 (SI 1994 No 2328), Reg 12*].

### Preparatory acts by producers and distributors

**P9005**    No producer or distributor may:

(*a*)    offer or agree to place on the market any dangerous product, or expose or possess such product for placing on the market, or

(*b*)    offer or agree to supply any dangerous product, or expose or possess same for supply.

Contravention is an offence, carrying the same maximum penalties as breach of *Reg 12* (see P9004 above).

### Offence by another person

**P9006**    As with breaches of *HSWA* and similarly-oriented legislation, where an offence is committed by 'another person' in the course of his commercial activity, that person can be charged, whether or not the principal offender is prosecuted. Similarly, where commission of an offence is consented to or connived at, or attributable to neglect, on the part of a director, manager or secretary, such persons can be charged in addition to or in lieu of the body corporate. [*General Product Safety Regulations 1994 (SI 1994 No 2328), Reg 15*].

### Defence of 'due diligence' – and exceptions

**P9007**    It is a defence for a person charged under these Regulations to show that he took all reasonable steps and exercised all due diligence to avoid committing the offence. [*General Product Safety Regulations 1994 (SI 1994 No 2328), Reg 14(1)*]. (See further ENFORCEMENT.)

The exceptions to the above are:

(*a*)    Where, allegedly, commission of the offence was due to:

(i)    the act or default of another, or

(ii)    reliance on information given by another,

a person so charged cannot, without leave of the court, rely on the defence of 'due diligence', unless he has served a notice, within, at least, seven days before the hearing, identifying the person responsible for the commission or default. [*General Product Safety Regulations 1994 (SI 1994 No 2328), Reg 14(2)(3)*].

(*b*)    A person so charged cannot rely on the defence of 'information supplied by another', unless he shows that it was reasonable in all the circumstances for him to have relied on the information. In particular, did he take steps to verify the information or did he have any reason to disbelieve the information? [*General Product Safety Regulations 1994 (SI 1994 No 2328), Reg 14(4)*].

(*c*)    A distributor charged with an offence cannot rely on the defence where he has contravened *Reg 9(b)* concerning passing on information. [*General Product Safety Regulations 1994 (SI 1994 No 2328), Reg 14(5)*].

A mere recommendation on the part of an importer that labels should be attached to boxes by retailers does not constitute 'due diligence' for the purposes of *Reg 14(1)*. (In *Coventry County Council v Ackerman Group plc [1995] Crim LR 140*, an egg boiler imported by the defendant failed to contain instructions that eggs should be broken into the container and yolks pricked before being microwaved. The defendant had learned of the problem and had printed instructions which were sent to all retailers, recommending that they be fixed to the boxes.)

Compliance with recognised standards (such as British Standards) will not amount to the defence of due diligence if a product is nevertheless unsafe for the user. In *Whirlpool (UK) Ltd and Magnet Ltd v Gloucestershire County Council (1993, unreported)* cooker hoods which were intrinsically safe and which met applicable standards for the purposes of the *Low Voltage Electrical Equipment (Safety) Regulations 1989* failed to meet the general safety requirement contained in the then applicable consumer protection legislation because they were liable to result in fires when used in conjunction with certain gas hobs.

# Regulations made under the Health and Safety at Work etc. Act

P9008    Various safety regulations are made under the umbrella of *HSWA 1974* and these often implement European health and safety directives. The *Provision and Use of Work Equipment Regulations 1998 (SI 1998 No 2306)* is one example which implemented European Directive 89/655/EEC.

The 1998 Regulations place obligations on employers and on certain persons having control of work equipment, or of persons who use or supervise or manage the use of work equipment or of the way in which the equipment is used. The key requirement is to ensure that that work equipment is maintained in an efficient state, in efficient working order and in good repair. [*Provision and Use of Work Equipment Regulations 1998 (SI 1998 No 2306), Reg 5(1)*]. It was recently confirmed that this requirement imposes strict liability on the employer (*Stark v The Post Office, The Times, 29 March 2000*) and that, where a workplace product injures someone, the employer will be liable even in situations where through wear and tear the product has become dangerous. The employer's duty to maintain translates into a duty to ensure that there are no latent defects.

## Industrial products

P9009

The *HSWA 1974* was the first Act to place a *general* duty on designers and manufacturers of industrial products to design and produce articles and substances that are safe and without health risks when used at work. Prior to this date legislation had tended to avoid this approach, e.g. the *Factories Act 1961*, on the premise that machinery could not be made design safe (see M1001 MACHINERY SAFETY). Statutory requirements had tended to concentrate on the duty to guard and fence machinery, and with the placement of a duty upon the user/employer to inspect and test inward products for safety. There is a general residual duty on the employers/users of industrial products to inspect and test them for safety under *HSWA 1974, s 2.*

These duties notwithstanding, the trend of legislation in recent years has been towards safer design and manufacture of products for industrial and domestic use. Thus, *HSWA 1974, s 6* as updated by the *Consumer Protection Act 1987, Sch 3* imposes general duties on designers, manufacturers, importers and suppliers of products ('articles and substances') for use at work, to their immediate users. Contravention of s 6 carries with it a maximum fine, on summary conviction, of £20,000 or an unlimited fine in the Crown Court (see ENFORCEMENT). In addition, a separate duty is laid on installers of industrial plant and machinery. However, because of their involvement in the key areas of design and manufacture, more onerous duties are placed upon designers and manufacturers of articles and substances for use at work than upon importers and suppliers, who are essentially concerned with distribution and retail of industrial products. However. under *HSWA 1974, s 6(8A)* importers are made liable for the first time for the faults of foreign designers/manufacturers.

## Criminal liability for breach of statutory duties

P9010

This refers to duties laid down in *HSWA 1974* as revised by the *Consumer Protection Act 1987, Sch 3*. The duties exist in relation to articles and substances for use at work and fairground equipment. There are no civil claims rights available to employees under these provisions except for breach of safety regulations. (For the specific requirements now applicable to machinery for use at work, see MACHINERY SAFETY.)

### Definition of articles and substances

P9011

An article for use at work means:

(*a*)    any plant designed for use or operation (whether exclusively or not) by persons at work; and

(*b*)    any article designed for use as a component in any such plant.

[*HSWA 1974, s 53(1)*].

A substance for use at work means 'any natural or artificial substance (including micro-organisms), whether in solid or liquid form or in the form of a gas or vapour'. [*HSWA 1974, s 53(1)*].

An article upon which first trials/demonstrations are carried out is not an article for use at work, but rather an article which *might* be used at work. The purpose of trial/demonstration was to determine whether the article could safely be later used at work (*McKay v Unwin Pyrotechnics Ltd, The Times, 5 March 1991* where a dummy mine exploded, causing the operator injury, when being tested to see if it would explode when hit by a flail attached to a vehicle. It was held that there was no breach of *HSWA 1974, s 6(1)(a)*).

### Duties in respect of articles and substances for use at work

P9012  *HSWA 1974, s 6* (as amended by the *Consumer Protection Act 1987, Sch 3*) places duties upon manufacturers and designers, as well as importers and suppliers, of (*a*) articles and (*b*) substances for use at work, whether used exclusively at work or not (e.g. lawnmower, hair dryer).

*Articles for use at work*

P9013  Any person who designs, manufactures, imports or supplies any article for use at work (or any article of fairground equipment) must:

(*a*)  ensure, so far as is reasonably practicable (for the meaning of this expression see E15031 ENFORCEMENT), that the article is so designed and constructed that it will be safe and without risks to health at all times when it is being (i) set, (ii) used, (iii) cleaned or (iv) maintained by a person at work;

(*b*)  carry out or arrange for the carrying out of such testing and examination as may be necessary for the performance of the above duty;

(*c*)  take such steps as are necessary to secure that persons supplied by that person with the article are provided with adequate information about the use for which the article is designed or has been tested and about any conditions necessary to ensure that it will be safe and without risks to health at all such times of (i) setting, (ii) using, (iii) cleaning, (iv) maintaining *and* when being (v) dismantled, or (vi) disposed of; and

(*d*)  take such steps as are necessary to secure, so far as is reasonably practicable, that persons so supplied are provided with all such revisions of information as are necessary by reason of it becoming known that anything gives rise to a serious risk to health or safety.

[*HSWA 1974, s 6(1)(a)–(d) as amended by the Consumer Protection Act 1987, Sch 3*].

(See P9015 and P9016 below for further duties relevant to articles for use at work.)

In the case of an article for use at work which is likely to cause an employee to be exposed to 85 dB(A) or above, or to peak action level (200 pascals) or above, adequate information must be provided about noise likely to be generated by that article. [*Noise at Work Regulations 1989 (SI 1989 No 1790), Reg 12*] (see further NOISE AND VIBRATION).

*Substances for use at work*

P9014  Every person who manufactures, imports or supplies any substance must:

(*a*)  ensure, so far as is reasonably practicable, that the substance will be safe and without risks to health at all times when it is being (i) used, (ii) handled, (iii) processed, (iv) stored, or (v) transported by any person at work or in premises where substances are being installed;

(*b*)    carry out or arrange for the carrying out of such testing and examination as may be necessary for the performance of the duty in (*a*);

(*c*)    take such steps as are necessary to secure that persons supplied by that person with the substance are provided with adequate information about:

(i)    any risks to health or safety to which the inherent properties of the substance may give rise;

(ii)    the results of any relevant tests which have been carried out on or in connection with the substance; and

(iii)    any conditions necessary to ensure that the substance will be safe and without risks to health at all times when it is being (*a*) used, (*b*) handled, (*c*) processed, (*d*) stored, (*e*) transported and (*f*) disposed of; and

(*d*)    take such steps as are necessary to secure, so far as is reasonably practicable, that persons so supplied are provided with all such revisions of information as are necessary by reason of it becoming known that anything gives rise to a serious risk to health or safety.

[*HSWA 1974, s 6(4) as amended by the Consumer Protection Act 1987, Sch 3*].

*Additional duty on designers and manufacturers to carry out research*

**P9015**    Any person who undertakes the design or manufacture of any article for use at work must carry out, or arrange for the carrying out, of any necessary research with a view to the discovery and, so far as is reasonably practicable, the elimination or minimisation of any health or safety risks to which the design or article may give rise. [*HSWA 1974, s 6(2)*].

*Duties on installers of articles for use at work*

**P9016**    Any person who erects or installs any article for use at work in any premises where the article is to be used by persons at work, must ensure, so far as is reasonably practicable, that nothing about the way in which the article is erected or installed makes it unsafe or a risk to health when it is being (*a*) set, (*b*) used, (*c*) cleaned, or (*d*) maintained by someone at work. [*HSWA 1974, s 6(3) as amended by the Consumer Protection Act 1987, Sch 3*].

*Additional duty on manufacturers of substances to carry out research*

**P9017**    Any person who manufactures any substance must carry out, or arrange for the carrying out, of any necessary research with a view to the discovery and, so far as is reasonably practicable, the elimination or minimisation of any health/safety risks at all times when the substance is being (*a*) used, (*b*) handled, (*c*) processed, (*d*) stored, or (*e*) transported by someone at work. [*HSWA 1974, s 6(5) as amended by the Consumer Protection Act 1987, Sch 3*].

*No duty on suppliers of industrial articles and substances to research*

**P9018**    It is not necessary to repeat any testing, examination or research which has been carried out by designers and manufacturers of industrial products, on the part of importers and suppliers, in so far as it is reasonable to rely on the results. [*HSWA 1974, s 6(6)*].

## Custom built articles

P9019 Where a person designs, manufactures, imports or supplies an article for or to another person on the basis of a written undertaking by that other to ensure that the article will be safe and without health risks when being (*a*) set, (*b*) used, (*c*) cleaned, or (*d*) maintained by a person at work, the undertaking will relieve the designer/ manufacturer etc. from the duty specified in *HSWA 1974, s 6(1)(a)* (see P9012 above), to such extent as is reasonable, having regard to the terms of the undertaking. [*HSWA 1974, s 6(8) as amended by the Consumer Protection Act 1987, Sch 3*].

## Importers liable for offences of foreign manufacturers/ designers

P9020 In order to give added protection to industrial users from unsafe imported products, the *Consumer Protection Act 1987, Sch 3* has introduced a new subsection (*HSWA 1974, s 6(8A)*) which, in effect makes importers of unsafe products liable for the acts/omissions of foreign designers and manufacturers. *Section 6(8A)* states that nothing in (*inter alia*) is to relieve an importer of an article/substance from any of his duties, as regards anything done (or not done) or within the control of:

(*a*) a foreign designer; or

(*b*) a foreign manufacturer of an article/substance.

[*HSWA 1974, s 6(8A)*].

## Proper use

P9021 The original wording of *HSWA 1974, s 6(1)(a), 6(4)(a) and 6(10)* concerning 'proper use' excluded 'foreseeable user error' as a defence, which had the consequence of favouring the supplier. Thus, if a supplier could demonstrate a degree of operator misuse or error, however reasonably foreseeable, the question of initial product safety was side stepped. Moreover, 'when properly used' implied, as construed, that there could only be a breach of *s 6* once a product had actually been *used*. This was contrary to the principle that safety should be built into design/ production, rather than relying on warnings and disclaimers. The wording in *s 6* is now amended so that only *unforeseeable* user/operator error will relieve the supplier from liability; he will no longer be able to rely on the strict letter of his operating instructions. [*Consumer Protection Act 1987, Sch 3*].

## Powers to deal with unsafe imported goods

P9022 *HSWA 1974* does not empower enforcing authorities to stop the supply of unsafe products at source or prevent the sale of products by foreign producers after they have been found to be unsafe, but enforcement officers have the power to act at the point of entry or anywhere else along the distribution chain to stop unsafe articles/substances being imported by serving prohibition notices (see ENFORCE-MENT).

Customs officers can seize any imported article/substance, which is considered to be unsafe, and detain it for up to two (working) days. [*HSWA s 25A (incorporated by Schedule 3 to the Consumer Protection Act 1987)*].

In addition, customs officers can transmit information relating to unsafe imported products to HSE inspectors. [*HSWA 1974, s 27A (incorporated by the Consumer Protection Act 1987, Sch 3)*].

# Civil liability for unsafe products – historical background

P9023    Originally at common law where defective products caused injury, damage and/or death, redress depended on whether the injured user had a contract with the seller or hirer of the product. This was often not the case, and in consequence many persons, including employees repairing and/or servicing products, were without remedy. This rule, emanating from the decision of *Winterbottom v Wright (1842) 10 M & W 109*, remained unchanged until 1932, when *Donoghue v Stevenson [1932] AC 562* was decided by the House of Lords. This case was important because it established that manufacturers were liable in negligence (i.e. tort) if they failed to take reasonable care in the manufacturing and marketing of their products, and in consequence a user suffered injury when using the product in a reasonably foreseeable way. More particularly, a 'manufacturer of products, which he sells in such a form as to show that he intends them to reach the ultimate consumer in the form in which they left him with no reasonable possibility of intermediate inspection, and with the knowledge that the absence of reasonable care in the preparation or putting up of the products will result in an injury to the consumer's life or property, owes a duty to the consumer to take reasonable care' (per Lord Atkin). In this way, manufacturers of products which were defective were liable in negligence to users and consumers of their products, including those who as intermediaries, repair, maintain and service industrial products, it being irrelevant whether there was a contract between manufacturer and user (which normally there was not).

*Donoghue v Stevenson* is a case of enormous historical importance in the context of liability of manufacturers, but although the principle has become well established and is still widely applied it did not give a reliable remedy to injured persons, who still had to satisfy the legal burden of proving that the manufacturer had not exercised reasonable care, a serious obstacle to overcome in cases involving technically complex products. In some instances it became possible to avoid this obstacle, by establishing liability on other bases.

### Defective equipment supplied to employees

P9024    At common law an employer obtaining equipment from a reputable supplier was unlikely to be found liable to an employee if the equipment turned out to be defective and injured him (*Davie v New Merton Board Mills Ltd [1959] AC 604*). Although it represented no bar to employees suing manufacturers direct for negligence, the effect of this decision was reversed by the *Employers' Liability (Defective Equipment) Act 1969* rendering employers strictly liable (irrespective of negligence) for any defects in equipment causing injury. (See E11004–E11005 EMPLOYERS' DUTIES TO THEIR EMPLOYEES). In such circumstances the employer would be able to claim indemnity for breach of contract by the supplier of the equipment.

### Breach of statutory duty

P9025    Whilst legislation and regulations dealing with domestic and industrial safety are principally penal and enforceable by state agencies (trading standards officers and health and safety inspectors) if injury, death or damage occurs in consequence of a breach of such statutory duty, it may be possible to use this breach as the basis of a civil liability claim. Here there may be strict liability if there are absolute requirements, or the duty may be defined in terms of what it is practicable or reasonably practicable to do (see E15031 ENFORCEMENT).

As far as workplace products are concerned, *HSWA 1974, s 47* bars a right of action in civil proceedings in respect of any failure to comply with *HSWA 1974, s 6* (or the other general duties under the Act). However a breach of a duty imposed by health and safety regulations will generally be actionable in this way, unless the particular regulations in question contain a proviso to the contrary.

The position is the same in relation to consumer safety regulations made under the *Consumer Protection Act 1987 (Consumer Protection Act 1987, s 41(1))*. No provision is made in the *General Product Safety Regulations 1994 (SI 1994 No 2328)* for any breach thereof to give rise to civil liability for the benefit of an injured person. Given that the Regulations stem from European law it is unlikely that they would be construed in such a way as to give more extensive rights than those contained in the Product Liability Directive (85/374/EEC) (see P9026).

# Consumer Protection Act 1987

P9026  At European level it was deemed necessary to introduce a degree of harmonisation of product liability principles between member states, and at the same time to reduce the importance of fault and negligence concepts in favour of liability being determined by reference to 'defects' in a product. Thus the nature of the product itself would become the key issue, not the conduct of the manufacturer. After protracted debate the Product Liability Directive (85/374/EEC) was adopted.

## Introduction of strict product liability

P9027  The introduction of strict product liability is enshrined in Britain within the *Consumer Protection Act 1987, s 2(1)*. Thus, where any damage is *caused* wholly or partly by a defect (see P9030 below) in a product (e.g. goods, electricity, a component product or raw materials), the following may be liable for damages (irrespective of negligence):

(*a*)   the producer;

(*b*)   any person who, by putting his name on the product or using a trade mark (or other distinguishing mark) has held himself out as the producer;

(*c*)   any person who has imported the product into a member state from outside the EU, in the course of trade/business.

[*Consumer Protection Act 1987, s 2(1)(2)*].

## Producers

P9028  Producers are variously defined as:

(*a*)   the person who manufactured a product;

(*b*)   in the case of a substance which has not been manufactured, but rather won or abstracted, the person who won or abstracted it;

(*c*)   in the case of a product not manufactured, won or abstracted, but whose essential characteristics are attributable to an industrial process or agricultural process, the person who carried out the process.

[*Consumer Protection Act 1987, s 1(2)(c)*].

## Liability of suppliers

P9029   Although producers are principally liable, intermediate suppliers can also be liable in certain circumstances. Thus, any person who supplied the product is liable for damages if:

(*a*)   the injured person requests the supplier to identify one (or more) of the following:

(i)    the producer,

(ii)   the person who put his trade mark on the product,

(iii)  the importer of the product into the EU; and

(*b*)   the request is made within a reasonable time after damage/injury has occurred *and* it is not reasonably practicable for the requestor to identify the above three persons; and

(*c*)   within a reasonable time after receiving the request, the supplier fails either:

(i)    to comply with the request, or

(ii)   identify his supplier.

[*Consumer Protection Act 1987, s 2(3)*].

Importers of products into the EU and persons applying their name, brand or trade mark will also be directly liable as if they were original manufacturers. [*Consumer Protection Act 1987, s 2(2)*].

## Defect – key to liability

P9030   Liability presupposes that there is a defect in the product, and indeed, existence of a defect is the key to liability. Defect is defined in terms of the absence of safety in the product. More particularly, there is a 'defect in a product . . . if the safety of the product is not such as persons generally are entitled to expect' (including products comprised in that product). [*Consumer Protection Act 1987, s 3(1)*].

Defect can arise in one of three ways and is related to:

(*a*)   construction, manufacture, sub-manufacture, assembly;

(*b*)   absence or inadequacy of suitable warnings, or existence of misleading warnings or precautions;

(*c*)   design.

The definition of 'defect' implies an entitlement to an expectation of safety on the part of the consumer, judged by reference to *general* consumer expectations not individual subjective ones. (The American case of *Webster v Blue Ship Tea Room Inc 347 Mass 421, 198 NE 2d 309 (1964)* is particularly instructive here. The claimant sued in a product liability action for a bone which had stuck in her throat, as a result of eating a fish chowder in the defendant's restaurant. It was held that there was no liability. Whatever her own expectations may have been, fish chowder would not be fish chowder without some bones and this is a general expectation.)

The court will require a claimant to be specific and be particular about exactly what the alleged defect is (*Paul Sayers and Others v Smithkline Beecham plc and Others (MMR/MR litigation) [1999] MLC 0117*).

### Consumer expectation of safety – criteria

P9031    The general consumer expectation of safety must be judged in relation to:

(*a*)    the marketing of the product, i.e.:

    (i)    the manner in which; and

    (ii)    the purposes for which the product has been marketed;

    (iii)    any instructions/warnings against doing anything with the product; and

(*b*)    by what might reasonably be expected to be done with or in relation to the product (e.g. the expectation that a sharp knife will be handled with care); and

(*c*)    the time when the product was supplied (e.g. a product's shelf-life).

A defect cannot arise retrospectively by virtue of the fact that, subsequently, a safer product is made and put into circulation. [*Consumer Protection Act 1987, s 3(2)*].

### Time of supply

P9032    Liability attaches to the *supply* of a product (see P9041 below). More particularly, the producer will be liable for any defects in the product existing at the time of supply (see P9040(*d*) below); and where two or more persons collaborate in the manufacture of a product, say by submanufacture, either and both may be liable, that is, severally and jointly (see P9038 below).

### Contributory negligence

P9033    A person who is careless for his own safety is probably guilty of contributory negligence and, thus, will risk a reduction in damages. [*Consumer Protection Act 1987, s 6(4)*]. (See also E11010 EMPLOYERS' DUTIES TO THEIR EMPLOYEES.) However, in the product liability context, carelessness of the user may mean that there is no liability at all on the part of the producer. If, for example, clear instructions and warnings provided with the product had been disregarded, when compliance would have avoided the accident, it is highly unlikely that the product would be found to be defective for the purposes of the Act. No off-setting of damages for contributory fault of the claimant would arise.

### Absence or inadequacy of suitable/misleading warnings

P9034    The common law required that the vendor of a product should point out any latent dangers in a product which he either knew about or ought to have known about. Misleading terminology/labelling on a product or product container could result in liability for negligence (*Vacwell Engineering Ltd v BDH Chemicals Ltd [1969] 3 AER 1681* where ampoules containing boron tribromide, which carried the warning 'Harmful Vapours', exploded on contact with water, killing two scientists. It was held that this consequence was reasonably foreseeable and accordingly the defendants should have researched their product more thoroughly). In a similar product liability action today, the manufacturers would be strictly liable (subject to statutory defences) and, if injury/damage followed the failure to issue a written/pictorial warning, as required by law (e.g. the *Chemicals (Hazard Information and Packaging for Supply) Regulations 1994 (SI 1994 No 3247)*), there would be liability.

The duty, on manufacturers, to research the safety of their products, before putting them into circulation (see *Vacwell Engineering Ltd v BDH Chemicals Ltd*) is even more necessary and compulsory now, given the introduction of strict product liability. This includes safety in connection with directions for use on a product. A warning refers to something that can go wrong with the product; directions for use relate to the best results that can be obtained from products, if the directions are followed. In the absence of case law on the point it is reasonable to assume that in order to avoid actions for product liability, manufacturers should provide both warnings, indicating the worst results and dangers, and directions for use, indicating the best results; the warning, in effect, identifying the worst consequences that could follow if directions for use were not complied with.

In the case of *Worsley v Tambrands Ltd (No 2) [2000] MCR 0280*, it was held that a tampon manufacturer had done what was reasonable in all the circumstances to warn a woman about the risk of toxic shock syndrome from tampon use. They had placed a clear legible warning on the outside of the box directing the user to the leaflet. The leaflet was legible, literate and unambiguous and contained all the material necessary to convey both the warning signs and the action required if any risk were present. The manufacturer could not cater for lost leaflets or for those who chose not to replace them. This give valuable guidance as to the extent that manufacturers are expected to warn users of their products of the risks associated with their products.

*Defect must exist when the product left the producer's possession*

**P9035**
This situation tends to be spotlighted by alteration of, modification to or interference with a product on the part of an intermediary, for instance, a dealer or agent. If a product leaves an assembly line in accordance with its intended design, but is subsequently altered, modified or generally interfered with by an intermediary, in a manner outside the product's specification, the manufacturer is probably not liable for any injury so caused. In *Sabloff v Yamaha Motor Co 113 NJ Super 279, 273 A 2d 606 (1971)*, the claimant was injured when the wheel of his motor-cycle locked, causing it to skid, then crash. The manufacturer's specification stipulated that the dealer attach the wheel of the motor-cycle to the front fork with a nut and bolt, and this had not been done properly. It was held that the dealer was liable for the motor-cyclist's injury (as well as the assembler, since the latter had delegated the function of tightening the nut to the dealer and it had not been properly carried out).

*Role of intermediaries*

**P9036**
If a defect in a product is foreseeably detectable by a legitimate intermediary (e.g. a retailer in the case of a domestic product or an employer in the case of an industrial product), liability used to rest with the intermediary rather than the manufacturer, when liability was referable to negligence (*Donoghue v Stevenson [1932] AC 562*). This position does not duplicate under the *Consumer Protection Act 1987*, since the main object of the legislation is to fix producers with strict liability for injury-causing product defects to users. Nevertheless, there are common law and statutory duties on employers to inspect/test inward plant and machinery for use at the workplace, and failure to comply with these duties may make an employer liable. In addition, employers, in such circumstances, can incur liability under the *Employers' Liability (Defective Equipment) Act 1969* (see E11005 EMPLOYERS' DUTIES TO THEIR EMPLOYEES) and so may seek to exercise contractual indemnity against manufacturers.

*Comparison with negligence*

P9037    The similarity between product liability and negligence lies in causation. Defect must be the material *cause* of injury. The main arguments against this are likely to be along the lines of misuse of a product by a user (e.g. knowingly driving a car with defective brakes), or ignoring warnings (a two-pronged defence, since it also denies there was a 'defect'), or – as is common in chemicals and pesticides cases – a defence based on alternative theories of causation of the claimant's injuries.

Product liability differs from negligence in that it is no longer necessary for injured users to prove absence of reasonable care on the part of manufacturers. All that is now necessary is proof of (*a*) defect (see P9030 above) and (*b*) that the defect caused the injury. It will, therefore, be no good for manufacturers to point to an unblemished safety record and/or excellent quality assurance programmes, or the lack of foreseeability of the accident, since the user is not trying to establish negligence. How or why a defect arose is immaterial; what is important is the fact that it exists.

Liability in negligence still has a role to play in cases where liability under the *Consumer Protection Act 1987* cannot be established because, for example, the defendant is not a 'producer' as defined, or because the statutory defence or time limit would bar a strict liability claim (see P9039 and P9043). There is greater scope under the law of negligence for liability to be established against distributors and retailers who may be held responsible for certain defects, especially where inadequate warnings and instructions have been provided (e.g. *Goodchild v Vaclight, The Times, 22 May 1965*).

*Joint and several liability*

P9038    If two or more persons/companies are liable for the same damage, the liability is joint and several. This can, for example, refer to the situation where a product (e.g. an aircraft) is made partly in one country (e.g. England) and partly in another (e.g. France). Here both partners are liable (joint liability) but in the event of one party not being able to pay, the other can be made to pay all the compensation (several liability). [*Consumer Protection Act 1987, s 2(5)*].

*Parameters of liability*

P9039    For certain types of damage including (*a*) death, (*b*) personal injury and (*c*) loss or damage to property liability is included and relevant to private use, occupation and consumption by consumers. [*Consumer Protection Act 1987, s 5(1)*]. However, producers and others will not be liable for:

   (*a*)    damage/loss to the defective product itself, or any product supplied with the defective product [*Consumer Protection Act 1987, s 5(2)*];

   (*b*)    damage to property not 'ordinarily intended for private use, occupation or consumption' e.g. car/van used for business purposes [*Consumer Protection Act 1987, s 5(3)*]; and

   (*c*)    damage amounting to less than £275 (to be determined as early as possible after loss) [*Consumer Protection Act 1987, s 5(4)*].

*Defences*

P9040    The following statutory defences are open to producers:

   (*a*)    the defect was attributable to compliance with any requirement imposed by law/regulation or a European Union rule/regulation [*Consumer Protection Act 1987, s 4(1)(a)*];

(*b*)   the defendant did not supply the product to another (i.e. did not sell/hire/lend/exchange for money/give goods as a prize etc. (see below 'supply')) [*Consumer Protection Act 1987, s 4(1)(b)*];

(*c*)   the supply to another person was not in the course of that supplier's business [*Consumer Protection Act 1987, s 4(1)(c)*];

(*d*)   the defect did not exist in the product at the relevant time (i.e. it came into existence after the product had left the possession of the defendant). This principally refers to the situation where for example a retailer fails to follow the instructions of the manufacturer for storage or assembly [*Consumer Protection Act 1987, s 4(1)(d)*];

(*e*)   that the state of scientific and technical knowledge at the relevant time was not such that a producer 'might be expected to have discovered the defect if it had existed in his products while they were under his control' (i.e. development risk) [*Consumer Protection Act 1987, s 4(1)(e)*] (see P9044 below);

(*f*)   that the defect was:

(i)   a defect in a subsequent product (in which the product in question was comprised); and

(ii)   was wholly attributable to:

(A)   design of the subsequent product; or

(B)   compliance by the producer with the instructions of the producer of the subsequent product.

[*Consumer Protection Act 1987, s 4(1)(f)*]. This is known as the component manufacturer's defence.


## The meaning of 'supply'

P9041    Before strict liability can be established under the *Consumer Protection Act 1987*, a product must have been '*supplied*'. This is defined as follows:

(*a*)   selling, hiring out or lending goods;

(*b*)   entering into a hire-purchase agreement to furnish goods;

(*c*)   performance of any contract for work and materials to furnish goods (e.g. making/repairing teeth);

(*d*)   providing goods in exchange for a consideration other than money (e.g. trading stamps);

(*e*)   providing goods in or in connection with the performance of any statutory function/duty (e.g. supply of gas/electricity by public utilities);

(*f*)   giving the goods as a prize or otherwise making a gift of the goods.

[*Consumer Protection Act 1987, s 46(1)*].

Moreover, in the case of hire-purchase agreements/credit sales the effective supplier (i.e. the dealer), and not the ostensible supplier (i.e. the finance company),is the 'supplier' for the purposes of strict liability. [*Consumer Protection Act 1987, s 46(2)*].

Building work is only to be treated as a supply of goods in so far as it involves provision of any goods to any person by means of their incorporation into the building/structure, e.g. glass for windows. [*Consumer Protection Act 1987, s 46(3)*].

## No contracting out of strict liability

P9042    The liability to person who has suffered injury/damage under the *Consumer Protection Act 1987*, cannot be (*a*) limited or (*b*) excluded:

(*a*)    by any contract term; or

(*b*)    by any notice or other provision.

[*Consumer Protection Act 1987, s 7*].

## Time limits for bringing product liability actions

P9043    No action can be brought under the *Consumer Protection Act 1987, Part I* (i.e. product liability actions) after the expiry of ten years from the time when the product was first put into circulation (i.e. the particular item in question was supplied in the course of business/trade etc.). [*Limitation Act 1980, s 11A(3); Consumer Protection Act 1987, Sch 1*]. In other words, ten years is the cut-off point for liability. An action can still be brought for common law negligence after this time.

However all actions for personal injury caused by product defects must be initiated within three years of whichever event occurs later, namely:

(*a*)    the date when the cause of action accrued (i.e. injury occurred); or

(*b*)    the date when the injured person had the requisite knowledge of his injury/damage to property.

[*Limitation Act 1980, s 11A(4); Consumer Protection Act 1987, Sch 1*].

But if during that period the injured person died, his personal representative has a further three years from his death to bring the action. (This coincides with actions for personal injuries against employers, except of course in that case there is no overall cut-off period of ten years.) [*Limitation Act 1980, s 11A(5)*].

## Development risk

P9044    This will probably emerge as the most important defence to product liability actions. Manufacturers have argued that it would be wrong to hold them responsible for the consequences of defects which they could not reasonably have known about or discovered. The absence of this defence would have the effect of increasing the cost of product liability insurance and stifle the development of new products. On the other hand, consumers maintain that the existence of this defence threatens the whole basis of strict liability and allows manufacturers to escape liability by, in effect, pleading a defence associated with the lack of negligence. For this reason, not all EU states have allowed this defence; the states in favour of its retention are the United Kingdom, Germany, Denmark, Italy and the Netherlands. The burden of proving development risk lies on the producer and it seems likely that he will have to show that no producer of a product of that sort could be expected to have discovered the existence of the defect. 'It will not necessarily be enough to show that he (the producer) has done as many tests as his competitor, nor that he did all the tests required of him by a government regulation setting a minimum standard.' (Explanatory memorandum of EC Directive on Product Liability, Department of Trade and Industry, November 1985).

Additionally, the fact that judgments in product liability cases are 'transportable' could have serious implications for the retention of development risk in the United Kingdom (see P9045 below).

### Transportability of judgments

P9045    The Brussels Convention of 17 September 1968 on Jurisdiction and Enforcement of Judgments in Civil and Commercial Matters requires judgments given in one of the original six EC member states to be enforced in another. The United Kingdom is bound by this Convention, which, by virtue of the *Civil Jurisdiction and Judgments Act 1982*, is part of United Kingdom law. Where product liability actions are concerned, litigation can be initiated in the state where the defendant is based or where injury occurred and the judgment of that court 'transported' to another member state. This could pose a threat to retention of development risk in the United Kingdom and other states in favour of it from a state against it, e.g. France, Belgium, Luxembourg.

## Contractual liability for substandard products

P9046    Contractual liability is concerned with defective products which are substandard (though not necessarily dangerous) regarding quality, reliability and/or durability. Liability is predominantly determined by contractual terms implied by the *Sale of Goods Act 1979* and the *Sale and Supply of Goods Act 1994*, in the case of goods sold; the *Supply of Goods (Implied Terms) Act 1973*, where goods are the subject of hire purchase and conditional and/or credit sale; and the *Supply of Goods and Services Act 1982*, where goods are supplied but not sold as such, primarily as a supply of goods with services; hire and leasing contracts are subject to the 1982 Act as well.

Exemption or exclusion clauses in such contracts may be invalid by virtue of the *Unfair Contract Terms Act 1977*, which also applies to such transactions. Moreover, 'standard form' contracts with consumers where the terms have not been individually negotiated, which contain 'unfair terms' – that is, terms detrimental to the consumer – will have such terms excised, if necessary, by the Director General of Fair Trading, under the *Unfair Terms in Consumer Contracts Regulations 1999 (SI 1999 No 2083)*. These Regulations extend to most consumer contracts between a seller or supplier and a consumer. [*Unfair Terms in Consumer Contracts Regulations 1999, (SI 1999 No 2083), Reg 4(1)*]. (See P9057 below.)

Contractual liability is strict. It is not necessary that negligence be established (*Frost v Aylesbury Dairy Co Ltd [1905] 1 KB 608* where the defendant supplied typhoid-infected milk to the claimant, who, after its consumption, became ill and required medical treatment. It was held that the defendant was liable, irrespective of the absence of negligence on his part).

### Sale of Goods Acts

P9047    Conditions and warranties as to fitness for purpose, quality and merchantability were originally implied into contracts for the sale of goods at common law. Those terms were then codified in the *Sale of Goods Act 1893*. However, this legislation did not provide a blanket consumer protection measure, since sellers were still allowed to exclude liability by suitably worded exemption clauses in the contract. This practice was finally outlawed, at least as far as consumer contracts were concerned, by the *Supply of Goods (Implied Terms) Act 1973* and later still by the *Unfair Contract Terms Act 1977*, the current statute prohibiting contracting out of contractual liability and negligence. Indeed, consumer protection has reached a height with the *Unfair Terms in Consumer Contracts Regulations 1999 (SI 1999 No 2083)*, invalidating 'unfair terms' in most consumer contracts of a standard form nature (see P9057 below).

More recently, the law relating to sale and supply of goods has been updated by the *Sale of Goods Act 1979* and the *Sale and Supply of Goods Act 1994*, the latter replacing the condition of 'merchantable quality' with 'satisfactory quality'. The difference between the 'merchantability' requirement, under the *1979 Act*, and its replacement 'satisfactory quality', under the *1994 Act*, is that, under the former Act, products were 'usable' (or, in the case of food, 'edible'), even if they had defects which ruined their appearance; now they must be free from minor defects as well as being safe and durable. Further, under the previous law, a right of refund disappeared after goods had been kept for a reasonable time; under current law, there is a right of examination for a reasonable time after buying.

## Sale of Goods Act 1979

P9048    In 1979 a consolidated *Sale of Goods Act* was passed and current law on quality and fitness of products is contained in that Act. Another equally important development has been the extension of implied terms, relating to quality and fitness of products, to contracts other than those for the sale of goods, that is, to hire purchase contracts by the *Supply of Goods (Implied Terms) Act 1973*, and to straight hire contracts by the *Supply of Goods and Services Act 1982*. In addition, where services are performed under a contract, that is, a contract for work and materials, there is a statutory duty on the contractor to perform them with reasonable care and skill. In other words, in the case of services liability is not strict, but it is strict for the supply of products. This is laid down in the *Supply of Goods and Services Act 1982, s 4*. This applies whether products are simultaneously but separately supplied under any contract, e.g. after-sales service, say, on a car or a contract to repair a window by a carpenter, in which latter case service is rendered irrespective of product supplied.

### *Products to be of satisfactory quality – sellers/suppliers*

P9049    The *Sale of Goods Act 1979* (as amended) writes two quality conditions into all contracts for the sale of products, the first with regard to satisfactory quality, the second with regard to fitness for purpose.

Where a seller sells goods in the course of business, there is an implied term that the goods supplied under the contract are of satisfactory quality, according to the standards of the reasonable person, by reference to description, price etc. [*Sale of Goods Act 1979, s 14(2) as substituted by the Sale and Supply of Goods Act 1994, s 1(2)*]. The 'satisfactory' (or otherwise) quality of goods can be determined from:

(*a*)    their state and condition;

(*b*)    their fitness for purpose (see P9052 below);

(*c*)    their appearance and finish;

(*d*)    their freedom from minor defects;

(*e*)    their safety; and

(*f*)    their durability.

However, the implied term of 'satisfactory quality' does not apply to situations where:

(i)    the unsatisfactory nature of goods is specifically drawn to the buyer's attention prior to contract; or

(ii)    the buyer examined the goods prior to contract and the matter in question ought to have been revealed by that examination.

[*Sale of Goods Act 1979, s 14(2) as substituted by the Sale and Supply of Goods Act 1994, s 1(2A), (2B) and (2C)*].

### Sale by sample

**P9050**  In the case of a contract for sale by sample, there is an implied condition that the goods will be free from any defect making their quality unsatisfactory, which would not be apparent on reasonable examination of the sample. [*Sale of Goods Act 1979, s 15(2) as substituted by the Sale and Supply of Goods Act 1994, s 1(2)*].

### Conditions implied into sale – sales by a dealer

**P9051**  The condition of satisfactory quality only arises in the case of sales by a dealer to a consumer, not in the case of private sales. The *Sale of Goods Act 1979, s 14(2)* also applies to second-hand as well as new products. It is not necessary, as it is with the 'fitness for purpose' condition (see P9053 below), for the buyer in any way to rely on the skill and judgment of the seller in selecting his stock, in order to invoke *s 14(2)*. However, if the buyer has examined the products, then the seller will not be liable for any defects which the examination should have disclosed. Originally this applied if the buyer had been given opportunity to examine but had not, or only partially, exercised it. In *Thornett & Fehr v Beers & Son [1919] 1 KB 486*, a buyer of glue examined only the outside of some barrels of glue. The glue was defective. It was held that he had examined the glue and so was without redress.

### Products to be reasonably fit for purpose

**P9052**  'Where the seller sells goods in the course of a business and the buyer, expressly or by implication, makes known

(*a*)    to the seller, or

(*b*)    where the purchase price or part of it is payable by instalments and the goods were previously sold by a credit-broker to the seller, to that credit-broker,

any particular purpose for which the goods are being bought, there is an implied condition that the goods supplied under the contract are reasonably fit for that purpose, whether or not that is a purpose for which such goods are commonly supplied, except where the circumstances show that the buyer does not rely or that it is unreasonable for him to rely, on the skill or judgment of the seller or credit-broker.' [*Sale of Goods Act 1979, s 14(3)*].

Reliance on the skill/judgment of the seller will generally be inferred from the buyer's conduct. The reliance will seldom be express: it will usually arise by implication from the circumstances; thus to take a case of a purchase from a retailer, the reliance will be in general inferred from the fact that a buyer goes to the shop in the confidence that the tradesman has selected his stock with skill and judgment (*Grant v Australian Knitting Mills Ltd [1936] AC 85*). Moreover, it is enough if the buyer relies partially on the seller's skill and judgment. However, there may be no reliance where the seller can only sell goods of a particular brand. A claimant bought beer in a public house which he knew was a tied house. He later became ill as a result of drinking it. It was held that there was no reliance on the seller's skill and so no liability on the part of the seller (*Wren v Holt [1903] 1 KB 610*).

Even though products can only be used normally for one purpose, they will have to be reasonably fit for that particular purpose. A claimant bought a hot water bottle and was later scalded when using it because of its defective condition. It was held that the seller was liable because the hot water bottle was not suitable for its normal purpose (*Priest v Last [1903] 2 KB 148*). But, on the other hand, the buyer must not be hypersensitive to the effects of the product. A claimant bought a Harris Tweed coat from the defendants. She later contracted dermatitis from wearing it. Evidence showed that she had an exceptionally sensitive skin. It was held that the coat was reasonably fit for the purpose when worn by a person with an average skin (*Griffiths v Peter Conway Ltd [1939] 1 AER 685*).

Like *s 14(2)*, *s 14(3)* extends beyond the actual products themselves to their containers and labelling. A claimant was injured by a defective bottle containing mineral water, which she had purchased from the defendant, a retailer. The bottle remained the property of the seller because the claimant had paid the seller a deposit on the bottle, which would be returned to her, on return of the empty bottle. It was held that, although the bottle was the property of the seller, the seller was liable for the injury caused to the claimant by the defective container (*Geddling v Marsh [1920] 1 KB 668*).

Like *s 14(2)* (above), *s 14(3)* does not apply to private sales.

### Strict liability under the Sale of Goods Act 1979, s 14

**P9053**    Liability arising under the *Sale of Goods Act, s 14* is strict and does not depend on proof of negligence by the purchaser against the seller (*Frost v Aylesbury Dairy Co Ltd* (see P9046 above)). This fact was stressed as follows in the case of *Kendall v Lillico [1969] 2 AC 31*: 'If the law were always logical one would suppose that a buyer who has obtained a right to rely on the seller's skill and judgment, would only obtain thereby an assurance that proper skill and judgment had been exercised, and would only be entitled to a remedy if a defect in the goods was due to failure to exercise such skill and judgment. But the law has always gone further than that. By getting the seller to undertake his skill and judgment the buyer gets . . . an assurance that the goods will be reasonably fit for his purpose and that covers not only defects which the seller ought to have detected but also defects which are latent in the sense that even the utmost skill and judgment on the part of the seller would not have detected them' (per Lord Reid).

### Dangerous products

**P9054**    As distinct from applying to merely substandard products, both *s 14(2)* and *(3)* of the *Sale of Goods Act 1979* can be invoked where a product is so defective as to be unsafe, but the injury/damage must be a reasonably foreseeable consequence of breach of the implied condition. If, for instance, therefore, the chain of causation is broken by negligence on the part of the user, in using a product knowing it to be defective, there will be no liability. In *Lambert v Lewis [1982] AC 225*, manufacturers had made a defective towing coupling which was sold by retailers to a farmer. The farmer continued to use the coupling knowing that it was unsafe. As a result, an employee was injured and the farmer had to pay damages. He sought to recover these against the retailer for breach of *s 14(3)*. It was held that he could not do so.

### Credit sale and supply of products

**P9055**    Broadly similar terms to those under the *Sale of Goods Act 1979, s 14* exist, in the case of hire purchase, credit sale, conditional sale and hire or lease contracts, by virtue of the Acts described above at P9046 having been modified by the *Sale and Supply of Goods Act 1994*.

# Unfair Contract Terms Act 1977 (UCTA)

**P9056**    In spite of its name, this Act is not directly concerned with 'unfairness' in contracts, nor is it confined to the regulation of contractual relations. The main provisions are as follows:

(a) Liability for death or personal injury resulting from negligence cannot be excluded by warning notices or contractual terms. [*UCTA 1977, s 2*]. (This does not necessarily prevent an indemnity of any liability to an injured person being agreed between two other contracting parties: if A hires plant to B on terms that B indemnifies A in respect of any claims by any person for injury, the clause may be enforceable (see *Thompson v T Lohan (Plant Hire) Ltd [1987] 2 All ER 631)*.)

(b) In the case of other loss or damage, liability for negligence cannot be excluded by contract terms or warning notices unless these satisfy the requirement of reasonableness.

(c) Where one contracting party is a consumer, or when one of the contracting parties is using written standard terms of business, exclusions or restrictions of liability for breach of contract will be permissible only in so far as the term satisfies the requirement of reasonableness [*UCTA 1977, s 3*]; as far as contracts with consumers are concerned, it is not possible to exclude or restrict liability for the implied undertakings as to quality and fitness for purpose contained in the *Sale of Goods Act 1979* (as amended) or in the equivalent provisions relating to hire purchase and other forms of supply of goods [*UCTA 1977, s 6(2)*]. Separate provisions make it an offence to include this type of exclusion clause in a consumer contract [*Consumer Transactions (Restrictions on Statements) Order 1976 (SI 1976 No 1813)*].

(d) In all cases where the reasonableness test applies, the burden of establishing that a clause or other provision is reasonable will lie with the person who is trying to rely on the term in question. The consequence of contravention of the Act is, however, limited to the offending term being treated as being ineffective; the courts will give effect to the remainder of the contract so far as it is possible to do so.

# Unfair Terms in Consumer Contracts Regulations 1999 (SI 1999 No 2083)

**P9057**   Consumers faced with standard form contracts are given more ammunition to combat terminological obscurity, legalese and inequality of bargaining power, by the *Unfair Terms in Consumer Contracts Regulations 1999 (SI 1999 No 2083)*. These regulations have the effect of invalidating any 'unfair terms' in consumer contracts involving products and services, e.g. sale, supply, servicing agreements, insurance and, as a final resort, empowering the Director General of Fair Trading to scrutinise 'standard form' terms, with a view to recommending, where necessary, their discontinued use. Contracts affected by the Act will remain enforceable minus the unfair terms (which will be struck out), in so far as this result is possible. [*Unfair Terms in Consumer Contracts Regulations 1999 (SI 1999 No 2083), Reg 8(2)*].

The contracts affected are only 'standard form' ones, that is, contracts whose terms have not been 'individually negotiated' between seller/supplier and consumer [*Unfair Terms in Consumer Contracts Regulations 1999 (SI 1999 No 2083), Reg 5*]; and a term is taken not to have been 'individually negotiated', where it has been drafted in advance and the consumer has not been able to influence the substance of the term [*Unfair Terms in Consumer Contracts Regulations 1999 (SI 1999 No 2083), Reg 5(2)*]. Significantly, it is incumbent on the seller/supplier, who claims that a term was 'individually negotiated' (i.e. not unfair) to prove that it so was. [*Unfair Terms in Consumer Contracts Regulations 1999 (SI 1999 No 2083), Reg 3(5)*]. However, if the terms of the contract are in plain, intelligible language, fairness, relating to subject matter or price/remuneration, cannot be questioned [*Unfair Terms in Consumer Contracts Regulations 1999 (SI 1999 No 2083), Reg 6(2)*].

The key provisions are:

(*a*)    an 'unfair term' is one which has not been individually negotiated and causes a significant imbalance in the parties' rights and obligations, detrimentally to the consumer, contrary to the underlying tenet of good faith [*Unfair Terms in Consumer Contracts Regulations 1999 (SI 1999 No 2083), Reg 5(1)*];

(*b*)    an 'unfair term' is not binding on the consumer [*Reg 5(1)*];

(*c*)    terms of standard form contracts must be expressed in plain, intelligible language and, if there is doubt as to the meaning of a term, it must be interpreted in favour of the consumer [*Unfair Terms in Consumer Contracts Regulations 1999 (SI 1999 No 2083), Reg 6*];

(*d*)    complaints about 'unfair terms' in standard forms are to be considered by the Director General of Fair Trading, who may bring proceedings for an injunction to prevent use of the terms in future if the proponent of the unfair terms does not agree to desist from using them [*Unfair Terms in Consumer Contracts Regulations 1999 (SI 1999 No 2083), Reg 8*];

(*e*)    instead of the Director General of Fair Trading, a qualifying body named in *Sch 1* (statutory regulators, trading standards departments and the Consumers' Association) may notify the Director that it agrees to consider the complaint and may bring proceedings for an injunction to prevent the continued use of an unfair contract term. [*Unfair Terms in Consumer Contracts Regulations 1999 (SI 1999 No 2083), Regs 10 and 12*].

## Examples of 'unfair terms'

**P9058**    Terms which have the object or effect of:

(*a*)    excluding or limiting the legal liability of a seller or supplier in the event of the death of a consumer or personal injury to the latter resulting from an act or omission of that seller or supplier;

(*b*)    inappropriately excluding or limiting the legal rights of the consumer vis-à-vis the seller or supplier or another party in the event of total or partial non-performance or inadequate performance by the seller or supplier of any of the contractual obligations, including the option of offsetting a debt owed to the seller or supplier against any claim which the consumer may have against him;

(*c*)    making an agreement binding on the consumer whereas provision of services by the seller or supplier is subject to a condition whose realisation depends on his own will alone;

(*d*)    permitting the seller or supplier to retain sums paid by the consumer where the latter decides not to conclude or perform the contract, without providing for the consumer to receive compensation of an equivalent amount from the seller or supplier where the latter is the party cancelling the contract;

(*e*)    requiring any consumer who fails to fulfil his obligation to pay a disproportionately high sum in compensation;

(*f*)    authorising the seller or supplier to dissolve the contract on a discretionary basis where the same facility is not granted to the consumer, or permitting the seller or supplier to retain the sums paid for services not yet supplied by him where it is the seller or supplier himself who dissolves the contract;

(*g*) enabling the seller or supplier to terminate a contract of indeterminate duration without reasonable notice except where there are serious grounds for doing so;

(*h*) automatically extending a contract of fixed duration where the consumer does not indicate otherwise, when the deadline fixed for the consumer to express this desire not to extend the contract is unreasonably early;

(*i*) irrevocably binding the consumer to terms with which he had no real opportunity of becoming acquainted before the conclusion of the contract;

(*j*) enabling the seller or supplier to alter the terms of the contract unilaterally without a valid reason which is specified in the contract;

(*k*) enabling the seller or supplier to alter unilaterally without a valid reason any characteristics of the product or service to be provided;

(*l*) providing for the price of goods to be determined at the time of delivery or allowing a seller of goods or supplier of services to increase their price without in both cases giving the consumer the corresponding right to cancel the contract if the final price is too high in relation to the price agreed when the contract was concluded;

(*m*) giving the seller or supplier the right to determine whether the goods or services supplied are in conformity with the contract, or giving him the exclusive right to interpret any term of the contract;

(*n*) limiting the seller's or supplier's obligation to respect commitments undertaken by his agents or making his commitments subject to compliance with a particular formality;

(*o*) obliging the consumer to fulfil all his obligations where the seller or supplier does not perform his;

(*p*) giving the seller or supplier the possibility of transferring his rights and obligations under the contract, where this may serve to reduce the guarantees for the consumer, without the latter's agreement;

(*q*) excluding or hindering the consumer's right to take legal action or exercise any other legal remedy, particularly by requiring the consumer to take disputes exclusively to arbitration not covered by legal provisions, unduly restricting the evidence available to him or imposing on him a burden of proof which, according to the applicable law, should lie with another party to the contract.

[*Unfair Terms in Consumer Contracts Regulations 1999 (SI 1999 No 2083), Sch 2*].

# Risk Assessment

## Introduction

R3001

Although the term 'risk assessment' probably first came into common use as a result of the *Control of Substances Hazardous to Health Regulations 1988* (commonly known as the *'COSHH Regulations'* and revised several times since), similar requirements had actually previously been contained in both the *Control of Lead at Work Regulations 1980* and the *Control of Asbestos at Work Regulations 1987*.

In practice a type of risk assessment had already been necessary for some years particularly as a result of the use of the qualifying clause 'so far as is reasonably practicable' in a number of the sections of the *Health and Safety at Work etc. Act 1974 ('HSWA 1974')*.

## HSWA 1974 requirements

R3002

*HSWA 1974, s 2* contains the general duties of employers to their employees with the most general contained within *s 2(1)*:

> *'It shall be the duty of every employer to ensure, so far as is reasonably practicable, the health, safety and welfare at work of all employees.'*

Other more specific requirements are contained in *s 2(2)* and these are also qualified by the term 'reasonably practicable'.

*HSWA 1974, s 3* places general duties on both employers and the self-employed in respect of persons other than their employees. *Section 3(1)* states:

> *'It shall be the duty of every employer to conduct his undertaking in such a way as to ensure, so far as is reasonably practicable, that persons not in his employment who may be affected thereby are not exposed to risks to their health or safety.'*

Employers thus have duties to contractors (and their employees), visitors, customers, members of the emergency services, neighbours, passers-by and the public at large. This may to a certain point extend to include trespassers. Self-employed persons are put under a similar duty by virtue of *s 3(2)* and must also take care of themselves. In each case these duties are subject to the 'reasonably practicable' qualification.

*HSWA 1974, s 4* places duties on each person who has, to any extent, control of non-domestic premises used for work purposes in respect of those who are not their employees. *HSWA 1974, s 6* places a number of duties on those who design, manufacture, import or supply articles for use at work, or articles of fairground equipment and those who manufacture, import or supply substances. Many of these obligations also contain the 'reasonably practicable' qualification.

## What is reasonably practicable?

R3003

The phrase 'reasonably practicable' is not just included within the key sections of *HSWA 1974* but is also contained in a wide variety of regulations. Lord Justice Asquith provided a definition in his judgement in the case of *Edwards v National Coal Board [1949] 1 AER 743* in which he stated:

*'Reasonably practicable' is a narrower term than 'physically possible" and seems to me to imply that a computation must be made by the owner in which the quantum of risk placed on one scale and the sacrifice involved in the measures necessary for averting risk (whether in money, time or trouble) is placed in the other, and that, if it be shown that there is a gross disproportion between them – the risk being insignificant in relation to the sacrifice – the defendants discharge the onus on them. Moreover, this computation falls to be made by the owner at a point in time anterior to the accident.'*

*HSWA 1974, s 40* places the burden of proof in respect of what was or was not 'reasonably practicable' (or 'practicable', see R3004 BELOW) on the person charged with failure to comply with a duty or requirement. Employers and other duty holders must establish the level of risk involved in their activities and consider the various precautions available in order to determine what is reasonably practicable i.e. they must carry out a form of risk assessment.

### Practicable and absolute requirements

R3004    Not all health and safety law is qualified by the phrase 'reasonably practicable'. Some requirements must be carried out 'so far as is practicable'. 'Practicable' is a tougher standard to meet than 'reasonably practicable' – the precautions must be possible in the light of current knowledge and invention (*Adsett v K and L Steelfounders & Engineers Ltd [1953] 1 WLR 773*). Once a precaution is practicable it must be taken even if it is inconvenient or expensive. However, it is not practicable to take precautions against a danger which is not yet known to exist (*Edwards v National Coal Board [1949] 1 AER 743*), although it may be practicable once the danger is recognised.

Many health and safety duties are subject to neither 'practicable' nor 'reasonably practicable' qualifications. These absolute requirements usually state that something 'shall' or 'shall not' be done. However, such duties often contain other words which are subject to a certain amount of interpretation e.g. 'suitable', 'sufficient', 'adequate', 'efficient', 'appropriate' etc.

In order to determine whether requirements have been met 'so far as is practicable' or whether the precise wording of an absolute requirement has been complied with, a proper evaluation of the risks and the effectiveness of the precautions must be made.

# The Management of Health and Safety at Work Regulations 1999

R3005    The Management Regulations were introduced in 1992 and revised by the 1999 Regulations. They were intended to implement the European Framework Directive (89/391) on the introduction of measures to encourage improvements in the safety and health of workers at work. The *Management of Health and Safety at Work Regulations 1999 (SI 1999 No 3242), Reg 3* require employers and the self-employed to make a suitable and sufficient assessment of the risks to both employees and persons not in their employment. The purpose of the assessment is to identify the measures needed 'to comply with the requirements and prohibitions imposed . . . by or under the relevant statutory provisions . . . ' i.e. identifying what is needed to comply with the law.

Given the extremely broad obligations contained in *HSWA 1974*, ss 2, 3, 4 and 6, all risks arising from work activities should be considered as part of the risk assessment process (although some risks may be dismissed as being insignificant). Compliance with more specific requirements of regulations must also be assessed, whether these are absolute obligations or subject to 'practicable' or 'reasonably practicable' qualifications. The requirement for risk assessment introduced in the Management Regulations simply formalised what employers (and others) should have been doing all along i.e. identifying what precautions they needed to take to comply with the law. More detailed requirements of the Management Regulations are covered later in the chapter.

Any such additional precautions must then be implemented (the *Management of Health and Safety at Work Regulations 1999 (SI 1999 No 3242), Reg 5* contains requirements relating to the effective implementation of precautions).

# Common regulations requiring risk assessment

R3006    An increasing number of codes of regulations contain requirements for risk assessments. Several of these regulations are of significance to a wide range of work activities and are dealt with in more detail elsewhere in the looseleaf. The main regulations are as follows.

### Control of Substances Hazardous to Health Regulations 1999 (COSHH)

R3007    The *Control of Substances Hazardous to Health Regulations 1999 (SI 1999 No 437), Reg 6* requires employers to make a suitable and sufficient assessment of the risks created by work liable to expose any employees to any substance hazardous to health and of the steps that need to be taken to meet the requirements of the regulations. See DANGEROUS SUBSTANCES I – AT THE WORKPLACE, which provides more details of the COSHH requirements.

HSE booklet L5, contains both the regulations and the associated Approved Code of Practice. There are many other relevant HSE publications including HSG97 '*A step by step guide to COSHH assessment*'.

### Noise at Work Regulations 1989

R3008    The *Noise at Work Regulations 1989 (1989 No 1790), Reg 4* requires employers to make a noise assessment which is adequate for the purposes of:

— identifying which employees are exposed to noise above defined action levels;

— providing information to comply with other duties under the Regulations ( e.g. reduction of noise exposure, provision of ear protection, establishment of ear protection zones and informing employees).

See NOISE AND VIBRATION which provides more details of the requirements of the Noise at Work Regulations 1989. HSE booklet L108 '*Reducing Noise at Work*' contains guidance both on the regulations and on the assessment process.

### Manual Handling Operations Regulations 1992

R3009    Employers are required by the *Manual Handling Operations Regulations 1992 (SI 1992 No 2793), Reg 4* to make a suitable and sufficient assessment of all manual handling operations at work which involve a risk of employees being injured, and to take appropriate steps to reduce the risk to the lowest level reasonably practicable (They must avoid such manual handling operations if it is reasonably practicable to do so).

See MANUAL HANDLING which provides further details of the Regulations and the carrying out of assessments. HSE booklet L23, *'Manual Handling: Manual Handling Operations Regulations 1992 – guidance on regulations'* provides detailed guidance on the Regulations and manual handling assessments.

## Health and Safety (Display Screen Equipment) Regulations 1992

R3010    The *Health and Safety (Display Screen Equipment) Regulations 1992 (SI 1992 No 2792), Reg 2* requires employers to perform a suitable and sufficient analysis of display screen equipment (DSE) workstations for the purpose of assessing risks to 'users' or 'operators' as defined in the Regulations. Risks identified in the assessment must be reduced to the lowest extent reasonably practicable.

See OFFICES AND SHOPS which contains further information on visual display units. HSE booklet L26, *'Display screen equipment work'* contains guidance on the Regulations and on workstation assessments.

## Personal Protective Equipment at Work Regulations 1992

R3011    Under the *Personal Protective Equipment at Work Regulations 1992 (SI 1992 No 2966), Reg 6* employers must ensure that an assessment is made to determine risks which have not been avoided by other means and identify personal protective equipment (PPE) which will be effective against these risks. The Regulations also contain other requirements relating to the provision of PPE; its maintenance and replacement; information, instruction and training; and the steps which must be taken to ensure its proper use.

See PERSONAL PROTECTIVE EQUIPMENT which provides further details of the requirements under the Regulations. HSE booklet L25, *'Personal protective equipment at work'* provides detailed guidance on the Regulations and the assessments of PPE needs.

## Fire Precautions (Workplace) Regulations 1997

R3012    The *Fire Precautions (Workplace) Regulations 1997 (SI 1997 No )* together with the *Management of Health and Safety at work Regulations 1999 (SI 1999 No 3242)*, make it quite explicit that employers must carry out an assessment of fire risks and fire precautions. Part II of the 1997 Regulations contains specific requirements relating to fire safety which must be included in the assessment.

Amendments to the 1997 Regulations in 1999 removed the exemption from risk assessment requirements originally given to holders of fire certificates (under the Fire Precautions Act 1971 and other legislation). They too are required to carry out fire risk assessments.

See FIRE AND FIRE PRECAUTIONS which contains further details both on the Regulations and on fire precautions generally. The HSE/Home Office publication *'Fire Safety: An employer's guide'* provides extensive guidance on factors to be taken into account during fire risk assessments.

## Specialist regulations requiring risk assessment

R3013    Some codes of regulations requiring risk assessments are of rather more specialist application, although some are still covered in some detail elsewhere in the looseleaf. References to relevant chapters of the looseleaf and to key HSE publications of relevance are included below. These regulations include:

- *Control of Lead at Work Regulations 1998*

  See DANGEROUS SUBSTANCES I – AT THE WORKPLACE.

  COP 2   Control of lead at work.

- *Control of Asbestos at Work Regulations 1987*

  See ASBESTOS.

  L 27       The control of asbestos at work: Control of Asbestos at Work Regulations 1987 – approved code of practice.

  L 28       Work with asbestos insulation, asbestos coating and asbestos insulating board: Control of Asbestos at Work Regulations 1987 – approved code of practice.

  L 11       A guide to the Asbestos (Licensing) Regulations 1983.

- *Genetic Manipulation Regulations 1989*

  L 29       A guide to the Genetically Modified Organisms (Contained Use) Regulations 1992.

- *Supply of Machinery (Safety) Regulations 1992*

  The Regulations include a variety of procedures which must be followed in assessing conformity of machinery with essential health and safety requirements set out in the Machinery Directive.

  See MACHINERY SAFETY.

  INDG 270   Supplying new machinery: Advice to suppliers, free leaflet.

  INDG 271   Buying new machinery: A short guide to the law, free leaflet.

- *Control of Major Accident Hazard Regulations 1999 (COMAH)*

  The Regulations only apply to sites containing specified quantities of dangerous substances.

  See DISASTER AND EMERGENCY MANAGEMENT SYSTEMS (DEMS).

  L 111      A guide to the Control of Major Accident Hazard Regulations 1999.

  HSG 190    Preparing safety reports: Control of Major Accident Hazard Regulations 1999.

  HSG 191    Emergency planning for major accidents: Control of Major Accident Hazard Regulations.

- *Ionising Radiation Regulations 1999*

  See DANGEROUS SUBSTANCES I – AT THE WORKPLACE.

  L 121      Work With Ionising Radiation: Ionising Radiations Regulations 1999 – approved code of practice and guidance.

# Related health and safety concepts

R3014   Risk assessment techniques are an essential part of other health and safety management concepts.

- *Safe systems of work*

  Employers are required under *HSWA 1974, s 2(2)(a)* to provide and maintain 'systems of work that are, so far as is reasonably practicable, safe and without risks to health'.'

  Both the *Confined Spaces Regulations 1997 (SI 1997 No 1713)* and the *Lifting Operations and Lifting Equipment Regulations 1998 (LOLER) (SI 1998 No 2307)* contain similar requirements for safe systems of work. A safe system of work can only established through a process of risk assessment.

- *'Dynamic risk assessment'*

  The term 'dynamic risk assessment' is often used to describe the day to day judgements that employees are expected to make in respect of health and safety. However, employers must ensure that employees have the necessary knowledge and experience to make such judgements. The employer's 'generic risk assessments' must have identified the types of risks which might be present in the work activities, established a framework of precautions (procedures, equipment etc.) which are likely to be necessary and provided guidance on which precautions are appropriate for which situations.

- *Permits to work*

  A permit to work system is a formalised method for identifying a safe system of work (usually for a high risk activity) and ensuring that this system is followed. The permit issuer is expected to carry out a dynamic risk assessment of the work activity and should be more competent in identifying the risks and the relevant precautions than those carrying out the work.

- *CDM health and safety plans*

  A key component of the *Construction (Design and Management) Regulations 1994 (CDM) (SI 1994 No 3140)* is the requirement for a health and safety plan. Essentially this process requires an assessment of risks involved in the project and the identification and eventual implementation of appropriate precautions. (The requirements of the CDM Regulations are covered in more detail in CONSTRUCTION AND BUILDING OPERATIONS.)

- *Method statements*

  Method statements usually involve a description of how a particular task or operation is to be carried out and should identify all the components of a safe system of work arrived at through a process of risk assessment.

## Management Regulations requirements

R3015     The general requirement concerning risk assessment is contained in the *Management of Health and Safety at Work Regulations 1999 ('the Management Regulations') (SI 1999 No 3242), Reg 3*. Changes to the original regulations passed in 1992 mean that the risk assessment must now include fire risks and precautions (see R3012 ABOVE) and also risks to both young persons (under 18's) (see R3022 below) and new and expectant mothers (see R3023 below). Other regulations require more specific types of risk assessment e.g. of hazardous substances (COSHH), noise, manual handling operations, display screen equipment and personal protective equipment (see R3006–R3013 ABOVE).

*Regulation 3(1)* of the Management Regulations states:

*'every employer shall make a suitable and sufficient assessment of:*

*(a)*   *the risks to the health and safety of his employees to which they are exposed whilst they are at work; and*

*(b)*   *the risks to the health and safety of persons not in his employment arising out of or in connection with the conduct by him of his undertaking,*

*for the purpose of identifying the measures he needs to take to comply with the requirements or prohibitions imposed upon him by or under the relevant statutory provisions and by Part II of the Fire Precautions (Workplace) Regulations 1997.'*

*Regulation 3(2)* imposes similar requirements on self-employed persons.

*Regulation 3(3)* requires a risk assessment to be reviewed if:

—   there is reason to suspect that it is no longer valid; or

—   there has been a significant change in the matters to which it relates.

*Regulation 3(4)* requires a risk assessment to be made or reviewed before an employer employs a young person, and *Regulation 3(5)* identifies particular issues which must be taken into account in respect of young persons (especially their inexperience, lack of awareness of risks and immaturity). Further requirements in respect of young persons are contained in *Regulation 19*. *Regulation 16* contains specific requirements concerning the factors which must be taken into account in risk assessments in relation to new and expectant mothers. These relate to processes, working conditions and physical, biological or chemical agents. Assessments in respect of young persons and new or expectant mothers are dealt within more detail later in the chapter.

*Regulation 3(6)* requires employers who employ five or more employees to record:

—   the significant findings of their risk assessments; and

—   any group of employees identified as being especially at risk.

Methods of recording assessments are described later in this chapter (see R3038 below).

HSE booklet L 21, *'Management of health and safety at work'*, contains the Management Regulations in full, the associated Approved Code of Practice (ACoP) and Guidance on the Regulations.

## Hazards and risks

**R3016**   The ACoP to the Management Regulations provides definitions of both hazard and risk.

A *hazard* is something with the potential to cause harm.

A *risk* is the likelihood of potential harm from that hazard being realised.

The *extent of the risk* will depend on:

—   the likelihood of that harm occurring;

—   the potential severity of that harm (resultant injury or adverse health effect);

—   the population which might be affected by the hazard i.e. the number of people who might be exposed.

As an illustration, work at heights involves a hazard of those below being struck by falling objects. The extent of the risk might depend on factors such as the nature of the work being carried out, the weight of objects which might fall, the distance to the ground below, the numbers of people in the area etc.

## Evaluation of precautions

R3017     The ACoP to the Management Regulations clearly states that risk assessment involves 'identifying the hazards present and evaluating the extent of the risks involved, taking into account existing precautions and their effectiveness.'

The evaluation of the effectiveness of precautions is an integral part of the risk assessment process. This is overlooked by some organisations who concentrate on the identification (and often the quantification) of risks without checking whether the intended precautions are actually being taken in the workplace and whether these precautions are proving effective.

Using the illustration in the previous paragraph, the risk assessment must take account of what precautions are required, such as:

—     use of barriers and/or warning signs at ground level;

—     use of tool belts by those working at heights;

—     provision of edge protection on working platforms;

—     use of head protection by those at ground level.

## 'Suitable and sufficient'

R3018     Risk assessments under the Management Regulations (and several other regulations) must be 'suitable and sufficient', but the phrase is not defined in the Regulations themselves. However, the ACoP to the Regulations states that 'The level of risk arising from the work activity should determine the degree of sophistication of the risk assessment.' The ACoP also states that insignificant risks can usually be ignored, as can risks arising from routine activities associated with life in general ('unless the work activity compounds or significantly alters those risks').

In practice, a risk can only be concluded to be insignificant if some attention is paid to it during the risk assessment process and, if there is any scope for doubt, it is prudent to state in the risk assessment record which risks are considered insignificant.

Winter weather (with its attendant rain, ice, snow or wind) may be considered to pose a routine risk to life. However, driving a fork lift truck in an icy yard or carrying out agricultural or construction work in a remote location may involve a far greater level of risk than normal and require additional precautions to be taken.

The risk assessment must take into account both workers and other persons who might be affected by the undertaking.

For example, a construction company would need to consider risks to (and from) their employees, sub contractors, visitors to their sites, delivery drivers, passers by and even possible trespassers on their sites.

Similarly a residential care home should take into account risks to (and from) their staff, visiting medical specialists, visiting contractors, residents and visitors to residents.

## Reviewing risk assessments

**R3019**    The *Management of Health and Safety at Work Regulations 1999 (SI 1999 No 3242)*, *Reg 3(3)* requires a risk assessment to be reviewed if:

'*(a)    there is reason to suspect it is no longer valid; or*

*(b)    there has been a significant change in the matters to which it relates ; and where as a result of any such review changes to an assessment are required, the employer or self-employed person concerned shall make them.*'

The ACoP to the Management Regulations states that those carrying out risk assessments 'would not be expected to anticipate risks that were not foreseeable.' However, what is foreseeable can be changed by subsequent events. An accident, a non-injury incident or a case of ill-health may highlight the need for a risk assessment to be reviewed because:

—    a previously unforeseen possibility has now occurred;

—    the risk of something happening (or the extent of its consequences) is greater than previously thought;

—    precautions prove to be less effective than anticipated.

A review of the risk assessment may also be required because of significant changes in the work activity e.g. changes to the equipment or materials used, the environment where the activity takes place, the system of work used or to the numbers or types of people carrying out the activity. The need for a risk assessment review may be identified from elsewhere e.g. from others involved in the same work activity, through trade or specialist health and safety journals, from the suppliers of equipment or materials or from the Health and Safety Executive or other specialist bodies. Routine monitoring activity (inspections, audits etc.) or consultation with employees may also identify the need for an assessment to be reviewed. A review of the risk assessment does not necessarily require a repeat of the whole risk assessment process but it is quite likely to identify the need for increased or changed precautions.

In practice workplaces and the activities within them are constantly subject to gradual changes and the ACoP states 'it is prudent to plan to review risk assessments at regular intervals'. The frequency of such reviews should depend on the extent and nature of the risks involved and the degree of change likely. It is advisable that all risk assessments should be reviewed at least every five years.

There are many activities where the nature of the work or the workplace itself changes constantly. Examples of such situations are construction work or peripatetic maintenance or repair work. Here it is possible to carry out 'generic' assessments of the types of risks involved and the types of precautions which should be taken. However, some reliance must be placed upon workers themselves to identify what precautions are appropriate for a given set of circumstances or to deal with unexpected situations. Such workers must be well informed and well trained in order for them to be competent to make what are often called 'dynamic' risk assessments (see R3014 ABOVE).

## Related requirements of the Management Regulations

**R3020**

A number of other requirements within the Management Regulations are closely related to the risk assessment process.

- *Regulation 4: Principles of prevention to be applied*

  The *Management of Health and Safety at Work Regulations 1999 (SI 1999 No 3242), Reg 4* and *Sch 1* require preventive and protective measures to be implemented on the basis of specified principles.

- *Regulation 5: Health and safety arrangements*

  Under the *Management of Health and Safety at Work Regulations 1999 (SI 1999 No 3242), Reg 5*, employers are required to have appropriate arrangements for the effective planning, organisation, control, monitoring and review of preventive and protective measures. Those employers with five or more employees must record these arrangements. This application of the 'management cycle' to health and safety matters is dealt with in greater detail in R3021 BELOW.

- *Regulation 6: Health surveillance*

  Under the *Management of Health and Safety at Work Regulations 1999 (SI 1999 No 3242), Reg 6*, where risks to employees are identified through a risk assessment, they must be 'provided with such health surveillance as is appropriate.' (Surveillance is also likely to be necessary to comply with the requirements of more specific regulations e.g. COSHH, *Control of Asbestos at Work Regulations 1997, Ionising Radiations Regulations 1999*). Surveillance may be appropriate to deal with risks such as colour blindness and other vision defects (e.g. in electricians and train or vehicle drivers) or blackouts or epilepsy (e.g. for drivers, operators of machinery and those working at heights).

  HSE guidance is available on this important area (see HSG 61 *'Health surveillance at work'*).

- *Regulation 8: Procedures for serious and imminent danger and for danger areas*

  The *Management of Health and Safety at Work Regulations 1999 (SI 1999 No 3242), Reg 8* requires every employer to 'establish and where necessary give effect to appropriate procedures to be followed in the event of serious and imminent danger to persons at work in his undertaking.' It also refers to the possible need to restrict access to areas 'on grounds of health and safety unless the employee concerned has received adequate health and safety instruction.'

  The need for emergency procedures or restricted areas should of course be identified through the process of risk assessment. Situations 'of serious and imminent danger' might be due to fires, bomb threats, escape or release of hazardous substances, out of control processes, personal attack, escape of animals etc. Areas may justify access to them being restricted because of the presence of hazardous substances, unprotected electrical conductors (particularly high voltage), potentially dangerous animals or people etc.

## Application of the management cycle

R3021     The time spent in carrying out risk assessments will be wasted unless those precautions identified as being necessary are actually implemented. The *Management of Health and Safety at Work Regulations 1999 (SI 1999 No 3242), Reg 5* requires the application of a five stage 'management cycle' to this process.

- Planning

  The employer must have a planned approach to health and safety involving such measures as:

  — a health and safety policy statement;

  — annual health and safety plans;

  — development of performance standards.

- Organisation

  An organisation must be put in place to deliver these good intentions e.g.:

  — individuals allocated responsibility for implementing the health and safety policy or achieving elements of the health and safety plan;

  — arrangements for communicating with and consulting employees (using such measures as health and safety committees, newsletters, noticeboards);

  — the provision of competent advice and information.

- Control

  Detailed health and safety control arrangements must be established. The extent of such arrangements will reflect the size of the organisation and the degree of risk involved in its activities but they are likely to involve:

  — formal procedures and systems e.g. for accident and incident investigation, fire and other emergencies, the selection and management of contractors;

  — the provision of health and safety related training e.g. at induction, for the operation of equipment or certain activities, for supervisors and managers;

  — provision of appropriate levels of supervision.

- Monitoring

  The effectiveness of health and safety arrangements must be monitored using such methods as:

  — health and safety inspections (both formal and informal);

  — health and safety audits;

  — accident and incident investigations.

- Review

  The findings of monitoring activity must be reviewed and, where necessary, the management cycle applied once again to rectify shortcomings in health and safety arrangements.

  The review process might involve:

  — joint health and safety committees;

  — management health and safety meetings;

  — activities of health and safety specialists.

## Children and young persons

R3022    Previous Acts and regulations identified many types of equipment which children and young persons were not allowed to use or processes or activities that they must not be involved in. Many of these 'prohibitions' were revoked by the *Health and Safety (Young Persons) Regulations 1997 (SI 1997 No 135)*, since incorporated into the *Management of Health and Safety at Work Regulations 1999 (SI 1999 No 3242)*. (A few 'prohibitions' still remain). The emphasis has now changed to restrictions on the work which children and young persons are allowed to do, based upon the employer's risk assessment.

The *Health and Safety (Training for Employment) Regulations 1990 (SI 1990 No 1380)* have the effect of giving students on work experience training programmes and trainees on training for employment programmes the status of 'employees'. The immediate provider of their training is treated as the 'employer'. (There are exceptions for courses at educational establishments, i.e. universities, colleges, schools etc.). Therefore employers have duties in respect of all children and young persons at work in their undertaking: full-time employees, part-time and temporary employees and also students or trainees on work placement with them.

The term 'child' and 'young person' are defined in the *Management of Health and Safety at Work Regulations 1999 (SI 1999 No 3242)*, Reg 1(2).

- *Child* is defined as a person not over compulsory school age in accordance with:

  —    the *Education Act 1996*, *s 8* (for England and Wales); and

  —    the *Education (Scotland) Act 1980*, *s 31* (for Scotland).

  (In practice this is just under or just over the age of sixteen)

- *Young Person* is defined as 'any person who has not attained the age of eighteen'.

Some of the prohibitions remaining from older health and safety regulations use different cut off ages.

See CHILDREN AND YOUNG PERSONS which provides much more detail on the requirements of the Management Regulations and the factors to be taken into account when carrying out risk assessments in respect of children and young persons. These factors centre around their:

—    lack of experience;

—    lack of awareness of existing or potential risks; and

—    immaturity (in both the physical and psychological sense).

That chapter also contains in Appendix C a checklist of 'Work presenting increased risks for children and young persons'.

## New or expectant mothers

R3023    Amendments made in 1994 to the previous Management Regulations implemented the European Directive on Pregnant Workers, requiring employers in their risk assessments to consider risks to new or expectant mothers. These amendments were subsequently incorporated into the 1999 Management Regulations. The *Management of Health and Safety at Work Regulations 1999 (SI 1999 No 3242)*, *Reg 1* contains two relevant definitions:

- '*New or expectant mother*' means an employee who is pregnant; who has given birth within the previous six months; or who is breastfeeding.

- '*Given birth*' means 'delivered a living child or, after twenty-four weeks of pregnancy, a stillborn child.'

The requirements for 'risk assessment in respect of new and expectant mothers' are contained in the *Management of Health and Safety at Work Regulations 1999 (SI 1999 No 3242), Reg 16* which states in *paragraph (1)*:

> '*(1)    Where —*
>
> *(a)    the persons working in an undertaking include women of child-bearing age; and*
>
> *(b)    the work is of a kind which could involve risk, by reason of her condition, to the health and safety of a new or expectant mothers, or to that of her baby, from any processes or working conditions, or physical, biological or chemical agents, including those specified in Annexes I and II of Council Directive 92/85/EEC on the introduction of measures to encourage improvements in the safety and health at work of pregnant workers and workers who have recently given birth or are breastfeeding,*
>
> *the assessment required by regulation 3(1) shall also include an assessment of such risk.*'

*Regulation 16(4)* states that in relation to risks from infectious or contagious diseases an assessment must only be made if the level of risk is in addition to the level of exposure outside the workplace. (The types of risk which are more likely to affect new or expectant mothers are described in R3024 below). *Regulation 16(2) and (3)* set out the actions employers are required to take if these risks cannot be avoided. *Paragraph (2)* states:

> '*Where, in the case of an individual employee, the taking of any other action the employer is required to take under the relevant statutory provisions would not avoid the risk referred to in paragraph (1) the employer shall, if it is reasonable to do so, and would avoid such risks, alter her working conditions or hours of work.*'

Consequently where the risk assessment required under *Reg 16(1)* shows that control measures would not sufficiently avoid the risks to new or expectant mothers or their babies, the employer must make reasonable alterations to their working conditions or hours of work.

In some cases restrictions may still allow the employee to substantially continue with her normal work but in others it may be more appropriate to offer her suitable alternative work.

Any alternative work must be:

— suitable and appropriate for the employee to do in the circumstances;

— on terms and conditions which are no less favourable.

*Regulation 16(3)* states:

> '*If it is not reasonable to alter the working conditions or hours of work, or if it would not avoid such risk, the employer shall, subject to section 67 of the 1996 Act, suspend the employee from work for so long as is necessary to avoid such risk.*'

(The 1996 Act referred to is the *Employment Rights Act 1996* which provides that any such suspension from work on the above grounds is on full pay. However, payment might not be made if the employee has unreasonably refused an offer of suitable alternative work.)

The *Management of Health and Safety at Work Regulations 1999 (SI 1999 No 3242), Reg 17* deals specifically with night work by new or expectant mothers and states:

> 'Where —
>
> (a)   a new or expectant mother works at night; and
>
> (b)   a certificate from a registered medical practitioner or a registered midwife shows that it is necessary for her health or safety that she should not be at work for any period of such work identified in the certificate,
>
> the employer shall, subject to section 46 of the 1978 Act, suspend her from work for so long as is necessary for her health or safety.'

Such suspension (on the same basis as described above) is only necessary if there are risks arising from work. The HSE do not consider there are any risks to pregnant or breastfeeding workers or their children working at night per se. They suggest that any claim from an employee that she cannot work nights should be referred to an occupational health specialist. The HSE's own Employment Medical Advisory Service are likely to have a role to play in such cases.

The requirements placed on employers in respect of altered working conditions or hours of work and suspensions from work only take effect when the employee has formally notified the employer of her condition. The *Management of Health and Safety at Work Regulations 1999 (SI 1999 No 3242), Reg 18* states:

> 'Nothing in paragraph (2) or (3) of regulation 16 shall require the employer to take any action in relation to an employee until she has notified the employer in writing that she is pregnant, has given birth within the previous six months, or is breastfeeding.'

*Regulation 18(2)* states that the employer is not required to maintain action taken in relation to an employee once the employer knows that she is no longer a new or expectant mother; or cannot establish whether this is the case.

## Risks to new or expectant mothers

R3024    The HSE booklet HSG 122 *'New and expectant mothers at work: A Guide for employers'* provides considerable guidance on those risks which may be of particular relevance to new or expectant mothers, including those listed in the EC Directive on Pregnant Workers (92/85/EEC). These risks might include:

### Physical Agents

● Manual handling.

● Ionising radiation.

● Work in compressed air.

● Diving work.

● Shock, vibration etc.

● Movement and posture.

● Physical and mental pressure.

- Extreme heat.

*Biological Agents*

Many biological agents in hazard groups 2, 3 and 4 (as categorised by the Advisory Committee on Dangerous Pathogens) can affect the unborn child should the mother be infected during pregnancy.

*Chemical Agents*

- Substances labelled with certain risk phrases.

- Mercury and mercury derivatives.

- Antimitotic (cytotoxic) drugs.

- Agents absorbed through the skin.

- Carbon Monoxide.

- Lead and lead derivatives.

*Working Conditions*

The HSE's frequently stated position in respect of work with display screen equipment (DSE) is that radiation from DSE is well below the levels set out in international recommendations, and that scientific studies taken as a whole do not demonstrate any link between this work and miscarriages or birth defects. There is no need for pregnant women to cease working with DSE. However, the HSE recommend that, to avoid problems from stress or anxiety, women are given the opportunity to discuss any concerns with someone who is well informed on the subject.

Other factors associated with pregnancy may also need to be taken into account e.g. morning sickness, backache, difficulty in standing for extended periods or increasing size. These may necessitate changes to the working environment or work patterns.

# Who should carry out the risk assessment?

R3025

The *Management of Health and Safety at Work Regulations 1999 (SI 1999 No 3242)*, *Reg 7* requires employers to appoint competent health and safety assistance. Such persons must have sufficient training and experience or knowledge together with other qualities, in order to be able to identify risks and evaluate the effectiveness of precautions to control those risks. (*Regulation 7(8)* expresses a preference for such persons to be employees as opposed to others e.g. consultants).

The HSE guidance on risk assessment states that in small businesses the employer or a senior manager may be quite capable of carrying out the risk assessment. Larger employers may create risk assessment teams who might be drawn from managers, engineers and other specialists, supervisors or team leaders, health and safety specialists, safety representatives and other employees. Many employers continue to utilise consultants to co-ordinate or carry out their risk assessments. Whether the assessments are to be carried out by an individual or by a team, others will need to be involved during the process. Managers, supervisors, employees, specialists etc. will all need to be consulted about the risks involved in their work and the precautions that are (or should be) taken.

## Assessment units

R3026    In a small workplace it may be possible to carry out a risk assessment as a single exercise but in larger organisations it will usually be necessary to split the assessment up into manageable units. If done correctly this should mean that assessment of each unit should not take an inordinate amount of time and also allows the selection of the people best able to assess an individual unit. Division of work activities into assessment units might be by department or sections, buildings or rooms, processes or product lines, or services provided.

As an illustration a garage might be divided into:

—    Servicing and repair workshop.

—    Body repair shop.

—    Parts department.

—    Car sales and administration.

—    Petrol and retail sales.

## Relevant sources of information

R3027    There is a wide range of documents which might be of value during the risk assessment process including:

●   Previous risk assessments

    (including risk assessments carried out to comply with specific regulations e.g. COSHH or Noise regulations).

●   Operating procedures

    (where these include health and safety information).

●   Safety handbooks etc.

●   Training programmes and records

●   Accident and Incident records

●   Health and safety inspection or audit reports

●   Relevant Regulations and Approved Codes of Practice

    (Risk assessment involves an evaluation of compliance with legal requirements and therefore an awareness of the legislation applying to the workplace in question is essential.)

●   Relevant HSE Guidance

    The HSE publishes a wide range of booklets and leaflets providing guidance on health and safety topics. Some of these relate to the specific requirements of regulations, others deal with specific types of risks whilst some publications deal with sectors of work activity.

    All of these can be of considerable value in identifying which risks the HSE regard as significant and in providing benchmarks against which precautions can be measured. The guidance on specific types of workplaces (which includes engineering workshops, motor vehicle repair, warehousing, kitchens and food preparation, golf courses, horse riding establishments and many others) should form an essential basis for those carrying out assessments in those sectors.

HSE Books regularly publishes a detailed catalogue of HSE publications. Their booklet '*Essentials of Health and Safety at Work*' provides an excellent starting point for those in small businesses needing guidance or carrying out risk assessment. The booklet also contains a useful reference section to other HSE publications which may be of relevance. To obtain these publications contact HSE Books, PO Box 1999, Sudbury, Suffolk CO10 2WA (tel: 01787 881165; fax: 01787 313995; website: www.hsebooks.co.uk).

- Trade Association codes of practice and guidance

- Information from manufacturers and suppliers

  (Equipment handbooks or substance data sheets).

- General health and safety reference books

## Consider who might be at risk

**R3028**     The risk assessment process must take account of all those who may be at risk from the work activities i.e. both employees and others. It is important that all of these are identified.

- *Employees*

  Different categories of employees to take into account might include:

  — production workers;

  — maintenance workers;

  — administrative staff;

  — security officers;

  — cleaners;

  — delivery drivers;

  — sales representatives;

  — others working away from the premises;

  — temporary employees.

  Some of these employees may merit special considerations:

  — children and young persons;

  — women of childbearing age (i.e. potential new or expectant mothers);

  — employees with disabilities;

  — people working alone;

  — those working at night or weekends;

  — inexperienced staff.

- *Contractors and their staff*

  Contracted services might involve:

  — construction or engineering projects;

  — routine maintenance or repair;

  — hire of plant and operators;

  — support services e.g. catering, cleaning, security, transport;

— professional services e.g. architects, engineers, trainers;

— supply of temporary staff.

(Contractors also have duties to carry out risk assessments in respect of their own staff.)

● *Others at risk*

The types of people might be put at risk by the organisation's activities will depend upon the nature and location of those activities. Groups of people to be considered include:

— volunteer workers;

— co-occupants of premises;

— occupants of neighbouring premises;

— drivers making deliveries;

— visitors (both individuals and groups);

— residents e.g. in the care or hospitality sectors;

— passers-by;

— users of neighbouring roads;

— trespassers;

— customers or service users.

## Identify the issues to be addressed

R3029    The issues which will need to be addressed during the risk assessment process should be identified. This may be done in respect of the assessment overall or separately for each of the assessment units and will be based upon the knowledge and experience of those carrying out the assessment and the information gathered together from the sources described earlier. This will create an initial list of headings and sub-headings for the eventual record of the risk assessment, although in practice this list is likely to be amended along the way. The sample assessment records contained later in the chapter (see R3046 and R3047) will demonstrate how such a list can be built up for typical workplaces.

These headings are likely to consist of the more common types of risk e.g. fire, vehicles, work at heights, together with some specialised types of risk associated with the work activities such as violence, lasers or working in remote locations. A checklist of possible risks to be considered during risk assessments is provided in R3031 BELOW. This includes some of the risks which have specific regulations associated with them.

In some situations particular notes may also be made to check on the effectiveness of the precautions which should be in place to control the risks e.g. standards of machine guarding, compliance with personal protective equipment (PPE) requirements or the quality and extent of training.

## Variations in work practices

R3030    Consideration should also be given at this stage to possible variations in work activities which may create new risks or increase existing risks. Such variations might involve:

— Fluctuations in production or workload demands.

— Reallocation of staff to meet changing workloads.

— Seasonal variations in work activities.

— Abnormal weather conditions.

— Alternative work practices forced by equipment breakdown/unavailability.

— Urgent or 'one-off' repair work.

— Work carried out in unusual locations.

— Difference in work between days, nights or weekends.

Further variations may emerge later on in the assessment process.

## Checklist of possible risks

R3031

This checklist is intended to assist in identifying which issues need to be addressed during risk assessments. In some cases the headings and/or sub-headings might be used in the form shown, in other cases it may be more appropriate to combine them or modify the titles.

*Work Equipment*

- Process machinery
- Other machines
- Powered tools
- Handtools
- Knives/blades
- Fork-lift trucks
- Cranes
- Lifts
- Hoists
- Lifting equipment
- Vehicles

*Access*

- Vehicle routes
- Rail traffic
- Pedestrian access
- Work at heights
- Ladders and stepladders
- Scaffolding
- Mobile elevating work platforms
- Falling objects

- Glazing

*Services/power sources*

- Electrical installation
- Compressed air
- Steam
- Hydraulics
- Other pressure systems
- Buried services
- Overhead services

*Storage*

- Shelving and racking
- Stacking
- Silos and tanks
- Waste

*Fire prevention*

- Flammable liquids
- Flammable gases
- Storage of flammables
- Hot work

*Work activity*

- Burning or welding
- Entry into confined spaces
- Electrical work
- Excessive fatigue or stress
- Handling cash/valuables
- Use of compressed gases
- Molten metal

*External factors*

- Violence or aggression
- Robbery
- Large crowds
- Animals
- Clients' activities

*Other factors*

- Vibration
- Lasers

- Ultra violet/infra red radiation
- Work related upper limb disorder

*Work locations*

- Heat
- Cold
- Severe weather
- Deep water
- Tides
- Remote locations
- Work alone
- Homeworking
- Poor hygiene
- Infestations
- Work abroad
- Work in domestic property
- Clients' premises
- Site security

| *Risks/issues subject to separate assessment requirements* | |
|---|---|
| Hazardous substances (COSHH) | Lead |
| Noise | Asbestos |
| Manual handling | Genetic manipulation |
| Display screen equipment workstations | Genetically modified organisms |
| PPE needs | Conformity of machinery |
| Fire precautions | Major accident hazards (COMAH) |
| | Ionising radiation |

## Making the risk assessment

R3032  Good planning and preparation can reduce the time spent in actually making the risk assessment as well as enabling that time to be used much more productively. However, it is essential that time is spent in work locations, seeing how work is actually carried out (as opposed to how it should be carried out).

### Observation

R3033  Observation of the work location, work equipment and work practices is an essential part of the risk assessment process. Where there are known to be variations in work activities a sufficient range of these should be observed to be able to form a judgement on the extent of the risks and the adequacy of precautions. Evaluations can be made of the effectiveness of fixed guards, the suitability and condition of access equipment, compliance with PPE requirements, the observance of specified operating procedures or working practices and many other aspects. It should also be borne in mind that work practices may change once workers realise they are under observation. Initial or undetected observation of working practices may be the most revealing.

### Discussions

R3034 Discussions with people carrying out work activities, their safety representatives and those responsible for supervising or managing them are also an essential part of risk assessment. Amongst aspects of the work that might be discussed are possible variations in the work activities, problems that workers encounter, workers' views of the effectiveness of the precautions available, the reasons some precautions are not utilised and their suggestions for improving health and safety standards.

### Tests

R3035 In some situations it may be appropriate to test the effectiveness of safety precautions e.g. the efficiency of interlocked guards or trip devices, the audibility of alarms or warning devices or the suitability of access to remote workplaces e.g. crane cabs, roofs. When carrying out such tests care must be taken by those carrying out the assessment not to endanger themselves or others, nor to disrupt normal activities.

### Further investigations

R3036 Frequently further investigations will need to be made before the assessment can be concluded. Such investigations may involve detailed checks on standards or records, or enquiries into how non-routine situations are dealt with. Examples of further checks or enquiries which might be appropriate are:

— Detailed requirements of published standards e.g. design of guards, thickness of glass.

— Contents of operating procedures.

— Maintenance or test records.

— Contents of training programmes or training records.

Once again the potential list is endless although lines of further enquiry should be indicated by the observations and discussions during the initial phase of the assessment.

### Notes

R3037 Rough notes should be made throughout the assessment process. It will be on these notes that the eventual assessment record will be based. It will seldom be possible to complete an assessment record 'on the run' during the assessment itself. The notes should relate to anything likely to be of relevance, such as:

— Risks discounted as insignificant.

— Further detail on risks or additional risks identified during the assessment.

— Risks which are being controlled effectively.

— Descriptions of precautions which are in place and effective.

— Precautions which do not appear to be effective.

— Alternative precautions which might be considered.

— Problems identified or concerns expressed by others.

— Related procedures, records or other documents.

## Assessment records

R3038    This phase of the risk assessment process concludes with the preparation of the assessment records. It may be preferable to record the findings in draft form initially, with a revised version being produced once the assessment has been reviewed more widely and/or recommended actions have been completed.

● Decide on the record format

Details of the content of assessment records and examples of one assessment record format are provided later in the chapter (see R3046 and R3047) but many alternatives are available. Different types of records may be appropriate for different departments, sections or activities. Use of a 'model' assessment might be relevant for similar workplaces or activities. Some (or all) of the assessment record might be integrated into documented operating procedures.

● Identify the section headings to be used

During the preparatory phase of the assessment a list of risks and other sources to be addressed in each assessment unit was prepared as an aide memoire. This list will now need to be converted into section headings for the assessment records. As a result of the assessment some of the headings may have been sub-divided into different headings whilst others may have been merged.

● Prepare the assessment records

The rough notes made during assessment must then be converted into formal assessment records. Preparing the records will normally require at least half of the time that was spent in the workplace carrying out the assessment and sometimes might even take longer. It is wise not to allow too long to elapse between assessing in the workplace and preparation of the assessment record. Notes will seem much more intelligible and memory will often be able to 'colour in' between the notes.

● Identify the recommendations

The assessment will almost inevitably result in recommendations for improvements and these must be identified. As can be seen later, some assessment record formats incorporate sections in which recommendations can be included but in other cases separate lists will need to be prepared. The use of risk rating matrices (see below) may assist in the prioritisation of recommendations.

## Risk rating matrices

R3039    The ACoP accompanying the *Management of Health and Safety at Work Regulations 1999 (SI 1999 No 3242)* describes how the risk assessment process needs to be more sophisticated in larger and more hazardous sites. Nevertheless it suggests that quantification of risk will only be appropriate in a minority of situations. Some organisations utilise risk-rating systems to assist in the identification of priorities.

Most involve matrices utilising a simple combination of the likelihood of a hazard having an adverse effect and the severity of the consequences if it did. Some use numbers to produce a risk rating, as in the example below:

| *Risk Assessment Matrix* | | | *Likelihood of adverse effect* | | |
|---|---|---|---|---|---|
| | | | Unlikely | Possible | Frequent |
| | | | 1 | 2 | 3 |
| *Severity of consequences* | Minor | 1 | 1 | 2 | 3 |
| | Moderate | 2 | 2 | 4 | 6 |
| | Severe | 3 | 3 | 6 | 9 |

The numbers can be replaced by descriptions of the level of risk as shown in the next example:

| *Risk Assessment Matrix* | | *Likelihood of adverse effect* | | |
|---|---|---|---|---|
| | | Unlikely | Possible | Frequent |
| *Severity of consequences* | Minor | Low | Low | Medium |
| | Moderate | Low | Medium | High |
| | Severe | Medium | High | Very high |

The author's view is generally against the use of such matrices on the basis that time is often spent considering risk values at the expense of evaluating the effectiveness of the controls which ought to be in place.

# After the assessment

R3040    Whilst the recording of the risk assessment is an important legal requirement, it is even more important that the recommendations for improvement identified during the assessment are actually implemented. This is likely to involve several stages.

## Review and implementation of the recommendations

R3041    There may be a need to involve others outside (and probably senior to) the risk assessment team. The reasoning behind the recommendations can be explained and various alternative ways of controlling risks can be evaluated. Changes to the assessment findings or recommendations may be made at this stage but the risk assessment team should not allow themselves to be browbeaten into making alterations that they do not feel can be justified. Similarly they should not hold back on making recommendations they consider are necessary just because they believe that senior management will not implement them. The assessment team should carry out their duties to the best of their abilities in identifying what precautions are necessary in order to comply with the law – the responsibility for achieving compliance rests with their employer.

Some recommendations may need to be costed in respect of the capital expenditure or staff time required to implement them. It is unlikely that all recommendations will be able to be implemented immediately; there may be a significant lead time for the delivery of materials or the provision of specialist services from external sources.

Once costings and prioritisation have been agreed, the recommendations should be converted into an action plan with individuals clearly allocated responsibility for each element of the plan, within a defined timescale. Some members of the risk assessment team (particularly health and safety specialists) may have responsibility for implementing parts of the plan or providing guidance to others.

### Recommendation follow-up

R3042    Even in well-intentioned organisations, recommendations for improvement that have been fully justified and accepted are often still not implemented. It is essential that the risk assessment process includes a follow-up of the recommendations made. The recording format provided later in the chapter includes reference to this. As well as establishing that the improvements have actually been carried out, consideration should also be given to whether any unexpected risks have inadvertently been created.

Once the follow-up has been carried out, the assessment record should be annotated or revised to take account of the changes made. If recommendations have not been implemented there is a clear need for the situation to be referred back to senior management for them to take action to overcome whatever are the obstacles to progress.

### Assessment review

R3043    The *Management of Health and Safety at Work Regulations 1999 (SI 1999 No 3242)* and the associated ACoP state that assessments must be reviewed in certain circumstances (see R3019 ABOVE). The ACoP also states that 'it is prudent to plan to review risk assessments at regular intervals.' The frequency for reviews should be established which relates to the extent and nature of the risks involved and the likelihood of creeping changes (as opposed to a major change which would automatically justify a review).

The review may, however, conclude that the risks are unchanged, the precautions are still effective and that no revision of the assessments is necessary. The process of conducting regular reviews of assessments and, where appropriate, making revisions may be aided by the application of document control systems of the type used to achieve compliance with ISO 9000 and similar standards.

## Content of assessment records

R3044    The *Management of Health and Safety at Work Regulations 1999 (SI 1999 No 3242)*, *Reg 3(6)* states:

'Where the employer employs five or more employees, he shall record —

(a)    the significant findings of the assessment; and

(b)    any group of his employees identified by it as being especially at risk.'

The accompanying ACoP refers to the record as representing 'an effective statement of hazards and risks which then leads management to take the relevant actions to protect health and safety.' It goes on to state that the record must be retrievable for use by management, safety representatives, other employee representatives or visiting inspectors. The need for linkages between the risk assessment, the record of health and safety arrangements (required by *Reg 5* of the Management Regulations) and the health and safety policy is also identified. The ACoP allows for assessment records to be kept electronically as an alternative to being in written form.

The essential content of any risk assessment record should be:

— Hazards or risks associated with the work activity.

— Any employees identified as especially at risk.

— Precautions which are (or should be) in place to control the risks (with comments on their effectiveness).

— Improvements identified as being necessary to comply with the law.

Other important details to include are:

— Name of the employer.

— Address of the work location or base.

— Names and signatures of those carrying out the assessment.

— Date of the assessment.

— Date for next review of the assessment

(These might be provided as a introductory sheet.)

## Illustrative assessment records

R3045    In the final pages of this chapter the risk assessment methodology described earlier is used to provide illustrations of how the process can be applied in two different types of workplace. In each case, relevant risks or issues to be addressed are listed, one of those risks or issues is selected, relevant regulations, references and other key assessment points relating to that risk or issue are identified and an illustration of how the completed assessment record might look is provided. The content of the form used is similar to that provided in the HSE's *'Five steps to risk assessment'* leaflet but the layout is felt to be more user-friendly.

The illustrations used are for a supermarket and a newspaper publisher.

## A supermarket

R3046    Relevant risk topics are likely to include:

- Food processing machinery – in the delicatessen.

- Knives – delicatessen and butchery.

- Fork-lift trucks – warehousing areas.

- Vehicle traffic – delivery vehicles, customer and staff vehicles.

- Vehicle unloading – in the goods inward area.

- Pedestrian access – external to and inside the store.

- Glazed areas – store windows, display cabinets.

- Electrical installation – the power system within the store.

- Electrical equipment – including tills, cleaning equipment, office equipment.

- Shelving – in the store.

- Racking – in warehouse areas.

- Refrigerators – in the store and warehouse.

- Fire – general risks only, precautions must take account of customers.

- Aggression – e.g. from unhappy customers.

- Possible robbery – the supermarket will hold large quantities of cash.

- WRULD – for checkout operators.

- Hazardous substances – cleaning materials, office supplies.

- Manual handling – e.g. shelf stacking, movement of trolleys.

- Display screen equipment – used at workstations in the office.

- PPE requirements – throughout the supermarket.

- Use of contractors – for maintenance and repair work.

A sample risk assessment record for **vehicle traffic** is provided below.

In conducting this risk assessment:

- The requirements of the *Workplace (Health, Safety and Welfare) Regulations 1992* must be complied with.

- HSE booklet HS(G) 136 *'Workplace Transport Safety'* is likely to be relevant.

- Particular attention should be paid to:

   — signage and road markings;

   — observation of vehicle movements and speeds;

   — conditions during busy periods and hours of darkness.

# ABC Supermarkets, Newtown

## Risk Assessment

| Reference number: 4 | Risk topic/issue: Vehicle traffic | Sheet 1 of 1 |
|---|---|---|
| Cross references: HSE booklet IND(G) 136 Risk assessments 5 (vehicle unloading) and 6 (pedestrian access) | | |
| **Risks identified** | **Precautions in place** | **Recommended improvements** |
| Vehicles making deliveries to the 'Goods inward' bay present risks to each other and to any pedestrians on the access road<br><br>There are also risks to other road users as they leave and rejoin the main road. | Prominent 10 mph are in place on the roadway. The speed limit is enforced effectively.<br><br>Signs prohibit use of the road by pedestrians and customer or staff vehicles.<br><br>There are give way signs and road markings at the junction with the main road.<br><br>Vehicles are parked in a holding area prior to backing up to the 'Goods Inward' bay.<br><br>Movement of vehicles is controlled by a designated member of the supermarket staff.<br><br>The area is well lit by roadside lamps and floodlights on the side of the building. | Reposition the advertising sign which partly blocks visibility on rejoining the main road.<br><br>Provide this designated staff member with a high visibility waterproof jacket. |
| Customer and staff vehicles circulating in the car park area present risks to each other and to pedestrians in the area.<br><br>There are also risks to other road users at the entrance from and access back into the main road. | The access road around the car park is one way and well indicated by signs.<br><br>The entrance and exit are well separated from each other and the good access road.<br><br>There are prominent 15 mph signs around the roadways (some vehicles exceed this speed).<br><br>There are also some give way markings and signs at all roadway junctions.<br><br>Parking bays are well marked.<br><br>Pedestrian crossing points are clearly marked and signed.<br><br>The area is well lit by lighting towers which are protected at the base.<br><br>Security staff inspect, and where necessary, salt roadways in icy or snowy weather | Provide clearly marked speed ramps at suitable locations.<br><br>The surface of some bays in the south west corner of the car park should be repaired.<br><br>Include the goods access road, Goods inward bay and car park in routine safety inspections. |
| **Signature(s)**<br>A Smith,<br>B Jones | **Name(s)**<br>A Smith,<br>B Jones | **Date** 11/12/00 |
| **Dates for** | Recommendation follow up March 2001 | Next routine review December 2003 |

## A newspaper publisher

R3047     A large workplace like this would need to be divided into assessment units (see R3025 ABOVE), which might consist of:

- Common facilities and services – e.g. fire, electrical supply, lifts, vehicle traffic.

- Reel handling and stands – e.g. supply of reels of newsprint to the press area.

- Platemaking – e.g. equipment and chemicals used to produce printing plates.

- Printing press – e.g. press machinery, solvents, noise etc.

- Despatch – e.g. inserting equipment, newspaper stacking, strapping and loading.

- Circulation and transport – e.g. distribution and other vehicles, fuel, waste disposal.

- Maintenance – e.g. workshops, garage, maintenance activities.

- Offices – e.g. editorial and administrative areas.

Selecting the **reel handling and stands** unit, risk topics are likely to include:

- Fork-lift trucks – used to unload, transport and stack reels.

- Reel storage – stability of stacks, access issues.

- Reel handling equipment – hoists, conveyors and the reel stands feeding the press.

- Wrappings and waste – removal of wrappings, storage and disposal of waste paper etc.

- Noise and dust – from the operation of the reel stands and nearby press.

A sample assessment record for **reel handling equipment** is provided below.

In conducting this risk assessment:

- The requirements of the *Provision and Use of Work Equipment Regulations 1998 (PUWER)*, the *Lifting Operation and Lifting Equipment Regulations 1998* and the *Manual Handling Operations Regulations 1992* must be complied with.

- Reference may need to be made to BS 5304:1988 'Safety of machinery' or to other standards for conveyors or specialist handling equipment.

- Particular attention should be paid to:

  — guarding standards and the possible presence of unguarded dangerous parts;

  — any need for manual handling of the reels;

  — training issues relating to the above;

  — statutory examination records (for the hoist).

# Newtown News

| Risk Assessment | | |
|---|---|---|
| Reference number: B3 | Risk topic/issue: **Reel handling and stands – reel handling equipment** | Sheet 1 of 1 |
| Cross references: Risk assessments B1 (Fork-lift trucks), B2 (Reel storage), B5 (Noise and dust) | | |
| **Risks identified** | **Precautions in place** | **Recommended improvements** |
| The equipment below presents risks to all staff working in the area. | | |
| *Reel hoist* – Carries reel down from the reels store to the reel stand basement. It is fed by fork-lift trucks and feeds onto the roller conveyor system. | Slow moving hoist protected by a substantial mesh guard. No need for access within the hoist enclosure. Sign states 'Do not ride on hoist'. | Replace this sign by one complying with the *Safety Sign Regulations*) |
| | Gap between base of hoist and roller conveyor (no shear trap). Statutory examinations by Insurance Engineers (kept by Work Engineer). | |
| *Roller conveyor* – This is in a T formation and consists of powered and free running rollers with a turntable at the junction. Reels are transferred to holding bays or floor-based trolleys by fork-lift truck. | All drives for the conveyor are fully enclosed and there are no in-running nips. The conveyor is protected by kerbs from fork-lift damage. Signs prohibit climbing on the conveyor system. | Replace these signs as above. |
| *Floor-based trolleys* – This system carries reels right up to the transfer carriages up to the reel stand. | Reels can be easily moved by one person using the trolley system. Reels can be safely rolled across the floor onto the trolleys if the correct technique is used. | Include formal training on correct techniques in the induction programme for new staff in the area. |
| Some reels must be transferred manually from the holding bays onto the trolleys. | Two persons are required to move the transfer carriages up to the reel stands. | |
| *Reel stands* – The reel stands rotate mechanically ensuring a constant web feed to the press. | There are no accessible in-running nips. Operatives do not need to approach the rotating reels. | |
| The rotating drive shaft for the reel stands is approximately 4 metres above the ground level. | This shaft is considered to be 'safe by position' for normal operating purposes. | Ensure a safe system of work for maintenance work near the shaft, e.g. by using a permit to work procedure. |
| **Signature(s)** J Young, K Old | **Names(s)** J Young, K Old | Date 26/3/00 |
| Dates for | Recommendation follow up June 2000 | Next routine review March 2002 |

# Safe Systems of Work

## Introduction

S3001      The importance attached by health and safety legislation to the provision of safe systems of work can be demonstrated by the *Health and Safety at Work etc. Act 1974 (HSWA 1974)), s 2(2)(a)*. This provision extends the general duty of every employer to ensure, so far as is reasonably practicable, the health, safety and welfare at work of all his employees to include in particular:

> *'the provision and maintenance of plant and systems of work that are, so far as is reasonably practicable, safe and without risks to health.'*

There is no statutory definition of a safe system of work, but the question of what is a safe system of work was considered by the Court of Appeal in *Speed v Thomas Swift Co Ltd [1943] 1 AER 539*. In that case, the Master of the Rolls, Lord Greene, said:

> *'I do not venture to suggest a definition of what is meant by a system. But it includes, or may include according to circumstances, such matters as the physical lay-out of the job . . . the sequence in which the work is to be carried out, the provision . . . of warnings and notices and the issue of special instructions.'*

> *'. . . A system may be adequate for the whole course of the job or it may have to be modified or improved to meet circumstances which arise: such modification or improvements appear to me equally to fall under the heading of system.'*

and

> *'. . . the safety of a system must be considered in relation to the particular circumstances of each particular job.'*

This means that a system of work must be tailored to the job to which it is intended to apply.

## Provision of safe systems of work

S3002      The provision of safe systems of work will generally involve the following steps:

(1)      carrying out a risk assessment;

(2)      identifying hazards and the steps that can be taken to remove them;

(3)      developing a safe system of work to deal with hazards that cannot be removed;

(4)      formalising the system of work into procedures, where hazards are serious; and

(5)      incorporating the use of permits-to-work into the procedures where necessary.

# Risk assessment

S3003    The requirement to carry out a risk assessment is now a familiar part of health and safety management, and is required in order to ensure compliance with the following regulations:

(1)    the *Control of Asbestos at Work Regulations 1987 (SI 1987 No 2115)*;

(2)    the *Noise at Work Regulations 1989 (SI 1989 No 1790)*;

(3)    the *Health and Safety (Display Screen Equipment) Regulations 1992 (SI 1992 No 2792)*;

(4)    the *Manual Handling Operations Regulations 1992 (SI 1992 No 2793)*;

(5)    the *Personal Protective Equipment At Work Regulations1992 (SI 1992 No 2966)*;

(6)    the *Control of Lead at Work Regulations 1998 (SI 1998 No 543)*; and

(7)    the *Control of Substances Hazardous to Health Regulations 1999 (SI 1999 No 437)*.

Under those regulations, employers are obliged to carry out a risk assessment in order to identify the steps that need to be taken to protect employees and others from harm that may arise from the subject matter of the regulations, eg asbestos.

However the overriding duty on all employers, whatever the nature of their undertaking, is imposed by the *Management of Health and Safety at Work Regulations 1999 (SI 1999 No 3242)*. The Regulations require an employer to make a suitable and sufficient assessment of the risks created by his undertaking for the purpose of identifying the measures he needs to have in place to comply with his duties under *HSWA 1974*:

'Every employer shall make a suitable and sufficient assessment of –

(a)    the risks to the health and safety of his employees to which they are exposed whilst they are at work; and

(b)    the risks to the health and safety of persons not in his employment arising out of or in connection with the conduct by him of his undertaking,

for the purpose identifying the measures he needs to take to comply with the requirements and prohibitions imposed upon him by or under the relevant statutory provisions and by Part II of the Fire Precautions (Workplace) Regulations 1997.'

[*Management of Health and Safety at Work Regulations 1999 (SI 1999 No 3242)*, *Reg 3(1)*].

There is a duty to review an assessment if:

'(a)    there is reason to suspect that it is no longer valid; or

(b)    there has been a significant change in the matters to which it relates; and where as a result of any such review changes to an assessment are required, the employer or self-employed person concerned shall make them.'

[*Management of Health and Safety at Work Regulations 1999 (SI 1999 No 3242)*, *Reg 3(3)*].

If there are 5 or more employees, significant findings of the assessment must be recorded in writing. [*Management of Health and Safety at Work Regulations 1999 (SI 1999 No 3242)*, *Reg 3(6)*].

## Appointment of competent persons

S3004    Every employer must:

'*appoint one or more competent persons to assist him in undertaking the measures he needs to take to comply with the requirements and prohibitions imposed upon him by or under the relevant statutory provisions and by Part II of the Fire Precautions (Workplace) Regulations 1997.*'

[*Management of Health and Safety at Work Regulations 1999 (SI 1999 No 3242), Reg 7(1)*].

'*A person shall be regarded as competent for the purposes of paragraphs (1) and (8) where he has sufficient training and experience or knowledge and other qualities to enable him properly to assist in undertaking the measures referred to in paragraph (1).*'

[*Management of Health and Safety at Work Regulations 1999 (SI 1999 No 3242), Reg 7(5)*].

'*Where there is a competent person in the employer's employment, that person shall be appointed for the purposes of paragraph (1) in preference to a competent person not in his employment.*'

[*Management of Health and Safety at Work Regulations 1999 (SI 1999 No 3242), Reg 7(8)*].

## Risk assessment in respect of young persons

S3005    There are particular duties in relation to the employment of young persons. An employer must not employ a young person unless he has, in relation to risks to the health and safety of young persons, made or reviewed a risk assessment, taking particular account of:

'*(a)    the inexperience, lack of awareness of risks and immaturity of young persons;*

*(b)    the fitting-out and layout of the workplace and the workstation;*

*(c)    the nature, degree and duration of exposure to physical, biological and chemical agents;*

*(d)    the form, range, and use of work equipment and the way in which it is handled;*

*(e)    the organisation of processes and activities;*

*(f)    the extent of the health and safety training provided or to be provided to young persons; and*

*(g)    risks from agents, processes and work listed in the Annex to Council Directive 94/33/EC on the protection of young people at work.*'

[*Management of Health and Safety at Work Regulations 1999 (SI 1999 No 3242), Reg 3(4), (5)*].

## Risk assessment in respect of new or expectant mothers

S3006    Where in an undertaking:

'*the work is of a kind which could involve risk, by reason of her condition, to the health and safety of a new or expectant mother, or to that of her baby, from any processes or working conditions, or physical, biological or chemical agents, includ-*

ing those specified in Annexes I and II of Council Directive 92/85/EEC on the introduction of measures to encourage improvements in the safety and health at work of pregnant workers and workers who have recently given birth or are breastfeeding, the assessment required by regulation 3(1) shall also include an assessment of such risk.'

[*Management of Health and Safety at Work Regulations 1999 (SI 1999 No 3242), Reg 16(1)(b)*].

Where necessary, the employer must:

'if it is reasonable to do so, and would avoid such risks, alter her working conditions or hours of work.'

[*Management of Health and Safety at Work Regulations 1999 (SI 1999 No 3242), Reg 16(2)*].

If it is not reasonable to do the above, or it would not avoid such risk, he must suspend her. [*Management of Health and Safety at Work Regulations 1999 (SI 1999 No 3242), Reg 16(3)*].

## Principles of prevention

S3007   The Regulations do not prescribe the steps that should be taken by the employer following the carrying out of a risk assessment. It is for the employer to determine what are, and to take, *'the preventive and protective measures'* necessary, meaning:

'... the measures which have been identified by the employer ... in consequence of the assessment as the measures he needs to take to comply with the requirements and prohibitions imposed upon him by or under the relevant statutory provisions and by Part II of the Fire Precautions (Workplace) Regulations 1997.'

[*Management of Health and Safety at Work Regulations 1999 (SI 1999 No 3242), Reg 1(2)*].

However employers should be mindful of the requirement of Regulation 4 of the 1999 Regulations which incorporates the *'principles of prevention to be applied'*:

'Where an employer implements any preventive and protective measures he shall do so on the basis of the principles specified in Schedule 1 to these Regulations.'

[*Management of Health and Safety at Work Regulations 1999 (SI 1999 No 3242), Reg 4*].

Schedule 1 specifies the general principles of prevention set out in Article 6(2) of Council Directive 89/391/EEC, which are as follows:

(*a*)   avoiding risks;

(*b*)   evaluating the risks which cannot be avoided;

(*c*)   combating the risks at source;

(*d*)   adapting the work to the individual, especially as regards the design of workplaces, the choice of work equipment and the choice of working and production methods, with a view, in particular, to alleviating monotonous work and work at a predetermined work-rate and to reducing their effect on health;

(*e*)   adapting to technical progress;

(*f*)   replacing the dangerous by the non-dangerous or the less dangerous;

(*g*)    developing a coherent overall prevention policy which covers technology, organisation of work, working conditions, social relationships and the influence of factors relating to the working environment;

(*h*)    giving collective protective measures priority over individual protective measures; and

(*i*)    giving appropriate instructions to employees.

### Statutory guidance – the approved code of practice

S3008    The Approved Code of Practice (ACoP), published in March 2000 to accompany the introduction of the *Management of Health and Safety at Work Regulations 1999 (SI 1999 No 3242)*, contains guidance on the changes that have been introduced, particularly relating to the area of risk assessment. It sets out:

(1)    the principles of prevention;

(2)    the principle that employers should use competent employees, where they exist, in preference to external sources, for competent advice and assistance on health and safety;

(3)    the need to establish contacts with emergency services to ensure the effective provision of external first-aid, emergency medical care and rescue work, in response to accidents and serious incidents; and

(4)    the fact that any act or omission, by an employee or by an appointed competent person, cannot be relied upon by an employer as a defence, should the employer be prosecuted for breaches of health and safety law.

The ACoP states that 'a suitable and sufficient risk assessment' is one that:

(*a*)    identifies significant risks arising out of work;

(*b*)    enables the employer to identify and prioritise measures that need to be taken to comply with relevant statutory provisions;

(*c*)    is appropriate to the nature of the work; and

(*d*)    remains valid for a reasonable period of time.

## Identifying hazards

S3009    Employers should identify the hazards that can reasonably be expected to occur in the workplace and the steps that can be taken to remove them. This must include checking that all statutory obligations are met, for example, the fitting of guards to dangerous machinery. The focus should be on trying to identify serious hazards that are likely to result in serious harm or affect a number of people. This process involves identifying who can be harmed by hazards, and should include consideration of potential hazards to members of the public if there is a risk that they may be injured in workplace activities. In overall terms, the objective should be to minimise risks by checking, and augmenting as necessary, the precautions that are already being taken so that the employer meets the general duty imposed by *HSWA 1974* to ensure, so far as is reasonably practicable, the health, safety and welfare at work of all his employees.

## Developing safe systems of work – HSE guidance

S3010    The HSE publication '*Safe work in confined spaces*, IND(G) 258 (L) contains guidance on developing safe systems of work. It emphasises the need for an employer to carry out a suitable and sufficient assessment of the risks for all work activities for the purpose of deciding what measures are necessary for safety. This means identifying the hazards present, assessing the risks and determining what precautions to take. In most cases the assessment will include consideration of:

- the task;

- the working environment;

- working materials and tools;

- the suitability of those carrying out the task; and

- arrangements for emergency rescue.

## Safe systems of work

S3011    The guidance advises on the need to have a safe system of work for hazards that cannot be avoided. An employer should use the results of his risk assessment to help identify the necessary precautions to reduce the risk of injury. These will depend on the nature of the working environment, the associated risk and the work involved. An employer should make sure that the safe system of work, including the precautions identified, is developed and put into practice. Everyone involved will need to be properly trained and instructed to make sure they know what to do and how to do it safely.

The guidance suggests elements to help prepare a safe system of work. These include the following.

### *Appointment of a supervisor*

S3012    Supervisors should be given responsibility to ensure that the necessary precautions are taken, to check safety at each stage and may need to remain present while work is underway.

### *Assessment of suitability of persons for the work*

S3013    Persons should have suitable training in and sufficient experience of the type of work to be carried out. The competent person may need to consider and seek medical advice on an individual's suitability.

### *Isolation*

S3014    Mechanical and electrical isolation of equipment is essential if it could otherwise operate, or be operated, inadvertently.

### *Provision of emergency arrangements*

S3015    This will need to cover the necessary equipment, training and practice drills.

### *Communication*

S3016    An adequate communication system is needed to enable those involved in the work to summon help in an emergency. This should take account of night and shift work, weekends and times when the premises are closed, e.g. holidays.

*Need for a 'permit-to-work'*

S3017 A permit-to-work ensures a formal check is undertaken to ensure all the elements of a safe system of work are in place before people are allowed to enter the hazardous area. It is also a means of communication between site management, supervisors and those carrying out the hazardous work. Essential features of a permit-to-work are:

- clear identification of who may authorise particular jobs (and any limits to their authority) and who is responsible for specifying the necessary precautions (e.g. isolation, air testing, emergency arrangements etc.):

- provision for ensuring that contractors engaged to carry out work are included;

- training and instruction in the issue of permits; and

- monitoring and auditing to ensure that the system works as intended.

*Emergency procedures*

S3018 Effective arrangements should be made for carrying out rescue operations in an emergency.

## Procedures for serious and imminent danger and for danger areas

S3019 Under the *Management of Health and Safety at Work Regulations 1999 (SI 1999 No 3242), Reg 8:*

'(1) *Every employer shall –*

(a) *establish and where necessary give effect to appropriate procedures to be followed in the event of serious and imminent danger to persons at work in his undertaking;*

(b) *nominate a sufficient number of competent persons to implement those procedures in so far as they relate to the evacuation from premises of persons at work in his undertaking; and*

(c) *ensure that none of his employees has access to any area occupied by him to which it is necessary to restrict access on grounds of health and safety unless the employee concerned has received adequate health and safety instruction.'*

The procedures established under *Reg 8(1)(a)* above must:

'(a) *so far as is practicable, require any persons at work who are exposed to serious and imminent danger to be informed of the nature of the hazard and of the steps taken or to be taken to protect them from it;*

(b) *enable the persons concerned (if necessary by taking appropriate steps in the absence of guidance or instruction and in the light of their knowledge and the technical means at their disposal) to stop work and immediately proceed to a place of safety in the event of their being exposed to serious, imminent and unavoidable danger; and*

(c) *save in exceptional cases for reasons duly substantiated (which cases and reasons shall be specified in those procedures), require the persons concerned to be prevented from resuming work in any situation where there is still a serious and imminent danger.'*

[*Management of Health and Safety at Work Regulations 1999 (SI 1999 No 3242), Reg. 8(2)*].

The attributes required of a competent person are the same as in *Reg.7(5)*:

*'A person shall be regarded as competent for the purposes of paragraph (1)(b) where he has sufficient training and experience or knowledge and other qualities to enable him properly to implement the evacuation procedures referred to in that sub-paragraph.'*

[*Management of Health and Safety at Work Regulations 1999 (SI 1999 No 3242), Reg. 8(3)*].

### Contacts with external services

S3020    *'Every employer shall ensure that any necessary contacts with external services are arranged, particularly as regards first-aid, emergency medical care and rescue work.' [Reg.9]*.

### Information for employees

S3021    *'(1)  Every employer shall provide his employees with comprehensible and relevant information on –*

  *(a)   the risks to their health and safety identified by the assessment;*

  *(b)   the preventive and protective measures;*

  *(c)   the procedures referred to in regulation 8(1)(a) and the* [equivalent] *measures referred to in regulation 4(2)(a) of the Fire Precautions (Workplace) Regulations 1997;*

  *(d)   the identity of those persons nominated by him in accordance with regulation 8(1)(b) and regulation 4(2)(b) of the Fire Precautions (Workplace) Regulations 1997; and*

  *(e)   the risks notified to him* [by another employer sharing the same work place, in respect of risks to his employees' health and safety arising out of or in connection with the conduct by the other employer of his undertaking] *in accordance with regulation 11(1)(c).'*

[*Management of Health and Safety at Work Regulations 1999 (SI 1999 No 3242), Reg 10(1)*].

### Permit-to-work systems

S3022    HSE publication, *'Pemits-to-work systems'*, IND(G) 98 (L) gives further guidance on the use of permit-to-work systems. It states that:

*'A permit-to-work system is a formal written system used to control certain types of work that are potentially hazardous. A permit-to-work is a document which specifies the work to be done and the precautions to be taken. Permits-to-work form an essential part of a safe system of work for many maintenance activities. They allow work to start only after safe procedures have been defined and they provide a clear record that all foreseeable hazards have been considered.*

*A permit is needed when maintenance work can only be carried out if normal safeguards are dropped or when new hazards are introduced by the work. Examples are, entry into vessels, hot work and pipeline breaking.'*

The guidance states that employers should consider the following questions.

## Information

**S3023**
- Is the permit-to-work system fully documented, laying down:
  - — how the system works;
  - — the jobs it is to be used for;
  - — the responsibilities and training of those involved; and
  - — how to check its operation?
- Is there clear identification of who may authorise particular jobs (and any limits to their authority)?
- Is there clear identification of who is responsible for specifying the necessary precautions (e.g. isolation, emergency arrangements, etc.)?
- Is the permit form clearly laid out?
- Does it avoid statements or questions which could be ambiguous or misleading?
- Is it designed to allow for use in unusual circumstances?
- Does it cover contractors?

## Selection and training

**S3024**
- Are those who issue permits sufficiently knowledgeable concerning the hazards and precautions associated with the plant and proposed work? Do they have the imagination and experience to ask enough 'what if' questions to enable them to identify all potential hazards?
- Do staff and contractors fully understand the importance of the permit-to-work system and are they trained in its use?

## Description of the work

**S3025**
- Does the permit clearly identify the work to be done and the associated hazards?
- Can plans and diagrams be used to assist in the description of the work to be done, its location and limitations?
- Is the plant adequately identified, e.g. by discrete number or tag to assist issuers and users in correctly taking out and following permits?
- Is a detailed work method statement given for more complicated tasks?

## Hazards and precautions

**S3026**
- Does the system require the removal of hazards and, where this is not reasonably practicable, effective control? Are the requirements of the *Control*

of Substances Hazardous to Health Regulations (COSHH) (SI 1999 No 437) and other relevant legislation known and to be followed by those who issue the permits?

● Does the permit state the precautions that have been taken and those that are needed while work is in progress? For instance, are isolations specified and is it clear what personal protective equipment should be used?

● Do the precautions cover residual hazards and those that might be introduced by the work, e.g. welding fume and vapour from cleaning solvents?

● Do the *Confined Spaces Regulations 1997* apply? If so, has a full risk assessment identified the significant risks and identified alternative methods of working or necessary precautions?

## Procedures

S3027    ● Does the permit contain clear rules about how the job should be controlled or abandoned in the case of an emergency?

● Does the permit have a hand-back procedure incorporating statements that the maintenance work has finished and that the plant has been returned to production staff in a safe state?

● Are time limitations included and is shift changeover dealt with?

● Are there clear procedures to be followed if work has to be suspended for any reason?

● Is there a system of cross-referencing when two or more jobs subject to permits may affect each other?

● Is the permit displayed at the job?

● Are jobs checked regularly to make sure that the relevant permit-to-work system is still relevant and working properly?

## Essentials of the permit-to-work form

S3028    The guidance states that the permit-to-work form must help communication between everyone involved. It should be designed by the company issuing the permit, taking into account individual site conditions and requirements. Separate permit forms may be required for different tasks, such as hot work and entry into confined spaces, so that sufficient emphasis can be given to the particular hazards present and precautions required.

The essential elements of a permit-to-work form are listed in the guidance:

(1)    *Permit title.*

(2)    *Permit number* (and reference to other relevant permits or isolation certificates).

(3)    *Job location.*

(4)    *Plant identification.*

(5)    *Description of work* to be done and its limitations.

(6)    *Hazard identification* – including residual hazards and hazards introduced by the work.

(7)  *Precautions necessary* – person who carries out precautions, e.g. isolations, should sign that precautions have been taken.

(8)  *Protective equipment.*

(9)  *Authorisation* – signature confirming that isolations have been made and precautions taken, except where these can only be taken during the work; date and time duration of permit.

(10)  *Acceptance* – signature confirming understanding of work to be done, hazards involved and precautions required. Also confirming permit information has been explained to all workers involved.

(11)  *Extension/shift handover procedures* – signatures confirming checks made that plant remains safe to be worked upon, and new acceptor/workers made fully aware of hazards/precautions. New time expiry given.

(12)  *Hand back* – signed by acceptor certifying work completed. Signed by issuer certifying work completed and plant ready for testing and re-commissioning.

(13)  *Cancellation* – certifying work tested and plant satisfactorily re-commissioned.

# Requirements for a safety policy statement

S3029

If an employer employs five or more people he must have a written statement of his health and safety policy. The *Management of Health and Safety at Work Regulations 1999 (SI 1999 No 3242), Reg 5* requires that:

> *'(1)  Every employer shall make and give effect to such arrangements as are appropriate, having regard to the nature of his activities and the size of his undertaking, for the effective planning, organisation, control, monitoring and review of the preventive and protective measures.*
>
> *(2)  Where the employer employs five or more employees, he shall record the arrangements referred to in paragraph (1).'*

HSE has published a guidance booklet *'Writing a Safety Policy Statement'*. This advises that the statement, which should be specific to the undertaking, should set out the employer's general *policy* for protecting the health and safety of his employees at work and the *organisation* and *arrangements* for putting that policy in to practice.

## Policy

S3030

This should state, in simple terms, what the employer's general aims are with regard to his employees' health and safety. The employer must demonstrate commitment to the policy, which must stress the importance of co-operation from the workforce and of good communications at all levels in the firm. It should identify the senior personnel who are responsible for implementing and monitoring the policy. The commitment should be demonstrated by the publication of an action programme which expresses the employer's proposals on matters such as:

(1)  works and equipment to provide safe and healthy working conditions;

(2)  training in health and safety and first-aid, and

(3)  consultation with employees;

## Organisation

**S3031**    The statement should describe the systems and procedures for ensuring employees' health and safety. This should be based on an analysis of the activities carried out by the undertaking, the hazards that may arise, together with the rules and precautions for avoiding them. It should also cover the arrangements for dealing with injury, fire and other emergencies and arrangements for providing the instruction, training and supervision necessary to ensure that safe systems are always adopted and adhered to. The arrangements for seeing that employees follow the rules and precautions should also be set out. The strategy for protecting other people who could be put at risk by work activities, such as contractors, customers, and the public should be covered, as should activities of others (e.g. those of contractors on the employer's site) which could put the employer's own employees at risk. If there is a safety committee, its constitution and terms of reference should be included in this section.

The guidance suggests that employers should consider the following checklist as an aid in writing and reviewing a safety policy statement.

- Does the statement express a commitment to health and safety and are your obligations towards your employees made clear?

- Does it say which senior officer is responsible for seeing that it is implemented and for keeping it under review, and how this will be done?

- Is it signed and dated by you or a partner or senior director?

- Have the views of managers and supervisors, safety representatives and of the safety committee been taken into account?

- Were the duties set out in the statement discussed with the people concerned in advance, and accepted by them, and do they understand how their performance is to be assessed and what resources they have at their disposal?

- Does the statement make clear that co-operation on the part of all employees is vital to the success of your health and safety policy?

- Does it say how employees are to be involved in health and safety matters, for example by being consulted, by taking part in inspections, and by sitting on a safety committee?

- Does it show clearly how the duties for health and safety are allocated and are the responsibilities at different levels described?

- Does it say who is responsible for the following matters (including deputies where appropriate)?:

  — reporting investigations and recording accidents;

  — fire precautions, fire drill, evacuation procedures;

  — first-aid;

  — safety inspections;

  — the training programme;

  — ensuring that legal requirements are met, for example regular testing of lifts and notifying accidents to the health and safety inspector.

## Arrangements

**S3032**    The guidance suggests that the following arrangements need to be considered.

*Workplace*

- Keeping the workplace, including staircases, floors, ways in and out, washrooms etc in a safe and clean condition by cleaning, maintenance and repair.

*Plant and substances*

- Maintenance of equipment such as tools, ladders etc.

- Maintenance and proper use of safety equipment such as helmets, boots, goggles, respirators etc.

- Maintenance and proper use of plant, machinery and guards.

- Regular testing and maintenance of lifts, hoists, cranes, pressure systems, boilers and other dangerous machinery, emergency repair work, and safe methods of doing it.

- Maintenance of electrical installations and equipment.

- Safe storage, handling and, where applicable, packaging, labelling and transport of dangerous substances.

- Controls on work involving harmful substances such as lead and asbestos.

- The introduction of new plant, equipment or substances into the workplace – by examination, testing and consultation with the workforce.

*Other hazards*

- Noise problems – alleviate by wearing ear protection, and control of noise at source.

- Preventing unnecessary or unauthorised entry into hazardous areas.

- Lifting of heavy or awkward loads.

- Protecting the safety of employees against assault when handling or transporting the employer's money or valuables.

- Special hazards to employees when working on unfamiliar sites. Therefore there should be discussion with site manager where necessary.

- Control of works transport, e.g. fork-lift trucks by restricting use to experienced and authorised operators or operators under instruction (which should deal fully with safety aspects).

*Emergencies*

- Ensuring that fire exists are marked, unlocked and free from obstruction.

- Maintenance and testing of fire-fighting equipment, fire drills and evacuation procedures.

- First-aid, including name and location of person responsible for first-aid and deputy, and location of first-aid box.

*Communication*

- Giving your employees information about the general duties under the *HSWA 1974* and specific legal requirements relating to their work.

- Giving employees necessary information about substances, plant, machinery, and equipment with which they come into contact.

- Discussing with contractors, before they come on site, how they can plan to do their job, whether they need equipment to help them, whether they can operate in a segregated area or when part of the plant is shut down and, if not, what hazards they may create for your employees and vice versa.

*Training*

- Training employees, supervisors and managers to enable them to work safely and to carry out their health and safety responsibilities efficiently.

*Supervising*

- Supervising employees so far as necessary for their safety – especially young workers, new employees and employees carrying out unfamiliar tasks.

*Keeping check*

- Regular inspections and checks of the workplace, machinery appliances and working methods.

*Monitoring*

- Monitoring the effectiveness of the arrangements and reviewing safety performance as a whole.

## Further information

S3033    The following information is available from HSE Books, PO Box 1999, Sudbury, Suffolk CO10 2WA (tel: 01787 881165; fax: 01787 313995).

- Five steps to risk assessment, IND(G) 163 (L).

- A guide to risk assessment requirements, IND(G) 218 (L).

- Management of Health and Safety at Work: Approved Code of Practice, L 21 2000.

- COSHH: The new brief guide for employers, IND(G) 136 (L).

- Safe work in confined spaces, IND(G) 258 (L).

- The safe isolation of plant and equipment, ISBN 0 7176 0871 9.

- Permit-to-work systems, IND(G) 98 (L).

- Guidance on permits-to-work systems in the petroleum industry, ISBN 0 7176 1281 3.

- Writing a Health and Safety Policy Statement, HSC 6.

# Statements of Health and Safety Policy

## Introduction

S7001 Employers have a statutory duty under *s 2(3)* of the *Health and Safety at Work etc. Act 1974 (HSWA 1974)* to prepare a written statement of their health and safety policy, including the organisation and arrangements for carrying it out, and to bring the statement to the attention of their employees. Employers with less than five employees are excepted from this requirement.

This section sets out the legal requirements for a policy, explains the essential ingredients that a policy should contain and provides checklists to assist in the preparation of policies.

## The legal requirements

S7002 *Section 2(3)* of the *HSWA 1974* states:

> '*Except in such cases as may be prescribed, it shall be the duty of every employer to prepare and as often as may be appropriate revise a written statement of his general policy with respect to the health and safety at work of his employees and the organisation and arrangements for the time being in force for carrying out that policy, and to bring the statement and any revision of it to the notice of his employees.*'

The *Employers' Health and Safety Policy Statements (Exception) Regulations 1975 (SI 1975 No 1584)* except from these provisions any employer who carries on an undertaking in which for the time being he employs less than five employees. In this respect regard is to be given only to employees present on the premises at the same time *(Osborne v Bill Taylor of Huyton Ltd [1982] IRLR 17)*.

Directors, managers and company secretaries can be personally liable for a failure to prepare or to implement a health and safety policy. (see further *Armour v Skeen at E15040 ENFORCEMENT*).

## Content of the policy statement

S7003 The policy statement should have three main parts:

— *The Statement of Intent*

This should involve a statement of the organisation's overall commitment to good standards of health and safety and usually includes a reference to compliance with relevant legislation. Whilst *s 2(3)* of the *HSWA 1974* only requires the statement to relate to employees, many organisations also make reference to others who may be affected by their activities e.g. contractors, clients, members of the public (This may be of particular relevance if the policy is being reviewed by other parties such as clients). In order to demonstrate that there is commitment at a high level, the statement should preferably be signed by the chairman, chief executive or someone in a similar position of seniority.

— *Organisation*

It is vitally important that the responsibilities for putting the good intentions into practice are clearly identified. This may be relatively simple in a small organisation but larger employers are likely to need to identify the responsibilities held by those at different levels in the management structure as well as those for staff in more specialised roles e.g. health and safety officers. In all cases the competent person who is to assist in complying with health and safety requirements should be identified [*Management of Health and Safety at Work Regulations 1999 (SI 1999 No 3242), Reg 7*].

— *Arrangements*

The practical arrangements for implementing the policy (e.g. emergency procedures, consultation mechanisms, health and safety inspections) should be identified in this section. It may not be practicable to detail all of the arrangements in the policy document itself but the policy should identify where they can be found e.g. in a separate health and safety manual or within procedure systems.

More detailed guidance on what should be included in each of these parts is contained later together with guidance on two other important issues:

- Communication of the policy to employees.

- Revision of the policy.

## The statement of intent

S7004    The statement should emphasise the organisation's commitment to health and safety. The detailed content must reflect the philosophical approach within the organisation and also the context of its work activities. Typically it might include:

—    a commitment to achieving high standards of health and safety in respect of its employees;

—    a similar commitment to others involved or affected by its activities (possibly specifying them e.g. contractors, visitors, clients, tenants, members of the public);

—    a recognition of its legal obligations under the *HSWA 1974* and related legislation and a commitment to complying with these obligations,

—    references to specific obligations e.g. to provide safe and healthy working conditions, equipment and systems of work;

—    reference to the importance of health and safety as a management objective;

—    a commitment to consultation with its employees.

Most employers keep the statement of intent relatively short – less than a single sheet of paper. This allows it to be prominently displayed (e.g. in reception areas or on noticeboards), or to be inserted easily into other documents such as employee handbooks.

Example:

The Midshires Development Agency (MDA) is committed to achieving high standards of health and safety not only in respect of its own employees but also in relation to tenants of the Agency's property, contractors working on the Agency's property or projects, visitors and members of the community who may be affected by the Agency's activities.

The Agency is well aware of its obligations under the Health and Safety at Work Act and related legislation and is fully committed to meeting those obligations. The successful management of health and safety is a key management objective.

MDA supports the concept of consultation with its staff on health and safety matters and has established a Health and Safety Committee to provide a forum for such consultation. This policy will be distributed to all staff and will be reviewed on an annual basis.

A Champion

Chief Executive

August 2000

## Organisation

**S7005**

The statement of intent is of little value unless the organisation for implementing these good intentions is clearly established. This usually involves identifying the responsibilities of people at different levels in the management organisation and also those with specific functional roles e.g. the health and safety officer. How these responsibilities are allocated will depend upon the structure and size of the organisation. The responsibilities of the managing director of a major company will be quite different from those of a managing director in a small business. The latter will quite often have responsibilities held by a supervisor in a larger organisation e.g. ensuring staff comply with PPE requirements.

Most organisations prefer to identify the responsibilities through job titles rather than by name as this avoids the need to revise the document when individuals change jobs or leave. Responsibilities might be allocated to levels in the organisation e.g.

— Managing Director/Chief Executive

— Senior Managers

— Junior Managers

— Supervisors/Foremen/Chargehands

— Employees

and also to those with specialist roles e.g.

— Health and Safety Officer

— Occupational Hygienist

— Occupational Health staff

— Personnel staff

— Maintenance Engineer

Where health and safety advice is provided from outside (e.g. a consultant or a specialist at a different location), this should be stated and the means of contacting this person for advice should be identified.

The following examples are provided as an illustration of how responsibilities might be allocated in a medium sized organisation. The allocation will undoubtedly be different for businesses of greater or lesser size.

Examples:

- Managing Director

  The Managing Director has overall responsibility for health and safety and in particular for:

  — ensuring that adequate resources are available to implement the health and safety policy;

  — ensuring health and safety performance is regularly reviewed at board level;

  — monitoring the effectiveness of the health and safety policy;

  — reviewing the policy annually.

- Works Manager

  The Works Manager is primarily responsible for the effective management of health and safety within the factory. In particular this includes;

  — delegating specific health and safety responsibilities to others;

  — monitoring their effectiveness in carrying out those responsibilities;

  — ensuring the company has access to adequate competent health and safety advice;

  — ensuring that safe systems of work are established within the factory;

  — ensuring that premises and equipment are adequately maintained;

  — ensuring that risk assessments are carried out;

  — ensuring that adequate health and safety training is provided;

  — chairing the health and safety committee.

- Supervisors

  Each Supervisor is responsible for the effective management of health and safety within his or her own area or function. In particular this includes:

  — ensuring that safe systems of work are implemented;

  — enforcing PPE requirements;

  — ensuring that staff are adequately trained for the tasks they perform;

  — monitoring premises and work equipment, reporting faults where necessary;

  — identifying and reporting health and safety related problems and issues;

  — identifying training needs;

  — investigating and reporting on accidents and incidents;

  — participating in the risk assessment programme;

  — setting a good example on health and safety matters.

- All employees

  All employees have a legal obligation to take reasonable care for their own health and safety and for that of others who may be affected by their actions e.g. colleagues, contractors, visitors, delivery staff. Employees are responsible for:

  — complying with company procedures and health and safety rules;

  — complying with PPE requirements;

  — behaving in a responsible manner;

  — identifying and reporting defects and other health and safety concerns;

  — reporting accidents and near miss incidents to their supervisor;

  — suggesting improvements to procedures or systems of work;

  — co-operating with the company on health and safety matters.

- Health and Safety Officer

  The Health and Safety Officer is responsible for co-ordinating many health and safety activities and for acting as the primary source of health and safety advice within the company. These responsibilities specifically include:

  — co-ordinating the company's risk assessment programme;

  — acting as secretary to the Health and Safety Committee;

  — administering the accident investigation and reporting procedure;

  — liaising with the HSE, the company's insurers and other external bodies;

  — submitting reports as required by RIDDOR;

  — co-ordinating the health and safety inspection programme;

  — identifying health and safety training needs;

  — providing or sourcing health and safety training;

  — providing health and safety induction training to new staff;

  — identifying the implications of changes in legislation or HSE guidance;

  — preparing and submitting progress reports on an annual health and safety action programme;

  — sourcing additional specialist health and safety assistance when necessary.

**Arrangements**

S7006    The duty to provide information on the arrangements for carrying out the health and safety policy overlaps with the duty imposed by *Regs 3* and *5* of the *Management of Health and Safety at Work Regulations (SI 1999 No 3242)* to record the results of risk assessments and of arrangements 'for the effective planning, organisation, control, monitoring and review of the preventive and protective measures'. Rather than providing all of the detail on arrangements within the health and safety policy many employers prefer to provide information on where these details can be found, for example in:

— risk assessment records;

—   health and safety manuals or handbooks;

—   formal health and safety procedures (e.g. within an ISO 9000 controlled system).

This has the benefit of keeping the policy document itself relatively short – an aid in the effective communication of the policy to employees. Some key aspects of health and safety arrangements which should be included or referred to in this section of the policy are those for:

—   conducting and recording risk assessments;

—   specialised risk assessments e.g. COSHH, Noise, Manual Handling, DSE workstations;

—   assessing and controlling risks to young persons and new or expectant mothers;

—   establishing PPE standards and the provision of PPE;

—   operational procedures (where these relate to health and safety);

—   permit to work systems;

—   routine training e.g. induction, operator training;

—   specialised training e.g. first aiders, fork lift drivers;

—   health screening e.g. pre-employment medicals, regular monitoring, DSE user eye tests;

—   statutory inspections;

—   consultation with employees e.g. health and safety committees, staff meetings, shift briefings;

—   health and safety inspections;

—   auditing health and safety arrangements;

—   investigation and reporting of accidents and incidents;

—   selection and management of contractors;

—   control of visitors;

—   fire prevention, control and evacuation;

—   dealing with other emergencies e.g. bomb threats, chemical leaks;

—   first-aid;

—   maintaining and repairing premises and work equipment.

## Communication of the policy

**S7007**   Employers must bring the policy (and any revision of it) to the notice of their employees. The most important time for doing this is when new employees join the organisation and communication of the policy should be an integral part of any induction programme. Young people in particular need to be reminded of their personal responsibilities at this stage, as well as any restrictions on what they can and can't do. Even experienced workers may need to be made aware that they are joining an organisation that takes health and safety seriously, as well as knowing what the PPE rules are and where they can obtain the PPE from.

Many employers provide their employees with a personal copy of the policy whilst others include it in a general employee handbook or display it prominently e.g. on noticeboards. In all cases communication will be aided by keeping the policy itself relatively brief and providing the detail (particularly in respect of 'arrangements') elsewhere.

## Review

**S7008**

The policy must be revised 'as often as may be appropriate' but the need for revision can only be identified through a review. In their free guidance leaflet for small firms on preparing a health and safety policy document (IND(G) 324 *'Stating your business'*) the HSE recommend an annual review and this should not be too onerous even for small employers, for whom it should be a fairly simple affair.

In larger organisations the policy could be subjected to an annual review by incorporating it within an ISO 9000 document control system or making the review an annual task of the health and safety committee. Alternatively the review could be made the responsibility of an individual (e.g. the Managing Director or the Health and Safety Officer), either formally through specifying this within the organisational responsibilities or informally through a simple diary entry.

The review may well conclude that there is no need for change but it may identify the need for revision such as:

—    A new Managing Director should make his personal commitment to the statement of intent by signing and re-issuing it.

—    Changes in the management structure necessitate a reallocation of responsibilities for health and safety.

—    New 'arrangements' for health and safety have been established (or existing ones have been altered) and the policy needs to be amended to match this.

A policy which is clearly well out of date does not reflect well on the organisation's commitment to health and safety, nor on the effectiveness of its health and safety management.

# Training and Competence in Occupational Safety and Health

## Introduction

T7001    Much of post-1992 safety at work legislation has emphasised 'training', or 'competence' as a key focus for the employer in improving safety performance and reducing accidents, ill-health and injury. Training is seen as a solution to most safety at work problems ranging from training employees in the safe use of electricity through to training to cope with violence at work. This chapter focuses on the legal, managerial, behavioural, economic and professional issues that safety and health practitioners as well as organisations need to consider in order to establish reliable and proactive safety training systems at work. It also considers the central issue of safety competence at work of employees and contractors.

## Definitions

T7002    Figure 1 depicts a framework that shows how key concepts within safety training systems are linked and also how they differ.

*Figure 1: Thinking Safety: a Systems Approach*

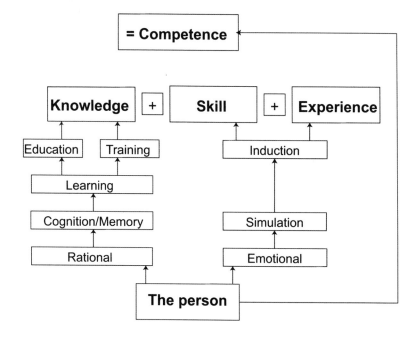

## Key concepts

T7003   The following table summarises the meanings of the key concepts identified in figure 1 based upon the '*The New Oxford Dictionary of English*', Oxford University Press 1999.

| Term | Definition | Interpretation |
|------|-----------|----------------|
| • **Competence** | 'the ability to do something successfully or efficiently' (page 374). | • The Dictionary also equates competency with competence.<br><br>• The completion of a task in a careful, thorough, resource saving manner that yields maximum benefits (e.g. to the person, group or environment).<br><br>• A person, whose performance – practical and/or theoretical, satisfies a criteria, standard or benchmark set by a body or society. |
| • **Competent** | 'having the necessary ability, knowledge, or skill to do something successfully' (page 374). | Comments:<br><br>1. It would seem 'competence' is a general concept, broadly used in judgmental terms whilst 'competent' is specific and relates to well defined actions to be assessed.<br><br>2. Competence/ competent refer to the 'end' or goal to be achieved.<br><br>3. Both concepts will be used interchangeably. |
| • **Educate**<br><br>• **Education** | 'give intellectual, moral, and social instruction to (someone, especially a child), typically at a school or university' (page 589).<br><br>'the process of receiving or giving systematic instruction, especially at a school or university' (page 589). | • Both terms combined: a broad psychosocial and institutional process involving the imparting of 'instructions' (i.e. theoretical, logical, sequential and systematic details) and interaction with the recipient(s), usually within a formal and structured environment. |

| Term | Definition | Interpretation |
|------|-----------|----------------|
| ● **Training** | 'the action of teaching a person or animal a particular skill or type of behaviour' (page 1966). | ● Training in contrast to education is more skill acquisition focused in relation to a well defined task ( rather than a broad/generic theoretical experience) with the view of solving a problem or acquiring new behaviour that reduces risk and improves efficiency.<br><br>● Both education and training are 'means' to achieving an 'end' namely competence. |
| ● **Induct**<br><br><br><br>● **Induction** | 'admit (someone) formally to a post or organisation' (page 932).<br><br><br>'the action or process of inducting someone to a post or organisation' (page 932). | ● Induction is a dual process of imparting factual information to a new entrant as to the organisation's norms, values and mores. As well as for the new entrant to acquire new experiences (thus, subjective, relative and normative) of seeing, feeling and being absorbed into a new/different working environment.<br><br>● Induction (together with education and training ) is also a means to an end (competence) |
| ● **Learn**<br><br><br><br><br><br><br><br>● **Learning** | 'gain or acquire knowledge of or skill in (something) by study, experience, or being taught' (page 1048).<br><br>'USAGE: In modern standard English, it is incorrect to use *learn* to mean *teach* . . .' (page 1048).<br><br>'the acquisition of knowledge or skills through experience, practice, study or by being taught' (page 1048). | ● Learning underpins training and education in particular. It is a structured process that is a function of time (hence 'learning curve') of methodically seeing, hearing, writing and vocalization whether in an institutional or societal context. |

| Term | Definition | Interpretation |
|------|-----------|----------------|
| • Cognition | 'the mental action or process of acquiring knowledge and understanding through thought, experience, and the senses. [count noun] a result of this: a perception, sensation, notion, or intuition' (page 355). | • Cognition is a psychological variable that enables conceptualisation and learning. A practical outcome of Cognitive processes is indexed by concepts such as know-how, knowledge, awareness, consciousness. |
| • Memory | 'a person's power to remember things' (page 1155). | • A cognitive and behavioural process of storing/retaining, retrieving and reviewing data/information held by the brain. It is also an reflective process of retrieving experiences and emotions built over time. In any case, memory involves recall and is a function of repetition. |
| • Simulate | imitate the appearance or character of' (page 1737). | • Simulation is a process of rehearsal, copying or to mimic behaviour and/or action in order to acquire key experiences, that correspond as far as possible to real world occurrences. It aims to bridge the 'actual' from the perceived |
| • Simulation | A derivative noun of 'simulate'. | |
| Additional: | | |
| • Teach | 'show or explain to (someone) how to do something' (page 1901). | • Teaching is a methodology and framework of/for imparting information and experience to a number of persons. It is a mode of delivery, a structured channel of communication. It provides the foundation and structure for education and training and involves and integrates key behavioural and social concepts and skills such as induction, learning, cognition etc. |
| • Supervise | 'observe and direct the execution of (a task, project, or activity' (page 1864). | • Supervision is a method of overt and/or covert observation of the actions and/or behaviour of another, to identify deviations from correct conduct. |

# Types of training and competence

T7004     The main types of training and competence are:

| | Training | Competence |
|---|---|---|
| **1. Continuous** | • regular, on-going training at intervals to update the person of latest best practice | • re-setting and revising key standards, benchmarks and competencies in line with industrial, socio-technical and academic change |
| **2. Specific** | • theoretical and practical knowledge in relation to a particular topic or problem e.g. first aid or fire | • testing skills, knowledge and experience in relation to a well defined task e.g. extinguishing a fire |
| **3. Professional** | • an entry level qualification in order to attain membership , recognition or accreditation | • the standards and ability to be attained before the person is allowed to practice at a defined level; such competencies cover the breadth and range of skills, knowledge and experience |
| **4. Bespoke** | • relevant and very specific to the needs of a particular organisation e.g. off-shore first aid training | • reaching a standard deemed adequate and appropriate by the organisation. |
| **5. 'On-the job'** | • very practical, primary and 'sense-focused' training by touching , seeing, experiencing at first hand the hazards and associated risk controls | • setting practical standards of 'do' and 'don't' |

|  | Training | Competence |
|---|---|---|
| **6. Induction** | ● for new entrants to brief them of the minimum standard of conduct and safety behaviour expected and showing them the working environment; this may be reinforced by a practical assessment either on the same day or later of information retained | ● ensuring the new entrant is aware of the standards and expectations of the organisation and the law |
| **7. Academic** | ● that which is regarded as necessary to obtain a certificate or diploma | ● the minimum theoretical, conceptual and pedagogic skills needed to satisfy the assessing body of academic ability |

## Training and competence: health and safety law

T7005   Below is a summary of the principal and industry wide legislation requiring employers and others to aspect training and competence into the workplace. Much of the post 1992 requirements have been driven by European law.

### Health and Safety at Work etc. Act 1974

T7006   *The Health and Safety etc at Work Act 1974 (HSWA)* is the principal, enabling legislation imposing duties on employers, employees, body corporates, manufacturers and others. It also established the Health and Safety Commission and Health and Safety Executive, giving powers to statutory inspectors to serve notices.

*(a)*   *Competence*

● The Act does not explicitly focus on 'competence'. Although, its creation was for the purpose of setting a 'benchmark' for British industry. For instance, the strict duty to possess a written Safety Policy (for those employing five or more) can be a standard against which arrangements can be compared.

● *s 19(1)* of the *HSWA 1974* does allude to competence of statutory inspectors, in that the enforcing authority appoints '. . . persons having suitable qualifications . . .'.

*(b)*   *Training*

● *s 2(2)(c)* of the *HSWA 1974* states 'the provision of such information, instruction, training and supervision as is necessary to ensure, so far as is reasonably practicable, the health and safety at work of his employees.' This provision requires the employer to assess the generic and specific workplace risk and consider training as a possible risk control measure. As this section does not impose a strict duty on the employer, training is one option and not compulsory.

## Management of Health and Safety at Work Regulations 1999

T7007    This Regulation up-dates the *HSWA 1974* and provide specific 'managerial' actions for employers to take and additional responsibilities to employees and contractors.

(*a*)    *Competence*

- *Reg 7* of the *Management of Health and Safety at Work Regulations 1999 (SI 1999 No 3242)* ('Health and Safety Assistance') is the main focus for many on discussions relating to competence in safety. *Reg 7* has shifted the focus to 'in-house competence' rather than simply relying on external consultants (the latter being an option of last resort). *Reg 7* can be summarised as follows:

    — Strict duty to appoint a competent person to assist the employer, to advice him/her of their statutory responsibilities and translate and transpose these into practical safety actions. The competent person is an 'advisor'.

    — Strict duty to ensure that such persons (e.g. more than one competent person in the organisation) co-operate amongst themselves.

    — Strict duty to ensure that the competent person has the time and resources to carry out their function, role and task.

    — Strict duty to disclose information by the employer to the competent person, whether he is an employee or otherwise.

    — *Reg 7(5)* states that a competent person is one who has '. . . sufficient training and experience or knowledge and other qualities to enable him properly to assist in undertaking the measures referred to in paragraph (1)'.

    — A self employed employer who possesses the qualities outlined in *Reg 7(5)* does not need to appoint a competent person. Likewise in a partnership setting, if one of the employer/partners has those qualities, then a competent person need not be appointed.

    — Preference for in-house competent persons rather than external sources (as a last resort).

- The Approved Code of Practice (L21) makes it clear that competence is not necessarily an academic matter; it should be contingent on the situation. More simple work/production processes may require practical understanding, awareness, access to information and assistance. Whilst, more complex situations may require a 'higher level of knowledge and experience'.

- *Reg 8(1)(b)* of the *Management of Health and Safety at Work Regulations 1999 (SI 1999 No 3242)* imposes a strict duty to nominate competent persons who have the desired understanding of the establishment to carry out an evacuation in the event of serious and imminent danger. *Reg 8(3)* adds that a competent person is one who has '. . . sufficient training and experience or knowledge and other qualities . . .'.

- *Reg 15* of the *Management of Health and Safety at Work Regulations 1999 (SI 1999 No 3242)* is concerned with 'temporary workers'. Employers for example, are under a strict duty to ensure that those employed on a fixed term contract and sub-contractors or their employees are given information on 'any special occupational qualifications or skills required to be held by that employee if he is to carry out his work safely'. This tells employers that recruitment is not a simple case of agreeing employment terms but also of informing and checking to see if the potential temporary employee has the competence to carry out the task. Neither *Reg 15* nor the ACOP guidance to *Reg 15* does not impose a duty to provide training to temporary workers, *Reg 13* of the 1999 Regulations does not discriminate between full-time and temporary workers.

*(b)    Training*

- *Reg 3(5)(f)* of the *Management of Health and Safety at Work Regulations 1999 (SI 1999 No 3242)* deals with 'the extent of the health and safety training provided or to be provided to young persons'. The employer is under a strict duty to carry out a risk assessment in relation to 'young persons'. This duty extends to consider the amount, duration, quality and value of safety training required by the young person in order to perform the tasks safely.

- *Reg 7* of the *Management of Health and Safety at Work Regulations 1999 (SI 1999 No 3242)* does not specify the form of training appropriate to be called 'competent'. Although it can be inferred from the ACOP (L21):

  — the employer recruiting a competent person or selecting one (in-house) ought not just to consider qualifications but practical capabilities, problem solving skills and experience. A balance needs to be drawn between theory and practical skills.

  — The Health and Safety Executive (HSE) in their 1995 Policy Statement on training (T7024) and their 1999 *'Strategy document'* (T7025) seem to view it is a 'vocational' activity. For example, National Vocational Qualifications in occupational health and safety level 3 or 4 or equivalent.

- *Reg 13(2)(a), 13(2)(b)(i)–(iv)* and *13(3)(a)–(c)* of the *Management of Health and Safety at Work Regulations 1999 (SI 1999 No 3242)* imposes strict duties with regards to safety training. In summary:

  — Provision of training upon recruitment and induction.

  — Training whenever the employee is exposed to new or increased risk from production, processes, plant, premises or people.

  — The training needs to be repeated/continuous, so that the employee is given information on the current best practice in safety at work.

  — The training needs to be adaptable and flexible to new working conditions and consequential risks.

—    Safety training is not a luxury but a necessity and needs to be undertaken during working hours.

● *Reg 19* of the *Management of Health and Safety at Work Regulations 1999 (SI 1999 No 3242)* ('Protection of Young Persons') does not impose a duty to provide safety training to the young person, other than being aware of their lack of training. *Reg 3* of the 1999 Regulations focuses on training in relation to identified and foreseeable risks and *Reg 13* of the same Regulations requires a capability assessment of the young person, with any 'gaps' as to the safety performance of a task being rectified by safety training.

## Provision and Use of Work Equipment Regulations 1998 (PUWER)

T7008    These Regulations focus on the safe use, handling, storage, maintenance and management of work equipment. Work equipment 'means any machinery, appliance, apparatus, tool or installation for use at work (whether exclusively or not) '.

*(a)    Competence*

● The ACOP guidance to *Reg 9(1)* of the *Provision and Use of Work Equipment Regulations 1998 (SI 1998 No 2306)* ('Training') highlights vocational standards as possible indices of competence.

*(b)    Training*

● *Reg 7(2)* of the *Provision and Use of Work Equipment Regulations 1998 (SI 1998 No 2306)* imposes a strict duty on the employer to ensure that those who will encounter specific risks whilst engaged in 'repairs, modifications, maintenance or servicing of that work equipment' are given 'adequate training. By implication this will be technical/engineering focused as well as covering key human factors, safe systems and risk assessing.

● *Reg 9* of the *Provision and Use of Work Equipment Regulations 1998 (SI 1998 No 2306)* addresses 'training' and the strict duties imposed on employers:

—    *Reg 9(1)* says 'Every employer shall ensure that all persons who use work equipment have received adequate training for purposes of health and safety, including training in the methods which may be adopted when using the work equipment, any risks which such use may entail and precautions to be taken'. Thus, 'adequate training' needs to account for the type of work equipment, the circumstances of use (lone or under supervision for example), the minimum standard of competence needed to operate the work equipment and technological change factors.

—    *Reg 9(2)* requires that those employees who manage or supervise work equipment themselves possess 'adequate' safety training encompassing the technical, risk assessments, safe systems and human factors.

● The ACOP to the Regulations also points out additional responsibilities that the employer has in relation to 'young persons' – to ensure they operate/use work equipment only once they have had complete safety training and that a phased approach in using work equipment may be more desirable, with the appropriate supervision.

## Workplace (Health, Safety and Welfare) Regulations 1992

T7009    The *Workplace (Health, Safety and Welfare) Regulations 1992 (SI 1992 No 3004)* deal with the working environment and infrastructure.

*(a)*    *Competence*

No explicit focus on competence – although there are cross references made to the *Management of Health and Safety at Work Regulations 1999 (SI 1999 No 3242)*.

*(b)*    *Training*

No explicit focus on training – although there are cross references made to the *Management of Health and Safety at Work Regulations 1999 (SI 1999 No 3242)*.

## Personal Protective Equipment at Work Regulations 1992

T7010    These Regulations deal with the supply of protective/ safety equipment and its safe usage, storage and maintenance.

(a)    *Competence*

- The *Personal Protective Equipment at Work Regulations 1992 (SI 1992 No 2966)* imply that competence will vary according to the personal protective equipment (PPE) in question and context, frequency and intensity of use. Nevertheless, a person using PPE needs to have a theoretical and practical understanding of the technical and behavioural consequences of using, misusing or not using PPE.

*(b)*    *Training*

- *Reg 9(1)* of the *Personal Protective Equipment at Work Regulations 1992 (SI 1992 No 2966)* says that if PPE has to be provided then there is a strict duty on the employer to provide information, instruction and training with regards to the risks the PPE aims to control; correct and safe usage; ways of retaining the PPE in a good state of repair and minimising defect. The training can be formal or informal so long as it comprehensive and relevant taking account of the working environment the work equipment will be used in.

- *Reg 10(2)* of the *Personal Protective Equipment at Work Regulations 1992 (SI 1992 No 2966)* imposes a strict duty on the employee to use the PPE in accordance with the instruction and training provided.

## Health and Safety (Display Screen Equipment) Regulations 1992

T7011    These Regulations generally concern computer work stations and ergonomic layout.

*(a)*    *Competence*

- Figure 1 and 2, as well as Annex A in the Guidance to the Regulations identifies the minimum standards that an ergonomic workstation needs to possess and knowledge, awareness and understanding the user needs to possess.

*(b)*    *Training*

- Reg 6(1) and (2) of the Health and Safety (Display Screen Equipment) Regulations 1992 (SI 1992 No 2792) imposes a strict duty on the employer to ensure that:

    — Users of display screen equipment are given training on the safe usage and structure of workstations at which they may work.

    — When the workstation undergoes change or modification, further training is provided.

    The training needs to focus on ergonomic layout and design of the workstation to avoid problems such as over reaching or variations between seat height and screen, identifying risks and welfare issues (breaks, eye sight tests etc.).

## Manual Handling Operations Regulations 1992

T7012    The *Manual Handling Operations Regulations 1992 (SI 1992 No 2793)* deal with safe handling, moving and lifting.

*(a)*    *Competence*

- The Guidance to the Regulations provide a methodology and anthropometric ratios for manual handling activities. This can be regarded as a benchmark/index of best practice.

*(b)*    *Training*

- The Regulations do not explicitly refer to training. However, as the Guidance to the Regulations alludes, the legislation is practical and requires training for its proper and successful implementation. *Reg 4(1)(b)(i)–(iii)* focuses on risk control measures to reduce injury from manual handling. Training is implied as a risk control measure (see Guidance).

## Construction (Design and Management) Regulations 1994

T7013    These Regulations apply the same logic as the *Management of Health and Safety at Work Regulations 1999 (SI 1999 No 3242)* to construction work.

*(a)*    *Competence*

- *Reg 8* of the *Construction (Design and Management) Regulations 1994 (SI 1994 No 3140)* requires the client to ensure a 'competent' planning supervisor (*Reg 8(1)*), 'competent' designer (*Reg 8(2)*) and 'competent' (principal) contractor (*Reg 8(3)*) are appointed before construction work commences and in respect of each project. The competence of such persons in construction design and management is with respect to performing the specific legislative requirements upon them and the ability 'to conduct his undertaking without contravening any prohibition'. In practice, the client would need to seek evidence of qualifications, experience in similar projects, safety track record, documentation and systems of work used etc.

*(b)*    *Training*

- *Reg 17* of the *Construction (Design and Management) Regulations 1994 (SI 1994 No 3140)* relates to 'information and training'. *Reg 17(2)* requires the principal contractor to ensure that all contractors that employ people provide such people with relevant training in accordance with the *Management of Health and Safety Regulations 1999*. The extent of this duty is as far as 'reasonably practicable' rather than a strict duty.

## Construction (Health, Safety and Welfare) Regulations 1996

T7014    The *Construction (Health, Safety and Welfare) Regulations 1996 (SI 1996 No 1592)* apply the same logic as the *Management of Health and Safety at Work Regulations 1999 (SI 1999 No 3242)* and the *Workplace (Health, Safety and Welfare) Regulations 1992 (SI 1992 No 3004)* to a construction working environment.

(a)    *Competence*

- The following Regulations require the construction work activity to be supervised or overseen or planned by a 'competent person' (like the *Construction (Design and Management) Regulations 1994*, this phrase is not defined):

    — *Reg 10(2)*, demolition and dismantling (strict duty).

    — *Reg 12(5)*, any 'installation, alteration or dismantling of any support for an excavation . . . ' (strict duty).

    — *Reg 13(2)*,'the construction, installation, alteration or dismantling of a cofferdam or caisson shall take place only under the supervision of a competent person' (strict duty).

    — *Reg 14(3)(c )*,competent person to be in charge of water based vessels that transport people to or from a place of work.

    — *Reg 29(1)*, construction work can only be carried out in a place if it has been inspected by a competent person and that person is satisfied that construction work can be safely undertaken. *Schedule 7* identifies the place of work and time(s) of the inspection by such competent persons.

(b)    *Training*

- *Reg 28* of the *Construction (Health, Safety and Welfare) Regulations 1996 (SI 1996 No 1592)* states that 'any person who carries out any activity involving construction work where training, technical knowledge or experience is necessary to reduce the risks of injury to any persons shall possess such training, knowledge or experience, or be under such degree of supervision by a person having such training, knowledge or experience, as may be appropriate having regard to the nature of the activity'. This is a strict duty although again, the legislation leaves the determination of the format and type of training to the organisation.

## Fire Precautions (Workplace) Regulations 1997; Fire Precautions (Workplace) (Amendment) Regulations 1999

T7015    Both Regulations are concerned with fire safety arrangements, fire risk assessments, evacuation, alarms, drills, testing, inspection and enforcement/ notices.

(a)    *Competence*

- The 1997 Regulations amended the Management of Health and Safety at Work Regulations 1992 (SI 1992 No 2051),which have now been updated and brought forward by the Management of Health and

Safety at Work Regulations 1999 (SI 1999 No 3242). Therefore, the statements above in relation to risk assessment (Reg 3) and health and safety assistance (Reg 7) of the Management of Health and Safety at Work Regulations 1999 would apply to ensuring that the competent person is also competent with regards to fire safety.

(*b*)    *Training*

- *Reg 4(2)(b)* of the *Fire Precautions (Workplace) Regulations 1997 (SI 1997 No 1840)* states in order to safeguard the safety of employees in the event of a fire, the employer shall (strict duty) 'nominate employees to implement those measures and ensure that the number of such employees, their training and the equipment available to them are adequate, taking into account the size of, and the specific hazards involved in, the workplace concerned'.

## Safety Representatives and Safety Committees Regulations 1977

T7016    These Regulations are concerned with the appointment, duties, function and rights of safety representatives from recognised trade unions.

(*a*)    *Competence*

- There is no guidance on the minimum competence that safety representatives need to possess. Many unions including the 'parent' i.e Trade Union Congress (TUC) have either adopted NVQs in Safety Practice as a benchmark or developed their own competencies which correspond to NVQs.

(*b*)    *Training*

- *Reg 4(2)* of the *Safety Representatives and Safety Committees Regulations 1977 (SI 1977 No 500)* permits the safety representative to undergo training so that he/she can acquire the appropriate understanding of legislation, human factors, occupational health etc. The employer must (strict duty) provide the time-off, with pay during normal working hours. The employer does not have to provide the training as usually it is the trade union that arranges it.

## Health and Safety (Consultation with Employees) Regulations 1996

T7017    Under these Regulations employers have a duty to consult with non-unionised employees directly or via appointment/ election of representatives of employee safety (ROES).

(*a*)    *Competence*

- There seems to be no generic standard for competence, given that ROES lack a parent body such as the TUC to set key competencies. However, the TUC and unions have either co-operated or ROES tend to follow the same format of training as safety representatives so would cover similar competencies.

(b)   *Training*

- Reg 7 of the Health and Safety (Consultation with Employees) Regulations 1996 (SI 1996 No 1513) is similar to Reg 4(2) of the Safety Representatives Safety Committees Regulations 1977 (SI 1977 No 500).

## Health and Safety (First-Aid) Regulations 1981, as amended

T7018   The *Health and Safety (First-Aid) Regulations 1981 (SI 1981 No 917)*, as amended, are concerned with the provision of facilities, first-aiders, equipment and ensuring adequate arrangements and assessments are made of first-aid needs.

(a)   *Competence*

- The Approved Code of Practice (L 74) with the Regulations provides various indices for both theoretical and practical competence for first-aiders and to a lesser extent 'appointed persons'. The competencies for first-aiders can range from the ability to administer CPR through to the safe carriage of the injured, as well as legal issues involved.

(b)   *Training*

- Reg 3 of the Health and Safety (First-Aid) Regulations 1981 (SI 1981 No 917) highlights 3 classes of 'first-aid personnel':

  — *Reg 3(2)* requires the employer (strict duty) to ensure that there exists an 'adequate number' of 'suitable persons' who possess recognised qualifications (approved/recognised by for instance the HSE), relevant first-aid training and any specialised training specific to the risks at the place of work.

  — The appointment of a non-first aider to take charge of first aid if for instance the first aider is ill (*Reg 3(3)*).

  — Finally, the employer can decide upon an 'appointed person'. Such a person is not a 'first-aider' . They would for instance call the emergency services or oversee first-aid facilities.

  Only the first-aider requires formal training under the legislation whilst for the other two categories it is implied that they will possess a minimum level of understanding of first-aid if they are to take charge of first-aid facilities.

## Noise at Work Regulations 1989

T7019   These Regulations deal with the assessment of noise pressure, exposure, risk and controls in the working environment to minimise hearing damage.

(a)   *Competence*

- *Reg 4(2)* of the *Noise at Work Regulations 1989 (SI 1989 No 1790)* requires the noise assessment (85 dB(A) or above or 200 Pascals or above) to be made by a competent person. Such a person is competent if he/she can identify the individuals at risk, the information they need to control the risk, can review the assessment and follow the latest best practice in noise assessment and management.

*(b)* Training

- Reg 11 of the *Noise at Work Regulations 1989 (SI 1989 No 1790)* requires the employer to provide training (as well as information and instruction) to those employees likely to be exposed to noise that is 85 dB(A) or above, or 200 Pascals or above .This Regulation focuses on risks of damage to hearing, minimising such risk, obtaining ear protectors from employees and employees responsibilities.

## Electricity at Work Regulations 1989, as amended

T7020    These Regulations cover inspection, testing, controlling, managing electrical hazards at work.

*(a)* Competence

- Reg 16 of the *Electricity at Work Regulations 1989 (SI 1989 No 635)*, as amended suggests (strict duty) that 'technical knowledge' or experience are necessary in order to work safely with electricity or at the very least supervision is necessary. In any case, personnel confronting electrical hazards must be 'competent'. The HSE's *'Memorandum of guidance'* (HSR25) on the 1989 Regulations gives more detail. Essentially, key competencies have to encompass the specific and real risks to the place of work (rather than just theoretical) and be regularly monitored.

*(b)* Training

- The legislation does not specify the mode, frequency and format of any training. Guidance may be available from the Institute of Electrical Engineers etc.

## Control of Substances Hazardous to Health Regulations 1999 (COSHH)

T7021    These Regulations are concerned with identifying chemicals that when exposed can give rise to health risks, the need for risk assessment and control that are reviewed.

*(a)* Competence

- No explicit statement on competence of COSHH assessor.

*(b)* Training

- Reg 12(1) of the *Control of Substances Hazardous to Health Regulations 1999 (SI 1999 No 437)* imposes a strict duty on the employer to provide training (as well as information and instruction) to employees who are exposed to substances hazardous to health, 'as is suitable and sufficient'.

- Reg 13(3) of the *Control of Substances Hazardous to Health Regulations 1999 (SI 1999 No 437)* says 'every employer shall ensure that any person (whether or not his employee) who carries out any work in connection with the employer's duties under these Regulations has the necessary information, instruction and training'.

## Other legislation

T7022    Generally, most regulations make reference to training and /or competence e.g. *Control of Lead at Work Regulations 1998 (SI 1998 No 543)*, *Confined Spaces*

Regulations 1997 (SI 1997 No 1713), Control of Asbestos at Work Regulations 1987 (SI 1987 No 2115)(as amended), Control of Major Accident Hazards Regulations 1999 (SI 1999 No 437), Carriage of Dangerous Goods by Road (Driver Training) Regulations 1996 (SI 1996 No 2094), Transport of Dangerous Goods (Safety Advisors) Regulations 1999 (SI 1999 No 257), Carriage of Dangerous Goods by Road Regulations 1996, (SI 1996 No 2095) and Carriage of Explosives by Road Regulations 1996 (SI 1996 No 2093) etc.

Most health and safety regulations are created under the enabling powers under the *HSWA* and reflect *s 2(2)(c )* 'information, instruction, training and supervision' of the 1974 Act.

## Training and competence: safety management

T7023    The HSC and the HSE have produced various guidance and advisory documentation on training and competence.

### 'Policy Statement on health and safety training' (HSC)

T7024    This policy statement was issued in 1991/2 and revised in 1995. It was subsequently withdrawn and replaced by the HSE's *'Health and Safety Training Strategy'*. However, it is valuable to summarise this original statement as much of it is still relevant and provided the basis for the competency based approaches e.g. National Vocational Qualifications (NVQs).

To summarise, the 1995 Policy Statement emphasises:

- The importance of quality health and safety training for all occupational groups, which reflects up to date ideas and best practice and which is continuously appraised in line with new legislation.

- Employers have statutory duties to provide training in line with risk exposure and such training needs to be continuous.

- 'For managers, employees and health and safety practitioners directly involved in work processes, training is necessary to achieve competence, and these groups therefore represent our priority.'

- The HSC has three strands to its strategy to achieving the above:

    (a)    the HSE to use its personnel and informational resources to promote and publicise with the focus being:

    (i)    Emphasising health and safety training for managers by showing the safety-cultural, financial and corporate benefits.

    (ii)    Internalising health and safety so it becomes a part of on-the-job training rather than a 'bolt on'.

    (iii)    Reminding employers and the self-employed of the statutory responsibilities to train.

    (b)    The promotion of health and safety training *per se* as a virtue. Thus:

    (i)    The HSE will continue to support health and safety training programmes (and providers) by sending their speakers, supporting initiatives such as 'European Health & Safety Week' as well as the promotion of safety in schools and colleges.

    (ii)    The HSE will work to promote health and safety issues and training within various 'lead bodies' (which produce key competencies for a particular industry or sector). This ensures general competencies do account for health and safety training. 'The HSE will play a 'full and active' role in the Occupational Health & Safety Lead Body (OHSLB). The increasing importance of competence based training which leads to accredited qualifications is recognised by the Commission and will continue to be encouraged.'

(iii)   The HSE will interface with employers, employees and other bodies to ensure they influence the content and direction of training material to account for health and safety.

*(c)*   'Legislative action' e.g:

(i)   'The Commission is committed to the removal or reform of all items of unnecessary or outdated legislation.'

(ii)   'Proposals for future legislation and guidance will increasingly take account of developments in training making use, for example, of the 'competencies' being established by lead bodies.'

## 'Health and Safety Training Strategy' (HSC)

**T7025**   This replaced the 1995 Policy Statement and came into force in 1999. It is a statement of intent by the HSC as to 'raise awareness and ensure that a better quantity and quality of training is available to all employees.'

The key features ('aims and objectives') of this Strategy are:

● to influence the education system so that risk issues are incorporated into teaching at schools and colleges which in turn will impact on safety attitudes of such children and young persons when they enter the world of work.

● To redress the imbalance of safety training; namely, very little takes place in those organisations with less than 50 employees.

● HSC seeks to promote the legal duty to train amongst employers and such promotion and influencing will continue via statutory inspectors.

● A 'joined up' approach is being advocated by the HSC so that they work in unison with other bodies and government departments.

● To encourage a competence based approach by working with employers and unions, statutory inspectors, the education system, government departments etc.

● In general, to link training and competence to wider corporate goals – to integrate it into organisational thinking.

## 'Successful Health and Safety Management' (HSG65)

**T7026**   In *'Successful Health and Safety Management'* (HSG65), the HSE present a safety management system with 5 key stages:

(1)   Policy

(2)   Organising

(3)   Planning

(4)   Monitoring

(5)   Audit/Review

Stage 2 is concerned with establishing a 'safety culture' to ensure that a positive environment is created where the safety policy and other safety messages will be readily accepted. Safety culture is defined as the '4 C's': communication, co-operation, control and competence. Training is a means of achieving competence. The HSE then present a 'training cycle' as a logical framework for deciding whether training is appropriate or not and the structure of any training. Figure 2 outlines the training cycle.

*Figure 2: Training Cycle (HSG65)*

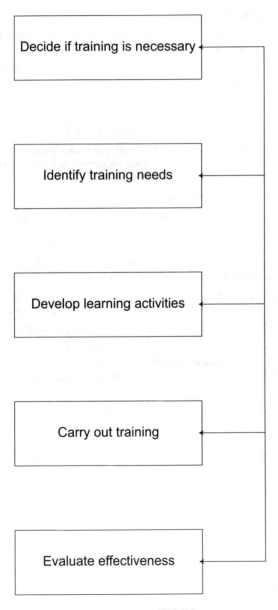

*Step 1: is training necessary?*

T7027     This means:

- Is training the only means of achieving competence? What alternatives are there e.g. recruitment, selection, supervision etc. How does training compare with such alternatives (advantages and disadvantages of each)?

- With regards to the organisation's size, is training a realistic option?

- Will the training assist in improving the safety management system and contribute positively to the wider corporate culture?

- Will the training reduce workplace risk, assist in legal compliance and improve economic efficiency?

*Step 2: identify training needs*

T7028     Step 1 asks broader, philosophical questions. Step 2 focuses on specific needs:

- Personal needs for training.

  Training can assist the individual to:

  — reduce 'human error' (e.g. number of mistakes per task);

  — improve risk awareness and perception;

  — assist in improving safety attitudes;

  — improve the communication skills;

  — improve safety knowledge and memory as well as boosting motivation;

  — improve the understanding to cope with change (new technology or new working structures).

  The training needs to benefit the individual positively in psychological, situational response and social interaction terms.

- Job needs for training.

  The training needs to positively impact on:

  — the safe use of plant and equipment;

  — the ability to understand and implement procedures (e.g. safe system);

  — the ability to understand the working environment – both generic and specific risks;

  — the ability to understand work and technology and the impact it can have on people (occupational stress, fatigue, ergonomic constraints on decision making, interaction with management etc.).

- Organisational needs for Training.

  These could include:

  — the need to get individuals to understand the Safety Policy and its implementation;

  — to improve the safety culture at work;

  — to improve productivity and economic performance;

  — to ensure harmonisation of work practices with other sectors, industries or possible take over/merger.

*Step 3: identify training objectives*

T7029      Assuming there is a genuine need for training, clear training objectives will need to be set:

- What are 'training objectives'? This refers to key targets of achievement that the attendees on a training programme need to have realised. They are the key competencies or 'intended learning outcomes'.

- How are objectives set?

  — Use the Safety Policy as a benchmark. For example, 'at the end of this session attendees will know the meaning and purpose of a Safety Policy as well as the key arrangements to be implemented . . . '.

  — Risk assessments: these will tell the organisation of key areas of concern and the need to understand and control such known and foreseeable risks.

  — Training Needs Analysis (TNA) using questionnaires and interviews to ascertain from the workforce the issues they have difficulty with.

  — Enforcement and legal advice: the objectives need to take account of any notices, information, advice or guidance given to the organisation by the enforcing officer, insurer or the courts.

  — Industry standards: key competencies from lead bodies can act as a benchmark as can manufacturers guidelines.

  — Changes in competencies: for instance with the introduction of NVQs in safety, this has led to changes in diploma programmes offered by the National Examination Board in Occupational Safety & Health (NEBOSH), the British Safety Council and university post graduate diplomas to reflect the new vocational competencies.

  — Other factors such as corporate needs, political considerations (unions, employers' groups), economic competition, resources etc. are also important.

- What are the generic objectives of any training programme? Whether the session lasts one hour or longer there are key underpinning targets the session needs to achieve:

  — for the attendee to understand the specific theoretical concepts, models or explanations;

  — for the attendee to understand the practical application within their job, task and/or occupation;

  — for the attendee to be able to realise the wider corporate and cultural implications of the training topic;

  — for the attendee to be able to relate it to specific key issues, problems and/or risks;

  — for the attendee to be able to communicate the key concepts to others;

  — for the attendee to be able to review, critique and understand the limitation to any model, theory, concept or explanation.

*Step 4: decide on training method*

T7030      The options are summarised below:

|  | Day Release (e.g. one day per week) | Block (e.g. one week per three months) | Distant Learning (e.g. at the learner's pace) | Sessional (e.g. as and when the learner can attend) |
|---|---|---|---|---|
| **In-house/ bespoke** |  |  |  |  |
| **External** (e.g. at a training centre) |  |  |  |  |
| **Remote e-learning** (e.g. on-line internet) |  |  |  |  |

Each option has its costs and benefits, whether financial, cognitive, behavioural, time and indeed administrative.

*Step 5: carry out training*

T7031   Key issues:

● where will the training be conducted from?

— Is it conveniently located for attendees and the trainer?

— Is it adequately resourced: flipchart/board, overhead projector, tables, chairs, ventilation, access/egress, a safe learning/working environment etc.

— Does the venue have welfare facilities such as toilets, drinking water, access for disabled, parking etc.?

— Is access to a practical demonstration/simulation site needed (e.g. fire extinguisher testing)?

● Who will do the training?

— Is the trainer qualified and competent in the topic to be discussed? Do they understand the latest legal, technical, managerial and behavioural issues in relation to the topic ?

— Has the trainer a good track record in that topic to be delivered and/or with that group?

— Are gender and linguistic issues important? (For instance should a man or woman deliver a programme on health, safety and welfare for pregnant/nursing mothers? What if the audience's English is limited, should someone with knowledge of the relevant language be used?).

— If the trainer is relatively new, will another monitor sit-in with the class?

— One should not equate qualifications with good training/teaching skills (there have been many 'highly qualified' people who have been poor at delivery). Therefore, ensure that the trainer has the qualities of an effective communicator and listener.

- When will the training be conducted?
  - Is the start-finish times realistic and achievable?
  - Is the time sufficient for attendees to reach the destination?
  - Time management issues: planning out the training day into sessions or blocks, so that the trainer and the attendees know the pace for the training.
- What will be covered?
  - Ensure the intended learning objectives are clear and that they are communicated at the outset to the attendees. That objectives should also conform to key competencies identified by the HSE, lead bodies or professional bodies. Also, issues that should not be covered should also be communicated to attendees so that their expectations are clearly set from the outset.
  - Decide on textbook, lecture notes, cases to be handed out to attendees (relevance, quality of material, user-friendliness, value for money etc.).
  - Ensure all documentation is accurate, up to date, genuine and not in breach of copyright. All statements and references cited must be verifiable.
- Why is the topic being covered? What reasons are there for its coverage? This can benefit the attendees and the trainer to be clear as to why they are all engaged in the session. Issues such as ethical, legal, behavioural, technical, managerial and environmental should be focused on.

### Step 6: evaluate and feedback

T7032
- Does the training achieve the objectives set out at the beginning of the session? Were all the topics covered?
- Issue a trainer/tutor 'evaluation form' to seek comments and constructive criticism. Ensure such forms are clear and objectively worded. If need be, explain to the attendees any questions. Such forms provide not only evidence as to the session but invaluable information to improve future training and delivery.
- The trainer needs to be given the feedback even if it is critical.
- Feedback/loop-back to any of the previous steps if the evaluations indicate failings in these areas. Ensure the failing is addressed before the next session.

## '5 Steps to Information, Instruction and Training' (HSE)

T7033    This short publication suggests that a 'training needs assessment' needs to focus on:
- Step 1: Determine who needs the training ? Which occupational group?
- Step 2: 'Decide what training is needed and what the objectives are – giving people the wrong training or too much is a waste of time and money'.
- Step 3: How should the training be carried out?
- Step 4: When should the training be carried out ?
- Step 5: Check to assess that the training has worked.

This approach corresponds to the fifth step in the Training Cycle (see T7031).

# Training and competence: safe behaviour at work

**T7034**   The HSE in *'Reducing Error and influencing behaviour'* (HSG48) say that education and training are means that ' . . .can successfully influence safe behaviour at work . . . ' (page 41). The HSE say that training needs to cover four key areas:

- Knowledge of the generic and specific risks at the individual's area of work and the wider working environment.

- The proper use/feedback of safety-related equipment as well as work procedures (such as permits to work, safe systems etc.).

- People need to know the personal, job and organisational benefits of training.

- Perception of risk and risk assessment methodology by different occupational groups.

The HSE also note that many of the major accidents and disasters have involved a lack of training or competence, for instance:

— Clapham Junction, London, UK (triple train crash in 1988): problems with the training in particular, communication skills of test engineers, up to date and latest skills and management knowledge of health and safety issues.

— Union Carbide, Bhopal, India (release of gas by plant with fatalities at work and in the city in 1984): Bhopal based staff had a complete lack of relevant training and competence in safety. The training was relevant to a North American setting rather than within the Indian context.

— Piper Alpha, North Sea, UK (fire and explosion on off-shore oil platform in 1988): whilst Occidental Petroleum had policy /procedures they were not effectively communicated. Ineffective emergency escape training given to staff.

— Chernobyl, former USSR (radioactive release due to reactor exploding, 1986): whilst the engineers and scientists possessed the scientific knowledge, they lacked systems, procedures and training in safety management, risk analysis and ergonomic design.

A common feature of all the major man-made disasters or major accidents has been the role of 'human error'. Following Rasmussan's classification (see DISASTER AND EMERGENCY MANAGEMENT SYSTEMS (DEMS)), of human error, one can relate this with training and competence:

| | Training aspects to reduce human error | Competencies to reduce human error |
|---|---|---|
| • **Skill based error** (not undergoing the routine/ repetition on sufficient occasions, so that it lacks familiarity). | • Continuous repetition under a variety of theoretical and practical simulations, ranging from 'normal' to 'dangerous' e.g. fire fighters or paramedics need the skill of a quick response in an emergency, which needs to be 'second nature' to the officer. | • The individual can recall without hesitation.<br><br>• They can implement the skill in practice and not just in class room environments.<br><br>• They can cope under extreme safety situations. |

| | Training aspects to reduce human error | Competencies to reduce human error |
|---|---|---|
| • **Rule based error** (involves learning a set of sequences, which need to be understood/ implemented as a complete set. Not knowing the sequences e.g. safe system or permit to work). | • Logical, step-by-step breakdown and explanation by the trainer and recall by the student.<br><br>• 'Reverse logic' training so that student understands the negative/reversal of the sequence as well as isolation of individual sequences. | • Theoretical understanding and familiarity of all sequences and sub-sequences in all possible permutations.<br><br>• Understand the likely causes of failure of a sequential system.<br><br>• Be able to develop emergency procedures/sequences at short notices if others fail. |
| • **Knowledge based error** (involves learning something new e.g. not knowing the legislation or switching procedures). | • Requires a patient approach reinforced by simulation. Learning for the first time will involve mistakes, which will decline with simulation relating to personal experience and practical examples. | • The individual can identify the key issues from the new concept/ topic being discussed and be able to see relevance for him/her, the job and organisation.<br><br>• Be able to appreciate the change required to adopt and adapt to new systems.<br><br>• Be flexible and critical of situations and concepts that are not understood. |

## Training and competence: human capital and choice

T7035    Economists apply 'capital investment appraisal' approaches to evaluating whether a student (or his/her organisation) should choose course A or B or another. For example:

- an individual with four years health and safety enforcement experience aims to obtain a one year, day release qualification in 'Occupational Health and Safety Management' so that he/she can be 'competent' with respect to *Reg 7* of the *Management of Health and Safety at Work Regulations 1999 (SI 1999 No 3242)* as well as obtain more income and status at work.

- The individual has two choices, either embark on a nationally accredited diploma which has key competencies recognised by the HSE/ Occupational Health and Safety Lead Body or following the specific and practical training offered by the employer through their autonomous, profit making training department. In either case, the courses have a 'shelf life' of five years after which they have to be re-designed and in one case seek accreditation again. Both providers charge a 'one off' fee including registration and lecture notes.

● The individual is self financing and has been offered a 'training loan' by the local bank at a 10% (0.1) rate of interest fixed over five years.

● After researching the various courses available, speaking to his/her line manager, calculating the net return from the two options (income minus costs such as books, travel, subsistence on the course, study time etc.) he/she concludes the following:

| | Course A: in-house, specific, job related (day release) | Course B : accredited and certified one year diploma (day release) |
|---|---|---|
| **Initial Fee** (Investment) | £4,000 | £5,200 |
| **Net Income Benefit** (expected income increment once holding the diploma *minus* costs associated with training – books, travel, etc): | | |
| Year 1 | £1,600 | £2,000 |
| Year 2 | £2,400 | £2,000 |
| Year 3 | £1,000 | £1,600 |
| Year 4 | £800 | £1,800 |
| Year 5 | £400 | £1,800 |

From the purely personal perspective of the individual (as distinct from the organisation he/she works for), which option is the best economic one?

There are three models that individual could use explained in the following paragraphs.

## Payback model

T7036    This approach suggests, choose the option that gives the quickest payback of the initial fees. The payback of Course A is by the end of Year 2 (£1,600+ £2,400 = Initial Fee) whereas for Course B it would be into Year 3.

## Accounting rate of return (ARR)

T7037    This calculates the percentage rate of return of each course by using the formula:

$$\text{ARR} = \frac{\text{Total estimated Net Income} - \text{Initial Fee}}{\text{Estimated life of course}} \times \frac{100}{\text{Initial Fee}}$$

$$\text{ARR Course A} = \frac{£6,200 - £4,000}{5} \times \frac{100}{£4,000}$$

$$= 440 \times 0.025 = 11\%$$

$$\text{ARR Course B} = \frac{£9,200 - £5,200}{5} \times \frac{100}{£5,200}$$

$$= 15.38\%$$

Therefore, on the ARR method, Course B offers the better return.

### Net present value approach

T7038     ● This is based on the discounted cash flow method. Given that the income benefits are in the future, this model says they need to be converted into present values. This is based on the economic assumption of 'time value', that the further in time one expects to receive money, the lower will be its present value.

● To make an accurate assessment of the current position (income benefits today) for both courses, the income streams for both courses has to be discounted (adjusted) to account for the interest paid (as a general rule £1 benefit at the end of year 1 is worth 0.909 pence now, using the formula £1 x 100/100 + rate of interest, thus £1 x 100/110 = 0.909. At the end of year 2 that £1 is worth even less noting our assumption of time value, thus £1 x 100/110 x 100/110 = 0.83 and by the end of year 5, that £1 is worth now only 0.621 pence: £1 x 100/110 x 100/110 x 100/110 x 100/110 x 100/110). Therefore:

Course A:

| Year | Net Income | Discounted Factor | Discounted Net Income |
|---|---|---|---|
| Year 0 | | | (£4,000) |
| Year 1 | £1,600 × | 0.909 = | £1,454.40 |
| Year 2 | £2,400 × | 0.826 = | £1,982.40 |
| Year 3 | £1,000 × | 0.751 = | £ 751 |
| Year 4 | £ 800 × | 0.683 = | £ 546.40 |
| Year 5 | £ 400 × | 0.621 = | £ 248.40 |
| Total Present Value | | | £4,982.60 |
| Net Present Value | | | £4,982.60 – £4,000 =£982.60 |

Course B:

| Year | Net Income | Discounted Factor | Discounted Net Income |
|---|---|---|---|
| Year 0 | | | (£5,200) |
| Year 1 | £2,000 × | 0.909 = | £1,818 |
| Year 2 | £2,000 × | 0.826 = | £1,652 |
| Year 3 | £1,600 × | 0.751 = | £1,201.60 |
| Year 4 | £1,800 × | 0.683 = | £1,229.40 |
| Year 5 | £1,800 × | 0.621 = | £1,117.80 |
| Total Present Value | | | £7,018.80 |
| Net Present Value | | | £7,018.80 – £5,200 =£1,818.80 |

All things remaining equal, Course A offers the individual an economic return of £982.60 and Course B £1,818.80. Therefore Course B offers a a better prospect.

## Comparison of three approaches

T7039    To compare the three approaches:

|  | Course A | Course B |
|---|---|---|
| 1. Payback | By end of year 2 | Into year 3 |
| 2. Accounting Rate of Return | 11% | 15.38% |
| 3. Net Present Value | £982.60 | £1,818.80 |

Assuming the individual uses all three methods, then Course B is the better choice.

It must be noted that:

- such approaches are *economic* ones and only account for quantifiable variables or those that can be estimated. However, training is not just about a 'return'. There are intangible behavioural benefits, status benefits etc. that cannot be quantified into pounds with a high degree of accuracy (although ordinal techniques exist to determine preferences which can be given an economic value).

- The approaches also assume that choice is purely an economic/rational one. However, the credibility of the course provider, their past performance, credibility of the accrediting body etc. are also significant.

- The above are economic variants of cost benefit analysis (CBA) .A 'simpler' approach maybe to carry out a qualitative CBA. This involves for example:

|  | Benefits | Costs |
|---|---|---|
| a. Economic/Financial | • future financial gains <br><br> • tax rebate (e.g. NVQs) <br><br> • improved 'market position' and economic choice | • fees involved <br><br> • travel costs <br><br> • books <br><br> • registration fees |
| b. Personal | • improved knowledge <br><br> • problem solving skills <br><br> • risk awareness <br><br> • enhanced competence | • stress <br><br> • time allocation and commitment <br><br> • opportunity cost (forsaking other activities) |

|  | **Benefits** | **Costs** |
|---|---|---|
| **c. Family** | • future benefits from enhanced income <br> • status <br> • the gain in terms of risk awareness | • less interaction <br> • increased probability of tension <br> • less income for other purposes as surplus funds used for training (unless borrowing) |
| **d. Corporate** | • organisation's human assets increase in value <br> • improved organisational response <br> • potential for 'Investor in People' status <br> • competitive advantage | • opportunity cost – find alternative personnel to fill work gap whilst other person is being trained <br> • indirect costs – administration, being available to take queries, continuity etc. |
| **e. Social** | • community/ profession benefits <br> • increased competence in society <br> • dissemination of best practice | • less short term output and increased chance of injury as manager for instance is not available whilst being trained <br> • involvement of technocrats in setting standards |

## Training and competence: European comparisons

T7040    The European Agency for Safety and Health at Work at Bilbao, Spain produced a comparative study called *'Priorities and Strategies in Occupational Safety and Health Policy in the Member States of the European Union'* (1998). This also evaluated the different training/competence regimes in the fifteen member states. This is summarised below:

| | To what extent has training been shown to be effective at the workplace level? How has this been evaluated?' | What ideas exist regarding the future role of training? |
|---|---|---|
| 1. Austria | • No data available. | • Sometimes labour inspectors train safety specialists and also provide information, support and guidance. |
| 2. Belgium | • Lack of relevant data. | • Training of 'prevention consultants' including re-training.<br><br>• Employee training as labour market becomes more flexible. |
| 3. Denmark | • Compulsory training for the 'safety group/ organisation'.<br><br>• Compulsory vocational training e.g. for scaffolders, those working with asbestos etc.<br><br>• Public-private involvement in training. | • Training should be sector based and modular.<br><br>• Integrate safety training into education and specialist schools such as architects etc. |
| 4. Finland | • Provided by various organisations. | • Emphasis on bespoke and specific training to the organisations needs. |
| 5. France | • All workers receive practical, safety training upon joining and regular updates as the conditions of work change. | • Priority to be given to temporary workers, construction site officers and safety officers.<br><br>• Integrate training into vocational training. |

|  | To what extent has training been shown to be effective at the workplace level? How has this been evaluated?' | What ideas exist regarding the future role of training? |
|---|---|---|
| 6. Germany | • Regular repetition of training used to increase awareness.<br><br>• More than 360,000 persons per annum trained by a 'statutory accident insurance funds'. | • Integration and make more relevant.<br><br>• Update standards regularly. |
| 7. Greece | • Improved safety conditions in industry and positive impact on accident ratios indicates the agency says that training has been effective. | • More need for training which will be undertaken by government or its agencies. |
| 8. Ireland | • No formal evaluation undertaken but Ireland has adopted a participative and multi-disciplinary approach to safety training. | • Distant learning to be considered.<br><br>• Sector specific training.<br><br>• Integrated approach. |
| 9. Italy | • Training is being carried out but its effectiveness is yet to be evaluated. | • Important component – emphasis on employee and first aid teams.<br><br>• Integration into vocational and private educational schemes. |
| 10. Luxembourg | • 'Training is considered to be an essential basis of the "knowing how to, wanting to, and being able to do" approach' | • Systematic training to be made compulsory/ and to be of a high standard. |
| 11. Netherlands | • Increasingly done with support from specialists. | • Special attention to members of works councils. |

|  | To what extent has training been shown to be effective at the workplace level? How has this been evaluated?' | What ideas exist regarding the future role of training? |
|---|---|---|
| **12. Portugal** | • Insufficient arrangements in place.<br><br>• Need to promote centrality of safety training. | • Link safety training with new work forms.<br><br>• Integrate it with education and vocational systems.<br><br>• A European level of specialists' support needed. |
| **13. Spain** | • No data. | • Emphasis on OSH in schools.<br><br>• Start vocational degree programmes.<br><br>• Support public/social bodies. |
| **14. Sweden** | • Several evaluations undertaken. | • Focus on schools.<br><br>• Evaluation of effectiveness of training required. |
| **15. United Kingdom** | • At the time of this report, UK viewed training as important and was planning a study. This was followed by the HSC/HSE as a part of its 'training strategy' which showed a greater need for small and medium sized enterprises to receive advice and training support. | • Emphasis on competence based approach linked with training. |

One can infer:

• Member states wish to see greater integration of safety into the wider education curriculum. In the UK this is reflected in the HSE's ' *The new general teaching requirements for health and safety*'.

• Training should be wide-scale and not just confined to practitioners or specific sectors.

- Training should be continuous and regularly evaluated.

- Linking training to other corporate and economic objectives rather than being a stand alone topic.

- There should be increased emphasis on vocational-academic interface.

## Training and competence: providers and sources of information

T7041    The following paragraphs focus on the main bodies and organisations involved in providing training and courses.

### NEBOSH (National Examination Board in Occupational Safety and Health)

T7042    This body is one of the principal forces in safety training. NEBOSH have a thorough Quality Assurance system to approve course providers (which must include highly trained/qualified tutors, adequate resources to deliver the training, sound internal financial management, marketing and administration to promote NEBOSH courses).

Programmes include:

- NEBOSH General Certificate – a broad introduction to the principles of OSH (Occupational Safety and Health). It covers legal, behavioural, managerial, occupational health and safety technology principles. Holding the certificate does not mean the person is 'competent' under *Reg 7* of the *Management of Health and Safety at Work Regulations 1999 (SI 1999 No 3242)*.

- NEBOSH Construction Certificate – a specialist construction safety certificate building upon the NEBOSH Certificate. It covers construction safety law, construction safety management and technical/engineering issues.

- NEBOSH Diploma Part 1 – is aimed at safety advisors and safety managers. It is a rigorous and more detailed exposition into OSH issues, case studies and practical implementation. There are five modules: 'Management of Risk', 'Legal and Organisational Factors', 'Work Equipment', 'Work Place' and 'Agents'. Also, communication skills are assessed in each module. There are five assignments accounting for 50% of the total marks. There are two exams – each lasting two and a half hours in length.

- NEBOSH Diploma Part 2 – as above but a further analysis of core issues and strategic safety management. Likewise, it has five modules, two Exams (each lasting three hours in length) and five assignments (50% of total marks).

- NEBOSH Specialist Diploma in Environmental Management – this is aimed at safety, health and environmental (SHE) practitioners, environmental advisors who need to know about the interface between OSH and the environment. It covers environmental law, EMAS/ISO 14001, European issues, pollution and waste management, case studies etc. There is a written exam of three hours and a report required of an environmental audit.

There are many ways in which NEBOSH courses are delivered – day release being the most popular (as well as block, distant learning etc.). The nearest NEBOSH provider can be identified by contacting NEBOSH on telephone number (0116) 263 4700 and/or viewing the NEBOSH website at www.nebosh.org.uk. It must be said that NEBOSH Diploma 1 and 2 are challenging. Individuals must make the time available for considerable study on top of class room attendance. In the past failure rates have been high although now improving. However, the NEBOSH Diploma is a 'status symbol' with excellent career opportunities for those holding it.

## NVQs (National Vocational Qualifications)

T7043  The NVQ has revolutionised OSH training. There are no exams as it is essentially work related assessing actual competence. NVQs in safety have been influenced by the HSE through their *'Policy Statement on health and safety training'* in 1991/2 and in 1995 (see T7024). NVQs are currently being re-examined to account for the latest competency standards from industry.

- NVQ Level 3 in Safety Practice – is for those in 'low risk environments' such as offices. There is a set performance criteria and the student must provide evidence via work documents to prove that they have met the breadth and range of skills being assessed. The student has an assessor appointed. NVQ 3 equates broadly to NEBOSH Diploma 1.

- NVQ Level 4 – is the next level up and more detailed and equated broadly to NEBOSH Diploma 2.

City and Guilds are the awarding body. Their website is www.city-and-guilds.co.uk.

## British Safety Council

T7044  The British Safety Council (BSC) has focused on practical OSH training. The BSC's 'Diploma in Safety Management' and 'Diploma in Environmental Management' cover similar topics to NEBOSH. BSC courses are more bespoke and are assessed via multiple choice tests and reports. The BSC is well known world wide with a large membership. Holding the DipSM or equivalent can lead to the Membership of the International Institute of Risk and Safety Management (IIRSM). The BSC can be contacted on telephone no. (020) 8741 0835.

## Degrees

T7045  There are many BSc/PG Dip/MSc degrees in OSH Management. They are more academic and theoretical and are well suited for those that want more detailed information. Indeed, the degree route is an alternative to NEBOSH etc. but can also compliment it; many universities give credits to NEBOSH Diploma holders leading directly onto the PGCert/PG Dip/MSc degrees. Some of the leading names include Universities of Surrey, Aston, Loughborough, Salford, Middlesex, South Bank to name a few.

## IOSH (Institution of Occupational Safety and Health)

T7046  IOSH and NEBOSH were one body and are still closely linked today. IOSH is one of Europe's premier safety professional bodies with over 25,000 members. IOSH does not offer degree or diploma equivalent training. Instead it offers short, practical and bespoke OSH training such as:

- IOSH Managing Safely

- IOSH Working Safely

- IOSH Safety for Senior Executives

- IOSH Managing the Environment

- Many other short programmes

IOSH can be contacted on telephone no. (0116) 257 3100 or alternatively on their website www.iosh.co.uk.

## Others

T7047     The Royal Society for the Prevention of Accidents (ROSPA), the Trade Union Congress (TUC), specific unions and employers federations will also offer some OSH courses aimed at their membership. In addition many professional bodies also offer safety training commensurate with their professional standards such as the Chartered Institute of Environmental Health, Fire Protection Association, Loss Prevention Council, Building Research Establishment, Institute of Personnel Development etc.

## Conclusion

T7048     Training and competence are evolving concepts. There are powerful legal, managerial, behavioural and economic reasons for ensuring key safety competencies are in place at work and that training is used as a means of achieving such standards. Organisations need to continuously monitor their standards to ensure they are conforming and complying with industry best practice. Finally, it must be remembered that training and competence are of little use if they do not benefit the individual in risk control, motivational, cognitive, behavioural and economic terms.

# Ventilation

## Introduction

Air being invisible and intangible, there is a dangerous tendency to take it for granted. As breathing is predominantly an involuntary activity, it underlines the need to be selective about what we breathe, with whom we do so, and in what conditions. The twin objectives of good ventilation are the elimination or dispersal of particulate matter (see V3010 below) and the replacement of stale, hot or humid air (often associated with production processes or equipment) with fresh air free from impurity, the aim being to induce a sense of individual comfort in employees. The *Workplace (Health, Safety & Welfare) Regulations 1992* guidance states that the fresh air supply rate to workplaces should not normally fall below 5 to 8 litres per second, per occupant. When considering the appropriate fresh air supply rate, the factors that should be considered include: the amount of floor space available for each occupant; the work actives being carried out; whether there is smoking allowed within the work areas; and whether there are other sources of airborne contamination, such as that arising from work activities, process machinery, heaters, furniture, furnishings, etc. In addition to air changes, the movement of air across the work area/occupant should also be taken into consideration. The CIBSE Guide '*Volume A: Environmental design*' recommends that 'At normal temperatures the air flow velocity should be between 0.1 to 0.15 metres per second and up to 0.25 metres per second during summer.' Draughts should be kept to a minimum. The composition of pure dry air is 20.94% oxygen, 0.03% carbon dioxide and 79.03% nitrogen and inert gases.

Satisfactory ventilation is normally achievable by means of windows (or other similar apertures), as well as by recycled air, particularly in warm weather or hot workplaces. Air recirculated via mechanical ventilation or air conditioning systems should be adequately filtered and impurities removed (see 'Legionella' at D1032 DANGEROUS SUBSTANCES I), and be impregnated with fresh air prior to recirculation. To that end, ventilation systems should be designed with fresh air inlets and kept open, regularly and properly cleaned, tested and maintained. In order to avoid uncomfortable draughts the velocity of ventilation systems may have to be controlled. Employers who fail to ventilate effectively and follow relevant official guidance on medical surveillance of workers can be liable at common law if an employee becomes sensitised to a respiratory sensitiser in the workplace, even in the absence of evidence that the relevant occupational exposure limits have been exceeded (*Douglas Reilly v Robert Kellie & Sons Ltd (1989) HSIB 166* where an employee contracted occupational asthma whilst working with low levels of isocyanate fumes. It was held that the employer was liable at common law for breach of the *Factories Act 1961, s 63* (now repealed), since the hazards associated with isocyanate fumes had been known about since the early 1980s).

This section deals with current statutory requirements, contained in the *Health and Safety at Work etc. Act 1974* (general) (see V3004 below), the *Workplace (Health, Safety and Welfare) Regulations 1992 (SI 1992 No 3004)* (specific) (see V3005 below), and certain specific processes where adherence to ventilation requirements is paramount (see V3006 below). (For requirements relating to ventilation on construction sites see C8047 CONSTRUCTION AND BUILDING OPERATIONS.) Origins of pollution of the working atmosphere, specific pollutants and their insidious effect on health, along with strategies for controlling them, are also covered.

## Pollution of the working environment and dangers of exposure to dust and fumes

V3002     Pollution of the working environment can occur through the generation of airborne particulates, such as dusts, fumes, mists and vapours (as defined in V3003 below). Of these, probably dust and fumes pose the principal hazard to workers, some of the situations being well documented, e.g. tungsten and silicon processes resulting in pneumonia followed by progressive fibrosis, milling cotton resulting in byssinosis, weaving hemp in chronic bronchitis, underground mining in emphysema and copper welding/electroplating with cadmium also causing emphysema (see further O1034 OCCUPATIONAL HEALTH AND DISEASES). Dusts can be fibrogenic, that is they can lead to fibrotic changes to lung tissue, or, alternatively be toxic, eventually leading to poisoning of body systems. Examples of fibrogenic dusts are: silica, cement dust and certain metals such as tungsten; toxic dusts include: arsenic, lead, mercury and beryllium. More particularly, dusts are classified according to the response on the worker, as follows:

(a)     benign pneumoconiosis, such as siderosis, associated with work with iron particles; here there is no permanent lung disorder;

(b)     pneumonitis or acute inflammation of lung tissue, caused by inhalation of metallic fumes, e.g. zinc oxide fumes; this can result in death;

(c)     extrinsic allergic alveolitis, e.g. farmer's lung; this can eventuate into a disabling condition;

(d)     tumour-forming, e.g. asbestosis, plural mesothelioma (caused by work with crocidolite); characterised by a high mortality rate;

(e)     nuisance particulates, e.g. dust from combustion of solid fuels; however causing no permanent lung damage.

Dust at the workplace has a variety of origins ranging from:

(i)     dust arising in connection with cleaning and treatment of raw materials, e.g. sandblasting in foundries;

(ii)     dust emitted in operations such as refining, grinding, milling, cutting, sanding; and

(iii)     dusts manufactured for specific treatments or dressings; to

(iv)     general environmental dust, e.g. caused by sweeping factory floors or by fuel combustion.

Fumes are formed through vaporisation or oxidation of metals, e.g. typically lead and welding fumes. Lead processes emitting dust and fume should be enclosed and maintained under negative pressure by an enclosing hood. Moreover, the fume should be treated before any escape into the atmosphere. Welding fume, caused by action of heat and ultraviolet light, produces carbon monoxide and ozone and is potentially harmful, leading to 'welder's lung'. For that reason, welding should only be carried out in ventilated areas. Welding workshops should be equipped with adequate mechanical ventilation, and local exhaust ventilation should be incorporated at the point of fume emission as a supplement to general ventilation. If welding is carried out in a confined space (see the *Confined Spaces Regulations 1997 (SI 1997 No 1713)*), a permit to work system should be in force. Welders should of necessity be familiar with various relevant forms of respiratory protection (see further PERSONAL PROTECTIVE EQUIPMENT).

## Polluting agents

V3003    Pollution of the workplace environment may take place through the generation of airborne particulates, such as dusts, fumes, mists and vapours. These are defined below.

*Particulate*: a collection of solid particles, each of which is an aggregation of many molecules.

*Dust*: an aerosol composed of solid inanimate particles. (Standard ILO definition).

*Fumes*: airborne fine solid particulates formed from a gaseous state, usually by vaporisation or oxidation of metals.

*Mist*: airborne liquid droplets.

*Vapour*: a substance in the form of a mist, fume or smoke emitted from a liquid.

## Statutory requirements

### General – HSWA 1974

V3004    The general duty upon employers under the *Health and Safety at Work etc. Act 1974* (*HSWA 1974*) to 'ensure, so far as reasonably practicable, the health, safety and welfare at work of all their employees' [*HSWA 1974, s 2(1)*], must be regarded as including a duty to provide employees with an adequate and renewable supply of pure and uncontaminated air. Employers must also provide and maintain a safe working environment. [*HSWA 1974, s 2(2)(e)*]. In consequence, employers may be in breach if the workplace is not adequately ventilated and specific dust and fume hazards not controlled. In addition, all employers must inform, instruct and train their employees in health and safety procedures. This means that they, or their representatives, must know how to use, test and maintain equipment for ensuring air purity and ventilation as well as dust control (*R v Swan Hunter Shipbuilders Ltd [1981] ICR 831*, where the deaths of the subcontractor employees might have been avoided, had they been properly instructed and trained in the use of respirators). (See further C8134 CONSTRUCTION AND BUILDING OPERATIONS.)

Facilities managers (i.e. those responsible for the well-being of occupants and visitors) are required to maintain a clean and healthy ventilation system in the workplace. This may mean the procurement of ventilation hygiene services from a specialist contractor which often demands a level of technical expertise outside the scope of the majority.

*'General ventilation guidance for employers'*, HSG202, is published by HSE Books.

The Heating and Ventilating Contractors' Association (HVCA) have published a Guide to Good Practice, *'Cleanliness of Ventilation Systems – TR/17'*. This Guide and others on ventilation are available from HVCA Publications (tel: 01768 864771).

Responding to industry needs, the Building Services Research and Information Association has developed a Standard Specification for Ventilation Hygiene* to allow competitive tenders to be provided by contractors on an equal basis. The client thereby achieves optimum value for money by securing complete but not excessive action by the contractor. Correspondingly, contractors face less ambiguity in performance expectations.

The Standard Specification is in two parts, the basic specification with accompanying detailed guidance. Supported by the Department of Environment Transport and Regions, this is the first of a range of specifications written for facilities managers. It provides straightforward, easy to use clauses of industry-standard performance requirements. The guidance document explains in detail the scope of work required to fulfil a ventilation hygiene contract.

* '*Guidance and Standard Specification for Ventilation Hygiene*', price £40, is available from BSRIA publications sales, tel: 01344 426511.

### Specific – Workplace (Health, Safety and Welfare) Regulations 1992 (SI 1992 No 3004)

V3005    Effective and suitable provision must be made to ensure that every enclosed workplace is ventilated by a sufficient quantity of fresh or purified air. Plant designed and used for such purposes must be accompanied with visible and/or audible means of warning of any failure, which might affect health or safety. [*Workplace (Health, Safety and Welfare) Regulations 1992 (SI 1992 No 3004), Reg 6*].

# Specific processes or industries

## Highly flammable liquids and liquefied petroleum gases

V3006    Where a dangerous concentration of vapours from a highly flammable liquid may be expected, the process must be carried on within a cabinet or other enclosure, which is:

(*a*)    effective to prevent the escape of such vapours into the general atmosphere;

(*b*)    adequately ventilated; and

(*c*)    fire-resistant.

[*Highly Flammable Liquids and Liquefied Petroleum Gases Regulations 1972 (SI 1972 No 917), Reg 10(2)*].

Where compliance with this requirement is not reasonably practicable the workroom must have exhaust ventilation adequate to remove vapours from the workroom. [*Highly Flammable Liquids and Liquefied Petroleum Gases Regulations 1972 (SI 1972 No 917), Reg 10(3)*].

## Lead processes

V3007    The *Control of Lead at Work Regulations 1998 (SI 1998 No 543)* came into force on 1 April 1998. They were introduced to ensure that work involving lead might be covered by a single set of regulations.

Regulations revoked include the *Control of Lead at Work Regulations 1980 (SI 1980 No 1248)*. See the *Control of Lead at Work Regulations 1998, Sch 3* for a full list of revocations. The *Factories Act 1961, ss 74, 128, 131 and 132* have been repealed by *Reg 14(1)* of the 1998 Regulations.

The aims of the new Regulations and Approved Code of Practice, Regulations and Guidance, (COP2) are to:

(*a*)    protect the health of people at work by preventing or, where this is not practicable, adequately controlling their exposure to lead;

(*b*)    monitor the amount of lead that employees absorb so that individuals whose work involves significant exposure (as defined by *Control of Lead at Work Regulations 1998 (SI 1998 No 543), Reg 2*) to lead at work can be taken off such work before their health is affected.

The Regulations apply to all work which exposes employees to lead in any form in which it may be inhaled, ingested or absorbed through the skin, for example as dust, fume or vapour.

The duties imposed by these Regulations extend not only to employers but also to self-employed persons. [*Control of Lead at Work Regulations 1998 (SI 1998 No 543), Reg 3(2)*].

## Control of Lead at Work Regulations 1998 (SI 1998 No 543)

**V3008**    An employer who is working with lead, or a substance or material containing it has a duty to ensure that his employees are not exposed to lead, or, where this is not reasonably practicable (see E15039 ENFORCEMENT), to ensure that appropriate control measures are adequately controlling the exposure to lead of his employees and of anyone else who may be affected by their work with lead and/or lead-based products – such persons may include:

—    persons working for other employers, such as maintenance staff or cleaners;

—    visitors to the work area; and

—    families of those exposed to lead at work who may be affected by lead carried home unintentionally on clothing and/or footwear.

Exposure to lead covers all routes of possible exposure, i.e. inhalation, absorption through the skin and ingestion.

Without prejudice to the *Management of Health and Safety at Work Regulations 1999 (SI 1999 No 3242, Reg 3*, employers must not carry on any work which is liable to expose any employees to lead at work unless they have first made an assessment as to whether the exposure of any employees to lead is liable to be significant. [*Control of Lead at Work Regulations (SI 1998 No 543), Reg 5*].

Measures for controlling exposure to lead may include one or more of the following:

(*a*)    using substitutes, i.e. lead-free or low-solubility lead compounds;

(*b*)    using lead or lead compounds in emulsion or paste form to minimise the formation of dust;

(*c*)    using temperature controls to keep the temperature of molten lead below 500°C, the level above which fume emission becomes significant, though the formation of lead oxide and the emission of dust is still possible below this temperature;

(*d*)    the containment of lead, lead materials, compounds, fumes or dust in totally enclosed plant and in enclosed containers such as drums and bags. The container must be so designed that no lead is allowed to leak out. Where it is necessary to open such containers, this should be carried out under exhaust ventilation conditions, if reasonably practicable;

(*e*)    where total enclosure is not reasonably practicable, an effective ventilation system must be in operation before work is allowed to commence. This may consist of:

(i)    partial enclosure such as booths designed to prevent the lead escaping – these should be fitted with exhaust ventilation;

(ii)    various types of exhaust hoods which should be as close to the lead source as is reasonably practicable so that they may take the lead dust, fume or vapour away from the employee's breathing zone;

(iii) an extract ductwork system that is adequate to remove the dust, fume or vapour from the source area;

(iv) a dust and/or fume collection unit with a sound and adequate filtration system that will both remove the lead source from the workplace and prevent it from re-entering;

(v) fans of a suitable type placed in the system after the collection and filtration units so that the units are kept under negative pressure, thus ensuring that any escape of lead is minimised;

(f) wet methods which include:

(i) the wetting of lead and lead materials, e.g. wet grinding and pasting processes. Wet methods should be used during rubbing and/or scraping lead-painted surfaces;

(ii) the wetting of floors and work benches whilst certain types of work are being carried out, e.g. work with dry lead compounds and pasting processes in the manufacture of batteries.

Wetting should be sufficiently thorough to prevent dust forming, and the wetted materials or surfaces should not be allowed to dry out since this can create dry lead dust which then is liable to be hazardous if it becomes airborne. Water sprays are not a fully effective method of controlling airborne dust.

Wetting methods should not be used when they are liable to be unsafe, such as:

(i) at furnaces where they could cause an explosion;

(ii) when lead materials containing arsenides or antimonides could, on contact with water, produce highly toxic arsine or stibine gases;

(g) providing and maintaining a high standard of cleanliness.

Special care and attention should be given to the design of plant and systems to eliminate possible areas which might increase the risk to the employee of exposure from lead.

Before any plant, equipment or systems are used in lead or lead compound work, there should be an adequate checking procedure in place to ensure that such plant, equipment or systems are as designed and that they meet the standard required under the *Control of Lead at Work Regulations 1998* for the safety of all those who could be affected by lead.

## Asbestos

V3009

No process must be carried on in any factory unless exhaust equipment is provided, maintained and used, which prevents the entry into air of asbestos dust. [*Control of Asbestos at Work Regulations 1987 (SI 1987 No 2115), Reg 13(2)*].

In addition, where it is not reasonably practicable to reduce exposure of employees to below the 'control limits', employers must provide employees concerned with suitable respiratory protective equipment. [*Control of Asbestos at Work Regulations 1987 (SI 1987 No 2115), Reg 8(2)*].

Moreover, where the concentration of asbestos is likely to exceed any 'control limit', the employer must designate that area a 'respirator zone' and ensure that only permitted employees enter/remain in that zone. [*Control of Asbestos at Work Regulations 1987 (SI 1987 No 2115), Reg 14(2)*]. (See further ASBESTOS.)

# Control of airborne particulates

V3010    Airborne particulates may be controlled in the following ways.

(*a*) *Substitution replacement*

The use of a less harmful toxic substance or modification to a process may minimise or totally eliminate the hazard. For example, substitution of soap solutions for organic solvents is sometimes possible in cleaning operations.

(*b*) *Suppression*

The use of a wet process for handling powders or other particulates is an effective form of control. In the cleaning process, it may be possible to damp down floors prior to removal of dust sooner than resorting to dry sweeping.

(*c*) *Isolation*

This form of control entails enclosure of all or part of a process or the actual point of dust production and may be incorporated in machinery/plant, in which case it is necessary to ensure seals are maintained. Total enclosure of large processes involving grinding of metals or other materials, linked to an extract ventilation system, is an effective method of isolating dust from the operator's breathing zone.

(*d*) *Extract/exhaust ventilation*

Removal of dust or fume at the point of emission by entraining it in a path of fresh air and taking it to an extract hood or other collection device is the role of extract/exhaust ventilation (see the HSE's guidance booklet HSG54: '*The maintenance, examination and testing of local exhaust ventilation*'). The air velocity required to provide this movement depends upon the type of material, varying from about 0.5 metres per second for gases to 10 metres per second or above for some dusts. In fact for large dense dust particles from grinding or cutting operations, it may be necessary to arrange for the trajectory of the emitted particles to be encompassed by the exhaust hood so that the material is literally thrown into the hood by its own energy.

Extract ventilation systems generally take three distinct forms:

(i)    *Receptor systems*: the contaminant enters the system without inducement, and is transported from the hood through ducting to a collection point by the use of a fan.

(ii)   *Captor systems*: in this system moving air captures the contaminant at some point outside the hood and induces its flow into it. The rate of air flow must be sufficient to capture the contaminant at the furthest point of origin, and the air velocity induced at this point must be high enough to overcome the effects of cross currents created by open doors, windows or moving parts of machinery.

(iii)  *High velocity low volume systems*: dusts from high speed grinding machines in particular require very high capture velocities. With an HVLV system high velocities at the source are created by extracting from small apertures very close to the source of the contaminant. These high velocities can be achieved with quite low air flow rates.

(*e*) *Dilution ventilation*

In certain cases, it may not be possible to extract particulates close to their point of origin. Where the quantity of contaminant is small, uniformly evolved and of low toxicity, it may be possible to dilute it by inducing large volumes of air to flow through the contaminated region. Dilution ventilation is most successfully used to control vapours from low toxicity solvents, but is seldom satisfactory in the control of dust and fumes.

(*f*) *Cleaning procedures*

Whilst the above methods may be effective in preventing environmental contamination of the workplace, there will inevitably be a need for efficient cleaning procedures wherever dusty processes are operated. Hand sweeping should be replaced by the use of industrial vacuum cleaning equipment, or in situ (ring main) systems which incorporate hand-held suction devices connected via ducting to a central collection point.

(*g*) *Air cleaning*

Air cleaning is often employed, either to prevent emission of noxious substances into the atmosphere or to enable some of the air to be recirculated during winter months, thus reducing heated air costs and lowering fuel bills. For particulates such as dusts and grit, air cleaning may involve some form of inertial separator, such as settling chambers or cyclones, usually followed by bag filters. For very fine dusts and fumes, bag filters are often used as the pre-filter, followed by absolute or electrostatic filters. For gases and vapours, the cleaning is usually achieved by wet scrubbers (device where the air is passed in close contact with a liquid) to take the gas into solution or react chemically with it. Scrubbers can also be used for particulate material. The selection of air cleaning types will depend upon the properties of the materials emitted and the size ranges of the particulates.

To generate air flow in the duct, various types of fans are available. The type of fan must be suitable for the system in which it is installed. This requires a knowledge of the system resistance and the fan characteristics in order to generate the desired air flow with minimum noise and power consumption.

For systems with little ducting and airflow resistance, axial fans may be used to generate high air flows. For ducted systems, centrifugal fans are often used, creating generally lower air flows per size, but at the higher air pressures required to overcome the resistances imposed by ducting and air cleaners. The fan should not be used outside its duty range. It should be sited either outside the building or as near to the discharge as possible, so that air cleaners and all ducting within the building are on the negative static pressure side of the fan, thus preventing leakage of the contaminant through cracks or defects in the duct.

New guidance* on the use of the dust lamp for observing the presence of airborne particles in the workplace has been published by the Health & Safety Executive (HSE) in the series 'Method for the Determination of Hazardous Substances' (MDHS). The guidance has been written for occupational hygienists, ventilation engineers, and health and safety practitioners. It briefly explains the principle of the dust lamp, its use in observing the presence of airborne particles and identifies its advantages and limitations. Despite its name, the dust lamp can be used to reveal the presence of many different types of airborne particulates both solids (dusts, fumes, fibres) and liquids (organic or inorganic mists). The dust lamp can be used to gauge the size and direction of movement of a particle cloud, but it does not give a quantitative measure of either concentration or particle size.

* '*MDHS 82: The dust lamp: A simple tool for observing the presence of airborne particles*', price £15.00, is available from HSE Books.

## Respiratory protection

V3011     Respiratory protection implies the provision and use of equipment such as dust masks, general purpose dust respirators, positive pressure powered dust respirators, self-contained breathing apparatus or other forms of such protection. Where dust emission is intermittent or other controls are not available (as above), then resort may be made to respiratory protection. The work and care required in the selection and establishment of a respiratory protection programme, including the training of operators in the correct use of the equipment, is likely to be at least as great as any other control system. The protection must be selected to give adequate cover and minimum discomfort and the need for other personal protective devices should not be ignored. (See also PERSONAL PROTECTIVE EQUIPMENT.)

# Work at Heights

## Introduction

Work at heights characterises many occupations – construction and maintenance workers, plant and equipment installers, personnel servicing passenger lifts, heating and air conditioning systems, window cleaners. The risk of a fall during such activities is common and can be fatal. Indeed, two-fifths of all reported major injuries are caused by falls from a height; as are half the fatal injuries to construction workers. It is the most common cause of fatal accidents to employees generally. Falls are usually associated with either (a) means of access to the workstation or (b) the system of work itself.

As regards means of access to the working position, this can be assisted by a portable ladder, roof ladder or powered working platform. In many cases, the means provided, or too often, assumed, have proved to be singularly inadequate or unsuitable for the task at hand, resulting in falls through fragile roofs, from a roof edge or from an item of plant above floor level. In this instance, all workplaces (temporary as well as permanent) must have suitable and effective safeguards for preventing people from being injured as a result of falling a distance likely to cause personal injury (see W9004 below). [*Workplace (Health, Safety and Welfare) Regulations 1992 (SI 1992 No 3004), Reg 13*]. (Construction works are covered separately by the *Construction (Health, Safety and Welfare) Regulations 1996 (SI 1996 No 1592)*. (See CONSTRUCTION AND BUILDING OPERATIONS.) However, the duty of architects etc. to pay adequate regard to the avoidance or reduction of risk to future maintenance workers when designing both new structures and repairs or alterations to existing ones should be noted, particularly as this duty will also protect many not usually thought to be construction workers. [*Construction (Design and Management) Regulations 1994 (SI 1994 as amended by SI 2000 No 2380), Reg 13*]. The Health and Safety Executive (HSE) are particularly concerned to reduce risk presented by fragile rooflights and other fragile roofing materials by requiring designers to stop specifying them. To assist designers, they have agreed standards of strength and durability with UK manufacturers' representatives.

A further point to be noted in relation to repair and new construction is that if the occupier intends to control the way that construction work is done he could well acquire typical and specific contractor duties including those relating to the prevention of falls. [*Construction (Health, Safety and Welfare) Regulations 1996 (SI 1996 No 1592), Reg 4*].

The second most common cause of accidents/fatalities arises from the system of work adopted once the working position is reached. If the system has been correctly planned, operators briefed beforehand on the system and the appropriate precautions to be taken, should be able to work safely at a height. Such systems, as well as incorporating precautions such as temporary guard-rails and toe boards and the wearing of safety harnesses etc., may also include a provision to wear safety helmets to protect those working at heights. [*Construction (Head Protection) Regulations 1989 (SI 1989 No 2209)*]. Reliance on the latter provision is legitimate only after precautions have been taken to prevent objects falling in the first place.

Sometimes work at heights is undertaken in a crisis situation. For instance, a fault may have developed on an item of plant which needs immediate attention for production to continue, or the factory roof may be leaking resulting in damage to stored products below. In both cases, there may be insufficient time to properly consider the precautions necessary to ensure safe working at height. Procedures should be planned and in force to deal with this sort of contingency.

Another aspect of work at heights is window cleaning. Windows in factories, workplaces and high-rise commercial and office blocks must be regularly and periodically cleaned [*Workplace (Health, Safety and Welfare) Regulations 1992 (SI 1992 No 3004), Reg 16*]. Frequency of cleaning depends on the type of establishment, whether office, shop or factory etc. (see W9039 below) – but in any case the method selected should ensure protection for window cleaners (see W9037, W9038 and W9040 below). Window cleaning, particularly in high-rise commercial properties has posed serious safety problems for contract window cleaning companies and self-employed window cleaners. On the one hand, contract cleaning companies need to use the best available window cleaning equipment and methods, and, on the other, building owners/occupiers need to make safety anchorage points, in so far as they are permitted to do so, conveniently accessible on the building (see further BS 8213 for guidance). Crucially, in this respect, buildings, windows and skylights on buildings may need to be fitted with suitable devices (see W9041–W9043 below) to allow windows and skylights to be securely cleaned to satisfy the safety requirements. [*Workplace (Health, Safety and Welfare) Regulations 1992 (SI 1992 No 3004), Reg 16(1)*]. More generally, the building designer has a duty to pay adequate attention to the avoidance or reduction of risk to those cleaning windows and any transparent or translucent wall, ceiling or roof where they might fall more than two metres. [*Construction (Design and Management) Regulations 1994 (SI 1994 No 3140 as amended by SI 2001 No 2380), Regs 2(1), 13(2)(a)*]. As falls from heights account for by far the greater majority of major injuries, the need to comply with fall-preventive statutory requirements and window cleaning regulations at all times is paramount.

## Current statutory requirements

Current statutory requirements relating to falls from heights are contained in the *Workplace (Health, Safety and Welfare) Regulations 1992 (SI 1992 No 3004)*. There are also specific requirements relating to prevention of falls on construction sites, in the form of the *Construction (Health, Safety and Welfare) Regulations 1996 (SI 1996 No 1592), Regs 5-8*. In addition, the *Management of Health and Safety at Work Regulations 1999 (SI 1999 No 3242), Reg 3*, specifies that there must be a proper risk assessment. Therefore individuals cannot be required to work at heights from which they may be injured or killed until this assessment has taken place. There is a clear duty, according to the degree of risk revealed, to avoid the risk altogether or to reduce the extent or potentially dangerous nature of the work, wherever reasonable, before adopting the precautions in the specific regulations referred to. [*Management of Health and Safety at Work Regulations 1999 (SI 1999 No 3242), Reg 4 and Sch 1*]. (See also paragraphs 30 and 31 of the Approved Code of Practice (ACoP) to the 1999 Regulations.) In practical terms this means asking at the outset 'do we have to do it at all?', 'do we only have to do so much of it?' or 'do we have to do it in that way?'.

Specific requirements relating to windows and window cleaning are contained in the *Workplace (Health, Safety and Welfare) Regulations 1992 (SI 1992 No 3004), Regs 14–16*. Designers should take into consideration window cleaning along with the risk implications of their designs for construction and maintenance workers. They have a duty under the *Construction (Design and Management) Regulations 1994 (SI 1994 No 3140 as amended by SI 2000 No 2380*) to avoid or reduce risk.

### Recent developments

W9003    New regulations on working at heights are expected within a year of the adoption the second amendment to the *Use of Work Equipment Directive 89/655/EEC* in the summer of 2001. A consultative document should appear by the end of 2001. Essentially the Directive will require Member States to introduce the kind of specific regulations that exist on working at heights in construction (for example in the UK the *Construction (Health Safety and Welfare) Regulations 1996 (SI 1996 No 1592), Regs 5–8*) generally across all industries. The Directive addresses the use of equipment for working at heights and an integral part of the resultant regulations is expected to proceed on the basis of assessment of risk .

The proposed temporary work at height Directive would require employers to:

● select the most suitable and safe equipment based on their risk assessment. Selection must take account of how often the equipment will be used, at what height and for how long;

● take steps to prevent or arrest falls from height, giving priority to collective measures, such as netting, over personal protection measures, such as lanyards;

● use ladders and rope access, such as abseiling, only where other safer equipment, such as scaffolding is not justified;

● ensure that the bearing components of scaffolding are prevented from slipping or from moving accidentally during work at height, and that the dimensions and layout of the decks are suitable for work and allow safe passage and use and;

● ensure ladders are used safely and positioned and secured to ensure that they are stable and do not slip in use.

The Directive may well require a more prescriptive approach than that of the corresponding construction regulations and it appears that the latter will have to be amended, particularly in relation to the order of preference of the preventative measures outlined in the *Construction (Health Safety and Welfare) Regulations 1996 (SI 1996 No 1592), Reg 6*. Where working platforms with guard rails and toe boards are not practicable or where because of the short duration of the work they are not reasonably practicable, means of personal suspension (safety harnesses) are preferred over means of arresting falls (safety nets) (see W9015 and W9016). This however contradicts the fundamental strategy of preventative measures of the *Framework Directive* set out in the *Management of Health and Safety at Work Regulations 1999 (SI 1999 No 3242), Reg 4 and Sch 1*, where collective measures, which include nets, must be considered before personal ones. The Directive follows the *Framework Directive*.

### Falls from a height – all workplaces (except construction sites)

W9004    As mentioned in W9002 above, the risks from work at heights must be assessed and considered in light of the fundamental principles of prevention and protection set out in the *Management of Health and Safety at Work Regulations 1999 (SI 1999 No 3242) (MHSWR), Sch 1*. Before deciding the type of precautions necessary, the approach explained in paragraphs 30 and 31 of the MHSWR ACoP must be followed. Once it is established what extent of the work that cannot be reduced or avoided altogether (the higher the risk the greater the case for elimination, or reduction at source), the precautions specified in the Regulations can be applied. Care must also be taken to give preference to collective precautions: fixed means of access, working platforms etc. over personal measures such as providing individuals with safety harnesses etc. Training cannot be a substitute for the physical precautions required but must complement them.

So far as reasonably practicable (for meaning, see E15039 ENFORCEMENT), suitable and effective measures must be taken (other than by provision of personal protective equipment, training, information, supervision etc.) to prevent:

(*a*)    any person falling a distance likely to cause personal injury; or

(*b*)    any person being struck by a falling object likely to cause personal injury.

Any area from which this might happen must be clearly indicated – particularly in the case of pits or tanks. [*Workplace (Health, Safety and Welfare) Regulations 1992 (SI 1992 No 3004), Reg 13*].

Suitable and effective measures are:

(i)    fencing;

(ii)    covering; and

(iii)    fixed ladders.

### Fencing

W9005    This should primarily prevent people falling from edges and objects falling onto people, and where it has to be removed temporarily (as where goods/materials are admitted), temporary measures should be put in train (e.g. provision of handholds). Except in the case of roof edges or other points to which there is no general legitimate access, secure fencing should be provided where a person might fall:

(*a*)    2 metres or more, or

(*b*)    less than 2 metres, where the risk of injury is otherwise greater (e.g. internal traffic route below).

Fencing should be sufficiently high to prevent falls, both of people and objects, over or through it. Minimally, it should consist of two guard-rails at suitable heights. The top of the fencing should generally be at least 1,100 millimetres above the surface from which a person might fall, be of adequate strength and stability to restrain any person or object liable to fall against it.

### Covers

W9006    Pits, tanks, vats, sumps, kiers etc. can be securely covered (instead of fenced). Covers must be strong and able to support loads imposed on them as well as passing traffic; nor should they be easily detachable and removable. They should be kept securely *in situ* except for purposes of inspection or access. Uncovered tanks, pits or structures must be fenced if there is a traffic route over them.

### Fixed ladders

W9007    Assuming a staircase is impractical, fixed ladders – sloping ones are safer than vertical ones – (which should be provided in pits etc.) should be:

(*a*)    of sound construction,

(*b*)    properly maintained,

(*c*)    securely fixed.

Rungs should be horizontal and provide adequate foothold without reliance on nails or screws. In the absence of an adequate handhold, stiles should extend to at least 1,100 millimetres above any landing (or the highest rung) to step or stand on. Fixed ladders with a vertical distance of more than 6 metres should normally have a landing at every 6 metre point. Where possible, each run should be out of line with the previous run to reduce falling distance. And where a ladder passes through a floor, the opening should be as small as possible, fenced (if possible) and a gate provided to prevent falls.

(For ladders on construction sites, see W9018 below and C8066 CONSTRUCTION AND BUILDING OPERATIONS.)

### Pits, tanks, vats, kiers etc. – new workplaces

W9008  Serious accidents have occurred as a result of workers, often maintenance workers, falling into or overreaching or overbalancing (and falling) into pits etc. containing dangerous corrosive or scalding substances. Thus, where there is a risk of a person or employee falling into a dangerous or corrosive or scalding substance, (so far as is reasonably practicable) pits, tanks (or similar vessels) must be either:

(*a*)  fenced, or

(*b*)  covered

[Workplace (Health, Safety and Welfare) Regulations 1992 (SI 1992 No 3004), Reg 13(5)]

and means of access/egress into pits/tanks – in the form (preferably) of fixed ladders (or the equivalent) – should be provided [*Workplace (Health, Safety and Welfare) Regulations 1992 (SI 1992 No 3004), Reg 13(6)*].

## Construction sites – the Construction (Health, Safety and Welfare) Regulations 1996 (SI 1996 No 1592)

W9009  Construction work is associated with a large number of falls, some of which are fatal. A fair proportion of serious accidents occur as a result of workers falling off (or through) working platforms, scaffolds, toe boards, fragile roofs and personal suspension equipment. This situation is addressed by the *Construction (Health, Safety and Welfare) Regulations 1996 (SI 1996 No 1592), Regs 6–8*. The *Management of Health and Safety at Work Regulations 1999 (SI 1999 No 3242), Regs 3, 4*, and *Sch 1* also address the situation whereby employers have a duty to assess risks and to avoid or reduce them at source. (See particularly the advice to *Reg 4* in paragraphs 30 and 31 of the ACoP). Designers too must pay adequate regard to the avoidance or reduction of risk. [*Construction (Design and Management) Regulations 1994 (SI 1994 No 3140 as amended by SI 2000 No 2380), Reg 13(2)(a)*].

These duties will entail such matters as reviewing the need firstly to have the work – or so much of it – done at heights; and where the work cannot be avoided or reduced, giving preference to collective measures such as secure working platforms over individual ones such as safety harnesses.

## Working platforms, scaffolds, toe-boards, guard-rails, personal suspension equipment – fall preventative requirements

W9010    Suitable and sufficient steps must be taken to prevent any person (direct or indirect employees) from falling, so far as is reasonably practicable. [*Construction (Health, Safety and Welfare) Regulations 1996 (SI 1996 No 1592), Reg 6(1)*]. This will usually involve the provision of:

(*a*)    suitable working platforms;

(*b*)    guard-rails, toe-boards (not required in respect of stairway or rest platforms of a scaffold used as a means of access or egress to or from a place of work) [*Construction (Health, Safety and Welfare) Regulations 1996 (SI 1996 No 1592), Reg 6(9)*]; and

(*c*)    barriers.

These can be removed for movement of materials, but must be replaced as soon as practicable. [*Construction (Health, Safety and Welfare) Regulations 1996 (SI 1996 No 1592), Reg 6(4)*].

Where working platforms etc. are not practicable, or are not reasonably practicable because the duration of the work is short, means of personal suspension should be used (see W9014 below). Where it is not practicable to provide neither platforms nor personal suspension, then other precautions should be taken as well as means of arresting falls (nets) (see W9016). It should be noted that this preference for personal suspension over safety nets – which are a collective means of preventing injury from falls – is contrary to the hierarchy within the *Management of Health and Safety at Work Regulations 1999 (SI 1999 No 3242), Reg 4* and *Sch 1*. This approach will be reversed as soon as the new regulations on the prevention of falls in non-construction situations are made in 2002 in accordance with the second amendment to the *Use of Work Equipment Directive*. The preference for collective over personal precautions stems from experience that the use of personal precautions depends upon constant human compliance, which is often absent. Collective precautions are more easily managed because they depend less on human behaviour and thus are more reliable.

HSE Guidance in Operational Circular 314/19 gives information on the matters inspectors take into account when considering mobile elevating work platforms. This covers safe systems of work; planning; training and experience.

High risk situations occur where:

●    there are protruding features which could catch or trap the carrier;

●    nearby vehicles or mobile plant could foreseeably collide with, or make accidental contact with the MEWP;

●    the nature of the work being done from the basket may mean operators are more likely to lean out or are handling awkward work pieces which may move unexpectedly; and

●    unexpected or rapid movement of the machine or overturning is possible.

These assessments will be of particular interest to architects and engineers considering MEWPS for window cleaners etc. since they are indications of the unsuitability of this means of access.

## Definition

W9011 A working platform refers to any platform used (*a*) as a place of work, or (*b*) a means of access or egress (to or from) a place of work, including:

(*a*)   a scaffold;

(*b*)   a suspended scaffold;

(*c*)   a cradle;

(*d*)   a mobile platform;

(*e*)   a trestle;

(*f*)   a gangway;

(*g*)   a run;

(*h*)   a gantry;

(*j*)   a stairway; and

(*k*)   a crawling ladder.

[*Construction (Health, Safety and Welfare) Regulations 1996 (SI 1996 No 1592), Reg 2(1)*].

## Requirements relating to guard-rails and toe boards

W9012 The Regulations require that:

(*a*)   guard-rails, toe-boards and barriers and other similar means of protection must be:

    (i)   suitable and of sufficient strength and rigidity for the purpose for which they are being used, and

    (ii)   so placed, secured and used as to ensure, so far as is reasonably practicable, the avoidance of accidental displacement;

(*b*)   structures supporting guard-rails, toe-boards, barriers and other means of protection, or a structure to which these are attached, must be of a suitable and sufficient strength for the purpose for which they are used;

(*c*)   main guard-rails must be at least 910 millimetres above the edge from which a person is liable to fall;

(*d*)   there must not be an unprotected gap of more than 470 millimetres between any guard-rail, toe-board or barrier and the walking surface;

(*e*)   toe-boards must be not less than 150 millimetres high; and

(*f*)   guard-rails, toe-boards, barriers and other similar means of protection must be so placed as to prevent, so far as is reasonably practicable, the fall of a person, material or objects from a place of work.

[*Construction (Health, Safety and Welfare) Regulations 1996 (SI 1996 No 1592), Sch 1*].

## Requirements relating to working platforms

W9013 The Regulations require work platforms to conform to the following requirements.

(*a*)   *Stability* – they must be:

(i)    suitable and of sufficient strength and rigidity for the intended use,

(ii)    erected and used to ensure, so far as is reasonably practicable, the avoidance of accidental displacement,

(iii)    remain stable and if modified or altered, remain stable after modification or alteration, and

(iv)    dismantled so as to avoid accidental displacement.

(*b*)    *Safety* – they must be:

(i)    of sufficient dimensions to permit free passage of persons and safe use of equipment and materials, and, so far as is reasonably practicable, be a safe working area,

(ii)    at least 600 millimetres wide,

(iii)    so reasonably constructed that the surface has no gap likely to cause injury, or from which there is any risk of any person below the platform being struck by falling objects,

(iv)    so erected, used and maintained to prevent, so far as is reasonably practicable, any slipping or tripping, or any person being caught between a working platform and an adjacent structure, and

(v)    provided with such handholds and footholds as are necessary to prevent, so far as is reasonably practicable, any person from slipping or falling from a working platform.

(*c*)    *Load* – they must not be so loaded as to give rise to danger of collapse or deformation which could affect its safe use.

(*d*)    *Supporting structures* – must be:

(i)    of suitable and sufficient strength and rigidity for the intended purpose,

(ii)    so erected and, where necessary, securely attached to another structure as to ensure stability,

(iii)    so altered or modified as to ensure stability when altered or modified, and

(iv)    erected on surfaces which are stable and of a sufficient strength and suitable composition to ensure the safe support of the structure, working platform and any load intended to be placed upon the working platform.

[*Construction (Health, Safety and Welfare) Regulations 1996 (SI 1996 No 1592), Sch 2*].

## Personal suspension equipment – fall preventative requirements

**W9014**    Personal suspension equipment refers to suspended access (other than a working platform) for use by an individual, including a boatswain's chair and abseiling equipment, but does not include a suspended scaffold or cradle. [*Construction (Health, Safety and Welfare) Regulations 1996 (SI 1996 No 1592), Reg 2(1)*].

Where compliance with guard-rail, toe-board or working platform duties (see above) is not reasonably practicable, (e.g. owing to short-term work), suitable personal suspension equipment must be provided and used. [*Construction (Health, Safety and Welfare) Regulations 1996 (SI 1996 No 1592), Reg 6(3)(c)*].

See also the discussion on the preference for personal suspension over means of arresting falls in W9003 and W9010 above.

### Requirements relating to personal suspension equipment

W9015 Personal suspension equipment must be:

(*a*) of suitable and sufficient strength, having regard to the work being carried out and the load, including any person it is intended to bear;

(*b*) securely attached to a structure or plant, and the structure or plant must be suitable and of sufficient strength and stability to support the equipment and load;

(*c*) installed or attached so as to prevent uncontrolled movement of equipment; and

(*d*) suitable and sufficient steps must be taken to prevent any person from falling or slipping from personal suspension equipment.

[*Construction (Health, Safety and Welfare) Regulations 1996 (SI 1996 No 1592), Sch 3*].

### Means of arresting falls

W9016 Where compliance with guard-rail, toe-board, working platform or personal suspension equipment requirements is not reasonably practicable, suitable and sufficient means for arresting falls must be (i) provided, and (ii) used. [*Construction (Health, Safety and Welfare) Regulations 1996 (SI 1996 No 1592), Reg 6(3)(d)*].

Equipment provided for arresting falls must adhere to the following requirements:

(*a*) The equipment must be suitable and of sufficient strength to safely arrest the fall of any person liable to fall.

(*b*) The equipment must be securely attached to a structure or to a plant, and the structure or plant (and the means of attachment) must be suitable and of sufficient strength and stability to safely support the equipment and any person liable to fall.

(*c*) Suitable and sufficient steps must be taken to ensure, so far as is reasonably practicable, that in the event of a fall, equipment does not cause injury to a person.

[*Construction (Health, Safety and Welfare) Regulations 1996 (SI 1996 No 1592), Sch 4*].

See also the discussion on the preference for personal suspension over means of arresting falls in W9003 and W9010 above.

### Installation and erection of scaffolds, personal suspension equipment and fall-arresting devices

W9017 Installation and erection of any scaffold, personal suspension equipment or fall-arresting devices, or substantial addition or alteration thereto (not including personal attachment of any equipment or fall-arresting devices to a person for whose safety such equipment or device is provided) must be carried out under the supervision of a competent person. [*Construction (Health, Safety and Welfare)*

*Regulations 1996 (SI 1996 No 1592), Reg 6(8)*]. Training to CITB standards in fall arrest safety equipment is now available. Guidance on the use of fall arrest equipment during the erection, dismantling and alteration of scaffolding is available from Construction Industry Publications, 60 New Coventry Road, Sheldon, Birmingham B26 3AY (tel: 0121 722 8200).

## Ladders

W9018    Owing to a growing number of fatalities and serious injuries to workers involving the use of ladders, ladders can no longer be used as:

(*a*)    a place of work, or

(*b*)    a means of access or egress, to or from a place of work, unless it is reasonable to do so, having regard to:

— the nature of work and the duration of work, and

— the risk to the safety of any person at work arising from the use of a ladder.

[*Construction (Health, Safety and Welfare) Regulations 1996 (SI 1996 No 1592), Reg 6(5)*].

Ladders must be:

(i)    of suitable and sufficient strength for their intended purpose;

(ii)    so erected as to avoid displacement;

(iii)    (where they are of three metres in height or more), secured, so far as is practicable, and where not practicable, a person must be positioned at the foot of the ladder to prevent it slipping during use (see further the case of *Boyle v Kodak Ltd [1969] 2 AER 439*, where an experienced painter failed to secure a ladder, contrary to the *Building (Safety, Health and Welfare) Regulations 1948, Reg 29* and was injured);

(iv)    (where used as a means of access between places of work), sufficiently secured to prevent slipping and/or falling.

In addition, ladders must also:

(v)    (where the top of the ladder is used as a means of access to another level), extend to a sufficient height above the level to which it gives access, so as to provide a safe handhold (unless a suitable alternative handhold is provided);

(vi)    (where a ladder or run of ladders rises vertically 9 metres or more above its base), be provided, where practicable, with a safe landing area or rest platform at suitable intervals;

(vii)    be erected on surfaces which are stable and firm, of sufficient strength, and of suitable composition safely to support the ladder and its load.

[*Construction (Health, Safety and Welfare) Regulations 1996 (SI 1996 No 1592), Sch 5*].

(For practical safety criteria in the use of ladders, see also C8066 CONSTRUCTION AND BUILDING OPERATIONS.)

## Maintenance of fall-preventative equipment

W9019     All scaffolds, working platforms, toe-boards, guard-rails, personal suspension equipment, fall-arresting devices and ladders must be properly maintained. [*Construction (Health, Safety and Welfare) Regulations 1996 (SI 1996 No 1592), Reg 6(7)*].

## Fragile materials

W9020     Suitable and sufficient steps must be taken to prevent any person falling through any fragile material. [*Construction (Health, Safety and Welfare) Regulations 1996 (SI 1996 No 1592), Reg 7(1)*]. In particular:

(*a*)     no person must pass or work on or from fragile material, through which he would be liable to fall 2 metres (or more), unless suitable and sufficient platforms, coverings or other similar means of support are provided and used so that the weight of any person so passing or working is supported by such supports;

(*b*)     no person must pass or work near fragile materials through which he would be liable to fall 2 metres (or more), unless suitable and sufficient guard-rails or coverings are provided and used to prevent any person working or passing from falling; and

(*c*)     in the above cases, prominent warning notices must be affixed to the place where the material is located.

[*Construction (Health, Safety and Welfare) Regulations 1996 (SI 1996 No 1592), Reg 7(2)*].

For the possible effect of such notices, see OCCUPIERS' LIABILITY.)

HSE are particularly concerned about reducing the risk from fragile materials and consider that designers, having regard to their duty to avoid or reduce risk under the *Construction (Design and Management Regulations 1994*, should not specify them. To assist designers they have agreed standards for strength and durability with manufacturers' representatives. (See Advisory Committee for Roofwork Material Standards: ACR (M) 001: 2000, available from The Fibre Cement Manufacturers' Association, Ghyll House Cock Road, Colton, Stowmarket IP14 4QA, Tel: 01449 781 577.)

## Falling objects

W9021     With relation to this hazard the Regulations require:

(*a*)     that in order to prevent danger to any person, suitable and sufficient steps must be taken to prevent, so far as is reasonably practicable, the fall of any material or object (e.g. the provision of working platforms or guard-rails etc.) [*Construction (Health, Safety and Welfare) Regulations 1996 (SI 1996 No 1592), Reg 8(1)*];

(*b*)     where compliance is not reasonably practicable, suitable and sufficient steps must be taken to prevent any person being struck by any falling material or object likely to cause injury (e.g. the provision of a covered traffic route or roadway) [*Construction (Health, Safety and Welfare) Regulations 1996 (SI 1996 No 1592), Reg 8(3)*];

(*c*)     that no material or object must be thrown or tipped from a height, where it is likely to cause injury [*Construction (Health, Safety and Welfare) Regulations 1996 (SI 1996 No 1592), Reg 8(4)*]; and (*d*) that materials or equipment must be so stored as to prevent danger to any person from:

    (i) collapse,

    (ii) overturning, or

    (iii) unintentional movement of such materials and equipment [*Construction (Health, Safety and Welfare) Regulations 1996 (SI 1996 No 1592), Reg 8(5)*].

### Inspection of working platforms etc.

W9022    Working platforms and personal suspension equipment must be inspected by a competent person:

(*a*) before being taken into use for the first time;

(*b*) after any substantial addition, dismantling or other alteration;

(*c*) after any event likely to have affected its strength or stability; and

(*d*) at regular intervals not exceeding seven days.

[*Construction (Health, Safety and Welfare) Regulations 1996 (SI 1996 No 1592), Reg 29(1), Sch 7*].

Also, the employer or person who controls the way that construction work is done by anyone using a scaffold must ensure that it is stable and complies with the safeguards required by the Regulations before it is used by such persons for the first time. [*Construction (Health, Safety and Welfare) Regulations 1996 (SI 1996 No 1592), Reg 29(2)*].

Where a person may fall more than two metres, the competent person must make a report within the working period in which the inspection is completed. The report must contain the following:

— the name and address of the person for whom the inspection was carried out;

— the location of the place of work inspected;

— a description of what was inspected;

— date and time of the inspection;

— details of anything that could cause risk;

— details of any consequent action;

— details of further action considered necessary;

— name and position of the person making the report.

[*Construction (Health, Safety and Welfare) Regulations 1996 (SI 1996 No 1592), Reg 30(1), (5), Sch 8*].

The report must be provided within 24 hours to the person for whom it was prepared. It must be kept on site until completion and for a further three months at the office of the person for whom it was prepared; in addition, it must be available to an inspector at all reasonable times and copies or extracts must be sent to an inspector if required. [*Construction (Health, Safety and Welfare) Regulations 1996 (SI 1996 No 1592), Reg 30(2)–(4)*].

No report is required on a mobile tower scaffold unless it has remained in the same place for seven days or more [*Construction (Health, Safety and Welfare) Regulations*

*1996 (SI 1996 No 1592), Reg 30(6)(a)]* and only report of an addition, dismantling or alteration (see *(b)* above) is required in any period of 24 hours. *[Construction (Health, Safety and Welfare) Regulations 1996 (SI 1996 No 1592), Reg 30(6)(b)].*

## Practical guidelines

**W9023**     Construction or extensive maintenance work will probably entail risks both to those carrying it out and to the ordinary worker. These risks must be assessed and any existing precautions reviewed *[Management of Health and Safety at Work Regulations 1999 (SI 1999 No 3242), Reg 3].* The *appropriate action should also be taken according to Schedule 1* of the 1999 Regulations *[Management of Health and Safety at Work Regulations 1999 (SI 1999 No 3242), Reg 4].*

Where work must be done at heights, suitable access equipment or other safeguards must be provided and attention paid to the following:

*(a)*     Who is in control and what is the amount of co-ordination necessary, i.e. have the responsibilities of the occupier, employer and contractor been clearly defined?

*(b)*     What level of supervision and training is required with regard to the type of hazard and level of risk? (including selection of the appropriate method, and the use of approved equipment).

*(c)*     What other considerations are necessary, e.g. is there any danger to works employees from the contractors' operations, or vice-versa?

Many of these matters may seem obvious, but lives have been lost because the contractor or maintenance worker did not appreciate the fragile nature of a roof or the fact that it had been weakened owing to the nature of the process. These considerations point to the need for careful preparation and planning of such work to ensure that there is proper co-ordination and co-operation *[Management of Health and Safety at Work Regulations 1999 (SI 1999 No 3242), Regs 11 and 12].* The contractor must be aware of any risks from the operations on the premises that might affect his workforce and of the precautions that the occupier is taking to control them. Furthermore, the occupier must ensure that comprehensible information about this has been passed on to the construction workers. *[Management of Health and Safety at Work Regulations 1999 (SI 1999 No 3242), Reg 12(1), (3)].* The contractor must be provided with the names of the relevant persons who have been appointed to ensure evacuation in an emergency, while the occupier must take all reasonable steps to ensure that the contractor's employees themselves know who is to implement their own evacuation. *[Management of Health and Safety at Work Regulations 1999 (SI 1999 No 3242), Reg 12(4)].*

Where the *Construction (Design and Management) Regulations 1994 (SI 1994 No 3140 as amended by SI 2000 No 2380)* apply, the occupier (as client) must give the planning supervisor information about the premises. This information should be taken into account by the designers in the avoidance or reduction of risk and in the subsequent preparation of the health and safety plan. It is important to note that this information must include anything that the client could find out by making reasonable enquiries. For instance, the obvious risks to construction workers of falling should not obscure the possible danger that work at heights may disturb any asbestos that might be there – it should not be forgotten that asbestos is a greater cause of death in the construction trades than falling.

Since the inception of the *Management of Health and Safety at Work Regulations 1999* and *Construction (Design and Management) Regulations 1994* (as amended), larger firms should have well-established systems to deal with these matters, including the appointment of competent principal and other contractors. Smaller firms, or those that do not regularly commission construction work, while they are entitled to the advice of the planning supervisor where the *Construction (Design and Management) Regulations 1994* apply, may care to consider the following as appropriate when selecting contractors or in subsequent dealings with them:

(*a*)   the time for the tendering contractor to respond to the initial (pre-tender) stage of the health and safety plan;

(*b*)   the time for the contractor's own investigation of health and safety matters (e.g. a survey) where the Regulations do not apply;

(*c*)   the response to the significant risks – knowledge of precautions; possession of advisory booklets etc; any safety training of managers and supervisors; signs that the impact of risks arising from the operations has been appreciated;

(*d*)   how the contractor checks his health and safety performance;

(*e*)   how staff (including casuals) engaged for this job are or will be trained;

(*f*)   the protective clothing and equipment that will be provided (see PERSONAL PROTECTIVE EQUIPMENT);

(*g*)   the resources to be devoted to health and safety management (ask to see the person who will actually do the managing);

(*h*)   the arrangements for necessary liaison throughout the job (not forgetting the contractor's arrangements for delivering file information to the planning supervisor);

(*j*)   potential risks associated with adverse weather conditions, such as a sudden downpour, dense fog, snow lying on a roof or high winds; in particular, the responsibility for calling operators off a roof or high-level position given adverse weather conditions;

(*k*)   the provision of safety harnesses and belts, including the necessary anchorage points for them, or safety nets in certain situations (see W9032 below).

In addition the occupier/employer should ensure that his maintenance supervisor or clerk of works, etc. has access to the information contained in the health and safety at work guidance/advisory booklets. He may also provide simple check lists to cover his own operations.

HSE has published an important new guidance booklet on safety in roof work. The booklet, the latest in HSE's revised guidance series for the construction industry, replaces an earlier version first published in 1987.

The new guidance is relevant not only to contractors and others who actually carry out work on roofs, but also to those who have an influence on workers' health and safety, such as planning supervisors, clients, designers and manufacturers.

It carries forward existing, well-known messages on basic safety precautions, such as the fundamental need for edge protection. Effective fall arrest equipment is essential during industrial roofing projects, HSE's preferred method being properly installed and maintained safety netting. The guidance also contains important new material on:

—   the use of safety nets, particularly in industrial roofing. HSE is convinced that there is a substantial role for a greater use of safety nets in industrial roofing. Although they are not the only way of arresting falls, it is inspectors' consistent experience that harnesses, for example, are frequently not provided or worn. Where they are used, more often than not they are used incorrectly;

—    the role of designers in creating roofs that are safe to build and subsequently to maintain. Designers can often eliminate risks by designing them out at source, but they need to understand the problems faced by contractors to realise these benefits. If not, they could be breaking the law, as well as helping to perpetuate one of the biggest workplace killers. The *Construction (Design and Management) Regulations 1994* require designers to have regard to health and safety risks for construction and maintenance workers in their designs. Their role in reducing the presence of fragile materials in roofs is clearly highlighted in the guidance as the most effective area in which they can contribute to improving health and safety;

—    the role of clients in providing relevant information ensuring that adequate resources are allocated for safety; and

—    the risks from fragile roofing material and how to manage them.

'*Health and safety in roof work*' (ref HSG33), price £8.50, is available from HSE Books, PO Box 1999, Sudbury, Suffolk CO10 2WA.

# Windows and window cleaning – all workplaces

**W9024**    Window cleaning hazards occur principally in high-rise properties such as office blocks and residential tower blocks. These contain vast areas of glass which should be maintained in a clean state on both inner and outer surfaces. Cleaning the interior surfaces generally presents no difficulties, though accidents have arisen from the unsafe practice of window cleaners reaching up to clean windows from step ladders which have not been securely placed on highly-polished office floors and, in consequence, falling through the glass windows and injuring themselves. Moreover, if windows can be cleaned from inside, company safety rules and procedures should prevent employees going out onto sills in cases where a window/windows, if in proper working order, can be cleaned from inside. Failure to operate this rule can involve the employer in both criminal and civil liability. Equally important, if not more so, the customer or client must ensure that his windows are in proper working order and regularly inspected and maintained, if they are capable of being cleaned from inside (*King v Smith [1995] ICR 339* (see W9035 below)).

It is the cleaning of outer surfaces that can present serious hazards if proper precautions are not taken, and this part of the section is concerned with the duties of workplace occupiers in relation to windows and window-cleaning on their premises (see W9032 below). In addition, liability of employers at common law in relation to window cleaning personnel is also covered (see W9035 below), and methods of protection for window cleaners as well as methods of cleaning (see W9037–W9043 below).

## Statutory requirements relevant to windows in all workplaces (except construction sites) – the Workplace (Health, Safety and Welfare) Regulations 1992 (SI 1992 No 3004)

*Composition of windows*

**W9025**    Every window (and every transparent/translucent surface in a door or gate) where necessary for reasons of health or safety must be:

(a)     of safety material (e.g. polycarbonates, glass blocks, glass which breaks safely (laminated glass) or ordinary annealed glass meeting certain minimal criteria),

(b)     protected against breakage of transparent/translucent material (e.g. by a screen or barrier); and

(c)     appropriately (and conspicuously) marked so as to make it apparent (e.g. with coloured lines/patterns).

[*Workplace (Health, Safety and Welfare) Regulations 1992, Reg 14*].

HSC in October 1996 approved a change to its publication 'Workplace health, safety and welfare', the Approved Code of Practice (ACoP) which supports the *Workplace (Health, Safety and Welfare) Regulations 1992 (SI 1992 No 3004)*. The change became necessary as the HSC acknowledged that there was confusion in the business world on what the law says about glazing in existing workplaces that became subject to the *Workplace Regulations* on 1 January 1996. The change relates to workplace glazing and now reads:

> *'In assessing whether it is necessary, for reasons of health and safety, for transparent or translucent surfaces in doors, gates, walls and partitions to be of a safety material or be adequately protected against breakage, particular attention should be paid to the following cases:*
>
> *(a)     in doors and gates, and door and gate side panels, where any part of the transparent or translucent surface is at shoulder height or below;*
>
> *(b)     in windows, walls and partitions, where any part of the transparent or translucent surface is at waist level or below, except in glasshouses where people there will be likely to be aware of the presence of glazing and avoid contact.*
>
> *This paragraph does not apply to narrow panes up to 250mm wide measured between glazing beads.'*

*Position and use of windows*

**W9026**     No window, skylight or ventilator, capable of being opened, must be likely to be:

(a)     opened,

(b)     closed,

(c)     adjusted, or

(d)     in a position when open,

so as to expose the operator to risk of injury. [*Workplace (Health, Safety and Welfare) Regulations 1992 (SI 1992 No 3004), Reg 15*].

In other words, it must be possible to reach openable windows safely; and window poles or a stable platform should be kept ready nearby. Window controls should be positioned so that people are not likely to fall out of or through the window. And where there is a danger of falling from a height, devices should prevent the window opening too far. In order to prevent people colliding with them, the bottom edge of opening windows should generally be 800 millimetres above floor level (unless there is a barrier to stop or cushion falls). Staircase windows should have controls accessible from a safe foothold, and window controls beyond normal reach should be gear-operated or accessible by pole (see BS 8213 and GS 25 1983). Manually operated window controls should not be higher than 2 metres above floor level.

*Cleaning windows*

W9027   All windows and skylights in workplaces must be designed and constructed to allow safe cleaning. [*Workplace (Health, Safety and Welfare) Regulations 1992 (SI 1992 No 3004), Reg 16(1)*]. If they cannot be cleaned from the ground (or similar surface), the building should be fitted with suitable safety devices to be able to comply with the general safety requirement (see W9026). [*Workplace (Health, Safety and Welfare) Regulations 1992 (SI 1992 No 3004), Reg 16(2)*].

**Civil liability in connection with fall-preventive regulations**

W9028   Because regulations give rise to civil liability when breached, even if silent (which the 1992 Regulations are), if breach leads to injury/damage, an action for breach of statutory duty would lie (see further INTRODUCTION).

**Window cleaners as employees or self-employed contractors**

W9029   Where window cleaners are employees of a contract window cleaning company, the company as employer owes a duty to its employees, under *HSWA 1974, s 2(1)* and *(2)*, to provide a safe method of work, and instruction and training in job safety, e.g. provision of information as to how to tackle the job and the use of safety harnesses etc. All workplaces, buildings, windows and skylights should be fitted with suitable devices to allow the window or skylight to be cleaned safely, to comply with the *Workplace (Health, Safety and Welfare) Regulations 1992 (SI 1992 No 3004), Reg 16* (see W9027 above).

Alternatively, window cleaners may be self-employed. In such cases they themselves commit an offence if they fail to provide themselves with adequate protection, e.g. safety harnesses, because of the requirement of *HSWA 1974, s 3(2)* (see INTRODUCTION).

# Who provides protection to window cleaners on high-rise properties?

W9030   Where multi-storey properties are concerned, the duty of protection may fall upon one of three parties (or, at least, there may be division of responsibility between them):

(*a*)   the contract window cleaning firm or the self-employed window cleaner;

(*b*)   the building owner;

(*c*)   the building occupier or business operator (i.e. the building occupier who is not the owner of the building).

**Contract window cleaning firms and self-employed window cleaners**

W9031   Both the contract window cleaning firm and the self-employed window cleaner have a statutory duty to provide protection (under *HSWA 1974, ss 2(1)(2), 3(2)*) and the employer/occupier, under the *Workplace (Health, Safety and Welfare) Regulations 1992 (SI 1992 No 3004), Regs 15 and 16* (see W9026, W9027 above). This applies to contract cleaning companies (not just of windows) in respect of equipment left on the occupier's premises and used by the occupier's employees, even though the contract cleaning company is not actually working (*R v Mara [1987] 1 WLR 87* where one of the occupier's employees was electrocuted when using polisher/scrubber, which had a defective cable, to clean loading bay on a Saturday afternoon, when cleaning company did not operate its undertaking. It was held that the director of the cleaning company was in breach of *HSWA 1974, s 3(1)*). In addition, if an accident arose from the work, the window cleaning company could, as employer, be liable at common law, if it failed to take reasonable care and exercise control. There is no action for damages for breach of statutory duty under *HSWA 1974* (see EMPLOYERS' DUTIES TO THEIR EMPLOYEES). In this connection, any employer, when prosecuted under the 1974 Act or sued at common law would have to show that he had clearly instructed employees not to clean windows where no proper safety precautions had been taken, in order to avoid liability. Also, window cleaning companies would have to satisfy themselves, before instructing employees to clean windows, as to what safety precautions (if any) were provided, and that, if necessary, employees were told to test for defective sashes (see further *King v Smith* at W9035 below).

## Division of responsibility between window cleaning firm or self-employed window cleaner and building owner or occupier (i.e. employer)

W9032    Although a window cleaner, whether an employee or self-employed, would be expected to have his own safety harness, it would be up to the contractor to provide fixing points for harness attachment. The responsibility for provision of harness anchorage points (e.g. safe rings, i.e. eyebolts) will be with either the building owner or building occupier (business operator) whose windows are being cleaned. Two situations are possible here:

(*a*)    the building occupier is the owner of the building; or

(*b*)    the building occupier (as is usual) is not the owner of the building.

*Where the building occupier is the building owner*

W9033    In this situation, the window cleaning contract is placed by the building occupier/owner and the latter, having control of the building, is therefore responsible under *HSWA 1974, s 3(1)* and the *Workplace (Health, Safety and Welfare) Regulations 1992 (SI 1992 No 3004), Regs 15 and 16*, and at common law (and under the contract) to protect window cleaning personnel on his premises. Courts may also be prepared to imply terms into such contracts that such premises be reasonably safe to work on.

This position (that is, where the building owner and the building occupier are the same person) is not, however, the norm. On the contrary, the normal position is that the building owner and business operator are separate persons or companies.

*Where the building occupier (that is, the employer) is not the building owner*

W9034    Given that the employee or self-employed window cleaner must provide his own safety harness (see W9032 above), the responsibility of providing a safe ring for harness attachment lies with the building owner or occupier. More precisely, where the building owner employs a contract window cleaning firm, then it is up to the building owner (*inter alia*, as an implied contractual term) to make safety anchorage provision. He cannot escape from this contractual obligation owing to the strictures of the *Unfair Contract Terms Act 1977* (see OCCUPIERS' LIABILITY). He would also be required to do so by virtue of *HSWA 1974, s 3(1)* – the duty towards persons working on premises who are not one's employees (see EMPLOYERS' DUTIES TO THEIR EMPLOYEES).

This is the exception, not the norm. Generally, window cleaning contracts are placed by building occupiers (business operators), and so in the great majority of cases it is the *building occupier* who is responsible under *HSWA 1974, s 3(1)* and under the *Workplace (Health, Safety and Welfare) Regulations 1992 (SI 1992 No 3004)*, under the express or implied terms of a contract, and/or at common law (should an accident occur) for ensuring the safety of window cleaning personnel. Thus, the building occupier would have to provide a safety ring for harness attachment. A problem could arise here if the building owner refused permission for such attachment – resort to legal action would be, it is thought, the only ultimate solution. And occupiers should be under no illusion that failure to provide safety anchorage points can (and will, in all probability) result in the imposition of heavy fines! (By way of consolation, however, the cost of making available certain types of protection to window cleaners may often be less than the penalty incurred for failing to provide it.)

## Common law liability to window cleaners

**W9035**   At common law (and under *HSWA 1974, s 2(2)*), an employer must provide and maintain a safe system of work. This extends to provision of safe appliances, tools etc. and giving information/training on how to carry out tasks safely (see EMPLOYERS' DUTIES TO THEIR EMPLOYEES). Nevertheless, there is a division of responsibility between employer and occupier of premises where a window cleaner is working. The former, the employer, must see that the employee is provided with a safe method of work; but this did not extend to defects in the premises (e.g. window sills) of the occupier causing injury to employees (*General Cleaning Contractors Ltd v Christmas [1952] 2 AER 1110* where an experienced employee window cleaner was injured whilst cleaning windows at a club. There were no fittings on the building to which safety belts could have been attached. A defective sash dropped onto the employee's hand, causing him to lose his handhold and fall. It was held that the employer was liable; he should have provided wedges to prevent sashes from falling and also instructed employees to test for dangerous sashes). Modern conventional wisdom suggests, however, that an employer does not provide a safe system of work if a window cleaner has to clean windows from an outside window sill, which are capable of being cleaned from inside if they are in proper working order. It is incumbent on the customer-occupier to ensure that such windows are in a good state of maintenance and proper working order. (In the case of *King v Smith [1995] ICR 339*, a window cleaner was injured when he fell from a sill on a local authority building. The court held both employer and customer liable, the former 70 per cent, the latter 30 per cent.)

Much of the earlier common law liability will, in all probability, be replaced in due course by case law arising in connection with breach of duty under the *Workplace (Health, Safety and Welfare) Regulations 1992 (SI 1992 No 3004)*, where such duties are strict.

In practice it is important that owners and occupiers of buildings assure themselves that the proposed method of cleaning the windows by the cleaning contractor is safe and in compliance with *Reg 16* of the 1992 Regulations, and the owners/occupiers should verify that the agreed system of work is being followed by the contractor's employees, or by a self-employed contractor, as the case may be.

## Accidents to window cleaners – typical causes

**W9036**   (*a*)   The most common fatal accident is that of a cleaner falling from an external window sill, ledge, or similar part of a building, due to loss of balance as the result of a slip, or the breakage of part of a sill, or the failure of a pull handle or part of a building being used as a handhold.

(*b*)     Other fatalities have been due to falls through fragile roofing where cleaners have relied upon the roof for support when cleaning or glazing windows, or gaining access for such work, and falls from suspended scaffolds or boat-swain's chairs due to failure of the equipment.

(*c*)     Falls from ladders, which account for a substantial proportion of injuries, are occasionally fatal; they include falls due to the unexpected movement of a ladder such as the top sliding sideways or the foot slipping outwards, failure of part of the ladder, and falls when stepping on or off it.

## Methods of protection for window cleaners

W9037     (*a*)     If the building was designed with totally self-pivoting windows, this is probably the ideal situation in terms of safeguarding the window cleaner. Note the qualified duty in this regard on the building designer in the *Construction (Design and Management) Regulations 1994 (SI 1994 No 3140* as amended by *SI 2000 No 2380), Reg 13(2)(a)*. However, a wide variety of window designs are used in buildings – sliding sashes, hinged casements and fixed lights. All require a slightly different technique for cleaning.

(*b*)     Ordinary ladders are not suitable (and should not be used) for multi-storey properties of more than two storeys.

(*c*)     Hydraulic platforms are effective but work can only safely proceed at a relatively slow rate; moreover, their maximum reach is sometimes limited, and they cause nuisance to passers-by.

(*d*)     Gondola cages are used on high-rise buildings with good results, but are of little use for low and medium-rise blocks. They can also be dangerous to window cleaning personnel, as they are inclined to sway about in high winds. Moreover, this method of window cleaning is expensive.

Probably the most practical and economical method of complying with legal requirements for the safety of window cleaning personnel is provision of safe ring/harness combinations. However, note the presumption in favour of collective over individual precautions that is contained within the *Management of Health and Safety at Work Regulations 1999 (SI 1999 No 3242), Reg 4* and *Sch 1* and the similar duty imposed upon building designers by the *Construction (Design and Management) Regulations 1994 (SI 1994 No 3140* as amended by *SI 2000 No 2380), Reg 13(2)(a)(iii)*. These bolts can be installed rapidly, without damaging the building structurally, and without impairing its aesthetic appearance. Such bolts must, however, comply with British Standard BS 970: 1980 Part 1 (high tensile carbon steel) or Part 4 (premium stainless steel); also the whole anchorage system must comply with BS 5845: 1980.

Safety rings should be installed by a specialist company operating in the field. In this way a window cleaner can clip his harness onto the ring and step onto the window ledge and clean the window safely. After proper installation, anchorage points should be professionally examined from time to time to ensure that they remain firm and safe.

Another (relatively inexpensive) device for use in cleaning outer surfaces on high-rise office blocks and industrial multi-storey properties is the new mobile safety anchor. The cost is often shared between the contract window cleaning company (or self-employed window cleaner) and the building owner or occupier.

Suspended scaffolds are commonly used for window cleaning in high-rise buildings. Guidance on the design, construction and use of suspended scaffolds is given in:

(i)    HSE guidance PM Machinery 30 'Suspended access equipment' (1983);

(ii)   BS 6037: 1981 'Code of Practice for permanently installed suspended access equipment'; and

(iii)  BS 5974: 1982 'Code of practice for temporarily installed suspended scaffolds and access equipment'; and

(iv)   GS 25 'Prevention of falls to window cleaners' (HSE Books).

Whether a suspended scaffold is used, either permanently or temporarily installed, it is essential to ensure that:

—    safe means of access to and egress from the cradle are provided;

—    properly planned inspection and maintenance procedures for each installation are carried out;

—    there are instructions that work shall be carried out only from the cradle; and

—    operatives are properly trained in the use of the cradle.

Where power-driven equipment is used, operatives should be familiar with:

—    relevant instructions from the manufacturer or supplier;

—    any limitations on use, for example, due to wind conditions or length of suspension rope;

—    the correct operation of the controls, particularly those affecting the raising or lowering of the cradle;

—    the safety devices fitted to the equipment; and

—    the procedure if the equipment does not work properly.

Precautions against the failure of a cradle having a single suspension rope at each end are described in BS 6037 (Clause 14.3), for example, the provision at each suspension point of a second rope (safety rope) and an automatic device to support the platform. In some cases, protection against suspension rope failure at the cradle end can be obtained by fitting a manually operated clamping device.

Travelling ladders are permanently installed in some buildings. In other cases a ladder can be suspended from a specially designed frame on the roof. In such cases, the cleaner should wear a safety harness or belt, attached to an automatic fall arresting device on the side of the ladder, and have a safe place at which he can step on or off the ladder.

## Cleaning methods

W9038    Window glass can normally be cleaned satisfactorily using plain water, liberally applied, followed by leather off and polishing with a scrim. The use of squeegees is on the increase and, although they cannot safely be used by a person standing on a window sill, they can be safely operated from the ground. Very dirty glazing in factories, foundries or railway premises may need treatment with ammonia or strong soda solution; and hydrofluoric acid in diluted solution may be necessary when cleaning skylights or roof glazing which has remained uncleaned for a long time. Here the working area should be adequately sheeted to protect passers-by, and, in the case of roof glazing, the interior of the building should be protected against penetrating drops. Stringent personal precautions are necessary when handling acids (e.g. eye shields, rubber gloves, boots (see further PERSONAL PROTECTIVE EQUIPMENT), which should only be used as a last resort) and such work should only be carried out by specialist firms. Hydrofluoric acid should never be used on vertical glazing.

## Frequency of cleaning

W9039    The recommended frequencies of external and internal cleaning, as dictated by current good practice, are as follows:

| | |
|---|---|
| Shops | weekly |
| Banks | twice a month |
| Offices/hotels | monthly |
| Hospitals | monthly |
| Factories – light industry | monthly |
| Heavy industry | every two months |
| Schools | every two months |

## Access for cleaning

W9040    There are three ways in which windows can be cleaned, affecting access:

(*a*)    external cleaning (with access exclusively from the outside);

(*b*)    internal cleaning;

(*c*)    a mixed system, whereby windows accessible from the inside are cleaned internally, and the rest are cleaned externally, access being through the opening lights of the facade.

Moreover, in factories and other industrial concerns windows are, not infrequently, obstructed by machines, reflecting in-plant lay-out at initial design – a matter for safety officers and safety representatives when carrying out safety audits (see JOINT CONSULTATION – SAFETY REPRESENTATIVES AND SAFETY COMMITTEES).

### *Cleaning from the outside*

W9041    Assuming windows cannot be cleaned from inside the workplace or building, as a matter of design, there should be safe external access in the form of permanent walkways, with guard-rails or other protective devices to prevent cleaners (and other users) from falling down. Such walkways should be at least 400 millimetres wide and guard-rails at least 900 millimetres above the walkway, with a knee rail. Safety of window cleaners is best guaranteed by installation of totally self-pivoting windows (see W9036 above). However, a wide variety of window designs is currently in use in buildings – sliding sashes, fixed lights and hinged casements, all requiring different cleaning techniques.

#### (*a*) *Cleaning from ladders*

Portable ladders, aluminium or timber, should rest on a secure base and reasonably practicable precautions, to avoid sliding outwards at the base and sideways at the top, should be taken to:

(i)   secure fixing at the top to preclude lateral or outward movement, e.g. by fastening to an eyebolt/ringbolt;

(ii)  fasten rung to eyebolt/ringbolt or other anchorage point (see further W9037 above) at a height of 2 metres;

(iii) failing this, a person should be stationed at the base in order to steady the ladder or an approved base anchoring device should be used.

The '1 out 4 up' rule (for ladders) suggests that ladders are safest when placed at an angle of 75° to the horizontal; lesser angles indicate that the ladder is more likely to slide outwards at the base. Moreover, window cleaners (and other users) should avoid:

—   overreaching (as this can unbalance the ladder);

—   proximity with moving objects either above or below (e.g. overhead travelling crane or vehicles operating in the workplace or delivering to the workplace);

—   positioning near to vats or tanks containing dangerous fluids/substances or near to unguarded machinery or exposed electrical equipment. (As for *in situ* travelling ladders, see W9037 above.)

*(b) Safety harnesses*

In the absence of other, more satisfactory means of cleaning windows, e.g. suspended scaffolds, hydraulic platforms etc., the other reasonably practicable alternative is a safety harness. However, this has the shortcoming that, if a window cleaner falls, he is still likely to be injured. For this reason, harnesses and safety belts must be up to 'free fall' distance (that is, the distance preceding arrest of fall) of, at least,

(i)   2 metres – safety harness, or

(ii)  0.6 metres – safety belt.

(BS 1397: 'Specification for industrial safety belts, harnesses etc.').

Because some walls may not be strong enough or otherwise suitable, inspection by a competent person should always precede selection of permanent fixed anchorage points. Permanent fixed anchorages should comply with BS 5845 (see W9037 above) and be periodically inspected and tested for exposure to elements. Failing this, temporary anchorage or even mobile anchorage, given the same built-in safeguards, may suffice (see W9037 above).

*Cleaning from the inside*

W9042

Outer surfaces by design should be able to be cleaned from inside the workplace without use of steps or stepladders. Also, size of aperture and weight of window is relevant. Different types of windows present different dangers; for example, in the case of reversible pivoted/projecting windows, a safety catch is necessary to maintain the window in a fully reversed position; in the case of louvres, there should be sufficient space for a cleaner's hand to pass between the blades, which should incorporate a positive hold–open position to avoid the danger of blowing shut (see BS 8213, Part 1 1991: 'Safety in use and during cleaning of windows').

Maximum safe reach to clean glass immediately beneath an open window is 610 millimetres downwards (that is, 2' 0"), 510 millimetres upwards (1' 8") and 560 millimetres sideways (1' 10"). Horizontally or vertically pivoted windows, reversible for cleaning purposes, are probably the best safety option (see W9037 above). Given that windows should be accessible without resort to a ladder, short-of-stature window cleaners should invariably make use of cleaning aids to reach further up glazing panels. Built-in furniture should never be placed near windows to obstruct access; nor should blinds or pelmets inhibit the operation of windows and window controls.

*Mixed system of cleaning*

W9043     Where window cleaners clean windows externally without facilities for ladders or cradles, the building designer should appreciate that the cleaner's safety depends on good foothold and good handhold. The practice of cleaners having to balance, like trapeze artists, on narrow sills or transoms, is patently dangerous. Owing to the frequency of failure of apparently safe and adequate footholds and handholds, it is imperative that suitable and convenient safety bolts or fixings, to which the cleaner may fix his safety belt, should be provided. Where possible, the safety eyebolt should be fitted on the inside of the wall. Moreover, internal bolts are not weakened by the weather. Where safety eyebolts are fitted to the window frame, architects should pay particular regard at design stage to the fixing of the frame to the building structure, so as to ensure that fixings can withstand the extra load, imposed on the frame, in the event of the cleaner falling.

Where glazing areas are incorporated in roofs, provision should be made for cleaning both sides of the glass, and, where possible, walkways should be provided, both externally and internally. Internal walkways can also be designed to serve for maintenance of electric lighting installations. Where walkways are not feasible, access by permanent travelling ladders should be considered.

The *Construction (Design and Management) Regulations 1994* place specific responsibility upon designers to ensure that their designs avoid or reduce health and safety risks in maintenance (including window cleaning) (see C8005 CONSTRUCTION AND BUILDING OPERATIONS). Practical advice for designers on this subject, and on cleaning buildings in general, will be found in CIRIA report 166, *CDM Regulations – work sector guidance for designers*, at section D6.

# Working Time

## Introduction

*The Working Time Regulations 1998 (SI 1998 No 1833)* (the Regulations) came into force on 1 October 1998. This is the first piece of English law which sets out specific rules governing working hours, rest breaks and holiday entitlement for the majority of workers (as opposed to those in specialised industries). The Regulations implement the provisions of the *Working Time Directive (93/104/EC)* and the *Young Workers Directive (94/33/EC)*. This chapter deals only with the Regulations as they govern adult workers, i.e. those aged 18 or over.

The Working Time Directive (the Directive) has led a fairly controversial life. It was adopted on 23 November 1993 as a health and safety measure under *Article 138* (formerly *118a*) of the *Treaty of Rome 1957*, requiring only a qualified majority, rather than a unanimous vote. As such, the UK Government, which was opposed to the Directive, was unable to avoid its impact. The UK Government challenged the Directive on the basis that it was not truly a health and safety measure and should, in fact, have been introduced under Article 100 as a social measure which would have required a unanimous vote. This argument was lost when, on 12 November 1996, the European Court of Justice upheld the status of the Directive as a health and safety measure. As a result, the UK Government was obliged to implement the Directive into national legislation by 23 November 1996. The Government published a consultative document and a set of draft Regulations in April 1998 and on 30 July the Regulations were laid before Parliament in their current form. On 1 October 1998, they came into force, and at the same time the DTI issued guidance to accompany the Regulations.

The Regulations (and guidance) were met with vociferous criticism from the business world. The government sought to address these concerns in 1999, just a year after the Regulations had become law. Following a limited consultation in July of 1999, amendments were tabled to two key areas of the Regulations (see below). The *Working Time Regulations 1999 (SI 1999 No 3372)* (which had the effect of amending the 1998 Regulations) became law on 17 December 1999. The 1999 Regulations also provided that the Secretary of State would publish information and advice concerning the operation of the Regulations. Thus, in March 2000, the DTI issued a second (more concise) version of its guidance, which contains many changes from the original. It is not known how much weight tribunals will attach to this publication, which does not have the force of law.

The stated purpose of the Working Time Directive, acknowledged by the European Court of Justice, is to lay down a minimum requirement for health and safety as regards the organisation of working time. This is, of course, significant to the extent that the English courts and tribunals will interpret the Regulations in accordance with the Directive by adopting the 'purposive' approach, which is now accepted under English law.

As of July 2000, there have been over 8000 cases lodged at Employment Tribunals under the Regulations, and at least a handful in the High Court. There have been very few reported cases, as only a few employment tribunal decisions have been appealed to the employment appeal tribunal. In only one case, has a question of interpretation of the UK Regulations been referred to the European Court of Justice (the *BECTU case*, see W10022). Accordingly, many of the cases referred to in this chapter are only first instance decisions. These are not, therefore, binding on other courts and tribunals but they serve to illustrate the tribunals' approach in the past.

The structure of the Regulations is to prescribe various limits and entitlements for workers and then to set out a sequence of exceptions and derogations from these provisions. The structure of this chapter will roughly follow that format.

# Definitions

W10002     *Regulation 2* sets out a number of basic concepts (some more familiar than others), which recur consistently and which underpin the legislation. These are as follows.

## Working time

W10003     Working time is defined, in relation to a worker, as:

(*a*)     any period during which he is working, *at his employer's disposal* and carrying out his activity or duties;

(*b*)     any period which he is receiving relevant training; and

(*c*)     any *additional* period which is to be treated as working time for the purposes of the Regulations under a relevant agreement (see W10006 below).

As was highlighted by the Labour Government's consultative document, this definition raises numerous uncertainties; for example, in relation to workers who are 'on call' or who operate under flexible working arrangements. The DTI, in the first version of their guidance to the Working Time Regulations took the fairly robust view that time when a worker is 'on call' but otherwise free to pursue their own activities would not be working time. Similarly if a worker was required to be at their place of work 'on call', but was sleeping though available to work if necessary, a worker would not be working and so the time spent asleep would not count as working time.

However, the Advocate General's opinion in the case of *SIMAP v Conselleria de Sanidad y Consumo de la Generalitat Valencia (C303/98)* has caused practitioners to exercise some caution in following the DTI's original advice and the DTI has rewritten their guidance so that it is now expressly silent on the point, pending the ECJ's ruling. The Advocate General suggests that time spent on call, in this case by doctors at health centres, is 'working time', provided the doctors are available and physically present. In addition, periods during which doctors are subject to the 'on-call' system, that is available to come in while being outside the health centre, but only for the time spent effectively exercising their professional responsibility, is working time. The ECJ's decision is awaited with interest.

The DTI has given examples of what it considers constitutes working time. In its latest guidance it states that 'time spent travelling outside normal working time' is not working time. This seems to address the difficult question of non-routine travel. For example, it has never been clear whether someone who is required to travel from London to Edinburgh on a Sunday, to be at a meeting in Edinburgh at 9am on Monday morning, can count that time as working time. The DTI's guidance would suggest that it would not be working time. In practice, however, it seems that it would depend on the facts.

It should be noted that the definition of working time can be clarified in a relevant agreement between the parties, but only by specifying any *additional* period which can be treated as working time. The relevant agreement cannot alter, in particular it cannot narrow, the absolute definition of working time.

## Worker

W10004    A worker is any individual who has entered into or works under (or where the employment has ceased), worked under:

(*a*)    a contract of employment; or

(*b*)    any other contract, whether express or implied and (if express) whether oral or in writing, whereby the individual undertakes to do or perform personally any work or services for another party to the contract whose status is not by virtue of the contract that of a client or customer of any profession or business undertaking carried on by the individual.

This definition is wider than just employees and covers any individuals who are carrying out work for an employer, unless they are genuinely self employed, in that the work amounts to a business activity carried out on their own account (see also the reference to agency workers below).

The Employment Tribunal in *Willoughby v County Home Care Ltd (1999) (unreported)* found that Willoughby, who provided care to CHC's clients on their behalf, was not an employee (there being, on the facts, no mutuality of obligation) but had agreed to provide work on a personal basis; she was not in business on her own account and, therefore, fell into the wider category of 'worker' contained in the Regulations.

## Agency workers

W10005    *Regulation 36* makes specific provision in relation to agency workers who do not otherwise fall into the general definition of workers. This provides that where (i) any individual is employed to work for a principal under an arrangement made between an agent and that principal, and (ii) the individual is not a worker because of the absence of a contract between the individual and the agent or principal, then the Regulations will apply as if that individual were a worker employed by whichever of the agent or principal is responsible for paying or actually pays the worker in respect of the work. Again, individuals who are genuinely self-employed are excluded from this definition.

## Collective, workforce and relevant agreements

W10006    These play a significant role in the Regulations as employers and employees can, by entering into such agreements (where the Regulations so allow), effectively supplement or derogate from the strict application of the Regulations. Employers and employees who need a certain amount of flexibility in their working arrangements may well find one or other of these agreements will facilitate compliance with the Regulations.

### *Collective agreement*

W10007    This is an agreement with an independent trade union within the meaning of the *Trade Union and Labour Relations (Consolidation) Act 1992, s 178.*

### *Workforce agreement*

W10008    This is a concept new to English law. It is an agreement between an employer and the duly elected representatives of its employees or, in the case of small employers (i.e. those with 20 or fewer employees), potentially the employees themselves. In order for a workforce agreement to be valid, it must comply with the conditions set out in *Schedule 1* to the Regulations, which provides that a workforce agreement must:

(*a*)    be in writing;

(*b*)    have effect for a specified period not exceeding five years;

(*c*)    apply either to

    (i)    all of the relevant members of the workforce, or

    (ii)    all of the relevant members of the workforce who belong to a particular group;

(*d*)    be signed by

    (i)    the representatives of the workforce or of the particular group of workers, or

    (ii)    where an employer employs 20 or fewer workers on the date on which the agreement is first made available for signature, either appropriate representatives or by a majority of the workers employed by him;

(*e*)    before the agreement was made available for signature, the employer must have provided all the workers to whom it was intended to apply with copies of the text of the agreement and such guidance as they might reasonably require in order to understand it fully.

'Relevant members of the workforce' are defined as all of the workers employed by a particular employer (excluding any worker whose terms and conditions of employment are provided for wholly or in part in a collective agreement). Therefore, as soon as a collective agreement is in force in respect of any worker, the provisions of any workforce agreement in respect of that worker would cease to apply.

*Paragraph 3 of Schedule 1* to the Regulations sets out the requirements relating to the election of workforce representatives. These are as follows:

(*a*)    the number of representatives to be elected shall be determined by the employer;

(*b*)    candidates for election as representatives for the workforce must be relevant members of the workforce, and the candidates for election as representatives of a particular group must be members of that group;

(*c*)    no worker who is eligible to be a candidate can be unreasonably excluded from standing for election;

(*d*)    all the relevant members of the workforce must be entitled to vote for representatives of the workforce and all the members of a particular group must be entitled to vote for representatives of that group;

(*e*)    the workers must be entitled to vote for as many candidates as there are representatives to be elected;

(*f*)    the election must be conducted so as to secure that (i) so far as is reasonably practicable those voting do so in secret, and (ii) the votes given at the election are fairly and accurately counted.

*Relevant agreement*

W10009    This is an 'umbrella provision' and means a workforce agreement which applies to a worker, any provision of a collective agreement which forms part of a contract between a worker and his employer, or any other agreement in writing which is legally enforceable as between the worker and his employer. A relevant agreement could, of course, include the written terms of a contract of employment. It would only include the provisions of staff handbooks, policies etc. where it could be shown that these were 'legally enforceable' as between the parties.

# Maximum weekly working time

## 48-hour working week

W10010 It is, of course, the 48-hour working week which has caused so much controversy. *Regulation 4* provides that an employer shall take all reasonable steps, in keeping with the need to protect the health and safety of workers, to ensure that a worker's *average* working time (including overtime) shall not exceed 48 hours for each 7-day period.

*Regulation 4(6)* provides a specific formula for calculating a worker's average working time over a reference period, which the Regulations have determined as 17 weeks (for exceptions, see below). This is as follows:

$$\frac{a + b}{c}$$

where

$a$      is the total number of hours worked during the reference period;

$b$      is the total number of hours worked during the period which

         (i)    begins immediately after the reference period, and

         (ii)    consists of the number of working days equivalent to the number of 'excluded days' during the reference period; and

$c$      is the number of weeks in the reference period.

'Excluded days' are days comprised of annual leave, sick leave or maternity leave and any period in respect of which an individual has opted out of the 48-hour limit (see below).

The case of *Barber and Others v RJB Mining (UK) Ltd [1999] IRLR 308* adds considerably to the importance of this provision. The facts of this case were as follows. For the 17 weeks from 1 October 1998 (the date the Regulations came into force), the plaintiffs worked more than the average of 48 hours per week. Letters seeking workers' agreement to opt out of the 48 hour limit were sent out on 7 December 1998. Each of the plaintiffs refused to sign the opt-out. On 25 January 1999, each plaintiff objected to further work until his average working hours fell to within the specified limit. Each was required to continue working and did so 'under protest' and without prejudice to their rights in the proceedings.

In his judgement, Mr Justice Gage said:-

> '*It seems to me clear that Parliament intended that all contracts of employment should be read so as to provide that an employee should work no more than an average of 48 hours in any week during the reference period. In my judgement, this is a mandatory requirement which must apply to all contracts of employment.*'

He stated that although *Regulation 4(1)* does not prohibit an employer from requiring his employee to work longer hours, it does not preclude this interpretation as the obligation is in keeping with the stated objective of the Directive, of providing for health and safety of employees.

The plaintiffs had clearly worked more than their 48 hour average. The judge continued:

> '*Having held that para.(1) of reg. 4 provides free-standing legal rights and obligations under their contract of employment, it must follow that to require the plaintiffs to continue to work before sufficient time has elapsed to bring the weekly average below 48 hours is a breach of reg. 4(1).*'

In practice, the ruling could add an extra string to the worker's bow in the form of a claim for breach of contract if their employer fails to comply with their obligations under *Regulation 4(1)*. They may be able to claim damages, a declaration or possibly an injunction in the event of a breach. However, it should be remembered that the case is a first instance decision and unfortunately, due to the 'politics' of the circumstances surrounding the cases will not be appealed.

The issue of an employer's obligations under the Regulations where they are not the only employer of the worker is problematic. *Regulation 4(2)* states 'an employer shall take all reasonable steps, in keeping with the need to protect the health and safety of workers, to ensure that the limit specified in paragraph (1) is complied with in the case of each worker employed by him in relation to whom it applies'. The DTI, in its guidance, recommends that an employer should agree an opt-out with a worker (see below) if they know the worker has a second job, if the total time worked is in excess of 48 hours a week. They also suggest that employers may wish to make an enquiry of their workforce about any additional employment. If a worker does not tell an employer about other employment and the employer has no reason to suspect that the worker has another job, it is extremely unlikely, the DTI suggest, that the employer would be found not to have complied.

In *Brown v Controlled Packaging Services Ltd (1999) (unreported)*, a worker who had another job in a bar on Tuesday and Thursday evenings was told at his interview that his basic working week would be 40 hours but that on occasion he would be required to work overtime. He soon discovered that the amount of overtime expected of him conflicted with the bar job, as on a number of occasions he was required to start work at 6 am instead of 8 am and he did not want to start work early on Wednesdays or Fridays. After the Regulations came into force, the worker was asked to sign an opt-out agreement which was viewed by his manager as a formality to ensure that existing overtime arrangements complied with the Regulations. Brown refused to sign the agreement because long hours would be incompatible with his evening job. Brown left and claimed constructive dismissal. The Employment Tribunal found that the dismissal was automatically unfair under the *Employment Rights Act 1996, s.101A* – i.e. for a reason connected with the employee exercising his rights under the Regulations.

### *Reference period*

W10011    The crucial issue in calculating the average number of hours worked is the question of when the reference period starts. The reference period is any period of 17 weeks in the course of a worker's employment, unless a relevant agreement provides for the application of successive 17-week periods (*Reg 4(3)*). This means that unless the parties specify that the reference period is a defined period of 17 weeks, followed by a successive period of 17 weeks, then the reference period will become a 'rolling' 17-week period. This could be significant where there is a marked variation in the hours that an individual works in a particular period, from week to week. In such a situation an employer would be recommended to include provision in a relevant agreement for successive 17-week reference periods to ensure that it can comply with the maximum weekly working requirements. Such a provision may be desirable in any event, for ease of administration.

For the first 17 weeks of employment, the average is calculated by reference to the number of weeks actually worked (*Reg 4(4)*).

*Exceptions and derogations to Regulation 4*

W10012    There are various exceptions to the maximum working week.

(*a*)    *Regulation 5* provides that an individual can agree with his employer to opt out of the 48-hour week (see W10013 below).

(*b*)    The 48 hour limit does not apply at all in the case of certain workers whose working time is unmeasured; in respect of other workers, part of whose working time is unmeasured, it only applies to that part of their working time which is not unmeasured (*Reg 20* – see W10028 below).

(c)    In special cases (as described in *Reg 21* – see W10029 below), the 17-week reference period over which the 48 hours are averaged will be automatically extended to 26 weeks (*Reg 4(5)*).

(*d*)    A collective or workforce agreement can extend the 17-week reference period to a period not exceeding 52 weeks, if there are objective or technical reasons concerning the organisation of work (*Reg 23*).

## Agreement to exclude 48-hour working week

W10013    The 48-hour limit on weekly working time will not apply where a worker agrees with his employer in writing that the maximum 48-hour working week should not apply in the individual's case, provided that certain requirements are satisfied. These are:

(*a*)    the agreement must be in writing;

(*b*)    the agreement may specify its duration or be of an indefinite length – however, it is always open to the worker to terminate the agreement by giving notice, which will be the length specified in the agreement (subject to a maximum of 3 months), or, if not specified, 7 days; and

(*c*)    the employer must keep up-to-date records of all workers who have signed such an agreement.

Until December 1999, employers were under controversial and onerous record keeping requirements in relation to workers who had signed opt out agreements. Since December 1999, employers only need to keep records of who has opted out.

The ability of employers to seek the agreement of workers to 'opt out' of the 48 hour week (which is specifically permitted by the Directive) arguably runs a 'coach and horses' through the spirit of the legislation. Only the UK and Ireland currently allow workers generally to opt-out of the maximum working week. Interestingly, there is to be a review by the EU Council of the use of the opt-out by 23 November 2003 (although Ireland will by this time no longer allow workers to opt-out).

However, a worker cannot be forced to sign an opt-out agreement. Moreover, the Regulations provide protection where an employee has suffered any detriment on the grounds that he has refused to waive any benefit conferred on him/her by the Regulations (*Employment Rights Act 1996, s 45A(1)(b)*, inserted by *Reg 31(1)(b)* – see W10036 below). Furthermore, a worker will always have the right to terminate the agreement and work no more than 48 hours on giving, at most, three months' notice.

On a practical note, the agreement by a worker to exclude the 48-hour working week must be a written agreement between the employer and the individual worker. It cannot take the form of or be incorporated in a collective or workforce agreement. However, it could, of course, be part of the contract of employment, (although it would be advisable for an employer to clearly delineate the agreement to work more than 48 hours from the rest of the contract of employment). It seems that employers' record keeping obligations in this regard would be satisfied by keeping an up-to-date list of workers who have signed opt-out agreements.

# Rest periods and breaks

## Daily rest period

W10014   Adult workers are entitled to an uninterrupted rest period of not less than 11 consecutive hours in each 24-hour period (*Reg 10*).

*Exceptions and derogations*

W10015   The provisions regarding daily rest periods do not apply where a worker's working time is unmeasured (*Reg 20(1)*).

Derogations from the rule may be made with regard to shift work (*Reg 22*), or by means of collective or workforce agreements (*Reg 23*) or where there are special categories of workers (*Reg 21*). However, in all cases (except for workers with unmeasured working time under *Reg 20(1)* – see W10028 below) compensatory rest must be provided (*Reg 24*).

## Weekly rest period

W10016   Adult workers are entitled to an uninterrupted rest period of not less than 24 hours in each seven-day period (*Reg 11*). However, if his employer so determines, an adult worker will be entitled to either two uninterrupted rest periods (each of not less than 24 hours) in each 14-day period or one uninterrupted rest period of not less than 48 hours in each 14-day period.

The entitlement to weekly rest is in addition to the 11-hour daily rest entitlement which must be provided by virtue of *Regulation 10*, except where objective or technical reasons concerning the organisation of work would justify incorporating all or part of that daily rest into the weekly rest period.

For the purposes of calculating the entitlement, the 7 or 14-day period will start immediately after midnight between Sunday and Monday, unless a relevant agreement provides otherwise. The Regulations do not require Sunday to be included in the minimum weekly rest period.

Derogations from the entitlement to weekly rest periods are the same as those for daily rest.

## Rest breaks

W10017   By virtue of *Regulation 12*, adult workers are entitled to a rest break where their daily working time is more than six hours. Details of this rest break, including duration and the terms on which it is granted, can be regulated by a collective or workforce agreement. If no such agreement is in place, the rest break will be for an uninterrupted period of not less than 20 minutes and the worker will be entitled to spend that break away from his work station, if he has one. In its latest guidance the

DTI states that the break should be taken during the six hour period and not at the beginning or end of it, at a time to be determined by the employer.

Derogations from the entitlement to rest breaks include cases specified in *Regulation 21* (see above), where working time is unmeasured and cannot be predetermined (*Reg 20(1)*), and also by means of a collective or workforce agreement (*Reg 23*). As before, compensatory rest must be provided other than where *Regulation 20* applies (*Reg 24*).

### Monotonous work

W10018    *Regulation 8* provides that where the pattern according to which an employer organises work is such as to put the health and safety of a worker employed by him at risk, in particular because the work is monotonous or the work rate is predetermined, the employer shall ensure that the employee is given adequate rest breaks. This Regulation is phrased in virtually identical terms to Article 13 of the Working Time Directive and unfortunately, its incorporation into the Regulations has not clarified its meaning in any way!

It is not clear how rest breaks in *Regulation 8* would differ from those under *Regulation 12*. It may be that in the case of monotonous work, an employer might have to consider giving employees shorter breaks more frequently as opposed to one longer continuous break. This was the suggestion in the Government's consultative document.

No derogations from these provisions apply except in the case of domestic workers.

# Night work

## Definitions

W10019    Before considering the detailed provisions in relation to night work contained in *Regulation 6*, an understanding of the definitions of 'night time' and 'night worker' contained in *Regulation 2*, is necessary. These are as follows.

*Night time* in relation to a worker means a period:

(*a*)    the duration of which is not less than 7 hours; and

(*b*)    which includes the period between midnight and 5 a.m.,

which is determined for the purposes of the Regulations by a relevant agreement or, in the absence of such an agreement, the period between 11 p.m. and 6 a.m.

*Night worker* means a worker –

(i)    who *as a normal course* works at least three hours of his daily working time during night time (for the purpose of this definition, it is stated in the Regulations that (without prejudice to the generality of that expression) a person works hours 'as a normal course' if he works such hours on a majority of days on which he works – a person who performs night work as part of a rotating shift pattern may also be covered); or

(ii)    who is likely during night time to work at least such proportion of his annual working time as may be specified for the purposes of the Regulations in a collective or workforce agreement.

The question of when someone works at least 3 hours of his daily working time 'as a normal course' was addressed in the case of *R v Attorney General for Northern Ireland ex parte Burns [1999] IRLR 315*. In this case the Northern Ireland High Court held that a worker who spent one week in each 3 week cycle working at least 3 hours during the night was a 'night worker'. The High Court said that 'as a normal course' meant nothing more than as a regular feature. The DTI in its guidance refers to this case and says that it expects further clarification from the European Court in due course. It states that occasional and or ad hoc work at night does not make you a 'night worker'.

The question is certainly open, following the *Burns* case, of how frequent something has to be to become "regular".

## Length of night work

W10020   If a worker falls within these definitions, then he or she is a night worker for the purposes of the Regulations. *Regulation 6* then goes on to provide that an employer shall take all reasonable steps to ensure that the normal working hours of a night worker do not exceed an average of 8 hours in any 24-hour period. This is averaged over a 17-week reference period which is calculated in the same way as in *Regulation 4* (see W10011 above).

As with the maximum working week, there is a formula for calculating a night worker's average normal hours for each 24-hour period as follows:

$$\frac{a}{b-c}$$

where:

*a*    is the normal (not actual) working hours during the reference period;

*b*    is the number of 24-hour periods during the applicable reference period; and

*c*    is the number of hours during that period which comprise or are included in weekly rest periods under *Regulation 11*, which is then divided by 24.

If the night work involves 'special hazards or heavy physical or mental strain', then a strict eight-hour time limit is imposed on working time in each 24-hour period and no averaging is allowed over a reference period. The identification of night work with such characteristics is by means of either a collective or workforce agreement which takes account of the specific effects and hazards of night work, or by the risk assessment which all employers are required to carry out under the *Management of Health and Safety at Work Regulations 1999 (SI 1999 No 3242)* (see RISK ASSESSMENT).

The derogations in *Regulation 21* (special categories of workers) apply to the provisions on length of night work. Workers whose working time is unmeasured or cannot be predetermined (and where it is only partly unmeasured or predetermined, to the extent that it is unmeasured) are also excluded (*Reg 20*). Other exemptions may be made by means of collective or workforce agreement (*Reg 23*).

## Health assessment and transfer of night workers to day work

W10021   An employer must, before assigning a worker to night work, provide him with the opportunity to have a free health assessment (*Reg 7*). The purpose of the assessment is to determine whether the worker is fit to undertake the night work. While there is no reliable evidence as to any specific health factor which rules out night work, a number of medical conditions could arise or could be made worse by working at night, such as diabetes, cardiovascular conditions or gastric intestinal disorders.

Employers are under a further duty to ensure that each night worker has the opportunity to have such health assessments 'at regular intervals of whatever duration may be appropriate in his case' (*Reg 7(1)(b)*).

The Regulations do not specify the way in which the health assessment must be carried out, nor is there specific reference to medical assessments, so that strictly speaking, such assessments could be carried out by qualified health professionals rather than by a medical practitioner. The latest DTI guidance contains a sample health questionnaire.

Contrast this with the position as regards the transfer from night to day work. If a night worker is found to be suffering from health problems that are recognised as being connected with night work, he or she is entitled to be transferred to suitable day work 'where it is possible'. In such a situation, the Regulations provide that a 'registered medical practitioner' must have advised the employer that the worker is suffering from health problems which the practitioner considers to be connected with the performance by that night worker of night work.

# Annual leave

## Entitlement to annual leave

W10022   The right under *Regulation 13* to paid holiday is the first time under English law that workers have had a statutory right to paid holiday. The right is available to all workers within the scope of the Regulations, providing that they have been continuously employed for 13 weeks. This requirement is satisfied if the worker's relations with his employer have been governed by a contract during the whole or part of each of those weeks.

The 13-week qualifying period has been challenged by BECTU in the case *R v Secretary of State for Trade and Industry ex parte BECTU, Case–173/99 (25 June 2001) (ECJ)*. The issue confronting the European Court of Justice was whether the UK had, in the then *Working Time Regulations 1998*, correctly transposed the provision in the *Working Time Directive 93/104/EC* stipulating that workers were entitled to at least four weeks' paid annual leave. In the 1998 Regulations, *Regulation 13(7)* specified that the right did not arise until the worker had been continuously employed for 13 weeks.

Most of the members of the Broadcasting, Entertainment and Cinematographic and Theatre Union (BECTU) were engaged on short-term contracts, frequently for less than 13 weeks with the same employer. Thus, although they worked on a regular basis, they did so for successive employers and were accordingly deprived by *Regulation 13* of the 1998 regulations of entitlement to paid annual leave.

BECTU applied to the High Court in 1999 for judicial review contending that *Regulation 13(7)* of the 1998 Regulations constituted an incorrect transposition of the provision of the directive in question i.e. *article 7*.

Because of the importance of the issue, the High Court referred the matter to the European Court for its ruling.

The European Court of Justice, in a preliminary ruling, held that *Regulation 13(7)* of the 1998 Regulations, specifying that workers were entitled to paid annual leave only after 13 weeks' continuous employment with the same employer was indeed contrary to the Directive.

In so ruling, the European Court rejected the UK's argument that the threshold limit laid down in *Regulation 13(7)* of the 1998 Regulations struck a fair balance between the protection of workers' safety and health, on the one hand, and, on the other hand, the need to avoid imposing excessive constraints on small and medium-sized undertakings. That was because the Directive stated that 'the improvement of workers' safety, hygiene and health at work is an objective which should not be subordinated to purely economic considerations.' The UK's argument was 'incontestably' such a consideration.

Other businesses most likely to be affected by the European Court's ruling will be those employing large numbers of seasonal workers, for example in agriculture, hotels, catering and tourism.

In *Wellicome v Kelly Services (UK) Ltd (1999) (unreported)*, the employer specified in the contract of employment that holiday accrued at the rate of 0.29 days per week. The Employment Tribunal held that this clause was caught by *Regulation 35(1)*, which states that a provision in an agreement is void insofar as it purports to exclude or limit the operation of the Regulations.

All qualifying workers are now entitled to 4 weeks' leave. This entitlement was in fact phased in. Qualifying workers were initially entitled only to 3 weeks annual leave, rising to 4 weeks on 23 November 1999 in each 'leave year'. The phasing in of 4 weeks' leave in 1999 was subject to transitional provisions. In case an issue arises concerning a historic entitlement, the transitional entitlements were as follows.

(*a*)    In any leave year beginning on or before 23 November 1998, the entitlement was 3 weeks.

(*b*)    In any leave year beginning after 23 November 1998 but before 23 November 1999, the entitlement was 3 weeks plus a proportion of a fourth week equivalent to the proportion of the year beginning on 23 November 1998 which had elapsed at the start of that leave year. This provision is logical if somewhat confusing. It is best demonstrated by means of an example. If an employee's leave year commenced on 1 January 1999, he was entitled to 3 weeks plus one day. If it commenced on 24 May 1999, he was entitled to 3 weeks and 4 days' annual leave. This is because holiday entitlement including a fraction of any day is rounded up to a whole day (*Reg 13(6)*).

(*c*)    Where the leave year begins after 23 November 1999, the entitlement to annual leave is 4 weeks.

For the purposes of *Regulation 13*, a worker's leave year begins on any day provided for in a relevant agreement, or, where there is no such provision in a relevant agreement, 1 October 1998 or the anniversary of the date on which the worker began employment (whichever is the later). In the majority of cases, written statements of terms and conditions contain a reference to the holiday or leave year. If they do not, employers are recommended to ensure that they do so. Failure in this regard could result in administrative confusion as each employee could have a different holiday year for the purposes of calculations under the Regulations.

The statutory leave entitlement may be taken in instalments, but it can only be taken in the leave year to which it relates and a payment in lieu of the statutory entitlement cannot be made except where the worker's employment is terminated. It should be noted that this relates only to the entitlement under the Regulations, so that if an employer provides for annual leave over and above the statutory entitlement, the enhanced element of the holiday can be carried forward or paid for in lieu as agreed between the parties. In *Miah v La Gondola Ltd (1999) (unreported)*, the Employment Tribunal found that a worker who was paid an additional week's pay instead of taking a week's holiday (due under the Regulations) during his employment, was entitled, on the termination of that contract, to payment for that proportion of annual leave which was due to him in accordance with *Regulation 14(3)(b)* and the payment paid to him during his employment in lieu of the week's statutory holiday had to be disregarded.

For many workers (and employers), the introduction of rights to paid annual leave was significant. It is understood that before the Regulations came into force some 2.5 million workers had no right to a holiday at all. Employment Tribunals have had to resolve many disputes arising from this right. Accordingly, it is no surprise that there have been several Employment Tribunal decisions concerning the (now historic) problem facing employers who sought to adjust workers' pay to take into account the extra expense of giving paid holiday, when the Regulations came into force, including *Chapman v Eurostaff Personnel Ltd (1999) (unreported)*, *Ackerman and Another v Stratton (1999) (unreported)*, *Davies and Others v MJ Wyatt (Decorators) Ltd (1999) (unreported)*, *Johnson v Northbroke College (1999) (unreported)*, and *Tompkins v Kurn (1999) (unreported)*.

Employers who give more than 4 weeks' holiday and who are obliged to pay their workers more for the statutory 4 weeks than they pay for the remaining leave will be interested in *Barton & Others v SCC Ltd (1999) (unreported)*. In this case, an employer sought to argue that monies paid by way of holiday pay for leave in excess of the statutory minimum leave under the Regulations can go towards the employer's liability to pay a week's pay for each week of leave taken under the Regulations (calculated under *Regulation 16*). In addition, the employer argued that they had the right to chose which days off would be paid at the statutory rate and which at the contractual rate. The Employment Tribunal found in favour of the workers on both issues. *Regulations 16(1)* and *(5)* make it clear that the Employment Tribunal have to focus on the individual holiday week in question and the payment made for that individual week. With regard to which holiday is paid at which rate, the Employment Tribunal said that the right to holiday pay is an entitlement and it is a matter for the worker to choose which holiday weeks he or she seeks to take pursuant to his or her statutory entitlement.

The right to paid holiday was not introduced by the UK as soon as it should have been. The Working Time Directive required implementation by member states by 23 November 1996. However, the UK implementing legislation came into force almost two years after this (on 1 October 1998). The Employment Appeal Tribunal in *Gibson v East Riding of Yorkshire Council [1999] ICR 622* had held that *Article 7* of the Directive, which obliges member states to ensure that workers are entitled to paid holiday, is sufficiently precise and unconditional that a worker of the state or an 'emanation of the state' is entitled to enforce that provision of the Directive against their employer from the earlier date of 23 November 1996 (see W10024). However, the Court of Appeal have recently overturned this decision (reported in The Times, 6 July 2000).

## Compensation related to entitlement to annual leave

W10023    Where an employee has outstanding leave due to him when the employment relationship ends, *Regulation 14* specifically provides that an allowance is payable in lieu. It states that in the absence of any relevant agreement to the contrary, the amount of such allowance will be determined by the formula

$(a \times b) - c$

where:

*a*    is the period of leave to which the worker is entitled under the Regulations;

*b*    is the proportion of the worker's leave year which expired before the effective date of termination;

*c*    is the period of leave taken by the worker between the start of the leave year and the effective date of termination (*Reg 14(3)*).

*Regulation 14(4)* provides that where there is a relevant agreement which so provides, an employee shall compensate his employer – whether by way of payment, additional work or otherwise – in relation to any holiday entitlement taken in excess of the statutory entitlement.

## Payment, and notice requirements, for annual leave

W10024    *Regulation 16* specifies the way in which a worker is paid in respect of any period of annual leave: this is at the rate of a week's pay in respect of each week of leave.

In order to calculate the amount of a 'week's pay', employers are referred to *s 221–224* of the *Employment Rights Act 1996* (although the calculation date is to be treated as the first day of the period of leave in question, and the relevant references to *ss 227 and 228* do not apply). The application of these provisions can lead to a disproportionately high level of holiday pay for workers paid on a commission only basis. This is because *s 223(2)* stipulates that if, during any of the 12 weeks preceding the worker's holiday, no remuneration was payable by the employer to the worker concerned, account should be taken of remuneration in earlier weeks so as to bring the number of weeks of which account is taken up to 12. In other words, it seems that the calculation of a 'commission only' worker's holiday entitlement will be based solely on the worker's earnings for any weeks (up to a maximum of 12) in which they received commission payments – any slow, unproductive weeks will be disregarded.

In the case of *Smith & Others v Chubb Security Personnel Ltd (1999) (unreported)*, employees who were obliged to work such hours as were detailed in their duty roster were paid holiday pay on the basis of a 40 hour week when in fact they worked a 3 week cycle of fourteen 12 hour days which averaged out at 56 hours per week. The Tribunal decided that their pay should be calculated on the basis of a 56 hour week.

*Regulation 15* deals with the dates on which the leave entitlement can be taken, and sets out detailed requirements as to notice. This Regulation is extremely complicated and before going into the details, it should be noted that alternative provisions concerning the notice requirements can be contained in a relevant agreement. Bearing in mind the detailed nature of the provisions, it is recommended that employers consider specifying such notice requirements in their contracts of employment, thereby avoiding the need for confusion at a later stage.

*Regulation 15* provides that a worker must give his employer notice equivalent to twice the amount of leave he is proposing to take. An employer can then prevent the worker from taking the leave on a particular date by giving notice equivalent to the number of days' leave which the employer wishes to prohibit. An employer can also, by giving notice equivalent to twice the number of days' leave in question, require an employee to take all or part of his leave on certain dates. This would, of course, be useful with regard to seasonal shutdowns over summer and Christmas holidays etc.

Another case on accrual of holiday was *Bowling v Grove Leisure Ltd (1999) (unreported)*. The employer unsuccessfully argued that the worker was not entitled to paid leave at the full rate until that leave entitlement had accrued throughout the leave year. The Employment Tribunal suggested there were two options open to employers: either they could serve a 'counter-notice' regulating the time at which leave was taken and paid for, or they could have made a relevant agreement pursuant to *Regulation 14(4)* requiring workers to repay excess holiday pay if their employment ended before they had 'earned' the holiday taken.

There have been two conflicting Employment Tribunal decisions on the question of a worker's entitlement to annual leave while on sick leave. In the first case, *Warnes v Situsec Contractors Ltd (1999) (unreported)*, the Employment Tribunal dismissed

Warnes' claim for payment for holiday on bank holidays and other leave which, when he was working, he had been obliged to take at fixed times, during a period of sick leave. The Employment Tribunal said that the purpose of the Regulations is to safeguard the health of workers and ensure they take adequate breaks from work. A person who is off sick cannot take leave from work. The tribunal said that entitlement to paid holiday leave under *Regulation 13* is governed by the definition of 'working time' in *Regulation 2*. A person who is off sick is not a person who is working within *Regulation 2(1)* and, therefore, could not be taking leave in accordance with the Regulation. Furthermore, they said, *Regulation 13* prohibits payment in lieu of leave accept where the contract is terminated.

The second, conflicting Employment Tribunal decision was *Brown v Kigass Aero Components Ltd (2000) (unreported)*. In this case, Mr Brown was involved in a road accident in January 1997. He never became well enough again to work but his employment was not terminated by Kigass. Mr Brown had exhausted his sick pay entitlement by December 1997 and his entitlement to statutory sick pay ended in January 1999. As a result, and in respect of the holiday year 1 April 1999 to 31 March 2000, Mr Brown was not entitled to any further sick pay. Mr Brown then notified Kigass (complying with the annual leave notification requirements in Regulation 15) that he wanted to take part of his annual leave entitlement during his sickness absence. Kigass refused but the Employment Tribunal allowed Mr Brown's claim (although the Tribunal agreed that an employee could not receive both statutory sick pay and holiday pay in respect of the same period). The appeal of this case is expected to be heard in around October 2000.

## Records

W10025    The publicity and controversy surrounding the introduction of the Regulations related primarily to the maximum working week and the annual leave entitlement. However, in practice the provisions relating to record keeping proved very significant for employers, in particular those with workers who had signed opt-outs, where the rigorous record keeping requirements arguably undermined the benefit to an employer of the freedom given by the opt-out. Accordingly, the UK Government significantly watered down the requirements for employers *vis a vis* opted out workers, and the current position is outlined below.

*Regulation 9* introduces an obligation on employers to keep specific records of working hours. All employers (except in relation to workers serving in the armed forces – *Reg 25(1)*) are under a duty to keep records which are adequate to show that certain specified limits are being complied with in the case of each entitled worker employed by him. These limits are:

(*a*)    the maximum working week (see W10010 above);

(*b*)    the length of night work (including night work which is hazardous or subject to heavy mental strain) (see W10020 above); and

(*c*)    the requirement to provide health assessments for night workers (see W10021 above).

These records are required to be maintained for two years from the date on which they were made.

In addition, where a worker has agreed to exclude the maximum working week under *Regulation 5* (see W10013 above), an employer is required to keep up-to-date records of all workers who have opted out. Note that, in contrast with the obligations under *Regulation 9*, no time limit is imposed for the maintenance of such records.

# Excluded sectors

## Total exclusions

W10026    By virtue of *Regulation 18*, the sectors of activities listed below are totally excluded from the terms of the Regulations:

(*a*)    air, rail, road, sea, inland waterway and lake transport;

(*b*)    sea fishing;

(*c*)    other work at sea;

(*d*)    the activities of doctors in training;

(*e*)    specified services, e.g. armed forces, the police, civil protection services, where the characteristics of these services inevitably conflict with the provisions of the Regulations.

When the Regulations came into force, it was not clear how *Regulation 18* would impact on a worker employed in one of these sectors but not directly involved in the targeted activity, for example, a baggage handler at an airport. This issue was addressed by the Employment Appeal Tribunal in the case of *Bowden & Others v Tuffnells Parcels Express Ltd (6 April 2000) (EAT 622/99)*.

In this case, Ms Bowden was a clerical worker employed by Tuffnells Parcels Express Ltd which operates a major parcel delivery service. She had no contact with the vans nor could contractually be required to work with any transport. She had no contractual entitlement to holidays. She could, however, take unpaid holiday. The Employment Appeal Tribunal found itself torn. On the one hand it wanted to adopt the view already taken up by several Community bodies, that a formal amendment is necessary to the Directive to extend protection to such workers, and, by implication, that until such an amendment comes, the exclusion is to be interpreted widely. On the other hand, it was reluctant to embrace a result which, in practical terms, was devoid of any support in economic, social, political or common sense terms (namely that a clerk in a shipping office should be treated any differently to one at a firm of solicitors). Accordingly, the Employment Appeal Tribunal has stayed the appeal pending the ruling of the ECJ on the matter. The case was lodged with the ECJ (reference C-133/00) on 10 April 2000. The Employment Tribunal had previously concluded that Ms Bowden fell within the transport exclusion in *Regulation 18* and that they had no jurisdiction to hear her claim.

In the DTI's new guidance, they advise workers that if they work for a road haulage, delivery or distribution firm, they are in the road transport sector and the Regulations will not apply to them, even if they are not a driver. Similarly, if they work for a railway operator, they are in the rail sector and excluded; and if they work for a retailer in a station or sell petrol at a garage the Regulations will apply to them. The guidance also deals with 'own account' transport services. For example, a transport division of a retail chain which delivers goods to its stores. The clear advice in the DTI's guidance is that such an operation, if it is part of an unidentifiable transport function, would form part of the transport sector.

In *Cornwall v McIntosh and Another T/A Aristocars Ltd (1999) (unreported)*, the Employment Tribunal held that a worker who had started as a driver but had since assumed greater management responsibility in the office, was directly involved with transport activities, even when he was not himself driving, and that the Regulations did not, therefore, apply.

Whilst whole sectors are currently exempt from the Directive and, therefore, exempt from the Regulations (see below), it has always been the intention for protection eventually to extend to workers in these excluded sectors. There has been a significant development in this area recently with the adoption by the European Parliament of the text of a directive amending the Working Time Directive.

The consolidated text has not yet been published, but it is understood that the main points of the proposed new law are as follows:-

- workers engaged in off-shore work, doctors in training, workers concerned with the carriage of passengers on regular urban transport services and certain railway transport workers may be exempted by member states from provisions regarding daily rest, rest breaks, weekly rest, length of night work and reference periods. However, they will be covered by all other provisions of the Directive, including annual leave and weekly working time;

- average weekly working time limits of 48 hours for doctors in training may be introduced over a 5 year transitional period;

- mobile workers, as defined, will not be covered by the Directive's provisions on daily rest, rest breaks, weekly rest and length of night work. Member states must, however, ensure that these workers are entitled to adequate rest.

- the amending directive must be implemented three years from whenever it comes into force (with an extra year for doctors in training).

Proposals have also been put forward for regulation of the road transport industry but it seems that progress on this matter has yet to be made, largely due to disagreement over the proposals to regulate self employed drivers. Proposals in the maritime sector and for seafarers on board ships using Community ports have been consolidated into two directives which have already been adopted.

## Partial exemptions

*Domestic service*

W10027 The following provisions of the Regulations do not apply in relation to workers employed as domestic servants in private households:

(*a*) the 48-hour working week (see W10010 above);

(*b*) length of night work (see W10020 above);

(*c*) health assessments for night workers (see W10021 above);

(*d*) monotonous work (see W10018 above).

*Unmeasured working time*

W10028 The requirements of the Regulations listed below are, by virtue of *Regulation 20(1)*, not applicable to workers where, on account of the specific characteristics of the activity in which they are engaged, the duration of their working time is not measured or pre-determined or can be determined by the workers themselves. The provisions excluded are:

(*a*) the 48 hour working week (see W10010 above);

(*b*) minimum daily and weekly rest periods and rest breaks (see W10014 above);

(*c*) length of night work (see W10020 above).

This would leave such workers with requirements relating to monotonous work, the requirement for health assessments for night workers, the requirement to keep records and annual leave. It should also be noted that there is no requirement to provide such workers with compensatory rest where the requirements of the Regulations are not complied with.

This provision is often thought to exclude the Regulations in relation to 'managing executives or other persons with autonomous decision-making powers'. However, it should be noted that this is simply *one* of the three examples given in *Regulation 20(1)*, as regards the type of worker with unmeasured working time. The application of the Regulation could be much wider than this, and will depend on whether the worker in question is genuinely able to control his work, to the extent of being able to determine how many hours he works.

The UK Government made an amendment to *Regulation 20* in December 1999 so that the working time of workers does not, effectively count towards their weekly working time, to the extent that it is unmeasured, even if their time is not wholly unmeasured. Prior to the amendment, workers were either within the *Regulation 20* 'unmeasured' exemption or they were outside it. The exemption provides a 'half way house' for workers who have some part of their working time set in advance (e.g. under their contract of employment) but choose on their own account to work longer hours. It is as yet unclear how widely this provision will be interpreted i.e. when extra hours can genuinely be said not to be 'required' by the employer.

### Special categories of workers

W10029     *Regulation 21* provides that in the case of certain categories of employees, the following Regulations do not apply:

(*a*)     length of night work (see W10020 above);

(*b*)     minimum daily rest and weekly rest periods and rest breaks (see W10014 above).

This leaves the 48-hour working week, requirements relating to monotonous work, the requirement for health assessments for night workers, the requirement to keep records and annual leave. However, it should be noted that where any of the allowable derogations are utilised, an employer will have to provide compensatory rest periods (see W10032 below).

Further, for these categories of workers, the reference period over which the 48-hour working week is averaged is 26 weeks and not 17 (*Reg 4(5)*).

The special categories of worker are as follows:

(i)     where the worker's activities mean that his place of work and place of residence are distant from one another, or the worker has different places of work which are distant from one another;

(ii)     workers engaged in security or surveillance activities, which require a permanent presence in order to protect property and persons – examples given are security guards and caretakers;

(iii)     where the worker's activities involve the need for continuity of service or production – specific examples are:

(A)     services relating to the reception, treatment or care provided by hospitals or similar establishments, residential institutions and prisons;

(B)     workers at docks or airports;

(C)     press, radio, television, cinematographic production, postal and telecommunications services, and civil protection services;

(D)    gas, water and electricity production, transmission and distribution, household refuse collection and incineration;

(E)    industries in which work cannot be interrupted on technical grounds;

(F)    research and development activities;

(G)    agriculture;

(iv)    any industry where there is a foreseeable surge of activity – specific cases suggested are:

(A)    agriculture;

(B)    tourism;

(C)    postal services;

(v)    where the worker's activities are affected by:

(A)    unusual and unforeseeable circumstances beyond the control of the employer;

(B)    exceptional events which could not be avoided even with the exercise of all due care by the employer;

(C)    an accident or the imminent risk of an accident.

## *Shift workers*

W10030    Shift workers are defined by *Regulation 22* as workers who work in a system whereby they succeed each other at the same work station according to a certain pattern, including a rotating pattern which may be continuous or discontinuous, entailing the need for workers to work at different times over a given period of days or weeks.

In the case of shift workers the provisions for daily rest periods (see W10014 above) and weekly rest periods (see W10016 above) can be excluded in order to facilitate the changing of shifts, on the understanding that compensatory rest must be provided (see W10032 below). In addition, those provisions also do not apply to workers engaged in activities involving periods of work split up over the day – the example given is that of cleaning staff.

## *Collective and workforce agreements*

W10031    By virtue of *Regulation 23(a)*, employers and employees have the power to exclude or modify the following provisions:

(*a*)    length of night work (see W10020 above);

(*b*)    minimum daily rest and weekly rest periods and rest breaks (see W10014 above),

by way of collective or workforce agreements. Compensatory rest must be provided (see W10032 below).

In addition, *Regulation 23(b)* allows the reference period for calculating the maximum working week to be extended to up to 52 weeks, if there are objective or technical reasons concerning the organisation of work to justify this.

This Regulation gives the parties a good deal of flexibility (on the understanding that they are prepared to consent with each other) to opt out of significant provisions contained in the Regulations.

## Compensatory rest

W10032   *Regulation 24* provides that where a worker is not strictly governed by the working time rules because of:

(*a*)   a derogation under *Regulation 21* (see W10029 above); or

(*b*)   the application of a collective or workforce agreement under *Regulation 23(a)* (see W10031 above); or

(*c*)   the special shift work rules under Regulation 22 (see W10030 above);

and as a result, the worker is required by his employer to work during what would otherwise be a rest period or rest break, then the employer must wherever possible allow him to take an equivalent period of compensatory rest. In exceptional cases, in which it is not possible for objective reasons to grant such a rest period, the employer must afford the employee such protection as may be appropriate in order to safeguard his health and safety.

# Enforcement

W10033   The Regulations divide the enforcement responsibilities between the Health and Safety Executive and the employment tribunals.

## Health and safety offences

W10034   *Regulation 28* provides that certain provisions of the Regulations (referred to as 'the relevant requirements') will be enforced by the Health and Safety Executive (except to the extent that a local authority may be responsible for their enforcement by virtue of Regulation 28(3)). The relevant requirements are:

(*a*)   the 48 hour working week;

(*b*)   length of night work;

(*c*)   health assessment and transfers from night work;

(*d*)   monotonous work;

(*e*)   record keeping; and

(*f*)   failure to provide compensatory rest, where the provision concerning the length of night work is modified or excluded.

Any employer who fails to comply with any of the relevant requirements will be guilty of an offence and shall be liable on summary conviction (in the magistrates' court) to a fine not exceeding the statutory maximum and on conviction on indictment (in the Crown Court) to a fine.

In addition, the Health and Safety Executive can take enforcement proceedings utilising certain provisions of the *Health and Safety at Work etc. Act 1974*, as set out in *Regulations 28* and *29*. Employers may face criminal liability under these provisions, the sanctions for which range, according to the offence, from a fine to two years' imprisonment. (For enforcement of health and safety legislation generally, see ENFORCEMENT.)

## Employment tribunals

*Enforcement of the Regulations*

W10035    By virtue of *Regulation 30*, certain provisions of the Regulations may be enforced by a worker presenting a claim to an employment tribunal where an employer has refused to permit him to exercise such rights. These are:

(*a*)    daily rest period;

(*b*)    weekly rest period;

(*c*)    rest break;

(*d*)    annual leave;

(*e*)    failure to provide compensatory rest, insofar as it relates to situations where daily or weekly rest breaks are modified or excluded;

(*f*)    the failure to pay the whole or any part of the amount relating to paid annual leave, or payment on termination in lieu of accrued but untaken holiday.

A complaint must be made within (i) three months (other than in the case of members of the armed forces – see below) of the act or omission complained of (or in the case of a rest period or leave extending over more than one day, of the date on which it should have been permitted to begin) or (ii) such further period as the tribunal considers reasonable, where it is satisfied that it was not reasonably practicable for the complaint to be presented within that time. (The time limit in respect of members of the armed forces is six months.)

Where an employment tribunal decides that a complaint is well-founded, it must make a declaration to that effect and can award compensation to be paid by the employer to the worker. This shall be such amount as the employment tribunal considers just and equitable in all the circumstances, having regard to (i) the employer's default in refusing to permit the worker to exercise his right and (ii) any loss sustained by the worker which is attributable to the matters complained of. With regard to complaints relating to holiday pay or payment in lieu of accrued holiday on termination, the tribunal can also order the employer to pay the worker the amount which it finds properly due.

There is no qualifying service period with regard to such complaints being presented to a tribunal.

*Protection against detriment, and against unfair dismissal*

W10036    *Regulation 31* inserts a new *section 45A* into the *Employment Rights Act 1996*, so as to provide protection for a worker against being subjected to any detriment, where the worker has:

(*a*)    refused (or proposed to refuse) to comply with a requirement which the employer imposed (or proposed to impose) in contravention of the Regulations;

(*b*)    refused (or proposed to refuse) to forgo a right conferred on him by the Regulations;

(*c*)    failed to sign a workforce agreement or make any other agreement provided for under the Regulations, such as an individual opt-out from the maximum weekly working time limit;

(*d*)    been a candidate in an election of work place representatives or, having been elected, carries out any activities as such a representative or candidate; or

(e)    in good faith, (i) made an allegation that the employer has contravened a right under the Regulations, or (ii) brought proceedings under the Regulations.

The right to bring these claims would (as with discrimination claims) allow an individual to pursue a claim relating to a breach of the Regulations whilst continuing in employment.

By virtue of the inserted *section 101A* of the *Employment Rights Act 1996*, the dismissal of an employee on all but ground (e) above is automatically unfair, although this will only apply to employees and not to the wider definition of worker (for the position of workers who are not employees, see below). The compensation available would be subject to any cap on unfair dismissal compensation (the current cap on unfair dismissal compensatory awards is £50,000). Employees whose contracts were terminated on ground (e) above would be protected from dismissal for assertion of a statutory right, by virtue of *section 104* of the 1996 Act.

An employee would also be protected if selected for redundancy on any of the grounds listed above. This would be automatically unfair selection, by virtue of *section 105* of the 1996 Act.

Workers (i.e. those who are not employees) whose contracts are terminated for any of the grounds set out above can claim that they have suffered a detriment, and they may claim compensation, which would be capped in the same way as an award for unfair dismissal.

### *Breach of contract claims*

W10037    Following the *RJB Mining case* (see W10010), workers may also be able to claim for breach of contract, if their employer breaches the obligations in *Regulation 4(1)*. If the claim is for damages and is outstanding at the termination of the employment, then the worker could in principle take their case to the Employment Tribunal (within 3 months of the effective date of termination of the contract giving rise to the claim). If the claim is for a declaration or an injunction, then the worker will have to apply to the High Court, where special rules apply.

### *Contracting out of the Regulations*

W10038    An agreement to contract out of the provisions of the Regulations can be made via a conciliation officer or by means of a compromise agreement, and the provisions are similar and consistent with the current provisions in the *Employment Rights Act 1996, s 203* (as amended by the *Employment Rights (Dispute Resolution) Act 1998*).

### *Conclusion*

W10039    The Regulations broke new ground in English law. Despite the adverse publicity surrounding them their introduction does not appear to have unduly changed current industrial practice. The proposed changes to the Directive which, in time, must be reflected in UK law will probably have a greater impact than the existing Regulations. The EU Commission's review of the use of opt-outs in 2003 could also be significant for the UK.

# Workplaces – Health, Safety and Welfare

## Introduction

W11001 The *Workplaces (Health, Safety and Welfare) Regulations 1992 (SI 1992 No 3004)* (set out a wide range of basic health, safety and welfare standards applying to most places of work. They largely replaced legislation like the *Offices, Shops and Railway Premises Act 1963* and the *Factories Act 1961*, although some provisions of the latter Act are still in force. The Workplaces Regulations cover not only offices, shops and factories covered by earlier legislation, but apply to a much wider range of workplaces, including schools, hospitals, theatres, cinemas and hotels, for example.

They set down detailed standards for premises used as places of work in the following areas:

(*a*)  maintenance [*(SI 1992 No 3004), Reg 5*] (see W11003);

(*b*)  ventilation [*(SI 1992 No 3004), Reg 6*] (see VENTILATION);

(*c*)  temperature [*(SI 1992 No 3004), Reg 7*] (see W11005);

(*d*)  lighting [*(SI 1992 No 3004), Reg 8*] (see LIGHTING);

(*e*)  cleanliness and waste storage [*(SI 1992 No 3004), Reg 9*] (see W11007);

(*f*)  room dimensions and space [*(SI 1992 No 3004), Reg 10*] (see W11008);

(*g*)  workstations and seating [*(SI 1992 No 3004), Reg 11*] (see W11009);

(*h*)  conditions of floors and traffic routes [*(SI 1992 No 3004), Reg 12*] (see W11010);

(*j*)  freedom from falls and falling objects [*(SI 1992 No 3004), Reg 13*] (see WORK AT HEIGHTS);

(*k*)  windows and transparent or translucent doors, gates and walls (see W11012);

(*l*)  windows, skylights and ventilators [*(SI 1992 No 3004), Reg 18*] (see W11013);

(*m*)  window cleaning [*(SI 1992 No 3004), Regs 14—16*] (see WORK AT HEIGHTS);

(*n*)  organisation of traffic routes [*(SI 1992 No 3004), Reg 17*] (see W11015);

(*o*)  doors and gates [*(SI 1992 No 3004), Reg 18*] (see W11016);

(*p*)  escalators and travelators [*(SI 1992 No 3004), Reg 19*] (see W11017);

(*q*)  sanitary conveniences/washing facilities [*(SI 1992 No 3004), Regs 20, 21*] (see W11019–W11023);

(*r*)  drinking water [*(SI 1992 No 3004), Reg 22*] (see W11024);

(*s*)  clothing accommodation and facilities for changing clothing [*(SI 1992 No 3004), Reg 23*] (see W11026–W11027); and

(*t*)  rest/meal facilities [*(SI 1992 No 3004), Reg 25*] (see W11027).

In addition to these Regulations, there is other legislation which contain health, safety and welfare standards for particularly high risk industries and workplaces, including construction sites, mines, quarries and the railway industry. This legislation is dealt with in other chapters. For typical hazards in offices and shops, see further OFFICES AND SHOPS.

This chapter looks at the provisions of the *Workplace (Health, Safety and Welfare) Regulations 1992*, together with guidance provided in the associated approved code of practice (ACOP). It outlines the requirements of the *Building Regulations 1991 (SI 1991 No 2768)*, which apply where workplaces are being built, extended or modified, and looks at the *Disability Discrimination Act 1995, s 6*, which requires that reasonable adjustments be made to workplaces where necessary to ensure that disabled workers are not put at a substantial disadvantage.

The chapter also outlines the residual application of the *Factories Act 1961* and its enforcement, and sets out the provisions of the *Health and Safety (Safety Signs and Signals) Regulations 1996 (SI 1996 No 341)*.

# Workplace (Health, Safety and Welfare) Regulations 1992 (SI 1992 No 3004)

## Definitions

W11002    A 'workplace' is any non-domestic premises available to any person as a place of work, including:

(*a*)    canteens, toilets;

(*b*)    parts of a workroom or workplace (e.g. corridor, staircase, or other means of access/egress other than a public road);

(*c*)    a completed modification, extension, or conversion of an original workplace;

but excluding

(i)    boats, ships, hovercraft, trains and road vehicles (although the requirements in *regulation 13*, which deal with falls and falling objects, apply when aircraft, trains and road vehicles are stationary inside a workplace);

(ii)    building operations/works of engineering construction;

(iii)    mining activities.

[*Workplace (Health, Safety and Welfare) Regulations 1992 (SI 1992 No 3004), Regs 2, 3 and 4*].

The definition of 'work' includes work carried out by employees and self-employed people and the definition of 'premises' includes outdoor places. The Regulations do not apply to private dwellings, but they do apply to hotels, nursing homes and to parts of premises where domestic staff are employed, for example in the kitchens of hostels.

*Regulations 20 to 25* (which deal with toilets, washing, changing facilities, clothing accommodation, drinking water and eating and rest facilities) apply to temporary work sites, but only so far as is reasonably practicable.

## General maintenance of the workplace

W11003    All workplaces, equipment and devices should be maintained

(*a*)    in an efficient state,

(*b*)    in an efficient working order, and

(*c*)    in a good state of repair.

[*Workplace (Health, Safety and Welfare) Regulations 1992 (SI 1992 No 3004), Reg 5*].

Dangerous defects should be reported and acted on as a matter of good housekeeping (and to avoid possible subsequent civil liability). Defects resulting in equipment/plant becoming unsuitable for use, though not necessarily dangerous, should lead to decommissioning of plant until repaired – or, if this might lead to the number of facilities being less than required by statute, repaired forthwith (e.g. a defective toilet).

To this end, a suitable maintenance programme must be instituted, including:

(*a*)    regular maintenance (inspection, testing, adjustment, lubrication, cleaning);

(*b*)    rectification of potentially dangerous defects and the prevention of access to defective equipment;

(*c*)    record of maintenance/servicing.

There are more detailed regulations dealing with plant and equipment used at work, including the *Provision and Use of Work Equipment Regulations 1998 (SI 1998 No 2306)*, which are examined in detail in MACHINERY SAFETY.

## Ventilation

W11004    *Workplace (Health, Safety and Welfare) Regulations 1992 (SI 1992 No 3004), Reg 6* deals with the provision of sufficient ventilation in enclosed workplaces. There must be effective and suitable ventilation in order to supply a sufficient quantity of fresh or purified air. If ventilation plant is necessary for health and safety reasons, it must give warning of failure.

The ACOP to the Regulations sets out that ventilation should not cause uncomfortable draughts, and that it should be sufficient to provide fresh air for the occupants to breathe, to dilute any contaminants and to reduce odour.

The Health and Safety Executive (HSE) publication, *General ventilation in the workplace: Guidance for employers*, provides detailed guidance in this area. It sets out that the fresh air supply rate to workplaces should not normally fall below 5 to 8 litres per second, per occupant, and that in deciding the appropriate rate, employers should consider factors including:

●    The amount of floor space available to each worker;

●    The type of work being carried out;

●    Whether people smoke in the workplace; and

●    What contaminants are being discharged by, for example, any process machinery, heaters, furniture and furnishings.

This guidance also lists sources of further information and help, from organisations including the Chartered Institution of Building Services Engineers (CIBSE) and the Heating and Ventilating Contractors Association (HVCA) and is available from HSE Books price £4.00.

Ventilation is dealt with in detail in VENTILATION.

## Temperature

W11005    The temperature in all workplaces inside buildings should be reasonable during working hours. [*Workplace (Health, Safety and Welfare) Regulations 1992 (SI 1992 No 3004), Reg 7*]. Workroom temperatures should enable people to work (and visit sanitary conveniences) in reasonable comfort, without the need for extra or special clothing. Although the Regulations themselves do not specify a maximum or minimum indoor workplace temperature, the approved code of practice (ACoP) sets out that the minimum acceptable temperature is 16°C at the workstation, except where work involves considerable physical effort, when it reduces to 13°C (dry bulb thermometer reading). Space heating of the average workplace should be 16°C, and this should be maintained throughout the remainder of the working day. However, this is a minimum temperature. The method of heating or cooling should not result in dangerous or offensive gases or fumes entering the workplace.

The following temperatures for different types of work are recommended by the Chartered Institute of Building Services Engineers (CIBSE):

(*a*)    heavy work in factories 13°C;

(*b*)    light work in factories 16°C;

(*c*)    hospital wards and shops 18°C; and

(*d*)    office and dining rooms 20°C.

Maintenance of such temperatures may not always be feasible, as, for instance, where hot/cold production/storage processes are involved, or where food has to be stored. In such cases, an approximate temperature should be maintained. With cold storage, this may be achievable by keeping a small chilling area separate or by product insulation; whereas, in the case of hot processes, insulation of hot plant or pipes, provision of cooling plant, window shading and positioning of workstations away from radiant heat should be considered in order to achieve a reasonably comfortable temperature. Moreover, where it is necessary from time to time to work in rooms normally unoccupied (e.g. storerooms), temporary heating should be installed. Thermometers must be provided so that workers can periodically check the temperatures.

Where, despite the provision of local heating or cooling, temperatures are still not reasonably comfortable, suitable protective clothing or rest facilities should be provided, or there should be systems of work in place, such as job rotation, to minimise the length of time workers are exposed to uncomfortable temperatures.

HSE guidance on the Regulations, *Workplace health, safety and welfare: A short guide for managers*, sets out how to carry out an assessment of the risk to workers' health from working in either a hot or cold environment. This advises that employers should look at personal factors, such as body activity, the amount and type of clothing and duration of exposure, together with environmental factors, including the ambient temperature and radiant heat, and if the work is outdoor, sunlight, wind velocity and the presence of rain or snow.

It sets out that any assessment needs to consider:

●    Measures to control the workplace environment, particularly heat sources;

●    Restriction of exposure by, for example, reorganising tasks to build in rest periods or other breaks from work;

●    Medical pre-selection of employees to ensure that they are fit to work in these environments;

●    Use of suitable clothing;

- Acclimatisation of workers to the working environment;

- Training in the precautions to be taken; and

- Supervision to ensure that the precautions the assessment identifies are taken.

HSE produces further guidance on temperature at work, *Thermal comfort in the workplace: Guidance for employers.* This is available from HSE Books, price £3.50.

For employers with outdoor workers there is a free leaflet, *Keep your top on*, which contains guidance on working outdoors in sunny weather, also available from HSE Books.

## Lighting

W11006    Every workplace must be provided with suitable and sufficient lighting. [*Workplace (Health, Safety and Welfare) Regulations 1992 (SI 1992 No 3004), Reg 8*]. This should be natural lighting, so far as is reasonably practicable. There should also be suitable and sufficient emergency lighting where necessary. The ACoP sets out that in order to be suitable and sufficient, lighting must enable people to work and move about safely. HSE guidance on the Regulations advises that where necessary, local lighting should be provided at individual workstations, and at places of particular risk such as crossing points on traffic routes.

An HSE booklet, *Lighting at work*, gives detailed guidance in this area and is available from HSE Books, price £9.25. LIGHTING also deals with this area in greater detail.

## General cleanliness

W11007    All furniture and fittings of every workplace must be kept sufficiently clean. Surfaces of floors, walls and ceilings must be capable of being kept sufficiently clean and waste materials must not accumulate other than in waste receptacles. [*Workplace (Health, Safety and Welfare) Regulations 1992 (SI 1992 No 3004), Reg 9*].

The level and frequency of cleanliness will vary according to workplace use and purpose. Obviously a factory canteen should be cleaner than a factory floor. Floors and indoor traffic routes should be cleaned at least once a week, though dirt and refuse not in suitable receptacles should be removed at least daily, particularly in hot atmospheres or hot weather. Interior walls, ceilings and work surfaces should be cleaned at suitable intervals and ceilings and interior walls painted and/or tiled so that they can be kept clean. Surface treatment should be renewed when it can no longer be cleaned properly. In addition, cleaning will be necessary to remove spillages and waste matter from drains or sanitary conveniences. Methods of cleaning, however, should not expose anyone to substantial amounts of dust, and absorbent floors likely to be contaminated by oil or other substances difficult to remove, should be sealed or coated, say, with non-slip floor paint (not covered with carpet!).

## Workroom dimensions/space

W11008    Every room in which people work should have sufficient

(*a*)    floor area,

(*b*)    height, and

(*c*)    unoccupied space

for health, safety and welfare purposes. [*Workplace (Health, Safety and Welfare) Regulations 1992 (SI 1992 No 3004), Reg 10*].

Workrooms should have enough uncluttered space to allow people to go to and from workstations with relative ease. The number of people who may work in any particular room at any time will depend not only on the size of the room but also on the space given over to furniture, fittings, equipment and general room layout. Workrooms should be of sufficient height to afford staff safe access to workstations. If, however, the workroom is in an old building, say, with low beams or other possible obstructions, this should be clearly marked, e.g. 'Low beams, mind your head'.

The total volume of the room (when empty), divided by the number of people normally working there, should be 11 cubic metres (minimum) per person, although this does not apply to:

(i)    retail sales kiosks, attendants' shelters etc.,

(ii)    lecture/meeting rooms etc.

[*Workplace (Health, Safety and Welfare) Regulations 1992 (SI 1992 No 3004), Sch 1*].

In making this calculation, any part of a room which is higher than 3 metres is counted as being 3 metres high.

Where furniture occupies a considerable part of the room, 11 metres may not be sufficient space per person. Here more careful planning and general room layout is required. Similarly, rooms may need to be larger or have fewer people working in them depending on the contents and layout of the room and the nature of the work.

### Workstations and seating

The Regulations stipulate the following.

*(a) Workstations*

Every workstation must be so arranged that:

(i)    it is suitable for

(*a*)    any person at work who is likely to work at the workstation, and

(*b*)    any work likely to be done there;

(ii)    so far as reasonably practicable, it provides protection from adverse weather;

(iii)    it enables a person to leave it swiftly or to be assisted in an emergency;

(iv)    it ensures any person is not likely to slip or fall.

[*Workplace (Health, Safety and Welfare) Regulations 1992 (SI 1992 No 3004), Reg 11(1)(2)*].

*(b) Workstation seating*

A suitable seat must be provided for each person at work whose work (or a substantial part of it) can or must be done seated. The seat should be suitable for:

(i)    the person doing the work, and

(ii)    the work to be done.

Where necessary, a suitable footrest should be provided.

[*Workplace (Health, Safety and Welfare) Regulations 1992 (SI 1992 No 3004), Reg 11(3)(4)*].

It should be possible to carry out work safely and comfortably. Work materials and equipment in frequent use (or controls) should always be within easy reach, so that people do not have to bend or stretch unduly, and the worker should be at a suitable height in relation to the work surface. Workstations, including seating and access, should be suitable for special needs, for instance, disabled workers. The workstation should allow people likely to have to do work there adequate freedom of movement and ability to stand upright, thereby avoiding the need to work in cramped conditions. More particularly, seating should be suitable, providing adequate support for the lower back and a footrest provided, if feet cannot be put comfortably flat on the floor.

Workstations with visual display units (VDUs) are subject to the *Health and Safety (Display Screen Equipment) Regulations 1992 (SI 1992 No 2792)* (see OFFICES AND SHOPS).

The Health and Safety Executive (HSE) revised its guidance on seating in 1998, and advises employers to use risk assessments in order to ensure that safe seating is provided. *Seating at Work*, HS(G)57 is available, price £5.95, from HSE Books.

## Condition of floors and traffic routes

W11010   The principal dangers connected with industrial and commercial floors are slipping, tripping and falling. Slip, trip and fall resistance are a combination of the right floor surface and the appropriate type of footwear. Employers should ensure that level changes, multiple changes of floor surfaces, steps and ramps etc. are clearly indicated. Safety underfoot is at bottom a trade-off between slip resistance and ease of cleaning. Floors with rough surfaces tend to be more slip-resistant than floors with smooth surfaces, especially when wet; by contrast, smooth surfaces are much easier to clean but less slip-resistant. Use of vinyl flooring in public areas – basically slip-resistant – is on the increase. Vinyl floors should be periodically stripped, degreased and resealed with slip-resistant finish; linoleum floors similarly.

Apart from being safe, floors must also be hygienically clean. In this connection, quarry tiles have long been 'firm favourites' in commercial kitchens, hospital kitchens etc. but can be hygienically deceptive. In particular, grouted joints can trap bacteria as well as presenting endless practical cleaning problems. Hence the gradual transition to seamless floors in hygiene-critical areas. Whichever floor surface is appropriate and whichever treatment is suitable, underfoot safety depends on workplace activity (office or factory), variety of spillages (food, water, oil, chemicals), nature of traffic (pedestrian, cars, trucks).

Thus, floors in workplaces must:

(*a*)   be constructed so as to be suitable for use. [*Workplace (Health, Safety and Welfare) Regulations 1992 (SI 1992 No 3004), Reg 12(1)*].

They should always be of sound construction and adequate strength and stability to sustain loads and passing internal traffic; they should never be overloaded (see *Greaves v Baynham Meikle [1975] 3 AER 99* for possible consequences in civil law).

(*b*)   (i)   not have holes or slopes, or

(ii)   not be uneven or slippery

so as to expose a person to risk of injury. [*Workplace (Health, Safety and Welfare) Regulations 1992 (SI 1992 No 3004), Reg 12(2)(a)*].

The surfaces of floors and traffic routes should be even and free from holes, bumps and slipping hazards that could cause a person to slip, trip or fall, or drop or lose control of something being lifted or carried; or cause instability or loss of control of a vehicle.

Holes, bumps or uneven surfaces or areas resulting from damage or wear and tear should be made good and, pending this, barriers should be erected or locations conspicuously marked. Temporary holes, following, say, removal of floorboards, should be adequately guarded. Special needs should be catered for, for instance, disabled walkers or those with impaired sight. (Deep holes are governed by *Workplace (Health, Safety and Welfare) Regulations 1992 (SI 1992 No 3004), Reg 13* (see W9003 WORK AT HEIGHTS).) Where possible, steep slopes should be avoided, and otherwise provided with a secure handrail. Ramps used by disabled persons should also have handrails.

(*c*)   be kept free from

(i)   obstructions, and

(ii)   articles/substances likely to cause persons to slip, trip or fall

so far as reasonably practicable. [*Workplace (Health, Safety and Welfare) Regulations 1992 (SI 1992 No 3004), Reg 12(3)*].

Floors should be kept free of obstructions impeding access or presenting hazards, particularly near or on steps, stairs, escalators and moving walkways, on emergency routes or outlets, in or near doorways or gangways or by corners or junctions. Where temporary obstructions are unavoidable, access should be prevented and people warned of the possible hazard. Furniture being moved should not be left in a place where it can cause a hazard.

(*d*)   have effective drainage. [*Workplace (Health, Safety and Welfare) Regulations 1992 (SI 1992 No 3004), Reg 12(2)(b)*].

Where floors are likely to get wet, effective drainage (without drains becoming contaminated with toxic, corrosive substances) should drain it away, e.g. in laundries, potteries and food processing plants. Drains and channels should be situated so as to reduce the area of wet floor and the floor should slope slightly towards the drain and ideally have covers flush with the floor surface. Processes and plant which cause discharges or leaks of liquids should be enclosed and leaks from taps caught and drained away. In food processing and preparation plants, work surfaces should be arranged so as to minimise the likelihood of spillage. Where a leak or spillage occurs, it should be fenced off or mopped up immediately.

Staircases should be provided with a handrail. Any open side of a staircase should have minimum fencing of an upper rail at 900mm or higher, and a lower rail.

It is important also to consider the dangers posed by snow and ice upon, for example, external fire escapes.

## Falls and falling objects

W11011 *Workplace (Health, Safety and Welfare) Regulations 1992 (SI 1992 No 3004), Reg 13* deals with falls and falling objects, which are covered in detail in WORK AT HEIGHTS.

It also requires that tanks, pits and other structures containing dangerous substances are securely covered or fenced where there is a risk of a person falling. Traffic routes over such open structures should also be securely fenced.

## Windows and transparent or translucent doors, gates and walls

W11012 Transparent or translucent surfaces in windows, doors, gates, walls and partitions should be constructed of safety material or be adequately protected against breakage, where necessary for health and safety reasons, where:

(*a*) any part is at shoulder level or below in doors and gates; or

(*b*) any part is at waist level or below in windows, walls and partitions, with the exception of glass houses.

Screens or barriers can be used as an alternative to the use of safety materials. Narrow panels of up to 250mm width are excluded from the requirement.

Transparent or translucent surfaces should be marked to make them apparent where this is necessary for health and safety reasons.

[*Workplace (Health, Safety and Welfare) Regulations 1992 (SI 1992 No 3004), Reg 14*].

## Windows, skylights and ventilators

W11013 Openable windows, skylights and ventilators must be capable of being opened, closed and adjusted safely. They must not be positioned so as to pose a risk when open.

They should be capable of being reached and operated safely, with window poles or similar equipment, or stable platforms, made available where necessary. Where there is the danger of falling from a height, devices should be provided to prevent this by ensuring the window cannot open too far. They should not cause a hazard by projecting into an area where people are likely to collide with them when open. The bottom edge of opening windows should normally be at least 800mm above floor level, unless there is a barrier to prevent falls.

[*Workplace (Health, Safety and Welfare) Regulations 1992 (SI 1992 No 3004), Reg 15*].

## Ability to clean windows etc. safely

W11014 *Workplace (Health, Safety and Welfare) Regulations 1992 (SI 1992 No 3004), Reg 16* deals with the safe cleaning of windows and skylights where these cannot be cleaned from the ground or other suitable surface. This is dealt with in detail in WORK AT HEIGHTS.

## Organisation of traffic routes

W11015 Traffic routes in workplaces should allow pedestrians and vehicles to circulate safely, be safely constructed, be suitably indicated where necessary for health and safety reasons, and be kept clear of obstructions.

They should be planned to give the safest route, wide enough for the safe movement of the largest vehicle permitted to use them, and they should avoid vulnerable items like fuel or chemical plants or pipes, and open and unprotected edges.

There should be safe areas for loading and unloading. Sharp or blind bends should be avoided where possible, and if they cannot be avoided, one-way systems or mirrors to improve visibility should be used. Sensible speed limits should be set and enforced. There should be prominent warning of any limited headroom or potentially dangerous obstructions such as overhead electric cables. Routes should be marked where necessary and there should be suitable and sufficient parking areas in safe locations.

Traffic routes should keep vehicles and pedestrians apart and there should be pedestrian crossing points on vehicle routes. Traffic routes and parking and loading areas should be soundly constructed on level ground. Health and Safety Executive (HSE) guidance in this area can be found in the publication, *Workplace transport safety – guidance for employers*, HS(G)136, price £7.50, available from HSE Books.

[*Workplace (Health, Safety and Welfare) Regulations 1992 (SI 1992 No 3004), Reg 17*].

This area is dealt with in detail in ACCESS, TRAFFIC ROUTES AND VEHICLES.

### Doors and gates

**W11016**     Doors and gates must be suitably constructed and fitted with safety devices. In particular,

(i)     a sliding door/gate must have a device to prevent it coming off its track during use;

(ii)     an upward opening door/gate must have a device to prevent its falling back;

(iii)     a powered door/gate must

      (*a*)     have features preventing it causing injury by trapping a person (e.g. accessible emergency stop controls),

      (*b*)     be able to be operated manually unless it opens automatically if the power fails;

(iv)     a door/gate capable of opening, by being pushed from either side, must provide a clear view of the space close to both sides.

[*Workplace (Health, Safety and Welfare) Regulations 1992 (SI 1992 No 3004), Reg 18*].

Doors and gates that swing in both directions should have a transparent panel, unless they are low enough to see over.

### Escalators and travelators

**W11017**     Escalators and travelators must:

(*a*)     function safely;

(*b*)     be equipped with safety devices;

(*c*)     be fitted with emergency stop controls.

[*Workplace (Health, Safety and Welfare) Regulations 1992 (SI 1992 No 3004), Reg 19*].

## Welfare facilities

W11018    'Welfare facilities' is a wide term, embracing both sanitary and washing accommodation at workplaces, provision of drinking water, clothing accommodation (including facilities for changing clothes) and facilities for rest and eating meals (see W11027 below). The need for sufficient suitable hygienic lavatory and washing facilities in all workplaces is obvious. Sufficient facilities must be provided to enable everyone at work to use them without undue delay. They do not have to be in the actual workplace but ideally should be situated in the building(s) containing them and they should provide protection from the weather, be well-ventilated, well-lit and enjoy a reasonable temperature. Where disabled workers are employed, special provision should be made for their sanitary and washing requirements. Wash basins should allow washing of hands, face and forearms and, where work is particularly strenuous, dirty, or results in skin contamination (e.g. molten metal work), showers or baths should be provided. In the case of showers, they should be fed by hot and cold water and fitted with a thermostatic mixer valve. Washing facilities should ensure privacy for the user and be separate from the water closet, with a door that can be secured from the inside. It should not be possible to see urinals or the communal shower from outside the facilities when the entrance/exit door opens. Entrance/exit doors should be fitted to both washing and sanitary facilities (unless there are other means of ensuring privacy). Windows to sanitary accommodation, showers/bathrooms should be obscured either by being frosted, or by blinds or curtains (unless it is impossible to see into them from outside).

This section examines current statutory requirements in all workplaces. For requirements relating to sanitary conveniences and washing facilities on construction sites see C8045 CONSTRUCTION AND BUILDING OPERATIONS.

### *Sanitary conveniences in all workplaces*

W11019    Suitable and sufficient sanitary conveniences must be provided at readily accessible places. In particular,

(*a*)    the rooms containing them must be adequately ventilated and lit;

(*b*)    they (and the rooms in which they are situated) must be kept clean and in an orderly condition;

(*c*)    separate rooms containing conveniences must be provided for men and women except where the convenience is in a separate room which can be locked from the inside.

[*Workplace (Health, Safety and Welfare) Regulations 1992 (SI 1992 No 3004), Reg 20*].

### *Washing facilities in all workplaces*

W11020    Suitable and sufficient washing facilities (including showers where necessary (see W11018 above)), must be provided at readily accessible places or points. In particular, facilities must:

(*a*)    be provided in the immediate vicinity of every sanitary convenience (whether or not provided elsewhere);

(*b*)    be provided in the vicinity of any changing rooms – whether or not provided elsewhere;

(*c*)    include a supply of clean hot and cold or warm water (if possible, running water);

(*d*)    include soap (or something similar);

(*e*)   include towels (or the equivalent);

(*f*)   be in rooms sufficiently well-ventilated and well-lit;

(*g*)   be kept clean and in an orderly condition (including rooms in which they are situate);

(*h*)   be separate for men and women, except where they are provided in a lockable room intended to be used by one person at a time, or where they are provided for the purposes of washing hands, forearms and face only, where separate provision is not necessary.

[*Workplace (Health, Safety and Welfare) Regulations 1992 (SI 1992 No 3004), Reg 21*].

*Minimum number of facilities – sanitary conveniences and washing facilities*

(*a*) *People at work*

**W11021**

| Number of people at work | Number of WCs | Number of wash stations |
|---|---|---|
| 1 to 5 | 1 | 1 |
| 6 to 25 | 2 | 2 |
| 26 to 50 | 3 | 3 |
| 51 to 75 | 4 | 4 |
| 76 to 100 | 5 | 5 |

(*b*) *Men at work*

| Number of men at work | Number of WCs | Number of urinals |
|---|---|---|
| 1 to 15 | 1 | 1 |
| 16 to 30 | 2 | 1 |
| 31 to 45 | 2 | 2 |
| 46 to 60 | 3 | 2 |
| 61 to 75 | 3 | 3 |
| 76 to 90 | 4 | 3 |
| 91 to 100 | 4 | 4 |

For every 25 people above 100 an additional WC and wash station should be provided; in the case of WCs used only by *men*, an additional WC per every 50 men above 100 is sufficient (provided that at least an equal number of additional urinals is provided). [*Workplace (Health, Safety and Welfare) Regulations 1992 (SI 1992 No 3004), Sch 1, Part II*].

*Particularly dirty work etc.*

**W11022**   Where work results in heavy soiling of hands, arms and forearms, there should be one wash station for every 10 people at work up to 50 people; and one extra for every additional 20 people. And where sanitary and wash facilities are also used by members of the public, the number of conveniences and facilities should be increased so that workers can use them without undue delay.

### Temporary work sites

W11023    At temporary work sites suitable and sufficient sanitary conveniences and washing facilities should be provided so far as is reasonably practicable (see E15039 ENFORCEMENT for meaning). If possible, these should incorporate flushing sanitary conveniences and washing facilities with running water.

### Drinking water

W11024    An adequate supply of wholesome drinking water must be provided for all persons at work in the workplace. It must be readily accessible at suitable places and conspicuously marked, unless non-drinkable cold water supplies are clearly marked. In addition, there must be provided a sufficient number of suitable cups (or other drinking vessels), unless the water supply is in a jet. [*Workplace (Health, Safety and Welfare) Regulations 1992 (SI 1992 No 3004), Reg 22*].

Where water cannot be obtained from the mains supply, it should only be provided in refillable containers. The containers should be enclosed to prevent contamination and refilled at least daily. So far as reasonably practicable, drinking water taps should not be installed in sanitary accommodation, or in places where contamination is likely, for instance, in a workshop containing lead processes.

### Clothing accommodation

W11025    Suitable and sufficient accommodation must be provided for:

(*a*)    any person at work's own clothing which is not worn during working hours; and

(*b*)    special clothing which is worn by any person at work but which is not taken home, for example, overalls, uniforms and thermal clothing.

[*Workplace (Health, Safety and Welfare) Regulations 1992 (SI 1992 No 3004), Reg 23(1)*].

Accommodation is not suitable unless it:

(i)    provides suitable security for the person's own clothing where changing facilities are required;

(ii)    includes separate accommodation for clothing worn at work and for other clothing, where necessary to avoid risks to health or damage to clothing; and

(iii)    is in a suitable location.

[*Workplace (Health, Safety and Welfare) Regulations 1992 (SI 1992 No 3004), Reg 23(2)*].

Work clothing is overalls, uniforms, thermal clothing and hats worn for hygiene purposes. Workers' own clothing should be able to hang in a clean, warm, dry, well-ventilated place. If this is not possible in the workroom, then it should be put elsewhere. Accommodation should take the form of a separate hook or peg. Clothing which is dirty, damp or contaminated owing to work should be accommodated separately from the worker's own clothes.

## Facilities for changing clothing

W11026  Suitable and sufficient facilities must be provided for any person at work in the workplace to change clothing where:

(*a*)  the person has to wear special clothing for work, and

(*b*)  the person cannot be expected to change in another room.

Facilities are not suitable unless they include:

(i)  separate facilities for men and women, or

(ii)  separate use of facilities by men and women.

[*Workplace (Health, Safety and Welfare) Regulations 1992 (SI 1992 No 3004), Reg 24*].

Changing rooms (or room) should be provided for workers who change into special work clothing and where they remove more than outer clothing; also where it is necessary to prevent workers' own clothes being contaminated by a harmful substance. Changing facilities should be easily accessible from workrooms and eating places. They should contain adequate seating and clothing accommodation, and showers or baths if these are provided (see W11018 above). Privacy of user should be ensured. The facilities should be large enough to cater for the maximum number of persons at work expected to use them at any one time without overcrowding or undue delay.

*Post Office v Footitt [2000] IRLR 243*, involved an employers' appeal against an improvement notice requiring the construction of a separate changing room for women postal workers to change into and out of their uniforms, and looked at the definition of 'special clothing' and at the concept of propriety.

An environmental health officer had served an improvement notice under the *Workplace (Health, Safety and Welfare) Regulations 1992 (SI 1992 No 3004), Reg 24* as she had found that any female employees wishing to change their clothing could only do so in the general area of the women's toilet facilities.

In the High Court, the judge held that the uniform worn by postal workers was 'special clothing' for the purposes of *Regulation 24*. It was held that 'special clothing' is not merely limited to clothing that is worn only at work. Therefore the fact that postal workers wear their uniform to and from work does not prevent it from being 'special clothing'. The changing facilities for women provided by the Post Office were therefore not 'suitable and sufficient' within the meaning of the Regulation.

The court also held that the fact that the changing facilities for men and women were separated was not in itself enough to satisfy the concept of propriety referred to in *Regulation 24(2)*. There is no reason why requiring one female to undress in the presence of another cannot be said to offend against the principles of propriety. The fact that many people would have no objection to changing in the company of others of the same sex does not absolve the employer from providing facilities for those who may prefer privacy.

## Rest and eating facilities

W11027  Suitable and sufficient rest facilities must be provided at readily accessible places. [*Workplace (Health, Safety and Welfare) Regulations 1992 (SI 1992 No 3004), Reg 25(1)*].

(*a*)  *Rest facilities*

A rest facility is:

(i)  in the case of a new workplace, extension or conversion – a rest room (or rooms);

(ii)  in other cases, a rest room (or rooms) or rest area; including

(iii)  (in both cases):

— appropriate facilities for eating meals where food eaten in the workplace would otherwise be likely to become contaminated;

— suitable arrangements for protecting non-smokers from tobacco smoke. The ACoP advises that this can be achieved by providing separate areas for smokers and non-smokers, or by prohibiting smoke in rest areas;

— a facility for a pregnant or nursing mother to rest in.

Canteens or restaurants may be used as rest rooms provided that there is no obligation to buy food there (ACoP). [*Workplace (Health, Safety and Welfare) Regulations 1992 (SI 1992 No 3004), Regs 25(2)—(4)*].

(*b*)  *Eating facilities*

Where workers regularly eat meals at work, facilities must be provided for them to do so. [*Workplace (Health, Safety and Welfare) Regulations 1992 (SI 1992 No 3004), Reg 25(5)*].

In offices and other workplaces where there is no risk of contamination, seats in the work area are sufficient, although workers should not be interrupted excessively during breaks, for example, by the public. In other cases, rest areas or rooms should be provided and in the case of new workplaces, this should be a separate rest room. Rest facilities should be large enough, and have enough seats with backrests and tables, for the number of workers likely to use them at one time.

Where workers regularly eat meals at work, there should be suitable and sufficient facilities. These should be provided where food would otherwise be contaminated, by dust or water for example. Seats in work areas can be suitable eating facilities, provided the work area is clean. There should be a means to prepare or obtain a hot drink, and where persons work during hours or at places where hot food cannot be readily obtained, there should be the means for heating their own food. Eating facilities should be kept clean.

## Smoking

W11028    Providing protection to non-smokers from tobacco smoke in rest areas is the only specific legal requirement concerning smoking at work, although the general duty to ensure the health, safety and welfare of the employees under the *Health and Safety at Work etc. Act 1974 (HSWA 1974), s 2* applies. However there have been a number of legal cases, and compensation awards have been made to employees who have claimed their health has been affected by breathing in tobacco smoke at work.

Stockport Metropolitan Council has made two out of court settlements of £25,000 and £15,000 to employees who claimed that their health was damaged as a result of passive smoking. In addition, an Employment Appeal Tribunal (EAT) case, *Dryden v Greater Glasgow Health Board [1992] IRLR 469*, held that a change to a complete smoking ban, which meant an employee who smoked had to leave her job, did not amount to constructive dismissal. In this case, the employer had consulted workers about the introduction of the ban.

In another EAT case, *Walton and Morse v Dorrington* [*1997*], a tribunal decision that an employee had been constructively dismissed when her employer failed to provide her with a smoke free environment or deal with her problems relating to passive smoking, was upheld.

In the first passive smoking case to reach the courts, in May 1998, a nurse lost her action for damages against her employer. Silvia Sparrow claimed that she had developed asthma as a result of exposure to environmental tobacco smoke in a residential care home for elderly people. But the court said she had failed to prove that her former employers, St Andrew's Homes Ltd, were negligent so as to cause injury to her.

The Health and Safety Commission (HSC) has recommended that an approved code of practice (ACoP) on passive smoking should be introduced. This would give authoritative guidance on the employer's legal obligation to protect their employees from exposure to environmental tobacco smoke (ETS).

As with other ACoPs, failing to follow the code would not in itself be an offence, but the employer would have to demonstrate that equally effective methods have been adopted to signal compliance with the law.

Under the code, employers will have to determine the most reasonably practical way of controlling ETS. This could involve:

• Banning smoking in the workplace completely or partially;

• Physically segregating non-smokers from tobacco smoke;

• Providing adequate ventilation; or

• Implementing a system of work to reduce the time an employee is exposed to ETS.

There will, however, be a two-year exemption for parts of the hospitality industry, such as bars, clubs and restaurants. They will need to instead comply with the Public Places Charter during this period.

The code is currently awaiting ministerial approval.

The current HSE publication, *Passive smoking at work*, IND(G)63(L), recommends that all employers should introduce a policy to control smoking in the workplace in full consultation with employees.

The guidance sets out that environmental tobacco smoke contains carbon dioxide, hydrogen cyanide and ammonia and that passive smoking has irritant effects on the eyes, throat and respiratory tract. In addition to aggravating asthma, research indicates that it can increase the risk of lung cancer and may increase the risk of heart disease.

The HSE agrees with the advice of the Independent Scientific Committee which says that employers should regard non-smoking as the norm in enclosed workplaces and make provision for smoking, rather than vice versa, and that smokers should be segregated from non-smokers.

The guidance advises employers that they should have a specific written policy on smoking in the workplace which gives priority to the needs of non-smokers. Any policy should be introduced with proper consultation of employees and their representatives and a minimum of three months' notice of its introduction should be given. It also advises that may employers provide help to smokers to reduce or give up smoking.

It outlines that the only effective ways to achieve a smoke-free environment for non-smokers are to:

● Introduce a complete ban on indoor smoking; or

● Ban smoking in all parts of the building with the exception of designated, enclosed smoking areas.

A less effective method, which employers may have to resort to if the constraints of the workplace do not allow the above, is to segregate smokers and non-smokers in separate rooms and ban smoking in common areas.

The guidance advises employers in buildings with mechanical ventilation to consider discharging air from smoking areas separately, and if this is not reasonably practicable, decontamination systems should be used to bring the re-circulated air up to an appropriate standard.

### Civil liability

W11029    There is no specific reference to civil liability in the Regulations. However, safety regulations are actionable, even if silent (as here), and, if a person suffered injury/damage as a result of breach by an employer, he could sue. Certainly, there is civil liability for breach of the *Building Regulations 1991 (SI 1991 No 2768)* (W11044 below).

## Safety signs at work – Health and Safety (Safety Signs and Signals) Regulations 1996 (SI 1996 No 341)

W11030    Traditionally, safety signs, communications and warnings have played a residual role in reducing the risk of injury or damage at work, the need for them generally having been engineered out or accommodated in the system of work – a situation unaffected by these Regulations.

### Types of signs

W11031    Safety signs and signals can be of the following types:

(*a*)    permanent (e.g. signboards);

(*b*)    occasional (e.g. acoustic signals or verbal communications – acoustic signals should be avoided where there is considerable ambient noise).

### Interchanging and combining signs

W11032    Examples of interchanging and combining signs are:

(*a*)    a safety colour (see W11033 below) or signboard to mark places where there is an obstacle;

(*b*)    illuminated signs, acoustic signals or verbal communication; and

(*c*)    hand signals or verbal communication.

[*Health and Safety (Safety Signs and Signals) Regulations 1996 (SI 1996 No 341), Sch 1, Part I, para 3*].

## Safety colours

| Colour | Meaning or purpose | Instructions and information |
|---|---|---|
| Red | Prohibition sign | Dangerous behaviour |
| | Danger | Stop, shutdown, emergency cut-out services |
| | | Evacuate |
| | Fire-fighting equipment | Identification and location |
| Yellow or Amber | Warning sign | Be careful, take precautions |
| | | Examine |
| Blue | Mandatory sign | Specific behaviour or action |
| | | Wear personal protective equipment |
| Green | Emergency escape, first-aid sign | Doors, exits, routes, equipment and facilities |
| | No danger | Return to normal |

[*Health and Safety (Safety Signs and Signals) Regulations 1996 (SI 1996 No 341), Sch 1, Part I, para 4*].

## Varieties of safety signs and signals

W11034    Safety signs and signals include, comprehensively:

(*a*)    safety signs – providing information about health and safety at work by means of a signboard, safety colour, illuminated sign, acoustic signal, hand signal or verbal communication;

(*b*)    signboards – signs giving information by way of a simple pictogram, lighting intensity providing visibility (these should be weather-resistant and easily seen);

(*c*)    mandatory signs – signs prescribing behaviour (e.g. safety boots must be worn);

(*d*)    prohibition signs – signs prohibiting behaviour likely to cause a health and safety risk (e.g. no smoking);

(*e*)    hand signals – movement or position of arms/hands for guiding persons carrying out operations that could endanger employees;

(*f*)    verbal communications – predetermined spoken messages communicated by human or artificial voice, preferably short, simple and as clear as possible.

[*Health and Safety (Safety Signs and Signals) Regulations 1996 (SI 1996 No 341), Reg 2*].

## Duty of employer

W11035    It is only where a risk assessment carried out under the *Management of Health and Safety at Work Regulations 1999 (SI 1999 No 3242)* (see EMPLOYERS' DUTIES TO THEIR EMPLOYEES) indicates that a risk cannot be avoided, engineered out or reduced significantly by way of a system of work that resort to signs and signals becomes necessary. In these circumstances, all employers (including offshore employers) must:

(*a*)    provide and maintain any appropriate safety sign(s) (see W11037–W11041 below) (including fire safety signals) but not a hand signal or verbal communication;

(*b*)    so far as is reasonably practicable, ensure that correct hand signals or verbal communications are used;

(*c*)    provide and maintain any necessary road traffic sign (where there is a risk to employees in connection with traffic); and

(*d*)    provide employees with comprehensible and relevant information, training and instruction and measures to be taken in connection with safety signs.

[*Health and Safety (Safety Signs and Signals) Regulations 1996 (SI 1996 No 341), Regs 4, 5*].

*Schedule 1* to the Regulations sets out the minimum requirements concerning safety signs and signals with regard to the type of signs to be used in particular circumstances, interchanging and combining signs, signboards, signs on containers and pipes, the identification and location of fire-fighting equipment, signs used for obstacles and dangerous locations, and for marking traffic routes, illuminated signs, acoustic signals, verbal communication and hand signals.


## Exclusions

W11036    Excluded from the operation of these Regulations are:

(*a*)    the supply of dangerous substances or products;

(*b*)    the transportation of dangerous goods;

(*c*)    road traffic signs (except where there is a particular risk to employees. Where there is a risk arising from the movement of traffic and the risk is addressed by a sign stipulated in the *Road Traffic Regulations Act 1984* (e.g. speed restriction sign), these signs must be used, whether or not the Act applies to that place of work. In effect this means that where road speed and other signs are needed on a company's road, these must replicate the signs used for the purpose on public roads; and

(*d*)    activities on board ship.

[*Health and Safety (Safety Signs and Signals) Regulations 1996 (SI 1996 No 341), Reg 3(1)*].


## Examples of safety signs

*Prohibitory signs*

W11037    Intrinsic features:

—    round shape

— black pictogram on white background, red edging and diagonal line (the red part to take up at least 35% of the sign area).

| No smoking | Smoking and naked flames forbidden | No access for pedestrians |

| Do not extinguish with water | Not drinkable | No access for unauthorised persons |

| No access for industrial vehicles | Do not touch |

*fig. 1 Safety signs (prohibitory)*

### Warning signs

W11038   Intrinsic features:

— triangular shape

— black pictogram on a yellow background with black edging (the yellow part to take up at least 50% of the area of the sign).

| Flammable material or high temperature | Explosive material | Toxic material |

*fig. 2 Safety signs (warning)*

*Mandatory signs*

W11039    Intrinsic features:

—    round shape

—    white pictogram on a blue background (the blue part to take up at least 50% of the area of the sign).

*fig. 3 Safety signs (mandatory)*

*Emergency escape or first-aid signs*

W11040    Intrinsic features:

—    rectangular or square shape

—    white pictogram on a green background (the green part to take up at least 50% of the area of the sign).

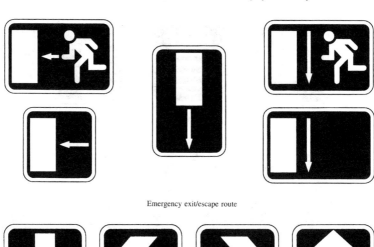

Emergency exit/escape route

This way
(supplementary information sign)

First-aid post          Stretcher          Safety shower          Eyewash

Emergency telephone for first-aid or escape

*fig. 4 Safety signs (emergency escape or first-aid)*

### Fire-fighting signs

W11041    Intrinsic features:

— rectangular or square shape

— white pictogram on a red background (the red part to take up at least 50% of the area of the sign).

| Fire hose | Ladder | Fire extinguisher | Emergency fire telephone |

This way
(supplementary information sign)

*fig. 5 Safety signs (fire-fighting)*

## Examples of hand signals

W11042  *Meaning*  *Description*  *Illustration*

### A. General signals

START
Attention
Start of
Command

both arms are extended
horizontally with the palms
facing forwards.

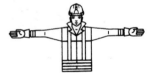

STOP
Interruption
End of movement

the right arm points
upwards with the palm
facing forwards.

END
of the operation

both hands are clasped at
chest height.

## B. Vertical movements

RAISE

the right arm points upwards with the palm facing forward and slowly makes a circle.

LOWER

the right arm points downwards with the palm facing inwards and slowly makes a circle.

VERTICAL DISTANCE

the hands indicate the relevant distance.

## C. Horizontal movements

MOVE FORWARDS

both arms are bent with the palms facing upwards, and the forearms make slow movements towards the body.

MOVE BACKWARDS

both arms are bent with the palms facing downwards, and the forearms make slow movements away from the body.

RIGHT
to the signalman's

the right arm is extended more or less horizontally with the palm facing downwards and slowly makes small movements to the right.

| | | |
|---|---|---|
| LEFT<br>to the signalman's | the left arm is extended more or<br>less horizontally with the palm<br>facing downwards and slowly<br>makes small movements to the<br>left. | 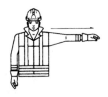 |
| HORIZONTAL<br>DISTANCE | the hands indicate the relevant<br>distance. |  |

### D. Danger

| | | |
|---|---|---|
| DANGER<br>Emergency stop | both arms point upwards with<br>the palms facing forwards. |  |
| QUICK | all movements faster. | |
| SLOW | all movements slower. | |

*fig. 6 Hand signals*

## Disability Discrimination Act 1995

W11043    The *Disability Discrimination Act 1995 (DDA 1995)* makes it unlawful for employers (who employ 15 or more people) to treat a disabled person less favourably, without a justifiable reason.

In order to gain protection under the *DDA 1995*, a person must have a substantial and long-term disability, affecting them (or which could affect them) for more than 12 months, impacting on their ability to carry out normal day-to-day activities, and affecting their mobility, dexterity, co-ordination, continence or memory. It covers mental as well as physical impairments, and applies to recruitment, selection, promotion and redundancy. It applies to all workers, including the self-employed, contract workers and agency workers, as well as employees. It does not currently apply to the police, prison and fire services nor to the armed forces.

The *DDA 1995, s 6* requires employers to make reasonable adjustments to working conditions or to the workplace to avoid putting disabled workers at a substantial disadvantage, and could therefore involve making adjustments to the physical features of workplace premises.

The Act gives examples of adjustments to the workplace that could be required, including access for wheelchairs and acquiring or modifying wheelchairs.

There is a provision in the Act to enable employers who lease their premises to obtain their landlord's permission to make alterations in order to make any necessary reasonable adjustments to the workplace.

The *Disability Discrimination (Employment Relations) Regulations 1996 (SI 1996 No 1456)* set out the duty to make adjustments in more detail. The Regulations specify that physical features of the employer's premises are:

(a) any feature arising from the design or construction of a building on the premises or any approach to, exit from or access to such a building;

(b) any fixtures, fittings, furniture, equipment or materials in or on the premises; and

(c) any other physical element or quality of land included in the premises.

Complaints about disability discrimination are heard in employment tribunals. In addition, the Disability Rights Commission, which came into effect in April 2000, can carry out formal investigations where it believes there is discrimination and can enter into legally binding agreements with employers where the employer can choose to comply with it's recommendations. It can also assist individuals taking cases to tribunals.

In *Tawling v Wisdom Toothbrushes Ltd*, a 1997 tribunal case, a woman who had a club foot and was experiencing sciatica and other pain and discomfort as a result of standing for long periods had to take increasing amounts of sickness absence.

Her employers sought advice from an organisation providing financial support for people with disabilities, the Shaw Trust. It recommended the purchase of one of two specific types of chair costing £500 and around £1000 respectively, to which the employer would have had to fund 20 per cent of the cost. The employer did not take the advice and instead provided her with a series of ordinary chairs, which did not meet her needs and then dismissed her for poor performance.

The tribunal found that the woman had been unfairly dismissed because the employer had failed to make reasonable adjustments in not providing a suitable chair for her.

# Building Regulations 1991 (SI 1991 No 2768)

**W11044** Where workplaces are built, extended or altered, or where fittings such as drains, heat-producing appliances, washing and sanitary facilities or hot water storage are provided, the *Building Regulations 1991 (SI 1991 No 2768)* normally apply.

The Regulations set down minimum standards of design and building work for the construction of buildings. They contain requirements designed to ensure the health and safety of people in and around buildings, to provide for energy conservation and to provide access for disabled people.

The requirements, which are set out in *Schedule 1* of the Regulations, concern:

● Structure

Buildings must be constructed to withstand loads and ground movement. Buildings of five or more storeys must be constructed in such a way that in the event of an accident it will not suffer collapse to an extent disproportionate to the cause. Where parts of a public building, shop or shopping mall have a roof with a clear span exceeding nine metres between supports, these should be constructed so that in the event of the failure of any part of the roof, the building will not suffer collapse to an extent disproportionate to that failure;

- Fire safety

  Buildings must be designed and constructed with a means of escape, in the case of fire, from the building to a place of safety outside the building. Internal linings of the building must inhibit the spread of fire and the building must be designed and constructed to maintain stability for a period of time in the event of fire. Party walls should resist the spread of fire between buildings and the spread of fire within buildings should be inhibited by sub-division with fire-resisting construction as appropriate to the size and intended use of the building. The building should be designed and constructed so that the unseen spread of fire and smoke within concealed spaces in the structure and fabric of the building is inhibited. The external walls and the roof of the building should resist the spread of fire, and the building should be designed and constructed to provide facilities for fire fighters and to enable fire fighting appliances to gain access to the building. Fire safety in workplaces is dealt with in detail in FIRE AND FIRE PRECAUTIONS.

- Site preparation and resistance to moisture

  The ground to be covered by the building should be reasonably free from vegetable matter, and precautions should be taken to avoid risks to health and safety from any dangerous or offensive substances found on or in this ground, and subsoil drainage should be provided where necessary to avoid damage to the fabric of the building or the passage of ground moisture to the interior of the building. The walls, floors and roof of the building should also prevent damp penetration.

- Toxic substances

  If cavity wall insulation is used, precautions should be taken to prevent any subsequent release of toxic fumes into any occupied parts of the building.

- Resistance to the passage of sound

  This part applies only to dwellings.

- Ventilation

  Rooms containing sanitary conveniences must be adequately ventilated, and provision must be made to prevent excessive condensation in a roof or a roof void above an insulated ceiling.

- Hygiene

  Adequate sanitary conveniences shall be provided in rooms provided for that purpose and they must be separated from places where food is prepared. Adequate wash basins must be provided in or next to rooms containing wcs, and again must be separated from areas where food is being prepared. There should be suitable installation for the provision of hot and cold water to washbasins, and wcs and washbasins should be designed and installed to allow them to be effectively cleaned. There are also requirements concerning the installation of hot water storage systems.

- Drainage and waste disposal

  There must be a waste water drainage system which takes foul water from toilets, washbasins and sinks to a sewer, or properly constructed cesspool or septic or settlement tank. There should be adequate rainwater drainage and adequate means of storing solid waste.

- Heat producing appliances

  Heat producing appliances designed to burn solid fuel, oil or gas and incinerators should have adequate air supply, and adequate provision for the discharge of combustion products to the outside air. Appliances should be installed, and fireplaces and chimneys constructed to reduce the risk of the building catching fire as a consequence of their use.

- Protection from falling, collision and impact

  Stairs, ladders and ramps should allow users to move safely between different levels of the building, and there should be barriers where necessary to protect people from falling. Vehicle ramps and floors and roofs with vehicular access should also be guarded with barriers where necessary to protect people in and around the building.

- Conservation of fuel and power

  Reasonable provision should be made for the conservation of fuel and power in buildings where the floor area exceeds 30 metres squared.

- Access and facilities for disabled people

  Reasonable provision should be made for disabled people to gain access to and use the building; and to use any sanitary conveniences provided. This applies to people who have an impairment which limits their ability to walk or requires them to use a wheelchair for mobility, or who have impaired hearing or sight. It excludes extensions which do not include a ground storey; material alterations and parts of a building used solely for the maintenance, inspection or repair of fittings or services.

- Glazing

  Glazing which people are likely to come into contact with must break on impact in a way unlikely to cause injury, or resist impact without breaking or be shielded or protected from impact. Transparent glazing with which people are likely to collide should be made apparent; and

- Materials and workmanship

  Any building work should be carried out with proper materials and in a workmanlike manner.

There are approved documents setting out detailed practical and technical guidance on how these requirements are to be met, although the requirements can be met in alternative ways if these are available.

The *Building Regulations 1991 (SI 1991 No 2768), Reg 11* requires that anyone intending to carry out building work or make a material change of use must give a building notice to, or deposit full plans with the local authority. This does not have to be done where gas appliances are being installed by, or are under the supervision of people approved under the Gas Safety Regulations. Full plans are only required where buildings are to be put to a use designated under the *Fire Precautions Act 1971* (see F5004 FIRE AND FIRE PRECAUTIONS).

An approved inspector can be chosen to ensure compliance with the Regulations rather than the local authority, in which case a building notice or deposit of full plans is not required. The list of approved inspectors is available from the Association of Corporate Approved Inspectors (see website: http://www.acai.org.uk

The Regulations and approved documents can be purchased from the Stationary Office on 0870 600 5522.

# Factories Act 1961

W11045    Although large parts of the *Factories Act 1961* have now been repealed and replaced by more recent legislation, some provisions are still in force, although the Health and Safety Commission (HSC) is considering complete repeal. Additionally, civil actions for injury, relating to breach of health and safety provisions of the *Factories Act* (though not welfare) may well continue for some time, since actions for personal injury can be initiated for up to three years after injury/disease has occurred. [*Limitation Act 1980, s 11*].

## Residual application of the Factories Act 1961

W11046    The *Factories Act 1961* applies to factories, as defined in *s 175*, including 'factories belonging to or in the occupation of the Crown, to building operations and works of engineering construction undertaken by or on behalf of the Crown, and to employment by or under the Crown of persons in painting buildings', e.g. hospital painters. [*Factories Act 1961, s 173(1)*].

## Enforcement of the Factories Act 1961 and regulations

W11047    Offences under the Act are normally committed by occupiers rather than owners of factories. Unless they happen to occupy a factory as well, the owners of a factory would not normally be charged. Offences therefore relate to physical occupation or control of a factory (for an extended meaning of 'occupier', see OCCUPIERS' LIABILITY). Hence the person or persons or body corporate having managerial responsibility in respect of a factory are those who commit an offence under *s 155(1)*. This will generally be the managing director and board of directors and/or individual executive directors. Moreover, if a company is in liquidation and the receiver is in control, he is the person who will be prosecuted and this has in fact happened (*Meigh v Wickenden [1942] 2 KB 160; Lord Advocate v Aero Technologies 1991 SLT 134* where the receiver was 'in occupation' and so under a duty to prevent 'accidents by fire or explosion', for the purposes of the *Explosives Act 1875, s 23*).

## Defence of factory occupier

W11048    The main defence open to a factory occupier charged with breach of the *Factories Act 1961* is that the Act itself, or more likely regulations made under it, placed the statutory duty on some person other than the occupier. Thus, where there is a contravention by any person of any regulation or order under the *Factories Act 1961*, 'that person shall be guilty of an offence and the occupier or owner . . . shall not be guilty of an offence, by reason only of the contravention of the provision . . . unless it is proved that he failed to take all reasonable steps to prevent the contravention . . .'. [*Factories Act 1961, s 155(2)*].

Before this defence can be invoked by a factory occupier or company, it is necessary to show that:

(a)    a statutory duty had been laid on someone other than the factory occupier by a regulation or order passed under the Act;

(b)    the factory occupier took all reasonable steps to prevent the contravention (a difficult test to satisfy).

*NB.* This statutory defence is not open to a building contractor (in his capacity as a notional factory occupier).

## Effect on possible civil liability

W11049   Whether conviction of an employee under the *Factories Act 1961, s 155(2)* would prejudice a subsequent claim for damages by him against a factory occupier, must be regarded as an open question. Thus, in *Potts v Reid [1942] 2 AER 161* the court said 'Criminal and civil liability are two separate things . . . The legislation (the *Factories Act 1937*) might well be unwilling to convict an owner who failed to carry out a statutory duty of a crime with which he was not himself directly concerned, but still be ready to leave the civil liability untouched'. Similarly in *Boyle v Kodak Ltd [1969] 2 AER 439* it was said, 'When considering the civil liability engrafted by judicial decision upon the criminal liability which has been imposed by statute, it is no good looking to the statute and seeing from it where the criminal liability would lie, for we are concerned only with civil liability. We must look to the cases' (per Lord Diplock). Moreover, a breach of general duties of *HSWA 1974* gives rise only to civil liability at common law and not under statute. (Though this is not the position where there is a breach of a specific regulation under *HSWA 1974*.) On the other hand, there is at least one isolated instance of an employee being denied damages where he was in breach of specific regulations (*ICI Ltd v Shatwell [1964] 2 AER 999*). It is thought, however, that this decision would not apply in the case of breach of a *general* statutory duty, such as *s 155(2)*.

*Appendix 1*

## Associations, organisations and departments connected with health and safety

**Advisory, Conciliation and Arbitration Service (ACAS)**
Brandon House
180 Borough High Street
London
SE1 1LW
Telephone: (020) 7210 3613

**Association of British Insurers (ABI)**
Head Office
51 Gresham Street
London
EC2V 7HQ
Telephone: (020) 7600 3333

**Association of Industrial Truck Trainers**
Huntingdon House
87 Market Street
Ashby-de-la-Zouch
Leicestershire
Telephone: (01530) 417 234

**Building Research Establishment**
Bucknalls Lane
Garston
Watford
Hertfordshire
Telephone: (01923) 664000

**British Chiropractic Association (BCA)**
Blagrave House
17 Blagrave Street
Reading
Berkshire
RG1 1QB
Telephone: (0118) 950 5950

**British Industrial Truck Association (BITA)**
Scammell House
High Street
Ascot
Berkshire
SL5 7JF
Telephone: (01344) 623 800

**British Occupational Hygiene Society**
Suite 2
Georgian House
Great Northern Road
Derby
DE1 1LT
Telephone: (01332) 298 101

**British Safety Council (BSC)**
National Safety Centre
70 Chancellors Road
London
W6 9RS
Telephone: (020) 8741 1231

**British Standards Institution (BSI)**
389 Chiswick High Road
London
W4 4AL
Telephone: (020) 8996 9000

**Chartered Institute of Environmental Health (CIEH)**
Chadwick Court
15 Hatfields
London
SE1 8DJ
Telephone: (020) 7928 6006

**Construction Industry Training Board (CITB)**
Bircham Newton
Kings Lynn
Norfolk
PE31 6RH
Telephone: (01485) 577 577

**Department for Transport, Local Government and the Regions (DTLR)**
Public Enquiries
Century Buildings
Great Smith Street
London
SW1P 3BT
Telephone: (0845) 609 9960

**Department of the Environment, Transport and the Regions (DETR)**
Public Enquiries
Ashdown House
123 Victoria Street
London
SW1E 6DE
Telephone: (020) 7890 3000

**Department of Health (DoH)**
Public Enquiries
Richmond House
79 Whitehall
London
SW1A 2NS
Telephone: (020) 7210 4850

**Department of Social Security (DSS)**
Richmond House
79 Whitehall
London
SW1A 2NS
Telephone: (020) 7712 2171

**Department of Trade and Industry (DTI)**
Public Enquiries
10-18 Victoria Street
London
SW1H 0NN
Telephone: (020) 7215 5000

**Environment Agency**
Apollo Court
2 Bishops Square Business Park
St Albans Road West
Hatfield
Hertfordshire
AL10 9EX
Telephone: (01707) 632 300

**Fire Protection Association (FPA)**
Bastille Court
2 Paris Garden
London
SE1 8ND
Telephone: (020) 7902 5300

**Health and Safety Commission (HSC)**
Rose Court
2 Southwark Bridge
London
SE1 9HS
Telephone: (020) 7717 6000

**Health and Safety Executive (HSE)**
Information Centre & Public Enquiry Point
Broad Lane
Sheffield
S3 7HQ
Telephone: (0541) 545 500

**Health and Safety Publications**
HSE Books
PO Box 1999
Sudbury
Suffolk
CO10 6FS
Telephone: (01787) 881 165

**Independent Training Standards Scheme and Register**
Second Floor Suite
Armstrong House
28 Broad Street
Wokingham
RG40 1AB
Telephone: (0118) 989 3229

**Institute of Occupational Hygienists**
Suite 2
Georgian House
Great Northern Road
Derby
DE1 1LT
Telephone: (01332) 298 087

**Institution of Occupational Safety and Health (IOSH)**
The Grange
Highfield Drive
Wigston
Leicester
LE18 1NN
Telephone: (0116) 257 3100

**Lantra National Training**
National Agricultural Centre
Stoneleigh
Near Kenilworth
Warwickshire
CV8 2LG
Telephone: (024) 7669 6996

**Loss Prevention Council**
(*see* Fire Protection Association above)

**Qualifications and Curriculum Authority (QCA)**
83 Piccadilly
London
W1J 8QA
Telephone: (020) 7509 5555

**Road Haulage and Distribution Training Council**
14 Warren Yard
Warren Farm Office Village
Stratford Road
Milton Keynes
MK12 5NW
Telephone: (01908) 313 360

**RTITB Ltd**
Ercall House
8 Pearson Road
Central Park
Telford
TF2 9TX
Telephone: (01952) 777 777

**Royal Society for the Prevention of Accidents (RoSPA)**
Edgbaston Park
35 Bristol Road
Birmingham
B5 7ST
Telephone: (0121) 248 2000

**Society for the Prevention of Asbestosis and Industrial Diseases (SPAID)**
39 Drapers Road
Enfield
Middlesex
EN2 8LU
Telephone: (020) 8388 1640

**Storage Equipment Manufacturers' Association (SEMA)**
MacLaren Buildings
35 Dale End
Birmingham
B4 7LN
Telephone: (0121) 200 2100

# Appendix 2

# Current HSE Publications

## Guidance Notes

There are 6 principal series of guidance notes available. These are: Chemical Safety (CS); Environmental Hygiene (EH); General Series (GS); Medical Series (MS); Plant and Machinery (PM), and Legal Series (L).

The following list indicates publications currently in print available from HSE Books.

### Chemical safety

| | |
|---|---|
| CS 3 | Storage and use of sodium chlorate and other similar strong oxidants. 1998 |
| CS 15 | The cleaning and gas freeing of tanks containing flammable residues. 1985 |
| CS 21 | Storage and handling of organic peroxides. 1991 |
| CS 22 | Fumigation. 1996 |
| CS 23 | Disposal of waste explosives. 1999 |
| CS 24 | The interpretation and use of flashpoint information. 1999 |

### Environmental hygiene

| | |
|---|---|
| EH 1 | Cadmium: health and safety precautions. 1995 |
| EH 2 | Chromium and its inorganic compounds: health and safety precautions. 1998 |
| EH 10 | Asbestos: exposure limits and measurement of airborne dust concentrations. 1995 |
| EH 13 | Beryllium: health and safety precautions. 1995 |
| EH 16 | Isocyanates: health hazards and precautionary measures. 1999 |
| EH 17 | Mercury and its inorganic divalent compounds. 1996 |
| EH 19 | Antimony and its compounds: health hazards and precautionary measures. 1997 |
| EH 38 | Ozone: health hazards and precautionary measures. 1996 |
| EH 40/00 | Occupational exposure limits. 2000 |
| EH 43 | Carbon monoxide. 1998 |
| EH 44 | Dust: general principles of protection. 1997 |
| EH 46 | Man-made mineral fibres. 1990 |
| EH 47 | Provision, use and maintenance of hygiene facilities for work with asbestos insulation and coatings. 1990 |
| EH 50 | Training operatives and supervisors for work with asbestos insulation and coatings. 1988 |
| EH 51 | Enclosures provided for work with asbestos. 1999 |
| EH 54 | Assessment of exposure to fume from welding and allied processes. 1990 |
| EH 55 | The control of exposure to fume from welding, brazing and similar processes. 1990 |
| EH 57 | The problems of asbestos removal at high temperatures. 1993 |
| EH 58 | Carcinogenicity of mineral oils. 1990 |
| EH 59 | Respirable crystalline silica. 1997 |

| | |
|---|---|
| EH 60 | Nickel and its inorganic compounds: health hazards and precautionary measures. 1997 |
| EH 63 | Vinyl chloride: toxic hazards and precautions. 1992 |
| EH 64 | Summary criteria for occupational exposure limits 1996. 1999 |
| EH 64supp | Summary criteria for occupational exposure limits. 2000 |
| EH 65/1 | Trimethylbenzenes – criteria document for an OEL. 1992 |
| EH 65/2 | Pulverised fuel ash – criteria document for an OEL. 1992 |
| EH 65/3 | N,N-Dimethylacetamide – criteria document for an OEL. 1992 |
| EH 65/4 | 1,2-dichloroethane – criteria document for an OEL. 1993 |
| EH 65/5 | 4.4-Methylene dianiline – criteria document for an OEL. 1993 |
| EH 65/6 | Epichlorohydrin – criteria document for an OEL. 1993 |
| EH 65/7 | Chlorodifluoromethane – criteria document for an OEL. 1994 |
| EH 65/8 | Cumene – criteria document for an OEL. 1994 |
| EH 65/9 | 1,4-dichlorobenzene – criteria document for an OEL. 1994 |
| EH 65/10 | Carbon tetrachloride – criteria document for an OEL. 1994 |
| EH 65/11 | Chloroform – criteria document for an OEL. 1994 |
| EH 65/12 | Portland cement dust – criteria document for an OEL. 1994 |
| EH 65/13 | Kaolin – criteria document for an OEL. 1994 |
| EH 65/14 | Paracetamol – criteria document for an OEL. 1994 |
| EH 65/15 | 1,1,1,2-Tetrafluoroethane HFC 134a – criteria document for an OEL. 1995 |
| EH 65/16 | Methyl methacrylate – criteria document for an OEL. 1995 |
| EH 65/17 | p-Aramid respirable fibres – criteria document for an OEL. 1995 |
| EH 65/18 | Propranolol – criteria document for an OEL. 1995 |
| EH 65/19 | Mercury and its inorganic divalent compounds – criteria document for an OEL. 1995 |
| EH 65/20 | Ortho-toluidine – criteria document for an OEL. 1996 |
| EH 65/21 | Propylene oxide – criteria document for an OEL. 1996 |
| EH 65/22 | Softwood dust – criteria document for an OEL. 1996 |
| EH 65/23 | Antimony and its compounds – criteria document for an OEL. 1996 |
| EH 65/24 | Platinum metal and soluble platinum salts – criteria document for an OEL. 1996 |
| EH 65/25 | Iodomethane – criteria document for an OEL. 1996 |
| EH 65/26 | Azodicarbonamide – criteria document for an OEL. 1996 |
| EH 65/27 | Dimethyl and diethyl sulphates – criteria document for an OEL. 1996 |
| EH 65/28 | Hydrazine – criteria document for an OEL. 1996 |
| EH 65/29 | Acid anhydrides – criteria document for an OEL. 1996 |
| EH 65/30 | Review of fibre toxicology – criteria document for an OEL. 1996 |
| EH 65/31 | Rosin-based solder flux fume – criteria document for an OEL. 1997 |
| EH 65/32 | Glutaraldehyde – criteria document for an OEL. 1997 |
| EH 66 | Grain dust. 1998 |
| EH 67 | Grain dust in maltings (maximum exposure limits). 1993 |
| EH 68 | Cobalt: health and safety precautions. 1995 |
| EH 69 | How to handle PCBs without harming yourself or the environment. 1995 |
| EH 70 | Control of fire-water run-off from CIMAH sites to prevent environmental damage. 1995 |
| EH 72/1 | Phenylhydrazine – risk assessment document. 1997 |
| EH 72/2 | Dimethylaminoethanol – risk assessment document. 1997 |
| EH 72/3 | Bromoethane – risk assessment document. 1997 |
| EH 72/4 | 3-Chloropropene – risk assessment document. 1997 |

| EH 72/5 | Chlorotoluene – risk assessment document. 1997 |
| EH 72/6 | 2-Furaldehyde. 1997 |
| EH 72/7 | 1,2-Diaminoethane (Ethylenediamine (EDA)) – risk assessment document. 1997 |
| EH 72/8 | Aniline _risk assessment document. 1998 |
| EH 72/9 | Barium sulphate – risk assessment document. 1998 |
| EH 72/10 | N-Methyl-2-Pyrrolidone – risk assessment document. 1998 |
| EH 72/11 | Flour dust – risk assessment document. 1999 |
| EH 72/12 | Bromochlromethane – risk assessment document. 2000 |
| EH 72/13 | Methyl and ethyl cyanoacrylate – risk assessment document. 2000 |
| EH 72/14 | Chlorine dixide. 2000 |
| EH 73 | Arsenic and its compounds: Health hazards and precautionary measures. 1997 |
| EH 74/1 | Exposure assessment: Dichloromethane. 1998 |
| EH 72/2 | Respirable crystalline silica. 1999 |
| EH 74/3 | Dermal exposure to non-agricultural pesticides. 1999 |
| EH 74/4 | Metalworking fluids: Exposure assessment document. 2000 |
| EH 75/1 | Medium density fibreboard: MDF. 1999 |
| EH 75/2 | Occupational exposure limits for hyperbaric conditions. 2000 |

## General series

| GS 4 | Safety in pressure testing. 1998 |
| GS 6 | Avoidance of danger from overhead electrical lines. 1997 |
| GS 6W | Avoidance of danger from overhead electrical lines – Welsh version. 1999 |
| GS 28/2 | Safe erection of structures: Part 2. Site management and procedures. 1985 |
| GS 28/3 | Safe erection of structures: Part 3. Working places and access. 1986 |
| GS 32 | Health and safety in shoe repair premises. 1984 |
| GS 38 | Electrical test equipment for use by electricians. 1995 |
| GS 46 | In situ timber treatment using timber preservatives: health, safety and environmental precautions. 1989 |
| GS 49 | Pre-stressed concrete. 1991 |
| GS 50 | Electrical safety at places of entertainment. 1997 |
| GS 51 | Façade retention. 1992 |
| GS 53 | Single-flue steel industrial chimneys: inspection and maintenance. 1997 |

## Medical series

| MS 7 | Colour vision. 1987 |
| MS 12 | Mercury: medical guidance notes. 1996 |
| MS 13 | Asbestos: medical guidance notes. 1999 |
| MS 17 | Biological monitoring of workers exposed to organo-phosphorus pesticides. 2000 |
| MS 24 | Health surveillance of occupational skin disease. 1998 |
| MS 25 | Medical aspects of occupational asthma. 1998 |
| MS 26 | A guide to audiometric testing programmes. 1995 |

## Plant and machinery

| PM 4 | High temperature textile dyeing machines. 1997 |

| PM 5 | Automatically controlled steam and hot water boilers. 1989 |
|---|---|
| PM 15 | Safety in the use of pallets. 1998 |
| PM 16 | Eyebolts. 1978 |
| PM 17 | Pneumatic nailing and stapling guns. 1979 |
| PM 24 | Safety at rack and pinion hoists. 1981 |
| PM 28 | Working platforms on fork-lift trucks. 2000 |
| PM 29 | Electrical risks from steam/water pressure cleaners. 1995 |
| PM 33 | Reducing bandsaw accidents in the food industry. 2000 |
| PM 38 | Selection and use of electric handlamps. 1992 |
| PM 39 | Hydrogen cracking of grade T(8) chain and components. 1998 |
| PM 48 | Safe operation of passenger carrying amusement devices: the octopus. 1985 |
| PM 55 | Safe working with overhead travelling cranes. 1985 |
| PM 56 | Noise from pneumatic systems. 1985 |
| PM 57 | Safe operation of passenger carrying amusement devices: the big wheel. 1986 |
| PM 59 | Safe operation of passenger carrying amusement devices: the paratrooper. 1986 |
| PM 60 | Steam boiler blowdown systems. 1998 |
| PM 61 | Safe operation of passenger carrying amusement devices: the chair-o-plane. 1986 |
| PM 63 | Inclined hoists used in building and construction work. 1987 |
| PM 65 | Worker protection at crocodile (alligator) shears. 1986 |
| PM 66 | Scrap baling machines. 1986 |
| PM 69 | Safety in the use of freight containers. 1987 |
| PM 70 | Safe operation of passenger carrying amusement devices: ark/speedways. 1988 |
| PM 71 | Safe operation of passenger carrying amusement devices: water chutes. 1989 |
| PM 72 | Safe operation of passenger carrying amusement devices: the trabant. 1990 |
| PM 73 | Safety at autoclaves. 1998 |
| PM 74 | Forced air filtration units for agricultural vehicles. 1991 |
| PM 75 | Glass reinforced plastic vessels and tanks: advice to users. 1991 |
| PM 76 | Safe operation of passenger carrying amusement devices: inflatable bouncing devices. 1991 |
| PM 77 | Fitness of equipment used for medical exposure to ionising radiation. 1998 |
| PM 78 | Passenger carrying aerial ropeways. 1994 |
| PM 79 | Power presses: thorough examination and testing. 1995 |
| PM 81 | Safe management of ammonia refrigeration systems: food and other workplaces. 1995 |
| PM 82 | The selection, installation and maintenance of electrical apparatus for use in and around buildings containing explosives. 1997 |
| PM 83 | Drilling machines: guarding of spindles and attachments. 1998 |
| PM 84 | Control of safety risks at gas turbines used for power generation. 2000 |

# Health and Safety: Guidance Booklets

The purpose of this series is to provide guidance for those who have duties under *HSWA* and other relevant legislation. It gives guidance on the practical application of regulations made under *HSWA*, but should not be regarded as an authoritative interpretation of the law.

| | |
|---|---|
| HS(G) 6 | Safety in working with lift trucks. 2000 |
| HS(G) 17 | Safety in the use of abrasive wheels. 2000 |
| HS(G) 28 | Safety advice for bulk chlorine installations. 1999 |
| HS(G) 31 | Pie and tart machines. 1986. |
| HS(G) 32 | Safety in falsework for in situ beams and slabs. 1987 |
| HS(G) 33 | Health and safety in rootwork. 1998 |
| HS(G) 37 | An introduction to local exhaust ventilation. 1993 |
| HS(G) 38 | Lighting at work. 1998 |
| HS(G) 39 | Compressed air safety. 1998 |
| HS(G) 40 | Safe handling of Chlorine from drums and cylinders. 1999 |
| HS(G) 42 | Safety in the use of metal cutting guillotines and shears. 1988 |
| HS(G) 43 | Industrial robot safety. 2000 |
| HS(G) 45 | Safety in meat preparation: guidance for butchers. 1988 |
| HS(G) 47 | Avoiding danger from underground services. 2000 |
| HS(G) 48 | Human factors in industrial safety. 1999 |
| HS(G) 51 | The storage of flammable liquids in containers. 1998 |
| HS(G) 54 | The maintenance, examination and testing of local exhaust ventilation. 1998 |
| HS(G) 55 | Health and safety in kitchens and food preparation areas. 1990 |
| HS(G) 57 | Seating at work. 1998 |
| HS(G) 60 | Work related upper limb disorders: a guide to prevention. 1990 |
| HS(G) 61 | Health Surveillance at Work. 1999 |
| HS(G) 62 | Health and safety in tyre and exhaust fitting premises. 1991 |
| HS(G) 63 | Radiation protection off site for emergency services in the event of a nuclear accident. 1991 |
| HS(G) 65 | Successful health and safety management. 1997 |
| HS(G) 66 | Protection of workers and the general public during the development of contaminated land. 1991 |
| HS(G) 67 | Health and safety in motor vehicle repair. 1991 |
| HS(G) 71 | Chemical warehousing: storage of packaged dangerous substances. 1998 |
| HS(G) 72 | Control of respirable silica dust in heavy clay and refractory processes. 1992 |
| HS(G) 73 | Control of respirable crystalline silica in quarries. 1992 |
| HS(G) 76 | Health and safety in retail and wholesale warehouses. 1992 |
| HS(G) 78 | Dangerous goods in cargo transport units: packing and carriage for transport by sea. 1998 |
| HS(G) 79 | Health and safety in golf course management and maintenance. 1994 |
| HS(G) 85 | Electricity at work: safe working practices. 1993 |
| HS(G) 87 | Safety in the remote diagnosis of manufacturing plant and equipment. 1995 |
| HS(G) 88 | Hand-arm vibration. 1994 |
| HS(G) 89 | Safeguarding agricultural machinery; advice for designers, manufacturers, suppliers and users. 1998 |
| HS(G) 90 | VDUs: an easy guide to the Regulations: how to comply with the Health and Safety (Display Screen Equipment) Regulations 1992. 1994 |
| HS(G) 92 | Safe use and storage of cellular plastics. 1996 |
| HS(G) 93 | The assessment of pressure vessels operating at low temperature. 1993 |
| HS(G) 94 | Safety in the use of gamma and electron irradiation facilities. 1998 |
| HS(G) 95 | The radiation safety of lasers used for display purposes. 1996 |
| HS(G) 96 | The costs of accidents at work. 1997 |

| HS(G) 97 | A step by step guide to COSHH assessment. 1992 |
| HS(G) 100 | Prevention of violence to staff in banks and building societies. 1993 |
| HS(G) 101 | The costs to Britain of workplace accidents and work-related ill health in 1995/96. 1999 |
| HS(G) 103 | Safe handling of combustible dusts: precautions against explosions. 1994 |
| HS(G) 107 | Maintaining portable and transportable electrical equipment. 1994 |
| HS(G) 109 | Control of noise in quarries. 1993 |
| HS(G) 110 | Seven steps to successful substitution of hazardous substances. 1996 |
| HS(G) 110W | Seven steps to successful substitution of hazardous substances. (Welsh version) 1996 |
| HS(G) 112 | Health and safety at motor sports events: a guide for employers and organisers. 1999 |
| HS(G) 113 | Lift trucks in potentially flammable atmospheres. 1996 |
| HS(G) 114 | Conditions for the authorisation of explosives in Great Britain. 1994 |
| HS(G) 115 | Manual handling: solutions you can handle. 1994 |
| HS(G) 116 | Stress at work: a guide for employers. 1995 |
| HS(G) 117 | Making sense of NONS: a guide to the Notification of New Substances Regulations 1993. 1994 |
| HS(G) 118 | Electrical safety in arc welding. 1994 |
| HS(G) 119 | Manual handling for drinks delivery. 1994 |
| HS(G) 120 | Nuclear site licences under the Nuclear Installations Act 1965: notes for applicants. 1994 |
| HS(G) 121 | A pain in your workplace? Ergonomic problems and solutions. 1994 |
| HS(G) 122 | New and expectant mothers at work: a guide for employers. 1994 |
| HS(G) 123 | Working together on firework displays: a guide to safety for firework display organisers and operators. 1999 |
| HS(G) 124 | Giving your own firework display: how to run and fire it safely. 1995 |
| HS(G) 125 | A brief guide on COSHH for the offshore oil and gas industry. 1994 |
| HS(G) 126 | CHIP 2 for everyone. 1995 |
| HS(G) 129 | Health and safety in engineering workshops. 1999 |
| HS(G) 131 | Energetic and spontaneously combustible substances: identification and safe handling. 1995 |
| HS(G) 132 | How to deal with sick building syndrome: guidance for employers, building owners and building managers. 1995 |
| HS(G) 133 | Preventing violence to retail staff. 1995 |
| HS(G) 135 | Storage and handling of industrial nitrocellulose. 1995 |
| HS(G) 136 | Workplace transport safety: guidance for employers. 1995 |
| HS(G) 137 | Health risk management: a practical guide for managers in small and medium-sized enterprises. 1995 |
| HS(G) 137W | Health risk management: a practical guide for managers in small and medium-sized enterprises. (Welsh version). 1996 |
| HS(G) 138 | Sound solutions: techniques to reduce noise at work. 1995 |
| HS(G) 139 | The safe use of compressed gases in welding, flame cutting and allied processes. 1997 |
| HS(G) 140 | Safe use and handling of flammable liquids. 1996 |
| HS(G) 141 | Electrical safety on construction sites. 1995 |

| | |
|---|---|
| HS(G) 142 | Dealing with offshore emergencies. 1996 |
| HS(G) 143 | Designing and operating safe chemical reaction processes. 2000 |
| HS(G) 144 | Safe use of vehicles on construction sites. 1998 |
| HS(G) 146 | Dispensing petrol: assessing and controlling the risk of fire and explosion at sites where petrol is stored and dispensed as a fuel. 1996 |
| HS(G) 148 | Sheeting and unsheeting of tipper lorries: guidance for the road haulage industry. 1996 |
| HS(G) 149 | Backs for the future: safe manual handling in construction. 2000 |
| HS(G) 150 | Health and safety in construction. 1996 |
| HS(G) 151 | Protecting the public – your next move. 1997 |
| HS(G) 153/1 | Railway safety principles and guidance: part 1. 1996 |
| HS(G) 153/2 | Railway safety principles and guidance: part 2 section A. Guidance on the infrastructure. 1996 |
| HS(G) 153/3 | Railway safety principles and guidance: part 2 section B. Guidance on stations. 1996 |
| HS(G) 153/4 | Railway safety principles and guidance: part 2 section C. Guidance on electric traction systems. 1996 |
| HS(G) 153/5 | Railway safety principles and guidance: part 2 section D. Guidance on signalling. 1996 |
| HS(G) 153/6 | Railway safety principles and guidance: part 2 section E. Guidance on level crossings. 1996 |
| HS(G) 153/7 | Railway safety principles and guidance: part 2 section F. Guidance on trains. 1996 |
| HS(G) 153/8 | Railway safety principles and guidance: part 2 section G. Guidance on tramways. 1997 |
| HS(G) 154 | Managing crowds safely. 2000 |
| HS(G) 155 | Slips and trips: guidance for employers on identifying hazards and controlling risks. 1996 |
| HS(G) 156 | Slips and trips: guidance for the food processing industry. 1996 |
| HS(G) 158 | Flame arresters: preventing the spread of fires and explosions in equipment that contains flammable gases and vapours. 1997 |
| HS(G) 160 | The carriage of dangerous goods explained: Part 1. Guidance for consignors of dangerous goods by road and rail (classification, packaging, labelling and provision of information). 1996 |
| HS(G) 161 | The carriage of dangerous goods explained: Part 2. Guidance for road vehicle operators and others involved in the carriage of dangerous goods by road. 1996 |
| HS(G) 162 | The carriage of dangerous goods explained: Part 4. Guidance for operators, drivers and others involved in the carriage of explosives by road. 1999 |
| HS(G) 163 | The carriage of dangerous goods explained: Part 3. Guidance for rail operators and others involved in the carriage of dangerous goods by rail. 1996 |
| HS(G) 164 | The carriage of dangerous goods explained: Part 5. Guidance for consignors, rail operators and others involved in the packaging, labelling and carriage of radioactive material by rail. 1996 |
| HS(G) 165 | Young people at work: a guide for employers. 2000 |
| HS(G) 166 | Formula for health and safety: guidance for small to medium-sized firms in the chemical manufacturing industry. 1997 |
| HS(G) 167 | Biological monitoring in the workplace: a guide to its practical application to chemical exposure. 1997 |

| HS(G) 168 | Fire safety in construction: guidance for clients, designers and those managing and carrying out construction work involving significant fire risks. 1997 |
| HS(G) 169 | Camera operations on location: guidance for managers and camera crews for work in news gathering, current affairs and factual programming. 1997 |
| HS(G) 170 | Vibration solutions: practical ways to reduce hand-arm vibration injury. 1997 |
| HS(G) 171 | Well handled: offshore manual handling solutions. 1997 |
| HS(G) 172 | Health and safety in sawmilling: a run-of-the-mill-business? 1997 |
| HS(G) 173 | Monitoring strategies for toxic substances. 1997 |
| HS(G) 174 | Anthrax: safe working and the prevention of infection. 1997 |
| HS(G) 175 | Fairgrounds and amusement parks: guidance on safe practice: practical guidance on the management of health and safety for those involved in the fairgrounds industry. 1997 |
| HS(G) 176 | The storage of flammable liquids in tanks. 1998 |
| HS(G) 178 | The spraying of flammable liquids. 1998 |
| HS(G) 179 | Managing health and safety in swimming pools. 1999 |
| HS(G) 180 | Application of electro-sensitive protective equipment using light curtains and light beam devices to machinery. 1999' |
| HS(G) 181 | Assessment principles for offshore safety cases. 1998 |
| HS(G) 182 | Sound solutions offshore: practical examples of noise reduction. 1998 |
| HS(G) 183 | Five steps to risk assessment: case studies. 1998 |
| HS(G) 184 | Guidance on the handling, storage and transport of airbags and seat pretensioners. 1998 |
| HS(G) 185 | Health and safety in excavations: be safe and shore. 1999 |
| HS(G) 186 | The bulk transfer of dangerous liquids and gasses between ship and shore. 1999 |
| HS(G) 187 | Control of diesel engine exhaust emissions in the workplace. 1999 |
| HS(G) 188 | Health risk management: a guide to working with solvents. 1999 |
| HS(G) 189/1 | Controlled asbestos stripping techniques for work requiring a licence. 1999 |
| HS(G) 189/2 | Working with asbestos cement. 1999 |
| HS(G) 190 | Preparing safety reports: Control of Major Accident Hazard Regulations 1999. 1999 |
| HS(G) 191 | Emergency planning for major accidents: Control of Major Accident Hazard Regulations 1999. 1999 |
| HS(G) 192 | Charity and voluntary workers: a guide to health and safety at work. 1999 |
| HS(G) 193 | COSHH essentials: easy steps to control chemicals. 1999 |
| HS(G) 194 | Thermal comfort in the workplace: guidance for employers. 1999 |
| HS(G) 195 | The event safety guide: a guide to health, safety and welfare at music and similar events. 1999 |
| HS (G) 196 | Moving food and drink: Manual handling solutions for the food and drink industries. 2000 |
| HS(G) 199 | Managing health and safety on work experience: a guide for organisers. 2000 |
| HS(G) 202 | General ventilation in the workplace: Guidance for employers. 2000 |
| HS(G) 203 | Controlling exposure to coating powders. 2000 |
| HS(G) 204 | Health and safety in arc welding. 2000 |

| HS(G) 205 | Assessing and managing risks at work from skin exposure to chemical agents: Guidance for employers and health and safety specialists. 2001 |
| HS(G) 207 | Choice of skin care products for the workplace: Guidance for employers and health and safety specialists. 2001 |
| HS(G) 209 | Aircraft turnaround: A guide for airport and aerodrome operators, airlines and service providers on achieving control, co-operation and co-ordination. 2000 |
| HS(G) 212 | The training of first-aid at work. 2001 |

## Legal – Approved Codes of Practice (COP series), HS(R) series and new L series

*Code numbers in the HS(R) series and the COP series are gradually being superseded by the L series. Publications in the L series contain guidance on Regulations and Approved Codes of Practice.*

### Approved Codes of Practice

| COP 2 | Control of lead at work (in support of SI 1980 No 1248) – approved code of practice. 1998 |
| COP 6 | Plastic containers with nominal capacities up to 5 litres for petroleum spirit: requirements for testing and marking or labelling (in support of SI 1982 No 830) – approved code of practice. 1982 |
| COP 14 | Road tanker testing: examination, testing and certification of the carrying tanks of road tankers and of tank containers used for the conveyance of dangerous substances by road (in support of SI 1981 No 1059) – approved code of practice. 1985 |
| COP 15 | Zoos: safety, health and welfare standards for employers and persons at work – approved code of practice and guidance notes. 1985 |
| COP 20 | Standards of training in safe gas installation – approved code of practice. 1987 |
| COP 25 | Safety in docks: Docks Regulations 1988 – approved code of practice with regulations and guidance. 1988 |
| COP 28 | Safety of exit from mines underground workings: Mines (Safety of Exit) Regulations 1988 – approved code of practice. 1988 |
| COP 34 | Use of electricity in mines: Electricity at Work Regulations 1989 – approved code of practice. 1989 |
| COP 35 | The use of electricity at quarries: Electricity at Work Regulations 1989 – approved code of practice. 1989 |

### HS(R) series

| HS(R) 17 | A guide to the Classification and Labelling of Explosives Regulations 1983. 1983 |
| HS(R) 25 | Memorandum of guidance on the Electricity at Work Regulations 1989. 1989 |
| HS(R) 27 | A guide to the Dangerous Substances in Harbour Areas Regulations 1987. 1988 |
| HS(R) 28 | Guide to the Loading and Unloading of Fishing Vessels Regulations 1988. 1988 |

HS(R) 29    Guide to the notification and marking of sites in accordance
            with the Dangerous Substances (Notification and Marking of
            Sites) Regulations. 1990

## L series

L 5     General COSHH ACOP, Carcinogens ACOP and Biological
        Agents ACOP. Control of Substances Hazardous to Health
        Regulations 1999 – approved code of practice. 1999
L 8     Legionnaires disease: The control of legionella bacteria in water
        systems. 2000
L 9     Safe use of pesticides for non-agricultural purposes. Control of
        Substances Hazardous to Health Regulations 1994 – approved
        code of practice. 1991
L 10    A guide to the Control of Explosives Regulations 1991: guidance
        on Regulations. 1991
L 11    A guide to the Asbestos (Licensing) Regulations 1983: guidance
        on Regulations. 1999
L 13    A guide to the Packaging of Explosives for Carriage Regulations
        1991: guidance on Regulations. 1991
L 21    Management of health and safety at work. Management of
        Health and Safety at Work Regulations 1999 – approved code
        of practice. 2000
L 22    Safe use of work equipment: Provision and Use of Work
        Equipment Regulations 1998 – approved code of practice and
        guidance. 1998
L 23    Manual handling: Manual Handling Operations Regulations
        1992 – guidance on regulations. 1998
L 24    Workplace health, safety and welfare. Workplace (Health, Safety
        and Welfare) Regulations 1992 – approved code of practice
        and guidance. 1992
L 25    Personal protective equipment at work. Personal Protective
        Equipment at Work Regulations 1992 – guidance on
        regulations. 1992
L 26    Display screen equipment work. Health and Safety (Display
        Screen Equipment) Regulations 1992 – guidance on
        regulations. 1992
L 27    The control of asbestos at work: Control of Asbestos at Work
        Regulations 1987 – approved code of practice. 1999
L 28    Work with asbestos insulation, asbestos coating and asbestos
        insulating board: Control of Asbestos at Work Regulations
        1987 – approved code of practice. 1999
L 29    A guide to the Genetically Modified Organisms (Contained
        Use) Regulations 1992. 2000
L 30    A guide to the Offshore Installations (Safety Case) Regulations
        1992. 1998
L 31    A guide to the Public Information for Radiation Emergencies
        Regulations 1992. 1993
L 42    Shafts and winding in mines: Mines (Shafts and Winding)
        Regulations 1993 – approved code of practice. 1993
L 43    First-aid at mines: Health and Safety (First-Aid) Regulations
        1981 – approved code of practice. 1993
L 44    The management and administration of safety and health at
        mines. Management and Administration of Safety and Health
        at Mines Regulations 1993 – approved code of practice. 1993

| | |
|---|---|
| L 45 | Explosives at coal and other safety-lamp mines. Coal and Other Safety-lamp Mines (Explosives) Regulations 1993 – approved code of practice. 1993 |
| L 46 | The prevention of inrushes in mines – approved code of practice. 1993 |
| L 47 | The Coal Mines (Owners' Operating Rules) Regulations 1993 – guidance on Regulations. 1993 |
| L 49 | Protection of outside workers against ionising radiations: The Ionising Radiations (Outside Workers) Regulations 1993 – approved code of practice. 1993 |
| L 50 | Railways Safety Critical Work: Railways (Safety Critical Work) Regulations 1994 – approved code of practice and guidance. 1996 |
| L 52 | Railway safety cases. Railways (Safety Case) Regulations 2000 – guidance on regulations. 2000 |
| L 54 | Managing construction for health and safety. The Construction (Design and Management) Regulations 1994 – approved code of practice. 1995 |
| L 55 | Preventing asthma at work: How to control respiratory sensitisers. 1994 |
| L 56 | Safety in the installation and use of gas systems and appliances. The Gas Safety (Installation and Use) Regulations 1998 – approved code of practice and guidance. 1998 |
| L 59 | A guide to the approval of railway works, plant and equipment. 1994 |
| L 60 | Control of substances hazardous to health in the production of pottery: The Control of Substances Hazardous to Health Regulations 1994. The Control of Lead at Work Regulations 1980 – approved code of practice. 1995 |
| L 62 | Safety datasheets for substances and preparations dangerous for supply: Guidance on regulation 6 of the CHIP Regulations 1994 – approved code of practice. 1995 |
| L 64 | Safety signs and signals: The Health and Safety (Safety Signs and Signals) Regulations 1996 – guidance on regulations. 1997 |
| L 65 | Prevention of fire and explosion, and emergency response on offshore installations. Offshore Installations Regulations 1995 – approved code of practice and guidance. 1997 |
| L 66 | A guide to the Placing on the Market and Supervision of Transfers of Explosives Regulations 1993 (POMSTER) 1993. 1995 |
| L 67 | Control of vinyl chloride at work. Control of Substances Hazardous to Health Regulations 1994 – approved code of practice. 1995 |
| L 70 | A guide to the Offshore Installations and Pipeline Works (Management and Administration) Regulations 1995 – guidance on regulations. 1995 |
| L 71 | Escape and rescue from mines. Escape and Rescue from Mines Regulations 1995 – approved code of practice. 1995 |
| L 72 | A guide to Borehole Sites and Operations Regulations 1995 – guidance on regulations. 1995 |
| L 73 | A guide to the Reporting of Injuries, Diseases and Dangerous Occurrences Regulations 1995. 1999 |
| L 74 | First aid at work: The Health and Safety (First-Aid) Regulations 1981 – approved code of practice and guidance. 1997 |

| | |
|---|---|
| L 75 | Guidance for railways, tramways, trolley vehicle systems and other guided transport systems on Reporting of Injuries, Diseases and Dangerous Occurrences Regulations 1995 – guidance on regulations. 1996 |
| L 77 | Guidance to the licensing authority on the Adventure Activities Licensing Regulations 1996. The Activity Centres (Young Persons' Safety) Act 1995 – guidance on regulations. 1996 |
| L 80 | A guide to the Gas Safety (Management) Regulations 1996. 1996 |
| L 81 | The design, construction and installation of gas service pipes: The Pipelines Safety Regulations 1996 – approved code of practice and guidance. 1996 |
| L 82 | A guide to the Pipelines Safety Regulations 1996 – guidance on regulations. 1996 |
| L 84 | A guide to the well aspects of amendments of the Offshore Installations and Wells (Design and Construction etc.) Regulations 1996 – guidance on regulations. 1996 |
| L 85 | A guide to the integrity, workplace environment and miscellaneous aspects of the Offshore Installations and Wells (Design and Construction etc.) Regulations 1996 – guidance on regulations. 1996 |
| L86 | Control of Substances Hazardous to health in fumigation operations: Control of Substances Hazardous to Health Regulations 1994 – approved code of practice. 1996 |
| L87 | Safety representatives and safety committees (the brown book) – approved code of practice and guidance on the regulations. 1996 |
| L 88 | Approved requirements and test methods for the classification and packaging of dangerous goods for carriage: Carriage of Dangerous Goods (Classification, Packaging and Labelling) and Use of Transportable Pressure Receptacles Regulations 1996. 1996 |
| L 89 | Approved vehicle requirements: Carriage of Dangerous Goods by Road Regulations 1996. 1999 |
| L 90 | Approved Carriage List: information approved for the carriage of dangerous goods by road and rail other than explosives and radioactive material. 1999 |
| L91 | Suitability of vehicles and containers and limits on quantities for the carriage of explosives: Carriage of Explosives by Road Regulations 1996 – approved code of practice. 1996 |
| L 92 | Approved requirements for the construction of vehicles intended for the carriage of explosives by road: Carriage of Explosives by Road Regulations 1996. 1999 |
| L 93 | Approved tank requirements: the provisions for bottom loading and vapour recovery systems of mobile containers carrying petrol. Carriage of Dangerous Goods by Road Regulations 1996. Carriage of Dangerous Goods by Rail Regulations 1996. 1996 |
| L 94 | Approved requirements for the packaging, labelling and carriage of radioactive material by rail: Packaging, Labelling and Carriage of Radioactive Material by Rail Regulations 1996. 1996 |
| L95 | A guide to the Health and Safety (Consultation with Employees) Regulations 1996 – guidance on regulations. 1996 |
| L96 | A guide to the Work in Compressed Air Regulations 1996. 1996 |

| | |
|---|---|
| L 97 | A guide to the Level Crossings Regulations 1997. 1997 |
| L 98 | Railway safety miscellaneous provisions: Railway Safety (Miscellaneous Provisions) Regulations 1997 – guidance on regulations. 1997 |
| L 100 | Approved guide to the classification and labelling of substances dangerous for supply: Chemicals (Hazard Information and Packaging for Supply) (Amendment) Regulations 1997 – guidance on regulations. 1999 |
| L 101 | Safe work in confined spaces: Confined Spaces Regulations 1997 – approved code of practice, regulations and guidance. 1997 |
| L 102 | A guide to the Construction (Head Protection) Regulations 1989. 1998 |
| L 103 | Commercial diving projects offshore: Diving at Work Regulations 1997 – approved code of practice. 1998 |
| L 104 | Commercial diving projects inland/inshore: Diving at Work Regulations 1997 – approved code of practice. 1998 |
| L 105 | Recreational diving projects: Diving at Work Regulations 1997 – approved code of practice. 1998 |
| L 106 | Media diving projects. Diving at Work Regulations 1997 – approved code of practice. 1998 |
| L 107 | Scientific and archaeological diving projects: Diving at Work Regulations 1997 – approved code of practice. 1998 |
| L 108 | Guidance on the Noise at Work Regulations 1989. 1998 |
| L 110 | A guide to the Offshore Installations (Safety Representatives and Safety Committees) Regulations 1989. 1998 |
| L 111 | A guide to the Control of Major Accident Hazard Regulations. 1999 |
| L 112 | Safe use of power presses. 1998 |
| L 113 | Safe use of lifting equipment: Lifting Operations and Lifting Equipment Regulations 1998 – approved code of practice and guidance. 1998 |
| L 114 | Safe use of woodworking machinery. 1998 |
| L 116 | Preventing accidents to children in agriculture – approved code of practice. 1999 |
| L 117 | Rider operated lift trucks: operator training – approved code of practice and guidance. 1999 |
| L 118 | Health and safety at quarries: Quarries Regulations 1999 – approved code of practice. 1999 |
| L 119 | The control of ground movement in mines – approved code of practice and guidance. 1999 |
| L 120 | Train protection systems and mark 1 rolling stock: Railway Safety Regulations 1999 – guidance on regulations. 1999 |
| L 121 | Work with ionising radiation: Ionising Radiations Regulations 1999 – approved code of practice and guidance. 2000 |
| L 122 | Safety of pressure systems: Pressure Systems Safety Regulations 2000 – approved code of practice. 2000 |
| L 123 | Health care and first-aid on offshore installations and pipeline works: Offshore Installations and Pipeline Works (First-aid) Regulations 1999 – approved code of practice and guidance. 2000 |
| L 124 | Approved supply list: Information approved for the classification and labelling of substances and preparations dangerous for supply Chemicals (Hazard Information and Packaging for Supply) Regulations 1994 – approved list. 2000 |

# Other Publications

## Accidents and emergencies

L73    A guide to the Reporting of Injuries, Diseases and Dangerous Occurrences Regulations. Revised 1999

HSE31    Everyones guide to RIDDOR (available in Welsh). 1999

HSE33    RIDDOR Offshore. Revised 1999

INDG214    First aid at work – your questions answered (available in Welsh). 1996

INDG215    Basic advice on first aid at work. Revised 1999

## Asbestos

INDG188    Asbestos alert for building maintenance, repair and refurbishment workers. 1995

INDG223    Managing asbestos in workplace buildings. Revised 1999

INDG255    Asbestos dust kills. 1999

INDG289    Working with asbestos in buildings. 1999

## Chemical Industry

–    Managing contractors – a guide for employers. 1997

–    Handle with care – assessing musculoskeletal risk in the chemical industry. 2000

HSG71    Chemical warehousing – storage of packaged dangerous substances. 1998

HSG166    Formula for health and safety – guidance for small and medium-sized firms in the chemical manufacturing industry. 1997

CHIS2    Emergency isolation of process plant in the chemical industry. 1999

CHIS3    Major accident prevention policies for lower-tier COMAH establishments. 1999

CHIS4    Use of LPG in cylinders. 1999

INDG98    Permit to work systems. Revised 1997

INDG186    Read the label – how to find out if chemicals are dangerous. 2000

INDG243    Computer control – a question of safety. 1997

INDG245    Biological monitoring for chemicals in the workplace. 1997

INDG246    Prepared for emergency. 1997

INDG254    Chemical reaction hazards and the risk of thermal runaway. 1997

## Construction

HSG33    Health and safety in roofwork. Revised 1998

HSG47    Avoiding danger from underground services. Revised 2000

HSG144    Safe use of vehicles on construction sites. 1998

HSG149    Backs for the future: safe manual handling in construction. 2000

HSG185    Health and safety in excavations: be safe and shore. 1999

L102    A guide to the Construction (Head Protection ) Regulations. Revised 1998

CIS17    Construction health and safety checklist. Revised 1996

CIS18    The provision of welfare facilities at fixed construction sites. Revised 1996

CIS24    Chemical cleaners. Revised 1998

| | |
|---|---|
| CIS27 | Solvents. Revised 1998 |
| CIS36 | Silica. 1999 |
| CIS37 | Handling heavy building blocks. 1999 |
| CIS39 | Construction (Design and Management) Regulations 1994: the role of the client. 1995 |
| CIS40 | Construction (Design and Management) Regulations 1994: the role of the planning supervisor. 1995 |
| CIS41 | Construction (Design and Management) Regulations 1994: the role of the designer. 1995 |
| CIS42 | Construction (Design and Management) Regulations 1994: the pre-tender stage health and safety plan. 1995 |
| CIS43 | Construction (Design and Management) Regulations 1994: the health and safety plan during the construction phase. 1995 |
| CIS44 | CDM Regulations 1994: The Health & Safety File. 1995 |
| CIS45 | Establishing exclusion zones when using explosives in demolition. 1995 |
| CIS46 | Provision of welfare facilities at transient construction sites. 1997 |
| CIS47 | Inspections and reports. 1997 |
| CIS49 | General access to scaffolds and ladders. 1997 |
| CIS50 | Personal Protective Equipment (PPE): safety helmets. 1997 |
| CIS51 | Construction fire safety. 1997 |
| CIS52 | Construction Site Transport Safety: safe use of compact dumpers. 1999 |
| CIS53 | Crossing high-speed roads on foot during temporary traffic management works. 2000 |
| CIS54 | Dust control on concrete cutting saws used in the construction industry. 2000 |
| INDG127 | Noise in construction: further guidance on the Noise at Work Regulations 1989. Revised 1995 |
| INDG212 | Workplace health and safety – Glazing: guidance on glazing for employers and people in control of workplaces. 1996. |
| INDG220 | A guide to the Construction (Health, Safety and Welfare) Regulations 1996. 1996 |
| INDG242 | In the driving seat: advice to employers on reducing back pain in drivers and machinery operators. 1997 |
| INDG258 | Safe work in confined spaces. (Available in Welsh) 1999 |
| INDG262 | Head protection for Sikhs wearing turbans: guidance for employers. 1998 (Available from Sikh Community and Youth Service, Birmingham *Tel:* 0121 523 0147) |
| INDG332 | Manual packing in the brick industry. 2000 |
| MISC193 | Having Construction Work Done? – duties of clients under the Construction (Design and Management) Regulations 1994. 1999 |

## Dangerous substances – general

| | |
|---|---|
| – | The technical basis for COSHH essentials: easy steps to control chemicals. 1999 |
| HSG188 | Health risk management: a guide to working with solvents. 1998 |
| HSG193 | COSHH essentials: easy steps to control chemicals. 1999 |
| L5 | General COSHH ACOP, Carcinogens ACOP and Biological Agents ACOP: Control of Substances Hazardous to health Regulations 1999. Approved Code of Practice. Revised 1999 |

| | |
|---|---|
| L100 | Approved guide to the classification and labelling of substances dangerous for supply. 1999 |
| INDG136 | COSHH: a brief guide to the Regulations. Revised 1999 |
| INDG181 | The complete idiot's guide to CHIP2: a guide to the Chemicals (Hazard Information and Packaging) Regulations. Revised 1999 |
| INDG182 | Why do I need a safety data sheet?: for those who use or supply dangerous chemicals. 1999 |
| INDG273 | Working safely with solvents: a guide to safe working practices. 1998 |

## Dangerous substances – by type

| | |
|---|---|
| COP2 | Control of lead at work in support of SI 1980 No 1248 – approved code of practice. 1998 |
| INDG66 | VCM and you. 1995 |
| INDG197 | Working with sewage: the health hazards – a guide for employers and employees. 1995. |
| INDG198 | Working with sewage: the health hazards – a guide for employers. 1995 |
| INDG230 | Storage and safe handling of ammonium nitrate. 1996 |
| INDG257 | Pesticides: use them safely. 1997 |
| INDG300 | Skin cancer by oil. 1999 |
| INDG307 | Hydrofluoric acid poisoning: recommendations on first aid treatment. 1999 |
| MISC076 | Cyanide poisoning: new recommendations on first aid treatment. 1997 |
| MSA7 | Cadmium and you: working with cadmium – are you at risk? Revised 1995 |
| MSA8 | Arsenic and you: arsenic is poisonous – are you at risk? 1996 |
| MSA14 | Nickel and you: working with nickel – are you at risk? Revised 1997 |
| MSA15 | Silica dust and you. Revised 1997 |
| MSA16 | Chromium and you: chromium can be dangerous – are you at risk? 1991 |
| MSA17 | Cobalt and you: working with cobalt – are you at risk. 1995 |
| MSA18 | Berylium and you: working with beryllium – are you at risk? 1995 |
| MSA19 | PCBs and you – do you know how to work safely with PCBs? 1995 |
| MSA21 | MbOCA and you: do you use MbOCA? 1996 |
| MSB4 | Skin cancer by pitch and tar. 1996 |

## Diving

| | |
|---|---|
| DVIS1 | General hazards. 1998 |
| DVIS2 | Diving system winches. 1998 |
| DVIS3 | Breathing gas management. 1998 |
| DVIS4 | Compression chambers. 1998 |
| DVIS5 | Exposure limits for air diving operations. 1998 |
| DVIS6 | Maintenance of diving bell hoists. 1998 |
| DVIS7 | Bell run and bell lock-out times in relation to habitats. 1998 |
| DVIS8 | Diving in benign conditions and in pools, tanks, acquariums and helicopter underwater escape training. 1999 |
| INDG266 | Are you involved in a diving project? 1998 |

## Electricity and electrical systems

| | |
|---|---|
| INDG68 | Do you use a steam/water pressure cleaner. 1997 |
| INDG139 | Electric storage batteries. 1993 |
| INDG231 | Electrical safety and you. 1996 |
| INDG236 | Maintaining portable electrical equipment in offices and other low-risk environments. 1996 |

## Engineering

| | |
|---|---|
| EIS1 | Hot work on vehicle wheels. 1992 |
| EIS2 | Accidents at metalworking lathes using emery cloth. 1993 |
| EIS3 | Monitoring requirements in the electroplating industry including electrolytic chromium processes. Revised 1998 |
| EIS4 | Workplace welfare in the electroplating industry. Revised 1998 |
| EIS5 | Health surveillance requirements in the electroplating industry. Revised 1998 |
| EIS6 | Electrical systems in the electroplating industry. Revised 1998 |
| EIS7 | Safeguarding 3-roll bending machines. Revised 1998 |
| EIS12 | Safety at manually-fed pivoting-head metal-cutting circular saws. 1998 |
| EIS13 | Safeguarding of combination metalworking machines. Revised 2000 |
| EIS14 | Skin creams and skin protection in the engineering sector. 1996 |
| EIS15 | Control of exposure to triglycidyl isocyanurate (TGIC) in coating powders. Revised 1998 |
| EIS16 | Preventing injuries from the manual handling of sharp edges in the engineering industry. 1997 |
| EIS18 | Isocyanates: health surveillance in motor vehicle repair. 1997 |
| EIS19 | Engineering machine tools: retrofitting CNC. 1997 |
| EIS20 | Maintenance and cleaning of solvent degreasing tanks. 1998 |
| EIS21 | Immersion and cold cleaning of engineering components. 1998 |
| EIS22 | Health and safety at degreasing operations: sources of guidance. 1998 |
| EIS26 | Noise in engineering. 1998 |
| EIS27 | Control of noise at metal cutting saws. 1998 |
| EIS28 | Safeguarding at horizontal boring machines. 1998 |
| EIS29 | Control of noise at power presses. 1998 |
| EIS30 | Safety in the use of hand and foot operated presses. 1999 |
| EIS31 | Cadmium in silver soldering or brazing. 1999 |
| EIS32 | Chromate primer paints. 1999 |
| INDG165 | Health surveillance programmes for employees exposed to metalworking fluids: guidance for the responsible person. 1994 |
| INDG167 | Health risks from metalworking fluids: aspects of good machine design. 1994 |
| INDG168 | Metalworking fluids: a guide to good management and practice for minimising risks to health. 1994 |
| INDG169 | Metalworking fluids and you. 1994 |
| INDG297 | Safety in gas welding, cutting and similar processes. 1999 |
| INDG313 | Safe unloading of steel stock. 2000 |
| INDG314 | Hot work on small tanks and drums. 2000 |
| INDG327 | Take care with acetylene. 2000 |
| WGIS1 | Supply of welding consumables. 1999 |

## Flammable and explosive substances

| | |
|---|---|
| – | Fire Safety: an employers guide. 1999 |
| CS23 | Disposal of waste explosives. 1999 |
| HSG51 | The storage of flammable liquids in containers. Revised 1998 |
| HSG71 | Chemical warehousing. 1998 |
| HSG103 | Safe handling of combustible dusts. 1994 |
| HSG114 | Conditions for the authorisation of explosives in Great Britain. 1994 |
| HSG131 | Energetic and combustible substances. 1995 |
| HSG135 | Storage and handling of industrial nitrocellulose. 1995 |
| HSG140 | Safe use and handling of flammable liquids. 1996 |
| HSG146 | Dispensing petrol. 1996 |
| HSG158 | Flame arresters. 1997 |
| HSG176 | The storage of flammable liquids in tanks. 1998 |
| HSG178 | The spraying of flammable liquids. 1998 |
| HSR17 | A guide to the Classification and Labelling of Explosive Regulations 1983. 1983 |
| L10 | A guide to the Control of Explosives Regulations 1991. 1991 |
| L13 | A guide to the Packaging of Explosives for Carriage Regulations 1991. 1991 |
| L66 | A guide to the Placing on the Market and Supervision of Transfers of Explosives Regulations (POMSTER) 1993. 1995 |
| HSE8 | Taking care with oxygen. 1999 |
| INDG115 | An introduction to the Control of Explosives Regulations. 1991 |
| INDG216 | Dispensing petrol as a fuel. 1996 |
| INDG227 | Safe working with flammable substances. 1996 |
| INDG314 | Hot work on small tanks and drums. 2000 |

## Foundries

| | |
|---|---|
| FNIS1 | Hazards associated with foundry processes. 1995 |
| FNIS2 | Foundry machine guarding: introductory sheet. 1995 |
| FNIS3 | Foundry machine guarding: mould and core-making machinery. 1995 |
| FNIS4 | Foundry machine guarding: sand handling equipment. 1995 |
| FNIS5 | Foundry machine guarding: shakeouts, sand mixer and shotblasts. 1995 |
| FNIS6 | Hazards associated with foundry processes: fettling. 1995 |
| FNIS7 | Hazards associated with foundry processes: rumbling – noise hazard. 1996 |
| FNIS8 | Hazards associated with foundry processes: hand-arm vibration – the current picture. 1996 |
| FNIS9 | Hazards associated with foundry processes: hand-arm vibration – symptoms and solutions. |
| FNIS10 | Hazards associated with foundry processes: hand arm vibration – assessing the need for action. 1999 |
| IACL83 | Is your hearing protection effective? Noise in foundries. 1994 |
| IACL104 | Health surveillance in foundries. 1998 |

## Health care

| | |
|---|---|
| HSG205 | Assessing and managing risks at work from skin exposure to chemical agents. 2001 |
| L55 | Preventing asthma at work. 1997 |
| INDG84 | Leptospirosis. 1990 |

| INDG91 | Drug misuse at work: a guide for employers. 1998 |
| INDG233 | Preventing dermatitis at work: advice for employers and employees. 1996 |
| INDG240 | Don't mix it! A guide for employers on alcohol at work. 1996 |
| INDG281 | Help on work-related stress. 1999 |
| INDG304 | Understanding health surveillance at work: an introduction for employers. 1999 |

## Health services

| IACL64 | Glutaraldehyde and you. Revised 1998 |
| HSIS1 | The Reporting of Injuries, Diseases and Dangerous Occurences Regulations 1995. 1998 |
| MISC186 | Safe use of pneumatic air tube transport systems for pathology specimens. 1999 |
| INDG320 | Latex and you. 2000 |

## Legislation and enforcement

| HSE4 | Employers Liability (Compulsory Insurance) Act 1969: a guide for employers. Revised 1998 |
| HSE5 | An introduction to the Employment and Medical Advisory Service. 2000 |
| HSC13 | Health and safety regulation: a short guide (available in Welsh). 1995 |
| HSC14 | What to expect when a health and safety inspector calls. 1998 |
| HSE36 | Employers Liability (Compulsory Insurance) Act 1969: a guide for employees and their represenatatives. 1998 |
| INDG184 | Signpost to the Safety Sign and Signals Regulations 1996: guidance on the regulations. 1996 |
| MISC030 | Enforcement policy statement (available in Welsh). 1995 |

## Major hazards

| – | Fire Safety: an employers guide. 1999 |
| HSG190 | Preparing safety reports: Control of Major Accident Hazards (COMAH) Regulations 1999. 1999 |
| HSG191 | Emergency planning for major accidents: Control of Major Accident Hazards Regulations 1999. 1999 |
| INDG196 | Safety reports: how HSE assesses these in connection with the Control of Industrial Major Accident Hazards Regulations. 1995 |
| L111 | A guide to the Control of Major Accident Hazards (COMAH) Regulations 1999. 1999 |

## Management of occupational health

| INDG163 | Five steps to risk assessment. Revised 1998 |
| INDG179 | Policy statement on open government. Revised 1998 |
| INDG208 | Be safe save money: the cost of accidents – a guide for small firms. 1995 |
| INDG213 | Five steps to information, instruction and training. 1996 |
| INDG218 | A guide to risk assessment requirements: common provisions in health and safety law. 1996 |
| INDG232 | Consulting employees on health and safety: a guide to the law. 1996 |

| | |
|---|---|
| INDG301 | Health and safety benchmarking. 1999 |
| MISC038 | The use of risk assessment in government departments. 1996 |
| MISC154 | Risk assessment and risk management. 1998 |

## Mines

| | |
|---|---|
| COP28 | Safety of exit of mines underground workings: Mines (Safety of Exit) Regulations 1988 – approved code of practice. 1988 |
| COP34 | The use of electricity in mines: Electricity at Work Regulations 1989 – approved code of practice. 1997 |
| L42 | Shafts and winding in mines: Mines (Shafts and Winding) Regulations 1993 – approved code of practice. 1993 |
| L43 | First aid at mines: Health and Safety (First Aid) Regulations 1981 – approved code of practice. 1993 |
| L44 | The management and administration of safety and health at mines: Management and Administation of Safety and Health at Mines Regulations 1993 – approved code of practice. 1993 |
| L45 | Explosives at coal and other safety-lamp mines: Coal and other Safety-lamp Mines (Explosives) Regulations 1993 – approved code of practice. 1993 |
| L46 | The prevention of inrushes in mines – approved code of practice. 1993 |
| L47 | The Coal Mines (Owners Operating Rules) Regulations 1993: guidance on regulations. 1993 |
| L71 | Escape and Rescue from Mines: Escape and Rescue from Mines Regulations 1995 – approved code of practice. 1995 |
| L119 | The control of ground movement in mines – approved code of practice and guidance. 1999 |
| QIS1 | Manager's guide to safe coal cleaning and the control of pedestrians at opencast coal sites. 1994 |
| TOP07 | Improving visibility on underground free steered vehicles. 1996. |

## Noise

| | |
|---|---|
| L108 | Guidance on the Noise at Work Regulations 1989. 1998 |
| INDG75 | Introducing the Noise at Work Regulations: a brief guide to the requirements for controlling noise at work. (Also available in Welsh). 1989 |
| INDG99 | Noise at work: advice to employees. 1995 |
| INDG193 | Health surveillance in noisy industries: advice for employers. 1993 |
| INDG263 | Keep the noise down: advice for purchasers of workplace machinery. 1997 |
| INDG298 | Ear Protection: employers duties explained. 1999 |
| INDG299 | Protect your hearing: pocket card. 1999 |
| MISC185 | Wear ear protection properly! Poster. 1999 |
| PBIS1 | Noise assessments in paper mills. 2000 |

## Nuclear

| | |
|---|---|
| INDG206 | Wear your dosemeter. Revised 1995 |
| IRIS2 | Radiation doses: assessment and recording. Revised 2000 |
| MISC148 | Safety audit of Dounreay 1998. 1998 |
| L31 | A guide to the Public Information for Radiation Emergncies Regulations 1992. 1993 |

## Oil Industry

| | |
|---|---|
| L110 | A guide to the Offshore Installations (Safety Representatives and Safety Committees) Regulations 1989. Revised 1998 |
| INDG94 | Offshore first-aid. 1990 |
| INDG119 | Safety representatives and safety committees on offshore installations. Revised 1999 |
| INDG219 | How offshore helicopter travel is regulated. 1996 |
| INDG239 | Play your part! 1996 |
| INDG250 | How HSE assesses Offshore Safety Cases. 1997 |
| INDG274 | Offshore health and safety legislation: your questions answered. 1998 |

## Personal Protective Equipment (PPE)

| | |
|---|---|
| INDG147 | Keep your top on: health risks from working in the sun – advise for outdoor workers. 1998 |
| INDG288 | Selection of suitable respiratory protective equipment for work with asbestos. 1999 |
| INDG330 | Selecting protective gloves for work with chemicals. 2000 |

## Quarries

| | |
|---|---|
| HSG73 | Control of respirable crystalline silica in quarries. 1992 |
| HSG109 | Control of noise in quarries. 1993 |
| L118 | Health and safety at quarries. 1999 |
| L119 | The control of ground movement in mines. 1999 |

## Vibration

| | |
|---|---|
| INDG126 | Health risks from vibration white finger: advice for employees and the self employed. Revised 1998 |
| INDG175 | Health risks from hand arm vibration: advice for employers. Revised 1998 |
| INDG242 | In the driving seat: advice to employers on reducing back pain in drivers and machinery operators. 1997 |
| INDG296P | Hand-arm vibration syndrome; pocket card for employees. 1999 |
| MISC112 | Reducing the risk of hand-arm vibration injury among stonemasons. 1998 |

## Woodworking

| | |
|---|---|
| INDG318 | Manual handling solutions in woodworking. 2000 |
| WIS6REV | COSHH and the woodworking industries. Revised 1997 |
| WIS7 | Accidents at woodworking machines. Revised 1999 |
| WIS13 | Noise at woodworking machines. 1997 |
| WIS15 | Safe working at woodworking machines. 1992 |
| WIS39 | Safe use of single-end tenoning machines. 2000 |

## Work Equipment

| | |
|---|---|
| L22 | Safe use of work equipment: Provision and Use of Work Equipment Regulations 1998 – approved code of practice and guidance. Revised 1998 |
| INDG290 | Simple guide to LOLER. 1999 |
| INDG291 | Simple guide to PUWER. 1999 |

| INDG317 | Chainsaws at work. 2000 |
| MISC241 | Fitting and use of restraining systems on lift trucks. 2000 |

## Workplace

| HSG199 | Managing health and safety on work experience: guide for organisers. 2000 |
| INDG36 | Working with VDUs. Revised 1998 (Also available in Welsh) |
| INDG173 | Officewise. (Also available in Welsh). 1994 |
| INDG226 | Homeworking: guidance for employers and employees on health and safety. 1996 |
| INDG333 | Back in work: managing back pain in the workplace. 2000 |
| OSR1 | Office, shop and railway premises. (Also available in Welsh). 1994 |

## Appendix 3

## Relevant British Standards

| | |
|---|---|
| Access equipment | BS 6037 |
| Agricultural machinery: combine and forage harvesters | BS EN 632 |
| Agricultural machinery: silage cutters | BS EN 703 |
| Airborne noise emission | |
| earth-moving machinery | BS 6812, BS ISO 6393, 6394 |
| hydraulic fluid power systems and components | BS 5944 |
| portable chain saws | BS 6916–6 |
| Ambient air: determination of asbestos fibres – direct-transfer transmission electron microscopy method | BS ISO 13794 |
| Anchorages | |
| industrial safety harnesses | BS EN 795 |
| self-locking, industrial | BS EN 353, 355, 36, 362, 365 |
| Arc welding equipment | BS 638, BS EN 609 |
| Artificial daylight lamps | |
| colour assessment | BS 950 |
| for sensitometry | BS 1380–4 |
| Artificial lighting | BS 8206–1 |
| Barriers, in and about buildings | BS 6180 |
| Bromochlorodifluoromethane | |
| fire extinguishing systems | BS 5306, BS EN 27201–1 |
| fire extinguishers | BS EN 27201 |
| Carbon steel welded horizontal cylindrical storage tanks | BS 2594 |
| Carpet cleaners, electric, industrial use | BS EN 60335–2–67 BS EN 60335–2–72 |
| Cellulose fibres | BS 1771–2 |
| Chain lever hoists | BS 4898 |
| Chain pulley blocks, hand-operated | BS 3243 |
| Chain slings | |
| alloy steel | BS 3458 |
| high tensile steel | BS 2902 |
| steel use and maintenance | BS 6968 |
| welded | BS 6304 |
| Chairs | |
| office furniture, performance | BS 5459–2 |
| office furniture, ergonomic design | BS 3044 |
| Chemical protective clothing | |
| against gases and vapours | BS EN 464 |
| liquid chemicals | BS EN 466, 467 |
| Circular saws | |
| hand-held electric | BS EN 50144–2–5 |
| woodworking | BS 411 |
| Cleaning and surface repair of buildings | BS 6270 |
| Closed circuit escape breathing apparatus | BS EN 400 |
| Clothing for protection against heat and fire | BS EN 366, 367 |
| Concrete cladding | BS 8297 |

Construction equipment

    hoists                                            BS 7212

    suspended safety chairs, cradles      BS 2830

Control of noise (construction and open sites)      BS 5228

Cranes, safe use      BS 5744, 7121

Disabled people, means of escape      BS 5588–8

Drill Rigs      BS EN 791

Dust

    high efficiency respirators      BS EN 136, 143

    particulate emission      BS 3405

Ear protectors, acoustics      BS EN 24869, BS EN ISO 4869

Earphones

    audiometry, calibration, acoustic couplers      BS 4668, BS EN 60318–2, 60318–3

    audiometry, calibration, artificial ears      BS 4669

Earthing      BS 7430

Earth moving equipment      BS 6912

Electrical equipment

    explosive atmospheres      BS 4683, 5501, 6941

    fire hazard testing      BS 6458

    guidance to wiring regulations      BS 7671

Electrical resistance materials

    bare fine resistance wires      BS 1117

    conductor sizes, low-voltage industrial switchgear and controlgear      BS EN 60947

    earth-leakage circuit-breakers

    — AC voltage operated      BS 842

    — current-operated      BS 4293

    — portable RCDs      BS 7071

    electric shock protection, construction of electrical equipment      BS 2754

    enclosures for high-voltage cable terminations, transformers and reactors      BS 6435

    fans for general purposes      BS 848

    industrial electric plugs      BS EN 60309

    industrial machines      BS 2771

    marking for low-voltage industrial switchgear/controlgear      BS 6272

    metallic      BS 115

    resistivity measurement      BS 5714

    static electricity      BS 5958

    switchgear      BS 5486, BS EN 60298

    test for resistance per unit length      BS 3466

Emergency exits      BS EN 179, 1125

Emergency lighting      BS 5266

Environmental management systems      BS EN ISO 14001

Ergonomics of the thermal environment      BS ISO 10551

Ergonomic requirements for office work with VDUs      BS EN 29241

Eye protection

    equipment for eye and face protection during welding operations      BS EN 175

    glossary of terms      BS EN 165

| | |
|---|---|
| specification for sunglare filters used in personal eye protectors for industrial use | BS EN 172 |
| Eye protectors | BS EN 169, 170, 171, 172, 207, 379, 1836 |
| Fabrics, curtains and drapes | BS 5867 |
| Falling-object protective structures | BS EN ISO 3164 |
| Falsework, code of practice | BS 5975 |
| Filters | |
| specification for infra-red filters used in personal eye protection equipment | BS EN 171 |
| specification for personal eye protection equipment in welding | BS EN 169 |
| specification for ultra-violet filters used in personal eye protection equipment | BS EN 170 |
| Fire blankets | BS EN 1869 |
| Fire classification | BS EN 2 |
| Fire detection/alarm systems | BS 5839 |
| Fire detection/alarm systems – design, installation and servicing of integrated systems | BS 7807 |
| Fire door assemblies | BS 8214 |
| Fire extinguishers | |
| disposable aerosol type | BS 6165 |
| media | BS 6535, BS EN 1568, 27201 |
| on premises | BS 5306 |
| portable | BS EN 3 |
| portable, recharging | BS 6643 |
| Fire hose reels | BS 5306–1 |
| Fire point determination, petroleum products | |
| Cleveland open cup method | BS EN 22592 |
| Pensky-Martens apparatus method | BS 2000–35 |
| Fire precautions in design/construction and use of buildings | BS 5588 |
| Fire protection measures, code of practice for operation | BS 7273 |
| Fire safety signs | BS 5499 |
| Fire terms | DS 4422 |
| Fire tests | BS 476 |
| Fire tests for furniture | BS 5852 |
| Firefighters gloves | BS EN 659 |
| First-aid reel/hoses | BS 3169 |
| Flameproof industrial clothing | BS EN 469, 531 |
| Footwear | |
| footwear fitted with toe caps | BS EN 345, 346 |
| lined industrialised vulcanised rubber boots | BS 5145 |
| methods of test for safety | BS EN 344–1 |
| occupational footwear for professional use | BS EN 347 |
| protective clothing for users of hand-held chain saws | BS EN 381 |
| requirements/test methods for safety protective and occupational footwear for professional use | BS EN 344 |
| specification for occupational footwear for professional use | BS EN 347 |
| Freight containers | BS 3951, BS 1SO 1496 |
| Gaiters and footwear for protection against burns and impact risks in foundries | BS 4676 |

| | |
|---|---|
| Gas detector tubes | BS 5343 |
| Gas fired hot water boilers | BS 6798 |
| Gas welding equipment | BS EN 731 |
| Glazing | BS 6262 |
| Gloves: medical gloves for single use | BS EN 455 |
| Gloves: rubber gloves for electrical purposes | BS 697 |
| Goggles, industrial/non-industrial use | BS EN 166, 167, 168 |
| Grinding machines | |
|     hand-held electric | BS 2769–2–3 |
|     pneumatic, portable | BS 4390 |
|     spindle noses | BS 1089 |
| Head protection — fire fighters | BS EN 443 |
| Headforms for use in testing protective helmets | BS EN 960 |
| Hearing protectors | BS EN 352 |
|     Part 1 Ear Muffs | |
|     Part 2 Ear Plugs | |
| High visibility warning clothing | BS EN 471 |
| Hoists | |
|     construction, safe use | BS 7212 |
|     electric, building sites | BS 4465 |
|     working platforms | BS 7171 |
| Hose reels with semi-rigid hose | BS EN 671–1 |
| Hose systems with lay-flat hose cloth | BS EN 671–2 |
| Hot environments | |
|     estimation of heat stress on the working man | BS EN 27243 |
| Household and similar electrical appliances | BS EN 60335 |
| Industrial gloves | BS EN 374, 388, 407, 420 |
| Industrial safety helmets, firemen's | BS EN 443 |
| Industrial trucks | |
|     hand-operated stillage trucks, dimensions | BS 4337 |
|     pallet trucks, dimensions | BS ISO 509 |
|     pedals, construction/layout | BS 7178 |
| Insulating material | BS 2844, 5691, 7737, 7822, 7831, BS EN 60383–2, |
| Ionising radiation | |
|     recommendation for data on shielding from ionizing radiation | BS 4094 |
|     units of measurement | BS 5775 |
| Jib cranes | |
|     high pedestal and portal | BS 2452 |
|     power-driven, mobile | BS 1757 |
| Ladders | |
|     code of practice | BS 5395 |
|     permanent for chimneys, high structures | BS 4211 |
|     portable aluminium | BS 2037 |
|     portable timber | BS 1129 |
| Life jackets | BS EN 394, 395, 396, 399 |
| Lifting chains | |
|     alloy, steel | BS 3113 |
|     high tensile steel | BS 1663 |
|     safe working on lifts | BS 7255 |
| Lifting slings | BS 6166 |

| | |
|---|---|
| safe use | BS 5744 |
| Packaging | |
| pictorial marking for handling of goods | BS EN ISO 780 |
| Particulate air pollutants | |
| in effluent gases, measurement | BS 3405 |
| Passenger hoists | |
| electric, building sites | BS 4465 |
| vehicular | BS 6109 |
| working platforms, mobile, elevating | BS 7171 |
| Patent glazing | BS 5516 |
| Pedestrian guardrails (metal) | BS 7818 |
| Performance of windows | BS 6375 |
| Personal eye protection | |
| filters for welding and related techniques | BS EN 169 |
| infrared filters | BS EN 171 |
| non-optical test methods | BS EN 168 |
| optical test methods | BS EN 167 |
| specifications | BS EN 166 |
| ultraviolet filters | BS EN 170 |
| vocabulary | BS EN 165 |
| Pipelines, identification marking | BS 1710 |
| Pneumatic tools | |
| portable grinding machines | BS 4390 |
| Portable fire extinguishers | BS EN 3, BS 7863 |
| Portable tools | |
| pneumatic grinding machines | BS 4390 |
| Powder fire extinguishers | |
| disposable, aerosol type | BS 6165 |
| extinguishing powders for | BS EN 615 |
| on premises | BS 5306 |
| portable, recharging | BS 6643 |
| Power take-off | |
| agricultural tractors, front-mounted | BS 6818 |
| agricultural tractors, rear-mounted | BS 5861 |
| Powered industrial trucks | |
| driverless, safety | BS EN 1525 |
| Process control – safety of analyser houses | BS EN 61285 |
| Protective barriers | BS 6180 |
| Protective cabs | |
| controls for external equipment | BS 5731 |
| Protective clothing | |
| against cold weather | DD ENV 342 |
| against foul weather | DD ENV 343 |
| against heat and fire | BS EN 366 |
| against heat and flame | BS EN 702 |
| against heat and flame – test method for limited flame spread | BS EN 532 |
| against molten metal splash | BS EN 373 |
| against risk of being caught up in moving parts | BS EN 510 |
| eye, face and neck protection, welding | BS EN 175 |
| flameproof | BS EN 469, 531 |
| for firefighters | BS EN 469 |
| for industrial workers exposed to heat | BS EN 531 |
| for use where there is risk of entanglement | BS EN 510 |
| for users of hand-held chain saws | BS EN 381 |

| | |
|---|---|
| for welders | BS EN 470 |
| for workers exposed to heat | BS EN 531 |
| gaiters for foundries | BS 4676 |
| general requirements | BS EN 340 |
| mechanical properties | BS EN 863 |
| protection against heat and fire | BS EN 366 |
| protection against intense heat | BS EN 366, 367 |
| protection against liquid chemicals | BS EN 369, 466, 467 |
| welding | BS EN 470 |
| Protective equipment | |
| against falls from a height | BS EN 341 |
| against falls from a height – guided fall type arresters | BS EN 353 |
| Protective footwear | |
| vulcanised rubber | BS 5145, 7193 |
| firemen's leather boots | BS 2723 |
| for foundries | BS 4676 |
| lined industrialised rubber boots | BS 5145 |
| polyvinyl chloride boots | BS 6159 |
| professional use | BS EN 346 |
| Protective gloves | |
| against chemicals and micro-organisms | BS EN 374 |
| against cold | BS EN 511 |
| against ionising radiation | BS EN 421 |
| against mechanical risks | BS EN 388 |
| against thermal hazards | BS EN 407 |
| for users of hand-held chain saws | BS EN 381 |
| general requirements | BS EN 420 |
| mechanical test methods | BS EN 388 |
| Protective helmets | BS EN 397 |
| Quality control | BS 5750, BS EN ISO 9000–9004 |
| | |
| Radiation measures | |
| detectors, nuclear reactors | BS 5548 |
| electroscope, exposure meters | BS 3385 |
| film badges | BS 3664 |
| neutron detectors | BS 5552 |
| personal photographic dosemeters | BS 6090 |
| Radiation protection, | |
| area radiation monitors, X-ray and gamma radiation | BS 5566 |
| Refrigeration systems | BS EN 378 |
| Resistance to ignition of upholstered furniture | |
| for non-domestic seating | BS 7176 |
| Respirators | |
| full masks for respiratory protective devices | BS EN 136 |
| Respiratory protective devices | BS EN 138, 139, 269, 270, 271 |
| | |
| Roll-over protective structures | |
| industrial trucks, stacking with masted tilt forward | BS 5778 |
| pallet stackers/high lift platform trucks | BS 5777 |
| reach and straddle fork trucks | BS 4436 |
| Rope pulley blocks | |
| gin blocks | BS 1692 |

| | |
|---|---|
| synthetic fibre | BS 4344 |
| Rope slings | |
| fibre rope slings | BS 6668–1 |
| wire rope slings | BS 1290, 6210 |
| Rubber/plastics injection moulding machines | BS EN 201 |
| Safety anchorages | |
| industrial safety harnesses | BS EN 795 |
| Safety distances to prevent danger zones being reached by upper limbs | BS EN 294 |
| Safety harnesses | |
| industrial | BS EN 354, 355, 358, 361–365 |
| industrial, manually operated positioning devices | BS 6858 |
| Safety helmets | BS EN 397 |
| Sampling methods | |
| airborne radioactive materials | BS 5243 |
| particulate emissions | BS 3405 |
| Scaffolds, code of practice | BS 5973, 5974 |
| Scalp protectors | BS EN 812 |
| Shaft construction and descent | BS 8008 |
| Specification for artificial daylight for colour assessment | BS 950 |
| Staging | |
| lightweight portable timber | BS 1129 |
| portable aluminium alloy | BS 2037 |
| Stairs, ladders, walkways | BS 5395 |
| Steam boilers | |
| electric boilers | BS 1894 |
| safety valves for | BS 6759–1 |
| welded steel low pressure boilers | BS 855 |
| Step ladders | |
| portable aluminium alloy | BS 2037 |
| portable timber | BS 1129 |
| Storage tanks | |
| carbon steel welded horizontal cylindrical | BS 2594 |
| vertical steel welded non-refrigerated butt-welded shells | BS 2654 |
| Suspended access equipment, permanently installed | BS 6037 |
| Suspended safety chairs | BS 2830 |
| Suspended scaffolds, temporarily installed | BS 5974 |
| Tables, office furniture, ergonomic design | BS 3044 |
| Textile floor coverings | BS 5287 |
| Textile machinery, safety requirements | BS EN ISO 11111 |
| Transportable gas containers | |
| acetylene containers | BS 6071 |
| periodic inspection, testing and maintenance | BS 5430 |
| welded steel tanks for road transport of liquefiable gases | BS 7122 |
| Travelling cranes, power-driven jib | BS 357, 5744 |
| Vertical steel welded non-refrigerated storage tanks, manufacture of | BS 2654 |
| Vibration measurement | |
| chain saws | BS 6916 |
| rotating shafts | BS ISO 7919 |
| Water absorption and translucency of china or porcelain | BS 5416 |
| Water services, installation, testing and maintenance | BS 6700 |

| | |
|---|---|
| Welders, protective clothing | BS EN 470 |
| Window cleaning | BS 8213–1 |
| Windows, performance of | BS 6375 |
| Woodworking noise | BS 7140 |
| Wool and wool blends | BS 1771–1 |
| Working platforms | |
|     mobile, elevating | BS 7171 |
|     permanent, suspended access | BS 6037 |
| Workplace atmospheres | |
|     performance of procedures for measurement of chemical agents | BS EN 482 |
|     size definitions for measurement of airborne particulates | BS EN 481 |
| Workwear and career wear | BS 5426 |

# Appendix 4

# A Summary of Risk Assessment Requirements

| Regulations<br><br>Features | Management of Health and Safety at Work Regulations 1999 | Manual Handling Operations Regulations 1992 | Personal Protective Equipment at Work Regulations 1992 (as amended most recently by SI 1999 No 860) | Health and Safety (Display Screen Equipment) Regulations 1992 |
|---|---|---|---|---|
| On whom duties placed | 1. Employers<br>2. Self-employed persons | 1. Employers<br>2. Self-employed persons | 1. Employers<br>2. Self-employed persons | Employers |
| Identity of those Assessed and Geographical Location | 1. Employees (at Work)<br>2. Persons not in the employer's employment who may face risks arising out of or in connection with the conduct by him of his undertaking.<br>3. New and expectant mothers.<br>4. Young persons.<br><br>The MHSW Regulations ACoP recommends that employers should identify groups of workers particularly at risk such as night workers, homeworkers, those who work alone and disabled staff. | Employees (at Work)<br><br>The HSE's Manual Handling Regulations Guidance emphasises that employers must make allowance for those who might be pregnant or have a disability or health problem. | Employees (at Work) | 1. Users (Employees who habitually use display screen equipment as a significant part of their normal work)<br>2. Operators (Self-Employed persons who habitually use display screen equipment as a significant part of their normal work) |
| Hazards or Risks to be Assessed | All Risks. A risk assessment carried out by a self-employed person in circumstances where he or she does not employ others does not have to take into account duties arising under Part II of the Fire Precautions (Workplace) Regulations 1999, as amended by the Fire Precautions (Workplace) (Amendment) Regulations 1999 (SI 1999 No 1877)<br><br>Physical, biological and chemical agents | All manual handling operations (with regard to factors – task, load, working environment, individual capability, other factors – listed in Schedule 1) | Any risks which have not been adequately controlled by other means | Workstations |

| Regulations<br><br>Features | Management of Health and Safety at Work Regulations 1999 | Manual Handling Operations Regulations 1992 | Personal Protective Equipment at Work Regulations 1992 (as amended most recently by SI 1999 No 860) | Health and Safety (Display Screen Equipment) Regulations 1992 |
|---|---|---|---|---|
| Purpose of Assessment | To identify measures needed to be taken to comply with the requirements and prohibitions imposed by or under the relevant statutory provisions and by Part II of the Fire Precautions (Workplace) Regulations 1999, as amended (see above) | To consider the questions set out in column 2 of Schedule 1 pertaining to the factors listed in that Schedule (see above) | To assess risks to health and safety which have not been avoided by other means | To assess workstations for health and safety risks to which users/operators are exposed |
| Qualification of Duty | Suitable and Sufficient | Suitable and Sufficient | | Suitable and Sufficient |
| When assessment has to be made | | Make assessment where it is not reasonably practicable to avoid the need for employees to undertake any manual handling operations which involve risk of injury | Assessment to be made *before* choosing any personal protective equipment | |
| Record Provision<br><br>(a) Threshold<br><br>(b) Contents<br><br>(c) How long to be kept? | (a) Five or more employees<br><br>(b) Significant findings of the assessment and any group of employees identified by it as being especially at risk | | | |
| Review Provision | Review assessment if:<br><br>– reason to suspect it is no longer valid (or can be improved)<br><br>– there has been a significant change | Review assessment if:<br><br>– reason to suspect it is no longer valid<br><br>– there has been a significant change | Review assessment if:<br><br>– reason to suspect it is no longer valid<br><br>– there has been a significant change | Review assessment if:<br><br>– reason to suspect it is no longer valid<br><br>– there has been a significant change |
| Action on Review | Risk assessment to be modified, as necessary | Changes to assessment to be made where required | Changes to assessment to be made where required | Changes to assessment to be made where required |

| Regulations | Management of Health and Safety at Work Regulations 1999 | Manual Handling Operations Regulations 1992 | Personal Protective Equipment at Work Regulations 1992 (as amended most recently by SI 1999 No 860) | Health and Safety (Display Screen Equipment) Regulations 1992 |
|---|---|---|---|---|
| **Features** | | | | |
| Details | | Employers shall<br><br>– take steps to reduce risk of injury to lowest level reasonably practicable<br><br>– take steps to provide (to employees) general indications, and, where reasonably practicable, precise information on:<br><br>– weight of load<br><br>– heaviest side of load where centre of gravity is not central | Assessment to include:<br><br>– definition of the characteristics which PPE must have in order to be effective against the risks (taking into account any risks which the equipment itself may create)<br><br>– comparison of the characteristics of the PPE available to the required characteristics | Employers shall reduce risks identified by assessment to lowest extent reasonably practicable |

| Regulations<br><br>Features | Noise at Work Regulations 1989 (as amended by SI 1997 No 1993 and SI 1999 No 2024) | Control of Substances Hazardous to Health Regulations 1999 | Control of Asbestos at Work Regulations 1987 (as amended by SI 1992 No 3068 and SI 1998 No 3235) |
|---|---|---|---|
| On whom duties placed | Employers and self-employed persons to ensure competent person makes assessment | 1. Employers<br>2. Self-employed persons<br>3. Employees | 1. Employers<br>2. Self-employed persons |
| Identity of those Assessed and Geographical Location | Employees (at Work) | Employees liable to be exposed to substances hazardous to health by any work<br><br>Other persons who may be affected by the employer's work | 1. Employees (at Work)<br>2. Other Persons |
| Hazards or Risks to be Assessed | Noise | Any substance hazardous to health | Asbestos |
| Purpose of Assessment | 1. To identify which employees are exposed<br><br>2. To provide such information, with regard to the noise, as will facilitate compliance with Regs 7,8,9 and 11 | To identify risk to enable a decision to be made on the measures to take to prevent or adequately control exposure | 1. To identify type of asbestos. The 1998 Amendment Regulations extend the ambit of the 1987 Regulations to include *all* types of asbestos work that may lead to exposure<br>2. To determine nature and degree of exposure<br>3. To set out steps to reduce exposure to lowest level reasonably practicable |
| Qualification of Duty | Adequate | Suitable and Sufficient<br><br>SFAIRP for other persons (whether at work or not) who may be affected by the employer's work<br><br>'Due diligence' defence | Adequate |
| When assessment has to be made | Assessment to be made when any employee is likely to be exposed to the first action level or above or to the peak action level or above. | Assessment to be made *before* work is commenced | Assessment to be made *before* work is commenced |

| Regulations / Features | Noise at Work Regulations 1989 (as amended by SI 1997 No 1993 and SI 1999 No 2024) | Control of Substances Hazardous to Health Regulations 1999 | Control of Asbestos at Work Regulations 1987 (as amended by SI 1992 No 3068 and SI 1998 No 3235) |
|---|---|---|---|
| Record Provision | Record to be kept until a further assessment is made | No specific recording requirement *but certain records related to assessment to be kept.* | No specific recording requirement but certain records related to assessment to be kept. |
| (a) Threshold | | (a) Health record to be made relating to each employee exposed | (a) Health record to be made relating to each employee exposed |
| (b) Contents | | (b) At least the information specified in the Appendix to the 1999 General COSHH ACoP | (b) The health record must contain at least the following information:<br>(i) name, sex, date of birth, address and NI No<br>(ii) types of work carried out with asbestos, its location, end and start dates and average duration in hours per week<br>(iii) any work with asbestos prior to present employment, and<br>(iv) dates of medical examination |
| (c) How long to be kept? | | *(c) To be kept for at least 40 years from last entry* | (c) To be kept for at least 40 years from last entry |
| Review Provision | Review assessment if:<br>– reason to suspect that it is no longer valid<br>– there has been a significant change | Review assessment:<br>– regularly; and forthwith if,<br>– reason to suspect assessment is no longer valid, and/or<br>– there has been a significant change | Review assessment:<br>– regularly; and if,<br>– reason to suspect it is no longer valid<br>– there has been a significant change |
| Action on Review | Changes to assessment to be made where required | Changes to assessment to be made where required | |
| Details | | Assessment should include the steps that need to be taken to comply with other requirements of the Regulations | |

| Regulations / Features | Control of Lead at Work Regulations 1998 | Genetically Modified Organisms (Contained Use) Regulations 2000 | Ionising Radiations Regulations 1999 |
|---|---|---|---|
| On whom duties placed | 1. Employers<br>2. Self-employed persons<br>3. Employees | Any person undertaking any activity involving genetic modification of micro-organisms and organisms other than micro-organisms | 1. Employers<br>2. Self-employed persons<br>3. Mine managers – in so far as the duties relate to the mine or part thereof which he is manager/operator and to matters within his control<br>4. Quarry operators – in so far as the duties relate to the quarry or part thereof which he is manager/operator and to matters within his control<br>5. The holder of a nuclear site licence – in so far as the duties relate to the licensed site |
| Identity of those Assessed and Geographical Location | 1. Employees<br>2. Other persons likely to be affected by the work. The HSC's ACoP on the Regulations states as well as an employer's own employees these include:<br>– other workers, including another employer's employees/other employees not working/working with lead, i.e. maintenance staff, cleaners etc.<br>– visitors to the work site<br>– families of those exposed to lead at work and who may be affected by lead carried home unintentionally on clothing and footwear | Persons and the environment put at risk by the above activity | 1. Employees<br>2. Persons other than an employer's employees, only in so far as the exposure of these persons to ionising radiation arises from work with ionising radiation undertaken by that employer<br>3. Self-employed persons<br>4. Trainees, as defined |
| Hazards or Risks to be Assessed | Exposure to lead | As above i.e. the risks created by the activity to human health and the environment | Any new activity involving work with ionising radiation – the 'Prior risk assessment' |

| Regulations<br><br>Features | Control of Lead at Work Regulations 1998 | Genetically Modified Organisms (Contained Use) Regulations 2000 | Ionising Radiations Regulations 1999 |
|---|---|---|---|
| Purpose of Assessment | To allow employer to make a valid decision about whether the work concerned is likely to result in any employees being 'significantly' exposed to lead and to identify the measures needed to prevent or control exposure | To identify those risks | To identify the measures needed to be taken to restrict the exposure of employees or other persons to ionising radiation |
| Qualification of Duty | Suitable and Sufficient | Suitable and Sufficient | Suitable and Sufficient |
| When assessment has to be made | Assessment to be made *before* work is commenced | Prior to undertaking any such activity | Before a duty holder commences a new activity involving working with ionising radiation |
| Record Provision | No specific recording requirement but certain records related to assessment to be kept. | | |
| (a) Threshold | (a) The MHSW Regulations require employers to record the 'significant' finding of the assessment if five or more employees. | | (a) No stipulation in the Regulations but ACoP and guidance says that it 'makes sense' to record the significant findings of the prior risk assessment where employers have five or more employees and/or where any group of employees is especially at risk |
| (b) Contents | (b) The HSC's ACoP and Guidance on the Lead Regulations states that the recorded findings of the assessment should include:<br><br>(i) the significant hazards identified by the assessment arising from exposure to lead<br><br>(ii) the existing control measures in place and the extent to which they control the risks<br><br>(iii) the people who may be affected by these significant risks and hazards, and<br><br>(iv) where appropriate, the type of protective clothing and respiratory equipment to be issued to employees | A record of the assessment relating to the activity, and any review of that assessment | (b) The significant findings |
| (c) How long to be kept? | (c) The MHSW Regulations do not set a period for retaining recorded assessments, but the ACoP and Guidance (see above) says that they should be kept for a minimum of five years | At least 10 years from the date of cessation of the activity | |

| Regulations / Features | Control of Lead at Work Regulations 1998 | Genetically Modified Organisms (Contained Use) Regulations 2000 | Ionising Radiations Regulations 1999 |
|---|---|---|---|
| Review Provision | The ACoP and Guidance (see above) says assessment should be reviewed if: <br> – evidence to suggest it is no longer valid <br> – significant change in the work | Review assessment if <br> – reason to suspect it is no longer valid <br> – there has been a significant change in the activity to which assessment relates | Review prior risk assessment if <br> – reason to suspect it is no longer valid (or can be improved) <br> – there has been a significant change |
| Action on Review Details | Changes to assessment to be made where required <br><br> Employer must take steps that need to be taken to comply with other requirements of the Regulations | Risk assessment to be modified, as necessary | Prior risk assessment to be modified, as necessary |

# Appendix 5
# A Summary of Requirements for the Provision of Information

| Legislation<br><br>Duties On | The Management of Health and Safety at Work Regulations 1999 | The Manual Handling Operations Regulations 1992 | Personal Protective Equipment at Work Regulations 1992 | Health and Safety (Display Screen Equipment) Regulations 1992 |
|---|---|---|---|---|
| Employer to provide for: own employees | Risks identified by the assessment<br><br>Preventive and protective measures as per Schedule 1<br><br>Procedures in event of serious and imminent danger<br><br>Competent persons re evacuation<br><br>Risks notified by other employers | Those undertaking m/h ops<br><br>(a) General indications, and where reasonably practicable, precise information on:<br><br>(i) Weight of each load,<br><br>(ii) Heaviest side | Such information as is adequate and appropriate on:<br><br>(i) Risks PPE will avoid/limit<br><br>(ii) Purpose/manner of use,<br><br>(iii) Action to be taken by employee | For his employees who are 'users' employer must provide information on:<br><br>– All aspects of health and safety relating to their workstation;<br><br>– Measures taken to comply with Regulations 2 (risk assessment), 3 (workstations), 4 (breaks), 5 (eyes and eyesight) and 6 (training) |
| Employer/self-employed person to provide for other workers | Risks to health and safety arising from the conduct of the undertaking<br><br>To enable them to identify competent persons re evacuation<br><br>Any special occ. qualifications or skills needed to work safely<br><br>Any health surveillance required | | | For 'users' employed by other employers, and 'operators', at work in his undertaking the employer must provide information on:<br><br>– All aspects of health and safety relating to their workstation;<br><br>– Measures taken to comply with Regulations 2 and 3 for 'users' only Regulations 4 and 6(2) (training when workstation modified) |
| Employer/self-employed person to provide for other employers, self-employed persons/others | Risks to health and safety arising from the conduct of the undertaking<br><br>Measures taken in compliance<br><br>To enable them to identify competent persons re evacuation<br><br>Any special occ. qualifications or skills needed to work safely<br><br>Specific features of jobs in relation to health and safety | | | |

| Legislation | The Provision and Use of Work Equipment Regulations 1998 (as amended by SI 1999 No 860 and SI 1999 No 2001) (new provisions replacing the revoked Power Press Regulations are incorporated in Part IV of these Regulations) | The Noise at Work Regulations 1989 (as amended by SI 1997 No 1993 and SI 1999 No 2024) | The Control of Substances Hazardous to Health Regulations 1999 | The Control of Asbestos at Work Regulations 1987 (as amended by SI 1992 No 3068 and SI 1998 No 3235) |
|---|---|---|---|---|
| **Duties On** | | | | |
| Employer to provide for: own employees | Every employer must ensure that all employees using work equipment are provided with adequate health and safety information and, where appropriate, written instructions about the use of such equipment. The employer must also ensure that any employee supervising or managing the use of work equipment has available adequate health and safety information and, as above, where appropriate, written instructions. The information and instructions required above must include information and, where appropriate, written instructions on:<br><br>(i) All health and safety aspects arising from the use of the work equipment including conditions in which and methods by which it can be used<br><br>(ii) Any limitations on these uses<br><br>(iii) Any foreseeable difficulties that could arise<br><br>(iv) The methods to deal with them<br><br>(v) Any conclusions to be drawn from experience in using the work equipment | Every employer shall provide any of his employees, who are likely to be exposed to the first action level or above, information on:<br><br>(i) Risk of damage to hearing<br><br>(ii) What steps can be taken to minimise risk<br><br>(iii) Steps that the employee must take in order to obtain personal ear protection<br><br>(iv) Employees' obligations | (a) Such information, instruction and training as is suitable and sufficient about the risks and precautions including:<br><br>(i) Results of monitoring of exposure and in particular, in the case of any substance hazardous to health for which a maximum exposure limit has been approved, the provision of that information to the employee or his representative<br><br>(ii) Health surveillance information<br><br>(b) Necessary information, instruction and training for person carrying out any work in connection with employer's duties | Adequate information, instruction and training for:<br><br>(a) Employees liable to be exposed so they are aware of risks/precautions<br><br>(b) Employees who carry out work in connection with employer's duties |

| | | |
|---|---|---|
| Employer/ self-employed person to provide for other workers | Employers and the self-employed are under a duty to provide information etc. to other workers only in so far as they have control, to *any* extent, of<br>(i) Work equipment<br>(ii) A person at work who uses or supervises or manages the use of work equipment<br>(iii) The way in which such equipment is used at work to the extent of that control.<br>*Note:* the Regulations do *not* apply to a person who has supplied work equipment by way of sale, agreement for sale, or hire purchase agreement | (c) Necessary information, instruction and training for person (whether or not an employee) carrying out any work in connection with employer's duties and information on risks and precautions SFAIRP. These obligations do *not* extend to non-employees unless they are on the premises where the work is being carried out |
| Employer/ self-employed person to provide for other employers, self-employed persons/others | See above | (d) Necessary information, instruction and training for person carrying out any work in connection with employer's duties and information on risks and precautions SFAIRP, subject to above |

| Legislation | Control of Lead at Work Regulations 1998 | Dangerous Substances in Harbour Areas Regulations 1987 (as amended most recently by SI 1998 No 2885) | Health and Safety Information for Employees Regulations 1989 (as amended by SI 1995 No 2923) | Carriage of Dangerous Goods by Road Regulations 1996 (as amended by SI 1998 No 2885 and SI 1999 No 303) |
|---|---|---|---|---|
| **Duties On** | | | | |
| Employer to provide for: own employees | Employer undertaking work liable to expose any employee to lead must provide such information, instruction and training as is suitable and sufficient to enable the employee to know: (a) The risks to health created by such exposure, and (b) The precautions which must be taken That information must include: (i) The results of any monitoring of exposure to lead carried out in accordance with the Regulations (ii) Information on the collective results of any medical surveillance carried out in accordance with the Regulations (iii) An explanation of the significance of (i) and (ii) above | Employer to provide information necessary to ensure his health and enable him to perform any operations in which he is involved with due regard to the health and safety of others | Employer to ensure that the approved poster is kept displayed in a readable condition at an accessible place to the employee while he is at work and must provide the employee with the approved leaflet. Employer has to have information of EMAS office and enforcing authority on poster | |
| Employer/ self-employed person to provide for other workers | An employer/self-employed person is under no duty to provide information etc. to a person other than an employee unless that person is on the premises where the work is being carried out | Self-employed person to ensure that he has information to ensure his and others' health and safety | | |

| | | |
|---|---|---|
| Employer/ self-employed person to provide for other employers, self-employed persons/others | See above | Consignor of dangerous substances to supply sufficient accurate written information to enable the operator to: |
| | Operator to provide persons present on the berth with information to ensure their and others' health and safety. | (a) comply with his duties under these Regs; and |
| | | (b) be aware of the hazards created by the substance to health and safety |
| | | (c) adequate information about identity, quantity and nature of hazards created by substance information to operator. This must be accurate, sufficient and so far as possible in writing |
| | | Operator to keep information for at least three months after completion of journey and must have information before carriage |

| Legislation | Carriage of Dangerous Goods by Road (Driver Training) Regulations 1996 (as amended by SI 1999 No 303) | Safety Representatives and Safety Committees Regulations 1977 (as amended by SI 1996 No 1513, SI 1997 No 840, SI 1999 No 860 and SI 1999 No 2024) | The Health and Safety (First-aid) Regulations 1981 (as amended by SI 1989 No 1674, SI 1993 No 1897 and SI 1997 No 2776) | The Pressure Systems Safety Regulations 2000 |
|---|---|---|---|---|
| **Duties On** | | | | |
| Employer to provide for: own employees | | To allow safety reps to carry out inspections to allow access to relevant documents to make available all the information necessary to allow fulfilment of functions | Inform his employees of the arrangements that have been made in connection with the provision of first-aid, including the location of equipment, facilities and personnel | 1. Any person who: (a) designs for another any pressure system or any article which is intended to be a component or part thereof; or (b) supplies (whether as manufacturer or importer or in any other capacity) any pressure system or any such article, shall provide sufficient information concerning its design, construction, examination, operation and maintenance as may reasonably foreseeably be needed to comply with the Regulations.2. The employer of a person who modifies or repairs any pressure system must provide sufficient information concerning the modification or repair as may reasonably foreseeably be needed to comply with the Regulations. |
| Employer/ self-employed person to provide for other workers | | Safety representatives to receive information from inspectors | | |
| Employer/ self-employed person to provide for other employers, self-employed persons/others | | | | |

| Legislation | The Work in Compressed Air Regulations 1996 (as amended by SI 1997 No 2776) | The Chemicals (Hazard Information and Packaging for Supply) Regulations 1994 (as amended most recently by SI 2000 No 2381) | Carriage of Dangerous Goods by Road Regulations 1996 (as amended by SI 1998 No 2885 and SI 1999 No 303) | Carriage of Explosives by Road Regulations 1996 (as amended by SI 1999 No 303) |
|---|---|---|---|---|
| **Duties On** | | | | |
| Employer to provide for: own employees | The 'compressed air contractor', as defined, is to ensure that adequate information etc. is given to *all* persons working in compressed air on the risks arising from such work and the precautions to be taken. The HSE Guidance to the 1996 Regulations stresses that the provision of information etc. in such circumstances may be carried out by anyone competent to do so, but the compressed air contractor is responsible for ensuring that it is carried out to standard. | | Sufficient accurate written information to enable the operator to:<br><br>(a) comply with his duties under these Regs; and<br><br>(b) be aware of the hazards created by the substance to health and safety Adequate information about identity, quantity and nature of hazards created by substance | The following information in writing at the start of the journey:<br><br>(a) in the case of classified explosives the Division and Compatibility Group of each type of explosive carried;<br><br>(b) the net mass of each type of explosive carried<br><br>(c) whether, in the case of explosives in Compatibility Group C, D or G, the explosives carried are explosive substances or explosive articles<br><br>(d) name and address of consignor, operator and consignee<br><br>(e) information to enable driver and attendant to know nature of danger and action to be taken in an emergency |
| Employer/ self-employed person to provide for other workers | See above | | | |
| Employer/ self-employed person to provide for other employers, self-employed persons/others | See above | Supplier of dangerous chemicals to communicate with recipients information on the hazards presented | | |

| Legislation / Duties on | Offshore Installations and Wells (Design and Construction, etc) Regulations 1996 | Construction (Design and Management) Regulations 1994 (as amended by SI 2000 No 2380) | Ionising Radiations Regulations 1999 |
|---|---|---|---|
| Well-operator or installation duty holder | Provision of appropriate information so that those carrying out well operations can carry them out competently | | |
| Principal contractor | | To provide:<br><br>(i) so far is reasonably practicable, every contractor with comprehensible information on the risks to the health or safety of that contractor or of any other employees or other persons under the control of that contractor arising out of or in connection with the construction work<br><br>To ensure:<br><br>(i) so far is reasonably practicable, that every contractor who is an employer provides his employees carrying out the construction work with the information the employer must provide to those employees under the Management of Health and Safety at Work Regulations 1999, namely: the risks identified by the risk assessment; the preventative and protective measures thereby made necessary; the procedures in event of serious and imminent danger; the 'competent persons' as regards evacuation; and, the risks notified by other employers | |

| | |
|---|---|
| Employer/ self-employed person to provide for own employees | Such information as is suitable for them to know:<br>(i) the health risks created by exposure to ionising radiation;<br>(ii) the precautions which should be taken; and<br>(iii) the importance of complying with the medical, technical and administrative requirements of the Regulations |
| Employer/ self-employed person to ensure | Adequate information is given to persons other than employees who are directly concerned with ionising radiation work carried on by the employer/self-employed person to ensure, so far is reasonably practicable their health and safety |

# Summary of the Requirements for Training/Instruction and Consultation

| Legislation | Management of Health and Safety at Work Regulations 1999 | Manual Handling Operations Regulations 1992 | Personal Protective Equipment at Work Regulations 1992 (as amended most recently by SI 1999 No 860) | Health and Safety (Display Screen Equipment) Regulations 1992 |
|---|---|---|---|---|
| **Duties On** | | | | |
| Employer provides training/instruction for employees | Adequate health and safety training: on recruitment on being exposed to new/increased risks e.g. on transfer/change of responsibilities; new work equipment; new technology; new system of work | | Adequate and appropriate training about risks the ppe will avoid/limit; purposes of ppe; action to be taken by employee | Employer shall provide adequate health and safety training in use of workstation to: <br> – his employees who are 'users' on date of coming into force of the regulations <br> – his employees about to become users employers also shall provide such training to employee 'users' when the organisation of their workstation is substantially modified <br><br> Current users of DSE. Adequate health and safety training in the use of workstation, and whenever organisation of workstation modified |
| Employer provides training/instruction for specified employees/others | Employees who have access to any area (where such access is subject to restriction): adequate instruction for evacuation procedures | | | |

| Legislation | The Provision and Use of Work Equipment Regulations 1998 (as amended by SI 1999 No 860 and SI 1999 No 2001) | The Noise at Work Regulations 1989 (as amended by SI 1997 No 1993 and SI 1999 No 2024) | The Control of Substances Hazardous to Health Regulations 1999 | The Control of Asbestos at Work Regulations 1987 (as amended by SI 1992 No 3068 and SI 1998 No 3235) |
|---|---|---|---|---|
| **Duties On** | | | | |
| Employer provides training/ instruction for employees | All persons who use work equipment:– adequate training for purposes of health and safety inc. training in the methods of use, risks and precautions. For employers' obligations regarding instruction see Provision of Information above | Every employer shall provide each of his employees, who is likely to be exposed to the first action level or above, instruction and training on:<br><br>(i) risk of damage to hearing<br><br>(ii) what steps can be taken to minimise risk<br><br>(iii) steps that employee must take in order to obtain personal ear protectors<br><br>(iv) employees' obligations | Employer to provide –<br><br>(a) such information, instruction and training as is suitable and sufficient about the risks to health created by exposure to substances hazardous to health and the precautions which should be taken.<br><br>Without prejudice to the above the information must include:<br><br>(i) information on the results of any monitoring of exposure at the workplace in accordance with the Regulations, and<br><br>(ii) in the case of any substance hazardous to health or for which a maximum exposure limit has been approved, the employee or his representative must be informed if the results of that monitoring show that the maximum exposure limit has been exceeded<br><br>(iii) information on the collective results of any health surveillance undertaken in accordance with the Regulations<br><br>(b) Necessary information, instruction and training for persons carrying out any work in accordance with the employer's duties<br><br>(c) Necessary information, instruction and training for person (whether or not an employee) carrying out any work in connection with employer's duties, subject to the proviso that the obligation does not extend to non-employees unless those persons are on the premises where the work is being carried out | Adequate information, instruction and training for –<br><br>(a) employees liable to be exposed so they are aware of risks/precautions<br><br>(b) who carry out work in connection with employer's duties |
| Employer provides training/ instruction for specified employees/ others | Obligations as above. The HSC's ACoP and Guidance on the Regulations emphasises that 'training and proper supervision of "young people" is particularly important because of their relative immaturity and unfamiliarity with the working environment' | | | |

| Legislation<br><br>**Duties On** | The Control of Lead at Work Regulations 1998 | The Dangerous Substances in Harbour Areas Regulations 1987 (as amended most recently by SI 1998 No 2885) | The Health and Safety Information for Employees Regulations 1989 (as amended by SI 1995 No 2923) | Health and Safety (Consultation with Employees) Regulations 1996 (as amended by SI 1997 No 1840) |
|---|---|---|---|---|
| Employer provides training/ instruction for employees | Employer undertaking work liable to expose employee to lead must provide employee with such information, instruction and training as is suitable and sufficient for the employee to know:<br><br>(i) the risk to health created by such exposure, and<br><br>(ii) the precautions that must be taken | Employer and self-employed person to provide instruction, training and supervisor necessary to ensure his health and safety and to enable him to perform any operations in which he is involved with due regard to the health and safety of | | Employer to consult either:<br><br>(a) with employees directly, or<br><br>(b) with representatives of employee safety in non-unionised workforces,<br><br>and to allow time-off for training |
| Employer provides training/ instruction for specified employees/ others | The above obligation subsists so long as the other persons are on the premises where the work is being carried out | Operator to provide instruction, as necessary, to persons present on the berth to ensure their health and safety | | |

| Legislation<br><br>Duties On | Carriage of Dangerous Goods by Road (Driver Training) Regulations 1996 (as amended by SI 1999 No 303) | The Safety Representatives and Safety Committees Regulations 1977 (as amended by SI 1996 No 1513, SI 1997 No 840, SI 1999 No 860 and SI 1999 No 2024) | The Work in Compressed Air Regulations 1996 (as amended by SI 1997 No 2776) | Construction (Health, Safety and Welfare) Regulations 1996 (as amended by SI 1998 No 494 and SI 1998 No 2306) |
|---|---|---|---|---|
| Employer provides training/instruction for employees | | | The 'compressed air contractor', as defined, to provide adequate training on risks and precautions. See entry for Regulations under Provision of Information | Adequate training of employees to avoid acts causing injury or damage |
| Employer provides training/instruction for specified employees/others | Operator must ensure driver of vehicle has received adequate instruction and training. This includes understanding his duties under other relevant h & s legislation | Allow time off with pay for training of safety reps (as may be reasonable); consult with safety reps and with other trade unions reps over establishment of safety committees; consult safety reps on: instruction of measures which may affect h & s of employees<br>– arrangements for appointing those who give health and safety assistance<br>– health and safety information provided to workforce<br>– planning and organisation of health and safety training for employee<br>– health and safety implications of new technologies | | |

| Legislation<br><br>Duties On | Ionising Radiations Regulations 1999 | Confined Spaces Regulations 1997 | Quarries Regulations 1999 | Offshore Installations and Wells (Design and Construction, etc) Regulations 1996 |
|---|---|---|---|---|
| Employer/ self-employed person to ensure | Those of his employees engaged in work with ionising radiation are given appropriate training in the field of radiation protection and receive instruction as is suitable and sufficient for them to know:<br><br>(i) the risks to health created by exposure to ionising radiation;<br><br>(ii) the precautions which should be taken; and<br><br>(iii) the importance of complying with the medical, technical and administrative requirements of the Regulations. | Persons likely to be involved in any emergency rescue to be trained for that purpose. The ACoP and guidance specifies the content of that training, where appropriate. | | |
| Quarry operator must | | | Ensure that no person undertakes any work in a quarry unless: that person is either competent to do the work or does so under the instruction and supervision of some other person who is competent to give instruction in and to supervise the doing of that work for the purpose of training him | |
| Well-operator or installation duty holder to ensure | | | | Well operations are not carried out unless persons carrying out the operation have received appropriate instruction and training |

| Legislation | Ionising Radiation (Medical Exposure) Regulations 2000 | | |
|---|---|---|---|
| **Duties on** | | | |
| Employer provides training/ instruction for 'practitioners or operators', as defined | Steps must be taken to ensure that every 'practitioner or operator' engaged by the employer to carry out medical exposures involving ionising radiation undertakes continuing education and training after qualification, as specified (where the employer is concurrently 'practitioner or operator' he must ensure that he undertakes such continuing education and training as may be 'appropriate') | | |

# Table of Cases

This table is referenced to paragraph numbers in the work.

# Table of Statutes

# Table of Statutory Instruments

# Index

References are to sections and paragraph numbers of this book.